Tributes
Volume 20

The Goals of Cognition
Essays in honour of Cristiano Castelfranchi

Volume 9
Acts of Knowledge: History, Philosophy and Logic.
Essays dedicated to Göran Sundholm
Giuseppe Primiero and Shahid Rahman, eds.

Volume 10
Witnessed Years. Essays in Honor of Petr Hájek
Petr Cintula, Zuzana Haniková and Vítězslav Švejdar, eds.

Volume 11
Heuristics, Probability and Causality. A Tribute to Judea Pearl
Rina Dechter, Hector Geffner and Joseph Y. Halpern, eds.

Volume 12
Dialectics, Dialogue and Argumentation. An Examination of Douglas Walton's
Theories of Reasoning and Argument
Chris Reed and Christoher W. Tindale, eds.

Volume 13
Proofs, Categories and Computations. Essays in Honour of Grigori Mints
Solomon Feferman and Wilfried Sieg, eds.

Volume 14
Construction. Festschrift for Gerhard Heinzmann
Solomon Feferman and Wilfried Sieg, eds.

Volume 15
Hues of Philosophy. Essays in Memory of Ruth Manor
Anat Biletzki, ed.

Volume 16
Knowing, Reasoning and Acting. Essays in Honour of Hector J. Levesque.
Gerhard Lakemeyer and Sheila A. McIlraith, eds.

Volume 17
Logic without Frontiers. Festschrift for Walter Alexandre Carnielli on the
occasion of his 60th birthday
Jean-Yves Beziau and Marcelo Esteban Coniglio, eds.

Volume 18
Insolubles and Consequences. Essays in Honour of Stephen Read.
Catarina Dutilh Novaes and Ole Thomassen Hjortland, eds.

Volume 19
From Quantification to Conversation. Festschrift for Robin Cooper on the
occasion of his 65th birthday
Staffan Larsson and Lars Borin, eds

Volume 20
The Goals of Cognition. Essays in Honour of Cristiano Castelfranchi
Fabio Paglieri, Luca Tummolini, Rino Falcone and Maria Miceli, eds.

Tributes Series Editor
Dov Gabbay   dov.gabbay@kcl.ac.uk

The Goals of Cognition
Essays in honour of Cristiano Castelfranchi

edited by

Fabio Paglieri,

Luca Tummolini,

Rino Falcone,

and

Maria Miceli

ISBN 978-1-84890-094-3

College Publications
Scientific Director: Dov Gabbay
Managing Director: Jane Spurr
Department of Computer Science
King's College London, Strand, London WC2R 2LS, UK

http://www.collegepublications.co.uk

Cover by Laraine Welch, based on an idea by Vania Castelfranchi
Printed by Lightning Source, Milton Keynes, UK

Contents

Part VI Communication

Part VII Norms, organizations, and institutions

Part VIII Cognitive and computational social science

Part IX Afterword

List of Contributors

Giulia Andrighetto
Laboratory of Agent-based Social Simulation (LABSS), Institute of Cognitive
Sciences and Technologies, CNR, Italy
Department of Political and Social Sciences, European University Institute of
Florence, Italy
e-mail: giulia.andrighetto@istc.cnr.it

Luis Antunes
Laboratory of Agent Modelling (LabMAg), Faculty of Sciences, University of
Lisbon, Portugal
e-mail: xarax@di.fc.ul.pt

Sebastiano Bagnara
Faculty of Architecture, University of Sassari-Alghero, Italy
e-mail: sebastiano.bagnara@gmail.com

Guido Boella
Department of Computer Science, University of Torino, Italy
e-mail: guido@di.unito.it

Samuel Bowles
University of Siena, Italy and Santa Fe Institute, USA
e-mail: samuel.bowles@gmail.com

Martin V. Butz
Cognitive Modeling, Department of Computer Science, University of
Tübingen, Germany
e-mail: martin.butz@uni-tuebingen.de

Cristiano Castelfranchi
Goal-Oriented Agents Lab (GOAL), Institute of Cognitive Sciences and
Technologies, CNR, Italy
e-mail: cristiano.castelfranchi@istc.cnr.it

Yurij Castelfranchi
Department of Sociology and Anthropology, Faculty of Philosophy and

Human Sciences, Universidade Federal de Minas Gerais, Brazil
e-mail: ycastelfranchi@gmail.com

Helder Coelho
Laboratory of Agent Modelling (LabMAg), Faculty of Sciences, University of
Lisbon, Portugal
e-mail: hcoelho@di.fc.ul.pt

Rosaria Conte
Laboratory of Agent-based Social Simulation (LABSS), Institute of Cognitive
Sciences and Technologies, CNR, Italy
e-mail: rosaria.conte@istc.cnr.it

Giorgio Coricelli
Department of Economics, University of Southern California, USA
e-mail: giorgio.coricelli@usc.edu

Mehdi Dastani
Intelligent Systems Group, Utrecht University, The Netherlands
e-mail: mehdi@cs.uu.nl

Francesca D'Errico
Department of Education, Roma Tre University, Italy
e-mail: fderrico@uniroma3.it

Frank Dignum
Department of Computing Sciences, Utrecht University, The Netherlands
e-mail: dignum@cs.uu.nl

Virginia Dignum
Faculty of Technology, Policy and Management, Delft University of
Technology, The Netherlands
e-mail: M.V.Dignum@tudelft.nl

Nicola Dimitri
Department of Political Economy and Statistics, University of Siena, Italy
e-mail: dimitri@unisi.it

Patrick Doherty
Department of Computer and Information Science, Linköping University,
Sweden
e-mail: Patrick.Doherty@liu.se

Aldo Franco Dragoni
Department of Electronics, Artificial Intelligence and Telecommunications,
Università Politecnica delle Marche, Italy
e-mail: a.f.dragoni@univpm.it

Tarek el Sehity
Institute for Science of Ethical Wealth and Wealth Psychology, Sigmund Freud
Private University of Vienna, Austria
e-mail: tarek.el-sehity@sfu.ac.at

Elisabetta Erriquez

Department of Computer Science, University of Liverpool, UK
e-mail: E.Erriquez@liverpool.ac.uk

Rino Falcone
Goal-Oriented Agents Lab (GOAL), Institute of Cognitive Sciences and
Technologies, CNR, Italy
e-mail: rino.falcone@istc.cnr.it

Dov M. Gabbay
Group of Logic, Language and Computation, Department of Computer
Science, King's College London, UK
e-mail: dov.gabbay@kcl.ac.uk

Amelia Gangemi
Department of Cognitive Sciences, University of Messina and Scuola di
Psicoterapia Cognitiva, and Associazione di Psicologia Cognitiva, Italy
e-mail: gangemia@unime.it

Francesca Giardini
Laboratory of Agent-based Social Simulation (LABSS), Institute of Cognitive
Sciences and Technologies, CNR, Italy
e-mail: francesca.giardini@istc.cnr.it

Herbert Gintis
Santa Fe Institute, USA and Central European University, Hungary
e-mail: hgintis@comcast.net

David M. Godden
Department of Philosophy, Old Dominion University, USA
e-mail: dgodden@odu.edu

Marco Gori
Department of Information Engineering, University of Siena, Italy
e-mail: marco@dii.unisi.it

Davide Grossi
Agent Applications, Research and Technology Group, University of Liverpool,
Italy
e-mail: d.grossi@liverpool.ac.uk

Marco Guerini
Center for Information Technology (FBK-Irst), Italy
e-mail: guerini@fbk.eu

Swati Gupta
Program in Computational Social Cognition, Institute of High Performance
Computing, Singapore
e-mail: guptas@ihpc.a-star.edu.sg

Andreas Herzig
Université de Toulouse, IRIT-CNRS, France
e-mail: andreas.herzig@irit.fr

Alessandra Jacomuzzi

Department of Philosophy and Cultural Heritage, University Ca' Foscari, Italy
e-mail: alessandra.jacomuzzi@unive.it

Mateus Joffily
Center for Mind Brain Sciences-CIMEC, University of Trento, Italy
e-mail: mateus.joffily@unitn.it

Paolo Legrenzi
Department of Philosophy and Cultural Heritage, University Ca' Foscari, Italy
e-mail: paolo.legrenzi@gmail.com

Emiliano Lorini
Université de Toulouse, IRIT-CNRS, France
e-mail: lorini@irit.fr

Francesco Mancini
Scuola di Psicoterapia Cognitiva, Associazione di Psicologia Cognitiva, Italy
e-mail: mancini@apc.it

Francesca Marzo
Libera Università Internazionale degli Studi Sociali "Guido Carli", Italy
e-mail: fmarzo@luiss.it

John-Jules Ch. Meyer
Department of Information and Computing Sciences, University of Utrecht, The Netherlands
e-mail: jj@cs.uu.nl

Maria Miceli
Goal-Oriented Agents Lab (GOAL), Institute of Cognitive Sciences and Technologies, CNR, Italy
e-mail: maria.miceli@istc.cnr.it

Frédéric Moisan
Université de Toulouse, IRIT-CNRS, France
e-mail: moisan@irit.fr

Andrea Omicini
Department of Computer Science and Engineering (DISI), University of Bologna, Italy
e-mail: andrea.omicini@unibo.it

Andrew Ortony
Program in Computational Social Cognition, Institute of High Performance Computing, Singapore
Northwestern University, USA
e-mail: ortony@northwestern.edu

Fabio Paglieri
Goal-Oriented Agents Lab (GOAL), Institute of Cognitive Sciences and Technologies, CNR, Italy

e-mail: fabio.paglieri@istc.cnr.it

Mario Paolucci
Laboratory of Agent-based Social Simulation (LABSS), Institute of Cognitive
Sciences and Technologies, CNR, Italy
e-mail: mario.paolucci@istc.cnr.it

Domenico Parisi
Institute of Cognitive Sciences and Technologies, CNR, Italy
e-mail: domenico.parisi@istc.cnr.it

Vittorio Pelligra
Department of Economics and Business, University of Cagliari, Italy
e-mail: pelligra@unica.it

Giovanni Pezzulo
Goal-Oriented Agents Lab (GOAL), Institute of Cognitive Sciences and
Technologies & Institute of Computational Linguistics, CNR, Italy
e-mail: giovanni.pezzulo@cnr.it

Michele Piunti
Reply Whitehall, Italy
e-mail: m.piunti@reply.it

Raffaella Pocobello
Institute of Cognitive Sciences and Technologies, CNR, Italy
e-mail: raffaella.pocobello@istc.cnr.it

Isabella Poggi
Department of Education, Roma Tre University, Italy
e-mail: poggi@uniroma3.it

Simone Pozzi
Faculty of Architecture, University of Sassari-Alghero, Italy and
Deep Blue Consulting and Research, Italy
e-mail: simone.pozzi@gmail.com

Rainer Reisenzein
Institute of Psychology, University of Greifswald, Germany
e-mail: rainer.reisenzein@uni-greifswald.de

Alessandro Ricci
Department of Electronics, Informatics and Systems (DEIS), University of
Bologna, Italy
e-mail: a.ricci@unibo.it

Kayo Sakamoto
Program in Computational Social Cognition, Institute of High Performance
Computing, Singapore
e-mail: sakamotok@ihpc.a-star.edu.sg

Giovanni Sartor
Law Faculty - CIRSFID, University of Bologna, Italy
Law Department, European University Institute of Florence, Italy

e-mail: giovanni.sartor@eui.eu

Jaime Simão Sichman
Laboratório de Técnicas Inteligentes (LTI), Escola Politécnica (EP),
Universidade de São Paulo, Brazil
e-mail: jaime.sichman@poli.usp.br

Maury Silver
Department of Psychology, Yeshiva University, USA
e-mail: stivelsilv@gmail.com

Munindar P. Singh
Department of Computer Science, North Carolina State University, USA
e-mail: singh@ncsu.edu

Oliviero Stock
Center for Information Technology (FBK-Irst), Italy
e-mail: stock@fbk.eu

Luca Tummolini
Goal-Oriented Agents Lab (GOAL), Institute of Cognitive Sciences and
Technologies, CNR, Italy
e-mail: luca.tummolini@istc.cnr.it

Paolo Turrini
Faculty of Sciences, Technology and Communication, University of
Luxembourg, Luxembourg
e-mail: paolo.turrini@uni.lu

Wiebe Van der Hoek
Department of Computer Science, University of Liverpool, UK
e-mail: Wiebe.Van-Der-Hoek@liverpool.ac.uk

Leendert van der Torre
Faculty of Sciences, Technology and Communication, University of
Luxembourg, Luxembourg
e-mail: leon.vandertorre@uni.lu

Serena Villata
WIMMICS team, INRIA Sophia Antipolis, France
e-mail: serena.villata@inria.fr

Michael Wooldridge
Department of Computer Science, University of Oxford, UK
e-mail: mjw@cs.ox.ac.uk

Introduction

Getting to know the pupils of a true master speaks volumes about the mind-set and skills of their mentor. So, before discussing Cristiano Castelfranchi's intellectual odyssey (still very much in progress, we are happy to say), let us mention a few things about people that had the good luck of working with him, at various stages of their own education and/or career. In place of the somewhat cumbersome and pompous label of "pupils of Castelfranchi", we will christen them (us) as "Castelfrankians".[1] Here are a few points worth mentioning about this odd group of people:

- *Castelfrankians live among us!* Over the years, Castelfranchi managed to spawn a veritable host of students, colleagues, collaborators, and the like. So, be warned: Castelfrankians are many and multifarious (see next point), and you might be sitting next to one of them – come to think of it, if you are reading this, you are probably a Castelfrankian yourself!
- *Castelfrankians are not like him!* When Castelfranchi feels the urge to look at himself, he gets in front of a mirror; when he wishes to converse with himself, he does just that – often loudly, truth be told. What he does not, and never did, is imposing his ways to his pupils. Quite the opposite: autonomy and argumentativeness are the two features that Castelfranchi prizes above all in his interlocutors. As a result of that, not a single Castelfrankian does research as Castelfranchi does – not in the sense that they are not as good as him (some are, in their own ways, which is indeed remarkable), but in the sense that they do research differently from him, sometimes even drastically so, in more or less open conflict with his ideas and methods. Oddly, he does not mind that – in fact, the more confrontational former pupils turn out to be, the prouder they make him.
- *Castelfrankians are always more conservative than Castelfranchi!* This is one of three things that all Castelfrankians share (the other two follow below): no matter how hard they try, they will never manage to outdo their mentor

---

[1] Let us take this opportunity to set the phonetic record straight: the "chi" in "Castelfranchi" is correctly pronounced \'ki\, as in "kitchen", and not \'chi\, as in "children". Thus, to avoid the misspelling and mispronunciation that often plagued their mentor, Castelfrankians have opted for using the k to remove any ambiguity in their name.

2

in terms of revolutionary ideas, unconventional style, and sheer (but kind) disregard for the rituals and etiquette of academia. This is especially disconcerting, and at times downright depressing, for relatively young Castelfrankians: they would love nothing more than play the role of the innovative genius who rebels against the oppressive and outdated rule of their academic father figure, yet this pleasure is forever denied them. On the contrary, already at an early age they must learn to embrace the opposite attitude, counseling prudence and greater academic decorum to the scientific daredevil they happen to be working with. Castelfranchi, who probably never watched a single episode of *Star Trek*, is nevertheless thoroughly committed "to boldly go where no man has gone before", as per the motto of the famous spaceship. In doing just that, his style cannot be imitated, his momentum cannot be matched: this makes for a wonderful scientific ride, but forces Castelfrankians to play the part of the reactionaries.

- *Calstelfrankians are disciplinary nomads!* This is one of the most lasting effects of working with Castelfranchi: after some time, you discover that you are no longer able to conceive your entire scientific life within just one discipline, not even if doing so would ensure better chances of "academic survival" – as it is often the case, alas! Even more drastically, Castelfrankians end up looking at disciplines as mere instruments: they learn from their mentor that all that really matters in research are problems, that is, phenomena in need of explaining, and what tools one uses to do the explaining are irrelevant, as long as they are well suited for the task and applied with scientific rigor. Thus, Castelfrankians do not feel a sense of belonging to any particular "disciplinary church", and they fail to understand what is all the fuss about that. It is not as if they were jacks of all trades (they are not), it is just that they feel the need to specialize on specific problems, rather than on specific methods. Sometimes, this makes for an awkward living in today academia, where interdisciplinarity is regularly paid lip service, but rarely helps anyone getting tenured. Yet, the benefits of a life full of problems outdo the discomforts of a career without disciplines – see next point.

- *Castelfrankians have fun!* Happiness, for Castelfranchi, is in the pursuit of one's goals, not in their attainment. It is no happenstance that one of his favorite quotes is the well-known quip by Richard Feynman: "Science is like sex: sometimes something useful comes out, but that is not the reason we are doing it"[2]. As a modern day Sherlock Holmes, Castelfranchi feels alive, professionally speaking, only when the game is afoot, that is, when there is some intellectual puzzle occupying all of his attention and strenuously evading his attempts to solve it. The end of problems to struggle with would be for him nothing short than intellectual death. Conversely, a scientific problem is not a personal threat, in the sense that failing to understand something is, for Castelfranchi, the beginning of an exciting adventure, instead of something to be feared or avoided – not because one is necessarily sure of finding the right solution (or any solution), but because looking hard for it will be rewarding whatever the outcome, and well beyond it.

[2] Often quoted in a slightly different version: "Physics is like sex: sure, it may give some practical results, but that's not why we do it". The meaning, though, is the same.

This playful attitude is something all true Castelfrankians share with their mentor: in fact, such an attitude is the only strict requirement for working with him – if you do not have it, you cannot fake it. Unless you love struggling with problems, a day with Castelfranchi is a day in hell! Even at the apex of some grand scientific revelation, or in the middle of some well-deserved public celebration of his achievements, he will always manage to remind you (and himself) that the problems yet to be solved vastly outnumber those we already dealt with. What is worse, he will say that with a twinkle in his eyes and a smile on his lips.

This brief sketch of the Castelfrankians might strike some reader as too quixotic to do justice to their mentor. Indeed, those who do not know Castelfranchi might very well picture him in the act of appropriating Carl Jung's famous (alleged) quote, and exclaiming: "Thank God I'm Castelfranchi and not a Castelfrankian!"[3]. But for those who do know him, it will be easier to imagine Castelfranchi recognizing himself in this description of his former pupils, which of course was meant to be humorous, yet not too far off the mark. And, just to avoid offending anyone, let us be clear: we, the editors of this volume, are Castelfrankians of the purest breed, and proud to be! With all our quirks and strange habits, we would not want to do research in any other way, and we feel nothing but honored to trace back part of our scientific DNA to Cristiano.

More to the point, the broad scope and problem-oriented nature of Castelfranchi's research is fully reflected in the thirty-nine essays gathered in this volume, to honor his incredible career. Some of them have been written by true Castelfrankians, but the vast majority is authored by many of the scholars who happened to collaborate with him over the years, and/or have been influenced by his ideas. Some others were invited but could not participate in this volume, for a variety of reasons: however, as editors, we were taken aback by how few people declined our invitation, always expressing genuine regret and mentioning truly insurmountable difficulties. For any one who declined, at least five more were eager to accept. This gave us the measure of how deep Castelfranchi's scientific influence and personal kinship is felt in all the academic circles where he ventured during his career – which are indeed many, as this volume demonstrates.

In spite of this diversity, the contents of this book are remarkably coherent, and even systematic. They exhibit the same kind of coherence which is found in the solar system, where all planets differ in size, mass, structure, motion, and much more, yet they all revolve around the same star. For the papers in this collection, this center of gravity is the notion of *goal*. We are reminded of its centrality not only by the very title of this volume, but also by Castelfranchi's own contribution, at the very end of it. In that final chapter, he discusses goals as "the true center of cognition", around which all the rest is built. Incidentally, taking that perspective allows him to recap most of his scientific endeavors, spanning decades of research, since he consistently devoted his distinguished

---

[3] The phrase "Thank God I'm Jung and not a Jungian!" is attributed to Jung in Yandell, J. (1978). The imitation of Jung. An exploration of the meaning of "Jungian". *Spring*, 54–76 (in particular, on p. 57).

career to *understand cognition as goal-directed*. In his own words, "it's all about goals: action is for goals (and goals are for potential actions), knowledge is for goals, intelligence is for goals (solving problems via mental representations), sociality is for goals and goal-based, [and] emotions are goal-centered".

Around this pivotal and multifaceted notion of goals, of which Castelfranchi has been one of the foremost pioneers, all contributions to this volume orbit. Part I, "Representation, action and cognition", provides some essential groundwork to the whole edifice: goals are analyzed as anticipatory representations, whose main function is precisely to bridge the gap between cognition and action – more exactly, to make sure that cognition is *for* action, rather than disjointed from it. Giovanni Pezzulo (chapter 1) outlines Castelfranchi's project of re-founding cognitivism on the cybernetic idea of goal-directed action, spelling out its implications for our understanding of the mind and its connections with many recent developments in cognitive science. Martin Butz (chapter 2) discusses how anticipatory agents form spatial representations for flexible, goal-directed decision making and behavioral control, thus laying the foundations for the development and grounding of higher-level, symbolic cognition and abstract thought. The issue of development is then taken up by Marco Gori (chapter 3), who considers the implications of stage-based cognitive development for the next generation of learning systems and models in Artificial Intelligence.

Part II, "Reasons, reasoning and rationality", discusses how Castelfranchi's goal-centered view of cognition impacts on issues of reasoning and rationality, providing a garden variety of test cases and applications. Aldo Franco Dragoni (chapter 4) details a computational structure for representing recursive mental states, intended to constitute the semantic level of a formal language to deal with cognitive dynamics. In a similar vein, Mehdi Dastani and Leendert van der Torre (chapter 5) revisits the well-known BOID architecture (beliefs, obligations, intentions, desires), to demonstrate how it can handle goal generation in agent systems. Fabio Paglieri (chapter 6) focuses on beliefs, using Peirce's notion of "the irritation of doubt" to highlight the goal-centered nature of belief dynamics, and to uncover a close kinship between pragmatism and goal theory. David Godden (chapter 7) shows how the psychology of belief, and the role goals play in it, should inform process-based accounts of argumentation, at the same time posing two problems for assessing the rationality of arguments. Paolo Legrenzi and Alessandra Jacomuzzi (chapter 8) discuss the goals of analogies, describing the mechanisms of transfer of the solution from one problem to another, as well as the main cognitive and computational theories of analogical reasoning. The attention shifts towards decision-making with Nicola Dimitri (chapter 9), who points out a behavioral duality in intertemporal choice regarding losses and gains, and suggests a more complex role of delay tolerance in explaining such choices. Time and decision are also central in Maury Silver's contribution (chapter 10), where he fleshes out an intriguing account of self-deception as procrastinating further investigation on current evidence, and then proceeds to illustrate the import of this view for the much debated notion of self-deception. Finally, Francesca Marzo (chapter 11) compares Castelfranchi's goal-centered view of rationality to the capability approach developed by Amartya Sen, highlights strong analogies between key concepts in both theories (e.g., goals, norm-driven behavior, functioning values), and uses this as a stepping stone to suggest a novel perspective on preference dynamics.

Part III, "Emotion and motivation", takes advantage of Castelfranchi's rich work on emotions as goal-centered constructs, to develop it in further details and unexpected directions. Rainer Reisenzein (chapter 12) contrasts the belief-desire compound theory of emotion, that he attributes to Castelfranchi, with his own causal feeling theory, and finds the former wanting in its ability to provide a convincing characterization of emotional states. Giorgio Coricelli and Mateus Joffily (chapter 13) focus on the neural correlates and the role of cognitive-based emotions in decision-making, arguing that cognitive processes, such as counterfactual thinking and social comparison, elicit a specific class of emotions, of which regret and envy constitute paradigmatic examples. Isabella Poggi and Francesca D'Errico (chapter 14) analyze pride in connection to the goals of power, image and self-image, thus distinguishing three types of pride (dignity, superiority, and arrogance pride), discussing their functions as displays of dominance, and connecting them to bodily expression in political debates. Francesco Mancini and Amelia Gangemi (chapter 15) illustrate the clinical implications of a goal-centered approach to cognition and emotions, in relation to depressive reaction and its two main paradoxes, pessimistic fixation (why do depressed people continue to dwell on what they believe to be unattainable and/or lost forever?) and lack of motivation (why do depressed people lose interest in alternative goals, instead of trying to compensate for the loss they suffered?). Emiliano Lorini (chapter 16) revisits and extends his own analysis of expectation and expectation-based emotions (e.g., hope and fear), which he originally co-authored with Castelfranchi, by distinguishing between goal value and belief strength in the anatomy of expectations, thus providing a formal analysis of the intensity of hope and fear. Samuel Bowles and Herbert Gintis (chapter 17), building on Castelfranchi's work on the relationship between norms and emotions, model the process by which social emotions (e.g., shame, guilt, pride) can positively affect social interaction, by favoring high levels of cooperation with minimal levels of costly punishment, and discuss under what conditions such emotions might have evolved.

This also serves to introduce the rest of the volume, which describes in great details how Castelfranchi's goal-centered view of cognition radically transforms and deepens our understanding of social phenomena. Part IV, "Power, dependence and social interaction", concentrates on power and dependence as the essential building blocks of social interaction – so much so, that they are found to be relevant for the most disparate domains and levels of analysis, from formal models to socio-cognitive theories, via social simulations. Vittorio Pelligra (chapter 18) identifies the greatest limit of game theory in its poor understanding of intersubjectivity, reviews empirical data highlighting the relevance of mentalizing and empathy in strategic interaction, and argues that conceptualizing a hierarchy of higher order beliefs in psychological game theory improves our formal understanding of the motivational structure of real social agents. Davide Grossi and Paolo Turrini (chapter 19) build on Castelfranchi's work on dependence theory to develop a full-fledged game-theoretical analysis of social interaction in terms of dependence and related notions, such as dependence cycle and reciprocity, thus revealing a close, unexpected kinship between game theory and dependence theory. Helder Coelho (chapter 20) puts the notion of power, in particular social power, in contact with that of leadership, distinguishes power-over from power-of, and dwells on the implications of such an analysis for understanding and transforming contemporary societies, be they real or artificial. Raffaella Pocobello and Tarek el Sehity (chapter 21) illustrate how Castelfranchi's goal-centered approach to cognition sheds light on the mental components of a new paradigm in the field of mental health, recovery, understood as the individual's capacity to develop a meaningful life and a self-concept beyond the illness, with a strong emphasis on autonomy and empowerment.

Part V, "Trust & delegation", deals with the theory of trust and delegation, one of the most influential contributions of Castelfranchi and his team to multi-agent systems and social science. Rino Falcone and Maria Miceli (chapter 22) analyze the complex relationships between trusting and being trustworthy, with special emphasis on how the fact that agent X trusts agent Y might be perceived by Y as a sign of X's trustworthiness, and how being trusted will also increase the likelihood that Y proves in fact to be worthy of that trust. Andreas Herzig, Emiliano Lorini and Frédéric Moisan (chapter 23) propose a simple logic of belief and action that allows to express the concepts of belief, goal, ability, willingness, and opportunity, upon which the socio-cognitive theory of trust is built, and then provide a decision procedure and a proof of completeness for such logic. Serena Villata, Guido Boella, Dov Gabbay and Leendert van der Torre (chapter 24) develop a cognitive model of conflicts in trust using argumentation, in which trust serves to minimize the uncertainty in the interactions of information sources, while argumentation is used to reason about trust and its two main dimensions, competence and sincerity. Elisabetta Erriquez, Wiebe van der Hoek and Michael Wooldridge (chapter 25) take distrust, rather than trust, as their primitive concept, and use it to model how agents in a society may form stable coalitions based on their mutually perceived level of trustworthiness, or lack thereof – an approach that they successfully apply to a fascinating case of complex trust and distrust relationships, namely, Shakespeare's *Othello*. Patrick Doherty and John-Jules Meyer (chapter 26) focus on the logic of delegation, proposing to extend its application, typically limited to multi-agent systems and social sciences, to collaborative robotic systems, by instantiating delegation as a speech act and then illustrating its usefulness in a running prototype, used in collaborative missions with multiple unmanned aerial vehicle systems.

Part VI, "Communication", brings together many different strands of Castelfranchi's work, such as persuasion, deception, gestures, and behavioral implicit communication, to highlight their mutual connections and shared roots. Oliviero Stock and Marco Guerini (chapter 27) take on Castelfranchi's frequent invitation to understand the ethical implications of building intelligent machines, *before* we build them, and apply it to persuasive systems, offering both a bird's eye view and a critical assessment of this thriving research area. Sebastiano Bagnara and Simone Pozzi (chapter 28) discuss the import of Castelfranchi's notion of behavioral implicit communication for the design of Natural User Interfaces, arguing that traces of human activity could be used to teach such interfaces what are the relevant gestures and what is their intended meaning for users – two aspects on which current systems are sadly lacking. Michele Piunti, Alessandro Ricci and Luca Tummolini (chapter 29) introduce a vision of agent-oriented Ambient Intelligence (AmI) systems, understood as not only mirroring but also augmenting the physical world, and discuss how to enable such systems to detect and digitally represent the traces left by humans in the physical world, in order to fully exploit the value of stigmergy as a coordination mechanism. The relevance of stigmergy for intelligent coordination is also the focus of Andrea Omicini (chapter 30), who reviews and classifies some of the main types of environment-based coordination, to discuss their impact on the engineering of self-organising socio-technical systems. Swati Gupta, Kayo Sakamoto and Andrew Ortony (chapter 31) endeavor to provide a comprehensive and systematic account of the ubiquitous phenomenon of verbal deception, building on the work done by Castelfranchi and many others on this topic, and ending up with two original taxonomies, one for the types of verbal deception, and one for the strategies used to verbally deceive.

Part VII, "Norms, organizations and institutions", focuses on another central aspect of Castelfranchi's theorizing: the nature, dynamics and evolution of norms and normative reasoning, as well as their role in the emergence of institutions and in the functioning of organizations. Pivotal to that theory is the notion of commitment, which is the topic addressed by Munindar Singh (chapter 32): he first provides a comprehensive and authoritative survey of the rich literature on this topic, with special focus on commitments in multi-agent systems, highlighting key concepts, lingering confusions, and promising directions for future research; then he endeavors to present the main points of disagreements between his own views and those of Castelfranchi, in spite of their largely shared background and interests. Giovanni Sartor (chapter 33) discusses norm compliance, arguing that complex normative systems, albeit very successful at directing people's thoughts and actions, cannot be, as a whole, objects of the individual agents' mental attitudes. Still, for Sartor this feature is not evidence against the mentalistic theory of norms developed by Castelfranchi and collaborators, if one acknowledges that the agents adopt a general policy-based intention to comply with the normative system as a whole, which can be based on different mental attitudes, ranging from self-interest to pro-social motivations. Giulia Andrighetto, Rosaria Conte and Francesca Giardini (chapter 34) use a simulation-based methodology to model how cognitive activities and representations affect institutional change, and play a decisive role in their selection and retention: as a relevant case study, they focus on enforcing institutions that are hypothesized to have evolved from retaliatory to punishing, and even sanctioning, systems, thanks to and by means of specific cognitive capacities. Jaime Simão Sichman (chapter 35) articulates and defends the idea that autonomous cognitive agents, immersed in an open environment, are more efficient and adaptive to changes if they can represent, elaborate and exploit information about other agents and or-

8

ganizations, since this enables a virtuous loop between agents interactions, coalitions, and organizations. Frank Dignum and Virgina Dignum (chapter 36) investigate how norms about having emotions, as well as sanctions for their violation, can exist and make sense, in spite of the fact that emotions are something that people cannot (easily) control, and therefore a very strange object of normative concern: nonetheless, they provide a formal description of these kinds of norms, to discuss whether they are the same as other norms or have special properties.

Part VIII, "Cognitive and computational social science", takes a more methodological and meta-theoretical stance on Castelfranchi's work, to consider the implications of agent-based modeling and simulation for the understanding of cognitive and social phenomena. Domenico Parisi (chapter 37) argues that scientific theories should be formulated and presented as computer-based artifacts, rather than verbally or even mathematically, in order to remove ambiguity, overcome disciplinary fragmentation, avoid value-laden implications and biases, and facilitate technological transfer and socially relevant application of those theories: he then exemplifies the benefits and potentialities of this method with his ongoing work on evolutionary robotics, discussing what we can learn about motivations, emotions, mental life, language, social interaction, economic dynamics, politics, and even culture, by trying to evolve robots capable of manifesting such phenomena in their artificial ecology. Mario Paolucci (chapter 38) presents social simulation as one of our best chances for breakthroughs in understanding society, and yet also discusses why social simulation so far largely failed to deliver substantial results on this big challenge: then he introduces the concept of crowdsourcing, elaborating on how it could positively reshape this methodology for computational social science. Luis Antunes (chapter 39) describes the epistemological challenges and risks entailed by a simulation-based research program, with an emphasis on what types of mistakes are most likely to occur at various stages of the process (from conceptual analysis to modeling, from simulation design to actual implementation, and on), and what methods are available to predict, minimize and correct them – an enterprise that, according to Antunes, has been central to Castelfranchi's approach, often focused on foundational issues both in multi-agent systems and in social science. Finally, Yurij Castelfranchi (chapter 40), starting from a small digression on the infamous micro-macro, agency-structure dilemma of social sciences, shows how insights coming from multi-agent systems and the theory of social functions could improve our understanding of two key societal issues: the politics and economy of science in the contemporary regime of knowledge production, and the functions and issues of the public communication of science and technology. This also uncovers a common core between Cristiano Castelfranchi's theoretical contributions (in particular, his ideas on social emergence and "immergence") and his political positions on science communication and science policies[4].

This last contribution is especially tinged with affection, which is no surprise, since the author is Castelfranchi's eldest son, a researcher himself (in sociology), as well as a science writer, journalist, traveler, and more – in sum, a true Castelfrankian. Exactly like his younger brother, Vania Castelfranchi, also a great traveler, as well as a professional actor, director, author, mime, juggler, teacher, etc. It is thanks to Vania that this volume is graced by such a nice cover, which we would have never had the talent to design or the competence to realize. Finally, our little conspiracy in putting together this volume, unbeknownst to Cristiano, would have not been possible without the generous help of Rosanna Bosi, psychotherapist, pedagogist, instrumentalist, and, most importantly, the love of his life. If Cristiano had edited this volume himself, he would have certainly dedicated it to her, as he did so often in the past. This time, we will take the liberty of acting on his behalf, and dedicate this volume for Cristiano to Ros, the worthy companion of our wonderful teacher, inspired colleague, and dear friend.

Rome, November 2012

THE EDITORS

---

[4] As mentioned, the volume is completed by Cristiano Castelfranchi's own contribution, in Part IX, "Afterword": there he offers an impressive summary of almost 40 years of research on goals and goal-directed behavior. However, we briefly sketched the contents of that chapter at the very beginning of this Introduction, and we would never presume to summarize his monumental contribution in just a few lines, nor we dare trying. Thus, no more is said about it here, except for a strong suggestion to readers to peruse Cristiano's paper *before* anything else, especially if they are not yet familiar with his work. Doing so, in fact, will offer them a favored standpoint to appreciate all other contributions, as well as a fresh angle on cognition in general.

Part I
Representation, action, and cognition

Chapter 1
Re-founding cognitivism based on the cybernetic idea of goal-directed action

Giovanni Pezzulo

Abstract Cristiano Castelfranchi's legacy is the re-foundation of cognitivism based on the Cybernetic notion of goal-directed action. I illustrate how the idea of the cognitive mind as a Cybernetic machine forms the backbone of almost all Castelfranchi's theories, across all the domains of behavioral, cognitive and social sciences. By analyzing this idea in the context of current cognitive science and neuroscience research, I suggest some key challenges to continue developing a novel cognitivism that has goal processing at its core.

1 Introduction

The "fil rouge" that links the theoretical incursions of Cristiano Castelfranchi in many disciplinary fields (philosophy, artificial intelligence, psychology, and the social sciences, among others) is the central notion of a cognitive mind that is autonomous, purposive and goal-directed, and operates as—or, better, *is a Cybernetic machine*. In Castelfranchi's view, all the diverse functions that cognitive science attributes to the mind are produced by the same Cybernetic mechanism that selects goals based on beliefs, matches discrepancies between goal and current states, and actuate patterns of action that achieve goals by minimizing the discrepancies.

The idea of the cognitive mind as a Cybernetic machine, which is central in all Castelfranchi's theories, is deeply rooted in an evolutionary argument that has two main parts. First, the main function of the mind is determining action success. Second, the (progressive) passage from primitive action control mechanisms to Cybernetic controllers has ultimately produced the cognitive revolution and an "autonomization" of the mind from the demands of situated action, in that (i) the function of the mind becomes achieving goals and not

Giovanni Pezzulo
Goal-Oriented Agents Lab (GOAL), Institute of Cognitive Sciences and Technologies & Institute of Computational Linguistics, CNR, Italy
e-mail: giovanni.pezzulo@cnr.it

obtaining rewards per se (ii) goal representations can be, and actually are, internally manipulated independent of overt action, and achieved independent of the rewards they determine.

Because goals (and the Cybernetic mechanisms for achieving them) are the cornerstones of the cognitive mind, Castelfranchi's view is a peculiar form of cognitivism: one in which the foundational notions of purpose and teleology [41] play (again) a key role in explaining behavior (including social behavior), cognition, and even brain organization. Similar to traditional cognitivism, a central role is played by the notion of *internal manipulation of representations*. Here "manipulation" has to be interpreted quite literally, in the sense Tolman [45] describes cognitive maps as internally navigable before (and without) actually moving, and Piaget [39] describes mental operations as "internal" counterparts of overt actions. A second aspect of traditional cognitivism that is maintained is that, although embodiment and situatedness might play a role in the arise and functioning of a cognitive mind, still it is an *autonomous* entity that is partially disengaged from the control of the body and associated constraints.

At the same time, Castelfranchi's view implies two main departures from traditional cognitivism: (i) the cognitive mind is organized around a Cybernetic mechanism rather than according to the perception-cognition-action "pipeline" of information processing; (ii) as cognitive and social activities are organized around satisfaction of goals (via Cybernetic mechanisms), the notions of goals, goal processing, and goal representations play a key role in any cognitive theory. Below I discuss these two aspects in more detail.

2 Cognitive mind as a Cybernetic mechanism

A key aspect of Castelfranchi's view, which distinguishes it from traditional cognitivism, is the idea that the cognitive mind is essentially a Cybernetic mechanism, and all the abilities traditionally studied in cognitive science (e.g., attention, memory, action selection, emotions, social skills) are parts of its functioning.

A well-known example of Cybernetic mechanism, which can serve as a basis for this discussion, is the TOTE (Test, Operate, Test, Exit) model of Miller, Galanter and Pribram [27]. As illustrated in fig. 1, in a TOTE unit, firstly a goal is tested to see if it has been achieved (the *test* component): if not, an operation is executed (the *operate* component) until the test on the goal's achievement is successful (*test* and *exit* components).

A TOTE unit offers a simplified but almost complete functional view of goal-directedness, as it interactively produces (sub)goals, projects them into patterns of actions and expected outcomes, and monitors their achievement. Castelfranchi has adopted and extended the TOTE model to explain how goals are selected based on beliefs, expectations and current affordances, how plans and actions are selected that achieve such goals, and also how parts of this

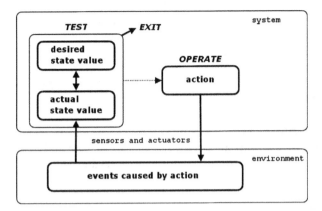

Fig. 1 The main features of the TOTE model [27]. Words in *Italics* are the main processes composing it (test, operate, test, exit). Thin arrows represent information flows. The double-headed arrow represents a process of comparison between the desired and the actual state value. The dashed arrow represents the fact that an action is selected and executed in the case the *Test* fails, but not how it is selected. The bold arrow represents a switch in the sequence of processes implemented by the system.

process can be delegated to other agents, thus linking individual and social mechanisms of cognition; see [34] for a discussion.

As it forms the core component of a full-fledged cognitive mind, the TOTE model would appear in the first chapter of a cognitive science textbook *a la* Castelfranchi (or better a "Theoretical Psychology" textbook). In such a textbook, the TOTE model would be the key organizing principle of cognitive processing, and help framing the discussion of all the (socio-)cognitive abilities that Castelfranchi has investigated; each of these abilities would appear as a chapter in the textbook, such as for instance: attention (to the events that are more relevant given the goal), memory retrieval (of previous episodes of goal achievement), anticipation (of the emotional consequences of goal achievement, of future opportunities for goal achievement, or of events that conflict with the goal), decision-making (what (sub)goal is worth pursuing), monitoring (of goal achievement), delegation (of a goal to another individual), help (as the realization of a goal of another individual), influence (as the change of the beliefs and goals of another individual), means-ends reasoning (selecting the means to achieve the desired goal), social reasoning (in which subgoals are achieved by other individuals), complex emotions such as relief or disappointment (as linked to the emotional and cognitive consequences of goal processing), sense of agency (as the self-attribution of choices and actions), problem solving (as the "internal" reuse of TOTE units, without overtly executing the actions), and psychopathology (as dysfunctional goal and social emotion processing).

This short and informal excursus reveals why Castelfranchi's theories maintain a unitary nature although they apply to the more diverse domains of cognition and interaction, and help making the case for an "Aristotelian methodology" that uses first principles to inspire multidisciplinary research.

Furthermore, an advantage of such an imaginary textbook is that all the aforementioned (individual and social) abilities would not appear as disconnected, as it is the case in many real cognitive science textbooks, but rather stem from the very same principles of organization of the mind, as they are all part of its functioning. In striking contrast with many rational-level descriptions, which analyze cognitive abilities as if they had individual and disconnected functions (e.g., what perception is for, what memory is for), Castelfranchi aims at an over-compassing "functional level" description of the cognitive mind, in which all abilities are part of a larger picture, as they all serve for goal achievement within the Cybernetic mechanism described so far.

3 Goal achievement as the key organizing principle of the cognitive mind

The second departure of Castelfranchi's view from traditional cognitivism is the key role assigned to *goals*, goal processing and goal representations in the cognitive mind.

In this respect, it is worth noting that Castelfranchi is principally interested in practical (means-ends) reasoning, such as for instance the decision to take the car or the train (the means) to go to the beach (the ends), and in other mental operations that link to planning and the selection of goal-directed actions, such as for instance the cognitive mechanisms that permit mechanics to assemble and dismantle a motor in their minds before doing the same thing in practice. For this reason, he has principally focused his research on *goal representations* rather than on other forms of representation that are less tied to the exigencies of action performance (e.g., how declarative representations afford deduction).

Goals have several facets, and play many roles in Castelfranchi's view of a cognitive mind. First and foremost, goal representations combine motivational and representational elements, linking to affective and predictive mechanisms in the brain, respectively. Castelfranchi's view is related to theories in social psychology and (neuro)economy, that link goals to motivation and value (e.g., [2, 26]), but puts more emphasis on the dependence of goals on beliefs, rather than directly on values and rewards.

This view is also well connected with action-based approaches in computational motor control (e.g. [44, 47]), cognitive neuroscience (e.g., [18, 22, 24]), ideomotor theory (e.g., [23]), and philosophy (e.g., [11, 31]), which emphasize predictive goal processing, internal modeling, and intentionality in action. However, in Castelfranchi's theories goals do not only serve for steering and controlling action (as recognized by action-based views), but are also active besides action control, such as for instance when desired and actual state of the environment are compared, or in the decision to trust or delegate a task to another person. This *autonomy* of goal processing from the demands of action control corresponds to an autonomization of the cognitive mind itself. Moreover, Castelfranchi draws a picture of goal selection and goal processing that is far richer than most of the accounts mentioned so far. In his models of individual and social phenomena, Castelfranchi has often "dissected" and taxonomized all the cognitive and affective ingredients—beliefs, expectations, emotions—that accompany goal selection and goal processing, in all their phases, analyzing for instance which are the necessary beliefs that an agent must have for selecting a certain goal, or what affective and anticipatory states are characteristic of the emotions that are associated to goal achievement or failure (e.g., relief or regret).

Using this "Linnean" methodology, Castelfranchi has applied a goal-based analysis to two contexts that are broader than those typically considered in the aforementioned literatures: achievement of distal intentions and social action. Relative to the former issue, goals become part of a sophisticated means-end reasoning process, in which not only the immediate action outcomes but also distal ones, side-effects (intended and non-intended), and how the world changes must be taken into account. Relative to the latter issue, in contrast with other views of social cognition that emphasize imitative or population-level dynamics, Castelfranchi highlights that goals are the "currency" of social cognition; this permits to develop sophisticated models of the micro-structure of sociality, such as for instance how an agent can help another agent by satisfying one of its goals, how an agent can have goals relative to another agent (e.g., changing its beliefs), how an agent can delegate one of its goals to another agent, on what bases an agent trusts another agent [8, 12]. Furthermore, Castelfranchi's notion of goal-directedness is highly heuristic in psychopathology, as it permits to link a broad range of pathologies to specific dysfunctional mechanisms of goal monitoring, selection, anticipation, and social emotion processing.

These considerations illustrate the pervasiveness of goals in Castelfranchi's picture of cognitive mind. However, there is more than that. From a (more speculative) evolutionary perspective, goals form an "ecology" in the mind in that they have become autonomous from basic drives and rewards. The main activity of a cognitive mind consists in achieving goals, not obtaining rewards (although of course in many cases the former entails the latter). This view permits to study choice episodes in which goals are achieved despite they are not rewarding (e.g., Muzio Scevola who puts his hand on fire, or the altruistic punishment of defectors).

Goal dynamics explain the autonomy of the cognitive mind. Goals are prescriptive of conducts, in that they constrain, monitor and regulate behavior toward the realization of some specific state of affairs. First, actions are selected on the basis of goals that are autonomously generated, rather than being dictated by current stimuli. Second, as already remarked, purposive behavior means that cognitive agents pursue their goals, not that they (only) maximize rewards; again, this entails that what the cognitive mind monitors is goal satisfaction, not (only) the obtainment of rewards (although of course goal achievement and increase of the fitness are related at the evolutionary level). Third, it is neither a stimulus nor a goal representation that steers action directly, but a mismatch between desired and actual states –a fully internal, autonomous operation of the mind. Overall, goals determine a *cognitive revolution* in that goal-directed agents do not simply adapt to their environments, but actively *change* it to make it more similar to its goals. This has lead profound changes in the ecological niches of goal-directed agents, which have become increasingly social and able to structure their environments to better satisfy their goals (in turn, these changes have determined profound modifications of individual cognition).

As I have emphasized, goal dynamics are (partially) autonomous from action dynamics. However, to be complete the theory has to explain how the two domains of goals and actions connect. Castelfranchi's solution to this problem uses, again, the notion of TOTE. Because of the demands of the Cybernetic controllers (e.g., the TOTE), goal representations cannot be only symbolic or pseudo-linguistic, but must relate to sensorimotor patterns that permit a matching with external states. This view of goal-directedness allows for hierarchical organizations in which higher levels provide constraints for lower levels (similar to [40]), and in which abstract goal representations (no matter how coded) link to concrete sensorimotor states that can be directly matched, and which act as "signs" that the abstract goal has been achieved. For instance, seeing one's picture on the Time magazine can indicate that the abstract goal of "becoming famous" has been achieved. Note however that goals can be specified and matched in multiple ways. For instance, one can assess that a glass is full by watching at the level of liquid, lifting it to sense its weight, or even ask another person. As all these operations can be used interchangeably, this example indicates (again) that goal processing is autonomous with respect to the modalities of its achievement and monitoring.

4 Current and future challenges

Cristiano Castelfranchi's research is (purposively) unrespectful of disciplinary boundaries, trends and authorities. He defends:

1. the notion of representation-based cognition from various "reductionisms" (from time to time incarnated in behaviorism, anti-representational connectionism, dynamicism, radical embodiment, etc.);
2. the importance of studying purpose and teleology of minds at the functional level, before (and even without) mechanistic and neuronal explanations;
3. the centrality of minds against the "brain reductionism" that only focuses on the *neural underpinnings of function x*, without first asking what *function x* is;
4. the importance of cognitive-level explanations, against emerging trends that only focus on biological bases and genetic determinants of behaviors;
5. the importance of theories against (early) formalizations, which bring the risk of changing the theory for adapting to the formalism, not vice versa;
6. the importance of conceptual clarifications, against the idea that no theory is possible without empirical confirmation.

Despite his refusal of current trends (or perhaps because so), several aspects of Castelfranchi's view put it in a favorable position to deal with current open issues in the cognitive and social sciences. Below I shortly discuss five examples of how Castelfranchi's ideas have the potential to bring substantial contributes to current and future hot-topics in these disciplines, and beyond.

Re-founding cognitivism based on the Cybernetic idea of goal-directed action

Castelfranchi's legacy is the re-foundation of cognitivism based on the Cybernetic notion of goal-directed action. The most important, high-gain challenge for Castelfranchi and the many researchers who were influenced by his theories consists in continuing his efforts towards a full fledged "goal theory": a goal-centered theoretical framework that can provide a theoretical foundation for future advancements in cognitive science and neuroscience, psychopathology, and the human and social sciences at large.

Action-based and embodied approaches to cognition are becoming a strong paradigm that will plausibly dominate the field in the next decades. Castelfranchi's idea of goal dynamics can enrich this paradigm, expanding its scope from action performance to goal processing (an entirely autonomous *mental* operation) and from on-line action performance to off-line thought, across individual and social cognitive domains. Goal-directedness, and the Cybernetic mechanisms for achieving goals in the cognitive mind, could really provide unifying principles for addressing the full complexity of cognitive phenomena, reconciling cognitive processes with bodily, brain, environmental and social dynamics.

Autonomy and embodiment: are they contrasting requirements?

A second, deeply interrelated advancement consists in studying autonomization of the mind from the demands and the dynamics of the body. As recent theories of grounded cognition are increasingly demonstrating, embodiment is important to explain cognition [4]. However, a cognitive mind *a la* Castelfranchi is essentially autonomous for what concerns its cognitive processing (operations that are not conducted for the sake of acting here and now), its agenda (overcoming current affordances in favor of intertemporal coordination and the realization of distal intentions [6]), and its representations (e.g., forming concepts such as "begin" and "end" that are about mental states and mental processing and not about the external world). Understanding how the constraints of embodiment and the necessity of autonomization of the mind combine is an open issue for future research [37, 35].

Explaining the loop between individual and social dimensions

A third important avenue for future research consists in studying the loop between individual and social dimensions in cognition, behavior and learning.
On the one hand, goals determine a mind-to-reality direction, and profoundly
change and structure the ecological niches of cognitive agents. Parallel to this
"externalization" process, there is an equally important process of "internalization" of intellectual and social practices, which takes many forms, from
cultural learning to the development of self-regulation skills as the internalization of face-to-face communication and interaction strategies. Castelfranchi
has already studied parts of these dynamics under the labels of micro-macro
(i.e., from individual cognition to social emergence, institutions and cultures)
and macro-micro (i.e., how social dynamics influence individual cognition and
behavior) determinants of behavior and cognition [12]. However, several important aspects of this process are unknown. For instance, although it is widely
believed that sociality and language change the mind and cognition, it is still
unknown how this precisely happen and if, as a consequence of this process,
the cognitive mind becomes *essentially* social and linguistic [19].

Grounding goal theory in the brain and its prediction and value systems

Goal theory *a la* Castelfranchi is firmly established as a functional-level theory.
As a fourth challenge, it has to be grounded in brain mechanisms to be further
specified and empirically tested. The cross-fertilization of functional, mechanistic and neuronal explanations can shed light on several aspects of brain
functioning and brain organization (of humans and other animals), as these
complementary aspects are rarely investigated in combination.

   Goal representations are described as a having complementary *motivational*
and *predictive* aspects; thus, mapping goal theory into neural mechanisms
should start from the analysis of brain codes for motivational and predictive dynamics. First, a deep investigation of the relations between goals and
values is necessary. Current research in cognitive neuroscience reveals that
value representations are pervasive in the brain, in all its perceptual, cognitive, motor and social aspects, and investigation of the neural underpinnings
of rewards lies at the foundations of animal cognition, neuroeconomics and
social neuroscience (e.g., [1, 21, 42]). Castelfranchi has always refuted reward-
(or preference-) based explanations of behavior in favor of more sophisticated
analyses of goal dynamics. To map goal theory into the brain substrate of value
representation, it is necessary to draw a complete picture of the affective and
motivational constructs that are linked to goals, such as urgency and value,
and to study how abstract goal representations link to the basic repertoire of
an organism's drives and affective states. Recent studies in neuroeconomics
try to establish links between goal and reward dynamics, suggesting that the
former could reuse mechanisms initially developed for the latter [29] and that
the selection between abstract goals could follow similar rules as the selection
between simpler actions that are directly linked to rewards [10, 9, 43]. These

and other ideas could constitute a starting point for linking goal processing (and ideally the TOTE) to brain substrate, including its functioning in social interactions and its malfunctioning in psychopathology [28].

The second aspect of brain functioning that is particularly relevant for goal theory is prediction. A parallel can be established between the idea that *the mind is essentially an anticipatory device* [6, 36], and current theories emphasizing that *prediction is the main organizing principle of brain functioning* is prediction, such as *proactive brain, predictive coding, prospective coding,* and the *Bayesian brain,* see e.g., [3, 13, 14, 15, 16]. Furthermore, the idea of *active inference* holds the promise to explain mechanisms of the TOTE in terms of predictive brain dynamics [17, 33]. These and other proposals could help explaining how the brain produces the expectations (and beliefs) that are part and parcel of Castelfranchi's theories.

In addition to those two aspects of brain processing, motivation and prediction, many other parts of goal theory can be grounded in neuroscience; two interesting directions of research are linking Castelfranchi's ideas of cognitive control and self-control to theories of executive functions in the brain [5, 25, 20, 46] and clarifying the "division of labour" between properly goal-directed actions and additional mechanisms, habitual and Pavlovian, that control behavior [30].

Explaining goal-directedness from simpler to complex organisms

A final challenge that I propose is relative to the evolution of the current architecture of cognition. Castelfranchi's view, which emphasizes goal-directness in low and high level cognition, naturally favors a continuity across the early architectures for the control of action of our far ancestors, and the sophisticated mechanisms of intentionality, proactivity, self-control and sociality of humans and other animals [32, 38]. Exploring how the former develop into the latter, and how this process is influenced by changes of bodies and environments (which become increasingly richer of tools, sociality and language during evolution) could help framing Castelfranchi's ideas in a sound evolutionary framework, and suggest how to design developmental and comparative studies to test them.

Finale: a call for multidisciplinary and multi-methodological research

The five challenges that I have shortly described are by no means the only possible ones. As Castelfranchi's ideas are so inspiring, multifaceted and broad in scope, they can exert a strong impulse for the braves to explore many more novel avenues of research, in as many disciplines as they can imagine (and create). All these challenges require a multi-methodological methodology, in which theoretical, empirical and computational means are used in combination.

In particular, I argue, computational modeling could be the "Rosetta stone" of the multi-methodological methodology, providing for instance the necessary "bridge" between functional explanations offered by Castelfranchi's theories, neuroscientific evidence on how the brain works, and evolutionary explanations, and ultimately revealing the full potential of Castelfranchi's seminal ideas.

References

1. B. W. Balleine and A. Dickinson. Goal-directed instrumental action: contingency and incentive learning and their cortical substrates. *Neuropharmacology*, 37(4-5):407–419, 1998.
2. A. Bandura. Social cognitive theory: An agentic perspective. *Annual review of psychology*, 52(1):1–26, 2001.
3. M. Bar. The proactive brain: memory for predictions. *Philos Trans R Soc Lond B Biol Sci*, 364(1521):1235–1243, May 2009.
4. L. Barsalou. Grounded cognition. *Annual Review of Psychology*, 59:617–645, 2008.
5. M. M. Botvinick, T. S. Braver, D. M. Barch, C. S. Carter, and J. D. Cohen. Conflict monitoring and cognitive control. *Psychol Rev*, 108(3):624–652, Jul 2001.
6. M. Bratman. *Intentions, Plans, and Practical Reason*. Harvard University Press, 1987.
7. C. Castelfranchi. Mind as an anticipatory device: For a theory of expectations. In *BVAI 2005*, pages 258–276, 2005.
8. C. Castelfranchi and R. Falcone. *Trust Theory: A socio-cognitive and computational model*. Wiley, 2010.
9. P. Cisek. Making decisions through a distributed consensus. *Curr Opin Neurobiol*, Jun 2012.
10. P. Cisek and J. F. Kalaska. Neural mechanisms for interacting with a world full of action choices. *Annu Rev Neurosci*, 33:269–298, 2010.
11. A. Clark and R. Grush. Towards a cognitive robotics. *Adaptive Behavior*, 7(1):5–16, 1999.
12. R. Conte and C. Castelfranchi. *Cognitive and Social Action*. University College London, London, UK, 1995.
13. K. Doya, S. Ishii, A. Pouget, and R. P. N. Rao, editors. *Bayesian Brain: Probabilistic Approaches to Neural Coding*. The MIT Press, 1 edition, January 2007.
14. A. K. Engel, P. Fries, and W. Singer. Dynamic predictions: oscillations and synchrony in top-down processing. *Nature Reviews Neuroscience*, 2(10):704–716, 2001.
15. K. Friston. A theory of cortical responses. *Philos Trans R Soc Lond B Biol Sci*, 360(1456):815–836, Apr 2005.
16. K. Friston. The free-energy principle: a unified brain theory? *Nat Rev Neurosci*, 11(2):127–138, Feb 2010.
17. K. J. Friston, J. Daunizeau, J. Kilner, and S. J. Kiebel. Action and behavior: a free-energy formulation. *Biol Cybern*, 102(3):227–260, Mar 2010.
18. C. Frith. *Making up the Mind. How the Brain Creates our Mental World*. Blackwell, 2007.
19. U. Frith and C. Frith. The social brain: allowing humans to boldly go where no other species has been. *Philos Trans R Soc Lond B Biol Sci*, 365(1537):165–176, Jan 2010.
20. J. M. Fuster. *The prefrontal cortex: anatomy, physiology, and neuropsychology of the frontal lobe*. Lippincott-Raven, Philadelphia, PA, 1997.
21. P. W. Glimcher and A. Rustichini. Neuroeconomics: the consilience of brain and decision. *Science*, 306(5695):447–452, Oct 2004.
22. P. Haggard. Human volition: towards a neuroscience of will. *Nature Reviews Neuroscience*, 9:934–946, 2008.

23. B. Hommel, J. Musseler, G. Aschersleben, and W. Prinz. The theory of event coding (tec): a framework for perception and action planning. *Behavioral and Brain Science*, 24(5):849–78, 2001.
24. M. Jeannerod. *Motor Cognition*. Oxford University Press, 2006.
25. E. Koechlin and C. Summerfield. An information theoretical approach to prefrontal executive function. *Trends Cogn Sci*, 11(6):229–235, June 2007.
26. A. Kruglanski, J. Shah, A. Fishbach, R. Friedman, et al. A theory of goal systems. *Advances in experimental social psychology*, 34:331–378, 2002.
27. G. A. Miller, E. Galanter, and K. H. Pribram. *Plans and the Structure of Behavior*. Holt, Rinehart and Winston, New York, 1960.
28. P. R. Montague, R. J. Dolan, K. J. Friston, and P. Dayan. Computational psychiatry. *Trends Cogn Sci*, 16(1):72–80, Jan 2012.
29. R. Montague. *Why Choose This Book? How We Make Decisions*. Penguin Group, New York, 2006.
30. Y. Niv, N. D. Daw, and P. Dayan. Choice values. *Nature Neuroscience*, 9:987–988, 2006.
31. E. Pacherie. The phenomenology of action: A conceptual framework. *Cognition*, 107:179–217, 2008.
32. G. Pezzulo. Grounding procedural and declarative knowledge in sensorimotor anticipation. *Mind and Language*, 26(1):78–114, 2011.
33. G. Pezzulo. An active inference view of cognitive control. *Frontiers in Theoretical and Philosophical Psychology*, 2012.
34. G. Pezzulo, G. Baldassarre, M. V. Butz, C. Castelfranchi, and J. Hoffmann. From actions to goals and vice-versa: Theoretical analysis and models of the ideomotor principle and tote. In M. Butz, O. Sigaud, G. Pezzulo, and G. Baldassarre, editors, *Anticipatory Behavior in Adaptive Learning Systems: Advances in Anticipatory Processing*, LNAI 4520, pages 73–93. Springer, 2007.
35. G. Pezzulo, L. Barsalou, A. Cangelosi, M. Fischer, K. McRae, and M. Spivey. The mechanics of embodiment: A dialogue on embodiment and computational modeling. *Frontiers in Cognition*, 2(5):1–21, 2011.
36. G. Pezzulo, M. V. Butz, C. Castelfranchi, and R. Falcone, editors. *The Challenge of Anticipation: A Unifying Framework for the Analysis and Design of Artificial Cognitive Systems*. LNAI 5225. Springer, 2008.
37. G. Pezzulo and C. Castelfranchi. The symbol detachment problem. *Cognitive Processing*, 8(2):115–131, 2007.
38. G. Pezzulo and C. Castelfranchi. Thinking as the control of imagination: a conceptual framework for goal-directed systems. *Psychological Research*, 73(4):559–577, 2009.
39. J. Piaget. *The Construction of Reality in the Child*. Ballentine, 1954.
40. W. T. Powers. *Behavior: The Control of Perception*. Aldine, Hawthorne, NY, 1973.
41. A. Rosenblueth, N. Wiener, and J. Bigelow. Behavior, purpose and teleology. *Philosophy of Science*, 10(1):18–24, 1943.
42. W. Schultz, P. Dayan, and P. Montague. A neural substrate of prediction and reward. *Science*, 275:1593–1599, 1997.
43. M. Shadlen, R. Kiani, T. Hanks, and A. Churchland. Neurobiology of decision making: An intentional framework. In C. Engel and W. Singer, editors, *Better than conscious?: decision making, the human mind, and implications for institutions*. The MIT Press, 2008.
44. R. Shadmehr and S. Mussa-Ivaldi. *Biological learning and control: How the brain builds representations, predicts events, and makes decisions*. MIT Press, Cambridge, MA, 2012.
45. E. Tolman. *Purposive Behavior in Animals and Men*. Appleton-Century-Crofts, New York, 1932.
46. S. P. Wise. Forward frontal fields: phylogeny and fundamental function. *Trends Neurosci*, 31(12):599–608, Dec 2008.
47. D. M. Wolpert and Z. Ghahramani. Computational principles of movement neuroscience. *Nature Neuroscience*, 3:1212–1217, 2000.

Chapter 2
Interactive spatial representations constitute a basis for cognition

Martin V. Butz

Abstract We propose that anticipatory agents, as introduced by Cristiano Castelfranchi and others, form spatial representations for flexible, goal-directed decision making and behavioral control. Moreover, we propose that these representations may constitute one essential foundation for the development and grounding of higher-level, symbolic cognition and abstract thought. First, we show that various research directions suggest that the brain develops sensorimotor, highly modular, spatial representations both for the generation of forward predictions and expectations as well as for inverse, goal-directed behavioral control. Next, we introduce several neuro-cognitive machine learning approaches that model the development of such spatial representations for adaptive and versatile behavioral control. Anticipatory, forward-inverse representations and learning biases seem essential to develop these representations. Based on Castelfranchi's take on cognitive agents, we conclude that such spatial representations may serve as the believe center of the agent, which eventually can be extended with an interactive decision making center, yielding an autonomous system that is cognition-ready. We conclude that separating spatial representations of behavioral interactions from decision- and goal-oriented representations may be the key to develop higher-level cognitive agents, which are able to learn grammatical structures and generate abstract, but sensorimotor-grounded thoughts.

1 Multi-Modular Spatial Representations in the Brain

Over the last decade, embodiment has been increasingly acknowledged to be a crucial factor for the realization of versatile, energy-efficient behavioral capabilities of animals and humans. *Morphologically intelligent* systems [38] exhibit complex behavioral patterns that are hardly actively controlled by motor forces and that are mainly the emergent result of a clever body morphology. While

Cognitive Modeling, Department of Computer Science, University of Tübingen, Germany
e-mail: martin.butz@uni-tuebingen.de

amazing emergent behavior can be generated by such systems – such as the passive walker robot [19] – the generation of higher-level cognitive and versatile behavioral structures out of morphologically intelligent systems remains a hard challenge.

Flexible decision making, planning, and behavior needs to be inevitably controlled by internal representations that self-organize based on the experienced sensorimotor flow, while the system interacts with its surrounding environment. In simple organisms, hardly processed sensory information might be linked to motor commands. However, mammals and particularly humans tend to utilize more than one type of sensor to analyze the environment for more complex decision making. Spaces are transferred into each other to utilize various sources of information for controlling the body in interaction with the environment goal-directedly [1]. Multiple sensory and also predictive, reafferent sources of information are bidirectionally associated to increase certainty about the current state of the body and the surrounding environment. In the brain, spatial representations of this kind can be found in parietal and premotor cortical areas [1, 20, 43], amongst others.

The body state, for example, appears to be maintained by integrating various sources of sensory, motor, and sensorimotor information weighted by its estimated information content and relative plausibility. The *rubber hand illusion* may illustrate this continuous process of body state maintenance in the most vivid way [4]. In the original experiments, participants experienced brush strokes that were simultaneously applied to their hidden left hand and the visible left hand-like rubber hand. The participants reported that the felt strokes appeared to come from the rubber hand, and, indeed, that the rubber hand seemed to be the own hand. The brain apparently "decided" that the available proprioceptive posture information must be inaccurate because (1) two other modalities (vision and touch) signaled highly coincident information and (2) vision signaled the corresponding (head-centered) spatial location where the rubber hand was located. Ehrsson et al. [24] confirmed the suspicion that the illusion is (at least partially) generated in multi-sensory brain areas (premotor cortex). The results suggest that the brain continuously maintains an internal body schema, which continuously integrates multiple sensory and motor sources of information and which is situated in the surrounding space.

Since each sensory and motor source of information is inevitably grounded in a different body-relative frame of reference, dependent on where the sensor or motor is located on the body, a highly modular cortical structure emerges that maintains multiple body and surrounding spatial representations in various frames of reference. *Somatotopic* representations of body-parts can be found in the somatosensory cortex and *muscletopic* representations are located in the motor cortex [49]. But also *peripersonal spatial representations* of the body in parietal and premotor cortical areas can be found – such as specialized modules for the manipulable space in front of us or skin-relative arm and face spaces [29, 32, 43]. In order to align and thus exchange the different sources of information maintained in the various frames of reference, the brain has to know how to match these different frames of reference body posture dependent. Only then phenomena like the rubber hand illusion can emerge.

2 Models of Spatial Representations

The brain represents these spatial codes by means of distributed population codes, which cover particular frames of reference [26, 40]. By monitoring the firing rates of different neurons, vector representations of the encoding can be derived [45]. It remains unclear, however, how these neural population codes develop and self-organize with respect to the available representation at hand.

Neural models of population codes suggest several important self-organization principles. Rao and Ballard [42] stress the importance of predictive encoding in the visual cortex, where a multiple layer neural network generates internal feedback loops between the successive layers, yielding visual receptive field structures comparable to those in V1. Later, similar mechanisms were related to Bayesian processing and were also associated with attention [41]. Gain fields can be found in various brain areas to translate information in sensory frames of reference into motor commands and also to exchange redundant sensory information between different spatial representations [1, 17]. In general, the brain appears to employ Bayesian principles to realize effective information exchange as well as to focus attention and learning [22].

Such spatial representations have been directly modeled to yield interactive, psychological plausible behavior of reaching movements with the *Sensorimotor Unsupervised Redundancy Resolving Architecture* (SURE_REACH) [9]. SURE_REACH learns to associate the angular, posture space of an arm with the location space of the end-effector, allowing flexible information exchange and the execution of anticipatory, goal-directed planning and behavior [9, 28]. In this case, another challenge is mastered, which is the challenge of redundant actuators: since the human arm has redundant degrees of freedom, a torso-relative location in space can be reached theoretically on infinitely many paths and with infinitely many end postures. SURE_REACH encodes posture- and location-spaces with distributed neural fields and thus associates one location neuron with multiple posture neurons – all those that yield a close by end-effector location. In this way, redundancy can be resolved flexibly on the fly, potentially taking other task constraints into account.

A big challenge is the scalability of spatial population codes. The higher dimensional the space, the exponentially larger the necessary local population code to cover the space exhaustively with a fixed distance between neural centers in each dimension. The population code of SURE_REACH in posture space, for example, scales exponentially in the number of degrees of freedom covered, thus rendering the simulation of a seven-degree of freedom arm nearly intractable. Current research modularizes the SURE_REACH approach with respect to the sensory-grounded frames of reference and the locally interactive arm limbs further, yielding modular posture space representations with maximally three dimensions each [23]. The realization of an artificial neural representation of this modular representation is pending.

Various approaches can be utilized to learn such neural spatial representation with self-organizing neural networks. While Kohonen networks [31] require the pre-definition of a particular dimensionality, the growing neural gas algorithm can technically cover any dimensionality [25]. Recent derivatives based on temporal Hebbian learning [3] can learn spatially distributed networks that can be used, for example, in maze navigation tasks [47, 11]. In this case, the learned neural distributions show similarities with Hippocampal place and head-direction cells [34], and essentially constitute a cognitive map of the surrounding environment [35].

Interestingly, temporal Hebbian learning algorithms can develop behavior manifold structures that may be embedded in higher dimensional sensory spaces [11]. For example, the location of the elbow with respect to the shoulder is restricted to a subsurface of a sphere, which is embedded in the three dimensional space surrounding the body. Such lower dimensional manifolds can be covered rather effectively, as long as noise in irrelevant spatial directions is small. Since the motor-dependent temporal Hebbian learning determines a motor-dependent locality in the manifold, such manifold spaces may be termed *sensorimotor representations of space* [7, 11]. Interestingly, a previous investigation without population codes even suggests that such sensorimotor spaces may reflect interaction manifolds that reflect the external spatial dimensionality [39].

While self-organization is an important aspect, the employed algorithms only re-present the encountered input distribution without any real purpose besides compression. Based on anticipatory behavior principles [12], however, the population codes can be expected to be structured purposefully for the effective control of goal-oriented behavior. Population codes that develop from scratch to yield accurate, local predictions are, for example, realized by the locally weighted projection regression (LWPR) architecture [48] or the XCSF learning system with Gaussian kernels [5, 10]. In this case, population codes develop that may be said to pro-present a particular input space for the generation of accurate, forward predictions, and potentially also for inverse, goal-directed control [8, 44].

Other pro-presentation drives may be incorporated, such as representations for the establishment of effective information exchange between different frames of reference or also for self-motivated decision making and planning purposes. Graziano [27] reviews the action repertoire in motor- and pre-motor cortex and shows that it is not only tuned to reach certain locations or move in certain directions, but also to execute particular ethologically relevant actions, such as hand-to-mouth movements or defensive movements. This insight confirms the propositions that the brain structures itself purposefully – probably based on internal, anticipatory drives that foster the formation of bidirectional, forward-inverse, sensorimotor structures for the flexible control of the body.

3 From Spatial Representations to Higher-Level Cognition

While the surveyed spatial representations form an integral part of the brain's architecture, they are certainly not sufficient to develop higher-level cognitive agents. Castelfranchi [13] suggests that:

A Cognitive agent [...] founds his decisions, intentions and actions on his beliefs. This bridge connects knowledge, and abstract mechanisms of "cognitive processing", to action and then to adaptation [13, p.234].

While beliefs about the own body and its perceived surrounding can be encoded within the discussed spatial representations, intentions are necessary to select goals that are currently believed to be achievable and available. Achievability and availability can be encoded in the spatial representations. Decision making, however, needs to be additionally driven by other, homeostatic-like drives, which induce goals and priorities. Castelfranchi proposes that this division may be the key to ground abstract, cognitive capabilities in the adaptive behavioral capabilities of an agent.

Interestingly, the division of labor in the dorsal and ventral streams of sensory processing suggest a somewhat similar division of *spatial beliefs*, which are essential for interaction, and *representational beliefs*, which are essential for decision making. Milner and Goodale [33] characterize this division by *vision for action* (dorsal) and *vision for representation* (ventral). While this separation of knowledge is certainly not as clear cut as it may sound at first sight, it needs to be noted that similar dorsal and ventral streams of sensory processing can also be found in other sensory modalities [21] – rendering the division a fundamental processing principle in the brain. Models of this division of labor, however, are still in their infancy. A most recent model in visual perception combines top-down attentional processing by modeling spatial (dorsal) and feature-based (ventral) priors [18]. It is shown that this separation can model saccadic eye movement and fixation behavior rather well – suggesting its plausibility.

A recent second-order neural network model with parametric bias neurons (sNNPB) separates spatial sensory-to-motor mappings from decision-oriented encodings [46] in a learning robotics experiment. The architecture yielded unique behavioral generalizations over trained types of object interactions. Moreover, the architecture developed a simple grammatical representation in the parametric bias neurons, represented by a self-organized geometrically-arranged manifold structure. It is suggested that separating spatial, body-relative representations from feature-based, decision-oriented representations may not only be useful for versatile decision making and planning, but also for the development of higher-level, cognitive capabilities.

While the latter study has shown how cognitive structures may be developed in interaction with spatial representations, the scalability of the method is limited. Thus, it remains unanswered which processes and learning biases may rigorously drive the brain to develop higher-level cognitive structures. In line with thoughts of Castelfranchi [15, 36], we believe that an anticipatory drive shapes the mind towards the development of increasingly more abstract pro-presentations and the detachment of symbolic thoughts from current reality [6, 37]. While such an anticipatory drive may be highly important in the development of self-representations [6], it seems to be also one of the driving forces for complex decision making, reasoning [13], and social interaction [16, 14]. Thus, this drive may first lead to the development of bodily-grounded, spatial representations for interaction and may then proceed to embed these representations also in social contexts. Once imitation stages are reached, higher-level cognitive stages may develop that enable social interaction and communication and ultimately may lead to the development of abstract thoughts [2].

While it remains unclear how distributed and coordinated such an anticipatory drive needs to be to enable the observed language evolution, it should be clear that all higher levels of cognition are ultimately grounded in spatial representations of behavioral interactions. Seeing that the brain also generalizes these spatial concepts to social interaction spaces and others [30], it seems essential to separate spatial interaction concepts from concepts for decision making. The result may be the next generation of cognitive, but sensorimotor-based spatially grounded intelligent, adaptive, and highly flexible agent architectures. These will on the one hand reveal how and why the brain processes information in the way it does and on the other hand enable the design of much more intelligent robotic and other agent platforms. An exciting way to proceed lies ahead – and Castelfranchi paved the way for the discovery of this next generation.

References

1. Andersen, R. A., Snyder, L. H., Bradley, D. C., and Xing, J. (1997). Multimodal representation of space in the posterior parietal cortex and its use in planning movements. *Annual Review of Neuroscience*, 20:303–330.
2. Arbib, M. A. (2005). From monkey-like action recognition to human language: An evolutionary framework for neurolinguistics. *Behavioral and Brain Sciences*, 28:105–167.
3. Bishop, C. M., Hinton, G. E., and Strachan, I. G. D. (1997). GTM through time. *Proceedings of the IEEE Fifth International Conference on Artificial Neural Networks*, pages 111–116.
4. Botvinick, M. and Cohen, J. (1998). Rubber hands 'feel' touch that eyes see. *Nature*, 391:756.
5. Butz, M. V. (2005). Kernel-based, ellipsoidal conditions in the real-valued XCS classifier system. *Genetic and Evolutionary Computation Conference, GECCO 2005*, pages 1835–1842.
6. Butz, M. V. (2008a). How and why the brain lays the foundations for a conscious self. *Constructivist Foundations*, 4(1):1–42.
7. Butz, M. V. (2008b). Sensomotorische Raumrepräsentationen. *Informatik-Spektrum*, 31:237–240.
8. Butz, M. V. and Herbort, O. (2008). Context-dependent predictions and cognitive arm control with XCSF. *Genetic and Evolutionary Computation Conference, GECCO 2008*, pages 1357–1364.
9. Butz, M. V., Herbort, O., and Hoffmann, J. (2007). Exploiting redundancy for flexible behavior: Unsupervised learning in a modular sensorimotor control architecture. *Psychological Review*, 114:1015–1046.
10. Butz, M. V., Lanzi, P. L., and Wilson, S. W. (2008). Function approximation with XCS: Hyperellipsoidal conditions, recursive least squares, and compaction. *IEEE Transactions on Evolutionary Computation*, 12:355–376.
11. Butz, M. V., Shirinov, E., and Reif, K. L. (2010). Self-organizing sensorimotor maps plus internal motivations yield animal-like behavior. *Adaptive Behavior*, 18(3-4):315–337.
12. Butz, M. V., Sigaud, O., and Gérard, P. (2003). Internal models and anticipations in adaptive learning systems. In Butz, M. V., Sigaud, O., and Gérard, P., editors, *Anticipatory Behavior in Adaptive Learning Systems: Foundations, Theories, and Systems*, pages 86–109, Berlin Heidelberg. Springer-Verlag.

13. Castelfranchi, C. (1996). Reasons: belief support and goal dynamics. *Mathware & Soft Computing*, 3(1-2):233–247.
14. Castelfranchi, C. (2001). The theory of social functions. challenges for multi-agent-based social simulation and multi-agent learning. *Cognitive Systems Research*, 2(1):5–38.
15. Castelfranchi, C. (2005). Mind as an anticipatory device: For a theory of expectations. In *BVAI 2005*, pages 258–276.
16. Castelfranchi, C. and Falcone, R. (1998). Principles of trust for mas: cognitive anatomy, social importance, and quantification. *Proc. of the Int. Conf. on Multi-Agent Systems (ICMAS'98), Paris*, pages 72–79.
17. Chang, S. W. C., Papadimitriou, C., and Snyder, L. H. (2009). Using a compound gain field to compute a reach plan. *Neuron*, 64:744 – 755.
18. Chikkerur, S., Serre, T., Tan, C., and Poggio, T. (2010). What and where: A Bayesian inference theory of attention. *Vision Research*.
19. Collins, S. H., Wisse, M., and Ruina, A. (2001). A three-dimensional passive-dynamic walking robot with two legs and knees. *The International Journal of Robotics Research*, 20:607–615.
20. Corradi-Dell'Acqua, C., Hesse, M. D., Rumiati, R. I., and Fink, G. R. (2008). Where is a nose with respect to a foot? The left posterior parietal cortex processes spatial relationships among body parts. *Cerebral Cortex*, 18(12):2879.
21. Dijkerman, H. C. and de Haan, E. H. F. (2007). Somatosensory processing subserving perception and action: Dissociations, interactions, and integration. *Behavioral and Brain Sciences*, 30(02):224–230.
22. Doya, K., Ishii, S., Pouget, A., and Rao, R. P. N. (2007). *Bayesian brain: Probabilistic approaches to neural coding*. The MIT Press.
23. Ehrenfeld, S. and Butz, M. V. (2011). A modular, redundant, multi-frame of reference representation for kinematic chains. In *IEEE International Conference on Robotics and Automation*, pages 141–147.
24. Ehrsson, H. H., Spence, C., and Passingham, R. E. (2004). That's my hand! Activity in premotor cortex reflects feeling of ownership of a limb. *Science*, 305(5685):875–877.
25. Fritzke, B. (1995). A growing neural gas network learns topologies. *Advances in Neural Information Processing Systems*, 7:625–632.
26. Georgopoulos, A. P., Pellizzer, G., Poliakov, A. V., and Schieber, M. H. (1999). Neural coding of finger and wrist movements. *Journal of Computational Neuroscience*, 6:279–288.
27. Graziano, M. S. A. (2006). The organization of behavioral repertoire in motor cortex. *Annual Review of Neuroscience*, 29:105–134.
28. Herbort, O. and Butz, M. V. (2007). Encoding complete body models enables task dependent optimal behavior. *Proceedings of International Joint Conference on Neural Networks, Orlando, Florida, USA, August 12-17, 2007*, pages 1424–1429.
29. Holmes, N. P. and Spence, C. (2004). The body schema and multisensory representation(s) of peripersonal space. *Cognitive Processing*, 5:94–105.
30. Johnson, M. (1987). *The body in the mind: The bodily basis of meaning, imagination and reason*. Chicago: University of Chicago Press.
31. Kohonen, T. (2001). *Self-Organizing Maps*. Springer-Verlag, Berlin Heidelberg, New York, 3rd edition.
32. Maravita, A., Spence, C., and Driver, J. (2003). Multisensory integration and the body schema: Close to hand and within reach. *Current Biology*, 13:531–539.
33. Milner, A. D. and Goodale, M. A. (2008). Two visual systems re-viewed. *Neuropsychologia*, 46(3):774 – 785. Consciousness and Perception: Insights and Hindsights - A Festschrift in Honour of Larry Weiskrantz.
34. Moser, E. I., Kropff, E., and Moser, M.-B. (2008). Place cells, grid cells, and the brain's spatial representation system. *Annual Review of Neuroscience*, 31(1):69–89.
35. O'Keefe, J. and Nadel, L. (1978). *The Hippocampus as a Cognitive Map*. Clarendon Press, Oxford.
36. Pezzulo, G., Butz, M. V., and Castelfranchi, C. (2008). The anticipatory approach: Definitions and taxonomies. In Pezzulo, G., Butz, M. V., Castelfranchi, C., and Falcone, R.,

editors, *The Challenge of Anticipation: A Unifying Framework for the Analysis and Design of Artificial Cognitive Systems*, LNAI 5225, pages 23–43. Springer-Verlag, Berlin Heidelberg.

37. Pezzulo, G. and Castelfranchi, C. (2007). The symbol detachment problem. *Cognitive Processing*, 8(2):115–131.

38. Pfeifer, R. and Bongard, J. C. (2006). *How the Body Shapes the Way We Think: A New View of Intelligence*. MIT Press, Cambridge, MA.

39. Philipona, D., O'Regan, J. K., and Nadal, J.-P. (2003). Is there something out there? Inferring space from sensorimotor dependencies. *Neural Computation*, 15:2029–2049.

40. Pouget, A., Dyan, T., and Zemel, R. (2000). Information processing with population codes. *Nature Reviews Neuroscience*, 1:125–132.

41. Rao, R. P. N. (2005). Bayesian inference and attentional modulation in the visual cortex. *Neuroreport*, 16:1843–1848.

42. Rao, R. P. N. and Ballard, D. H. (1997). Dynamic model of visual recognition predicts neural response properties in the visual cortex. *Neural Computation*, 9:721–763.

43. Rizzolatti, G., Fadiga, L., Fogassi, L., and Gallese, V. (1997). Enhanced: The space around us. *Science*, 277:190–191.

44. Salaün, C., Padois, V., and Sigaud, O. (2009). Control of redundant robots using learned models: An operational space control approach. *Proceedings of the 2009 IEEE/RSJ international conference on Intelligent robots and systems*, pages 878–885.

45. Salinas, E. and Abbott, L. F. (1994). Vector reconstruction from firing rates. *Journal of Computational Neuroscience*, 1:89–107.

46. Sugita, Y., Tani, J., and Butz, M. V. (2011). Simultaneously emerging Braitenberg codes and semantic compositionality. *Adaptive Behavior*. submitted.

47. Toussaint, M. (2006). A sensorimotor map: Modulating lateral interactions for anticipation and planning. *Neural Computation*, 18:1132–1155.

48. Vijayakumar, S., D'Souza, A., and Schaal, S. (2005). Incremental online learning in high dimensions. *Neural Computation*, 17:2602–2634.

49. Ward, J. (2006). *The student's guide to cognitive neuroscience*. Psychology Press, New York, NY.

Chapter 3
Natural laws of developmental intelligence

Marco Gori

Abstract The impact of AI in real-world applications has been remarkable and somewhat surprising, especially for those tasks that are truly regarded of human pertinence. The impressive results in some grand challenges, like chess, linguistic skills, and robotics seem to suggest that other big achievements are just behind the corner. The position supported in this chapter is that, on the opposite, some truly human - and animal - skills, especially connected with learning, are far away from being captured by nowadays approaches. When focusing on the interplay between learning and reasoning, the solutions based on most of the AI side explored so far are at least arguable, and likely unsuitable to really achieve human-like performance. Following a recent wave of thoughts, mostly connected with the philosophy of mind, it is pointed out that the principles of cognitive development behind stage-based learning are likely to open the doors to another side of AI, where the focus is on the gradual achievements of pursued skills by proper developmental plans. Most importantly, it is claimed that the way biology breaks complexity, by dictating stages in the child development, is an instance of general principles at the basis of natural laws from which the need of development stages and of the induction/deduction loop emerges as the outcome of simple interactions with examples and constraints that express relations on semantic attributes. Hence, stage-based learning, as discussed in developmental psychology, is not the outcome of biology, but it is instead the consequence of optimization principles and complexity issues that hold regardless of the "body." Apart from the interest in itself, this might have an enormous impact in the conception of a new models strongly based on developmental plans.

Marco Gori
Department of Information Engineering, University of Siena, Italy
e-mail: marco@dii.unisi.it

1 Introduction

The popular Sam Loyd's fifteen puzzle and Rubik's cube share surprisingly something in common with optical character recognition of written and hand-written chars: They can be successfully faced by processing the information "all at once" and by setting the final goal to reach at the beginning of the task. In the puzzles, most of the approaches deriving from problem solving with proper heuristics (see e.g. $IDA^\star$ [1]), do not operate by scheduling intermediate steps, but they focus only on the final goal, which gives rise to amazingly intelligent solutions especially during the final steps, in which a few moves lead to the solution from an apparently far away configuration. Likewise, most of the learning algorithms for OCR rely on the global optimization of an error function composed of all the learning examples processed all at once. The classic on-line learning schemes are not a truly exception, since they merely increase gradually the training examples, but they do not typically set intermediate goals. Interestingly, the clean formulation within the framework of optimization that is behind most of the methods used to tackle the mentioned tasks is the key of success in many concrete problems. However, in spite of extraordinary achievements in specific tasks, nowadays intelligent agents are still striving for acquiring a truly ability to deal with many challenging human cognitive processes, especially when a mutable environment is involved and perceptual information has to be processed jointly with symbolic knowledge. In the last few years, the progressive awareness on that critical issue has led to develop interesting bridging mechanisms between symbolic and sub-symbolic representations and to develop new theories to reduce the huge gap between most approaches to learning and reasoning. While the search for such a unified view of intelligent processes might still be an obliged path to follow in the years to come, in this chapter, we claim that we are still trapped in the insidious paradox that feeding the ravenous agent with the available information, all at once, might be the major reason of failure when aspiring to achieve certain human-like cognitive capabilities. Their emulation in the mentioned framework gives rise to an instant feeling of déjà vu that is recurrently summarized by the presence of computational complexity barriers. Therefore, the solution offered in nature must contain some key ingredients that are not necessarily interwound with biology.

When water moves, mollusks open shell and when something touches membrane, then shell closes. Animals are able to coordinate perception with action, which is especially clear during the hunt. In the children cognitive development, the transition from sensorimotor to more abstract representations of reality follows a stage-based principle. Regardless of the extent to which animal, human, and machines share biological principles, one might be interested in studying human and artificial cognitive processes under the same umbrella. While this is of interest in itself, the consequences of discovering such natural laws might offer the key to access a new side of AI, in which the role of developmental plans plays a crucial role. When observing human and nowadays artificial minds on the same play, one early realizes that especially learning machines do not take into account most of the rich human communication protocols and, most importantly, do not follow any developmental path in order to acquire cognitive abilities. In most of the studies of AI, the agent does exploit all the information available in the environment at once. While this seems to be a sort of axiomatic engineering principle dictated by efficiency unarguable requirements, in this chapter, it is pointed out that trusting this principle has led, on the opposite, to bounce against computational complexity barriers. Human learning experiences witness the importance of asking questions and of learning under a of teaching plan. What is often neglected is that most intriguing human learning skills are due, to a large extent, to the acquisition of relevant semantic attributes and to their relations. This makes learning a process which goes well beyond pure induction; the evidence provided by the induction of a semantic attribute is typically propagated to other attributes by formal rules, thus giving rise to a sort of reinforcement cyclic process.

While the studies in the symbolic domain have already clearly recognized the role of a gradual acquisition of knowledge, in the case of perception and of complex behavior, that involve symbolic and sub-symbolic representations, the role of developmental plans, behind most cognitive tasks, has not be understood yet. Developmental plans are crucial to attack the optimization problem associated with most of those tasks, since they can cut dramatically the computational complexity. It is claimed that the children developmental path, as well as that of primates, mammals, and most animals might not be primarily the outcome of biologic laws, but that it could be instead the consequence of a more general complexity principle, according to which the environmental information must properly be filtered out so as to focus attention on "easy tasks." This leads necessarily to stage-based developmental strategies that any intelligent agent must follow, regardless of its body. Most importantly, we claim that the way biology breaks complexity barriers, by dictating stages in the child development, seems to be an instance of a general information-based principle that holds regardless of the "body." Hence, the rooting in computational complexity of stage-based learning gives us an important warning also on AI methods for learning and reasoning. The focus on developmental plans might just enable the access to on another side of AI which has not been explored carefully so far and that is of crucial importance when aspiring to acquire most interesting human-like cognitive abilities.

This chapter is organized as follows. In the next section, the paradox of ravenous agents, which process all the information at once, is introduced. In 3, it is shown that when processing symbolic knowledge the need to devise revision of belief has been extensively studied in the last few years. In Section 4, the effect of developmental plans is discussed in perception and, especially, in vision, which in 5 a discussion is proposed on the interplay between learning and reasoning at the light of developmental plans. Finally, some conclusions are drawn in 7.

2 Constraint machines and the paradox of the ravenous agent

We think of an intelligent agent acting in the perceptual space $X \subset \mathbb{R}^d$ as a vectorial function $f = [f_1, \ldots, f_n]'$, where $\forall j \in \mathbb{N}_n : f_j \in W^{k,p}$ belongs to a Sobolev space, that is to the subset of L^p whose functions f_j admit weak derivatives up to some order k and have a finite L^p norm. The functions $f_j : j = 1, \ldots, n$, are referred to as the "tasks" of the agent. We can introduce a norm on f by the pair (P, γ), where P is a pseudo-differential operator ([2]) and $\gamma \in \mathbb{R}^n$ is a vector of non-negative coordinates [1]. We are interested in *parsimonious agents* aimed at keeping small the functional

$$E(f) = \| f \|_{P_\gamma}^2 = \sum_{j=1}^n \gamma_j < Pf_j, Pf_j >, \tag{1}$$

when interacting in their own environment. This is a generalization to multi-task learning of what has been proposed in ([3]) for regularization networks. The definition is rooted in Tikhonov's regularization theory ([4]) and related studies on spline functions ([5, 6]). In physics, this is a generalized version of the *Dirichlet integral* and it plays a fundamental role in many classic physic laws. In the case of $n = 1$, the operator P has also been related to the notion of kernel ([7, 8]), while in ([9]) there are some relevant links between regularization networks and kernel machines. An additional connection was pointed out in [10] on the effect of the boundary condition in the variational formulation to address the well-posedness ([11]) of the learning problem. An interesting case is the one in which we choose $\alpha_r(x) \equiv \alpha_r \geq 0$ constant and the derivative operator is such that $D^{2r} = \Delta^r = \nabla^{2r}$ and $D^{2r+1} = \nabla\nabla^{2r}$, where Δ is the Laplacian operator and ∇ is the gradient, with the additional condition $D^0 f = f$ ([3, 12]). For instance, a smoothness function that yields an interaction that has the spatial behavior of a Gaussian kernel (with variance σ^2) can be obtained when posing $\alpha_r = (-1)^r \sigma^{2r}/(r!2^r)$ ([12]).

When $n > 1$ the pseudo-differential operator P acts on all coordinates of f, that is $Pf := [Pf_1, Pf_2, \ldots, Pf_n]'$. The input space on which the agent operates is generally composed of tuples, since any object that is handled is composed of at most p different parts which may be attached a different meaning. An object is any entity picked up in

$$X^{p,\star} = \bigcup_{i \leq p} \bigcup_{|\alpha_i| \leq p^{\underline{i}}} X_{\alpha_{1,i}} \times X_{\alpha_{2,i}}, \ldots, X_{\alpha_{i,i}}$$

where $\alpha_i = \{\alpha_{1,i}, \ldots, \alpha_{i,i}\} \in \mathcal{P}(p,i)$ is any of the $p^{\underline{i}} = p(p-1)\ldots(p-i+1)$ (falling factorial power of p) i-length sequences without repetition of p elements. We propose to build an interaction amongst different tasks by introducing con-

---

[1] The proof that $\| \cdot \|_{P_\gamma}$ is a norm in $W^{k,p}$ in given in the Appendix on pseudo-differential operators.

straints of the following types [2]

$$i. \quad \chi_i \sim \left\{\forall x \in \mathcal{X}_i \subset \mathcal{X}^{p,\star} : \varphi_i(x, f(x), Pf(x), y(x)) = 0, \ i = 1, \dots, m_\forall\right\}, \quad (2)$$

$$ii. \quad \chi_i \sim \{\exists v_i : \Phi_i(f, Pf, y, v_i) = 0), \ i = 1, \dots, m_\exists,\}$$

$$iii. \quad \chi_i \sim \left\{\forall x \in \mathcal{X}_i \subset \mathcal{X}^{p,\star} : \breve{\varphi}_i(x, f(x), Pf(x), y(x)) \geq 0, \ i = 1, \dots, \breve{m}_\forall\right\}$$

$$iv. \quad \chi_i \sim \left\{\exists v_i : \breve{\Phi}_i(f, Pf, y, v_i) \geq 0), \ i = 1, \dots, \breve{m}_\exists\right\},$$

where $y : \mathcal{X}_i \to \mathbb{R}^n$ is a given *target function* and $v_i \in \mathcal{E}_i$ is an *existential parameter*, and $\varphi \in C$, $\Phi \in \bar{C}$. Notice that $\mathcal{E}_i$ might be empty. Constraints i and iii will be referred to as *universally-quantified constraints*, (*u-constraints*), while ii and iv will be referred to as *existentially-quantified constraints* (*e-constraints*). In both cases $\chi_i : \mathcal{F} \to \{0,1\}$ can be thought of as the characteristic function of the functional set $\mathcal{F}_i$, that is $f \in \mathcal{F}_i \Leftrightarrow \chi_i(f) = 1$. Alternatively, one can give $\mathcal{F}_i$ a fuzzy description by replacing the above characteristic function with a membership function $\chi_i : \mathcal{F} \to [0,1]$.

Definition 1 *Let $\chi(\cdot)$ be a collection of constraints, where $\forall f \in \mathcal{F} : \chi(f) \in \{0,1\}^m$. Furthermore, let $\mathcal{P}$ be a proposition on $\{0,1\}^m$ associated with χ and consider the space $\mathcal{F}_{\mathcal{P}} \subset \mathcal{F} = \{f \in \mathcal{F} : \mathcal{P}(\chi(f)) = 1\}$. The problem of determining $f^\star \in \mathcal{F}_{\mathcal{P}}$, that minimizes $\| f \|_{P_y}$ is referred to as* learning from constraints.

Once the task functions f_j have been learned, a *constraint machine* can check new constraints constructed on f_j, that turns out to be the arguments of the constraints. Of course, while a similar machine can perform constraint check, it is not entitled to perform any form of reasoning, which necessarily involves a formal description of the way constraints are transformed.

A different formulation of learning considers the case in which the collection of constraints is ordered and the agent interacts on-line with in-coming constraints.

In the above definition, the tasks of the agent (function f_j) and the constraints (functions φ_i or Φ_i) are distinct entities with clearly different attached semantics. However, the removal of this barrier opens new very interesting scenarios in which the parsimonious agent we are studying might be able to deal better in high level tasks. The interchangeability of f_j and φ_i makes it possible to perform recursive computational scheme where the inputs is not distinguished w.r.t. the functions (see e.g. [13], [14]). However, the analysis of this relevant case is outside the scope of this paper.

An abstract interaction of the parsimonious agent with the environment arises in a multi-task environment when involving the quantifiers to express logic properties, like the following example.

Example 1 *Let $\mathcal{X} = \mathbb{R}^2$ and $r(x, y) = 1$ if and only if $y = [0,1]' + x$ and let $f_a, f_b, f_c : \mathcal{X} \to \mathbb{R}$ be three tasks subjected to the following constraints*

---

[2] For the sake of simplicity, throughout the paper, we use the same symbols for denoting the constraints also when the corresponding functions are defined on a restricted domain, so as the dependency on some variables is dropped. Most of the analyses need not to involve the general object space $\mathcal{X}^{p,\star}$ and focus on $\mathcal{X} \in \mathbb{R}^d$.

$$i. \ \forall x: \ \min_{x \in \mathcal{X}} f_a(x) f_b(x) (f_c(x) - 1) = 0 \tag{3}$$

$$ii. \ \forall x \, \exists y: \ \min_{y \in \mathcal{X}} f_a(x) f_b(x) f_c(x) r(x, y) = 0.$$

These are constraints that involve both the universal and existential quantifier expressed as functionals of the tasks f_a, f_b, f_c. Interestingly, even if the universal quantifier is involved, unlike what has been seen for the constraint deriving from the probabilistic normalization, the constraint is not of holonomic type. It is easy to see that the above constraints exhibit a inherent logic structure that, in this case, can be represented by the FOL clauses by

$$\forall x: \ a(x) \wedge b(x) \Rightarrow c(x)$$
$$\forall x: a(x) \wedge b(x) \Rightarrow \exists y: \ c(y) \wedge r(x, y)$$

The equivalence is induced by the product t-norm and is also discussed for this and related examples in ([15, 16]).

There a number of converging indications that most of nowadays approaches to learning and reasoning have been bouncing against the same wall. This is especially clear when facing cognitive tasks that involve both learning and reasoning capabilities, that is when symbolic and sub-symbolic representations of the environment need to be properly bridged. Now, let us consider an agent which operates dynamically in a mutable environment where, at each time t, it is expected to access only to a limited subset $C_t \subset C_U$ of constraints, where C_U can be thought of as the *universal set of constraints*. At any time, an agent might be restricted to acquire a limited set of constraints C, so as $\forall t \in \mathcal{T}: C_t \subset C \subset C_U$. Alternatively, instead of following a *developmental path*, one could think of agents that acquire C all at once.

Definition 2 *A ravenous agent is one which accesses to the whole constraint set at any step, that is one for which $\forall t \in \mathcal{T}: C_t = C_U$.*

At first a glance, ravenous agents seem to have more chances to develop an efficient and effective behavior, since they can access all the information expressed by C at any time. Basically, ravenous agents lack of any *developmental path*. Interestingly, when bridging symbolic and sub-symbolic representations of information and developing intelligent agents that operate accordingly, one faces the problem of choosing a developmental path. It turns out that accessing all the information at once is not a sound choice in terms of complexity issues, which is concisely stated as follows:

The paradox of ravenous agents[3] *Ravenous agents are not the most efficient choice to achieve a parsimonious constraint consistency.*

To support the paradox, we start noting that hierarchical modular architectures used in challenging perceptual tasks like vision and speech are just a way to introduce intermediate levels of representation, so as to focus on simplified tasks. For example, in speech understanding, phonemes, and words

---

[3] This paradox was previously pointed out in [17].

could be intermediate steps for understanding and take decisions accordingly. Similarly, in vision, SIFT features could be an intermediate representation to achieve the ability to recognize objects. However, when looking for deep integration of sub-symbolic and symbolic levels the issue is more involved and mostly open. Clearly, a developmental agent based on a unified computational scheme at any representational level would regard those intermediate levels as temporal steps to achieve in a definite ordering. In the following, we discuss three different contests that involve different degree of symbolic and sub-symbolic representations.

3 Beyond ravenous agents in reasoning

In the symbolic domain, non-ravenous agents have been early recognized and thoroughly investigated for years. This emerges clearly when thinking of circumscription [18] and, in general, of non-monotonic reasoning, which involve a behavior that is outside the perimeter of ravenous agents. It might be convenient to start from a default assumption, e.g. the typical "bird flies." This leads to conclude that if a given animal is known to be a bird, and nothing else is known, it can be assumed to be able to fly. The default assumption can be retracted in case we subsequently learn that the considered animal is a penguin. Something similar happens during the learning of the past tense of English verbs [19], that is characterized by three stages: memorization of the past tense of a few verbs, generalization of the rules for regular verbs to all verbs and, finally, acquisition of the exceptions. Related mechanisms of retracting previous hypotheses arise when performing abductive reasoning. For example, the most likely explanation when we see wet grass is that it rained. This hypothesis, however, must be retracted if we get to know that the real cause of the wet grass was simply a sprinkler. Again, we are in presence of a from of non-monotonic reasoning. Likewise, if a logic takes into account the handling of something which is not known, it should not be monotonic. A logic for reasoning about knowledge is autoepistemic logic, which offers a formal context for the representation and reasoning of knowledge about knowledge. Once again, we rely on the assumption of not to construct ravenous agents which try to grasp all the information at once but, on the opposite, we assume that the agent starts reasoning with a limited amount of information on the environment, and that there is a mechanism for growing up additional granules of knowledge. Belief revision is the process of changing beliefs to accommodate a new belief that might be inconsistent with the old ones. In the assumption that the new belief is correct, some of the old ones have to be retracted in order to maintain consistency. This retraction in response to an addition of a new belief makes any logic for belief revision to be non-monotonic. In [6], two separate threads in the formal study of epistemic change, namely belief revision and argumentation, are seen as two sides (cognitive and social) of the same epistemic coin. Data and beliefs, are introduced to account for the distinction between pieces of information that are simply gathered and stored by the agent (data), and pieces of information that the agent considers reliable bases for action, decision, and specific reasoning tasks, e.g. prediction and explanation (beliefs).

Amongst others, the studies on non-monotonic reasoning seem to be motivated by the need to create a framework to incorporate common-sense reasoning, a distinctive human ability that has not been fully grasped in AI, yet. On the other hand, this kind of truly human reasoning is interwound with learning and with the temporal dimension and, therefore, it seems to be the natural direction for studies aimed at bridging symbolic and sub-symbolic representations. Interestingly, the introduction of forms of non-monotonic reasoning may lead to computational schemes that are even simpler than classical reasoning [21]. In particular, the complexity of non-monotonic reasoning can be reduced by disallowing some constructs and by requiring the knowledge base to be stratified [22].

4 Developmental paths in perception

The need of developmental plans have beeing emerging clearly, and perhaps primarily, also in the acquisition of perceptual skills, which are strongly rooted on learning. For example, nowadays significant achievements in the field of speech recognition rely on stratified architectures, in which models like HMMs express phoneme, words, and language models. In a sense, such a stratification can be read as the sign of an underlying developmental plan of the agent.

Fig. 1 Tagging single pixels with multiple labels. This task is still open and it is often regarded as a truly human ability.

Here we focus on vision, not only because of its relevance, but mostly because it is essentially an open problem and, therefore, once for which the other side of AI invoked in this paper, might open the doors to new challenging approaches. Most of the studies on vision have not been focused on its own nature and, especially, have neglected the importance of motion in the whole process of scene understanding. Like other animals[4], frogs could starve to death if given only a bowlful of dead flies, whereas they catch and eat moving flies [23]. This suggests that their excellent hunting capabilities depend only on the acquisition of a very good vision of moving objects. Saccadic eye movements play an important role in facilitating human vision and, of course, the autonomous motion is of crucial importance for any animal in vision development. Birds, some of which exhibit proverbial abilities to discover their preys (e.g. eagles, terns), are known to detect slowly moving objects, an ability developed during evolution, since the objects they typically see are far away when flying. A detailed investigations on fixational eye movements across vertebrate indicates that micro-saccades appear to be more important in foveate than afoveate species and that saccadic eye movements seem to play an important role in perceiving static images [24]. When compared with other animals, humans are likely to perform better in static - or nearly static - vision simply because they soon need to look at objects and pictures thoughtfully. However, this arises at a late stage during child development, jointly with the emergence of other symbolic abilities. The same is likely to hold for amodal perception and for the development of strange perceptive behavior like popular Kanizsa triangle [25]. The vision mechanisms experimented in different animals is the outcome of complex evolutive paths and, like for other cognitive skills, its acquisition follows rigorous stage-based schemes [26]. This might be not be simply a biologic issue, but it could be instead the consequence of more general optimization principles and complexity issues that hold regardless of the "animal body."

Computer vision has achieved impressive results in specific real-world problems, yet the studies on truly vision systems capable of reacting like most animals in their environment are still in their infancy. Humans can attach labels to any pixel of a given picture, thus providing an impressively accurate description of the entities to which it belongs to (see Fig 1). This cognitive ability is essentially independent of rotations, translations, and changes of scale. In spite of the relevant achievements of the last few years in neuroscience, the associated computational mechanisms are not fully understood yet, and computer vision is far away from even figuring out similar cognitive skills. The nearest challenge is mostly faced on image collections using variational approaches for image segmentation with some interesting results (see e.g. [27, 28]). However, in these and related studies, the labels are thought of as entities used for discovering clusters with homogeneous chromatic features, not for performing object segmentation, which requires involving higher cognitive levels. The problem of tagging objects is considered so hard that other smart solutions to collect labeled images and video have been devised which are based on human labeling initiatives like pixadus (pixdaus.com) and gwap (espgame.org/gwap). Most efforts in computer vision have not focused on the

---

[4] In addition to their infrared vision, snakes are also known to react much better to quick movements.

deep analysis of video, but mostly on sophisticated studies on images. While in the past few years this choice was mostly dictated by limitations of computational resources, the perspective has been changing significantly, especially if we consider that there are strong reasons to shift the emphasis to video.

The most significant claim of paper is in fact that if we want to start facing the above described labeling problem, we need to abandon image analysis and focus on visual analysis. We claim that image understanding is very hard to attack, and that the fact that humans brilliantly solve it might be mostly due to their natural embedding of pictures into visual scenes. Human perception of static images seems to be a higher level skill that might have been acquired only after having gained the ability of detecting moving objects. In addition, the saccadic eye movements might suggest that static images are just an illusory perception, since human eyes always perceive moving objects. The impressive literature accumulated so far in the area of natural image understanding might have faced a problem on which there is no evidence of solution in nature. This suggests to develop a vision theory in terms of functional requirements so as to discover hidden computational mechanisms that might not necessarily need to emerge from the neuronal structure of animals' visual cortex. In order to be efficient, the learning scheme must follow a developmental plan, so as we start with very simple vision tasks and gradually increase the difficulty as time goes by. The first step is basically associated with the growth of learning mechanisms that emerge while looking at moving objects in a fixed background. The focus on this specific kind of movements simplifies dramatically the objection recognition problem. The detection of the same objects in a cluttered environment requires a segmentation process that takes place thanks to the previously developed ability of recognizing objects regardless of translations, rotations, and change of scale. However, supervised learning schemes aimed at solving the pixel labeling problems are likely to fail if they do not process higher level features than the simple brightness. The development of such features is expected to be the outcome of a developmental plan in which the role of motion in perception is gradually decreased.

5 Developmental issues in the interplay of learning and reasoning

In the previous two sections, the discussion has centered around the gradual growth of skills in both reasoning and perceptual tasks. Interestingly, agents based on the proposed *constraint machine*, outlined in Section 2, encompass both learning and reasoning, provided that some logic formalism is attached to the constraints. At the light of this representation of intelligent agents, one early recognizes that non-monotonic reasoning and stage-based learning are nothing else that two sides of the same medal, and that the conception of developmental plan has to play a crucial role also in cases in which we expect a significant interplay of learning and reasoning. This corresponds with most challenging human abilities that grows up as the time goes by. The detailed analysis of the simple artificial learning task shown below suggests that the role of the temporal dimension and the stratification of knowledge is not of unique human pertinence.

Example 2 *Let us consider the learning task sketched in Fig. 2. Interestingly, the examples and the predicates can be expressed in the common formalism of constraints. We can neatly distinguish supervised learning pairs and FOL predicates. There is experimental evidence to claim that a ravenous agent which makes use of C is not as effective as one which focuses attention on the supervised examples and, later on, continues by incorporating the predicates [29]. Basically, the developmental path which first favors the development of sub-symbolic representations leads to a more effective solution. The effect of this developmental step is to break up the complexity of learning jointly examples and predicates. Learning turns out to be converted into an optimization problem, which is typically plagued by the presence of sub-optimal solutions. The developmental path which enforces the learning from examples at the first stage is just a way to circumvent local minima.*

6 Stage-based learning

The studies in developmental psychology can provide insights on the structure of models of intelligent agents. Along this research guideline we can frame the recent research on developmental AI by [30, 31]. The gradual exposition to knowledge granules or, equivalently, the birth of mechanisms of focussing of attention is rooted in general principles that hold for humans and machines. This becomes clear when considering supervised learning as posed in Definition 1. Within the given framework, the learning process is given a functional interpretation that makes no assumption on the agent body. However, for complex tasks, when optimizing the functional 1, we are likely to end up into poor sub-optimal solutions. The blind search in similar functional spaces is hopeless, unless some the learning process is properly fragmented into simpler stages. The functions f_j introduced in Section 2 have an attached semantics and can be properly labelled, but can be hardly learned in the input space. The emergence of deep structures is the only possible way to escape to the trap of local minima, provided that the different representation layers that emerge are associated with an appropriate developmental plan. For example, in vision a developmental agent is expected to construct intermediate layers that remind us of V1 and V2 in the visual neural cortex (see Fig. 3). Apart from the self-organizing mechanisms for learning these internal features, a central problem is that of devising a plan that is likely to succeed.

A general principle that seems to be at the basis of human cognition is to focus on easy constraints at any state of the learning process. In vision, this the translation of this principle is start to learn from quickly moving objects, and continue by focussing on slower moving objects later. Interestingly, the motion offers a way of restricting significantly the portion of the retina to be processed,

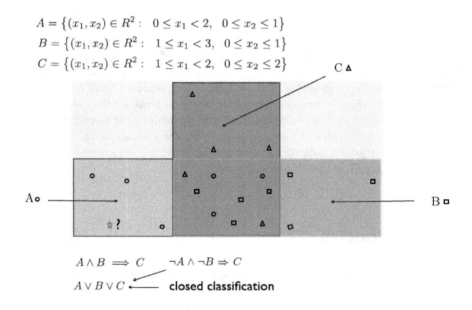

$$A = \{(x_1, x_2) \in R^2 : \ 0 \le x_1 < 2, \ \ 0 \le x_2 \le 1\}$$
$$B = \{(x_1, x_2) \in R^2 : \ 1 \le x_1 < 3, \ \ 0 \le x_2 \le 1\}$$
$$C = \{(x_1, x_2) \in R^2 : \ 1 \le x_1 < 2, \ \ 0 \le x_2 \le 2\}$$

$$A \wedge B \implies C \qquad \neg A \wedge \neg B \Rightarrow C$$
$$A \vee B \vee C \longleftarrow \ \text{closed classification}$$

Fig. 2 The task consists of learning three classes from examples and from a set of FOL predicates. The ordering of presentation does matter: First, learning of supervised examples and then injection of FOL predicates is more effective than using a ravenous agent.

thus postponing the recognition of structured objects at higher levels, where the corresponding features can span larger area of the retina.

7 Conclusions

It has been claimed that reasoning and learning in perceptual tasks, like vision, strongly benefit from a developmental path. This becomes increasingly more important when approaching tasks in which symbolic and sub-symbolic representations co-exist. This paper supports the position that stage-based learning, as discussed in developmental psychology is not the outcome of biology, but is instead the consequence of optimization principles and complexity issues that hold regardless of the body. This position is supposed to re-enforce recent

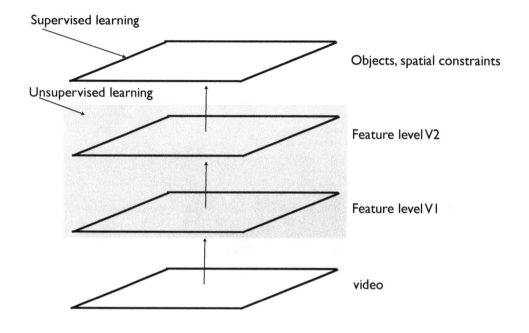

Supervised learning

Objects, spatial constraints

Unsupervised learning

Feature level V2

Feature level V1

video

Fig. 3 Stage-based learning and a corresponding deep architecture for vision.

studies on developmental AI more inspired to studies in cognitive development (see e.g. [31]) and is somehow coherent with the growing interest in deep architectures and learning [32].

Acknowledgements We thank M. Diligenti and M. Maggini, L. Serafini, and G. Palm for fruitful discussions.

References

1. Korf, R.: Depth-first iterative-deepening: An optimal admissible tree search. Artificial Intelligence **27** (1985) 97–109
2. Taylor, M.: Pseudo-differential operators. Princeton University Press (1981)
3. Poggio, T., Girosi, F.: A theory of networks for approximation and learning. Technical report, MIT (1989)
4. Tikhonov, A., Arsenin, V., John, F.: Solutions of ill-posed problems. VH Winston Washington, DC (1977)
5. Wahba, G.: Smoothing noisy data by spline functions. Num. Math. **23** (1975) 183–194

6. Wahba, G.: Spline models for observational data. Society for Industrial Mathematics (1990)
7. Schoelkopf, B., Smola, A.: From regularization operators to support vector kernels. In Kaufmann, M., ed.: Advances in Neural Information Processing Systems. (1998)
8. Smola, A., Schoelkopf, B., Mueller, K.: The connection between regularization operators and support vector kernels. Neural Networks **11** (1998) 637– 649
9. Evgenious, T., Pontil, M., Poggio, T.: Regularization networks and support vector machines. Avances in Computational Mathematics (1999)
10. Gori, M.: A variational framework for kernel machines. Technical report, University of Sienna (2009)
11. Hadamard, J.: Sur les problemes aux derivees partielles et leur signification physique. Princeton University Bulletin (1902) 49–52
12. Yuille, A., Grzywacz, N.: A mathematical analysis of the motion coherence theory. International Journal of Computer Vision **3** (1989) 155–175
13. Kataoka, N., Kaneko, K.: Functional dynamics. i: Articulation process. Physica D: Nonlinear Phenomena **138** (2000) 225–250
14. Kataoka, N., Kaneko, K.: Functional dynamics ii: Syntactic structure. Physica D: Nonlinear Phenomena **149** (2001) 174–196
15. Diligenti, M., Gori, M., M. Maggini, M., Rigutini, L.: Multitask kernel-based learning with logic constraints. In: Proceedings of the 19th European Conference on Artificial Intelligence. (2010)
16. Diligenti, M., Gori, M., M. Maggini, M., Rigutini, L.: Multitask kernel-based learning with first-order logic constraints. In: Proceedings of the 20th International Conference on Inductive Logic Programming. (2010)
17. Diligenti, M., Gori, M., Maggini, M.: Towards developmental ai: The paradox of ravenous intelligent agents. In: 7th International Workshop on Neural-Symbolic Learning and Reasoning - IJCAI 2011. (2011)
18. McCarthy, J.: Circumscription's a form of non-monotonic reasoning. Artificial Intelligence **13** (1980) 27–39
19. Rumelhart, D., McClelland, J.: On learing the pat tense of english verbs. In: Parallel Distributed Processing, Vol. 2. (1986) 216–271
20. Paglieri, F., Castelfranchi, C.: Revising Beliefs Through Arguments: Bridging the Gap Between Argumentation and Belief Revision in MAS. Volume 3366. Springer, Lecture Notes in Computer Science (2005)
21. Cadoli, M., Donini, F., Schaerf, M.: Is intractability of non-monotonic reasoning a real drawback? In: Proceedings of the AAAI-2004. (2004)
22. Niemela, I., Rintanen, J.: On the impact of stratification on the complexity of nonmonotonic reasoning. Volume 810. Springer, Lecture Notes in Computer Science (1994)
23. Lettvin, J., Maturana, H., McCulloch, W., Pitts, W.: What the frog's eye tells the frog's brain. In: Reprinted from - The Mind: Biological Approaches to its functions - Eds Willian C. Corning, Martin Balaban. (1968) 233–358
24. Martinez-Conde, S., Macknik, S.: Fixational eye movements across vertebrates: Comparative dynamics, physiology, and perception. Journal of Vision **8** (2008) 1–16
25. Kanizsa, G.: Margini quasi-percettivi in campi con stimolazione omogenea. Rivista di Psicologia **49** (1955) 7–30
26. Piaget, J.: La psychologie de l'intelligence. Armand Colin, Paris (1961)
27. Ishikawa, H.: Exact optimization for random markov fields with convex priors. IEEE Trans. on Pattern Anal. and Machine Intell. **25** (2003) 1333–1336
28. Pock, T., Schoenemann, T., Graber, G., Bishop, H., Cremers, D.: A convex formulation of continuous multilabel problems. In Forsyth, D., Torr, P., A. Zisserman, S.V., eds.: European Conference on Computer Vision. (2008)
29. Diligenti, M., Gori, M., Maggini, M.: Bridging logic and kernel machines. Machine Learning **83** (2011)
30. Guerin, F.: Constructivism in ai: Prospects, progress and challenges. In: Computing and Phylosophy: AISB 2008 Proceedings, Vol. 12. (2008) 20–28

31. Sloman, A.: Ontologies for baby animals and robots. from baby stuff to the world of adult science: Developmental ai from a kantian viewpoint. Technical report, University of Birmingham (2009)
32. Bengio, Y., Louradour, J., Lollobert, R., Weston, J.: Curriculum learning. In: 26th Annual International Conference on Machine Learning, Montreal, Canada (2009) 41–48

Part II

Reasons, reasoning, and rationality

Chapter 4
A formalism to represent mental states

Aldo Franco Dragoni

Abstract This chapter provides simple computational structure for representing recursive mental states that could constitute the semantic level of a formal language to deal with mental states' dynamics. For the sake of simplicity, we base our conception of *mental state* on only two primitive attitudes: *beliefs* (for the cognitive sphere) and *desires* (for the volitional sphere).

1 Introduction

As far as I know, the term "intentional systems" was coined by the philosopher Daniel Dennett to describe entities whose behavior can be predicted by attributing them beliefs, desires and rational acumen [Dennett, 1987]. Many researchers, as John McCarthy and Yoav Shoham, have substantially agreed in believing that agents are conveniently described (and ontologically "defined") by their intentional stance, and that two major categories of mental skills may characterize an agent: those related to *cognition* and those related to *action*. "Cognition" and "Action", *information-related* vs. *pro-active* mental attitudes. The first category includes knowledge and beliefs (regarding the world in which the agent resides). The second one takes into account everything else, i.e. desires, intentions, obligations, commitments, choices etc. In Artificial Intelligence it is commonly accepted that it is these *pro*-attitudes that drive the actions of the agent, but there is still no clear consensus about which "magic" combination of information-related and pro-active attitudes is more appropriate to characterize a rational agent. While the BDI paradigm conceives an equal role for Beliefs, Desires and Intentions in the ontology of "rational agenthood", and while the rest of the AI community shares a *knowledge-centered* vision of the "intelligence", throughout his scientific life Castelfranchi argued

Aldo Franco Dragoni
Department of Electronics, Artificial Intelligence and Telecommunications, Università Politecnica delle Marche, Italy
e-mail: a.f.dragoni@univpm.it

against the prevalent tolemaic view of *cognition*- towards a *goal-centered* view of agenthood.

Cristiano has been the most influential scientist in my research. When I met him I was just an AIÂηenthusiastic graduate in electronic engineering, while he was already leading a community of researchers in "Distributed Artificial Intelligence". He drove my attention towards two problems:

Question 1: Why an artificial agent should *believe* information coming from other agents, including humans? (*gullible agent* assumption)

Question 2: Why an artificial agent should stop pursuing their goals to adopt another agent's goal? (*benevolent agent* assumption)

These two weaknesses of the nascent research on Multi-Agent Systems (MAS) were perfectly focused on the dual nature of rational agenthood, the cognitive and the deliberative ones, the knowledge-based and the volitional.

I was very impressed by the actual urgency to answer these two questions, so I immediately approached the first one, trying to figure out what might be the reasons that could lead a rational agent to disbelieve an information in case of conflict with others. More generally, one could disbelieve some information even if it does not cause conflicts with known pieces of information, but these position seemed to me (as an engineer) somewhat strange and irrational, so not desirable to be introduced in our artificial *rational* agents. I sketched then a couple of "rational criteria for the cognitive change" [Dragoni 1992][Dragoni 1996]. That problem was regarded as a "belief revision" process, i.e. a process that a rational agent should follow to solve conflicts inside its cognitive state. While I was trying to understand how to solve these cognitive conflicts (for the advantage of my artificial agents) I experienced my first conflict with Cristiano, (for the disadvantage of my scientific carrier...). Actually, on my side, I concentrated my attention on two common *logical errors* in the cognitive revision:

• the *partial acceptance*: the new information is eventually accepted without *all* its logical implications (all the logical consequences of the combination *new∪known* pieces of information)

• the *excessive rejection*: to accommodate a *new* conflicting piece of information one should get rid of no more knowledge than strictly necessary (the ancient *Occam's razor principle*, i.e., the principle of parsimony).

Instead, Cristiano, in some private conversations, proposed to add the following three principles, that I refused, since they seemed to me not "*logical criteria*" but "*psycho*logical errors"!

• *conservation of objectives*: people tend to feel more credible information which, if true, would make it possible the achievement of desired objectives

• *retention of knowledge*: people tend to feel less credible information which, if accepted, would lead to a more drastic and tiring change of the cognitive state

• *chronological dependence*: people tend to feel more credible information gained from more time, even if they never had a real confirmation.

The first point made me clear how much important were *goals* to Cristiano. It seemed to me that much of Cristiano's interests in MAS was motivated by the need to deepen into the nature of human conflicts; *goal* conflicts among "rational" agents; how do they raise, how do they evolve (*goal dynamics*) and, eventually, how could a human community deal with them. This is a genuine scientific interest that can be approached from many perspectives since the issue is inherent to human nature and can be dealt with under the light of different scientific disciplines. Cristiano chose the light of Artificial Intelligence, thus contributing so much to the development of Distributed Artificial Intelligence all over the world.

But, as an engineer, I had to be more interested in *defining* the relationships between the cognitive and volitional levels, for the design of future *intelligent* artificial agents, rather than *studying* those same relationships for understanding the current *deficient* human agents ... . Under my *normative* perspective things seemed quite different since, while the knowledge level should actually affect the deliberative one, the opposite should not. In my point of view the volitional sphere should not affect cognition but *action*. Eventually, an action may acquire new knowledge thus modifying the knowledge level, so the deliberative sphere could really affect the cognitive state, but only in an indirect manner, through the mediation of that action (eventually a speech-act) as depicted in Fig. 1.

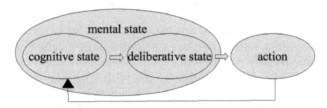

Fig. 1 Desires should not affect Beliefs, unless through the mediation of Actions

So, to answer Question 1 (*gullible agent* assumption), I committed myself to understand the relationships between the *credibility* of the information provided by a given source and the *reliability* of that source. I supposed that the reliability of a source of information affects the credibility of those pieces of information and *viceversa*, but I hardly could understand how. I finally converged on a model that is based on the following elements [Dragoni 1997]:

1. *assumption-based deduction*, to avoid the "partial acceptance"
2. *maximal consistency*, to avoid the "excessive rejection"
3. *bayesian conditioning*, to revise the various sources' degrees of reliability after contradictions among them
4. *dempster-shafer theory of evidence*, to correlate the credibility of a piece of information with its source's reliability

Such a model for "belief revision" is be applied to solve conflicts between data coming from different sensors [Dragoni 1998] or between information coming from different expert systems or neural networks [Dragoni 2010], since *all these do not have goals nor desires* (or, better, since *it seems there is no need to think them as having goals or desires*)! But humans do have intentions, whether overt or hidden! so it should be a nonsense to apply this method to police investigations [Dragoni 1994][Dragoni 2003] or to model the cognitive process of jury deliberation in a trial court [Dragoni 2001]. However, although the reliability of a witness depends on its desires and that of a defendant depends on its motive, it is safer to ground the jurors' opinions about their reliability only on the information provided, regardless of their goals, because these latter are just "presumed" and because their intentions do not *necessarily* affect their testimonies.

Cristiano's Question 2 (*benevolent agent* assumption) was much harder for me to deal with. The psychology of sociality, the emergence of collective goals from a collection of selfish interests and utilitarian behaviour, the relationship of these social phenomena with the personal and collective memory (and therefore with the cognitive spheres, both social and individual), the onset and change of these interests, etc., all these were phenomena too complex to understand for a computer programmer like me. Furthermore, when I was trying to approach these problems, after Cristiano's steps, I was a bit frustrated by formulas like this:

$$GOAL_x : (Do\ X\ A) \Rightarrow GOAL_x : p \Rightarrow GOAL_x : (Obtain\ Y\ p) \Rightarrow GOAL_x : \quad (1)$$

with an undefined syntax and, of course, semantics. So I experienced my second (and last) conflict with Cristiano's scientific approach. For him, the formal symbols were merely a means to express concepts in a schematic way, but unfortunately I did not know what to do with formulas written in an undefined pseudo-language with ambiguous meanings. I realized that even if I had been successful in defining a syntax for that language, without a mechanized semantics I couldn't ever build any automatic proof procedure that could be used to implement an artificial reasoner. At best, I'd reach a point as Modal Logic would be today if Kripke hadn't provided a semantics for it, i.e. the *possible-worlds semantics*; we would had a language for expressing concepts, but not for programming theorem-provers that could be eventually proved to be *correct* and *complete* (w.r.t. the underlying semantics).

In those days Modal Logic was already used in various scientific and technical disciplines, for instance it was interpreted as a "Temporal Logic", a "Deontic Logic" or an "Epistemic Logic", by simply changing the interpretations of its modal operators. Cohen and Levesque extended its use to represent and model not only the *cognitive state* of an artificial mind (with the cited epistemic logic), but also its *volitional state*, introducing their *"logic of intentions"*. [Cohen 1990] has been one of the best-known and most influential contributions to the area of Agent Theory. Their logic has been useful for the analysis of conflicts and cooperation in multi-agent dialogue, but it was originally conceived to develop a theory of intention as a pre-requisite for a theory of speech acts (from intention to action, to *speech*-action). I was excited to use their logic to formalize the causal relation from a mental state (the cause) and a speech-act (the effect). However, while I was trying to use that theory to understand how the receiver of a speech-act could infer, through abduction, the speaker's mental state that caused the speech-act [Dragoni, 1993][Dragoni, 1994], it seemed to me that the Kripke style *desirable-world semantics* for intentional modal logic was too rigid and not so useful to deal with the inherent recursive structure of mental states, which plays an essential role when modelling high level interaction between intelligent agents. Quoting from [Bradshaw 1997]:

"each agent might possess to a greater or lesser degree attributes like the ones enumerated in [Etzioni and Weld 1995] and [Franklin and Graesser 1996]:...

- Autonomy: goal-directedness, proactive and self-starting behavior
- Collaborative behavior: can work in concert with other agents to achieve a common goal
- "Knowledge-level" [Newell 1982] communication ability: the ability to communicate with persons and other agents with language more resembling humanlike "speech acts" than typical symbol-level program-to-program protocols"
- Inferential capability: can act on abstract task specification using prior knowledge of general goals and preferred methods to achieve flexibility; goes beyond the information given, and may have explicit models of self, user, situation, and/or other agents.

It is clear that these capabilities cannot be performed without making our agents able to represent the others' mental state, which in turn should represent the others' mental state and so on, in a *recursive* manner; of course, this implies that agents need also to represent their own mental state, thus opening the way to implement a form of *consciousness*.

The rest of the paper is structured as follows.

Sect. 2 describes the recursive structure that provides semantics to the formalism for the representation of mental states.

Sect. 3 introduces the syntax and the semantics of the formalism.

Sect. 4 explains how the formalism could provide a basis for reasoning with the dynamics of mental states, i.e. how act follow a certain mental condition.

In Sect. 5 we introduce two important limitation of the formalism described in this paper and give some suggestions abut how to overcome them; we also foresee here what will be our work in the immediate future.

2 The mental structure of an artificial agent

We needed a computational structure as simple as possible for representing recursive mental states that could constitute the semantic level of a formal language to deal with mental states' dynamics. For the sake of simplicity, we base our conception of *mental* state on only two primitive attitudes: *beliefs* (for the cognitive sphere) and *desires* (for the volitional sphere). "Believing" just means "having a symbolic representation of a *real* state of the world", while "desiring" means "having a symbolic representation of an *ideal* state of the world", where "ideal" means "preferable over all the possible states of the world". Other attitudes, as "knowledge" and "intention", might either be added or eventually derived from these primitives (see the discussion in [Rao-Georgeff, 1995]).

Let us introduce the *mental* structure of our artificial agent Adam. It *believes* a certain state of affairs **B** of the world while it *desires* a state **D**. Both **B** and **D** might be partitioned into an external (**E**) and an internal (**I**) continents, the latter referring to the agent's own mental world. Thus we have four continents, **BE**, **BI**, **DE** and **DI**. Normally **BE≠DE**; in fact, **BE=DE** would mean that Adam is completely satisfied with the external world where he *believes* to live in. Analogously, **BI** and **DI** might be different, meaning that *Adam desires* to change what he *believes* its own mental state is (Fig. 2).

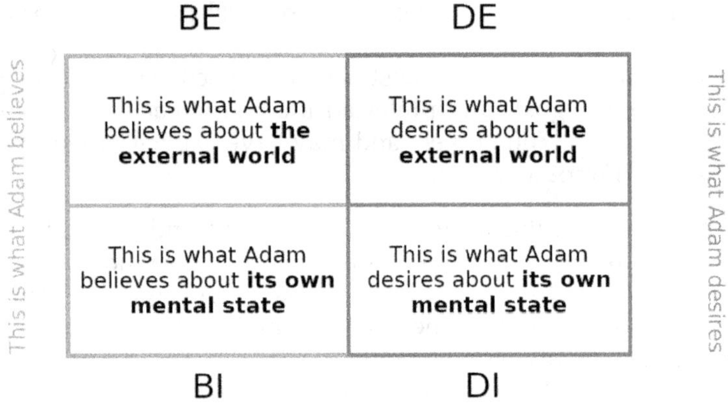

Fig. 2 Partitioning mental *worlds* into *internal* and *external* continents

Both the continents **BI** and **DI** may be recursively mapped into four sub-continents, two of which are meant to be "known" (internal and external) and the other two are intended to be "desired" (internal and external, Fig. 3). Clearly, this notion of mental state is recursive: mental attitudes may have other mental attitudes as arguments and so on. Although recursion is theoretically infinite, three or four levels of depth should be sufficient to describe most of the psychologically plausible human mental dynamics (see also the discussion in [Gmytrasiewicz-Durfee-Wehe, 1995]) (Fig. 4).

When Adam is engaged in a conversation with Eve, both its internal continents take into account also Eve's mental structure. On her side, Eve's internal continents must map also Adam's mental structure and so on (Fig. 5).

Adam's and Eve's scenario might be generalized to a group of agents. Let us denote with $\Sigma_{i,G}$ the mental structure of the agent i as part of the group G. Since mental structures are trees, pathnames are the obvious way to identify nodes.

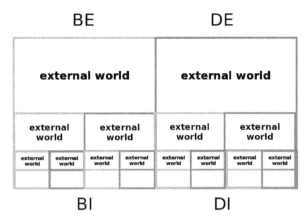

Fig. 3 Internal continents are nested recursively ...

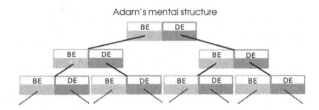

Fig. 4 ...and the recursion is potentially infinite, but three levels are sufficient for most reasoning

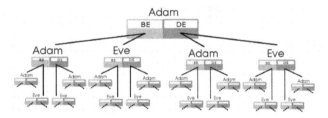

Fig. 5 Adam's mental state after the creation of Eve

2.1 The multi-contextual representation of a mental state

Multi-language formalisms [Giunchiglia-Serafini, 1994] gave us new opportunities to represent mental states. We base the semantics on the notion of mental structure given in the previous section. The formalism is modular; its elementary brick is a triangular structure made of three contexts (i.e. three different sets of formulae, Fig. 6 right side):

- x: represents the agent x's mental state as a whole
- B: represents x's beliefs
- D: represents x's desires

Sentences in B and in D represent, respectively, something which is "consciously believed" or "consciously desired". Instead, some non-atomic formulae in x (e.g., implications between beliefs and desires) may represent mental attitudes and correlations that affect unconsciously the agent's cognitive behaviour, i.e. the agent is not aware of them. Each context is a decidable theory (possibly empty) expressed in an appropriate formal language (see next section). Each of the four arrows represents a "*bridge-rule*": B_down, B_up, D_down and D_up. Informally, their effect is as follows:

- if it is provable in x that a formula is *believed*, then that formula is provable in B (*B_down*) and vice-versa (*B_up*)
- if it is provable in x that a formula is *desired*, then that formula is provable in D (*D_down*) and vice-versa (*D_up*)

These bridge rules' semantics will be formally described in the next section. The *x-module* is then replicated and assembled in a hierarchical manner, from the first level, down to the second and so on. Fig. 7 shows the multi-contextual representation of Adam's mental state when engaged in a communication with Eve, again truncated at the third level of depth.

Let us denote with $MS_{i,G}$ the multi-contextual representation of the agent i's mental state, being i part of the group G. The correspondence between $MS_{i,G}$ and $\Sigma_{i,G}$ is quite evident, and pathnames are again the obvious way to label the contexts. Just to give an intuitive idea of the meaning of the various contexts:

- a/D/a: represents what a desires its own mental state would be
  - (in particular) a/D/a/B: represents what a desires to believe
  - (in particular) a/D/a/D: represents what a desires to desire
- a/D/e: represents what a desires e's mental state would be
  - (in particular) a/D/e/B: represents what a desires that e believes
  - (in particular) a/D/e/D: represents what a desires that e desires
- aa/B/a: represents what a believes its own mental state is
  - (in particular) a/B/a/B: represents what a believes to believe
  - (in particular) a/B/a/D: represents what a believes to desire
- a/B/e: represents what a believes e's mental state is
  - (in particular) a/B/e/B: represents what a believes that e believes
  - (in particular) a/B/e/D: represents what a believes that e desires

3 Languages and Semantics

Let us define now the languages adopted in the contexts and their semantics.

3.1 *Sintax*

To cope with the complexity of this formalism we need three kinds of languages. At the basic level there are the *external languages,* i.e. those which agents adopt to *represent the external world,* not their own mental attitudes. Each agent *i* has its own external language *ELi*. Although the essential requirement for each *ELi* is decidability, we suppose these languages to be propositional. Referring to the mental structure depicted in Fig 5, *ELa* describes the continents *$*a$/**BE** and *$*a$/**DE** (where * stands for "any path") and *ELe* describes the continents *$*e$/**BE** and *$*e$/**DE**.

Definition 1 *For each agent i, the* external language *ELi is the propositional language associated to i.*

External languages are the basis for the *argument languages* adopted in the contexts *$*i$/B and *$*i$/D.

Definition 2 *For each agent i ∈ G, its* argument language *ALi is defined as follows:*

1. *α is an* atomic *formula of ALi iff:*

   a. *either it is a formula of the external language ELi*
   b. *or it is a formula of a mental language MLj (see the next definition) for an agent j ∈ G*

2. *¬α is a formula of ALi iff α is a formula of ALi*
3. *α∨β, α∧β and α→β are formulae of ALi iff α and β are formulae of ALi*
4. *nothing else is a formula of ALi.*

Argument language *ALi* borrows the atoms from its correspondent external language *ELi* and from a third kind of language, *MLj*, that we call *"mental language"* of the agent *j*. *MLi* is the language adopted in any context of the type *$*/i$. Each *MLi* is a first order language with no functional symbols and only two unary predicates, *iB* and *iD*, denoting, respectively, the beliefs and the desires of agent *i*. They have as arguments the reified versions of argument language formulae as follows:

Definition 3 *For each agent i, its mental language MLi is defined as follows:*

- *iB(δ) and iD(δ) are atomic sentences of MLi iff δ is a sentence of ALi*
- *¬α is a formula of MLi iff α is a formula of MLi*
- *α∨β, α∧β and α→β are formulae of MLi iff α and β are formulae of MLi*
- *nothing else is a formula of MLi.*

Although $iB(_\delta)$ and $iD(_\delta)$ are atomic, we distinguish between the "mental level" $iB(\cdot)$ or $iD(\cdot)$, and the "argument-level" $_\delta$, where the subscript $_\delta$ is an individual constant of *MLi* denoting the name of a formula $\delta \in ALi$. As a matter of fact, these reified formulae are the only constants of *MLi*. There are no quantifiers because there are no variables. The interleaving between *MLi* and *ALi* is to avoid that sentences of the form $iiB(-\alpha)$ (or $iD(_\alpha)$), with $\alpha \in ELj$ and $i \neq j$ could belong to *MLi* and appear in the contexts *$*/i$; thus it is not possible that an agent i's mental attitude has as argument a state of the external world described through the language of another agent j. Even if all the external languages would be identical, mental languages would be completely disjoint from each others. In other words, there does not exist a formula belonging to more than one mental language. This is just because each MLi relies on its own set of atomic sentences built upon its own couple of unary predicates $iB(\cdot)$ and $iD(\cdot)$. The argument language of the various agents differ only in the part relative to their external language. For any agent i, any formula of MLi is also a formula of ALi. Fig. 10 shows some examples of mental and argument formulae built upon two propositional languages, $ELadam=\{a,b\}$ and $ELeve=\{a\}$ (meaning that Eve has a poorer dictionary to represent the external world where she lives in). Line 6 in Fig. 10 says that "Eve believes that either Adam desires b or herself desires a". That formula belongs to Eve's mental language even if the propositional letter b is not in her dictionary, but in Adam's one. "Eve believes b" cannot be represented as a formula of Eve's mental language, but "Eve believes that Adam believes b" do can.

3.2 Semantics

As anticipated, theories in contexts *i are expressed through MLi, while theories in contexts *i/B and *i/D are expressed through ALi. The fact that a formula α belongs to the theory contained in a context C will be expressed by prefixing the name of that context as a label to the formula, i.e. C:α. These *labelled formulae* are of the following two kinds:

- *i:α, where $\alpha \in MLi$
- *i/B:α and *i/D:α, where $\alpha \in ALi$

As we'll see in a while, the semantic of the formers, which we call *mental formulae*, relies upon the semantic of the latter, that we call *argument formulae*. To simplify definitions and proofs we'll refer to a generic predicate iP, instead of iB or iD, and to a generic context P, instead of B or D.

Let us start by defining the semantics of *atomic* mental formulae, i.e., the semantics of *i:$iP(_\delta)$ where $\delta \in ALi$. This is related to the multi-context representation of mental states introduced in the previous section. In fact, the intended meaning of predicates $iP(_\delta)$ in a context *i is that $\delta \in ALi$ is true in the context *i/P.

Definition 4 *An* atomic *mental formula of MLi* *i:$iP(_\delta)$, with $\delta \in ALi$, is true iff the argument formula *i/P:δ is true.*

The semantics of *non-atomic* mental formulae is defined as usual:

Definition 5 *Given two mental formulae α and β of MLi:*

- *i:¬α *is true iff* *i:α *is false.*
- *i:$\alpha \lor \beta$ *is true iff either* *i:α *is true, or* *i:β, *or both*

- *i:α∧β is true iff both *i:α and *i:β are true
- *i:α→β is true iff *i:¬α∨β is true.

As anticipated, definition 4 grounds the semantics of mental formulae (i.e., formulae of the kind i:α, where α∈MLi) upon the semantics of argument formulae (i.e., *i/P:δ where δ∈ALi). From definition 2 we see that the semantic of argument languages ALi needs, in turn, to be built upon that of atoms of ELi and MLi. The semantic of this multi-language formalism stands essentially on the atoms *i/P:α with α∈Eli, which are related to the notion of "mental structure" introduced in the previous section. This mental structure maps on the multi-context representations of mental states since contexts of the type *i/B maps into continents of the type *i/BE, while context of the type *i/D maps into continents of the type *i/DE (Fig. 6). Let **PE** denote either **BE** or **DE**. Let Ω_i denote the set of all the "truth functions" over the propositional letters of ELi.

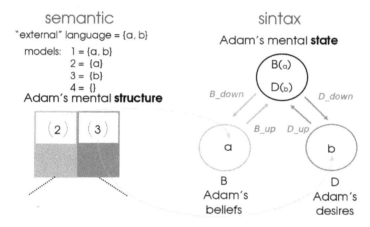

Fig. 6 Our multi-context formalism for representing mental states and its semantics

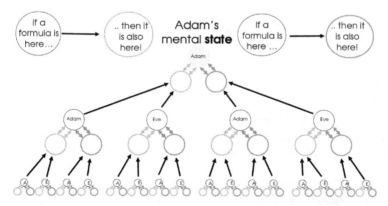

Fig. 7 The triangular module is the elementary brick of an infinite recursive syntactic structure

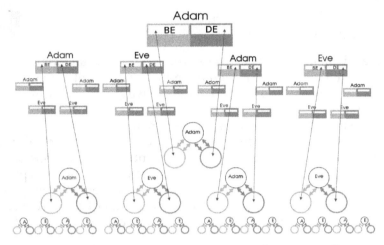

Fig. 8 Our multi-context form*ALi*sm bases its semantic on the corresponding mental structure

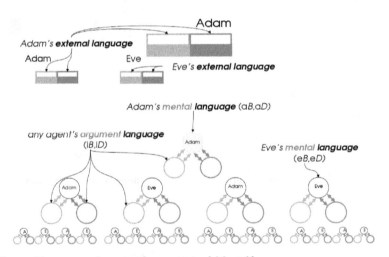

Fig. 9 *External* language, *Argument* language and *Mental* language

Definition 6 *An* interpretation *of ELi is an element of* Ω_i. *A* model *of a continent* **i/PE in* Σ_i, G *is a subset of* Ω_i, *i.e. a set of interpretations of ELi.*

The interpretations play the role of "possible worlds" in our system. As a default each continent **i/*PE in Σ_i, G should have the overall Ω_i as a model, so that nothing can be derived in the corresponding context **i/P in MS_i, G, apart from tautologies. By doing so our agents will have a void mental state at birth! In our examples, the fact that the model of a continent is not represented, or that the continent itself is not represented, means that its model is Ω_i.

A mental structure is a theoretically infinite tree (Fig. 5), so we need to provide semantics for any element of that tree.

ELadam and ELeve are two propositional languages built, respectively, on
the propositional letters $\{a,b\}$ and $\{a\}$

		MLadam	ALadam	MLeve	ALeve
1	a		•		•
2	$a \vee b$		•		
3	$adamB_{(a)}$	•	•		•
4	$adamB_{(a \vee b)}$	•	•		•
5	$a \vee adamB_{(b)}$		•		•
6	$eveB(adamD_{(b)} \vee eveD_{(a)})$		•	•	•
7	$\neg adamB_{(a)} \wedge adamD_{(b)}$	•	•		•
8	$adamD_{(a)} \vee eveD_{(a)}$		•		•

Fig. 10 Examples of *Argument* and *Mental* formulae from two *External*

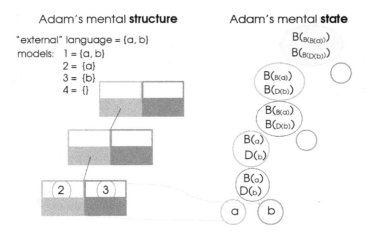

Fig. 11 Example a Mental State from a *Truth Tree*

Definition 7 *A* Truth Tree $TT_{i,G}$ *for an agent i in a group G, is the assignment of a model to each* continent *$*i/PE$ in Σ_i, G.*

In the rest of the paper we always refer to an agent i as member of a group
G, so that we undertake both the agent and the group by writing TT, MS and
Σ instead of TT_i, G, MS_i, G and Σ_i, G.

Let Ω (without the index) denote the set of all the *Truth Trees* TT. The semantics of argument atoms $*i/P:\alpha$, where $\alpha \in ALi$ is a formula of ELi, is defined as
follows:

Definition 8 *Let $*i/P^{TT}$ denote the model associated by the truth tree TT to the continent $*i/PE$. We say that $TT \in \Omega$ is a* model *for a labelled formula $*i/P:\alpha$, where $\alpha \in ALi$
is an atomic formula of ELi, iff α is true in* all *the interpretations of the set $*i/P^{TT}$.
In this case we write $*i/P^{TT} \models \alpha$ and $TT \models *i/P:\alpha$.*

Note that $*i/P:\alpha$ and $*i/P:\neg\alpha$ may both be false since $TT \in \Omega$ could not be a
model either for $*i/P:\alpha$ or for $*i/P:\neg\alpha$. In this case the following definition holds:

Definition 9 *Let* $*i/P^{TT}$ *denote the model associated by the truth tree* TT *to the continent* $*i/\textbf{PE}$*. We say that* $TT{\in}\Omega$ *is a model for* $*i/{\neg}P : \alpha$*, where* $\alpha{\in}ALi$ *is an atomic formula of ELi, iff it is not the case that* α *is true in all the interpretations of the set* $*i/P^{TT}$*. In this case we write* $*i/P^{TT} \not\models \alpha$ *and* $TT \not\models *i/P{:}\alpha$*.*

Even if a mental structure is potentially infinite, for practical purposes we suppose Σ made up of a finite number of continents. To be more precise, we suppose that only a limited number of continents of a mental structure have a model different from Ω_i.

The semantics of argument atoms $*i/P{:}\alpha$, where $\alpha{\in}ALi$ is a mental formula of MLj, for any agent j, is related to MS in a very simple way:

Definition 10 *An attitudinal formula* $*i/P{:}\alpha$*, where* $\alpha{\in}ALi$ *is a formula of some mental language MLj, is true iff* α *is true in the context* $*i/P/j$*.*

This definition makes recursive the semantic of mental formulae of MLi in $*i$. In fact, it depends on the semantics of argument formulae of ALi in $*i/P$, which in turn may depend on the semantics of mental formulae of MLi in $*i/P/i$ and so on. The example in Fig. 11 supposes that G={*Adam*} and that *ElAdam* is built upon two propositional letters: a and b.

Comment 1. This multi-context formalism departs from conventional modal approaches to BDI architectures, and its semantics has little in common with classical "Kripke-style" possible worlds one. There is no notion of "accessibility relation" here and truth trees do not make any commitment on the interpretations of their continents. The unconstrained nature of this formalism implies that it does not make much a sense puzzling about which axioms of classical modal logic apply here since, in general, the answer is negative. For instance, S4:$K\alpha{\rightarrow}KK\alpha$, which is a controversial axiom in epistemic modal logic, does not hold here. The price to pay for this freedom is implausible configurations of beliefs and desires, as in the trivial case illustrated in Fig. 12. In classical modal logic, epistemic properties are related to various degrees of constraints imposed over the accessibility relation on possible worlds. In this form*AL*ism, epistemic axioms could be proved on the backstage of opportune constraints imposed over the possible paths/interpretations in the mental structure's hierarchy. However, this complex matter is far out of the scope of this introductory paper and we hope it will be a fruitful line of research for future work.

The semantics of non-atomic attitudinal formulae $*i/P{:}\alpha$, where $\alpha{\in}ALi$, is as usual:

Definition 11 *Given two formulae* α *and* β *of ALi:*

- $*i/P{:}{\neg}\alpha$ *is true iff* $*i/P{:}\alpha$ *is false.*
- $*i/P{:}\alpha{\vee}\beta$ *is true iff either* $*i/P{:}\alpha$ *is true, or* $*i/P{:}\beta$*, or both*
- $*i/P{:}\alpha{\wedge}\beta$ *is true iff both* $*i/P{:}\alpha$ *and* $*i/P{:}\beta$ *are true*
- $*i/P{:}\alpha{\rightarrow}\beta$ *is true iff* $*i/P{:}{\neg}\alpha{\vee}\beta$ *is true.*

In [Dragoni 2008] the following theorems were proved.

Theorem 1 *For any context* *i, *the equivalence* *i:iP(α) $\vee$ iP(β) $\equiv$ *i:iP$(\alpha\vee\beta)$ *does not hold. It holds instead the material implication:* *i:iP(α) $\vee$ iP(β) $\rightarrow$ *i:iP$(\alpha\vee\beta)$

Theorem 2 *For any context C, if C:α, C:β and C:χ are syntactically correct labelled formulae, then the following classical equivalence rules are preserved:*

- C:$\neg(\alpha\wedge\beta)$ $\equiv$ C:$\neg\alpha\vee\neg\beta$ *(De Morgan)*
- C:$\neg(\alpha\vee\beta)$ $\equiv$ C:$\neg\alpha\wedge\neg\beta$ *(De Morgan)*
- C:$\alpha\wedge(\beta\vee\chi)$ $\equiv$ C:$(\alpha\wedge\beta)\vee(\alpha\wedge\chi)$ *(Distributive of $\wedge$ over $\vee$)*
- C:$\alpha\vee(\beta\wedge\chi)$ $\equiv$ C:$(\alpha\vee\beta)\wedge(\alpha\vee\chi)$ *(Distributive of $\vee$ over $\wedge$)*

With these definitions, the semantics of any labelled formula C:α (for any C) is completely grounded on the notion of truth-tree.

Definition 12 *A truth tree TT is a* model *for a set of labelled formulae S, written as TT$\models$S, iff TT is a model for any element of S.*

Definition 13 *Given a set S of labelled formulae, let [S] denote the set of its models. C:α is defined a* logical consequence *of S, written S$\models$C:α, iff [S]$\subseteq$[{C:α}].*

The previous definition means that all the models of S are also models of the (singleton) set {C:α}. In the following, when S is singleton, i.e. S={C:α}, we will write [C:α] instead of [{C:α}]. Let us notice the difference between the two symbols:

$\models$ means "is a model", for istance "TT is a model for *i/P:α", while:

$\models$ means "is a logical consequence", for instance "C:α is a logical consequence of a set S of labelled formulae".

Definition 14 *Two labelled formulae C:α and C:β are* logically equivalent, *written C:α $\equiv$ C:β, iff C:α $\models$ C:β and C:β $\models$ C:α, i.e., iff [C:α]=[C:β]. Analogously, two sets of labelled formulae S and R are logically equivalent iff [S]=[R]. A labelled formula C:α is* valid *if [C:α]=Ω, i.e. iff $\forall_{TT}$ TT $\models$ C:α.*

We think of a mental state as a collection of mental attitudes (beliefs, intentions and logical relations among them), hence the *representation* of a mental state should be a collection of *representations* of mental attitudes. So we need to represent mental attitudes, with a definition like this:

"a representation of a *mental attitude* of the agent *i* is a *formula of MLi*"

and, as the opposite:

"any formula of *MLi* represents a mental attitude of the agent *i*".

However, this definitions are insufficient, from a cognitive point of view, since we conceive mental states as *recursive* structures. Hence, to represent precisely a mental attitude it is necessary to specify the *position* of the formula of *MLi* in the multi-contextual structure MS. If we consider also the label of the formula as part of the representation of the mental attitude, then we can relax the requisite that the formula α must belong to *MLi* and require simply that α belongs to *ALi*. In fact, the label renders unique the sense of the formula as representation of a mental attitude.

Definition 15 *Any* mental attitude *of the agent i can be represented as a* labelled *formula C:α, where α∈ALi, and vice-versa.*

As long as we represent mental attitudes as labelled formulae, we can represent mental states as *sets* of labelled formulae. From definition 12 we see that a truth tree TT is a model for a mental state, iff TT is a model for any of its mental attitudes. This definition looks quite like the semantics of the logical connective "∧". One may be tempted to conclude that "a mental state is a logical conjunction of mental attitudes". Unfortunately, we didn't define a language to which a pseudo-formula like C1:α1 ∧ . . . ∧ Cn:αn could belong to, but we can define a particular conjunctive labelled formula to which a mental state is logically equivalent.

Theorem 3 *For any set of labelled formulae* $\{C_1 : \alpha_1, \ldots, C_n : \alpha_n\}$ *of the multi-contextual representation MS of the agent i's mental state, there exists a labelled formula* $i:\beta_1 \wedge \cdots \wedge \beta_n$ *such that* $\{C_1 : \alpha_1, \ldots, C_n : \alpha_n\} \equiv i:\beta_1 \wedge \cdots \wedge \beta_n$.

Corollary 3.1. Any agent i's mental state can be completely represented by a single labelled formula i:α, where α∈MLi.

Comment 2. We are all interested in the dynamics of agent's mental states. In particular, we want to model changes of mental states after communication. For this purpose, collapsing a mental state into a single labelled formula is not much computationally appealing. This would force every speech act to change the overall mental states of the agents engaged in the communication. It would be much better splitting that single labelled formula into syntactically smaller parts which could be handled separately in a semantically correct way.

Comment 3. Now that we have a well-grounded semantics, we need an efficient syntactic theorem-prover, which has to be *sound* and *complete*. "Sound" means that if it proves a labelled formula to be valid, that must actually be true semantically or, which is the same, that every time it proves that a labelled formula derives from others that formula must be a logical consequence of the latter. "Complete" means that for every valid labelled formula there should be somewhere a derivation of that formula from a void set of labelled formulae (i.e. from a void mental state, which means also from *any* mental state) or, which is the same, that every time a labelled formula is a logical consequences of some others the theorem prover is able to prove that in some way.

The previous comment can be rephrased more formally.

Definition 16 *A theorem-prover ⊢ for labelled formulae is* **sound** *and* **complete** *iff for any C:α:*

- *⊢ C:α iff* $\forall_{TT}TT \models C:\alpha$

or, which is the same:

- $C_1 : \alpha_1 \vdash C_2 : \alpha_2$ *iff* $C_1 : \alpha_1 \models C_2 : \alpha_2$

In Dragoni [2008] we provided an answer to both the previous comments. For the consideration in comment 2 we provided a clausal representation of mental states that brings to a *canonical representation* which is a set of labelled clauses each placed at the lowest possible level in the mental structure. For the consideration in comment 3 we provided the definition of a theorem-prover that was proved to be correct and complete w.r.t. the previous definition.

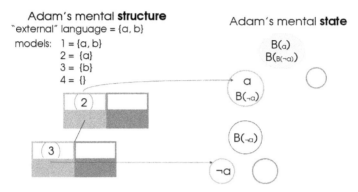

Fig. 12 A psychologically implausible case in which Adam believes *a* and also believes to believe *not a*

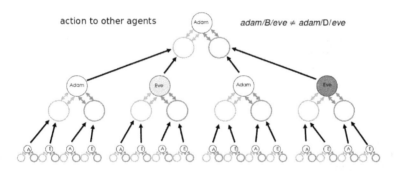

Fig. 13 Action toward other agents

4 Dynamics of mental states

Now that we have a simple but semantically well founded formalism to represent mental states, we can adopt it to model their dynamics, i.e. cognitive changes and volitional actions.

4.1 Mental states as causes of actions

"Dynamics" is the study of how forces change the state of the world and produce movements. In our "mental states physics", we need to understand what a "force" is and which effects it produces. Probably, an intentional force is nothing but the innate need to achieve "objectives" and/or "needs". At its simplest, this concept implies a temporal projection: one wants to meet a "future" goal that "now" he believes will be not satisfied in that future. After you reach the desired/needed state in the external world, then the state you want and the state you believe should be identical (unless in the meanwhile, another "deus ex machina" has come again to change the state of affairs), at which point the force ceases. The the best metaphor is that of the electric field, in which the current flows (and performs actions) from the two poles until the voltage difference levels off between the two; in the same way, actions will be deliberated until there persist some differences between a certain "desired" mental state and its corresponding "believed" mental state.

When we consider our agent isolated as a hermit, his actions affect only the passive outside world (not the mental states of other agents), but his actions are still caused by his mental state and will modify indirectly it. But when our agent is interacting with other agents, the "external" world that he wants to change may actually be the mental state of other agents or even its own actual mental state! In the first case the agent wants to change beliefs and/or desires of other agents, in the second case the agent wants to change its own beliefs and/or desires. We believe that these forces produces speech acts, so they stands to communicative acts as the causes to their effects, and these dynamics can easily be supported by our formalism for representing mental states.

Let's go back to Adam and Eve (Fig. 7). We see this basic taxonomy of actions.

1. $adam/B/eve \neq adam/D/eve$ causes and "ad extra" act

    a. $adam/B/eve/B \neq adam/D/eve/B$ causes a *speech* act
- $adam/B/eve/B/adam \neq adam/D/eve/B/adam$
- $adam/B/eve/B/eve \neq adam/D/eve/B/eve$

    b. $adam/B/eve/D \neq adam/D/eve/D$ causes a proactive act
- $adam/B/eve/D/adam \neq adam/D/eve/D/adam$
- $adam/B/eve/D/eve \neq adam/D/eve/D/eve$

2. $adam/B/adam \neq adam/D/adam$ causes a "ad intra" act

    a. $adam/B/adam/B \neq adam/D/adam/B$ causes a *cognitive* act
- $adam/B/adam/B/adam \neq adam/D/adam/B/adam$
- $adam/B/adam/B/eve \neq adam/D/adam/B/eve$

    b. $adam/B/adam/D \neq adam/D/adam/D$ causes a *convertive* act
- $adam/B/adam/D/adam \neq adam/D/adam/D/adam$
- $adam/B/adam/D/eve \neq adam/D/adam/D/eve$

The first category of mental causes is the difference between what an agent believes the mental state on another agent *is* and what *he desires* it would be. This kind of differences yields actions toward the other agent. The second category of mental causes is the difference between what an agent believes his own mental state *is* and what *he desires* it would be. This kind of differences yields a sort of introspective actions.

4.2 Example

Probably the best way to illustrate how the formalism supports mental states' dynamics is through an example.

Let's turn on Adam and Eve, and suppose to limit the external language to the two propositions taken from Genesis:

$ElAdam \stackrel{def}{=} \{a, b\}$

where:

$a \stackrel{def}{=}$ eating the apple

$b \stackrel{def}{=}$ staying in the Eden

Ω_{Adam} is made of four possible interpretations (i.e., possible worlds):

1. $\{a, b\}$
2. $\{a,\}$
3. $\{b\}$
4. $\{\}$

Here are some notable compound propositions:

$a \wedge b$: eating the apple *and* staying in the Eden

$a \vee b$: eating the apple *or* staying in the Eden

$a \underline{\vee} b \stackrel{def}{=} (a \vee b) \wedge \neg(a \wedge b)$: eating the apple or staying in the Eden, *and not both*

$\neg(a \underline{\vee} b)$: *it is false that* one can either eat the apple or stay in the Eden but not both

Their possible interpretations (possible world) are illustrated in the following table (where 0 means "false" and 1 means "true").

Ω_{Adam}	a	b	¬a	¬b	a∧b	a∨b	a$\underline{\vee}$b	¬(a$\underline{\vee}$b)	¬(a∧b)	¬a∨b
1	0	0	1	1	0	0	0	1	1	1
2	0	1	1	0	0	1	1	0	1	1
3	1	0	0	1	0	1	1	0	1	0
4	1	1	0	0	1	1	0	1	0	1

There are 16 possible subsets of Ω_{Adam}: each one may be a model of a formula, as illustrated in the following table, where in gray background are represented the maximal models (i.e. the *maximal* subset of Ω_{Adam} such that its elements makes true that formula).

$2^{\Omega_{Adam}}$	1	2	3	4	a	b	¬a	¬b	a∧b	a∨b	a⊻b	¬(a⊻b)	¬(a∧b)	¬a∨b
					this is the model of a CONTRADICTION (no world is possible)									
	■						1	1		1		1	1	1
		■					1	1			1		1	1
	■	■						1					1	1
			■		1			1		1	1		1	
	■		■				1						1	
		■	■						1	1		1		
	■	■	■									1		
				■	1	1			1	1		1		1
	■			■			1				1			1
		■		■	1					1				1
	■	■		■										1
			■	■	■	1				1				
	■		■	■										
		■	■	■					1					
Ω_{Adam}	■	■	■	■	this is the model of a TAUTOLOGY (every world is possible)									

The fact that Adam wants to stay in the Eden, i.e.:

adam:adamD($_b$)

comes from this mental structure:

(everything else being unspecified). If Adam also wants that Eve wants to stay in the Eden, i.e.:

adam:adamD($_b$)∧adamD($_{eveD(_b)}$)

then his mental structure becomes:

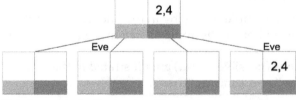

If Adam also believes that Eve wants to eat the apple:

adam:adamD($_b$) ∧adamD($_{eveD(_b)}$) ∧adamB($_{eveD(_a)}$)

then his mental structure is:

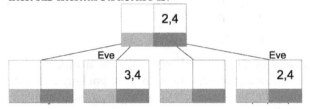

Since there is a difference between *adam/B/eve/D* and *adam/D/eve/D*, then Adam performs a *proactive* act whose effect will be that of changing his mental structure into the following:

$adam{:}adamD(_b) \wedge adamD(_{eveD(_b)}) \wedge adamB(_{eveD(_a)})$

On the cognitive side, let's suppose that Adam also believes that eating the apple is not compatible with staying in the Eden:

$adam{:}adamD(_b) \wedge adamD(_{eveD(_b)}) \wedge adamB(_{eveD(_b)}) \wedge adamB(_{a \vee b})$

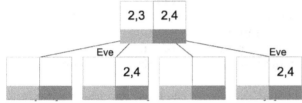

and that he also believes that Eve disagrees with him, believing that it is possible to eat the apple and remain in the Eden:

$adam{:}adamD(_b) \wedge adamD(_{eveD(_b)}) \wedge adamB(_{eveD(_b)}) \wedge$
$adamB(_{a \vee b}) \wedge adamB(_{eveB(_{\neg(a \vee b)})})$

then Adam may desires that Eve changes her beliefs as follows:

$adam{:}adamD(_b) \wedge adamD(_{eveD(_b)}) \wedge adamD(_{eveB(_{a \vee b})}) \wedge$
$adamB(_{eveD(_b)}) \wedge adamB(_{a \vee b}) \wedge adamB(_{eveB(_{\neg(a \vee b)})})$

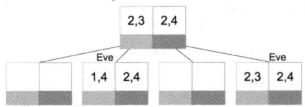

Since there is a difference between *adam/B/eve/B* and *adam/D/eve/B*, then Adam performs a communicative act (speech act) whose effect will be that of changing his mental structure into the following one:

$adam{:}adamD(_b) \wedge adamD(_{eveD(_b)}) \wedge adamD(_{eveB(_{a \vee b})}) \wedge$

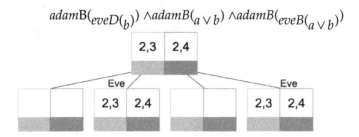

$$adamB(eveD_{(b)}) \wedge adamB(_{a \vee b}) \wedge adamB(eveB(_{a \vee b}))$$

5 Conclusions and future work

We have introduced a formalism to represent mental states. It is equipped with a precise semantics that captures and fully exploits the inherent recursive structure of a mental state. We also mentioned that this formalism can be taken as a basis for modeling the dynamics of mental states, that is how it is possible to rely on a theory of mental states the production of actions, whether directed towards the outside world, to other agents (speech-acts, for example) or to themselves.

However, we have omitted some 'problems. The most important is the fact that ontologically separating the cognitive and volitional spheres prevents to include in a single theory the relationships between these two spheres. Of course, the two spheres are much related to each others as we discussed in the introduction. For instance, from the "belief" in a context B that *it is raining*, the "desire" *bring-umbrella* should derive in the corresponding context D. This means that we should have a formula such:

$$i: iB_{(raining)} \rightarrow iD_{(bring-umbrella)}$$

or:

$$i: \neg iB_{(raining)} \vee iD_{(bring-umbrella)}$$

but unfortunately these kinds of formula do not have a semantics in our formalism, since theorem 3 admits only *conjunctions of mental* attitudes, like this:

$$i: \neg iB_{(raining)} \wedge iD_{(bring-umbrella)}$$

This is a very important limitation that, luckily, seems to have also a solution; and this solution seems to solve also another problem, which is that of dealing with psychologically implausible mental states, as the following:

$$i: iB_{(raining)} \wedge iB(\neg iB_{(raining)})$$

which should be *avoided*, i.e. formula of this kind should implicitly be true (as tautologies):

$$i: iB_{(raining)} \rightarrow \neg iB(\neg iB_{(raining)})$$

The common solution seems to be that of providing constraints over the truth-trees. Constraints over the models at different levels of a same mental attitude should solve the latter problem and embody some psychological plausible "rationality postulates", while constraints at the same level of the truth-tree should provide a semantics for the *disjunction* of different mental attitudes, as implications between beliefs and desires.

Another important step will be that of defining operators to *change* mental states after the reception of a communication or the arrival of new information from sensorial apparatus. We will apply the abductive operators defined in [Dragoni, 1994] for revising mental states after the reception of a speech act to this novel formalization of mental structures.

Our last step will be that of bringing revision algorithm [Dragoni, 1997] over these mental structure to solve eventual contradictions (conflicts between beliefs and/or desires) generalizing the notion of "belief revision" to that of "mental state revision".

References

1. Bradshaw, J., Introduction to Software Agents, in "Software Agents", AAAI Press/The MIT Press, 1997
2. Cohen, P. R., Levesque, H. J. (1990). Intention is choice with commitment. *Artificial Intelligence*, 42:213-261
3. Dragoni, A.F. (1992). A Model for Belief Revision in a Multi-Agent Environment (abstract). SIGOIS BULLETIN, vol. 13, 3; p. 133-137, ISSN:0894-0819, doi:10.1145/152683.152688
4. Dragoni, A.F., Puliti P., Perception of Mental States from Communication, in V. Roberto (Ed.), *Intelligent Perceptual Systems, New Directions in Computational Perception*, Springer-Verlag, Berlin-Heidelberg, vol. 745, pp. 263-272, 1993.
5. Dragoni, A.F., Di Manzo, M. (1994). Supporting Complex Inquiries. International Journal of Intelligent Systems, vol. 10(11); p. 959-986, ISSN:0884-8173, doi:10.1002/int.4550101104
6. Dragoni, A.F., Puliti, P., "Mental States Recognition from Speech Acts through Abduction", Proceedings of the *11th European Conference on Artificial Intelligence* (ECAI 94), Amsterdam August 8-12. John Wiley & Sons. 1994.
7. Dragoni, A.F. (1996). Norme e Metodi Razionali per il Cambiamento di Stato Cognitivo. Sistemi Intelligenti, ISSN:1120-9550, ed. "Il Mulino" (in italian)
8. Dragoni, A.F., "Belief Revision: From Theory to Practice", in *The Knowledge Engineering Review*, vol. 12(2), p. 147-179. Cambridge University Press, June 1997.
9. Dragoni, A.F., Giorgini, P. (1998). Self-Monitoring Distributed Monitoring Systems for Nuclear Power Plants. Computers and Artificial Intelligence, vol. 17, 2-3; p. 152-168, ISSN:0232-0274
10. Dragoni, A.F., Giorgini, P., Nissan, E. (2001). Distributed Belief revision as Applied Within a Descriptive Model of Jury Deliberations. Information & Communications Technology Law, vol. 10(1); p. 53-65, ISSN:1360-0834, doi:10.1080/13600830123621
11. Dragoni, A.F., Animali, S. (2003). Maximal Consistency and Theory of Evidence in the Police Inquiry Domain. Cybernetics and Systems, vol. 34, 6-7; p. 419-465, ISSN:0196-9722, doi:10.1080/01969720302863
12. Dragoni, A.F., Vallesi, G., Baldassarri, P. (2010). Multiple Neural Networks and Bayesian Belief Revision for a Never-ending Unsupervised Learning. In: Proceedings of the 10th International Conference on Intelligent Systems Design and Applications (ISDA 10). Cairo, Egypt.
13. Dennett, D., *The Intentional Stance*, Cambridge, Mass.:The MIT Press. 1987.
14. Etzioni, O., Weld, D. S. 1995. Intelligent Agents on the Internet:Fact, Fiction, and Forecast. IEEE Expert 10(4):44–49.

15. Franklin, S., Graesser, A. 1996. Is It an Agent or Just a Program? A Taxonomy for Autonomous Agents. In Proceedings of the Third International Workshop on Agent Theories, Architectures, and Languages. New York:Springer-Verlag.
16. Giunchiglia, F., Serafini, L., Multilanguage Hierarchical Logics (or: How we can do without modal logic), Artificial Intelligence, vol. 65, pp. 29-70, 1994.
17. Gmytrasiewicz, P.J., Durfee, E.H., Wehe, D.K., The Utility of Communication in Coordinating Intelligent Agents, Formalisms for Coordination, Proc. of the Ninth National Conference on Artificial Intelligence, 1991.
18. Gmytrasiewicz, P.J., Durfee, E.H., A Rigorous, Operational Formalization of Recursive Modeling, in Proc. of the First International Conference on Multi-Agent Systems (ICMAS), pp 125-132, 1995.
19. Newell, A., 1982. The Knowledge Level. Artificial Intelligence 18:87–127.
20. Rao, A.S., Georgeff, M., "BDI Agents:from theory to practice". In *Proceedings f the First International Conference on Multi-Agent Systems* (ICMAS-95), pp 312-319, S. Francisco, CA, June 1995.

Chapter 5
The BOID architecture revisited: Goal generation in agent systems

Mehdi Dastani and Leendert van der Torre

Abstract Cristiano Castelfranchi emphasizes that goals are a key concept in understanding as well as designing autonomous, proactive, and normative agents. Goals constitute an agent's motivational attitude and denote the states an agent aims to achieve. Castelfranchi and colleagues argue that goals are not only first class citizens in the design and development of software agents, but also that desires, obligations and intentions are goals at different stages of processing. One of the first approaches to generate goals based on more fundamental concepts such as desires, norms, and intentions is the BOID framework proposed a decade ago. The introduction of the BOID architecture has influenced the work in the area of agent design and development, as well as the development of normative multiagent organizations of interacting BOID agents. In the field of agent programming, goals have been recognized as an essential concept that can be used to program an agent's autonomy as well as its pro-active and normative behavior. The idea is that the execution of an agent program generates plans in order to reach its goals, depending on what it believes about the world. In this chapter, we provide an overview of the BOID research project and discuss the development and influences of this framework in the field of agent research, in particular in the area of the design and development of autonomous, proactive, and normative agent systems.

Mehdi Dastani
Intelligent Systems Group, Utrecht University, The Netherlands
e-mail: mehdi@cs.uu.nl

Leendert van der Torre
Faculty of Sciences, Technology and Communication, University of Luxembourg, Luxembourg
e-mail: leon.vandertorre@uni.lu

1 Introduction

Cristiano Castelfranchi [15] identifies autonomy as an essential characteristic of individual agents, and he emphasizes that goals are a key concept in understanding as well as designing autonomous, proactive, and normative agents. Without getting into the exact nature of autonomy, in this paper we consider an agent autonomous if it has a decision making component that governs its decisions based on its informational (beliefs / distributions / knowledge), motivational (desires / preferences / obligations / norms), and deliberational (intentions / commitments) attitudes. One can argue that any computational system interacting with other systems (e.g., other agents or environment) can be seen as autonomous, at least from an external and behavioral point of view.

The BOID framework [12] considers the autonomy of agents from a design and development perspective. From this internal point of view, an autonomous agent is required to have an architecture that comprises an explicit decision making component. Such a component should be specified, designed, or implemented in terms of the agent's informational, motivational, and deliberational attitudes. In particular, the decision making component should involve different issues related to an agent's decisions such as decision strategies, resolving decision conflicts, and rationality of decisions. In this sense, the architectures that are proposed for the design and development of autonomous agents consist of components supporting the design and development of concepts and issues involved in an agent's decision process.

In this paper we give an overview of goal generation in the BOID architecture, including its origins in the work of Castelfranchi and colleagues, and its impact on normative multiagent systems and agent programming. In particular, we address the following questions.

1. How does the work of Castelfranchi and colleagues influence the development of the BOID architecture?
2. What is goal generation as developed in the BOID architecture?
3. How to develop normative multiagent organizations with interacting BOID agents?
4. How to develop agent programming languages to program BOID agents and organizations?

The BOID architecture extends a wide class of architectures for autonomous agents based on the BDI (Beliefs, Desires, Intentions) model of agency [30, 31, 18]. The BDI model has been considered as a qualitative decision model that explains an agent's rational decision in terms of the agent's information about the current state of the world (Beliefs), the states the agent wants to achieve (Desire), and its commitments to already made choices (intentions) [22]. The BDI model has proven to be an efficient model for reactive planning and for the agents that have complex goals interacting with highly dynamic environments. A majority of the existing BDI-based (computational) agent architectures provide components to model an agent's beliefs, goals, and conditional plans (e.g., [21, 24, 10, 29]). The conditions that are assigned to plans are specified in terms of beliefs, goals, and events such that a plan can be decided/selected if these conditions are satisfied, i.e., an agent can decide a plan if the agent believes the belief condition of the plan and has a goal that entails the goal condition of the plan (or has received an event or a message). The reasoning engine of the BDI agents is often a process that continuously decides a plan to execute. Following the BDI models, where an agent's decisions depend also on its previous decisions, the choice for a plan in some BDI-based agent architectures depends on the agent's previously generated plans in the sense that a plan is selected if there are no already selected plans that aim at achieving either the same or a conflicting goal. Moreover, in the BDI models the relation between beliefs and goals is formulated by means of rationality axioms in the BDI logics [31, 18]. For example, an agent cannot pursue an achieve goal if the agent believes the state denoted by the achieve goal is the current state.

Castelfranchi and colleagues make many contributions to the development of cognitive and social agent theory, and they point to various omissions and limitations of the dominant BDI theory developed by Bratman and colleagues, such as the role of emergence and immergence. In this paper we highlight their contribution to the role of goal generation in BDI theory. In particular, the aim of Castelfranchi and Paglieri [17] is to detail a model in which specific types of beliefs act as filters and triggers from goal activation to goal execution. According to this view, in order to activate, promote, drop, or suspend a goal, an intention, or an intentional action, one has to provide or modify the appropriate beliefs.

BOID is an architecture for autonomous agents. It is designed to model an agent's decision making process is terms of cognitive concepts such as beliefs, obligations, intentions and desires. Beliefs are informational attitudes, which model what the world is expected to be like. Intentions are previously generated goals or plans [11]. Desires model internal motivations. Obligations model external motivations such as norms. In the BOID architecture [12], an agent decision making process comprises a goal and a plan generation component. The goal generation component determines the goals an agent aims at achieving and the plan generation component determines the actions the agent has to perform for achieving the goals. In particular, a BOID agent continuously perceives its surrounding environment, updates its cognitive state based on the sensed data, determines the goals to be achieved based on the updated state, generates plans for achieving its selected goals, and finally executes the plans to act in its environment. The overall structure of the BOID architecture is outlined in Figure 1.

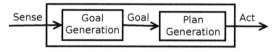

Fig. 1 The BOID architecture.

Normative multiagent organizations represent besides the BOID agents also the environment in which the BOID agents interact. Such an environment contains a normative system regulating the interaction of the agents, which is the source of the obligations of the agents, and thus of their normative goals. Such a normative multiagent system is also called an institution, organization, or more generally a society. The architecture of a normative system contains constitutive norms as well as regulative norms, including permissive norms, and it determines the institutional facts of the society, as well as the obligations and permissions of the agents. Moreover, the agents can play roles in the normative system, such as legislators, judges and policemen.

2APL [21] is designed to implement multi-agent systems consisting of autonomous agents. It provides two sets of programming constructs to implement multi-agent and individual agent concerns. The multi-agent programming constructs are designed to create individual agents (based on their specifications as will be explained later in this section), external environments, and to specify the agents' access relations to the external environments. Environments in 2APL are implemented as Java objects. In particular, the state of an environment is implemented by the state of its corresponding java object and the effect of an action in the environment is implemented by a method of the java object. As the focus of this paper is on individual agents, we ignore programming constructs for multi-agent concerns and explain only how individual autonomous agents can be developed in 2APL.

In Section 2, we first explain goal generation in the work of Castelfranchi and colleagues. In Section 3 we discuss how the BOID framework unifies external and internal motivational sources into one single abstraction called the agent's goals. In Section 4 we discuss norms as an external motivational source that can motivate an agent to decide a specific plan. Then, in Section 5 we explain 2APL, an existing computational architecture for the BDI agents. In this framework, goals and events are the only motivational abstractions that are used to generate/decide plans.

2 Goal generation by Castelfranchi and Paglieri

Cristiano Castelfranchi develops the foundations of his agent model together with Rosaria Conte in the 90s [19, 15], but we believe that goal generation becomes most sophisticated in his work on belief dynamics together with Paglieri [17]. They see goal processing as the cognitive transition that leads from a mere desire to a proper intention, and they strive to provide a detailed and principled analysis of the role of beliefs in goal processing. In this section we give a brief summary of their work, but for the details we refer the reader to [17].

2.1 *Goals versus other classes of motivational states*

The theory of Castelfranchi and Paglieri can be adequately labelled as a form of cognitive functionalism: the significant and heuristic categories of beliefs and goals are defined by their functions, rather than by their format, content, or other intrinsic features. Their understanding of belief is fairly common in the literature. The word "belief" indicates any mental representation that is used as a plausible substitute for a certain aspect of reality, and that is supposed to be referentially true, i.e. to provide a description that is assumed to correspond, and used as corresponding, to how things actually are. Properly speaking, the notion of belief defines a specific cognitive function that is absolved by a mental representation–in the same way in which a goal indicates a (different) functional role played by a mental representation.

The class of goals considered by Castelfranchi and Paglieri is rather broad, and it encompasses several other concepts familiar both in Artificial Intelligence (e.g. desires and intentions), in cognitive psychology (e.g. motivations, wishes, aims), and in social sciences (e.g. preferences). Essentially, a goal is defined as an anticipatory internal representation of a state of the world that has the potential for and the function of (eventually) constraining/governing the behaviour of an agent towards its realization. The defining function of goals is to shape, to direct in a teleological sense the actual behaviour of the system. As for the typical anticipatory nature of goals, this is meant to capture the fact that goals prefigure a certain state of affairs, as opposed to representing a state of the world which is believed to be the case. This remains true (and rational) even when a certain goal is already realized: this is the case with the so-called "maintenance goals", i.e. goals about keeping things as they are, which have been sometimes opposed to "achievement goals", i.e. goals about state of things not yet realized. This distinction, although significant for some specific purposes, should not hide the fact that both kinds of goal share the same basic anticipatory nature. More generally, the function of a goal is to serve as a frame of reference for driving the agent's conduct towards an anticipated state of things. In this sense, goals, either for maintaining the current status quo or for achieving a new one, are anticipatory representations by definition. To summarize, a goal is not a representation currently and necessarily orienting and guiding an action; instead, it is a representation endowed with this potential function, so that it is somehow "destined" to play this role but whether or not this role is actually fulfilled depends on the agent's beliefs.

Many authors use "desires" instead of "goals." Castelfranchi and Paglieri do not do so for three reasons. First, desires have an unavoidable connotation of expected pleasure: we cannot desire something if it fails to give us some kind of pleasure, or if it entails a prevalent displeasure. Second, desires have an unavoidable mark of endogenous pro-attitudes, possibly as a consequence of their hedonistic character: they cannot originate from a duty or an order, possibly even one that we dislike. Third, desires have a strong connotation as non pursued or even "non pursuable" states of affairs. This is one of the reasons in BDI for not using the term in more advanced stages of practical reasoning and deliberation, introducing a new theoretical entity, i.e. intention, as a new primitive. On the contrary, the technical notion of goal used by Castelfranchi and Paglieri can be applied both before, without, and after the decision to act, as well as during the persecution of one's aim and the performance of an action. Thus the notion of goal emphasizes the continuity between (what in BDI are called) desires and intentions, opening the way for an operational model of intention formation. Behind the process that leads from a desire to an intention, they claim that there is always a goal from the beginning to the end, which is transformed in its functional properties by subsequent accretions of relevant belief patterns.

Ultimately, the main reason to prefer the notion of goal over that of desire is that it yields a richer model of motivational dynamics. Indeed, since the notion of goal is deliberately designed to cover a wide variety of motivational states, several internal distinctions are introduced, and they are matched with different stages in goal-processing, i.e. the process that brings the agent from a general interest for a potentially relevant outcome to the subjective commitment to bring it about through adequate planning and action. In BDI models, this process is known as intention formation, and only two stages are considered: desires, i.e. states of the world that agents find desirable but that they are not yet committed to act upon, and intentions, i.e. desires that agents are committed to make real through their plans and actions. One of the basic assumptions of the analysis of Castelfranchi and Paglieri is that this view of intention formation, although basically correct in its outline, is still oversimplified, and that both formal models and computational systems might benefit from a more refined model of goal processing.

2.2 Goal-supporting beliefs: a tentative ontology

The analysis of the interaction between belief dynamics and goal dynamics is based on the following principle formulated by Castelfranchi:

Postulate of Cognitive Regulation of Action: The goals of a cognitive agent have to be supported and justified by the agent's beliefs (i.e. reasons). Cognitive agents can not activate, maintain, decide about, prefer, plan for, or pursue any goal which is not grounded (implicitly or explicitly) on pertinent beliefs.

Castelfranchi and Paglieri draw a comprehensive list of different types of goal-supporting beliefs, arranged according to the different functional role they play in goal-processing, from activation to action:

Motivating beliefs: aside from the case of bodily activation of goals or emotional arousal, goals are often activated by beliefs on the current state of the world. Two sub-classes are considered. Triggering beliefs are beliefs that reactively activate goals on the basis of a preestablished association, and conditional beliefs are beliefs that activate a goal on the basis of the conditional nature of the goal itself.

Assessment beliefs: in order to consider a goal as candidate for being pursued, one cannot believe that such a goal is either already realized, self-realizing, or plainly impossible. Self-realization beliefs concern the fact that one of the goals will come to be realized in the world autonomously and without my direct intervention, satisfaction beliefs concern the fact that one of the goals is already realized, and that it will remain as such without intervention, and impossibility beliefs concern the fact that one of the goals is impossible at a given time, or it will never be possible.

Cost beliefs: beliefs concerning the costs that the agent expects to sustain as a consequence of pursuing a certain goal, in terms of the necessary resources that will be allocated to that end.

Incompatibility beliefs: beliefs concerning different forms of incompatibility between goals, that can force the agent to chose among them, either in absolute terms or for the time being.

Preference beliefs: beliefs concerning what (incompatible) goals should be given precedence over others in the current context. Value beliefs concern the subjective value of a certain goal, given current interests, and urgency beliefs concern when (if ever) a given goal will "expire", i.e. it will be no more possible to achieve it.

Precondition beliefs: beliefs concerning the necessary preconditions for successfully pursuing a given goal by executing the appropriate action. Incompetence beliefs of "internal attribution" (Weiner, 1974), self-efficacy, and confidence that mainly concern both the basic know-how and competence, and the sufficient skills and abilities needed to reach the goal, given convictions on how the goal can be reached. Lack of conditions beliefs of "external attribution" concern external conditions, opportunities, and resources; they cover both conditions for the execution of the appropriate actions, and conditions for the success of a correctly performed action.

Means-End beliefs: beliefs concerning the instrumental relation between a given goal and an action or an event which is considered to serve to achieve the former, and therefore can be assumed as a means (sub-goal) to that end.

2.3 Goal-supporting beliefs: a dynamic model

Castelfranchi and Paglieri take active goals (akin to BDI desires) as their primitive of choice, and define all other goal types, down to executive goals, in terms of such a primitive plus presence/absence of some specific beliefs, roughly as follows:

Active goal (desire): GOAL(p)
Pursuable goal: P-GOAL(p)=
     GOAL(p)
     AND no assessment belief on p
Chosen goal (necessary for future-directed intention): C-GOAL(p) =
     P-GOAL(p)
     AND no cost belief on p such as to prevent pursuing it
     AND no incompatibility belief on p
          OR no goal r preferred over p given preference beliefs
Executed goal(necessary for present-directed intention): E-GOAL(p)=
     C-GOAL(p)
     AND no precondition belief on p

Besides the taxonomy and the dynamic model of the belief structure that supports our goals, from their inception as mere desires to their realization through intentional action, Castelfranchi and Paglieri also provide the following.

- Some working hypotheses on the consequences of this structural interaction between goals, beliefs, and actions, with special reference to the dynamics of these notions. In particular, they emphasize the principles of cognitive integration typical of intelligent behaviour, and the role of belief tests in goal processing and intention formation.
- An original conception of intentions as double-faced teleological entities, which is argued to be interestingly related to other important contributions in this area, including Sellars' observations on the link between intention-that and intention-to, Bratman's functional analysis of future-directed intentions, and the desire-belief theory of intentions endorsed, in several variants, by Anscombe, Davidson, Goldman, and Audi.
- A detailed discussion of the standing of their model with respect to other theories of intentional action, in particular Bratman's planning theory of intention. Intentions, although playing a crucial role in practical reasoning, can still be precisely defined in terms of beliefs and goals.

See [17] for examples and further details. The whole model of belief-based goal processing, although quite well specified in its details, is not yet formalized or implemented. Moreover, Castelfranchi and Paglieri conclude that at present it remains unclear what could be the best way to formalize and implement it.

3 BOID: Beliefs, Obligations, Intentions and Desires

In this section we summarize the main ideas underlying the BOID architecture.

3.1 *Goal generation component*

The characterizing feature of the BOID architecture is its goal generation component. In contrast to other cognitive agent architectures where a goal is seen
as a primitive motivational attitude, the BOID architecture considers a goal
as derived from the interaction between other, more fundamental, cognitive
attitudes such as beliefs, desires, obligations, and intentions. In particular, the
goal generation component is responsible for the generation of an agent's
goals based on the interaction between the agent's informational attitude (beliefs), internal motivational attitude (desires), external motivational attitude
(obligations), and deliberational attitude (intentions). The idea is that an agent
who attempts to satisfy its desires, to fulfill its obligations, and to commit to
its intentions, needs to decide which of the desires, obligations, or intentions
to follow as these cognitive attitudes may conflict. The conflicts may emerge
within one cognitive attitude or because of the interaction between different
cognitive attitudes. The goal generation component of the BOID architecture
is responsible for detecting and resolving both kinds of conflicts between cognitive attitudes such as desires, obligations, and intentions.

In order to illustrate the goal generation component of the BOID architecture
and possible conflicts that may emerge from and between cognitive attitudes,
consider the following example. Imagine an agent that intends to go to a
conference. The agent believes there are no cheap hotel rooms close to the
conference site. The agent desires to stay in a hotel close to the conference site,
if he attends the conference. Finally, the agent is obliged to take a cheap room
if he goes to the conference. The goals of this agent depend on its conflicting
cognitive attitudes and how these conflicts are resolved. For example, the
agent may want to attend the conference if he is committed to its intentions.
Moreover, the agent may want to stay in a cheap hotel and probably far from
the conference site, if the agent follows its obligation. Otherwise, the agent
may follow its desire and stay in a possibly expensive hotel, but as close to the
conference site as possible. This example illustrates that the goals of an agent
are derived from its underlying conflicting cognitive concepts such as beliefs,
obligations, intentions and desires. Note that conflicts can also emerge within
one cognitive attitude. For example, the agent in our example may also have
a desire to stay in a large room while believing that there are no large hotel
rooms close to the conference site. In this case, the desire to stay in a large room
conflicts the desire to stay as close as possible to the conference site.

Conflicts within a single cognitive attitude have been studied in the literature by for example van Fraassen [39]. However, conflicts between different
cognitive attitudes as illustrated in the abovementioned example have received
less attention. A cognitive attitude conflicts with another cognitive attitude if
both cannot be used to generate a consistent set of goals. The agent thus has to
choose which of the two attitudes it should use at the expense of the other one.
For such a choice, we say that the former overrides the latter. The overriding
mechanism is the method that is used in the BOID architecture to solve conflicts
and generate goal sets. As observed by Thomason [36], overriding desires by
beliefs reflects that the agent does not suffer from wishful thinking. A similar

argument applies to obligations and intentions. For example, the overriding of intentions by beliefs reflects that an intended state can no longer be pursued due to a belief changes (e.g., caused by environmental changes). In such a case, an intention should not generate a goal. Also overriding obligations or desires by intentions reflects that agents do not reconsider their intentions, which brings stability [11].

In the BOID architecture, the process of generating goals from different mental attitudes is biased by the type of agents. Agent types are an idea developed in BDI logics to distinguish, classify and compare agent behaviors [18, 30]. For example, a blindly committed agent will not drop its intentions due to changes in its beliefs or desires and maintain its intentions until they are achieved. However, a single minded agent drops its intentions as soon as it believes the intentions are no option anymore. In the BOID architecture, this notion of agent types is applied to goal generation, where agent types correspond to ways to resolve conflicts. Agent types for goal generation are given intuitive names. If the agent's beliefs override its obligations, intentions or desires, then the agent is called realistic. If its intentions override its desires and obligations, then the agent is called stable. Moreover, if its desires override its obligations, then the agent is called selfish and if its obligations override its desires, then the agent is called social. These agent types can also be combined. For example, in stable social agents intentions override obligations or desires, and obligations override desires. A useful notion here is that some agent types are more specific than other agent types. Of course not all agent types are comparable. For example, the realistic agent type is neither more specific than the social agent type, nor vice versa. Goal generation of more specific agents is more predictable than goal generation of general ones.

3.2 *Computational Architecture of BOID*

In the BOID architecture, an agent's mental attitudes are considered to be conditional and context dependent. In the computational model for the goal generation component, mental attitudes are formalized as sets of defeasible rules in a prioritized default logic [32]. In the following, we use $\overset{X}{\hookrightarrow}$ to represent a defeasible rule for mental attitude X and ρ to indicate the priority of a rule. Using this representation, the conference visiting agent can be formalised as follows. The first rule represents the agent's beliefs that there are no cheap rooms close to the conference site he is going to attend and the final rule represents the agent's desire to stay close to the conference site if he goes to the conference. The BOID architecture implements agent types as constraints on the priority function. The priority values that are assigned to these rules indicate that the agent's beliefs are the most important attitude and that the agent's desires are the least important one.

$$goToConference \wedge cheapRoom \xrightarrow{B} \neg closeToConfSite \qquad (\rho = 5)$$
$$goToConference \wedge closeToConfSite \xrightarrow{B} \neg cheapRoom \qquad (\rho = 4)$$
$$\top \xrightarrow{I} goToConference \qquad (\rho = 3)$$
$$goToConference \xrightarrow{O} \neg cheapRoom \qquad (\rho = 2)$$
$$goToConference \xrightarrow{D} \neg closeToConfSite \qquad (\rho = 1)$$

The goals are generated based on the derivation of so-called extensions in default logic [32]. Default logic extends the inference rule modus ponens with two new mechanisms. First, there is a consistency constraint on the inference process, such that rules are applied only if they do not lead to an inconsistency. Second, the application of defeasible rules may result in conflicting outputs and thus in conflicting goal sets. They lead to alternative sets of logic formulas. However, to resolve the conflict we have to consider the whole extension, because agents should consider the effects of goals before they commit to them. In the BOID architecture, goal generation is based on prioritized default logic. The specification of goal generation process - the instantiation of a default theory - contains the specification of a set of facts, a set of rules, and the specification of a priority function ρ on the rules.

The specification of goal generation process is given in Definition 1. The goal generation process starts with a set of observations Obs, which cannot be overridden, and initial sets of default rules for B, O, I, and D. The procedure then determines a sequence of sets of extensions $S_0, S_1, \ldots$. The first element in the sequence is the set of observations: $S_0 = \{Obs\}$. A set of extensions S_{i+1} is calculated from a set of extensions S_i by checking for each extension E in S_i whether there are rules that can extend the extension. There can be none, in which case nothing happens. Otherwise each of the consequents of the applicable rules with highest ρ-value are added to the extension separately, to form distinct extensions in S_{i+1}. The operator $Th(S)$ refers to the logical closure of S, and the syntactic operation $Lit(b)$ extracts the set of literals from a conjunction of literals b. In practice not the whole set of extensions is calculated, but only those that are calculated before the agent runs out of resources.

Definition 1 (Generate goal process) *Let $\Delta = \langle Obs, B, O, I, D, \rho \rangle$ be the specification of the goal generation process for propositional logic L, and let an extension E be a set of L literals (an atom or its negation). We say that:*
- a rule $(a \hookrightarrow b)$ is strictly applicable to an extension E, iff $a \in Th(E)$, $b \notin Th(E)$ and $\neg b \notin Th(E)$;
- $\max(E, \Delta) \subseteq B \cup O \cup I \cup D$ is the set of rules $(a \hookrightarrow b)$ strictly applicable to E such that there does not exists a $(c \hookrightarrow d) \in B \cup O \cup I \cup D$ strictly applicable to E with $\rho(c \hookrightarrow d) > \rho(a \hookrightarrow b)$;
- $E \subseteq L$ is an extension for Δ iff $E \in S_n$ and $S_n = S_{n+1}$ for the following procedure:
    $i := 0; S_i := \{Obs\};$
  repeat
      $S_{i+1} := \emptyset;$
      for all $E \in S_i$ **do**
        if exist $(a \hookrightarrow b) \in B \cup O \cup I \cup D$ strictly applicable to E **then**
          for all $(a \hookrightarrow b) \in \max(E, \Delta)$ **do**

$$S_{i+1} := S_{i+1} \cup \{ E \cup Lit(w) \};$$
        end for
      else
$$S_{i+1} := S_{i+1} \cup \{E\};$$
      end if
    end for
    $i := i + 1;$
  untill $S_i = S_{i-1};$

3.3 BOID agent types

Agent types are used to distinguish, classify and compare agent decision making behavior. In this paper, we consider agent types that are defined in terms of
the goal generation process. These agent types are based on overriding, such
that in realistic agents beliefs override other mental attitudes, and in social
agents obligations override desires. Agent types based on goal generation are
conflict resolution methods. An agent has a conflict if the goal generation process in Definition 1 derives multiple extensions. A conflict is resolved if the
priority function is adapted such that no alternative extensions are generated.
A mental attitude conflicts with another mental attitude if two rules from different attitudes are applicable, but applying both leads to an inconsistent set.
A rule overrides another rule if it has a higher priority. Finally, agent types
based on goal generation are formalized in Definition 2 as constraints on the
set of available priority functions. When the process starts the selected priority
function obeys the constraints corresponding to the agent type. An agent type
is called primitive if it contains only one constraint, and complete if it induces
a total strict ordering on the components.

Definition 2 *An agent type based on goal generation is a consistent set of constraints*
on priority function ρ. A constraint, which is of the form $X > Y$ for set of rules
$X, Y \in \{B, O, I, D\}$, is defined as follows:

$$X > Y \quad iff \quad \forall r_x \in X \, \forall r_y \in Y : \; \rho(r_x) > \rho(r_y)$$

    A primitive agent type contains a single constraint. A complete agent type is a
maximal consistent set of constraints.

There are twelve primitive agent types, which are listed in Table 1 together
with the corresponding constraint. They are ordered in six pairs, each agent
type A together with its inverse $\{X > Y \mid Y > X \in A\}$. An agent type is a set
of primitive agent types. For example, the realistic agent type is $\{B > O, B >$
$I, B > D\}$, the stable agent type is $\{I > O, I > D\}$, the social stable agent type is
$\{I > O, I > D, O > D\}$, etc. Moreover, agent types can be derived. For example,
since orderings are transitive we can derive that an agent which is unstable
with respect to obligations $(O > I)$ and stable with respect to intentions $(I > D)$
is social $(O > D)$. There are twenty-four complete agent types, of which the six

Constraint	Agent type
$B > O \, (O > B)$	Realistic with respect to obligations (dogmatic)
$B > I \, (I > B)$	Realistic with respect to intentions (over-committed)
$B > D \, (D > B)$	Realistic with respect to desires (wishful thinker)
$O > I \, (I > O)$	(Un)Stable with respect to obligations
$O > D \, (D > O)$	Social (selfish)
$I > D \, (D > I)$	(Un)Stable with respect to desires

Table 1 Twelve primitive agent types

realistic ones are listed in Table 2. The definition of agent types leads to a simple

Constraints	Agent type
$B > O\,O > I\,I > D$	Realistic, unstable-O, stable-D, social
$B > O\,O > D\,D > I$	Realistic, unstable-O, unstable-D, social
$B > I\,I > O\,O > D$	Realistic, stable-O, stable-D, social
$B > I\,I > D\,D > O$	Realistic, stable-O, stable-D, selfish
$B > D\,D > O\,O > I$	Realistic, unstable-O, unstable-D, selfish
$B > D\,D > I\,I > O$	Realistic, stable-O, unstable-D, selfish

Table 2 Six complete realistic agent types

way in which agent types can be compared. Agent type A is at least as general as agent type B if all the priority functions that respect constraints of agent type A, also respect the constraints of agent type B. The generality relation between realistic agent types forms the lattice visualized in Figure 2 if we add a top element. This figure should be read as follows. The level in this hierarchy indicates the generality of agent types. The bottom of this lattice is the realistic agent type. Each higher layer adds additional constraints resulting in more specific agent types. The top of this lattice is the falsum which indicates that adding any additional constraint to the ρ function results in an inconsistent ordering. Just below are the six complete realistic agent types.

There are also other constraints on priority functions. One of them is the following unique extension property, which says that ρ associates with each rule a unique integer. It induces a strict total order on the rules.

Definition 3 (Unique goal set) *A goal generation process that generates unique goal sets is specified by a tuple $\langle Obs, B, O, I, D, \rho \rangle$ with ρ a function from $B \cup O \cup I \cup D$ to the integers such that $\rho(x) = \rho(y)$ implies $x = y$.*

Another constraint on priority function ρ is the following attitude order property.

Definition 4 (Attitude order) *A goal generation process specified by a tuple $\langle Obs, B, O, I, D, \rho \rangle$ induces a strict attitude order if ρ is a function from $B \cup O \cup I \cup D$ to the integers such that for all $X, Y \in \{B, O, I, D\}$ with $X \neq Y$ we have either $X > Y$ or $Y > X$.*

The only agent types that satisfy the attitude order property are the complete agent types. Lack of the attitude order property is illustrated by the realistic

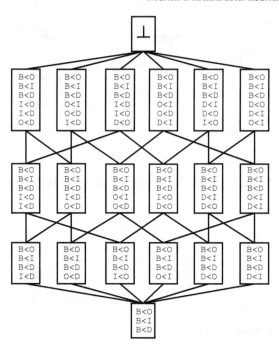

Fig. 2 The lattice structure of realistic agent types.

agent. It starts with the observations and calculates belief extensions by iteratively applying belief rules. When no belief rule is applicable anymore, then the set of either O, the I, or the D rules are chosen arbitrarily. The chosen set is called the active set of rules. If a rule from the active set of rules is applicable, then the rule is selected and applied. When the rule is applied successfully, the belief rules are attended again and belief rules are applied. If there is no rule from the active set of rules O, I, or D is applicable, then another set of rules becomes the active set of rules. If there is no rule from any of the O, I, or D applicable, then the process terminates – a fixed point is reached – and extensions are calculated.

4 Normative Multi-BOID organizations

Castelfranchi observes that autonomy comes from the combination of auto and nomos, and therefore that agents are autonomous only when they can decide on their own norms. The BOID architecture has inspired Boella and van der Torre to develop an architecture for normative systems [7, 8], as discussed in this section. Moreover, for decision making in such normative multiagent systems, Boella and van der Torre [9] develop a game theoretic approach to norms.

4.1 Types of norms

Searle [33, 34] distinguishes two types of norms: "Some rules regulate antecedently existing forms of behavior. For example, the rules of polite table behavior regulate eating, but eating exists independently of these rules. Some rules, on the other hand, do not merely regulate an antecedently existing activity called playing chess; they, as it were, create the possibility of or define that activity. The activity of playing chess is constituted by action in accordance with these rules. Chess has no existence apart from these rules. The institutions of marriage, money, and promising are like the institutions of baseball and chess in that they are systems of such constitutive rules or conventions" [33, p. 131].

Thus far the two kinds of norms have mainly been studied in isolation, which raises the question how regulative and constitutive norms are related. In the deontic logic literature, the interaction among obligations and permissions has been studied in some depth, see, e.g., [40, 14, 28]. In most formalizations, obligations, prohibitions and permissions have a conditional nature. Their conditions could directly refer to entities and facts of the commonsense world, but they often refer to a legal and more abstract classification of the world, making them more independent from the commonsense view. E.g., they refer to money instead of paper sheets, to properties instead of houses and fields. This more natural and economical way to model the relation between commonsense reality and legal reality uses constitutive norms, and allows regulative norms to refer to the legal classification of reality. In this way, it is not necessary that each regulative norm refers to all the conditions involved in the classification of paper as money or of houses and fields as properties. A constitutive norm has been defined by Searle as "X counts as Y in context C", and has been formalized as a counts-as conditional [26, 3, 23, 5].

Since all kinds of norms are represented by conditionals, we can represent them as subsystems within the normative system, or as input/output components in architecture. This raises the question what kind of input and output these components have. According to Searle, institutional facts like marriage, money and private property emerge from an independent ontology of "brute" natural facts through constitutive norms of the form "such and such an X counts as Y in context C" where X is any object satisfying certain conditions and Y is a label that qualifies X as being something of an entirely new sort. Examples of constitutive norms are "X counts as a presiding official in a wedding ceremony", "this bit of paper counts as a five euro bill" and "this piece of land counts as somebody's private property". Thus, the propositions describing the world are distinguished in two categories. First, "brute facts" are natural facts and events produced by actions of agents. Second, "institutional facts" are a legal classification of brute facts; they belong only to the beliefs of the normative system and have no direct counterpart in the world. We call a set of brute literals a brute description, a set of institutional literals an institutional description, and a set of both brute and institutional literals a mixed description.

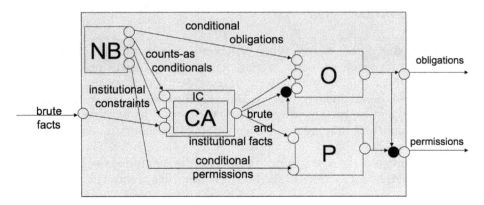

Fig. 3 The Architecture of the Normative System.

4.2 Normative components

We follow the definition of normative systems of Alchourrón and Bulygin [1], inspired by Tarski's definition of deductive systems. They consider as input factual descriptions and as output a classification of obligatory and permitted situations. Permissions are not closed under logical consequence, in the sense that a permission for p and a permission for $\neg p$ do not imply a permission for a contradiction. For technical reasons, we describe the permissions by sets of mixed descriptions. In our architecture, visualized in Figure 3, the input of the normative system is a context, a brute description, and the output is a set of obligations, a mixed description, and a set of permissions, a set of mixed descriptions.

There are four components in the architecture. Besides the components for counts-as conditionals (CA), obligations (O) and permissions (P), there is a component containing the norms (NB). The counts-as component has a wrapper (IC) to enable the connection with the other components. The components are connected by channels. The data flowing over the channels is not indexed by modal operators. So if a proposition p is flowing over a permission channel it is interpreted as a permission, usually represented in deontic logic by $P(p)$, and when it is flowing over an obligation channel it is interpreted as an obligation, usually represented by $O(p)$.

The norm database does not have any input, we therefore assume that the norms of the normative system are fixed. E.g., it can be extended with an input to update the norm database. We also assume that there can be background knowledge in the form of institutional constraints. The output contains sets of conditional obligations, conditional permissions, counts-as conditionals, and institutional constraints, four sets of pairs of mixed descriptions.

The counts-as component directly encodes Searle's "X counts as Y in context C". The input contains counts-as conditionals, X, a brute description, and C, a mixed description. The output is Y, an institutional literal.

The input of the wrapper for counts-as conditionals are the brute facts, the counts-as conditionals, and the institutional constraints. The output are the brute and institutional facts, a mixed description.

The notorious contrary-to-duty paradoxes such as Chisholm's and Forrester's paradox have led to the use of constraints in deontic logic [27]. The strategy is to adapt a technique that is well known in the logic of belief change - cut back the set of norms to just below the threshold of making the current situation inconsistent. Therefore, the input of the obligation component contains conditional obligations, a set of pairs of mixed descriptions, a context, a mixed description, and constraints, a set of mixed descriptions. The output contains obligations, a mixed description.

The permission component is like an obligation component without constraints, since the issue of contrary-to-duty does not play a role for permissions. The input of the permission component is a set of conditional permissions, and a context of brute and institutional facts. As mentioned above in the description of the whole normative system, another distinction is that the output is a set of mixed descriptions. The input contains conditional permissions, a set of pairs of mixed descriptions, and a context, a mixed description. The output contains permissions, a set of mixed descriptions.

Finally, consider again the whole architecture. When designing a normative system, there is a tradeoff between obligations, permissions and counts-as conditionals, in the sense that there are many norm bases which have the same global output. For example, the same output can be obtained for example using many counts-as conditionals, or no counts-as conditionals at all. Likewise there is a tradeoff between obligations and permissions. Consequently, there is a need for a methodology to represent normative systems in our architecture. It is relatively straightforward to represent a piece of legal code in the architecture, as in legal code the three kinds of norms are usually clearly distinguished, but in general it is more problematic.

4.3 Logical specifications

The architecture is a bridge between logical specifications, for example based on deontic logic, and normative multi-agent systems. In a normative multi-agent system the components can be implemented in a variety of ways. The abstract behavior of the components and channels can be given in terms of real-timed timed data streams [2], based on general results in the Reo coordination language. The principles of deontic logic can be interpreted as functionality descriptions of the components [38, 13].

By varying the logics to describe the components, we can use the architecture to study the interaction among the logics. For example, we can use either the logic for counts-as conditionals of Jones and Sergot [26], Artosi et al. [3], Grossi et al. [23], or our own proposal [5], and study its interaction with input/output logic [27], or some other deontic logic. To do so, we just have to find the flat conditional fragment of the logics, and ignore the modal operator. The architecture can thus be used as a logical architecture to study this interaction among logical systems [8].

4.4 Decision making in normative multiagent systems

Boella and van der Torre [9] develop a game theoretic approach to norms. Norms should satisfy various properties to be effective as a mechanism to obtain desirable behavior. For example, the system should not sanction without reason, as for example Caligula or Nero did in the ancient Roman times, as the norms would loose their force to motivate agents. Moreover, sanctions should not be too low, as in the daycare example, but they also should not be too high, as shown by argument of Beccaria. Otherwise, once a norm is violated, there is no way to prevent further norm violations. Boella and van der Torre [6] list the following requirements for such an analysis.

The first requirement is that norms influence the behavior of agents. However, they only have to do so under normal or typical circumstances. For example, if other agents are not obeying the norm, then we cannot expect an agent to do so. This norm acceptance has been studied by Castelfranchi and colleagues [20], and in a game-theoretic setting for social laws by Tennenholtz [35].

The second requirement is that even if a norm is accepted in the sense that the other agents obey the norm, an agent should be able to violate the norms. A normative multi-agent system is a "set of agents [...] whose interactions can be regarded as norm-governed; the norms prescribe how the agents ideally should and should not behave. [...] Importantly, the norms allow for the possibility that actual behavior may at times deviate from the ideal, i.e., that violations of obligations, or of agents' rights, may occur" [25]. In other words, the norms of global policies must be represented as soft constraints, which are used in detective control systems where violations can be detected, instead of hard constraints restricted to preventative control systems in which violations are impossible. The typical example of the former is that you can enter a train without a ticket, but you may be checked and sanctioned, and an example of the latter is that you cannot enter a metro station without a ticket. Moreover, detective control is the result of actions of agents and therefore subject to errors and influenceable by actions of other agents. Therefore, it may be the case that violations are not often enough detected, that law enforcement is lazy or can be bribed, there are conflicting obligations in the normative system, that agents are able to block the sanction, block the prosecution, update the normative system, etc. A game-theoretic analysis can be used to study these issues of fraud and deception.

The third requirement is that norms should apply to a variety of agent types, since agents can be motivated in various ways, as the daycare example illustrates. A norm is a mechanism to obtain desired multi-agent system behavior, and must therefore under normal or typical circumstances be fulfilled for a range of agent types. Castelfranchi argues that sanctions are only one of the means which motivate agents to respect obligations, besides "pro-active actions, prevention from deviation and reinforcement of correct behavior, and then also 'positive sanctions', social approval" [16]. Castelfranchi [16] argues that an agent should fulfill an obligation because it is an obligation, not because there is a sanction associated with it.

> "True norms are aimed in fact at the internal control by the addressee itself as a cognitive deliberative agent, able to understand a norm as such and adopt it. [...] The use of external control and sanction is only a sub-ideal situation and obligation." [16]

Boella and van der Torre therefore use the distinction between violations and sanctions to distinguish between the agent's interpretation of the obligation, and its personal characteristics or agent type. The agent types are inspired by the use of agent types in the goal generation components of Broersen et al.'s BOID architecture [12]. *Roughly*, Boella and van der Torre distinguish among *norm internalizing agents*, *respectful* agents that attempt to evade norm violations and that are motivated by what counts and does not count as a violation, and *selfish* agents that obey norms only due to the associated sanctions, i.e. that are motivated by sanctions only. An obligation without a sanction *should* be fulfilled, as Castelfranchi argues. But if fulfilling the obligations has a cost then it *is* only fulfilled by respectful agents, not by selfish agents, unless some incentives are provided or the agents dislike some social consequences of the violations. A respectful agent fulfills its obligations due to the existence of the obligation, whereas a selfish agent fulfills its obligations due to fear of consequences.

Respectful agents: agents that base their decisions solely on whether their behavior respects the goals of the normative agents. They put their duties before their own goals and desires: they maximize the fulfilment of obligations regardless to what happens to its own goals; even if the agent **n** did not sanction them, the agent **a** would prefer to respect the obligation. It is said that respectful agents *adopt* the goal of the normative agent as their preference.

Selfish agents: agents that base their decisions solely on the consequences of their actions. If the obligation is respected, it is because agent **a** predicts that the situation resulting from the fulfillment is preferred according to its own goals and desires only: e.g., if it does not share its files, it knows that it can be sanctioned, a situation it does not desire or want. But it is possible also that there are not only material reasons, that is, not only for the damage caused by the sanction. Nothing prevents that the content of the norm is already a goal of the agent; moreover, agent **a** could have the desire not to be considered a violator, or it knows that being considered a violator gives it a bad reputation, so that it would not be trusted by other agent. However, to stick to the obligation, the goal of not being a violator or of not being sanctioned must be preferred by the agent to the desire or goal not to respect the obligation (obligations usually have a cost): a weak sanction, as it often happens, does not enforce the respect of a norm (e.g., the sanction is that the access to a website is forbidden, but the agent has already downloaded what it wanted).

To distinguish these cases, Boella and van der Torre distinguish between the decision to count behavior as a violation, and the decision to sanction it.

Of course, most agents are mixed types of agents between these two extremes. Sometimes an agent is respectful and in other cases it is selfish. Balancing these two extremes is an important part of the agent's deliberation. The adoption of the obligation as a goal can be considered as an additional factor when the different alternatives are weighed according to its own goals and desires: so that the newly added motivations can affect the decision of agent **a** and move it towards an obligation-abiding behavior besides its own attitude towards that goal and the possible consequences of its alternative decisions. However, if a norm is effective in each case of the agent types, it is also effective for mixed agents. therefore we can restrict ourselves to the extreme agent types in a game-theoretical analysis.

Given possible conditions for a norm, the fourth requirement is that norms are as weak as possible, in the sense that the norms should not apply in cases where this is undesired, and that sanctions should not be too severe. The latter is motivated by a classical economic argument due to Beccaria, which says that if sanctions are too high, they can no longer be used in cases where agents already have violated a norm. Sanctions should be high enough to motivate selfish agents, but they should not be too high.

Designing norms satisfying these requirements is an area of game theory called mechanism design. In, amongst others, [6] Boella and van der Torre provide the following informal definition of obligation, extending Boella and Lesmo [4]'s proposal. According to legal studies what distinguishes norms from mere power to damage an agent is that sanctions are possible only in case of violations and which situations can be considered as violations is defined by the law: *"nullum crimen, nulla poena sine lege"*. In their definition a norm specifies what will be considered as a violation by the normative agent (item 2) and that the normative agent will sanction only in case of violations (item 3). Given a set of norms N, agent **a** is obliged by the normative agent **n** to do x with sanction s, iff there is a norm n of N such that:

- The content x of the obligation is a desire and goal of **n** and agent **n** wants that agent **a** adopts this as its decision since it considers agent **a** as responsible for x.
- agent **n** has the desire and the goal that, if the obligation is not respected by agent **a**, a prosecution process is started to determine if the situation "counts as" a violation of the obligation and that, if a violation is recognized, agent **a** is sanctioned.
- Both agent **a** and agent **n** do not desire the sanction: for agent **a** the sanction is an incentive to respect the obligation, while agent **n** has no immediate advantage from sanctioning.

This definition is extended in various papers in a number of ways. For example, goals and desires are formalized as conditional rules, because norms and obligations are typically represented by conditional rules.

5 A Practical Agent Programming Language: 2APL

In order to facilitate the implementation of BOID like autonomous agents, Dastani [21] has proposed a programming language, called 2APL (A Practical Agent Programming Language). The general architecture of individual agents in 2APL is based on the BDI model. A 2APL agent is designed and implemented in terms of beliefs, goals , events, plans, and three different types of practical reasoning (or decision) rules. An agent's beliefs, goals, and events which constitute the agent's informational and motivational attitude, are implemented in a declarative way, while plans are implemented in an imperative style. As we explain later in this section, the plans of an agent constitute the agent's commitments and influence the agent's decision making behaviour. The practical reasoning (decision) rules enable an agent to decide/generate plans at runtime. In particular, a practical reasoning rule implements a plan together with some conditions under which the plan should be decided/generated. An agent's beliefs, goals, events, plans, and practical reasoning rule constitute the agent's state. Although the state of an agent can change during the agent's execution, we assume that practical reasoning rules are not subject of change.

2APL provides three types of practical reasoning (decision) rules. The first type of rules are called *planning goal rules* (or simply PG-rules). A PG-rule can be applied to decide plans for achieving goals. The second type of practical reasoning rules are called *procedural call rules* (or simply PC-rules) and are designed to decide plans for reacting to external events or messages. Finally, the third type of practical reasoning rules are called *plan repair rules* (or simply PR-rules), which are designed to decide alternative plans for those plans whose executions have failed. A 2APL agent decides its plans through its so-called deliberation process, which is a cyclic process. At each cycle, the agent senses its environment (receives its events and messages), updates its beliefs, goals, and events based on the sensed information, checks the conditions of its practical reasoning rules and decides/generates plans if the conditions of rules are satisfied, and finally executes its generated plans. The general architecture of a 2APL agent is illustrated in Figure 4.

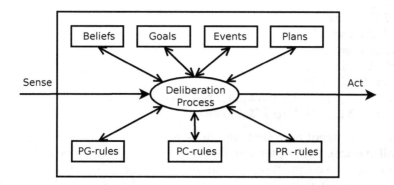

Fig. 4 The 2APL architecture.

2APL agents are assumed to have consistent beliefs, goals, and events. They are also assumed to have PG-rules for deciding plans that contribute to the achievement of goals (i.e., partially achieve goals). For example, consider a 2APL agent that is going to a conference as in section 3. The agent may believe that hotels nearby the conference site or hotels with large rooms are expensive. The agent may have a goal to have a flight ticket and a cheap hotel. Finally, the agent has a decision rule for booking hotels and a decision rule for booking flight tickets. Each rule can be applied to achieve a part of the agent's goal. It is important to note that the agent may have different rules for booking a hotel. In such case, the agent can apply a second rule if the application of the first cannot achieve its intended goal.

5.1 Computational Architecture of 2APL

In this section, we provide a short exposition of 2APL to illustrate the use of goals by this type of agents. A detailed presentation of 2APL can be found in [21]. A 2APL agent program specifies the initial state of an agent's beliefs, goals, plans, and practical reasoning (decision) rules. A 2APL program provides also the specification of belief update actions. The specification of such an action indicates when the action can be performed and what is the effect of executing the action (see below for more details about belief update actions). The initial state of an agent's events is considered to be empty as events are assumed to be received during the agent's execution at runtime.

The beliefs of an agent represent information the agent has about itself and its surrounding world including other agents. The implementation of the initial beliefs is a Prolog program. The following example illustrates the implementation of the initial beliefs of a 2APL agent, called ag1. This beliefs represents the information of ag1 about possible accommodations for the ijcai conference. In particular, ag1 has information about three hotels and believes that hotels nearby the conference site or hotels with large rooms are expensive.

```
Beliefs:
    hotel(h1,large).
    hotel(h2,small).
    hotel(h3,small).
    nearby(h1,ijcai).
    nearby(h2,ijcai).
    expHotel(X,Y) :- hotel(X,_), nearby(X,Y).
    expHotel(X,_) :- hotel(X,large).
```

The goals of an agent represent situations the agent wants to realize (not necessary all at once). The implementation of the initial goals is a list of formulas, each of which is a conjunction of ground atoms. The following example is the implementation of an initial goal of ag1. This goal represents the desired situation where ag1 has a flight ticket and has booked a cheap hotel for the ijcai conference.

```
Goals:
    flightTicket(ijcai) and cheapHotel(ijcai)
```

The beliefs and goals of an agent are governed by a rationality principle. According to this principle, if an agent believes a certain fact, then the agent does not pursue that fact as a goal. This means that if an agent modifies its beliefs, then its goals may be modified as well. An agent's beliefs and goals change during the agent's execution.

A plan in 2APL consists of basic actions composed by sequence operator, conditional choice operator, and conditional iteration operator. 2APL agents can perform different types of basic actions such as belief update actions, belief and goal test actions, external actions, communication actions, and actions to manage the dynamics of goals. A belief update action updates an agent's beliefs when it is executed, and it is specified by a of the action name, together with its pre- and post-conditions (formulas consisting of atoms). Note that the specification of belief update actions are given by 2APL agent programs. An agent can execute a belief update action if its pre-condition is entailed by the agent's beliefs. The execution of a belief update action modifies the beliefs such that it entails the post-condition of the action. A belief and goal test actions check whether a formula consisting of atoms is entailed by the agent's beliefs and goals. External actions are performed in the agent's environment to change its state, and communication actions are performed to send information to other agents. Finally, the goal dynamic actions can be used to modify an agent's goals. The following example is the implementation of an initial plan of agent ag1 consisting of an external action followed by a belief update action. The external action will be performed in a yellow page database (which is assumed to be an environment) and will search for the contact information of a travel agency in the yellow page. The found contact information will be returned to the agent by the output parameter A. The subsequent belief update action adds the contact information A to the beliefs of ag1. This information can be used for buying a flight ticket. Note the use of variable A which passes the contact information from the external action to the belief update action.

```
Plans:
    @yellowPage(findTravelAgency(),A);AddBeliefs(A)
```

A PG-rule consists of a goal condition (a formula consisting of atoms), a belief condition (same as the goal condition), and a plan. A PG-rule can be applied if 1) its goal condition is satisfied by the agent's goals (which means that the agent has a goal that satisfies the goal condition), 2) its belief condition is satisfied by the agent's beliefs (which means that the agent's beliefs satisfies the belief condition), and 3) the agent has not already decided a plan for the same goal (if the agent has no existing plan for achieving the same goal).[1] For example, the following PG-rule specifies that a cheap accommodation for a conference X can be booked (represented by the goal condition cheapHotel(X)) by sending a request message to the conference site to book a room in hotel

---

[1] The current version of 2APL cannot cope with conflicting goals. An operational analysis of conflicting goals is given in [37].

Y (represented by the plan `send(X,request,book(Y))`). In order to apply this PG-rule, the agent need to know the name of a hotel which is not expensive (represented by the belief condition `hotel(Y,_)` and not `expHotel(Y,X)`).

```
PG-rules:
    cheapHotel(X) <- hotel(Y,_) and not expHotel(Y,X) |
                          { send(X,request,book(Y)) }
```

Given agent `ag1` with initial beliefs and goals as specified above, the application of this planning goal rule proceeds as follows. First, the goal condition is checked against the goal of `ag1`. This condition is satisfied under the substitution `[X/ijcai]`. Second, this substitution is applied to the belief condition of the rule resulting a more concrete belief condition `hotel(Y,_)` and not `expHotel(Y,ijcai)`. Third, the new belief condition is checked against the beliefs of `ag1` and satisfied under the substitution `[Y/h3]`. Fourth, the application of these substitutions to the plan results in the communication action `send(ijcai,request,book(h3))`. Finally, this plan is generated and added to the plans of `ag1`. We would like to emphasize that the plan can only be generated if there is no plan yet generated for the goal `cheapHotel(ijcai)`. We assume that generated plans are enriched with the goals they aim at achieving.

In this short exposition of 2APL, we will not discuss PC-rules and PR-rules in detail, but explain their syntax and intuitive semantics. A procedure call rule (PC-rules) can be used to respond to the received messages and to handle external events. In fact, a procedure call rule can be used to generate plans as a response to 1) the reception of messages that are received from other agents, and 2) the reception of events generated by the external environments. Like planning goal rules, the specification of procedure call rules consist of three entries. The only difference is that the head of the procedure call rules can be a message template or an event. The following is an example of a procedure call rule that generates a plan to update an agent's beliefs about a booking confirmation when it receives a message from sender X informing that the hotel booking is confirmed (represented by `bookingConfirmed`). We assume that the belief update action `Confirm(X,Y)` is specified such that its execution updates an agent's beliefs with the fact `cheapHotel(X,Y)`. Note that because of the rationality principle between beliefs and goal, then the goal `cheapHotel(X,Y)` is assumed to be achieved after this update. Note also that the goal of agent `ag1` in the above example will not be dropped until `ag1` also believes that it has a flight ticket.

```
PC-rules:
    message(X,inform,bookingConfirmed(Y)) <- (X = ijcai)|
                          { Confirm(X,Y) }
```

Finally, a plan repair rule specifies that a plan whose execution has been failed should be replaced by an alternative plan. A plan repair rule consists of three entries: two plans and one belief condition. A plan repair rule of an agent can be applied if 1) the execution of one of its plan fails, 2) the failed plan can be unified with the plan in the head of the rule, and 3) the belief condition of the rule is satisfied by the agent's beliefs. The satisfaction of these three conditions results in a substitution for the variables that occur in the alternative plan. The following is an example of a plan repair rule. This rule specifies that if the execution of a plan that unifies `send(X,request,book(Y))` fails and the agent knows an alternative recipient Z, then the agent should replace the failed plan with a new plan `send(Z,request,book(Y))`, i.e., sending the same booking request to the alternative recipient Z.

```
PR-rules:
  send(X,request,book(Y)) <- alternativeAddress(X,Z)  |
                        { send(Z,request,book(Y)) }
```

In order to execute a 2APL agent, the deliberation process (which is a cyclic process) follows a certain order of deliberation steps repeatedly and indefinitely. Each cycle starts by applying all applicable PG-rules followed by executing only the first actions of all plans. This is in order to make the deliberation process fair with respect to the execution of all plans. The next deliberation steps are to process all events received from the external environment, all internal events indicating the failure of plans, and all messages received from other agents, respectively. An event from external environment is processed by applying the first applicable PC-rule. An internal event, which identifies a failed plan, is processed by applying the first applicable PR-rule to the failed plan. A received message is processed by applying the first applicable PC-rule. Note that the application of rules to process events generates and add plans to the corresponding agent's plans. After these deliberation steps, it is checked if it makes sense to do a new cycle of deliberation steps. In fact, if in a deliberation cycle no rule could be applied, no plan could be executed, and no event could be processed, then it makes no sense to try again a new cycle of deliberation steps, except when a new event or message has arrived. The 2APL deliberation cycle is illustrated in Figure 5.

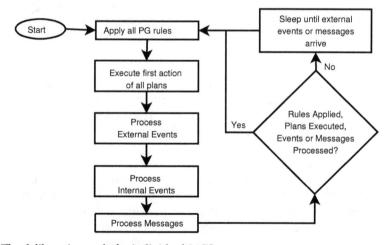

Fig. 5 The deliberation cycle for individual 2APL agents.

6 Conclusions

In this paper we give an overview of ten years of research in BOID theory, including its origins in the work of Castelfranchi and colleagues, and its impact on normative multiagent systems and agent programming. Castelfranchi emphasizes that goals are not only first class citizens in the design and development of software agents, but also that desires, obligations and intentions are goals at different stages of processing. In particular, the aim of Castelfranchi and Paglieri [17] is to detail a model in which specific types of beliefs act as filters and triggers from goal activation to goal execution. According to this view, in order to activate, promote, drop, or suspend a goal, an intention, or an intentional action, one has to provide or modify the appropriate beliefs. cognitive functionalism: the significant and heuristic categories of beliefs and goals are defined by their functions, rather than by their format, content, or other intrinsic features. Goal change is a consequence of belief change. Many kinds of beliefs, and whether or how all of them can be modeled in the BOID architecture remains to be studied.

The characterizing feature of the BOID architecture is its goal generation component, coordinating sub-components that represent cognitive attitudes. The mechanism of the goal generation component is a conflict resolution mechanism that resolves conflicts within and among its sub-components. In the computational model for the goal generation component, mental attitudes are formalized as sets of defeasible rules in a prioritized default logic. In the BOID architecture, the process of generating goals from different mental attitudes is biased by the type of agents, such as realistic, stable and social.

Often, the BOID like agents operate in a normative setting comprising other agents and a set of norms that should be respected by the agents. There are four components in the architecture of a normative system. Besides the components for counts-as conditionals (CA), obligations (O) and permissions (P), there is a component that contains the norms (NB). In normative decision making, Boella and van der Torre model the normative system as a normative BOID agent. In their recursive definition a norm specifies what will be considered as a violation by the normative agent and that the normative agent will sanction only in case of violations.

The BOID project has influenced BDI-based agent programming languages, which are designed to facilitate the implementation of autonomous agents. One of such programming languages is 2APL. The general architecture of individual agents in 2APL is based on the BDI model. 2APL provides three types of practical reasoning (decision) rules. The first type of rules are called *planning goal rules* (or simply PG-rules). A PG-rule can be applied to decide plans for achieving goals. The second type of practical reasoning rules are called *procedural call rules* (or simply PC-rules) and are designed to decide plans for reacting to external events or messages. Finally, the third type of practical reasoning rules are called *plan repair rules* (or simply PR-rules), which are designed to decide alternative plans for those plans whose executions have failed.

There are many topics for further research in goal generation. First, we have ignored the types of goals. There have been many studies proposing various goal types such achieve goals, maintain goals, perform goals, and temporally extended goals (subset of LTL formula). It is the question how various goal types can be generated based on internal and external motivational attitudes. Second, the role on other cognitive attitudes such as emotions in the generation of goals and vice versa. According to the existing emotion theories such as OCC model, an agent's emotions is influenced by an agent's motivations and goals can be studied, and conversely an agent's motivations and goals is effected by an agent's goals. For example, an agent who wants to be have his thesis finished before a deadline may be hopeful if the agent's believes it will achieve this goal. If the agent starts to fear his health, the agent may drop his goal to finish his thesis. Future work can focus on how emotions influence an agent's goal and how emotions can be incorporated in an agent's goal generation process.

References

1. C.E. Alchourrón and E. Bulygin. *Normative Systems*. Springer, Wien, 1971.
2. F. Arbab. Reo: a coordination language. *Mathematical structures in computer science*, 2004.
3. A. Artosi, A. Rotolo, and S. Vida. On the logical nature of count-as conditionals. In *Procs. of LEA 2004 Workshop*, 2004.
4. G. Boella and L. Lesmo. A game theoretic approach to norms. *Cognitive Science Quarterly*, 2(3-4):492–512, 2002.
5. G. Boella and L. van der Torre. Regulative and constitutive norms in normative multiagent systems. In *Procs. of 10th International Conference on the Principles of Knowledge Representation and Reasoning KR'04*, pages 255–265, Menlo Park (CA), 2004. AAAI Press.
6. G. Boella and L. van der Torre. Game-theoretic foundations for norms. *Proceedings of Artificial Intelligence Studies*, 3(26):39–51, 2006.
7. G. Boella and L.W. N. van der Torre. An architecture of a normative system: counts-as conditionals, obligations and permissions. In Hideyuki Nakashima, Michael P. Wellman, Gerhard Weiss, and Peter Stone, editors, *AAMAS*, pages 229–231. ACM, 2006.
8. G. Boella and L.W. N. van der Torre. A logical architecture of a normative system. In Lou Goble and John-Jules Ch. Meyer, editors, *DEON*, volume 4048 of *Lecture Notes in Computer Science*, pages 24–35. Springer, 2006.
9. G. Boella and L.W. N. van der Torre. A game-theoretic approach to normative multiagent systems. In Guido Boella, Leendert W. N. van der Torre, and Harko Verhagen, editors, *Normative Multi-agent Systems*, volume 07122 of *Dagstuhl Seminar Proceedings*. Internationales Begegnungs- und Forschungszentrum für Informatik (IBFI), Schloss Dagstuhl, Germany, 2007.
10. R. Bordini, M. Wooldridge, and J. Hübner. *Programming Multi-Agent Systems in AgentSpeak using Jason (Wiley Series in Agent Technology)*. John Wiley & Sons, 2007.
11. M.E. Bratman. *Intention, plans, and practical reason*. Harvard University Press, Cambridge Mass, 1987.
12. J. Broersen, M. Dastani, J. Hulstijn, and L. van der Torre. Goal generation in the BOID architecture. *Cognitive Science Quarterly*, 2(3-4):428–447, 2002.
13. J. Broersen, M. Dastani, and L. van der Torre. Beliefs, obligations, intentions and desires as components in an agent architecture. *International journal on intelligent systems*, 2005.
14. E. Bulygin. Permissive norms and normative systems. In A. Martino and F. Socci Natali, editors, *Automated Analysis of Legal Texts*, pages 211–218. Publishing Company, Amsterdam, 1986.

15. C. Castelfranchi. Modeling social action for AI agents. *Artificial Intelligence*, 103(1-2):157–182, 1998.
16. C. Castelfranchi. Engineering social order. In *LNCS n.1972: Procs. of ESAW'00*, pages 1–18, Berlin, 2000. Springer.
17. C. Castelfranchi and Fabio Paglieri. The role of beliefs in goal dynamics: prolegomena to a constructive theory of intentions. *Synthese*, 155:237–263, 2007.
18. P.R. Cohen and H.J. Levesque. Intention is choice with commitment. *Artificial Intelligence*, 42:213–261, 1990.
19. R. Conte and C. Castelfranchi. *Cognitive and Social Action*. UCL Press, 1995.
20. R. Conte, C. Castelfranchi, and F. Dignum. Autonomous norm-acceptance. In *Intelligent Agents V (ATAL'98)*, volume 1555 of *LNCS*, pages 99–112. Springer, Berlin, 1998.
21. M. Dastani. 2APL: a practical agent programming language. *International Journal of Autonomous Agents and Multi-Agent Systems*, 16(3):214–248, 2008.
22. M. Dastani, J. Hulstijn, and L. van der Torre. How to decide what to do? *European Journal of Operational Research*, 160 (3):762–784, 2005.
23. D. Grossi, F. Dignum, and J.-J.Ch. Meyer. Contextual taxonomies. In *LNCS n. 3487: Procs. of CLIMA'04 Workshop*, pages 33–51, Berlin, 2004. Springer.
24. K. Hindriks. Programming rational agents in GOAL. In *Multi-Agent Programming: Languages and Tools and Applications*, page 119–157. Springer, 2009.
25. A. Jones and J. Carmo. Deontic logic and contrary-to-duties. In D. Gabbay and F. Guenthner, editors, *Handbook of Philosophical Logic*, volume 3, pages 203–279. Kluwer, Dordrecht (NL), 2001.
26. A. Jones and M. Sergot. A formal characterisation of institutionalised power. *Journal of IGPL*, 3:427–443, 1996.
27. D. Makinson and L. van der Torre. Constraints for input-output logics. *Journal of Philosophical Logic*, 30(2):155–185, 2001.
28. D. Makinson and L. van der Torre. Permissions from an input-output perspective. *Journal of Philosophical Logic*, 32(4):391–416, 2003.
29. A. Pokahr, L. Braubach, and W. Lamersdorf. Jadex: A BDI reasoning engine. In *Multi-Agent Programming: Languages, Platforms and Applications*. Kluwer, 2005.
30. A. Rao and M. Georgeff. Modeling rational agents within a BDI architecture. In *Proceedings of the KR91*, 1991.
31. A.S. Rao and M.P. Georgeff. BDI agents: From theory to practice. In J. Allen, R. Fikes, and E. Sandewall, editors, *Proceedings of the First International Conference on Multi-Agent Systems (ICMAS'95)*, 1995.
32. R. Reiter. A logic for default reasoning. *Artificial Intelligence*, 13:81–132, 1980.
33. J.R. Searle. *Speech Acts: an Essay in the Philosophy of Language*. Cambridge University Press, Cambridge (UK), 1969.
34. J.R. Searle. *The Construction of Social Reality*. The Free Press, New York, 1995.
35. M. Tennenholtz. On stable social laws and qualitative equilibria. *Artificial Intelligence*, 102(1):1–20, 1998.
36. R. Thomason. Desires and defaults:. In *Proceedings of the KR2000*. Morgan Kaufmann, 2000.
37. N. Tinnemeier, M. Dastani, and J.J. Meyer. Goal selection strategies for rational agents. In *Proceedings of the workshop LAnguages, methodologies and Development tools for multi-agent systemS (LADS'07)*, 2007.
38. J. Treur. Functionality descriptions. *International journal on intelligent systems*, 2002.
39. B. van Fraassen. Values and the heart command. *Journal of Philosophy*, 70:5–19, 1973.
40. G. Henrik von Wright. *An Essay in Modal Logic*. North-Holland, Amsterdam, 1951.

Chapter 6
The irritation of doubt: When is it OK to scratch your beliefs?

Fabio Paglieri

Abstract Building upon Peirce's notion of "the irritation of doubt", I outline the role doubts play in belief formation, drawing a distinction between two different phenomena: Peircean doubts and scary doubts. I argue that the former are an essential and useful ingredient in our belief dynamics, whereas the latter are potentially dangerous and yet unavoidable biases, even though they might occasionally be redeemed by their practical merits. This analysis is intertwined with Castelfranchi's views on belief formation and goal processing, with the aim of highlighting a common root between pragmatism and goal theory, and to provide a unifying picture of the mind as a goal-directed, coherence-seeking control system.

1 Introduction

In one of his many illuminating passages, Peirce observed that «the action of thought is excited by the irritation of doubt, and ceases when belief is attained; so that the production of belief is the sole function of thought» (1958, p. 118).[1] Nowadays "thought" is called cognition and is no longer conceived as pertaining solely or even mainly to the production of belief. Nevertheless, there is still much to be learned from Peirce's remark, as well as good chances of misunderstanding its meaning. In what follows I try to elucidate both Peirce's insight and some misconception that might plague it, and to stress its connections with Cristiano Castelfranchi's own views on belief dynamics and, to a minor extent, goal dynamics. This will serve not only to build a bridge between

Fabio Paglieri
Goal-Oriented Agents Lab (GOAL), Institute of Cognitive Sciences and Technologies, CNR, Italy
e-mail: fabio.paglieri@istc.cnr.it

[1] Originally published as "How to make our ideas clear" in Popular Science Monthly 12 (January 1878), pp. 286–302.

the father of semiotics and the father of goal theory, but also to formulate a general hypothesis on the main function of the mind.

So, what kind of doubt works as an irritant for cognition, according to Peirce? As it has been noted before (Thagard 2004; Magnani 2009; Magnani and Bertolotti 2011), and as it is clear from the rest of Peirce's essay, he is not referring to some kind of Hamletic doubt on ontological or moral dilemmas ("To be or not to be?"), nor to the all-encompassing Skeptical doubt, but rather to mundane doubts concerning practical matters: it is the kind of doubt we encounter when we are presented with any ambiguous or unclear situation that requires us to form an opinion[2] on the facts in order to act accordingly and, if we are right, adequately. It is the doubt we face when we wonder about the nature of tonight's party to decide what to wear, or about the likelihood of rain in the afternoon to choose whether to take the umbrella in the morning, or about the meaning of our boss' remark to find a suitable response, or about the relative merits and shortcomings of various candidates in an election to establish how to vote. These are the kind of doubts that, according to Peirce, prompt our cognition to operate and move towards a certain state of belief. Let us call them *Peircean doubts*, for the sake of simplicity.

Now, it should be clear that Peircean doubts are an irritant insofar as they are impractical: the subject needs to know what to do, and for that s/he must move beyond the current state of doubt and reach some belief on the issue at hand, no matter how temporary. It should also be clear, though, that there is another type of doubts, which are not those contemplated by Peirce here, and that these doubts can also work as an irritant, but in a very different (and stronger) sense. I am referring to those doubts that threaten one's self image and/or social image, such as doubting one's professional or relational adequacy, moral fiber, religious faith, ethical values, personal engagements with family and friends, and the like. Let us call them *scary doubts*, because that is what they do: they scare the person into believing something, often (not always) with little regard for evidence, because the persistence of doubt would be painful or otherwise distasteful for the subject.

This distinction is relevant because Peircean doubts are not scary doubts, and their respective effects on cognition should not be confused. Yet it is easy to confuse them, since both types of doubt pressure the mind towards belief: but they do so in different ways, for different reasons, and serving different functions. While the exact differences between Peircean doubts and scary doubts will be the topic of the next sections, I want to anticipate their crucial difference. The influence of Peircean doubts is a fact of life, and Peirce was absolutely right to remind us that our strife for belief is essentially a response to the (practical) irritation they cause to our cognitive system: we need to reach a somewhat stable assessment of reality, even if precarious and fallible, in order to operate effectively, so it is unsurprising and certainly adaptive that our cognition evolved to answer that need. But the influence of scary doubts on belief formation and change (or lack thereof) is something that needs to be proven, and indeed I will review some evidence about it. Moreover,

---

[2] To Peirce, famously, this process was mainly one of abduction: for present purposes, however, it is unimportant what kind of inferential mechanism is involved in belief formation.

even after establishing that some of our beliefs are born out of fear rather than reason, this does not imply at all that fear-induced belief formation is a "good thing", either morally, rationally, or adaptively. Arguments are needed for each of these claims, and in what follows I will try to assess their merits and limits. For the time being, let us just emphasize that Peirce's thesis on the role of doubt in prompting cognition towards belief was intended for (and makes sense of) practical doubts on mundane matters, not scary doubts on issues of personal relevance.

2 Peircean doubts, epistemic bubbles and degrees of belief

Let us define a Peircean doubt as follows:

PROPOSITION 1 (Peircean doubt) *An agent X has a Peircean doubt on the issue P when (i) X is undecided regarding whether P or not-P is the case, and (ii) X needs to reach a temporary conclusion on P in order to act in the pursue of X's goals.*

Most emphatically,

COROLLARY 1 *It is not required that X has anything of importance at stake in resolving the current state of doubt one way or another, aside from being able to act.*

Peircean doubts are minor inconveniences that we encounter in the ongoing transition from ideation to realization of our daily deeds: for a variety of reasons (ignorance, uncertainty, forgetfulness, perceptual limits, etc.), we find ourselves with some gaps in the list of things we need to command in order to plan a certain action, and these gaps have to be fixed immediately and without much conscious effort or reflection. Repairing Peircean doubts typically does not involve any sophisticated reasoning task: agents take them in stride and simply assign a value to the previously undecided item, based on other relevant knowledge and (if pertinent) past experience. Interestingly, the agent treats the solution to a Peircean doubt as something well established (well enough to warrant acting upon it), and yet has no reservation in reconsidering it – that is, the kind of belief prompted by the irritation of Peircean doubts is not particularly resistant to update and change.

As a case in point, imagine that Luigi goes to the train station in Rome with the aim of taking the 11:00 am express train to Naples: upon entering the station at 10:45 am, Luigi looks up at the electronic board listing all departing trains and their platforms. To his dismay, the 11:00 am is listed as on time, but no platform is yet indicated, leaving Luigi in the dark on where to go (a typical instance of Peircean doubt). Since Luigi frequently takes this train from this station, he happens to know that (i) the train typically leaves from platform 20B, and (ii) the electronic board is often defective and does not show the platform until the very last moment. Without hesitation, Luigi solves his Peircean doubt by assuming that today the train will leave from platform 20B, and thus proceeds in that direction. At this point, Luigi is quite firm in his conviction that he is moving in the right direction, and he is certainly willing to act upon this notion. But clearly this would not preclude him from changing his mind in the blink of an eye, should further considerations come into play – e.g., an audio announcement informing passengers that the 11:00 am train to Naples is leaving from platform 7C. Even more importantly, we find nothing to object in Luigi's beliefs and actions, and in fact there would be nothing to fault in his reasoning even if the right platform number turned out not to be 20B.

As the example shows, there are several typical features of Peircean doubts and of the beliefs originated by them:

1. Peircean doubts need to be solved as a matter of practical necessity;
2. solving them does not serve to alleviate any special concern of the agent, but merely to enable some practical course of action;
3. the resulting belief is sufficient to warrant acting upon it – in fact, warranting action is the reason why the irritation of Peircean doubt has to be satisfied;
4. the resulting belief is perfectly defeasible, and the agent has no special resistance to change it, if given reasons to do so.

Considering the strong emphasis placed on practical reasoning and action execution in this analysis of Peircean doubts, one might be tempted to suggest that perhaps belief is not the right mental attitude to invoke as their solution – contra Peirce's original suggestion. If all that really matters in these cases is to take as granted something (temporarily) in order to act, then it would seem that these are instances of *acceptance* rather than belief, in the sense proposed, among others, by Cohen (1989) and Bratman (1992). Elsewhere (Paglieri 2009) I have argued that this pragmatic notion of acceptance is not especially helpful, since it is redundant with respect to explanations based on beliefs and goals: whenever it is tempting to say that the agent is in a state of acceptance of p (in our example, accepting that the train will leave on platform 20B), it is also the case that the agent's actions can be as easily (and more parsimoniously) explained in terms of doxastic and motivational attitudes – in Luigi's case, it would be natural to say that he wants to catch the train and, based on his past knowledge of Rome train station, he believes running to platform 20B is the most sensible course of action. So making too much of pragmatic acceptance does not grant us any special insight on the agent's cognitive practices – or so I claim (for further arguments and details, see Paglieri 2009).

Another tempting equivocation of Peircean doubts is the idea that our tendency to quench their irritation creates a special *vulnerability* to our doxastic practices, making us prone to believe much more than we should, given extant evidence. This interpretation would become especially pernicious if paired with John Woods' notion of *epistemic bubbles* (2005), that is, the observation that knowledge and belief are, in many cases, indistinguishable from a first person perspective. If Peircean doubts made us prone to generate hasty beliefs, and if epistemic bubbles made us mistake such beliefs for knowledge, then our predicament would seem dire indeed. Fortunately, neither Peircean doubts nor epistemic bubbles have anything to do with any special vulnerability of our cognitive practices. Let us see why.

Woods' reflections on epistemic bubbles stems from an observation on the phenomenology of knowledge: whenever we think we know that p, this state is indistinguishable for us from the state of actually knowing that p. There is nothing to tell apart the experience of knowing that p from the experience of thinking to know that p: in fact, these two experiences are identical, from a first-person perspective. Of course, from a third-person perspective it is perfectly clear (with variations, depending on your favored epistemology) what is that distinguishes thinking to know that p from actually knowing that p: but a third-person perspective is precisely what we cannot have concerning our own knowledge states, and the point Woods is making is that, no matter your preferred epistemology, you will remain blind on whether you actually know that p or you just think you know it. In his apt metaphor, we are all caught in an epistemic bubble, defined as follows:

> A cognitive agent X occupies an epistemic bubble precisely when he is unable to command the distinction between his thinking that he knows P and his knowing P. Corollary: When in an epistemic bubble, cognitive agents always resolve the tension between their thinking that they know P and their knowing P in favour of knowing that P (2005, p. 740).

A careless reader might interpret the epistemic bubble thesis as simply saying that people often mistake beliefs for knowledge, thus overestimating the quality of their doxastic states. But nothing of the sort is implied here. First of all, the thesis is restricted to those beliefs that are experienced as knowledge by the agent (as in "I know the bus will arrive", "I know what is best for my children", "I know you cannot mean harm to me", and the like), and it is not meant to be true for all senses of the word "belief" – most notably, it is not meant to be true for (weak) gradual beliefs, suspicions, hunches, and the like (on this point, see Woods 2005, p. 744).[3] Secondly, experiencing something as being known does not necessarily imply being entrenched in this conviction, according to Woods (and I agree): it is a common experience to take something as being known one moment, and then abandon it without regret as soon as its inadequacy becomes apparent. That is, finding out that something we thought to know was actually mistaken (hence not known at all) is no big surprise for any minimally self-reflective agent, and does not typically cause any major discomfort. In fact, we are so jaded with respect to the volatility of our claims to knowledge precisely because we are accustomed to living in an epistemic bubble, and we have learned to tolerate well our incapacity to tell apart true knowledge from the mere appearance of it.

---

[3] Actually, Woods would probably go further and claim that many things often labeled as beliefs in the literature do not deserve that label, and would instead be better classified as other kinds of mental attitudes, e.g. suspecting that p, being willing to bet on p, finding plausible that p, and so on (2005, p. 744-745). This view is consistent with Bas van Fraassen's invitation to endorse a more liberal descriptive epistemology, one that admits of greater variety than just belief, disbelief or neutrality (2001, p. 165). While I agree that we should remain open-minded on what mental states to include in our epistemology, I also think that Ockham's razor should shave our liberal inclinations here, and that mental attitudes should not be multiplied without cause. Since using "belief" in its more general sense has no significant repercussion for current purposes, here I will stick to this traditional usage.

The crucial point is that the subjective strength of our convictions does not depend on them being experienced as knowledge rather than belief – contra the epistemologist's prejudice according to which knowledge is something more/better than belief (e.g., true justified belief, in the most widespread recipe). Woods' notion of epistemic bubbles is not committed to such prejudice: it is a thesis on the fact that the distinction between belief and knowledge, perfectly intelligible in a third-person perspective, is immaterial from a first-person perspective, but it does not imply that the agent will become fixated on whatever beliefs s/he misattributes as knowledge.

So, what is the right way of connecting Peircean doubts with epistemic bubbles, if any? There is a thin but clear link: it could very well be the case that our tendency to take belief as knowledge is inspired by the practical need for a partially stable (and quick) assessment of reality, as emphasized by Peircean doubts. Second-guessing what we think to know is, in general, the wrong way of reacting to a Peircean doubt: whether that knowledge will turn out to be correct or not is relevant only to the extent that the resulting action will end up being successful – and if it does, that is all that matters to the agent. This is why issues of justification (in the sense of having a good case for p, not just a cause for believing p; see Woods 2005, pp. 759-761) becomes typically irrelevant to consider, or at least secondary.

But it is certainly *not* the case that Peircean doubts plus epistemic bubbles imply belief rigidity. This is not the case because knowledge does not differ from belief in terms of doubt-resolution: believing that p solves Peircean doubts about p as effectively as knowing that p, from a first-person perspective (precisely due to our epistemic embubblement). The difference between belief and knowledge is in terms of objective truth and valid justification, and it is a difference that, according to Woods, we have trouble grasping in a first-person perspective. So Peircean doubts and epistemic bubbles can happily co-exist, without engendering any special risk of tunnel vision or cognitive fixation. For the same reasons, Peircean doubts and epistemic bubbles do not (and are not meant to) offer an explanation to extant cases of unreasonable resistance to changes in one's beliefs. For a diagnosis of such cases, one has to look at scary doubts and their impact on belief formation: this will be the business of the next section.

Before moving on to that, however, it is interesting to put Peircean doubts in contact with the idea that, in believing that p, extant evidence on p produces a lower and an upper boundary for our *degree* of belief in p, and the interval between such boundaries represents the agent's ignorance on p – in the vein of Dempster (1967) and Shafer (1976). The interesting psychological twist in looking at beliefs that way is that whatever assignment of confidence x to p within p's ignorance interval is compatible with the existing evidence, hence legitimate. In other words, it is not a matter of evidence whether the agent believes more or less strongly that p, within the current ignorance interval for p. What is the import of that for Peircean doubts? Simply put, it allows us to speculate the following:

PROPOSITION 2 (Peircean confidence) *When faced by a Peircean doubt on p and with an ignorance interval for p equal to [A, Z], solve the doubt by setting the degree of belief in p to the upper boundary Z.*

Let us see how Peircean confidence might work in our train example. We will stipulate that Luigi's past experience in taking the 11:00 am train to Naples from Rome provides a lower boundary for the belief "The train will leave from platform 20B" equal to 0.5: that is, current evidence does not justify being more skeptical than that on platform 20B being the right one. On the other hand, Luigi did experience unexpected last-minute changes of platform in the past, so let us say that his upper boundary for that belief is equal to 0.9: that is, current evidence does not justify being more certain than that about the rightness of that belief. Peircean confidence predicts that Luigi will automatically set his belief to the highest justified degree – in this case, 0.9. Interestingly, this view explains both the fact that the agent is ready to act on beliefs prompted by Peircean doubts (unless there is strong evidence against them, i.e. the upper boundary is too low to warrant action), the fact that doing so is perceived as fully rational (as it is, in the sense of being within the boundaries of what is permissible, given current evidence), and the fact that even discovering such beliefs to be false is not so shocking, since they were conceived from the start as an informed guess under conditions of partial ignorance. Indeed, a subsequent change of belief would be surprising for the agent only if it revealed the original boundaries to be mistaken: for instance, if Luigi discovered from a train assistant that the 11:00 am train to Naples in fact *never* or *rarely* leaves from platform 20B, this would give him pause, and rightly so. But the conflict here would not be with the belief that today the train is leaving from platform 20B, but rather with the past evidence that Luigi used to reach that belief. And Luigi would have solid reasons to be puzzled, because in this case either the new information is mistaken, or what he thought was good evidence in fact wasn't.

Even if Peircean confidence works well in this example, it might be defective as a generalization of how we react to Peircean doubts. For instance, one might object that Peircean confidence, once applied to issues on which there is no evidence for or against, delivers the counterintuitive verdict that we should have full belief in such matters, since their ignorance interval is [0, 1]. To this, there are two answers: first, complete ignorance on an issue relevant for Peircean doubt occurs more rarely than one might expect; secondly, it is reasonable to assume that, when faced with contradictory beliefs, one will endorse only those with the higher degree, and none at all if they are all evenly matched. Under this assumption, full credence for states we are ignorant about becomes unproblematic, as we shall see.

Let us start from the first point, using again Luigi's predicament as a case in point. A critic of Peircean confidence may be tempted to reason as follows: Luigi is completely ignorant on whether the 11:00 am train to Naples may leave from any platform *different* from 20B, hence he should believe (for Peircean confidence) that the train will leave from any of those platforms with degree 1, which is greater than 0.9 – hence Luigi should prefer to run for any platform, except the one he knows it is likely the train will leave from. This is paradoxical, thus Peircean confidence is mistaken as a general criterion. However, this argument is clearly flawed, because Luigi is not at all ignorant on whether the train will leave from any of the other platforms: the very fact that he has evidence of platform 20B being the right one is evidence *against* the train leaving from another platform; conversely, whatever evidence against the train leaving from platform 20B is evidence *in favor of* the train leaving from somewhere else. In short, the belief "The train will leave from platform X", with X being any platform other than 20B, in this example has the ignorance interval [0.1, 0.5], hence it is to be believed, by Peircean confidence, with degree 0.5, which is lower than 0.9 and explains why Luigi runs towards platform 20B and nowhere else.

The second point is more delicate. Imagine an issue p for which there is indeed full ignorance, and yet such as it raises a Peircean doubt – for instance, you are considering whether to buy at a certain price a toy for your niece, and you do not have any clue on whether that price is appropriate or not.[4] Now, in this case your ignorance interval on "The price is right" is [0, 1], so Peircean confidence would have you giving full credence to it, hence buying the toy without a moment of hesitation – which does not seem the right option, given your utter ignorance on the matter (after all, the toy may be outrageously over-priced, for all you know). But on further reflection, it is obvious that also the ignorance interval for the contrary belief "The price is *not* right" is [0, 1], hence Peircean confidence would command full credence for this belief too. But you cannot have it both ways, hence Peircean confidence leaves you with no clue on what to do – which is precisely what should happen, assuming you are indeed totally ignorant on the matter. That is, Peircean doubts under conditions of complete ignorance are *not* meant to be solved.

To see why, consider the following variation of Luigi's predicament: imagine now that Luigi has never taken the 11:00 am train to Naples from Rome and has no prior information on what platform the train is supposed to leave from – he is in a state of full ignorance on this issue. Upon looking at the electronic board and realizing that no platform is indicated there, what should Luigi do, to behave rationally? Even more crucially, what would *you* do, if you were in that situation with a pressing need to catch that train? You would certainly not start running towards a random platform, nor should Luigi. What you would do is to accept that your Peircean doubt on the train's platform currently has no satisfactory solution, and thus proceed to look for more information – either waiting in front of the electronic board, hoping the platform number will soon appear, or going in search of someone who might point you in the right direction. This is what any reasonable person would (and should) do in a state of total ignorance, and this is why it is OK for Peircean confidence to leave you in the dark on what to believe in such cases. Otherwise, Peircean confidence

---

[4] Once again, it is worth emphasizing how unnatural the assumption of total ignorance is, in matters of Peircean doubts: even if you did not enter a toy shop in your whole life and were never exposed to the prices of toys (which is unlikely), you would still have a lot of background experience on what is the value of commodities in general. You would know, for instance, that a price of 1 billion dollars is excessive for a doll, while a price of 1 cent is unrealistically cheap – comparisons with the price of other goods would be enough to give you evidence for such rough estimates.

would in fact become *overconfidence*, which is not a reasonable reaction to Peircean doubts.

In light of these considerations, it is possible to propose a revised version of Peircean confidence, to better accommodate cases of complete ignorance:

PROPOSITION 3 (Peircean confidence revised) *When faced by a Peircean doubt on p, consider all the candidate beliefs p^i that would solve that doubt, each of them with a respective ignorance interval $[A^i, Z^i]^i$. Then take only the candidate (or the internally consistent subset of candidates) that has the highest upper boundary, and believe it with a degree equal to such upper boundary. If there are two or more conflicting candidates that share the same upper boundary, do not believe anything at all on the issue at hand and look for more information.*

The morale of these reflections is that Peircean doubts are not solved by any sleight of hands, such that states of complete ignorance can be magically turned into full-blown beliefs, while retaining a valid claim to rationality. What happens is both more mundane and more healthy: Peircean doubts are solved, whenever possible (to wit, in the absence of total ignorance), by taking a carefully optimistic outlook on the evidence we already possess and acting on it.[5] This is both *optimistic*, insofar as we pick the upper boundary of the current ignorance interval, and *careful*, because that boundary is still within what is rational to surmise in light of present evidence. Importantly, this way of forming defeasible beliefs as a reaction to the irritation of Peircean doubts is both automatic and effortless – hence the simplicity of the principle of Peircean confidence.

3 Scary doubts, defensive beliefs and biases

In order to emphasize their difference with Peircean doubts, let us define scary doubts as follows:

---

[5] It may seem natural to think that this carefully optimistic stance is modulated by personal inclinations and contextual factors. After all, a very prudent person would be naturally more reserved in giving credence to things that are uncertain, while special circumstances (e.g. urgent matters where one lacks better alternatives) may justify acting on wild guesses, even beyond the upper boundary of one's ignorance interval. However, I think it is more natural and more parsimonious to think that these effects concern what we do with our beliefs, rather than how we form them. Imagine the train scenario happens to Luisa instead of Luigi, and let us say that Luisa is much more prudent than Luigi: as a result, she does not rush to platform 20B, but rather waits until the latest possible moment to see what number will appear on the electronic board. I see no reason to claim that Luisa is any less confident than Luigi on whether the train will in fact leave from platform 20B, assuming they have the same evidence: the point is rather that she does not want to take the small risk of running to the wrong platform, while Luigi accepts it. Even more clearly, the fact that on occasion acting on a wild guess may be the rational (or even only) option has nothing to do with the doxastic status of that guess: that is, we do not become any more convinced of a wild guess just because we decide or are forced to act upon it.

PROPOSITION 4 (Scary doubt) *An agent X has a scary doubt on the issue P when (i) X is undecided regarding whether P or not-P is the case, and (ii) at least one of these options would, if believed, undermine some important goals of X.*

A scary doubt has no neutral solution for the subject: when I wonder whether or not my wife loves me, how I answer this doubt deeply affects my well-being, besides and beyond how it affects my conduct. More generally, with scary doubts at least one[6] of the candidates for belief has a negative impact on the agent's goals – more precisely, on some *important* goal of the agent. This is very different from what happens with Peircean doubts, where solving the doubt is a matter of practical necessity, but nothing relevant for the agent is at stake in solving it one way or another (provided such solution turns out to be pragmatically right).

Scary doubts entertain important relations with a special class of beliefs, defined as follows:

PROPOSITION 5 (Defensive belief) *An agent X has a defensive belief p if believing p avoids undermining an important goal of X and prevents X from being in a state of scary doubt on p.[7]*

In order to avert any equivocation, let us first clarify that a belief can be defensive even if it is held on the ground of legitimate evidence, and not because of whatever scary doubt it helps keeping at bay. To get back to the previous example, the belief that my wife loves me is a defensive belief, with respect to my goal of being loved by her, even if I have perfectly sound reasons to endorse it: her daily manifestations of devotion, our mutual happiness, the harmony of our family, and so on. Dropping that belief would hurt me, while maintaining it prevents that from happening: this fact is independent from whatever other reason I might have to hold that belief.

In other words, defensive beliefs are a broader category than *fear-induced beliefs*, defined as follows:

PROPOSITION 6 (Fear-induced belief) *An agent X has a fear-induced belief p if p is a defensive belief which was formed and/or is maintained, partially or solely, to avoid undermining an important goal of X and to prevent X from being in a state of scary doubt on p.*

The distinction between defensive beliefs and their sub-class of fear-induced beliefs captures the fact that not all defensive beliefs are irrational, in the sense of lacking proper reasons for being held. Conversely, having proper epistemic backing does not make a defensive belief any less defensive, since what makes

---

[6] The "at least" specification is needed to cover also cases where many or even all answers to the doubt are damaging for the agent: e.g., imagine a 50-years-old unemployed man who never had a sentimental partner in his life, seriously wondering whether his misfortunes indicate lack of character or some congenital cognitive deficit. We might label these extreme instances as "scary dilemmas", and treat them as severe instances of scary doubts.

[7] Defensive beliefs are only a type of self-serving beliefs: another obvious candidate are fulfilling beliefs, that is, beliefs that actually satisfy some important goal of the agent. Since here I am interested in scary doubts, I will confine my analysis to defensive beliefs, even though many considerations relevant for them apply also to fulfilling beliefs.

it so is a relationship with the agent's goals, not with evidence. Regardless, the presence of scary doubts create an influence on belief formation that is very different from the pressure towards belief countenanced by Peircean doubts.

Before discussing the specifics of such influence, there is an interesting question worth considering, albeit only cursorily: Is it better to live in a state of scary doubt or to face the worst possible outcome? More precisely: Is a scary doubt more or less scarier than the conclusion we fear to draw from it? The question is not idle, as the wife example immediately reveals: it is not at all clear that a man constantly wondering about his wife's affection is better off than another man who firmly believes his wife to be no longer in love with him. After all, we all have experiences (both first-hand and reported) on how sometimes fearing something is much worse than facing it – or, as the saying goes, "the devil is not so black as he is painted". The same could well apply to scary doubts: it is perfectly possible that persisting in a state of scary doubt is no better, subjectively speaking, than reaching a negative conclusion on the matter in doubt. However, this does not change the basic relation between scary doubts and defensive beliefs, since the latter solve both the uncertainty *and* the fear of the worst. My belief in the love of my wife prevents me both from worrying about it and from believing that she doesn't.

But is there any evidence that scary doubts, so defined, have an influence on our beliefs? Indeed, social psychology abounds of such evidence, and entire theories have been developed to study and articulate similar effects: in different guises and with different emphasis, cognitive dissonance (Festinger 1957; Aronson 1969), confirmation bias (Wason 1960), motivated reasoning (Kunda 1990), self-verification (Swann and Read 1981; Swann 1999), self-enhancement (Alicke and Sedikides 2011), self-perception (Bem 1967), adaptive preference formation and "sour grapes" effects (Elster 1983), and good old fashioned wishful thinking (Greenwald 1980; Taylor and Brown 1988), they all deal with various aspects of the influence of scary doubts on belief formation. The strength and the scariness of such doubts may vary, from the relatively severe (e.g. in self-verification) to the comparatively mild (e.g. in cognitive dissonance), yet all these approaches have in common the basic view that beliefs can be shaped by a pressure to avoid undesirable consequences – that is, a pressure to avoid jeopardizing one's goals by coming to believe something we would not like. Moreover, in all these contexts, albeit with variations, it is assumed that this influence is partially independent from, and potentially in contrast with, evidence-based reasons to hold or not a given belief.

My point here is not to review this large literature, but rather to mention it as proof of the extent to which scary doubts influence belief formation, and also of the difference between such influence and the impact of Peircean doubts on our beliefs. In a nutshell, the key distinction is in that scary doubts pressure us to reach a *specific* conclusion on the matter under consideration, whereas Peircean doubts only demand that we reach *some* conclusion, with no constraint on which one it should be. This difference is capital, since it defines scary doubts as *biases*, whereas Peircean doubts are revealed as mere expressions of a *practical need* for information to act upon. Granted, scary doubts may induce, on occasion or even typically, very beneficial biases, as I shall discuss in a moment. But this does not change the fact that their effects are biases, insofar as they systematically pressure belief formation in a direction unrelated with considerations of accuracy or evidence.[8]

Also the converse is true, of course: not all biases are necessarily liabilities for our cognitive processes – indeed, some biases can be highly advantageous. This point is often missed in cognitive psychology, where the terms "bias" carries an indisputable negative connotation. For instance, much of the current tension between the heuristics and biases approach of Kahneman and Tversky (Kahneman et al. 1982) and the adaptive toolbox idea championed by Gigerenzer (Gigerenzer et al. 1999) hinges on considering biases either a negative or a positive asset for cognition. However, it is possible (and I believe desirable) to use a neutral notion of bias, as a systematic influence over a certain disposition which is independent from the typical and/or normatively correct reasons to hold such disposition – in the case of belief, these typical/correct reasons would roughly amount to evidence-sensitivity and internal consistency. All influences that are independent from such considerations and yet typically affect belief formation can legitimately be defined as biases, with no evaluative judgment attached to this label. In fact, such judgment can only be applied meaningfully to specific biases or, more precisely, to applications of certain biases in specific contexts.

This is true also for the kind of defensive biases discussed here, and in particular for fear-induced beliefs. The general point is rather obvious: defending something can be good or bad depending on *what* you defend, and *why*. For instance, tampering with one's own beliefs in order to avoid impairing the capacity to function effectively (e.g. due to a depressive crisis induced by low self-esteem) may be a very wise thing to do. More generally and less dramatically, the fact that our goals have a biasing influence on our beliefs can have beneficial effects on our behavior even when no psychopathology is looming over us, e.g. in terms of coherence of conduct. As argued in details by Miceli and Castelfranchi (2012), a more or less acute obsession with preserving a coherent self-image is a powerful motive to avoid excessive deviations from one's typical conduct, thus ensuring greater behavioral stability: whether or not this turns out to be a good thing depends on whether a given individual is set upon a virtuous or vicious path of conduct. But the mere fact that our aspirations can bias our actions, as well as our assessment of such actions, is an important mechanism to ensure self-reflective forms of action control (Paglieri and Castelfranchi 2008; Castelfranchi, 2012). And Castelfranchi has argued (1995), with good reason, that such higher mechanisms for behavioral regulation enables human beings to achieve feats that would be impossible for simpler (and thus less biased) creatures.

---

[8] Genuine instances of defensive beliefs should be kept apart from other non-evidential constraints over belief formation and change, such as ensuring minimal change (Alchourrón, Gärdenfors and Makinson 1985; Harman 1986). The parsimonious tendency to minimize the amount of cognitive restructuring required to accommodate new information certainly exerts a biasing influence over belief dynamics, and this might on occasion have pernicious effects, even if it is highly convenient on average. But such bias, and others like it, depends on an imperfect attempt to optimize efficacy and is not born out of fear: thus it does not relate to scary doubts at all.

The pragmatic defense of motivationally biased beliefs presented by Castel-franchi and colleagues is not new, albeit its details are. The basic rationale of it is similar to that of William James' much celebrated essay on "The will to believe" (1895/1979), and indeed this line of reasoning is deeply rooted in and inspired by pragmatism. In short, undertaking the best possible course of action is seen as rationally superior to believing the truth, at least when these two values come into conflict, as exemplified by Pascal's famous wager. The standard counterargument against this defense of defensive beliefs (pun intended) is that the pragmatic efficacy of such biases do not make them any more evidence-based or truth-preserving, hence it does not constitute a valid form of epistemological justification. A mistake of reasoning remains a mistake of reasoning, even if it happens to save your life.

A way out of this objection is to make the legitimacy of motivational biases conditional on the lack of better epistemological alternatives: when you do not have ways to solve your doubt on the grounds of evidence, it is rationally legitimate to let your goals shape your beliefs. This is the position James himself endorses, when he writes:

> Our passional nature not only lawfully may, but must, decide an option between propositions, whenever it is a genuine option that cannot by its nature be decided on intellectual grounds; for to say, under such circumstances, "Do not decide, but leave the question open", is itself a passional decision – just like deciding yes or no –, and is attended with the same risk of losing the truth (James 1895/1979, p. 11).

In addition to that, James also suggests that instances where belief can be reached on purely intellectual grounds (i.e. based solely on evidence) are much rarer than what is usually assumed, even in science,[9] so that most of our beliefs must in fact rely, to some extent, on our volitional dispositions – that is, on our goals and values.[10] Whether or not one agrees with James regarding the relative infrequency of pure evidence-based belief, it is still possible to endorse his circumscribed defense of motivation-biased belief: insofar as evidence do not suggest either belief or disbelief, there is nothing epistemologically wrong in letting our goals settle our convictions. To which a stalwart critic might object that lack of epistemological fault does not imply presence of epistemological merit: granted, there is nothing wrong in letting your goals bias your beliefs in the absence of evidence, but this is not to say that there is something *right* in that process – apart from whatever pragmatic benefits you might achieve, which is beside the point for our imaginary critic. In this view, proper justification requires that a belief forming procedure has some epistemic virtue, whereas

---

[9] Although it does not bear on the present discussion, it is worth recalling James' penetrating caricature of scientific method, as presented in his essay, since it is still actual nowadays, possibly more than ever: «The most useful investigator, because the most sensitive observer, is always he whose eager interest in one side of the question is balanced by an equally keen nervousness lest he become deceived. Science has organized this nervousness into a regular technique, her so-called method of verification; and she has fallen so deeply in love with the method that one may even say she has ceased to care for truth by itself at all. It is only truth as technically verified that interests her. The truth of truths might come in merely affirmative form, and she would decline to touch it».

[10] For in depth analysis of the complex relationship between goals and values, see Miceli and Castelfranchi (1989).

lack of obvious epistemic vice is not a sufficient condition. Hence, the will to believe would not qualify as proper justification, not even in the absence of evidence, contra James.

This debate, far from being settled, concerns the normative validity (or lack thereof) of cognitive biases, in this case the role of scary doubts in prompting the formation of defensive beliefs: as such, it pertains more to philosophical epistemology than to psychology. However, also psychologists could (and often do, see for instance Gigerenzer and colleagues) wonder about the merits and shortcomings of such biases. For them, the debate is more naturally framed in terms of efficacy and adaptation.[11] To what extent defensive beliefs happen to be correct and thus successful in supporting one's behavior? And is it possible to track the evolutionary processes that might have produced these belief-formation practices as an adaptation to certain selective pressures? In order to address these questions, it is not enough to establish that, in general, goals do exert a systematic influence over our beliefs: we also need to specify more clearly what kind of influence is exerted, and what mechanisms are responsible for it.

Without entering in too much details here, it is fair to say that the work of Castelfranchi and collaborators provides some guidance in this respect. In a series of papers devoted to analyze belief dynamics and their interaction with goals (Castelfranchi 1996; 1997; 2004; Paglieri 2004; 2005; 2006; Paglieri and Castelfranchi 2005; 2006; 2007), they indicate two distinct ways in which goals might affect belief:[12] *relevance* and *likeability*. These are conceived as properties of information, that is, of data that the agent is aware of without yet being committed to. Both the relevance and the likeability of an information are dependent upon the agent's goals and might influence the likelihood of believing that information, but they do so in very different ways. More exactly, relevance is defined as the *pragmatic utility* of an information, i.e. the number and value of the (pursued) goals that depend on reaching a conclusion, i.e. a belief, on that matter; in contrast, likeability is understood as the *motivational appeal* of an information, that is, the value of the pursued goal(s) directly fulfilled by believing it. Likeability arises because, subjectively speaking, a goal *p* is satisfied only when the agent believes *p*, whether or not such belief is factually correct – in short, goals are satisfied by beliefs, not by states of the world. This puts a definite pressure on believing certain things to be true, insofar as doing so would directly and immediately satisfy the agent's current goals. Relevance, on the other hand, works very differently: it directs our attention towards certain information rather than others, depending on current needs, but without pressuring us to believe them. This still has a definite influence on belief formation, since it determines what contents come to be

---

[11] It is worth emphasizing that there is an intriguing, yet largely unexplored continuity between the pragmatist focus on practical success and the evolutionary concern with the adaptive value of certain behaviors or traits. Even though these are different notions used in different debates within different disciplines, they share the same core: the idea that success (pragmatic in one case, evolutionary in the other) is the ultimate end, whereas truth is just a means for it.

[12] For the converse path of influence, i.e. from beliefs to goals, see Castelfranchi and Paglieri (2007).

considered as candidates for belief, but does not make us any less prone to wishful thinking (for further discussion on this distinction, see Paglieri 2005).

The distinction between relevance and likeability provides us with a simple framework to analyze the different impact that Peircean doubts and scary doubts have on belief formation, and also to question separately the adaptive value of these different mechanisms of goal-directed belief formation. It is easy to see that Peircean doubts, and our reaction to them, concerns relevance alone: in fact, relevance is precisely a measure of how much a certain information is needed to advance the agent's current plans, that is, of how many Peircean doubts would be quenched by the corresponding belief, and how important they are for the agent. It is also apparent that this bias is adaptively beneficial, since beliefs are meant to serve as "maps by which we steer" (Ramsey 1931), and the general direction of our behavior is obviously determined by goals. So it is certainly a good thing that relevance prompt us to focus on goal-related matters, thus keeping goals and beliefs in sync. Were it not so, we would find ourselves ill equipped to pursue our current interests: for instance, we might end up walking down the aisle at our own wedding with the head full of thoughts on differential equations, but without a clue on how to behave with our spouse-to-be. Indeed, when similar incidents happen, they are universally regarded as disastrous, and diagnosed as bad cases of epistemic distraction.[13] I suggest that their root cause is a failure of relevance.

Likeability, on the other hand, is uniquely tied to scary doubts and defensive beliefs: it is precisely when an information happens to be likeable or distasteful for us (i.e. prone to satisfy or frustrate our goals) that we feel the pressure to either believe or disbelieve it, independently from whatever evidence we might have on the matter. Whether or not this tendency is adaptive constitutes a thorny issue, that I would spell out as follows: Assuming likeability-induced belief formation works as supposed, is it an effective mechanism, and in which sense? It is certainly not infallible, since it can easily lead us to entertain false beliefs (e.g. an overinflated opinion of ourselves, or a mistaken faith in the love of our relatives). But is it typically fallacious, that is, does it produce more false beliefs than true ones? This is an empirical question, one which will be very difficult to answer and far exceeds the purpose of the present contribution.[14]

By way of mere speculation, I just want to stress that from the (evident) fact that likeability often biases belief formation we should *not* immediately infer that such process must have some evolutionary relevance or adaptive value.

---

[13] By epistemic distraction I mean here an instance where the agent has a unique or dominant goal, but fails to focus on the beliefs needed to pursue it effectively. Another type of distraction can be labeled as motivational, and refers to instances where more than one goal compete to catch the agent's attention, so s/he ends up switching back and forth between different tasks – cyber-slacking being a clear example of this phenomenon.

[14] According to Mercier and Sperber (2011), this question is actually besides the point, because the function of reasoning is not to deliver true belief, but to make us capable of producing good arguments and assessing poor ones. This would make our belief system highly adaptive, even if it turned out to produce a substantial body of falsehoods – that would not been its purpose, after all. I am somewhat skeptical of this radical proposal, but I acknowledge that it provides an interesting alternative to the standard account of belief, worthy of greater attention in future work.

This is of course true in general when we reason in evolutionary terms (not all current traits are adaptations, for sure), but there are also special reasons to be extra careful in assessing scary doubts and defensive beliefs. This is why: as mentioned, the likeability bias is a side product of a basic feature of goal-directed behavioral control, namely, the fact that *goals are subjectively satisfied by beliefs*, not by facts. This is unavoidable, insofar as our perception of external reality is filtered by our representational system. But it also creates a vulnerability, because the belief that originally serves as a mere means to check that the world has been changed according to plan, can later become an end in itself, since goal satisfaction is in fact dependent on it. This is an instance of a more general phenomenon in the dynamics of signs: once a stable association is determined between a sign and its referent, so that we start reacting to the sign as we would to the referent itself, then producing the sign is sufficient to elicit our behavioral response. When we run out of the building to save our life, we are reacting to the alarm, not to the fire – even if of course the reason for doing so is because we assume the fire is there. Beliefs suffer the same fate: insofar as they are conceived as reliable signs of the attainment or failure of our goals (and we cannot help but conceiving them so), then the danger of likeability bias immediately lurks in their shadow.

If this is correct, then the quest for an evolutionary justification of scary doubts and defensive beliefs might well be a fool's errand. Regardless of how often such beliefs end up being correct or incorrect, the mechanism that produces them would be more parsimoniously understood as a side effect of a much larger adaptation – namely, our goal-oriented, cognitively mediated action control system (Pezzulo and Castelfranchi 2009; Pezzulo this volume).

4 No doubts: the mind as a coherence-seeking device

Phenomenologically speaking, there is a sharp difference between a state of doubt and a condition of ignorance. When in doubt, we are typically presented with a finite number of competing options, all of which appear to us equally plausible – or, at least, close enough in plausibility as to preclude a principled choice in favor of one of them. Ignorance feels different: when we ignore something, we are mostly in the dark about it, so that no option at all presents itself as a candidate for belief or action. In spite of this phenomenological difference, doubt and ignorance share something important: they both carries a *potential for internal inconsistency*, that is, for the possibility of holding two or more conflicting mental states. Such inconsistency is more manifest in our doubts and more hidden in our ignorance, but the potential for it is present in both cases. The ignorant is by definition open to multiple possibilities (typically far more than those entertained by a doubtful mind), and most of these options are known to be mutually incompatible. Hence both doubt and ignorance can be the harbinger of inconsistency.

This is relevant for our cognitive practices, not because our mind is or should be free of contradictions, but because for some classes of mental states, and only for them, we have a natural tendency to strive for coherence by removing inconsistencies.[15] On this view (Castelfranchi 2004; Paglieri 2006), the mind is conceived as a *coherence-seeking device*, which is different from a coherence-bounded machine: in particular, the quest for coherence regards both epistemic and motivational attitudes, but is also limited to those attitudes that entail some sort of commitment for the agent, i.e. beliefs and intentions, respectively; with regard to more basic attitudes, such as data and desires, contradictions do not pose any problem for our mind. Figure 1 summarizes this parallel between the dynamics of epistemic and motivational states, whereas the details of each process has been discussed in details elsewhere (see Paglieri 2004 for an account of data-oriented belief formation, and Castelfranchi and Paglieri 2007 for an analysis of belief-based goal processing).

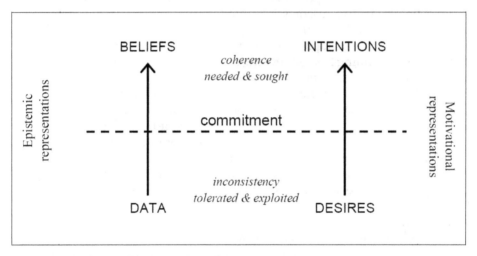

Fig. 1 The mind as a coherence-seeking device

It is the need to act effectively upon reality that prompts us to commit ourselves to certain intentions and to endorse certain beliefs, moving beyond ignorance and doubt – sometimes by an act of will, but mostly as a reaction to whatever evidence we are presented with. It is in this sense that Peircean doubts work as an irritant for cognition: they simultaneously indicate that something needs to be ascertained in order to act, and also that there is the potential for an inconsistency in our belief system, unless the matter is settled.

---

[15] This is typically achieved either by making a choice among multiple conflicting candidates, or by compartmentalizing, that is, segregating conflicting mental states into rigidly separated areas of our mind (see Cherniak 1986 for in-depth discussion of the role of compartmentalization in human rationality).

5 Conclusions

In this paper I took advantage of Peirce's apt metaphor to distinguish two types of doubt, and to analyze their different impact on belief formation. In particular, I argued that Peircean doubts work as a beneficial irritant to instigate informed guesses that are necessary for effective action, even though they lead us occasionally astray. In contrast, scary doubts pressure us towards self-serving beliefs, often regardless of factual evidence: this might or might not be warranted on practical or prudential grounds, but it is certainly risky business as a general epistemic habit. However, it is a vulnerability in our belief formation system that we have to live with, insofar as it originates from the practical need to (fallibly) determine whether a certain goal is attained. This implies that "scratching our beliefs" (that is, letting our goals influence our convictions) is always reasonable in the face of Peircean doubts, while it might be a ruinous path down a slippery slope in matters of scary doubts. Unfortunately, Peirce's metaphor turns out to be devilishly accurate: as for most irritations, refraining from scratching our beliefs in the presence of doubts is extremely hard, regardless of what made us itchy.

In unfolding this view of the connection between doubts, beliefs, and actions, I also tried to weave it within the rich fabric of Castelfranchi's theory of cognition and, more precisely, within his analysis of belief formation and goal processing. The purpose of this exercise was not only to honor Castelfranchi's contribution to this area of inquiry, as it is customary on such an occasion, but also to unearth a conceptual root that Peirce's pragmatism and Castelfranchi's goal theory have in common. This is the *primacy of action* in our understanding of the mind. For both these scholars, possibly for different reasons, cognition is *for* action, first and foremost. It is so not only because goals are mental attitudes on a par with beliefs (a lesson Castelfranchi never tires of hammering into the mind of students and colleagues), but also because belief formation itself is motivated and shaped by goals. Peirce's irritation of doubt, far from being the intellectual, methodological doubt advocated by Descartes, is precisely a manifestation of how goals initiate and guide all our cognitive undertakings, including the formation and revision of beliefs. Thus I dare to say that Peirce and Castelfranchi would have shared the same doubts on any theory of cognition that takes truth, rather than success, as its cornerstone.

References

1. Alchourrón, C., Gärdenfors, P., & Makinson, D. (1985). On the logic of theory change: partial meet contraction and revision functions. *Journal of Symbolic Logic* 50, pp. 510-530.
2. Alicke, M., & Sedikides, C. (2011). *Handbook of self-enhancement and self-protection.* New York: Guilford Press.
3. Aronson, E. (1969). The theory of cognitive dissonance: a current perspective. In L. Berkowitz (Ed.), *Advances in experimental social psychology, vol. 4* (pp. 1-34). New York: Academic Press.

4. Bem, D. (1967). Self-perception: an alternative interpretation of cognitive dissonance phenomena. *Psychological Review, 74*, 183-200.
5. Bratman, M. (1992). Practical reasoning and acceptance in a context. *Mind, 101*, 1-15.
6. Castelfranchi, C. (1995). Self-awareness: notes for a computational theory of intrapsychic social interaction. In G. Trautteur (Ed.), *Consciousness* (pp. 55-80). Napoli: Bibliopolis.
7. Castelfranchi, C. (2004). Reasons to believe: cognitive models of belief change. Manuscript. Ws *Changing minds: cognitive, computational and logical approaches to belief change*, Amsterdam 29/10/2004. http://www.unisi.it/ricerca/dip/fil_sc_soc/dot-sc/castelfranchi.pdf. Accessed 8 June 2011.
8. Castelfranchi, C. (2012). "My mind": reflexive sociality and its cognitive tools. In F. Paglieri (Ed.), *Consciousness in interaction: the role of the natural and social context in shaping consciousness* (pp. 125–149). Amsterdam: John Benjamins.
9. Castelfranchi, C., & Paglieri, F. (2007). The role of beliefs in goal dynamics: prolegomena to a constructive theory of intentions. *Synthese, 155*, 237-263.
10. Castelfranchi, C. (1996). Reasons: belief support and goal dynamics. *Mathware & Soft Computing, 3*, 233-247.
11. Castelfranchi, C. (1997). Representation and integration of multiple knowledge sources: issues and questions. In V. Cantoni, V. Di Gesù, A. Setti & D. Tegolo (Eds.), *Human & machine perception: information fusion* (pp. 235-254). New York: Plenum Press.
12. Cherniak, C. (1986). *Minimal rationality*. Cambridge: MIT Press.
13. Cohen, L. (1989). Belief and acceptance. *Mind, 98*, 367-389.
14. Dempster, A. (1967). Upper and lower probabilities induced by a multivalued mapping. *Annals of Mathematical Statistics, 38*, 325-339.
15. Elster, J. (1983). *Sour grapes: studies in the subversion of rationality*. Cambridge: Cambridge University Press.
16. Festinger, L. (1957). *A theory of cognitive dissonance*. Stanford: Stanford University Press.
17. Gigerenzer, G., Todd, P., & the ABC Research Group (1999). *Simple heuristics that make us smart*. New York: Oxford University Press.
18. Greenwald, A. (1980). The totalitarian ego: fabrication and revision of personal history. *American Psychologist, 35*, 603-618.
19. Harman, G. (1986). *Changes in view: principles of reasoning*. Cambridge: MIT Press.
20. James, W. (1895/1979). *The will to believe and other essays in popular philosophy*. Cambridge: Harvard University Press.
21. Kahneman, D., Slovic, P., & Tversky, A. (1982). *Judgment under uncertainty: heuristics and biases*. Cambridge: Cambridge University Press.
22. Kunda, Z. (1990). The case for motivated reasoning. *Psychological Bulletin, 108*, 480-498.
23. Magnani, L. (2009). *Abductive cognition. The epistemological and eco-cognitive dimensions of hypothetical reasoning*. Berlin: Springer.
24. Magnani, L., & Bertolotti, T. (2011). Cognitive bubbles and firewalls: epistemic immunizations in human reasoning. In L. Carlson, C. Hölscher & T. Shipley (Eds.), *Proceedings of CogSci 2011*. Accepted poster, forthcoming.
25. Mercier, H., & Sperber, D. (2011). Why do humans reason? Arguments for an argumentative theory. *Behavioral and Brain Sciences, 34 (2)*, 57-74.
26. Miceli, M., & Castelfranchi, C. (1989). A cognitive approach to values. *Journal for the Theory of Social Behaviour, 19*, 169-193.
27. Miceli, M., & Castelfranchi, C. (2012). Coherence of conduct and the self-image. In F. Paglieri (Ed.), *Consciousness in interaction: the role of the natural and social context in shaping consciousness* (pp. 151–177). Amsterdam: John Benjamins.
28. Paglieri, F. (2009). Acceptance as conditional disposition. In A. Hieke & H. Leitgeb (Eds.), *Reduction: between the mind and the brain* (pp. 29-49). Berlin: Ontos-Verlag.
29. Paglieri, F., & Castelfranchi, C. (2008). Cambiare la mente: mindreading, azione intenzionale e coscienza. *Sistemi Intelligenti, 20 (3)*, 489-520.
30. Paglieri, F. (2004). Data-oriented belief revision: towards a unified theory of epistemic processing. In E. Onaindia & S. Staab (Eds.), *Proceedings of STAIRS 2004* (pp. 179-190). Amsterdam: IOS Press.

31. Paglieri, F. (2005). See what you want, believe what you like: relevance and likeability in belief dynamics. In L. Cañamero (Ed.), *Agents that want and like: motivational and emotional roots of cognition and action* (pp. 90-97). Hatfield: AISB.

32. Paglieri, F. (2006). *Belief dynamics: from formal models to cognitive architectures, and back again*. PhD dissertation, University of Siena. http://www.media.unisi.it/cirg/fp/Paglieri_phd_thesis.pdf. Accessed 8 June 2011.

33. Paglieri, F., & Castelfranchi, C. (2005). Revising beliefs through arguments: bridging the gap between belief revision and argumentation in MAS. In placeI. Rahwan, P. Moratïs & C. Reed (Eds.), *Argumentation in multi-agent systems* (pp. 78-94). Berlin: Springer-Verlag.

34. Paglieri, F., & Castelfranchi, C. (2006). The Toulmin test: framing argumentation within belief revision theories. In D. Hitchcock & B. Verheij (Eds.), *Arguing on the Toulmin model* (pp. 359-377). Berlin: Springer.

35. Paglieri, F., & Castelfranchi, C. (2007). Belief and acceptance in argumentation. Towards an epistemological taxonomy of the uses of argument. In J. A. Blair, F. H. van Eemeren & C. A. Willard (Eds.), *Proceedings of ISSA 2006* (pp. 1011-1018). Amsterdam: Sic Sat.

36. Peirce, C. S. (1958). *Charles S. Peirce: selected writings*. New York: Dover.

37. Pezzulo, G., & Castelfranchi, C. (2009). Thinking as the control of imagination: a conceptual framework for goal-directed systems. *Psychological Research, 73,* 559-577.

38. Pezzulo, G. (in press). Re-founding cognitivism based on the cybernetic idea of goal-directed action. This volume.

39. Ramsey, F. (1931). Truth and probability. Reprinted in H. E. Kyburg & H. E. Smokler (Eds.) (1964), *Studies in subjective probability* (pp. 61-92). New York: Wiley.

40. Shafer, G. (1976). *A mathematical theory of evidence*. Princeton: Princeton University Press.

41. Swann, W. Jr., & Read, S. (1981). Self-verification processes: how we sustain our self-conceptions. *Journal of Experimental Social Psychology, 17,* 351-372.

42. Swann, W. Jr. (1999). *Resilient identities: self, relationships, and the construction of social reality*. Basic Books: New York.

43. Taylor, S., & Brown, J. (1988). Illusion and well-being: a social psychological perspective on mental health. *Psychological Bulletin, 103 (2),* 193-210.

44. Thagard, P. (2004). What is doubt and when is it reasonable? In M. Ezcurdia, R. Stainton & C. Viger (Eds.), *New essays in the philosophy of language and mind* (pp. 391-406). Calgary: University of Calgary Press.

45. van Fraassen, B. (2001). Constructive empiricism now. *Philosophical Studies, 106,* 151-170.

46. Wason, P. (1960). On the failure to eliminate hypotheses in a conceptual task. *Quarterly Journal of Experimental Psychology, 12 (3),* 129-140,

47. Woods, J. (2005). Epistemic bubbles. In S. Artemov, H. Barringer, A. Garcez, L. Lamb & J. Woods (Eds.), *We will show them: essays in honour of Dov Gabbay, vol. 2* (pp. 731-774). London: College Publications.

Chapter 7
The role of mental states in argumentation: Two problems for rationality from the psychology of belief

David M. Godden

Abstract This chapter recognizes the contributions made to the theory of argument by the work of Cristiano Castelfranchi, together with Fabio Paglieri, by situating their work in the development of social, or process-based accounts of argumentation. It is argued that this orientation to the social requires grounding in the psychological, and thus calls for a belief-based perspective on argumentation. It is shown how Castelfranchi's work on the ontology of belief in relation to goals and intentions, together with the Data-oriented Belief Revision model contributes to this approach by bridging the gap between the social and the psychological. The paper concludes by raising two problems for standard models of argument arising from the psychology of belief: (i) that we seem to lack adequate voluntary control over our beliefs to be rationally responsible for them, and (ii) that we seem not to be reason trackers in the way required by standard accounts of rationality employed in argumentation.

1 Introduction

In pioneering work, Castelfranchi and, more recently, Castelfranchi and Paglieri, have brought together two parallel but previously disparate research traditions: formal theories of rational belief revision and theories of argumentation understood as inter-individual systems of commitment management and rational dispute resolution. In doing so they have brought argumentation theorists to recognize the central role of belief, and other doxastic attitudes, in argumentation. By and large, formal theories of belief revision consider beliefs as theoretical entities – components of constructed formal systems. Yet, beliefs are mental, psychological states of boundedly-rational agents, and this presents a variety of problems for belief-oriented theories of argumentation.

David M. Godden
Department of Philosophy, Old Dominion University, USA
e-mail: dgodden@odu.edu

After making the case for the need for belief-centered theories of argument, the paper considers the contributions that the formal theory of belief revision, specifically Castelfranchi and Paglieri's Data-oriented Belief Revision (DBR) theory, has made to argumentation. The paper then considers two, related problems arising from the psychology of belief, which have important consequences for theories of rationality and belief revision, as well as any theories of argumentation connected thereto: (i) doxastic voluntarism, the causal efficacy of reasons, and our rational accountability for belief, and (ii) our cognitive capacities as reason trackers.

A brief comment on each is in order. On the deontological conception, to be rational is to be epistemically responsible. A rational agent is one who can be held accountable for her doxastic attitudes. She is rational to the extent that her doxastic attitudes are rightly connected to reason. Yet, our beliefs are not the sorts of things over which we have conscious, voluntary control. Thus, it is difficult to understand how believers can be held rationally responsible for them.

Secondly, to rightly connect our beliefs to reasons, it would seem that any target doxastic attitude ought to change correlatively with, and proportionately to, changes in the relevant evidential beliefs. Yet beliefs are not causally connected to their reasons; the evidential relations that occur amongst our beliefs are not mirrored at a causal, psychological level. So, it seems that, on the deontological conception of rationality, we must be reason-trackers. Indeed, Brandom (1994, 2000) contends that in order to be sapient, concept-users we must be scorekeepers (i.e., commitment and entitlement trackers) in the game of giving and asking for reasons. Yet, empirical research indicates that our capacity for reason tracking does not bring us close to the standards of epistemic rationality to which we typically hold ourselves accountable in normal argumentative practice.

I contend that these psychological features of belief, and issues consequent to them, present significant obstacles for theories of argumentation and belief revision that aspire to provide a normative component.

2 An historic perspective shift in the study og argument

Argumentation studies, in its present state, may be viewed as a disciplinary collective which seeks to study argumentation as an essentially situated activity engaged in by autonomous, cognitive and rational agents. This disciplinary collective emerged from a set of reactions to a logical approach to argument, which conceived of its subject matter as a purely semantic entity. Arguments were defined as sets of propositions, one of which was designated as the conclusion the remainder of which were the premises. These abstract entities were interpreted and evaluated purely on the basis of their formal and semantic properties of premise truth and inferential validity. Pragmatic and situational properties were considered descriptively and normatively irrelevant and deliberately ignored. For example, arguments were interpreted and evaluated independently of their (i) intentionality (purpose or function) – e.g., that the argument was offered in an effort to rationally persuade, (ii) agent-relatedness (or audience) – e.g., that the propositions are instantiated by arguers as speech-acts directed to audiences, and (iii) situation (or context) – e.g., that the argument was offered in a public, institutionalized setting rather than a private, personal one. Such an approach not only neglected the rhetorical dimensions of argument, but its pragmatic dimensions as well.

In the late 1970's, a fundamental perspective shift occurred in the study of argument. This shift may be roughly identified by Brockriede's (1975, p. 179) methodological hallmark that "people will find arguments in the vicinity of people." Responding to O'Keefe (1977)[1], Brockriede (1977) distinguished between two senses of "argument," as (i) *product* (argument$_1$) and (ii) *process* (argument$_2$) to which Joseph Wenzel added a third perspective of *procedure* (1979).[2] Rather than being conceived of as abstract entities essentially devoid of contextual features, arguments were now conceived of as essentially situated artifacts deployed by agents engaged in purposeful activities.

Not only did this occasion a methodological shift in focus from product-oriented, to process-oriented approaches. Additionally, the very subject matter of argument was recast. Arguments were no longer abstract semantic objects (sets of propositions), but *doings* (or attempts at doings); they were *communicative actions.*[3]

Arguments, on this new conception, became activities defined according to their goals (typically demonstrative or persuasive) and their means (typically rational).

---

[1] O'Keefe (1977) distinguished two concepts of argument:

(i) *argument$_1$*, or "arguing-*that* " which is "a kind of utterance or a sort of communicative act;" and "something one person makes (or gives, or presents or utters)."
(ii) *argument$_2$*, or "arguing-*about* " which is "a particular kind of interaction;" "something two or more persons have (or engage in)."

[2] Wenzel(1979, pp. 115-116) paired these three perspectives to the Aristotelian branches of the study of argument as follows: logic (product-based), rhetoric (process-based), and dialectic (procedure-based).

[3] For example, consider the following list of definitions of "argument":

"a reasoned attempt to justify a conclusion" (Govier 2005, p. 2)
"an attempt to justify or prove a conclusion." (LeBlanc, 1998)
"an attempt to prove or establish a conclusion." (Ennis,1996)
"any unit of discourse (oral, written, or non-verbal) that gives one or more reasons in support of a claim." (Groarke, Tindale & Fisher, 1996)
" 'to give an argument' means to offer a set of reasons or evidence in support of a conclusion." (Weston, 2000)

Notice that, while argument has become an action (a doing or an attempt) the standard of success (justify, prove, establish, provide a reason), while partly constitutive of the action itself, is independent and primitive. What it is to justify, prove, establish or be a reason, is not given in terms of the activity. Rather these concepts form independent standards of success for the activity of arguing. It is noted below that the shift to a process-based view of argumentation as a subject matter brought with it procedural accounts of argumentative norms. Importantly, procedural normativity is not a necessary consequence of a process-based view.

In addition to characterizing arguments pragmatically rather than semantically, the perspective shift fundamentally humanized the study of argument
by focusing on the inherently social or interpersonal aspect of argument. From
a rhetorical perspective, Willard (1989, p. 1), claimed "Argument is a form of
interaction in which two or more people maintain what they construe to be
incompatible positions." Dialectical perspectives defined argument in terms
of a verbal, social activity. For example Walton (1990, p. 411) defined an argument as "a social and verbal means of trying to resolve, or at least contend
with, a conflict or difference that has arisen between two parties engaged in
a dialogue." Similarly, from the Pragma-Dialectical perspective: "Argumentation is a verbal and social activity of reason aimed at increasing (or decreasing)
the acceptability of a controversial standpoint for the listener or the reader, by
putting forward a constellation of propositions intended to justify (or refute)
the standpoint before a rational judge" (van Eemeren et al. 1996, p. 5). Even
traditionally product-based approaches, such informal logic, embraced a dialectical approach which conceived of the argument-product as the outcome
of a situated practice. For example, Blair and Johnson (1987, p. 45) wrote that
"An argument understood as *product* ... cannot be properly understood except against the background of the process which produced it – the process of
argumentation" (cf. Johnson 2000, p. 12).

Clearly this shift from product to process affected the interpretative task
of argument analysis, which now focused on pragmatic doings (speech acts)
rather than semantic things (sentences). Perhaps more importantly, concomitant changes also occurred in the normative task of argument evaluation.
Process-based, dialectical approaches to argumentation reconceived argument
norms as essentially procedural rather than structural (e.g., logical or epistemic). Johnson and Blair (1994, p. 13) describe this shift as follows:

> The dialogue logician assigns to logic the task of prescribing rights and duties in
> the transaction of a rational dialogue. The [product-based] informal logician assigns
> to logic the task of developing the criteria or standards for use in the evaluation of
> arguments. (cf. Johnson, 2000, p. 291)

Typically these procedural norms were taken to derive (a) from the type of
activity (read "argumentative discussion") engaged in – specifically the overall goal or purpose ascribed to that activity – and (b) from the type of act
performed in the course of that activity (Hamblin 1970; Walton & Krabbe 1995;
Walton 1998). For example in Pragma-Dialectics (van Eemeren and Grootendorst 2004, pp. 17, 132) the rules governing a critical discussion (a normative
ideal for argumentative dialogues which seek to rationally resolve a difference
of opinion) are justified by their *problem validity* (an instrumental standard of
how successfully the rules bring about the goal of the discussion) and *intersubjective validity* (an anthropological standard of reasonableness, external to
any particular instance of argumentation). Fallacies, on such accounts, are conceived of as discussion moves which impede the resolution of the discussion.

By contrast, the *design* approach (Goodwin 2002; 2007) to argument does
not presuppose or impose an overarching purpose upon the activity (read
"dialogue") itself, but instead focuses on the goals of individual, situated and
autonomous actors acting strategically. Instead of as a rule-governed dialogue,

design theory (Goodwin 2002, p. 6) conceives of the activity of arguing as (paradigmatically) a *transaction* – understood (as per *Webster's*) as "a communication or activity involving two parties or two things reciprocally affecting or influencing each other."

Argumentative norms, on this view, are located and applied from a bottom-up, rather than a top-down, approach.

> Instead of deriving norms from the standards set by some social function external to arguing, design theories contend that the argumentative transaction is internally self-regulating. Each arguer, to achieve her goals, tries to establish for herself and the other participants a normative environment within which their arguing can proceed. (Goodwin 2002, p. 6)

On the design approach, norms come to bear on argumentative situations as arguers act so as to manifestly undertake, discharge, impose and enforce certain commitments (or responsibilities) attached to the ordinary pragmatics of speech acts.

3 The legacy of commitment in argumentation

One of the legacies of the shift to the pragmatic, dialectical, process-based perspective on argumentation, where the basic components of arguments are viewed not as a propositions, or sentences (e.g., premises or conclusions), but speech acts, or utterances (e.g., moves in a language game or dialogue), has been that commitment has become the central locus of argument interpretation and evaluation. Commitments arise out of, and are attached to, the public doings of arguers, and have become not only the units in which argumentative positions are described (since utterances both instantiate and generate commitments),[4] but the markers or argumentative responsibilities.

Commitments are understood as "proposition[s] one has gone on record as accepting [i.e., verbally (see below)]" (Walton 2010, p. 23). So, in one sense, commitments are simply speech acts – bits of verbal behavior. Yet, they also have an inherently normative dimension which is cashed out as sets of responsibilities one undertakes in respect to some particular claim. Commitments, in this sense, are obligations. Agents incur these obligations by doing certain kinds of things, specifically by making speech acts in the right sorts of circumstances. For example, if an agent asserts that c, she has undertaken a set of responsibilities to do things like (i) support c with sufficient and acceptable reasons if challenged, and (ii) retract c in the event that she cannot meet her first responsibility. Similarly, the commitments that arise from conceding that c might include things like the following: (i) revising one's other commitments such that they are consistent with c, (ii) not making assertions one takes to

---

[4] In one sense, the utterance-to-commitment relationship is many:one, since there can be many different tokens for, or even ways of instantiating, a particular commitment. In another sense, there is a one:many relationship between utterances and commitments, since a single utterance can generate several different commitments (see below).

be inconsistent with c, (iii) allowing c to be used as a premise, and (iv) not arbitrarily abandoning c.

Importantly, these responsibilities are inherently public and social. They derive not only from the nature of the speech act itself, but often also from the particular rules governing the activity (read "argumentative discussion") in which one is engaged at the time of making the speech act. In addition to the overarching *telos* of the argumentative discussion (if any), these commitments also serve – at the local level – as the locus, and sometimes even the basis, for argumentative norms, understood as procedural obligations arguers have to themselves and one another.

As Walton (1998, p. 31) writes, "The concept of commitment is the basic idea behind all dialogue as a form of reasoned argumentation." This focus on commitment can be found in formal approaches to argument dialogues (e.g., Hamblin 1970), pluralistic goal-driven and speech-act approaches (Walton & Krabbe 1995, Walton 1998), highly idealized and normalized approaches to argumentative dialogue (such as the Pragma-Dialectical approach; van Eemeren & Grootendorst 1984, 2004), and even design approaches (Goodwin 2002, 2005). By focusing on the essentially social and behavioral aspects of argumentation, the perspective shift to the process-based view of argument has resulted in a commitment-oriented view of it.

While humanistic, this process-based, commitment-oriented conception ignores the cognitive and psychological dimensions of argument. It is not only that the producers and consumers of arguments are psychological as well as situated and social beings. More specifically, their doxastic life has both a causal and an explanatory relationship to their social and behavioral life, and as such it seems both primary and ineliminable to a properly humanized study or argument. Persuasive argument seeks to affect its audience's behavior by changing their minds with reasons. As such, arguments contain or represent inferences, and the stakes in argument are cognitive attitudes. Thus it would seem that the move to the social ought to have resulted in a move to the psychological. These ideas are explored below in the context of the role belief should play in explaining and evaluating argumentative behavior, and in analyzing and appraising arguments.[5]

4 The primacy of belief in argumentation

4.1 Belief and acceptance

Godden (2010, p. 399) proposed an account of belief with minimal metaphysical 'freight,' on which beliefs have two defining characteristics. First, beliefs have what Searle (1979, pp. 7-9) called a *world to mind fit*; second, they are what

---

[5] Belief is here intended only to be a representative of the conscious mental attitudes which are advanced as being the proper focus of theories of argument (see Godden 2010, p. 398, fn1).

Ramsey (1931, p. 28) called the *maps by which we steer*. Together, these properties are sufficient to distinguish beliefs from commitments and acceptances.

Acceptance comes in two varieties: verbal acceptance (conceding), understood as a speech act of assent, and mental acceptance (accepting proper). Pinto (2003, p. 8) describes (mentally) accepting a proposition as "being prepared to use it as a premiss in my reasonings or inferences (or in cases of public discussion being prepared to tolerate its use by others)." This account roughly coincides with Cohen's (1992, p. 4) definition: "to accept that *p* is to have or adopt a policy for deeming, position, or postulating that *p*" (cf. Stalnaker 1984, pp. 79-80).

Paglieri and Castelfranchi (2006a) distinguish belief and acceptance according to the "different functional roles . . . [they] play in the cognitive economy of the subject." Belief has an *alethic function* which "is meant to provide a veridical representation of the world," while acceptance has a *pragmatic function*, "its role is to provide a representation of the world that is suitable for supporting successful deliberation and effective action." While belief and acceptance are not exclusionary (indeed in normal cases they coincide), they are not coextensive either.

For Cohen (1992, p. 4), beliefs are dispositions of a certain sort; they are inclinations towards feeling that a certain proposition is true: to believe that *p*, is to, upon introspection, "normally . . . feel it true that *p* and false that *not-p*." As such, our beliefs play a premissory role in our inferences and practical reasoning, they have a causal role in determining our actions, and they contribute significantly to a rational explanation of our behavior. Davidson (1980, pp. 4-5, fn. 2) describes *actions* as the intentional doings of agents – acts which, under some description, can be said to be done *for a reason*. Roughly, then, to attribute actions to agents is to take what Dennett has called the *intentional stance* towards them; this involves explaining their behavior in terms of beliefs and desires which are taken to causally determine the outward behavior.

4.2 Belief as the locus of persuasion

Given these conceptions of belief, acceptance and commitment, Godden (2010, pp. 404-406) then argued that belief, not commitment, is the primary target at which persuasive argumentation should be directed. The argument presented there ran roughly as follows. Commitment-based theories of argument (e.g., Hamblin 1970; Walton and Krabbe 1995; van Eemeren and Grootendorst 1984, 2004) tend to share a commitment to the following three claims:

1. *Goal*: The goal of persuasive argumentation is to settle a difference of opinion by rational means.
2. *Independence of belief and commitment*: Commitment and belief are logically and causally independent; a change in one does not always result in a corresponding change in the other.

3. *Resolution*: A difference of opinion is resolved when the commitments of the disputants have reached a state of agreement with respect to the claim at issue. (Godden 2010, p. 404)

Yet, a paradigm of failure of persuasive argumentation occurs whenever an arguer concedes a position in argument (e.g., as a speech act or as a move in an argumentative dialogue) but subsequently (perhaps following the argumentative exchange) acts as though no such concession had been made. Because such argumentation fails to determine, or even to affect, the future actions of arguers, a *genuine* resolution to a difference of opinion is not achieved, despite the *appearance* of a resolution having been achieved through the concession.

Whatever the agent's motives for making such a concession, that it fails to subsequently inform her behavior indicates that her beliefs are not aligned with her commitments on the matter at issue. Since, by definition, an agent's actions are shaped by her beliefs, to be effective resolutions of differences of opinion must occur at the level of belief and not merely at the level of verbal commitment. Even though we may be able, sometimes, to hold agents answerable to commitments they made in argumentation, when the agent's own beliefs do not coincide with those commitments she well not hold *herself* accountable to them. Yet, that she does so is normally necessary for the resolution of a difference of opinion to be effective, since interlocutors in argumentation will not normally be present to hold each other accountable to commitments undertaken in argumentation much beyond the argumentative exchange.

4.3 Belief as the foundation for action

A second argument, touched upon in that paper (p. 401, fn. 6), might now be offered in greater detail. This argument also hinges on the point that beliefs are causally related to actions. Importantly, the normal competitors to belief as the locus of argumentation and persuasion – acceptance and commitment – are each actions in Davidson's sense: they are intentional acts, consciously and voluntarily performed, which may be described as having been done *for a reason*. As intentional acts, acceptance and commitment are subject to intentional explanation, and such explanations are given in terms of the agent's beliefs and desires.

Insofar as acceptance is like a Cartesian *judgement* – the conscious and deliberate endorsement of a claim – an agent's acceptance of a claim is both explained by and justified in terms of her beliefs about the acceptability (be it alethic or pragmatic) of that claim. Similarly with speech acts, such as assertion and concession. That an agent asserts, concedes or retracts a claim in her commitment-store is explained by recourse to her beliefs concerning the relevant properties of that claim. For example, standard analytical explanations (Grice 1989; Searle 1979) of acts of assertion hold as constitutive that assertions are expressions of beliefs through uttering sentences. Thus Hindriks (2004, p. 136) gives the following condition as a criterion for assertion: "An utterance of u counts as an assertion of p just if the person who utters it expresses her belief that p."

5 From the social to the cognitive

The perspective shift from product to process, and from argument to arguer, reflected an attempt to humanize the study of argument and an awareness of the essential place of social and situational factors in the nature of the very subject matter under investigation in argumentation studies. Yet, it would seem that this perspective has neglected the cognitive, psychological dimensions of argument – dimensions which seem to be both ineliminable and basic.

In lamenting the lack of integration of theories of argumentation with theories of belief change, Paglieri and Castelfranchi (2005, pp. 359-360) portray belief revision and argument as distinguished only according to audience, with both aiming at what Harman (1986) has called *reasoned change in view*. One useful way to conceive of the *activity* of arguing which includes its essential, cognitive dimension is found in Campolo's (2005, p. 41) idea that arguing is *reasoning together*. This conception emphasizes not only the interpersonal and cognitive aspects of argumentation, but views argument as an activity whose function is inherently reflective, reparative or remedial. The activity of reasoning is invoked when some other activity in which we are otherwise smoothly engaged is somehow interrupted. Like any other activity, our reasoning abilities (and therefore our argumentative abilities) are founded in training (socialization) as well as capacity (natural endowments). Each of these factors serves to further set limits to the prospects of reason. "[R]easoning together," Campolo reminds us (p. 41), "is not some sort of magically creative act that always produces efficacious results. It is rather a way of drawing on shared resources, and as those resources get thinner, reasoning loses traction." This conception begins to raise important questions concerning the effect that the cognitive limitations of arguers might have on not only the efficaciousness of argument, but also on how argumentative norms ought to be formulated and relate to arguer's cognitive capacities.

6 Formal theories of belief revision

The increased appreciation of the cognitive bases and ineliminable doxastic dimensions of the social and behavioral aspects of argumentation has provided one catalyst for the re-introduction of beliefs into theories of argumentation. Accepting the centrality of belief to argumentation, it is worthwhile to consider where theorists might turn to gain a working understanding of how belief operates in argumentation. One such direction is to formal models of belief revision.

In this context, the work of Castelfranchi, and more recently Castelfranchi and Paglieri [hereafter "C&P"], have contributed substantial advances in the theoretical understanding and representation of the operation of belief in argumentation. The theoretical framework adopted by C&P takes seriously the relevance of belief to argumentation argued for above. Indeed, on many occasions they have been outspoken advocates for the integration of theories of argumentation with theories of belief revision. For example, they (P&C 2005, p. 360) comment on the necessity of belief-talk in explaining the behavior – including their verbal behavior – of arguers.

> Argumentation theories remain incomplete, if they cannot be grounded in belief revision models: they describe interesting dialogical patterns and their effects, but cannot explain *why and how such effects are produced*. Without an underlying model of belief dynamics, argumentation theories are forced to remain 'out of the black box'.

Indeed, previously Castelfranchi (1996, p. 234) had argued that the causal connection between belief and action necessitates the incorporation of theories of rational belief (revision) into rational action theory. "A Cognitive agent, as a matter of fact, is an agent who founds his decisions, intentions and actions on his beliefs. . . . rationality in believing contributes to rationality in behaving. . . . Rational beliefs are a necessary condition for rational behaviour, since irrational beliefs are a sufficient condition for irrational behaviour." Thus, Castelfranchi (1996, p. 235; cf. 1995) proposed the *Autonomous Cognitive Agent Postulate*:

> It is impossible to directly modify the goals (and then the intentions and actions) of an Autonomous Cognitive Agent. In order to influence him (i.e. to modify his goals), another agent should modify his beliefs supporting those goals.

According to this postulate, the intentional, goal-directed behavior of agents cannot be properly explained or affected (e.g., through argument) without reference to, or effecting, corresponding changes or states in the agent's belief structure.

6.1 Data-oriented belief revision (DBR)

In this context, Paglieri and Castelfranchi developed a Data-oriented Belief Revision (DBR) model (Paglieri 2004), which is offered as an alternative to the AGM approach (Gärdenfors 1988). DBR effectively models a two-system, two-stage process of belief revision. The model (P&C 2005, p.80) distinguishes between *data* and *beliefs* where data are conceived of as "pieces of information *gathered and stored*" by a cognitive agent, while beliefs are data that "the agent considers *reliable bases for action, decision, and specific reasoning tasks* e.g., prediction and explanation."

This distinction leads P&C to conceive of belief change as a two-step process. First, information received as data may have initial and direct effects on other pieces of data stored by the agent. Second, data that is subsequently endorsed as a belief (a process characterized as *belief selection*) may have secondary and *indirect* effects on other beliefs (pp. 80-81). Importantly, data-management is a process independent of belief revision, and involves processes such as (i) information update, (ii) data properties and assessment, and (iii) belief selection.

P&C (pp. 81 ff.) propose that data are selected or rejected as beliefs on the basis of four properties conceived as cognitive reasons to believe. These are: relevance, credibility, importance and likeability. Relevance and likeability measure a relation between data and goals, while credibility and importance are structural relations between data. P&C propose that the properties of credibility, importance and likeability determine the outcomes of belief selection (adoption) in algorithmic ways according to whether their combined value (which gives the strength of the datum) meets or exceeds a certain threshold, understood as a minimal threshold of belief. Information update, as a kind of data management, occurs independently of belief revision.

Belief revision can occur in two principal ways. First, it can be triggered *externally* as a result of information update and belief selection. Secondly, it can occur *internally* as a result of inference from existing (or selected) beliefs. Importantly, data are managed in ways that are categorically different than the ways in which beliefs are revised. Data are organized according to three relations of support, contrast and union (p. 84). Data are managed in a connectionist, parallel, and coherentist way, while beliefs are revised in a computationalist, serial and foundationalist manner according to rule-governed algorithms.

6.2 *Applications of DBR*

The DBR model was developed in the context of existing work by Castelfranchi which had already established a working notion of belief, and explored its relationship not only to intentional behavior but also to other cognitive entities informing behavior such as goals, intentions and commitments. For example, Castelfranchi (1996) contributed to an understanding of the relationship between theoretical and practical reasoning by demonstrating that there is a support relation between beliefs and goals whereby beliefs provide the reason for goals such that goals should change when supporting beliefs do, and supporting beliefs should be maintained when their goals are. This work is developed in C&P (2007) into a model of belief-based goal processing which provides the core for a constructive theory of intentions. In more recent work P&C (2010) this theme is revisited through a consideration of the strategic and instrumental, goal directed reasoning involved in deciding to argue based on a cost-benefit analysis.

Within the overall framework of the DBR model, the accomplishments of Castelfranchi and Paglieri have been remarkable, and their contributions to theories of argument impressive. P&C (2006b) show how the essentially coherentist AGM model cannot express or represent the basing relations at the core of argument – and reasoning, or inference – where conclusions based on reasons. They proceed to show how DBR can model argumentative relations when understood on Toulmin's Data-Warrant-Claim structure. Importantly, this includes showing how DBR can accommodate defeasible reasoning, including premise defeaters, undercutting (warrant) defeaters, and direct (conclusion) rebutters.

Overall, Castelfranchi and Paglieri's Data-oriented Belief Revision model provides a comprehensive and powerful model capable of representing not only argument as a kind of other-directed, inferential-based belief revision, but also the connection between belief and argumentatively relevant behaviors from speech acts and strategic maneuvering within and prior to argument, to an arguer's actions following argumentation. Yet, in understanding belief as a component of a formal model, it is important to see how well the assumptions informing these models, and our theories of argument more generally, correspond to the actual operation of belief. The final sections of this paper turn to two psychological characteristics of belief and its operation which seem problematic to standard accounts of the role of belief in argument.

7 Belief, rationality and reactive attitudes

Rationality is the basic evaluative ideal of argument, and virtually all theories of argumentation, whether rhetorical, dialectical or epistemic, suppose, either implicitly or explicitly, some theory of rationality. As Willard (1989, p. 152) observed "Not all rationality theories include argument in their definitions, but virtually all argument theories include rationality in theirs."

Basically, to be rational is to respond rightly to reasons. That is, "rational beliefs must be based on reasons" (Brown 1988, p. 38; cf. Siegel 2004, p. 598). "To be a critical thinker," Siegel writes, "is to be appropriately moved by reasons. To be a rational person is to believe and act on the basis of reasons" (1988, p. 32). Similarly, rational persuasion occurs when the Other is persuaded to accept a conclusion "on the basis of the reasons and considerations cited [in the argument], and those alone" (Johnson 2000, p. 150); thus persuasive success depends not only on the overall rationality of the result but on the *apparentness* of that rationality (*ibid.* and passim). What is it for our views to be based on reasons? Roughly, this occurs when our degree of commitment or attachment to our views somehow accords with the reasons we have for those views. Siegel (1997, p. 2) puts it this way: "to say that one is *appropriately* moved by reasons is to say that one believes, judges, and acts in accordance with the probative force with which one's reasons support one's beliefs, judgments and actions." Similarly, Pinto (2006, p. 287) explains rationality along the lines of a *qualitative evidence proportionalism* whereby "rationality is a matter of making our *attitudes* towards propositions or propositional contents *appropriate to the evidence* which shapes them."

Roughly, this picture amounts to a deontological conception of rationality. It is based on the idea that rational agents have a basic epistemic duty to know (relevant) truths and avoid error. This, combined with the idea that being rational – i.e., rightly connecting our cognitive attitudes to reason and evidence – is essential and instrumental in fulfilling our epistemic duties, forms the basis of our argumentative norms. As believers, we have a duty to be rational, and argumentative norms and obligations flow from these rational norms and obligations. Importantly, then, on this account, our beliefs and other cognitive attitudes are rightly subject to what Strawson (1962; cf. Jäger 2004, p. 1) called *reactive attitudes*; we rightly praise and blame people not only for what they do, but for what they believe.

On the picture we have been advancing, belief plays an essential role in argument. Beliefs feature centrally in explaining an agent's behavior, including her argumentative behavior. Ultimately, beliefs are what is *at stake* in argumentation; arguers seek to affect their interlocutors behavior *by changing their minds with reasons*. Further, beliefs are rightly subject to rational evaluation and to our reactive attitudes. In some cases, irrationality or error is blameworthy and irrational believers can rightly be held accountable.

Yet, when considered as purely abstract, formal entities, as beliefs are in formal theories of belief revision, various contingent qualities of beliefs arising from their psychological nature, and the nature of believers as psychological beings, are glossed over or neglected. Regrettably, several of these qualities raise important problems for normative theories of belief revision, and hence to belief-centric theories of argumentation.

8 Volition, belief and rational accountability

A first problem is this. Beliefs do not seem to be subject to voluntary control. That is, as a contingent matter of fact, by and large, believers lack the ability to voluntarily form or revise their beliefs (cf. Feldman 2000, p. 670). To demonstrate: consider whether, at this moment, you can come to believe that the United States are still a colony of Great Britain. (If it will help, suppose you are offered the additional incentive of a large cash reward if you are successful) (cf. Alston 1989, p. 122). As it turns out, this is just something that, as believers, we are unable to do. As Alston (1986, p. 196) writes:

> For the most part my beliefs are formed willy-nilly. When I see a truck coming down the street, I am hardly at liberty to either believe that a truck is coming down the street or refrain from that belief . . . it is clear that for the most part we lack such powers.

It is not merely that we cannot form or change our beliefs purely at will, but rather that, choice seems to play no part in the process whatsoever. For the most part, belief formation and revision does not seem as though it could go otherwise than as it does.

Yet, as Alston proceeds, if believers lack basic voluntary control over their beliefs, it is *prima facie* implausible that they should be held accountable for them. Again Alston (1986, p. 196) writes:

> All this talk [of deontological conceptions of rationality] has application only if one has direct voluntary control over whether one believes that *p* at any given moment. If I lack such control, I cannot believe or refrain from believing that *p* at will, then it is futile to discuss whether I am *permitted* to believe that *p* at *t* or whether I would be

irresponsible in choosing to believe that *p* that *t*. And it seems that we just don't have any such control, at least not in general.

In general, this line of thinking has been named *the voluntarism argument*, a standard formulation of which is:

P1. Doxastic voluntarism is false.
P2. If doxastic voluntarism if false, then the deontological conception of rationality (epistemic justification) is false.
C: Therefore, the deontological conception of rationality and epistemic justification is false. (cf. Feldman 1988, p. 237; Jäger 2004; Kim 1994, p. 282)

If correct, this line of argument affects not only deontological theories of rational belief (revision), but also all theories of argument which depend on such a theory. Yet, as argued above, it would seem that theories of argument do and should rely on such deontological theories.

As Feldman observes (1988, p. 238) there are two primary strategies of refutation available. One is to reject P1. Moves of this sort begin by considering the kinds of voluntary control agents can have over their actions, a standard list (cf. Alston 1989, pp. 122 ff.; Feldman 2000, pp. 670-671) of which goes as follows in order of strength:

  (i) *Basic voluntary control*: things we can just do (e.g., raise own hand)
 (ii) *Non-basic immediate voluntary control*: things we can straightforwardly do by doing other things which, ultimately, will be under basic voluntary control. (e.g., opening doors, turning on lights)
(iii) *Long-range voluntary control*: things we can accomplish over time by doing other things (e.g., paying off debts)
(iv) *Indirect voluntary influence*: things which we can affect over time by doing other things (e.g., controlling our weight)

Both sides of the debate tend to agree that we lack basic or direct voluntary control over our beliefs, and that the kind of control we have over our beliefs is indirect. Advocates of the voluntarism argument (Alston 1989) have claimed that at best we generally have only indirect voluntary influence over our beliefs, and that this is not sufficient to claim that beliefs are appropriately subject to reactive attitudes. Kim (1994) accepts Alston's claim concerning the degree of control we have, but claims that all that is required in order for us to be epistemically responsible is that we critically reflect on our beliefs, and this is surely something over which we have sufficient voluntary control. Although Feldman (2000, pp. 671 ff.) has argued that many ordinary beliefs are subject to non-basic immediate voluntary control (e.g., I can come to believe that the lights are on by turning on the light-switch), Jäger (2004, p. 5) has argued that this is not to the point: "The (alleged) problem is not that *under different epistemic conditions*, in different epistemic worlds, we could not believe otherwise than we actually do. The problem is that, in light of the grounds we actually have for and against a given belief, we cannot but adopt or reject it." Instead, Jäger (2004) opts for a compatibalist view which claims that even though there may not be any alternate possibilities for believing in some given epistemic circumstance, it remains the case that our beliefs can be said to be voluntary so long as they can be caused in the right sorts of ways, such as on the basis of the evidence.[6]

A second refutation strategy is to reject P2, by claiming that obligations can still attach to behavior over which we have no control or alternatives. Unlike the compatibalist approach, this move rejects the *ought implies can* principle, and claims that we can be held responsible even in cases where we cannot meet our obligations (regardless of whether we could have done other than what we did). Feldman (1988, 2000) offers examples of several obligations which are like this. Some of these (e.g. contractual obligations) are not sufficiently like epistemic obligations to make the point, while others (e.g., obligations to meet performative norms when engaging in certain roles) are. Thus, Feldman concludes (2000, p. 676) that "It is our plight to be believers. We ought to do it right. It doesn't matter that in some cases we're unable to do so."

Yet another line of response to the voluntarism argument is to retreat from belief to the view that acceptance, which is clearly voluntary, should be the locus of argument evaluation. Lehrer (1981, pp. 79-80; cf. Feldman 1988, p. 240) suggests this route, writing: "Sometimes a person cannot decide what to believe at a moment, but can decide what to accept. ... Believing is not an action. Accepting is." While this escapes the immediate problem raised by the voluntarism argument, it does so at the cost of providing meaningful intentional explanations of actions. That is to say, it gives up Castelfranchi's (1996, p. 235) Autonomous Cognitive Agent Postulate, and in doing so it fails to adequately explain the intentional behavior of agents.

So, it would seem that there are a series of important conceptual, ontological and empirical questions at the bottom of this debate. The question of whether our beliefs are properly subject to reactive attitudes, seems to depend either on the degree of voluntary control required to properly hold believers responsible for their beliefs, or on whether our having an obligation entails that we can meet it.

9 Belief revision, argumentation and reason tracking

A second problem arising from the psychology of belief concerns our competence as reason trackers. Belief-centric theories of argumentation hold that argument involves inference, and that rational persuasion occurs when arguers base their cognitive attitudes on reasons. Thus, patterns of inference map out, or represent, episodes in the cognitive lives of reasoners.

As Pinto (2001, p. 10) writes, persuasive argumentation can usefully be understood as "the attempt to modify conscious attitudes through rational means." Pinto (2001, pp. 37, 32) describes arguments as "invitations to inference" where inference is explained as "the mental act or event in which a person draws a conclusion from premises, or arrives at a conclusion on the basis of the consideration of a body of evidence." Similarly, Johnson (2000, p. 150)

---

[6] See Feldman (2000, pp. 673-674) for an assessment of this view.

describes persuasive argument as "discourse directed toward rational persuasion," where rational persuasion is taken to mean "that the arguer wishes to persuade the Other to accept the conclusion on the basis of the reasons and considerations cited [in the argument] and those alone." Yet, previously Johnson (2000, p. 24) introduced the term "inference" to mean "a movement (of the mind) from one item (usually a thought) to another, where the former serves as the basis for and leads to the later." These accounts do not differ significantly from Castelfranchi's (1996, p. 238) conception of inference as a "knowledge acquisition process," "by which a cognitive system is able to generate, internally, new pieces of knowledge from already existing pieces of knowledge explicitly represented." (Here, the normative aspect of inference is implicit in its ability to generate *knowledge*.) Thus, in order for the reasons cited in the argument to provide the genuine bases for an arguer's acceptance of the conclusion, the basing relations of an argument's premises and conclusions must accurately represent the basing relations between reasons and claims in the arguer's beliefs. That is, arguments must represent and occasion (or bring about) the corresponding and actual inferences which arguers make.

Arguments, on this view, contain or represent inferences – i.e., mental acts on the part of their audiences. On the traditional picture, inference has a dual-nature. On the one hand, inference is a mental process – that is, it is an episode in the psychological history of a cognitive agent. Indeed, as Harman (1986, p. 207) points out, "We normally think of inference as a *causal process*, in which the premises are all *causally operative* in producing a new belief (or other doxastic change)." But, not just any kind of mental act, or causal movement of the mind from one idea to another, will qualify as an inference. Purely associationistic causal relations of ideas will not count. Rather, to count as an inference, some thoughts must serve as the basis of others, from which the latter are taken to follow. These basing relations are intrinsic and distinguishing features of inference as a mental process. Thus, Johnson (2000, p. 94; cf. 98) describes inference as "the transition of the mind from one proposition to another in accordance with some principle." The principle articulates the basing relation that is taken to hold between reasons and conclusions and which *justifies* or *warrants* the inferential move. Inference, then, seems to have a dual character on which it is both essentially psychological and causal and on the other hand inherently normative and justificatory. Thus, it would seem that arguers and reasoners must track basing relations among their beliefs in order to infer successfully.

This picture of the nature of inference and its relationship to argument has important consequences for which theories of justification will count as acceptable. In *Change in View* (1986, pp. 29 ff.) Harman considers two models of ideal belief revision: the *foundations* theory and the *coherence* theory. These models are distinguished according to the theory of justification each adopts, and the key feature is whether rationality requires tracking reasons (or the basing-relations among beliefs). Foundationalists say "yes" while coherentists say "no." As Harman (p. 30) writes, "the theories are most easily distinguished by the conflicting advice they occasionally give concerning whether one should *give up* a belief P ... when P's original justification has to be abandoned." On the foundational view justification requires reason-tracking, and to the extent that reasons are not tracked – let alone not cogent – beliefs become irrationally held. By contrast, the coherence view rejects reason-tracking in favor of a kind of principle of conservatism whereby merely having a belief counts as a reason entitling one to keep it, so long as there is no special reason for abandoning it. It would seem that the inferentialist picture described above is committed to something like the foundationalist picture of rationality.

Paglieri and Castelfranchi (2006b, p. 362) write that one of the problems with all coherence theories of belief revision, such as the AGM model, is that they

> do not take into account such 'reasons to believe' – and that is precisely the reason why they cannot capture argumentation structures effectively. . . . Argumentation theories capture the ways in which a desired change in the audience's beliefs is brought about by the arguer: therefore, without an explicit theory of *the reasons to believe* something, the main point of argumentation is lost.

Indeed, in previous work Castelfranchi (1996, p. 238) had already postulated the *trace hypothesis* that "we maintain in our memory a trace of the derivation of the cognitive item: its story. . . . A trace means a link, a relation between the *source* of the knowledge acquisition or elaboration, and the result. This link maintains also the kind of derivation: perception, communication, reasoning." The satisfaction of this trace hypothesis, Castelfranchi (*ibid.*) takes to be an "important cognitive property" of "any process of knowledge acquisition."

Yet, as crucial as this idea that reasoners and arguers are reason-trackers is to standard (indeed, one might say, informative) accounts of inference and argument, there is reason to think that it is empirically false. As, Harman (1986) observes, when we consider actual cases of belief perseverance in the face of the manifest undermining of their original evidential basis, as experimentally demonstrated in Ross, Lepper and Hubbard's (1975) debriefing paradigm, it becomes clear that our actual and typical behavior presents significant problems for foundationalist theories.[7] It is found that people regularly retain beliefs even after the positive and manifest refutation of all the evidence upon which their beliefs were originally based. That is, studies such as the debriefing paradigm seem to show that reasoners aren't reason-trackers. Yet, if this is the case, then it seems that the foundational theory fails by *reductio*. Harman (1986, p. 39) writes, "since people rarely keep track of their reasons, the [foundational] theory implies that people are unjustified in almost all their beliefs. This is an absurd result" (39). Harman's critique not only challenges the causal elements of the traditional picture whereby beliefs are established *on the basis of* the reasons supplied in argument, but it challenges the very picture of rationality on which argumentation theory may depend.

---

[7] See Godden (2012) for an extended discussion of this problem.

10 Conclusion

This chapter has sought to recognize contributions made to the theory of argumentation by the work of Castelfranchi, together with Paglieri, by situating their efforts in the context of recent developments in argumentation studies market by the shift in focus from argument to argumentation. Within the last generation it has been realized that in order to properly understand arguments they must be studied not as decontextualized, abstract objects, but rather in the context of their use and application in concrete situations by social and cognitive beings. This process-based approach conceives of argument as an activity, deliberately and often strategically engaged in by intentional agents seeking to affect each other's behavior by employing reasons to change each other's minds. It was argued that the process-based view of argument entails the necessity of a psychological dimension in our theories of it. Explanations of intentional, argumentative behavior as well as the inherently cognitive aspects of arguing understood as involving inference and reasoned change in view require a belief-based approach to the theory of argumentation as an activity, as well as the structure of argument as an artifact.

The work of Castelfranchi, together with Paglieri, has contributed substantially to these ends. Pioneering work by Castelfranchi set forth an ontology of beliefs in relation to other mental states such as goals and intentions such that the connection between belief and action can be better explained and understood. With this, the argumentative behavior of rational agents of can be better understood and explained. Further, the Data-oriented model of Belief Revision proposed by Paglieri and Castelfranchi provides theorists with a robust model of rational belief change in relation to the processes of information management which precede and inform belief revision. The DBR model recognizes these processes to be effectively independent, though data management processes can result in inputs, through belief selection, to the processes of belief revision such as inference and argument. In addition to being able to represent such well-established models of argument as Toulmin's Data-Warrant-Claim model, DBR promises substantial contributions to the theory of argument in ways largely unexplored. For example by formalizing the process of belief selection, it is able to provide an explanation of how and why arguers make determinations of premise adequacy.

There are, though, a variety of problems facing all belief-based approach to argument, many of which come from the psychology of belief. Two of these were raised in the paper.

(i) If beliefs are properly subject to the praise and blame of our reactive attitudes, then it seems as though rational believers must have sufficient control over their beliefs such that they can be rightly held accountable for them. Yet, arguably, believers do not have sufficient voluntary control over their beliefs that they should be held responsible for them. Thus, it seems as though belief is not properly subject to rational appraisal.

(ii) Foundationalist accounts of rationality commonly employed in argumentation theory presuppose that arguers track reasons on the basis of which they draw the conclusions of their inferences and arguments. Yet, empirical studies tend to suggest that reasoners are not reason-trackers in anything like the manner or degree required by such foundationalist accounts of rationality. If so, then it would seem as though either we are much less rational than we ordinarily take ourselves to be, or foundationalism is the wrong picture of rationality to apply to belief revision and argument.

By failing to focus on the inherently doxastic dimensions of argumentation, social, process-based accounts were able to avoid addressing pressing concerns such as these. Yet, when the relationship between belief and argument is articulated, problems such as these come to light – problems which seem to challenge many of the core assumptions on which standard theories of rational belief change, and their attendant accounts of argumentation are based. These problems must be faced squarely, since a retreat to a view of argument which fails to incorporate belief is neither plausible nor viable.

No solution to these problems is here offered. Rather, I raise them merely because they are troubling to me – to my own projects – and it seems to me that they are shared by any theory which seeks to adequately describe, explain and evaluate what is going on when people argue. The turn towards the humanized, process-oriented, situated and concrete view of argument opens not only the doxastic door, but the empirical one as well. Theories hoping to succeed at this level, whether in projects of a descriptive and explanatory nature, or in the normative and evaluative ones with which I am primarily concerned, must aim at a much higher standard. Purely social and behavioral approaches contented themselves to 'work outside the black box' of belief and cognition, and were the worse-off for it. Yet, once the 'black box of belief' is opened the picture becomes not only more informative but more complicated and challenging.

References

1. Alston, W.P. (1986). Internalism and externalism in epistemology. *Philosophical topics*, 14, 179-221.
2. Alston, W.P. ([1988] 1989). The deontological conception of epistemic justification. In *Epistemic justification: Essays in theory of knowledge* (pp. 115-152). Ithaca, NY: Cornell University Press.
3. Blair, J.A. & Johnson, R. (1987). Argumentation as dialectical. *Argumentation*, 1, 41-56. Reprinted in Johnson (1996).
4. Brandom, R. (1994). *Making it explicit*. Cambridge, MA: Harvard University Press.
5. Brandom, R. (2001). *Articulating reasons: An introduction to inferentialism*. Cambridge, MA: Harvard University Press.
6. Brockriede, W. (1975). Where is argument? *Journal of the American Forensic Association*, 11, 179-182.
7. Brockriede, W. (1977). Characteristics of arguments and arguing. *Journal of the American Forensic Association*, 13, 129-132.
8. Brown, H. (1988). *Rationality*. London: Routledge.
9. Campolo, C. (2005). Treacherous ascents: On seeking common ground for conflict resolution. *Informal Logic*, 25, 37-50.

10. Castelfranchi, C. (1995). Guarantees for autonomy in cognitive agent architecture. In M. Woolridge & N. Jennings (Eds.), *Intelligent agents: Theories, architec-tures and languages* LNAI 890 (pp. 56-70). Berlin: Springer-Verlag.
11. Castelfranchi, C. (1996). Reasons: Belief support and goal dynamics. *Mathware and soft computing*, 3, 233-247.
12. Castelfranchi, C. & Paglieri, F. (2007). The role of beliefs in goal dynamics: Prolegomena to a constructive theory of intentions. *Synthese*, 155, 237-263.
13. Cohen, L.J. (1992). Belief and acceptance. *Mind*, 98, 367 – 389.
14. Davidson, D. (1980). Actions, reasons and causes. In *Essays on actions and events* (pp. 3-20). Oxford: Clarendon Press.
15. Eemeren, F.H. van & Grootendorst, R. (1984). *Speech acts in argumentative discourse.* Dordrecht: Foris.
16. Eemeren, F.H. van & Grootendorst, R. (2004). *A systematic theory of argumentation: The pragma-dialectical approach.* Cambridge: Cambridge University Press.
17. Eemeren, F.H. van, Grootendorst, R., Snoeck Henkemans, F. et al. (1996). *Fundamentels of argumentation theory. A handbook of historical backgrounds and contemporary developments.* Mahwah, NJ: Lawrence Erlbaum.
18. Ennis, R. H. (1996). *Critical thinking.* Upper Saddle River, NJ: Prentice Hall.
19. Feldman, R. (1988). Epistemic obligations. *Philosophical Perspectives*, 2, 235-256.
20. Feldman, R. (2000). The ethics of belief. *Philosophy and Phenomenological Research*, 60, 667-695.
21. Gärdenfors, P. (1988). *Knowledge in flux.* Cambridge, MA: MIT Press.
22. Godden, D.M. (2010). The importance of belief in argumentation: Belief, commitment and the effective resolution of a difference of opinion. *Synthese*, 172, 397-414.
23. Godden, D.M. (2012). Rethinking the debriefing paradigm: The rationality of belief perseverance. *Logos & Episteme*, 3, 51–74.
24. Goodwin, J. (2002). One question, two answers. In H.V. Hansen et al. (Eds.), *Argument and its Applications: Proceedings of OSSA 2001*, CD-ROM (pp. 1-17). Windsor,ON: OSSA.
25. Goodwin, J. (2007). Argument has no function. *Informal Logic*, 27, 69-90.
26. Govier, T. (2005). *A practical study of argument*, 6th ed. Toronto: Wadsworth.
27. Grice, P. (1989). *Studies in the ways of words.* Cambridge, MA: Harvard UP.
28. Groarke, L., Tindale, C. & Fisher, L. (1996). *Good reasoning matters! A constructive approach to critical thinking*, 2nd ed. Toronto: Oxford University Press.
29. Hamblin, C.L. (1970). *Fallacies.* London: Methuen & Co.
30. Harman, G. (1986). *Change in view: Principles of reasoning.* Cambridge, MA: MIT Press.
31. Hindriks, F.A. (2004). Knoweldge, belief, and assertion. In W. Löffler & P. Weingartner (Eds.), *Knowledge and belief: Proceedings of the 26th international Wittgenstein symposium* (pp. 135-137). Wein.
32. Jäger, C. (2004). Epistemic deontology, doxastic voluntarism, and the princi-ple of alternate possibilities. In W. Löffler & P. Weingartner (Eds.), *Knowl-edge and belief: Proceedings of the 26th international Wittgenstein symposium.* Wein. Available online at: http://www.abdn.ac.uk/philosophy/staff/documents/ EpistemicDeontologyFinalVersion.pdf (Accessed 15/4/2011, pp. 1-15.)
33. Johnson, Ralph H. (1996). *The rise of informal logic: Essays on argumentation, critical thinking, reasoning and politics*, John Hoaglund (Ed.). Newport News, VA: Vale Press.
34. Johnson, R.H. (2000). *Manifest rationality: A pragmatic theory of argument.* Mahwah, NJ: Lawrence Erlbaum Associates.
35. Johnson, R.H. & Blair, J.A. (1994). Informal logic: Past and present. In R.H. Johnson & J.A. Blair (Eds.), *New Essays in Informal Logic* (pp. 1-19). Windsor,ON: Informal Logic. Reprinted in Johnson (1996).
36. Kim, K. (1994). The deontological conception of epistemic justification and doxastic voluntarism. *Analysis*, 54, 282-284.
37. LeBlanc, J. (1998). *Thinking clearly: A guide to critical reasoning.* Toronto: W.W. Norton.
38. Lehrer, K. (1981). A self profile. In R. Bogdan (Ed.), *Kieth Lehrer* (pp. 3-104). Dordrecht: D. Reidel.

39. O'Keefe, D.J. (1977). Two concepts of argument. *Journal of the American Forensic Association*, 13, 121-128.
40. Paglieri, F. (2004). Data oriented belief revision: Towards a unified theory of epistemic processing. In E. Onaindia & S. Staab (Eds.), *Proceedings of STAIRS 2004* (pp. 179-190). Amsterdam: IOS Press.
41. Paglieri, F. & Castelfranchi, C. (2005). Revising beliefs through arguments: Bridging the gap between argumentation and belief revision in MAS. In I. Rahway et al. (Eds.), *ArgMAS 2004, LNAI 3366* (pp. 78-94). Berlin: Springer.
42. Paglieri, F. & Castelfranchi, C. (2006a). Belief and acceptance in argumentation: Towards an epistemological taxonomy of the uses of argument. In F.H. van Eemeren et al. (Eds.), *Proceedings of the sixth international conference on argumentation*. Amsterdam: SicSat.
43. Paglieri, F. & Castelfranchi, C. (2006b). The Toulmin test: Framing argumentation within belief revision theories. In D. Hitchcock & B. Verheij (Eds.), *Arguing on the Toulmin model: New essays in argument analysis and evaluation* (pp. 359-377). Dordrecht: Springer.
44. Pinto, R.C. (2001). *Argument, inference and dialectic*, H.V. Hansen (Ed.). Dordrecht: Kluwer.
45. Pinto, R.C. (2003). Reasons. In F.H. van Eemeren et al. (Eds.), *Anyone who has a view: Theoretical contributions to the study of argumentation* (pp. 3-16). Dordrecht: Kluwer.
46. Pinto, R.C. (2006). Evaluating inferences: The nature and role of warrants. *Informal Logic*, 26, 287-318.
47. Ramsey, F. (1931). *The foundations of mathematics and other logical essays*. London: Routledge & Kegan Paul.
48. Ross, L., Lepper, M.R., & Hubbard, M. (1975). Perseverance in self-perception and social perception: Biased attributional processes in the debriefing paradigm. *Journal of Personality and Social Psychology*, 32, 880-892.
49. Searle, J. (1979). *Intentionality: An essay in the philosophy of mind*. Cambridge: Cambridge University Press.
50. Siegel, H. (1988). *Educating reason: Rationality, critical thinking and education*. New York: Routledge.
51. Siegel, H. (1997). *Rationality redeemed: Further dialogues on an educational ideal*. New York: Routledge.
52. Siegel, H. (2004). Rationality and judgment. *Metaphilosophy*, 35, 597-613.
53. Stalnaker, R. (1984). *Inquiry*. Cambridge: MIT Press.
54. Strawson, P. (1962). Freedom and resentment. *Proceedings of the British Academy*, 48, 1-25. Reprinted in J.M. Fischer & M. Ravizza (Eds.), *Perspectives on moral responsibility* (pp. 45-66). Ithaca, NY: Cornell University Press.
55. Walton, D. (1990). What is reasoning? What is an argument? *Journal of Philosophy*, 87, 399-419.
56. Walton, D. (1998). *The new dialectic: Conversational contexts of argument*. Toronto: University of Toronto Press.
57. Walton, D. (2010). A dialogue model of belief. *Argument and Computation*, 1, 23-46.
58. Walton, D. & Krabbe, E.C.W. (1995). *Commitment in dialogue: Basic concepts of interpersonal reasoning*. Albany, NY: State University of New York Press.
59. Wenzel, J.W. (1979). Perspectives on argument. In *Proceedings for the 1979 Summer Conference on Argumentation* (pp. 112-133). Alta, UT: NCA/AFA.
60. Weston, A. (2000). *A rulebook for arguments*, 3rd ed. Indianapolis, IA: Hackett.
61. Willard, C.A. (1989). *A theory of argumentation*. Tuscaloosa, AL: University of Alabama Press.

Chapter 8
The goals of analogies

Paolo Legrenzi and Alessandra Jacomuzzi

Abstract We will present the mechanisms of transfer of the solution from one problem to the other and the cognitive and computational theories of analogical reasoning. Both transitive inference and analogical inference have been held to require a process of relational integration that have been localised to a left lateral region of frontopolar cortex. A more adequate task analysis is essential when attempting to interpret the imaging results.

1 Analogical reasoning

The analogies of human thought are based on the use of invariants in the fields of both perception and thought. When we are able to individuate a common structure in a visual or mental model, this helps us to see analogies between phenomena which at a first glance appear different.

Let's imagine you need to loosen a screw and you can't find a screwdriver, but you remember that there is a blunt knife in the kitchen drawer. There you are! You now have an instrument with a handle that you can get a good grip on and which has a flat surface that you can wedge into the head of the screw. You have exploited an invariant function, shared by a sharp screwdriver and a blunt knife; you have constructed prosthesis for your hand, which is not a normal screwdriver, but a blunt knife. No problem, both serve to loosen that screw.

This is an example of problem solving through what we call "analogical reasoning". We take our knowledge of a specific domain as the "source", which in this case was the screwdriver, and transfer it to a different domain,

Paolo Legrenzi
Department of Philosophy and Cultural Heritage, University Ca' Foscari, Italy
e-mail: paolo.legrenzi@gmail.com

Alessandra Jacomuzzi
Department of Philosophy and Cultural Heritage, University Ca' Foscari, Italy
e-mail: alessandra.jacomuzzi@unive.it

the blunt knife. By exploiting the invariance of functions we attain our goal: loosen that screw without a screwdriver (Holyoak, 2005).

The history of science is constellated with examples of this transfer mechanism. Probably the most well-known is the comparison between the composition of the atom and the solar system, which was first formulated by the Danish physicist Niels Bohr (1885-1962). Bohr represented the hydrogen atom as a planetary system, with the sun in the centre and the planets rotating around it. The hydrogen atom has a nucleus which contains protons. Bohr hypothesized the electrons rotate around the nucleus in well-defined orbits: the orbit closest to the nucleus is assigned the lowest energy level.

Just like in the solar system, the distance from the nucleus (in other words, the range of the orbit described by the electron) is defined by the number "n", which can be any value. As long as it maintains its assigned orbit, the electron neither absorbs nor emits energy. If however it moves to an orbit closer to the nucleus, it emits energy, and, vice-versa, if it moves to an orbit which is further away, it absorbs the amount of energy equivalent to the distance between the two orbits.

Therefore a conceptual analogy corresponds to the visual analogy, which is the invariant between the solar system and Bohr's model of the hydrogen atom. The visual analogy, which is immediately perceptible and easy to memorize, acts as a guide to understanding the conceptual invariant.

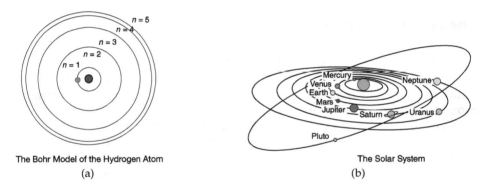

The Bohr Model of the Hydrogen Atom   The Solar System
                    (a)   (b)

Fig. 1 The atom (a) and the solar system (b). The comparison of the atom and the solar system. Bohr explained the hydrogen emission spectrum by picturing the hydrogen atom as a solar system. The power of Bohr's analogy transformed scientific thinking about the atom.

Invariants are also used in more abstract analogy reasoning processes, which are not based on visual models. Just think for a minute about how we protect our computer, a machine made of sand, petrol and metals, from viruses. When we think of a virus, we think of viral infections that attack biological organisms, for which vaccines have been developed over the years. The same can be done for computers, by writing software with an analogous protective function. True, there are differences between the viruses that attack computers and those that attack man. A computer with a virus doesn't run a temperature, for example. But all the same the structure is similar: both are contagious, both can reproduce themselves once they have entered the host and both can cause serious damage to that host. Therefore if we want to build an analogy between the two phenomena, we have to transfer what we know of a familiar system (in this case biological viruses) to an unfamiliar system (computer viruses).

If we take this step by step, we find that there are five sub-processes involved in analogical reasoning:

1. Retrieval: we must conserve a target in the working memory (computer viruses) while we retrieve a more familiar case in our long term memory (where the information on biological viruses is conserved).
2. Mapping: keeping both the source (biological viruses) and the target (computer viruses) in our working memory, we must align the two. The mind builds a bridge which rests on the properties that the source and the target have in common: they are contagious, they can replicate, they are harmful.
3. Evaluation: we must then decide if the analogy we have selected is viable and efficacious.
4. Abstractions: at this point, the invariants between the source and the target have to be isolated.
5. Explanations and Predictions: finally we have to develop hypotheses regarding the behaviour or the characteristics of that target, on the basis of what we know about the source (e.g., the way that viruses hide in order to replicate within the human organism and within the software of a computer).

Over the last twenty years these five operations on which analogical reasoning is based have been studied in numerous experiments and have been simulated using computational models. One of the first studies of this kind was conducted by Mary Gick and Keith Holyoak. It was in 1980. These two researchers devised an experiment, a problem and a solution, which they presented to the participants in story form. After having dedicated an appropriate period of time to what seemed like an irrelevant task, the students were given a second problem, but this time without the solution.

The first story told of a general who had to attack a fortress held by a dictator. There were several approaches to the fortress, but the dictator had had them all mined, to make the passage of a heavy army impractical. The general, having understood this, divided his troops into small groups, distributing them over all the access roads. In this way the soldiers were able to reach the fortress safely and capture the dictator.

The second story was about a patient with cancer of the stomach. The cancer could be cured by a laser ray, which was potent enough to destroy the cancer cells, but unfortunately would also destroy all the healthy surrounding tissue. The solution was to fragment the laser ray into smaller rays aimed at various points, which would then converge on the tumour without damaging the healthy cells. Just as the general split up his forces to ensure they would reach the fortress intact, so the ray was split up to destroy the tumour without causing further damage to the patient.

The analogy between these two stories – i.e., the invariance between the structures of the two – is not easy to see at a first glance. However, while keeping the conceptual invariance unchanged, we can modify the superficial resemblance to make the solution easier to find.

A great number of studies have focused on the interaction between the superficial similarities and structure of a problem, not only when a solution has to be found, but also when a decision has to be taken. The persuasive powers of analogies have swayed many an important political decision before now.

Following the Second World War, American politicians have more than once justified American intervention abroad on the basis of the situation that emerged from that terrible conflict. The usual story of the second world war has a central 'bad guy', Hitler, while the 'good guys', Winston Churchill and Franklin Delano Roosevelt, set things to rights after the bumbling attempts by the British prime minister Neville Chamberlain to negotiate a peace treaty. This story simplifies the course of history, reducing it to a stereotype, with the participation of Germany and Japan as the evil invaders, Austria, Czechoslovakia and Poland as the victims, and of course Britain and the United States of America, the heroic defenders, struggling for a better world.

This story leads to the following hypothesis: "If Great Britain and the United States hadn't stepped in, violence and injustice would have won the day", the reasoning being that if we don't use military force in these situations which appear analogous to World War II, then violence and injustice will set in.

It is a very convincing story, with emotional overtones, which many believe in. Various US presidents have used it to justify military intervention abroad: Harry Truman, 1950 (Korea), Lyndon Johnson, 1965 (Vietnam), George Bush senior, 1991 (Kuwait and Iraq) and, last but not least, George W. Bush, 2003 in Iraq again, a military operation which is still on-going.

Now the Second World War was extremely complex and it is not easy to draw parallels between that conflict and subsequent scenarios; the usual bad guy/good guy distinction does not always work in these cases, and can even by counterproductive.

Take the war in Vietnam, for example. It was 'also' the continuation of the uprising against the French colonialism in Indochina and not just a struggle against communist invasion, which characterized the Korean intervention. However, using the same analogy over and over again was effective in convincing the people back home on an emotional level, as it was easy for them to summon up the cognitive framework that appears to explain how things stand and evoke the appropriate sentiments, a call for justice to be done and help for the underdog. But in many cases, the analogy was so strong as to throw a shadow over the real situation. The problem is that the similarities on the surface of a situation are often much easier to see, and therefore very convincing, then the structural differences.

This mechanism was analysed for the first time by Markman and Gentner in an elegant experiment in 1993. The participants were given a number of stories to read. In one of these stories, a falcon is attacked by a hunter, but wins his friendship by making him a present of some feathers. The hunter, in exchange, allowed the falcon to live. After a week, the same participants were given other stories to read. Some of these new stories had a similar structure, others resembled the previous week's story only superficially.

One story with a similar structure, for example, told a tale of two nations. One of the two, Zerdia, is attacked by the other: Gagrach. Zerbia offers Gagrach the use of its computer system and the two nations become allies. Another story, which superficially resembled the hunter-falcon story, told of a hunter who liked to fish and eat wild boar.

When the participants were asked which story reminded them of the original story heard the week before, their answers were predominantly the stories that shared superficial similarities. However, when asked which stories were analogically similar, they cited the stories with similar structures. On a general plane, people are convinced, and get emotionally involved, by superficial analogies 'offered' to them by third parties, as was the case in the US military interventions, inspired by the second world war. When, on the other hand, they construct their analogies themselves, they tend to use the invariants based on deep-seated structures. A recent example of this is the migration of North Africans to the south of Italy, by boat. If you think of this situation in the light of the moving story of the poor Italians from the South of Italy who crossed the Atlantic in search of a better life in the United States, as recounted in Emanuele Crialese's film Nuovomondo, the analogy "Just as half a million Sicilians dreamt of a new life in America and migrated there a century ago in spite of the dangers and uncertainty, so today the North Africans dream of a better future in Europe" is absolutely natural and spontaneous.

This is emotively compelling. And it is the reason that the media are using the Italian emigration to the United States as an analogy to convince the local population to accept the influx of North Africans (try googling "emigrati in Italia come Italiani in America", http://www.instoria.it/home/migranti_consolo_lampedusa.htm).

2 Working memory and neuropsychology

We have already examined the role that memory plays in constructing analogies. We have seen that analogical reasoning uses long term memory: we have to know and have committed to memory the story of the Second World War, with its triad "the good, the bad and the victims", so that we can retrieve it at the right moment. If we have forgotten the story, the mechanism won't work. If the public doesn't remember the story of the Second World War, then politicians won't be able to convince them that the victim of the situation, for example, South Korea, has to be protected from the bad guy, not Hitler this time but the rabid communists of North Korea. This second comparison, based on presumed invariants, is possible due to the efforts of our working memory where old and new information is re-processed and compared.

Markman and Genter (1993) did important work in this area too. This time, their participants had to look at two drawings. The first drawing was a sketch of a man with a dog on a lead, in which the dog is trying to get at a cat (see

Fig. 2 One of the many pairs of drawings used to study the difference between relational and superficial analogies. The arrows indicate the answers evoked by adopting the two strategies: superficial similarities and relational correspondence.

Figure 2). The sketch shows the exact instant in which the lead breaks. The second sketch, in the lower part of Figure 2, shows a dog on a lead which is tied to a tree, a boy and the same cat. This sketch too shows the exact moment in which the lead breaks. The task was to compare the two drawings, for example: in the drawing below, what corresponds to the man in the drawing above?

When the participants proceed item by item, asking themselves what corresponds to the man? to the dog? to the cat? their reply is based on the similarities: the boy corresponds to the man, the dog to the dog and so on. However, when they have to make a global comparison between the two drawings, and not take one item at a time, their opinions change. The participants are obliged to make an integrated representation and so make matches on the basis of the relations between the various elements in the two drawings. In doing so, they realise that the function of the man in the first drawing is done by the tree in the second (both impede the dog from moving). Now the roles and relationships are important, not the superficial matches. It follows that when we make an analogy from a picture taken as a whole, our reasoning is different to when we examine the individual items of the same picture.

Relational analogies, which take the overall picture into consideration, require a greater cognitive effort than when we take the individual items one by one. Holyoak, Waltz, Lau and Greval (Holyoak, 2005, p. 128), demonstrated this by an experiment in which they asked their participants to execute a task in parallel with the drawing comparison task described above. While comparing the two sketches, the one with the dog barking at the cat and the other, in which the dog is barking at the boy, the participant had also to generate numbers at random. Having to do two mental tasks at once significantly increased the cognitive load and so the participants tended to limit themselves to superficial analogies, which are simpler and less taxing. Being easier to grasp and transmit explains why they spread more rapidly, but unfortunately they also tend to be less accurate and lead to erroneous reasoning.

The mechanism which induces us to limit ourselves to superficial analogies also kicks in when we have to make a decision quickly or are under pressure. Holyoak et al. (2005) devised a series of experiments in which the level of anxiety of the participants was increased by a stratagem, which confirmed this. Therefore superficial analogies are the most suitable to convince a number of people who are in a state of anxiety that a certain action is beneficial and necessary to set things right, as we have seen done in the recent military operations carried out by the United States.

To conclude, it appears these analogical operations require a lot of working memory, and the best results are obtained if this latter is completely free. This conclusion is corroborated by neuropsychological studies based on PET scans, which show that the areas of the brain involved in attention processes, in working and long term memory, i.e., the prefrontal cortex, are the areas activated during performance of this type of task (Wharton et al., 2000).

Analogical reasoning is one of the fields of research in which behavioural data were strongly confirmed by psychobiological findings, at least as far as studies concerning thought processes were concerned.

Geometrical shapes are used in Wharton et al.'s experiments; the participants are asked to examine various shapes and deduce the invariant structure, as in the example of Hitler and the Second World War (the good, the bad and the victims, etc.). Once the participant has individuated the visual variant present in all the initial stimuli (which is not easy) they have to transfer it to new and different shapes (i.e., as in the conflicts following the second world war, where the invariants were transferred to justify the use of military force in a situation which was only apparently similar). The execution of various tasks allows the researcher to subtract the activation of the cortical areas involved in the superficial similarity test from those activated in the relational similarity test and so identify the areas specialized in processing actual relational and structural analogies (see Legrenzi, Umiltà, 2011, pp. 23-28).

The fMRI technique has also been used to individuate the sites of the mental operations used to extract invariants, starting from the visual configurations. Take for example the analogy we have just looked at: Roosevelt is to Hitler as Bush is to.... Now, if we apply the usual analogical text to the American military operations based on the triangle of aggressor (Saddam), defender (President of the United States) and victim (Kuwait), the answer in this case should be

Kuwait. If you prefer, we can use analogies that are not so bloodthirsty and controversial, and accepted by everyone such as: the adult is to the child as the dog to the . . . (puppy). Silvia Bunge et al. (2005) used this type of task based on daily inferences made by analogical reasoning to study the corresponding neural activity.

The participants were presented with a pair of semantically related words (e.g., bouquet and flowers) and a cue indicating which of the two following tasks, an analogical reasoning task and a semantic task, was to be performed.

The analogical task consisted in two couples of words, one presented after the other and the participant had to say whether the second pair of words was connected analogically to the first pair (e.g.: first pair = adult-child, second pair = dog-puppy: correct answer = yes; second pair = adult-child, dog-cat: correct answer = no). The semantic task consisted in saying whether the meanings of the words of the second pair were related. The associative strength of the word pairs varied so as to separate the effect of the semantic similarity from that of the analogical reasoning, and this allowed the researchers to discover that the frontopolar cortex is activated in the analogical reasoning task but not in the semantic task which activated a different area of the brain.

Green et al. (2006) conducted another study based on analogical reasoning and localization using fMRI, using an experiment similar to that of Silvia Bunge. In this experiment the participants were asked to decide if four words were connected by analogy or similarity of meaning not based on analogy. Green also used word pairs that were not analogical such as cow/milk; duck/water, where the individual components of both pairs are semantically connected. The terms cow and duck are both members of the same category (animals), as are milk and water (liquids), but they do not form analogies: a cow is NOT related to milk in the same way as a duck is related to water. The fMRI scan indicated that only the left side of the frontopolar cortex was involved in the integration of the abstract relation that lead to the analogy. The other tasks activate other areas.

These and other more recent studies described by Shallice and Cooper (2011), show that there are areas of the brain which are highly specialized in the various analogical reasoning tasks, however similar these might appear. These are very interesting discoveries as they validate sophisticated models which require that the diverse cognitive processes are as separate as their cerebral sites.

They also demonstrate the need to obtain behavioural data through different types of analogical reasoning, as it has been seen that it is only possible to find the cerebral sites of the various mental processes involved by the different tasks if a detailed model of inference forms is used. If this is not done, it would be no easy matter to disentangle the experimental task from the control task, which have to be defined appropriately and correctly so that the cerebral activations relative to the two tasks can be subtracted (Legrenzi and Umiltà, op. cit.).

And so it has been definitively demonstrated that the logical notion of relation, to which philosophers and psychologists have dedicated years of study convinced that it is the result of a process of abstraction has "a specific material basis and so the A is to B statement is held to result in priming not only the concepts A and B but also of the operation of the relation that maps A to B" (Shallice and Cooper, 2011, p. 472).

3 The goals of analogy and computational models

As well as being studied in experiments, analogies are simulated in computational models. Analogical mapping can be performed by algorithms based on a partial graph matching (Holyoak, 2005, p. 132). The basic knowledge representation for the input is based on a notation in the style of predicate calculus. Consider the example based on the World War II analogy as it was used by President George Bush Senior. The Source of the analogy and the Target are the following:

SOURCE

Führer of (Hitler, Germany)
occupy (Germany, Austria)
evil (Hitler)
cause [evil (Hitler), occupy (Germany, Austria)]
prime-minister-of (Churchill, Great Britain)
cause [occupy (Germany, Austria), counterattack (Churchill, Hitler)]

TARGET

President-of (Hussein, Iraq)
invade (Iraq, Kuwait)
evil (Hussein)
cause [evil (Hussein), invade (Iraq, Kuwait)]
president-of (Bush, United States)

The goal of the algorithm is a procedure for finding graph matches that satisfy certain criteria. More in general, the procedures of the algorithm must simulate the cerebral processes.

Study of the analogy shows that these three methods are complementary:

- Experiments, by which we infiltrate the mind to see how it works
- Simulations, to construct integrated models on which to base previsions
- Cerebral locations, which allow us to ascertain that the differences in the model and the experimental data correspond to differences in the localization of the processes.

Lately, for reasons which would take too long to analyse here (see Legrenzi and Umiltà, 2011), the cerebral location method has come into vogue. However there is a general lack of a clear understanding as to how this method really works: it requires that the subtractive method be applied and therefore the study of the differences between two tasks. The issue is that the only way to individuate these tasks is by experimenting.

The study of analogy can share the same methodological and epistemological conclusions reached by Castelfranchi and Falcone (2010, p. 361):

> Trust cannot be reduced to a simple, vague, unitary notion and activation: it is a complex structure of representations, related feelings, dispositions, decisions and actions.

There is an even narrower parallel between analogical reasoning and trust which makes reductionism even more hazardous. We have seen that the analogies used in many political decisions have been exploited to convince the public of the pertinence of a certain strategy. If these analogies are used in bad faith, or to manipulate, then the risk is that the public's trust will be undermined. Once again, Castelfranchi and Falcone have hit the nail on the head:

> Trust in politics and institutions are (or better, should be) relative to collective achievements, public interests, ideal attainments. So the frustration of these achievements over a long duration can have different solutions.

Needless to say, at the origins of this frustration there is frequently a misused analogy.

References

1. Bunge, S.A., & Wallis, J.D. (Eds.) (2008). *Neuroscience of rule-governed behaviour*. Oxford: Oxford University Press.
2. Bunge, S.A., Wendelken, C., Badre, D., & Wagner, A.D. (2005). Analogical reasoning and prefrontal cortex: Evidence for separable retrieval and integration mechanisms. *Cerebral Cortex*, 15, 239-249.
3. Castelfranchi, C., & Falcone, R. (2010). *Trust theory. A socio-cognitive and computational model*. Chichester: Wiley.
4. Green, A.E., Fugelsang, J.A., Kraemer, D.J., Shamosh, N.A., & Dunbar, K.M. (2006). Frontopolar cortex mediates abstract integration in analogy. *Brain Research*, 1096, 125-137.
5. Holyoak, K.J. (2005). Analogy. In K.J. Holyoak & R.G. Morrison (Eds.), *The Cambridge Handbook of Thinking and Reasoning* (pp. 117-142). Cambridge: Cambridge University Press.
6. Legrenzi, P., & Umiltà, C. (2011). *Neuromania. On the limits of brain science*. Oxford: Oxford University Press.
7. Markman, A.B., & Gentner, D. (1993). Structural alignment during similarity comparison. *Cognitive Psychology*, 23, 431-467.
8. Shallice, T., & Cooper, R.P. (2011). *The organisation of mind*. Oxford: Oxford University Press.
9. Wharton, C.M., Grafman, J., Flitman, S.S., Hansen, E.K. Brauner, E.K., Marks, J., Honda, M. (2000). Toward neuroanatomical models of analogy: A positron emission tomography study of analogical mapping. *Cognitive Psychology*, 40, 173-197.

Chapter 9
A note on the reward-loss duality in time consistent decisions

Nicola Dimitri

Abstract In a simple dynamic framework with two payoffs this note considers time consistent decision making for symmetric rewards and losses, when individuals preferences for future payoffs are not affected by their sign. In pointing out a behavioral duality, implying that consistent individuals either choose higher rewards later and smaller losses earlier, or smaller rewards earlier and higher losses later, the paper suggests that further work is needed for a full understanding of the role of time patience, *vs* payoff concern, in explaining dynamic choice.

1 Introduction

Individuals choosing among payoffs available at different points in time are considered to be rational if they are dynamically consistent (DC), namely if their choices match their action plans (Frederick at al. 2002, Rick and Loewenstein, 2008). For example, consider a person facing today the choice between $2€$ in *10* days and $3€$ in *15* days. She is DC if prior to reaching the 10th day she either (i) plans to choose $2€$, which she effectively chooses when the 10th day comes or else (ii) she plans to choose, and indeed opts for, $3€$ at the 15th day.

As a consequence, a received wisdom emerged that consistency of plans and actions has to do with the individual's *willingness to wait* for future payoffs (Mc Lure et al. 2004, 2007) In the above example, DC is the case when either the person is *"relatively impatient"*, and favours the earlier payoff $2€$, or else is *"sufficiently patient"* opting for $3€$.

Nicola Dimitri
Department of Political Economy and Statistics, University of Siena, Italy

Honorary Professor, Maastricht School of Management, The Netherlands

Visiting Professor, IMT Institute for Advanced Studies Lucca, Italy
e-mail: dimitri@unisi.it

However, a person's degree of patience does not necessarily lead to consistent choice of payoffs which are located at the same point in time. In particular, this communication discusses how symmetric rewards and losses (positive and negative payoffs, with the same absolute value) give rise to an interesting *dual* manifestation of DC. In the previous example, a person consistently choosing 3€ later will consistently prefer –2€ earlier while an individual preferring 2€ will consistently opt for –3€.

This is so when an individual dynamic preferences are not fundamentally affected by the payoffs sign. By this we simply mean, for example, that if an individual is indifferent between receiving +2€ in *10* days or +1€ now, it would also be indifferent between losing -2€ in *10* days or -1€ now.

In its simplicity, this *duality* raises the question as to whether DC should be mainly explained by payoff concern rather than degree of patience, as in the received view. In the light of some recent contributions, we also briefly discuss how brain imagining might help shedding light on this issue.

2 The results

Consider three consecutive time instants $t = 0,1,2$, and monetary payoffs $x(1)$ and $x(2)$, available at $t = 1$ and $t = 2$, though monetary payoffs are not necessarily the main motivating driver behind dynamic choice (Elbert 2009). And indeed, in what follows payoffs have a general connotation and should be considered as welfare levels. A person is asked to choose, at $t = 0$ and $t = 1$, between $x(1)$ and $x(2)$. Moreover suppose the discounting function (DF), namely the sequence of weights through which future payoffs are transformed into equivalent present welfare levels is given by $d(t)$, where it is standard to assume that $1 = d(0) \geq d(1) \geq d(2)$.

The weights $d(t)$ represent "shares" of the relevant payoffs, formalizing the idea that immediately available payoffs receive full weight while those located at future dates are assigned lower weights, decreasing with time. Hence, DF models a person's preferences with respect to payoffs available over time; we assume DF to be payoff-independent, in particular to be the same over rewards and losses.

Then $d(1)x(1)$ and $d(2)x(2)$ represent the payoff level that at $t = 0$ a person considers equivalent to $x(1)$ and $x(2)$. For example, if $x(1) = 2, x(2) = 6, d(1) = 1/2$ and $d(2) = 1/3$ then he would be indifferent between having $d(1)x(1) = (1/2)2 = 1$ at $t = 0$ and 2 at $t = 1$. Analogously, he will be indifferent between $d(2)x(2) = (1/3)6 = 2$ at $t = 0$ and $x(2) = 6$ at $t = 2$. By the same reasoning, $d(1)x(2) = 3$ is the payoff that the person, at time $t = 1$, considers equivalent to 6 available at time $t = 2$.

Dynamic Consistency (DC) *A person is dynamically consistent if she prefers x(1) (or else x(2)) at both t=0 and t=1*

According to the standard way to model decision making over time, in what follows we discuss the conditions for dynamic consistency.

Consider positive payoffs, rewards, $x(2) \geq x(1) > 0$ and their symmetric losses given by $0 > -x(1) \geq -x(2)$. Then, it is immediate to see that with these gains and losses DC is the case if the following conditions are satisfied

Table 1 The reward-loss duality of time consistent decision making

	DC with respect to $x(1)$ and $-x(2)$	DC with respect to $x(2)$ and $-x(1)$
$t = 0$	$x(1)d(1) \geq x(2)d(2)$	$x(1)d(1) < x(2)d(2)$
$t = 1$	$x(1) \geq x(2)d(1)$	$x(1) < x(2)d(1)$

Since the discounting function is payoff-independent, from the above two sets of conditions we can draw the following conclusion,

Conclusion 1 *In the three-periods, two-payoffs, framework considered a person is dynamically consistent towards $x(1)$ if and only if she consistently prefers $-x(2)$, and a person is dynamically consistent towards $x(2)$ if and only if she is dynamically consistent towards $-x(1)$.*

Hence, a person consistently preferring a *delayed*, higher, positive reward (higher payoff) would also consistently prefer an *earlier* smaller loss (again higher payoff), and viceversa. With three or more payoffs individual preferences would be much more articulated; yet the following general conclusion could still be made.

Conclusion 2 *With more than three periods and more than two payoffs a person consistently choosing payoff $x(t)$ will never consistently choose $-x(t)$.*

It is however worth noting that the temporal discounting of gains and losses is subject to an anomaly, known as the *sign effect*. Gains are typically discounted more than losses (Thaler 1981), and in many studies negative discounting was observed for losses (e.g. Loewenstein 1987), that is, subjects prefer to incur the same loss immediately rather than delay it (for a discussion, see Frederick et al. 2002, pp. 362-363). This indicates that real subjects systematically violate the assumption of payoff-independence in their DF. The standard interpretation of this fact is in terms of prospect theory (Loewenstein and Prelec 1992): it is assumed that DF applies not to the objective worth of the reward but rather to its value function, which assigns greater weight to losses in comparison to gains of equal magnitude. Under this assumption, the same DF can produce the asymmetry observed in experimental studies. But what mechanisms are likely to explain this differential concern for positive and negative payoffs?

Recent work (McLure et al. 2004, Hariri et al. 2006) with monetary payoffs, as well as with primary non-monetary rewards (McLure at al. 2007), based on fMRI imaging identified two main brain structures which activate when people choose between immediate and delayed positive rewards. When immediate rewards are chosen the activation of a limbic system area prevails, while in the latter case the activation of lateral prefrontal cortex structures prevails. Based on the above observations, with symmetric losses we ask whether we should observe activation of the same brain areas? Existing neuroscientific evidence is not conclusive on this issue (Xu et al. 2009, Faralla et al. 2010). The question is of interest for a better understanding of the determinants underlying dynamic choice. In particular, if the same areas would activate should we induce that consistent behaviour is mostly due to the degree of patience, while could activation of different areas be interpreted by a concern for the (higher-lower) payoff? The issue is open and its full understanding will require further investigation to appreciate whether similar, or different brain mechanisms, underlie choice between gains and losses. The answer may have important bearings on economic issues such as saving decisions, since individuals who decide to save accept losses today against future gains (Dimitri 2008), but also on the stability of intentional conduct in general, since many long-term plans (e.g. submitting oneself to painful medical treatment) require the same kind of present sacrifices in light of future rewards (Paglieri and Castelfranchi 2008).

References

1. Dimitri N. (2008). Decisioni intertemporali e risparmio. *Giornale Italiano di Psicologia, 35,* 783-788
2. Ebert J. (2009). The surprisingly low motivational power of future rewards: Comparing conventional money-based measures of discounting with motivation-based measures. *Organizational Behavior and Human Decision Processes, forthcoming*
3. Faralla V., Benuzzi F., Lui F., Baraldi P., Nichelli P., Dimitri N. (2010). Gains and losses: A common neural network for economic behavior. *LabSI Working Papers, 33.*
4. Frederick S., Loewenstein G., O'Donoghue T. (2002). Time discounting and time preference: A critical review. *Journal of Economic Literature., 40,* 351-401.
5. Hariri A., Brown S., Williamson D., Flory J., de Wit, H., Manuck S., (2006) Preference for immediate over delayed rewards is associated with magnitude of ventral striatal activity, *The Journal of Neuroscience,* 26, 13213-13217.
6. Loewenstein G. (1987). Anticipation and the valuation of delayed consumption. *The Economic Journal, 97,* 666-684.
7. Loewenstein G., Prelec D. (1992). Anomalies in intertemporal choice: Evidence and interpretation. *The Quarterly Journal of Economics, 107,* 573-597.
8. McLure S. M., Laibson D. L., Loewenstein G., Cohen J.D., (2004). Separate neural systems value immediate and delayed monetary rewards. *Science, 306,* 503-507
9. McLure S.M., Ericson K.M., Laibson D., Loewenstein G., Cohen J. (2007). Time discounting for primary rewards. *Journal of Neuroscience, 27(21),* 5796-5804.
10. Paglieri F., Castelfranchi C. (2008). Decidere il futuro: scelta intertemporale e teoria degli scopi. *Giornale Italiano di Psicologia, 35,* 743-776.
11. Rick S., Loewenstein G., (2008), Intangibility in intertemporal choice, *Philosophical*
12. *Transactions of the Royal Society B, 363,* 3813-3824.
13. Thaler R.H. (1981). Some empirical evidence on dynamic inconsistency. *Economic Letters, 8,* 201-207.
14. Xu L., Liang Z.Y., Wang K., Li S., Jiang T. (2009). Neural mechanism of intertemporal choice: From discounting future gains to future losses. *Brain Research, 1261,* 65-74.

Chapter 10
Self-deception and weak will: Fooling oneself as a form of procrastination *

Maury Silver

Abstract The issue of "self-deception" arises when one suspects that someone (a) is oblivious to obvious evidence, (b) has motives that are sincerely believed to be dominant while having conflicting subordinate motives, (c) avoids finding out about things that would require abandoning his subordinate motives in order to honor his dominant ones, (d) follows an "avoidance rule" that inhibits such a discovery from being made, and (e) is unaware of doing so and believes he is adhering to his dominant motive. The avoidance rule states: "If something is seen to potentially be evidence then 'don't notice it' or neutralize its import. If applying the rule fails to disable the evidence then reapply it until the evidence disappears." The avoidance rule mandates an active project of self-deception as opposed to passive motivated bias. It does not require that a person knows and does not know x simultaneously, but rather that the person recognizes evidence as increasing the probability that x is the case and then avoiding following up on it. Self-deception involves procrastinating investigations. Just as a student procrastinating writing a paper postpones writing while knowing this will reduce the chance of completing the paper and despite his intending to write the paper, the individual procrastinating an investigation postpones following a lead to x while knowing this will reduce the probability of discovering x despite his intention to ultimately discover x.

Maury Silver
Department of Psychology, Yeshiva University, USA
e-mail: stivelsilv@gmail.com

* This paper is, of course, dedicated to Cristiano. For the last thirty years he has been amused by our style if not our conclusions. What this paper lacks in wit and succinctness is John Sabini's fault since he is no longer able to supply it. I would like to thank Fabio Paglieri who alerted me to the relevance of George Ainslie's work to the analysis of procrastination and Judy Stivelband for not tolerating my grammatical errors.

1 Introduction

We sometimes remark that people are "fooling themselves" when they believe that they are more intelligent, beautiful, moral, witty, than they really are, especially if there is good evidence to the contrary. Let's call this sort of self-serving bias, "weak self-deception". Sometimes we use "self-deception" to denote something odder. A person appears to be deceitful, as if she were actively trying, sometimes successfully, to get someone to believe something untrue – this in itself is not nice, but it isn't puzzling; but if the someone she is trying to deceive is herself, that is puzzling, indeed[2]. This is the sense of self-deception that we shall be concerned with in this paper.

If you are deceiving yourself then as deceiver you must know, and as deceived you can't know, what you are hiding from yourself and that you are hiding it. Or so it would seem. This is the conceptual puzzle of self-deception. But self-deception is interesting for other reasons, moral and psychological, as well as conceptual. Morally: Deceivers deserve opprobrium and the deceived sympathy; the self-deceived merit both. Psychologically: What is the self-deceiver trying to achieve? How are the conflicting motives of self-deception related? In what sense does the self-deceiver as deceived want the truth? On the other hand, what is the cover up's payoff? If, by definition, someone in self-deception is not merely wavering or ambivalent, then what is her state of mind?

In everyday life when people gossip about someone else's self-deception or lament their own they are not primarily interested in examining a logical puzzle: the moral and motivational, psychological, aspects of what was done, or not done, believed, or not believed, is what is most important to them. Thus, an analysis of self-deception adequate to commonsense must include a solution to the psychological and moral issues as well as to the conceptual one. That is, if one's goal is an analysis of something real and not an illusion. As of late "deflationary analyses" have been the rage, and, at least in regard to the strong sense of self-deception, their task has been, as Mele (Mele, 2001) puts it, to unmask "self-deception", that is, to show why it is an illusion, and why, despite this, people believe in its reality[3]. We shall not consider unmasking accounts since they should be repaired to only if realist accounts fail.

In our analysis we follow Goffman's lead (1959, 1972) and construct ideal types of situations that people often see as demanding an explanation in terms of self-deception. For instance, despite patent evidence to the contrary: A father does not see the evidence of his daughter's drug addiction; a wife does

---

[2] On the face of it self-deception appears as odd and unlikely as the White Queens project in *Through the Looking Glass* (Carroll, 1865/1960). Alice sensibly tells the queen: "There's no use trying," she said; "one can't believe impossible things." The Queen answered, "I daresay you haven't had much practice. When I was younger, I always did it for half an hour a day. Why, sometimes I've believed as many as six impossible things before breakfast." In regard to self-deception our aim is to explain how Alice is right and the Queen's practice is unnecessary.

[3] Another sort of account is deflationary only as regarding the idea of self-deception within a unitary consciousness, for instance, Pears (1982). Invoking unconscious dynamics, a "divided mind," is appropriate if, but only if, a simpler account limited to conscious processes fails.

not notice her husband's affair, a mortally ill patient does not believe he is dying and thus does not write his will; a faded beauty denies to herself that her beauty is past; a dishonest merchant is convinced of his probity. In all of these cases, we are tempted to see a person as having fooled him or herself. For convenience, throughout this paper we will use "the father of the junkie" as an illustration of, and, test case for, our analysis. When necessary we will supplement this example with these other traditional stories of self-deception.

2 Criteria for and signs of self-deception

What would cause us, as ordinary people and not philosophers, to suspect a person of having fooled him or herself, rather than merely being ignorant or shamming ignorance? What are the criteria of, and the signs pointing to, someone being self-deceived?

If we see a person as self-deceived, then

– he seems to be oblivious to something that he should find obvious. If the facts are not of the sort he would know or be able to infer, we see him as ignorant, and the issue of self-deception does not arise;
– he has conflicting motives. For instance, in the case of "the father of the junkie", it is not surprising that someone who wants to do whatever is necessary to protect his daughter would still want to avoid the stress and disruption entailed by intervening in a sticky situation; but it is surprising that he never notices it when these motives clash;
– he sees himself as giving priority to his dominant motive where it is relevant. He does not see himself as ambivalent or wavering in his commitment to his dominant motive but rather wholehearted in his commitment. For instance, the father in our running example does not see himself as wavering or ambivalent in his belief that pursuing his daughter's welfare is more important than the pursuit of a nonstressful life. He might be resting on the divan as opposed to checking up on his daughter, but he would not perceive that he had chosen pleasure over duty. Rather, he would see that checking up on his daughter at present was irrelevant since she didn't have any problems at the moment, or any serious problems, or any problems that required immediate attention. If the father were to perceive that his daughter was a junkie given his dominant motive he would have to abandon his subordinate one;
– he is sincere. Given his values and past history we believe that he sincerely believes that he gives priority to this motive;
– he is not merely unaware of the conflict, but appears to be *working* to avoid this awareness, that is, in so far as he becomes aware of facts that would require someone with his dominant motive to follow up, investigate, or act, he neutralizes or avoids this potential evidence. In this way he does what a deceiver would do. Yet because we believe he is sincere about his concern for his daughter we simultaneously believe that he must be ignorant and not a deceiver. The notion of "working" is at the heart of the logical and

psychological paradox. For this reason we need to examine more closely what the concept of "working" implies.

2.1 "Working"

What is the difference between saying that the father is "working" to avoid the evidence rather than just saying that he is unaware of the evidence? When we claim that the father is working to avoid evidence as opposed to merely overlooking evidence we imply that the father is following a *rule*: "If something is seen to potentially be evidence then 'don't notice it' or neutralize its import. If applying the rule fails to disable the evidence then reapply it until the evidence disappears". Let's call this *"the avoidance rule"*. Notice that in such a rule the unwanted conclusion is what determines whether otherwise disparate facts are evidence or not. Since the only thing that these facts have in common is that they are potential evidence, the father must recognize that they are leads in order to avoid them or neutralize them.

In this sense the father not only misses the evidence but works at missing it.

2.2 Summary

In brief, the issue of "self-deception" arises when one suspects that someone

1. is oblivious to obvious evidence;
2. has motives that are sincerely believed to be dominant while having conflicting subordinate motives;
3. avoids finding out about things that would require abandoning his subordinate motives in order to honor his dominant ones;
4. follows an avoidance rule that inhibits such a discovery from being made;
5. is unaware of doing so and believes he is adhering to his dominant motive[4].

Let's consider some common examples of what the father might do if he were following an avoidance rule. Notice that the only things the following behaviors have in common is that they serve to prevent following up on leads. To avoid leads pointing to an unwanted conclusion the father might:

– avoid entering her room although previously he had done so;

---

[4] Other examples also are in accord with these criteria. For instance the faded beauty: 1. is oblivious to facts that would force her to realize that she is no longer beautiful; 2. she sincerely believes that she most wants to discover what she really looks but wants to believe that she is beautiful; 3. following up on her dominant motive will lead to a conclusion that precludes reaching her subordinate motive; 4. she works, that is follows an avoidance rule, to avoid this conclusion; 5. she is unaware of doing so.

– not notice that daughter's old friends don't stop by anymore and that some people who do don't look like students – at least not like wholesome ones;
– attribute her wearing long sleeves in summer to a new style – even though he doesn't check whether other teenagers are doing so;
– rationalize her new "listlessness" and shivering, as symptoms of a cold, even though she doesn't have other symptoms;
– blow off the "danger signal" of his daughter's withdrawal and touchiness as just typical examples of ordinary adolescent sulkiness.

These are all things that a deceiver who wanted to mislead others into believing that he was ignorant about his daughter's involvements might do. Yet, insofar as we are also convinced that concern for his daughter is his highest value we can not believe he is a deceiver. Perhaps there are symptoms of self-deception that would allow us to distinguish it from deception. Psychology might help.

3 Differences between self and other deception

It would be reasonable to assume that the behavior of a deceiver and of a self-deceiver is the same except that one is aware that his game is a con game and the other is not. But because the self-deceiver must be unaware of certain facts in order to avoid coming to a particular conclusion he is handicapped in his presentation and less flexible than a deceiver in his handling or manhandling the evidence. The father who knows his daughter is a junkie and is merely trying to hide this fact from others can use his knowledge to ferret out the facts he needs to best deceive them. For instance, he might hunt for his daughter's stash to make sure it's well concealed and thereby make sure that houseguests do not make embarrassing discoveries. If the father is self-deceived he could not make use of such specifics because he needs to be unaware of them in order to maintain his self-deception. The self-deceived, for this reason, risk blundering into unwanted truths or unknowingly betraying these truths to others. The deceiver does not have this problem.

Although the self-deceiver is handicapped by his need for evidence to be ambiguous he is dependent on ambiguity to maintain his self-deception. The more ambiguous the evidence the easier it is to deny or overlook its import. The more patent the evidence the harder it is to deny. Without ambiguity there can be no self-deception. If after coming across my daughter shooting up I claim that she has never used drugs then I'm trying to deceive others or I suffer from something much more unfortunate than self-deception.

3.1 *Payoff*

There are many obvious reasons why it would benefit one to deceive others, but what is the payoff for deceiving oneself? I can con you into believing that the money I am paying you for this diamond ring is genuine and not counterfeit. The payoff is obvious. I get a free ring. But deceiving myself that the diamond is genuine does not get me a diamond ring. We have mentioned one payoff: self-deception allows me to realize my secondary motives while believing that I am living up to my dominant motive. The father can think himself a good father while continuing to keep his comfortable routine. But why should he care about *believing* that he is a good father? Self-esteem can be propped up by belief as well as reality. The father trades being a good father for *believing* that he is one (Silver et al, 1989; Sabini and Silver, 1998). At the very least this will quell the anxiety of knowing that one has strayed from one's ideals.

3.2 *Which leads does a self-deceiver follow up and which does he avoid*

The father wants to *see* himself as a good father. To do so he need not avoid all evidence. Of course, he need not avoid following up a lead that points to his daughter's being "clean", but he also does not need to avoid all incriminating evidence if the evidence is not likely to be very incriminating. Following such leads pays off in that it is a way to "demonstrate" to himself that he is actively protecting his daughter's welfare without much risk that what he finds will disrupt his quiet life. Since he is indeed following up on leads it is not difficult for him to convince himself that he would follow hotter leads if they were to appear. And even if he is forced to realize that there are good leads that he is not following, who is to say that eliminating less plausible clues does not clear the ground for more probative investigations. Or that he will not investigate all leads in their time.

The demands of self-presentation are different for the deceiver and the self-deceiver. The deceiver needs to bear in mind how his behavior looks to others. Carrying out a less informative investigation when it should be obvious that a more informative one is readily at hand may look suspicious to his audience so he takes care to fashion a convincing presentation. The self-deceiver's primary audience – herself – is more tolerant, she can trust it to accept even a mediocre presentation. Since she does not prepare for a presentation to an audience of others she is more likely than a deceiver to inadvertently leak out information as to what her concerns really are[5].

---

[5] For analytic purposes we have made the distinction between other and self-deception sharper than it is. We usually use the term "rationalization" to cover insincere justifications of our behavior to others. But the line between justifications as pretexts and sincere justifications is unclear. Rationalization is one tool of the deceiver as well as the self-deceiver, but not all self-deception involves rationalization. The goal of a rationalization is to justify behavior;

3.3 *Deceiving oneself without self-deception*

We trust that we have shown that "self-deception" is potentially a rich psychological concept, but the riches are just an illusion if the concept is self-contradictory. But even if a non-contradictory sense of self-deception can be found it may not be able to carry the psychological and moral weight that made it of interest to common sense in the first place.

As Champlain (1977) points out, some sorts of deceiving oneself aren't logically contradictory, but rather they are just tricky to pull off. Champlain compares the difficulty of deceiving oneself with the seeming impossibility of strangling yourself – as you pass out you release the grip. Yet with a couple of props, a noose and a chair, for instance, self-strangulation is not so difficult after all. Likewise, counterfeiters can be taken in by their counterfeit. The counterfeiter is surely a deceiver and if he is in the supermarket and unknowingly changes his own real money for his own fake he has been taken in by his own deceit. In this sense he is self-deceived. This self-deception does not quite capture what is implied by strong self-deception since the counterfeiter does not use his suspicion that the "money" might be his handiwork to avoid evidence of this fact. That is, his behavior cannot be described by the avoidance rule. But putting this objection aside, using a case of deception caused by the self as a model does not capture what is of psychological and moral interest in self-deception. The counterfeiter wants money not the belief that he has money (Silver et al, 1989 and Sabini and Silver, 1998). He is not torn between conflicting motives. He just wants the money. We would not see his accepting the bill as an example of some flaw of character, except, perhaps, the flaw of weak eyesight. The self-deceiver is unwilling to face the truth; the counterfeiter has no hesitation in facing the truth. He is just taken in by his own handiwork.

Is an account of self-deception that is both non-contradictory and psychologically informative possible?

3.4 *Self-deception without self-contradiction*

To repeat: The self-deceiver is not in the same position as the deceiver. If the father in our example is a deceiver, then he knows, or thinks he knows, that his daughter is using drugs and he is attempting to hide this fact. If the father is a self-deceiver he does not *know* that his daughter is a junkie but he *suspects* that she may be. He may have clues, but a clue needs substantiation, requires following up. A clue is not proof.

Let us say that the father unreservedly believed that his daughter's keeping her door locked was proof that she was using drugs. If he simultaneously

---

the role of self-deception, on the other hand, involves strategies to avoid knowing what one would one would rather not know. For instance, the father might as part of his self-deception "just not notice" that his child was acting more withdrawn than usual. Once his child's behavior was pointed out he might rationalize his lack of vigilance.

unreservedly believed that she was not using drugs then he would be mired in self-contradiction. But this is not the case. He thinks that her keeping her door shut is a *clue* that she is a drug user. He does not believe however that it *proves* that she is. There is no contradiction between his believing at the very same moment that a particular clue makes a conclusion more likely and yet believing that all things considered the conclusion is false. The puzzle at the heart of self-deception, then, is not about the father's simultaneously knowing and not knowing that his daughter is a user. The puzzle is, why would a father who had his daughter's best interest at heart, and who suspects that she is using drugs, not investigate?

4 Self-deception as a form of weak will

The father's self-deceiving behavior can be described in the following way: He believes that his following a certain lead is the best way to find out if his daughter is in trouble, he desires above all else to help his daughter, but he doesn't follow up on the lead. Because of this inactivity he does not discover what as a concerned father he needs to discover. Aristotle considered this sort of behavior to be an example of *akrasia*, that is, "weakness of will". When a person displays weak will he wants to do something, can do it, has the opportunity to do it and does not do it. Procrastination is a form of weak will involving irrational delay. We hypothesize that *self-deceiving behavior can be explained as procrastinating following up on a suspicion. Self-deception is the result of such behavior.*

4.1 Would-be writers and concerned fathers: Some parallels between procrastinating work on a paper and deceiving oneself by procrastinating an investigation

If self-deception is a form of procrastination then there should be parallels between the behavior of a student procrastinating a paper and the father deceiving himself about his daughter's situation. For instance:

- Both the student and the father know what they should do in order to be likely to bring off successfully that which they most desire. The student knows he must start working on his paper and the father knows that he must find out what his daughter is up to and that this involves investigating his daughter's behavior.
- Both the student and the father have conflicting motives with one motive being dominant. The most important motive for the student is to get the paper done and for the father it is to protect his daughter's welfare, yet these motives conflict with the subsidiary motive of enjoying a tranquil life.

- Both the student and the father are not engaging in the tasks most likely to advance their most important goal – the student avoids the work needed to write a paper, the father avoids the work of investigating his daughter's behavior.
- Neither the student nor the father believes they have abandoned their intentions to write the paper or to look out for the welfare of the daughter.
- They both suspect that their procrastinating writing or delaying investigating will make success less likely.
- Neither the student nor the father, up to the last moment, believes that his delay in writing or his delay in following up on his suspicions about his daughter will cause them to fail to achieve their dominant desire. The student doesn't believe that he will get a failing grade and the father doesn't believe he will let down his daughter.
- If the student believed that he had so little time that if he did not work at the present moment, he would fail to write the paper, he would stop procrastinating and start working –or he would give up on writing the paper; if the father believed that if he did not follow a certain lead immediately, he would fail to discover whether his daughter was a junkie in time to help her, then he would stop delaying –or he would admit to himself that he didn't intend to help her.
- Both the student and father bring about that which they most want to avoid.

4.2 The ambiguity of the distinction between procrastinating and postponing

If the parallel between procrastination and self-deception holds then the determinants of procrastination more generally should also be determinants of self-deception as well[6].

Ambiguity is a primary determinant of procrastination. We start by examining the role of ambiguity in ordinary procrastination and then examine to what extent ambiguity plays the same role in self-deception.

Rational postponing is a necessary part of organizing, planning, and establishing priorities so that the most important tasks are the most likely to be completed. Trying to do everything at once is a way to not get anything done. On the other hand the line between rationally postponing and irrationally putting off work until it is too late to finish it at an acceptable level is often not obvious. It is not only ambiguous as to whether a postponing is really procrastination but also as to the nature and effects of the procrastination. The degree of ambiguity and the effects of being ambiguous on procrastination are crucially affected by the nature of the deadline set for the task. For this reason we shall contrast two stories of procrastinating writers one with and one

---

[6] Our account of procrastination relies on Silver and Sabini's (1981, Sabini and Silver, 1982) ideal type analysis. Since Silver and Sabini (1982) there has been little nonclinical work on procrastination. Happily this is now changing as can be seen in the recently published, "The thief of time" (Andreou and White, 2010). Also see Tice (1997).

without a fixed deadline. We shall then show that the effects of ambiguity on self-deception are closely parallel to its effects on procrastination. Obviously it is not possible to present all the varieties of procrastination. People are creative. We trust that our two examples are sufficiently representative to convince the reader of the close parallel between procrastinating and self-deceiving.

4.3 *Procrastinating when one has a firm deadline*

Let's say that a student, call him Dave, has a term paper due by the end of the semester. He knows that he has some tendency to procrastinate assignments. Still, based on past experience he realizes that he has plenty of time to complete his paper by the due date. He puts off starting to work. If he reflects on why he is "putting off" working on his paper he most probably would see himself as postponing a task rather than procrastinating. And he would do so with reason: He has more than enough time to complete the paper and immediately starting to work would cause him to forgo responsibilities and pleasures that require more immediate attention. Still he realizes that starting earlier is safer, and an observer, or Dave in a reflective mood, might question his priorities. Even at this stage it is to some extent ambiguous to him and others as to whether he is postponing or procrastinating. Time passes and he doesn't start working. Whether he is procrastinating or postponing starting to work is less ambiguous. Still, he may very well be right when he decides that he has other more urgent things to do instead of the paper. But now when he agrees to go to the movies with his friends, Dave, and an observer, might wonder if he really might be procrastinating. Time passes and he still doesn't start working. The focal issue now becomes not whether he is rationally postponing or procrastinating but whether he can make up for his delay by putting in extra hours and working harder than is his wont. If he thinks that this will not be a problem he can almost convince himself that he is not "really" procrastinating. Soon he realizes that postponing any more threatens his getting an acceptable grade. Whether he is procrastinating or not is not an issue. He knows that he is surely procrastinating. What *is* ambiguous is whether he can continue to put off work and still get an acceptable grade if he puts in extra hours. Must he get an "A" or does a "B" suffice? But what if Dave is uncertain which grade is acceptable? If it's a "B", then he can harmlessly postpone a bit more. But either way the point at which not working translates into forgoing that grade is unclear. For this reason Dave may discover that his putting off work has all but determined that he is working for a "B" even though he had not made up his mind that it was acceptable to get a "B." At some point Dave realizes that he must start working. But now a new ambiguity comes into play. He knows that he must start working but what topic it would be best to write on may not be obvious[7]. After several false starts Dave decides on a topic. Now he is faced

---

[7] Teachers inadvertently increase this ambiguity when they leave the topic of the paper open: "Any topic is acceptable as long as it is creatively takes off from what we've covered in class". Leaving the length of the paper unspecified has a similar although smaller effect.

with new ambiguities: How much reading and note taking needs to be done before starting to write the paper. Persevering on one part of a task – intensely reading and taking notes – and not shifting to writing until the last moment is a typical pitfall of procrastination. At some point it becomes clear to Dave that he has postponed writing so long that if he postpones any longer he will not get the paper done by the deadline. At this point ambiguity vanishes. Dave knows that he must start writing or decide not to submit the paper. When ambiguity disappears he works – even if he realizes that at best his paper will receive a poor grade – or accepts the consequences of not handing in his term paper. Where certainty begins procrastination ends.

4.4 Procrastinating when one has no firm deadline

One thing about Dave's assignment was not ambiguous – its due date. Not having a due date, or not believing that the due date will be enforced, makes it particularly difficult to determine whether one is procrastinating or not. For this reason procrastination is more severe at each stage when the deadline is ambiguous than when it is firm. Indeed, the notion of a stage, that is, an orderly passage from one state to another without regressing or skipping ahead, is not fully applicable to tasks with ambiguous deadlines. At most points in this sort of procrastination's trajectory it is possible to change one's mind and decide that the procrastination can be made up for or even question whether one is "really" procrastinating.

Consider the case of Jill who is working on her first novel. If she has no contract, then from the moment she embarks on her project, she knows that there is no set date by which she must complete the novel. Dave knows when he should get the paper in and that he risks unfortunate consequences if he does not get the paper in by that date. Jill does not have either of these goads. Still there is no such thing as the complete absence of a deadline. Jill is likely to realize, if only vaguely, that deadlines requiring her to finish her novel are likely to crop up; for instance, a job opportunity or having her third child might not allow her sufficient free time to finish her novel. But she does not know the form the deadline will take, or when it will pop up, or how serious the consequences of not having the work finished by this time will have for the possibility of ever finishing her novel. She is also likely to realize that if she postpones writing long enough, then at some point in the future she is likely to lose heart and find that her project has slid from unfinished into unfinishable. But she cannot predict when disenchantment will step in. Hence she can never be sure as to whether she is postponing or procrastinating, or whether it's time to stop researching and start writing. She will frequently be nagged by the suspicion that she is procrastinating, and this disheartening suspicion may contribute to making the thought of work less than pleasant. This may lead to even further procrastination. Of course she can always set herself a deadline. But self-set deadlines are likely to be unenforceable and easy to revise.

4.5 Self-deception and procrastinating without a deadline: Fleeting thoughts, suspicions, and knowledge

The father in our story of "the father of the junkie" is in the same situation as Jill, only worse. Jill knows the specific outcome she is trying to avoid – having an uncompleted novel – but the father does not. He must have some reason to believe that his daughter is in trouble. If this were not the case, the issue of whether to investigate or not would never have come up. Still, he does not know specifically what kind of trouble his daughter is in. Despite this ambiguity he could decide to base an investigation on the worst possible outcome. But this would be costly, in time, effort, and probable disruption, as well as being damaging to his relationship with his daughter. What would you think of someone who upon discovering that his child had cut a class, would without further reason start investigating the possibility that she had become a junkie. Paranoia is not concern. Of course the father might have a fleeting thought that his daughter who had cut a class might be a junkie. People often entertain fleeting thoughts involving worst possible outcomes. For instance, many parents have the fleeting thought that their child who is an hour late in coming home has been hurt in an accident. They typically dismiss this thought in the absence of further evidence. Fleeting thoughts are not the same as suspicions. *Suspicions* have grounds sufficient to raise the question of whether an investigation might be in order, *fleeting thoughts* do not.

4.6 Procrastinating without a deadline: "I never knew", "I never suspected", or "I was surprised."

In addition to not knowing *what* is wrong the father has no fixed deadline by which he can decide to measure his behavior. Dave, the student who must hand in a paper, at least knows where he stands in respect to his deadline; the father does not. If he has plenty of time to intervene then stirring things up by an investigation might be a poor idea and his inactivity would be a form of rational postponing. If not it is irrational procrastination. In the absence of a fixed deadline he cannot be sure. After all, problems do sometimes resolve themselves without interference and investigations may be disruptive of family life. Still he may realize that a deadline of sorts can crop up at any time, for instance, if his daughter is using drugs and is about to graduate from sampling the contents of the medicine cabinet to shooting up heroin. His situation is the same as that of the would-be novelist, Jill. Like her he knows that at some point action – writing or investigating – might become necessary, but he doesn't know when. Of course, as time passes and his daughter still seems troubled, or even more troubled than she had been previously, a sort of deadline emerges; but the ambiguous deadline that her gradually worsening condition over time provides is more obvious in retrospect than prospect.

These ambiguities go to the heart of a central issue in the explanation of self-deception: What sense does it make for a self-deceiver to sincerely say that "she did not know," or "she did not even suspect," or "was surprised," that x was the case?

4.6.1 Knowledge

Well, in fact, she does not *know*. Those who know that it's futile to write or investigate don't procrastinate. They know it's too late to do so.

4.6.2 Suspicion

The issue of "suspicion" is more difficult. The father must believe he has some reason to consider investigating possible drug use or not. If not, the issue of "procrastination" wouldn't come up. On the other hand, the line between "suspicion" and "fleeting thought" is vague, especially when the situation itself is unclear. Secondly suspecting that something is wrong is not the same as suspecting that one's daughter is using drugs; suspecting that one is procrastinating writing is not the same as believing that one won't finish a novel. Further, even if the father thinks that there is a possibility that his daughter is using drugs, it still may be ambiguous as to whether an immediate investigation is warranted. An investigation may provoke a scene and problems sometimes solve themselves on their own. And the father might have many suspicions in addition to "she may be using drugs" – that she is depressed, that she is having trouble at school, that she is upset because of some trouble in her romantic life. If his suspicion that she is using drugs is one suspicion among others, in retrospect, he can dismiss it as a "fleeting thought" and not really a suspicion at all.

As the evidence that an immediate investigation would be prudent accumulates the claim that "I never suspected" becomes more and more dubious. At some point self-deception slides into deception of others. (Or for the "blocked" term paper writer, Dave "I'm sorry that I procrastinated writing the paper; I was really interested in doing it" becomes just an excuse to mitigate a penalty.) At some point the father will have to realize that he must investigate or give up the belief that protecting his daughter was his dominant concern. For instance, if we knew that the father had seen his daughter putting a needle into her arm and did not ask what she was putting in her arm we would not see him as deceiving himself. If he said that he never knew his daughter was using drugs we would accuse him of lying and not self-deception.

4.6.3 Surprise

Jill and the father have a reason *to be surprised* when something occurs that forces Jill to abandon her novel or when the father stumbles upon his daughter "shooting up". Unlike Dave they could not predict when or in what form such an event would occur or what form it might take. Still, they did know that some such event would be likely to crop up.

5 An Evaluation

Our hypothesis is that self-deceiving behavior is a form of procrastinating an investigation. The result of that procrastination is self-deception. Has our analysis adequately explained the psychological and moral as well as the conceptual issues involved? Let's treat the conceptual issue first.

5.1 *The conceptual issue*

5.1.1 Simultaneously knowing and not knowing x

Does the concept of self-deception involve a self-contradiction? The simplest form of the question as to whether self-deception is contradictory or not, is whether it makes sense to say that a self-deceiver simultaneously knows and does not know x. Epistemologically "know" is, on some accounts, in a different category than "believe." Saying that someone "knows", asserts, on these accounts, that x is true. If we take the psychologically more plausible interpretation that saying that one knows something about x is to make a warranted assertion about x, then there is no specific point demarcating "suspicion" from "knowledge". Questions concerning "suspicion" and "knowledge" involve the question of how good the evidence for an assertion is. Hence one can translate the paradoxical sounding "know but not know" into "having enough evidence to warrant some investigation" and "having enough evidence to warrant a particular conclusion". In this sense one can suspect and not know in that one can have credible suspicions – believe that something is worth investigating - but still believe that in the end these suspicions will not be borne out – that the evidence will not turn out to be sufficient to draw a conclusion.

5.1.2 Simultaneously being the deceived and the deceiver

"Know but not know" does not, in itself, capture what we mean by the "self-deception". The notion that to be a self-deceiver one must simultaneously be deceived and be a deceiver does. On our account a person who is deceiving herself is *working* to not follow leads to knowing that x is the case even though she does not wish to abandon her dominant motive that would require her to find this out. She is doing this because discovering that x is the case would require her to give up an important but subsidiary motive. "Working" was interpreted as following the avoidance rule: "If something is seen to potentially be evidence then 'don't notice it' or neutralize its import. If applying the rule fails to disable the evidence then reapply it until the evidence disappears".

Let's examine how the notion of "simultaneously being deceived and a deceiver" as we have glossed it can be applied to "the father of the junkie":

The father encounters a lead that has the potential to demonstrate that his daughter is a junkie. Following this lead is in accord with his sincerely held dominant motive of protecting his daughter; however, following this lead would require him to give up realizing his secondary motive of maintaining a tranquil life. He puts off following the lead. He must be aware that something is a potential lead in order to put it off. This implies that he realizes that this will inhibit, although he does not believe it will preclude, finding out whether his daughter is a junkie or not. Hence he has intentionally done something that he knows is likely to maintain, at least temporarily, the ignorance that his adherence to his dominant motive requires him to dispel. What the father has done is analogous to someone taking down a sign saying, "Danger! Bridge out," when he believes that there is at least a minimal chance that the warning sign is correct. The driver since he is ignorant of the warning drives into the river. It would be sensible to say that the person who removed the sign had deceived the driver. How does this example apply to the case of the father of the junkie? Let's call the father in his role as deceiver, "A", and in his role as deceived, "B." A recognizes that something is a lead, that is, a possible indicator that his daughter is a junkie. His intentionally procrastinating following up on a lead causes B to lack information that he may need to determine whether his daughter is a junkie or not. For this reason B does not learn that his daughter is a junkie and misfortune results. What A has done is analogous to what the person who has removed the sign has done. He is a deceiver. Since the father is both A and B he has deceived himself. There is a possible disanalogy between these two cases. The driver is not aware that someone removed the sign. B because he is the same person as A is aware that B has prevented him from knowing something. Can A then be a deceiver if he knows that A knows that he has sat on potential evidence by his intentional procrastination. Of course, A's intentional procrastination is not an attempt to prevent the discovery of the daughter's drug use but he is aware that it may have this effect and still does it. None the less the father in his role as B, the deceived, is aware that B is procrastinating – in effect, "taking down the sign." We must alter our bridge example a bit, what if the person who takes down the sign does so not in order to hurt a motorist but because he wishes to repaint it; however, he is fully aware of what the result of the removal of the sign might be. Further let us assume that the driver sees the person taking down the sign but decides that someone taking down the sign most probably indicates that the bridge is finished - even though it is not. We could still say that the person who took down the sign had deceived the driver even though it was not his specific intention and the fact that the deception succeeded was partially the driver's fault. The case of the father is similar. As B he knows that A has intentionally "withheld" a possibly probative lead while knowing what the results might be. A has deceived B even though B is partly responsible for his own deception because he was aware of what A was doing. Since the father is both A and

B he is both the deceiver and the deceived; he is self-deceived. Because he is a deceiver who has caused harm by what he has intentionally done we condemn him; because he is deceived and thus been harmed he commands our sympathy. We see him simultaneously as victim and victimizer.[8] This is the moral import of self-deception.

5.2 *Are the criteria for self-deception captured by this account?*

Putting the issue of self-contradiction aside, does our analysis capture the criteria we laid out for something to qualify as self-deception? Once again we shall use "the father of the junkie" as an illustration. The self-deceived:

1. *is oblivious to obvious evidence:* Since the father puts off investigating he does not know what the results of the investigation would be. If he had the evidence the conclusion might be obvious. We accuse the father of "self-deception" when it is obvious in retrospect what leads he should have followed and what they would have told him;
2. *has motives that he sincerely believed to be dominant and conflicting subordinate motives.* The father sincerely wants to be a good father and protect his daughter as his primary motive and yet does not want to disrupt his routine;
3. *avoids finding out about things that would require abandoning his subordinate motives in order to honor his dominant ones.* If he does not know that his daughter is in serious trouble than there is no contradiction between taking his ease and being a vigilant father. Hence he procrastinates investigations that have a good chance of leading to a conclusion that would require action, such as would be the case if he were to discover that his daughter was a junkie. The payoff for such behavior is that he can fulfill his secondary motive without disrupting his belief that he is loyal to his primary motive. Besides the payoff of being able to maintain his ease he has the payoff that he can maintain his self-esteem as a vigilant father;
4. *he follows an avoidance rule that inhibits such a discovery from being made.* The father must recognize something as a potentially a good lead in order to procrastinate investigating it. He also needs to recognize a lead as not likely to be very informative in order that he may follow the lead without much risk and yet demonstrate to himself that he is vigilant. Insofar as he

---

[8] The father is clearly morally blameworthy. He did not intend to hurt his daughter but he did the sort of thing that he had to have known could hurt his daughter. In so far as self-deception effects our obligations to other people it is a moral flaw. Of course the extent of our condemnation of the self-deceived depends on the damage they have brought about. Still we condemn someone who on a dare drives down a highway blindfolded. He may luckily not run into anyone but he had done the sort of thing that could plausibly do so. Sometimes the only victim of self-deception is the deceived. The self-deceived faded beauty hurts no one but herself and she may not even hurt herself. Perhaps she is happier self-deceived. Goleman (1985) believes that the self-deceived are often the better for it. Still the self-deceived faded beauty, even the happy self-deceived faded beauty, displays a flaw, if not a moral one: She is weak, too weak to face reality.

believes that his motives are compatible he need not be ambivalent, nor wavering in his belief that he is doing what he intends to do;

5. *he is unaware of doing so and believes he is adhering to his dominant motive.* Since he has made himself believe that his goals are compatible by preventing himself from finding out that they are not he can continue to believe that he is adhering to his dominant motive although he is acting in accord with his subsidiary motive. This is reinforced by his investigating leads that are not likely to be probative.

Self-deception on our account is conceptually, psychologically, and morally complex[9]. It is not self-contradictory, nor mystifying. It bears analysis rather than unmasking. And most of all it does not need deflating.

6 A postscript on Ainslie's theory of weak will

We have reduced self-deception to weak will. Have we just taken two conceptual puzzles and bundled them into one? We think not. George Ainslie (2001) has shown how weak will, including procrastination, may derive from some basic psychological processes[10]. While the correctness of our account does not depend on the correctness of Ainslie's the compatibility of our account with this reductive analysis reinforces our confidence that our theory is correct.

In Ainslie's account (2001) irrational behavior is to be expected, basic, while rational behavior need be explained. For behavior to be rational, all things being equal, choices should be consistent. For example: After careful consideration you decide that you prefer one brand of radio, even though you would have to wait a week to pick it up, to another that is immediately available. If you are rational when the time comes and your need for a radio and your

---

[9] Does our analysis fit the other cases we mentioned at the start of the paper as well as it does that of "the father of the Junkie". Consider:In the case of "the woman who does not notice her husband's affair" the woman has conflicting motives. She desires to preserve her marriage and to avoid a wrenching confrontation. Presumably the first is dominant. If the woman were to follow the "lipstick on the collar" class of clues she would discover that he had a lover and given her dominant motive would have to confront her husband to save the marriage but she would also have to endure a wrenching confrontation. By not following up on these leads she will not know that her husband is having an affair so that she will experience no conflict between preserving her marriage and avoiding a messy scene.In the case of "the faded beauty" an actress who is known for her beauty but is aging has a dominant desire to find out if she is still beautiful but unfortunately since her beauty has indeed faded fulfilling this desire will conflict with a desire to still feel that she is a beauty. If she keeps procrastinating clues that would lead her to answer her question she would, at least for a while, believe that feeling and reality do not conflict. For instance she might avoid asking critics and only ask fans or hangers-on "how she looks".In the case of "the mortally ill man who does not wish to know that he is dying" the man really wishes to know what his condition is, this is his dominant desire; but he wants the comfort of believing that he is not about to die. Since finding out about his true condition will make these two desires incompatible he procrastinates asking the direct questions that would give him the answer.

[10] Ainslie (2010) has recently written his own analysis of procrastination as a form of weak will.

information about the radio hasn't changed you should stick to your choice. According to Ainslie (2001) when a choice is immediate people often do not do this. Indeed pigeons faced with an analogous situation do not do this. Rather they experience a "preference reversal." We sometimes say that they have "given in to an impulse". Why is this reversal irrational? Taking delay into account isn't irrational; delay is aversive and decreases the value of an option. When you chose in the morning you took account of how long you would have to wait for delivery of the radio, but the imminence of the choice produced a preference reversal. Preferences can be described by a hyperbolic curve, that is, the more imminent the opportunity to choose an option the steeper is the increase in my desire for it. When one decided which radio was preferable ten hours in advance the difference between waiting ten hours and a week and ten hours wasn't sufficient to prefer the radio that would be available immediately after purchase. But in the store the difference between waiting one second or a week for the radio is comparatively much greater than the difference between waiting ten hours and a second, or one week for its delivery. Since choice is hyperbolic we reverse our preference even though nothing but the imminence of the choice has changed. When you look back at your choice at a distance, imminence is no longer a factor and you regret your weakness[11]. This analysis of weak will applies in the same way to procrastinating on a paper. In the morning it is obvious that studying for an exam is preferable to watching a mildly pleasant TV show. When the moment of decision comes the goal of a good paper is still distant but the opportunity to watch TV is right at hand. You watch rather than work. Procrastinating an investigation, self-deception, has a similar dynamic. In the morning the father may decide that he should more seriously investigate what is wrong with his daughter even though he knows that such an investigation is likely to produce some disruption. When the choice of entering his daughter's room or just choosing a less upsetting but less probative investigation the annoyance caused by investigating is at hand while the fruits of helping one's daughter is still comparatively distant. The father "changes his mind" and puts off sneaking into his daughter's room.

What needs to be explained on Ainslie's account is why we do we not always act irrationally, always procrastinate. Sometimes the less imminent alternative serves a goal that is more attractive even in the face of the spike in attractiveness that enhances the imminent option. When this is not the case we have to do things to avoid succumbing to the short term spike. Let's say that you want

---

[11] On Ainslie's model (2001) because of delay has a hyperbolic effect on choice people genuinely prefer the imminent alternative. Why call this temporary preference reversal an example of "weak will" as opposed to just changing one's mind and then changing back upon reflection? In Ainslie's model the person choosing has no additional information about the two options nor does his values change. Presumably if asked he would give you the same compelling arguments for resisting temptation that he did originally. His preference reversal was also made without new evidence. It's tempting to say that there was new evidence provided by the imminence of the choice. However, delay was factored in when the person made her original choice. Hardie (1971) in a discussion of Aristotle's *akrasia*, points out that a preference reversal of this sort fall short of what we ordinarily mean by giving in to weak will since it does not capture the experience of struggling and losing the struggle to not give in to temptation.

to stay on your diet but know how tempting cookies are. How might you arrange now to restrain yourself then? You might arrange to prevent yourself from being able to indulge in the still attractive cookies – avoid snack parties, you might reduce the pleasure of eating the cookie – who knows, maybe there is an antibuse for cookies, you might brag to your friends about your "will power" in order to recruit potential embarrassment, or you might decide on a "bright line": "No cookies" is easier to enforce that "an occasional cookie."

Ainslie suggests that the most useful and also the most common strategy would be a form of reframing, bundling, that is, shifting one's focus from particular choice, say indulging in one cookie, to seeing a particular choice as part of a larger category - the first step in abandoning one's diet and not being able to wear that new suit for the upcoming wedding. As one raises a cookie to one's mouth one can see it as just "eating a cookie" or one can see the act as an instance of "going off one's diet" and predict that once you give in you are likely to keep giving in. Ainslie's analysis (2001) of weak will, especially in regard to the role of rationalization in resisting and giving in to temptation is considerably more sophisticated than what I have presented. But this much will do[12]. Self-deception then is reducible to procrastination, a form of weak will, and weak will is reducible to an irrationality that is inherent in human nature. Our account of procrastination is in part reducible to Ainslie's account of weak will (2001). Weak will and its variants procrastination and self-deception are omnipresent temptations only to be overcome by cognitive and behavioral strategies.

References

1. Andreou, C., & White, M. (Eds.) (2010). *The thief of time: Philosophical essays on procrastination*. New York: Oxford University Press.
2. Ainslie, G. (2001). *Breakdown of will*. New York: Cambridge University Press.
3. Ainslie, G. (2010). Procrastination: The basic impulse. In C. Andreou & M. White (Eds.), *The thief of time: Philosophical essays on procrastination*. New York: Oxford University Press.

---

[12] The correctness of our analysis does not depend on the success of Ainslie's account. Ainslie's account always remains on the level of a struggle between long term and short term choices. His theory has no place for notions such as self or character. He believes that these notions are not explanatory but, are in Ryle's (1949) phrase, "ghosts in a machine". Notions such as going against "one's real values" or "character" or "self" have no place in Ainslie's account, hence Ainslie's theory does not fully capture the ordinary sense of "giving in to weak will". We suspect that some modification of Frankfurt's theory of personhood and the will (1988) might help to fill this gap without letting in any ghosts. Baumeister's (1996) much sketchier theory of the will does have room for concepts such as "self" and "character". Even if no present theory is fully adequate, the existence of these accounts demonstrate that "weak will" is amenable to a reductive analysis. One way that procrastination may not neatly fit into the Ainslie account has been brought up by Fabio Paglieri (personal communication). He has argued that since according to Silver and Sabini (1981) procrastinators not only make choices based on comparative time intervals but choose time intervals before they make choices, Ainslie's theory may be circular. Ainslie's concept of "bundling" may be able to handle this objection.

4. Aristotle (330 BCE). *Nichomachean Ethics*. Translated by Crisp, R. (2000). New York: Cambridge University Press.
5. Carroll, L. (1865). *Alice's adventures in wonderland and Through the looking glass*. New York: New American Library, 1960.
6. Champlain,T.S. (1977). Self-Deception–A reflexive dilemma. *Philosophy*, 52, 281-299.
7. Frankfurt, G. (1988). *Freedom of the will and the concept of the person*. New York: Cambridge University Press.
8. Goffman, E. (1959). *The presentation of self in everyday life*. New York: Doubleday-Anchor Books.
9. Goffman, E. (1971). *Relations in public*. New York: Harper & Row.
10. Goleman, D. (1985) *Vital lies, simple truths: The psychology of self-deception*. New York: Simon & Schuster.
11. Hardie, W. (1971). Aristotle on moral weakness. In G. Mortimore (Ed.), *Weakness of will*. London and Basingstoke: MacMillan and Co.
12. Mele, A.R. (2001). *Self-deception unmaked*. New Jersey: Princeton University Press.
13. Pears, D. (1982). Motivated irrationality, Freudian theory and cognitive dissonance. In R. Wollheim & J. Hopkins (Eds.), *Philosophical essays on Freud*. New York: Cambridge University Press.
14. Ryle, G. (1949). *The concept of mind*. Chicago: University of Chicago Press.
15. Sabini, J., & Silver, M. (1982). *Moralities of everyday life*. New York: Oxford University Press.
16. Sabini, J., & Silver, M. (1998). *Emotion, character, and responsibility*. NewYork: Oxford University Press.
17. Silver, M., & Sabini, J. (1981). Procrastinating. *Journal for the Theory of Social Behaviour*, 11, 207-221.
18. Silver, M., Sabini, J., & Miceli, M. (1989). On knowing self-deception. *Journal for the Theory of Social Behaviour, 19*, 213-227.
19. Tice, D. (1997) A longitudinal study of the effects of procrastination, performance strength and health. *Psychological Science*, 8, 454-458.

Chapter 11
Goals evaluation and preferences dynamics: Amartya Sen's approach and a cognitive interpretation

Francesca Marzo

Abstract Amartya Sen's criticism of the mainstream microeconomic view of preference ordering will be proposed as a starting point to develop a cognitive model of preferences dynamics. In fact, following Sen's reasoning, we end up talking about 'cognitive agents', namely about 'belief based goal-governed systems'. This means that cognitive agents pursue a certain objective, following a certain plan to achieve a certain aim, because and as long as they rely on specific assumptions. Far from solving the problem of preference dynamics, this work aims to suggest an approach to the issue by highlighting a correspondence between some concepts developed by Amartya Sen and the cognitive perspective, in order to track a possible path for improving the theory of preferences in future works. First of all, a brief overview of the theory of rationality developed in cognitive economics, traced back to cognitive goal theory, will be offered. Then, the concepts of rationality and preferences as proposed by Sen will be presented. Both these overviews will allow us to show the strict link between the two ways of addressing the problem of rational choice. Finally, an application of Sen's Capability Approach will be proposed for future work: by taking into account the strong analogy between some concepts of cognitive theory and some basic issues of this approach, such as norm-driven behavior and functionings values, a suggestion on how to address the study of preferences dynamics will be originated.

1 Introduction

Taking the substantive rationality approach, and starting from the assumption that utility as profit is what *moves* human action, decision theorists have often fallen into erroneous interpretations of human behavior, wondering why people act 'irrationally' and do not conform to the predictions of rational deci-

Francesca Marzo
Libera Università Internazionale degli Studi Sociali "Guido Carli", Italy
e-mail: fmarzo@luiss.it

sion theory. By assuming that 'utility' is the actor's own ordering of preferences among outcomes and that it is consistent, but arbitrary, we can conclude something about his behaviors only if we know what he is trying to accomplish, that is, what his utility function is (Simon 1991). Nevertheless, following the theory of "revealed preferences", first formulated by Paul Samuelson (1948), rational choice theorists have typically pursued the aim of understanding and explaining the regularities of human behaviour as instances of self-centred utility-maximization (Colman 2002). But lacking any clear distinction between the concepts of utility and self-centred rationality, any deviations from a self-interest maximizing behaviour, when contemplated, have been considered as systematic errors in decision making due to biases and imperfections in human cognition (Connelly et al 2000).

Although biases in cognition and bounded rationality are fundamental factors in decision-making, they are not enough. Neglecting subjective goals and values behind strategic consideration about self-centred maximization entails the risk of leaving unexplained certain regularities, which can systematically affect decision-making (Castelfranchi et al 2004). Or, even worse, by modelling the decision process in a wrong way, we can incur the mistake of considering some characteristics of human preferences as common errors of cognition, although sometimes they can lead to better solutions of social games and to more successful interactions (Bazerman et al 2002). A possible way to avoid this risk is to develop models that take into account a clear distinction between "utility function" and "preferences".

This work, far from solving such a problem, aims to suggest an approach to the issue of preferences by highlighting a correspondence between some concepts developed by Amartya Sen in his work and the cognitive perspective, in order to track a possible path for improving the theory of preferences in future works.

First of all, a brief overview of the theory of rationality developed in cognitive economics, traced back to cognitive goal theory, will be offered. Then, the concepts of rationality and preferences as proposed by Sen will be presented. Both these overviews will allow us to show the strict link between the two ways of addressing the problem of rational choice. Finally, a cognitive view of Sen's Capability Approach will be proposed for future work: by taking into account the strong analogy between some concepts of cognitive theory and some basic issues of this approach, such as norm-driven behavior and functionings values, a suggestion on how to address the study of preferences dynamics will be originated.

2 Goal-Centered Rationality

Moving from the assumption that we cannot predict anything at all about human behavior without assuming in the subjects some specific *motivation* (goals, values, subjective rewards), a Cognitive Theory of Goals has been developed (see Conte and Castelfranchi 1995 and, for a recent survey of the theory, Castelfranchi's keynote lecture at ICAART 2011). The basic idea is that there are long term, rather abstract or 'universal' goals and values, or generic motivations that must be implemented into specific objectives and plans depending on the context and individual experience; and even 'impossible' goals that will never produce an intention to be achieved, thus remaining mere aspirations, utopias, and hopes. Goal-directed action and its motives and objectives must be taken into account in their being the only ground of utility, interpreted as a quantitative measure of these qualitative aspects of mind. The inputs of any decision process are multiple conflicting goals and the related beliefs about conflict, priority, value, means, conditions, plans, risks, etc. This 'quality' - the explicit account of the multiple and specific goals of the agent (from which agents' competition or cooperation follow) and the agent's related beliefs must be reintroduced into the model of the social and economic actor's mind.

Cognitive agents have representations of the world, of the effects of their own actions, of themselves, and of other agents. Beliefs (the agent's explicit knowledge), theories (coherent and explanatory sets of beliefs), expectations, desires, plans, and intentions are relevant examples of these representations that can be internally generated, manipulated, and also be subject to inferences and reasoning. The agents act on the basis of their representations, which play a crucial role since they both cause the action and guide it. The behavior of cognitive agents is a teleonomic phenomenon, directed toward a given result that is pre-represented or anticipated in their minds. A cognitive agent exhibits a 'representation-driven behaviour'. In this framework, the success (or failure) of his actions depends on the adequacy of his limited knowledge and on his decisions, as well as on objective resources and conditions, including unpredicted events.

However, a variety of non-instrumental goals (motives) is not enough for explaining human behavior, there are also different *mechanisms* for driving behavior and even different *decision mechanisms*. Psychological research shows that humans use different strategies, apply several rules, and consider different aspects of the same problem, depending on the circumstances, the context, and the way the problem is described (Payne et al, 1992; Payne et al, 1993). Since Kahneman and Tversky (1979) developed their Prospect Theory, countless studies have demonstrated that human beings do not behave as formal models would predict, and that is necessary to take into account several mechanisms.

The impressive literature about heuristics and biases in decision making shows that it is impossible to look for only one decision mechanism, suitable for every kind of decision process and situation. For example Slovic (2002) shows that when the decisions to be taken are quite complex while mental resources are limited, people resort to more economic strategies mainly based on intuitive affective appraisals of situations and scenarios - something close to Damasio's (1994) "somatic markers" (affect heuristic). These evoked affective connotations may actively enter the decision process together with the analytical evaluations (Miceli and Castelfranchi, 2000).

Not only the deliberation process does not follow a single model, but several times deliberation is bypassed. In some instances the decision is not due to a process of reasoning and comparing options, but is more a matter of recognizing the appropriate response. In other instances, the deliberation can be completely bypassed, as happens when physiological needs (as hunger, thirst, pain, or even addiction) or emotions trigger an action. Loewenstein (Loewenstein, 1996; Loewenstein and Schkade, 1999) calls them 'gut feelings', and describes how they can avoid cognitive processing and directly trigger a behavioral response, even when this irrational behavior can be harmful for the subject.

It should be clear that utility maximization cannot be considered as a true motive, but as just an algorithm, a procedure for dealing with multiple goals. We can define it as a meta-goal: a regulatory principle concerning the management of the explicitly represented goals and beliefs (Miceli and Castelfranchi, 1997).

For instance, the goal of avoiding and solving contradictions, and maintaining coherent and integrated knowledge, or the goal of believing the most believable and sufficiently supported alternative are meta-goals. It is by no means necessary to formulate these teleonomic effects as goals explicitly represented and processed in the mind, whereas it is sufficient to consider them as functional principles or adaptive procedures used to deal with mental representations. In the same vein, the goal of assuring the best allocation of resources, of attaining the greatest possible number of goals with the overall highest value at the lowest cost, is not a goal proper, explicitly represented in the system and governing its everyday choices: individuals act with concrete and specific goals in mind, rather than pursuing a single totalizing goal (Castelfranchi, 1997; Castelfranchi, 2003). Of course it is true that, to the extent allowed by their limited knowledge, agents normally choose the most appropriate goal (action) among the active ones that cannot be pursued simultaneously. However, this result is not necessarily guaranteed by an explicit goal of profit maximization: it is enough to be endowed with a mechanism or procedure for choosing among active goals on the basis of their value coefficients.

In this perspective, self-interested or self-motivated agents are simply agents endowed with and guided by their own internal goals and motives. They can choose among those goals thanks to some rational principle of optimizing expected utility on the basis of their beliefs. The fact that they are unavoidably driven by their internal motives, once considered their value, does not make them *selfish* agents. This is a matter of motives, not of mechanisms (Castelfranchi 2003). They may have any kind of motives: together with selfish or competitive motives, they may have motives defined as moral, pro-social, altruistic, in favor of the group and self-sacrificial, etc. Agents' attitudes toward others can be only due to specific motives in specific contexts. The comparison between these motives makes them formulate their preferences as considered value judgments.

For these reasons, agents playing a game and not behaving in the prescribed manner are not necessarily irrational: they may be simply considering other aspects of the game or, in Binmore's (1994) words, they are playing another game.

Therefore, before searching for different mechanisms, we need to consider that subjects have different goals, that they process them in order to reach the most important ones or to compromise the lowest value ones.

Decision processes may be affected by strategic reasons as well as by cultural factors, giving rise to different preferences, that in turn lead to specific behaviors. This is, according to us, the way to overcome the interpretational gap between the game theoretic approach and the 'social norms' one. More explicitly, different goals are generated in the agent's mind by cultural factors and weighted (considered) differently. In this way, different value judgments become the very bases for the strategic reasoning that characterizes decision processes in interaction. What we need to study is how these value judgments can change in different contexts.

Extending the arguments of preferences and permitting the preferences to change with context in a systematic way enables theorists to expand the scope of the theory.

3 Sen's Concept of Preferences

Following a parallel trail, Amartya Sen, who never found himself quoted as a cognitive economist, has developed his theories starting from a notion of rationality different from that of mainstream economics.

He views rationality as a power each individual possesses (without necessarily exercising it), of subjecting goals and values to reasoned scrutiny. In contrast with mainstream approach in Economics, to be rational does not mean to respond to some ordered preferences, but to be able to reason about preferences, goals and values (Sen 2002). According to this new point of view, optimization is no longer what guide everything else involved in decision and concepts such as social commitment, norms, moral consideration cannot be reduced to the maximization of utility functions.

In Sen's opinion different motivations, goals, values and reasons for choice cannot be described by the same preference ordering: human behaviour is the result of several motivations (sometimes in competition between each other) that cannot always be described by ordering preferences (Sen and Nussbaum 1993); when this should be possible, anyway, such a description can be appropriate but not necessarily complete (Sen 1997). Therefore, in Sen's approach, since there are none exact regularities of behavior, optimization, as well as other mathematical methods, is not the instrument to understand rational choice and to predict actual behavior: even adopting a rational decision framework we can postulate in our agents any kind of possible motive/goal: benevolence, group concern, and so on.

While the conventional use of the term "preference" in economics implies the assumption that an agent's welfare is self-centered, that her goal is limited to maximizing her own welfare, and that she makes choices in accordance with her goal, Sen (1987) develops a theory in which welfare, goals, and choice are concepts that cannot be reduced to a single one (they do not coincide with each other). In order to understand Sen's proposal, it is useful to report a survey that Sandbu (2003) wrote on traditional point of view and a new concept of "preferences".

It is possible to consider preference with respect to well-being: preferring x to y means that x produces more well-being to the agent than y. In this point of view, well-being is synonymous of pleasure, happiness, desire-satisfaction etc. Preferring x to y can mean desiring x more strongly than y, or obtaining more happiness or pleasure or satisfaction from the realization of x than of y. In any case, feelings, not beliefs, are central in this point of view, allowing preferences to be inconsistent and, then, a-rational rather than irrational. Therefore it cannot be taken into account if our aim is to investigate rationality.

The notion of "revealed preference", at the bases of economic definition of rationality, is exactly at the opposite of this well-being consideration: "preference" is just the ranking of alternatives that can be derived from observed choice behavior. Preferring x to y, on the revealed preference view, means choosing x when y is available. From this point of view preferences are rational when choices are conform to an internal consistency of choice. But there can be no coherent notion of purely internal consistency of choice: in order to claim that there is something inconsistent or contradictory about choices, we need to know something about the agent's non-revealed preferences, so that we may correctly describe the choice set (Sen and Nussbaum, 1993, Sen, 1995).

Both the well-being-based and the choice-based interpretations of the word "preference" have correlates in common uses of the word "utility". The difference has been recognized by employing the more specific labels "experience-utility" and "decision-utility", respectively (Kahneman et al, 1991).

We actually need another concept of preference, different from both the interpretations presented above: preference as considered value judgment. Interpreting preferences in this way, we can say that the fact that an agent prefers x to y means that she values x more highly than y.

Formally, the notion of considered valuation is still a binary relation: the main difference from the traditional economic idea of preference is that, in this case, preference is not synonymous neither with welfare nor with choice. It is a concept related to well-being since the aim of producing well-being may itself lead one to value something, but for the same reason it does not coincide (there may be other sources of value in competition with that one related to well-being). On the other way, if we value something we recognize that it can contribute to our own well-being (if we get it or we bring about it). Nevertheless, it is possible that what we value has nothing to do with pleasure and that to reach what we value most highly we need to pass through displeasure.

At the same time, preference as considered value judgment is also related to choice since I will choose something I value highly and act in order to achieve it; but, again the two concept do not coincide (there can be cases in which, due to human features, bias and wickness, most highly valued things are not chosen) Also on this perspective, there is another way around: there can be values discovered by behaving and choosing.

It is evident that, following this approach, we end up talking about 'cognitive agents', namely about 'belief based goal-governed systems'. This means that cognitive agents pursue a certain objective, following a certain plan to achieve a certain aim, because and as long as they rely on specific assumptions.

These assumptions are about what has been achieved and what not, about what is achievable, what is in conflict with what, whether agents are able and in condition to do something or something else, what is better and preferable relative to their aims, and so on.

Taking into account these considerations, we can see that the way the decision is presented, the way the alternatives are described, and also the order of appearance of the different solutions may lead to different choices thanks not only to different strategies, but also to different consideration of value judgments (different preferences in different decision contexts).

In the following we will try and show how this evaluation process can be analyzed cognitively by using the basic elements of Sen's most famous theory: the Capability Approach. This will allow us to figure out how to exploit such powerful concepts not only for studying society at the macro-level, but also to explore what happens at the micro-level, once the mainstream economics idea of rationality is left for a more correct interpretation of human choices and preferences.

4 Capability set, functionings values and preference change

4.1 Introducing the Capability Approach

In judging the quality of life we should consider what people are able to achieve. Different people and societies are different in their capacity to convert income and commodities into valuable achievements: the commodity requirements for complex social achievements typically depend on cultural factors such as norms and social conventions.

Therefore, far for being explained by the concept of utility, human behavior must be analyzed on the basis of what can be called agent satisfaction. That is why Sen (1993) introduced a more direct approach that focuses on human functionings and on the capability to achieve those funtionings that agents value most.

A "functioning" is, in Sen's approach, an achievement of an agent: it is what she manages to do or to be, given some commodities and depending on a range of personal and social factors. A capability, instead, can be considered the ability of the agent to achieve a given functioning (for instance, to use commodities).

Given this atomistic definition, we can understand two other crucial concepts in the Capability Approach: functioning n-tuple, which is the description of the agent's life (the set of what she is and does); and capability set, which represents the set of functioning n-tuple an agent can achieve: capabilities, then, reflect the agent's real opportunities of choice (often in literature the notion of capability is actually used as synonym for the capability set).

One of the strengths of this framework is its flexibility and the possibility of being applied in many different ways.

Two points are quite interesting for our purpose of understanding preferences dynamics: (1) there is no fixed or definitive list of capabilities, but their selection and weighting depend on personal value judgments, influenced by the nature and the purpose of the evaluative act (2) the Capability Approach can be used to asses individual advantage in a range of different spaces.

Furthermore, Sen's Capability Approach proposes a concept of a human agent situated in a complex social structure of ethical norms and conventional rules, which conditions and facilitates human agency and is not reducible to the interaction of agents engaged in optimizing behaviour. In fact, Sen's approach somehow brought back to economics some of the basic anthropological ideas of Adam Smith, long abandoned by the mainstream, and whose philosophical background can be found in Aristotle.

All human groups have a culture consisting of shared values and norms (not necessarily explicitly stated or imposed on the group by external authority); individuals act in their social reality on the bases of values and rules. There is then a very strong relationship between social action and those mental phenomena which prompt, guide and constrain that action: every behaviour in a social environment can only be evaluated when compared and weighted (both at micro and at macro level) on what is the "norm".

This social structure constituted by values and norms, on our view, concurs to delimit both the capability set and the functionings evaluations, taking part in the process of organizing preferences.

While several factors intervene in influencing the solution of different social dilemmas (i.e. objective attributes, environmental features etc.) shared norms are mental objects that directly intervene to limit the choice among solutions.

Indeed, it is possible to comprise four major categories of social norms: moral rules, legal rules, rules of practice and values as generators of goals While rules are object that clearly function as constrains in the choice of goals to be reached and actions to be performed, we need to consider not only the merely constrictive nature of norms if we want to analysis what happen from a mental point of view (not just behaviorally). In other terms, we need to consider their specific nature of cognitive mediators of social phenomena; (Conte, Castelfranchi, 1995). Therefore, assuming value as a belief that generates goals, we can overcome the limited point of view of considering only beliefs to be involved and concluding that norms, at cognitive level, are connected with motivation. Thus, value may be identified as a normative object in agents' mind that functions by restricting the set of goals to be adopted.

4.2 Evaluating Functionings and Choosing Capability set to change preferences

What is needed is a systematic model and a well-grounded theory of human preferences, with the purpose of studying the bases of their specific dynamics and processing in future works. To start with, on the grounds of what has been discussed about goal-oriented rationality and Sen's concept of preferences, we can claim that preferences can change: preferences are a context dependent construct because a preferential evaluation or decision always occurs in a given context and is influenced by the context. What we need to know is how, why and when this happens.

Our aim in this work is to suggest a possible development of this theory (on the basis of goal-oriented rationality) thanks to the concepts we have presented above (namely, capability set, functionings and norms) and to the ideas that in time have come out of private conversations between the author and Cristiano Castelfranchi.

Preference change can be described as follows. At time t1 the agent had at least two aims: achieving functioning 1 and achieving functioning 2. She was preferring 2 to 1, meaning that she was giving precedence, was choosing or would have been choosing to achieve 2 over achieve1 because she was giving more value to 2 than to 1. At time t2, she has changed her mind about her aims, and now she prefers to achieve functioning 1 over achieving functioning 2. But we can also put it in other terms, so that we have something different in defining preference change: at time t2 the agent has completely changed her aims: at t1 she was considering both functioning 1 and functioning 2, while at t2 she has changed her aims, either eliminating 2, or substituting it with another objective that was not there before.

Both these scenarios can be rewritten by using "goal" instead of "functioning" (as in a Castelfranchi's personal conversation on this issue), but we preferred to take this terminology on one hand to explicit the analogy between the two theories we are considering, and on the other, to be able to introduce in the analysis also the concept of capability.

Still reporting the idea of Castelfranchi about changing preferences, there can be at least three cases of this phenomenon.

First case: agent changes her preference from G2 > G1 to G1 > G2, because she sees or considers, at t2, new aspects or features, of the motivating outcomes. In Sen's terms we can say that this happens because new components of the functionings she preferred have been added to the outcome (expected results) and some of them are "negative" and decrease the functioning's value. It can be also the case that she sees additional components of the other functioning's outcome and some of them are considered "valuable", thus increasing the functioning's value. Thus, now (in this new mental setting) her preferences are reversed. Although it seems that her goals are the same, it is not so: additional features changed the perception of functionings and so the goals of achieving them. Norms, as Sen introduces them, intervene, in this case, in the process of changing the features and, consequently, the value of the functionings to be achieved. It can be said that, in certain cases, a new goal, behind the ones of achieving the functionings, is activated by rules of behaving leading the agent to reconsider the evaluation in the new context.

Second case: agent changes preferences on the basis of a change of prediction. In a more general sense, as suggested by Castelfranchi, this can mean that the agent's beliefs have changed. Viewing it from Sen's perspective, either her beliefs about functionings have changed (which reminds of the first case) or her beliefs about her capability set. This latter case is exemplified by the following scenario, suggested by Castelfranchi: before going to the cafè our agent has decided that a sandwich will be ok today for her because of the desired flavor (G1), for its ability of satisfying her hunger (G2) and for its being cheap (G3); she would prefer it to a big salad, good for G2, less good as for G1 (today), and as for G3 (since it is more expensive). But, once at the cafè, she realizes that sandwiches are rather small and one sandwich will not satisfy her hunger. So the sandwich's value relative to G2 is decreased, bringing down even the global evaluation. This will make the salad win, since the agent's previous preferences between sandwich and salad are reversed. In this case the agent's predictions (beliefs) about features of means to reach goals were wrong; therefore, because the commodities' features were subjected to wrong expectations, the capability set is changed, although the goals to achieve the functionings taken into account have remained stable. This interpretation can also fit for the sub-case of wrong evaluation of values/costs rate: in order to achieve funtionings we need some capabilities that have costs to be born: when we discover that they will be higher than the value of funtionings they allow us to pursue, our preferences between "doing/pursuing" and "not doing/pursuing" can be reversed. Also in this case social norms can play a role: when rules change, some capabilities can be considered as no longer suitable for achieving certain functionings, making it necessary to change preferences. For example, consider the possibility of becoming rich and famous by having sex with the premier of a state: in a society in which meritocracy and respect are very important values, the aimed functionings cannot be achieved by using such capabilities as being good looking and sexually smart. A change in the systems of values and norms leads agents to change their capability set.

Third case: independent of new beliefs or new salient features in the comparison of functionings, an agent's goal is abandoned or is activated: just goals changed, making relevant some features of the previous alternative functionings. This can lead either to a change of preference order, or to the search of new functionings. As a consequence, not only the agent can re-evaluate the functionings she aims to achieve, but she can also reconsider the capability set available to her. In this latter case, being everything under reconsideration, values and norms will be involved in the building of new strategies and plans of action.

5 Concluding remarks

The many uses to which the terms "preference" and "utility" have been put are a reflection of how useful the concepts are to social theorists of various disciplines. Yet this profusion of interpretations can be a source of confusion if not of serious fallacy. We believe that the concept of preference must be studied in its own characteristics, once we abandon the idea of a match with the concept of utility (idea at the basis of the revealed preferences theory).

We have tried to show a possible way to interpret the phenomenon of preference change, based both on Castelfranchi's cognitive approach to rational choice and on Sen's Capability Approach.

Assuming that the problem of preferences dynamics cannot be solved without solving more basic problems of cognitive processes, we aimed to suggest an analysis of what can happen to preferences when agents are dealing with the evaluation of functionings and with the choice of capability set (concepts incorporated for the first time in a cognitive analysis), in order to have a more precise idea of what to model in future works.

References

1. Bazerman, M.H., Baron, J., Shonk, K. (2002). You can't enlarge the pie: the psychology of ineffective government. New York: Basic Books.
2. Binmore, K.G. (1994). Playing Fair (Game Theory and the Social Contract). Cambridge: The MIT Press.
3. Castelfranchi C. (1997). Individual Social Action. In G. Holmstrom-Hintikka and R. Tuomela (Eds), Contemporary Theory of action, vol. II. Dordrecht: Kluwer.
4. Castelfranchi C. (2003). For a 'Cognitive Program': Explicit Mental Representation for Homo Oeconomicus (the Case of Trust)". In M. Basili, N. Dimitri, I. Gilboa (Eds), Cognitive Processes and Economic Behaviour. London: Routledge.
5. Castelfranchi C., Giardini F., Marzo F. (2004). The relationship between rational decision, human motives and emotions. *Mind & Society*, 5.
6. Castelfranchi C. (2010). Private conversation.
7. Collett, P. (1976). Social Rules and Social Behaviour. Oxford: Basil Blackwell.
8. Colman, A.M. (2002). Cooperation, psychological game theory, and limitations of rationality in social interaction. Behavioral and Brain Sciences. Cambridge: Cambridge University Press.
9. Connelly, T., Arkes, H. R. Hammond, K. R. (2000). Judgment and decision making: An interdisciplinary reader. Cambridge: Cambridge University Press.
10. Conte, R., Castelfranchi, C. (1995). Cognitive and Social Action. London: UCL Press.
11. Damasio, A. (1994). Descartes' Error: Emotion, Reason, and the Human Brain. New York: Avon Books.
12. Kahneman, D. and Frederick, S., (2002). Representativeness revisited: Attribute substitution in intuitive judgment. In T. Gilovich, D. Griffin and D. Kahneman (Eds.), Heuristics and Biases: The Psychology of Intuitive Judgment. New York: Cambridge University Press.
13. Kahneman, D. and Tversky, A. (1979). Prospect theory: An analysis of decision under risk. Econometrica, 47.
14. Kahneman, D., Knetsch J.L. and Thaler, R.H. (1991). Anomalies: The Endowment Effect, Loss Aversion, and Status Quo Bias. *Journal of Economic Perspectives*, 5(1).

15. Loewenstein, G. (1996). Out of control: visceral influences on behavior, Organizational Behavior and Human Decision Processes, 65(3).
16. Loewenstein, G. and Schkade, D. (1999). Wouldn't it be nice? Predicting future feelings. In D. Kahneman, E. Diener and N. Schwarz (Eds.), Well-being: The foundations of hedonic psychology. New York: Russell Sage Foundation.
17. Miceli, M., Castelfranchi, C. (1997). Basic principles of psychic suffering: A preliminary account. Theory & Psychology, 7.
18. Miceli, M., Castelfranchi, C. (2000). The Role of Evaluation in Cognition and Social Interaction. In Dautenhahn K. (Ed.), Human Cognition and Social Agent Technology. Amsterdam: John Benjamins.
19. Payne, J.W., Bettman, J.R. and Johnson, E.J. (1992). Behavioral decision research: A constructive processing perspective. *Annual Review of Psychology*, 43.
20. Payne, J.W., Bettman, J.R. and Johnson, E.J. (1993). The adaptive decision maker. Cambridge: Cambridge University Press.
21. Samuelson, P.A., (1948). Economics: An introductory analysis. (revised edition, 1985), New York: McGraw Hill.
22. Sandbu, M.E. (2003). Explorations in Process-Dependent Preference Theory. Ph.D dissertation. Harvard University.
23. Sen, A. and Nussbaum, M. (1993). The Quality of Life. Oxford: Clarendon Press.
24. Sen, A. (1987). On Ethics and Economics. Oxford: Basil Blackwell.
25. Sen, A. (1993). Development as freedom. New York: Knopf.
26. Sen, A. (1996). Maximization and the Act of Choice. *Econometrica*, 65 (4).
27. Sen, A. (1995). Choice, Welfare and Measurement. Cambridge, MA: Harvard University Press.
28. Sen, A. (2002). Rationality and freedom. Cambridge, MA: Harvard University Press.
29. Simon, H.A. (1991). Nonmonotonic reasoning and causation: comment. *Cognitive Science*, 16.
30. Sloman, S.A. (1996). The Empirical Case for Two Systems of Reasoning. *Psychological Bulletin*, 119(1).
31. Slovic, P. (2002). Rational actors or rational fools: Implications of the affect heuristic for behavioral economics. *Working paper*, University of Oregon.
32. Tyler, T. (1994). Psychological Models of the Justice Motive: Antecedents of Distributive and Procedural Justice. *Journal of Personality and Social Psychology*, 67(5).

Part III
Emotion and motivation

Chapter 12
What is an emotion in the belief-desire theory of emotion?

Rainer Reisenzein[*]

Abstract Let us assume that the basic claim of the belief-desire theory of emotion is true: What, then, is an emotion? According to Castelfranchi and Miceli (2009), emotions are mental compounds that emerge from the gestalt integration of beliefs, desires, and hedonic feelings (pleasure or displeasure). By contrast, I propose that emotions are affective feelings caused by beliefs and desires, without the latter being a part of the emotion. My argumentation for the causal feeling theory proceeds in three steps. First, I argue that affective feelings should be regarded as components of emotions because this assumption provides the best available explanation of the phenomenal character and the intensity of emotional experiences. Second, I examine the two main arguments for regarding beliefs and desires as emotion components – that doing so is needed to explain the finer distinctions among emotions and their object-directedness – and argue that they are unconvincing: Emotions can be distinguished by referring to their cognitive and motivational causes, and their appearance of object-directedness could be an illusion. Third, I present three objections against the hypothesis that beliefs and desires are components of emotions: This hypothesis fails, at second sight, to explain the directedness of emotions at specific objects; it has difficulty accounting for the duration of emotional reactions caused by the fulfillment of desires and the disconfirmation of beliefs; and there are reasons to question the existence of the postulated emotional gestalts and the process that presumably generates them. The causal feeling theory avoids these problems. I therefore recommend abandoning the belief-desire compound theory of the nature of emotions in favor of the causal feeling theory. However, a partial reconciliation of the two theories is possible with respect to the concept of "affectively tinged" thoughts.

Rainer Reisenzein
Institute of Psychology, University of Greifswald, Germany
e-mail: rainer.reisenzein@uni-greifswald.de

[*] I thank Maria Miceli and Martin Junge for their comments on a previous version of the manuscript.

1 The Belief-Desire Theory of Emotion

1.1 Basic Assumptions of BDTE

The task of emotion psychology is to develop an accurate, reasonably detailed, and comprehensive model of the human emotion system, including its interactions with other subsystems of the mind. I believe that, of the different theoretical approaches to emotion, the cognitive approach holds the greatest promise for attaining this goal. This belief is shared by many of my fellow psychologists, which partly explains why cognitive theories have dominated the psychological discussion of emotions during the past 30 years (e.g., Frijda, 1986; Lazarus, 1991; Oatley & Johnson-Laird, 1987; Ortony, Clore & Collins; 1988; Scherer; 2001; review in Ellsworth & Scherer, 2003). The same is true for philosophy (e.g., Lyons, 1980; Roberts, 2003; Solomon, 1976; review in Goldie, 2007). Likewise, cognitive theories of emotion dominate artificial intelligence research on emotions (e.g., Marsella, Gratch, & Petta, 2010).

However, the cognitive approach to emotions is not homogeneous. Rather, there are different cognitive emotion theories, and some are more plausible than others (see e.g., Reisenzein & Döring, 2009). In this article, I restrict my attention to what I regard as the most plausible version of cognitive emotion theory: the *cognitive-motivational*, or *belief-desire theory of emotion* (BDTE). Originally proposed by philosophers (e.g., Davis, 1981; Green, 1992; Marks, 1982; for an early version, see Meinong, 1894 [summarized in Reisenzein, 2006]), BDTE is attracting increasing interest in psychology and artificial intelligence research (e.g., Reisenzein, 2001a; 2009a; 2009b; Mellers, 2000; Marsella et al., 2010). Writing at the intersection of these areas, Maria Miceli and Cristiano Castelfranchi have been long-standing proponents of BDTE (e.g., Miceli & Castelfranchi, 1997; 2002; 2007; Castelfranchi & Miceli, 2009).

Seen from up close, BDTE itself turns out to be a family of theories rather than a single, uniform theory. What unites the members of the BDTE family is a basic assumption about the "psychological preconditions" (Meinong, 1894) of emotions. The assumption can be formulated as follows: A central subset of the mental states presystematically regarded as emotions – roughly, those that seem to be directed at propositional objects (i.e., actual or possible states of affairs) – presuppose, for their existence, beliefs and desires concerning these objects.[2] Beliefs and desires, in turn, are regarded in BDTE as basic kinds of representational mental states that cannot be reduced to one another: Beliefs aim at truth and have a cognitive or information-providing function, whereas desires aim at satisfaction and have a motivational function (Green, 1992, p. 18).

---

[2] Strictly speaking, this is true only for emotional reactions to events considered to be real (Meinong [1910] called them "serious emotions"), not for emotional reactions to fictions (Meinong's "fantasy emotions"). However, BDTE can be extended to deal with fantasy emotions, by replacing beliefs with assumptions (Meinong, 1910; Reisenzein, Meyer, & Schützwohl, 2003; Reisenzein, 2012).

To illustrate, according to BDTE, Mary feels *happy* that *Mr. Schroiber was elected chancellor* (only[3]) if she comes to believe that this state of affairs *p* is the case, and if she desires *p*; whereas Mary feels *unhappy* that Schroiber was elected chancellor if she is averse to *p* or "diswants" *p* to happen (which I shall here analyze as: she desires not-*p*), and comes to believe that *p* is the case. Hope and fear can be analyzed by allowing for beliefs held with uncertainty: Mary *hopes* for *p* if she desires *p* but is uncertain about *p* (i.e., her subjective probability that *p* is the case is between 0 and 1), and she *fears p* if she desires not-*p* and is uncertain about *p*. Several other emotions can be brought into the scope of BDTE if one takes the experiencer's pre-existing beliefs into consideration (Reisenzein, 2009a): Mary is *surprised* that *p* if she up to now believed *not-p* and now comes to believe *p*; she is *disappointed* that not-*p* if she desires *p* and up to now believed *p*, but now comes to believe *not-p*; and she is *relieved* that not-*p* if she is averse to *p* and up to now believed *p*, but now comes to believe not-*p*. Social and moral emotions such as joy and pity for another, or guilt and moral elevation, can be analyzed in BDTE by introducing other-regarding desires – desires that concern the fate and actions of other agents (see Reisenzein, 2010; and Castelfranchi and Miceli, 2009; Miceli & Castelfranchi, 2007).

Although the belief-desire theory of emotion has been around for some time, it has so far been only partially explored, both theoretically and empirically. At least it has been much less explored than the belief-desire theory of action, BDTE's cousin in the domain of goal-directed behavior. Just as BDTE assumes that beliefs and desires are the mental preconditions of emotion, the belief-desire theory of action assumes that beliefs and desires – in this case, beliefs about means-ends relations, and desires for the ends – are the mental preconditions of action (e.g., Conte & Castelfranchi, 1995). The belief-desire theory of action has, under a variety of different names and in several conceptual disguises, become the object of an extensive research program in several disciplines spanning philosophy, psychology, sociology, and artificial intelligence (for a selective sample of this literature, see e.g., Bratman, 1987; Conte & Castelfranchi, 1995; Feather, 1982; Fox & Poldrack, 2009, Goldthorpe, 1998; Mele, 1992; Reisenzein, 2001b; Wooldridge, 2002). No comparably extensive research program exists to date for BDTE, although several explorations of the theoretical domain have been made (e.g., Castelfranchi & Miceli, 2009; Davis, 1981; Green, 1992; Mellers, 2000; Miceli & Castelfranchi, 1997; Reisenzein, 2009a; 2009b; 2010; Reisenzein & Junge, 2012). As Castelfranchi and Miceli (2009) note, further exploration of BDTE is needed.

---

[3] As far as I can see, all BDTE theorists assume that under normal conditions (roughly, in the normally functioning, awake adult), the co-occurrence of the beliefs and desires required for an emotion is also, at least causally, sufficient for the occurrence of that emotion. Given normal circumstances, the "if" in the following if-then laws of BDTE can therefore be read as "if and only if" rather than just as "only if."

1.2 Emotions: Belief-and-desire-caused Feelings or Compounds of Beliefs, Desires, and Feelings?

In this article, I focus on one of the issues that divide the members of the BDTE family: the question of what an emotion is in BDTE. The answer to this question – the question of the nature of emotion – is intimately connected to the interpretation of the basic claim of BDTE, that beliefs and desires are necessary preconditions of emotions (see also, Reisenzein, 1994a; 2000). Three main proposals regarding the more precise relation between beliefs/desires and emotions, and corresponding to these, three main proposals regarding the nature of emotion in BDTE have been made. Illustrated for the case of happiness about p, they are as follows.

1. The *causal view* holds that the belief that p and the desire for p are (necessary) causes of happiness about p, whereas the emotion is a separate mental state, such as a feeling of pleasure or displeasure (e.g., Reisenzein, 2009a).
2. The *part-whole view* claims that the belief that p and the desire for p are not, or at least not only, the causes of the emotion, but parts of the emotion. Correspondingly, the emotion is conceived of as a complex mental state consisting of the co-occurrence of (2a) the belief that p and the desire for p (e.g., Marks, 1982); or (2b) the belief and desire plus other components (e.g., a feeling of pleasure or displeasure).
3. The *fusion view* maintains that happiness about p is a new mental state that emerges through a process of "fusion" (Green, 1992) or mental integration from (3a) the belief that p and the desire for p (Green, 1992) or from (3b) these two and further components (e.g., feelings of pleasure or displeasure; Castelfranchi and Miceli, 2009).[4] Characteristic of the fusion view is not only the assumption that the output of the fusion process—the emotion—is a phenomenally unitary mental state; but also the assumption that this state has emergent properties, such as a unique experiential quality (Castelfranchi & Miceli, 2009; Green, 1992).

In this article, I compare two specific versions of the causal view and the fusion view of the nature of emotions in BDTE: the *causal feeling theory* proposed by Reisenzein (2009a; 2009b), and the *belief-desire compound*, or *emotional gestalt theory* proposed by Castelfranchi and Miceli (2009).

---

[4] Philosophers typically classify the causal version of BDTE as a "noncognitive" theory of emotion. The reason is that their criteria for classifying emotion theories are the theories' assumptions about the nature of emotion. The causal theory, although assuming that emotions presuppose cognitions as their causes, takes the emotion itself to be a noncognitive mental state—at least in the sense that it is not, and does not include, a belief. (Note, however, that this still allows the emotion to be cognitive in the wider sense of being a representational mental state). Theories of types 2b and 3b are sometimes called "hybrid" theories of emotion, because they assume that emotions contain both cognitive and noncognitive components (e.g., Reisenzein, 1994a). By contrast, theories of types 2a and 3a are called "pure" cognitive (or cognitive-motivational) theories of emotion. For further discussion, see e.g., Green (1992), Prinz (2004), Reisenzein (1994a), and Reisenzein and Döring (2009).

1.2.1 The Causal Feeling Theory

Reisenzein (2009a) proposed a computational (C) model of the belief-desire theory of emotion called CBDTE, according to which emotions are the products of two hardwired comparator mechanisms that service the belief-desire system, the belief-desire comparator (BDC) and the belief-belief comparator (BBC). These mechanisms constantly compare, at an unconscious level of information processing, newly acquired beliefs about the world or the self with, respectively, pre-existing desires (BDC) and beliefs (BBC). If a match (p; p) or a mismatch (p; not-p) between the contents of a new belief and those of an existing belief or desire is detected, the comparator mechanisms generate non-propositional, sensation-like output signals that communicate the information about the detection of the match or mismatch to other cognitive subsystems. Based on this computational explication of BDTE, I then proposed that emotions should be identified with the output signals generated by the BDC and the BBC (see also, Reisenzein, 2009b). This proposal implies that emotions, although caused by certain belief-desire constellations, are distinct from the latter and do not contain them as components. Specifically, emotions are nonconceptual and nonpropositional mental states that are, when conscious, experienced as feelings of pleasure and displeasure, surprise and expectancy confirmation, combinations of these feelings (e.g., disappointment, relief), and hope and fear. A main reason for proposing this theoretical (theory-based; see Section 2) definition of emotion – the identification of emotions with the output signals of the BDC and BBC – was causal-functional: These signals recommended themselves as the scientific referents of the term "emotion" because, assuming that CBDTE is a correct description of the emotion-generating mechanisms, they constitute the "causal hub in the wheel of emotion" (Reisenzein, 2009a): They are proximately caused by beliefs and desires (the inputs of the emotion mechanisms) and they are in turn (partial) causes of all emotional effects postulated in the theory – emotional experience, shifts of attention, updates of the belief-desire system, emotional actions, expressions, and physiological changes. In addition, I argued that the proposed theoretical definition of emotion provides a natural explanation of the salient properties of emotional experiences, in particular their phenomenal quality and intensity (see also, Reisenzein, 2009b).

1.2.2 The Belief-Desire Compound (Emotional Gestalt) Theory

In contrast to the causal feeling theory, Castelfranchi and Miceli (2009) propose that emotions are mental *gestalts* in the sense of the Gestalt theorists (e.g., Köhler, 1947). As the authors explain, these emotional gestalts

> "result from the 'fusion' [Gestalt integration] of the BD [belief-desire] compound with affect (feelings of pleasure or displeasure). In this process, the BD compound is hedonically colored by affect, while the latter is specified and qualified by the BD compound. The emotional experience resulting from this fusion is...an emergent property which cannot be traced back to any single component of the emotion" (Castelfranchi & Miceli, 2009, p. 228).

To illustrate this theory, Mary's happiness that Schroiber was elected chancellor would result from the fusion, or gestalt integration, of Mary's belief that this state of affairs p is the case, her desire for p, and the pleasant feeling generated by the co-occurrence of these two mental states. According to Castelfranchi and Miceli (2009), the resulting emotional gestalt, although being a causal effect of the belief that p and the desire for p, can also be said to contain these mental states as parts.[5] Thus, the gestalt theory of emotion combines assumptions of the causal and the part-whole theory. It may be noted that the gestalt theory represents one of two existing explications of the idea that emotions result from a fusion or integration of several components. The other explication of this idea holds that the fusion process is a process of categorization in which the different components of an emotion instance or token are subsumed under an emotion schema (e.g., Mandler, 1984; Barrett, 2006). For discussions about this alternative, see Castelfranchi and Miceli (2009) and Reisenzein (1994a).

My aim in this article is to compare the two described theories concerning the nature of emotion in BDTE, the causal feeling theory and the emotional gestalt theory. This comparison is facilitated by the fact that, apart from their different assumptions about the nature of emotion, the versions of BDTE endorsed by Castelfranchi and Miceli and myself are close. Most important for the following discussion, both versions of BDTE assume that "emotional" belief-desire configurations (those considered to be necessary for an emotion; e.g., in the case of happiness about p, the desire that p plus the belief that p) cause feelings of pleasure or displeasure, and that these hedonic feelings are an essential component of emotions (in CBDTE: for all emotions but hedonically neutral surprise). Furthermore, we agree that the computational processes that underlie the causal link between belief and desire on the one hand, and hedonic feelings on the other hand, involve a comparison of belief and desire (on this point, see also Miceli & Castelfranchi, 1997). However, whereas I propose to identify emotions with the output signals generated by the belief-desire comparator – as well as the belief-belief comparator, which is not explicitly considered a part of the emotion mechanism by Miceli and Castelfranchi – Castelfranchi and Miceli (2009) identify the emotion with a mental gestalt that integrates belief, desire, and hedonic affect. These differences in the theoretical definition of emotion imply another, causal or processual difference between our respective versions of BDTE: Whereas Castelfranchi and Miceli are committed to the existence of the hypothesized gestalt formation process and its outcomes, the emotional gestalts, CBDTE assumes neither a gestalt formation

---

[5] At first sight, a component α of a complex mental state $\gamma = (\alpha \,\&\, \beta)$ cannot also be the cause of γ, for that would imply self-causation, something generally regarded as impossible (see e.g., Mackie, 1974; Reisenzein & Schönpflug, 1992). Castelfranchi and Miceli (2009, p. 229) concede this point but argue as follows: "the BD [belief-desire] compound. . . (α). . . together with affect (β) causes the emotional gestalt (γ). . . when α is included into γ, it is no longer there as such; rather, in virtue of its being part of the whole (γ), it changes into α'. This is analogous to a line segment that, when it merges with other lines into the gestalt of a triangle, is no longer perceived as a (mere) line segment but as a side of the triangle. If this is accepted, one can legitimately talk about the BD compound as being both a cause (α) and a constituent (α') of emotions."

process nor emotional gestalts.[6] Castelfranchi and Miceli's version of BDTE is therefore, in this respect at least, more complex than CBDTE.

2 What is a Definition of Emotion?

Before proceeding, I need to address an antecedent issue. This issue concerns the metatheoretical status of the problem under discussion, the question "What is an emotion in BDTE?"

The issue addressed by the question "What is an emotion?" is traditionally called the problem of the *nature* of emotion. Alternatively, it is called the problem of the *definition* of emotion (e.g., Scherer, 2005). I will use the latter formulation because it is more general. As usually understood, a definition is a specification of the essential or necessary (or, if such don't exist, at least the typical) features of a class of objects. Since Aristotle, two different bases of definitional necessity have been distinguished: linguistic conventions and the structure of language-independent reality. These two bases of necessity are reflected in the traditional distinction between nominal and real definitions (e.g., Boyd, 2002). As traditionally understood, *nominal definitions* reflect conventions about how a term is to be used, whereas *real definitions* capture the pre-existing essential properties of a class of objects.

In terms of this distinction, the question "What is an emotion?" seems to be prima facie asking for a real definition: a description of the nature of emotions, their pre-existing essential features. And this is how the question has been understood by most classical (e.g., James, 1890/1950; Meinong, 1894; Wundt, 1896) and many contemporary emotion theorists (e.g., Arnold, 1960; Schachter, 1964), at least in psychology.[7] However, during the heyday of logical empiricism, the view became popular that the concept of real definition is obscure and unscientific (e.g., Hempel, 1965). For the adherents of this view, the question "What is an emotion?" and parallel questions about specific emotions, such as "What is fear?", which prima facie seem to ask for real definitions, are either nonsensical or need to be reinterpreted in ways consistent with the

---

[6] Apart from the question of the nature of emotion, there are several other differences between our respective versions of BDTE. For example, Miceli and Castelfranchi (1997) assume that at least for some kinds of emotions, the belief-desire comparison process involves meta-beliefs about the presence of a discrepancy between belief and desire, whereas I reject this idea (Reisenzein, 2009a). I distinguish between emotions and emotional experience, whereas Castelfranchi and Miceli largely equate the two. And whereas I assume that the emotions covered by BDTE require a propositional representation system (a language of thought; Fodor, 1987), Castelfranchi and Miceli (personal communication) find this assumption too restrictive and prefer a more liberal view of the format of the mental representations that may underlie the emotions covered by BDTE. In this article, I will ignore these differences because they are not decisive for the present discussion of the nature of emotions in BDTE.

[7] Supporting this view, the history of emotion psychology is full of attempts to empirically test proposed definitions of emotion (e.g., those of James, 1890; or Schachter, 1964). The view that an emotion definition is a nominal definition would make this research activity look utterly irrational. These empirical tests, however, make perfect sense if an emotion definition is a real definition – an empirical claim about the essence of emotions (Reisenzein, 1994a).

idea of a nominal definition. One such way is to reinterpret the problem of the definition of emotion as a problem of terminological standardization, that is, of getting emotion researchers to agree to a stipulation about how to use the term "emotion" (Scherer, 2005). Another way is to reinterpret the question "What is an emotion?" as asking for the meaning of emotion words in ordinary language (e.g., "What do people mean by 'fear'?") (Hempel, 1965), with the implicit assumption being that the ordinary language definitions of emotions are themselves nominal (i.e., based on linguistic conventions).

However, since the demise of logical empiricism and the rise of the "new scientific realism" philosophies of science, the idea that some definitions – in fact, those of greatest interest to science – are after all a form of real definitions has gained renewed respectability (for details, see Boyd, 1991; 2002; Griffith, 1997). According to the modern view, a real definition is a hypothesis about the "deep structure" or core constitution of the objects in the class picked out, more or less precisely, by an extension-fixing device, such as a list of examples or a set of typical features. The paradigm case is the scientific definition of water, identified by a set of features such as "the clear, odorless liquid found in lakes and rivers, essential for animal and plant life (etc.)" as "H_2O."

In line with others (e.g., Griffith, 1997; see also Charland, 2002), I believe that this "real definition" view is the correct model for the definition of emotions (Reisenzein, 1994a; 2007; Reisenzein & Schönpflug, 1992). According to this understanding, a definition of emotion is an empirical hypothesis about the nature or constitution of the states identified, more or less precisely, with the help of a list of paradigmatic examples (e.g., joy, sadness, fear, hope, disappointment, pity, joy for another. . .) and a set of typical features of the items on this list (a "working definition" of emotions; see Meyer, Reisenzein, & Schützwohl, 2001). This hypothesis about the nature of emotion is always formulated against the background of a theory of emotion generation (and the effects of emotions). Hence, the definition of emotions always presupposes such a causal theory, and it stands and falls with this theory (Reisenzein & Schönpflug, 1992; Reisenzein, 2007).

Accordingly, the title question of this article, "What is an emotion *in BDTE?*" asks for a theoretical identification of emotions while presupposing the truth of BDTE. This means at minimum that the *basic assumption* of BDTE – beliefs and desires are necessary for emotions – is accepted. However, when comparing Castelfranchi and Miceli's (2009) view of the nature of emotion in BDTE with my own view, a richer version of BDTE can be presupposed that includes additional shared assumptions; in particular, the assumption that beliefs and desires cause feelings of pleasure and displeasure.

Given this understanding of the problem of the definition of emotion, how can this problem be solved? In principle, I propose, it can be solved by means of an inference to the best explanation (e.g., Lipton, 2004). That is, different proposals concerning the nature of emotion in BDTE – different proposals for the theoretical definition of emotions – are compared in terms of their ability to explain various accepted properties of emotions, such as their type distinctions (happiness, fear, etc.), their experiential quality, their intensity, their (apparent) object-directedness, and their temporal course; and the theoretical definition of emotions that best explains these properties of emotions is (provisionally) accepted.

One last point: Although I have discussed the question of the definition of emotion for emotions *in general*, it cannot be *directly* answered on this level. The reason is that emotions always come in more or less specific qualities (happiness, fear, etc.), and that the set of emotions demarcated by a working definition has fuzzy boundaries and may comprise several distinct subgroups (e.g., "cognitive" versus "sensory" emotions). What one can do, however, is to try to answer the definition question for as many paradigmatic emotions as possible and try to make plausible that parallel answers can be given in other similar cases (see also, Ortony et al., 1988). Furthermore, provided that the presupposed theory of emotion accounts well for paradigmatic emotions, one can and should use the theory itself to help decide on its range of application (Reisenzein & Schönpflug, 1992; Reisenzein, 2009b). This may lead to certain theoretically motivated reclassifications. For example, in CBDTE, surprise is classified as an emotion (Reisenzein, 2009a; 2009b).

In the remainder of this article, I will put the proposed method to work with the aim of deciding which of the two described theories of the nature of emotion in BDTE is more plausible. My conclusion will be that the gestalt theory of emotion is less successful overall in explaining salient properties of emotions than the causal feeling theory. My argumentation for this conclusion proceeds in three steps. In the first step, I present two arguments for the assumption, made by both Castelfranchi and Miceli and myself, that the feeling of pleasure or displeasure is a necessary component of emotions: I argue that this assumption is the best explanation of the phenomenal character of emotional experiences and their intensity. In the second step, I examine the two main arguments for regarding beliefs and desires as emotion components – that doing so is required to explain the finer distinctions among emotions and their object-directedness – and argue that they are unconvincing. In step three, I present three objections against the hypothesis that beliefs and desires are components of emotions. The causal feeling theory avoids these objections. I therefore recommend abandoning the belief-desire compound theory of the nature of emotion in favor of the causal feeling theory.

3 Why Hedonic Feelings (Pleasure and Displeasure) are Necessary for Emotions

Castelfranchi and Miceli (2009) and I agree on an "affect-enriched" version of BDTE: We assume that "emotional" belief-desire constellations cause feelings, most importantly of pleasure or displeasure, and that these feelings are essential for emotional experience. What we disagree on is the more precise theoretical definition of emotion, given these shared assumptions. I propose to identify emotions with the output signals of the emotion-generating mechanisms assumed in CBDTE (the BDC and the BBC) that, when conscious, are experienced as feelings of pleasure and displeasure, surprise and expectancy confirmation, mixtures of these, and hope and fear (Reisenzein, 2009a; 2009b). By contrast, Castelfranchi and Miceli (2009) propose to identify emotions – which they essentially equate with emotional experiences – with "mental compounds," which they claim emerge from beliefs, desires, and hedonic feelings through a further information-processing step, a process that integrates beliefs, desires, and feelings into an emotional gestalt. Which of these theoretical definitions of emotion is more plausible?

As the first step in trying to answer this question, I will present arguments for the *shared assumption* of the two compared views of the nature of emotion: the assumption that feelings of mental pleasure or displeasure are (at least) a necessary component of (most) emotional experiences. Castelfranchi and Miceli (2009) do not argue for this assumption, probably because it was introspectively evident to them, as it was to numerous classical (e.g., Bentham, 1889/1970; Külpe, 1893; Meinong, 1906; Wundt, 1896) and contemporary emotion researchers (e.g., Barrett, 2006; Cabanac, 2002; Goldstein, 2002; Mellers, 2000; Ortony, Clore, & Collins, 1988; Reisenzein, 1994b; 2009b; Russell, 2003). As a matter of fact, however, not everybody is convinced that emotions contain a hedonic feeling component; therefore, it *is* necessary to present arguments for this claim. The strongest arguments are, I believe, that this assumption provides the best available explanation for (a) the phenomenal character of emotions and (b) their intensity. Note that, to the degree that these arguments are successful, they place an important constraint on theories of the nature of emotions: Any plausible theory of the nature of emotions would then have to assume that (most) emotions contain a hedonic feeling component.

3.1 Explaining the Phenomenal Character of Emotions

Probably the most salient property of emotions, from the perspective of the experiencing person, is their phenomenality, the fact that it "is like" or "feels" a particular way for the person to have an emotion (e.g., Reisenzein & Döring, 2009). Although there is a longstanding and still ongoing debate about how many different affective feeling qualities there are, both everyday experience and more formally collected psychological data suggest that, barring hedonically neutral surprise (which is included in CBDTE, for theoretical reasons, as a limiting case of emotions), all emotional experiences are at least among others characterized by a pleasurable or displeasurable quality, a positive or negative hedonic tone (see e.g., Barrett, Mesquita, Ochsner, & Gross, 2007; Külpe, 1893; Mellers, 2000; Reisenzein, 1994b; Russell, 2003; Reisenzein & Junge, 2006; Wundt, 1896). The phenomenal quality, specifically the hedonic tone of emotional experiences, thus needs to be accounted for by any plausible theory of emotion.

The assumption that "emotional" constellations of beliefs and desires cause feelings of pleasure or displeasure, and that these feelings are necessary components of emotional experiences, provides a natural explanation for the hedonic tone of emotions (Reisenzein, 2009b). A feeling of mental pleasure or pain, conceived of as a sensation-like mental state similar to sensations of color, tone, or temperature, explains the hedonic quality of emotions in a natural way because it belongs to the essence of sensations to have a phenomenal quality (Külpe, 1893; Wundt, 1896). In fact, I believe that the assumption that emotions contain – or even are – feelings of mental pleasure or mental pain provides the *best available* explanation of the hedonic tone of emotions. However, I will first argue for a weaker claim: To account for the hedonic tone of emotions in BDTE, one must assume that "emotional" belief-desire configurations cause *a separate mental state that carries the hedonic tone*. The main argument for this conclusion is that attempts to explain the hedonic character of emotions in terms of belief and desire alone seem to meet with insuperable difficulties. To see this, let us consider how BDTE theorists might try to account for the hedonic character of emotions in terms of belief and desire (for additional discussions, see Pugmire, 1998; Salmela, 2002). In principle, these theorists have two options. First, they can try to explain the hedonic quality of emotions by appealing to the phenomenal properties of beliefs and desires. Second, they can assume that hedonic tone is an emergent property of the fusion of "emotional" belief-desire configurations (Green, 1992). Let us examine these two options in turn.

3.1.1 Explaining Hedonic Quality by Appealing to the Phenomenal Properties of Beliefs and Desires

The first stepping stone for BDTE theorists who try to explain the experiential quality of emotions by appealing to the phenomenal qualities of beliefs and desires is the intuition that these mental states do not have any experiential quality (e.g., Green, 1992; Smith, 1987; for a recent overview of this debate about "cognitive phenomenology," see Bayne & Montague, 2011). According to this intuition, being conscious of our occurrent beliefs or desires consists exclusively of our being immediately (noninferentially) aware of them when they occur; but there is nothing it is like to have them.

However, even assuming that beliefs and desires do have phenomenal character, as some have argued (see Bayne & Montague, 2011; I concede this possibility in Reisenzein, 2009a), it is questionable whether this character is *of the right kind* to explain the experiential and specifically the hedonic quality of emotions.

(1) The phenomenal qualities of belief and desire, considered separately, seem unsuited to explain the hedonic tone of emotions. Beliefs – at least the factual beliefs regarded as preconditions of emotions in BDTE – do not have any intrinsic pleasure-pain quality. With respect to conscious desires, it is more plausible to argue that they are occasionally characterized by hedonic tone (e.g., Marks, 1982). However, often they are not, and when they are, they seem to be mainly unpleasant, particularly when they are intense (e.g., cravings). Furthermore, the hedonic tone of an emotion is sometimes the opposite of the hedonic tone most plausibly attributed to the underlying desire. The satisfaction of unpleasant cravings is still pleasurable; likewise, the hedonic tone of relief about the non-occurrence of an undesired state of affairs p is

pleasurable, whereas the hedonic tone of the underlying desire (the aversion to p) is, if anything, negative.[8] Finally, the pleasure of desire fulfillment cannot be the hedonic tone of the desire because desires are extinguished upon their subjective fulfillment (see Section 5.2).

(2) If these intuitions are correct, then the hedonic quality of emotions also cannot be explained in terms of a mixture of the experiential qualities of beliefs and desires—if only because the belief, lacking hedonic tone, cannot contribute anything useful to that mixture.

3.1.2 Hedonic Quality as an Emergent Property

To overcome the difficulties of explaining the hedonic quality of emotions in terms of the phenomenal qualities of beliefs and desires, Green (1992) proposed that emotions are the products of a fusion of "emotional" belief-desire constellations, and that hedonic quality is an emergent property of the resulting mental states.[9] If we assume, as I think we must, that the proposed fusion process is a causal process, Green's suggestion combines two claims: (a) "Emotional" belief-desire constellations cause another mental state with hedonic properties, and (b) this mental state is a holistic compound of beliefs and desires. Of these two claims, the second remains largely metaphorical until the details of the proposed fusion process are spelled out. However, about all that is said about this process is that its inputs are beliefs and desires, whereas its output is a mental compound, which contains beliefs and desires as parts, and has emergent properties including hedonic quality and intensity.[10] Hence, this second claim is at best a promissory note of future explanation.[11] Therefore, we are left with the first claim. However, the first claim is identical to the hy-

[8] When reflecting on the hedonic tone of desires, one should keep in mind that one becomes aware of a desire mainly when one acquires the belief that a state of affairs that fulfills or frustrates the desire is possible or certain – that is, at the time when an emotion occurs. There is thus the danger of attributing the hedonic quality of emotions to the desire, in which case the desire account of the hedonic tone of emotions would be circular (see also Stocker, 1983).

[9] Hence, Green assumes that hedonic tone is a property of the output of the fusion of "emotional" belief-desire constellations. By contrast, Castelfranchi and Miceli (2009) assume that feelings of pleasure or displeasure are one of several inputs to the fusion process that results in the emotion.

[10] In addition, Green (1992, p. 97) draws an analogy with the process of chemical bonding (e.g., of hydrogen and oxygen into water). However, this analogy is presumably meant only to document the existence of physical compounding processes whose products have emergent properties, and thereby to raise the probability that analogous processes might exist in the mental realm; it is not meant to imply any deeper similarity of the intervening processes.

[11] Attempts to provide this explanation suggest that the proposed fusion process is actually something else entirely. Specifically, CBDTE suggests two things about this process: (a) It includes the comparison of newly acquired beliefs with existing beliefs and desires, for without the detection of a belief-desire match or mismatch, no emotion will result (Reisenzein, 2009a); (b) beyond the belief-desire comparison, no further process is needed to explain the hedonic quality, as well as the intensity, of emotions. Hence, CBDTE suggests that the process in question is one of comparing beliefs and desires, not of fusing them into a new mental state.

pothesis I presently seek to establish: The carrier of hedonic tone is a mental state caused by beliefs and desires.

The discussed options seem to exhaust the possibilities of explaining the hedonic quality of emotions in terms of the beliefs and desires that, according to BDTE, are necessary conditions of emotions. The failure of these explanatory attempts implies that beliefs and desires alone are insufficient to explain the hedonic quality of emotions; an additional mental state caused by "emotional" belief-desire constellations needs to be assumed. This conclusion does not per se entail that this additional component of emotion, the carrier of hedonic tone, is a sensation-like, intrinsically objectless feeling, as Reisenzein (2009a; 2009b) and Castelfranchi and Miceli (2009) assume. There is at least one alternative possibility. Illustrated for the case of happiness about p, this is the proposal that the belief that p and the desire for p cause another intentional mental state directed at p, $F(p)$, that is *simultaneously* a feeling of pleasure. The theory that emotions are, or at least comprise, "intentional feelings" (specifically, of pleasure or displeasure) was originally advanced by Franz Brentano and his students, in particular, Alexius Meinong (1894; 1906) and Carl Stumpf (1899; see Reisenzein and Schönpflug, 1992) and has recently been reproposed by several philosophers (e.g., Goldie, 2000; Helm, 2001). Although attractive in other respects—in particular because it offers a neat explanation of the intentionality of emotions—the theory of intentional pleasure feelings has to cope with a number of difficulties: It has been debated whether propositional attitudes have phenomenal character (see Bayne & Montague, 2011), and it is not clear what the semantic properties (conditions of satisfaction; see Green, 1992) of object-directed feelings would be. The hypothesis that the carrier of the hedonic tone of emotions is an objectless sensation-like feeling of pleasure or displeasure avoids these problems. For this and other reasons (Reisenzein, 2009a; b), I prefer this hypothesis to the "intentional feeling" theory. However, it should be noted that the "intentional feeling" theory is similar enough to the "sensory feeling" theory to be regarded, at least in the present context, as a variant of the latter: Both theories assume that the affective component of emotions is a hedonic feeling, but in one case this feeling is intrinsically objectless, whereas in the other case, it is directed at the object of the emotion.

3.2 *Explaining the Intensity of Emotions*

Emotions are not just present or absent; rather, they can be instantiated in different degrees or gradations, ranging from just noticeable to extremely intense. For example, one can be a little, moderately, or very happy; or mildly, somewhat, or extremely surprised. Intensity has been neglected in theoretical discussions of emotion. Nevertheless, it is an undisputed, salient feature of emotions that, therefore, any plausible theory of emotion must explain (Frijda, Ortony, Sonnemans, & Clore, 1992; Green, 1992; Pugmire, 1998; Reisenzein, 1994b). I submit that, just like the phenomenal quality of emotions, the intensity of emotions cannot be explained in terms of belief and desire alone. To account for the intensity of emotions, another component of emotions needs to be posited; and the best candidate for this additional component, I submit, is a sensation-like feeling.

In CBDTE, this idea is implemented as follows: It is assumed that "emotional" constellations of beliefs and desires cause sensation-like feeling qualities, and that the intensity of these feelings is a quantitative function of belief and desire strength (Reisenzein, 2009a; 2009b). Because quality and intensity are essential properties of sensations (Külpe, 1893; Wundt, 1896), these assumptions allow CBDTE to simultaneously explain the phenomenal quality and the intensity of emotions in a natural way: Emotions are signals produced by the belief-desire and belief-belief comparator mechanisms that are experienced as feelings, and the intensity of the emotions is simply the intensity of these feelings (Reisenzein, 2009b). Again, although I believe that this is the best available explanation of emotion intensity, I will first argue for a weaker claim: To account for the intensity of emotions in BDTE, it is necessary to posit a separate mental state caused by beliefs and desires, one that carries emotional intensity.

One argument for this conclusion can be obtained by an extension of the preceding argument concerning the explanation of hedonic quality. The hedonic quality of emotions itself has an intensity; it can occur in different degrees (Reisenzein, 1994b). If the carrier of the hedonic tone of emotions is a separate mental state caused by beliefs and desires, then the different intensities of pleasure and displeasure must be carried by (different specifications of) this separate mental state.

However, the conclusion that the intensity of emotions is carried by a separate mental state can also be arrived at independently of the phenomenal quality argument, by considering the problems that confront BDTE theorists who attempt to explain the intensity of emotions in terms of belief and desire alone. Again, these theorists have two principal options: They can try to explain the intensity of emotions by appealing to the intensities of beliefs and desires, or they can assume that emotion intensity is an emergent property of the fusion of "emotional" belief-desire constellations (Green, 1992).

3.2.1 Explaining Emotion Intensity by Appealing to the Intensities of Beliefs and Desires

(1) The intensities of belief and desire, considered separately, are unsuited to explain the intensity of emotions. Equating emotion intensity with belief strength does not work for the simple reason that belief strength has a clear upper bound (certainty), whereas the intensity of emotions has no definite upper bound. Furthermore, if emotion intensity were identified with belief strength, then emotions connected to beliefs held with certainty (the "emotions of certainty"; Green, 1992; Meinong, 1894), such as joy, could not vary in intensity. Neither can emotion intensity be equated with the strength of desire. In the case of the "emotions of certainty," this idea may at first seem to have some plausibility: Mary feels more joy about Schroiber being elected

chancellor the more she desires this event to happen; so perhaps the intensity of Mary's happiness is simply the intensity of the desire. However, the intensity of the "emotions of uncertainty" (Green, 1992; Meinong, 1894), hope and fear, depends on *both* belief strength and desire strength. For example, Mary is more strongly afraid that she may miss her connecting plane the more probable this event appears to her and the more averse she is to it. Analogously, the intensities of disappointment and relief depend on both belief and desire strength (for empirical evidence, see e.g., Reisenzein & Junge, 2006).

(2) The intensity of emotion also cannot be equated with the intensity of "emotional" belief-desire configurations. The intensity of these configurations is, minimally, a two-dimensional magnitude of the kind $<b(p), d(p)>$, whereas the intensity of emotion is a one-dimensional quantity, and is at least in some cases (e.g., hope, fear, disappointment, and relief) a joint function of the intensities of the involved beliefs and desires (Reisenzein, 2009a).

3.2.2 Emotion Intensity as an Emergent Property

To overcome these difficulties, one could again propose that emotions result from a fusion of "emotional" belief-desire constellations, and that the intensity of emotions is an emergent property of the resulting mental states (Green, 1992). However, this proposal provokes objections exactly parallel to those raised against the "emergentist" explanation of hedonic quality. One part of the proposal – "emotional" belief-desire constellations cause another mental state that is the carrier of emotion intensity – is identical to the hypothesis I presently seek to establish, and thus grants this hypothesis. The second part of the proposal claims that the new mental state, the carrier of emotion intensity, is a compound of beliefs and desires. This claim is at best a promissory note for an explanation as long as the fusion process is not spelled out, and CBDTE suggests that this process is actually one of comparing, rather than fusing, beliefs and desires.

The failure of the attempts to explain the intensity of emotions in terms of the intensities of belief and desire suggests that the latter are insufficient to explain the intensity of emotions. To explain emotion intensity in BDTE, an additional mental state, caused by "emotional" belief-desire constellations, needs to be posited. This conclusion does not per se entail that this mental state, the carrier of emotion intensity, is a sensation-like, intrinsically objectless feeling. An alternative is again that emotions are a class of mental states *sui generis*, which are simultaneously feelings *and* object-directed. As mentioned in Section 3.2.1, the "intentional feeling" hypothesis has a number of problems that make me prefer the sensory feeling hypothesis. However, in the present context, the "intentional feeling" and the "sensory feeling" hypotheses of the nature of emotions can be regarded as variants of one and the same proposal.

4 Two Unconvincing Arguments for the Belief-Desire Compound Theory of Emotion

Because phenomenal quality and intensity are essential properties of sensations, the assumption that emotions contain a sensory feeling component makes it possible to explain both the phenomenal quality and the intensity of emotional experiences in a natural way. Why then not simply assume that emotions *are* the feelings of pleasure and displeasure (and a few others, such as surprise) caused by the detection of, inter alia, desire-fulfillment and desire-frustration, as assumed by CBDTE? Why assume that beliefs and desires, too, are *components* of the emotion, as Castelfranchi and Miceli (2009) propose? Two main arguments have been advanced for this theory of the nature of emotions: the *emotion differentiation* argument and the *intentionality* argument. It has been claimed that only by conceiving of beliefs and desires as parts of the emotion can one explain (a) the finer distinctions between emotions – possibly all distinctions beyond positive and negative – and (b) the intentionality or object-directedness of emotions. However, although these arguments have been influential, they are ultimately unconvincing (see also Reisenzein, 2000; Reisenzein & Döring, 2009).

4.1 Why the Emotion Differentiation Argument Fails

Castelfranchi and Miceli (2009) refer to the emotion differentiation argument to motivate their theory that emotions are compounds of beliefs, desires, and affect. They argue that, although "the feeling of pleasantness and unpleasantness [is] . . . one essential component of emotional experience", beliefs and desires need to be added "to produce distinct emotions" (pp. 223-224). However, one can accept that beliefs and desires are necessary to distinguish between emotions without assuming that emotions contain beliefs and desires as (ontological) parts. A main reason for this is that mental states need not – and, if causal-role functionalism about mental states (e.g., Block, 1980) is right, cannot – be defined and distinguished from one another exclusively in terms of their intrinsic or nonrelational properties; they can also be defined and distinguished in terms of their relational features, in particular, their causes and consequences. Partly causal definitions are in fact common in everyday language. To mention a standard example, "sunburn" is defined as an "inflammation of the skin caused by over-exposure to sunlight" (Gordon, 1978, p. 125). Analogously, emotions could be defined as the feelings (e.g., of pleasure or displeasure) that are caused by particular constellations of beliefs and desires (see also Reisenzein, 1994a; 1994b; Reisenzein & Schönpflug, 1992). For example, happiness about p could be defined as the feeling of pleasure caused by the desire for p and the belief that p is the case. In fact, this is how emotional experiences are defined in CBDTE (Reisenzein, 2009a).[12] In adopting a (partly) causal definition of emotions, CBDTE finds itself in agreement with the position of causal-role functionalism in the philosophy of mind, the metaphysical backbone of contemporary cognitivism (e.g., Block, 1980; Fodor, 1975). It also finds itself in agreement with the views of many cognitive emotion theorists from Aristotle (about 350 B.C.) to Arnold (1960)[13] and with the folk-psychological understanding of mentalistic terms in general (Lewis, 1972) and emotion terms in particular (e.g., Reisenzein & Junge, 2012; Siemer, 2008).

The existence of causal-functional definitions of emotions (in both scientific and common-sense psychology) means that the emotion differentiation argument is invalid: The claim that beliefs and desires are necessary to distinguish between emotions does not entail that beliefs and desires are components of emotions. The belief that this inference is logically valid may have been due to an inadvertent confusion of the conceptual-linguistic and ontological levels of analysis: the *concepts* "belief," "desire," "happiness," "fear," etc., and the *referents of these concepts*. This confusion could have been facilitated by the fact that part-whole relations exist on both levels. Suppose that an emotion researcher sets out to clarify the nature of emotions and presents the results of this analysis in the form of a theoretical definition that states necessary features. To illustrate, suppose that the researcher defines or analyzes the concept "being happy about p" using the concepts "believing p" and "desiring p." In this case, the latter concepts are components of the former concept in the sense that they (or the terms that express them) are parts of the proposed definiens or analysans of "being happy about p." It might then be concluded that the *referents* of "believing p" and "desiring p" (the mental states of believing and desiring) are likewise parts of the *referent* of "being happy about p" (the mental state of happiness). However, this would be too quick: The concept "being happy about p" could be defined functionally, for example, as "the feeling of pleasure caused by the belief that p and the desire for p."

---

[12] To be precise, emotions and emotional experiences are defined in CBDTE on the computational level of system analysis. Emotions are the output signals of hardwired mechanisms that compare new beliefs with existing beliefs and desires (Reisenzein, 2009a, b). These signals can remain unconscious (e.g., when they are below a minimum level of intensity), but usually, they give rise to emotional experiences, which are conscious feelings of pleasure and displeasure, surprise and expectancy-confirmation, mixtures of these, plus hope and fear. On the phenomenological or intentional level of system analysis—that knows nothing about the representational codes and computational mechanisms underlying beliefs and desires—these experiences can be defined as emotional feelings that are caused by particular belief-desire configurations.

[13] In his *Rhetoric*, Aristotle defined fear as a kind of displeasure or perturbation arising from the idea of impending evil. Descartes (1649) defined several of his nonbasic emotions as subtypes of basic feelings whose distinguishing features consist of their being caused by particular types of appraisals. Stumpf (1899) proposed that emotions are belief-caused pro- or con-evaluations of states of affairs (see Reisenzein & Schönpflug, 1992). Arnold (1960) defined emotions as felt action tendencies caused by cognitive appraisals. In previous work, I proposed a causalist version of appraisal theory, according to which emotions are appraisal-caused mixtures of pleasure or displeasure and activation or deactivation (Reisenzein, 1994b). Further examples of functional definitions of emotion are referenced in Reisenzein and Schönpflug (1992).

Some proponents of the thesis that emotions contain beliefs and desires (or other mental states) as parts may in fact only have had a conceptual part-whole relation in mind, with no implications for the ontological level. In previous writings on emotion, Miceli and Castelfranchi (e.g., 2002), too, seem to use the expression "belief B and desire D are components of emotion E" in the conceptual part-whole sense only. Understood in this way, the claim that beliefs and desires are parts of emotions does not go beyond the basic claim of BDTE, that beliefs and desires are necessary for emotions, and is thus compatible with different ontological interpretations. However, in their 2009 article, Castelfranchi and Miceli take a stronger stance on the issue: There, they assume that beliefs and desires are ontological parts of the emotion.

In taking this stronger position, Castelfranchi and Miceli (2009) could have been motivated by the consideration that, even though the assumption that beliefs and desires are ontological parts of emotions is not needed to explain the differences between emotions *in general*, it may be needed to explain their differences in *phenomenal quality*. That is, it could be argued that conceiving of beliefs and desires as mere causes of emotions does not explain how different emotions can *feel* different to the experiencer in ways that go beyond pleasure and displeasure (and perhaps a few other feelings). To explain, for example, why happiness *feels* different from pride, one must appeal to the components of emotional experiences, rather than to their causes.

However, this argument is also unconvincing. For one reason, its implicit general premise – nothing short of a proper part of an experience can contribute to that experience's phenomenal character – can be doubted. The mental context of an emotional feeling, including its causes and consequences, might conceivably change the experience of that feeling (Reisenzein, 2009b). For another reason, even if one accepts the general premise of the argument, the conclusion does not follow. First, there may in fact be nothing to explain: The argument may rest on a confusion of the differences between *emotions* with differences in the *phenomenal quality of emotions*. There is no question that, for example, happiness and pride differ – they differ, in particular, in their cognitive-motivational preconditions. However, this does not necessarily mean that happiness and pride *feel* different: Not every difference between emotions needs to be a felt difference, a difference in experiential quality. In terms of experiential quality, happiness and pride might be exactly alike: both feel pleasant (e.g., Bentham, 1789/1970; Külpe, 1893); any cognized differences between happiness and pride could be due to differences in the perceived causes (and consequences) of the feeling of pleasure. Second, regarding beliefs and desires as emotion components may not be of much help in explaining the phenomenal quality of emotions, for as mentioned before (3.1.1), beliefs and desires may not have phenomenal properties, or at least none that could explain differences in emotional experience. In this context, it is important to note that the subtler distinctions between "emotional" belief-desire constellations concern differences in their *contents* – differences in *what* is believed and desired (see Castelfranchi and Miceli, 2009, for examples). To explain presumed subtle experiential differences between emotions in terms of belief and desire, one must therefore assume that at least some differences in the contents of beliefs and desires are reflected in phenomenal experience (see Bayne & Montague, 2011).

4.2 *Why the Intentionality Argument Fails*

The second introspectively salient property of emotional experiences, apart from their phenomenal quality (including their intensity) is their (apparent) intentionality or object-directedness: Typically at least, emotions present themselves to the experiencer as being directed at certain objects. For the emotions that fall within the purview of BDTE, these objects are propositions or states of affairs (e.g., Mary feels happy about the fact that Schroiber was elected chancellor). The intentionality argument holds that, to account for the object-directedness of emotions, one must assume that beliefs and desires are not just causes but components of emotions (see e.g., Green, 1992; Pitcher, 1965; Reisenzein & Schönpflug, 1992; Solomon, 1976). The intentionality argument is arguably the strongest argument for regarding cognitions (as well as, in the case of BDTE, desires) as components of emotions (Green, 1992; see also, Whiting, 2011). Nevertheless, this argument is not waterproof either. There are at least two ways in which the causal feeling theorist can avoid the conclusion of the intentionality argument.

The first way out is to accept the initial premise of the argument, that emotions are object-directed, but argue that emotions are a separate kind of object-directed mental states, distinct from but caused by beliefs and desires. In Sections 3.1.2 and 3.2.2, I mentioned a special version of this idea: the hypothesis that the feeling of pleasure caused by the belief that p and the desire for p is intrinsically directed at p.[14] However, as also mentioned there, it is debatable whether propositional attitudes can have phenomenal quality, and it is unclear what the semantic properties of object-directed feelings would be. For these reasons, I prefer the second option available to the causal feeling theorist; one that avoids these problems. This option consists of denying the initial premise of the intentionality argument, that emotions are object-directed. Note that this is not meant to deny that emotions *appear to be*, in a presystematic sense of the term, "directed at" objects; for example, that Mary's happiness appears to her to "focus" on Schroiber's election victory. Rather, the argument is that this subjective appearance of focus does not reflect a genuine intentional relation (Reisenzein, 2009a). That is, whereas the experienced object focus of emotions may be *reminiscent* of true intentional (i.e., representational) relations such as believing p or desiring p, closer examination reveals that it is not a genuine representational relation after all.

The plausibility of this suggestion depends, among others, on whether a plausible explanation of the illusion of intentionality of emotions can be

---

[14] The gestalt theory of emotion, too, implies that emotions (emotional gestalts) are caused by beliefs and desires (Castelfranchi & Miceli, 2009). However, the resultant emotional gestalts are still thought to contain beliefs and desires as components. Therefore, this proposal is not sufficiently different from the part-whole theory to be regarded as a real alternative.

given. CBDTE offers an explanation: According to this theory, the illusion of object-directedness can be traced to the special way the emotion-generating mechanisms operate (Reisenzein, 2009a). For example, when the belief-desire comparator detects that the contents of a newly acquired belief $Bel(p)$ match the contents of an existing desire $Des(p)$, it generates a feeling of pleasure and, simultaneously, focuses attention on the responsible proposition p. It then appears to the person that she is *pleased about p*. Furthermore, it seems conceivable that subsequent cognitive processes bind feelings to the representations of the objects of the beliefs that proximately caused them, transforming these initially neutral thoughts into "affectively tinged" thoughts about these objects (Reisenzein, 2009a; 2009b; see also James, 1890/1950). For example, the feeling of pleasure caused by Mary's belief that Schroiber won the election might get attached to the mental representation of Schroiber's election victory, resulting in Mary's thought of a pleasurable victory. Alternatively, the appearance of object-directedness might be due to an implicit causal attribution of the feeling (Reisenzein, 1994a; Schachter, 1964).

I conclude that the two main arguments in favor of the idea that beliefs and desires are components of emotions – the emotion differentiation argument and the intentionality argument – are unconvincing.

5 Three Problems for the Belief-Desire Compound Theory of Emotion

I argued that the two main arguments for the belief-desire compound theory of the nature of emotions are not compelling. However, this does not necessarily mean that this theory is wrong and the causal feeling theory is correct. It only means that, to decide this issue, we must turn to other arguments. In the following section, I present three arguments that speak directly against the belief-desire compound theory of emotion.[15]

5.1 The Problem of Emotional Intentionality – Still Unsolved

In Section 4.2, I argued that one need not regard beliefs and desires as ontological parts of emotions to explain the (apparent) intentionality of emotions: One can either deny that emotions are truly intentional (representational), in which case their object-directedness need not be explained; or one can argue that emotions are a separate class of intentional mental states caused by beliefs and desires. However, none of this touches the claim of the belief-desire compound theorists, that taking beliefs and desires to be components of emotions provides *another* viable explanation for the intentionality of emotions.

---

[15] The first two arguments also speak against a categorization account (e.g., Barrett, 2006; Mandler, 1984) of the "fusion" of beliefs and desires into an emotion.

Furthermore, belief-desire compound theorists could argue that their explanation is preferable because it neither requires questioning the intentionality
of emotions nor introducing new questionable mental entities (object-directed
feelings). I will now argue that the belief-desire compound theory of emotion,
at least in its original form, is in fact *unable* to explain the intentionality of emotions. The reason is that this theory does not allow for correctly identifying
the objects of emotions – "correctly" here meaning "the way we intuitively
identify them in everyday life."

Suppose Oscar is sad that he was not invited to a party. According to the
belief-desire compound theory of emotion, Oscar's sadness is a compound
mental state that emerges, via a gestalt formation process, from Oscar's belief
that he was not invited to the party, and his desire to be invited (plus, in
Castelfranchi and Miceli's version of the theory, a feeling of displeasure). The
object of Oscar's sadness is the state of affairs described, from the first-person
perspective, by the sentence "I am *not* invited to the party" (not-p), which is
identical to the object of Oscar's belief. The object of Oscar's desire, however,
is the state of affairs described by "I am invited to the party" (p). Hence, if
Bel(not-p) and $Des(p)$ are both components of Oscar's sadness, it would seem
that the emotion has *two* different objects that in addition, are contradictory
opposites: p and not-p. But although Oscar is sad that he was not invited to
the party (not-p), it is not the case that he is sad that he was invited (p); nor is
it the case that he is sad about a contradiction (not-p & p). In fact, since Oscar
does not believe p, he cannot – according to BDTE – be sad about p. And if he
believed p, he would be happy rather than sad about p.

Parallel cases can be constructed for other emotions including surprise –
in general, for all emotions that occur when a desire is frustrated by a newly
acquired belief, or when a previous belief is disconfirmed by a new belief.
Take surprise: If Oscar expects to be invited to the party (p), and then comes
to believe that he was not invited (not-p), he will be surprised about not-p.
If belief-desire compound theorists of emotion analyze surprise in a way that
parallels their analysis of hedonic emotions – that is, by including the necessary
cognitive preconditions of surprise into the emotional compound – they have
to regard both the belief that not-p and the belief that p as components of
surprise. However, it is not the case that Oscar is surprised that he was invited
to the party (p), nor is it the case that he is surprised about a contradiction
(not-p & p). Likewise, if Oscar both desires and expects to be invited to the
party (p), and then learns that he is not invited (not-p), he will be disappointed
about not-p; he will not be disappointed about p, nor about not-p & p.

In sum, emotions on the one hand, and their cognitive and motivational
preconditions on the other hand, have the same propositional objects only in
part. The object of the emotion corresponds to that of the proximate (according
to CBDTE, the most recently acquired) emotion-relevant belief, such as in
the present example, Oscar's belief that he is not invited to the party. By
contrast, the propositional objects of the emotion-relevant desires and pre-
existing beliefs can be contradictory opposites of the object of the emotion
(e.g., Oscar's desire to be invited to the party, and his belief that he would be).
Therefore, it seems that emotions cannot be identified with compounds that

include the cognitive and motivational preconditions of the emotions – *at least not all of them*.[16]

To solve this problem, Castelfranchi and Miceli (2009) might appeal to the proposed gestalt formation process: They could argue that one effect of this process consists precisely of providing the emotional gestalt with a single appropriate object. However, without further elaboration, this escape is too simple. Similar to the attempt to explain the hedonic quality and intensity of emotions by postulating that emotions are the outcomes of a process of a fusion of beliefs and desires whose details are left unspecified (see 3.1.2 and 3.2.2), the gestalt formation process here plays the role of a *deus ex machina* – it is simply ascribed whatever causal powers are needed to yield an output with desired properties (in the present case, a mental state with a particular object). We still do not understand *why* the emotion has only one object and why that object is identical to the object of the "proximate" belief, rather than to the object of the desire, or that of a pre-existing belief. Shall we assume that the desire and the pre-existing belief lose their objects when they become part of the emotional gestalt? But in this case, they would cease to exist; it belongs to the essence of beliefs and desires to be directed at objects. Furthermore, if the object of the emotional gestalt is the object of its belief component, can one really say that the *emotion*, rather than just its belief component, is directed at this object?

Even assuming that the problem of providing the emotional compound with the appropriate intentional object can be solved, another problem remains for Castelfranchi and Miceli's (2009) gestalt theory. Recall that according to this theory, emotions are mental gestalts that integrate beliefs, desires, *and hedonic feelings* (pleasure or displeasure). These hedonic feelings are regarded as intrinsically nonintentional. This raises the following question: Do the feelings become object-directed in the process of being integrated into the emotion? If yes, how is this feat achieved (Green, 1992)? If no, can one truly say that the *emotion* is directed at an object?

The more natural conclusion to draw from Oscar's case, it seems to me, is that at least desires and pre-existing beliefs are *not* parts of the emotion, but only their causes. Accepting this conclusion would mean, for Castelfranchi and Miceli's (2009) theory, that only the proximate belief and affect remain as components of the emotion (with the belief being a partial cause of the affect). This modified version of the belief-desire compound theory of emotion is

---

[16] Maria Miceli (personal communication) suggested that the object of Oscar's sadness might in fact not be not-p, but q = "my desire for p was frustrated." However, intuitively this seems wrong: Oscar is first and foremost sad that he was not invited to the party (not-p); he is not, or at least not only, sad that his desire for p was frustrated. Analogously, Oscar is surprised that he was not invited to the party; he is not, or at least not only, surprised that his belief that p would occur was disconfirmed (Reisenzein, 2009a). Independent of this issue, because q is different from both the object of the belief (not-p) and the object of the desire (p) underlying Oscar's sadness, Miceli's proposal makes it even more difficult for belief-desire compound theorists to explain the specific object-directedness of the emotion. And if they assume that Oscar is sad about q because he desired not-q and then came to believe that q, the original problem arises again: Oscar is sad only about q; he is not sad about not-q, nor about q & not-q.

already fairly close to the causal feeling theory. The main remaining difference concerns the question of whether the *proximate belief* is part of the emotion or not. I come back to this question at the end of the article.

5.2 *Problems with Emotion Duration*

A necessary requirement for the correctness of the belief-desire compound theory of emotion is that the elements of the compound are present during the emotion while it lasts. This is clear for the part-whole version of the belief-desire theory proposed by Marks (1982), where the emotion is *defined* as the co-existence of appropriate beliefs and desires. However, it is also the case for the gestalt theory version of BDTE (Castelfranchi & Miceli, 2009; see also Green, 1992, p. 81), for the gestalt-forming process produces an emotional gestalt only as long as it receives adequate inputs, the emotion components. To use Castelfranchi and Miceli's example of perceptual gestalt formation, the perception of a triangle exists only as long as the lines representing the sides of the triangle are perceived. If one of the lines is no longer visible, the perception of the triangle disintegrates.

I submit that this implication of the belief-desire compound theory of emotion – emotions are present only while their components are present – is not in line with the empirical facts. The discrepancy between theory and data is perhaps most apparent for desire-fulfillment emotions such as joy, but parallel discrepancies also exist for surprise and other emotional reactions to belief disconfirmation (e.g., disappointment, relief). In the case of the desire-fulfillment emotions, the problem is that, due to the updating of the belief-desire system that follows the detection of desire-fulfillment, the desire is usually deleted while the emotion still lasts. In the case of the expectancy-disconfirmation emotions, the problem is that the pre-existing belief with which a newly acquired belief is compared is changed while the emotion still persists. Another way of phrasing the problem is therefore that the temporal course, specifically the duration, of some emotions is not well explained by the belief-desire compound theory.

According to BDTE, Mary experiences happiness about p if she desires p and comes to believe that p is the case. Computationally speaking, happiness occurs if a cognitive subsystem (in CBDTE, the belief-desire comparator) detects that a desire has been fulfilled. However, according to the usual understanding of "desire", desires are extinguished by their detected fulfillment. As Meinong (1917, p. 96) put it, as soon as one comes to believe that a desired state of affairs exists, "the desire is destroyed; this is the subjective aspect of what is called... the fulfillment of the desire" (my translation). But if the desire for p is extinguished by the detection of its fulfillment, then the belief that p and desire for p are co-present in the cognitive system only as long as it takes to detect their congruence and to delete the desire (Reisenzein, 2009a). These are presumably primitive operations of the belief-desire updating mechanism that should accordingly take only minimal time (perhaps 300 ms; see Madl, Baars,

& Franklin, 2011). Furthermore, strictly speaking, the emotion comes into existence only *after* desire-congruence has been detected. As a consequence, the emotion of joy should in general be an extremely short-lived occurrence, perhaps too short to be subjectively noticeable, rather than lasting for a while, as it typically seems to do (e.g., Frijda et al., 1992).

A parallel objection can be raised in the case of surprise. Surprise is experienced if a cognitive module (in CBDTE, the belief-belief comparator) detects that a newly acquired belief is contrary to an existing belief. For example, Mary expects Schroiber will not win the election, but then learns that he, in fact, won. As soon as the belief-belief comparator detects that the newly acquired belief contradicts the old, the old belief is deleted; a process that presumably takes only a fraction of a second. By contrast, according to subjective tracings of the temporal course of surprise, the experience of surprise typically lasts for several seconds (Reisenzein, Bördgen, Holtbernd, & Matz, 2006). And in the case of pleasant surprise, both the pre-existing desire and the pre-existing belief are updated while the emotion still persists.

Belief-desire compound theorists of emotion could try to solve this problem, in the case of the desire-fulfillment emotions, by bringing in other desires, such as, in our example, Mary's desire that Schroiber will remain chancellor for as long as possible or that he will keep his campaign promises. But apart from the fact that it is not plausible that one experiences joy only if, at the subjective fulfillment of a desire, other related desires spring into existence, the problem is thereby not solved but only deferred. The desire that Schroiber will keep his campaign promises is different from the desire that Schroiber will win the election; correspondingly, the joy experienced when learning that Schroiber has kept his promises is different from the joy about Schroiber's election victory. And the former feeling of joy should be experienced only when the corresponding wish is subjectively fulfilled and as a consequence, extinguished. Analogous objections can be raised against the attempt to explain the duration of surprise by bringing in additional disconfirmed beliefs.

A more promising strategy of dealing with the present objection would be to argue that, notwithstanding the above-mentioned theoretical considerations, fulfilled desires are in fact not extinguished immediately, and disconfirmed beliefs are not immediately deleted, but that the process of desire and belief updating takes time – just enough time for joy or surprise to occur and subside again. Emotions are experienced only while the desire and belief, or the old and new belief, are simultaneously present in the cognitive system, as assumed by the belief-desire compound theory. This seems to be an empirically testable difference between the belief-desire compound theory and the causal feeling theory; however, I do not know of firm empirical data that would allow for a decision regarding this issue. In the absence of supporting data, these auxiliary assumptions about the relative duration of belief and desire updates, and of the associated emotions, strike me as ad hoc. In any case, it should be realized that the belief-desire compound theory entails strong empirical assumptions about the relative duration of emotions and belief-desire updates. The causal feeling theory does not require making these assumptions; it is equally well compatible with a variety of empirical data concerning this issue.

5.3 Are There Emotional Gestalts?

Castelfranchi and Miceli's (2009) gestalt theory of emotion would be on firmer ground if there were independent evidence that the emotional gestalts with which they identify emotions do exist (although they would then still have to argue for the *identity* of emotions and emotional gestalts). However, the existence of emotional gestalts is by no means certain. Emotional gestalts could be theoretical constructs that lack empirical referents. If so, the belief-desire compound theory of the nature of emotion cannot be correct, for surely, emotions cannot be identified with nonexistents (Reisenzein, 2007).

Whereas Castelfranchi and Miceli (2009) appeal to introspection to support the existence of emotional gestalts, I must admit that I do not share their intuitions. According to my introspection, when I am happy about some state of affairs p that fulfills a wish of mine, I am not experiencing a complex mental state that comprises the desire for p and the belief that p. Rather, I become aware that p is the case, and this thought is immediately followed and accompanied by an upsurge of pleasant feeling, that after a shorter or longer while, subsides again. I would also be willing to admit to an impression of phenomenal causality (Heider, 1958), in that the feeling appears to be caused by the thought that p. These introspective intuitions agree with those of others who have considered the issue (e.g., Meinong, 1906; Whiting, 2011). However, I am not aware of a fusion of belief and desire taking place (and as argued in 5.2, such an integration *cannot* take place because the desire is extinguished by its fulfillment). To the degree that anything like an integration occurs at all, it seems to concern only the object of the emotion p and the feeling: When thinking of the state of affairs p that I believe to be the case, it presents itself to me not just as a state of affairs that is real, but also as a pleasurable state of affairs (cf. James, 1890/1950).

These introspective worries about the existence of emotional gestalts of the kind required by Castelfranchi and Miceli's (2009) theory are reinforced by theoretically motivated concerns about the proposed gestalt formation process. As mentioned, the claim that emotions are the outcome of a process that integrates different components into a whole with suitable emergent properties runs the risk of being a pseudo-explanation – one simply imputes to the fusion process whatever causal powers are needed to produce outputs with the desired properties (e.g., intensity, a specific object). To avoid this danger, one must become more specific about the integration process. Castelfranchi and Miceli (2009) go some way toward explicating the integration process by proposing that it is analogous to gestalt-forming processes known from perception (e.g., Köhler, 1947). However, it should be acknowledged that the inputs of the emotional gestalt formation process (beliefs, desires, and hedonic feelings) differ significantly from the typical inputs of the perceptual gestalt formation processes (e.g., visual perceptions of lines), and so do their outputs (emotions versus e.g., the perception of geometrical figures). Given these peculiarities of the gestalt formation process in the case of emotions, it would be helpful to know that analogous gestalt formations, involving similar mental elements, occur in other, less controversial domains. However, gestalt formation processes have been nearly exclusively studied in the domain of perception. It therefore remains at present uncertain whether their extension to emotions really works.

6 The Causal Feeling Theory Vindicated

To recapitulate, I first argued that sensation-like feelings are a necessary component of emotions: This assumption is an inference to the best explanation of the phenomenal character (specifically the hedonic quality) of emotions and their intensity. Second, I argued that the two main arguments for regarding beliefs and desires as components of emotions – the emotion differentiation argument and the intentionality argument – are unconvincing. Third, I presented three objections to the hypothesis that beliefs and desires are components of emotions: This hypothesis fails, at second sight, to explain the directedness of emotions at specific objects; it has difficulty accounting for the duration of emotional reactions to the fulfillment of desires and the disconfirmation of beliefs; and there are reasons to question the existence of the postulated emotional gestalts and the process that presumably generates them.

The causal feeling theory of the nature of emotions avoids these problems. By assuming that emotional experiences are nonpropositional signals that, when conscious, are experienced as feelings, this theory accounts in a natural way for the phenomenal character of emotions and their intensity. It also vindicates our everyday talk of beliefs and desires as causes of emotions – something the belief-desire compound theory of emotion achieves only with some difficulty (see Footnote 4). The finer distinctions among emotions – those not attributable to differences in feelings – can be explained by assuming that emotions are, in part, distinguished by their cognitive and motivational causes (and consequences).

The price one may have to pay for these explanatory virtues of the causal feeling theory is the concession that – counter to linguistic practices and first phenomenological intuitions – emotions are *not* modes of representing propositional objects like beliefs and desires are. However, this may just be how things are. Furthermore, as mentioned, the belief-desire compound theory is incapable of explaining the specific object-directedness of emotions; it therefore presents no real advantage to the causal feeling theory in this respect. And by assuming that emotional feelings can be bound to the objects of the beliefs that cause them, resulting in "emotionally tinged" thoughts about them – or even more simply, that people form beliefs about the causes of their emotional feelings (Schachter, 1964; Reisenzein, 1994a; 1994b) – the cognitive (information-providing) and motivational functions of emotions can be saved without assuming that emotions themselves have propositional objects (Reisenzein, 2009b).

The last-mentioned elaboration of the causal feeling theory points to a possible reconciliation with the belief-desire compound theory: To solve the problems with explaining the intentionality and duration of emotions, and to avoid the uncertainties surrounding the postulated gestalt formation process and its outcomes, Castelfranchi and Miceli could modify their theory of the nature of emotions by proposing that only hedonic feelings and their proximate cognitive causes (beliefs), but not pre-existing beliefs and desires, are components of the emotion; the latter are only its causes. According to this revised version of the gestalt theory of emotion, Mary's happiness about p would be a mental state that emerges from the integration of the belief that p, with the pleasure caused by this belief plus Mary's desire for p. In the next step, the integration process could be explicated as the binding of sensory and propositional representations into an "affectively tinged" thought (Reisenzein, 2009a). The remaining difference to the causal feeling theory would then concern the question of whether the emotion is to be identified with the (signal underlying the) affective feeling, or with the "affectively tinged" thought resulting from the binding of the feeling to the representation of p (in CBDTE, the sentence sin the language of thought representing p). I continue to believe that the former theoretical definition of emotion is more adequate because it accounts better, overall, for the different properties of emotions. In particular, the signal underlying the emotional feelings is the common cause of both emotional experience and the physiological and expressive effects of emotions (Reisenzein, 2009a; 2009b). However, an in-depth discussion of this question must be left to another occasion.

References

1. Aristotle. (1980). *Rhetorik*. München: Fink. (Original work published about 350 b. c.).
2. Arnold, M. B. (1960a). *Emotion and personality* (Vols. 1 & 2). New York: Columbia University Press.
3. Barrett, L. F. (2006). Solving the emotion paradox: Categorization and the experience of emotion. *Personality and Social Psychology Review, 10*, 20–46.
4. Barrett, L. F., Mesquita, B., Ochsner, K. N., & Gross, J. J. (2007). The experience of emotion. *Annual Review of Psychology, 58*, 373–403.
5. Bayne, T., & Montague, M. (2011, in press). Cognitive phenomenology: An introduction. In T. Bayne & M. Montague (eds.) *Cognitive Phenomenology*. Oxford: Oxford University Press.
6. Bentham, J. (1789/1970). *An introduction to the principles of morals and legislation*. London: Athlone Press.
7. Block, N. (1980). Introduction: What is functionalism? In N. Block (Ed.), *Readings in philosophy of psychology* (Vol. 1, pp. 171–184). Cambridge, MA: Harvard University Press.
8. Boyd, R. (1991). Realism, Anti-Foundationalism, and the enthusiasm for natural kinds. *Philosophical Studies, 61*, 127–48.
9. Boyd, R. (2002). Scientific realism. *Stanford Encyclopedia of Philosophy*. http://plato.stanford.edu/archives/spr2011/entries/scientific-realism/
10. Bratman, M. E. (1987). *Intentions, plans, and practical reason*. Cambridge, StateMA: Harvard University Press.
11. Cabanac, M. (2002). What is emotion? *Behavioural Processes, 60*, 69–84.
12. Castelfranchi, C. & Miceli, M. (2009). The cognitive-motivational compound of emotional experience. *Emotion Review, 1*, 223–231.
13. Charland, L. (2002). The natural kind status of emotion. *British Journal for the Philosophy of Science, 53*, 511–537.

14. Conte, R., & Castelfranchi, C. (1995). *Cognitive and social action*. London: University College London Press.
15. Davis, W. (1981). A theory of happiness. *Philosophical Studies, 39*, 305–317.
16. Descartes, R. (1984). *Les passions de l'ame* [The passions of the soul]. Hamburg, Germany: Meiner. (Original work published 1649)
17. Ellsworth, P. C., & Scherer, K. R. (2003). Appraisal processes in emotion. In R. J. Davidson, K. R. Scherer, & H. H. Goldsmith (Eds.), *Handbook of Affective Sciences* (pp. 572–595). Oxford: Oxford University Press.
18. Feather, N. T. (Ed.). (1982). *Expectations and actions: Expectancy-value models in psychology*. Hillsdale, NJ: Erlbaum.
19. Fodor, J. A. (1975). *The language of thought*. New York: Crowell.
20. Fodor, J. A. (1987). *Psychosemantics: The problem of meaning in the philosophy of mind*. Cambridge, StateMA: MIT Press.
21. Fox, C. R., & Poldrack, R. A. (2009). Prospect theory and the brain. In Glimcher, P. W., Camerer, C. F., Fehr, E., & Poldrack, R. A. (Eds.), *Neuroeconomics: Decision making and the brain* (pp. 145–174). London: Elsevier/Academic Press.
22. Frijda, N. H. (1986). *The emotions*. Cambridge: Cambridge University Press.
23. Frijda, N. H., Ortony, A., Sonnemans, J., & Clore, G. L. (1992). The complexity of intensity: Issues concerning the structure of emotion intensity. In M. S. Clark (Ed.), *Review of Personality and Social Psychology* (Vol. 13, pp. 60–89). Newbury Park: Sage.
24. Goldie, P. (2000). *The emotions: A philosophical exploration*. Oxford: Clarendon Press.
25. Goldie, P. (2007). Emotion. *Philosophy Compass, 2*, 928–938.
26. Goldie, P. (2009). Getting feelings into emotional experience in the right way. *Emotion Review, 1*, 232–239.
27. Goldstein, I. (2002). Are emotions feelings? A further look at hedonic theories of emotions. *Consciousness & Emotion, 3*, 21–33.
28. Goldthorpe, J. H. (1998). Rational action theory for sociology. *British Journal of Sociology, 49*, 167–192.
29. Gordon, R. M. (1978). Emotion labeling and cognition. *Journal for the Theory of Social Behaviour, 8*, 125-135.
30. Green, O. H. (1992). *The emotions: A philosophical theory*. Dordrecht: Kluwer.
31. Griffith, P. E. (1997). *What emotions really are*. Chicago: University of Chicago Press.
32. Heider, F. (1958). *The psychology of interpersonal relations*. New York: Wiley.
33. Helm, B. (2001). *Emotional reason*: Deliberation, motivation, and the nature of value. Cambridge: Cambridge University Press.
34. Hempel, C. G. (1965). *Aspects of scientific explanation*. New York: Free Press.
35. James, W. (1884). What is an emotion? *Mind, 9*, 188-205.
36. James, W. (1950). *Principles of Psychology* (Vol. 1 & 2). New York: Dover. (Original work published 1890).
37. Köhler, W. (1947). *Gestalt Psychology* (2nd ed.). New York: Liveright.
38. Külpe, O. (1893). *Grundriss der Psychologie. Auf experimenteller Grundlage dargestellt* [Outlines of psychology]. Leipzig: Wilhelm Engelmann.
39. Lazarus, R. S. (1991). *Emotion and adaptation*. New York: Oxford University Press.
40. Lewis, D. (1972). Psychophysical and theoretical identifications. *Australasian Journal of Philosophy, 50*, 249-258.
41. Lipton, P. (2004). *Inference to the best explanation*. London: Routledge.
42. Lyons, W. (1980). *Emotion*. Cambridge: Cambridge University Press.
43. Mackie, J. (1974). *The cement of the universe: A study of causation*. Oxford: Clarendon Press.
44. Madl, T., Baars, B. J., Franklin, S. (2011). The timing of the cognitive cycle. *PLoS ONE, 6*: e14803. doi:10.1371/journal.pone.0014803
45. Mandler, G. (1984). *Mind and body*. New York: Norton.
46. Marks, J. (1982). A theory of emotion. *Philosophical Studies, 42*, 227–242.
47. Marsella, S., Gratch, J., & Petta, P. (2010). Computational models of emotion. In K. R. Scherer, T. Bänziger, & E. Roesch (Eds.) *Blueprint for affective computing: A sourcebook* (pp. 21–46). Oxford: Oxford University Press.

48. Meinong, A. (1894). *Psychologisch-ethische Untersuchungen zur Wert-Theorie* [Psychological-ethical investigations in value theory]. Graz, Austria: Leuschner & Lubensky. Reprinted in R. Haller & R. Kindinger (Eds.). (1968). *Alexius Meinong Gesamtausgabe* [Alexius Meinong's complete works] (Vol. III, pp. 3–244). Graz, Austria: Akademische Druck- und Verlagsanstalt.
49. Meinong, A. (1910). *Über Annahmen* [On assumptions] (2nd ed.). Leipzig, Austria: Barth. Reprinted in R. Haller & R. Kindinger (Eds.). (1977). *Alexius Meinong Gesamtausgabe* [Alexius Meinong's complete works] (Vol. IV). Graz, Austria: Akademische Druck- und Verlagsanstalt.
50. Meinong, A. (1917). Über emotionale Präsentation [On emotional presentation]. In *Sitzungsberichte der Kaiserlichen Akademie der Wissenschaften in Wien, Philosophisch-Historische Klasse* (Vol. 183, pp. 1–181). Wien: Hölder. Wiederabdruck in: R. Haller & R. Kindinger (Hrsg.) (1968), Alexius Meinong Gesamtausgabe [Alexius Meinong's complete works] (Vol III) (pp. 285–465). Graz: Akademische Druck- und Verlagsanstalt.
51. Mele, A. R. (1992). *Springs of action: Understanding intentional behavior.* NY: Oxford University Press.
52. Mellers, B. A. (2000). Choice and the relative pleasure of consequences. *Psychological Bulletin, 126,* 910–924.
53. Mellers, B. A., Schwartz, A., Ho, K., & Ritov, I. (1997). Decision affect theory: Emotional reactions to the outcomes of risky options. *Psychological Science, 8,* 423-429.
54. Meyer, W.-U., Reisenzein, R. and Schützwohl, A. (2001). *Einführung in die Emotionspsychologie, Band I* [Introduction to the psychology of emotions, Vol 1]. Bern: Huber. (2nd edition)
55. Miceli, M., & Castelfranchi, C. (1997). Basic principles of psychic suffering: A preliminary account. *Theory & Psychology, 7,* 769–798.
56. Miceli, M., & Castelfranchi, C. (2002). The mind and the future: The (negative) power of expectations. *Theory & Psychology, 12,* 335–366.
57. Miceli, M., & Castelfranchi, C. (2007). The envious mind. *Cognition and Emotion, 21,* 449–479.
58. Oatley, K., & Johnson- Laird, P. N. (1987). Towards a cognitive theory of emotions. *Cognition and Emotion, 1,* 29–50.
59. Ortony, A., Clore, G. L. & Collins, A. (1988). *The cognitive structure of emotions.* Cambridge: Cambridge University Press.
60. Pitcher, G. (1965). Emotion. *Mind, 74,* 326-346.
61. Prinz, J. (2004). *Gut reactions: A perceptual theory of emotion.* Oxford: Oxford University Press.
62. Pugmire, D. (1998). *Rediscovering emotion.* Edinburgh: Edinburgh University Press.
63. Reisenzein, R. (1994a). Kausalattribution und Emotion [Causal attribution and emotion]. In F. Försterling & J. Stiensmeier-Pelster (Eds.), *Attributionstheorie: Grundlagen und Anwendungen* (pp. 123–161). Göttingen: Hogrefe.
64. Reisenzein, R. (1994b). Pleasure-arousal theory and the intensity of emotions. *Journal of Personality and Social Psychology, 67,* 525–539.
65. Reisenzein, R. (2000). Einschätzungstheoretische Ansätze [Appraisal theories]. In J. H. Otto, H. A. Euler, & H. Mandl (Eds.), *Emotionspsychologie: Ein Handbuch* (pp. 117–150). Beltz: Psychologie Verlags Union.
66. Reisenzein, R. (2001a). Appraisal processes conceptualized from a schema-theoretic perspective: Contributions to a process analysis of emotions. In K. R. Scherer, A. Schorr, & T. Johnstone (Eds.), *Appraisal processes in emotion: Theory, methods, research* (pp. 187–201). New York: Oxford University Press.
67. Reisenzein, R. (2001b). Die Allgemeine Hedonistische Motivationstheorie der Sozialpsychologie [The General Hedonistic Motivation Theory of Social Psychology]. In R. K. Silbereisen & M. Reitzle (Eds.), *Bericht über den 42. Kongress der DGPs in Jena 2000* (pp. 649–661) Lengerich: Pabst Science Publishers.
68. Reisenzein, R. (2006). Arnold's theory of emotion in historical perspective. *Cognition and Emotion, 20,* 920–951.

69. Reisenzein, R. (2007). What is a definition of emotion? And are emotions mental-behavioral processes? *Social Science Information, 46,* 424–428.
70. Reisenzein, R. (2009a). Emotions as metarepresentational states of mind: Naturalizing the belief-desire theory of emotion. *Cognitive Systems Research, 10,* 6–20.
71. Reisenzein, R. (2009b). Emotional experience in the computational belief-desire theory of emotion. *Emotion Review, 1,* 214–222.
72. Reisenzein, R. (2010). Moralische Gefühle aus der Sicht der kognitiv-motivationalen Theorie der Emotion [Moral emotions from the perspective of the cognitive-motivational theory of emotion]. In M. Iorio & R. Reisenzein (Hg.), *Regel, Norm, Gesetz. Eine interdisziplinäre Bestandsaufnahme* [Rule, norm, law: An interdisciplinary survey] (pp. 257–283). Frankfurt am Main: Peter Lang Verlag.
73. Reisenzein, R. (2012). Extending the belief-desire theory of emotions to fantasy emotions. *Proceedings of the ICCM 2012,* 313–314.
74. Reisenzein, R., & Bördgen, S., Holtbernd, T., & Matz, D. (2006). Evidence for strong dissociation between emotion and facial displays: The case of surprise. *Journal of Personality and Social Psychology, 91,* 295–315.
75. Reisenzein, R., & Döring, S. (2009). Ten perspectives on emotional experience: Introduction to the special issue. *Emotion Review, 1,* 195-205.
76. Reisenzein, R., & Junge, M. (2006). *The intensity of disappointment and relief as a function of belief and desire strength.* Talk presented at the 45th Congress of the German Association of Psychology, Nuremberg, 2006.
77. Reisenzein, R., & Junge, M. (2012). Language and emotion from the perspective of the computational belief-desire theory of emotion. In P. A. Wilson (Ed.) *Dynamicity in emotion concepts (Lodz Studies in Language, 27,* pp. 37–59). Frankfurt am Main: Peter Lang.
78. Reisenzein, R., Meyer, W.-U., & Schützwohl, A. (1995). James and the physical basis of emotion: A comment on Ellsworth. *Psychological Review, 102,* 757–761.
79. Reisenzein, R., Meyer, W.-U., & Schützwohl, A. (2003). *Einführung in die Emotionspsychologie, Band III: Kognitive Emotionstheorien.* [*Introduction to the psychology of emotions, Vol 3: Cognitive emotion theories*]. Bern: Huber.
80. Reisenzein, R., & Schönpflug, W. (1992). Stumpf's cognitive-evaluative theory of emotion. *American Psychologist, 47,* 34–45.
81. Roberts, R. C. (2003). *Emotions: An essay in aid of moral psychology.* Cambridge: Cambridge University Press.
82. Russell, J. A. (2003). Core affect and the psychological construction of emotion. *Psychological Review, 110,* 145–172.
83. Salmela, M. (2002). The problem of affectivity in cognitive theories of emotion. *Consciousness & Emotion, 3,* 159–182.
84. Schachter, S. (1964). The interaction of cognitive and physiological determinants of emotional state. In L. Berkowitz (Ed.), *Advances in experimental social psychology* (Vol. 1, pp. 49–80). New York: Academic Press.
85. Scherer, K. R. (2001). Appraisal considered as a process of multilevel sequential checking. In K. R. Scherer, A. Schorr, & T. Johnstone (Eds.), *Appraisal processes in emotion: Theory, Methods, Research* (pp. 92-129). Oxford: Oxford University Press.
86. Scherer, K. R. (2005). What are emotions? And how can they be measured?. *Social Science Information, 44,* 693–727.
87. Siemer, M. (2008). Beyond prototypes and classical definitions: Evidence for a theory-based representation of emotion concepts. *Cognition and Emotion, 22,* 620–632.
88. Smith, M. (1987). The Humean theory of motivation. *Mind, 96,* 36-61.
89. Solomon, R. C. (1976). *The passions.* Garden City, NY: Anchor Press/Doubleday.
90. Stumpf, C. (1899). über den Begriff der Gemüthsbewegung [On the concept of emotion]. *Zeitschrift fur Psychologie und Physiologie der Sinnesorgane, 21,* 47–99.
91. Stocker, M. (1983). Psychic feelings: Their importance and irreducibility. *Australasian Journal of Philosophy, 61,* 5–26.
92. Whiting, D. (2011). The feeling theory of emotion and the object-directed emotions. *European Journal of Philosophy, 1,* 281–303.
93. Wooldridge, M. J. (2002). *Reasoning about rational agents.* Cambridge, MA: MIT Press.

94. Wundt, W. (1896). *Grundriss der Psychologie* [Outlines of Psychology]. Leipzig: Engelmann.

Chapter 13
Cognitive-based emotions: Theory and evidence from the brain

Giorgio Coricelli and Mateus Joffily

Abstract We analyze here the neural correlates and the role of cognitive-based emotions in decision-making. Our main hypothesis is that cognitive processes, such as counterfactual thinking and social comparison, elicit a specific class of emotions. Paradigmatic examples are regret ("I would have been better off by choosing another option") and envy ("I would have been better off by choosing the option he chose"). Evidence from behavioral and neuroscientific research show how these emotions play a crucial role in adaptive behavior. Thus, demonstrating how the interplay between cognition and emotion contributes to determine individual and social decision-making.

1 Introduction

Cristiano Castelfranchi is certainly one of the most influential theoreticians of the belief-desire approach of emotions. One distinctive aspect on his effort is to unveil the complexity of emotion experience in its finest nuances (Castelfranchi and Miceli, 2009; Lorini and Castelfranchi, 2007; Miceli and Castelfranchi, 1997). His approach doesn't limit to describe how belief-desire theory can account for families of emotions, but he explicitly dissects the emotion complexity to show how belief-desire can account for the subtlety among members of a same emotion family.

Castelfranchi has also a long-term commitment of research in cognition and social interactions (Castelfranchi and Paglieri, 2007; Castelfranchi, 2000; Conte and Castelfranchi, 1995). His recent control-theoretic model of goal-directed action integrates action, perception, attention and motivation within the same

Giorgio Coricelli
Department of Economics, University of Southern California, USA
e-mail: giorgio.coricelli@usc.edu

Mateus Joffily
Center for Mind Brain Sciences-CIMEC, University of Trento, Italy
e-mail: mateus.joffily@unitn.it

computational framework, and makes reference to the most advanced models in computational neuroscience (Pezzulo and Castelfranchi, 2009).

A common quantity among control-theoretic models of the brain is prediction error, loosely defined as the difference between a reference (desired) and a measured (sensed) signal (Dayan and Abbott, 2001). In our perspective, the belief-desire theory offers an appealing formulation to fill the gap between cognitive theories and neural based theories of emotion, if one attempts to relate belief-desire (mis)match to prediction error. A free energy theory of the brain has been recently proposed that seems to offer an adequate computational framework to integrate these ideas (Friston, Kilner and Harrison, 2006).

In what follows, we illustrate the impact that Castelfranchi's ideas had on our own research and on neuroscience in general. We outline the neural basis of a class of cognitive-based emotions and their fundamental role in adaptive behavior. We address the following questions: What are the neural underpinnings of cognitive-based emotions such as regret (based on counterfactual thinking) and envy (based on social comparison)? What are the theoretical implications of incorporating cognitive-based emotions into the process of choice, and into adaptive models of decision-making? In line with recent work on emotion-based decision making, we attempt to characterize the brain areas underlying decision processes in individual and social settings and, more specifically, define the functional relationship between "rational" decision making and emotional influences that impact on these decisional processes. Our focus, by way of illustration, is on the contribution of cortical (orbitofrontal cortex, OFC) and subcortical areas (amygdala, striatum) in both the experience and anticipation of cognitive-based emotions, such as regret.

2 Cognitive-based emotions in decision-making

We consider regret as a paradigmatic example of cognitive-based emotions. Regret is elicited by a counterfactual comparison (Roese and Olson, 1995; Byrne, 2002; Zeelenberg and van Dijk, 2004) between the outcome of a choice and the better outcome of a foregone rejected alternatives (what might have been). Regret differs from disappointment in its abstract point of reference: it arises from a discrepancy between the actual outcome and an outcome that would have pertained had an alternative choice been taken. Regret is an emotion characterized by the feeling of responsibility for the negative outcome of our choice (Bell, 1982; Loomes and Sugden, 1982; Gilovich and Melvec, 1994); while, disappointment is the emotion related to an unexpected negative outcome independently of the responsibility of the chooser (Loomes and Sugden, 1986; Bell, 1995; Miceli and Castelfranchi, 2010).

One important question is whether regret and disappointment are encoded by specific cerebral regions. Camille et al. (2004) studied the relationship between decision-making and emotion in normal subjects and in patients with selective lesions to the orbitofrontal cortex (OFC). The experimental task (regret gambling task) required subjects to choose between two gambles, each having different probabilities and different expected outcomes. After being exposed to a number of trials where they experienced regret, control subjects subsequently begun to choose the gambles with probable outcomes likely to produce minimal regret, indicating that they learnt from their prior emotional experience and integrated consideration about future emotional responses to the outcome of their choice. By contrast, patients with lesions of the orbitofrontal cortex did not report regret and did not anticipate negative affective consequences of their choices. The absence of regret in orbitofrontal patients suggests that these patients fail to grasp this concept of liability for one's own decision that characterized the emotion experienced by normal subjects. It is important to highlight the fact that OFC patients are not emotionally flat or unresponsive. For instance, these patients expressed a normal level of disappointment in Camille et al. (2004), and a higher than normal level of anger in response to unfairness in social situations (unfair offers in an Ultimatum Game)(Koenigs and Tranel, 2007; Conte and Castelfranchi, 1995).

Coricelli et al. (2005) measured brain activity using functional magnetic resonance imaging (fMRI) while subjects participated in the regret gambling task. Increasing regret was correlated with enhanced activity in the medial orbitofrontal region, the dorsal anterior cingulate cortex (ACC) and anterior hippocampus. Furthermore, the activity in response to experiencing regret (OFC/ACC/medial temporal cortex) is distinct from activity seen with mere outcome evaluation (ventral striatum), and in disappointment elicited by the mismatch between actual and expected outcome of choice. Indeed, the magnitude of disappointment correlated with enhanced activity in middle temporal gyrus and dorsal brainstem, including periaqueductal gray matter, a region implicated in processing aversive signal such as pain. This suggests distinctive neural substrates in reward processing, and the fact that the OFC and medial temporal cortex areas can bias basic dopamine mediated reward responses (De Martino et al., 2006).

But we live in a social environment, and many if not most of our choices are not made in isolation: we observe others that make similar choices, and we can observe their outcome as well. The same logic suggesting that using the information on the outcome of the actions we did not choose is useful in improving our future performance also suggests that we should use the information on the outcome of actions that others chose. The counterfactual reasoning extends from private to social learning. This is Festinger's idea, presented in his theory of Social Comparison (Festinger, 1954; Miceli and Castelfranchi, 2007). In this view, regret has a social correspondent, envy. Just as regret derives from the comparison between what we received from an action, and what we could have received from action that we did not take, so envy may simply derive from the comparison between the outcome from the action we chose and the outcome from an action we did not choose but someone else did. However, emotional evaluation of social rewards is more complex, because outcomes that are socially observable also affect the relative ranking of individuals, and so this evaluation is the result of social learning and social ranking.

Bault et al. (2008) conducted a study to investigate whether social and private emotions influence monetary decisions in different ways. The experimental task was similar to the lottery described in Camille et al (2004), except for the fact that participants could also observe the choice that others have made. Results showed that emotions in the social condition (envy and gloating), for the events in which participants made different choices, are stronger than in the single player condition (regret and relief). Thus, envy and gloating matter more because they are socially competitive emotions not just interpersonal ones. The second result is that social emotions operate differently from private ones: while regret looms larger than relief, gloating looms larger than envy. The effect is not induced by any social emotion (as opposed to non-social) as shared regret and shared relief received weaker ratings than regret and relief experienced in a non-social context. Indeed, many environments follow the rule winner-takes-all, and being first is much better than being second, while the latter is not much different from being third, gains might loom larger than losses.

3 The adaptive function of Cognitive-based emotions

Regret embodies the painful lesson that things would have been better under a different choice, thus inducing a disposition to behavioral change (Ritov, 1996). People, including those with a deep knowledge of optimal strategies often try to avoid the likelihood of future regret even when this conflicts with the prescription of decisions based upon rational choice, which predicts that individuals faced with a decision between multiple alternatives under uncertainty will opt for the course of action with maximum expected utility, a function of both the probability and the magnitude of the expected payoff (Von Neumann and Morgenstern, 1944).

In the theory of regret as a form of adaptive learning (Megiddo, 1980; Foster and Vohra, 1999; Hart and Mas-Colell, 2000; Foster and Young, 2003; Hart, 2005), learning adjusts the probability of choosing an action depending on the difference between the total rewards that could have been obtained with the choice of that action and the realized rewards. For example, in the Hart-MasColell (Hart and Mas-Colell, 2000) regret- matching rule model the regret for having chosen the action k instead of j is the difference between the total reward obtained if action j had been chosen instead of k in the past, and the total realized value. The probability of choosing an action is determined in every period by adjusting upwards the probability of choosing the action j by an amount proportional to the regret. This type of procedures have optimality properties just as the adjustment process based on prediction error: the Megiddo theorem (Megiddo, 1980) for the single player case, and the Foster-Vohra-Hart-MasColell theorems for games show that this procedure converges to optimal choices in the single player case and to correlated equilibria in the case of games.

Coricelli et al. (2005) reported that, across their fMRI experiment subjects became increasingly regret aversive, a cumulative effect reflected in enhanced activity within ventro-medial orbitofrontal cortex and amygdala. Under these circumstances the same pattern of activity that was expressed with the experience of regret was also expressed just prior to choice, suggesting the same neural circuitry mediates both direct experience of regret and its anticipation. OFC activity related to the effect of experienced emotions in relation to potential behavioral adjustment has been also found in a recent study by Beer et al. (2006). Thus, the OFC and the amygdala contribute to this form of high level learning based on past emotional experience, in a manner that mirrors the role of these structures in acquisition of value in low-level learning contexts (Gottfried et al., 2003).

Moreover, the affective consequences of choice, such as the experience of regret, can induce specific mechanisms of cognitive control. Coricelli et al. (2005) observed enhanced responses in brain structures related to cognitive control, such as right dorsolateral prefrontal cortex, right lateral OFC and inferior parietal lobule during a choice phase after the experience of regret (Coricelli et al., 2005), where subsequent choice processes, induced reinforcement, or avoidance of, the experienced behavior (Clark et al., 2004). Corroborating results from Simon-Thomas et al. (Simon-Thomas et al., 2005) show that negative emotions can recruit cognitive-based right hemisphere responses. Thus, negative affective consequences (e.g., regret) induce specific mechanisms of cognitive control on subsequent choices.

These data suggest a mechanism through which comparing choice outcome with its alternatives (counterfactual comparison), and the associated feeling of responsibility, promotes behavioral flexibility and exploratory strategies in dynamic environments so as to minimize the likelihood of emotionally negative outcomes.

4 Conclusions

We are still scratching the surface of the emotion organization in the brain. We are certainly very far from the refinement that Castelfranchi's theoretical analysis offers, but we can already start to appreciate the importance of his ideas to guide us in this quest (Coricelli et al, 2005). Experimental and theoretical results demonstrate an adaptive role of cognitive-based emotions, such as regret and envy. These emotions also figure prominently in the literature of learning in games (Hart, 2005; Conte and Castelfranchi, 1995). A remarkable result in this literature is that if players in a game minimize regret, the frequency of their choices converges to a correlated equilibrium (i.e., the rational solution) of the game. This has a general implication for our understanding of the role of emotions in decision making and rejects the dual/conflict view of 'emotion vs. cognition' (rationality) by showing the powerful consequences of full integration between those two components of human decision making. Within this hypothesis, emotions do not necessarily interfere with rational decision making, and on the contrary they may implement it: they are a way of evaluating past outcomes to adjust choices in the future.

Advancements in brain imaging methods and improvements in signal detection are progressing fast nowadays. Soon, neuroscientists will find the required technical conditions to explore the subtlety of emotion experience in much more detail. Cristiano Castelfranchi's theoretical work provides an extraordinary guide.

References

1. Bault N, Coricelli G, Rustichini A (2008) *Interdependent utilities: how social ranking affects choice behavior*. PLoS ONE 3:e3477.
2. Beer JS, Knight RT, D'Esposito M (2006) *Controlling the integration of emotion and cognition: the role of frontal cortex in distinguishing helpful from hurtful emotional information*. Psychol Sci 17:448-453.
3. Bell DE (1982) *Regret in decision-making under uncertainty*. Operations Research 30:961-981.
4. Bell DE (1995) *Disappointment in decision making under uncertainty*. Operations Research 33:1-27.
5. Byrne RM (2002) *Mental models and counterfactual thoughts about what might have been*. Trends Cogn Sci 6:426-431.
6. Camille N, Coricelli G, Sallet J, Pradat-Diehl P, Duhamel JR, Sirigu A (2004) *The involvement of the orbitofrontal cortex in the experience of regret*. Science 304:1167- 1170.
7. Castelfranchi C (2000) *Through the agents' minds: Cognitive mediators of social action*. Mind and Society. 1:109-140.
8. Castelfranchi C, Miceli M (2009) *The Cognitive-Motivational Compound of Emotional Experience*. Emotion Review 1:223 -231.
9. Castelfranchi C, Paglieri F. (2007) *The role of beliefs in goal dynamics: prolegomena to a constructive theory of intentions*. Synthese 155:237-263.
10. Clark L, Cools R, Robbins TW (2004) *The neuropsychology of ventral prefrontal cortex: decision-making and reversal learning*. Brain Cogn 55:41-53
11. Conte R, Castelfranchi C (1995) *Cognitive And Social Action*. Garland Science.
12. Coricelli G, Critchley HD, Joffily M, O'Doherty JP, Sirigu A, Dolan RJ (2005) *Regret and its avoidance: a neuroimaging study of choice behavior*. Nat Neurosci 8:1255-1262.
13. Dayan P, Abbott LF (2001) *Theoretical Neuroscience: Computational and Mathematical Modeling of Neural Systems (1st ed.)*. The MIT Press.
14. De Martino B, Kumaran D, Seymour B, Dolan RJ (2006) *Frames, biases, and rational decision-making in the human brain*. Science 313:684-687.
15. Festinger L (1954) *A theory of social comparison processes*. Human Relations 7:117-140.
16. Foster DP, Vohra R (1999) *Regret in the On-Line Decision Problem*. Games and Economic Behavior 29:7–35
17. Foster DP, Young HP (2003) *Learning, Hypothesis Testing, and Nash Equilibrium*. Games and Economic Behavior 45:73–96.
18. Friston K, Kilner J, Harrison L (2006) *A free energy principle for the brain*. Journal of Physiology Paris 100:70-87.
19. Gilovich T, Melvec VH (1994) *The temporal pattern to the experience of regret*. Journal of Personality and Social Psychology 67:357-365.
20. Gottfried JA, O'Doherty J, Dolan RJ (2003) *Encoding predictive reward value in human amygdala and orbitofrontal cortex*. Science 301:1104-1107.
21. Hart S (2005) *Adaptive Heuristics*. Econometrica 73:1401–1430.
22. Hart S, Mas-Colell A (2000) *A simple adaptive procedure leading to correlated equilibrium*. Econometrica 68:1127-1150.

23. Koenigs M, Tranel D (2007) *Irrational economic decision-making after ventromedial prefrontal damage: evidence from the Ultimatum Game*. J Neurosci 27:951-956.
24. Loomes G, Sugden R (1982) *Regret theory: An alternative theory of rational choice under uncertainty*. Economic Journal 92:805-824.
25. Loomes G, Sugden R (1986) *Disappointment and dynamic inconsitstncy in choice under uncertainty*. Review of Economic Studies 53:271-282.
26. Lorini, E, Castelfranchi C (2007). *The cognitive structure of surprise: looking for basic principles*. International Review of Philosophy 26:133:149.
27. Megiddo N (1980) *On Repeated Games with Incomplete Information Played by Non- Bayesian Players*. International Journal of Game Theory 9:157–167.
28. Miceli M, Castelfranchi C (1997) *Basic Principles of Psychic Suffering*. Theory and Psychology 7:769 -798.
29. Miceli M, Castelfranchi C (2007) *The envious mind*. Cogntion and Emotion 21:449-479
30. Miceli M, Castelfranchi C (2010) *Hope The Power of Wish and Possibility*. Theory and Psychology 20:251-276
31. Pezzulo G, Castelfranchi C (2009) *Thinking as the control of imagination: a conceptual framework for goal-directed systems*. Psychological Research 73:559-577.
32. Ritov I (1996) *Probabilities of regret: Anticipation of uncertainty resolution in choice*. Organizational Behavior and Human Decision Processes 66:228-236.
33. Roese NJ, Olson JM (1995) *What might have been: The social psychology of counterfactual thinking*. Mahwah, NJ: Erlbaum.
34. Simon-Thomas ER, Role KO, Knight RT (2005) *Behavioral and electrophysiological evidence of a right hemisphere bias for the influence of negative emotion on higher cognition*. J Cogn Neurosci 17:518-529.
35. Von Neumann J, Morgenstern O (1944) *Theory of Games and Economic Behavior*. Princeton NJ: Princeton University Press.
36. Zeelenberg M, van Dijk E (2004) *On the comparative nature of the emotion regret*. In: The Psychology of Counterfactual Thinking (Mandel D, Hilton J, Castellani P, eds). London: Routledge.

Chapter 14
Pride and its expression in political debates

Isabella Poggi and Francesca D'Errico

Abstract The paper analyses pride, its nature, expression and functions, according to a model in terms of goals and beliefs, by connecting it to the goals of power, image and self-image. Starting from a semantic analysis of the lexicon of pride, image and self-image in Italian, it defines the trait of "pride" and the emotion of "being proud of" in terms of their mental ingredients, the beliefs and goals represented in the mind of a proud person, and distinguishes three types of pride: dignity, superiority and arrogance pride. Then it overviews the body expressions of the affective states under analysis, and their function as a display of dominance during TV broadcasted political debates, finding that the three types of pride differ in terms of their gaze and smile behavior.

Index Terms: Pride, image, self-image, social emotions, mental ingredients, social signals, gaze, facial expression, political debates

1 Introduction

Pride is a positive emotion that we feel as we focus on positive qualities of ourselves, or on some achievement that we consider due to our own capacities or efforts, or anyhow linked to our own identity; it has an important effect over how other people view us and how we view ourselves, hence over our relationships with others. Thus studying pride implies exploring the areas of image and self image, and the relations of power between people.

In this work we analyse the expression of pride in political debates, and its functions as an expression of dominance. Before going into the body signals

Isabella Poggi
Department of Education, Roma Tre University, Italy
e-mail: poggi@uniroma3.it

Francesca D'Errico
Department of Education, Roma Tre University, Italy
e-mail: fderrico@uniroma3.it

that display the emotion of pride, we provide an analysis of the mental states that characterize pride both as a transient emotion and as a steady personality trait, and we do so by making reference to a model of mind and social interaction and communication in terms of goals and beliefs. We thus show how the mental state of pride is linked to the goals of image and self-image, and what is its place in the social relations of concurrence and competition.

After an overview of related works (Sect. 2), we present the notions of power, image and self-image in terms of goals and belief (Sect. 3 – 4). Then, based on a semantic analysis of the lexicon of pride, image and self-image in Italian (Sect. 5), we define the emotion of being "proud of" and the trait of being "proud", while looking for its "mental ingredients": the beliefs and goals that are represented in the mind of a proud person (Sect. 6). Finally we analyse the body expressions of those affective states and their function as a display of dominance during TV broadcasted political debates (Sect. 7 – 8).

2 Previous work on pride

"Pride has no other mirror for admire itself except pride, because knees bent feed the arrogance and are the proud man's fees" (Troilus and Cressida, III, 3; Shakespeare, 1601).

Shakespeare's aphorism captures the prevailing interpretation that for centuries has accompanied the emotion of pride. In particular, religious speculation, aimed to teach followers the supreme virtue of humility, has traditionally labeled as sinful and bad the emotions that privileg the "self" to the detriment of the "Highest Good".

Starting from the Christian tradition, where for Augustine [1] and Aquinas [2] pride was one of the worst sins, "at the root of all evil", up to the interpretation of Buddhism, with Dalai Lama [3] warning from the excesses of "destructive" pride, pride is seen as strongly correlated to the vanities of the human nature. However, the possibility of exaggeration in the opposite direction, i.e. a depreciation of its value, was seen as a risk by both Buddhists and Aristotle [4]. From these considerations two different approaches stem for the concept of "self-evaluation" that is behind this emotion: a kind of pride defined by Aristotle ([4]; cit. in Tracy, 2010) as "the crown of Virtues", and another opposite kind, that he defines as "hybris", or "going with thought beyond the right fit": the first called "megalopsychia" or proper pride, the other "hyperephanos", or over-appearing.

As noted by Tracy [5], the emotion of pride has been an object of attention more in ancient speculation (Greek myth, religion, moral philosophy) than in psychological literature. Within this, Darwin [6] and then Lewis [7] included pride among the "complex", more specifically the "self-aware" emotions: those emotions, like embarrassment, shame and guilt, that can be felt only by someone who has a concept of self, like a child of a least two years and a half, or some great apes. Later, Tracy and Robins [8] investigated nature, function and communication of this emotion. They distinguish two types of pride, authentic and hubristic. Authentic pride, mainly represented in words like *accomplished* and *confident*, is positively associated with "extraversion, agreeableness, conscientiousness, and genuine self-esteem, whereas hubristic pride"; related to words like *arrogant* and *conceited*, it "is negatively related to these traits but positively associated with self-aggrandizing narcissism and shame-proneness" [[8]; p.149]. The latter "may contribute to aggression, hostility and interpersonal problems" (p.148), while the former can favour altruistic action, since the most frequent behavioural responses to pride experience are seeking and making contact with others. From a cognitive point of view, "authentic pride seems to result from attributions to internal but instable, specific, and controllable causes, such as (...) effort, hard work, and specific accomplishments" [5], whereas hubristic pride results from attribution to "internal but stable, global, and uncontrollable causes", such as "talents, abilities, and global positive traits".

Concerning the adaptive function of pride, they propose that the feeling "might have evolved to provide information about an individual's current level or social status and acceptance" [[8]; p.149], thus being importantly liked to self-esteem. Tracy and Robins also investigated the nonverbal expression of pride, demonstrating its universality and singling out its constituting elements: small smile, head slightly tilted back, arms raised and expanded posture. The nonverbal expression of pride may serve to "alerting one's social group that the proud individual merits increased status and acceptance" (p.149-150).

Tracy, Shariff & Cheng [5], by adopting a functionalist view of emotions, propose that pride serves the adaptive function of promoting high status, and does so because the pleasant reinforcing emotion of pride due to previous accomplishments enhances motivation and persistence in future tasks, while the internal experience, by enhancing self-esteem, informs the individual, and the external nonverbal expression informs others, of one's achievement, indicating one deserves a high status in the group. While wondering if the two facts of pride, authentic and hubristic, have different adaptive functions, they remind that humans seek two distinct forms of high status – dominance, that can be acquired mainly through force, threat, intimidation, aggression, and prestige, a respect-based status stemming from demonstrated knowledge, skill, and altruism – and they posit that hubristic pride and its expression serves the function of dominance while authentic pride the function of prestige. In fact, the feature of expanded posture is very close to the bluff display before contests between animals, and hubristic pride seems to correlate with high levels of testosterone. Authentic pride, instead, is sustained by high levels of the neurotransmitter serotonine, and looks linked to prestige – a way to gain a higher status by demonstrating one's real skills and social and cooperative ability.

To sum up, for Tracy and Robins [8], "Authentic pride might motivate behaviours geared toward long-term status attainment, whereas hubristic pride provides a 'short cut' solution, promoting status that is immediate but fleeting and, in some cases, unwarranted"; it might have "evolved as a 'cheater' attempt to convince others of one's success by showing the same expression when no achievement occurred" (p.150).

3 A new perspective on pride

This view of pride, its two contrasting facets, and their function, looks in a great part correct, but incomplete. For example, according to Gladkova [10] this is too anglo-centric a view of pride in that it only sticks to the meaning of the word in English, while not taking into account other aspects of this emotion: for example, compared to the meaning of the English words *pride* and *to take pride in*, the Russian *gordit'sja* implies a more intense emotional experience, and one due to the realization not only of the goodness of one's actions, but also of one's innate qualities and characteristics; and these actions or characteristic have to be recognized as outstanding by other people. Thus Gladkova points at a kind of pride referred not only to self- esteem, but also to esteem by others.

Moreover, the picture provided by Tracy and others is somehow not well balanced, given the clearly negative connotation of *"hubristic"* pride, and the idea that its expression is necessarily "cheating" whereas the other is not, as stated by the very adjective *"authentic"* pride. Actually, these two (or more?) facets of pride might all have a positive function, and all might (why not?) be simulated and used to cheat. Why shouldn't it be possible to simulate also the so called *"authentic"* pride? And might one not be *"authentically"* arrogant?

In this work we analyse pride and its expression according to a model of mind an social interaction in terms of goals and beliefs. After defining the notions of power, dominance, evaluation, image and self image in terms of this theoretical framework, we provide a conceptual analysis of pride, starting from a semantic analysis of the Italian words in this area, and trying to outline an articulated net of dimensions to disentangle their nuances of meaning. This analysis is a first step to find out the "ingredients" of pride, that is, the beliefs and goals represented in the mind of the proud individual. Finally we analyse the nonverbal signals of pride in TV broadcast political debates, to explore the relationship between dominance and the expression of pride.

4 Power, evaluation, image and self-image

According to a model of mind, social interaction and emotions in terms of goals and beliefs [11, 12, 13, 14, 15, 16, 17, 18, 19, 20, 21], the life of a natural or artificial, individual or collective system consists of pursuing *goals*. A goal is a regulatory state not realized in the world: as long as the system perceives a discrepancy between the actual state of the world and the regulatory state, to realize that goal it projects and performs a plan where each action aims at one goal and possibly to one or more supergoals, with all goals and supergoals finally aiming at the final goal to achieve.

In this framework, *power* can be first defined as a notion concerning a single Agent [19]. A has the *"power of"* goal g if A is likely to achieve g. A's "power of" g depends on external and internal resources, i.e. favourable world conditions (e.g., presence of material resources), and A's action capacities and knowledge. If world conditions are favourable and A can perform the necessary plan of action, A has *"power of"* with respect to goal g. The notion of *evaluation* can be defined in terms of *"power of"* [16, 22]: an *evaluation* is a belief about how much some object, event, person have or provide one with the "power of" necessary to some goal. A system conceives of evaluations about world conditions, adequacy of actions, and the respective importance of goals, necessary to choose which goal to pursue between incompatible ones. So one may lack the power to achieve some goal due to lack of resources, but also due to the necessity of choice. If achieving goal g prevents A from achieving goal q, A must choose between them, and lacks the "power of" for either of the two. If A lacks the capacities or resources to achieve g, while another Agent B is endowed with them, A "depends on" B to achieve g. From this *dependency* the social devices stem of *adoption* and *influence*. If A depends on B, A can achieve g only if B "adopts" A's goal g, i.e., if B puts one's actions and resources to the service of A's goal. So, A and B may have the goal to influence each other: A may want to influence B to adopt A's goal gA, and B may want to influence A to pursue B's goal gB in exchange. As A depends on B, B has the *"power to influence"* A. This gives B *"power over"* A. "Power to influence" and "power over" are *social* notions of power, in that they necessary entail two agents, A and B.

Adoption multiplies people's "power of" to achieve their goals, thanks to resource exchange; but to decide what goals of what people to adopt we need to evaluate people as to their dependency on us, their capacity and willingness to reciprocate: we form an image of them. Our *image* is the set of evaluative and non-evaluative beliefs that others conceive of about us. We strive to present a positive image of ourselves to have others adopt our goals, and thus to gain more "power of". The image we present is generally functional to the type of adoption we aim at: to hire me as a real-estate seller you evaluate me as to my extraversion or argumentation skills, to choose me as a friend, as to my affective qualities. In rare cases do we obtain adoption by presenting an image of lack of power (e.g. when people help us out of compassion); but in general to be adopted we must elicit a positive evaluation, i.e., show an image of power in some areas (e.g. when they adopt our goals because they esteem us). In choosing whether to adopt the goal of A or B, C will compare their respective values, to establish who has more power as against a particular goal. Thus we can count one more type of power, stemming from power comparison: to have *"more power than"* another. And the notion of dominance referred to in ethological and social psychological studies can be translated, in this model, just as this notion: if I am dominant with respect to you, this means that "I have more power than you" concerning some particular goal [23].

So, we all have a *"goal of image"* and a *"goal of positive image"* (goal of esteem); and all the goals against which we want to be evaluated positively by others make part of our *goal of* (positive) *image*. But we also have the goal of being evaluated better than others – of showing we have more power than others.

Besides projecting an image of us to others, we also have a *self-image*: a set of evaluative and non-evaluative beliefs about ourselves. Having evaluations about our own actual worth – beliefs concerning our power to achieve goals – is necessary for us to decide which goals to pursue, leaving aside ones out of our reach. [13, 24]. And having positive self-evaluations (a high *self-esteem*) gives us confidence that we will achieve the goals for which we have power. So we also have a *goal of* (positive) *self-image*.

What is the role of emotions in this framework? Emotions are multifaceted subjective states, encompassing internal feelings but also cognitive, physiological, expressive, motivational aspects, that are triggered any time an important adaptive goal is, or is likely to be, achieved or thwarted. In this, emotions are functionally linked to goals: they are adaptive devices that monitor the achievement or thwarting of important adaptive goals, like survival and wellbeing, acquisition of knowledge, acquiring and keeping resources, but also the goals of equity, attachment and affiliation, image and self-image [25, 26, 27, 28, 29]. We feel positive emotions for the achievement and negative ones for the thwarting of these goals, hence emotions can be clustered in families depending on the type of goal they monitor. For instance, shame monitors the goals of image and of self-image: we feel shame when we think that what we are or we do may cause others or ourselves to have a negative evaluation of us [30].

5 Dimensions in the lexicon of pride

Our first goal in this paper is to provide a conceptual analysis of pride. The end point of this is to find those that, within the model above, has been called, exploiting first a gastronomic [31] and then a medical metaphor [27, 32], the "ingredients" or the "anatomy" of pride: conceptual analysis means to single out the mental elements which combine in our mind to make up a particular emotion or other mental state. Yet, to reach this end, an intermediate useful step is ethno-semantic analysis. As shown in various works [32] a natural language reflects the way in which specific mental states are represented in our mind; hence a semantic analysis of words in the lexical area at issue provides a deep insight in the very structure of mental representations.

To start our conceptual analysis of pride, we collected 96 words and idioms that in Italian refer to the semantic area of image, self-image and power comparison (see Table 1). From a grammatical point of view, this area includes verbs (like *vantarsi* = to boast), adjectives (*presuntuoso* = cocky), nouns (*orgoglio* = pride) and adverbs (*graziosamente* = graciously). On the meaning side, according to the semantic elements they contain, these words can be distinguished in terms of various dimensions.

5.1 State/trait

A first dimension to set apart words in this lexical area is the difference between a single event and a steady state. As well as in anxiety one can be anxious just in a specific event or be an anxious person (see the difference between state and trait anxiety, Cattell and Scheier [33], pride too can be both an emotion felt in a specific situation and an enduring personality trait. In Italian, the adjective *"orgoglioso"* (proud) tends to refer to a personality trait, while the emotion is better mentioned by expressions like *"orgoglioso di"* or *"fiero di"* (proud of).

We may define the emotion *"essere orgoglioso di"* (to be proud of, to take pride in) as a positive emotion that A feels when A believes, with a high degree of certainty, that he achieved a goal, but did so thanks to one's own resources, without resorting to help from other people. This allows him to achieve his own goal of having a positive self-image, mainly in that he evaluates himself an autonomous person. Coming to the trait side, if personality can be viewed as a different importance attributed by different persons to the same goals [34], the term *"orgoglioso"* (proud) as a personality trait is referred to a person for whom his goal of self-image of being autonomous, i.e. not depending on others' help, has a priority before all other goals.

5.2 Image/self-image

Some words in the area of pride refer to feelings, communicative acts or personality traits connected to the goal of image, others to the goal of self-image, others to both.

For instance, *vantarsi* (to boast) is a communicative action aimed at presenting a positive image to other people, while one who *"si sente superiore"* (feels superior) simply has a high opinion of oneself, a very high self-esteem. He attributes a high importance to his goal of self-esteem, and in fact does have a high self-esteem. Yet, not necessarily does he want others to have the same high opinion as he does: his goal of image (at least, of his image before those others) is not so salient as his goal of self-image.

On the other hand, the words concerning pride both as an emotion and as a personality trait may refer to both image and self-image. One who is *"fiero di"* ("proud of") something, but also one who is *"orgoglioso"* believe that their goal of self-image is achieved, and for both this may be also accompanied by fulfilment of the goal of image before others. Yet, while the former is always and necessarily present, the latter may or may not (see Sect. 6.1).

5.3 Presence/absence of power comparison

Words in the first two categories of Table 1, like *sicuro di sé* (self-confident), *orgoglio* (pride) and *dignità* (dignity) differ from all others since they do not necessarily imply a power comparison: the Actor is viewed as someone feeling an emotion or exhibiting a trait, without consideration of his being in the up or down side of a dyad; whereas words of other categories all refer to someone feeling, claiming or aspiring to superiority.

5.4 Feeling/communicating superiority

Some words simply mention the feeling of someone who thinks to be superior
to (more powerful than) others: *sentirsi superiore* (to feel superior), *pieno di
sé* (full of oneself), *esaltato* (elated), *megalomane* (megalomaniac), *presuntuoso*,
sopravvalutarsi (to overrate oneself) *narcisista* (narcissistic), *immodesto* (immod-
est) *affetto da ipertrofia dell'io*)(suffering from hypertrophic ego). Others refer to
the person's communicating this feeling of superiority: *vanitoso* (vain), *vana-
glorioso* (vainglorious), *spocchia* (swagger), *impettito* (stiff-necked) *darsi delle arie*
(to boast), *pavoneggiarsi* (to strut around like a peacock), *atteggiarsi* (to pose),
snob (snobbish), while wanting others to acknowledge it.

For instance, *sentirsi superiore* (feeling superior) may be represented as the
fact that a person believes she has more power than other people, more than
the majority or the average of them. Instead, in *vantarsi di* (boasting about) A
informs others of an action or feature of oneself, while implying that knowing
of this action or feature will cause other people to have a highly positive image
of A. So the goal of boasting is to have someone have an image of you more
positive than the image he has of others.

In these two groups of words (one of *sentirsi superiore*, feeling superior, and
one of *vantarsi*, to boast) the Actor feels or communicates, respectively, that he
has more power – hence deserves a higher image – than others; but he does
not communicate his superiority directly to the one with respect to whom he
feels superior.

This is what happens, on the contrary, in another group of expressions, like
guardare dall'alto in basso, (look down to others), *avere la puzza sotto il naso* (toffee-
nose), *saccente* (know-it-all), *disprezzo* (contempt), *sprezzante* (contemptuous),
sussiego (hauteur), *alterigia* (haughtiness), *scostante*, (distant), *supponente* (assuming), where the presumptuous person wants to show how much his value
is higher than the other's, in some cases even exhibiting that he scorns the
other and wants to keep distance from him. In some way, here the focus is not
only on the Actor's superiority, but also on the Other's inferiority.

5.5 Actor's/Observer's view

Curiously enough, all the words of the third group, like *"sentirsi superiore"*,
refer to the one who feels superior, but as described by a critical third person,
an Observer who does not agree about that superiority, in that he thinks the
Actor does not in fact deserve to be credited with such a high image.

Moreover, in another bunch of words the Observer does not simply find
the subject's beliefs unrealistic, but utterly considers them deceptive or self-
deceiving: this is the case for adjectives like *spaccone* (braggart) or*gradasso*
(bully). A *spaccone* boasts about his own potential; he assures he has so high
capacities as to be able to do very difficult things, to meet great challenges. If
one *si vanta* (boasts) about the past, about some already achieved accomplish-

ments, one is *spaccone* (braggart) about the future, he is sure he will win over someone else.

At first sight, in both groups of words the Observer does not agree on the highly positive evaluation claimed by the Actor. But there is a difference: in *"vantarsi"* (boasting) the Actor may well obtain a highly positive evaluation, but what the Observer does not approve is the criterion of the evaluation: the goal against which the Actor communicates his high value is a silly, vain or not relevant one, in the opinion of the Observer[1]. In *spaccone* (braggart), instead, the Observer may agree with the criterion of evaluation, but he does not believe the Subject really has such a high potential against that criterion; he believes the Actor is worse than he tries to convey.

5.6 High/high-low/low-high

In the words seen so far, the Actor feels, or communicates, or is seen as feeling, that he is at a higher level, one that has more power than the Other. But another group of words concerns a scenery of challenge, of defiance to power. In words like *impudente* (impudent), *sfrontato* (cheeky), *sfacciato* (bronze-face) the Subject communicates that he does not bow in front of power. The etymology of these words has clearly to do with the area of shame, pride and image. *Impudente* (impudent, one who does not show submission) derives from latin, prefix *in-* (negation) and *pudor* (a form of shame), while *sfrontato* (cheeky) and *sfacciato* (bronze-face) in Italian literally mean "without forehead" and "without face", respectively. Face symbolically stands for image: one who has no face has no image, he has no worth and does not care the others' judgement. And if one does not have this sensitivity to norms and values, he does not display shame when he should, keeping his head upright. To make things even more strictly entangled, also these words, like *presuntuoso* (cocky) and *sentirsi superiore* (to feel superior) appear as a description from an external Observer, who attaches them a very negative connotation. Finally, by referring to the bodily expression of someone who flaunts he does not feel shamed when he should, they communicate an attitude of challenge to power through non-compliance with conventional values. One who shows these attitudes communicates that he does not intend to submit to power, and communicates, in an ostentatious manner, that he is not afraid of it, nor does he feel shame when violating the rules imposed by that power; he does so by keeping his head upright and by avoiding bowing [34].

In the meaning of other words, like *provocazione* (provocation), *sfida* (challenge, defiance), *spavaldo* (boisterous), and at least in one sense of *arrogante* (arrogant) the Actor does not simply refuse to submit, but may be trying to climb the pyramid of power: he does not acknowledge the other's power because he claims he has – or has the right to have – more power than the other. The difference between high-low and low-high direction of the feeling or communicative action in these words may well correspond to the distinction

---

[1] This subtle difference was specifically pointed out by Cristiano.

between so-called "authentic" and "hubristic" pride; the former claims actual superiority, the latter denies inferiority – or even claims a potential to become superior – with a consequent challenge to one who is presently on the upper level.

Table 1 Italian words in the area of pride(see appendix below)

6 The mental ingredients of pride

After examining the "emic" aspects of pride and image, that is, the semantic elements crystallyzed in the words of this area in a natural language, we come to investigate the "etic" level, the cognitive elements that constitute the mental state or trait of pride.

For each emotion or personality trait we aim to find out their mental ingredients [35, 36], i.e., the beliefs and goals represented in the mind of someone who feels that emotion or exhibits that trait.

To find out the ingredients of some mental state one we should find out examples and counterexamples of the mental state under study, to discover its necessary and sufficient conditions. In doing so, the issue of prototypicality must be taken into account. For every emotion there are some prototypical cases in which a relatively high number of ingredients are present, and some "peripheral" cases in which only occur. The ingredients present in both prototypical and peripheral cases are the "core" ingredients of the emotion, to which others may add from case to case, whereas the prototypical cases contain both the "core" and other characterizing ingredients.

In the following, we analyse two different mental states connected to the emotion of pride, expressed by the words *"orgoglioso di"* (proud of) and *"orgoglioso"* (proud) respectively, one mentioning a feeling about a single event and the other a steady state: we view being *"proud of"* something as an emotion felt in a specific situation, and being a *"proud"* person as a personality trait.

6.1 The ingredients of "being proud of"

The "core" ingredients of an emotion can be seen as the necessary conditions to feel it. In this case, to find the ingredients of *"being proud of"* we must wonder what can one be proud of, and why. Here are, in our hypothesis, the "core" ingredients of this emotion

1. *A believes that ((A did p) or (A is p) or (p has occurred))*
2. *A believes p is positive*
3. *A believes p is connected to / caused by A*

4. *A wants to evaluate A as to p*
5. *A wants to evaluate A as valuable*
6. *A believes A is valuable (because of p)*

Let us see these ingredients in detail, with corresponding examples.

1. one may feel proud of an *action* (e.g., you ran faster than others) or a *property* (you are stubborn, you have long dark hair), or simply an *event* (your party has won the elections);
2. this action, property or event is evaluated by A as *positive*, i.e., as something which is a useful means for some goal of A's;
3. p is seen by A as caused by oneself, or anyway as an important *part of one's identity*. I can be proud of my son because I see what he is or does as something, in any case, stemming from myself; I can be proud of the good climate and nice weather of my country, just because I feel it as *my own* country. Additional ingredients, possibly present only in the prototypical cases, are that one can be proud only of things one attributes to internal controllable causes [10, 11]; but in less prototypical cases it is sufficient that the action, property or event is simply connected to, not necessarily caused by oneself;
4. a necessary condition is, instead, that the positive evaluation refers to something that not only makes part of one's identity, but of one's *goal of self-image*: something with respect to which one wants to evaluate oneself positively;
5. A has the goal of evaluating oneself positively as a whole.
6. the positive evaluation of p causes a more positive evaluation of oneself as a whole: it has a *positive* effect on one's *self-image*;

If conditions 1 – 4 are fulfilled, A's goal of self-image (ingredient n.5) is achieved (n.6), and A feels a positive emotion: A is "proud of" p.
So far this emotion is viewed as only linked to the goal of self-image. But it may also be connected to the goal of image: being *"proud of"* something also necessarily entails that one feels evaluated positively by others, not only by oneself. Here are then two more ingredients:

7. *A wants B to evaluate A as to p*
8. *A believes B believes A is valuable (because of p)*

These ingredients, though, are not necessarily contained in all possible cases of this emotion. In some cases they are: one feels *"proud of"* something not only before oneself but also because the positive fact, property or action enhances one's own image before others. Before my colleagues in a foreign college, I can be proud of Italia's victory in the football championship since this gives me the image of one belonging to a champion country.

But if the goal of image is sometimes a condition for feeling proud of something, we may wonder if it is always a necessary condition: if being "proud of" also necessarily entails that one feels evaluated positively by others, not only by oneself.

In this, pride is exactly symmetrical to shame. One is sincerely ashamed before others only if one is ashamed before oneself [30], that is, only if the value one is evaluated against makes part not only of one's goal of image before others but also of the image one wants to have of oneself. For instance, if I do not share some value (say, to be a very macho man) and others evaluate me against it, but for my own self-mage this is not a relevant value, one that I want to live up to, I do not feel shame if I don't look very macho to others. In the same vein, if I happen to look so, I will not feel proud of it. So much so that showing proud of something that goes against conventional/traditional values is a means for provocation, a way to challenge those values and to propose/impose new unconventional ones opposite to them. [34, 13].

In conclusion, one is *proud of* something that fulfils his goal of image only if it also fulfils his goal of self-image. Both goals of image and self-image are monitored by the emotion of *"being proud of"*.

Another ingredient possibly present in cases entailing actions or properties is victory. Sometimes, doing or being p makes you *win* over someone else, i.e. it implies showing others and yourself that you have been stronger or better than another. Furthermore, if your having more power than another comes to be assumed as not a single occurrence but as a steady property, this results in the assumption that you are *superior to others*. So the following ingredients can respectively be added for these cases:

9. *A believes A once has been superior to B with respect to p*
10. *A believes A is always superior to B with respect to p*

Ingredient 9. means that A has more power than B as to p in a specific situation, while 10. means that A feels in general superior to B with respect to p. But furthermore, the bare fact that A believes to be superior to B as to p may induce him to believe he is superior to B in general.

11. *A believes A is in general superior to B*

In conclusion, being *"proud of"* something is a positive emotion that A feels when A believes that something happened, or that he was or did something, which causes him to have a positive image of himself. And if he attributes this achievement to himself, he evaluates himself as an autonomous person, one who does not depend on others – even one superior to others.

6.2 The ingredients of "proud" and "pride"

So far we have seen the emotion of *being proud of* something. Yet, the adjective *proud* and the noun *pride* do not refer to a single emotion felt about some specific event, but to a steady state of a person, a personality trait. Coherently with the semantic content of *being proud of*, *proud* as a personality trait is referred to a person for whom his goal of self-image of being autonomous, i.e. not depending on others' help, has a priority before all other goals.

As mentioned above, emotions are linked to goals in that they monitor their state of achievement or thwarting. But also personality traits can be viewed as linked to goals [35, 21]: having a particular personality means that you, as opposed to others, consider a particular goal as more important than others do, to such an extent that should that goal be in conflict with another goal, you would certainly choose to pursue it, even if at the expense of the other. For instance, an extraverted person is one for whom the goal of communicating to others has a higher value than one of protecting one's privacy.

If being *proud* is seen as a personality trait, a *proud* person will have a steady tendency to attribute a high value to a particular goal. To establish what are the goals that a proud person values most, we should remind what are his/her typical behaviours: the *proud* one does not want to beg or make requests, to thank and to apologize, and often refuses offers and invitations. This means that he is strongly regulated by his goals of image and of self-image, and within these, more specifically, the goal of being believed by others, and of believing oneself, an autonomous person.

We may consider two sides of autonomy: self-sufficiency and self-regulation. An Agent is self-sufficient when he possesses all the (material and mental) resources he needs to achieve his goal by himself, that is, when he does not depend on others' help. On the other hand, you are self-regulated when you can decide which goals to pursue, when and how, by yourself: in a word, when your are free. And if someone has power over you, you are not free. Think of the pride of growing nations, when they finally conquer their independence. Freedom is the bulk of pride. But these two sides of autonomy are strictly connected: if you are self-sufficient – you have all the resources you need, and you do not need the others' adoption – you can afford self-regulation – you have the right to be free.

This kind of pride does not imply a sense of superiority, nor necessary one of challenge. Our hypothesis, then, is that a third type of pride exists, beside the "authentic" and "hubristic" ones posited by Tracy and al. [5, 8, 9]. A pride that does not ask for having power over others, or more power than others, but simply to be respected in one's human dignity. Another kind of pride, not linked in itself to the idea of a "proper" or "hubristic" pride, but inherent in a view of man characterized by his capacity for self-sufficiency and self-regulation, that is sublimely highlighted in a famous poem by Robert Burns, *"A man's a man for all that"*. This is the pride of "the man of independent mind" who "looks and laughs" at the ostentatious signs of the powerful, and bases pride on sense and good faith. *"A prince can mak' a belted knight / A marquise, duke an'a'that / But an honest man's aboon his might"*, since *"the pith o' sense an' pride o' worth / Are higher rank than a' that"* [37]. The kind of pride we refer to is one that escapes formal hierarchies but only feeds the bulk of being human: human *dignity*; the pride of someone who thinks, with Burns, that *"the rank is but the guinea stamp; the man's the gowd for a' that!"*.

6.2.1 Dignity pride

A *proud* person has a goal of image and of self-image both of self-sufficiency and of self-regulation.

On the one hand he wants to appear self-sufficient as to resources, that is, one able to achieve anything he needs all by himself. And, since he is not dependent on others, he does not want anyone to have power over him: he claims his right to be free. This is a first facet of *pride*, that we call the "pride of human dignity", or *dignity pride*. In this basic sense of pride there is no superiority; at most there is the goal of not being (treated as) inferior. The proud person in this case simply claims to his right of being treated as a peer, with same status, same rights, same freedom as the other. He wants to be acknowledged his worth as a human being, and the consequent right to be addressed respectfully and not to be a slave to anybody.

The ingredients characterizing this type of pride are the following:

12. *A wants A/B believes A has all the resources A needs*
13. *A wants A/B believes A does not depend on B*
14. *A wants A/B believes A has not less power than B*
15. *A wants A/B believes B has not power over A*
16. *A wants B believes A has the dignity of a human*

Coherent with this image and self-image of self-sufficiency and self-regulation are the *proud* person's typical behaviours; his refraining from begging, making requests, accepting offers and invitations, thanking or apologizing, can be accounted for by the definition above: asking, but also accepting offers or invitations would imply he needs the others' help, hence he is not autonomous. Thanking would mean acknowledging he is indebted, hence someone who needs others' help. Apologizing implies that he acknowledges his faults, and that to be forgiven he humiliates himself in front of the other; but being humiliated, or humiliating oneself typically implies that you have less power than another, or even that the other has power over you.

6.2.2 Superiority pride

In other cases, the proud person also holds an assumption of superiority as against other people. He believes he has a higher worth than others, and in some cases also wants his worth to be known and acknowledged by others. We call this *"superiority pride"*, and we distinguish two subtypes of it, a communicative and a non-communicative one. Some proud persons – for example the Italian poet and tragedy writer Vittorio Alfieri – feel superior to others to such an extent that they think others are not even able to understand their superiority, so they give up to communicating this (and possibly to communicating with them at all). But other proud persons do communicate their conviction of being superior, for instance by boasting, or by expressing contempt or haughtiness. Both communicative and non-communicative cases entail ingredient n.11

11. *A believes A is in general superior to B*

But only the "communicative" *pride* contains an additional ingredient

17. *A wants B believes A is superior to B*

In both communicative and non-communicative pride, the proud person's behaviour is characterized by taking distance from the other. Like in *"dignity
pride"*, he also does not want to ask, thank or apologize, he sometimes refuses offers and invitations, he likes being praised, and shows very sensitive
to offense. The reasons for his not asking, thanking or apologizing are, like
for *"dignity pride"* that such behaviours would imply dependency. Offers or
invitations are not accepted if he assumes they are not worth of him – for
instance, if he thinks he is considered as a "second choice". The other should
look for him, invite him, make offers to him as a first choice, because he is the
best, and all these behaviours would count as a symbolic acknowledgement of
his worth. Finally, his low threshold for feeling offended – due to the principle
that the higher the status, the heavier the offence [23] – implies he feels very
important, and superior to others.

These typical behaviours, as for the non-communicative case, mainly point
to the importance of the goal of self-image, but for the communicative case
they point to both goals of image and self-image. As to the latter, the "non-
communicative" *proud* person is one who highly cares his own goal of self-
image, particularly his goal of feeling autonomous, one who has all the resources he needs. As to the former, the "communicative" proud considers his
goal of image very important too; in fact he suffers if in situations of power
comparison he results as having less power than another. In this, being *proud*
is connected to a competitive attitude, that is, typically, to situations of power
comparison. But further, should someone have power over him, thus being
able to influence him, the goal of self-regulation, an important part of the
self-image of autonomy, would be thwarted for the *proud* person.

6.2.3 Arrogance pride

Of the types of *pride* seen above, in *superiority pride* the proud person pretends
he is superior to the other, while in *dignity pride* he only claims to being at the
same level as the other, not inferior to him. But there is a third type in which
the *proud* person is, at the start, on the "down" side of the power comparison:
A has less power than B, but wants to challenge, to defy the power of B. This
is the "hubristic pride" distinguished by Tracy [8], and is often linked to the
provocation, seen above, of showing *proud of* some anti-conventional property
or action. In these cases the *proud* person, in front of a power acknowledged
by others or institutionalized, may ostentatiously show he doesn't feel shame
when violating the rules imposed by that power, to convey he does not want
to submit. Thus he climbs the pyramid of power: he does not acknowledge the
other's power because he claims he has (or has the right to have) more power
than the other.

This, that we call *arrogance pride*, is the pride of one who blatantly displays he is autonomous and not submitted to another: the arrogance of the Angels who rebel to God in the Bible, the "hybris" of the kingdoms which, becoming more and more powerful, trigger the "phthonos theòn" (Gods' envy) in Herodotus' history. In these cases the *proud* one challenges another person or institution that has *more power than* he and possibly *power over* him.
Arrogance pride has ingredient n.15 in common with *dignity pride*. In both, the proud one wants to communicate to the other he has no power over him

15. *A wants B believes B has not power over A*

But *arrogance pride* also shares ingredients n.11 and n.17 with *superiority pride* (in the "communicative" version).

11. *A believes A is in general superior to B*
17. *A wants B believes A is superior to B*

Thanks to this superiority, the arrogant will be even able to overcome the other's power, and to finally have power over him. The distinctive ingredients of *arrogance pride* are, in fact, that the arrogant wants (n.18), and can (n.19), turn down fortunes, and become the one who has power over the other.

18. *A wants to have power over B*
19. *A believes A can have power over B*

The arrogant communicates: I am not afraid of you, though you claim to have more power than I, and even power over me; since actually I have more power than you (I am superior to you, n.17), I want to have power over you (n.18) and I have the power to do so (n.19).
In some cases the challenge to power, at least apparently, does not come from one who is the less powerful in a dyad, but from the more powerful one. This is the case of the so-called "arrogance of power": one who is powerful is arrogant when he abuses of his power. For example, a politician from the government who insults an interviewer of a TV channel of the opposite side, or who blatantly violates general rules while displaying his not being subject to any other power. Here the powerful one does something more than he would be entitled to, according to the principle that rules and laws are for people who have not power, while one who has the power can establish rules himself. So, also in this case there is, in a sense, a challenge to power: to the power of law.

6.2.4 Dignity, superiority, arrogance

The three types of pride differ for the different combination of actual and ideal power relations between the proud person and the other: the present relation and the one aimed at Table 2.
In dignity, the proud one has less power than the other but aims at be considered equal to him; in superiority, A wants (considers right) to be considered superior, whether or not he actually is; in arrogance, A may be either equal or inferior to B, but wants to become superior.

Table 2 Power relations in dignity, superiority and arrogance pride

Pride	Real power relation	Ideal power relation
Dignity	A < B	A = B
Superiority	A = B	A > B
Arrogance	A = B	A > B

From the differences and similarities evidenced by the ingredient analysis we can see the adaptive functions of these three types of pride. The function monitored by *arrogance pride* corresponds to the goal of the individual's "climbing the pyramid", i.e., of acquiring *power over* others. The function of *superiority pride* is to show, or be contented with, one's superiority, and in general to motivate to excellence, to enhance one's image and self-image, and to have *more power than* others. The function of *dignity pride* is to fight for a world of equity and equality, where one wants neither to command over others nor to be commanded by others: a world of respect and cooperation.

All types of pride share the goals of being autonomous, not to have less power than another and, primarily, not to be commanded by the other. *Superiority* and *arrogance pride* share the goal of competing, of having more power than the other, but in *arrogance* there is also the goal of having power over the other.

Provocation may be used in both *dignity* and *arrogance pride*, but the message in *dignity* is "I am not ashamed of being/doing so", while in *arrogance* it is "I am not afraid of you". In *dignity pride* provocation is used to challenge traditional values, showing that your values are not inferior or immoral as against others': you fight to impose your own values, but not only for yourself, rather, on behalf of all those who already share them but do not have the force to impose them. In *arrogance* instead one fights against the other's power; in a sense only on behalf of oneself.

7 Pride expression and mental ingredients

As shown by Tracy and Robins [9], the emotion of pride is generally expressed by a small smile, expanded posture, head tilted backward, and arms extended out from the body, possibly with hands on hips.
Our hypothesis is that one can find a correspondence between each of these signals and single ingredients of pride. For example, *a smile* is in general a signal of happiness, but in this case the positive feeling conveyed is one triggered by ingredients n.2 and n.6

2. *A believes p is positive*

6. *A believes A is valuable (because of p)*

The *expanded posture* is, as reminded by Tracy et al. [5], a way to enlarge the person's body, like in the dominance display. Yet, expanding one's chest is also a way to make *oneself* more visible. If one calls me, while answering I expand my chest as if showing myself, like in saying: "here I am, it's me!". In this, *expanding chest* might be seen as making reference to oneself, to one's own *identity*: an allusion to one's self-image mentioned by ingredient 5.

5. *A wants to evaluate A as valuable*

The *head tilted back* is a way to look taller, hence to symbolically communicate ingredient 11.

11. *A believes A is in general superior to B*

But if you tilt your head back, you necessary *look down to the other*: one more communicative signal of superiority. Moreover, if someone wants others to know and acknowledge his superiority, and boasts, he *looks around* to see if others are seeing him; as stated by ingredient 13.

13. *A wants B believes A is superior to B*

In a sense, these signals together make a multimodal discourse [30, 20].

Smile → I am happy
Expanded chest → of myself
Head tilted back → I am superior to you
Looking around → you should acknowledge this

Tracy, Shariff & Cheng [5] did not find a clear difference in the two facets of pride they posit – authentic and hubristic – as to their respective expressive patterns. But our hypothesis is that our three types of pride – dignity, superiority, arrogance – actually have different patterns of expression, resulting from different combinations of the same signals. Table 3 presents our hypotheses about these combinations, to be tested in a subsequent study.

8 Pride expressions in political debates

In this section we analyse some expressions of pride during political debates. We carried out a qualitative analysis of the multimodal communication of politicians during six political debates in talk shows broadcast in Italian TV.

The investigates the multimodal expression of pride, while exploring the three different facets of dignity, superiority and arrogance pride. The analysis is based on a model of multimodal communication [20] according to which communication is a social action whereby a Sender S has the (conscious, unconscious or biological) goal of having an Addressee A assume some belief B, and in order to this produces a communicative act (a sentence, gesture, facial expression, gaze, posture, body movement) that conveys belief B as its meaning. Each communicative act has a goal, and possibly one or more supergoals, i.e. indirect meanings that the Sender wants the Addressee to understand through inference.

Table 3 Combination of signals in Dignity, Superiority and Arrogance pride

	Dignity	Superiority	Arrogance
Eyes	*Fixed to interlocutor* = I am addressing you	*Half-closed eyelids* = I can afford not looking at you, not controlling you, since I am superior to you	*Fixed to interlocutor* = I am addressing you, I am defying you
	Frown = I am serious, this is an important thing	*Asymmetrically raised eyebrow* = I am haughty	*No frown* = I am not worried
			possibly raised eyebrows = I am superior
Mouth	*No smile* = I am not friendly	*Small smile*; if communicative, ironic smile = I contemn you	*Laughter* = I laugh at you, I am not afraid of you, I am stronger than you
Head	*Head upright* = I do not bow, I do not submit	*Chin up* = I am superior	*Chin up* = I am superior
Chest	*Expanded chest* = my identity	*Relaxed posture* = I am not afraid, I do not worry	*Expanded posture* = I am bigger than you
Hands	*Tense gestures* = I am willing to fight for this	*Calm gestures* = I do not worry	*Hands on hips* = I am larger, I make a barrier, you cannot invade

We analysed our data through an annotation scheme (see Table 3) that describes each signal in each modality as to both its physical aspects (Columns 2 and 3) and to its (direct and possibly indirect) meanings (Col.4).

In our analysis, we chose three crucial moments of political debates in which the three conditions described in Table 2 were fulfilled.

(1) While answering the Moderator in a political talk show, Vendola says: "*Vorrei essere giudicato, per esempio, è lì che mi ribello. . . su quello che ho fatto!*"
(I would like to be judged, for example, that is where I rebel. . . for what I have done!)

Here Vendola wants to be acknowledged the same status as other candidates, and expresses his pride for what he has done so far as a President of the Region, saying "I would like to be judged for what I have done". Expressing pride for his previous achievements as a President of his region is a way for Vendola to re-establish and reinforce his position as a national leftist candidate (Fig. 1).

The multimodal analysis of Table 4 (1'min. 23'sec.) helps us to interpret (col.4) the meanings underlying the pride expression: anger and determination, and challenge towards the party who does not want Vendola as a candidate.

In this case the expression of pride, like in the hypothesis of Table 3, presents the prototypical signals of the *head tilted upward*, but also signals of anger and determination such as *vertical wrinkles on the forehead* [38] terms, the Action Unit AU4) and *high intensity of voice*. In addition, his *eyes fixed to the interlocutor* and his *lowered eyebrows*, along with the total *absence of smile* signal the importance and seriousness of the verbal message.

Table 4 Multimodal analysis of Vendola's communication

1. Time Speaker	2. & Speech	3. Signal or action	4. Goal or Meaning
1.23 Vendola	*Vorrei essere giudicato, per esempio* I would like to be judged, for example	*High intensity of voice* *Eyebrows lowered – vertical wrinkles (AU4)*	I remark I am angry and determined
		Gaze fixed to interlocutor	I address you (PD Party)
	E' lì che mi ribello This is where I rebel	*Squints eyes and frowns* *Shakes head*	I feel annoyed by this I do not like this
	su...(on. . .)		
	pause		I want to remark I am proud (of what I have done)
	quello che ho fatto *what I have done*	*Head upward, chin up*	
		Gaze fixed to interlocutor	I address you with dignity and without fear
		Eyebrows lowered – vertical wrinkles (AU4)	I am serious and determined

Fig. 1 Vendola: a case of dignity pride

(2) Eugenio Scalfari, the founder of "La Repubblica", one of the most important Italian newspapers, politically taking stance for the leftist parties, is replying to Roberto

Castelli, a minister of the Government of the right, who is challenging Scalfari's expertise in the domain of business and companies. Scalfari expresses disappointment but also his pride by reminding Castelli: *"Voglio dire all'... Onorevole.... Eh... io conosco le aziende, sa? Io ne ho fatta una, di azienda... E adesso ha... cinquecento giornalisti"*. (I want to tell the... Honourable... (Parliament Lord) that I know companies, you know? I founded one ... and at the moment it has... 500 reporters).

His first sentence is "I would like to tell the honourable"... because in the Italian Parliament deputees are call "honourable". Yet, after saying "I would like to tell...", he makes an hesitation that might be interpreted either as "I do not even remember his name" or as "I hesitate to call him honourable". Both interpretations point at an attitude of superiority. This is also conveyed by the fact that Scalfari at first looks at the Moderator, and only in the crucial part of his reply does he gaze at Castelli: a way not to credit him with so much consideration. Also his voice intensity is low and voice rhythm slow, meaning he is not worried nor afraid, hence indirectly conveying superiority. Yet, at minute 3'46", while Scalfari is saying: "I know companies, you know?", i.e. while the sender is recalling his past achievements, he has a *higher voice intensity*, a *small smile* and *head-tilt back*, prototypical of pride. Generally, all his signals, like *gaze toward the interlocutor, frowning, low rhythm and intensity of voice*, correspond to an expression of pride from a high position, stemming from high self-confidence, and his remarking the importance of what he has done by *stressing syllables* he indirectly remarks his own value and competence. Considering the power relations between Sender and Addresse of these signals, Scalfari starts from a higher position (based on his past prestige, generally acknowledged in Italy, and only challenged in this talk-show) and through his pride expression he aims to re-establish dominance and to be re-acknowledged. As he is not starting from a lower status he can afford expressing pride in a calm way, quite different from Nichi Vendola who, from a lower status, is trying to be acknowledged as a national candidate and puts much more energy in his speech.

Fig. 2 Scalfari: a case of superiority pride

(3) Renato Brunetta, a minister of the right wing governement, while talking of the opposite party, during a convention of his own party, says (1'36"): *"Li stiamo facendo*

Table 5 Scalfari: multimodal analysis

1. Time Speaker	2. & Speech	3. Signal or action	4. Goal or Meaning
3.39 Scalfari	*Vorrei dire all...* I would like to tell...	*Does not look at Castelli*	I am so superior that I do not even consider you
		Low intensity of voice	I'm calm, I am not worried nor afraid
	Eh...	*Hesitation*	I'm not sure he is so honourable Or I do not even remember his name
	Onorevole honourable		
3.46 Scalfari	*Io conosco le aziende, sa?* I know companies, you know?	*Gaze to interlocutor*	I address you I sustain your gaze
	Io ne ho fatta una I founded one	Higher voice intensity Small smile	I remark this I am proud of it
3.57 Scalfari	*Che* *adesso* *ha... cinquecento* *gior-* *nalisti* That at the moment has 500 reporters	*Small head nods stress tonic syllables* *Slow rhythm*	I remark this I am self-confident

morire! (We are making them die!) *Gli stiamo facendo un mazzo così"*, an Italian idiom that uses an obscene phallic metaphor to mean "We are winning over them".

Brunetta, while defeating even the most basic norms of politeness, uses a cacophemistic [12] lexicon with a provocative intent, challenging the opposite party with an obscene sentence, to increase his image of a dominant politician. Thus he intends to put himself and his party at a higher level than the other party, rejecting a peer position and longing for a superior one. While uttering the sentence meaning "We are winning over them", with its vulgar expression and *high intensity of voice* expressing aggressiveness, Brunetta *opens his arms wide*, with an Italian obscene symbolic gesture that accompanies his idiom by iconically representing the effects of (metaphorical) penetration. The gesture is finally *repeated three times*, with *hands and arms moved downward*, in a movement of *high energy and amplitude* that, beside its iconic representation, at the same time fulfils a batonic function by scanning the rhythm of the concomitant obscene sentence to give it more enphasis; this, along with his repeated head nodding and shaking, that expresses high energy, conveys a meaning of a total and violent victory over the "enemy".

At the same time, the multimodal analysis highlights the *smile* (even a large one, probably close to an aggressive *laughter* aimed at humiliating the opponent) and the *expanded posture*; two typical signals of pride.

In this case, then, Brunetta is expressing arrogance pride, but this clearly is the arrogance of power. In fact, he is a Minister, so he is presently holding the power, different from the opposite party. But he is not contented of having power yet; he wants to completely destroy the opponents.

Table 6 Brunetta: multimodal analysis

1. Time Speaker	2. & Speech	3. Signal or action	4. Goal or Meaning
1.32	*Li stiamo facendo morire* We are making them die	*Smile*	I am happy and satisfied
1.34 Brunetta	*Gli stiamo facendo un mazzo così* We are winning over them (vulgar expression)	*Large Smile*	I am making fun of them
1.36 Brunetta		*High intensity of voice* *Head upward* *Head nods and shake*	We are strong I am triumphant (of our victory against them) I am energetic
1.41 Brunetta		*Symbolic gesture used as batonic gestures* *Smile*	I am energetic → We are winning over them in a violent way I am proud of myself and of my provocation

Fig. 3 Brunetta: Arrogance Pride

The three fragments analysed were selected by taking into account on the one side the actual power relation between the Sender and the Adreessee of the pride expressions (*real power relation*), and on the other side their *ideal power relation* – the kind of relation of power that the Sender of the expression of pride wants to establish: the goal of the pride expression. A first difference resulting from the comparison of these cases is in the use of smile. In the expression of pride of Nich Vendola smile is not present, because he is not the "good" position in the dyad but on the "down" side of the power relationship, being engaged in pretending an acknowledgement of his position, and necessarily putting all his concentration and determination in this. Scalfari only exhibits a very light smile, that may have ironic nuances about Castelli not acknowledging what everybody else knows; and irony is a way to show superiority [[39], after, after [13]). Finally Brunetta – a case of "arrogance of power" – uses a large smile quite similar to a laughter of triumph.

Also the role of gaze is different in the three contexts. In the expression of both dignity and arrogance pride (Vendola and Brunetta), the real interlocutor to whom the pride expression is addressed is not present. Vendola is answering the moderator of the talk show, but in fact he is addressing the leaders of the DP party who do not want him as a candidate. Brunetta is talking to an assembly of his own party, but his obscene threatening repeated gesture is addressed to the opposite party. So in both cases the Interlocutor is only virtually present. Yet, the Sender of the pride expression is gazing straight to the (albeit virtual) Addressee. In the case of superiority pride, instead, Scalfari directly gazes to his interlocutor only in the second part of his sentence, while in other moments he directs his gaze away from him, as if he hardly wanted to see him. Another difference is that in dignity and superiority pride the Sender is more likely to frown as compared to arrogance pride: in dignity and superiority you are more serious because you pretend the other's respect, while in the third type of pride you may even laugh at the target of your arrogance; like Brunetta clearly does.

Other parts of the body which differentiate the three expressions of pride are chest and hands: in the arrogance case the posture is expanded and gestures are ample and highly stretched, possibly not only due to their metaphorical meaning but to the high energy generally exhibited by Brunetta. In dignity pride, instead, the politician presents nervous gestures, while his posture is not expanded and rather unstable. Finally, in the case of superiority pride we find a relaxed posture and calm gestures.

9 Conclusion

We have analysed the emotion of "being proud of" something and the trait of "pride": both have in common the ingredient of a highly positive self-evaluation, and are functional to the goals of image and self-image and to the goal of being (and feeling) an autonomous person. We have also distinguished dignity, superiority and arrogance pride as three types of pride that are felt and exhibited, depending on whether the proud person simply wants his human dignity to be acknowledged, or he feels and wants to be considered superior by others, or if he finally wants to overcome the other's power and become dominant. By analyzing some pride displays in political talks, we have found that dignity pride is characterized by gaze to the interlocutor, no smile, no conspicuous gestures, and a serious frown. Superiority pride includes low gaze to the other, a light smile, and a distant posture. Arrogance entails ample gestures, gaze to the target, and a large smile, similar to a laughter of scorn.

All these expression of pride, along with the emotion itself, fulfil very important functions both in monitoring the goals of a person's identity and image towards oneself and other people, and to regulate the reciprocal relations of power.

Acknowledgements This research is supported by the 7th Framework Program, European Network of Excellence SSPNet (Social Signal Processing Network), Grant Agreement Number 231287.

For all the topics tackled in this paper, and the methods to approach them, from the specific emotion investigated to the importance of image and self-image in human life, from the lexico-semantic analysis to its end point, the conceptual analysis of mental states into their ingredients, for all of this we are indebted to Cristiano's seminal research works and methods and to his patient mentoring in doing research together. But also our multimodal analysis owes much to the principles of research on communication that we have learnt from him. Actually, if you have worked with him once, you never feel alone in your research, because his insight ahead always leads and accompanies you in your work, and you often discover that a solution to your present problem lies in an apparently insignificant idea he has launched long time before. Still, nothing can equal the admiration for the creativity of his hypotheses and the subtlety of his reasoning, nor the intense intellectual pleasure you feel while talking, discussing and making research with him.

References

1. O'Donnell, J. J. (2005). *Augustine: A new biography*. New York: Ecco.
2. Pope, S. J. (2002). *The ethics of Thomas Aquinas*.Washington, DC: Georgetown University Press.
3. Dalai Lama, & Cutler, H. C. (1998). *The art of happiness: A handbook for living*. New York: Riverhead Books.
4. Aristotle. (1925). *The Nicomachean ethics*(D. Ross, Trans.). New York: Oxford University Press.
5. Tracy, J.L. Shariff, A.F., Cheng, J.T. (2010). A Naturalist's View of Pride. *Emotion Review*, 2 (2), 163-177.
6. Darwin, C. (1872). *The Expression of the Emotions in Man and Animals*. New York and London: Appleton and Company.
7. Lewis, M. (2000). Self-conscious emotions: Embarrassment, pride, shame, and guilt." In M. Lewis & J. M. Haviland-Jones (Eds.), *Handbook of emotions* (2nd ed.; (pp. 623–636). New York: Guilford Press.
8. Tracy, J.L. and Robins, R.W. (2007) The prototypical pride expression: development of a nonverbal behavior coding system. *Emotion*. 7, 789-801.
9. Tracy, J.L.& Robins, R.W. (2004). Show your pride: Evidence for a discrete emotion expression. Psychological Science, 15, 194–197.
10. Gladkova, A. (2010) A Linguist's View of Pride. *Emotion Review*, 2 (2), 178-179.

11. Parisi, D., Castelfranchi, C. (1984) Appunti di scopistica. In R.Conte e M.Miceli (Eds.), *Esplorare la vita quotidiana.* (pp. 26-79), Roma: Il Pensiero Scientifico.
12. Castelfranchi, C. & Parisi, D. (1980). *Linguaggio, conoscenze e scopi.* Bologna: Il Mulino.
13. Castelfranchi, C. (1988). *Che figura. Emozioni e immagine sociale.* Bologna: Il Mulino.
14. Conte R., Castelfranchi, C. (1995). Cognitive and social action. London: University College.
15. Miceli, M. and Castelfranchi, C. (1994). *Le difese della mente.* Roma: Nuova Italia Scientifica.
16. Miceli, M., & Castelfranchi, C. (1992). *La cognizione del valore.* Milano: Franco Angeli
17. Castelfranchi, C., Poggi I. (1998). *Bugie, finzioni, sotterfugi. Per una scienza dell'inganno.* Carocci: Roma.
18. Castelfranchi, C. (2000). Affective appraisal versus cognitive evaluation in social emotions and interactions. In A. Paiva (Ed.), *Affective Interactions.* Springer: Berlin.
19. Castelfranchi, C. (2003). Micro-Macro Constitution of Power. ProtoSociology, *International Journal of Interdisciplinary Research*, 18-19, 208-265.
20. Poggi, I. (2007). *Mind, hands, face and body. Goal and belief view of multimodal communication.* Berlin: Weidler.
21. Poggi, I. (2008) *La mente del cuore.* Roma: Armando Editore.
22. Miceli, M., Castelfranchi, C. (1989). A cognitive approach to values. *Journal for the Theory of Social Behaviour*, 19 (202) 169-193.
23. Poggi, I., D'Errico, F. (2010). Dominance signals in debates. In A.A. Salah et al. (Eds.), *Human Understanding Behavior* LNCS 6219, (pp. 163—174). Heidelberg: Springer.
24. Miceli, M. (1998). *L'autostima.* Bologna: Il Mulino.
25. Castelfranchi, C. (1991). Emozioni e regolazione del comportamento. In T. Magri, F. Mancini (Eds.), *Emozione e conoscenza*, Roma: Editori Riuniti.
26. Frijda, N.H. (1986). *The emotions.* Cambridge and New York: Cambridge University Press.
27. Scherer, K. (2003). *Handbook of Affective Sciences*, Oxford: Oxford University Press.
28. Poggi, I. (2008). Types of emotions and types of goals. *Proceedings of the Workshop AFFINE: Affective Interaction in Natural Environment*, Proc. ACM 2008, Chania, Crete
29. Castelfranchi, C., Poggi, I. (1990 a). Blushing as a Discourse: Was Darwin Wrong?" R. Crozier (Ed.) *Shyness and Embarrassment. Perspectives from social Psychology.* (pp. 230-251) New: York: Cambridge University Press.
30. Castelfranchi, C., & Poggi, I. (1990 b). Ingredienti per una macchina che si vergogna. In V.D'Urso (Ed.), *Imbarazzo, vergogna e altri affanni.* (pp.115-138) Milano: Raffaello Cortina.
31. Castelfranchi, C. (2011). For a 'Cognitive Anatomy' of Human Emotions and a Mind-Reading Based Affective Interaction. In D. Gökçay, G. Yildirim. (Eds.). *Affective Computing and Interaction: Psychological, Cognitive and Neuroscientific Perspectives.*, pp. 110-131.
32. Miceli, M., Castelfranchi, C., Parisi, D. (1983). Verso una etnosemantica delle funzioni e dei funzionamenti: "rotto", "guasto", "non funziona", "malato". *Quaderni di Semantica*, 4, 179-208.
33. Cattell, R.B., Scheier, I.H. (1961). *The meaning and measurement of Neuroticism and Anxiety.* New York: Ronald Press.
34. D'Errico, F., Castelfranchi, C., Pocobello, R. & Poggi, I. (2010) Expressions of pride, haughtiness, provocation. 4th Conference of the International Society for Gesture Studies (ISGS) July 25 – 30, 2010 – European University Viadrina Frankfurt/Oder, Germany.
35. Castelfranchi, C., Miceli, M. (2009). The cognitive-motivational compound of emotional experience. *Emotion Review*, 1, 223-231.
36. Poggi I., D'Errico, F. (2009). The mental ingredients of Bitterness. *Journal of multimodal user interface*, 3, 79-86.
37. Burns, R. (2011). *The Complete Works of Robert Burns.* Montana- Usa: Kessinger Publishing.
38. Ekman, P., Friesen, W., Hager, J. (2002). *Facial Action Coding System (FACS): A Human Face.* Salt Lake City, USA.
39. Poggi, I. (2011). Irony, humour ad ridicule. Power, image and judicial rhetoric in an Italian political trial In: R. Vion, A. Giacomi et C. Vargas (Eds). *La corporalité du lan-*

gage: Multimodalité, discours et écriture, Hommage à Claire Maury-Rouan. Aix en Provence: Presses Universitaires de Provence.

Appendix

Table 1. Italian words in the area of pride

Semantic Dimensions	Verb	Adjective	Noun
Positive Self-Image	*essere fiero di* to take pride over	*sicuro di sé* self-assured *fiero* proud	*sicurezza* self-assurance *fierezza* pride
Goal of a Self-Image of autonomy		*orgoglioso* proud *dignitoso* * decent	*orgoglio* pride *dignità* dignity
Feeling superior (= very positive self-image) + Observer's disagreement	*sentirsi superiore* to feel superior *credersi onnipotente* to feel all-powerful	*narcisista* narcissistic *immodesto* immodest *pieno di sé* self sufficient, full of oneself *esaltato* elated *megalomane* megalomaniac *affetto da ipertrofia dell'io*, suffering from hypertrophic ego,	*narcisismo* narcissism *immodestia* immodesty *esaltazione* (*) elation *megalomania* megalomania

		presuntuoso presumptuous, cocky *pallone gonfiato* very full of himself	*presunzione* presumption, cockyness
	sopravvalutarsi to overrate oneself		
Communicating superiority + goal to have it acknowledged (= goal of positive image)	*vantarsi* to boast, to brag	*vanitoso* vain, boastful	*vanità* vanity
		vanaglorioso boastful, vainglorious	*vanagloria* boastfulness
		borioso bumptious	*boria* arrogance
	darsi delle arie to put on airs		
	pavoneggiarsi to strutt around like a peacock	*pavone* vain as a peacock	
	atteggiarsi to pose		
	tirarsela to give oneself airs		
	darsi un contegno to give oneself airs	*contegnoso* dignified, staid, aloof	
		Impettito stiff-necked, as a ramrod	

		pomposo assuming	
		superbo superb, haughty	*superbia* haughtiness
Communicating one's superiority (and the other's inferiority) to the other	*guardare dall'alto in basso* to look down on others		
	avere la puzza sotto il naso to be toffee-nosed		
		altero high and mighty	*alterigia* haughtiness
		altezzoso arrogant	
		sussiegoso condescending, haughty	*sussiego* hauteur, haughtiness
			albagia conceit
		saccente all-knowing, know-it-all, high-brow	
		Snob snob, snobbish,	*snobismo* snobbery
		blasé blase'	
		spocchioso boaster	*spocchia* swagger
		supponente opinionated, assuming	*supponenza* haughtiness

		scostante distant, forbidding	
		sdegnoso dismissive	sdegno (*) disdain
		sprezzante contemptuous	dispregio scorn
	disprezzare to despise, scorn		disprezzo contempt graziosamente (AD-VERB) graciously
Communicating that one is not inferior and/or can become superior		spavaldo boisterous	spavalderia boast-fulness
		arrogante arrogant	arroganza arro-gance
		impudente impudent	impudenza impudence
	sfidare to challenge, to defy		
	provocare to provoke	provocatorio (*) provoking	provocatore (*) provoker
		tracotante overbearing	tracotanza arrogance
		sfrontato cheecky	sfrontatezza effrontery, cheek
		sfacciato bronze-faced	sfacciataggine shamefulness
		strafottente insolent	strafottenza insolence
		insolente insolent	insolenza insolence

Communicating (through bluff or self-delusion) one will win over someone powerful		*spaccone* braggart	
		sbruffone blusterer	
		gradasso bully	

Chapter 15
The paradoxes of depression: A goal-driven approach

Francesco Mancini and Amelia Gangemi

Abstract Depressive reaction (DR) is a common and normal reaction to loss and failures when there isn't subjective hope of recovery or valid substitution. DR has two main features: pain and inactivity. The latter is due to anhedonia and pessimism. DR presents two paradoxical aspects. From the premise that pain reveals investment in the lost good, derives a first question: why do people continue to invest in something they know is unreachable and irreplaceable? When it becomes clear that reaching the goal is impossible, they should de-activate it and move to another goal. Why does a mind invest in something it knows is unreachable? Why cry over spilled milk? From the premise that anhedonia and pessimism reduce motivation to pursue goals, derives a second question: why, in case of DR, there is a reduction of motivation instead of an increase that could be useful to improve the goal balance and compensate for the loss? Our response is based on the idea that, in DR, there is an increase in investment in the lost good and that the investment is not for its recovery but to avoid losing it even more. A deceased loved one can be further lost, for example, through forgetting, losing interest and becoming interested in other things.
Did DR imply some evolutionary advantage? And, in case of a positive an-swer, which one? Our solution starts from the premise that the psychological mechanisms of DR have the function of stabilizing investments in adverse situations. This function is advantageous primarily in unpropitious soft situa-tions and can be disadvantageous in hard situations. Nevertheless, the former are much more frequent than the latter and therefore it is plausibile that in-

Francesco Mancini
Scuola di Psicoterapia Cognitiva, Associazione di Psicologia Cognitiva, Italy
e-mail: mancini@apc.it

Amelia Gangemi
Department of Cognitive Sciences, University of Messina and Scuola di Psicoterapia Cogni-tiva and
Associazione di Psicologia Cognitiva, Italy
e-mail: gangemia@unime.it

dividuals who have the ability to react with DR to adversity have had more evolutionary advantages than disadvantages.

1 Introduction

The aim of this chapter is twofold: to identify the characteristics of a mind that reacts with depression (depressive reaction, DR) to losses and failures, and to discuss the possible developmental avantages of DR.

1.1 The depressive reaction (DR)

Depression is an ambiguous term. It can refer to the emotion of sadness, to a complex psychological state involving a normal reaction to loss or failure or to a psychopathological state, i.e., major depression (Gut, 1989; Welling, 2003).

In this paper we refer to depression as a normal complex psychological state, i.e., "depressive reaction" (DR), caused by loss or failure without subjective hope of recovery or valid substitution.

DR may also arise from disappointment of an expectation or perception that the distance between an individual's perceived state and the pursued goal is not closing as fast as expected (Carver and Scheier, 1983, 1990; Miceli and Castelfranchi, 2002a, b). Loss of a good has to be distinguished from missed gains. Loss implies that the good was not just desired, but was owned or at least expected. A loss is not a missed gain. A missed gain is a good considered extra, something that could have been added to what one already has or is entitled to. We can have an affective loss, such as the death of a close family member, or a loss at the material level, such as the loss of physical beauty or a house. Loss can also be at a conceptual level, i.e., the loss of self-esteem, the hope of attaining happiness, faith in God or trust in people (see Welling, 2003). According to Welling (2003), DR is a complex reaction with affective, cognitive and behavioral components. At the affective level, depressed people suffer and feel sad and sometimes experience anxiety, irritability and guilt feelings. At the behavioral level, they lack motivation, are less active and usually lose their appetite and sexual drive. At the cognitive level, they are more pessimistic in estimating their success in influencing the environment. An order can be found in the different manifestations of DR starting from the two that are most evident upon observation: pain for the lost good and reduced activity.

Feeling pain, which accompanies tears and lamentation, means that the lost good is still desired and that its importance has not decreased following the loss. Desire for the lost good also manifests with systematic rumination and difficulty (evident in mourning) in detaching oneself from whatever brings it to mind (Parkes, 1972).

Reduced activity is due more to a sense of uselessness than to anticipation of a threat. For example, imagine two people, one timid and one with a DR due to mourning, both of whom refuse an invitation to go to the movies with friends. The timid person refuses because he fears he will not be well received because he will seem like an extra or will seem embarrassed or will be judged badly. Characteristically, the second person refuses becaues he thinks it's not worth it, that it's a useless effort. A sense of uselessness at the base of reduced activity is typical of DR. And the sense of uselessness seems due to anhedonia, i.e., to the inability to enjoy pleasures and interests, and to pessimism. In DR, pessimism is about the probability of reaching goals: obstacles are overevaluated and external resources and personal abilities are underevaluated. Pessimism is also related to the value of the results obtained, or that could be obtained, so that positive ones are demeaned and negative ones are emphasized.[1]

DR usually resolves with recovery of the loss or with its acceptance. Acceptance implies investment in substitutive goods, or goods that are part of the lost good, such as a minor success (i.e., individual contents himself), or in goods that can lead to attaining other goals, as may happen, for example, to those who dedicate themselves to success at work following a disappointment in love. Thus, DR can be considered a process, not a state, starting with the representation of a hopeless loss and ending with its recovery or acceptance. This process usually involves different phases: alarm, searching, mitigation, anger, depression and finally acceptance and reorganization (Parkes,1972). Although we will not give a detailed description of these phases, we wish to stress that the two fundamental aspects of DR, pain and inactivity, can be present in different proportions in each phase. Pain is usually more present in the initial phases and inactivity in the later ones (Bowlby, 1980). It is quite plausible that individual differences exist, so that some individuals experience DR with more pain than inactivity and vice versa. The possibility of differences linked to age must also be considered. Finally, some data suggest that DR is characterized primarily by pain if it is the result of affective loss and by inactivity if it is the result of failure (Keller et al., 2007; Keller and Nesse, 2005, 2006; Couyoumdjian et al., 2011 a, b). DR can be characterized by other emotions besides sadness, for example, by surprise when people are still not totally aware of what is happening, by anger if the loss is considered unjust, by guilt if they hold themselves responsible for the loss, and by anxiety if they have the impression that the loss is still going to happen or will be repeated (Parkes, 1972) or if its implications appear threatening.

2 The psychological paradoxes of DR

It is difficult to provide a psychological explanation of DR because, in many respects, it seems paradoxical.

---

[1] For the purposes of our analysis of DR, whether the pessimistic evaluations in DR are more or less realistic of the optimistic evaluations present in normal conditions is irrelevant, what counts is that the former are more negative than the latter.

2.1 *The first paradox: investment without hope*

The most obvious paradox is that in DR people invest in a good they assume is definitively lost. Pain for the lost good, rumination and difficulty detaching oneself from it strongly suggest that the lost good continues to be an object of desire and investment, even though it is considered unreachable and irreplaceable. Note that the desire in question is neither an abstract ("I would like my grandfather to still be alive and see my children") nor a simple preference ("imagine how great it would be if I had won the lottery"), but involves investment in emotional resources. How can we explain that people continue not only to desire but also to invest in something they know is unreachable and irreplaceable? When it becomes clear that reaching the goal is impossible, they should deactivate it and move to another goal. Why do people invest in something they know is unreachable? Why cry over spilled milk?

It could be that in reality hope is not completely lost or at least not in a stable manner. This seems true in two senses. First, it is true that people can have a DR even if they have suffered a disappointment or have discovered that reaching a goal is slower than expected or cannot see how to reach it; therefore, it is not necessary to consider the loss definitive. Indeed, a DR is possible when there is a glimmer of hope or at least when there is no certainty that there is no hope. Nevertheless, it is equally true that, besides cases of DR in which there is no representation of the impossibility of having what one has lost, there are cases of DR in which it is certain that the loss is irretrievable and irreplaceable; the clearest example is mourning. Second, in the case of great losses and in the time periods closest to them, representation of their irreparability is not necessarily integrated with the person's entire system of knowledge. Individuals with DR know that the lost good is irretrievable but at the same time their belief system has not yet completely adapted to the novelty; therefore, in many circumstances and due to consolidated automatisms, they tend to assume that the good is still reachable. Thus, two non-integrated representations turn over or coexist in the minds of individuals with DR, one of irreparabile loss and the other of the possibility of recovery. Pain for the loss should be present when the representation of irretrievability is active but investment in the lost good and desire for it should be active when hope for its recovery is active. However, pain due to the loss and awareness of its irretrievability are also present simultaneously. In fact, desperation is the characteristic form of pain in DR. The following question still remains, however: How can we explain continuation of the desire and investment in something known to be unreachable?

2.2 *The second paradox: inactivity due to sense of uselessness*

Generally speaking, inactivity may be due to fear of danger or to the intention to avoid unmerited success and gratification, which would involve a sense of guilt. Although both are found in DR, neither is necessarily present in it. Instead, in DR, inactivity is usually due to sense of uselessness. For example, depressed individuals stop trying to make friends, going on vacations and engaging in sports not only because these activities foreshadow a danger or because they believe they do not deserve these gratifications, but because they think "it's not worth it", "why should I go?" "it's exhausting", "it's a useless effort." What stops individuals with DR from undertaking an activity is their evaluation of its uselessness, not danger.[2]

Sense of uselessness can be traced to two phenomena: anhedonia and pessimism. Both pose difficulties for an explanation in terms of goals.

2.2.1 Anhedonia

Anhedonia can be defined as lack of interests and inability to enjoy and appreciate pleasures and satisfactions one was positively sensitive to before the loss and will again be sensitive to if he overcomes DR. For example, if one has DR due to failure at work he no longer enjoys the victories of his soccer team, as much as he did before. Capacity to appreciate sexual pleasure diminishes and disappears, for example, in those in mourning. Anhedonia in DR corresponds to a true disinvestment in goods, pleasures and interests, so that, for example, faced with the successes of his team the depressed person seems to be in a situation similar to that of a starving person whose thirst is quenched. Now, why, in DR, people disinvest in goals not involved in the loss? Note that disinvestment also involves goods that have been obtained; therefore, then, it is not a disinvestment due to pessimism about the possibility of obtaining what one wants. In case of irreparable loss, the opposite should occur: To improve the goal balance and compensate for the loss, other goals should be activated more often, primarily those with greater possibility for success. By contrast, we see the deactivation of goals that are alternatives to the frustrated one and therefore a worsening of the goal balance. How can this be explained?

2.2.2 Pessimism

Pessimism in DR regards the probability of favorable outcomes, both those that depend on one's efforts and those that do not; it also regards the value of the outcomes one believes can be obtained or have been obtained. The probability of outcomes and their value tends to be evaluated pessimistically. For example, those with DR due to a disappointment in love tend to deprecate possible alternative partners they would have appreciated if they were not in a state of DR. Pessimism increases sense of uselessness, which increases inactivity; therefore, it increases the risk of letting favorable situations slip or of diminishing results obtained. Pessimism, then, implies the risk of unjustifiably worsening one's goal balance. In part, pessimism can be explained on a strictly cognitive basis. DR presupposes a frustrating representation of reality, which in spite of favorable evidence can be maintained or strengthed by means of a confirmation

---

[2] In the area of negative evaluations, Miceli and Castelfranchi (1995) distinguish evaluations in terms of damage and uselessness.

bias and can extend to different domains thanks to a process of generalization (Beck, 2008). This explanation suggests that the dysfunctioning of pessimism in DR may depend on laws that normally regulate cognitive processes (de Jong et al., 1998; Friedrich, 1993; Gilbert, 1998; Johnson-Laird et al., 2006; Mancini et al., 2007). We know, however, that emotions, and more generally, goals orient the cognitive processes so as to minimize the risk of more costly errors. The choice of the focal hypothesis, the tendency to falsify or confirm personal beliefs, depends not only on their initial credibility but also and primarily on person's goals. As example, if a person perceives that he is in a threatening context then he tends to falsify the safety hypotheses and confirm those of danger. The result is that it is easier to become alarmed for nothing but more difficult to not be alarmed when this could be fatal. Individuals are largely optimistic in their hypothesis testing if they perceive themselves in a positive context. In this case, they tend to draw conclusions that overestimate their chances of success and underestimate difficulties (i.e., positive cognitive illusions; see Taylor and Brown, 1988). The optimistic orientation involves reduction of the risk of losing positive opportunities. Therefore, cognitive processes are practical instruments in the service of individual's goals and are particularly oriented toward reducing risk of crucial errors. It is not clear, however, in what sense depressed people's pessimism can be in the service of their goals. Remember that the pessimism of depressed individuals emphasizes difficulty and scarcity of resources and also diminishes results already obtained.

3 Possible solutions for the paradoxes of DR.

Various questions arise concerning an explanation of DR in terms of goals:

1. Why invest in a good if known to be lost forever?
2. Why disinvest in other goals i.e., that even the depressed person considers reachable or reached?
3. Why is there a tendency to diminish the results obtained, i.e., those concerning other goals and consolatory goals with respect to the compromised goal?
4. Why is there pessimism about the possibility of reaching goals other than the one irremediably compromised by the loss?

3.1 Why invest in a good known to be lost forever?

The first question regards investment in the good assumed to be lost forever. How is such an investment possible? This is a fundamental question because it regards the core of the depressive paradox and its answer will influence our response to the other questions. The existence of the investment is demonstrated by pain, rumination and difficulty in detaching oneself from all that regards the lost good, e.g., in the case of mourning active resistance to leaving the places habitually shared with the loved one (Parkes, 1972). But what is really being invested in? Note that the investment is not to recuperate the good, but rather to avoid losing it in a more complete and definitive sense. As a woman with DR following the death of her husband explained, "if I were to put away his clothes, his shoes and his ties, it would be like losing him a second time"; and then she added "If I were to stop keeping his clothes clean and in order it would be like closing our story and I would definitively lose even what had been between us." The woman's explanation reveals different, closely associated points: first, that her investment was not to have her husband back, but to avoid losing him "a second time", and that disinvesting in what concerned her husband was the same as sanctioning his definitive loss and losing what had been. This is like saying that disinvesting or detaching would have created an additional cost for her. Certainly, there seems to be some sort of confusion between preserving the affective investment toward her husband and not losing him, that is, between a subjective and an objective state. In any case, these types of confusion, which are part of the magical confusion between the subjective world of representations and the world of objective facts, are frequent and their existence and normality is widely documented in cognitive psychology. Note also that humans seem to give value not only to what is and will be, but also to what has been and is no longer. In fact, it is not difficult to put oneself in the shoes of another woman who, after the death of her husband, experienced as a further loss the discovery that during the years of their marriage he had had an important love story with another woman. The fact that humans give value to past investments emerges also in the well-known sunk cost phenomenon. [3]

In conclusion, the idea of not losing further the lost good is at the base of the emotional investment, not that of being able to recover it. Even a deceased person can be lost further if we consider affective disinvestment as a distancing from the memory of the lost person and from what the relationship with her had been. Note also that there are probably individual differences in the tendency to engage in magic-type confusion; for example, it has been documented that phenomena of affect as information (Arntz et al., 1995) are subject to individual differences. On the basis of available data, it seems possible to hypothesize that dysthymic people are more prone to confusing subjective and objective states (Buonanno et al., 2009).

But, except for individual differences, it seems that investment in the lost good is aimed at not losing what remains of it and what it was and that in

---

[3] The sunk cost phenomenon, is well known in general psychology. Much literature on the "sunk cost fallacy" (Arkes and Blumer, 1985) shows that when people make a hopeless investment they sometimes reason as follows: I can't stop now, otherwise what I've invested so far will be lost. Although this is true it is irrelevant to whether they should continue to invest in the project. In any case, everything they have invested in is lost. If there is no hope for success from the investment in the future, then the fact that they have already lost a bundle should lead them to conclude that the rational thing to do is withdraw from the project. But stopping could be seen as a further loss, probably leading to persistence with the investment, even though continuing to invest in a hopeless project is irrational. But, as stopping could be seen as a further loss, they will probably continue to invest despite the irrationality of investing in a hopeless project. It is likely that the idea of giving up the investment, even if it is considered hopeless, increases the feeling of loss.

the eyes of the person who has experienced the loss disinvesting is a way of making the loss more serious and definitive. Therefore, disinvesting has a further subjective cost.

3.2 *Why does the depressed person disinvest in other goals he considers reachable or already reached?*

How can we explain the disinvestment that underlies anhedonia, that is, the tendency to have no desire or interest in results and activities that gave pleasure and satisfaction before the DR? For example, a 22-year-old young woman lost her fiancé in a car accident. She was studying at the University and it had always been very important for her, but while she was in DR this interest disappeared. Indeed, studying no longer attracted her and she was unable to concentrate. In fact, her mind was completely taken up with thoughts of her dead fiancé. Anhedonia seems to be a consequence of investment in the lost good, which involves deactivation of alternative goals. It is rather obvious that in a goal system the most important goals are activated more than the others. We have to ask ourselves, however, why the young woman's desire to be with her fiancé before his death did not impede activation of her interest in studying. The answer may lie in the psychological mechanism known as the endowment effect or the framing effect (Kahneman and Tversky, 1979; Khaneman et al., 1990), in which the same outcome increases in value if it is considered in the domain of losses rather than in the domain of gains. First, not being with her fiancé and being away from him were most often a lost gain she could renounce to dedicate herself to studying. After his death, distancing herself from the thought of him was a loss; thus, dedicating herself to studying involved a greater cost.

3.3 *In the case of DR ,why does a goal system diminish the results obtained?*

When faced with a positive result, why does person in DR think, "yes, it's good, but it could have been better", "it's actually not much", "it's not really what I wanted", "it wasn't worth it"? When individuals with DR evaluate the results they have obtained, they likely have the lost good in their mind as a point of reference and compare the result with it; in other words, how much does what they have obtained compensate for their loss? The response will probably be negative if the standard of reference is high, that is, if the value attributed to the lost good is high (Scott and Cervone, 2002). Furthermore, the negativity of the response will tend to be greater if the question is formulated within the domain of losses ("how much does the result compensate for the loss?") rather than in that of gains ("how much does the result add to my current balance?"). What diminishes the outcome of the evaluation even more is that the orientation also comes into play, i.e., whether the person is focusing on the negative hypothesis and seeking its confirmation or whether he is seeking disconfirmation of the positive hypothesis. We have already pointed out that the orientation of the evaluative processes depends on doxastic factors, such as the initial credibility of beliefs, the confirmatory bias and the tendency to generalize. Therefore, an individual who has experienced losses, failures and disappointments will not easily believe in a positive result and will belittle it. However, we have also shown that strictly doxastic factors are insufficient to account for the orientation of the cognitive processes; indeed, goals have to be considered that influence the evaluative processes in a direction which minimizes the risk of more costly errors. What is the cost of not erroneously diminishing the results gained, more simply, of deceiving onself? If the main goal of individuals with DR is to avoid further and definitive losses of the good and if they believe that disinvesting is a way of losing the good further and definitively, then disinvesting, when it's not really worth, it is a costlty error that should be avoided. To avoid the error, evaluation of the results should be oriented toward reducing the risk of deceiving oneself, but this implies the tendency (also exaggerated) to belittle, which we often observe in individuals with DR.

3.3.1 Refused consolations

The tendency to belittle results explains the diffidence of people with DR toward consolations, that is, toward partial or substitute satisfactions for the lost good.

Let's consider, for example, the case of the already-cited 22-year-old woman who lost her fiancé in a car accident. She stayed with him for two days in the hospital until he died. Some weeks later, she seemed to find comfort by thinking of him as he was before the accident, that is, smiling, healthy and full of life. The possibility of recalling this image and communicating with it, helped alleviate her pain. Later, a question came into her mind, "Is this fantasy realistic or am I fooling myself?" She found her answer in starkly realistic images of her fiancé as he was at that moment, i.e., in a coffin, dead and decomposing. This image definitevely substituted the consoling image, annulling its beneficial effect. The young woman vainly attempted to restore the positive image. She had the impression she was fooling herself. It seems that her mind destroyed a consolation that worked. Why? If we consider the self-reports of people in analogous situations, their desire is to avoid illusions. In our case, if the young woman deceived herself she would have been distracted and, therefore, detached and distanced from how her fiancé really was.

3.4 Why are people pessimistic about the possibility of attaining their goals, even those that belong to different domains than the one in which they experienced the loss?

In DR, why does a goal-oriented system favor pessimistic expectations when evaluating the probability that a personal initiative will be successful or that events will develop positively? Presumably, doxastic and motivational factors intervene analogously to the preceding case. The role of doxastic factors is rather clear: Repeated failures make pessimistic beliefs more credible. By means of the confirmatory bias, the latter tend to be reinforced in spite of contrary evidence, and thanks to the generalization they also tend to influence evaluations in domains other than the one in which the loss was experienced. Which motivational factors influence pessimistic evaluations of the possibility for success? Note that these pessimistic evaluations are negative evaluations of uselessess, rather than damage. As already stated, depressed people renounce most activities because they evaluate them as useless more than dangerous or damaging, because they do not seem worth the effort. In other words, it is not worth investing resources in that direction because they would be wasted. Again, why do people want to avoid wasting resources? The answer is usually that it serves to optimize their investments. This solution gives rise to two objections. The first is that depressed people do not seem concerned with optimizing their investments. What kind of optimization is despairing and crying over spilled milk instead of dedicating oneself to something else? Indeed, it seems a waste of resources to cry or ruminate for days over the lost good. The second objection refers to the functioning of the mind. Are people interested in optimizing their investments when they avoid waste? The goal of ensuring better allocation of resources and attaining the highest number of goals (highest value for the lowest cost) is not explicitly represented in the mind that rules everyday life choices (Miceli and Castelfranchi, 2002a). "Individuals are not "economic actors"; they act in view of concrete and specific goals (to publish a book, to get married, to be loved). They do not act in view of a single totalizing goal, such as utility or pleasure. Agents usually choose the goal (action) that is more convenient (with respect to their own limited knowledge), between different and active, but not jointly pursuable, goals. Our thesis is that to achieve this result it is sufficient a procedure of choice between active goals that is based on their coefficients, and not on an explicit goal to maximize utility. Cognitive agents do not have the explicit goal to choose the more convenient goal, but their choice apparatus is built to produce this result. They behave as if they had this goal" (Miceli and Castelfranchi, 2002a). On the other hand, if people actually pursued optimization in the use of resources, they would have a complete representation of all possibilities and would compare them and choose the best ones, which is an impossible task. As suggested by Miceli and Castelfranchi (2002a), people simply choose to act or not, based on the different options and goals active at that moment. Therefore, if they choose not to act, it is not with the view of an abstract and overall saving of resources and optimization of their use, but to achieve a goal represented in their minds. Therefore, when depressed people evaluate that a certain initiative "isn't worth it" which goal is in their mind? Which goal is pursued when no action is taken? The goal could be the desire to not disinvest in the lost good and therefore, subjectively, to not lose it further or definitively. Briefly, the pessimistic orientation in evaluating the possibilities of success may be justified by the goal of avoiding choices that could unjustifiably distance the person from the lost good and therefore contribute to its further loss.

4 An alternative but unsatisfactory solution: DR as self-punishment

One hypothesis for explaining the psychological paradoxes is that DR is an expression of the need for self-punishment. This is the psychoanalytical explanation. In this framework, the person who has suffered a loss attributes it to aggressive feelings towards the loved object. Thus, the person has feelings of guilt and anger toward himself, and DR is the consequence of the need for self-punishment. This explanation seems to provide good solutions for the psychological paradox of DR: Suffering for the loss, pessimism and anhedonia may help the individual attain his goal of self-punishment because of guilt. This explanation also helps clarify cases in which depression and guilt are co-present, in particular cases in which patients boycott their own successes because they feel survivor guilt. It is not, however, adequate for explaining some clinical observations. For example, according to Beck (2008) the dreams of depressed patients contain less hostility than those of non-depressed people, but contain themes of loss, defeat, rejection and abandonment. Moreover, the dreamer is represented as defective or diseased. The idea that these negative themes in dream content express the need for self-punishment is also falsified by the fact that when encouraged to express hostility, patients become more, not less, depressed. Further, in some experiments they reacted positively to successful experiences and positive reinforcement, when the "self-punishment" hypothesis predicted the opposite (Beck, 2008). Finally, feelings of guilt and self-contempt are not always present but appear mainly in cases of clinical DR and seem to be secondary to the depression; that is, the patient belittles and reproaches himself for being depressed. So, guilt and contempt might better explain the maintenance and aggravation of depression than its determinants (Beck, 2008). Moreover, studies on the relationship between guilt and depression show only a very weak association (e.g., Kim et al., 2011).

5 The evoluzionist paradoxes of DR

In the preceding section, we attempted to understand how a mind, i.e. a system of goals and representations, can produce an apparently paradoxal reaction like DR. Now we would like to consider DR from an evolutionist point of view. Why did a species evolve that has a DR when faced with loss or failure? (McGuire et al., 1997; Nesse, 1990, 2000; Welling, 2003). Unlike other psychological reactions, for example, the tendency to react with fear when faced with a threat, that of DR is not obvious. In fact, the costs of DR in terms of subjective suffering and inactivity make it disadvantageous for the individual's survival. DR also seems disadvantageous for the group one belongs to. In fact, because of his inactivity the depressed person becomes a burden for others. Furthermore, reduced activity and libido do not favor propagation of the species. When faced with a loss or a failure, it would seem much more advantageous to simply forget and go on living instead of losing oneself, and to become active, optimistic and energetic rather than inactive, pessimistic and anhedonic.1

5.1 Is DR maladaptive?

One possible answer is that DR is like it appears and thus is "maladaptive and has no function at all, and has come into existence as a by-product of selection on a correlated trait or as an adaptation that has gone away" (p. 3, Welling, 2003). The following arguments (see Nesse, 2000) counter this position:

- Pain, fear, guilt, nausea and fatigue are aversive but useful;
- DR usually follows a loss or a failure and its intensity tends to be proportional to the severity of the loss. This suggests that DR is regulated by specific situations, and this is a characteristic of functional reactions;
- DR is a very common experience. The frequency of DR in addition to the obvious costs of inactivity suggest that it has a function, otherwise the disadvantages would outweigh the advantages. Could a species have survived that is predisposed to react with DR to losses and failures if the advantages were not greater than the disadvantages? (Welling, 2003).

5.2 DR as an interpersonal signal

A second group of students attributes a function to DR, but due to lack of agreement among the authors the function is not clear. Now we will critically examine the hypotheses considered by Welling (2003) and Nesse (2000).[4]

A common hypothesis is that depression serves to communicate the need for help (Hagen, 1999; Klerman, 1974). Crying certainly communicates this need and inspires compassion (Barr, 1990; Lummaa et al., 1998). Depressed people often cry and this certainly has a communicative effect. Nevertheless, passive withdrawal and loss of appetite or sexual drive are not necessary to communicate this need and are thus unexplained. Moreover, depressed people are usually considered unpleasant (Coyne et al., 1987), which contradicts this

---

[4] Nesse (2000) used the term " low mood" and gave it the same meaning as that of DR.

hypothesis. Another group-dynamic explanation is that depression may signal yielding in a hierarchy conflict (Price et al., 1994; Sloman et al., 1994). " (p. 4. Welling, 2003). One criticism of the latter hypothesis is that in many cases DR is free of interpersonal power conflicts. But apart from what DR signals, it is the idea that it is a signal that has some weak points. "There are many less costly alternatives, and behaviors with a signaling function are usually short (see van de Waal, 1998) and momentary communicative acts, while depression is a longer-lasting state" (p. 4. Welling, 2003). Moreover, the signaling function would be incompatibile with the fact that people with DR often tend to avoid others and isolate themselves and to speak little even with the people closest to them. If DR were a signal, it would manifest differently.

5.3 DR inhibits futile efforts

A third group of hypotheses revolve around the idea that "just as anxiety inhibits dangerous actions, depression inhibits futile efforts" (p. 17. Nesse, 2000). This idea is has been expressed in several ways.

5.3.1 DR preserves energy

"One of the most common explanations of the existence of depression revolves around the idea that DR helps to preserve energy (e.g., Schmale and Engel, 1975; Thierry et al., 2000)" (p. 4. Welling, 2003). Beck also "emphasizes a role for depression in conserving resources" (p. 15; Nesse, 2000). One problematic aspect of this hypothesis is that it is not very clear why saving energy after loss would be favorable. In fact, it would seem better to increase activity to compensate for the loss and find substitute resources (Nesse, 2000).

5.3.2 DR is useful for coping with unpropitious situations.

Nesse (2000) resolved this objection by suggesting that decreased motivation and activity would obviously be useful in situations characterized not only by loss or failure but also by a more general lack of alternatives in which every action would be futile and dangerous (p.16; Nesse, 2000). As DR is characterized by decreased motivation and activity, he hypothesized that DR "is adaptive for dealing with unpropitious situations: those situations in which the individual is confronted with an unreachable goal, and no alternatives with a positive pay-off are available". When the cost of every action is higher than its yield, it is better to do nothing at all. Depression is "a state shaped to cope with unpropitious situations and it could be useful both to decrease investments in the current unsatisfying life enterprise and to prevent the premature pursuit of alternatives" (p.17; Nesse, 2000). Several objections can be raised.

DR is characterized, not only by decreased motivation and activity, but also by crying, rumination over the lost good and reluctance to renounce anything that regards it. This activity seems opposite to that of decreasing investments in the current unsatisfying life enterprise and reducing futile efforts. DR does not seem like a useful state for reducing costs compared with circumstances that yield little, such as lethargy (Nesse, 2000). The relationship people in DR have with the lost good, nor does it resemble the serene attitude of one who has already accepted the loss or failure. A second problem with Nesse's version is that situations without any positive alternatives seem rather rare to justify the high incidence of DR (Welling, 2003). Nesse's examples of these situations, such as the absence of a viable life plan, insufficient internal reserves or the lack of a crucial resource are not very convincing (Welling, 2003). The third problem is that Nesse's version does not explain the presence of anhedonia in DR, that is, the depressed person's decreased ability to enjoy the goods he obtains and is aware of obtaining. How can losing interest in the wins of one's favorite team, or enjoying a sexual relationship less, be useful in preventing the premature pursuit of alternatives? The reduction of interests (including vital ones), which can be satisfied and that the person knows he can satisfy, does not seem to have the function of inhibiting futile efforts but rather to be a waste of gratifications. Fourth, note that Nesse's explanation revolves around the notion of cost: "When the cost of every action is higher than its yield, it is better to do nothing at all." But does the human mind really calculate the costs of every action and arrive at the conclusion that it is better to do nothing? This seems unlikely, because calculating the costs and benefits of every action and then comparing them would surely surpass working memory capacity. Therefore, as suggested by Castelfranchi and Miceli (in the already-cited work of 2002), humans do not try to maximize what is useful and therefore minimize damages, because this would require the ability to perform highly complex calculations. Instead, humans "choose the goal (action) that is most convenient (with respect to their own limited knowledge) from among different and active, but not jointly pursuable, goals" (Castelfranchi and Miceli, 2002). Therefore, "doing nothing" is a line of conduct at the service of a goal, not of minimizing the damage. Which goal? In the preceding section, dedicated to the psychological paradoxes of depression, we suggested that the goal is to avoid losing, or further and definitevly compromising, the lost good. It is not very relevant whether our suggestion is adeguate or not, the critical point is that Nesse's proposal presupposes an unrealistic capacity and functioning of the mind. In conclusion, for various reasons the function of DR does not seem to be that of decreasing investments in the current unsatisfying life enterprise, saving energy, conserving resources or uselessly inhibiting costly efforts in an unpropitious environment.

5.3.3 DR is useful for reorientation

A fourth group of authors share the idea that DR may foster disengagement from unreachable goals; but, unlike Nesse, they hold that "disengagement would have the function of reassessment or reorientation of where to direct one's motivation (Gut, 1989; Hamburg, 1974; Klinger, 1975; Wortman and Brehm, 1975). The insufficiency of this hypothesis is that the pessimism of depression lacks specificity for this purpose; it causes disengagement from all activities, not only from unfruitful but from all activies. It leads to helplessness (Seligman, 1975) rather than a functional and adaptive re-evaluation of reachable and unreachable goals." (p. 5, Welling, 2003). Furthermore, as we already stated with regard to Nesse, pain, rumination and refusal to distance oneself from the lost good suggest there is no disengagement from unreachable goals in DR; in fact, it seems that the opposite occurs, at least in the initial phases of DR. Finally, in agreement with Nesse, Welling(2003) argues that DR protects against futile and dangerous actions. But unlike Nesse, he believes that this protection would not be justified by the fact that the individual finds himself in an unpropitious world, but by the fact that following a loss or large failure the individual has no habits or reference points, lacks adequate cognitive maps and is therefore disoriented and vulnerable. In this view, DR provides the necessary time for updating the individual's cognitive maps, which have completely changed because of the loss (Welling, 2003). According to Pinker (1997), one must take time to plan how to cope with a world that has been turned upside-down. A weakness of this explanation is that if it were true we would observe efforts to construct a map of the new situation and attention, thoughts, and fantasies would be constructive and turned toward the present and future rather than the past. In DR the opposite occurs, e.g., rumination is mostly turned toward the past.

The two hypotheses also have another defect. It is true that in most cases DR is followed by reorientation and reorganization of investments and cognitive maps, but post hoc does not mean propter hoc. DR precedes the acceptance but is not necessarily its cause.

5.4 A proposal to explain the evolutionary paradox of DR

Attempts to answer the question, "Does DR have an advantageous role in evolution?", are limited because the psychological mechanisms, that generate DR, are not considered. A second limit is that scholars considered the "hardest" DR, those in which the damage, loss or failure were very severe and subjectively and objectively irreparable. In fact, they neglected the "softer" DR, which are obviously much more frequent in daily life. It is quite plausibile that the management of losses and failures takes place by means of analogous mechanisms in both hard and soft DR. We suggest that scholars have looked for the evolutionary function of DR, in the least opportune place. If, as Nesse (2000) suggests, DR is a way facing unpropitious situations, and if, as it seems reasonable to suppose, soft unpropitious situations are much more frequent than hard ones, then it is reasonable to hold that DR is chosen because it functions in managing soft unpropitious situations but not hard ones. A third aspect is that the disadvantages of DR are overrated. This is probably because the frame of reference of those who deal with this problem is usually clinical depression. Briefly and using an analogy, when they speak of the evolutionary advantages of DR, they seem to be looking more the evolutionary advantages of allergic reactions than those of the immune system. To get around these limitations, we must ask ourselves about the evolutionary advantages of DR, starting from the psychological mechanisms that generate it and considering the most frequent and everyday cases, i.e., soft DR.

In the preceding section, we suggested that the following psychological mechanisms are at the base of DR:

- an increase in the subjective value of a good when it is considered in the domain of losses;
- an investment aimed at reducing the possibility of a more severe loss of the good, in particular of distancing and distraction from the good;
- and connected with this, orienting functional cognitive processes toward reducing the risk of wasting resources in different, less important investments.

These mechanisms seem to have the function of stabilizing investments. In turn, stabilizing investments seems to be a basic function of systems that have many, often divergent goals, which could guide behavior in different and even opposing directions, primarily if one is in an environment able to activate such goals in rapid succession. It is easy to imagine that without adequate stabiliziing mechanisms one can end up in a distracting chaos, able to nullify all attempts to reach any goal. This risk would become even higher in the presence of a frustration (when these investments do not produce the expected result), if one cannot see how to reach the goal, and above all if hope is drastically reduced or lost. A system with many goals would have difficulty surviving without stabilizing mechanisms. In particular, having mechanisms able to stabilize investments in adverse conditions, in which optimism and hope are lost, is useful for maintaining strategic programs, that would otherwise risk being abandoned at the first difficulty.

Investments in discrete goods would be more affected by the lack of a stabilizing mechanism (Paglieri and Castelfranchi, 2008), such as investments in affective relationships in which the same desire, e.g., a desire for love, can be satisfied by several persons. The stabilization of investments in specific persons provides numerous evolutionary advantages, such as the strength of a group. Relationships would surely be more chaotic if there wasn't fidelity. And it is opportune that fidelity be maintained even in aderse conditions in which hope is lost. A lack of this type of mechanism would result in affective disinvestment and a break in the relationship every time one is separated from a loved person, without being supported by the hope of reunification. Many other factors useful to stabilize investment exist. Among these, it is worth citing moral factors, both in the sense of commitment to remain faithful to one's homeland, even when everything falls apart and there is no hope of avoiding its distruction, and in the altruistic sense, e.g., feeling guilty when one is detached from the memory of a deceased loved one. Another factor that stabilizes investments, even in the case of loss of hope, is the desire to maintain one's sense of identity. These factors and others intervene in DR. They can enrich its phenomenology and reinforce its stabilizing mechanisms, but they cannot necessarily explain it.

In conclusion, stabilizing investments (primarily affective ones), and above all when faced with frustrations, difficulties and obstacles, seems to have evolutionarily important advantages. The functioning of the stabilizing mechanisms that underlie DR is probabily maximal in unpropitious situations, which are soft and more frequent in daily life, and becomes minimal or null in the case of severe, objectively irrecuperabile losses. But the dysfunctionality of DR in unpropitious hard situations is probably not as severe as it is in psychopathological cases.

6 Conclusions

In the first part of this chapter we looked at the psychological paradoxes of DR and posed the following question: how can a mind produce a DR? Our response was based on the idea that there is an increase in investment in the lost good in DR and that the investment is not for its recovery but to avoid losing it even more. A deceased loved one can be further lost, for example, through forgetting, losing interest and becoming interested in other things. We have tried to show that the particular investment of DR, together with strictly doxastic factors, can explain the anhedonia and pessimism that are at the base of its characteristic inactivity.

In the second part of the chapter, we dealt with the evolutionary paradoxes of DR. The solution we proposed starts from the premise that the psychological mechanisms of DR have the function of stabilizing investments in adverse situations. This function is advantageous primarily in unpropitious soft situations and can be disadvantageous in hard situations. Nevertheless, the former are much more frequent than the latter and therefore it is plausibile that individuals who have the ability to react with DR to adversity have had more evolutionary advantages than disadvantages.

There are other important questions. The first regards acceptance of a loss: in which conditions, with which capacities and through which psychological processes is disinvestment in lost goods and investment in other goods accomplished? In other words, how is DR overcome? The second question concerns clinical depression: Do different mechanisms intervene in clinical depression than in DR or is the difference only quantitative? Does the endophenotype of depression involve some of the mechanisms of DR? How can we explain that most relapses seem to occur without adverse triggering events? Are the mechanisms of acceptance compromised in clinical depression?

References

1. Arntz, A., Rauner, M., & Van den Hout, M. (1995). "If I feel anxious, there must be danger": ex-consequentia reasoning in inferring danger in anxiety disorders. *Behaviour Research and Therapy*; 33: 917-925.
2. Barr, R.G. (1990). The crying paradox: A modest proposal. *Human Nature*, 1, 355–389.
3. Beck, A.T. (2008). The evolution of the cognitive model of depression and its neurobiological correlates. *American Journal of Psychiatry*, 165, 969–977.
4. Bowlby, J. (1980). *Attachment and loss, Vol. 3: Sadness and depression*. New York: Basic Book.
5. Buonanno, C., Frezza, P., Romano, G., & Gangemi, A. (2009). Il Ruolo del Ragionamento Emozionale come fattore di mantenimento degli stati depressivi: la tristezza come informazione di perdita. Psichiatria dell'Infanzia e dell'Adolescenza. 76 (2), 396-405.
6. Carver, C.S., & Scheier, M.F. (1983). A control-theory approach to human behavior, and implications for problems in self-management. In P. C. Kendall (Ed.), *Advances in cognitive-behavioral research and therapy* (Vol. 2, pp. 127-194). New York: Academic Press.
7. Carver, C.S., & Scheier, M.F. (1990). Origins and functions of positive and negative affect: A control-process view. *Psychological Review, 97*, 19-35.
8. Coyne, J.C., Kessler, R.C., Tal, M., & Turnbull, J. (1987). Living with a depressed person. *Journal of Consulting and Clinical Psychology, 55*, 347–352.
9. Couyoumdjian, A., Trincas, R., Ottaviani, C., Tenore, K., Spitoni, G., & Mancini, F. (2011a). Depression as a multifaceted condition: appraisals mediate the relationship between life events and different patterns of symptoms. Poster presented at the 7th ICCP Congress, Istanbul, Turkey, June 2-5, 2011.
10. Couyoumdjian, A., Trincas, R., Ottaviani, C., Tenore, K., Spitoni, G., & Mancini, F. (2011b). Extending the Situation–Symptom Congruence Hypothesis in Depression: the Role of Appraisals. Manuscript sumbitted for publication
11. de Jong, P. J., Haenen, M., Schmidt, A., & Mayer, B. (1998). Hypochondriasis: The role of fear-confirming reasoning. *Behaviour Research and Therapy, 36*, 65–74.
12. Friedrich, J. (1993). Primary error detection and minimization (PEDMIN) strategies in social cognition: A reinterpretation of confirmation bias phenomena. *Psychological Review, 100*, 289 – 319.
13. Gilbert, P. (1998). The evolved basis and adaptive functions of cognitive distortions. *British Journal of Medical Psychology, 71*, 447–463.
14. Gut, E. (1989). *Productive and unproductive depression*. Basic Books: New York.
15. Hamburg, D.A. (1974). Coping behavior in life-threatening circumstances. *Psychotherapeutic Psychodynamics, 23*, 13–25.
16. Hagen, E.H. (1999). The functions of postpartum depression. *Evolution and Human Behavior, 20*, 325–359.
17. Johnson-Laird, P.N., Mancini, F., & Gangemi, A. (2006). A theory of psychological illnesses. *Psychological Reviews, 113*, 822-842.
18. Kahneman, D. & Tversky, A. (1979). Prospect theory: An analysis of decisions under risk. *Econometrica, 4*, 313–327.
19. Kahneman, D., Knetsch, J. L., & Thaler, R. (1990). Experimental tests of the endowment effect and the coase theorem. *Journal of Political Economy, 98*, 1325-1348.
20. Keller, M.C., Neale, M.C., & Kendler, K.S. (2007). Association of different adverse life events with distinct patterns of depressive symptoms. *American Journal of Psychiatry*,164,1521-1529
21. Keller, M.C., & Nesse, R.M. (2005). Is low mood an adaptation? Evidence for subtypes with symptoms that match precipitants. *Journal of Affective Disorders, 86*, 27-35.
22. Keller, M.C., & Nesse, R.M. (2006). The evolutionary significance of depressive symptoms: different adverse situations lead to different depressive symptom patterns. *Journal of Personality and Social Psychology, 91*, 316-330.
23. Kim, S., Thibodeau, R, & Jorgensen,R.S. (2011). Shame, guilt, and depressive symptoms: A meta-analytic review. *Psychological Bulletin, 137*, 68-96.

24. Klerman, G.L. (1974). Depression and adaptation. In R. J. Friedman & M. M. Katz (Eds.), *The psychology of depression* (pp. 127–156). Washington: Winston & Sons.
25. Klinger, E. (1975). Consequences to commitment to and disengagement from incentives. *Psychological Review, 82*, 1–25.
26. Lummaa, V., Vuorisalo, T., Barr, R.G., & Lehtonen, L. (1998). Why cry? Adaptive significance of intensive crying in human infants. *Evolution and Human Behavior, 19*, 193–202.
27. Mancini, F., Gangemi, A., & Johnson-Laird, P.N. (2007). Il ruolo del ragionamento nella Psicopatologia secondo la Hyper Emotion Theory. *Giornale Italiano di Psicologia, 4*, 763-793.
28. McGuire, M. T., Troisi, A., & Raleigh, M. M. (1997). Depression in an evolutionary context. In S. Baron- Cohen (Ed.), *The maladapted mind: Classic readings in evolutionary psychopathology* (pp. 255-282). London: Erlbaum/Taylor and Francis.
29. Miceli, M., & Castelfranchi, C. (1995). *Le difese della mente*. Roma: La Nuova Italia Scientifica,
30. Miceli, M., & Castelfranchi, C. (2002a). La sofferenza psichica In C. Castelfranchi, M. Miceli & F. Mancini (Eds.), *Fondamenti di cognitivismo clinico*. Torino: Bollati Boringhieri.
31. Miceli, M. & Castelfranchi, C. (2002b). The mind and the future: The (negative) power of expectations. *Theory & Psychology, 12*, 335-366.
32. Nesse, R.M. (1990). Evolutionary explanations of emotions. *Human Nature, 1*, 261–289.
33. Nesse, R.M. (2000). Is depression an adaptation? *Archives of General Psychiatry, 57*, 14–20.
34. Paglieri, F., & Castelfranchi, C. (2008). Decidere il futuro: scelta intertemporale e teoria degli scopi. *Giornale Italiano di Psicologia, 4*, 739-771
35. Parkes, C. (1972). Components of the reaction to loss of a lamb, spouse or home. *Journal of Psychosomatic Research, 16 (5)*, 343-349.
36. Pinker, S. (1997). *How the mind works*. New York: Norton.
37. Price. J., Sloman, L., Gardner, R., Gilbert, P., & Rohde, P. (1994). The social competition hypothesis of depression. *British Journal of Psychiatry, 164*, 309–315.
38. Schmale, A., & Engel, G. (1975). The role of depression withdrawal in depressive reactions. In T. Benedek, & E. G. Anthony (Eds.), *Depression and human existence* (pp. 183–198). Boston: Little Brown & Co.
39. Seligman, M.E.P. (1975). *Helplessness: On depression, development and death*. San Francisco: Freeman & Co.
40. Scott, D.S., & Cervone, D. (2002) The Impact of Negative Affect on Performance Standards: Evidence for an Affect-as-Information Mechanism. *Cognitive Therapy and Research, 26*, 19–37.
41. Sloman, L., Price. J, Gilbert, P., & Gardner, R. (1994). Adaptive function of depression: Psychotherapeutic implications. *American Journal of Psychotherapy, 48*, 401–416.
42. Taylor, S.E., & Brown, J.D. (1988). Illusion and well-being: A social psychological perspective on metal health. *Psychological Bulletin, 103*, 193–210.
43. Thierry, B., Steru, L., Chermat, R., & Simon, P. (2000). Searching waiting strategy: A candidate for an evolutionary model of depression? *Archives of General Psychiatry, 57 (1)*, 14–20.
44. van de Waal, M. (1998). *Chimpanzee politics: Sex and power among the apes* (revised ed.). Baltimore: Johns Hopkins University Press.
45. Welling, H. (2003). An evolutionary function of the depressive reaction: the cognitive map hypothesis. *New Ideas in Psychology, 21*, 147–156.
46. Wortman, C.B., & Brehm, J.W. (1975). Responses to uncontrollable outcomes: An integration of reactance theory and the learned helplessness model. In L. Berkowitz (Ed.), *Advances in experimental social psychology* (pp. 277–336). New York: Academic Press.

Chapter 16
The cognitive anatomy and functions of expectations revisited

Emiliano Lorini

Abstract Some years ago (in 2003) I wrote my first paper in collaboration with Cristiano Castelfranchi who at that time was the supervisor of my Master project in Cognitive Science. The work was aimed at providing a logical formalization of the notion of expectation and of expectation-based emotions such as hope, fear, disappointment and relief. In this paper I will revisit and extend the analysis we did in 2003. I will propose a refinement of the notion of expectation by formalizing its two primitive components: the value of the goal and the strength of the belief. Thanks to this refinement, I will provide a formal analysis of the intensity of hope and fear.

1 Introduction

Cristiano Castelfranchi has been a great teacher and a constant source of inspiration. During the years of my PhD in Rome he taught me to love scientific research and how to find beautiful connections among different aspects of human mind and of social interaction. We had very intense discussions on several different topics: on the relationships between beliefs and motivations (*e.g.* goals, intentions *etc.*); on the concepts of intentional action and attempt; on the theory of altruism and pro-social attitudes; on the theory of social trust, power, delegation; on the cognitive theory of surprise, and on many many others. In 2003 I wrote my first scientific paper together with him who at that time was the supervisor of my Master project in Cognitive Science. The work - published in [7][1] - was aimed at providing a logical formalization of the notion of expectation and of expectation-based emotions such as hope, fear, disappointment and relief.

In this paper I will revisit and extend the analysis we did in 2003 into two directions. First of all, I will introduce a new logical framework which

Emiliano Lorini
Université de Toulouse, IRIT-CNRS, France

[1] A longer version of this work can be found in [8].

allows to formalize in a simple way some basic concepts for a formal theory of expectation-based emotions: the notion of graded belief and the notion of graded goal. Secondly, I will propose a refinement of the notion of expectation by formalizing its two primitive components: the value of the goal and the strength of the belief. Thanks to this refinement, I will provide a formal analysis of the cognitive structures of hope and fear and of their intensities. With cognitive structure of an emotion, I mean the emotion's triggering conditions, that is, the agent's mental states (beliefs, goals, intentions, *etc.*) that trigger the agent's emotional reaction (*e.g.*, action tendencies and physiological reactions) and 'cause' the agent to feel the emotion.

The rest of the paper is organized as follows. Section 2 is devoted to present a logical representation language for the formalization of expectation-based emotions. I will explain the syntax and the semantics of this logic which allows to represent different kinds of an agent's mental states such as knowledge, graded belief and graded goal. In Section 3, the logical framework of Section 2 will be applied to the formalization of the cognitive structures of hope and fear and of their intensities. I will consider the concepts of hope and fear. In Section 4 I will discuss some related works in the area of logical modeling of emotions. Then, I will conclude.

2 A simple logic of graded beliefs and graded goals

The logic **LGA** (*Logic of Graded mental Attitudes*) presented in this section is a BDI-like logic in the sense of [10, 32] which allows to represent formally different kinds of mental attitudes of an agent including knowledge, graded beliefs (*i.e.*, believing with a certain strength that a given proposition is true) and graded goals (*i.e.*, wanting with a given force or strength a given proposition to be true). I will present the syntax and the semantics of the logic **LGA**. I will only consider the single-agent case, postponing to future work an extension of the logic to the multi-agent case.

2.1 Syntax

Assume a finite set of propositional variables $Prop = \{p, q, \ldots\}$ and a finite set of positive integers $Num = \{0, \ldots, \mathsf{max}\}$ with $\mathsf{max} \geq 1$. The language $\mathcal{L}$ of the logic LGA is the set of formulae defined by the following grammar in Backus-Naur Form (BNF):

$$Atm : \chi ::= p \mid \mathsf{exc}_h \mid \mathsf{des}_h$$
$$Fml : \varphi ::= \chi \mid \neg\varphi \mid \varphi \wedge \varphi \mid \mathsf{K}\varphi$$

where p ranges over $Prop$ and h ranges over Num. The other Boolean constructions $\top, \bot, \vee, \rightarrow$ and $\leftrightarrow$ are defined from p, $\neg$ and $\wedge$ in the standard way.

Atm is the set of atomic formulae. The latter includes propositional variables and special constructions which are used to represent the agent's mental state (the agent's beliefs and goals).

The special atoms exc_h are used to identify the degree of *plausibility* of a given world according to the agent. Indeed, possible worlds are ordered according to their plausibility degree for the agent in such a way that the agent is capable of assessing whether a given world is more plausible than another world. Starting from [22], ranking among possible worlds have been extensively used in belief revision theory in order to define a selection mechanism (*i.e.*, a revision function) which can tell how to decide rationally which sentences to give up and which to keep when revising a knowledge base. I here use the notion of plausibility first introduced by Spohn [38]. Following Spohn's theory, the worlds that are assigned the smallest numbers are the most plausible, according to the beliefs of the individual. That is, the ordinal h assigned to a given world rather captures the degree of *exceptionality* of this world, where the exceptionality degree of a world is nothing but the opposite of its plausibility degree (*i.e.*, the exceptionality degree of a world decreases when its plausibility degree increases). Therefore, formula exc_h can be read alternatively as "according to the agent, the current world has a degree of exceptionality h" or "the current world has a degree of plausibility $max - h$".

The special atoms des_h are used to identify the degree of *desirability* (or the degree of *goodness*) of a given world for the agent.[2]

Contrary to plausibility, the worlds that are assigned the biggest numbers are the most desirable for the agent. The degree of undesirability (or degree of a badness) of a given world is the opposite of its desirability degree (or degree of goodness). Therefore, formula des_h can be read alternatively as "the current world has a degree of desirability h" or "the current world has a degree of undesirability $max - h$".

The formula $K\varphi$ has to be read "the agent knows that φ is true". This concept of knowledge is the standard S5-notion, partition-based and fully introspective, that is commonly used both in computer science [17] and economics [4]. If a proposition is part of the agent's knowledge then it means that the agent considers it a well-established truth [42]. The dual of the operator K is denoted by $\widehat{K}$, that is, we define:

$$\widehat{K}\varphi \overset{\text{def}}{=} \neg K \neg \varphi$$

$\widehat{K}\varphi$ has to be read "the agent thinks that φ is possible" or "the agent envisages a situation in which φ is true".

2.2 Semantics

The model-theoretic semantics of the logic LGA is a possible world semantics.

---

[2] The term 'goodness' is perhaps more convenient because one may ascribe to the terms 'desire' and 'desirability' a hedonistic connotation that I do not want to use here.

Definition 1 (Model) *LGA-models are tuples* $M = \langle W, \sim, \kappa_{exc}, \kappa_{des}, \mathcal{V} \rangle$ *where:*

- W *is a nonempty set of possible worlds or states;*
- $\sim$ *is an equivalence relation between worlds in W;*
- $\kappa_{exc} : W \longrightarrow Num$ *and* $\kappa_{des} : W \longrightarrow Num$ *are functions from the set of possible worlds into the set of integers Num;*
- $\mathcal{V} : W \longrightarrow 2^{Prop}$ *is a valuation function.*

As usual, $p \in \mathcal{V}(w)$ means that proposition p is true at world w.

The accessibility relation $\sim$, which is used to interpret the epistemic operator K, can be viewed as a function from W to 2^W. Therefore, we can write $\sim(w) = \{v \in W : w \sim v\}$. The set $\sim(w)$ is the agent's *information state* at world w: the set of worlds that the agent considers possible at world w or, the set of worlds that the agent cannot distinguish from world w. As $\sim$ is an equivalence relation, if $w \sim v$ then the agent has the same information state at w and v (*i.e.*, the agent has the same knowledge at w and v).

The function κ_{exc} represents a plausibility grading of the possible worlds and is used to interpret the atomic formulae exc_h. $\kappa_{exc}(w) = h$ means that, according to the agent the world w has a degree of exceptionality h or, alternatively, according to the agent the world w has a degree of plausibility $max - h$. (Remember that the degree of exceptionality of a world is nothing but the opposite of its plausibility degree.) The function κ_{exc} allows to model the notion of belief: among the worlds the agent cannot distinguish from a given world w (*i.e.*, the agent's information state at w), there are worlds that the agent considers more plausible than others. For example, suppose that $\sim(w) = \{w, v, u\}$, $\kappa_{exc}(w) = 2$, $\kappa_{exc}(u) = 1$ and $\kappa_{exc}(v) = 0$. This means that at world w the agent cannot distinguish the three worlds w, v and u (*i.e.*, $\{w, v, u\}$ is the set of worlds that the agent considers possible at world w). Moreover, according to the agent, the world v is strictly more plausible than the world u and the world u is strictly more plausible than the world w (as $max - 0 > max - 1 > max - 2$).

The function κ_{des} is used to interpret the atomic formulae des_h. $\kappa_{des}(w) = h$ means that, according to the agent the world w has a degree of desirability (or goodness) h or, alternatively, according to the agent the world w has a degree of undesirability (or badness) $max - h$. (Remember that the degree of undesirability of a world is the opposite of its desirability degree.)

LGA-models are supposed to satisfy the following additional *normality* constraints for the plausibility grading and for the desirability grading:

($NORM_{\kappa_{exc}}$) according to the agent, there exists a world with maximal degree of plausibility (or with minimal degree of exceptionality): for every $w \in W$, there is v such that $w \sim v$ and $\kappa_{exc}(v) = 0$;

($NORM_{\kappa_{des}}$) according to the agent, there exists a world with minimal degree of desirability 0 (or with maximal degree of undesirability): for every $w \in W$, there is v such that $w \sim v$ and $\kappa_{des}(v) = 0$.

As I will show in Section 2.4, these should be interpreted as a sort of *rationality* requirements that ensure that an agent cannot have inconsistent beliefs or conflicting goals.

Definition 2 (Truth conditions) *Given a* **LGA***-model M, a world w and a formula* φ, $M, w \models \varphi$ *means that* φ *is true at world w in M. The rules defining the truth conditions of atomic formulae, negation, conjunction and the epistemic operators are:*

- $M, w \models p$ *iff* $p \in \mathcal{V}(w)$
- $M, w \models \mathsf{exc_h}$ *iff* $\kappa_{\mathsf{exc}}(w) = \mathsf{h}$
- $M, w \models \mathsf{des_h}$ *iff* $\kappa_{\mathsf{des}}(w) = \mathsf{h}$
- $M, w \models \neg\varphi$ *iff not* $M, w \models \varphi$
- $M, w \models \varphi \wedge \psi$ *iff* $M, w \models \varphi$ *and* $M, w \models \psi$
- $M, w \models \mathsf{K}\varphi$ *iff* $M, v \models \varphi$ *for all v with* $w \sim v$

In the sequel I write $\models_{\mathsf{LGA}} \varphi$ to mean that φ is *valid* in **LGA** (φ is true in all **LGA**-models).

2.3 *Definitions of graded belief, certain belief, goal and graded goal*

Following [38], I extend the plausibility degree of a possible world to a plausibility degree of a formula viewed as a set of worlds (the worlds where the formula is satisfiable).

Definition 3 (Exceptionality degree of a formula) *Let* $\|\varphi\|_w = \{v \in W : M, v \models \varphi$ *and* $w \sim v\}$ *be the set of worlds envisaged by the agent at world w in which* φ *is true. The exceptionality degree of a formula* φ *at world w, denoted by* $\kappa^w_{\mathsf{exc}}(\varphi)$*, is defined as follows:*

$$\kappa^w_{\mathsf{exc}}(\varphi) = \begin{cases} \min_{v \in \|\varphi\|_w} \kappa_{\mathsf{exc}}(v) & \text{if } \|\varphi\|_w \neq \emptyset \\ \mathsf{max} & \text{if } \|\varphi\|_w = \emptyset \end{cases}$$

As expected, the *plausibility* degree of a formula φ is defined as $\mathsf{max} - \kappa^w_{\mathsf{exc}}(\varphi)$.
   I do a similar manipulation for the desirability degree.

Definition 4 (Desirability degree of a formula) *The desirability degree of a formula* φ *at world w, denoted by* $\kappa^w_{\mathsf{des}}(\varphi)$*, is defined as follows:*

$$\kappa^w_{\mathsf{des}}(\varphi) = \begin{cases} \min_{v \in \|\varphi\|_w} \kappa_{\mathsf{des}}(v) & \text{if } \|\varphi\|_w \neq \emptyset \\ 0 & \text{if } \|\varphi\|_w = \emptyset \end{cases}$$

The *undesirability* degree of a formula φ is defined as $\mathsf{max} - \kappa^w_{\mathsf{des}}(\varphi)$.
   Again following [38], I define semantically the concept of belief as a formula which is true in all worlds that are maximally plausible (or minimally exceptional) according to the agent.

Definition 5 (Belief, Bel) *At world w the agent believes that* φ *is true, i.e.,* $M, w \models \mathsf{Bel}\varphi$, *if and only if, for every v such that* $w \sim v$, *if* $\kappa_{\mathsf{exc}}(v) = 0$ *then* $M, v \models \varphi$.

The following concept of graded belief is taken from [24, 23]: the strength of the belief that φ is equal to the exceptionality degree of $\neg\varphi$.[3]

Definition 6 (Graded belief, Bel^h) *At world w the agent believes that φ with strength equal to h, i.e., $M,w \models \text{Bel}^h\varphi$, if and only if, $\kappa_{\text{exc}}^w(\neg\varphi) = h$.*

I moreover define the following concept of certain belief in the sense of believing that φ is true with maximal strength max.

Definition 7 (Certain belief, Certain) *At world w the agent is certain that φ is true, i.e., $M,w \models \text{Certain}\varphi$, if and only if $\kappa_{\text{exc}}^w(\neg\varphi) = \text{max}$.*

The following concept of graded goal is the motivational counterpart of the notion of graded belief. I say that at world w the agent wants (or wishes) φ to be true with strength equal to h if and only if, the desirability of φ is equal to h.

Definition 8 (Graded goal, Goal^h) *At world w the agent wants/wishes φ to be true with strength equal to h (or the agent has the goal that φ with strength equal to h), i.e., $\text{Goal}^h\varphi$, if and only if, $\kappa_{\text{des}}^w(\varphi) = h$.*

Note that previous definition captures a 'pessimistic' notion of graded goal: when assessing how much φ is desirable, the agent focuses on his epistemic alternatives with a minimal degree of desirability in which φ is true. In this sense, the preceding notion of graded goal that φ consists in a kind of worst case analysis of the epistemic alternatives in which φ is true. It is also worth noting that the previous operator of graded goal is an operator of strong possibility (or actual possibility) in the sense of possibility theory [14]. In the context of possibility theory it is also called operator Δ.[4]

The reason why the definition of graded goal is not symmetric to the definition of graded belief is that these two concepts satisfy different logical properties. As I will show below in Section 2.4, Definition 6 and Definition 8 allow to capture interesting differences between graded belief and graded goal, in particular on the way they distribute over conjunction and over disjunction.

The notion of goal is a just a special case of the notion of graded goal. I say that the agent wants (or wishes) φ to be true with strength equal to h if and only if, the agent wants (or wishes) φ to be true with strength higher than 0.

Definition 9 (Goal, Goal) *At world w the agent wants/wishes φ to be true (or the agent has the goal that φ), i.e., $\text{Goal}\varphi$, if and only if $\kappa_{\text{des}}^w(\varphi) > 0$.*

As the following proposition highlights the concepts of belief, graded belief, certain belief, goal and graded goal semantically defined in Definitions 5-9 are all syntactically expressible in the logic LGA.

Proposition 1 *For every model M, world w and $h \in Num$:*

- $M,w \models \text{Bel}\varphi$ *iff* $M,w \models \text{K}(\text{exc}_0 \rightarrow \varphi)$

---

[3] Similar operators for graded belief are studied in [3, 43].

[4] See also [1] for a recent application of the operator Δ to modeling desires.

- $M, w \models \mathsf{Bel}^h\varphi$ iff $\begin{cases} M, w \models \widehat{\mathsf{K}}(\mathsf{exc}_h \wedge \neg\varphi) \wedge \mathsf{K}(\mathsf{exc}_{<h} \to \varphi) & \text{if } h < \max \\ M, w \models \mathsf{K}(\mathsf{exc}_{<h} \to \varphi) & \text{if } h = \max \end{cases}$

- $M, w \models \mathsf{Certain}\varphi$ iff $M, w \models \mathsf{K}(\mathsf{exc}_{<\max-1} \to \varphi)$

- $M, w \models \mathsf{Goal}^h\varphi$ iff $\begin{cases} M, w \models \widehat{\mathsf{K}}(\mathsf{des}_h \wedge \varphi) \wedge \mathsf{K}(\mathsf{des}_{<h} \to \neg\varphi) & \text{if } h < \max \\ M, w \models \mathsf{K}(\mathsf{des}_{<h} \to \neg\varphi) & \text{if } h = \max \end{cases}$

- $M, w \models \mathsf{Goal}\varphi$ iff $M, w \models \mathsf{K}(\mathsf{des}_0 \to \neg\varphi)$

where $\mathsf{exc}_{<Numinalb} \overset{def}{=} \bigvee_{Numinale \in Num : 0 \leq Numinale < Numinalb} \mathsf{exc}_{Numinale}$ *and* $\mathsf{des}_{<k} \overset{def}{=}$ $\bigvee_{y \in Num : 0 \leq y < k} \mathsf{des}_y$ *for all* $k \in Num$ *such that* $k \geq 1$, $\mathsf{exc}_{<0} \overset{def}{=} \bot$ *and* $\mathsf{des}_{<0} \overset{def}{=} \bot$.

2.4 Some properties of mental attitudes

The following are some examples of LGA-validity which capture the basic relationships between knowledge, belief, graded belief, graded goal and certain belief. For every $h \in Num$ we have:

$$\models_{\mathsf{LGA}} \mathsf{Bel}^h\varphi \to \mathsf{Bel}\varphi \text{ if } h > 0 \tag{1}$$

$$\models_{\mathsf{LGA}} \mathsf{Certain}\varphi \leftrightarrow \mathsf{Bel}^{\max}\varphi \tag{2}$$

$$\models_{\mathsf{LGA}} \mathsf{Goal}\varphi \leftrightarrow \bigvee_{h \in Num : h > 0} \mathsf{Goal}^h\varphi \tag{3}$$

$$\models_{\mathsf{LGA}} \neg(\mathsf{Bel}\varphi \wedge \mathsf{Bel}\neg\varphi) \tag{4}$$

$$\models_{\mathsf{LGA}} \neg(\mathsf{Goal}\varphi \wedge \mathsf{Goal}\neg\varphi) \tag{5}$$

According to the validity 1, believing φ with force higher than 0 implies believing φ. According to the validity 2, being certain that φ is true is the same as believing φ with maximal degree max. Finally, according to the validity 3, having the goal that φ is true is the same as having a goal that φ is true with some strength higher than 0. Validities 4 and 5 are consequences of the constraints $(NORM_{\kappa_{exc}})$ and $(NORM_{\kappa_{des}})$ given in Section 2.2. Their meaning is that agent are assumed to be rational, in the sense that they cannot have at the same time logically inconsistent beliefs or logically inconsistent goals.

The following four valid formulae capture the basic decomposability properties of the operators of graded belief and graded goal:

$$\models_{\mathsf{LGA}} (\mathsf{Bel}^h\varphi \wedge \mathsf{Bel}^k\psi) \to \mathsf{Bel}^{\geq\max\{h,k\}}(\varphi \vee \psi) \tag{6}$$

$$\models_{\mathsf{LGA}} (\mathsf{Goal}^h\varphi \wedge \mathsf{Goal}^k\psi) \to \mathsf{Goal}^{\min\{h,k\}}(\varphi \vee \psi) \tag{7}$$

$$\models_{\mathsf{LGA}} (\mathsf{Bel}^h\varphi \wedge \mathsf{Bel}^k\psi) \to \mathsf{Bel}^{\min\{h,k\}}(\varphi \wedge \psi) \tag{8}$$

$$\models_{\mathsf{LGA}} (\mathsf{Goal}^h\varphi \wedge \mathsf{Goal}^k\psi) \to \mathsf{Goal}^{\geq\max\{h,k\}}(\varphi \wedge \psi) \tag{9}$$

where:

$$X^{\geq h}\varphi \overset{def}{=} \bigvee_{k \in Num : k \geq h} X^k\varphi \text{ with } X \in \{\mathsf{Bel}, \mathsf{Goal}\}$$

According to the validity 6, the degree of belief of $\varphi \vee \psi$ is at least equal to the maximum of the degree of belief of φ and ψ. According to the validity 7, the strength of the goal that $\varphi \vee \psi$ is equal to the minimum of the strength of the goal of φ and ψ. According to the validity 8, the degree of belief of $\varphi \wedge \psi$ is equal to the minimum of the degree of belief of φ and ψ. According to the validity 9, the strength of the goal that $\varphi \wedge \psi$ is at least equal to the maximum of the strength of the goal of φ and ψ.

The interesting aspect of the preceding valid formulae is that graded goals distribute over conjunction and over disjunction in the opposite way as graded beliefs. Consider for instance the validity (8) and compare it to the validity (9). The joint occurrence of two events φ and ψ cannot be more plausible than the occurrence of a single event. This is the reason why in the right side of the validity (8) we have the min. On the contrary, the joint occurrence of two desirable events φ and ψ is more desirable than the occurrence of a single event. This is the reason why in the right side of the validity (9) we have the $\geq$ max. For example, suppose Peter wishes to go to the cinema in the evening with strength h (*i.e.*, $\mathsf{Goal}^h goToCinema$) and, at the same time, he wishes to spend the evening with his girlfriend with strength k (*i.e.*, $\mathsf{Goal}^k stayWithGirlfriend$). Then, according to the validity (9), Peter wishes to to go the cinema with his girlfriend with strength at least max{h,k} (*i.e.*, $\mathsf{Goal}^{\geq \max\{h,k\}}(goToCinema \wedge stayWithGirlfriend)$).

Note that the following formula is valid in the logic LGA:

$$\models_{\mathsf{LGA}} \mathsf{K}\neg\varphi \rightarrow \mathsf{Goal}^{\max}\varphi \tag{10}$$

This means that if in all situations that an agent envisages φ is false, then the agent wants φ to be true with maximal strength max. This property follows from the fact that the graded goal operator Goal^h represents a 'pessimistic' notion of goal, that is to say, it is assumed that when assessing how much φ is desirable, the agent focuses on his epistemic alternatives with a minimal degree of desirability in which φ is true. Therefore, if the agent does not envisage a situation in which φ is true, he will consider φ maximally desirable. Nonetheless one might find the preceding property counterintuitive. For this reason, I define the following concept of *realistic goal*, which does not satisfy the same property:

$$\mathsf{RGoal}^h\varphi \overset{\mathrm{def}}{=} \mathsf{Goal}^h\varphi \wedge \widehat{\mathsf{K}}\varphi$$

This means an agent has a realistic goal that φ of strength h, denoted by $\mathsf{RGoal}^h\varphi$, if and only if the agent wants φ to be true with strength h and envisages at least one situation in which φ is true. Obviously if the agent does not envisage a situation in which φ is true then he does not have φ as a realistic goal. That is, for any $h \in Num$:

$$\models_{\mathsf{LGA}} \mathsf{K}\neg\varphi \rightarrow \neg\mathsf{RGoal}^h\varphi \tag{11}$$

2.5 *The concept of goal: some remarks*

In this work I assume that an agent's goal has two dimensions: (1) its content, and (2) its strength or value. Following Castelfranchi's theory of goals [6, 11], with the term 'value of a goal' I mean the subjective importance of the goal for the agent strictly dependent on context conditions and mental attitudes. In the graded goal formula $\text{Goal}^h \varphi$, φ is the goal content while h is the goal strength (or goal value).

Most appraisal models of emotions (see, *e.g.*, [25, 36]) assume that explicit evaluations based on evaluative beliefs (*i.e.*, the belief that a certain event is desirable or undesirable, good or bad, pleasant or unpleasant) are a necessary constituent of emotional experience. Other appraisal models (see, *e.g.*, [37, 19, 21, 9]) assume that emotions are triggering by specific combinations of beliefs and goals (or desires), and that the link between cognition and emotion is not necessarily mediated by evaluative beliefs. Reisenzein [34] calls *cognitive-evaluative* the former and *cognitive-motivational* the latter kind of models. For example, according to cognitive-motivational models of emotions, a person's happiness about a certain fact φ can be reduced to the person's belief that φ obtains and the person's desire (or goal) that φ obtains. On the contrary, according to cognitive-evaluative models, a person feels happy about a certain fact φ if she believes that φ obtains and she evaluates φ to be desirable (or good) for her. A similar distinction has been discussed in philosophy on whether motivational mental states such as goals and desires are derived from and reduced to evaluative beliefs or, viceversa, whether evaluative beliefs are derived from goals or desires (*i.e.*, are desires and goals more primitive than evaluative beliefs, or viceversa?) (see, *e.g.*, [26, 27, 5]).

In the present work, I stay closer to cognitive-evaluative models. In fact, I reduce the notion of goal - involved in the appraisal configuration of a given emotion - to the agent's evaluation of the desirability (or goodness) of a given state of affairs.[5] That is, I assume that an agent has φ as a goal *if and only if* the situations envisaged by the agent in which φ is true are desirable for him. Consequently, I assume that an agent's positive/negative emotion requires the agent's evaluation of the desirability of a certain event, situation or object. One might argue that evaluative beliefs are not primitive mental states, but they are just derived from goals. That is, an agent evaluates a given situation or event to be desirable (or good) for him, *because* he believes that in this situation he will achieve his goals or *because* he believes that the event has positive implications on his goals. I here take a different point of view by assuming that evaluations and goals somehow coincide.

---

[5] Note that, in most cases, the assessment of the desirability of φ has a somatic component, that is, the agent considers φ desirable because while thinking and imagining a situation in which φ holds, the agent has a positive *feeling* or *sensation*.

3 Formalization of expectation-based emotions and their intensity

The modal operators of graded belief and graded goal defined in Section 2.2 are used here to provide a logical analysis of expectation-based emotions such as hope and fear and of their intensities. An expectation-based emotion is an emotion that an agent experiences when having either a positive or a negative expectation about a certain fact φ, that is, when believing that φ is true with a certain strength but envisaging the possibility that φ could be false and either (1) having the goal that φ is true (positive expectation) or (2) having the goal that φ is false (negative expectation).

According to some psychological models [34, 35, 25, 31] and computational models [20, 15] of emotions, the intensity of hope with respect to a given event is a monotonically increasing function of: the degree to which the event is desirable and the likelihood of the event. That is, the higher is the desirability of the event φ, and the higher is the intensity of the agent's hope that this event will occur; the higher is the likelihood of the event φ, and the higher is the intensity of the agent's hope that this event will occur.[6] Analogously, the intensity of fear with respect to a given event is a monotonically increasing function of: the degree to which the event is undesirable and the likelihood of the event. That is, the higher is the undesirability of the event φ, and the higher is the intensity of the agent's fear that this event will occur; the higher is the likelihood of the event φ, and the higher is the intensity of the agent's fear that this event will occur. There are several possible merging functions which satisfy these properties. For example, I could define the merging function *merge* for calculating emotion intensity as an average function, according to which the intensity of hope about a certain event φ is the average of the strength of the belief that φ will occur and the strength of the goal that φ will occur. That is, for every $h, k \in Num$ representing respectively the strength of the belief and the strength of the goal, I could define *merge*(h,k) as[7]

$$\begin{cases} \frac{h+k}{2} & \text{if } h > 0 \text{ and } k > 0 \\ 0 & \text{if } h = 0 \text{ or } k = 0 \end{cases} \tag{12}$$

Another possibility is to define *merge* as a product function (also used in [20]), according to which the intensity of hope about a certain event φ is the product of the strength of the belief that φ will occur and the strength of the goal that φ will occur. That is, for every $h, k \in Num$ I could define *merge*(h,k) as

$$h \times k \tag{13}$$

---

[6] According to Ortony et al. [31] the intensity of hope and fear is determined by a third parameter: the (temporal and spatial) *proximity* to the expected event (the higher is the proximity to the expected event, and the higher is the intensity of hope/fear). This third dimension is not considered in the present analysis.

[7] The second condition is necessary to ensure that intensity of emotion is equal to zero when one of the two parameters (belief strength or goal strength) is set to zero.

Here I do not choose a specific merging function, as such choice would require an experimental validation and would much depend on the domain of application in which the formal model has to be used.

Let me now define the notion of hope and fear with their corresponding intensities. As pointed out in the introduction of the paper, I only characterize the emotion's triggering conditions, that is, the agent's mental states (beliefs and goals) that are responsible for triggering the agent's emotional reaction and that 'cause' the agent to feel the emotion. I define

$$ISCALE = \{x : \text{there are } h, k \in Num \text{ such that } merge(h,k) = x\}$$

to be the emotion intensity scale (*i.e.*, the set of values over which the intensity of hope or fear can range).

An agent is experiencing a hope with with intensity x about φ if and only if there are $h, k \in Num$ such that $h < max$, h is the strength to which the agent believes that φ is true, k is the strength to which the agent realistically wants φ to be true and $x = merge(h,k)$. That is:

$$\text{Hope}^x\varphi \stackrel{\text{def}}{=} \bigvee_{h,k \in Num: h < max \text{ and } merge(h,k)=x} (\text{Bel}^h\varphi \wedge \text{RGoal}^k\varphi)$$

The notion of fear can be defined in a similar way, after assuming that an event φ is undesirable for the agent if and only if the agent wants φ to be false.[8] An agent is experiencing a fear with with intensity x about φ if and only if there are $h, k \in Num$ such that $h < max$, h is the strength to which the agent believes that φ is true, k is the strength to which the agent realistically wants φ to be false and $x = merge(h,k)$. That is:

$$\text{Fear}^x\varphi \stackrel{\text{def}}{=} \bigvee_{h,k \in Num: h < max \text{ and } merge(h,k)=x} (\text{Bel}^h\varphi \wedge \text{RGoal}^k\neg\varphi)$$

The reason why in the definitions of hope and fear I use the notion of *realistic goal* RGoal^k instead of a *simple goal* Goal^k is that I want to avoid that if an agent does not envisage a situation in which φ is true (*i.e.*, K$\neg\varphi$) then he necessarily feels fearful about $\neg\varphi$.[9]

Moreover, in the preceding definitions, the strength of the belief is supposed to be less than max in order distinguish emotions such as hope and fear implying some form of uncertainty from emotions such as happiness and sadness (or unhappiness) which are based on certainty. In order to experience hope (or fear) about φ, the agent should have a minimal degree of uncertainty

---

[8] I am aware that this is a simplifying assumption, as the undesirability of an event φ does not always coincide with the desirability of its negation. For example, an agent might desire 'to gain 100 €', even though 'not gaining 100 €' is not undesirable for him (the agent is simply indifferent about this result).

[9] In fact, K$\neg\varphi$ implies both Goal$^{max}\varphi$ (see the equation 10 in Section 2.4.) and Bel$\neg\varphi$. Therefore, if I had used Goal^k in the preceding definition of fear, K$\neg\varphi$ would have implied Fear$^x\neg\varphi$ for some number $x \in ISCALE$ which is counterintuitive.

that φ might be false (*i.e.*, the agent should not know that φ is true). Indeed, from the previous definitions, it follows that:

$$\models_{\mathsf{LGA}} \mathsf{Hope}^x\varphi \to \neg\mathsf{Certain}\varphi \tag{14}$$

$$\models_{\mathsf{LGA}} \mathsf{Fear}^x\varphi \to \neg\mathsf{Certain}\varphi \tag{15}$$

This means that if an agent hopes (resp. fears) φ to be true, then he is not certain that φ (*i.e.*, he does not have the strong belief that φ). For example, if I hope that my paper will be accepted for publication in a prestigious journal, then it means that I am not certain that my paper will be accepted. The preceding two validities are consistent with Spinoza's quote "Fear cannot be without hope nor hope without fear". Indeed, if an agent hopes that φ will be true then, according to the validity 14, he envisages the possibility that φ will be false. Therefore, he experiences some fear that φ will be false. Conversely, if an agent fears that φ will be true then, according to the validity 15, he envisages the possibility that φ will be false. Therefore, he experiences some hope that φ will be false.

REMARK. It has to be noted that hope and fear, and more generally expectations, are not necessarily about a *future* state of affairs, but they can also be about a *present* state of affairs or a *past* state of affairs. For example, I might say 'I hope that you feel better now!' or 'I fear that you did not enjoy the party yesterday night!'. On the contrary, to feel happy (resp. sad) about φ, the

agent should be *certain* that φ is true. For example, if I am happy that my paper has been accepted for publication in a prestigious journal, then it means that I am certain that my paper has been accepted. More precisely, an agent is experiencing happiness with intensity h about φ if and only if, the agent strong believes (is certain) that φ is true and h is the strength to which the agent wants φ to be true. That is:

$$\mathsf{Happiness}^h\varphi \stackrel{\mathrm{def}}{=} \mathsf{Certain}\varphi \wedge \mathsf{RGoal}^h\varphi$$

Moreover, an agent is experiencing sadness with intensity h about φ if and only if, the agent strongly believes (is certain) that φ is true and h is the strength to which the agent wants φ to be false. That is:

$$\mathsf{Sadness}^h\varphi \stackrel{\mathrm{def}}{=} \mathsf{Certain}\varphi \wedge \mathsf{RGoal}^h\neg\varphi$$

4 Related works

Emotion is a very active field not only in psychology but also in AI. Several computational architectures of affective agents have been proposed in the last few years (see, *e.g.*, [33, 16, 13, 15]). The cognitive architecture EMA (Emotion and Adaption) [20] is one of the best example of research in this area. EMA defines a domain independent taxonomy of appraisal variables stressing the many different relations between emotions and cognition, by enabling a wide range of internal appraisal and coping processes used for reinterpretation, shift of motivations, goal reconsideration *etc.*

There are also several researchers who have developed formal languages for reasoning about emotions and for modelling affective agents. I discuss here some of the most important formal approaches to emotions and compare them with the approach presented in this paper.

One of the most prominent logical analysis of emotions is the one proposed by Meyer and coll. [29, 39, 41]. In order to formalize emotions, they exploit the logical framework KARO [30]: a framework based on a blend of dynamic logic with epistemic logic, enriched with modal operators for motivational attitudes such as desires and goals. In Meyer et al.'s approach each instance of emotion is represented with a special predicate, or fluent, in the jargon of reasoning about action and change, to indicate that these predicates change over time. For every fluent a set of effects of the corresponding emotions on the agent's planning strategies are specified, as well as the preconditions for triggering the emotion. The latter correspond to generation rules for emotions. For instance, in [29] generation rules for four basic emotions are given: joy, sadness, anger and fear, depending on the agent's plans. More recently [41], generation rules for social emotions such as guilt and shame have been proposed.

Contrarily to Meyer et al.'s approach, in the logic **LGA** there are no specific formal constructs, like special predicates or fluents, which are used to denote that a certain emotion arises at a certain time. I just *define* the appraisal pattern of a given emotion in terms of some cognitive constituents such as goal and knowledge. For instance, according to the definition of hope proposed in Section 3, an agent experiences hope about φ if and only if, he believes φ and he wants φ to be true with a certain strength. In other words, following the so-called appraisal theories in psychology, in this work I only consider the appraisal variables of emotion which can be defined through the basic concepts of a BDI logic (*e.g.*, knowledge, belief, desire, goal).

In a more recent work [40] Meyer et al. have integrated quantitative aspects in their logical model of emotions. However, differently from the present approach, they do not study the variables determining intensities but instead focus on the integration of intensities into a qualitative model of emotions. For example, they propose a function describing how the intensity of an emotion decreases over time.

Lorini & Schwarzentruber [28] have recently proposed a logical model of counterfactual emotions such regret and guilt, *i.e.*, those emotions based on counterfactual thinking about agents' choices and actions. Adam et al. [2] have exploited a BDI logic in order to provide a logical formalization of the emotion types defined in Ortony, Clore and Collins's model (OCC model) [31]. Similar to the approach presented in this paper, in Lorini & Schwarzentruber's approach and in Adam et al.'s approach emotion types are defined in terms of some primitive concepts (and corresponding modal operators) such as the concepts of belief, desire, action and responsibility which allow to capture the different appraisal variables of emotions. However, Lorini & Schwarzentruber's approach and Adam et al.'s approach are purely qualitative and do not consider emotion intensity.

5 Conclusion

The logical analysis of expectation-based emotions presented in this paper is obviously very simplistic. It misses a lot of important psychological aspects. For example, the fact that mental states on which emotions such as hope and fear are based are usually joined with bodily activation and components, and these components shape the whole subjective state of the agent and determine his action tendencies [18].[10] I have only focused on the cognitive structure of emotions, without considering the *felt* aspect of emotions. This is of course a limitation of the model presented in this paper, as the intensity of emotion also depends on the presence of these somatic components (*e.g.*, the intensity of fear is amplified by the fact that, when experiencing this emotion I feel my stomach contracted, my throat dry, *etc.*)

However, an analysis of the cognitive structure of emotions (*i.e.*, identifying the mental states which determine a given type of emotion), as the one presented in this paper, is a necessary step for having an adequate understanding of affective phenomena. I postpone to future work a logical analysis of the basic relationships between emotion and action (*i.e.*, how an emotion with a given intensity determines the agent's future reactions),[11] and of the relationships between cognitive structure and somatic aspects of emotions (*i.e.*, how somatic components affect emotion intensity).

References

1. L. Godo A. Casali and C. Sierra. A graded BDI agent model to represent and reason about preferences. *Artificial Intelligence*, 175:1468–1478, 2012.
2. C. Adam, A. Herzig, and D. Longin. A logical formalization of the OCC theory of emotions. *Synthese*, 168(2):201–248, 2009.
3. G. Aucher. A combined system for update logic and belief revision. In *Proceedings of PRIMA 2004*, volume 3371 of *LNAI*, pages 1–18. Springer-Verlag, 2005.
4. R. Aumann. Interactive epistemology I: Knowledge. *International Journal of Game Theory*, 28(3):263–300, 1999.
5. R. Bradley and C. List. Desire as belief revisited. *Analysis*, 69(1):31–37, 2009.

---

[10] According to Frijda, actions tendencies are [18, pp. 75] "...states of readiness to achieve or maintain a given kind of relationship with the environment. They can be conceived of as plans or programs to achieve such ends, which are put in a state of readiness." For example, the action tendency associated to fear is escape. According to Lazarus [25], there is an important difference between action tendencies and coping strategies. While the former are innately programmed unconscious reflexes and routines, the latter are the product of a conscious deliberation process.

[11] A first step in this direction has been taken in [12].

6. C. Castelfranchi. Mind as an anticipatory device: For a theory of expectations. In M. De Gregorio, V. Di Maio, M. Frucci, and C. Musio, editors, *Proceedings of the First International Symposium on Brain, Vision, and Artificial Intelligence (BVAI 2005)*, volume 3704 of *LNCS*. Springer, 2005.
7. C. Castelfranchi and E. Lorini. Cognitive anatomy and functions of expectations. In F. Schmalhofer, R. M. Young, and G. Katz, editors, *Proceedings of the First European Cognitive Science Conference (EuroCogSci 2003)*, pages 377–379, Mahwah, NJ, 2003. Lawrence Erlbaum Associates.
8. C. Castelfranchi and E. Lorini. Cognitive anatomy and functions of expectations. In R. Sun, editor, *Proceedings of IJCAI'03 Workshop on Cognitive modelling of Agents and Multi-Agent Interactions*, pages 29–36, 2003.
9. C. Castelfranchi and M. Miceli. The cognitive-motivational compound of emotional experience. *Emotion Review*, 1(3):223–231, 2009.
10. P. R. Cohen and H. J. Levesque. Intention is choice with commitment. *Artificial Intelligence*, 42:213–261, 1990.
11. R. Conte and C. Castelfranchi. *Cognitive and social action*. London Univ. College of London Press, London, 1995.
12. M. Dastani and E. Lorini. A logic of emotions: from appraisal to coping. In *Proceedings of the Eleventh International Conference on Autonomous Agents and Multi-Agent Systems*, pages 1133–1140 . ACM Press, 2012.
13. F. de Rosis, C. Pelachaud, I. Poggi, V. Carofiglio, and B. D. Carolis. From Greta's mind to her face: modelling the dynamics of affective states in a conversational embodied agent. *International Journal of Human-Computer Studies*, 59(1-2):81–118, 2003.
14. D. Dubois and H. Prade. Possibility theory: qualitative and quantitative aspects. In D. Gabbay and P. Smets, editors, *Handbook of Defeasible Reasoning and Uncertainty Management Systems*, volume Quantified Representation of Uncertainty and Imprecision, volume 1, pages 169–226. Kluwer, 1998.
15. M. S. El-Nasr, J. Yen, and T. R. Ioerger. FLAME: Fuzzy logic adaptive model of emotions. *Autonomous Agents and Multi-Agent Systems*, 3(3):219–257, 2000.
16. C. Elliot. *The Affective reasoner: A process model for emotions in a multi-agent system*. PhD thesis, Northwestern University, Institute for Learning Sciences, 1992.
17. R. Fagin, J. Halpern, Y. Moses, and M. Vardi. *Reasoning about Knowledge*. MIT Press, Cambridge, 1995.
18. N. Frijda. *The emotions*. Cambridge University Press, 1986.
19. R. M. Gordon. *The structure of emotions*. Cambridge University Press, Cambridge, 1987.
20. J. Gratch and S. Marsella. A domain independent framework for modeling emotion. *Journal of Cognitive Systems Research*, 5(4):269–306, 2004.
21. O. H. Green. *The emotions*. Cambridge University Press, Cambridge, 1992.
22. A. Grove. Two modellings for theory change. *Journal of Philosophical Logic*, 17:157–170, 1988.
23. N. Laverny and J. Lang. From knowledge-based programs to graded belief-based programs, part i: on-line reasoning. In *Proceedings of the Sixteenth European Conference on Artificial Intelligence (ECAI'04)*, pages 368–372. IOS Press, 2004.
24. N. Laverny and J. Lang. From knowledge-based programs to graded belief-based programs, part ii: off-line reasoning. In *Proceedings of the Nineteenth International Joint Conference on Artificial Intelligence (IJCAI'05)*, pages 497–502. Professional Book Center, 2005.
25. R. S. Lazarus. *Emotion and adaptation*. Oxford Univ. Press, New York, 1991.
26. D. Lewis. Desire as belief. *Mind*, 97:323–332, 1988.
27. D. Lewis. Desire as belief II. *Mind*, 105:303–313, 1996.
28. E. Lorini and F. Schwarzentruber. A logic for reasoning about counterfactual emotions. *Artificial Intelligence*, 175(3-4):814–847, 2011.
29. J.-J. Ch. Meyer. Reasoning about emotional agents. *International Journal of Intelligent Systems*, 21(6):601–619, 2006.
30. J.-J. Ch. Meyer, W. van der Hoek, and B. van Linder. A logical approach to the dynamics of commitments. *Artificial Intelligence*, 113(1-2):1–40, 1999.

31. Andrew Ortony, G.L. Clore, and A. Collins. *The cognitive structure of emotions*. Cambridge University Press, Cambridge, MA, 1988.
32. A. S. Rao and M. Georgeff. Decision procedures for BDI logics. *Journal of Logic and Computation*, 8(3):293–344, 1998.
33. W. S. Reilly and J. Bates. Building emotional agents. Technical report, CMUCS -92-143, School of Computer science, Canergie Mellon University, 1992.
34. R. Reisenzein. Emotional experience in the computational belief-desire theory of emotion. *Emotion Review*, 1(3):214–222, 2009.
35. R. Reisenzein. Emotions as metarepresentational states of mind: naturalizing the belief-desire theory of emotion. *Cognitive Systems Research*, 10:6–20, 2009.
36. K. Scherer. Appraisal considered as a process of multilevel sequential checking. In K. R. Scherer, A. Schorr, and T. Johnstone, editors, *Appraisal Processes in Emotion: Theory, Methods, Research*. Oxford University Press, Oxford, 2001.
37. J. Searle. *Intentionality: An Essay in the Philosophy of Mind*. Cambridge University Press, New York, 1983.
38. W. Spohn. Ordinal conditional functions: a dynamic theory of epistemic states. In W. L. Harper and B. Skyrms, editors, *Causation in decision, belief change and statistics*, pages 105–134. Kluwer, 1998.
39. B. R. Steunebrink, M. Dastani, and J.-J. Ch. Meyer. A logic of emotions for intelligent agents. In *Proceedings of the 22th AAAI conference on Artificial Intelligence (AAAI'07)*, pages 142–147. AAAI Press, 2007.
40. B. R. Steunebrink, M. Dastani, and J.-J. Ch Meyer. A formal model of emotions: integrating qualitative and quantitative aspects. In *Proceedings of the 18th European Conference on Artificial Intelligence (ECAI 2008)*, pages 256–260. IOS Press, 2008.
41. P. Turrini, J.-J. Ch. Meyer, and C. Castelfranchi. Coping with shame and sense of guilt: a dynamic logic account. *Journal of Autonomous Agents and Multi-Agent Systems*, 20(3):401–420, 2009.
42. J. van Benthem. Dynamic logic for belief revision. *Journal of Applied Non-Classical Logics*, 17:129–155, 2007.
43. H. van Ditmarsch. Prolegomena to dynamic logic for belief revision. *Synthese*, 147(2):229–275, 2005.

Chapter 17
Social cooperation: The role of emotions

Samuel Bowles and Herbert Gintis [*]

Abstract Social emotions – guilt, shame, pride, empathy, and others – are partly responsible for the civil and caring acts that enrich our daily lives and render living, working, shopping, traveling among strangers, sustaining social order, even conducting scientific research, feasible and efficient. As Conte and Castelfranchi (1995) have convinced a generation of socio-psychological researchers, adherence to social norms is underwritten not only by cognitively mediated decisions, but also by emotions (Frank, 1987, 1988; Ekman, 1992; Damasio, 1994; Elster, 1998; Boehm 2012). In this chapter, we will suggest that shame, guilt, and other social emotions function like pain, in providing personally beneficial guides for action that bypass the explicit cognitive optimizing process that lies at the core of the standard behavioral model in economics and decision theory. We first model the process by which an emotion such as shame may affect behavior in a simple public goods game. We then show that shame and guilt along with internalized ethical norms allow high levels of cooperation to be sustained with minimal levels of costly punishment, resulting in mutually beneficial interactions at limited cost. Finally, we ask how prosocial emotions such as shame might have evolved. We show that if the benefits associated with the public good are sufficiently high and if the reciprocity motive of one's fellow group members is strong, becoming more susceptible to shame will increase one's material payoffs.

Samuel Bowles
University of Siena, Italy and Santa Fe Institute, USA
e-mail: samuel.bowles@gmail.com

Herbert Gintis
Santa Fe Institute, USA and Central European University, Hungary
e-mail: hgintis@comcast.net

 [*] We would like to thank the Behavioral Sciences Program of the Santa Fe Institute for financial support. The material in this paper is partially drawn from Chapter 11 of Samuel Bowles and Herbert Gintis, *A Cooperative Species: Human Reciprocity and its Evolution* (Princeton University Press, 2011).

Social emotions – love, guilt, shame, and others – are responsible for the host of civil and caring acts that enrich our daily lives and render living, working, shopping, traveling among strangers, sustaining social order, even conducting scientific research, feasible and pleasant. As Conte and Castelfranchi (1995), have convinced a generation of socio-psychological researchers, adherence to social norms is underwritten not only by cognitively mediated decisions, but also by emotions (Frank, 1987, 1988; Ekman, 1992; Damasio, 1994; Elster, 1998; Boehm 2012). When the feelings of respondents in an ultimatum game are assayed, it is often found that low offers by the proposer provoke anger, contempt and sadness in the respondents, and that the intensity of the self-reported emotions predict the respondents' behavior, stronger emotions inducing rejections of low offers. Interestingly, the introduction of a "cooling off" period between the offer and the respondent's choice of an action tends to have no effect on either reported emotions or on the rejection behaviors of the respondents. Indeed, Sanfey et al. (2003) found that those rejecting low offers in an ultimatum game experienced heightened levels of activation in the brain areas associated with disgust and anger.

One of the most important emotions sustaining cooperation is *shame*, the feeling of discomfort at having done something wrong not only by one's own norms but also in the eyes of those whose opinions matter to you. Shame differs from guilt in that, while both involve the violation of a norm, the former but not the latter is necessarily induced by others' knowing about the violation and making their displeasure known to the violator (Miceli and Castelfranchi, 1998).

We will suggest that shame, guilt, and other social emotions may function like pain, in providing personally beneficial guides for action that bypass the explicit cognitive optimizing process that lies at the core of the standard behavioral model in economics and decision theory. Pain is one of the six so-called basic emotions, the others being pleasure, anger, fear, surprise, and disgust. Shame is one of the seven so-called social emotions, of which the others are love, guilt, embarrassment, pride, envy, and jealousy (Plutchik, 1980, Ekman, 1992). Basic and social emotions are expressed in all human societies, although their expression is affected by cultural conditions. For instance, in all societies one may be angered by an immoral act, or disgusted by an unusual foodstuff, but what counts as an immoral act or a disgusting foodstuff is, at least to some extent, culturally specific.

Antonio Damasio (1994) calls an emotion a "somatic marker," that is, a bodily response that "forces attention on the negative outcome to which a given action may lead and functions as an automated alarm signal which says: Beware of danger ahead if you choose the option that leads to this outcome... the automated signal protects you against future losses" (p. 173). Emotions thus may contribute to the decision-making process by working with, not against, reason. Damasio continues, analogizing emotions to physical pain: "suffering puts us on notice... it increases the probability that individuals will heed pain signals and act to avert their source or correct their consequences" (p. 264).

To explore the role of guilt and shame in inducing social behaviors we will consider a particular interaction having the structure of a public goods game.

In the public good setting, contributing too little to the public account may evoke shame if one feels that one has appropriated "too much" to oneself. Because shame is socially induced, being punished when one has contributed little triggers the feeling of having taken too much. In this case, the effect of punishment on behavior may not operate by changing the material incentives facing the individual, that is, by making clear that if he continues to free ride his payoffs will be reduced by the expected punishments in future rounds. Rather it evokes a different evaluation by the individual of the act of taking too much, namely, shame. This is the view expressed by Jon Elster (1998) "material sanctions themselves are best understood as vehicles of the emotion of contempt, which is the direct trigger of shame" (p. 67). Thus, self-interested actions, per se, may induce guilt, but not shame. If one contributes little and is not punished, one comes to consider these actions as unshameful. If, by contrast, one is punished when one has contributed generously, the emotional reaction may be spite toward the members of one's group. This is one of the reasons why the "antisocial" punishment of high contributors in public goods experiments has such deleterious effects on the level of cooperation in a group.

We assume individuals maximize a utility function that includes five distinct motives: one's individual material payoffs, how much one values the payoffs to others, this depending on both one's unconditional altruism and one's degree of reciprocity, as well as one's sense of guilt or shame in response to one's own and others' actions. To this end, we will amend and extend a utility function derived from the work of Geanakoplos et al. (1989), Levine (1998), Sethi and Somanathan (2001), and Falk and Fischbacher (2006).

There is considerable experimental evidence consistent with the view that punishment not only reduces material payoffs of those who transgress norms, but also may recruit emotions of shame toward the modification of behavior (Bowles and Gintis, 2011, Ch. 3). Indeed, in some societies many defectors react to being punished by increasing their contribution to the group, even when the punishment does not affect material payoffs, consistent with the shame response, while in other societies they react by counter-punishing contributors, consistent with an anger response (Herrmann et al., 2008). Social emotions in response to sanctions can thus either foster or undermine cooperation. Reacting to sanctions, then, is often not a dispassionate calculation of material costs and benefits, but rather involves the deployment of culturally specific social emotions. Indeed, one can show that the altruistic punishment of shirkers by strong reciprocators can proliferate in a population and sustain high levels of cooperation, provided those punished would react selfishly or prosocially rather than antisocially (Bowles and Gintis, 2011, Ch. 9). Here, we focus on the manner in which social emotions and punishment of miscreants may be synergistic, each enhancing the effects of the other.

We first model the process by which an emotion such as shame may affect behavior in a simple public goods game. We then show that shame and guilt along with internalized ethical norms allow high levels of cooperation to be sustained with minimal levels of costly punishment, resulting in mutually beneficial interactions at limited cost. In Section 2, we ask how prosocial emotions such as shame might have evolved. We show that if the benefits associated with the public good are sufficiently high and if the reciprocity motive of one's fellow group members is strong, becoming more susceptible to shame will increase one's material payoffs.

1 Reciprocity, Shame, and Punishment

Consider two individuals who play a one-shot public goods game in which each has a norm concerning the appropriate amount to contribute to the public project, and each (a) values his own material payoff, (b) may prefer to punish others who contribute insufficiently, (c) feels guilt if he contributes less than the norm; and finally (d) experiences shame if he is sanctioned for having contributed less than the norm. This psychological repertoire captures some of the motives that explain cooperation in behavioral experiments. The results that follow for a dyadic interaction generalize to an n-person interaction.

In what follows, we represent the two players as i and j, where $j \neq i$.

We assume each individual starts with a personal account equal to one unit. Each individual contributes to the public project an amount a_i, $0 \leq a_i \leq 1$, where $i = 1, 2$ refer to the two individuals, and each receives $\chi(a_1 + a_2)$ from the project, where $1/2 < \chi < 1$. Thus, the individuals do best when both cooperate $(a_i, a_j = 1)$, but each has an incentive to defect $(a_i, a_j = 0)$ no matter what the other does. In the absence of punishment, this two-person public goods game thus would be a prisoner's dilemma. But at the end of this cooperation period there is a punishment period, in which the individuals are informed of the contribution of the other individual, and each individual may impose a penalty μ on the other individual at a cost

$$c(\mu) = c\frac{\mu^2}{2}. \tag{1}$$

This, and the other functional forms below, are chosen for expositional and mathematical convenience.

Letting μ_{ij} be the level of punishment of individual j by individual i, the material payoff to i is then given by

$$\pi_i = 1 - a_i + \chi(a_1 + a_2) - \mu_{ji} - c(\mu_{ij}). \tag{2}$$

In 2, the first two terms give the amount remaining in i's private account after contributing, the third term is i's reward from the public project, the fourth term is the punishment inflicted by j upon i, and the final term is the cost to i of punishing j.

We assume that the norm is that each should contribute the entire endowment to the public project. The results generalize to the case where the norm is less stringent. Individual i may wish to punish j by reducing j's payoffs, if i is a reciprocator (that is $\lambda_i > 0$) and j contributes less than the entire endowment. To represent the propensity of i to punish j for not contributing, we assume that i's valuation of j's payoff is

$$\beta_{ij} = \lambda_i(a_j - 1) \tag{3}$$

where we assume $0 < \lambda_i < 1$, so that unless j contributed his entire endowment, i receives a psychic benefit from lowering j's material payoff that is proportional to j's shortfall. The parameter λ_i, $0 < \lambda_i < 1$, is the strength of i's reciprocity motive. The condition that $\lambda_i < 1$ ensures that individual i cannot value j's payoffs negatively more than he values his own positively. Thus should both payoffs increase proportionally, individual i cannot be worse off.

The shame experienced by i is a psychic cost proportional to the product of the degree to which he is punished by j, and the extent to which his contribution falls short of the norm, and is equal to $v_i(1 - a_i)\mu_{ji}$. Thus, punishment triggers shame, which is greater the more the individual has kept for himself rather than contributing to the public project, and the larger is v_i, the susceptibility of individual i to feeling shame. Finally, i may feel guilt simply for having violated his internal standards of moral behavior. We represent this feeling by $-\gamma_i(1 - a_i)$, which is negative for $\gamma_i > 0$ unless i contributes the full amount to the project.

The utility function i is then given by

$$u_i = \pi_i + \beta_{ij}(1 - a_j + \chi(a_1 + a_2) - \mu_{ij}) - (\gamma_i + v_i\mu_{ji})(1 - a_i). \tag{4}$$

The first term is i's material payoffs, which are those from the public project net of his own contribution and minus the cost of being punished by j and the cost of punishing j, from equation (2) and the second term is (using equation 3) i's evaluation of j's material payoffs, which are those from the project net of his own contribution and minus i's punishment of j.

We have not included the cost to j of punishing i, in the material payoffs of j that i takes account of when choosing his contribution level because we think it is unrealistic to imagine that i would seek to reduce j's payoffs by inducing j to punish i. The third term is the guilt and punishment-induced shame that i experiences when i contributes less than the amount that would maximize the well being of the two players, namely 1.

Given any level of j's contribution, we can represent the individual's behavior as the joint maximization of two objective functions. The first is, given j's contribution, how much to punish j. The answer is to select μ_{ij} so as to equate the marginal cost of punishment $(dc/d\mu_{ij})$ with the marginal benefit of punishing j, which is β_{ij}. Given the level of punishment, i will then select the level of contribution that equates the marginal benefits of contributing, which are reduced punishment, guilt and shame, and the marginal costs of contributing, which involve forgoing some of one's endowment and contributing to the material payoffs of j, even though i values these negatively. Note that because the susceptibility to shame and the level of punishment received appear multiplicatively in this last term, punishment and shame are what economists call complements. This means that an increase in the susceptibility to shame increases the marginal effect of punishment on the individual's utility and therefore raises the marginal benefit that i will receive by contributing more. Similarly, an increase in the level of punishment raises the marginal effect of an enhanced susceptibility to shame on the actor's utility. Shame thus enhances what is termed the "punishment technology," the effectiveness of which is measured by the ratio of the utility loss inflicted on the target, including both the subjective costs and the reduction in payoffs from equation 2, to the marginal cost to the punisher of undertaking the punishment, which from 1 is $c\mu_{ij}$. This punishment effectiveness ratio for i's punishment of j is thus

$$\frac{1+v_j(1-a_j)}{c(\mu_{ij})}, \tag{5}$$

from which it is clear that the punishment of j is more effective the more susceptible to shame is j.

Because each individual's valuation of the payoffs of the other depends on the actions the other takes, it is clear that the actions taken by each will be mutually determined. For any given value of j's action, there will be an action – a best response – by i that maximizes his utility as expressed in equation 4. The best response function for individual i is shown in Figure 1, along with the analogous best response function for j. Their intersection is the mutual best response, and is therefore the Nash equilibrium. In Figure 1 we see that the best response a_i, because of reciprocity, is an increasing function of a_j, and the a_i schedule shifts up when susceptibility to shame or guilt, or j's degree of reciprocity $(v_i, \gamma_i, \lambda_j)$ increases, corresponding to our intuitions concerning the model. There is also a minimal level of susceptibility to shame supporting positive contributions. The minimal level of shame that will induce a positive contribution is increasing in the cost of punishment and decreasing in i's susceptibility to guilt γ_i, j's level of reciprocity λ_j, and the productivity of the public project, again confirming our intuitions.

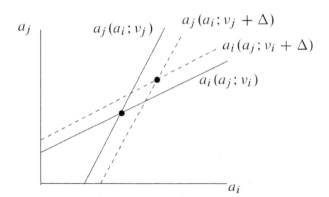

Fig. 1 Mutual determination of contributions to a public project. Thefunctions slope upwards because the individuals are reciprocators and shift as shown when susceptibility to shame, v increases, because this enhances the effects of punishment. There is no reason to think that the function would take the linear form shown here.

Suppose the level of shame of both individuals were to increase. This is shown in Figure 1 by the dashed lines. The result is a displacement of the mutual best response so that both individuals contribute more, and as a result the level of punishment is less. This is the sense in which we mean that because shame enhances the effectiveness of punishment: it economizes on the cost of punishment. When one individual's susceptibility to shame increases the other individual benefits and when this occurs for both, as in Figure 1, both benefit. Payoffs therefore are higher in a population that has inculcated a sense of shame in its members, as could be the case for example through the kinds of population-wide internalization of norms (Bowles and Gintis, 2011, Ch. 10).

2 The Evolution of Social Emotions

Human behaviors systematically deviate from the model of the self-interested actor, and we think the evidence is strong that social emotions account for much of the discrepancy. But this description of behavior would be more compelling if we understood how social emotions might have evolved, culturally, genetically, or both. There are two puzzles here. First, social emotions are often altruistic, indicating actions benefiting others at a cost to oneself, so that in any dynamic in which the higher payoff trait tends to increase in frequency, social emotions would eventually disappear. In Bowles and Gintis (2011, Chs. 7–10), we addressed this puzzle, showing that by the process of group competition, reproductive leveling, and norm internalization, vertically transmitted altruistic traits may evolve.

The second puzzle concerns social emotions per se. How could it ever be evolutionarily advantageous to bypass one's cognitive decision making capacities and let behavior be influenced by the visceral reactions associated with one's emotions? Internalizing norms may be a way of economizing the costs of calculating benefits and costs in each situation, and of averting costly errors when the calculations go wrong. A related argument, we think, helps explain the evolutionary viability of social emotions.

Humans tend to be impatient, a condition we share with other animals (Stephens et al., 2002). We tend to discount future costs and benefits myopically, that is, more than either a fitness-based or a lifetime welfare-based accounting would require. The mismatch between our impatience and our fitness is in part due to the payoff to patient behaviors that resulted from the extended life histories and prolonged period of learning the skills associated with the distinctive skill-intensive human feeding niche based on hunted and extracted foods. Prior to this period in human history, the importance of the future was more limited and largely concerned the survival of one's offspring. A genetically transmitted disposition to assist one's relatives may have produced a selective degree of patience as a by-product of kin-based selection, resisting stealing food from one's offspring, for example. But even if our genetic development in a cooperative social context has mitigated the extreme short-term benefits of lying, cheating, killing, stealing, and satisfying immediate bodily needs, such as wrath, lust, greed, gluttony, sloth, we nevertheless have a fitness-reducing bias toward behaviors that produce immediate satisfaction at the expense of our long-run well-being.

The internalization of norms and the expression of these norms in a social emotion such as guilt addresses this problem by inducing the individual to place a contemporaneous value on the future consequences of present behavior, rather than relying upon an appropriately discounted accounting of its probable payoffs in the distant future. One curbs one's anger today not because there may be harmful effects next month, but because one would feel guilty now if one violated the norms of respect for others and the dispassionate adjudication of differences. One punishes others for behaving antisocially not because there are future benefits to be gained thereby, but because one is angered at the moment.

Do the social emotions thus function in a manner similar to pain? Complex organisms have the ability to learn to avoid damage. A measure of damage is pain, a highly aversive sensation the organism will attempt to avoid in the future. Yet an organism with complete information, an unlimited capacity to process information, and with a fitness-maximizing way of discounting future costs and benefits would have no use for pain. Such an individual would be able to assess the costs of any damage to itself, would calculate an optimal response to such damage, and would prepare optimally for future occurrences of this damage. The aversive stimulus, pain, could then be strongly distorting of optimal behavior. If you sprain your ankle while fleeing from a lethal predator, you might have a better chance of survival if you could override the pain temporarily. Because pain per se clearly does have adaptive value, it follows that modeling pain presupposes that the individual experiencing pain must have incomplete information and/or a limited capacity to process information, and/or an excessively high rate of discounting future benefits and costs. Are guilt and shame social analogues to pain?

If being socially devalued has fitness costs, and if the amount of guilt or shame that a given action induces is closely correlated with the level of these fitness costs that would otherwise not be taken account of, then the answer is affirmative. The same argument will hold not only for fitness costs, but for any effect, possibly operating through cultural transmission, that reduces the number of replicas an individual will generate. Shame and guilt, like pain, are aversive stimuli that lead the individual experiencing them to repair the situation that led to the stimulus, and to avoid such situations in the future.

3 The Great Captains of Our Lives

Shame and guilt, like pain, dispense with an involved optimization process by means of a simple message: whatever you did, undo it if possible, and do not do it again. Two types of selective advantage thus may account for the evolutionary success of shame and related social emotions. First, social emotions may increase the number of replicas, by either genetic or cultural transmission, of an individual who has incomplete information (e.g., as to how damaging a particular antisocial action is), limited or imperfect information-processing capacity, and/or a tendency to undervalue costs and benefits that accrue in the future. Probably all three conditions conspire to induce people to respond insufficiently to social disapprobation in the absence of social emotions. The visceral reactions associated with these emotions motivate a more adequate response, one that will avert damage to the individual. Of course the role of social emotions in alerting us to negative consequences in the future presupposes that society is organized to impose those costs on norm violators. The social emotions thus may have coevolved with the reciprocity-based emotions motivating punishment of antisocial actions.

The second selective advantage favoring the evolution of social emotions refers specifically to shame. The fact that higher levels of shame among members of a group, the higher (in equilibrium) will be the sum of their payoffs also suggests that shame may evolve through the effects of group competition. As we have seen, where the emotion of shame is common, punishment of antisocial actions will be particularly effective and as a result seldom used. Thus groups in which shame is common can sustain high levels of group cooperation at limited cost and will be more likely to survive environmental, military and other challenges, and thus to populate new sites vacated by groups that failed.

As a result, selective pressures at the group level will also favor religious practices and systems of socialization that support susceptibility to shame for failure to contribute to projects of mutual benefit of the type modeled in the previous two sections. Moreover, where the returns to cooperation and levels of reciprocity are sufficiently great, an individual who acquires an enhanced sense of shame may increase his own individual payoff. Under these conditions an individual that acquired enhanced shame by chance (a mutation, developmental accident or other) could invade a large population of individuals with lesser levels of shame. Thus, a genetic or cultural predisposition to shame could increase in a population even in the absence of group competition.

It is quite likely, then, that the "moralistic aggression" that is involved in the altruistic punishment of miscreants and that motivate the punishment of shirkers by strong reciprocators also created a selective niche favorable to the emergence of shame and other social emotions, or what Christopher Boehm calls a conscience:

> Prehistorically humans began to make use of social control so intensively that individuals who were better at inhibiting their own antisocial tendencies, either through fear of punishment or through absorbing and identifying with their group's rules, gained superior fitness. By learning to internalize rules, humankind acquired a conscience (Boehm, 2011, p. 17).

Combining the model of this paper with one of norm internalization (Gintis, 2003), the emergence of shame would have reduced the costs of punishing transgressors incurred by the strong reciprocators. The reason for this is that gossip and ridicule could then suffice where physical, often violent, elimination from the group had been necessary in the absence of shame. The proliferation of strong reciprocators engaging in altruistic punishment that this cost reduction allowed would then have enhanced the advantages of shame.

Thus the moralistic aggression motivating the altruistic punishment of defectors, and shame, may have coevolved, each providing the conditions favoring the proliferation of the other. The groups in which this occurred initially, perhaps among our foraging ancestors in Africa, would have enjoyed survival advantages over other groups.

References

1. Boehm, Christopher, *Moral Origins: The Evolution of Virtue, Altruism, and Shame* (New York: Basic Books, 2011).
2. Bowles, Samuel and Herbert Gintis, *A Cooperative Species: Human Reciprocity and its Evolution* (Princeton: Princeton University Press, 2011).
3. Conte, Rosaria and Cristiano Castelfranchi, *Cognitive and Social Action* (London: University College of London Press, 1995).
4. Damasio, Antonio R., *Descartes' Error: Emotion, Reason, and the Human Brain* (New York: Avon Books, 1994).
5. Ekman, Paul, "An Argument for Basic Emotions," *Cognition and Emotion* 6 (1992):169-200.
6. Elster, Jon, "Emotions and Economic Theory," *Journal of Economic Perspectives* 36 (1998):47-74.
7. Falk, Armin and Urs Fischbacher, "A Theory of Reciprocity," *Games and Economic Behavior* 54,2 (2006):293-315.
8. Geanakoplos, John, David Pearce, and Ennio Stacchetti, "Psychological Games and Sequential Rationality," *Games and Economic Behavior* 1 (March 1989):60-79.
9. Gintis, Herbert, "The Hitchhiker's Guide to Altruism: Genes, Culture, and the Internalization of Norms," *Journal of Theoretical Biology* 220,4 (2003):407-418.
10. Herrmann, Benedikt, Christian Thoni, and Simon Gachter, "Anti-Social Punishment across Societies," *Science* 319 (7 March 2008):1362-1367.
11. Levine, David K., "Modeling Altruism and Spitefulness in Experiments," *Review of Economic Dynamics* 1,3 (1998):593-622.
12. Miceli, Maria and Cristiano Castelfranchi, "How to Silence One's Conscience: Cognitive Defenses Against the Feeling of Guilt," *Journal for the Theory of Social Behavior* 28,3 (1998):287-317.
13. Plutchik, R., *Emotion: A Psychoevolutionary Synthesis* (New York: Harper Row, 1980).
14. Sanfey, Alan G., James K. Rilling, Jessica A. Aronson, Leigh E. Nystrom, and Jonathan D. Cohen, "The Neural Basis of Economic Decision-Making in the Ultimatum Game," *Science* 300 (13 June 2003):1755-1758.
15. Sethi, Rajiv and E. Somanathan, "Preference Evolution and Reciprocity," *Journal of Economic Theory* 97 (2001): 273-297.
16. Stephens, W., C. M. McLinn, and J. R. Stevens, "Discounting and Reciprocity in an Iterated Prisoner's Dilemma," *Science* 298 (13 December 2002):2216-2218.

Part IV

Power, dependence, and social interaction

Chapter 18
The permeable limit: Constructing a shared intersubjective space in strategic interactions

Vittorio Pelligra

Abstract This chapter focuses on the relational aspects of strategic interactions. First, we highlight how some of the limitations of the classical theory of games can hinder a deeper understanding of two fundamental dimensions of the interpersonal relations, which are essential to our social epistemology: the mentalizing and empathizing processes. Secondly, we present the results of a series of experiments that stress the role of these two elements in the realm of strategic interactions. Finally, we argue that, by conceptualizing a hierarchy of higher order beliefs, psychological game theory seems to constitute a promising step forward towards the introduction of relational elements in the motivational structure of social agents.

1 Introduction

In its original project, Game Theory represents an attempt to ground the understanding of social dynamics and interpersonal relations on purely rational bases. The theory provides a set of descriptive mathematical structures and a series of solution concepts that can be applied to the whole class of strategic interactions, that is, those interactions where the consequences of an individual action depend on the combination of the choices made by *all* the interacting agents. These situations are defined as 'games' and are described as played by rational individuals. From the two assumptions of 'individualism' and 'rationality', plus a number of additional secondary assumptions, a number of algorithms can be derived that may lead to the solution(s) of the games. A solution can be thought of as the set of optimal (in many different meanings) choices that each player would choose, given the other players' optimal choices. Considering this structure and objective, it is not difficult to see that in a game, the most important ability that a player could show is the ability to

Vittorio Pelligra
Department of Economics and Business, University of Cagliari, Italy
e-mail: pelligra@unica.it

correctly anticipate other players' behavior. Whether she wants to cooperate or she intends to compete with her opponent, the player needs to form a series of conjectures about the other player's intentions, motives, beliefs and desires in order to select her optimal choice.

That said it should appear natural that the understanding of the mechanism through which anticipations and expectations are formed would lie at the core of the theory of strategic choices. However, in the last fifty years most theoretical progress has pointed to other directions. In particular, it seems as though the problem of intersubjective understanding has been more eluded and avoided, than explained. It is also worth noting that most of the 'anomalous' patterns of behavior that emerged in laboratory studies (see. Camerer, 2003), have been frequently interpreted as signs of the descriptive inadequacy of the concept of rationality but almost never as evidence against the assumption of 'individualism'[1]. This position has recently raised many criticisms that are very well summarized by the following quotation by Herbert Gintis (2009):

> "The most fundamental failure of game theory is its lack of a theory of when and how rational agents share mental constructs. The assumption that humans are rational is an excellent first approximation. But, the Bayesian rational actors favored by contemporary game theory live in a universe of subjectivity and instead of constructing a truly social epistemology, game theorists have developed a variety of subterfuges that make it appear that rational agents may enjoy a commonality of belief (. . .), but all are failures. Humans have a social epistemology, meaning that we have reasoning processes that afford us forms of knowledge and understanding, especially the understanding and sharing of the content of other minds, that are unavailable to merely "rational" creatures. This social epistemology characterizes our species. The bounds of reason are thus not the irrational, but the social" (Gintis, 2009, p. xvi).

This and other similar positions (see Pelligra, 2011c) point out that one of the still missing and most needed categories in the study of strategic and interpersonal relations refers to the notion of 'intersubjectivity'. Hence, undertaking this interesting path should lead to a better understanding of how 'encounters' between individuals (or better, *persons*), produce what can be defined as *interpersonal space* where the agents come to reciprocally share and to know each other's mental states, and thus beliefs, desires and intentions. By relaxing the assumption of 'individualism', these developments tend to pass over the epistemological individual boundary and enter the realm of a shared intersubjective space.

In this chapter I shall discuss, first, the limits of the classic approach of game theory in describing and analyzing the interpersonal dimension and, secondly, present the results of a series of experiments that highlight the crucial role played by eminently relational factors such as the 'theory of mind' (TOM) and the ability to 'empathize'. Finally, we argue that, by conceptualizing a hierarchy of higher order beliefs, psychological game theory seems to constitute a promising step forward towards the introduction of relational elements in the motivational structure of social agents.

---

[1] With the noticeable exception of Bacharach (1999, 2006) and Sugden (1993, 2000); see also Gui and Sugden (2005).

2 *Ich und Du* and the Theory of Games

In his famous book *Ich und Du* (1937/2004) the philosopher Martin Buber develops the idea that human life finds its meaningfulness in a series of 'I-Thou' relationships. This way he moves the focus from the agents, *ego* and *alter*, to the 'relationship' between them. In the theory of action, in psychology and especially in the social neurosciences, we are experiencing a similar shift of attention from the individual agents to the 'dyads' they form when interacting. I speculate that game theory could also greatly benefit from considering the 'relationship' between agents as a new level of analysis, and not only their individual behavior.

In this section I briefly describe the way in which classical game theory describes and utilizes the concepts of 'agent' and 'interaction'. I maintain that this description will be helpful to better understand how the theory conceives the idea of 'otherness': who is the 'other' with whom I interact in a strategic relationship?

The departing point of this story is, of course, Von Neumann and Morgenstern's theory and the *minimax* solutions. In this idea, in fact, we can find embedded their peculiar conception of rational agent. In Von Neumann and Morgenstern's framework, a given plan of action is thought to be rational if it leads to minimize (*min*) the maximum losses (*max*) that she can experience, *irrespective* of what the other players do. This condition of independence, that appears quite at odds with a theory of interdependent behavior, finds its rationale in the hostility, shared by both authors, towards any kind of recourse to psychological concepts. In this regard let me quote Nicola Giocoli (2003) who notices how Von Neumann and Morgenstern oriented their work towards a particular characterization of rational behavior and social interactions - "capable of setting the players free from the necessity to form an expectation about the rivals' actions and thoughts" (p. 282); again a concept where all the details are expunged except the mathematical properties of the payoffs.

This approach was harshly criticized already in the '60s by Thomas Schelling, among others, who remarked how absurd is that a player, like in Von Neumann and Morgenstern's perspective: "does not need to communicate with his opponent, he does not even need to know who the opponent is or *whether there is one*. (. . .) with a minimax criterion, a zero-sum game is reduced to a completely *unilateral* affair" (1960:105, emphasis added). A similar point is made against the interpretation of the concept of mixed-strategy: "A randomized strategy – continues Schelling - is a deliberate means of destroying any possibility of communication, especially communication of *intentions*" (Ivi).

Nash's approach, which is in many respects an alternative to Von Neumann and Morgenstern's, is built upon a solution, the Nash equilibrium, that is radically new, but in some ways not much more 'relational' than the *minimax*. According to Nash, in fact, rational behavior leads to actions that are optimal given the optimal actions of all the other agents she is interacting with. To arrive at that choice, each player has to form a series of conjectures about other players' behavior, and to do that she must attribute some goals, desires, beliefs and intentions to the others. The intrinsic complexity of this process is resolved by Nash through the strongly reductionist assumption that others' intentions are limited only to the pursuing of their maximum utility. Within this framework, each player forms conjectures about other players' behavior and they also know that the other players form similar conjectures as well. The convergence to the equilibrium point, which must satisfy the requirement of conjectures' (or beliefs') mutual consistency, is in the end assured by the two additional assumptions of optimizing behavior and common knowledge of optimizing conduct. To appreciate the restrictiveness of these assumptions, one may note, for example, that the theory implies the coordination of expectations, that is, that two players' beliefs about how a third player would play the game must necessarily be the same.

According to Nash himself, his own (non-cooperative) approach to the analysis of strategic interactions - "is based on the absence of coalitions in that it is assumed each participant act independently, without collaboration or communication with any of the others" (Nash, 1996:22). Philip Mirowski harshly criticized this fundamental assumption expressing his doubts about the very identity of players in such a theory: "What would mean to play a game without any open acknowledgment of an opponent whatsoever did seem to be a paradox; unless of course, the opponent was a machine" (2002:342). The ensuing developments of Bayesian game theory, and especially the contributions of John Harsanyi, do not modify much the idea of agent and the notion of 'relation' with others (see on this point Pelligra, 2011c).

This brief review, inevitably superficial though it may be, should have made it clear that the idea of social relations implied by classical game theory is extremely simplistic and grounded on a series of rather problematic assumptions.

This is especially true with respect to the role of intentions and to the consequentialist structure of the reasoning process described. This element, as I shall try to show, imposes strong limitations to the descriptive and prescriptive adequacy of the theory itself.

3 Intentions and consequences: some experimental results

One of the areas of inquiry where such limitations emerged most markedly is the explanation of cooperative behaviors. This is an important domain in which the insufficiency of the classical approach seems to derive more from a deficit of sociality, than from one of rationality. In this sense the introduction of relational concepts such as trust and reciprocity has resulted in significant steps towards the elaboration of a more adequate theory for the description of a genuinely 'social' agent. In the continuing, I shall consider only a few examples of 'anomalous' findings (compared to the standard perspective) that stimulated both theoretical and empirical developments.

The first example is an experiment proposed by McCabe, Smith and Rigdon (2003) in which the authors compare people's behavior in two different variants of the so-called 'trust-game'. In the first version, known as the 'voluntary trust-game' (VTG) (see figure 1a), player A can get \$20 for her and for player B, by playing 'right'. Alternatively she can choose 'down' and give player B the opportunity to choose. In this case he can get $25 both for him and for player A by choosing 'down' or get $30 for himself and $15 for player A. By backward induction, standard theory predicts that B plays 'down' and, therefore, A plays 'right'. The involuntary version of the game (figure 1b) is similar to the previous one, apart from the fact that here A has no 'right' outside option. As B is the only active player, the theory predicts, as in the VTG, that B plays 'down'.

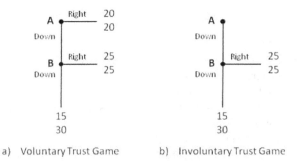

a) Voluntary Trust Game   b) Involuntary Trust Game

Fig. 1 "Voluntary trust-game (a); Involuntary trust-game (b)"

If we now consider two models that amend the classical theory introducing the idea of altruism (Margolis, 1982) and equity (Fehr and Schmidt, 1999) into the players' motivational structure, we will see how the theoretical predictions change radically. A certain percentage of both altruist and inequality-averse agents, in the role of B, could be willing to play 'right' in order to benefit player A or to reduce inequality. It is important to note, however, that both theories predict approximately the same percentage of B players choosing 'right' in both the VTG and the ITG. Anticipating this fact, a certain number of A players would then play 'down'. Things have now changed. Cooperation can be considered 'rational' if we consider agents with some degree of concern for the other.

The results of the experiment, however, are even more surprising. In fact, we observe a good number of As playing 'down' and Bs playing 'right', but the number of those playing 'right' is higher in the VTG (94.11%), than in the ITG (40.74%), even though, from B's standpoint, the consequences of his actions are exactly the same in both games. This result implies that neither the standard theory, nor altruism- and equity-based models are able to fully account for the motivations that drive player B's choice in the two games. What is missing then?

According to the authors of the study, what these models cannot describe is the agents' crucial ability to ascribe intentions to each other on the basis of observed actions. Although, in fact, both the VTG and the ITG are identical from B's point of view, in the VTG he has the possibility to infer A's intentions and expectations. Knowing A could have chosen the outside option, B knows, first, that A expects to get more than $20 and secondly, that she willingly exposed herself to the risk of opportunistic behavior. The combination of these two elements represents for B an *additional* reason to cooperate, not letting A down. While this argument is transparent in the VTG, it disappears in the ITG because of the absence of the outside option. "By eliminating Player A's opportunity cost associated with playing down, we have restricted Player B's ability to read his counterpart's intentions unambiguously. In the voluntary trust game, an intentional move down the tree by Player A can be interpreted by Player B as an act of trust. In the involuntary game, however, a down move carries no such information because Player A had no choice but to move down in the game" (2003: 273).

A second example draws from a study by Falk, Fehr and Fischbacher (2003). In their experiment they consider four different versions of a mini ultimatum game. In the mini UG there are two players, a proposer (P) and a respondent (R). P is endowed with 10 euros, and can offer R either 2 ('Left') or X euros ('Right'), keeping either 8 or (10 – X) euros for himself. R, in turn, can either 'Accept' or 'Reject' P's offer. If he accepts, the payoff distribution resulting from P's offer is implemented. If he rejects, both get nothing. In the four variants considered by Falk, Fehr and Fischbacher, X takes the values 5, 8, 2, and 0, respectively. These games are represented in Figure 2 a)–d). In the Figure, the top number indicates P's payoff, while the bottom number indicates R's payoff.

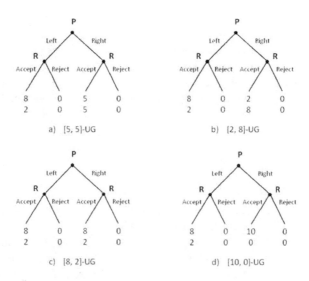

Fig. 2 "The mini ultimatum games"

Similarly to the previous experiment, here the standard theory and the model of altruistic behavior predict that the B players *always* accept the (8,2) offer. Inequality-aversion theory, instead, predicts that a B player who is sensitive enough to equity should prefer (0,0) to (8,2) and thus, should *always* reject the offer. However, as in the previous case, note how the predictions are the same across the four games. We do not know what we will observe, but we know that we will observe approximately the same behavior in each of the four games.

However, Falk and coauthors find that the number of rejections for the (8,2) offer is always positive, but also that it decreases as we move from game a) to b), c) and d). The percentage of rejection is equal to 44.4%, 26.7%, 18%, and 8.9% respectively.

The authors of the study interpret this result as showing that real agents are not purely consequentialists. That is, they do not order their preferred set of actions according to the outcomes that those actions lead to. Instead, they take into account the intentions that each action incorporates. In this sense, then, to offer 2 when the alternative not chosen is 5, as in the game a), is completely different from offering 2 when the alternative option is 0, as in game d). The former is interpreted as signaling mean intentions, whereas, the latter signals kind intentions. The experiment shows how agents systematically reply to those intentions in very different ways.

Intentions can be ascribed to a certain action only considering both the choice and what the agent could have done and did not do. However, this counter-factual reasoning which implies a form of 'forward induction' cannot be technically described within the formal framework of classical game theory, nor with the altruism- and equity-based models; precisely because those theories are consequentialist by their very nature. This explains why the behavioral patterns observed in the two experiments above cannot be rationalized by those theories. My argument here is that such limitations derive from a lack of understanding of the reasoning processes that, to quote again Herbert Gintis: "afford us forms of knowledge and understanding, especially the understanding and sharing of the content of other minds, that are unavailable to merely rational" creatures" (2009, p. xvi). In other words, game theory lacks a reliable and well-developed explanation of how our theory of mind (TOM) works.

4 The permeable limit I: thinking others' thoughts.

To be able to ascribe intentions to others allows us to understand others' actions, goals and ends. To do that we must be able to know that others have mental states and to predict their content; we must, in other words, try to think the others' thoughts. That is precisely what our Theory of Mind (ToM) does. ToM is made up by a series of abilities that simians and human beings have developed (Rizzolatti, et al., 2001) perhaps as a side effect of our linguistic abilities (Tommasello, 2000). This potential develops in an early stage of our lives. By the age of 4, children can infer what people know, think or believe on the basis on what they say or do: this ability is known as "mind-reading" (McCabe et al., 2000:4404). Neuroscientists are still debating on the details of the working of this process, commonly referred to as ToM.

Two main classes of explanations have emerged from this long and profound dialogue: the "theories of theory of mind", also known as "theory-theory" (TT) and the so-called "simulation theories" (ST).

The TT maintains that agents explain and predict other people's behavior by means of a set of causal laws that form a sort of folk psychology (Carruthers & Smith, 1996). According to TT, agents use simple explanatory laws to link the (unobservable) determinants of behavior (desires, beliefs and intentions) to external (observable) stimuli in order to predict people's actions. This attribution process works on the basis of theoretical reasoning that involves (tacitly) shared causal laws.

The ST, on the other hand, posits that the attribution of mental states to other people works through mental representation: agents are able to simulate the reasoning process, pretending to be, literally, in the "mental shoes" of the other agents whose behavior they are observing or want to predict (Davis and Stone, 1995). "First you create in yourself pretend desires and beliefs of the sort you take [the other] to have (...) these pretend preferences and beliefs are fed into your own decision-making mechanism, which outputs a (pretend) decision" (Gallese and Goldman, 1998:496).

The main difference between TT and ST, is that while the former describes mind-reading as a neutral, objective and detached theoretical process, the latter considers it as an actual replication of the same neural activities implied in the action the subject is trying to interpret or predict. According to ST, thus, social cognition is not only reasoning about others' mental states, it is more like 'experiential insight' of other minds and a matter of 'embodied simulation'. According to physiologist Vittorio Gallese, to understand 'the actions of others means to enter their world, not just metaphorically but 'physically' (2006). Within this perspective, we use our ToM to build our intersubjective reality, which is thus grounded not only on our cognitive abilities, but more fundamentally on a sort of mechanism by which we are able to share our subjectivity, emotions, thoughts, goals and ends. A crucial part is played in this process by human beings' ability to produce, share and understand emotional states, in other words, to empathize.

5 The permeable limit II: sharing emotions.

Our potential to understand the mental states of others is at the core of our empathizing faculties. As I said at the beginning, the rational analysis of strategic behavior is based on the assumption that agents are capable of predicting the actions of others. This ability, in turn, relies not only on the cognitive mechanisms of the ToM (mentalizing), but also on other processes that have more to do with the emotional dimension (empathizing). If we accept that human actions are, at least partially, motivated by the desire to experience and avoid certain classes of emotional states, the possibility to anticipate the insurgence and to share the content of such emotions, becomes a crucial part of this more general predictive mechanism. Empathy or *perspective-taking*, is generally defined as the possibility to understand the feelings of others (Preston and de Waal, 2002; Gallese, 2003). A more specific definition is provided by de Vignemont and Singer (2006). In their view empathy can be defined by a set of four conditions: we "empathize" with others when we have (a) an affective state, (b) which is isomorphic to another persons affective state, (c) which was induced by observation or imagination of another person's affective state, and (d) when we know that the other person's affective state is the source of our own affective state. Condition (a) is particularly important as it helps to differentiate empathy from mentalizing. Empathy is different from mentalizing because it determines an emotional state in the observer, which is not present in the mere mentalizing; it is also different from the simpler emotional contagion since in the empathic experience we know what the other feels but we may not experience the feelings.

Preston and de Waal (2002) develop a model of empathy that explains how we can understand what someone else feels when he or she experiences simple emotions such as anger, fear, sadness, joy or pain, or even more complex ones such as disappointment, shame or guilt. They suggest that the mere observation or imagination of another person's emotional state automatically triggers a representation of that state in the observer. This model is supported by recent neuroscientific evidence that shows how the observation or imagination of another person in a given emotional state activates a representation of a similar state in the observer through an unconscious and effortful process (Singer et al., 2004a). Further fMRI studies (Singer *et al.*, 2004) have shown that such a process is indeed, unconscious and automatic. The same affective pain circuits that are activated when we experience pain are also active when we observe someone else is a similar situation. That suggests that if another person suffers pain: "our brains also make us suffer from this pain." (Singer and Fehr, 2005, p.342).

In the context of an economic interaction this ability is useful both from a self-interested point of view and in motivating other-regarding behavior. Empathy enables to predict and to take into account others' emotional responses to our perspective actions. This way a self-interested agent can be able to best-reply to the expected reaction of the other agents in order to maximize her material payoff. On the other hand, the ability to empathize may also promote other-regarding behavior by inhibiting courses of action that may induce negative emotional states in others and consequent feelings of guilt in the agent.

6 Psychological Games.

We saw that classical game theory cannot formalize the *forward looking* reasoning that would be necessary to account for the intention-detection process involved in the ToM. A series of promising theoretical proposals have been recently advanced in the area of 'psychological game theory' (PGT). PGT differs from the classical theory because it is capable of describing human interactions at a deeper level. In a psychological game the decision-making process takes into account not only the actions of others and beliefs about those actions, as in the classical theory, but also higher order beliefs, that is, beliefs about beliefs about beliefs, and so on (Geneakoplos, Pearce and Stacchetti,1989; Battigalli and Dufwenberg, 2009). This epistemic device allows us to describe and formalize the set of strategic reasons for action that are emotional and relational in nature. We know, in fact, that a large set of emotions are beliefs-based or relational, as they depends on the expectations that others have on our behavior as well as on our beliefs about those expectations. The joy we derive from a surprise we successfully arranged for a friend, depends on the fact that we know that she was expecting something different from what actually happened. In the same way, we feel guilt when we know that someone counts on us and we consciously betray those expectations. Other emotions such as pride, resentment, gratitude, anger, have all the same motivational power and the same epistemic structure, which can be easily described within PGT. While classical game theory and the models based on altruism and inequality-aversion are built upon an oversimplified concept of intentionality, mainly because of the assumption of consequentialism, PGT and the models that use its tools describe agents capable of ascribing intentions to each other by observing or even imagining others' actions.

This process of intentions-detection is surprisingly similar to that described by the simulation theories, and for this reason, PGT is apt, to some extent, to take into account our mentalizing and empathizing abilities.

7 Intentions, empathy and pro-social behavior.

In this section we report on a series of experiments that along with co-authors, I designed to directly explore the role of ToM and empathy in driving pro-social behavior.

In the first study (Pelligra *et al.*, 2011c) we tried to analyze the effect of ToM, and, more specifically, of the intention-detection process, in explaining choices aimed at punishing unfair behaviors. We used the design devised by Falk *et al.* (2003), but considered the mentalizing abilities as a treatment variable. To do this, we enrolled two different groups of subjects and made them play the four variant of the mini-ultimatum game (see fig. 2). Normal Developing subjects (ND) made up the first group, while in the second group we considered individuals affected by Autistic Spectrum Disorders (ASD). Among many other characteristics, ASD subjects are 'mind-blind', that is, they have a strong deficit in their mentalizing abilities, and hence they are quite often unable to ascribe intentions to others on the basis of what the others do. Our research question, in this case, was focused on the different rate of rejection that we expected to observe in the two groups (ND vs. ASD) if the choices were really driven by intention-detection. In the high-ToM group we expected to observe a patter of rejection similar to that found by Falk and colleagues, and in the low-ToM group a rate of rejection approximately constant across games. The results of the experiment are depicted in figure 3.

Data show that although the members of both groups are sensitive to inequality concerns (see the rejection rates in game [8-2]), subjects from the ND group behave as in Falk *et al.* study. On the other hand, members of the ASD group show a very different pattern of choice, much more homogeneous with differences in the rejection rates across games that are not statistically significant. In light of these results we can conclude that from a *direct* exploration of the role of mentalizing in strategic behaviors, its strong involvement in the explanation of observed behavior emerges quite clearly, especially with choices aimed at punishing unfair behavior.

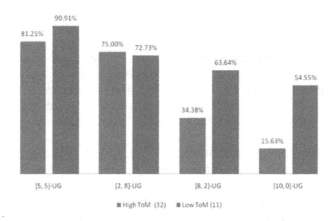

Fig. 3 "Rejection rates across the 4 UGs - High-ToM vs. Low-ToM" (source: Pelligra et al. 2011c)

A second relevant result refers to the relation between pro-social behavior and empathizing abilities and emerges in the experiment designed by Becchetti and Pelligra (2011). In this study we analyzed the choices made in a modified version of the dictator game. In this game the 'dictator' is given an endowment of 10 euros that she can give to a recipient, in any amount between 0 and 10. In this case the recipient is a well-known non-profit organization that the dictator can select from a list of nine. What is not given, is paid in cash to the subjects, while the total donations are paid to the respective organizations. The results show a high propensity to give, and, more interestingly, they show that such a propensity increases with a number of other variables, such as the number of family members, (1 euros more, on average, for each family member), the number of friends in the subject's Facebook profile (4 percent more for each friend) and, more relevant to the argument of this chapter, the individual's empathy quotient and guilt-propensity.

These findings are consistent with a model of strategic action based on the idea of *guilt-aversion* (Battigalli and Dufwenberg, 2007). In this model each agent reads others' intentions by considering what they do together with what they could have done. The alternatives not taken are, thus, an element that can be used to assess an agent's expectation. The idea of the guilt-aversion model is that if you consciously betray the expectation of others you will experience a psychological cost associated to the felling of guilt, that will be higher the more the others were expecting you to make the choice you did not make. If you think the non-profit organization expect a donation from you and you take all the money you will experience guilt. Our experiment seems to show that the higher the level of empathy, that is your ability to share or anticipate others' disappointment, the larger your donation will be. The same should be true in a trust game like the VTG we discussed a few sections earlier.

In a third experiment (Pelligra, 2011a), I tried to verify this last hypothesis. By analyzing different variants of the binary trust game it emerges that the probability of a trustworthy response, while not affected by the level of material reward it can bring to the trustee, is positively correlated with her level of empathy, as measured by the *Cambridge Empathy Quotient* (Baron-Cohen *et al.*, 2004). The greater my ability to anticipate and share the disappointment you could feel as a result of my opportunistic choice, the higher the likelihood of my trustworthy choice. That could be explained because to a higher level of empathy is associated stronger guilt stemming from the choice of letting the other down. Thus, *ceteris paribus*, empathy leads to greater guilt, that is to a psychological cost that the subject tries to avoid behaving as expected by the trustor.

In a fourth study (Pelligra, 2011b) we explored subjects' behavior in a more complex form of the trust game, the so-called 'investment-game' (Berg et al., 1995). In the investment-game, a trustor has to decide how much of its initial endowment, if any, to send to the trustee. Any positive amount is tripled by the experimenter and passed to the trustee, who in turn, has to decide how much of the tripled amount to send back to the proposer. The amount sent by the trustor and the return by the trustees are usually interpreted as measures of trust and trustworthiness, respectively. In the perfect Nash equilibrium of the game both the trustor and the trustee send nothing to the other. On the contrary, the results of our experiment show that the trustors send on average 59.76 percent of their endowments and that only 5 out of 53 trustees decide to keep all the money and to give back nothing (see figure 4). If we associate those choices (amount sent and payback) to individuals' level of empathy, no significant correlation emerges.

However, the effect of empathy clearly appears when we consider not the amount returned but the fraction of the amount sent which is returned, in other word the ratio between the investment and the restitution (figure 5). If we consider this variable, in fact, we can clearly distinguish two different kinds of subjects: those who send back a positive amount but always as a *constant* fraction of the received amount, and those who send back increasing fractions as the investment increases.

The former obey to the norm of 'balanced' reciprocity, while the latter can be defined as 'conditional' reciprocators (Greig and Bohnet, 2008).

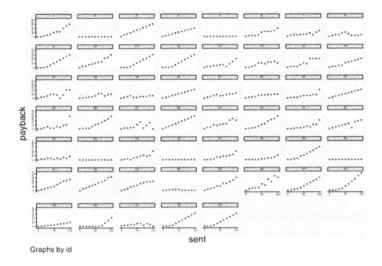

Graphs by id

Fig. 4 "Amount sent and payback" (source: Pelligra 2011b)

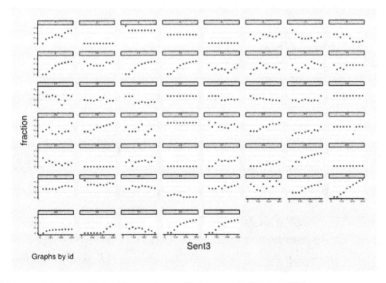

Graphs by id

Fig. 5 "Amount Sent and Fraction Returned" (source: Pelligra 2011b)

If we measure the empathy quotient of those who obey to the different norms we notice that the 'conditional' reciprocators score an average of 47.55, while the 'balanced' reciprocators have an average EQ of 42.15.

This result seems to show that for many players the decision to repay others' trust in the investment game is more closely associated to the compliance of an imperative norm, than to a complex psychological and material cost-benefit calculation. Individuals' empathy affects the choice of the norm to follow: the "balanced' form of reciprocity is a sort of 'no-loss' rule, which leads the subject both to maximize her material wealth and not to make the trustor worse off. A high level of empathy produces even greater results, as it pushes the trustee to send back more than necessary to conform to a 'no-loss' rule, and to share more equally the gains resulting from trustor's trust. Conditional reciprocity, according to which greater trust is rewarded with proportionally larger returns, is what is usually found in experiments with students in developed countries (see Greig and Bonhet, 2008). Balanced reciprocity, on the other hand, is a form of "no-loss" norm, that induces the trustee to maximize her material gain while refraining from making the trustor worse off with respect to the status-quo. This norm has been extensively observed in reciprocal-exchange economies from less developed countries (e.g., Platteau, 1997; Thomas and Worrall, 2002), where contracts are informally enforced by norms that obligate future quid-pro-quo (balanced) repayment of loans and gifts.

The investment game that we considered in our experiment has an intrinsic element of 'superadditivity' that leads a positive investment to generate social surplus. This game represents a typical exchange situation where trust and trustworthiness produce gains from trade. A conditional reciprocator shares with the trustee part of the surplus generated in the interaction, providing, this way, a good reason to invest a positive amount of her endowment. For this reason conditional reciprocity tends to promote a trusting attitude towards exchanges.

In the balanced reciprocity norm, on the other hand, the trustee retains the entire surplus. The problem with this pattern of behavior is that a mere "no-loss rule" may not be sufficient to induce the trustor to invest a positive amount of her endowment, and because of this, the potential gains of a successful trusting interaction may be lost.

One may speculate that our results, if corroborated by further researches, could link empathy, the ability to anticipate and share others' emotional states, to the social capital literature. The prevalence of one norm or the other, in fact, may affect a community 's ability to extract gains from trade. Only highly empathic subjects that are willing to reciprocate in a conditional way, are able to induce trust and contribute to lay the ground for the social benefits associated to high-trust communities, notably, the presence of large organizations (La Porta et al., 1997), a sustained rate of growth (Knack and Keefer, 1997), a higher degree of financial development (Guiso et al., 2004), and better quality of law enforcement (Zak and Knack, 1999).

8 Towards a Shared Intersubjective Space.

In the previous pages I tried to stress some of the limitations of the classical theory of games that may hinder a deeper understanding of fundamental dimensions that are intrinsic to the interpersonal relations. First of all, the possibility to describe the 'others' as agents with an identity, that is with heterogeneous intentions and goals. Secondly, the possibility to conceptualize a form of communication between agents that has not only cognitive but also emotional content.

These two elements constitute, I believe, two important building blocks of the social epistemology, the understanding of the world of others that any theory of strategic behavior cannot leave aside.

I discussed both theoretically and empirically the functioning of the process that allows us to mentalize and empathize with others, and I presented the results of a series of experiments that emphasize the role of these two processes in the realm of strategic interaction. I also argued how the conceptualization of a hierarchy of higher order beliefs in psychological game theory seems to constitute a promising step forward in the introduction of those relational elements in the motivational structure of social agents.

These are, of course, just preliminary indications that we can hint at. But they mark rather clearly the path to follow. The convergence of game theory, philosophy of action and social neuroscience towards an idea of agent as subject-in-relation, seems to support my analysis. It looks like different perspectives, more or less independently, are leading us to realize that the study of the interpersonal phenomena cannot be merely grounded on the analysis of individual subjects that interact in a 'cold' way. A perspective is emerging in which the unit of analysis is moving from the 'ego' to the dyad 'I-thou'. How the individual agent constructs itself in the relational space, in the encounter with the other, is in fact becoming clearer

When an agent 'encounters' another agent, he is 'changed'. In the relation they contribute to construct they inhabit a shared intersubjective space where the individual agent does not 'evaporate', but changes, becoming 'person', to employ a more philosophical term. The mentalizing and empathizing abilities are two of the main mechanisms that contribute to constructing such a space.

According to many, the mirror neuron system represents the physiological ground where the 'embodied simulation' process is built upon, giving us access to the sub-personal world of the others. This way, not only we become capable of understanding the others, but also, by assuming another person's perspective, to look at ourselves in a non ego-centric way, allowing us to see details of our personality and behavior that would have been precluded otherwise.

In this chapter we encountered and tried to trespass different boundaries: the disciplinary boundary, that urges us to go beyond the separations among languages and disciplines; the limit that exists between objective and perceptive reality; I tried to stress how much objective reality is built upon our interpersonal perceptions of others' objective reality. Lastly, the subjectivity limit: I argued that the personal identity originates not from the distinction across agents, but from the construction of a shared intersubjective space where we live our interpersonal lives, which makes the boundaries of our own subjectivity permeable.

References

1. Bacharach, M., (1999). Incorporating Game Theory in the Theory of Action. Paper presented at Workshop on Strategic Rationality in Economics, Associazione Sigismondo Malatesta, Rocca Malatestiana, Sant'Arcangelo di Romagna, August 26-27.
2. Bacharach, M., (Edited by Gold, N. & Sugden, R.), (2006). *Beyond Individual Choice: Teams and Frames in Game Theory. Princeton.* Princeton University Press.
3. Baron-Cohen, S., and Wheelwright, S., (2004). The Empathy Quotient: An Investigation of Adults with Asperger Syndrome or High Functioning Autism, and Normal Sex Differences. *Journal of Autism and Developmental Disorders* 34 (2), 164–175.
4. Battigalli, P., Dufwenberg, M., (2007). Guilt in Games. *American Economic Review, Papers & Proceedings* 97, 170-76.
5. Battigalli, P., Dufwenberg, M., (2009). Dynamic psychological games. *Journal of Economic Theory,* 144, 1–35.
6. Berg, J., Dickhaut, J., McCabe, K., (1995). Trust, Reciprocity, and Social History. *Games and Economic Behavior,* 10, 122-142.
7. Buber, M., (1937/2004), I and Thou. Charles Scribner's Sons. Reprint Continuum International Publishing Group.
8. Camerer, C., (2003). *Behavioral Game Theory. Experiments in Strategic Interaction.* Princeton, Princeton University Press.
9. Carruthers, P., Smith, P. (eds), (1996). *Theories of Theories of Mind.* Oxford: Basil Blackwell.
10. Davis, M., Stone, T. (eds.) (1995). *Mental Simulation.* Oxford: Basil Blackwell.
11. de Vignemont, F., Singer, T., (2006). The empathic brain: how, when and why? *Trends in Cognitive Science,* 10 , 435-441
12. Fehr E., Schmidt, K.M., (1999). A Theory of Fairness, Competition and Cooperation. *Quarterly Journal of Economics* 114, 817-868.
13. Gallese, V., (2006). "Corpo Vivo, Simulazione Incarnata e Intersoggettività", in Cappuccio, M., (ed.), *Neurofenomenologia.* Milano, Bruno Mondadori.
14. Gallese, V., Goldman, A., (1998). Mirror neurons and the simulation theory of mind-reading. *Trends in Cognitive Sciences* 2 (12), 493-501.
15. Geanakoplos, J., Pearce, D., Stacchetti, E., (1989). Psychological Games and Sequential Rationality. *Games and Economic Behavior* 1:60–79.
16. Gintis, H., (2009). *The Bounds of Reason, Game Theory and the Unification of the Behavioral Sciences.* Princeton, Princeton University Press.
17. Giocoli, N., (2003). *Modelling Rational Agents.* Cheltenham: Edward Elgar.
18. Greig, F., Bohnet, I., (2008). Is There Reciprocity In A Reciprocal-Exchange Economy? Evidence Of Gendered Norms From A Slum In Nairobi, Kenya. *Economic Inquiry* 46 (1), 77-83.
19. Gui, B., Sugden, R. (Eds.), (2005), *Economics and Social Interaction: Accounting for Interpersonal Relations.* Cambridge University Press, Cambridge.
20. Guiso, L., Sapienza, P. Zingales, L., (2004). The Role of Social Capital in Financial Development. *American Economic Review,* 94 (3), 526-556.
21. Knack, S., Keefer, P., 2007. Does Social Capital Have an Economic Payoff? A Cross-Country Investigation. *Quarterly Journal of Economics,* 112, 1251-88.
22. La Porta, R., Lopez de Silanes, F., Shleifer, A., Vishny, R., (1997). Trust in large organizations. *American Economic Review,* 87 (2), 333-338.
23. McCabe, K.A., Rigdon, M.L., Smith, V.L., (2003). Positive Reciprocity and Intentions in Trust Games. *Journal of Economic Behavior and Organization* 52, 267-275.
24. McCabe, K. Smith, V., Lepore, M., (2000). Intentionality and "mindreading": Why does the game form matter? *Proceedings of the National Academy of Science* 97 (8), 4404-4409.
25. Margolis, H., (1982). *Selfishness, Altruism, and Rationality. A Theory of Social Choice.* Chicago: Chicago University Press.
26. Mirowski, P., (2002). *Machine dreams.* Cambridge: Cambridge University Press.
27. Nash, J., (1951). Non-Cooperative Games. *Annals of Mathematics* 54, 286-295.
28. Nash, J., (1996). *Essays in Game Theory.* Cheltenham: Edward Elgar.

29. Pelligra, V., (2011a). Reciprocating Kindness. An Experimental Analysis. Mimeo, Università di Cagliari.
30. Pelligra, V., (2011b). Empathy, Guilt-Aversion, and Patterns of Reciprocity. *Journal of Neuroscience, Psychology, and Economics*, 4(3), pp. 161–173.
31. Pelligra, V., (2011c). Intentions, Trust and Frames: A note on Sociality and the Theory of Games, *Review of Social Economy*, 69(2), pp. 163–188.
32. Becchetti, L., Pelligra, V., (2011b) Don't Be Ashamed to Say You Didn't Get Much: Redistributive Effects of Information Disclosure in Donations and Inequity Aversion in Charitable Giving, Working Paper AICCON n. 88, University of Bologna (Forlì).
33. Pelligra, V., Isoni, A., Fadda, R., Doneddu, I., (2010). Social Preferences and Perceived Intentions. An experiment with Normally Developing and Autistic Spectrum Disorders Subjects. CRENoS, Working Paper Number 2010_10.
34. Platteau, J., (1997). Mutual Insurance as an Elusive Concept in Traditional Rural Communities. *Journal of Development Studies*, 33, 764-796.
35. Preston, S. and de Waal, F. (2002). Empathy: Its ultimate and proximate bases. *Behavioral and Brain Sciences*, 25 (1), 1-72.
36. Rizzolati, G., Fogassi, L., Gallese, V. (2001). Neurophysiological mechanisms underlying the understanding and imitation of action. *Nature Reviews of Neuroscience* 2:661–70
37. Schelling, T., (1960). The Strategy of Conflict. Cambridge: Boston MA., Harvard University Press.
38. Singer, T., Seymour, B., O'Doherty, J.P., Kaube, H. Dolan, R.J., Frith, C. D., (2004). Empathy for Pain Involves the Affective but not Sensory Components of Pain. *Science*, 303(5661), 1157-62.
39. Sugden R., (1993), "Thinking as a Team; Towards an explanation on non-selfish behaviour", *Social Philosophy and Policy*, 10:69-89.
40. Sugden R., (2000), "Team Preferences", *Economic and Philosophy*, 16:175-204.
41. Thomas, J.P., Worrall, T., (2002). Gift-giving, Quasi-credit and Reciprocity. *Rationality and Society*, 14, 308-352.
42. Tommasello, M., (2000). *The Cultural Origins of Human Cognition*. Cambridge, MA: Harvard University Press.
43. Zak P. J., Knack, S., (2001). Trust and growth. *Economic Journal*, 111, 295-321.

Chapter 19
The game of dependence *

Davide Grossi and Paolo Turrini

> To understand *an idea or a phenomenon— or even something like
> a piece of music—is to relate it to familiar ideas or experiences,
> to fit it into a framework in which one feels* at home.
>
> Robert J. Aumann, *What is game theory trying to accomplish?* [1]

Abstract The present chapter builds on Castelfranchi's influential work on dependence theory and takes up his challenge to develop a full-fledged formal theory of dependence. The upshot of such a theory is to set up the mathematical machinery necessary to analyze agent interaction in terms of dependence and related notions, such as the ones of dependence cycle and reciprocity. The method we follow approaches the study of dependence by borrowing and adapting standard notions from the theory of games. Concretely, the chapter presents two main results: first, it shows how the proposed formal analysis of dependence allows for an elegant characterization of a property of reciprocity for outcomes in strategic interaction; and second, it shows how this notion of reciprocity can be used to ground the definition of new classes of coalitional games, where coalitions can force outcomes only in the presence of reciprocal dependencies. As a result, the chapter reveals a close, though perhaps surprising, kinship between game theory and dependence theory.

· Davide Grossi
Agent Applications, Research and Technology Group, University of Liverpool, Italy
e-mail: d.grossi@liverpool.ac.uk

Paolo Turrini
Faculty of Sciences, Technology and Communication, University of Luxembourg, Luxembourg
e-mail: paolo.turrini@uni.lu

* The authors would like to thank the anonymous reviewers of AAMAS'10, COMSOC'10 and JAAMAS, where previous versions of the work have been submitted. Their remarks have been of great help for developing the present version of the work. Davide Grossi wishes to acknowledge support by the *Netherlands Organisation for Scientific Research* (NWO) under the VENI grant 639.021.816.

1 Introduction

The importance of dependence in multi-agent systems (henceforth MAS) was not recognized until the publication of a series of papers by Castelfranchi and colleagues [6, 5], who developed it into a powerful and suggestive paradigm to understand social interaction. Their work emphasized the necessity of building a formal theory of dependence modeling the role that cognitive phenomena such as beliefs and goals play in its definition. In the last decade, the notion of dependence has made its way into several research lines (e.g., [19, 2, 3, 14]), but still today dependence theory has several versions and no unified theory. However, the aim of the theory is clear:

> "One of the fundamental notions of social interaction is the *dependence* relation among players. In our opinion, the terminology for describing interaction in a multi-player world is necessarily based on an analytic description of this relation. Starting from such a terminology, it is possible to devise a calculus to obtain predictions and make choices that simulate human behavior" [6, p. 2].

In this view, dependence theory addresses two main issues:

- the representation of dependence relations among the players in a system;
- the use of such information as a means to obtain predictions about the behavior of the system.

While all contributions to dependence theory have thus far focused on the first point, the second challenge, "[to] devise a calculus to obtain predictions", has been mainly addressed by means of computer simulation methods (e.g., [14]) and no analytical approaches have yet been developed. The present contribution takes up these two challenge from an analytical point of view and outlines a theory of dependence based on standard game-theoretic notions and techniques.

The theory moves from the following definition of dependence, extracted from the discussion of the notion provided in [6]:

> *Player i depends on player j for strategy σ_j, within a given game, if and only if σ_j is a dominant strategy (or a best response in some profile σ) not for j itself, but instead for i.*

Our aim here is to provide a thorough analysis of the above definition, which will be made formal in Definition 9. Concretely, the chapter presents two results. First, it shows that this notion of dependence allows for the characterization of an original notion of reciprocity for strategic games (Theorem 1), i.e., of how players in a strategic interaction can profitably make use of their dependence relation. Second, it shows that the notion of dependence can be fruitfully applied to ground coalition formation. The class of coalitional games where coalitions can force outcomes only in the presence of dependence cycles—here called *dependence games*—can be directly linked to standard solution concepts used in cooperative game theory. The present contribution will dispense the reader with many technical details (such as proofs) which can be found in [11, 10].

	L	*R*
U	2,2	0,3
D	3,0	1,1

Prisoner's dilemma

	L	*R*
U	3,3	2,2
D	2,2	1,1

Full Convergence

	L	*R*
U	1,1	0,0
D	0,0	1,1

Coordination

	L	*R*
U	3,3	2,2
D	2,5	1,1

Partial Convergence

Fig. 1 Examples of two player strategic games in game matrices. Ordinal preferences are represented, as usual, by means of numerical payoffs. *U* and *D* denote the strategies 'up' and, respectively, 'down' for the row player. *L* and *R* denote the strategies 'left' and 'right' for the column player.

Our study is meant to lay a bridge between game theory and dependence theory that, within the MAS community, are erroneously considered to be alternative, when not incompatible, paradigms for the analysis of social interaction. An impression that was recently been reiterated during the AA-MAS'2009 panel discussion "Theoretical Foundations for Agents and MAS: Is game theory sufficient?". It is our conviction that the theory of games and that of dependence are highly compatible endeavors. On the one hand dependence theory can be incorporated into the highly developed mathematical framework of game theory, obtaining the sort of mathematical foundations that it is still missing. On the other hand, game theory can fruitfully incorporate a novel dependence-theoretic perspective on the analysis of strategic interaction.

Outline of the chapter

Section 2 briefly introduces the basic notions of game theory with which we will work in the rest of the chapter. Section 3 introduces our formal analysis of the concept of dependence, relating it to informal definitions available in the literature on dependence theory. It then moves on to the characterization of reciprocal outcomes in games. Starting from the notion of reciprocity, Section 4 introduces a notion of agreement among players in a game, and on this ground it defines and studies a specific class of coalitional games. Section 5 discusses related and future work concluding the chapter.

2 Preliminaries: game theory

The present section introduces the basic game-theoretic notions used in the chapter. All definitions will be based on an ordinal notion of preference. Main sources for this preliminary section are [16] and [15].

2.1 Strategic games and solution concepts

Let us start with the definition of a game in strategic form.

Definition 1 (Game) *A (strategic form) game is a tuple* $G = (N, S, \Sigma_i, \succeq_i, o)$ *where:*

- N *is a non-empty set of players;*
- S *is a non-empty set of outcomes;*
- Σ_i *is a non-empty set of strategies for player* $i \in N$*;*
- $\succeq_i$ *is a total preorder on* S*;*
- $o : \bigtimes_{i \in N} \Sigma_i \to S$ *is a function from the set* $\bigtimes_{i \in N} \Sigma_i$ *of strategy profiles to the set of outcomes* S.[2]

Examples of games represented as payoff matrices are given in Figure 1. The terms 'agent' and 'player' will be used interchangeably. Before we continue with the next definition, let us first introduce some further notation. Strategy profiles will be denoted $\sigma, \sigma' \dots$. Given a strategy profile σ and a player i, σ_i denotes the strategy chosen by i in σ, i.e., the ith projection of σ, and σ_{-i} denotes the profile consisting of all the strategies of the players except i. So, a profile σ can be seen as the juxtaposition of σ_i and σ_{-i}, in symbols, $\sigma = (\sigma_i, \sigma_{-i})$. More generally, σ_C, for a coalition $C \subseteq N$, denotes the tuple of strategies performed by the agents in C in profile σ, i.e. an element of $\bigtimes_{i \in C} \Sigma_i$. Given a coalition C, in order to denote the set of agents not belonging to C we use notation $\overline{C}$. We now define the notion of sub-game of a game in strategic form.

Definition 2 (Sub-game) *Let* $G = (N, S, \Sigma_i, \succeq_i, o)$ *be a game,* σ *be a strategy profile, and* $C \subseteq N$. *The subgame of* G *defined by* σ_C *is a game* $G \downarrow \sigma_C = (N', S', \Sigma_i', \succeq_i', o')$ *such that:*

- $N' = \overline{C}$*;*
- $S' = S - \{s \mid \exists \sigma' \text{ s.t. } s = o(\sigma') \text{ AND } \sigma_C' \neq \sigma_C\}$*;*
- *for all* $i \in \overline{C}$, $\Sigma_i' = \Sigma_i$*;*
- *for all* $i \in \overline{C}$, $\succeq_i' = \succeq_i \cap S' \times S'$*;*
- $o' : \bigtimes_{i \in N'} \Sigma_i \to S'$ *is a function from the strategy profiles to outcomes such that for all* $\sigma' \in \bigtimes_{i \in N'} \Sigma_i$, $o'(\sigma') = o(\sigma', \sigma_C)$.

A sub-game $G \downarrow \sigma_C$ of G is obtained from G once the coalitional strategy σ_C of the set of players in C is fixed. Intuitively, it as a snapshot of what is still 'left to play' once the players in C have made their choice. Therefore, in a sub-game, the only players actually playing are the ones outside C (first item in the definition); the available outcomes are only those that can be reached once the strategies of C are fixed (second item); the strategies available to the players remain the same (third item); players' preferences are restricted to the available outcomes (fourth item); and the outcome function corresponds to the one of the original game for that part of profiles which are available in the

---

[2] The outcome function is often assumed to be a bijection and it is consequently dispensed with [16]. However in the field of social choice theory several contributions exist where bijectivity is considered a restrictive constraint [15]. As different scenarios may require different assumptions, we study the outcome function in its most general form.

sub-game (fifth item). It is worth stressing that a sub-game is still a game in the sense of Definition 1.

As to the solution concepts, we will work with the Nash equilibrium, which we will typically refer to as best response equilibrium (BR-equilibrium), and the dominant strategy equilibrium (DS-equilibrium). Let us first introduce the notions of best response and dominant strategy.

Definition 3 (Best response and dominant strategy) *Let $G = (N, S, \Sigma_i, \succeq_i, o)$ be a game, and σ a profile. We say that:*

- *strategy σ_i is a best response for i in σ iff $\forall \sigma_i' \in \Sigma_i : o(\sigma) \succeq_i o(\sigma_i', \sigma_{-i})$;*
- *strategy σ_i is a dominant strategy for i iff $\forall \sigma' \in \bigtimes_{i \in N} \Sigma_i : o(\sigma_i, \sigma_{-i}') \succeq_i o(\sigma')$.*

In words, a strategy of i is a best response for i, in a given profile, whenever i has no strategy available that would lead to a strictly better outcome for him/herself, provided the rest of the players stick to their choices. The notion of dominant strategy is stronger. A strategy is a dominant strategy for i whenever no other choice of i would guarantee him/her a strictly better outcome, no matter what the rest of the players chooses to do. It is easy to see that a dominant strategy is a best response under any strategy profile.

With these auxiliary notions in place, we can now introduce the two solution concepts of interest for the chapter.

Definition 4 (Equilibria) *Let G be a game. A strategy profile σ is:*

- *a BR-equilibrium (Nash equilibrium) if σ_i is a best response in σ for all players i in N;*
- *a DS-equilibrium (dominant strategy equilibrium) if σ_i is a dominant strategy for all players i in N.*

In words, a Nash or BR-equilibrium is a profile in which no player can do strictly better for him/herself by deviating from his/her current strategy, i.e., by changing his/her strategy while assuming the other players stick to theirs. A DS-equilibrium is a stronger solution concept. It is a profile in which all players choose a strategy which is preferable no matter what all the other players choose.

Example 1 (Solution concepts) *Consider the four games given in Figure 1. We will illustrate Definition 4 by looking at their equilibria. In the Prisoner's dilemma the profile (D, R)—the profile commonly known as 'defect-defect' profile—is both a BR and a DS-equilibrium. The same is the case for profile (U, L) in the full convergence and partial convergence games. The coordination game has two BR-equilibria, namely (U, L) and (D, R), but no DS-equilibrium as players do not have a strategy which under any circumstance would lead to a preferable outcome.*

2.2 Coalitional games and the core

In addition to the games in strategic form (Definition 1) we will also work with cooperative, or coalitional, games. Unlike the games in strategic form, coalitional games, which have been extensively studied already in [20], model interactive situations by explicitly representing the possibility of cooperation among coalitions of agents. In particular, we will work with coalitional games with non-transferable payoffs [16], that is, with ordinal versions of coalitional games. These are represented abstractly by means of so-called effectivity functions [15].

Definition 5 (Coalitional game) *A coalitional game is a tuple $C = (N, S, E, \succeq_i)$ where:*

- *N is a non-empty set of players;*
- *S is a non-empty set of outcomes;*
- *E is function $E : 2^N \to 2^{2^S}$ (the effectivity function) from sets of players to sets of sets of outcomes;*
- *$\succeq_i$ is a total preorder on S.*

Just like games in strategic form, coalitional games consist of a set of players endowed with preferences over a set of outcomes. But unlike games in strategic form, interaction is here modeled via the effectivity function. An effectivity function associates to a coalition a set of sets of outcomes and the fact that a set of outcomes X belongs to the effectivity $E(C)$ of C is usually understood as the coalition C being able to force the interaction to end up in an outcome in X.

In this chapter we are interested in coalitional games only in as much as they provide a representation of games in strategic form which explicitly allows for cooperation. In other words, we use coalitional games only to describe the cooperative possibilities of players in strategic interaction. We now recall how to obtain a coalitional game from a strategic one (cf. [15]). These games in particular will be the object of study in Section 4.

Definition 6 (Coalitional games from strategic ones) *Let $G = (N, S, \Sigma_i, \succeq_i, o)$ be a strategic game. The coalitional game $C^G = (N, S, E^G, \succeq_i)$ of G is a coalitional game where the effectivity function E^G is defined as follows:*

$$X \in E^G(C) \Leftrightarrow \exists \sigma_C \forall \sigma_{\overline{C}} \, o(\sigma_C, \sigma_{\overline{C}}) \in X.$$

So the coalitional game C of a given game G in strategic form consists of G's set of agents, G's set of outcomes and G's agents' preferences. The effectivity function E^G is then defined in such a way that, for any coalition C, $E^G(C)$ consists of all those sets of outcomes within which C can force the game G to end up, no matter what the rest of the players do.

Example 2 (Effectivity function of the prisoner's dilemma) *Consider again the prisoner's dilemma (Figure 1). From a cooperative point of view there are four coalitions available: {column}, {row}, {column, row} and the empty coalition $\emptyset$. Let us abbreviate the set $\{(U,L),(U,R),(D,L),(D,R)\}$ with W. By applying Definition 6 we obtain the following effectivity function E:*

$$E(\emptyset) = \{W\}$$
$$E(\{column\}) = \{X \subseteq W \mid \{(U,L),(D,L)\} \subseteq X \; or \; \{(U,R),(D,R)\} \subseteq X\}$$
$$E(\{row\}) = \{X \subseteq W \mid \{(U,L),(U,R)\} \subseteq X \; or \; \{(D,L),(D,R)\} \subseteq X\}$$
$$E(\{column,row\}) = \{X \subseteq W \mid X \neq \emptyset\}$$

Intuitively, as the coalition grows, so grow its possibilities. Trivially, the empty coalition has no way of 'restraining' the game to any particular set of outcomes. Each player can either force the game to end up in the sets of outcomes consisting of the rows of the game matrix—by choosing U or D—or, respectively, the ones consisting of the columns of the game matrix—by choosing L or R. The coalition consisting of both players can not only force the game to end up in the sets belonging to the effectivity function of each player, but it can also force the game towards any of the four singleton sets. In other words, by coordinating their actions, the two players together can decide which outcome should result from the game.

Finally, we consider the most common solution concept for coalitional games, the core. This is inspired by the same sort of rationale behind the notion of Nash equilibrium in games in strategic form: an outcome is stable—and hence belongs to the core of the game—if no coalition can profitably deviate obtaining an outcome which is better for all the members of the coalition.

Definition 7 (The Core) *Let $C = (N,S,E,\geq_i)$ be a coalitional game. We say that a state $s \in S$ is dominated in C if for some C and $X \in E(C)$ it holds that $x >_i s$ for all $x \in X, i \in C$. The core of C, in symbols $CORE(C)$ is the set of undominated states.*

As an illustration, we show how the notion of core rationalizes the cooperative solution of the prisoner's dilemma.

Example 3 (The core of the coalitional version of the prisoner's dilemma) *Recall the effectivity function E described in Example 2. The coalitional version of the prisoner's dilemma scenario is then a coalitional game consisting of the two players column and row, the four set of outcomes $\{U,D\} \times \{L,R\}$, the effectivity function E, and the preferences given in the top left game matrix in Figure 1. The core of such game is the set $\{(U,L)\}$ in which the two players cooperate. This is so because neither can the coalition $\{column,row\}$ guarantee a better outcome for both players, nor can either of the players guarantee outcomes that are all strictly better than (U,L). To appreciate this notice, for example, that none of the sets of outcomes in $E(\{column\})$ (see Example 2) consists of outcomes that are all strictly preferred to (U,L) by column.*

We have now concluded the introduction of the game-theoretic machinery which will be used in the rest of the chapter, and can move to the presentation of our formal theory of dependence.

3 Dependence in games

Dependence theory, as developed within artificial intelligence and MAS, has been mainly inspired by work in the social sciences such as [7]. It moves from presuppositions that are clearly shared by the theory of games—eminently the fact that the outcome of social interaction depends on the choices of different agents—but it emphasizes, rather than the strategic aspect of agents' choices, the interdependencies existing between them in terms of what they want and what they choose. To put it in Castelfranchi's words:

> "Sociality obviously presupposes two or more players in a common shared world. A 'Common World' implies that there is interference among the actions and goals of the players: the effects of the action of one player are relevant for the goals of another: i.e., they either favour the achievement or maintenance of some goals of the other's (positive interference), or threat some of them (negative interference)" [5, p. 161-162]

In this view, what underpins the analysis of social interaction is the idea that agents can favour or hinder each other's goals.

The present section shows how, by tweaking some basic game-theoretic notions, this perspective on social interaction can be accommodated within the theory of games. The section proceeds with a formal definition and analysis of the notion of dependence in games.

3.1 Dependence relations

The literature on dependence theory features a number of different relations of dependence. Yet, in its most essential form, a dependence relation is a relation occurring between two players i and j with respect to a certain state (or goal) which i wants to achieve but which it cannot achieve without some appropriate action of j.

> "x depends on y with regard to an act useful for realizing a state p when p is a goal of x's and x is unable to realize p while y is able to do so." [6, p.4]

The definition in [6] acquires a variety of meanings applicable to different contexts. We start out by emphasizing the strategic aspects of dependence by reformulating its definition as follows:

> A player i depends on a player j for the strategy σ_j when σ_j is a favour by j to i, that is, the choice by j of σ_j is in i's interest.

Let us compare this reading with Castelfranchi's. This will make clear what the assumptions are upon which the theory will be developed. In fact, it might be argued that the focus of Castelfranchi's formulation seems to slightly differ from ours in a few points. Such differences, we claim, are not essential and do not lie at the core of the notion:

- Castelfranchi stresses the fact that one of the actors is not able to realize the goal which he is dependent for ("[...] while y is able to do so." [6, p.4]).

An attentive reading of our formulation will reveal that the requirement is encoded in the fact that strategy σ_j, played by j in i's interest, is by definition not under control of player i.

- Castelfranchi talks about playing to reach someone else's goal, while we adopt the more immediate notion of favor. Once again, clear formulations of favor or of play to reach someone else's goal are not available in the literature, and different cognitive accounts provide different solutions. As will be clear from Definition 8, a generalization of the stantard definitions of best response and dominant strategy can naturally formalize a game-theoretic notion of favour.
- Finally, while our formulation of dependence consists of a three-place relation, Castelfranchi's one incorporates further ingredients such as act, while some other accounts even adopt the notion of plans (e.g. [19]). We reckon a treatment of actions and plans separate from strategies not to be fundamental for a formal theory of dependence in games and we consequently abstract away from them by using the sole notion of strategy.

So let us now focus on the notion of favor. In order to formalize it, we generalize the notions of best response and dominant strategy, that are applied to strategies that a player plays in his own interest, to the notions of best response and dominant strategy *for someone else*.

Definition 8 (Best for someone else) *Let $G = (N, S, \Sigma_i, \succeq_i, o)$ be a game and σ a profile, and let $i, j \in N$. We say that:*

- *strategy σ_j is a best response for i in σ iff $\forall \sigma'_j \in \Sigma_j : o(\sigma) \succeq_i o(\sigma'_j, \sigma_{-j})$;*
- *strategy σ_j is a dominant strategy for i iff $\forall \sigma' \in \bigtimes_{i \in N} \Sigma_i : o(\sigma_i, \sigma'_{-i}) \succeq_i o(\sigma')$.*

It is easy to see that Definition 8 is a generalization of the definitions of best response and dominant strategy given in Definition 3. We simply allow the player holding the preference to be different from the player whose strategies are considered. We take this to be natural formalizations, within a standard game theoretic setting, of notions such as "doing a favour to" or "playing in the interest of".

On the basis of Definition 8 we can formulate a precise game-theoretic notion of dependence in the following way.

Definition 9 (Dependence) *Let $G = (N, S, \Sigma_i, \succeq_i, o)$ be a game and let $i, j \in N$. We say that:*

- *i BR-depends on j in profile σ iff σ_j is a best response for i in σ;*
- *i DS-depends on j in profile σ iff σ_j is a dominant strategy for i.*

That i BR-depends on j for σ will often be denoted $iR_\sigma^{BR} j$. Similary, that i DS-depends on j for σ is often schematically denoted $iR_\sigma^{DS} j$.

Intuitively, i depends on j for profile σ in a best response sense if, in σ, j plays a strategy which is a best response for i given the strategies in σ_{-j} (and hence given the choice of i itself). It depends in a dominant strategy sense if, in σ, j plays a dominant strategy for i.

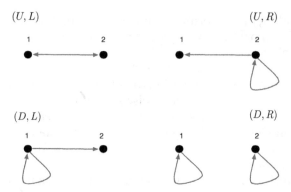

Fig. 2 The BR-dependence graph of the prisoner's dilemma: 1 and 2 denote player *row* and, respectively, player *column*.

Definition 9 deserves a few remarks. The first thing to notice is that the notion of dependence arising from it is based on an underlying notion of rationality. In our case we opted for the ones that are, arguably, most standard in a pure strategy setting like ours: best response and dominant strategy. But it must be clear that other choices are possible (e.g. strict best response, strict dominance) and that Definition 9 could be easily extended to accommodate them.

Secondly, a consequence of the definition is that, given any game, we can always associate to any profile σ a binary relation—R_σ^{BR} or R_σ^{DS}—on the set of players which describes who depends on whom for the realization of that profile. In other words, we can associate to each profile σ a graph $\langle N, R_\sigma^{BR} \rangle$, or a graph $\langle N, R_\sigma^{DS} \rangle$, which provide a structural description of the sort of dependencies at work in the underlying game. We call these graphs *dependence graphs*.

Example 4 (The dependence graph of the prisoner's dilemma) *Consider again the prisoner's dilemma in Figure 1. Its best response dependence graph is depicted in Figure 2. There we notice that, for instance, the relation $R_{(U,R)}^{BR}$ depicted in the up-right corner is such that column depends on him/herself (it is a reflexive point), as it plays its own best response, but also on row, as row does not play its own best response but a best response for column. Therefore (U,R) displays some kind of 'unbalance'. On the contrary, the graph associated to (U,R) depicts a cycle of BR-depdendence in which row plays a best response for column and, vice versa, column for row.*

The last remark worth making is that, in general, relations R_σ^{BR} and R_σ^{DS} do not enjoy any particular structural property. However, when they do, such structural properties can have a precise game theoretic meaning. The following simple fact gives a simple example of how structural properties of dependence graphs relate to game-theoretic properties of the underlying games.

Fact 1 (Reflexive dependencies and equilibria) *Let $\mathcal{G}$ be a game and let $x \in \{BR, DS\}$. It holds that: for any profile σ, R_σ^x is reflexive iff σ is an x-equilibrium.*

	g	$\neg g$
g	3,3,3	2,4,2
$\neg g$	4,2,2	1,1,0

g

	g	$\neg g$
g	2,2,4	0,1,1
$\neg g$	1,0,1	1,1,1

$\neg g$

Fig. 3 A three person game. Player 1 denotes *row*, player 2 *column*, and player 3 chooses between the right and left matrices.

In other words, any profile in which players depend on themselves—either in a best response or in a dominant strategy sense—is an equilibrium of the corresponding type—BR or DS. Figure 2 offers a good pictorial example. The 'defect-defect' profile (D,R), the Nash equilibrium, gives indeed rise to a BR-dependence relation which is reflexive.

3.2 Cycles

We have seen above how the reflexivity of dependence is related to the existence of equilibria (Fact 1). In this section we move to a more general property of dependence relations, the existence of cycles. The literature on dependence theory in MAS puts particular emphasis on this property as cycles intuitively suggest that there exist common ground for cooperation: if an individual depends on an other individual, and the latter depends in turn on the first to achieve a specific outcome, the choice of that outcome means that the individuals are doing each other a favour. This perspective is very clearly expressed, for instance, in [2, 3], where dependence cycles are taken to signal the possibility of social interaction between players of a *do-ut-des* (give-to-get) type.

In that literature, however, dependence relations are considered as given—they do not arise from underlying structures such as games—and so are cycles, whose importance is not motivated in terms of some underlying rationale, but is taken for granted. In this and the following sections (Sections 3.2-3.4) we show how, starting from dependence relations that arise from an underlying game (Definition 9), we can give precise game-theoretic reasons for the significance of dependence cycles in strategic settings. So let us start with a definition of what a dependence cycle is.

Definition 10 (Dependence cycles) *Let* $G = (N,S,\Sigma_i,\succeq_i,o)$ *be a game,* (N,R_σ^x) *be its dependence structure for profile* σ *with* $x \in \{BR,DS\}$, *and let* $i,j \in N$. *An* R_σ^x-*dependence cycle* $\mathfrak{c}$ *of length* $k-1$ *in* G *is a tuple* $(a_1,\ldots,a_k)$ *such that:*

1. $a_1,\ldots,a_k \in N$;
2. $a_1 = a_k$;
3. $\forall a_i,a_j$ *with* $1 \leq i \neq j < k,\ a_i \neq a_j$;
4. $a_1 R_\sigma^x a_2 R_\sigma^x \ldots R_\sigma^x a_{k-1} R_\sigma^x a_k$.

Given a cycle $\mathfrak{c} = (a_1,\ldots,a_k)$, *its orbit* $O(\mathfrak{c}) = \{a_1,\ldots,a_{k-1}\}$ *denotes the set of its elements.*

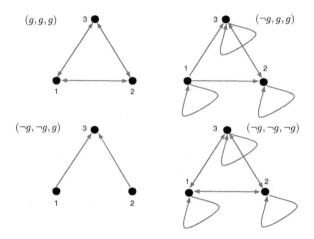

Fig. 4 Some BR-dependencies from the game matrix in Figure 3 (Example 5).

In other words, cycles are sequences of pairwise different players, except for the first and the last which are equal, such that all players are linked by a dependence relation. Note that the definition allows for cycles of length 1, whose orbit is a singleton, i.e., reflexive arcs. Those are the cycles occurring at reflexive points in the graph.

We have already seen in Example 4 that the cooperative outcome of the prisoner's dilemma exhibits a cycle linking *row* and *column* (see Figure 2). Even more interesting are cycles in games with more than two players.

Example 5 (Cycles in a three-person game) *Consider the following three-person game.[3] A committee of three jurors has to decide whether to declare a defendant in a trial guilty or not. All the three jurors want the defendant to be found guilty, however, all three prefer that the others declare the defendant while she declares her innocent. Also, they do not want to be the only ones declaring the defendant guilty if the other two vote for innocence. They all know each other's preferences. Figure 3 gives a payoff matrix for such game. Figure 4 depicts some cyclic BR-dependencies inherent in the game presented. Player 1 is row, player 2 column, and player 3 picks the right or left matrix. Among the ones depicted, (g,g,g) display s six cycles of length 3 and so does $(\neg g, \neg g, \neg g)$, which also contains three reflexive arcs—and hence, by Fact 1, is a Nash equilibrium. Also $(\neg g, g, g)$ is a Nash equilibrium, it does not contain any cycle of length 3, but it does contain two of length two between players 2 and 3. Finally, $(\neg g, \neg g, g)$ does not contain any cycle.*

---

[3] It can be viewed as a weak three-person variant of the prisoner's dilemma, where defection, although not being a dominant strategy, can turn out being a best response for all players, making it—like in the prisoner's dilemma—a Nash equilibrium.

3.3 Reciprocity

We now proceed to isolate some specific forms of cycles. These will be used to define several variants of a property of strategic games which we call *reciprocity*. The idea is that, depending on the properties of the dependence cycles of a given profile, we can isolate some significant ways in which players are interconnected via a dependence relation. These will be linked, in the next section, to the existence of equilibria in appropriately transformed games.

Definition 11 (Reciprocity) *Let G be a game, σ a profile, and $\langle N, R_\sigma^x \rangle$ the corresponding dependence graph with $x \in \{BR, DS\}$. We say that:*

1. *a profile σ is x-reciprocal if and only if there exists a partition $P(N)$ of N such that each element p of the partition is the orbit of some R_σ^x-cycle in $\langle N, R_\sigma^x \rangle$;*
2. *for $C \subseteq N$, a profile σ is partially x-reciprocal in C (or C-x-reciprocal) if and only if there exists a partition $P(C)$ of C such that each element p of the partition is the orbit of some R_σ^x-cycle in $\langle N, R_\sigma^x \rangle$;*
3. *a profile σ is trivially x-reciprocal if and only if $\langle N, R_\sigma^x \rangle$ is reflexive, that is, it contains $|N|$ x-cycles whose orbits are singletons;*
4. *a profile σ is fully x-reciprocal if and only if $\langle N, R_\sigma^x \rangle$ contains at least one x-cycle with orbit N (i.e., a Hamiltonian cycle).*

Let us explain the above definitions by considering the case of best response dependence (BR-dependence). A profile σ is BR-reciprocal if all players belong to some cycle of BR-dependence. This is the case in both the (U, L), i.e., 'cooperate-cooperate', and (D, R), i.e., 'defect-defect', outcomes in the prisoner's dilemma (see Figures 1 and 2). The other two outcomes are not BR-reciprocal as one of the two players does not belong to the orbit of any cycle.

Along the same lines, a profile σ is partially BR-reciprocal in coalition C (or C-BR-reciprocal) if all the members of C are partitioned by cycles of BR-dependence. This means, intuitively, that independently on whether the players outside of coalition C are linked by dependencies or not, the members of C are in a situation of reciprocity in which everybody plays a best response strategy for somebody else in the coalition. So, in the prisoner's dilemma, outcome (D, L)—maximally preferred by *row*—is {*row*}-BR-reciprocal as *row* is playing a best response for herself, hence being in a dependence relation with herself. A perfectly symmetric consideration can be made about (U, R) and *column*.

Finally, trivial and full BR-reciprocity are special cases of BR-reciprocity. In the first case all players belong to a reflexive arc, that is, all players play their own best response strategy. In the second case there exists one Hamiltonian cycle, that is, all players are connected to one another by a path of BR-dependence. For example, inspecting the BR-dependencies in the Prisoner Dilemma (Figure 2) it can be observed that: (U, L) is fully BR-reciprocal as it contains two Hamiltonian cycles: *row* $R_{(U,L)}^{BR}$ *column* $R_{(U,L)}^{BR}$ *row* and *column* $R_{(U,L)}^{BR}$ *row* $R_{(U,L)}^{BR}$ *column*. On the other hand, (D, R) is trivially BR-reciprocal as the only cycles are *column* $R_{(D,R)}^{BR}$ *column* and *row* $R_{(D,R)}^{BR}$ *row*.

To sum up, a profile is reciprocal when the corresponding dependence relation, be it a BR- or DS-dependence, clusters the players into non-overlapping groups whose members are all part of some cycle of dependencies (including degenerate ones such as reflexive links). It is partially reciprocal if its dependence graph contains at least one cycle. Trivial and full reciprocity refer to two extreme cases of reciprocity. In the first case the cycles are reflexive arcs and in the second case all players are 'visited' by one and the same cycle.

Before moving to the next section, we first provide one further illustrative example and then study the relation between the two types of reciprocity that arise from Definition 11: best response and dominant strategy reciprocity.

Example 6 (Reciprocity in the three person game) *Let us go back to Example 5 and to its BR-dependence graph given Figure 4. The graph of profile (g,g,g) contains cycles which all yield the partition $\{\{1,2,3\}\}$ of the set of players. It is then a fully BR-reciprocal profile. The cycles of profile $(\neg g,g,g)$, instead, yield two partitions: $\{\{1\},\{2\},\{3\}\}$ and $\{\{1\},\{2,3\}\}$. So that profile is BR-reciprocal, but not fully BR-reciprocal. As its graph is reflexive, it is trivially BR-reciprocal, and also partially BR-reciprocal with respect each nonempty coalition. Interestingly, profile $(\neg g,\neg g,\neg g)$ it is both fully and trivially BR-reciprocal. Intuitively, in that profile each player acts in favour of some other player by playing his/her own best response strategy. Finally, profile $(\neg g,\neg g,g)$ does not exhibit any form of reciprocity.*

Here below we report a few relevant facts concerning the interplay between DS- and BR-reciprocity.

Fact 2 (DS- vs. BR-reciprocity) *Let G be a game, σ a profile, $C \subseteq N$, and $\langle N, R_\sigma^x \rangle$ be its dependence graph with $x \in \{BR, DS\}$. The following holds:*

1. *σ is C-BR-reciprocal iff σ_C is BR-reciprocal $G \downarrow \sigma'_{\overline{C}}$;*
2. *σ is C-DS-reciprocal iff σ_C is DS-reciprocal in $G \downarrow \sigma'_{\overline{C}}$ for any profile σ';*
3. *if σ is C-DS-reciprocal, then σ is C-BR-reciprocal, but not vice versa;*
4. *if σ is DS-reciprocal, then σ is BR-reciprocal, but not vice versa.*

In words, the first claim states that a profile σ is partially BR-reciprocal in a coalition C if and only if the restriction σ_C of σ to C is BR-reciprocal with respect to the subgame (recall Definition 2) obtained from G by fixing the strategy of the complement $\overline{C}$ of coalition C. More concisely, a profile is partially BR-reciprocal in a given coalition if and only if it is BR-reciprocal in the subgame obtained by fixing what the players do who do not belong to the coalition. The second claim is similar and states that a profile is partially DS-reciprocal in a given coalition if and only if it is DS-reciprocal in all subgames obtainable by fixing the strategies of the players who are not in the coalition. These two claims show a first interesting difference between partial BR- and DS- reciprocity: partial BR-reciprocity is bound by the dependence structure of the current profile while partial DS-reciprocity is not. This is not surprising as the two forms of reciprocity build one on the notion of best response, and the other on the stronger notion of dominant strategy. A second important difference is pointed out by the third and fourth claims, which show that, as expected, that (partial) DS-reciprocity is a stronger notion than (partial) BR-reciprocity.

We now proceed to give a game theoretic interpretation of these definitions of reciprocity based on the notion of dependence cycle.

	L	R
U	0,0	1,0
D	0,1	1,0

$\mathcal{G}$

	L	R
	0,0	0,1
	1,0	1,0

$\mathcal{G}^\mu$

Fig. 5 The two horsemen game matrix and its permutation modeling the horse-swap.

3.4 Reciprocity and equilibrium

We provide a characterization of reciprocity as defined in Definition 11 in terms of standard solution concepts. However, we first have to complement the set of notions provided in Section 2 with the notion of permuted game.

Definition 12 (Permuted games) *Let* $G = (N, S, \Sigma_i, \succeq_i, o)$ *be a game,* σ *a profile, and* $\mu : N \mapsto N$ *a bijection on* N. *The* μ-*permutation of game* G *is the game* $G^\mu = (N^\mu, S^\mu, \Sigma^\mu, \succeq_i^\mu, o^\mu)$ *such that:*

- $N^\mu = N$;
- $S^\mu = S$;
- *for all* $i \in N$, $\Sigma_i^\mu = \Sigma_{\mu(i)}$;
- *for all* $i \in N$, $\succeq_i^\mu = \succeq_i$;
- $o_\mu : \times_{i \in N} \Sigma_{\mu(i)} \to S$ *is such that* $o_\mu(\mu(\sigma)) = o(\sigma)$, *where* $\mu(\sigma)$ *denotes the permutation of* σ *according to* μ.

Intuitively, a permuted game G^μ is therefore a game where the strategies of each player are redistributed according to μ in the sense that i's strategies become $\mu(i)$'s strategies, where players keep the same preferences over outcomes, and where the outcome function assigns same outcomes to same profiles.

Example 7 (Two horsemen [17]) *"Two horsemen are on a forest path chatting about something. A passerby M, the mischief maker, comes along and having plenty of time and a desire for amusement, suggests that they race against each other to a tree a short distance away and he will give a prize of $100. However, there is an interesting twist. He will give the $100 to the owner of the slower horse. Let us call the two horsemen Bill and Joe. Joe's horse can go at 35 miles per hour, whereas Bill's horse can only go 30 miles per hour. Since Bill has the slower horse, he should get the $100. The two horsemen start, but soon realize that there is a problem. Each one is trying to go slower than the other and it is obvious that the race is not going to finish. [...] Thus they end up [...] with both horses going at 0 miles per hour. [...] However, along comes another passerby, let us call her S , the problem solver, and the situation is explained to her. She turns out to have a clever solution. She advises the two men to switch horses. Now each man has an incentive to go fast, because by making his competitor's horse go faster, he is helping his own horse to win!"* [17, p. 195-196].

Once the game of the example is depicted as the left-hand side game matrix in Figure 5, it is possible to view the second passerby's solution as a bijection μ which changes the game to the right-hand side version. Now *row* can play *column*'s moves and *column* can play *row*'s moves. The result is a swap of (D, L)

with (U,R), since (D,L) in G^μ corresponds to (U,R) in G and vice versa. On the other hand, (U,L) and (D,R) stay the same, as the exchange of strategies do not affect them. As a consequence, profile (D,R), in which both horsemen engage in the race, becomes a dominant strategy equilibrium.

On the ground of these intuitions, it is possible to obtain a simple characterization of the different notions of reciprocity given in Definition 11 as the existence of equilibria in appropriately permuted games.

Theorem 1 (Reciprocity in equilibrium) *Let G be a game and $\langle N, R_\sigma^x \rangle$ be its dependence graph with $x \in \{BR, DS\}$ and σ be a profile. It holds that:*

1. *σ is x-reciprocal iff there exists a bijection $\mu : N \mapsto N$ s.t. σ is a x-equilibrium in the permuted game G^μ;*
2. * σ is partially BR-reciprocal in C (or C-BR-reciprocal) iff there exists a bijection $\mu : C \mapsto C$ s.t. σ_C is a BR-equilibrium in the permuted subgame $(G \downarrow \sigma_{\overline{C}})^\mu$;*
   * σ is partially DS-reciprocal in C (or C-DS-reciprocal) iff there exists a bijection $\mu : C \mapsto C$ s.t. σ_C is a DS-equilibrium in all permuted subgames $(G \downarrow \sigma'_{\overline{C}})^\mu$ for any profile σ';*
3. *σ is trivially x-reciprocal iff σ is an x-equilibrium in G^μ where μ is the identity over N;*
4. *σ is fully x-reciprocal iff there exists a bijection $\mu : N \mapsto N$ s.t. σ is a x-equilibrium in the permuted game G^μ and μ is such that $\{(i,j) \mid i \in N \ \& \ j = \mu(i)\}$ is a Hamiltonian cycle in N.*

Intuitively, the theorem connects all cycle-based forms of reciprocity identified in Definition 11 with equilibria in (sub-)games that could be obtained by appropriate permutations of the underlying game. Furthermore, the instructions for such permutations—which strategies go to which player—are provided by the existent cycles. For example, if the profile is trivially reciprocal (third claim), then it is already an equilibrium, and if it is fully reciprocal (fourth claim), it then becomes an equilibrium via a permutation that follows one of the available Hamiltonian cycles over the set of players.

We hold Theorem 1 to be of particular interest for two reasons. First, it provides a clear connection between intuitions developed in the theory of dependence—such as the significance of cycles—with notions which lie at the hart of game theory—such as the one of equilibrium. Second, it provides a systematic dependence-based rationale for modifications of games that allow desirable but unstable outcomes—such as the cooperative outcome in the prisoner's dilemma—to become equilibria.

3.4.1 Implementation via permutation

As just discussed, in view of Theorem 1, permutations can be fruitfully viewed as ways of *implementing*—in a social software sense [17]—reciprocal profiles. This terminology is worth casting in a definition.

<table>
<tr><td></td><td>L</td><td>R</td></tr>
<tr><td>U</td><td>2,2</td><td>0,3</td></tr>
<tr><td>D</td><td>3,0</td><td>1,1</td></tr>
</table>

$\mathcal{G}$

<table>
<tr><td></td><td>L</td><td>R</td></tr>
<tr><td>U</td><td>2,2</td><td>3,0</td></tr>
<tr><td>D</td><td>0,3</td><td>1,1</td></tr>
</table>

$\mathcal{G}^\mu$

Fig. 6 The prisoner's dilemma matrix and its permutation swapping *row* with *column* according to the cycle of profile (U,L).

Definition 13 (Implementation as game permutation) *Let $\mathcal{G}$ be a game, σ a profile and $\langle N, R_\sigma^x \rangle$ be its dependence graph. Let also $\mu : N \mapsto N$ be a bijection with $C \subseteq N$. We say that:*

1. *μ BR-implements σ iff σ is a BR-equilibrium in $\mathcal{G}^\mu$;*
2. *μ DS-implements σ iff σ is a DS-equilibrium in $\mathcal{G}^\mu$;*
3. *μ partially BR-implements σ in C iff σ_C is an BR-equilibrium in $(\mathcal{G} \downarrow \sigma_{\overline{C}})^\mu$;*
4. *μ partially DS-implements σ in C iff σ_C is a DS-equilibrium in $(\mathcal{G} \downarrow \sigma'_{\overline{C}})^\mu$ for any profile σ'.*

Intuitively, implementation is here understood as a way of transforming a game in such a way that the desirable outcomes, in the transformed game, are brought about at an equilibrium point. In this sense we talk about BR- or DS-implementation. Analogously, partial BR- or DS-implementation consist in the realization of the desirable outcomes as equilibria in one subgame (partial BR-implementation) or all possible sub-games (partial DS-implementation).

Example 8 (Implementation of cooperation in the prisoner's dilemma) *Just like the two-horsemen example (Example 7) we can think of implementing the cooperative outcome (U,L) of the prisoner's dilemma (Figure 1) by permuting the game according to the permutation μ dictated by one of the Hamiltonian cycles present in the dependence graph of that profile (Figure 2): $\mu(row) = column$ and $\mu(column) = row$. In the resulting game where, essentially, row decides whether column plays L or R and column whether row plays U or D, the cooperative outcome is a Nash equilibrium by Theorem 1 (see Figure 6). An example of partial BR-implementation is provided by Example 5 (see also Figure 3). There, profile $(\neg g, g, g)$ is partially BR-reciprocal in coalition $\{1,2\}$ (see Example 6). A permutation between 2 and 3 would yield a game such that (g,g) is a Nash equilibrium in the sub-game obtained by fixing the strategy of player 1 to $\neg g$ (notice, however, that in this case the identity permutation would also guarantee such result). In other words, was it so that 1 had already made his/her choice, swapping the strategies of 2 and 3 would lead to a stable outcome.*

4 Solving dependencies: dependence games

The previous sections have shown how reciprocity can be given two corresponding formal characterizations: existence of cycles in a dependence structure, and existence of equilibria in a suitably permuted game (Theorem 1). In the present section, we apply the notion of reciprocity to obtain a refinement of coalitional games. The intuition behind such refinement consists, in a nutshell, to allow coalitions to form only in presence of some sort of reciprocity. This will allow us to study a form of dependence-based cooperation which arises in strategic settings when the players' interests are somehow aligned.

A similar intuition can already be found in [20]:

> "As soon as there is a possibility of choosing with whom to establish parallel interests, this becomes a case of choosing an ally. When alliances are formed, it is to be expected that some kind of mutual understanding between the two players involved will be necessary. [...] One can also state it this way: A parallelism of interests makes a cooperation desirable, and therefore will probably lead to an agreement between the players involved." [20, p. 221]

Once this intuitive notion of "parallelism of interests" is taken to mean "mutual dependence" [6] or "dependence cycle" [19] a bridge is laid between the theory of cooperative games and dependence theory, as a special case of cooperation. By pursuing this research line, we intend to show that dependence theory can feed original insights into the theory of games.

4.1 Agreements

We now introduce the notion of players' agreement. The key idea behind it is that, given a reciprocal profile (of some sort according to Definition 11), the players can fruitfully *agree* to transform the game by some suitable permutation of sets of strategies.

Definition 14 (Agreements and partial agreements) *Let G be a game, (N, R_σ^x) be its dependence structure in σ with $x \in \{BR, DS\}$, and let $i, j \in N$. A pair (σ, μ) is:*

1. *an x-agreement for G if σ is an x-reciprocal profile, and $\mu : N \mapsto N$ a bijection which x-implements σ;*
2. *a partial x-agreement in C (or a C-x-agreement) for G, if σ is a C-x-reciprocal profile and $\mu : C \mapsto C$ a bijection which C-x-implements σ.*

The set of x-agreements of a game G is denoted x-AGR(G) and the set of partial x-agreements, that is the set of pairs (σ, μ) for which there exists a C such that μ C-x-implements σ, is denoted x-pAGR(G).

Intuitively, a (partial) agreement, of BR or DS type, can be seen as the result of coordination (endogenous, via the players themselves, or exogenous, via a third party like in Example 7) selecting a desirable outcome and realizing it by an appropriate exchange of strategies.

Example 9 (Agreements in the prisoner's dilemma) *Let us go back to the prisoner's dilemma. Agreement $((D, R), \mu)$ with $\mu(i) = i$ for all players, is the standard DS-equilibrium of the strategic game. But there is another possible agreement, where the players swap their strategies: it is $((U, L), v)$, for which $v(i) = N \setminus \{i\}$. Here row plays cooperatively for column and column plays cooperatively for row. Of the same kind* *is the agreement arising in Example 7. Notice that in such example, the agreement is the result of coordination mediated by a third party (the second passerby). Analogous considerations can also be done about Example 5 where, for instance, $((g, g, g), \mu)$ with $\mu(1) = 2, \mu(2) = 3, \mu(3) = 1$ is a BR- agreement.*

In what follows we will focus only on DS-agreements and partial DS-agreements so, whenever we talk about agreements and partial agreements, we mean DS-agreements and partial DS-agreements, unless stated otherwise.

4.2 Dependence-based coalitional games

Agreements could be seen as a *cooperative solutions* of strategic games that exploit the dependence relations between the players. As such agreements can be used to study strategic games as coalitional games, where players form coalitions whenever they are in some appropriate relation of reciprocity. This intuition leads us to the definition of classes of coalitional games based on the notion of dependence.

We proceed as follows. First, starting from a game G, we consider its representation C^G as a coalitional game as illustrated in Section 2 (Definition 6). As Definition 6 abstracts from dependence-theoretic considerations we refine it in two ways, corresponding to the two different sorts of dependence upon which we want to build the coalitional game:

1. The first refinement is obtained by defining a coalitional game C^G_{DEP} capturing the intuition that coalitions form only by means of *agreements* (Definition 14). Such games are called *dependence games*.
2. The second one is obtained by defining a coalitional game C^G_{pDEP} capturing the intuition that coalitions form only by means of *partial agreements* (Definition 14). Such games are called *partial dependence games*.

These games can then be studied from the point of view of stability concepts such as the core, which we refrain from doing here in detail (the interested reader is referred to [11, 10]).

4.2.1 Dependence games

Definition 15 (Dependence games from strategic ones) *Let $G = (N, S, \Sigma_i, \succeq_i, o)$ be a game. The dependence game $C^G_{DEP} = (N, S, E^G_{DEP}, \succeq_i)$ of G is a coalitional game where the effectivity function E^G_{DEP} is defined as follows:*

$$X \in E^G_{DEP}(C) \Leftrightarrow \exists \sigma_C, \mu_C \text{ s.t.}$$
$$\exists \sigma_{\overline{C}}, \mu_{\overline{C}} : [((\sigma_C, \sigma_{\overline{C}}), (\mu_C, \mu_{\overline{C}})) \in AGR(G)]$$
$$\text{AND } [\forall \sigma_{\overline{C}}, \mu_{\overline{C}} : [((\sigma_C, \sigma_{\overline{C}}), (\mu_C, \mu_{\overline{C}})) \in AGR(G)$$
$$\text{IMPLIES } o(\sigma_C, \sigma_{\overline{C}}) \in X]].$$

where $\mu : N \rightarrow N$ is a bijection. The core of a dependence game $C^{\mathcal{G}}_{DEP}$ is denoted $CORE(C^{\mathcal{G}}_{DEP})$.

This somewhat intricate formulation states nothing but that the effectivity function $E^{\mathcal{G}}_{DEP}(C)$ associates with each coalition C the states which are outcomes of agreements (and hence of reciprocal profiles), and which C can force via partial agreements (σ_C, μ_C) regardless of the partial agreements $(\sigma_{\overline{C}}, \mu_{\overline{C}})$ of $\overline{C}$.

4.2.2 Partial dependence games

Definition 16 (Partial dependence games from strategic ones) *Let $\mathcal{G} = (N, S, \Sigma_i, \succeq_i$, o) be a game. The partial dependence game $C^{\mathcal{G}}_{pDEP} = (N, S, E^{\mathcal{G}}_{pDEP}, \succeq_i)$ of $\mathcal{G}$ is a coalitional game where the effectivity function $E^{\mathcal{G}}_{pDEP}$ is defined as follows:*

$$X \in E^{\mathcal{G}}_{pDEP}(C) \Leftrightarrow \exists \sigma_C, \mu_C \text{ s.t.}$$
$$(\sigma_C, \mu_C) \in pAGR(\mathcal{G})$$
$$\text{AND } [\forall \sigma_{\overline{C}} : o(\sigma_C, \sigma_{\overline{C}}) \in X]].$$

where $\mu_C : C \rightarrow C$ is a bijection. The core of a partial dependence game $C^{\mathcal{G}}_{DEP}$ is denoted $CORE(C^{\mathcal{G}}_{DEP})$.

Partial dependence games are defined by just looking at the set of outcomes that each coalition can force by means of a partial agreement. Unlike Definition 15, Definition 16 is much closer to the standard definition of coalitional games based on strategic ones (Definition 6).

4.3 Coalitional, dependence, partial dependence effectivity

The coalitional game $C^{\mathcal{G}}$ built on a strategic game $\mathcal{G}$ and its dependence-based counterparts $C^{\mathcal{G}}_{DEP}$ and $C^{\mathcal{G}}_{pDEP}$ are clearly related. The following fact shows how.

Fact 3 (Effectivity functions related) *The following relations hold:*

1. *For all $\mathcal{G}$: $E^{\mathcal{G}}_{pDEP} \subseteq E^{\mathcal{G}}$;*

2. *It does not hold that for all $\mathcal{G}$: $E^{\mathcal{G}}_{DEP} \subseteq E^{\mathcal{G}}_{pDEP}$; nor it holds that for all $\mathcal{G}$: $E^{\mathcal{G}}_{pDEP} \subseteq E^{\mathcal{G}}_{DEP}$;*

3. *It does not hold that for all $\mathcal{G}$: $E^{\mathcal{G}}_{DEP} \subseteq E^{\mathcal{G}}$; nor it holds that for all $\mathcal{G}$: $E^{\mathcal{G}} \subseteq E^{\mathcal{G}}_{DEP}$.*

The fact shows that dependence-based effectivity function considerably modify the powers assigned to coalitions by the standard definition of coalitional games on strategic ones (Definition 6). Partial dependence effectivity functions instead really weaken the notion of coalitional ability, reducing the coalitional strategy at players' disposal. An important formal consequence of Fact

$$
\begin{array}{c|c|c|c|}
 & N & S & O \\
\hline
N & 2,2 & 2,0 & 9,1 \\
\hline
S & 0,2 & 0,0 & 0,1 \\
\hline
O & 1,9 & 1,0 & 8,8 \\
\hline
\end{array}
$$

Fig. 7 Strangers on a train.

3 is the establishment of the relation between $CORE(C^{\mathcal{G}})$, $CORE(C^{\mathcal{G}}_{DEP})$ and $CORE(C^{\mathcal{G}}_{pDEP})$, as a direct consequence of the inclusion relation among their corresponding effectivity functions.

Summing up, the results in this section have shown that agreements and partial agreements are a form of coalitional power that can be related to cooperative game theory. In particular, partial agreements can be seen as a weakened forms of coalitional strategies (Fact 3), i.e. those strategies that can be executed only in presence of mutual reciprocity among the members of a coalition. As such partial dependence games, that generalize dependence games, should be understood as an intermediate level between the individualistic perspective studied in strategic games and the unconstrained coalitional perspective analyzed in cooperative games.

4.4 *A recapitulative example:* **Strangers on a train**

In this section we illustrate the building blocks of our theory of dependence within one all-encompassing example.

Example 10 (Strangers on a Train) *In Patricia Highsmith's novel[4], Strangers on a Train [13], that Alfred Hitchcock turned in 1951 into a movie with the same title, the following story takes place:*

> *Two protagonists wish to get out of an unhappy relationship. Architect Guy Haines wants to get rid of his unfaithful wife, Miriam, in order to marry the woman he loves, Anne Faulkner. Charles Anthony Bruno, a psychopathic playboy, deeply desires his father's death. On a train to see his wife, Guy meets Bruno, who proposes the idea of exchange murders: Bruno will kill Miriam if Guy kills Bruno's father; neither of them will have a motive, and the police will have no reason to suspect either of them.*

We can illustrate our protagonists' setting, before any agreements are taken, with the two persons' matrix in Figure 7.

In the example, both players have the same possibilities: either do nothing (N), commit the murder of their own significant other (S), or commit the murder of the other persons' significant other (O). Let Guy be the row player and Bruno the column player. Focusing on the choices of Guy, we notice that N is a *dominant strategy* for Guy (Definition 3), as whatever strategy Bruno plays, N is a best response to that strategy. For Bruno the reasoning pattern is symmetric,

---

[4] We thank Paul Harrenstein for having brought this example to our attention.

	N	S	O
N	2,2	0,2	1,9
S	2,0	0,0	1,0
O	9,1	0,1	8,8

Fig. 8 Swapping murders.

therefore his strategy N is also a dominant strategy. These two facts taken together mean that the strategy profile (N,N) is a *dominant strategy equilibrium* (Definition 4).

However the story takes an interesting twist once we consider what players could do for each other. The strategy O, by Guy, is a *dominant strategy for Bruno* (Definition 8), as it is good for Bruno whatever Bruno himself decides to do. Same for Guy: the strategy O by Bruno is a *dominant strategy for Guy*. Once we identify what players can do for each other, the dependence relations can be automatically drawn: Guy *DS-depends* on Bruno for strategy O and on himself for strategy N (Definition 9), while Bruno *DS-depends on Guy* for strategy O and on himself for strategy N. Dependence *cycles* (Definition 10) suggests the possibility of reciprocal play: the profile (N,N), that is associated with two dependence cycles of lenght 1, is *trivially DS-reciprocal* (Definition 11), i.e. the only possible way for players to agree is to play for themselves, while the profile (O,O), that is associated with an hamiltonian dependence cycle, is *fully DS-reciprocal* (Definition 11), i.e. players can profit by playing for each other.

In this situation two *agreements* would be possible (Definition 14): $((N,N),\mu)$ and $((O,O),\nu)$, where μ is the identity permutation and ν is the players' transposition. However notice that the outcome resulting from (O,O) is preferred by both players to the outcome resulting from (N,N). The former is in fact *stable* as it belongs to the core of the resulting *dependence game* (Definition 15). Therefore $((O,O),\nu)$ can be considered as a *rational* outcome of the dependence game: Guy would find it reasonable to kill Bruno's father only if he knew that Bruno would kill his wife, and the same for Bruno. This would be possible if Guy could *lend* is action of killing *in exchange to* Bruno's one. The proposal of swapping murders, i.e. a simultaneous exchange of favours between the strangers, suggests itself. If this agreement could take place then the game would be transformed in the one pictured in Figure 8, the transposition of the matrix in Figure 7 under swap of strategies. The swap of players shown in this game *DS-implements* (O,O) (Definition 13).

5 Discussion

In this final section, we discuss related work, point at future directions of research, and conclude the paper.

5.1 *Related work*

Before concluding it is worth spending a few words trying to relate our game-theoretic view of dependence to existing literature in MAS. Actually, to the best of our knowledge, almost no attention has been dedicated up till now to the relation between game theory and dependence theory. There are, however, two noteworthy recent exceptions: [4] and [18].

In [4], the authors study the sort of dependence relations between players which arise within a specific class of games called Boolean games [12]. In a nutshell, Boolean games are n-player games where players act by controlling the truth value of a propositional variable, and where players' preferences are dichotomous, that is, each player has a single goal—expressed by a propositional formula—which is either fulfilled or not. The work presented in [18] then extends some of the results presented in [4] to the class of cooperative Boolean games [9], that is, a coalitional version of Boolean games. Like in our case, the authors of [4] and [18] look at dependence relations as graph-theoretical information hidden within the game structure. However, there are several important differences.

First of all the simple structure of Boolean games, and in particular the fact that players' preferences are dichotomous, allows for a definition of dependence which is considerably simpler than ours (Section 3.1):

> *Player i depends on player j if and only if j controls some propositional variables which are relevant for the satisfaction of i's goal.*

It is easy to see that such definition cannot be straightforwardly generalized to the case in which players have non-dichotomous preferences, as in that case it becomes unclear what the 'goal' of player *i* actually is. In fact, this is precisely the sort of issue that we went around by proposing Definition 9. Notice that, as a consequence, the two definitions of dependence differ radically in that the one proposed by [4] and [18] views dependence as a property of a game, while ours views dependence as a property of the outcome of a game.

Secondly, it is worth mentioning an underlying difference in motivation between our work and the one presented in [4] and [18]. The latter develops the analysis of dependence relations essentially as a means to extract graphical information which eases the complexity of computing Nash equilibria in Boolean games and the core in cooperative Boolean games. What motivates our analysis instead, is rather the attempt to provide a game-theoretical foundation to dependence theory as such. This lead us to consider strategic games in their generality—rather than Boolean games—and to look at dependence as a means to characterize interesting properties of games (e.g., reciprocity) and to define a specific class of coalitional games, which is the aim of Section 4.

5.2 *Future work*

The formalization of dependence relations and agreements provided here does not consider a variety of subtleties that might play a role in interaction. We list a few of them, sketching how to extend our framework in order to incorporate these more complex features.

5.2.1 Partial strategy permutation

Agreements are implemented by strategy permutation among stakeholders. If this operation fits perfectly games where players are endowed with a small number of strategies, such as those of Figures 1 and 5, it seems more problematic when players are endowed with a larger number of strategies. Therefore, players may be interested in favors without necessarily having to lend control of all their actions. To this purpose, it would make sense to restrict possible permutations—exchanges of favors—to subsets of the available strategies. This could be done via a function that, when applied to a game G, yields a game identical to G, but where profiles are restricted to the available strategies, and where the outcome function is restricted accordingly. The intuition behind restricting the game is that players decide in advance the type of strategies that they allow to be agreed upon.

5.2.2 AND and OR dependence

Our definition of players' dependence allows for situations, as the one illustrated in Figure 3, where a player can be simultaneously dependent on several other players, suggesting the possibility of many possible agreements. In the literature on dependence theory (cfr. [19]) this form of dependence is usually referred to as *OR dependence*, as opposed to *AND dependence*, where instead a player is dependent on the *combined strategy* of other players, i.e. a sort of dependence not on a player but on a coalition. While the first can be easily accomodated in our framework, for the latter a generalization is required, that allows a dependence relation between a player and a coalition. The informal account in [19] suggests that AND dependencies and OR dependencies have different consequences for the stability of coalitions. If a situation of AND dependence of player i on players j and k grants the latter two players a power position (as i needs both), a situation of OR dependence allows player i to choose among the possible stakeholders in a possible agreement: in some sense players profit from OR dependencies. A desirable feature of a generalized definition of dependence is to be able to account for this feature.

5.2.3 Extensive interaction

Dependence and agreements have been formulated for strategic games, where decisions have one-shot nature and no temporality is involved. However dependencies are naturally present in extensive interaction as well and agreements make perfect sense there. In order to analyze dependence in extensive games we can always adopt the standard translation of an extensive game into a strategic one [16]. Dependence relations and agreements can then be retrieved in the usual way, by resorting to the strategic game we have obtained. However extensive games have special features. Their typical solution concept, for instance, is that of *subgame perfect equilibrium*, i.e. a Nash-equilibrium that rules out incredible threats [16]. What is interesting for a theory of dependence in extensive interaction is whether analogue solution concepts can be obtained for dependence relations. A straightforward generalization of subgame perfect equilibria for someone else could be studied as an analogue to Nash-equilibrium for someone else that rules out incredible *favors*.

5.3 Conclusions

Our chapter has shown that a theory of agent dependence, first introduced by Castelfranchi and colleagues, can be fully incorporated within the theory of games, where it gives rise to forms of rationality that lie between the individual perspective of strategic games and the coalitional perspective of cooperative games. Concretely what we have shown can be articulated in two directions:

- First and foremost the intuitive notion of dependence relation originating from social and cognitive science literature [7, 5] can be given a game-theoretical semantics, contributing to the construction of solution concepts that account for its underlying dynamics. The standard solution concepts of best response and dominant strategies first provided in Definition 3 have been generalized to best response and dominant strategy for someone else in Definition 8, providing a basis for formalizing reciprocity in games.
- Second, once the game-theoretical account has been laid, central dependence-theoretic notions such as the notion of cycle have natural game-theoretic correspondents (Theorem 1). Furthermore, dependence theory has been demonstrated to give rise to types of cooperative games where solution concepts such as the core can be applied. The relation between the various forms of cooperative games where coalitions undertake agreements (dependence and partial dependence) have been analyzed. The results suggest the presence a full spectrum of cooperative solution concepts for dependence structure, that form a partial order under the inclusion relation, whose further investigation pose an interesting research challenge.

The possibility of incorporating a complex cognitive model of agent dependencies within a game-theoretical framework is no coincidence. It is our conviction that an account of social interaction based on goal governed entities that Castelfranchi calls *agents* has much in common with an account of interaction based on rational entities that von Neumann and Morgenstern call *players*. Nevertheless, Castelfranchi has often rejected a game-theoretical approach to social interaction on the grounds that it could not account for altruism. In games, he has argued, players act to maximize their utilities, ruling out the possibility of acting in someone else's interest [8]. We hope that our contribution has shown that games can naturally accomodate the notion of *playing for someone else*, countering the last criticism to an adoption of game-theoretical models in the cognitive and social sciences, which can in turn contribute to enriching game theory with more structured and realistic descriptions of social interaction.

References

1. R. Aumann. What is game theory trying to accomplish? In K. Arrow and S. Honkapohja, editors, *Frontiers of Economics*. Blackwell, 1985.
2. G. Boella, L. Sauro, and L. van der Torre. Admissible agreements among goal-directed agents. In *Proceedings of 2005 IEEE/WIC/ACM International Conference on Intelligent Agent Technology (IAT'05)*, pages 543—554. IEEE Computer Society, 2005.
3. G. Boella, L. Sauro, and L. van der Torre. Strengthening admissible coalitions. In *Proceeding of the 2006 conference on ECAI 2006: 17th European Conference on Artificial Intelligence*, pages 195—199. ACM, 2006.
4. E. Bonzon, M.-C. Lagasquie-Schiex, and J. Lang. Dependencies between players in boolean games. *International Journal of Approximate Reasoning*, 50:899—914, 2009.
5. C. Castelfranchi. Modelling social action for AI agents. *Artificial Intelligence*, 103:157—182, 1998.
6. C. Castelfranchi, A. Cesta, and M. Miceli. Dependence relations among autonomous agents. In E. Werner and Y. Demazeau, editors, *Decentralized A.I.3*. Elsevier, 1992.
7. J. Coleman. *Foundations of Social Theory*. Belknap Harvard, 1990.
8. R. Conte and C. Castelfranchi. *Cognitive and Social Action*. UCL Press, 1995.
9. P. Dunne, W. van der Hoek, S. Kraus, and M. Wooldridge. Cooperative boolean games. In *Proceedings of AAMAS 2008*, pages 1015—1022. ACM, 2008.
10. D. Grossi and P. Turrini. Dependence in games and dependence games. Under submission.
11. D. Grossi and P. Turrini. Dependence theory via game theory. In W. van der Hoek and G. Kaminka, editors, *Proceedings of AAMAS 2010*, 2010.
12. P. Harrenstein, W. van der Hoek, J.-J.Ch. Meyer, and C. Witteveen. Boolean games. In J. van Benthem, editor, *Proceedings of TARK'01*, pages 287–298. Morgan Kaufmann, 2001.
13. P. Highsmith. *Strangers on a Train*. W.W.Norton, 1950.
14. J.Sichman. Depint: Dependence-based coalition formation in an open multi-agent scenario. *Journal of Artificial Societies and Social Simulation*, 1(2), 1998.
15. H. Moulin and B. Peleg. Cores of effectivity functions and implementation theory. *Journal of Mathematical Economics*, 10:115—145, 1982.
16. M. J. Osborne and A. Rubinstein. *A Course in Game Theory*. MIT Press, 1994.
17. R.Parikh. Social software. *Synthese*, 132(3):187—211, 2002.
18. L. Sauro, L. van der Torre, and S. Villata. Dependency in cooperative boolean games. In A Håkansson, N. Nguyen, R. Hartung, R. Howlett, and L. Jain, editors, *Proceedings of KES-AMSTA 2009*, volume 5559 of *LNAI*, pages 1—10. Springer, 2009.
19. J. Sichman and R. Conte. Multi-agent dependence by dependence graphs. In *Proceedings of AAMAS 2002*, ACM, pages 483—490, 2002.

20. J. von Neumann and O. Morgenstern. *Theory of Games and Economic Behavior*. Princeton University Press, 1944.

Chapter 20
Power and leadership in virtual societies

Helder Coelho

Abstract We need smart and social agents, with good qualities, to come to the top of power, be it the macro-power of a social network and electronic corporation or the micro-power of organizations of all sorts. Power may be seen as based on dependency relations (power-over), or based on the direct control of communication and information (power-of), but an insurgent may have something more than potency to act. He is able to take initiatives, to lead, and to drive a collective to better dreams.

1 Introduction

«Quantitative differences are transformed into qualitative ones.»

K. Marx

Michael Hardt and Antonio Negri wrote, in the beginning of this century, that "The Empire emerges today as the center that supports the world wide globalization of the production networks and weaves a large and envolving web, in order to include all the power relations in its world order" (Hardt and Negri, 2001). This quotation shows that we need to invest more effort on studying the two forms of power (potestas versus potentia), namely in thinking in depth on individual power (power-of), the potency to lead and drive plans (sequence of goals and actions) to overthrow the present state of affairs. The past events on north Africa 2011 (Tunisia, Egypt, Libya) are an example of experiments and procedural essays tried for the first time to change the current state of affairs.

Helder Coelho
LabMAg,
Laboratory of Agent Modelling (LabMAg), Faculty of Sciences, University of Lisbon, Portugal
e-mail: hcoelho@di.fc.ul.pt

We need a different sort of smart and social agents (Coelho, Rocha and Trigo, 2010), with qualities (will) and character (purposefulness), to come to the top of power, be it the macro-power of an electronic corporation or the micro-power of organizations of all sorts, and be able to transform it. And, also to reflect on the ethics of collective passions, of the imagination and desire of the multitude.

Power may be seen as based only on dependency relations (power-over), or based on the direct control of communication and information (power-of). Along the present paper our focus is on the second situation (Castells, 2009), and our idea is to discover the agent architecture to grasp power-of, ie. to sketch a kind of an active agent, in the middle of an insurrection, aiming for social change and capable of acting by influencing and leading the minds of others.

In all societies, rules that govern institutions and organizations manifest power relationships (Castelfranchi, Falcone and Piunti, 2006; Castelfranchi, 2011), as a result of process struggles and compromises among conflicting social actors who mobilize for their interests under the banner of their values. The process of institutionalizing norms and rules by actors who do not feel adequately represented in the workings of a certain system go on simultaneously in a movement of representation of society and production of social transformations.

In which part of the mind of an agent lies the force of power-of? What sort of devices are behind the will of an agent? Which are the mechanisms necessary to break the communication power? How is shaped the morality of the insurgent agent? Is it possible to have a morality without ethics?

2 On the forms of power

Agent's behaviour may be studied looking to individuals in isolation, in society (social classes), or in group (organizations, institutions, teams). Each group is composed by elements (members, such as agents) and by coordination and control mechanisms, such as assign agents to roles, choose group's roles and distribute them among members, negotiate or plan, punish agents that violate norms, or promote active agents to power (Pörn, 1970; Jones, 1996). Each agent does actions, has goals, abilities (skills), explores resources, and it can be trusted or not. So, the conduct of an agent is described by actions and the required resources, or by achieving goals and sub-goals through plans (Smith, 2010).

Agents may have three kinds of power, according to be individuals (executional with can_do, deontic with entitled_to, and full powers when there is a mix of executional and deontic ones), viewed from a social perspective, or considered group related (Carabelea, Boissier and Castelfranchi, 2004).

From bottom-up we can arrange several types of power in a hierarchy, such as power-of, power-over, power-influence, separating personal (individuals) from social (institutional) power, and showing the role of dependence (the other side of power). And, in order to enlarge other networks of categories connected with power, we may introduce links for covering interfering, re-warding, negotiating, cooperating, and whithout forgetting also arcs for the notions of value and trust (Castelfranchi, 2003).

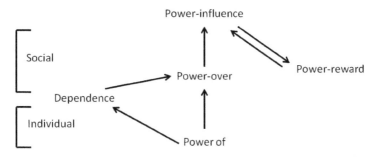

Fig. 1 Network of power forms

Figure 2 shows two different layers: at the bottom the individuals (individual power), and at the top the organization and the institutions (social power). Adopting a different perspective, we get a top-down point of view of power, and, in the first place, we focus on an institution, but leaving out its layers and the dynamics of distributed and local powers: no visual image of the leadership or of the insurgency is adopted in figure 2, because regular agents have no will.

3 Power-of and will

Agents may be bureaucrats, assigned to specific roles, living well in a society with dependencies, and with no autonomy. In this case, power is considered as pure domination (eg. corruption) and topics such as conflict resolution and alliance (coalition) formation are important. Howerver, we are now in a period of globalization which suggests fast transitions and regular changes, and the relevance of another class of agents, more energetics (activists) and intervenients, with will, is real. Now, power is more seen as direct action, followed by mass demonstrations, rebellions, surprise attacks, guerrila warfare or take overs.

In figure 3 we sketch the individual power, associated to the ability of an agent execute an action, attain a goal, or get a result. An organization is a network of relations to support interactions (coordination, cooperation, collaboration, or negotiation). And, by having leadership, an agent is capable to articulate the communications along the whole net. When these relations are modified or interfered, the leader looses control, power to dominate and, also, the possibility to give orders and commands (Bassler, 2005), as it occurs in a sea of bacteria. The activity of damaging communications supports the

Power of

Leadership

Power-driving

Fig. 2 A look to direct action

boycotts of all relations, and when it occurs all their energy is dissipated (and, the idea of probiotics arises).

The example of a multitude is interesting (Hardt and Negri, 2004), such as the one in Egypt during the February 2011 revolution. We have a multiple, a network of individuals, singularities or ones, where there is no movement to transform this set into an one or appoint a chief or leader (the ones are not attracked to the center in a centripetal way in order to constitute an one like in western democracy). The network operates as a produtive unit where each element is self-organized, autonomous, capable of initiative and power-of, and at the same time is a member of a multiple with collective power through cooperation.

The collective has no need to get unity based upon the dependence of its ones versus a chief, or to suppress the differences of those ones. There is also no strong hierarchy (in stead of, there is a net) and a boss imposing his will and the possibility to generate a counter power based upon a centralized form and some direction of ruling. The multitude is founded upon communication and collaboration, with a language, image and affects. Behind, there is a public good (knowledge, information, relations). The One is not anonymous, it composes the Multiple without disappearing and via cooperation, because the movement of the Ones is not centripetal (towards the center). The One has qualities, potency to be itself, yet it is member of the Multiple. What kind of democratic apparatus is it? How is built this kind of centralized power?

The example of bacteria (Bassler, 2005) is suitable to show this form of power and the need of the associated mechanisms, such as language (AI-1, AI-2) and quorun-sensing. A group of bacteria gets some authority when the number of its members attains a certain quorum (the group gets a majority, ie. it is stronger than its ennemies within some host). The mechanism of quorum-sensing computes a figure, by allowing communication among all the members, which means the group has enough power-of to attack its host. When there is no communication among members, or some links are broken or disconnected, the quorum is not computed or it is computed with a lesser figure, and no decision to fight is taken. Then, coalitions are possible by getting groups to-gether. Let us look now to the BDI (Belief-Desire-Intention) model of an agent

(Corrêa and Coelho, 2010) where we can find two computational processes supporting practical reasoning and directing proper action: 1) to decide what goal state may be reached, by deliberation and a choice mechanism, and 2) to decide how that state may be reached, by means-ends analysis and a planning mechanism, ie. by combining beliefs and desires:

$$Action = Beliefs + Desires$$

The intention is the mental attitude capable to drive the behaviour of the agent, as the following essential algorithm shows:

1. while true
2.   observe the world;
3.   actualize the internal model;
4.   deliberate about the intention that may be attained next;
5.   use means-end reasoning to get a plan for that intention;
6.   execute the plan;
7. end-while.

where the control cycle has three main components:

Belief revision function (brf): $f(B) \times Per \rightarrow f(B)$
Deliberation process (deliberate): $f(B) \rightarrow f(I)$
Means-ends reasoning (plan): $f(B) \times f(I) \rightarrow plan$

However, there is no will in this BDI model, and the claim "will can exist without desire, but desire requires will which is always behind desire", by (Spinoza, 2005), is not fulfilled. It lacks an energy device able to distinguish an active agent (intervention) from a passive one (spectator), ie. the idea of potency.

Grice (1975) proposed to define intention by one of two options:

$$Intention = Will + Belief \quad and \quad Intention = Volition$$

And, Cohen and Levesque (1990) introduced an apparatus to fix when and how intentions fall down, via the equation:

$$Intention = Choice + Commitment$$

where we have two implicit dimensions, will (relation between intention and action) and reasoning (directed to the future intention). But, where is the effort (potency), and how is it generated? An answer is to extend the equation of action by adding explicit will as another mental state:

$$Action = Beliefs + Will + Desires \quad Intention^{+} = Choice + Commitment + Action$$

Let us inspect what means an active behaviour:

1. Someone wants to do A on account of enveloping environment and self beliefs;
2. He gets energy to undo some desires and to choose the right commitments;

3. He weights the options and chooses his preference to intervene;
4. And, he acts, realizing A, intentionally.

A first draft of an algorithm with will is the following (Coelho, 2006):

```
1.    :=Do; /* Do are initial desires */
2.    Pi:=Pio; /* Pio are initial plans */
3.    while true do
4.        get next perception P;
5.        B:=brf(P);
6.        G:=filter_will(B,D);
7.        I:=rational_machine(G,B,Pi);
8.        Action_selec:=filter_values(B,I);
9.            execute(Action_selec)
10. end-while
```

But, the choice of goals is not focused. And, we have still the question "how can we build volition"? A possible answer consists of regenerating the BDI model, along the chain of practical reasoning, or subverting it. Let us look to an alternative: pick up PRS (Procedural Reasoning System) architecture of BDI model, which combines the goal-oriented reasoning with reactive behaviour. PRS is best suitable to uncertain, dynamic and real time environments, and we may advance with two comments about PRS. We have two cycles, where execution is embedded in a sub-cycle. The computation of commitment is set up in the big cycle of the choice of action, making the agent slower to react. And, the structure of the two cycles does not allow good local agents, because the associated calculus is more complex. What is needed for more complicate environments? An agent with local and global capabilities.

The solution is the new algorithm LGS (Coelho and Coelho, 2009):

```
1. bB:= Initial_beliefs( )
2. bD:= initial_goals( )
3. bP:= initial_plans( )
4. bS:= initial_solvers( )
5. while true do
6.    bB:= belief_revision(bB,stimulus);
7.    <aB,aD,aP,s>:= will(bB);
8.    C:= possibilities(aB,aP); can do
9.    N:= needs(aD,aP); need do
10.    I:= choice(s,C,N);
11.    execute(I)
12. end-while
```

(aB= activeBeliefs; s=choice strategy; L=Local, G=Global)

Now, in the LGS algorithm, the computation of commitment is not done in the big cycle (like in the PRS), but in the interior of will. All the cycle of choosing actions, in the PRS, is changed. The individual power (potency) of an agent depends on the computational cost of processing an intention, and it is not related with the process for executing a desire.

4 Power-of and leadership

The agent with qualities (Coelho and Costa, 2009; 2010) is unable to stand indifferent facing what cannot be held and his potency is directed to rise in opposition against the established authority in a knowledge driven world.

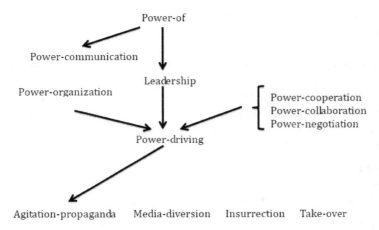

Fig. 3 A perspective on leadership

Leadership is one quality linked with promoting new directions (strategies) and advocating better ways. It is based on the power of his personality to dominate and take charge of the group, to innovate and promote new ideas, to free the energy of the other agents, to challenge the status, to direct the collective intelligence and to occupy positions of authority.

A framework of leadership is linked not only to cognition, but also to emotional intelligence, to a capability to stand in a leverage game, and to constitute a be-know-do unit. A leader is capable to set the vision, inspire and motivate, and elevate people to the highest values. Therefore, he may be ambitious first and foremost for the cause, have determination, empowerment, but also be modest and wilful, shy and fearless. Skills such as command, renew the organisational democracy, see advise signals, improvise changes, inovate solutions are very common in a leader candidate. Some authors (Collins, 2009) advocate that at the top of the leadership we may find:

Leadership Top Level = Humility + Will

A leader behaves as an architect, involving not only series of capabilities and levels of maturity, but also creativity, time spam, and scale. Therefore, a model of a leader is not a simple BDI, because it needs traits of personality, a mix of epistemic and motivational states (Lorini and Castelfranchi, 2006), belief and expectation revision (Castelfranchi, Falcone, and Piunti, 2006), invention, will, and moral supremacy (Coelho, Rocha and Trigo, 2010).

Software applications have been developed around the RoboSoccer (Cascalho, 2007) and the RoboRescue workbenches (Trigo, 2007), respectively for the game of soccer (definition of specific synthetic players) and for crisis management (eg. forest fires, earthquakes). This last example allowed two competing decision approaches were mixed, BDI, for monitoring and creating explanations, and POMDP (Partially Observable Markov Decision Problems), for using stochastic models for fixing agent behaviours (generating policies of role-taking and role-execution actions).

Our past experiments with individual mental states of several intelligent agent architectures, designed with the Extended Mental States Framework (EMSF), shown a suitable methodology in which the construction of agents with complex behaviour can be obtained from their mental states specification. The EMSF points toward the modelling of social behaviour of autonomous agents and to the design of stronger agencies with also collective mental states (Corrêa and Coelho, 1998; 2010). This is consistent with the framework for individual mental states which dynamics is also defined with the same framework. The EMSF challenges the way we think about the agent architecture design process. There are two distinctive features that sustain the EMSF framework:

- The set of mental state entities informing an agent's mind, and
- The relationships among those entities which dictate the creation of different artificial agent's architectures.

Artificial agents supported under the same framework share the same type of architectural primitive elements. The complexity inherent to their creation was studied in recent years, in which the role of particular attributes was dissected. Yet, several research issues are still open, such as, the direct tuning of attribute values during the Attribute Layer definition process, the aggregation of different attributes which contribute to the definition of agent's characters (types of personalities), and the interaction between those aggregated attributes and the mental states attributes in the top of our overall architecture. A contribution was done by (Cascalho, 2007), regarding how agent character can be changed (and, so its composed personality), but there still research to carry further on.

Emotions and moods are governed by different factors in addition to one's own thinking and behaviour. One of the means to access our moods and emotions are the cognitive and the behaviour routes, and in order to change how we feel we have to go about it indirectly. In human and social sciences, the relations between individual and collective mentalities are also a key for the comprehension and simulation of social behaviours. Otherwise, artificial agent design requires also a suite of development environments to precise the specifications of agent characters, with an extra capability to tune personalities and types of agents. In a way, our table of mental states behind the EMSF framework can be a suitable tool to help mind and character designs.

5 Power dynamics

Power-over is alone when facing the hidden influence of the dynamics of social networks. By electronic means and the Internet, it is possible today to generate mini donations that help those in need and involve those who always wanted to help. Using power of collaboration, solidarity ways, we can boost crowdsource learning, moving from tweet to street, along a continuous process of nourishing and sustaining nodes where we may find a connected life (net as a living organism). This is a diferent style of community building, by having group direction among like-minds striving to reach a collective common goal. A rational desire emerges from those connected minds (mind potency) to form a shared social consciousness, because humans at best are social species loving sharing (Hardt, 2011).

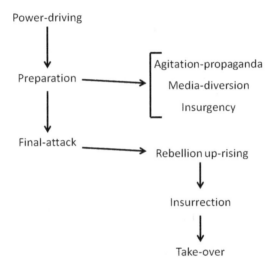

Fig. 4 Dynamics of power moves

Social power is not focused on individuals and one-to-one connections, but on constructing groups (hubs), on bringing people together. By reorienting priorities, focusing on getting connected with people with similar goals, surprising things can be accomplished with relative ease (emotional contagion: emotions are a primitive form of communication).

Power-over faces revolt when there is a feeling of a lack of liberties. And, the resistance is built bottom-up with singular power-of's spreading along. With the Internet, and through interaction, patterns of social networks are arranged to react against, triggered by desires, emotions, envy, altruism or solidarity. According to (Christakis, 2010), "ideas, germs and obesity underlie the creation of social ties to begin with", "if your friends are obese, your risk of obesity is 45% higher", ie. his work sheds light on how we might take advantage of an understanding of social networks to make the world a different place or not (see the turn moil of several arab countries).

When the amount of energy is enough to encourage development and generation of ideas but constraints are imposed on individuals (repression), further forces are accumulated in the societal level without each one being aware of. Two options are possible 1) a global one, rupture and revolution (hard path) and 2) a local one, accumulation and gradual change (soft path). Each case requests a leader able to drive the forces from some counter space to the idea of active resistance, knowing that there is a gap between those two levels of action, or another pathway where the collective acts by collaboration of all its elements (multitude).

In hard activism, those in struggle are subjugated by power relations (domination), and stay in a direct position to confront them. In soft activism it occurs a different situation because the participants are outside the power relations and on the side of exploitation. Further research with MABS tools may support inquiry around the forms of power and the different roles played by artificial agents. For example, suppose an arena for the experimentation of political struggles, in which the reproduction of organized life (social, political), in all its dimensions, is controlled, captured and exploited: circulation of money, police presence, life normalization, exploitation of productivity, repression, reining in of subjectivities, and services (housing, water, gas and energy supply, telephone, knowledge access).

6 Conclusions

We live today a period called age of information, and globalisation is one of its attributes, ie. the dispersion of knowledge, skills, viewpoints, experiences, innovations and norms (Castells, 2010). This does not mean Empire is dead, democracy is the unique regime, or empowerment (power to the people) is common. Power can be concentrated in networks, and by dependence relations in just a few, and of course later on in autocratic persons or committees.

By looking to the anatomy of power we followed Spinoza by distinguishing potestas from potentia, ie. separating, as Marx did, the power of capitalist relations of production from the power of proletarian productive forces, and the centralized, mediating, transcendental force of command from the local, immediate, actual force of constitution. Empowerment is connected with delegation of authority and influence, and it is based upon power, motivation, development and leadership. Through empowerment, decision taking, autonomy and participation is distributed, increasing the power-of individuals. Also, it involves the empowered increasing of confidence in their own capabilities. It is wise, when looking to power, to make a distinction between forms of authority and organization, or by other words between theological and political authority of Hobbes and democratic and republican Spinoza (freedom of thought). Spinoza was responsible to introduce the idea of multitude, against the old concept of people due to Hobbes, and this move was crucial to make us thinking again about the meaning of democracy in these days. The concept multitude introduces the collective social subject that is unified inasmuch as it manifests common desires through common social behaviour. As a matter of fact, potentia does not exist in Spinoza's democracy as except to the extent that it is a constituent power, completely and freely constituted by the power of the multitude. Therefore, the Spinoza concept of constitution is also necessary to cover the construction of social norms and rights, from the base of society, through a logic of immediate, collective and associative relations. Power is still elusive. It can turn into a single agent (dictator, prince) or a collective agency (multitude) eager to achieve thousand plans, with advantage for everybody or only for the one in power. On the opposite, on the side of exploitation, domination and oppression counter-forces based upon actions and active resistance may emerge, through situations of conflict and moments of becoming aware, to break the previous relations of dependence and overthrow the authority, introducing again new forms of domination and oppression.

Acknowledgements Cristiano Castelfranchi was a pioneer in studying the power of artificial agents, from the beginning of the 90's, and I would like to thank him for his great contribute to DAI at large. His influence was so big that no one can become addict to this topic without forgetting his major role in opening new alleys and making new steps forward, inspired by Hobbes tradition. My approach to this topic was motivated by Spinoza and Negri, yet it was always triggered by his enthousiasm and new ideas brought to the discussion of major breakthroughs, mainly around power-over and the theory of dependence.

References

1. Bassler, B. Quorum Sensing: Cell-to-Cell Communication in Bacteria, Annual Review of Cell and Developmental Biology, Vol. 21: 319–346, November 2005.
2. Carabelea, C., Boissier, O. and Castelfranchi, C. Using Social Power to enable Agents to Reason about being Part of a Group, Proceedings of ESAW, pp. 166–177, 2004.
3. Cascalho, J. The Role of Attributes for Mental States Architectures, PhD Thesis (in Portuguese), University of Açores, 2007.
4. Castelfranchi, C. The Micro-Macro Constitution of Power, ProtoSociology, An International Journal of Interdisciplinary Research, Volume 19(19), pp. 208–265, 2003.
5. Castelfranchi, C., Falcone, R. and Piunti, M. Agents with Anticipatory Behaviours: To Be Cautious in a Risky Environment, Proceedings of ECAI, 2006.
6. Castelfranchi, C. The Logic of Power. How my Power Becomes his Power, ICST/CNR Working Report, 2011.
7. Castells, M. Communication Power, OUP Oxford, 2009.
8. Castells, M. The Information Age, Economy, Society and Culture, Wiley and Blackwell, 2nd. Edition, 2010.
9. Christakis, N. The Hidden Influence of Social Networks, YouTube TED Talk, 2010.
10. Coelho, F. Emergency and Collapse of Power (in Portuguese), UL PhD Thesis, FCUL, 2006.
11. Coelho, F. and Coelho, H. Meta Agency and Individual Power, Web Intelligence and Agent Systems: An International Journal (WIAS), Volume 7(4), pp. 333–346, 2009.
12. Coelho, H. and Costa, A. R. On the Intelligence of Moral Agency, Proceedings of the Encontro Português de Inteligência Artificial (EPIA-2009), October 12-15 Aveiro (Portugal), in L. S. Lopes, N. Lau, P. Mariano e L. M. Rocha (eds.), New Trends in Artificial Intelligence, pp. 439–450, 2009.

13. Coelho, H., Costa, A. R. and Trigo, P. On the Complexity of Moral Decision, FCUL and DI Working Report, 2010.
14. Coelho, H. and Trigo, P. On the Operationality of Moral-Sense Decision Making, FCUL and DI Working Report, 2010.
15. Coelho, H., Rocha, A. R. and Trigo, P. Moral Minds as Multiple Layer Organizations, Proceedings of IBERAMIA 2010, Bahia Blanca (Argentine), November 1-5, Springer LNAI 6433, 2010.
16. Cohen, P. R. and Levesque, H. J. Intention is Choice plus Commitment, Artificial Intelligence, Volume 34(1), pp. 39–76, 1990.
17. Collins, J. How the Mighty Fall: And Why Some Companies Never Give In, Random House Business, 2009.
18. Corrêa, M. and Coelho, H. From Mental States and Architectures to Agents' Programming, Proc. of the 7th Iberoamerican Congress on Artificial Intelligence (IBERAMIA98), Lisbon 6-9, Springer-Verlag LNAI 1484, pp. 64–85, 1998.
19. Corrêa, M. and Coelho, H. Abstract Mental Descriptions for Agent Design, Intelligent Decision Technologies, an International Journal, Volume 4(2), 2010.
20. Grice, P. Logic and Conversation, in Cole, P. and Morgan, J. (eds.) Syntax and semantics, Volume 3, Academic Press, 1975.
21. Hardt, M. Reclaim the Common in Communism, Guardian, February 3, 2011.
22. Hardt, M. and Negri, A. Empire, Harvard University Press, 2001.
23. Hardt, M. and Negri, A. Multitude, War and Democracy in the Age of Empire, Penguin Press, 2004.
24. Jones, A. J. and Sergot, M. A Formal Characterization of Institutionalized Power, Journal of the Interest Group in Pure and Applied Logic, Volume 4(3), pp. 427–443, 1996.
25. Lorini, E. and Castelfranchi, C. The Unexpected Aspects of Surprise, International Journal of Pattern Recognition and Artificial Intelligence, Volume 20(6), pp. 817–835, 2006.
26. Negri, A. The Savage Anomaly, The Power of Spinoza's Metaphysics and Politics, University of Minnesota Press, 1999.
27. Pörn, I. The Logic of Power, Basil Blackwell, 1970.
28. Smith, A. The Theory of Moral Sentiments, Penguin Classics, 2010.
29. Spinoza, B. Ethics, Penguin Classics, 2005.
30. Trigo, P. Joint Work in Complex Environments (in Portuguese), UL PhD Thesis, FCUL, 2007.

Chapter 21
The recovered subject: A socio-cognitive snapshot of a new subject in the field of mental health

Raffaella Pocobello and Tarek el Sehity

Abstract Recovery represents a new paradigm in the field of mental health. It refers hereby less to the possibility of relief from symptoms than to the individual's capacity to develop a meaningful life and a self-concept beyond the illness. Several countries adopted recovery oriented approaches to implement mental health service reforms and attracted considerable scientific interest on that subject matter. A comprehensive theory of the recovery process is however still missing. The present article argues for an analytic approach to the socio-cognitive components in the different stages of the subject's recovery process. By the means of narratives from mental health patients, a dramatic loss of internal territoriality ("locus") is evidenced in psychiatric treatment, whereby a subject in crisis renounces its internality to the professionals' authority. The eventual process of a subject's recovery, we suggest, has to be regarded as an inverse process, in which internality is privately and socially reclaimed and defended in terms of ownership and responsibility. The phenomenon of users' social movements, such as Madpride, is suggested as a form of re-conquest of social territory by the means of emancipatory pride. The mental components of the recovery process represent, in a large part, concepts from the theoretic framework of Cristiano Castelfranchi and his associates. A conception of the subject emerges whereby recovery is ideated literally as a process of "re-covering" aka protecting the subject's internality against the psychiatric/institutional gaze and rule of private affairs.
Keywords: Recovery, Ownership, Responsibility, Self-trust, Pride, Internality

Raffaella Pocobello
Institute of Cognitive Sciences and Technologies, CNR, Italy
e-mail: raffaella.pocobello@istc.cnr.it

Tarek el Sehity
Institute for Science of Ethical Wealth and Wealth Psychology, Sigmund Freud Private University of Vienna, Austria
e-mail: tarek.el-sehity@sfu.ac.at

The explanatory power of the concepts Cristiano Castelfranchi developed with his group in the field of artificial intelligence extends as far as to the realm of mental health, a field of research where Cristiano made occasional interventions and contributions since the start of the anti-psychiatric movement in Italy led by Franco Basaglia. While his main focus of activity has remained over the years on AI and theoretic psychology his work is getting growing attention in fields as various as economic psychology, sociology, clinical psychology and philosophy. The contribution at hand reports to a large extent a theoretic draft on recovery from mental illness as discussed and elaborated with Cristiano in various occasions. In the past years, we had the great opportunity to exchange with Cristiano on several issues, ranging from recovery from serious mental illness up to the psychology of money. We have gradually metabolized (the process is still ongoing) and appreciate the significance of the large theoretic body of Cristiano's work and even more learned to esteem him as an admirable tutor and generous friend. Besides the evident use of a theory of recovery which we will draft here, we present this work as a case of how his theoretic approach allows for the understanding of almost any domain of human action. How and under what conditions does the goal of recovery emerge and be achieved will be the guiding question of the paper at hand.

1 Recovery: a new paradigm in mental health

Recovery is a key concept of the new mental health approach to mental illness and to reorient mental health services. In the last years, the recovery oriented paradigm has been adopted in many countries for the implementation of mental health service reforms (e.g. UK, Australia, USA). The Care Services Improvement Partnership, the Royal College of Psychiatrists, and the Social Care Institute for Excellence (2007), announced Recovery as a common purpose for the future of mental health services, emphasizing the need for a better understanding of the recovery approach. Definitions, methods, the role of agents in the process as well as its measurement stand and fall with the conceptual strength of the underlying theory (see hereto also chapter X in the policy manual as published by the American Psychological Association (2009); and the same published by the American Association of Community Psychiatrist: Sowers (2005)). Even if researchers have investigated the field and proposed intuitive models to grasp the recovery process, its components and conditions (e.g. Anthony, 1993; Jacobson & Greenley, 2001), explanation and description of the phenomenon have remained ambiguous.

    First, a clear definition of recovery is missing (Farkas, 2007; Sowers, 2005). It is worthwhile noting that the origins of the Recovery approach had and still have a considerable difficulty to cross the Anglo-Saxon-language borders. This difficulty might be due to a missing correspondence of the recovery term in other languages without losing its rich semantic and metaphoric sense which might constitute an element to the success of the recovery approach's spread:

"*to re-cover*: 1) To obtain again after losing; regain, as property, self-control, health, ect. 2) To make up for; retrieve, as a loss. 3) To restore (oneself) to natural balance, health, etc. 4) In sports, to regain (one's normal position of guard, balance, etc.). 6) *Law* **a** To gain in judicial proceedings: to recover judgment. **b** To gain or regain by legal process." (Webster Comprehensive Dictionary, 2003).

"Etymological dictionaries: c.1300, "to regain consciousness," from Anglo-Fr. rekeverer (late 13c.), O.Fr. recovrer, from L. recuperare "to recover" (see recuperation). Meaning "to regain health or strength" is from early 14c.; sense of "to get (anything) back" is first attested mid-14c.

The academic literature on mental health distinguishes at least three facets of recovery. It is conceptualized as

1. a spontaneous event of recovery from all the symptoms after illness;
2. a symptomatic recovery caused by treatment;
3. an experience of revitalization of proper life in a state of illness even in the persistence of symptoms (Ralph and Corrigan, 2005) – some authors refer to the last form of recovery as "social recovery" to distinguish it from "clinical recovery".

Clinical recovery concerns the alleviation of symptoms and the return to premorbid functioning (Young and Ensing, 1999), whereas social recovery implies neither symptom remission nor necessity of a return to the premorbid state (W. Anthony, Rogers, & Farkas, 2003; Deegan, 1996). Analyzing first-person narratives of recovered persons, the Center for Psychiatric Rehabilitation at Boston University has developed a working definition of recovery as "a deeply personal, unique process of changing one's attitudes, values, feelings, goals, skills and roles. It is a way of living a satisfying, hopeful, and contributing life even with limitations caused by the illness. Recovery involves the development of new meaning and purpose in one's life as one grows beyond the catastrophic effects of mental illness" (W. A. Anthony, 1993). Very similar but based on personal experience, Deegan (1988) defines recovery as "a process, a way of life, an attitude, and a way of approaching the day's challenges". In both perspectives a basic agreement on the conceptualization of recovery exists as a social process, as an outcome and both. However, both definitions imply a number of unspecified concepts such as attitudes, values, feelings and goals.

An influential model of recovery developed for the state of Wisconsin experimentation was proposed by Jacobson and Greenley (2001) in which they undertook a principal division of recovery's key conditions into internal and external factors:

• Internal key conditions: hope, healing, empowerment and connection;
• external key conditions: human rights, a positive culture of healing, recovery-oriented services.

The "model", however, provides no clear definitions of the concepts describing these conditions, nor sufficient explanations of their functioning, but just gives an account of a number of fuzzy concepts.

Farkas (2007) identifies four "core recovery values" that support the recovery process and which appear to be commonly reflected and referred to in consumer and recovery literature:

1. Person-orientation has emerged from the narratives of the consumers since most of them report damages due to the non holistic approach of the services. Hence, a recovery oriented service is based on the strength instead of the deficits of the persons. With respect to the design of recovery oriented mental health services Farkas recommends the consideration of
2. Person-involvement in the planning and delivery of the services to develop a sense of empowerment;
3. Self-determination and self-choice are considered the cornerstones of a recovery process to strengthen the self;
4. Hope is an essential ingredient for the recovering user and not least for the professionals who need to support the aspirations of recovery especially during the setbacks. "Hope means remembering, (...), that recovery can be a long-term process with many setbacks and plateaus along the way." (Farkas, 2007, p. 68).

Clearly, these "core values" refer to recovery-oriented services more than to the recovery process per se. There is an agreement in the literature on mental healthcare that the disregard of personal aspects is necessarily ruinous so that person-centered models are mandatory. A person-centered model of care is considered to be based on the needs and preferences of the person, involves its primary relationships as sources of support, focuses on capacities and strengths, and accepts risks, failures, uncertainties, and setbacks as natural and expected parts of learning and self-determination (Davidson et al, 2003; O'Brien & Lovett, 1992). In such a model, professionals learn to respect the users will and start to "involve" them in each decision of their process to recovery.

Ron Coleman's autobiographic description of his recovery published in "Recovery An Alien Concept" (2004) presents important material for a socio-cognitive theory. He identifies "people", "self" and "ownership" as the three stepping stones to recovery:

• People, since "Recovery is by definition wholeness and no one can be whole if they are isolated from the society in which they live and work" (Coleman, 2004, p.14); further,
• "Recovery requires self-confidence, self-esteem, self-awareness and self-acceptance without this recovery is not just impossible, it is not worth it." (ibd, p.15); and
• Ownership "For it is only through owning the experience of madness can we own the recovery from madness" (ibd, p.16).

In his view to achieve recovery, a shift in the paradigm from biological reductionism to one of societal and personal development is necessary. As other recovery key issues he elaborates on the reclamation of power and the demand of acceptance.

Taking into account the narratives of Ron Coleman (2004) and other recovered voice hearers, Marius Romme (2009) defines recovery as the "taking life back into your own hands (...) using one's own capabilities and making one's own dreams come true.(...) Recovery means take back power and use it to cope with own voices and problem, (...) create choices that make it possible to take responsibility for their life and emotions, and by doing so heighten their self-esteem" (Romme, 2009 p. 9, p. 27).

Other researchers which have analyzed the narratives of recovered persons (Topor, 2001; 2006; 2011; Davidson, 2003) stress the role of "the others" for the recovery process. Particularly, friendships before the start of an illness and family members create the red thread in a person's life, often guarantying affective and even material support. The peculiar emphasis on the relations with others which share the same experiences can be traced in the biographies as well as in academic literature. In biographies the role of peers is central: peers facilitate the renewing of a sense of hope for the future; create the climate of support and solidarity which helps the person in the feeling of mutual understanding and help for the others and reduces loneliness. For so called "schizophrenic" patients the "discovery" that voices are a reality for others as well, allows for a reframing of the voice hearers' personal condition. Peers also have a positive effect on the self-management of symptoms. They have a privileged position in teaching the know-how of managing the symptoms, since they can convey the lessons they have learned from personal experience, whereas professionals cannot.

Besides these empirical and autobiographic accounts of the recovery process, an interesting contribution has been provided by Hopper (2007). He proposes Amartya Sen's (1993) notion of capabilities as an alternative framework for the analysis of recovery. The capabilities approach

> "(...) reworks recovery not from within (where it remains hostage to a rhetoric of suffering) but from without (informed by an idiom of opportunity). Not healing but equality becomes the operant trope (...). This arms us to undress both immediate grievances experiences of humiliation and shame (...) and long-term prospects for growth and development." (Hopper, 2007, p.875).

The capability approach serves indeed an interesting reference point for our analysis, since it readdresses recovery as a question of resources, agency and opportunities. Nevertheless, we should keep in mind that the capabilities approach originates from, and is dedicated to structural problems of resource distribution and the opportunities for education etc. It misses however the adequate theoretic tools to grasp issues, in those cases in which structural factors are less involved in the conditioning of the individual's capabilities, whereas a major role is played by an acute personal crisis of loss of power which impairs the subject's capabilities and functionings. We will focus on the recovery process in precisely this sense, analyze the socio-cognitive components with the theoretic tools of Cristiano Castelfranchi's framework. This means that the actual beliefs and goals involved, the emotions implied in the subject's journey from mental illness to recovery, will be sought for, in order to draft a social cognitive model of recovery. Starting point must be the impaired subject's suffering from mental illness.

2 Suffering from Mental Illness

According to Maria Miceli and Cristiano Castelfranchi "psychic suffering is defined as the suffering implied by a frustrating assumption, that is, a particular
kind of discrepancy between a belief and a goal, embedding a time specification for both the goal and the belief representation" (Miceli and Castelfranchi.
1997 p. 769).

The frustrating assumptions implicated in the phenomenon of mental illness
are multiple. Several narratives of people with severe mental illness focus on
frustration assumptions which concern the belief and feeling to be unable to
trust in one's own perception and capabilities, or, its self-trust.

> "Slowly I descend into a paranoid state, of course afraid to tell anyone about it.
> The feelings become possessive and I feel myself without a sense of knowing who
> I am. Am I a vent for the fear in humanity? Is it the unconscious fear in humanity
> or am I just afraid my humanity has become? Perhaps there is no difference. These
> intellectualizations do not distract me from my worry." (Paul Hewitt, 2001; p.5)

The loss of self-trust has a huge impact on the system of beliefs and goals
of the agent, since it represents an instrumental capability for the totality of an
agent's goals. What happens can be conceptualized as a vicious circle of a loss
of powers (Castelfranchi, 2003):

> "There is either a virtuous or a vicious circle between (. . .) personal power (. . .) (i.e.
> being able and in condition to achieve goals) and Social Power. Any lack of personal
> power (lack of abilities, competence, knowledge, controlled resources) reduces the
> various forms of social power, and the probabilities of having goal-adoption relation-
> ships able to increase that power." (Castelfranchi, 2003, p. 232)

Not surprisingly, people with experience of mental disease are exposed to
conditions of disadvantage on multiple levels (e.g. HEA, 1997; Lahtinen, 1999;
Wilkinson and Marmot, 1998; Eaton and Harrison, 1998; Hosman and Llopis,
2004; Patel and Kleinman, 2003). As outlined by Castelfranchi above, both the
inherent nature of mental health problems and the discriminatory responses to
them have ruinous effects on interpersonal relationships, causing a significant
reduction of social contacts (Huxley and Thornicroft, 2003). Psychiatric patients
are four times more likely than the average not to have a close friend, and more
than one-third of patients say that they have no one to turn to for help (Meltzer
et al, 1995; Evan and Huxley, 2000).

Mental illness goes hand in hand with the process of psychiatric treatment.
Starting from the first diagnosis, to the actual therapeutic treatment mainly
based on pharmacological interventions and the support provided by mental
health facilities, the individual becomes an object of treatment by professionals.

2.1 Psychiatric treatment

> "For the majority (. . .) the first contact with psychiatry represents a further turn on
> the downward spiral. It is confirmation of one's worthlessness, an extension of the
> experience of neglect in early life" (Topor, 2001, p.182).

Despite the number of longitudinal studies (Ciompi, 1980; Bleuer, 1978; Harding et al, 1987; WHO, 1973; WHO, 1979; Leff et al, 1992) documenting the positive development of mental illness mostly in the absence of psychiatric institutions, a large share of psychiatric professionals still considers it incurable (Bachrach, 1996).

"I was a schizophrenic, they said "please remember that, oh, and while you are it, remember to stop thinking there is a cure, you are a chronic, a chronic schizophrenic, a biological defect with an incurable disease." (Runciman in Romme et al., 2009, p. 256).

This kind of prognosis, and the contact with psychiatric facilities create negative expectations for the future, disappointments and existential delusions:

"At the day centre I got a picture about expectations of what life was going to be like. I was then only fifteen and I spent my day with older people (. . .). I was given a diagnosis of schizophrenia and different professionals- nurses, social workers, psychologist and psychiatrists- all gave the same sort of message, time and time again: my prospect for the future were "not great": I shouldn't have expectations about school, or work, or having any relationships" (Hendry in Romme et al., 2009 p. 310).

Psychiatric care is experienced as

"Going round in circles and not going anywhere. It was very frightening and I felt such hopelessness. No one in the psychiatric services gave me any hope, in fact, it was the opposite" (Reid, in Romme et al., 2009, p. 119).

Hopelessness is due to the establishment of the belief about the impossibility to recover. The goal to recover becomes a mere wish:

"In other words, hopelessness still implies wish or desire. What is lacking is precisely the belief of possibility, which is replaced by its opposite: a belief of impossibility. It is the persistence of the desire, coupled with the belief of impossibility that accounts for the suffering of hopelessness." (Miceli and Castelfranchi, 2010, p.258)

2.1.1 Compliance

"To my astonishment the psychiatrists that I tried to tell (abuses in childhood) either denied my experience or told me that I would never, ever recover from what had happened. They told me that I had an illness. I was mentally ill. I was expected to be the passive recipient of treatment for a disorder I had; that medications was the only option open to me, and that, actually, I would never really get better anyway. No one ever asked me what I thought might help" (Dillon in Romme et al., 2009 p.189).

Psychiatry offers treatment in exchange for compliance. Compliance refers to the subject's "acceptance" of the role of the patient in its relation with the mental health professional. Due to the enormous legal powers (even coercion) of the psychiatrist as an institutional agent, the significance and implications of compliance are substantial for the life of the patient. To consider is here that the psychiatrist potentially decides where the patient should live (stationary or hospitalized treatment), the psychotropic substances for the treatment, whether or not to work, the patient's legal accountability, etc. Consider further the desperate mental state of a person turning to psychiatry for help to get treatment under the condition of compliance:

"I got the message that I was a passive victim of pathology. I wasn't encouraged
to do anything to actively help myself. Therapy meant drug therapy. It was hugely
disempowering. It was all undermine my sense of self, exacerbating all my doubts
about myself." (Longden, in Romme et al., 2009, p. 143).

Evidently, what is at stake with compliance, regards a large part of a person's natural ownership, where a significant portion of existential decisions is
delegated to the hands of the professional:

When I became a client of psychiatry I <u>lost</u> everything job, studies, friends not to
mention my self-respect, self-worth, hope and dreams. When I got back my life I
thought it was only temporary as I had been taught and told that schizophrenia was
chronic and incurable." (Runciman in Romme et al., 2009, p. 259).

2.1.2 Medication: a reductionist annihilation

The impact of medication in the context of mental illness is not limited to
its mental effects and its "side-effects" on the mental as well as physiological
level, but touches upon the conceptual level of agency and the self. The medical
intervention implicitly or explicitly conveys a reductionist message:

- "Your compliance (taking the medication) is essential for the success of
  the treatment" → "the plan for your treatment is not yours but part of
  professional expertise"
- "The cause of your mental suffering does not depend on you but on your
  physiological state" → "you do not control your body, but the body controls
  you"

The administration of psychotropic drugs as a principal focus of the professional intervention combined with the patient's compliance to the treatment
lead to the often described annihilation of the person. The reductionist approach is methodologically and even epistemologically based on the assumption of strict upwards causation[1]. The reductionist approach to mental illness
is for this reason necessarily an approach which transgresses the subject as
an arbitrary entity of social life, since the search and focus of the treatment
is centered on the elementary constituents of the same. What might be a cu-
rious (however legal) technicality of treatment from the "objective" point of
view of the medicating therapist, becomes a peculiar experience for the subject of mental illness and even paradox when the subject's compliance is taken
into account: through compliance, both, the therapist as well as the patient
"decide" to act *as if* the subject were complying. From the reductionist point
of view – and what is even more dramatic – from a legal point of view, the
"decision" itself is to be regarded a formal (though legal) technicality, given
that the subject is regarded as subjected (caused) by its mental illness, a cause
beyond the subject's "control". From a consequent reductionist point of view
on the relation between the medicating therapist and the medicated patient

---

[1] Consequently, the notion of downwards causation, or even mental causation represents
for the reductionist the inacceptable notion of a *causa sui*.

there remains only one reasonable instance of observation *for both parties*: the monitoring eyes of the therapist.

3 Recovery

3.1 *"Recovery exists": Surprise and Admiration*

Probably the most important starting point in the recovery process lies in some form of surprise:

> "(...) a fellow voice hearer who at my first hearing voices group asked me if I heard voices and when I replied that I did, told me that they were real. It does not sound much, but that one sentence has been a compass for me showing me the direction I needed to travel and underpinning my belief in the recovery process." (Coleman, 2004, p.12)

Often the surprise consists in the evidence that equal others (peers) have managed to recover from the same kind of disease, despite all expectations, and even severer, against all expert prognosis. The surprise leads to a belief revision process (Lorini and Castelfranchi, 2007) necessary to initiate the recovery process.

> "My recovery started when I met another service user who worked for a charity. It was a real eye-opener, because she was also a user but she had a job, a partner, a house, all things I was led to believe I couldn't have, things that were beyond me." (Steward Hendry in Romme et al, 2009, p.11)

In fact, the belief on which the personal hopeless condition was previously based gets questioned, and generates desires and goals which have been compromised by the beliefs of incurability and chronicity. The belief revision process represents an essential turning point in the career of the survivor where the aspirations for a meaningful life beyond the illness regain momentum.

Evidently, a crucial condition lies in the trusted source of the information, characterized by a large body of shared experiences. By the example of a *trusted* equal, the subject gains an awareness of its own powers and its "real" chances to recover. Even if the source for the initiation of the recovery process lies external to the subject, the fact that it comes from an evaluated "equal" changes the objective uncertainty into a felt degree of certainty, *as if* it were a repetition task in the form of a script of something already achieved. The powerful cognitive shortcut whereby another's successful goal achievement evaluated as if it were one's own achievement, brings about an interesting emotional shift concerning the self: from a sense of helpless inferiority (wanting p [meaningful life] alike Y [another] but not being able to achieve p) to a sense of admiration (esteeming Y for achieving p unlike X [oneself]) to emulation (evaluating Y equal to X and deducing that X can achieve p) (see Castelfranchi and Miceli, 2009, p.225ff). This is why especially self-help groups need to be considered of fundamental value for the recovering subject.

Mutual understanding in the exchange of experiences provokes more than just the insight of new possibilities – it creates a mind-frame in which recovery is experienced *as if* it were already happening to oneself. It is not theory and reasoning which convinces about a "probability of recovery" as it might even be presented from mental health professionals, but the actual evidence of its *real* possibility.

3.2 *From Hope to Trust*

As presented in our recovery review above, the hope to recover forms the conceptual core in many accounts of recovery. Hope as the motivational base of the recovery process is however overstressed. As evidenced in Miceli and Castelfranchi's (2010) analysis of hope, though referring to a desired goal, the individual's expectations of its actual achievement are not certain at all. Hope is characterized by an uncertainty which does not allow to engage in the actual planning of actions or decisions, since the hoping individual has no "clue" about what to do or how to decide in order to achieve the desired goal. For this reason, hope is characterized by temporal permanence, since it misses the actual criteria which would allow for the "falsification" of the goal it refers to. Further, the hoped for goal achievement concludes almost necessarily in a positive surprise, similar to the receiving of a gift which is obtained without a deeper understanding of the circumstances which have brought it about. While forming the positive ground for the mere possibility of recovery to exist, and as such constituting a necessary condition for the recovery process to take place, hope is insufficient for the activation of the recovery process, for it lacks a plan execution, the know-how for acting to achieve the desired goal (Castelfranchi and Pocobello, 2007). Rather, external circumstances might be vaguely assumed to bring about the hoped for goal.

> "If we did not distinguish what is most likely to happen from our wishes about mere possibilities, we might undergo serious consequences in terms of planning, commitment to, and pursuit of unfeasible goals." (Miceli and Castelfranchi, 2010, p266)

A form of efficiency rationalization, whereby probable goals are distinguished from possible ones, presents a class of goals which can be taken into account, however not be counted on. As such, hoped-for-goals remain in the hands of unknown factors and powers and would not only be insufficient to maintain the recovery process, but also contraindicated since this feeling induces some sort of passivity due to lack of (action-) plans an agent could be committed to. Therefore, rather than hope, it is trust (Castelfranchi, 1998; Castelfranchi and Falcone, 2010) which must be considered an essential form of motivation for the goal of recovery. The role of trust in the recovery process should be considered two-ways:

- As a trustor, when the subject has to evaluate the source of the recovery information as a trustworthy evidence of recovery ("trust-that" recovery).

At this level the subject has to act as a social trustor – the ability to trust and believe what was formerly assumed impossible (social trust as a key-element of the belief revision process after the initial surprise);
- As a trustee:
    - at the individual level, when the person needs to trust *in* its own capabilities – the capabilities which need to be trusted and appropriated, that is, recovered (trust-in);
    - at the social level, when the individual has to recover its role as a valuable trustee. At this level the evident complex of problems originating from stigmatization have to be confronted.

In both roles – as a trustor as well as a trustee – the resumed power to decide and not to comply, the commitment to pursue one's own trusted goals and to decide to count on trusted others rather than entitled professionals, constitute instances towards the reestablishment of ownership and responsibility.

3.3 "Recovery happens": Ownership as the Core of Recovery

"Ownership is the key to recovery. We must learn to own our experiences whatever they are. Doctors cannot own our experiences, psychologist cannot own our experiences, nurses, social workers, support workers, occupational therapist, psychotherapists, carers, and friends cannot own our experiences. Even our lovers cannot own our experiences. We must own our experiences. For it is only true owning the experience of madness can we own the recovery from madness." (Coleman, 2004, p.16)

Coleman's emphasis on the role of ownership in the recovery process is shared by many survivors in one form or another as a core piece on the journey to recovery. Formulations such as "regaining one's life", "taking your life in your own hands", "claiming responsibility for one's decisions and actions", indicate essential parts of ownership in the survivors' description of the recovery process.

To grasp some of the essential components of the appropriation process generally, and re-appropriation more specifically, it is necessary to consider ownership as a socio-cognitive process in various stages: from recognition and acceptance of the object of ownership to its social claim and defense against others to the taking of responsibility and its social recognition.

3.3.1 Recovering the resources: Acceptance

Next to the surprise trigger in the belief revision process, acceptance forms a substantial mental settling process in which a gradual change of perspectives takes place:

"An acceptance attitude can serve adaptive functions (...). The acceptance of the problem, and hence, its inclusion in the reality perceived by the person, permits a form of adaptation that extends beyond dealing with, and possibly solving, that specific problem. Even when one's goals are irrevocably thwarted, acceptance of these facts permits to readjust one's plans, project, and aspirations. By recognizing the harm suffered, the person can, in fact, not only avoid useless persistence (by accepting things that cannot be changed) but also ascertain whether the existing situation also presents some unexpected positive aspects and take advantage of them" (Miceli and Castelfranchi, 2001, p.294)

What is considered inacceptable, the targeted object of an effort at elimination, the mental source of suffering and frustration, has to be reframed and reevaluated as a form of resource. Especially in the case of mental illness, where the perceived source of suffering constitutes an intrinsic part of the self which is continuously objectified and externalized ("singled out", "identified") for treatment purpose ("symptom control"), a radical belief revision process dedicated to the inversion of the clinical estrangement process has to take place, whereby symptoms become accessible resources:

"I accepted my voices as real
I stopped trying to get rid of them, but accepted them as personal
I became conscious of ownership of my voices
I stopped looking for a cause outside myself
I looked for solutions in my self
I explored what had happened in my life that might have a relationship with my voices
I accepted those emotions which I did not like and could not easily master"
(Sue Clarkson in Romme et al, 2009, p 316f)

The acceptance of what was a mere symptom as something "real" plays a fundamental role in the acceptance process, for what is not real should not be there and cannot form a reliable resource for whatever goal. For Coleman (see p. 357 above) this reframing was the starting point of the recovery process. What is at stake here is the subject's essence in the power to claim its own reality, not in the form of a delirium, but as a fact it can actually share with equals (e.g. voice hearers). Once this fundamental question is settled, the resources can be accessed and employed, in a search for their use, and even more, in a search for their use for the recovering subject.

Thus, the motivational dimension – as outlined when discussing trust – builds an essential prerequisite in the means-ends-reasoning, for means are to be defined by the goals they serve for. Due to the emergence of a feasible scheme through the emulation of the recovery process as demonstrated by a trusted survivor, instrumental goals and the necessary means for their achievement are recognized. The guiding example of recovered individuals as well as the technique of recovery oriented training interventions provide valuable evidence for the way in which the object of suffering is reevaluated and accepted as a part of oneself, rather than fought as a symptom. Instructive are here the first steps towards the re-appropriation of voices in the voice-hearer trainings which are based on the principle of giving sense to voices (Romme and Escher, 1993, 1996) and working towards the recognition of voices as a personal and deeply connected part with one's life-story. The accidental nature of the symptom, a view inherently expressed through the medication treatment in the reductionist approach to mental illness, is necessarily elaborated as a *causal* part of the personal life-story. The symptoms are recognized as a part of one's self. The deficit is recovered as a source of information for the subject to accept and meaningfully incorporate it in its self-conception.

3.3.2 The social grounding of Recovery: Responsibility

Even if responsibility as a concept does not form an explicit part in many accounts of recovery from mental illness, it needs to be regarded as the constitutive frame of ownership on which the whole complex of mental illness and recovery rests. It is for the loss of accountability that mental illness is represented as a sever threat to the society and forms the reason for neglecting the subject's rights of ownership in the court of legal judgment. The legal system defines and prescribes accountability as a necessary condition for the individual to be judged as a subject of responsibility. The legal consequences for the subject of mental illness, often considered a sort of collateral to its mental suffering, builds necessarily the forefront of the recovery process.

Reclaiming the ownership of resources, be they cognitive, social or material, internal or external, is not just a claim of access to their use, but implies a social justification process for their use. Counting on the owner of resources to have awareness about the potential effects of their use is what account-*ability* refers to. The impressive consequences on the subject, once accountability is psychologically and even legally disapproved, give plain evidence of the significance of ownership, and more precisely, the psychological significance of responsibility.

The psychological literature treats responsibility mainly against the background of Heider's (1958) attribution theory, evidencing the mental components of responsibility such as internal attribution of the cause, intention of the actual effect, foreseeability of the effect and social justification of the cause (Hamilton, 1978). The more existential implications which are at stake with the judgment of responsibility have however remained in the backdrop of this conception of responsibility. Responsibility is not just about the question of whom to address for guilt and merit of effects, about the social *coverage* of actual and potential risks and events, but about a *social* frame of reference whereby a subject's *significance* as an agent is included or excluded, present or absent, declared or denied. The social negation of responsibility is therefore not just the negation of ownership (object of responsibility), but must be considered as the negation of a "true" locus of decision or intention (el Sehity, 2011). In its generalized form, as in the case of severe mental illness, the complete negation of accountability cannot but bring about a progressive annihilation of the subject.

Let us consider here the case where responsibility is not just denied to the subject ("we know, it is not your fault. . . ") but personally given up by a subject in crisis:

> "It was clear to me then, too, that I wanted someone else to take over the responsibility. I couldn't do it on my own. I desperately wanted someone else to do it." (Narratives in Topor, 2001, p.183)

By renouncing responsibility, the subject transfers the ownership of its powers to the "custody" of a more powerful/competent party. This transfer can be regarded as a standard component of tutorial relations (Conte & Castelfranchi, 1995; Castelfranchi & Falcone, 2010): The subject itself lacks sufficient awareness of its true interests so that another party is put in charge to decide for it. In the subject's state of acute mental crisis, the tutor takes over the full powers of the individual and is charged with the responsibility for the same. From there on the subject finds itself in a situation of "structured irresponsibility" where the tutor forms a socio-cognitive shield not only against failure and blame but also success and merit.

As stressed by Castelfranchi, the tutor should have the active goal to restitute the delegated powers to the individual as soon as possible. This would be natural, given the overwhelming weight of responsibility the tutor assumes. The tragedy of the transfer of responsibility in the psychiatric context lies however in the fact (1) that the tutorial relation is embedded in an institutional frame, where the subjects are confined to their roles based on "responsibility" (professional) and "non-responsibility" (client), and (2) that the delegated responsibility cannot be recovered from "the" professional, but must be claimed in the social arena by the means of trusted exchanges, and more specifically, in the subject's role as a veritable trustee[2]. Reclaiming responsibility represents the main struggle of the recovering subject, a struggle that is ventured socially in the sense of gaining back the right of ownership as a trusted subject of responsibility, and individually, through the reestablishment of an internal as well as stable "locus of control".

3.3.3 Recovering internality: The social claim

The acceptance of proper resources and the claim of responsibility for these formulate a social claim, for what is considered to be responsibly owned by one cannot be meaningfully claimed by another. The social claim of ownership addresses an essential component of the recovering individual as an autonomous subject. The recovery process necessarily conflicts with the patient role which is defined by the subject's compliance to the expert treatment it is submitted/committed to. The social claim of ownership represents therefore an essential emacipatory act towards the subject's full rights as a citizen:

> "Even if I am an unlucky person, I'm still a free citizen and no one can make me take anything. They can say "why don't you try to get better?" and Dr. M. is a doctor who cures people with medicine, all doctors cure people with medicine. (...) I definitely needed something more complete, a more complete course of treatment. When we disagreed on this, I practically bared my teeth at him and said: "we're not going to get into legal things here, are we? Or give me social assistance which I have a right to, remembering that I'm, to all intends and purposes, a free citizen or I'm going to call

---

[2] A socio-cognitive account of responsibility could find seminal foundation within the theoretic framework of the trustee as recently presented in Castelfranchi and Falcone's comprehensive monograph "Trust Theory" (2010). Of specific interest for the analysis of responsibility has to be considered their chapter "On the Trustee's Side: Trust as Relational Capital" (2010, Chap 10).

a lawyer, what do you want from me?" ... And now I don't take anything." (Luca in Mezzina et al., 2006, p.50)

Without the social claim of one's own decisions, own rights, agency powers, the individual's ownership would turn into mere properties in the sense of an object's qualities, but not constitute potentials at full disposition of the individual. Ownership in general, and more specifically in the recovery process from mental illness, leads necessarily to an emancipatory act, whereby the subject's internality is (re)established and socially claimed as the definite *locus* (a claim implicitly and explicitly undermined by the medical approach to mental illness, when the focus is set on the pharmacological treatment). This claim requires not only the personal commitment to control but also depends on the social recognition and acceptance of the same.

The aggressive attitude shown in Luca's statement above further indicates an instrumental emotive component of the recovery process where the subject's struggle for personal power becomes palpable. Recovering from a long-standing career of "structured dis-empowerment" (medication, manipulation, coercion to-, persuasion to-, suggestion to- and conviction to comply), a fundamental rearrangement of social dependencies and power-balances has to be considered as an almost inevitable part of the recovery process in which the emotive dimension is decisive. We will address two forms of this dimension relevant for the reclaim of the individual power-to and the social reclaim of power-over respectively: self-trust and emancipator pride.

Self-trust and Recovery Exchange

On the individual level a self-trust task is the necessary condition for the recovering subject to challenge the socially recognized powers of experts and professionals, and their prognostic judgments about its future.

"Within the realms of psychiatric practice it is accepted that the most powerful practitioner is the psychiatrist. Their power is rooted not only in the authority given to them by the state, but also in their singular right to make diagnosis. It is this ownership of a supposed expert knowledge that gives them so much power over their clients. I would content that the real expert of the client's experience is the client and it is they not the psychiatrist that own the knowledge that makes recovery a possibility." (Coleman, 2004, p.56)

The belief that one's recovery is not just possible but even probable is necessarily based on self-trust, that is, trust in one's own powers, for:

"It is not enough 'to be able to': in order to really be able, having the power of, the agent must also belief (be aware) of having the 'power of', otherwise they will renounce, they will nor exploit their skills nor resources." (Castelfranchi & Falcone, 2010, p.48)

The attitude of acceptance, its underlying cognitive process of belief-revision, provides an essential cognitive output which needs to be trusted in order to form a solid base for the social claim of ownership to be ventured. Self-trust is likely best initiated and promoted by the experience of being socially considered a veritable trustee. To be counted on, to be entrusted with real values, such as the case in significant economic exchange relations, provides the individual with an evidence based belief in its formerly lost accountability.

It is well recognized that reciprocation plays an important role for the individual's health and well-being in interpersonal relationships in self-help groups (Buunk & Schaufeli, 1999). Different to the implicit or explicit subjection to professional expertise (power), help is offered by request and not by default. Equally, there is no social role by default which might lead to the subject's subalternity. This reciprocity leads to the reestablishment of meaningful relationships repairing the social damage inflicted by the isolation and discrimination of mental health users. Through self-help groups the subject recreates a network of mutual dependencies accounting for its powers as well as its needs:

> "The main function of pro-social or positive sociality is the multiplication of the power of the participating agents. (. . .) Any agent, while remaining limited in its capabilities, skill and resources, finds the number of goals it can pursue and achieve increased by virtue of its "use" of others' skills and resources." (Castelfranchi, 2003, p. 228f)

With each step in the reciprocal exchange the subject regains confidence in its powers leading to the rehabilitation of its identity:

> "Positive experiences prepare the groundwork for improving one's self-image. As the person's self-image becomes increasingly more positive, it becomes a resource for coping with symptoms and the stigma that the person now has to contend with. The new self-image begins more and more to function as a protective shield against residual signs of illness and detrimental aspects of the environment and living conditions. The insight that one can influence one's environment provides a foundation for managing the illness." (Topor, 2001 p. 122)

The conquest of self-trust inevitably brings about a growing conquest of social ground, rejecting on one hand the unjust presumptions and on the other hand challenging the community with the subject's unexpected powers. The latter finds its open expression in the form of emancipatory pride as evidenced by social movements such as Mad-pride.

Mad-pride

The experience of mental illness is unfortunately too often connected to an experience of shame and humiliation. Shame represents hereby an experience with painful and devastating effects on the subject as a whole and not only just a specific behavior. Shame is a moral emotion, in the sense that it acts as an element of self-assessment with profound relational implications (Castelfranchi and Poggi, 1988 [2005]). Humiliation refers to an action (humiliate or being humiliated) and the experience of the subject (to feel oneself humiliated). It is a mental process of subjugation that damages or dampens pride, honor or dignity since the negative evaluation of the humiliator is shared by the humiliated subject (Silver et al, 1986).

For the subject's recovery process it is indispensable that the originally shared humiliating evaluation is reevaluated and disagreed upon at a certain stage. The subject perceives the unjust evaluation as expressed by others as an offensive act to which it wrongfully agreed upon. Through hindsight, the recovering subject reframes the humiliating events of its negative evaluation as direct evidence of social injustice and discrimination, as an offence against its social integrity it needs to oppose to.

> "We make a radical demand, one of the most difficult to fulfill: we insist that people get inside our heads and skins and try to empathize. This is something that all outsider groups have demanded, yet the experience of psychosis may be the most forbidding of all. Our plea cannot be "we are just like you" because that isn't true. On the other hand it is not completely untrue." (Stephen Weiner, in Hatfield & Levley, 1993, p. 4)

Anti-stigma movements are devoted to the change of their participants' social identity by the construction of a "political identity". Anspach (1979) describes how the participation of former psychiatric patients in political movements generates an experience of self-determination, which replaces the feeling of powerlessness and helplessness. The movement's objective transfers into a new self-conception, a process which implies the development of a feeling of pride.

When the subject stops to believe that its experience of mental illness is something to be ashamed of, accepting and reevaluating it, several emotions are likely to emerge: anger and revenge for the personal experience of social discrimination, and indignation for this kind of social injustice. This is the emotive base of a form of pride that we call "emancipatory pride" which has an internal as well as social reparative function (Pocobello and Castelfranchi, 2009):

- Internally, emancipatory pride is functional to the subject to recover from shame. Not necessarily the subject is truly convinced that "madness" is something to be proud of, but it needs to be convinced that it is something for which it unjustly felt ashamed of, that it is not justified to be judged negatively for mental illness. The emergence of this form of pride promotes the key-elements of the recovery process such as self-acceptance, self-trust and reduces the sense of inferiority caused by the experience of stigmatization.
- Socially, the exhibition of a "mad-pride" is functional and probably even strategic to the change of the social evaluation of "madness" and the social conditions in which persons with mental disease live. This pride implies a message of non subjugation - "I do not care about your judgment" and a provocation challenging the societal evaluation of madness.

4 The re-covered Subject

> "I had a longing to come back to myself. I had almost left my good house for good, to see it as such, so to speak." (Richard in Topor, 2001, p.181)

The semantic core of re-covery in terms of to-cover offers a rich metaphoric message concerning the actual situation of the subject of mentally illness: the psychiatric patient's condition as a nude existence vis-à-vis a reductionist search to un-cover the subject's dysfunctional components, cannot be better captured than in the subject's claim for a "cover" to re-cover. The deprivation of internality due to the investigative clinical procedure, due to the transparent existence in the clinic, due to the continuous exhibition of its pathology in the therapeutic activity, due to delegated or even negated personal accountability, due to growing unilateral dependencies, due to the justification of means and needs etc. a literal re-covering is mandatory for a subject to reclaim "a life in its own rights".

The processes and stages from mental illness to recovery as outlined in this draft unfold along the narrative of an uncovered/discovered human subject and its need for its own cover. The last act of this drama of the re-covered subject touches upon the social context, the social admiration – even if silent – of the shameless subject of madpride.

Evidently, the whole story of the subject's recovery process can be recounted more coherently in terms of power relations, against the background of disempowerment as well as empowerment processes. Hopefully you remain available to this chapter of the recovered subject, Cristiano?

Acknowledgements Special thanks are to Maria Miceli and Mrs. E. R. for their valuable suggestions and comments on the draft and to Ron Coleman, who inspired us in this work.

References

1. American Psychological Association. (2009). Resolution on APA Endorsement of the Concept of Recovery for People with Serious Mental Illness. Chapter X. Professional Affairs (Part 2). Retrieved April 14, 2011, from http://www.apa.org/about/governance/council/policy/chapter-10b.aspx{\#}apa-endorse
2. Anspach, R. R. (1979). From stigma to identity politics: Political activism among the physically disabled and former mental patients. *Social Science & Medicine. Part A: Medical Psychology & Medical Sociology, 13*, 765-773. doi:10.1016/0271-7123(79)90123-8
3. Anthony, W. A. (1993). Recovery from Mental Illness: The Guiding Vision of the Mental Health Service System in the 1990s. *Psychosocial Rehbilitation Journal, 16*(4), 11-23.
4. Anthony, W., Rogers, S. E., & Farkas, M. (2003). Research on Evidence-Based Practices: Future Directions in an Era of Recovery. *Community Mental Health Journal, 39*(2), 101-114. doi:10.1023/A:1022601619482
5. Bachrach, L.(1996) *Deistitutionalization: promises, problems and prospects* In Knudsen, H. C. and Thornicroft, G. (Eds) (1996) *Mental Health Service Evaluation* . Cambridge University Press
6. Bleuler, M (1978). *The schizophrenic disorders – Long-term patient and family studies.* New Haven and London: Yale University Press.
7. Buunk, B. P., & Schaufeli, W. B. (1999). Reciprocity in Interpersonal Relationships: An Evolutionary Perspective on Its Importance for Health and Well-being. *European Review of Social Psychology, 10*, 259. doi:10.1080/14792779943000080
8. Castelfranchi, C. (2003). The Micro-Macro Constitution of Power. *ProtoSociology - An International Journal and Interdisciplinary Project, 18-19*, 208-265.
9. Castelfranchi, C., & Falcone, R. (2010). *Trust Theory: A Socio-Cognitive and Computational Model.* West Sussex: John Wiley and Sons.
10. Castelfranchi, C., & Miceli, M. (2009). The Cognitive-Motivational Compound of Emotional Experience. *Emotion Review, 1*(3), 223-231. doi:10.1177/1754073909103590
11. Castelfranchi, C., & Poggi, I. (2005). Vergogna. In C. Castelfranchi (Hrsg.), *Che figura. Emozioni e immagine sociale* (S 13-45). Milano: Il Mulino.

12. Ciompi, L (1980). The natural history of schizophrenia in the long term, *British Journal of Psychiatry*, Vol 136, May, p 413–420.
13. Conte, R., & Castelfranchi, C. (1995). *Cognitive and social action*. London: Routledge.
14. Coleman, R. (2004). *Recovery. An Alien Concept?* P & P Press: Isle of Lewis.
15. Deegan, P. E. (1988). Recovery: the lived experience of rehabilitation. *Psychosocial Rehbilitation Journal, 11*, 11-19.
16. Deegan, P. E. (1996). "Recovery as a Journey of the Heart." *Psychiatric Rehabilitation Journal, 19*(3), 91-97.
17. Eaton, WW. and Harrison, G. (1996). *Prevention priorities*. Current Opinion in Psychiatry,9, 141–143.
18. el Sehity, T. (2011). Eigenvermögen: Ein sozialkognitiver Grundriss. In T. Druyen (Hrsg.), *Vermögenskultur* (S 101-111). Wiesbaden: VS Verlag für Sozialwissenschaften.
19. Farkas, M. (2007). The vision of recovery today: what it is and what it means for services. *World Psychiatry, 6*(2), 68-74.
20. Fishbein, M., & Ajzen, I. (1973). Attribution of responsibility: A theoretical note. *Journal of Experimental Social Psychology, 9*(2), 148-153. doi:10.1016/0022-1031(73)90006-1
21. Hamilton, V. L. (1978). Who is Responsible? Toward a Social Psychology of Responsibility Attribution. Social Psychology, 41(4), 316-328.
22. Hatfield, A. B., & Lefley, H. P. (1993). Surviving mental illness: stress, coping, and adaptation. New York: Guilford Press.
23. HEA (1997). Mental health promotion: a quality framework. Health Education Authority: London.
24. Heider, F. (1958). *The psychology of interpersonal relations*. New York: John Wiley & Sons.
25. Hopper, K. (2007). Rethinking social recovery in schizophrenia: what a capabilities approach might offer. Social Science & Medicine, 65, 868-879.
26. Huxley, P. and Thornicroft, G. (2003). *Social inclusion, social quality and mental illness*, British Journal of Psychiary, 182, 289-290.
27. Jacobson, N., & Greenley, D. (2001). What Is Recovery? A Conceptual Model and Explication. *Psychiatr Serv, 52*(4), 482-485. doi:10.1176/appi.ps.52.4.482.
28. Kallen, H. M. (1942). Responsibility. Ethics, 52(3), 350-376.
29. Kawachi, I. and Kennedy B (1997). *Socioeconomic determinants of health: health and social cohesion. Why care about income inequality?* British Medical Journal,314, 1037–1040.
30. Keller, M. (1996). Verantwortung und Verantwortungsabwehr (The Attribution and Denial of Responsibility). *Zeitschrift fur Padagogik, 42*(1), 71-81.
31. Lahtinen, E. (eds.). (1999). *Framework for promoting mental health in Europe*. Hamina, (STAKES) National Research and Development Centre for Welfare and Health, Ministry of Social Affairs and Health: Finland.
32. Leff, J & Sartorius, N & Jablensky, A & Korten, A & Ernberg, G (1992). The international pilot study of schizophrenia: five-year follow-up findings. *Psychological medicine*, Vol 22, 1, p 131–145.
33. Lorini, E., & Castelfranchi, C. (2007). The cognitive structure of surprise: looking for basic principles. *Topoi, 26*(1), 133-149. doi:10.1007/s11245-006-9000-x
34. Meltzer, H., Gill, B. and Petticrew, M. (1995). *Economic Activity and Social Functioning of Adult with Psychiatric Disorders*. Office of population Censuses and Surveys, Survey of Psychiatric Morbidity in Great Britain , Report 2. HMSO: London.
35. Miceli, M., & Castelfranchi, C. (1997). Basic Principles of Psychic Suffering: A Preliminary Account. *Theory Psychology, 7*(6), 769-798. doi:10.1177/0959354397076003
36. Miceli, M., & Castelfranchi, C. (2001). Acceptance as a Positive Attitude. *Philosophical Explorations: An International Journal for the Philosophy of Mind and Action, 4*(2), 112-134. doi:10.1080/10002001058538711
37. Miceli, M., & Castelfranchi, C. (2002). The Mind and the Future: The (Negative) Power of Expectations. *Theory Psychology, 12*(3), 335-366. doi:10.1177/0959354302012003015
38. Miceli, M., & Castelfranchi, C. (2010). Hope: The Power of Wish and Possibility. *Theory & Psychology, 20*(2), 251 -276. doi:10.1177/0959354309354393
39. O'Brien, J. & Lovett, H. (1992). Finding a way toward everyday lives: The contribution of person-centered planning. Harrisburg, PA: PA Office of Mental Retardation.

40. Patel, V. and Kleinman, A. (2003). *Poverty and common mental disorders in developing countries*. Bulletin of the World Health Organization, 81, 609–615.
41. Pocobello, R., & Castelfranchi, C. (2009). Pride: Cognitive Aspects and Social Implications. *The 17th Annual Meeting of the European Society for Philosophy and Psychology* (Bd. 17, S 37). Presented on the European Society for Philosophy and Psychology, Budapest: Wiley.
42. Ralph, R. and Corrigan, P. (eds) (2005) *Recovery in mental illness: Broadening our understanding of wellness*, Washington, DC: American Psychological Association.
43. Romme M., Escher S., Dillon J., Corstens D., Morris M. (2009) Living with Voices. 50 Stories of Recovery, PCCS Books, Ross-on-Wye.
44. Shaw, M. E., & Sulzer, J. L. (1964). An empirical test of Heider's levels in attribution of responsibility. *Journal of Abnormal and Social Psychology, 69*(1), 39–46. doi:10.1037/h0040051
45. Silver, M., Conte, R., Miceli, M., & Poggi, I. (1986i). Humiliation: Feeling, Social Control and the Construction of Identity. *Journal for the Theory of Social Behaviour, 16*(3), 269-283. doi:10.1111/j.1468-5914.1986.tb00080.x
46. Sowers, W. (2005). Transforming Systems of Care: The American Association of Community Psychiatrists Guidelines for Recovery Oriented Services. *Community Mental Health Journal, 41*(6), 757-774. doi:10.1007/s10597-005-6433-4
47. The Care Services Improvement Partnership, Royal College of Psychiatrists, & Social Care Institute for Excellence. (2007). *A common purpose: Recovery in future mental health services*. A Joint Position Paper. London: Social Care Institute for Excellence.
48. Topor, A. (2001). Managing the contradictions: Recovery from severe mental disorders. SSSW no 18, Stockholm, Department of Social Work, Stockholm University.
49. Topor, A., Borg, M., Mezzina, R., Sells, D., Marin, I. & Davidson, L. (2006). Others: The role of family, friends and professionals in the recovery process. American Journal of Psychiatric Rehabilitation. 9, 17-38.
50. WHO (1979). Schizophrenia – an international follow-up study. Chichester: Wiley.

Part V
Trust and delegation

Chapter 22
The complex relationships between trusting and being trustworthy

Rino Falcone and Maria Miceli

Abstract In this work we aim to explore the complex relationships existing between trusting and being trustworthy. On the one hand, after considering the possible signs of trustworthiness, we will focus on trust itself as a special sign of the *trustor's* trustworthiness. On the other hand, we will analyze how the trustor's trustful attitude can actually increase the *trustee's* trustworthiness. We will identify three distinct mental paths which may lead a trustee to being (more) trustworthy in response to a trustor's trust.

1 Introduction

Trust has been – and still is – a topic of great interest to Cristiano Castelfranchi. We are lucky enough to share a path of work with Cristiano in this frontier research area in which social, psychological, economical, computational and technological approaches confront with each other. Cristiano provides fascinating insights and a sharp reasoning to our common work, being able to capture the more essential aspects of a phenomenon, even when they are hidden in some minor facet of it. We have learnt to understand that even his "shallow" remarks hide in fact some crucial intuition.

From his first approaches to trust, Cristiano has argued in favor of a view of it in terms of a complex structure of beliefs and goals, also implying that the trustor should have a "theory of the mind" of the trustee, and vice versa. Following in his footsteps, this paper addresses the complex relationships

Rino Falcone
Goal-Oriented Agents Lab (GOAL), Institute of Cognitive Sciences and Technologies, CNR, Italy
e-mail: rino.falcone@istc.cnr.it

Maria Miceli
Goal-Oriented Agents Lab (GOAL), Institute of Cognitive Sciences and Technologies, CNR, Italy
e-mail: maria.miceli@istc.cnr.it

between trusting and being trustworthy, which entail some exploration into the trustor's and the trustee's theory of each other's mind. We also wish to remark that this work is, so to say, modelled after our relationship with Cristiano. The route from trust to trustworthiness in fact evokes to us our personal relationship with him, and the significant impact of his trustful attitude on our own trustworthiness.

Thus, we try to build upon our socio-cognitive model of trust (e.g., Castel-franchi & Falcone, 1998; Castelfranchi & Falcone, 2010), to show in particular how trust may be both a *sign of the trustor's trustworthiness* and a *facilitator of the trustee's trustworthiness*. It is worth specifying from the beginning that we do not claim that the relationships we hypothesize between trust and trust-worthiness necessarily or typically hold in any context or circumstance. While assuming that one's trust *may* be, on the one hand, a sign of one's own trust-worthiness, and, on the other hand, a facilitator of another's trustworthiness, we just intend to explore *how* a trusting behavior may favor the ascription of trustworthiness to the trustor, and *how* it may facilitate the trustee's trustwor-thiness.

In the following, after presenting a few basic features of Castelfranchi and Falcone's model of trust and trustworthiness, we will consider the possible signs of trustworthiness, and focus on trust as a special sign of the trustor's trustworthiness. That is, we will argue that y's trusting attitude may favor x's inference about y's trustworthiness, either in virtue of x's previous positive experience with "high trustors" or through some implicit reasoning that traces y's choice to risk being disappointed by x back to y's trustworthiness. Then, moving to trust as a facilitator of the trustee's trustworthiness, we will identify three distinct mental paths leading the trustee to being (more) trustworthy in response to the trustor's trusting attitude. The first path starts from y's (the trustee's) inference about x's (the trustor's) trustworthiness: if y assumes x to be trustworthy, y also comes to believe either that she can incur the costs associated with being trustworthy towards x or that x deserves reciprocation; in either case y's trustworthiness is likely to increase. (From now on, for the sake of clarity, we will refer to x as a he and to y as a she.) The second mental path prescinds from y's possible inference about x's trustworthiness: here, y merely considers x's willingness to risk being disappointed by her; such a "willing vulnerability" on x's part may induce y to feel committed to display a caregiving and trustworthy behavior, motivated by either altruistic or self-interested goals. The third path requires that y believes x to be a competent evaluator of y herself: if y believes she is trusted by such a competent evaluator, y is also likely to believe she deserves x's trust; as a result, y's self-confidence increases, and she feels encouraged to behave (more) trustworthily.

2 Trust and Trustworthiness: Basic Features

According to Castelfranchi and Falcone (2010), trusting somebody entails not only feeling confident in predicting his or her behavior, but also *expecting* such a behavior, that is, having both the *goal* and the *belief* that the trustee will show a certain conduct, and relying on it. In fact, a simple *prediction* can be defined as a belief that a certain future event p is (more or less) probable, and it involves no necessary personal concern or goal about p. In contrast, by *expectation* we mean an internally represented wish or goal about p together with the belief that p has a certain probability. In other words, an expectation is a prediction the subject is concerned about (Miceli & Castelfranchi, 2002). In particular, a *positive* expectation implies congruence between one's goal and one's prediction, whereas a negative expectation implies incongruence between one's goal and one's prediction.

A trustor x has *positive expectations* about his trustee's y conduct. These positive expectations are grounded on some *positive evaluations* of y, namely about her *competence* and *willingness* to pursue and achieve certain goals; moreover x's positive expectations imply his perceived *dependence* on y: that is, he needs the provision of a resource or action from her (this is precisely the goal implied in his expectation), and relies on her competence and willingness to obtain what he needs. Actually, any goal attainment, as well as any goal-directed action, may have some part that is perceived as outside one's own control and is delegated to another agent, who can be object of trust (Castelfranchi, 1998).

Trust is particularly relevant in conditions of ignorance or uncertainty (e.g., Gambetta, 2000). However, in comparison with other anticipatory mental attitudes such as mere *hope*, it implies greater confidence – namely, as already stressed, a positive expectation about the delegated agent's capability and willingness to realize p. (Conversely, hoping does not necessarily imply any positive expectation; while still hoping that y will realize p, x might even harbor a negative expectation about her capability or willingness to bring about p; see Miceli & Castelfranchi, 2010).

Still, trust is not equal to positive expectation. In trust there is something more: a sort of *commitment* to the positive expectation (see Luhmann, 2000). Going back to that part in the process leading to goal attainment which is outside x's control, when this delegated part (d) is object of trust, x relies on d and on the delegated agent y (Falcone & Castelfranchi, 2000), which implies not only acknowledging his dependence on y, but also *committing himself to expect that d will be realized by y*. This "commitment to expect" is something more than a mere positive expectation because it implies x's decision to rely on y (which entails some risk), and his doing something—namely, including d in his general plan, coordinating his own actions with d, and abstaining from interfering with it.

As far as trustworthiness (TW) is concerned, it is worth, first of all, distinguishing between *objective* and subjective or *perceived* TW of a certain agent y (Castelfranchi & Falcone, 2010). Whereas objective TW basically coincides with what y is actually able and willing to do,[1] perceived TW refers to x's *evaluations* and *expectations* about y's competence and willingness relative to some kind of task.

---

[1] We are neglecting here that objective TW is in general a function of the different trustors and of their relationships with y.

As in Castelfranchi and Falcone (1998), we introduce a set of agents (Ag) and consider trust as a relational construct between the trustor (x, with $x \in Ag$) and the trustee (y, with $y \in Ag$), about a specific task (τ) in a given context (c):

$$Trust(x, y, c, \tau, g_x) \tag{1}$$

where x's goal (g_x, with respect to which x's trust is tested/activated) is also explicitly mentioned.

The degree to which x trusts y (degree of trust: $DoT_{x,y,c}(\tau))^2$ will depend on both the perceived TW of y – in a given context (c) about a specific task (τ) – and x's own propensity to trust (e. g., Schoorman, Mayer, & Davis, 1996), which is also contingent upon the value of the specific goal pursued.

Thus, y's subjective TW identifies some properties of y (the trustee) as perceived by x (the trustor) when a relationship is established between y and x relative to the accomplishment of some task τ on behalf of x, within a certain context. Such properties amount to y's competence and willingness. "Competence" refers to y's capabilities (skills, know-how, know-that, etc.) relative to τ or to a class of tasks τ belongs to; these capabilities may be viewed as *dependent* on the context at hand, whereas they are generally considered as *independent* of the trustor, that is, not contingent upon x's identity or behavior. "Willingness" refers to y's motivations, namely her intention and commitment to accomplish τ; y's willingness may be to some extent *independent* of the task at hand (that is, it may be a general motivational disposition), though some tasks may happen to elicit y's willingness more than others; conversely, it is often trustor-specific, that is, it is likely to depend on the identity, characteristics, and behavior exibited by x, or the class of agents x belongs to, though it may also stem from an undifferentiated prosocial attitude.

Thus, y's *trustworthiness* as perceived by x in context c about task τ can be expressed as:

$$TW_{y,c}^x(\tau) = f(Competence_{y,c}^x(\tau), Willingness_{y,c}^x(\tau)) \tag{2}$$

where:

- f is in general a function that preserves monotonicity;
- $Competence_{y,c}^x(\tau)$ is y's competence as perceived by x about task τ in context c, and
- $Willingness_{y,c}^x(\tau)$ is y's willingness as perceived by x about task τ in context c.

But, what are the possible signs of y's trustworthiness? That is, what are y's features that favor x's perception of her TW? This important issue would require a work of its own. Here, we will limit ourselves to outline a few basic signs or criteria, and then focus on a special sign of y's TW: her own trusting attitude and behavior.

---

[2] From now by $DoT_{x,y,c}(\tau)$ we will mean, simplifying the original model, not just the degree of trust but also the trust action in the case in which this degree is over a certain threshold (dependent on the trustor). With $0 \le DoT_{x,y,c}(\tau) \le 1$.

3 Signs of Trustworthiness

As stressed by Castelfranchi and Falcone (2010), the nature of TW is inherently attributional: both y's competence and y's willingness (relative to τ) are internal properties or "kripta" (Bacharach & Gambetta, 2000) that x ascribes to y by inferring them from external signs.

These internal properties (Competence, Willingness) can be inferred from several information sources:

- y's previous behavior (as observed by x);
- y's categorization, that is, the category of agents y belongs to (as identified by x);
- y's reputation or other agents' recommendation about y.

A first general source of information is no doubt y's *previous behavior*, namely her previous successes or failures in accomplishing τ or similar tasks. However, y's actual performance is not sufficient for inferring her *internal* qualities (both her competence and willingness) because such successes or failures might have been favored by *external* and contingent factors. Therefore, as explained by attribution theory (e.g., Kelley, 1967) an observer (in our case, a potential trustor x) needs to discriminate between internal causes (ability or effort) and external ones (task difficulty or luck) of y's performance. Basically, x will rely on three factors:

1) The *consistency* of y's performance, that is, whether y behaves the same way in the same circumstances; considering that:

$\tau \in T$ (T is the set of possible tasks), and

$$Ag_1 = \left\{ z | z \in Ag \cap delegated^x_{z,y,c}(\tau) \right\} \qquad (3)$$

i.e., Ag_1 – a subset of Ag – is composed by those agents (possibly including x himself) who – according to x's observations – have delegated task τ to y ($delegated^x_{z,y,c}$) in previous situations.

Thus, *high consistency* is attributed when for each fixed couple (τ, Ag_1) and the same kind of context c, y's performance is significantly constant.[3]

Also interesting is the case in which τ is a class of tasks, and y behaves in the same way in different contexts relative to the same class of tasks.

2) The *distinctiveness* of y's performance, that is, whether y behaves differently in different cicumstances; *high distinctiveness* is attributed when for each different couple (τ, Ag_1), $y's$ performance is significantly different,[4] (with both the context and the delegating agent either constant or changing). Ag_1 is defined in (3).

3) Others' *consensus* about y's performance, that is whether other people (different from y) would behave the same way in similar circumstances; *high*

---

[3] By "significantly constant" we mean that, given $\forall (z_1, z_2) \in Ag_1$ (with $z_1 \neq z_2$), we have $Perform^x_{y,z_1,c}(\tau) = Perform^x_{y,z_2,c}(\tau)$, where $Perform^x_{y,z_i,c}(\tau)$ indicates the world states (in x's view) produced by y's performance of task τ delegated by z_i.

[4] By "significantly different" we mean that, given $\forall (z_1, z_2) \in Ag_1$ we have $Perform^x_{y,z_1,c}(\tau) \neq Perform^x_{y,z_2,c}(\tau)$.

consensus is attributed when for each fixed couple (τ, Ag_1), a set of agents (Ag_2) exists with Ag_1 defined in (3) and:

$$Ag_2 = \left\{ w | z, w \in Ag \cap delegated^x_{z,w,c}(\tau) \right\} \qquad (4)$$

(where it is also possible that $z = x$); such that, as observed by x, y and w have the same performance. The larger Ag_2, the higher the consensus about y's performance.

In order for x to attribute y's performance to internal factors, the relevant signs will be its *high consistency, low distinctiveness* and *low consensus*.

In fact, if y repeatedly behaves the same way relative to the same kind of task, context, and delegating agents (high consistency) there is some reason to ascribe her behavior to her (lack of) competence and/or (lack of) willingness, rather than to external factors.

If y behaves the same way in different circumstances (low distinctiveness), this is also a sign that her performance can be attributed to internal factors. In particular, it is a sign that such internal factors play a major role, for better or worse, in determining her performance. For instance, if y complies with her commitments to help z (or x himself) as well as other people by accomplishing τ as well as other kinds of task, this is a clear sign of her high and versatile competence, as well as of her generalized willingness to help others; conversely, if y fails to meet most of her commitments in different circumstances, this is a clear sign of her general lack of competence and/or general unwillingness, independent of specific tasks or delegating agents.

Finally, if y behaves differently from how other people tend to behave in similar circumstances (low consensus), this is a further sign that her performance is the effect of some internal factor. For instance, if other people are likely to accomplish τ on x's behalf whereas y fails to do the same; or conversely, if y is the only agent who accomplishes τ on x's behalf, x (as well as an external observer) will infer that y's behavior depends on y's (lack of) competence and/or willingness, rather than on external factors.

We can conclude, then, that as far as y's previous performance is concerned, the signs of her trustworthiness $\left(TW^x_y(\tau) \right)$ relative to τ as perceived by x will be the *high consistency* and *low consensus* of her *success* in accomplishing τ (or similar tasks) on the trustor's behalf; whereas the *low distinctiveness* of y's successful performance can be viewed as a sign of a more versatile competence and generalized willingness.

However y's past successful performance and the criteria for ascribing it to internal causes (thus inferring positive evaluations and expectations about y's competence and willingness) are just one source of information x may rely on. Incidentally, this information is not always available, in that x may lack experience with y and her behavior.

Other sources of information are the category of people y belongs to (e.g., Levin, Whitener, & Cross, 2006), and in particular the socially recognized role(s) y accomplishes.

Thus, given a set of agents $\left(Ag = \{x_1 \ldots x_n\}\right)$ and a set of classes of agents $\left(Class = \{Class_1 \ldots Class_n\}\right)$ (and supposing the trivial case in which each agent belongs to just one class), the trustworthiness transfer from a category (i.e. $Class_i$) to an agent (i.e. y) (in a given context c for a given task τ) is based on the following general rule:

$$\text{If} \quad y \in Class_i \quad \text{Then} \quad TW^x_{y,c}(\tau) = TW^x_{Class,c}(\tau) \tag{5}$$

There may also be a more specific attribution with respect to the particular components of trustworthiness:

$$Competence^x_y(\tau) = Competence^x_{Class_i}(\tau) \qquad \text{and/or}$$
$$Willingness^x_y(\tau) = Willingness^x_{Class_i}(\tau)$$

For instance, a policeman is expected to be competent about traffic rules; a nun is expected to be considerate of others' needs, and thus willing to help people (Falcone et al., in press).

The third kind of information sources consists in *other people's evaluations* or *recommendation* (Yu & Singh, 2003; Yolum & Singh, 2003) about y's TW. In fact, especially when neither relevant evidence of y's behavior nor information about her social role is available or pertinent to the task at hand, x is likely to resort to such "second-hand" experience, which recursively poses the problem of *the evaluators' trustworthiness*, in terms of both their competence and willingness. (About the problem of *trust transitivity* see Falcone and Castelfranchi (2010).) In particular as far as *recommendation* is concerned, we can say that:

$$TW^x_{y,c}(\tau) = f_1\left(TW^x_{z,c}(DoT_{z,y,c}(\tau)) \cap TW^x_{z,c}\left(comm_{z,x,c}(DoT_{z,y,c}(\tau))\right)\right) \tag{6}$$

in cases of *direct recommendation*; and

$$TW^x_{y,c}(\tau) = f_1\left(TW^x_{z,c}\left(DoT_{z,y,c}(\tau)\right)\right) \tag{7}$$

in cases of *indirect recommendation*; f_1 is a function that preserves monotonicity, and the operator $comm_{z,x,c}(\tau)$ indicates z's communication to x about τ in context c. In other words, y's TW about task τ as perceived by x is a function of z's TW (as perceived by x) about the task of trusting y about task τ, combined with z's trustworthiness in communicating this value. In the case of *indirect recommendation* we have just the first term.

Others' evaluations of y's TW may also be "frozen" into such special artefacts as various possible kinds of certificate, attesting y's competence and/or willingness.

Finally, the "experience" x may resort to can even be of the "third-hand" type, as when others who have no personal evidence of y's TW just report to x about y's "reputation" (Conte & Paolucci, 2002; Sabater & Sierra, 2001) within her reference group. This case of *reputation* can be represented as:

$$TW^x_{y,c}(\tau) = f_2\Big(TW^x_{RG,c}(DoT_{RG,y,c}(\tau)) \cap TW^x_{z,c}\big(comm_{z,x,c}(DoT_{RG,y,c}(\tau))\big)\Big) \quad (8)$$

where f_2 is a function that preserves monotonicity and RG is the group of agents in which that value of trust is shared/spread (*reputation*), while z is the "informant", that is, the agent who informs x about the reputation value.

Another, fairly different, source of information about y's TW may be y's appearance, body posture, eye contact, and facial properties and expressions. These nonverbal cues have been found to exert a powerful impact on our perceptions of others' mental attitudes and affective states (e.g., Aguinis, Simonsen, & Pierce, 1998; DePaulo, Rosenthal, Green, & Rosenkrantz, 1982), by inducing rapid and automatic "evaluations" of others' competence and willingness, with special reference to such traits as power, dominance, hostility, sincerity, and credibility. As pointed out by Castelfranchi and Falcone (2010), we are here in the realm of very special "evaluations"—namely, *intuitive appraisals*, which are not based on justifiable arguments, but on some "feeling" that is directly and automatically elicited by such external signs.

A few interesting findings are worth mentioning in this regard. For instance, facial resemblance between y and a potential trustor has been found to significantly raise the incidence of the latter's trusting behavior (e.g. DeBruine, 2002). In other words, all other things (context, kind of task, etc.) being equal, when y's face resembles x's face, x is more likely to perceive y as trustworthy, and to behave accordingly. Another study (Schlicht, Shimojo, Camerer, Battaglia, & Nakayama, 2010) has shown that in a competitive game (a simulated and simplified poker game), the participants relied on their opponents' facial expressions (simulated faces whose expressions were systematically modified) when deciding how to play. "Trustworthy faces" – that is, faces with u-shaped mouth and large eyes with a slightly surprised look, which can be roughly described as expressing a very quiet and mild happiness – had a powerful impact on the participants' choices, in comparison with either "untrustworthy" or neutral faces. In particular, the participants tended to make mistakes and folded more frequently when playing with "trustworthy" opponents (who, appearing "trustworthy", were probably supposed to have good hands when they betted).[5]

Understandably, such findings have elicited evolutionary explanations. Actually, face-"reading" seems to be deeply rooted in the human brain. As shown by a number of studies (e.g., Johnson, 2005; Lavie, Ro, & Russell, 2003; Vuilleumier, 2000), the human face is prioritized for attention selection. In particular, facial resemblance is a plausible cue of genetic relatedness in humans, and organisms are expected to be sensitive to genetic relatedness, especially when making decisions about how to deal with others (DeBruine, 2002). As far as facial expressions of affective states are concerned, their "universality" is well-known (e.g., Ekman & Friesen, 1986), as well as the human ability to recognize

---

[5] Even some stable facial properties, such as male facial width (a testosterone-linked trait, predictive of male aggression) also seem to be related to perceived trustworthiness (Stirrat & Perret, 2010): men with wider faces are perceived as less trustworthy, especially by women – and actually, they have been found to behave in an untrustworthy manner (that is, they are more likely to exploit their partners' trust)!

a variety of emotional expressions, the early acquisition of such ability, its neural correlates, and its plausible functional value (e.g., Leppäner & Nelson, 2009). What is interesting to note about the "trustworthy" face is that it is an almost "neutral" face, in that it does not express any evident emotion, but just vaguely reminds of a mildly happy (or "friendly") face. As argued by Oosterhof and Todorov (2008), in the absence of clear emotional cues signalling somebody's attitudes and dispositions, faces are appraised in terms of their *similarity* to the basic expressions of happiness and anger.

It is worth stressing that appraisals of trustworthiness are *not* necessarily accurate (which, in evolutionary terms, is not so puzzling, if one assumes that the appraisal of emotionally neutral faces involves *overgeneralization* from facial cues that have evolutionary significance), and they play a major role only in the absence of other evaluative information about the person (Engell, Haxby, & Todorov, 2007). In other words, people are likely to resort to, and rely on, such cues especially when no other kind of information about the candidate trustee is available.

4 A Special Sign of Trustworthiness: Trust

We view trust as a possible sign of TW. That is, we suggest that if y shows a trusting attitude and behavior (either generalized or x-specific), x is likely to perceive her as trustworthy. Let us try to explain why.

To start with, it is worth observing that, as a matter of fact, trust has been found to be positively associated with TW (e.g., Rotter, 1980). That is, "high trustors" actually tend to be trustworthy. Such TW is primarily described in terms of *willingness* (in particular, sincerity and honesty), rather than *competence*. This is fairly common in psychological approaches to trust, which typically focus on the motivational facet of TW – prosocial disposition, truthfulness, observance of one's own commitments – though in various instances the competence facet is more or less tacitly implied. (For instance, keeping one's promise to accomplish a certain task implies both one's willingness and *ability* to accomplish it.) High trustors have also been found to be distinct from gullible or exploitable people (e.g., Gurtman, 1992; Rotter, 1980): high trustors show a propensity to trust in the absence of evidence to the contrary; however, unlike gullible people, they do *not* trust others when there is some clear-cut evidence of their untrustworthiness.

In more formal terms: given $y \in Ag$, $Ag_3 \subset Ag$, $\tau \in T$, and $\sigma_{y,min}$ ($0 \le \sigma_{y,min} \le 1$) expressing y's *minimum threshold* for trusting any trustee in the given set of agents Ag about task τ (a specific task or a class of tasks); and

$$Ag_3 = \left\{ z \mid z \in Ag \cap \left(\neg untrustworthy_z^y(\tau) \right) \right\} \tag{9}$$

that is, each z is an agent who is not explicitly untrustworthy for y, we may say:

If for each $z \in Ag_3,$ $DoT_{y,z,c}(\tau) \geq \sigma^y_{min}$ Then $TW_{y,c}(\tau) \geq \Sigma^{Ag}_{min}$ (10)

where $TW_{y,c}(\tau)$ indicates y's trustworthiness on task τ in context c; while Σ^{Ag}_{min} $(0 \leq \Sigma^{Ag}_{min} \leq 1)$ is *the minimum threshold* for considering an agent as trustworthy (as established in the community of agents Ag).

In other words, if y is a high trustor (that is, one who trusts all the agents in Ag unless they are explicitly untrustworthy), then y is trustworthy in the Ag community. This is an objective representation of y's trustworthiness (whether or not y is perceived as trustworthy by any agent in Ag).

But where does y's propensity to trust come from? In our view, it comes precisely from her own TW. (In other words, it is y's trustfulness that follows from y's trustworthiness and not vice versa; better, y's willingness and competence that make her trustworthy imply her trusting behavior.) In particular, y's trusting attitude may be favored by her own TW in two possible ways.

4.1 Projection of One's Trustworthiness onto Others

On the one hand, y may be likely to *project* her TW onto others. Projection is a special case of ascription. While ascription just entails the attribution of some mental attitudes to others (Ballim & Wilks, 1991; Wilks & Ballim, 1987), projection consists in the ascription of *one's own* mental attitudes. This general cognitive bias of egocentric ascription, that leads one to believe to be the "measure of all things", and to take one's own mind as the prototype of mind, is a fundamental heuristics, a *default ascriptional rule*, according to which one assumes that "another person's view is the same as one's own except where there is explicit evidence to the contrary" (Ballim & Wilks, 1991, p. 156). The same attributional bias accounts for our tendency to believe that others share what we think, feel, and do. This is known, in Piagetian terms, as a form of assimilation (Piaget, 1929), and in attributional terms as the *false consensus effect* (e.g., Marks & Miller, 1987; Ross, Greene, & House, 1977). [6]

Thus, a trustworthy y is likely to project her own characteristics and dispositions, including her own TW, onto others. Such a default ascription of TW to others favors her trusting attitude: Since she considers others as trustworthy (unless there is explicit evidence to the contrary), she tends to trust them.

In more formal terms:

$\forall z \in Ag_3$, where Ag_3 is defined in (8)

If $TW_{y,c}(\tau) \geq \Sigma^{Ag}_{min}$ Then (through projection) $TW^y_{z,w,c}(\tau) \geq \Sigma^y_{min}$ (11)

---

[6] Some cognitive advantages compensate for the costs of possible mistakes induced by egocentric ascription. Since people actually share a great number of mental attitudes, "it is not necessary to store all the common beliefs of agents, as they can be inferred through the ascriptional rule... Rather, we generally only need to store those beliefs of other agents that we believe a priori to differ from our own" (Ballim & Wilks, 1991, p. 162).

with w included in $Ag_4 = \left\{ w | w \in Ag \cap \left(\neg untrustworthy_w^z(\tau) \right) \right\}$;

and, as a consequence of this projected trustworthiness attributed to z, y will trust z:

$$DoT_{y,z,c}^y \geq \sigma_{min}^y \qquad (12)$$

4.2 "Strategic" Trust for Promoting Others' Trustworthiness

On the other hand, a trustworthy y may trust others independent of any projective process. Suppose y holds the *value* of TW. Values can be defined as beliefs of a special kind: those concerning desirable states or behaviors, transcending specific situations, and guiding the evaluation of other states, events, and behaviors (e.g., Schwartz, 1992). More specifically, a value is in our view a special type of *evaluation* (Miceli & Castelfranchi, 1989, 2000).

Evaluations are beliefs about "what is good/bad for what". An evaluation (for instance, "these scissors are sharp") implies the assignment of some (positive or negative) valence to an object, event, or state of the world, because the latter is viewed as a good or bad means for some goal (in our example, the goal of cutting something, or of hurting someone). In contrast, a value can be viewed as a *"cut off" evaluation* giving the goodness or badness of an entity, event or state *tout court*, without specifying what for. For example, having TW as a value is tantamount to saying that TW is judged a good thing in itself.

Evaluations generate goals: If an object o or a state or event p is held good for achieving some goal, there will possibly arise the further goal of acquiring o or bringing about p. Values too will generate goals according to the same functional principle: if something is good, it will be sought, pursued, etc.; if bad, it will be eschewed, opposed, and so on. However, whereas a goal generated by an evaluation is an *instrumental* goal, subordinate to the original one, a goal generated by a value is *terminal*, i.e. an end in itself. Moreover, the terminal goals generated by values are likely to be perceived in *normative terms*: If TW is a positive value of y's, y feels she *should* pursue the goal of being trustworthy. In particular, value-generated goals are functionally instrumental to maintaining or enhancing y's self-image; as a consequence y feels a need to be coherent with her values by pursuing the goals stemming from them (Miceli & Castelfranchi, 2012). Finally, the normative character of value-generated goals is likely to be extended to other people; that is, y will believe that, since TW is a value (something good in itself), this value and the consequent goal of being trustworthy are to be shared by others.

But, how to promote such a value in others? A trustworthy y may trust others *as a means for favoring their trustworthiness*. In fact, as we will discuss in greater detail in the next session, if others realize that they are trusted, their TW may increase. Thus, if y is aware of the influencing power of trust on others' TW, y may show a trusting attitude in order to promote others' TW.

Such a strategic or "therapeutic" use of trust (see Horsburgh, 1960) implies that trust is an attitude one may *choose* to adopt, which is a controversial issue in the trust domain (see e.g., Baier, 1986). However, as pointed out by

Castelfranchi and Falcone (2010), a distinction is in order here between trust as a belief structure (the trustor's evaluations and expectations) and trust as an action. Whereas the former, as any other kind of belief, cannot be a matter of decision, the latter can be a choice: that is, even in the absence of trust as a belief structure, one may behave *as if* one had the sufficient positive evaluations and expectations, and decide to delegate some task, and accept to be vulnerable, to the other person. This choice may be motivated by a variety of goals, like showing one's positive qualities, or testing the other person's TW, or, as in the case at hand, promoting others' TW.

In more formal terms:

Given $Goal_y$ the set of y's goals,

$$\text{If} \quad \exists g_1 \in Goal_y | g_1\left(TW^y_{z,w,c}(\tau) \geq \Sigma^y_{min}\right) \quad \text{(for each } z, w \in Ag) \tag{13}$$

(in words: y has the goal that each agent in Ag be trustworthy towards any other agent)

and

$$\text{If} \quad Bel_y\left((DoT^z_{y,z,c}(\tau) \geq \sigma^y_{min}) \rightarrow (TW_{z,y,c}(\tau) \geq \Sigma^y_{min})\right) \tag{14}$$

(where "$\rightarrow$" is the classical "logical implication")

Then

$$DoT_{y,z,c}(\tau) \geq \sigma^y_{min} \quad \text{and} \quad Bel_y(DoT^z_{y,z,c}(\tau) \geq \sigma^y_{min}) \tag{15}$$

In words: because y has goal g_1(13) and believes (14), she will trust z and believe that z is aware of her trust act.

So y's trusting attitude derives again from y's trustworthiness, but in a way different from the previous case.

4.3 How x Infers y's TW from Her Trusting Attitude

Going back to trust as a *sign* of TW, x's inference about y's TW from her trusting attitude may depend either on x's past experience with "high trustors" or on some reasoning by which he is able to reconstruct the abovementioned causal relationships between trust and TW.

In the first case x, having good evidence of the TW of high trustors in general, may feel likely to (more or less consciously) ascribe TW to y as a supposed member of the class of high trustors. (See trustworthiness transfer from a category.)

In the second case, x may ascribe TW to y independent of his past experience with high trustors. An implicit reasoning of the following kind will support his inference: Since y shows a trusting disposition, y is willing to risk having her own positive expectations disappointed. Who is disposed to run this risk is likely to believe the risk to be acceptable. Who believes that this risk is acceptable is also likely to believe either that others are trustworthy or that TW should be promoted in others. Who believes either of these things (or both) is likely to be trustworthy. So, y is likely to be trustworthy.

Starting from (10), but considering now x's point of view, we have that given $DoT^x_{y,z,c}(\tau) \geq \sigma^y_{min}$ it can be inferred that

$$TW^x_{y,w,c}(\tau) \geq \Sigma^x_{min} \qquad (16)$$

with $z, w \in Ag_3$ (where it is possible that $z = w$)

In words: if x perceives that y trusts z, then x can assume that y is in general trustworthy.

5 Trust as a Facilitator of the Trustee's Trustworthiness

As already mentioned, x's trust in y may positively affect y's trustworthiness. By y's TW we mean here her *objective* TW, that is, what y is actually able and willing to do (not just y's TW as perceived by x). This is quite a widespread assumption in the trust domain. For instance, trust is likely to foster coopera-tion and teamwork (e.g., Chenhall & Langfield-Smith, 2003; Gambetta, 2000; Harding, 2009), which can be explained by its power to increase others' TW. Yet trust may also make individuals vulnerable to others' opportunistic and exploitative behavior. As stressed by Castelfranchi and Falcone (2010), x's trust may affect y's TW by either increasing or decreasing it, depending on a variety of factors and circumstances. However, we do not intend to address here these factors and circumstances. Our task is a different one: assuming that x's trust may be a facilitator of y's trustworthiness, we intend to explore *how* this facil-itation may be brought about. That is, we wish to explore the *possible mental paths* leading y to being (more) trustworthy in response to x's trust.

In our view, there are at least *three distinct paths* from x's trust to y's TW. The first one starts from y's inference about x's TW; the second one starts from y's inference that x has chosen to become vulnerable to her; and the third path has as a crucial step y's inference that x evaluates her as trustworthy.

5.1 The First Path: y Believes that x is Trustworthy

This process relies on x's trust as a sign of his TW. As just discussed (see section 4), a person's trusting attitude may favor people's ascription of TW to this person. So, if x shows a trusting attitude (towards y or other people), y may infer that x is a trustworthy agent. Once y has drawn this inference, at least two possible mental sub-paths may stem from it.

On the one hand, believing that she can trust x, y also comes to believe that *she can incur the costs associated with being trustworthy* towards him – that is, she can spend some of her resources and skills as well as her effort and commitment to accomplish some task on x's behalf – because such "expenditures" are likely to be reciprocated by a trustworthy agent. In other words, y's trust in x is focused on x's *likelihood to reciprocate*. In fact, among the basic features of a trustworthy agent there is precisely the likelihood to reciprocate others' trust (e.g., Chang, Doll, van't Wout, Frank, & Sanfey, 2010). Therefore, y may feel confident that her expenditures are a good investment rather than a waste of resources. As a consequence, y will feel inclined to be trustworthy towards x.

Let us express this in a more formal way. Suppose that y perceives x's trust action:

$$DoT^y_{x,y,c}(\tau) \geq \sigma^y_{min} \tag{17}$$

and considering (16), y can assume:

$$TW^y_{x,y,c}(\tau') \geq \Sigma^y_{min} (\text{with } \tau = \tau' \text{ or } \tau \neq \tau') \tag{18}$$

That is, y perceives the opportunity of trusting x about task τ'.[7]

Suppose that y considers her efforts for realizing τ as comparable to the benefits to achieve τ' through x. In this case we can have:

$$Perform^x_{y,x,c}(\tau) \tag{19}$$

As a consequence, y makes the following true:

$$TW^x_{y,x,c}(\tau) \geq \Sigma^x_{min} \tag{20}$$

On the other hand, once y has inferred that x is a trustworthy agent, she may come to believe that x's expenditures of his own resources (in terms of both skills and motivational dispositions) on others' behalf *deserve* to be reciprocated. In such a case, y's sense of equity plays a major role. In fact, as claimed by equity theorists (Adams, 1965; Homans, 1961; Walster, Berscheid, & Walster, 1976), people are sensitive to the balance of benefits and contributions in their interactions and relationships. Inequitable social exchanges cause inequity distress and consequent attempts to restore equity, by reestablishing a balance between benefits and contributions. In this way, people's sense of equity acts as a powerful norm influencing social behavior: each member of the group *should get what he or she deserves* (either positive or negative outcomes), depending on his or her contributions. Going back to y, if she believes that x's TW deserves to be reciprocated, she will tend to be trustworthy with him.

In a similar but more general way, y may focus on a positive global evaluation of x: perceiving him as trustworthy, y may also view him as a valuable agent (reliable, responsible, considerate of others, honest, etc.), whose moral worth deserves to be acknowledged and rewarded through reciprocation.[8] (Incidentally, the definition itself of *trustworthiness* as "the trait of deserving trust and confidence" implies deservingness.)

In more formal terms, suppose that y has the goal g_2:

---

[7] We are considering here for the first time the case in which the task delegated by the trustor (in this case x) and the task on which the trustor could be considered trustworthy are explicitly different (or belonging to different classes). Of course this could be true also in the previous treatments but here this is particularly useful for better clarifying the specific case.

[8] Also in this case one may trace back y's reaction to her equity concerns, though in more global terms, that is, without a specific attention to the proportionality of x's benefits to x's contributions.

$$\exists g_2 \in Goal_y | g_2 = (RA_{z,y} \to RA_{y,z}) \tag{21}$$

that means that y has the goal of reciprocation with respect to a special class of social actions (called RA). In other words, if an agent $z \in Ag$ realizes a social action RA that benefits y, then – if y can reciprocate this action (that is, if y can realize the RA benefiting z) – y has the goal of realizing RA for z.

More generally, y has the more abstract goal of reciprocation between any two agents $(z, w \in Ag)$:

$$\exists g_3 \in Goal_y | g_3 = (RA_{z,w} \to RA_{w,z}) \tag{22}$$

Suppose in addition that:

$$Bel_y \left(\left(TW_{z,w,c}(\tau) \to Perform_{z,w,c}(\tau) \right) \cap \left(Perform_{z,w,c}(\tau) \in RA_{z,w} \right) \right) \tag{23}$$

(y believes that trustworthiness $(TW_{z,w,c})$ is a social attitude producing actions $\left(Perform_{z,w,c}(\tau) \right)$ of the RA type).

From (21), and (22) it follows that:

$$(\text{for each } z, w \in Ag) \quad \left(TW^y_{z,w,c}(\tau) \geq \Sigma^y_{min} \right) \to \left(TW_{y,z,c}(\tau) \geq \Sigma^y_{min} \right) \tag{24}$$

As shown above, from $DoT^y_{x,y,c}(\tau) \geq \sigma^x_{min}$ it follows that $TW^y_{x,y,c}(\tau) \geq \Sigma^y_{min}$. Then, if it is true that $DoT^y_{x,y,c}(\tau) \geq \sigma^x_{min}$, from (20) and (24) we will have:

$$TW^y_{y,x,c}(\tau) \geq \Sigma_{min} \tag{25}$$

It is interesting to note that in either of the abovementioned sub-paths the issue of reciprocation plays a crucial role. But, whereas in the former sub-path reciprocation was expected by y from x as a likely response to y's TW, in the latter sub-path reciprocation is an equitarian or moral imperative y imposes on herself, in response to x's TW.

In any case, however, y will feel inclined to be trustworthy towards x as a consequence of y's original inference about x's TW.

5.2 The Second Path: y Believes that x is Willing to be Vulnerable to Her

As already pointed out, trust is particularly relevant in conditions of ignorance or uncertainty (e.g., Gambetta, 2000). Actually, trust is a form of risk-taking (Coleman, 1990). More precisely, it implies a *willingness* to take risk, or to be vulnerable to the trustee's behavior. Some authors (Mayer, Davis, & Schoorman, 1995) define trust precisely in such terms: "a willingness of a party to be vulnerable to the actions of another party based on the expectation that the other will perform a particular action important to the trustor, irrespective of the ability to monitor or control that other party" (p. 712).

Perceptions of a target's vulnerability – elicited by the latter's appearance (for instance, his or her childlike features) or behavior – are likely to provoke an emotional reaction of "tenderness" in an observer (Lishner, 2003). Tenderness has been closely related to caregiving: according to Kalawski (2010), it elicits caregiving, whereas according to Frijda (1986) tenderness and caregiving basically coincide with each other: "tenderness can be regarded as the impulse toward tender– that is, caregiving – behavior; or else as the acute act of recognition of an object as a fit object for such behavior" (p. 83). In any case, such an impulse is very basic, and its evolution has been taced back not only to mammals (Panskepp, 2000) but also to premammalian reptiles (Bell, 2001).

We suggest that x's trusting attitude, being a sign of x's vulnerability, is likely to elicit a caregiving disposition in y. In other words, x's trust acts as an "appeal" to y to take care of him. Moreover, this is an appeal of a special kind, for at least two reasons. First, x's vulnerability is not just a matter of fact, but it is to some extent *chosen* by x himself, in that x is both aware of his vulnerability and willing to be vulnerable. Second, x's choice may be person-specific: that is, x is willing to be vulnerable *to* y (and not necessarily to some other person or to anybody). Therefore, y is likely to infer that x *expects* a caregiving behavior *from her*. As a consequence of such an intentional and individualized "appeal", y may feel a more cogent *responsibility* to show a caregiving behavior towards x.

In other words, y feels not only the spontaneous caring impulse that is typically elicited by another's vulnerability, but also the responsibility to take care of somebody who is willing to be vulnerable to her and expects her caregiving behavior. She is likely to reason as follows: "Since x is voluntarily risking some harm by relying on me, I *should not* harm him, and in any case I *should not* disappoint his expectation". Thus, y feels *committed* to show a caregiving behavior, and consequently to be trustworthy with x. (See also the notion of "trust-responsiveness" as described by Pettit, 1995.)

It is worth observing that this mental path prescinds from y's ascription of TW to x. That is, y makes no necessary inference about x's TW, x's possible reciprocating behavior towards her or, conversely, some reciprocation he would deserve from her. Here, *what counts is just x's vulnerability*: that is, x's dependence and reliance on y may be sufficient to elicit y's caregiving, and in particular her TW, implying the accomplishment of some task on x's behalf.

Thus, x's trust in y elicits y's goal of *not disappointing his trust*. However, a variety of distinct motivations (not necessarily alternative to each other) may underlie such a goal. On the one hand, y may focus on *preventing the harm x* would incur if she disappointed x's trust in her; that is, y wants to meet x's expectations *because* she wants that x is not exposed to any damage caused by his vulnerability to her. Or, y may focus on preventing a very special harm x would incur, namely the psychological suffering of disappointment itself. In both cases, y wants to avoid that x suffers some (material or immaterial) harm. Such a goal may be favored by y's benevolent disposition towards x, be it a form of individualized concern for x's well-being (for instance, she knows x and loves him) or a more general prosocial attitude.

On the other hand, y's goal of not disappointing x's trust may be motivated by more self-centered concerns. In this case, rather than focusing on x's harm, y will focus on the negative evaluations or self-evaluations she might incur by disappointing x's trust. That is, y might be primarily interested in defending either her image (before x or other people) or her self-image (or both).

Actually, disappointing others' trust is liable to a variety of negative (self-) evaluations, relative to y's competence or willingness. However, whereas lack of ability is typically perceived as uncontrollable, and consequently as something one is not responsible for (e.g., Weiner, 1995), unwillingness (or lack of effort) calls into play one's responsibility, and elicits negative (self)evaluations of a moral kind. Not surprisingly, ascriptions of failure to lack of effort result in more punishment from others than do ascriptions to lack of ability (Weiner, 1994). Though y's "commitment" to meet x's expectations does not necessarily depend on any explicit agreement or contract with x, still y may represent it as a commitment proper, grounded on the moral obligation to assist, whenever possible, those who depend on her help and trustfully expect it. In this perspective, in fact, not meeting x's expectations would take on the taint of a "betrayal" (rather than mere disappointment) of x's trust.

Therefore, y may feel urged to meet x's expectations in order to show (to x himself and/or other people) that she is that kind of person who does not betray others' trust; or she may want to live up to her own moral values and commitments (Holton, 1994), and show her moral worth to herself, thus maintaining or enhancing her self-esteem.

In any case, regardless of y's specific concerns, this second path from x's trust to y's TW starts from, and is set up by, y's perception of x's vulnerability and its implications.

In more formal terms we can say that:

$$\left(DoT^y_{x,y,c}(\tau) \geq \sigma^x_{min} \right) \rightarrow Dependence_{x,y,c}(\tau) \rightarrow Vulnerability_{x,y,c}(\tau) \qquad (26)$$

where

- $Dependence_{x,y,c}(\tau)$ means that in x's trusting y about task τ and for accomplishing task τ, x needs y's good performance. Therefore we can say that $Dependence_{x,y,c}(\tau)$ implies $GoodPerform_{y,x,c}(\tau)$, that is, the performance in which all the world states intended by x as a consequence of the realization of task τ are brought about while its unintended and/or undesired world states are not achieved.
- $Vulnerability_{x,y,\tau}$ means that given such dependence relationship, if y does not perform the task or her performance is not a *good performance* the result will be some harm for x (H_x).

In general

$$Perform_{y,x,c}(\tau) = f\left(Competence_y(\tau), Willingness_y(\tau)\right) \qquad (27)$$

So, as just observed, y's bad performance or her abstaining from any performance results in a harm for x:

$$\left(\neg GoodPerform_{y,x,c}(\tau)\right) \cup \left(NoPerform_{y,x,c}(\tau) \rightarrow H_x^y\right) \tag{28}$$

We assume that in general an agent (y) has the following goals:

$$\exists g_4 \in Goal_y | g_4 = \neg BadEvaluation_y^w \tag{29}$$

($\forall w \in Ag$ included $w = y$); (in words: y has the goal of avoiding bad evaluations from both others and herself); and

$$\exists g_5 \in Goal_y | g_5 = \neg H_w^y \quad (\forall w \in Ag_f) \tag{30}$$

(where Ag_f is the set of agents towards whom y has no pre-existing hostile motivation).

In addition, y believes:

$$Bel_y(\neg H_z^y \rightarrow \neg BadEvaluation_y^{z,w}) \quad (\forall w, z \in Ag) \tag{31}$$

(y believes that not to cause harm to z implies avoiding bad evaluations from z and also from potential witnesses like w).

So, If $(DoT_{x,y,c}^y(\tau) \geq \sigma_{min}^x)$ and (29), (30), and (31) are satisfied

$$\text{Then} \quad \exists g_6 \in Goal_y | g_6 = GoodPerform_{y,x,c}(\tau) \tag{32}$$

that is, y will have goal g_6 to make a good performance, which will increase the likelihood of y's trustworthy behavior.

5.3 The Third Path: y Believes that x Evaluates Her as Trustworthy

Though, as already observed, trust as an action can be chosen even in the absence of trust as a belief structure, y is likely to infer from x's trusting behavior that x considers her as trustworthy. To be sure, y may at times suspect that x's demonstrations of trust are motivated by some particular intention (for instance, promoting her TW, or testing her TW; see Castelfranchi & Falcone, 2010). However, we assume that, unless y has some reason to suspect such particular intentions on x's part, her default inference will be that x actually evaluates her as trustworthy.

Such an inference may exert a positive impact on y's beliefs about her own TW. However, to be influenced by x's positive evaluations about her, y should consider such evaluations credible. As a consequence, y *should consider x a good judge of her own TW*. In a word, y should *trust x* as an accurate and sincere evaluator of both her competence and willingness, with special reference to the delegated task.

Provided that y trusts x's supposed evaluations of her TW, such evaluations will favor her self-confidence about her own TW: that is, y will be more likely to believe she is endowed with the ability and willingness required for accomplishing the delegated task.

As far as willingness is concerned, it may appear strange that y takes into account another person's judgment about her own motivations: in fact, it may be argued that nobody can evaluate such motivations and their strength better than y herself; and, more importantly, willingness (including effort, persistence, commitment) is something unstable and controllable, that is, something one can *choose*, and be responsible for.

However, willingness may acquire some "ability" connotation – and conversely, ability may acquire some "willingness" connotation – depending on the perspective one takes. Think for instance of the notion of "weakness of will" (e.g., Davidson, 1980), which explicitly refers to some (lack of) "power" or ability. In the same vein, persistence (or perseverance) is typically viewed as a personality trait or character disposition (e.g., Hancock & Szalma, 2008; John & Srivastava, 1999), and generally "character" is not chosen.[9] Moreover, the evaluations about y's effort, persistence, and commitment concern not only the absolute values of these attitudes but also their specific relationships with the particular task (or tasks' classes) in question. For example a certain task may require a degree of effort, persistence and commitment which is very different from that required by another task; and often the right degree of such requirements can be better evaluated by an external and expert agent.

In any case, to the extent that y views her own willingness as something she is relatively unable to assess and/or act upon, she may want to resort to the evaluations of (trustworthy) others in order to assess whether she is adequately "willing" or not.

Once y's self-confidence about her own competence and willingness is increased through x's (implicit) positive evaluations, y's TW is also likely to grow, and y will behave (more) trustworthily, thus increasing the probabilities that she will accomplish the delegated task.

In fact, self-confidence is a powerful predictor of a successful performance, in particular if it is relative to the (class of) task at hand. Though global self-confidence or self-esteem may also be associated with a good performance (Scheier & Carver, 1988), task-specific self-confidence is no doubt a more reliable predictor.[10] This specific self-confidence is akin to Bandura's (1997) self-efficacy beliefs, defined as "beliefs in one's capability to organize and execute the courses of action required to produce given attainments" (p. 3). Though self-efficacy beliefs just concern one's competence, they strongly impact on one's willingness. In fact, believing that one can achieve a certain goal increases one's motivation to pursue it. Not surprisingly, the stronger one's sense of self-efficacy, the higher is one's effort, persistence in the face of obstacles, and resilience (Bandura, 1997).

---

[9] We assume most depends on the particular temporal perspective and focus of attention one takes. One can look at one's (lack of) skills, (good or bad) dispositions, tendencies and traits from different perspectives. One can view most of one's character as liable to change, improvement, acquisition, or vice versa as a "given", i.e., an unmodifiable set of stable traits. Consider for instance people's different implicit theories of intelligence, in terms of either a fixed entity or a malleable and incremental quality (e.g., Dweck, 1991).

[10] The association between global self-esteem and actual performance is presently a matter of debate (e.g., Baumeister, Campbell, Krueger, & Vohs, 2003), and in any case this association is weaker than that between domain-specific self-esteem and performance.

The notion of *empowerment* is also relevant in this regard. The construct of empowerment basically involves an increased intrinsic task motivation (e.g., Spreitzer, 1995), which is closely linked to a sense of self-efficacy (e.g., Conger & Kanungo, 1988) or belief in one's (task-specific) competence (Spreitzer, 1995; Thomas & Velthouse, 1990). Some studies have already shown a relationship between trust and psychological empowerment (Moye & Henkin, 2006). In particular, the "transformational style" of a leader (Burns, 1979) includes trust as one of its fundamental components (Martins, 2002; Connell, Ferres, & Travaglione, 2003), and is characterized by the ability to "empower" his or her team (e.g., Kuo, 2004; Sofarelli & Brown, 1998).

To sum up, this third path from x's trust to y's TW starts from y's belief that x evaluates her as trustworthy. Such a belief is likely to foster y's self-confidence about her own TW relative to the delegated task; and y's self-confidence is in turn a powerful predictor of y's actual trustworthy behavior. However, in order to impact on her self-confidence, y's belief that x evaluates her as trustworthy should be accompanied by y's trust in x as a good evaluator of her TW. It is worth noticing that the importance of such precondition is also acknowledged in the self-efficacy domain: one of the sources of the individual's self-efficacy beliefs is in fact *social persuasion*; but the effectiveness of the "persuasive" message is deemed to depend on the credibility and expertise the individual attributes to the "persuader" (e.g., Bandura, 1977; Gist & Mitchell, 1992).

In more formal terms, we can say that in general $DoT_{x,y,c}(\tau) \geq \sigma^x_{min}$ has as one of its main premises the fact that

$$TW^x_{y,x,c}(\tau) = \Sigma^x \geq \Sigma^x_{min} \tag{33}$$

We also suppose that y has her own evaluation about her trustworthiness: $TW^y_{y,x,c}(\tau) = \Sigma^y$.

So if y is aware of (33) and assumes x to be a competent evaluator about the requirements (both competence and willingness) for accomplishing τ; that is,

$$Bel_y\big((DoT_{x,y,c}(\tau) \geq \sigma^x_{min}) \rightarrow (TW^x_{y,x,c}(\tau) = \Sigma^x \geq \Sigma^x_{min})\big) \tag{34}$$

and

$$Bel_y(HighEvaluator_{x,c}(\tau)) \tag{35}$$

If $\Sigma^x > \Sigma^y$ then y will change her evaluation of her own trustworthiness about task τ, assuming the new value Σ'^y with:

$$\Sigma^x \geq \Sigma'^y > \Sigma^y \tag{36}$$

and this new Σ'^y may be over y's threshold for evaluating herself trustworthy enough for accomplishing τ:

$$TW^y_{y,x,c}(\tau) = \Sigma'^y \geq \Sigma^y_{min} \quad (\text{while} \quad TW^y_{y,x,c}(\tau) = \Sigma^y \leq \Sigma^y_{min})$$

This new evaluation of $TW_{y,x,c}^{y}(\tau) = \Sigma'^{y}$ will influence the $DoT_{y,y,c}(\tau)$ and its main components (in particular y's degrees of willingness), and positively impact on y's actual performance.

6 Concluding Remarks

Trusting and trustworthy behaviors appear to be much more widespread than it would be expected according to the standard model of self-interested agents of economic game theory (Camerer, 2003). Actually, the results of many experiments that study behavior in the "trust game" (Berg, Dickhaut, & McCabe, 1995) challenge the predictions of classical game theory, in that, despite the risk intrinsic to trust, players tend to trust their partners, and, despite the "expensiveness" of TW, trustees tend to reward the trust they receive by behaving trustworthily.

However, as already mentioned, we neither claim that the relationships we have hypothesized between trust and TW necessarily hold in any context or circumstance, nor we make specific predictions about their likelihood. With this work, we intended to accomplish a different task: on the one hand, assuming that one's trust *may* be a sign of one's own trustworthiness, we have tried to explore *how* a trusting behavior may favor an inference of trustworthiness; on the other hand, assuming that one's trust *may* be a facilitator of another's trustworthiness, we have tried to explore *how* this facilitation may be brought about.

We in fact acknowledge that one's trusting attitude is not *necessarily* a sign of one's own TW, and it does not *necessarily* favor another's TW (e.g., Kiyonari, Yamagishi, Cook, &Cheshire, 2006). As also shown in the formal parts of the paper, the agents' choices depend on the goals these agents have to satisfy and on their degree of priority. We intended to model some specific attitudes and behaviors in trusting or being trustworthy and some of their relationships; but, changing the agents' goals or their priorities, some other attitudes and behaviors could be modelled.

Actually, going back to the hypothesized paths from x's trust to y's TW, we even admit that there may be cases in which y's TW is *reduced*, rather than increased, by x's trusting attitude. A paradigmatic example is offered by y's belief about x's vulnerability (which we have supposed to be the starting point of our second path). Such a belief may in fact favor y's exploitative intentions. That is, an unscrupolous trustee may feel tempted to take advantage of x's vulnerability, without any concern either for x's needs or for his expectations or for the likely negative evaluations she would receive (from x or other people). Moreover, even when immune from exploitative intentions, y may react negatively to x's "willing vulnerability" to her if she perceives x's attitude as a form of psychological blackmail. In other words, she may suspect that x displays his helplessness and trustful expectations in order to take advantage of either her caring impulse or her feeling of moral obligation to assist those who depend on, and expect, her help. As a consequence, y may "rebel" against such an imposed commitment to meet x's expectations – a commitment that, after all, does not result from any agreement with x – in that she views it as implying a threat to her freedom. Actually, when one feels pressured to adopt a certain attitude, one may experience what in psychology is called *reactance*, an emotional reaction characterized by the attempt at restoring one's freedom through an attitude or behavior that is the opposite of what was expected (e.g., Brehm, 1966; Wicklund, 1974). However, it is worth remarking that such a reactive response testifies to the existence and strength of the pressure y feels to meet x's trustful expectations.

With regard to the three paths from x's trust to y's TW, another question we have not addressed in the present work is what factors may favor the "choice" of one path over the others. This issue would indeed require a separate work. Here we limit ourselves to a few hints.

No doubt, y's personal dispositions are likely to guide her towards one path (or sub-path) or another. Consider for instance our first path and its sub-paths. Provided that y infers x's TW from his trusting attitude, she will be likely to believe that x *deserves* reciprocation *if* she holds the value of reciprocation. That is, a trustee who holds the value of reciprocation will behave trustworthily towards her trustor in order to comply with the self-imposed imperative to reward his TW (second sub-path), rather than because she expects some reward from him (first sub-path). As for our second path (which starts from y's perception of x's vulnerability), it is likely to be followed by a trustee with a caregiving disposition (that is, one who is very considerate of others' needs and/or holds the value of altruistic and prosocial behavior). Finally, a trustee who harbors doubts about her own self-efficacy and is in search of reassurance about her competence or willingness will be sensitive to our third path, provided that she considers her trustor a good judge of her TW: once her self-confidence about her own TW (relative to the delegated task) is increased through the (implicit) positive evaluations received from her trustor, she is likely to behave more trustworthily.

However, situational factors may also play a contributing role. For instance, y may be oriented toward the first path because of her past experience with "high trustors", that favors her inference about x's trustworthiness. But, when confronted with a trustor's extreme neediness, she may "choose" the second path. When the delegated task is a difficult one, and in particular y has no or little previous evidence of her specific skills, she may be more likely to follow the third path, even independent of dispositional factors such as lack of self-confidence.

References

1. Adams, J.S. (1965). Inequity in social exchange. In L. Berkowitz (Ed.), *Advances in experimental social psychology*, *Vol.* 2 (pp. 267-300). New York: Academic Press.
2. Aguinis, H., Simonsen, M.M., & Pierce, C.A. (1998). Effects of nonverbal behavior on perceptions of power bases. *The Journal of Social Psychology*, 138, 445-469.

3. Bacharach, M., & Gambetta, D. (2001). Trust in signs. In K. Cook (Ed.), *Trust and society* (pp. 148-184). New York: Sage.
4. Baier, A. (1986). Trust and antitrust. *Ethics, 96*, 231-260.
5. Ballim, A., & Wilks, Y. (1991). *Artificial believers*. Hillsdale, NJ: Erlbaum.
6. Bandura, A. (1977). Self-efficacy: Toward a unifying theory of behavioral change. *Psychological Review, 84*, 191-215.
7. Bandura, A. (1997). *Self-efficacy: The exercise of control*. New York: Freeman.
8. Baumeister, R.F., Campbell, J.D., Krueger, J.I., & Vohs, K.D. (2003). Does high self-esteem cause better performance, interpersonal success, happiness, or healthier lifestyles? *Psychological Science in the Public Interest, 4*, 1-44.
9. Bell, D.C. (2001). Evolution of parental caregiving. *Personality and Social Psychology Review, 5*, 216-229.
10. Berg, J., Dickhaut, J., & McCabe, K. (1995). Trust, reciprocity, and social history. *Games and Economic Behavior, 10*, 122-142.
11. Brehm, J.W. (1966) *A theory of psychological reactance*. San Diego, CA: Academic Press.
12. Burns, J.M. (1979). *Leadership*. New York: Harper & Row.
13. Camerer, C. (2003). *Behavioral game theory*. New York: Sage.
14. Castelfranchi, C. (1998). Modelling social action for AI agents. *Artificial Intelligence, 103*, 157-182.
15. Castelfranchi, C., & Falcone, R. (1998), Principles of trust for MAS: Cognitive anatomy, social importance, and quantification. *Proceedings of the International Conference of Multi-Agent Systems (ICMAS'98)*, pp. 72-79, Paris, July.
16. Castelfranchi, C., & Falcone, R. (2010). *Trust theory: A socio-cognitive and computational model*. Chichester, UK: Wiley.
17. Chang, L.J., Doll, B.B., van't Wout, M., Frank, M.J., & Sanfey, A.G. (2010). Seeing is believing: Trustworthiness as a dynamic belief. *Cognitive Psychology, 61*, 87-105.
18. Chenhall, R.H., & Langfield-Smith, K. (2003). Performance measurement and reward systems, trust, and strategic change. *Journal of Management Accounting Research, 15*, 117-143.
19. Coleman, J.S. (1990). *Foundations of social theory*. Cambridge, MA: Harvard University Press.
20. Conger, J., & Kanungo, R. (1988). The empowerment process: Integrating theory and practice. *Academy of Management Review, 13*, 471-482.
21. Connell, J., Ferres, N., & Travaglione, T. (2003). Engendering trust in manager-subordinate relationships: Predictors and outcomes. *Personnel Review, 32*, 569–587.
22. Conte, R., & Paolucci, M. (2002). *Reputation in artificial societies: Social beliefs for social order*. Dordrecht: Kluwer.
23. Davidson, D. (1980). How is weakness of the will possible? In D. Davidson (Ed.), *Essays on actions and events* (pp.21–42). Oxford: Oxford University Press.
24. DeBruine, L.M. (2002). Facial resemblance enhances trust. *Proceedings of the Royal Society B, 269*, 1307-1312.
25. DePaulo, B.M., Rosenthal, R., Green, C.R., & Rosenkrantz, J. (1982). Diagnosing deceptive and mixed messages from verbal and nonverbal cues. *Journal of Experimental Social Psychology, 18*, 433-446.
26. Dietz, G., & Den Hartog, D.N. (2006). Measuring trust inside organisations. *Personnel Review, 35*, 557-588.
27. Dweck, C.S. (1991). Self-theories and goals: Their role in motivation, personality, and development. In R. Dienstbier (Ed.), *Nebraska symposium on motivation, Vol. 38* (pp. 199-235). Lincoln: University of Nebraska Press.
28. Ekman, P., & Friesen, W.V. (1986). A new pan-cultural facial expression of emotion. *Motivation and Emotion, 10*, 159–168.
29. Engell, A.D., Haxby, J.V., & Todorov, A. (2007). Implicit trustworthiness decisions: Automatic coding of face properties in human amygdala. *Journal of Cognitive Neuroscience, 19*, 1508-1519.

30. Falcone, R., & Castelfranchi, C. (2000). Social trust: A cognitive approach. In C. Castel-franchi & Y.-H. Tan (Eds.), *Trust and deception in virtual societies* (pp. 55-90). Dordrecht, The Netherlands: Kluwer.
31. Falcone, R., Castelfranchi, C. (2010). Trust and transitivity: A complex deceptive rela-tionship. *International Workshop on Trust in Agent Societies*, c/o AAMAS 2010, Toronto.
32. Falcone, R., Piunti, M., Venanzi, M., & Castelfranchi, C. (in press). From manifesta to kripta: The relevance of categories for trusting others. *ACM Transaction on Intelligent Systems and Technology*.
33. Gambetta, D. (2000). Can we trust trust? In D. Gambetta (Ed.), *Trust: Making and break-ing cooperative relations* (pp. 213-237). Retrieved Nov. 8, 2006, from University of Ox-ford, Department of Sociology Web site: http://www.sociology.ox.ac.uk/papers/trustbook.html (Original work published 1988).
34. Gist, M.E., & Mitchell, T.R. (1992). Self-efficacy: A theoretical analysis of its determinants and malleability. *Academy of Management Review*, 17, 183-211.
35. Gurtman, M.B. (1992). Trust, distrust, and interpersonal problems: A circumplex analy-sis. *Journal of Personality and Social Psychology*, 62, 989-1002.
36. Hancock, P.A., & Szalma, J.L. (2008). Stress and performance. In P.A. Hancock & J.L. Szalma (Eds.), *Performance under stress* (pp. 1-18). Cornwall: MPG Books.
37. Harding, M. (2009). Manifesting trust. *Oxford Journal of Legal Studies*, 29, 245-265.
38. Holton, R. (1994). Deciding to trust, coming to believe. *Australasian Journal of Philosophy*, 72, 63-76.
39. Homans, G. (1961). *Social behaviour: Its elementary forms*. New York: Harcourt, Brace & World.
40. Horsburgh, H.J.N. (1960). The ethics of trust. *Philosophical Quarterly*, 10, 343-354.
41. John, O.P., & Srivastava, S. (2001). The big five trait taxonomy: History, measurements, and theoretical perspectives. In L.A. Pervin, & O.P. John (Eds.), *Handbook of personality: Theory and research* (pp. 102-138, 2nd ed.). New York: Guilford.
42. Johnson, M.H. (2005). Subcortical face processing. *Nature Reviews Neuroscience*, 6, 766-774.
43. Kalawski, J.P. (2010). Is tenderness a basic emotion? *Motivation and Emotion*, 34, 158-167.
44. Kelley, H.H. (1967). Attribution theory in social psychology. In D. Levine (Ed.), *Nebraska symposium on motivation, Vol. 15* (pp. 192-238). Lincoln: University of Nebraska Press.
45. Kiyonari, T., Yamagishi, T., Cook, K.S., & Cheshire, C. (2006). Does trust beget trust-worthiness? Trust and trustworthiness in two games and two cultures: A research note. *Social Psychology Quarterly*, 69, 270-283.
46. Kuo, C.C. (2004). Research on impacts of team leadership on team effectiveness. *Journal of American Academy of Business*, 5, 266-277.
47. Lavie, N., Ro, T., & Russell, C. (2003). The role of perceptual load in processing distractor faces. *Psychological Science*, 14, 510-515.
48. Leppänen, J.M., & Nelson, C.A. (2009). Tuning the developing brain to social signals of emotions. *Nature Reviews Neuroscience*, 10, 37-47.
49. Levin, D.Z., Whitener, E.M., & Cross, R. (2006). Perceived trustworthiness of knowledge sources: The moderating impact of relationship length. *Journal of Applied Psychology*, 91, 1163-1171.
50. Lishner, D.A. (2003). *The components of empathy: Distinguishing between tenderness and sympathy*. Unpublished doctoral dissertation, University of Kansas, Lawrence.
51. Luhmann, N. (2000). Familiarity, confidence, trust: Problems and alternatives. In D. Gambetta (Ed.), *Trust: Making and breaking cooperative relations* (pp. 94-107). Retrieved Nov. 8, 2006, from University of Oxford, Department of Sociology Web site: http://www.sociology.ox.ac.uk/papers/trustbook.html (Original work published 1988).
52. Marks, G., & Miller, N. (1987). Ten years of research on the false consensus effect: An empirical and theoretical review. *Psychological Bulletin*, 102, 72-90.
53. Martins, N. (2002). A model for managing trust. *International Journal of Manpower*, 23, 754-769.
54. Mayer, R.C., Davis, J.H, & Schoorman, F.D. (1995). An integrative model of organiza-tional trust. *Academy of Management Review*, 20, 709 – 734.

55. Miceli, M., & Castelfranchi, C. (1989). A cognitive approach to values. *Journal for the Theory of Social Behaviour*, 19, 169-193.
56. Miceli, M., & Castelfranchi, C. (2000). The role of evaluation in cognition and social interaction. In K. Dautenhahn (Ed.), *Human cognition and social agent technology* (pp. 225-261). Amsterdam, The Netherlands: John Benjamins.
57. Miceli, M., & Castelfranchi, C. (2002). The mind and the future: The (negative) power of expectations. *Theory & Psychology*, 12, 335-366.
58. Miceli, M., & Castelfranchi, C. (2010). Hope: The power of wish and possibility. *Theory & Psychology*, 20, 251-276.
59. Miceli, M., & Castelfranchi, C. (2012). Coherence of conduct and the self-image. In F. Paglieri (Ed.), *Consciousness in interaction* (pp. 151–177). Amsterdam, The Netherlands: John Benjamins.
60. Moye, M., & Henkin, A. (2006). Exploring associations between employee empowerment and interpersonal trust in managers. *Journal of Management Development*, 25, 101-117.
61. Oosterhof, N.N., & Todorov, A. (2008). The functional basis of face evaluation. *Proceedings of the National Academy of Sciences*, 105, 11087-11092.
62. Panksepp, J. (2000). Emotions as natural kinds within the mammalian brain. In M. Lewis & J.M. Haviland-Jones (Eds.), *Handbook of emotions* (pp. 137-156, 2nd ed.). New York: Guilford.
63. Pettit, P. (1995), The cunning of trust. *Philosophy and Public Affairs*, 24, 202-225.
64. Piaget, J. (1929). *The child's conception of the world*. New York: Harcourt Brace.
65. Ross, L., Greene, D., & House, P. (1977). The false consensus phenomenon: An attributional bias in self-perception and social perception processes. *Journal of Experimental Social Psychology*, 13, 279-301.
66. Rotter, J.B. (1980). Interpersonal trust, trustworthiness and gullibility. *American Psychologist*, 26, 1-7.
67. Sabater, J., & Sierra, C. (2001), Regret: A reputation model for gregarious societies. *Fourth workshop on deception and fraud in agent societies* (pp. 61-70). Montreal, Canada.
68. Schlicht, E.J., Shimojo, S., Camerer, C.F., Battaglia, P., & Nakayama, K. (2010). Human wagering behavior depends on opponents' faces. *PLoS ONE*, 5, e11663.
69. Scheier, M.F., & Carver, C.S. (1988). A model of behavioral self-regulation: Translating intention into action. In L. Berkowitz (Ed.), *Advances in experimental social psychology, Vol. 21* (pp. 303-346). San Diego, CA: Academic Press.
70. Schoorman, F.D., Mayer, R.C., & Davis, J.H. (2007). An integrative model of organizational trust: Past, present and future. *Academy of Management Review*, 32, 344-354.
71. Schwartz, S.H. (1992). Universals in the content and structure of values: Theoretical advances and empirical tests in 20 countries. In M. P. Zanna (Ed.), *Advances in experimental social psychology, Vol. 25* (pp. 1-65). San Diego, CA: Academic Press.
72. Sofarelli, M., & Brown, R. (1998). The need for nursing leadership in uncertain times. *Journal of Nursing Management*, 6, 201-207.
73. Spreitzer, G.M. (1995). Psychological empowerment in the work place: Dimensions, measurement, and validation. *Academy of Management Journal*, 38, 1442-1465.
74. Stirrat, M., & Perret, D.I. (2010) Valid facial cues to cooperation and trust: Male facial width and trustworthiness. *Psychological Science*, 21, 349-354.
75. Thomas, K., & Velthouse, B. (1990). Cognitive elements of empowerment: An interpretive model of intrinsic task motivation. *Academy of Management Review*, 15, 666-681.
76. Vuilleumier, P. (2000). Faces call for attention: evidence from patients with visual extinction. *Neuropsychologia*, 38, 693–700.
77. Walster, E., Berscheid, E., & Walster, G.W. (1976). New directions in equity research. In L. Berkowitz & E. Walster (Eds.), *Advances in experimental social psychology, Vol. 9* (pp. 1-42). New York: Academic Press.
78. Weiner, B. (1994). Integrating social and personal theories of achievement striving. *Review of Educational Research*, 64, 557-573.
79. Weiner, B. (1995). *Judgments of responsibility: A foundation for a theory of social conduct*. New York: Guilford.
80. Wicklund, R.A. (1974). *Freedom and reactance*. Wiley and Sons, New York.

81. Wilks, Y., & Ballim, A. (1987). Multiple agents and the heuristic ascription of belief. In J. McDermott (Ed.), *Proceedings of the 10th international joint conference on artificial intelligence, Vol. 1* (pp. 118-124). Los Altos, CA: Morgan Kaufmann.
82. Yolum, P., & Singh, M.P. (2003). Emergent properties of referral systems. *Proceedings of the 2nd International Joint Conference on Autonomous Agents and MultiAgent Systems (AAMAS)*. Melbourne: ACM Press.
83. Yu, B., & Singh, M.P. (2003). Searching social networks. *Proceedings of the 2nd International Joint Conference on Autonomous Agents and MultiAgent Systems (AAMAS)*. Melbourne: ACM Press.

Chapter 23
A simple logic of trust based on propositional assignments

Andreas Herzig, Emiliano Lorini and Frédéric Moisan

Abstract Cristiano Castelfranchi and Rino Falcone introduced an influential cognitive theory of social trust that is based on the concepts of belief, goal, ability, willingness and opportunity. In this paper we propose a simple logic of belief and action that allows to express these concepts. While our logic of belief is standard, our logic of action has a very simple kind actions: actions setting the truth value of a propositional variable to either true or false. We call such actions propositional assignments and argue that our logic provides a framework that is simple but expressive enough to account for Castelfranchi and Falcone's concept. We prove its completeness and give a decision procedure.

1 Introduction

Cristiano Castelfranchi and Rino Falcone introduced an influential cognitive theory of social trust that is based on the concepts of belief, goal, ability, willingness and opportunity [1, 6, 2]. According to that theory, "agent i trusts agent j to perform action δ_j to achieve i's goal φ" is defined as follows:

1. i has the goal that φ;
2. i believes that j is able to perform δ_j;
3. i believes that j is willing to perform δ_j;
4. i believes that j has the opportunity to achieve φ by performing δ_j.

Andreas Herzig
Université de Toulouse, IRIT-CNRS, France
e-mail: andreas.herzig@irit.fr

Emiliano Lorini
Université de Toulouse, IRIT-CNRS, France
e-mail: lorini@irit.fr

Frédéric Moisan
Université de Toulouse, IRIT-CNRS, France
e-mail: moisan@irit.fr

We here consider a generalisation of the definition where an agent may trust a group of agents J to perform a joint action δ_J to achieve φ.

Castelfranchi and Falcone's theory of trust was the starting point of the ForTrust project[1] that was funded by the French *Agence Nationale de la Recherche* from 2007 to 2010. One of the aims of ForTrust was to design a formal logical framework for their theory.

In previous work we had defined a logic of time, action, belief and choice where the above concepts of goal, belief, ability, willingness and opportunity can be expressed and within which one can therefore formally reason about trust [7]. That logic combined temporal, dynamic and epistemic logic and led to a rather complex formalism. While we were able to state a completeness result we were not able to prove its decidability or to characterise its complexity.

The aim of the present paper is to simplify our account and in particular to state a decidability result. We introduce a simple logic in the style of dynamic epistemic logics [5].

In what concerns actions our account of action is based on the concepts of *propositional assignment* and of *propositional control*. Basically, the idea is that the agents' actions consist in setting the truth values of a propositional variable to either true or false. In order to be able to set variable p to true an agent must have that action in his repertoire, and likewise for the action of setting p to false. As we have shown in [8] this allows to reason about propositional control in van der Hoek and Wooldridge's sense [10, 9]. The latter have used the logic of propositional control in order to talk about an agent's capability to achieve some property (whatever the other agents do). We moreover integrate protocols prescribing what action is going to take place next. This allows not only to talk about what agents *can do* but also about what they actually *do* (according to the current protocol). In previous work agents acted one at a time; we here move to a more game-theoretic account where all agents act in parallel.

Our concept of belief is in terms of the standard logic of belief KD45: we identify belief with truth in all the worlds that are possible for the agent. We also integrate the concept of weak belief and the concept of agent preference. We identify weak belief with truth in the most plausible worlds among those worlds that are possible for the agent; and we identify preference with truth in the most preferred worlds among those worlds that are possible for the agent.

We show that in our logic we can express Castelfranchi and Falcone's relevant concepts of goal, belief, ability, willingness and opportunity as follows:

1. Agent i has the goal that φ if and only if i prefers that φ will be true at the next time step.
2. Agent j is able to perform an action δ_j (of setting p to true or false) if and only if the performance of δ_j by j is possible.
3. Agent j is willing to perform action δ_j if and only if j prefers that j performs δ_j next.
4. Agent j has the opportunity to achieve φ by doing δ_j if and only if φ is true after every possible performance of δ_j by j, whatever the other agents do.

---

[1] www.irit.fr/ForTrust

Note that the last three components are logically independent: an agent may be willing to perform δ_j without being able to perform it, etc.

2 DDL–PA: dynamic doxastic logic of propositional assignments

In this section we define syntax and semantics of the basic dynamic doxastic logic of propositional assignments DDL–PA. We give its language and semantics and establish decidability of DDL–PA validity.

2.1 Language

Let $\mathbb{P}$ be a finite set of propositional variables and let $\mathbb{I}$ be a finite set of individuals, alias agents. An *assignment* is of the form $p \leftarrow \top$ or $p \leftarrow \bot$, where p is a propositional variable. The set of all assignments is

$$\mathsf{ASS} = \{p \leftarrow \top \ : \ p \in \mathbb{P}\} \cup \{p \leftarrow \bot \ : \ p \in \mathbb{P}\}.$$

The simultaneous performance of assignments by agents is an *event*. We model events as mappings from $\mathbb{I}$ to ASS. Hence the set of all events is $\mathsf{EVT} = \mathsf{ASS}^{\mathbb{I}}$. We denote the elements of EVT by δ, δ', etc. The restriction of a mapping δ to a set of agents $J \subseteq \mathbb{I}$ is noted δ_J. Hence the restriction of δ to the set of all agents $\mathbb{I}$ is nothing but δ itself: $\delta_{\mathbb{I}} = \delta$. It is convenient to write δ_i instead of $\delta_{\{i\}}$, δ_{-J} instead of $\delta_{\mathbb{I} \backslash J}$, δ_{-i} instead of $\delta_{-\{i\}}$. (Hence we can identify $\delta(i)$ with δ_i.) Observe that EVT is finite because both $\mathbb{P}$ and $\mathbb{I}$ are finite.

The language of DDL–PA is defined by the following grammar:

$$\varphi ::= p \mid \top \mid \bot \mid \mathsf{Hpn}(\delta_i) \mid \neg\varphi \mid \varphi \vee \varphi \mid \mathsf{Bel}_i\varphi \mid \mathsf{Next}\varphi \mid \langle\delta\rangle\varphi$$

where p ranges over $\mathbb{P}$, i ranges over $\mathbb{I}$ and δ ranges over the set of events EVT.

$\mathsf{Hpn}(\delta_i)$ reads "agent i is going to perform δ_i", or "δ_i is going to happen next"; $\mathsf{Bel}_i\varphi$ reads "i believes that φ"; $\mathsf{Next}\varphi$ reads "φ is going to be true next"; $\langle\delta\rangle\varphi$ reads "δ may occur, and φ is going to be true immediately afterwards". The modal operator $[\delta]$ is the dual of the modal operator $\langle\delta\rangle$ that is defined by:

$$[\delta]\varphi \stackrel{\mathrm{def}}{=} \neg\langle\delta\rangle\neg\varphi$$

Hence $[\delta]\varphi$ can be read "if δ occurs then φ is going to be true immediately afterwards".

We define $\mathbb{I}_\varphi$ to be the set of agents of $\mathbb{I}$ occurring in formula φ, and we define $\mathbb{P}_\varphi$ to be the set of propositional variables of $\mathbb{P}$ occurring in φ.

2.2 *Semantics*

An *epistemic PC model* is made up a set of possible worlds plus mappings associating to every possible world a valuation, a next state function, a repertoire function, and a belief state per agent. Formally, they are quadruples of the form $M = (W, B, R, N, V)$, where:

- W is a nonempty set of possible worlds;
- $B : W \longrightarrow (\mathbb{I} \longrightarrow 2^W)$ associates to every possible world w and to every agent i the set of worlds that are possible for i at w;
- $R : W \longrightarrow ((\mathsf{EVT}^* \times \mathbb{I}) \longrightarrow 2^{\mathsf{ASS}})$ associates to every possible world a repertoire function mapping a sequence of events and an agent to a set of assignments;
- $N : W \longrightarrow (\mathsf{EVT}^* \longrightarrow \mathsf{EVT})$ associates to every possible world a protocol function mapping sequences of events to events;
- $V : W \longrightarrow (\mathbb{P} \longrightarrow \{\mathtt{tt}, \mathtt{ff}\})$ associates to every possible world a valuation mapping propositional variables to truth values.

It is convenient to write $B_w(i)$, R_w, N_w, and V_w instead of $B(w)(i)$, $R(w)$, $N(w)$, and $V(w)$.

We require that B satisfies the following constraint, for all agents i and possible worlds w, w_1, w_2:

$$\text{if } w_1, w_2 \in B_w(i) \text{ then } B_{w_1}(i) = B_{w_2}(i) \tag{1}$$

We moreover require that R and N satisfy the following constraint, for all possible worlds w and sequences of events μ:

$$\text{if } N_w(\mu) = \delta \text{ then for every } i \in \mathbb{I}, \delta_i \in R_w(\mu, i) \tag{2}$$

The function B models the agents' uncertainty: $B_w(i)$ is the set of possible worlds that i cannot distinguish from the actual world w. Constraint 1 is nothing but transitivity and Euclideanity of the accessibility relations corresponding to the function B that is defined as $B_i = \{(w, w') : w' \in B_w(i)\}$.[2] It will make principles of positive and negative introspection valid. The tuple (W, B, V) is therefore a model of the standard logic of belief **K45**. The set of assignments $R_w(\mu, i)$ models agent i's control after the sequence of event $\mu \in \mathsf{EVT}^*$ took place at w. The event $N_w(\mu)$ is the event that is going to happen after the sequence of events μ took place at w. For every possible world w, the 'next state' function maps sequences of events $\mu \in \mathsf{EVT}^*$ to events $N_w(\mu)$: if the sequence μ occurs then $N_w(\mu)$ is the next event that is going to happen afterwards. Constraint 2 is therefore a 'do implies can' principle. Note that it implies that for every i, $R_w(\mu, i)$ is non-empty. Finally, the valuation function V associates to every possible world a valuation: a mapping from the set of propositional variables to the set $\{\mathtt{tt}, \mathtt{ff}\}$.

---

[2] The relation B_i is transitive if and only if $(w, w') \in B_i$ and $(w', w'') \in B_i$ implies $(w, w'') \in B_i$. It is Euclidean if and only if $(w, w') \in B_i$ and $(w, w'') \in B_i$ implies $(w', w'') \in B_i$.

For the subsequent definitions we need a bit of notation for the event sequences of EVT^*: we note nil the empty sequence of events, and we note $\delta;\mu$ the sequential composition of the event δ with the sequence of events μ.

Then the *update* of M by δ is defined as $M^\delta = (W, B, R^\delta, N^\delta, V^\delta)$, where R^δ, N^δ and V^δ are defined by:

$$R^\delta_w(\mu, i) = R_w((\delta;\mu), i), \quad \text{for } \mu \in \mathsf{EVT}^* \text{ and } i \in \mathbb{I}$$

$$N^\delta_w(\mu) = N_w(\delta;\mu), \quad \text{for } \mu \in \mathsf{EVT}^*$$

$$V^\delta_w(p) = \begin{cases} \mathtt{tt} & \text{if } \exists i, \delta_i = p{\leftarrow}\top \text{ and } \nexists j, \delta_j = p{\leftarrow}\bot \\ \mathtt{ff} & \text{if } \exists i, \delta_i = p{\leftarrow}\bot \text{ and } \nexists j, \delta_j = p{\leftarrow}\top \\ V_w(p) & \text{otherwise} \end{cases}$$

Hence updates neither change the set of possible worlds nor the agents' possibilities (the belief accessibility relation). Both the repertoire function and the protocol function are incremented by δ. The valuation function after the update gives to the variables that are assigned by δ their new truth values according to δ and leaves the other variables unchanged. The only subtlety is that we have to deal with contradicting assignments, i.e. when $\delta_i = p{\leftarrow}\top$ and $\delta_j = p{\leftarrow}\bot$, for some i and j. We here suppose that such contradicting assignments have no effect on p: the valuation $V^\delta_w(p)$ after the update is identical to the valuation before the update.

The truth conditions are standard for $\top$, $\bot$, negation and disjunction, plus:

$$M, w \Vdash p \qquad \text{iff } Val_w(p) = \mathtt{tt}$$

$$M, w \Vdash \mathsf{Hpn}(\delta_i) \quad \text{iff } (N_w(\mathsf{nil}))_i = \delta_i$$

$$M, w \Vdash \mathsf{Bel}_i \varphi \quad \text{iff } M, w' \Vdash \varphi \text{ for every } w' \in B_w(i)$$

$$M, w \Vdash \mathsf{Next}\,\varphi \quad \text{iff } M^{N_w(\mathsf{nil})}, w \Vdash \varphi$$

$$M, w \Vdash \langle\delta\rangle\varphi \qquad \text{iff } \delta_i \in R_w(\mathsf{nil}, i) \text{ for all } i \in \mathbb{I} \text{ and } M^\delta, w \Vdash \varphi$$

We say that a formula φ is *valid in the model M*, noted $M \Vdash \varphi$, if and only if $M, w \Vdash \varphi$ for every possible world w in M. The formula φ is *valid in the class of epistemic PC models* if and only if $M \Vdash \varphi$ for every epistemic PC model M. Finally, the formula φ is a *(global) logical consequence* of the set of formulas Γ, noted $\Gamma \models \varphi$, if and only if for every epistemic PC model M, if $M \Vdash \psi$ for every $\psi \in \Gamma$ then $M \Vdash \varphi$. Hence φ is valid if and only if $\emptyset \models \varphi$.

2.3 Reduction axioms and decidability

Basically, our semantics allows to eliminate the temporal operator Next and the dynamic operators $\langle\delta\rangle$. First, Next can be eliminated because the formula

$$\mathsf{Next}\,\varphi \leftrightarrow \bigvee_{\delta \in \mathsf{EVT}} \left(\langle \delta \rangle \varphi \wedge \bigwedge_{i \in \mathbb{I}} \mathsf{Hpn}(\delta_i) \right)$$

is valid. Note that finiteness of the set EVT warrants that the formula on the right is well-formed. Second, as customary in dynamic epistemic logics without the common belief operator, the dynamic operators $\langle \delta \rangle$ have reduction axioms.

Proposition 1 *The following equivalences are* **DDL–PA** *valid.*

$$\langle \delta \rangle \neg \varphi \qquad \leftrightarrow \langle \delta \rangle \top \wedge \neg \langle \delta \rangle \varphi$$

$$\langle \delta \rangle (\varphi_1 \vee \varphi_2) \leftrightarrow \langle \delta \rangle \varphi_1 \vee \langle \delta \rangle \varphi_2$$

$$\langle \delta \rangle \mathsf{Bel}_i\, \varphi \qquad \leftrightarrow \langle \delta \rangle \top \wedge \mathsf{Bel}_i\, [\delta]\varphi$$

The above equivalences allow to 'push inwards' the modal operators $\langle \delta \rangle$ until they are no longer in the scope of the Boolean and the belief operators.

Proposition 2 *The equivalence*

$$\langle \delta \rangle p \leftrightarrow \begin{cases} \langle \delta \rangle \top & \text{if } \exists i \in \mathbb{I}, \delta_i = p \leftarrow \top \text{ and } \nexists j \in \mathbb{I}, \delta_j = p \leftarrow \bot \\ \bot & \text{if } \exists i \in \mathbb{I}, \delta_i = p \leftarrow \bot \text{ and } \nexists j \in \mathbb{I}, \delta_j = p \leftarrow \top \\ \langle \delta \rangle \top \wedge p & \text{else} \end{cases}$$

is **DDL–PA** *valid.*

In order to formally define the set of resulting formulas we recursively define *dynamic modalities*, noted μ, as abbreviations of sequences of dynamic operators:

$$\langle \mathsf{nil} \rangle \varphi \overset{\mathrm{def}}{=} \varphi$$

$$\langle \mu;\delta \rangle \varphi \overset{\mathrm{def}}{=} \langle \mu \rangle \langle \delta \rangle \varphi$$

Let us say that a *dynamic atom* is either a propositional variable from $\mathbb{P}$, or of the form $\langle \mu \rangle \top$, or of the form $\langle \mu \rangle \mathsf{Hpn}(\delta_i)$, where μ is a dynamic modality. The above propositions allows us to transform every **DDL–PA** formula φ into an equivalent formula in *reduced form*: a formula that is built from dynamic atoms by means of the Boolean and the Bel_i operators. Let $red(\varphi)$ be the *reduction* of φ that is obtained in this way.

Proposition 3 *The equivalence* $\varphi \leftrightarrow red(\varphi)$ *is* **DDL–PA** *valid.*

PROOF. The result follows from Proposition 1, Proposition 2, and the fact that the rule of replacement of equivalents preserves validity. ∎

If we consider dynamic atoms as propositional variables then every formula in reduced form is a formula of the logic of belief K45. This will be exploited now in order to give a decision procedure for our logic.

For every formula φ that is in reduced form, let $DM(\varphi)$ be the set of dynamic modalities of φ, i.e. the set of event sequences μ such that φ contains a dynamic atom of the form either $\langle\mu\rangle\top$, or $\langle\mu\rangle\mathsf{Hpn}(\delta_i)$ for some δ_i. Let Γ_φ be the set of formulas defined as follows.

$$\Gamma_\varphi = \left\{ \neg\big(\langle\mu\rangle\mathsf{Hpn}(\delta_i) \wedge \langle\mu\rangle\mathsf{Hpn}(\delta_i')\big) \ : \ \mu \in DM(\varphi), \delta \in \mathsf{EVT}, i \in \mathbb{I}, \text{ and } \delta_i \neq \delta_i' \right\} \cup$$

$$\{ \, (\textstyle\bigwedge_{i\in\mathbb{I}}\langle\mu\rangle\mathsf{Hpn}(\delta_i)) \rightarrow \langle\mu\rangle\langle\delta\rangle\top \ : \ \mu \in DM(\varphi), \delta \in \mathsf{EVT}\} \cup$$

$$\{ \, \langle\mu\rangle(\textstyle\bigvee_{\delta\in\mathsf{EVT}}\bigwedge_{i\in\mathbb{I}}\mathsf{Hpn}(\delta_i)) \ : \ \mu \in DM(\varphi) \, \}$$

Γ_φ axiomatises the properties of models and the semantic constraints that are relevant for φ: the first line says that N is a function, and the last line says that it is total.[3] The second line expresses the 'do implies can' constraint 2. The formula $\langle\mu\rangle\langle\delta\rangle\top$ has to be understood as a dynamic atom (i.e. it is of the form $\langle\mu'\rangle\top$ for an appropriate μ'). Observe that every Γ_φ is finite.

Proposition 4 *Let φ be a DDL–PA formula in reduced form. Then*

$$\varphi \text{ is DDL–PA valid in epistemic PC models if and only if } \Gamma_\varphi \models_{K45} \varphi,$$

where $\models_{K45}$ is the global consequence relation of the modal logic K45 and where in the latter check each dynamic atom is considered to be an atomic formula of the language of K45.

PROOF. Let φ be a DDL–PA formula in reduced form. Define the set DA_φ of dynamic atoms that are relevant for φ as follows:

$$DA_\varphi = \mathbb{P} \cup \{\langle\mu\rangle\top \ : \ \mu \in DM(\varphi)\} \cup \{\langle\mu\rangle\mathsf{Hpn}(\delta_i) \ : \ \mu \in DM(\varphi), \delta \in \mathsf{EVT}, i \in \mathbb{I}\}$$

Suppose φ is invalid, i.e. $M, w \not\models \varphi$ for some epistemic PC-model
$$M = (W, B, R, N, V)$$
and possible world $w \in W$. We are going to build a K45 model
$$M^{K45} = (W, B, V^{K45})$$
such that $M^{K45} \models \psi$ for every $\psi \in \Gamma_\varphi$ and such that $M^{K45} \not\models_{K45} \varphi$, where the valuation V^{K45} of M^{K45} is for the set of propositional variables DA_φ. We define V^{K45} such that $V_w^{K45}(\pi) = \mathtt{tt}$ iff $M, w \Vdash \pi$, for every dynamic atom $\pi \in DA_\varphi$. M^{K45} is a legal K45 model because B is transitive and Euclidean. We check that $M, v \Vdash \psi$ for every $\psi \in \Gamma_\varphi$:

1. $M, v \Vdash \neg\big(\langle\mu\rangle\mathsf{Hpn}(\delta_i) \wedge \langle\mu\rangle\mathsf{Hpn}(\delta_i')\big)$ for every $\mu \in DM(\varphi)$, $\delta \in \mathsf{EVT}$, and $i \in \mathbb{I}$ such that $\delta_i \neq \delta_i'$ because N is a function.
2. $M, v \Vdash (\bigwedge_{i\in\mathbb{I}}\langle\mu\rangle\mathsf{Hpn}(\delta_i)) \rightarrow \langle\mu\rangle\langle\delta\rangle\top$ for every $\mu \in DM(\varphi)$ and $\delta \in \mathsf{EVT}$ because M satisfies the semantic constraint 2.
3. $M, v \Vdash \langle\mu\rangle(\bigvee_{\delta\in\mathsf{EVT}}\bigwedge_{i\in\mathbb{I}}\mathsf{Hpn}(\delta_i))$ for every $\mu \in DM(\varphi)$ because the function N is total.

---

[3] Note that the last constraint in Γ_φ can be dropped if $\mathbb{P}_\varphi \neq \mathbb{P}$: then it is not necessary to reflect the fact that the 'next' function N is total because then K45 models can always be arranged such that this is the case (by setting N_w to some δ such that say $\delta_i = p{\leftarrow}\top$ for some variable p not occurring in φ).

We finally prove by induction on the form of ψ that for every possible world $v \in W$ and for every formula ψ we have $M, v \vdash \psi$ iff $M^{\mathsf{K45}}, v \vdash \psi$. The base case of the induction where ψ is a dynamic atom is clear by the definition of V^{K45}; and the induction step is obvious.

Suppose $\Gamma_\varphi \not\models_{\mathsf{K45}} \varphi$, i.e. there is a $\mathsf{K45}$ model

$$M^{\mathsf{K45}} = (W, B, V^{\mathsf{K45}})$$

such that $M^{\mathsf{K45}} \models \psi$ for every $\psi \in \Gamma_\varphi$ and such that $M^{\mathsf{K45}}, w \not\models_{\mathsf{K45}} \varphi$ for some $w \in W$ (where the valuation V^{K45} of M^{K45} is for the set of propositional variables DA_φ). We build an epistemic PC model

$$M = (W, B, R, N, V)$$

by defining R, N, and V as follows:

$$
R_w(\mu, i) = \begin{cases} \{\delta_i \ : \ V_w^{\mathsf{K45}}(\langle \mu \rangle \langle \delta \rangle \top) = \mathsf{tt}\} & \text{if } \mu \in DM(\varphi) \\ \{\delta_i^0\} & \text{if } \mu \notin DM(\varphi) \end{cases}
$$

$$
N_w(\mu) = \begin{cases} \delta & \text{if } \mu \in DM(\varphi) \text{ and for every } i \in \mathbb{I}_\varphi, V_w^{\mathsf{K45}}(\langle \mu \rangle \mathsf{Hpn}(\delta_i)) = \mathsf{tt} \\ \delta^0 & \text{else} \end{cases}
$$

$$
V_w(p) = V_w^{\mathsf{K45}}(p) \text{ for } p \in \mathbb{P}
$$

In the definition of R and N, δ^0 is an arbitrary fixed event from EVT. Observe that N is well defined: it is a function because of the first item of the definition of Γ_φ, and it is total because of the third item. Moreover, M satisfies constraint 2 because of the second item of the definition of Γ_φ and because we have enforced it when $\mu \notin DM(\varphi)$. Finally, M's accessibility relation B is transitive and Euclidean because the relation B of M^{K45} is so. It remains to establish that $M, w \not\Vdash \varphi$. We do so by proving inductively that for every formula ψ such that $DM(\psi) \subseteq DM(\varphi)$ and for every possible world $v \in W$ we have $M, v \Vdash \psi$ if and only if $M^{\mathsf{K45}}, v \Vdash \psi$. It follows that φ is invalid in epistemic PC models. ∎

It follows from Proposition 3 and Proposition 4 that checking validity of φ in our logic reduces to checking whether $red(\varphi)$ is a global consequence of Γ_φ in $\mathsf{K45}$. Furthermore, it follows from the decidability of the $\mathsf{K45}$ global consequence relation that $\mathsf{DDL-PA}$ validity is decidable.

Theorem 1 *The $\mathsf{DDL-PA}$ validity problem is decidable.*

PROOF. Let φ be a $\mathsf{DDL-PA}$ formula. By Proposition 2 φ is valid iff $red(\varphi)$ is valid. As the latter is in reduced form, by Proposition 4 it is valid iff $\Gamma_\varphi \models_{\mathsf{K45}} \varphi$, i.e. iff φ is a global logical consequence of Γ_φ in $\mathsf{K45}$. As the latter problem is decidable, it follows that the problem of validity in epistemic PC models is decidable. ∎

The reduction schemas of Proposition 1 and Proposition 2 might increase formula size exponentially. Reduction therefore only provides a suboptimal decision procedure, and it remains to establish the complexity of validity checking.

2.4 *Axiomatisation*

An axiomatisation of DDL−PA can be obtained by putting together:

- some axiomatisation of multiagent K45
- the schemas of Proposition 1 and Proposition 2
- the axiom schemas:

$$\neg(\mathsf{Hpn}(\delta_i) \wedge \mathsf{Hpn}(\delta_i')) , \quad \text{for } \delta_i \neq \delta_i'$$

$$\mathsf{Hpn}(\delta_i) \rightarrow \langle \delta_i \rangle \top$$

$$\bigvee_{\delta \in \mathsf{EVT}} \bigwedge_{i \in \mathbb{I}} \mathsf{Hpn}(\delta_i)$$

- the inference rule:

$$\text{from } \varphi \leftrightarrow \psi \text{ infer } \langle \delta \rangle \varphi \leftrightarrow \langle \delta \rangle \psi$$

The above three axiom schemas generalise the formulas in Γ_φ of our reduction from DDL−PA to K45.

3 Defining trust in **DDL−PA**

By now we have the ingredients we need in order to capture Castelfranchi and Falcone's relevant concepts. We have already seen that our logic directly accounts for belief. It remains to define the concepts of goal, willingness, ability and opportunity.

But first of all let us have a closer look at the concept of belief.

3.1 *Belief and probability*

In epistemic logic, "*i* believes that φ" is identified with "φ is true in all worlds that are possible for *i*". This is a strong form of belief. We also need a weaker form where belief is identified with truth in the most plausible possible worlds. We therefore have:

- the strong belief in some physical properties of the world, which can be objectively verified, such as an agent's own beliefs and intentions or the belief that some agent is able to perform some action, or that some action will achieve some outcome;
- the weak belief in some non verifiable properties such as another agent's beliefs and intentions.

We are going to model an agent's weak beliefs in terms of a subset of the set of worlds possible for *i*.

We suppose that $\mathbb{P}$ contains special propositional variables poss, that we read "the current state is plausible/probable". Note that poss being a propositional variable, its truth value can be changed: the events poss$\leftarrow\top$ and poss$\leftarrow\bot$ modify the evaluation of the current state (whether the current state is plausible/probable or not). We then introduce modal operators of *probability* Prob_i as follows:

$$\mathsf{Prob}_i\varphi \stackrel{\text{def}}{=} \mathsf{Bel}_i(\mathsf{poss} \to \varphi)$$

We therefore identify "it is probable for agent i that φ" with "φ is true in all worlds that i considers plausible/probable". Our definition leads to both positive and negative introspection principles for weak belief: the formula schemas $\mathsf{Prob}_i\varphi \to \mathsf{Bel}_i\mathsf{Prob}_i\varphi$ and $\neg\mathsf{Prob}_i\varphi \to \mathsf{Bel}_i\neg\mathsf{Prob}_i\varphi$ are both valid. It also leads to the natural principle $\mathsf{Bel}_i\varphi \to \mathsf{Prob}_i\varphi$.

3.2 Goal and Willingness

In the same vein as before, we suppose that $\mathbb{P}$ contains special propositional variables good(i), one for every $i \in \mathbb{I}$. good(i) reads "the current state is good for i". Note that i's evaluation of the current state can be modified by assignments.
    We introduce preference operators Pref_i that are defined as follows:

$$\mathsf{Pref}_i\varphi \stackrel{\text{def}}{=} \mathsf{Bel}_i(\mathsf{good}(i) \to \varphi)$$

We therefore identify "agent i prefers that φ" with "φ is true in all of i's possible worlds that are good for i". Our definition leads to positive and negative introspection principles for preferences: the formula schemas $\mathsf{Pref}_i\varphi \to \mathsf{Bel}_i\mathsf{Pref}_i\varphi$, and $\neg\mathsf{Pref}_i\varphi \to \mathsf{Bel}_i\neg\mathsf{Pref}_i\varphi$ are both valid. Moreover the principle of strong realism $\mathsf{Bel}_i\varphi \to \mathsf{Pref}_i\varphi$ is valid [3, 4].
    We identify j's *willingness* to perform δ_j with j's preference that δ_j happen next, formally: $\mathsf{Pref}_j\mathsf{Hpn}(\delta_j)$.
    We finally identify "agent i has goal that φ" with "i prefers that $\mathsf{Next}\varphi$ is true", formally: $\mathsf{Pref}_i\mathsf{Next}\varphi$.

3.3 Ability and opportunity

We start by defining the concept "group J is capable to achieve φ by doing δ_J, if the agents outside J cooperate".

$$\langle\delta_J\rangle\varphi \stackrel{\text{def}}{=} \bigvee_{\delta'_{-J}} \langle\delta_J\cdot\delta'_{-J}\rangle\varphi$$

where $\delta_J\cdot\delta'_{-J}$ is the function that is obtained in the obvious way by combining the functions δ_J and δ'_{-J} (whose domains are disjoint):

$$(\delta_J \cdot \delta'_{-J})(i) = \begin{cases} \delta_J(i) & \text{if } i \in J \\ \delta'_{-J}(i) & \text{if } i \notin J \end{cases}$$

Observe that $\langle \delta_{\mathbb{I}} \rangle \varphi = \langle \delta \rangle \varphi$.

We define the *ability* of a group J to perform a joint action δ_J as $\langle \delta_J \rangle \top$.

Opportunity of J to achieve φ by doing δ_J is defined by means of the dual modal operator as: $[\delta_J]\varphi \overset{\text{def}}{=} \neg\langle \delta_J \rangle \neg \varphi$.

3.4 Trust

Now we are in a position to define the trust predicate $\mathsf{Trust}(i, J, \delta_J, \varphi)$, read "agent i trusts group J to do δ_J in order to achieve i's goal φ", as the conjunction of the following four formulas:

1. $\mathsf{Pref}_i \mathsf{Next}\, \varphi$: agent i has the goal that φ;
2. $\mathsf{Bel}_i \langle \delta_J \rangle \top$: i believes J is able to perform δ_J;
3. $\mathsf{Prob}_i \bigwedge_{j \in J} \mathsf{Pref}_j \mathsf{Hpn}(\delta_j)$: i expects the members of J to be willing to perform their part δ_j;
4. $\mathsf{Bel}_i [\delta_J]\varphi$: i believes J has the opportunity to achieve φ by performing δ_J, no matter what other agents do.

Actually we might drop the second argument J from the trust predicate because the third argument δ_J contains already that information.

Proposition 5 *The implication*

$$\bigwedge_{j \in J} \mathsf{Trust}(i, j, \delta_j, \varphi) \rightarrow \mathsf{Trust}(i, J, \delta_J, \varphi)$$

is DDL−PA valid.

Note that the converse does not hold. (This is due to the fourth item in the definition of trust.)

Proposition 6 *Let $J_1 \cap J_2 = \emptyset$. The implication*

$$\mathsf{Trust}(i, J_1, \delta_{J_1}, \varphi) \wedge \mathsf{Trust}(i, J_2, \delta_{J_2}, \psi) \rightarrow \mathsf{Trust}(i, J_1 \cup J_2, \delta_{J_1} \cdot \delta_{J_2}, \varphi \wedge \psi)$$

is DDL−PA valid.

4 A more general definition of trust

The evaluation of the trust predicate involves universal quantification over the complement set $-J = \mathbb{I} \setminus J$. If the truster i is not in J then that quantification includes all possible actions that i may perform. This is not realistic. More generally, we might wish to fix the behaviour of some of the agents outside J. The following definition achieves this, moving to a 5-ary predicate $\mathsf{Trust}(i, J, \delta_J, \varphi, \delta_K)$, where J and K are disjoint subsets of $\mathbb{I}$. It reads "i trusts J to do δ_J in order to achieve i's goal φ, given that the agents of K perform δ_K".

It is only the opportunity condition of the previous definition that has to be redefined:

4'. $\mathsf{Bel}_i[\delta_J \cdot \delta_K]\varphi$: i believes J has the opportunity to achieve φ by performing δ_J, given that the agents in K do δ_K, and no matter what other agents outside of J and K do.

Our previous definition of trust is a particular case of the new definition.

Proposition 7 *The equivalence*

$$\mathsf{Trust}(i, J, \delta_J, \varphi) \leftrightarrow \mathsf{Trust}(i, \delta_J, \varphi, \delta_\emptyset)$$

is DDL−PA valid.

5 Why we need strong and weak beliefs

A natural requirement to be added to our logic is the following axiom of intentional action:

$$\big(\langle \delta_j \rangle \top \wedge \mathsf{Pref}_j \mathsf{Hpn}(\delta_j)\big) \rightarrow \mathsf{Hpn}(\delta_j)$$

It follows that when i trusts j to perform δ_j then i believes that j is actually going to perform δ_j.

The above requirement allows us to give a technical explanation why we need two different kinds of belief. Let us suppose that the willingness condition is not

$$\mathsf{Prob}_i \bigwedge_{j \in J} \mathsf{Pref}_j \mathsf{Hpn}(\delta_j),$$

but $\mathsf{Bel}_i \bigwedge_{j \in J} \mathsf{Pref}_j \mathsf{Hpn}(\delta_j)$. With the ability condition $\mathsf{Bel}_i \langle \delta_J \rangle \top$ it follows that

$$\mathsf{Bel}_i \bigwedge_{j \in J} \mathsf{Hpn}(\delta_j).$$

Then with the opportunity condition $\mathsf{Bel}_i[\delta_J]\varphi$ it follows that $\mathsf{Bel}_i \mathsf{Next}\varphi$. But the latter implies the goal condition $\mathsf{Pref}_i \mathsf{Next}\varphi$, which would therefore be redundant with the goal condition of the above definition of trust!

We therefore chose to weaken the willingness condition.

6 Conclusion

We have defined a simple modal logic of belief and action DDL−PA. The actions of DDL−PA are assignments of propositional variables that are simultaneously performed by the agents. We have shown that our logic is decidable.

Our logic captures the spirit of Castelfranchi and Falcone's theory of trust. We have argued that a distinction between strong and weak belief is needed in order to keep the four items defining trust independent.

Acknowledgements The work of the authors was supported by the ANR VERSO 2010 project "Personal Information Management through Internet" (PIMI, ANR-10-VERS-0014).

References

1. C. Castelfranchi and R. Falcone. Principles of trust for MAS: Cognitive anatomy, social importance, and quantification. In *Proceedings of the Third International Conference on Multiagent Systems (ICMAS'98)*, pp. 72–79, 1998.
2. C. Castelfranchi and R. Falcone. *Trust Theory: A Socio-Cognitive and Computational Model*. John Wiley and Sons, Chichester, UK, 2010.
3. Philip R. Cohen and Hector J. Levesque. Intention is choice with commitment. *Artificial Intelligence*, 42(2–3):213–261, 1990.
4. Philip R. Cohen and Hector J. Levesque. Persistence, intentions, and commitment. In Philip R. Cohen, Jerry Morgan, and Martha E. Pollack, editors, *Intentions in Communication*, chapter 3, pages 33–69. MIT Press, Cambridge, MA, 1990.
5. Hans P. van Ditmarsch, Wiebe van der Hoek, and Barteld Kooi. *Dynamic Epistemic Logic*. Kluwer Academic Publishers, 2007.
6. R. Falcone and C. Castelfranchi. Social trust: A cognitive approach. In C. Castelfranchi and Y. H. Tan, editors, *Trust and Deception in Virtual Societies*, pages 55–90. Kluwer, 2001.
7. A. Herzig, E. Lorini, J. F. Hübner, and L. Vercouter. A logic of trust and reputation. *Logic Journal of the IGPL*, 18(1):214–244, 2010.
8. A. Herzig, E. Lorini, F. Moisan, and N. Troquard. A dynamic logic of normative systems. In *Proceedings of IJCAI 2011*, pp. 228–233 2011.
9. Wiebe van der Hoek, Dirk Walther, and Michael Wooldridge. On the logic of cooperation and the transfer of control. *J. of AI Research (JAIR)*, 37:437–477, 2010.
10. Wiebe van der Hoek and Michael Wooldridge. On the logic of cooperation and propositional control. *Artif. Intell.*, 164(1-2):81–119, 2005.

Chapter 24
A cognitive model of conflicts in trust using argumentation*

Serena Villata, Guido Boella, Dov M. Gabbay and Leendert van der Torre

Abstract Trust minimizes the uncertainty in the interactions of information sources. To express the possibly conflicting motivations about trusting or not information sources, we reason about trust using argumentation theory. First, we present a model for representing evidence provided in support of the sources' arguments, and we show how to model the information sources and how to attack untrustworthy sources. Second, we provide a representation of trust about the sources in which trust concerns not only the sources but also the information items and the relation with other information. Finally, we introduce the feedback on the trustworthiness among the sources and the information items they propose, and we distinguish two dimensions of trust, namely competence and sincerity.

Serena Villata
WIMMICS team, INRIA Sophia Antipolis, France
e-mail: serena.villata@inria.fr

Guido Boella
Department of Computer Science, University of Torino, Italy
e-mail: guido@di.unito.it

Dov M. Gabbay
Group of Logic, Language and Computation, Department of Computer Science, King's College London, UK
e-mail: dov.gabbay@kcl.ac.uk

Leendert van der Torre
Faculty of Sciences, Technology and Communication, University of Luxembourg, Luxembourg
e-mail: leon.vandertorre@uni.lu

* This chapter is an extended version of the paper "Arguing about the Trustworthiness of the Information Source" published at ECSQARU-2011.

1 Introduction

Trust is a mechanism for managing uncertain information in decision making, considering the information sources. In their interactions, the information sources have to reason whether they should trust or not the other sources, and on the extent to which they trust those other sources. This is important, for example, in medical contexts, where doctors have to inform the patient of the pro and con evidence concerning some treatment, or in decision support systems where the user is not satisfied by an answer without explanations.

Castelfranchi and Falcone [8] provide a definition of trust both as a mental state and as a social attitude and relation. Castelfranchi argues that "what is needed is a general and principled theory of trust, of its cognitive and affective components, and of its social functions. Such a theory has to be developed to answer questions like: When is trust rational? When is it over-confidence and risky? When is trust too weak and when do we waste time on redundant control mechanisms or loose good opportunities by not taking advantage of sufficient trust levels?..." To answer these questions, Castelfranchi presents a cognitive model of trust in term of necessary mental ingredients, i.e., beliefs and goals, and decision to delegate. In particular, Castelfranchi stresses the importance of this explicit cognitive account for trust in three ways. First, he criticizes the game-theoretic view of trust which is prisoner of the Prisoner Dilemma mental frame and reduces trust simply to a probability or perceived risk in decisions. Second, he finds the quantitative aspects of trust (its strength or degree) on those mental ingredients (beliefs and goals) and on their strength. Third, he claims that this cognitive analysis of trust is fundamental for distinguishing between internal and external attribution which predict very different strategies for building or increasing trust; for founding mechanisms of image, reputation, persuasion, and argumentation in trust building.

In Castelfranchi's model, the word "trust" means different things, but they are systematically related with each other. In particular, three crucial concepts have been recognized and distinguished. Trust is at the same time: (i) a mere mental attitude (prediction and evaluation) towards another agent; (ii) a decision to rely upon the other, i.e. an intention to delegate and trust, which makes the trustier "vulnerable"; (iii) a behavior, i.e. the intentional act of trusting, and the consequent relation between the trustier and the trustee. In each of the above concepts, different sets of cognitive ingredients are involved in the trustier's mind.

In this paper, we rely on the cognitive model of trust introduced by Castelfranchi and Falcone [8], and we present a cognitive model of conflicts in trust using argumentation. In particular, the reasoning process addressed by the information sources concerning the extent to which they trust the other sources leads to the emergence of conflicts among the sources. When an information source explicitly expresses a negative evaluation of the trustworthiness of another source, it can be seen as an "attack" to the trustworthiness of the second source. To deal with the dimension of conflict in handling trust, we propose to use argumentation theory, since it is a mechanism to reason about conflicting information [10]. The challenge is to use argumentation theory not only to model the sources and their conflicts based on trust, but also to understand the reasons, represented under the form of arguments, behind these conflicts. Moreover, we need to distinguish the conflicts about the content of the arguments, and the conflicts about the different opinions of the sources on the trustworthiness of the other sources. These are two separate reasoning levels, and the challenge is to model both of them by using only argumentation.

In this paper, a way to deal with the conflicts about trust using Dung's abstract argumentation framework is presented. A Dung argumentation framework [11] aims at representing conflicts among elements called *arguments*. It allows to reason about these conflicts in order to detect, starting by a set of arguments and the conflicts among them, which are those arguments which can be considered acceptable. The acceptable arguments are arguments which are considered as believable by an external evaluator, who has a full knowledge of the argumentation framework. A Dung argumentation framework [11] can be instantiated by the arguments and attacks defined by a knowledge base, and the knowledge base inferences are defined in terms of the claims of the justified arguments, e.g., the ASPIC+ framework instantiates Dung argumentation with accounts of the structure of arguments, the nature of attack and the use of preferences [24]. In such a kind of framework, arguments are instantiated by sentences of a single knowledge base, without reference to the information sources. Moreover, it is difficult to distinguish between the object level and the meta-level. In reasoning about trust, the information about the trustworthiness relations among the sources are meta-level information, and they cannot be inserted directly into the argumentation framework. They influence the behavior of the argumentation framework in the sense that they lead to further conflicts among the sources and their information items.

The following example presents an informal dialogue illustrating conflicts about trust among the sources and the pieces of information they provide, where the external evaluator is a judge:

- *Witness1: I suspect that the man killed his boss in Rome. (a)*
- *Witness1: But his car was broken, thus he could not reach the crime scene. (b)*
- *Witness2: Witness1 is a compulsive liar. (c)*
- *Witness3: I repaired the suspect's car at 12pm of the crime day. (d)*
- *Witness4: I believe that Witness3 is not able to repair that kind of car. (e)*
- *Witness5: The suspect has another car. (f)*
- *Witness6: Witness5 saw that the suspect parked 2 cars in my underground parking garage 3 weeks ago. (g)*
- *Witness2: Witness5 was on holidays 3 weeks ago. (h)*
- *Witness7: Witness5 cannot go on holidays because of his working contract. (i)*
- *Witness3: Witness7 is not competent about the working contracts of the underground parking garage. (l)*
- *Witness1: Witness7 does not really think that Witness5 cannot go on holidays because of his working contract. (m)*

In this dialogue, different kinds of conflicts are highlighted among the sources. First, the agents can attack the trustworthiness of the other sources, e.g., argument (c) of the dialogue. These attacks are addressed by means of arguments which attack the sources' trustworthiness at all. Second, the sources provide evidence in support of their arguments or attacks, and they can provide evidence also concerning the other sources' arguments, e.g., argument (g) provides evidence for argument (f). Third, conflicts can be restricted only to some particular argument or attack proposed by a source which is not considered untrustworthy in general, e.g., argument (h) expresses concerns about the trustworthiness of argument (g). Fourth, conflicts about the trustworthiness of the sources can be further specified in order to deal with the sincerity of the sources, e.g., argument (m), and their competence, e.g., argument (l). Fifth, there is a feedback between the trustworthiness of the sources and the trustworthiness of the information items they propose.

The problem is that it is difficult to formalize the example above with sentences from a single knowledge base only, e.g., to model it in ASPIC+ style instantiated argumentation. Moreover, meta-level information such as the distinction about conflicts based on sincerity and conflicts based on competence cannot be represented in those frameworks, but these two trust dimensions might be independently evaluated in the argumentation process: x's sincerity/honesty (y believes that x has told him the truth) vs. x's competence (y trusts the judgment of x). It is different in argumentation if I doubt about x's honesty, reliability, or if I have doubts about x's having access to the information, or being competent. Finally, it has to be modeled that attacking x's argument means attacking x and his credibility and trustworthiness as source. This is fundamental, both in the case in which it is intentional and it is the real objective of the move, or when is not intended but is a consequence of the invalidation of the arguments. There is a bidirectional link between the source and its information items: the provided item is more or less believable on the basis of the source trustworthiness, but the invalidation of the data feedbacks on the source's credibility [8]. We address the following research question:

- How to define a cognitive model of conflicts in trust using argumentation?

  This breaks down into the following subquestions:

  1. How to represent the information sources and attack their trustworthiness?
  2. How to represent pro and con evidence, as done in Carneades [15]?
  3. How to attack the sources' trustworthiness about single information items?
  4. How to represent the trust feedback between the sources and their information items?
  5. How to distinguish different dimensions of trust such as sincerity and competence?

To answer the research questions, we propose meta-argumentation [16, 20, 3, 6]. Meta-argumentation provides a way to instantiate abstract arguments, i.e., abstract arguments are treated as meta-arguments. It allows us not only to reason about arguments such as sentences from a knowledge base indexed by the information source, but also to introduce in the framework, at the meta-level, other instances like arguments about the trustworthiness of sources. The advantage of adopting meta-argumentation is that we do not extend Dung's framework in order to introduce trust but we instantiate his theory with meta-arguments. For a further discussion about meta-argumentation, see [27].

The idea is that the sources are introduced into the argumentation framework under the form of meta-arguments of the kind *"agent i is trustable"*. Each source supports the information items it proposes by means of meta-arguments representing evidence. An attack to the trustworthiness of a source is modeled as an attack to the meta-argument *"agent i is trustable"*. In meta-argumentation, both arguments and attacks are represented as meta-arguments. Also in this case, an attack to the trustworthiness of an item is modeled as an attack to the meta-argument representing that item. The representation of the feedback from the sources to the information items and back is modeled again by introducing a meta-argument. It represents the fact that a certain number of attackers of the information items proposed by a source is accepted, i.e., trustable, thus the attacked source cannot be considered trustworthy. Finally, the two dimensions of sincerity and competence are modeled using a meta-argument representing the fact that the argument is believed by the sources and thus the source is sincere in proposing *arg*. This meta-argument supports the "content" meta-argument associated to the argument *arg*. A conflict about sincerity is modeled as an attack towards the meta-argument representing the belief while a conflict about competence is modeled as an attack towards the support of the "belief" meta-argument and the meta-argument representing the content of the argument.

Note that we do not claim that argumentation is the only way to model trust, but we underline that, when the sources argue, they are strongly influenced by the trustworthiness relations with the other sources. Moreover, we do not assign a numerical value associated to trust, because we are more interested in analyzing the motivations behind the beliefs of the sources, e.g., in the case of Witness1 we have that he explains that he does not believe *a* and that this is due to argument *b*. In this paper, we do not treat converging and diverging beliefs sources, and the source's subjective uncertainty introduced by Catelfranchi and Falcone [8]. This is left as future work.

The paper follows the research questions. After a brief introduction on meta-argumentation, we describe our cognitive model of conflicts in trust. Conclusions end the paper.

2 Argumentation theory

2.1 Abstract argumentation

A Dung argumentation framework [11] is based on a binary *attack* relation among arguments, which are abstract entities whose role is determined only by their relation to other arguments.

Definition 1 (Argumentation framework AF **[11])** *An argumentation framework is a tuple* $\langle A, \rightarrow \rangle$ *where A is a finite set of elements called arguments and* $\rightarrow$ *is a binary relation called attack defined on* $A \times A$.

Definition 2 (Defence) *Let* $\langle A, \rightarrow \rangle$ *be an argumentation framework. Let* $S \subseteq A$. *S defends a if* $\forall b \in A$ *such that* $b \rightarrow a$, $\exists c \in S$ *such that* $c \rightarrow b$.

All Dung's semantics are based on the notion of defence. A semantics of an argumentation theory consists of a conflict free set of arguments, i.e., a set of arguments that does not contain an argument attacking another argument in the set.

Definition 3 (Conflict-free) *Let* $\langle A, \rightarrow \rangle$ *be an argumentation framework. The set* $S \subseteq A$ *is conflict-free if and only if there are no* $a, b \in S$ *such that* $a \rightarrow b$.

Like Baroni and Giacomin [1] we use a function $\mathcal{E}$ mapping an argumentation framework $\langle A, \rightarrow \rangle$ to its set of extensions, i.e., to a set of sets of arguments. Since they do not give a name to the function $\mathcal{E}$, and it maps argumentation frameworks to the set of accepted arguments, we call $\mathcal{E}$ the *acceptance function*.

Definition 4 *Let* $\mathcal{U}$ *be the universe of arguments. An acceptance function* $\mathcal{E} : 2^{\mathcal{U}} \times 2^{\mathcal{U} \times \mathcal{U}} \rightarrow 2^{2^{\mathcal{U}}}$ *is a partial function which is defined for each argumentation framework* $\langle A, \rightarrow \rangle$ *with finite* $A \subseteq \mathcal{U}$ *and* $\rightarrow \subseteq A \times A$, *and maps an argumentation framework* $\langle A, \rightarrow \rangle$ *to sets of subsets of A:* $\mathcal{E}(\langle A, \rightarrow \rangle) \subseteq 2^{A}$.

The following definition summarizes the most widely used acceptability semantics of arguments [11]. Which semantics is most appropriate in which circumstances depends on the application domain of the argumentation theory.

Definition 5 (Acceptability semantics) *Let* $AF = \langle A, \rightarrow \rangle$ *be an argumentation framework. Let* $S \subseteq A$.

- *S is an* admissible *extension if and only if it is conflict-free and defends all its elements.*
- *S is a* complete *extension if and only if it is conflict-free and we have* $S = \{a \mid S \text{ defends } a\}$.
- *S is a* grounded *extension of AF if and only if S is the smallest (for set inclusion) complete extension of AF.*
- *S is a* preferred *extension of AF if and only if S is maximal (for set inclusion) among admissible extensions of AF.*
- *S is a* stable *extension of AF if and only if S is conflict-free and attacks all arguments of* $A \backslash S$.

2.2 Meta-argumentation

Meta-argumentation instantiates Dung's theory with meta-arguments, such that *Dung's theory is used to reason about itself* [4, 3]. Meta-argumentation is a particular way to define mappings from argumentation frameworks to extended argumentation frameworks: arguments are interpreted as meta-arguments, of which some are mapped to "argument a is accepted", $acc(a)$, where a is an abstract argument from the extended argumentation framework *EAF*. Moreover, auxiliary arguments are introduced to represent, for example, attacks, so that, by being arguments themselves, they can be attacked or attack other arguments. The meta-argumentation methodology is summarized in Figure 1.

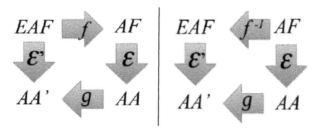

Fig. 1 The meta-argumentation methodology.

The function f assigns to each argument a in the *EAF*, a meta-argument "argument a is accepted" in the basic argumentation framework. The function f^{-1} instantiates an *AF* with an *EAF*. We use Dung's acceptance functions $\mathcal{E}$ to find functions $\mathcal{E}'$ between *EAFs* and the acceptable arguments AA' they return. The accepted arguments of the meta-argumentation framework are a function of the *EAF*, $AA' = \mathcal{E}'(EAF)$. The transformation function consists of two parts: the function f^{-1}, transforming an *AF* to an *EAF*, and a function g which transforms the acceptable arguments of the *AF* into acceptable arguments of the *EAF*. Summarizing $\mathcal{E}' = \{(f^{-1}(a), g(b)) \mid (a,b) \in \mathcal{E}\}$ and $AA' = \mathcal{E}'(EAF) = g(AA) = g(\mathcal{E}(AF)) = g(\mathcal{E}(f(EAF)))$.

The first step of the meta-argumentation approach is to define the set of *EAFs*. The second step consists of defining flattening algorithms as a function from this set of *EAFs* to the set of all basic *AF*: $f : EAF \to AF$. The inverse of the flattening is the instantiation of the *AF*. See [3, 27] for further details. We define an *EAF* as a set of partial argumentation frameworks of the sources $\langle A, \langle A_1, \to_1 \rangle, \ldots, \langle A_n, \to_n \rangle, \to \rangle$ [9].

Definition 6 *An extended argumentation framework EAF is a tuple* $\langle A, \langle A_1, \to_1 \rangle, \ldots, \langle A_n, \to_n \rangle, \to \rangle$ *where for each source* $1 \le i \le n$, $A_i \subseteq A \subseteq \mathcal{U}$ *is a set of arguments,* $\to$ *is a binary attack relation on* $A \times A$, *and* $\to_i$ *is a binary relation on* $A_i \times A_i$. *The universe of meta-arguments is* $MU = \{acc(a) \mid a \in \mathcal{U}\} \cup \{X_{a,b}, Y_{a,b} \mid a, b \in \mathcal{U}\}$, *where* $X_{a,b}, Y_{a,b}$ *are the meta-arguments corresponding to the attack* $a \to b$. *The flattening function* f *is given by* $f(EAF) = \langle MA, \longmapsto \rangle$, *where MA is the set of meta-arguments and* $\longmapsto$ *is the meta-attack relation. For a set of arguments* $B \subseteq MU$, *the unflattening function* g *is given by* $g(B) = \{a \mid acc(a) \in B\}$, *and for sets of subsets of arguments* $AA \subseteq 2^{MU}$, *it is given by* $g(AA) = \{g(B) \mid B \in AA\}$.

Given an acceptance function $\mathcal{E}$ *for an AF, the extensions of accepted arguments of an EAF are given by* $\mathcal{E}'(EAF) = g(\mathcal{E}(f(EAF)))$. *The derived acceptance function* $\mathcal{E}'$ *of the EAF is thus* $\mathcal{E}' = \{(f^{-1}(a), g(b)) \mid (a,b) \in \mathcal{E}\}$. *We say that the source i provides*

evidence in support of argument a when a ∈ A$_i$, and the source supports the attack
a → b when a → b ∈→$_i$.

Note that the union of all the A$_i$ does not produce A because A contains also those arguments which are not supported by the sources, and are just "put on the table." Definition 7 presents the instantiation of a basic AF as a set of partial argumentation frameworks of the sources using meta-argumentation.

Definition 7 *Given an EAF = ⟨A, ⟨A$_1$, →$_1$⟩, ..., ⟨A$_n$, →$_n$⟩⟩ where for each source*
$1 \le i \le n$, A$_i$ ⊆ A ⊆ 𝒰 *is a set of arguments, →⊆ A×A, and →$_i$⊆ A$_i$×A$_i$ is a binary*
relation over A$_i$. MA ⊆ MU is {acc(a) | a ∈ A$_1$ ∪ ... ∪ A$_n$}, and ⟼⊆ MA×MA is a
binary relation on MA such that: acc(a) ⟼ X$_{a,b}$, X$_{a,b}$ ⟼ Y$_{a,b}$, Y$_{a,b}$ ⟼ acc(b) if and
only if there is a source $1 \le i \le n$ such that a, b ∈ A$_i$ and a → b ∈→$_i$.

Intuitively, the X$_{a,b}$ auxiliary argument means that the attack a → b is "in-active", and the Y$_{a,b}$ auxiliary argument means that the attack is "active". An argument of an *EAF* is acceptable iff it is acceptable in the flattened *AF*.

3 Modelling trust in meta-argumentation

A number of authors have highlighted that the definition of trust is difficult to pin down precisely, thus in the literature there are numerous distinct definitions.

The socio-cognitive model of trust presented by Castelfranchi and Falcone [7] is based on a portrait of the mental state of trust in cognitive terms of beliefs and goals. This is not a complete account of the psychological dimensions of trust: it represents the most explicit reason-based, and conscious form. The model does not account for the more implicit forms of trust, for example, trust by default which is not based upon explicit evaluations, beliefs, derived from previous experiences or other sources, or for the affective dimensions of trust, based not on explicit evaluations but on emotional responses and an intuitive, unconscious appraisal. Castelfranchi and Falcone [7, 8] define trust as *"a mental state, a complex attitude of an agent x towards another agent y about the behaviour/action a relevant for the goal g"*.

In sociology, Gambetta [14] states that *"trust is the subjective probability by which an individual A expects that another individual B performs a given action on which its welfare depends"*. Castelfranchi and Falcone [7] observe that this definition is correct, and they stress that trust is basically an estimation, an opinion, an evaluation, i.e. a belief. However, it is also quite a poor definition, since it just refers to one dimension of trust (predictability), while ignoring the "competence" dimension; it does not account for the meaning of "I trust B" where there is also the decision and the act of relying on B; and it does not explain what is such an evaluation made of and based on: the subjective probability melts together too many important parameters and beliefs, which are very relevant in social reasoning.

Common elements of these definitions are a consistent degree of uncertainty and conflicting information associated with trust. Trust is tied up with the relationships between individuals and it is related to the actions of the individuals and to the effects these actions have on the others. Castelfranchi and Falcone [8] identify what ingredients are really basic in the mental state of trust, namely the "competence" belief and the "willingness" belief. In particular, "competence" belief, i.e., a positive evaluation of source y is necessary, source x should believe that y is useful for this goal of its, that y can produce/provide the expected result, that y can play such a role in x's plan/action, that y has some function, and "willingness" belief, i.e., x should think that y not only is able and can do that action/task, but y actually will do what x needs.

Another approach to model trust using modal logic is proposed by Lorini and Demolombe [18] where they present a concept of trust that integrates the truster's goal, the trustee's action ensuring the achievement of the truster's goal, and the trustee's ability and intention to do this action. In this paper, we do not refer to the actions of the sources, but we provide a model for representing the conflicts the sources have to deal with trust. The introduction of the actions in our cognitive model is left as future work, and it will allow also to model willingness. In this paper, we represent only the competence and sincerity mental states of trust.

We follow also the proposal of Liau [17] where the influence of trust on the assimilation of information into the source's mind is considered: *"if agent i believes that agent j has told him the truth on p and he trusts the judgement of j on p, then he will also believe p."* Extending the model by introducing goals to model the presented definitions is left for future work.

3.1 Information sources

The reason why abstract argumentation is not suited to model trust is that an argument, if it is not attacked by another acceptable argument, is considered acceptable. This prevents us from modeling the situation where, for an argument to be acceptable, it must be related to some sources which provide the evidence for such an argument to be accepted. Without an explicit representation of the sources, it becomes impossible to talk about trust: the argument can only be attacked by conflicting information, but it cannot be made unacceptable due to the lack of trust in the source.

Thus a challenge is how to model evidence, where sources are a particular type of evidence. Arguments needing evidence are well known in legal argumentation, where the notion of burden of proof has been introduced [15]. Meta-argumentation provides a means to model burden of proof in abstract argumentation without extending argumentation. The idea is to associate to each argument $a \in A$ put on the table, which is represented by means of meta-argument $acc(a)$, an auxiliary argument $W_{acc(a)}$ attacking it. Being auxiliary this argument is filtered out during the unflattening process. This means that without further information, just as being put on the table, argument a is not acceptable since it is attacked by the acceptable argument $W_{acc(a)}$ and there is no evidence defending it against this "default" attack, as visualized in Figure 2.a for arguments a and b. This evidence is modeled by arguments which attack auxiliary argument $W_{acc(a)}$, thus reinstating meta-argument $acc(a)$. Attacks are modeled as arguments as well. For each auxiliary argument $Y_{a,b}$, representing the activation of the attack, we associate an auxiliary argument $W_{Y_{a,b}}$.

Each argument a in the sources' mind is supported by means of an attack on $W_{acc(a)}$. Sources are introduced in the meta-argumentation framework under the form of meta-arguments "*source i is trustable*", $trust(i)$, for all the sources i. We represent the fact that one or more information sources support the same argument by letting them attack the same $W_{acc(a)}$ auxiliary argument. An example of multiple evidence is depicted in Figure 2.b. In the figures, we represent the information sources as boxes, and the arguments as circles where grey arguments are the acceptable ones. As for arguments, an attack to become active needs some trusted agent.

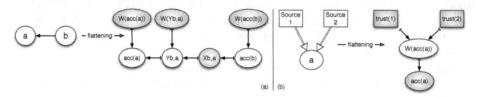

(a) | (b)

Fig. 2 (a) arguments and attack without evidence, (b) multiple evidence.

Notice that the assumption that there must be evidence for an argument to be accepted is a very general and often used reasoning pattern, e.g., in causal reasoning, where everything needs to be explained, i.e., to have a cause / to be caused, as in the Yale shooting problem for instance. For more details about causal reasoning, see [2].

We have now to discuss which semantics we adopt for assessing the acceptability of the arguments and the sources. For example, suppose that two sources claim they are each untrustworthy. What is the extension? We adopt admissibility based semantics. We do not ask for completeness because if one wants to know whether a particular argument is acceptable, the whole model is not needed, just the part related to this particular argument is needed.

The reader should not be confused by the similarity between evidence and support [5]. Support exploits an auxiliary argument Z, but with some difference with the auxiliary argument W. First, given a supporting b, there is a $Z_{a,b}$ such that b attacks $Z_{a,b}$ and $Z_{a,b}$ attacks a, while, here, $W_{acc(a)}$ attacks the argument needing evidence. The meaning of support is that if a is acceptable then b is acceptable too. Note that the supported argument b is acceptable (if not attacked) even without the support of a. Second, there is a Z for each supporting argument, while, here, there is only one W attacked by all arguments and agents providing evidence.

We extend the *EAF* proposed in Definition 6 by adding evidence provided by information sources and second-order attacks, such as attacks from an argument or attacks to another attack. For more details about second-order attacks in meta-argumentation, see [20, 3]. The unflattening function g and the acceptance function $\mathcal{E}'$ are defined as above.

Definition 8 *An EAF with second-order attacks is a tuple $\langle A, \langle A_1, \rightarrow_1, \rightarrow_1^2 \rangle,$ $\dots, \langle A_n, \rightarrow_n, \rightarrow_n^2 \rangle, \rightarrow \rangle$ where for each source $1 \le i \le n$, $A_i \subseteq A \subseteq \mathcal{U}$ is a set of arguments, $\rightarrow \subseteq A \times A$, $\rightarrow_i$ is a binary relation on $A_i \times A_i$, $\rightarrow_i^2$ is a binary relation on $(A_i \cup \rightarrow_i) \times \rightarrow_i$.*

Definition 9 presents the instantiation of an *EAF* with second-order attacks as a set of partial frameworks of the sources using meta-argumentation.

Definition 9 *Given an $EAF = \langle A, \langle A_1, \rightarrow_1, \rightarrow_1^2 \rangle \dots, \langle A_n, \rightarrow_n, \rightarrow_n^2 \rangle, \rightarrow \rangle$, the set of meta-arguments MA is $\{trust(i) \mid 1 \le i \le n\} \cup \{acc(a) \mid a \in A_1 \cup \dots \cup A_n\} \cup \{X_{a,b}, Y_{a,b} \mid a,b \in A_1 \cup \dots \cup A_n\} \cup \{W_{acc(a)} \mid a \in A_1 \cup \dots \cup A_n\}$ and $\longmapsto \subseteq MA \times MA$ is a binary relation on MA such that:*

- $acc(a) \longmapsto X_{a,b}$ *iff* $a,b \in A_i$ *and* $a \rightarrow_i b$, *and* $X_{a,b} \longmapsto Y_{a,b}$ *iff* $a,b \in A_i$ *and* $a \rightarrow_i b$, *and* $Y_{a,b} \longmapsto acc(b)$ *iff* $a,b \in A_i$ *and* $a \rightarrow_i b$, *and*
- $trust(i) \longmapsto W_{acc(a)}$ *iff* $a \in A_i$, *and* $W_{acc(a)} \longmapsto acc(a)$ *iff* $a \in A$, *and*
- $trust(i) \longmapsto W_{Y_{a,b}}$ *iff* $a,b \in A_i$ *and* $a \rightarrow_i b$, *and* $W_{Y_{a,b}} \longmapsto Y_{a,b}$ *iff* $a,b \in A_i$ *and* $a \rightarrow_i b$, *and*
- $acc(a) \longmapsto X_{a,b \rightarrow c}$ *iff* $a,b,c \in A_i$ *and* $a \rightarrow_i^2 (b \rightarrow_i c)$, *and* $X_{a,b \rightarrow c} \longmapsto Y_{a,b \rightarrow c}$ *iff* $a,b,c \in A_i$ *and* $a \rightarrow_i^2 (b \rightarrow_i c)$, *and* $Y_{a,b \rightarrow c} \longmapsto Y_{b,c}$ *iff* $a,b,c \in A_i$ *and* $a \rightarrow_i^2 (b \rightarrow_i c)$, *and*
- $Y_{a,b} \longmapsto Y_{c,d}$ *iff* $a,b,c \in A_i$ *and* $(a \rightarrow_i b) \rightarrow_i^2 (c \rightarrow_i d)$.

We say that source i is trustworthy when meta-argument trust(i) is acceptable, and we say that i provides evidence in support of argument a (or attack $a \rightarrow b$) when $a \in A_i$ (when $a \rightarrow b \in \rightarrow_i$), and trust(i) $\longmapsto W_{acc(a)}$ (trust(i) $\longmapsto W_{Y_{a,b}}$).

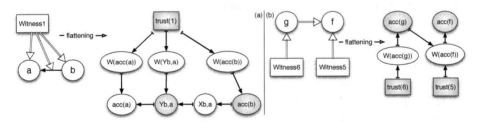

Fig. 3 Introducing (a) the sources, (b) evidence for the arguments.

Example 1 *Consider the informal dialogue in the introduction. We represent the sources in the argumentation framework, as shown in Figure 3.a. Witness1 proposes a and b and the attack $a \rightarrow b$. Using the flattening function of Definition 9, we add meta-argument trust(1) for representing Witness1 in the framework and we add meta-arguments acc(a) and acc(b) for the arguments of Witness1. Witness1 provides evidence for these arguments, and the attack $b \rightarrow a$ by attacking the respective auxiliary arguments W. In the remainder of the paper, we model the other conflicts highlighted in the dialogue.*

Let $trust(i)$ be the information source i and $acc(a)$ and $Y_{a,b}$ the argument a_i and the attack $a \rightarrow_i b$ respectively, as defined in Definitions 6 and 7. $trust(i)$ can provide evidence for $acc(a)$ and $Y_{a,b}$. Sources can attack other sources as well as their arguments and attacks. With a slight abuse of notation, we write $a \in \mathcal{E}'(EAF)$, even if the latter is a set of extensions, with the intended meaning that a is in some of the extensions of $\mathcal{E}'$. We now provide some properties of our model. Some of the proofs are omitted due to the lack of space.

Proposition 1 *Assume admissibility based semantics, if an argument $a \in A$ is not supported by evidence, i.e., $a \notin A_i$ for all i, then a is not accepted, $a \notin \mathcal{E}'(EAF)$.*

Proof. We prove the contrapositive: if argument a is accepted, then argument a is supported. Assume argument a is accepted. Then auxiliary argument $W_{acc(a)}$ is rejected due to the conflict-free principle. Meta-argument $acc(a)$ is defended, so $W_{acc(a)}$ is attacked by an accepted argument using admissible semantics. Auxiliary argument $W_{acc(a)}$ can only be attacked by meta-argument $trust(i)$. We conclude that a is supported.

Proposition 1 is strengthened to Proposition 2.

Proposition 2 *If an argument a is not supported, $a \notin A_i$, then the extensions $\mathcal{E}'(EAF)$ are precisely the same as the extensions of the $AF = \langle A, \rightarrow \rangle$ in which $a \notin A$, and the attacks on a or from a do not exist, i.e., $b \rightarrow a \notin \rightarrow$ and $a \rightarrow c \notin \rightarrow$.*

Proposition 3 *If an attack $a \rightarrow b$ is not supported, i.e., $a \rightarrow b \notin \rightarrow_i$, then the extensions $\mathcal{E}'(EAF)$ are precisely the same as the extensions of the $AF = \langle A, \rightarrow \rangle$, in which the attack does not exist, $a \rightarrow b \notin \rightarrow$.*

Proposition 4 *Assume EAF is a framework in which argument a is supported by the trustworthy source i, and there is another trustworthy source j. In that case, the extensions are the same if also j provides an evidence in support of a.*

3.2 Evidence for arguments

The evidence in favor of the arguments is evidence provided by the agents for the arguments/attacks they propose. At the meta-level, this is modeled as an attack from meta-argument $trust(i)$ to W auxiliary arguments. However, there are other cases in which more evidence is necessary to support the acceptability of an argument. Consider the case of Witness1. His trustworthiness is attacked by Witness2. What happens to the evidence provided by Witness1? Since the source is not trustworthy then it cannot provide evidence. Meta-argument $trust(1)$ becomes not acceptable and the same happens to all its arguments and attacks. What is needed to make them acceptable again is more evidence. This evidence can be provided under the form of another argument which reinstates the acceptability of these information items.

Definition 9 allows only the sources to directly provide evidence for the information items. As for Witness5 and Witness6 in the dialogue, sources can provide evidence also by means of other arguments. This cannot be represented using Definition 9, this is why we need to extend it with an evidence relation $\leftrightarrow$ representing evidence provided under the form of arguments for the information items of the other sources.

Definition 10 *An EAF with evidence* $TEAF^2 = \langle A, \langle A_1, \rightarrow_1, \rightarrow_1^2, \leftrightarrow_1 \rangle, \ldots,$ $\langle A_n, \rightarrow_n, \rightarrow_n^2, \leftrightarrow_n \rangle, \rightarrow \rangle$ *where* $\leftrightarrow_i$ *is a binary relation on* $A_i \times A_j$ *and the set of meta-arguments MA is* $\{trust(i) \mid 1 \leq i \leq n\} \cup \{acc(a) \mid a \in A_1 \cup \ldots \cup A_n\} \cup \{X_{a,b}, Y_{a,b} \mid a, b \in A_1 \cup \ldots \cup A_n\} \cup \{W_{acc(a)} \mid a \in A_1 \cup \ldots \cup A_n\}$ *and* $\longmapsto \subseteq MA \times MA$ *is a binary relation on MA such that hold the conditions of Definition 9, and:* $acc(a) \longmapsto W_{acc(b)}$ *iff* $a, b \in A_i$ *and* $a \leftrightarrow_i b$, *and* $W_{acc(b)} \longmapsto acc(b)$ *iff* $b \in A$ *and* $a \leftrightarrow_i b$. *We say that a source j supports the evidence provided by other sources to argument a when* $a \notin A_j, b \in A_j$, *and* $acc(b) \longmapsto W_{acc(a)}$.

The following properties hold for Definition 10.

Proposition 5 *If there are multiple arguments* $a_1 \in A_1, \ldots, a_n \in A_n$ *providing evidence for an argument* $b \in A_k$ *(or an attack), and there are no attacks on the arguments,* $c_1 \rightarrow a_1 \notin \rightarrow_1, \ldots, c_n \rightarrow a_n \notin \rightarrow_n$, *then b (or the attack) is accepted,* $b \in \mathcal{E}'(EAF)$, *iff at least one of the sources is trustworthy, i.e.,* $trust(j) \in \mathcal{E}(f(EAF))$ *with* $j \in 1, \ldots, n$.

Proposition 6 *Suppose two sources i and j provide evidence for the same argument a, i.e.,* $a \in A_i$ *and* $a \in A_j$, *then it is the same whether a source k supports the evidence provided by i or j, i.e.,* $b \in A_k$ *and* $acc(b) \longmapsto W_{acc(a)}$.

Example 2 *Consider the dialogue in the introduction. Argument g by Witness6 is an evidence for argument f by Witness5. This evidence is expressed in meta-argumentation in the same way as evidence provided by the sources, such as an attack to* $W_{acc(f)}$ *attacking* $acc(f)$. *In this case, it is meta-argument* $acc(g)$ *which attacks* $W_{acc(f)}$, *as visualized in Figure 3.b.*

3.3 Focused trust relationships

In our model, trust is represented *by default* as the absence of an attack towards the sources or towards the information items and as the presence of evidence in favor of the pieces of information. On the contrary, the distrust relationship is modeled as a lack of evidence in support of the information items or as a direct attack towards the sources and their pieces of information.

In the informal dialogue, Witness2 attacks the trustworthiness of Witness1 as a credible witness. In this way, she is attacking each argument and attack proposed by Witness1. Witness4, instead, is not arguing against Witness3 but she is arguing against the attack $d \rightarrow b$ as it is proposed by Witness3. Finally, for Witness2 the untrustworthiness of Witness6 is related only to the argument g. We propose a focused view of trust in which the information sources may be attacked for being untrustworthy or for being untrustworthy only concerning a particular argument or attack. Definition 11 presents an *EAF* in which a new relation *DT* between sources is given to represent distrust.

Definition 11 *A trust-based extended argumentation framework TEAF is a tuple* $\langle A, \langle A_1, \rightarrow_1, \rightarrow_1^2, \leftrightarrow_1, DT_1 \rangle, \ldots, \langle A_n, \rightarrow_n, \rightarrow_n^2, \leftrightarrow_n, DT_n \rangle, \rightarrow \rangle$ *where for each source* $1 \leq i \leq n$, $A_i \subseteq A \subseteq \mathcal{U}$ *is a set of arguments,* $\rightarrow \subseteq A \times A$, $\rightarrow_i \subseteq A_i \times A_i$ *is a binary relation,* $\rightarrow_i^2$ *is a binary relation on* $(A_i \cup \rightarrow_i) \times \rightarrow_i$, $\leftrightarrow_i$ *is a binary relation on* $A_i \times A_j$ *and* $DT \subseteq A_i \times \vartheta$ *is a binary relation such that* $\vartheta = j$ *or* $\vartheta \in A_j$ *or* $\vartheta \in \rightarrow_j$.

Definition 12 shows how to instantiate an *EAF* enriched with a distrust relation with meta-arguments. In particular, the last three points model, respectively, a distrust relationship towards an agent, towards an argument and towards an attack. The unflattening function g and the acceptance function $\mathcal{E}'$ are defined as above.

Definition 12 *Given a TEAF* $=$ $\langle A, \langle A_1, \rightarrow_1, \rightarrow_1^2, \leftrightarrow_1, DT_1 \rangle, \ldots,$ $\langle A_n, \rightarrow_n, \rightarrow_n^2, \leftrightarrow_n, DT_n \rangle, \rightarrow \rangle$, *see Definition 11, the set of meta-arguments MA is* $\{trust(i) \mid 1 \leq i \leq n\} \cup \{acc(a) \mid a \in A_1 \cup \ldots \cup A_n\} \cup \{X_{a,b}, Y_{a,b} \mid a, b \in A_1 \cup \ldots \cup A_n\} \cup \{W_{acc(a)} \mid a \in A_1 \cup \ldots \cup A_n\}$ *and* $\longmapsto \subseteq MA \times MA$ *is a binary relation on MA such that hold the conditions of Definitions 9 and 10, and:*

- $acc(a) \longmapsto X_{a,b}$ *iff* $a, b \in A_i$ *and* $a \rightarrow_i b$, *and* $X_{a,b} \longmapsto Y_{a,b}$ *iff* $a, b \in A_i$ *and* $a \rightarrow_i b$, *and* $Y_{a,b} \longmapsto acc(b)$ *iff* $a, b \in A_i$ *and* $a \rightarrow_i b$, *and*

- $trust(i) \longmapsto X_{trust(i),W_{acc(a)}}$ *iff* $a \in A_i$, *and* $X_{trust(i),W_{acc(a)}} \longmapsto Y_{trust(i),W_{acc(a)}}$ *iff* $a \in A_i$, *and* $Y_{trust(i),W_{acc(a)}} \longmapsto W_{acc(a)}$ *iff* $a \in A_i$, *and* $W_{acc(a)} \longmapsto acc(a)$ *iff* $a \in A_i$, *and*

- $trust(i) \longmapsto X_{trust(i),W_{Y_{a,b}}}$ *iff* $a, b \in A_i$ *and* $a \rightarrow_i b$, *and* $X_{trust(i),W_{Y_{a,b}}} \longmapsto Y_{trust(i),W_{Y_{a,b}}}$ *iff* $a, b \in A_i$ *and* $a \rightarrow_i b$, *and* $Y_{trust(i),W_{Y_{a,b}}} \longmapsto W_{Y_{a,b}}$ *iff* $a, b \in A_i$ *and* $a \rightarrow_i b$, *and* $W_{Y_{a,b}} \longmapsto Y_{a,b}$ *iff* $a, b \in A_i$ *and* $a \rightarrow_i b$, *and*

- $trust(i) \longmapsto W_{acc(a)}$ *iff* $a \in A_i$ *and* $aDT_i trust(j)$, *and* $W_{acc(a)} \longmapsto acc(a)$ *iff* $a \in A$ *and* $aDT_i trust(j)$, *and* $acc(a) \longmapsto X_{acc(a),trust(j)}$ *iff* $a \in A_i$ *and* $aDT_i trust(j)$, *and* $X_{acc(a),trust(j)} \longmapsto Y_{acc(a),trust(j)}$ *iff* $a \in A_i$ *and* $aDT_i trust(j)$, *and* $Y_{acc(a),trust(j)} \longmapsto trust(j)$ *iff* $a \in A_i$ *and* $aDT_i trust(j)$, *and*

- $trust(i) \longmapsto W_{acc(a)}$ *iff* $a \in A_i, b \in A_j$ *and* $aDT_i b$, *and* $W_{acc(a)} \longmapsto acc(a)$ *iff* $a \in A, b \in A_j$ *and* $aDT_i b$, *and* $acc(a) \longmapsto X_{acc(a),Y_{trust(j),W_{acc(b)}}}$ *iff* $a \in A_i, b \in A_j$ *and* $aDT_i b$, *and* $X_{acc(a),Y_{trust(j),W_{acc(b)}}} \longmapsto Y_{acc(a),Y_{trust(j),W_{acc(b)}}}$ *iff* $a \in A_i, b \in A_j$ *and* $aDT_i b$, *and* $Y_{acc(a),Y_{trust(j),W_{acc(b)}}} \longmapsto Y_{trust(j),W_{acc(b)}}$ *iff* $a \in A_i, b \in A_j$ *and* $aDT_i b$, *and*

- $trust(i) \longmapsto W_{acc(a)}$ *iff* $a \in A_i, b, c \in A_j$ *and* $aDT_i(b \rightarrow_j c)$, *and* $W_{acc(a)} \longmapsto acc(a)$ *iff* $a \in A, b, c \in A_j$ *and* $aDT_i(b \rightarrow_j c)$, *and* $acc(a) \longmapsto X_{acc(a),Y_{trust(j),W_{Y_{b,c}}}}$ *iff* $a \in A_i, b, c \in A_j$ *and* $aDT_i(b \rightarrow_j c)$, *and* $X_{acc(a),Y_{trust(j),W_{Y_{b,c}}}} \longmapsto Y_{acc(a),Y_{trust(j),W_{Y_{b,c}}}}$ *iff* $a \in A_i, b, c \in A_j$ *and* $aDT_i(b \rightarrow_j c)$, *and* $Y_{acc(a),Y_{trust(j),W_{Y_{b,c}}}} \longmapsto Y_{trust(j),W_{Y_{b,c}}}$ *iff* $a \in A_i, b, c \in A_j$ *and* $aDT_i(b \rightarrow_j c)$.

We say that a source i is untrustworthy when there is an attack from an argument $a_j \in A_j$ to i, $a_j DT_j i$. We say that an argument $a_i \in A_i$ or attack $a \rightarrow_i b \in \rightarrow_i$ is untrustworthy when there is an attack from an argument $a_j \in A_j$ to a_i or $a \rightarrow_i b$, $a_j DT_j a_i$ or $a_j DT_j(a \rightarrow_i b)$.

Proposition 7 *Assume that source* i *is the only source providing evidence for argument* $a \in A_i$ *and attack* $c \rightarrow b \in \rightarrow_i$, *and assume admissibility based semantics. If* *the information source i is considered to be untrustworthy, then a and c → b are not acceptable.*

Proof. We prove the contrapositive: if the arguments and attacks supported by an information source i are acceptable then the information source i is considered to be trustworthy. Assume the source supports argument a and the attack $c \to b$ and assume that this argument and this attack are acceptable. Then auxiliary arguments $W_{acc(a)}$ and $W_{Y_{c,b}}$ are rejected due to the conflict-free principle. Meta-arguments $acc(a)$ and $Y_{c,b}$ are defended, thus $W_{acc(a)}$ and $W_{Y_{c,b}}$ are attacked by an acceptable argument, using admissible semantics. We assumed that this argument and this attack have no other evidence, so auxiliary arguments $W_{acc(a)}$ and $W_{Y_{c,b}}$ can only be attacked by meta-argument $trust(i)$. Since they are attacked by an acceptable argument, we conclude that the source i is acceptable.

Example 3 *Figure 4.a shows that Witness2 attacks the trustworthiness of Witness1 by means of argument c. In meta-argumentation, we have that trust(2) provides evidence for acc(c) by attacking meta-argument $W_{acc(c)}$ and, with meta-arguments X,Y, it attacks trust(1). This means that if Witness1 is untrustworthy then each of his arguments and attacks cannot be acceptable either, if there is no more evidence. The set of acceptable arguments for the meta-argumentation framework is $\mathcal{E}(f(focus1)) = \{trust(2), acc(c), Y_{acc(c),trust(1)}\}$. In Figure 4.b-c, instead, the attack is directed against a precise information item provided by the source. In particular, Witness4 attacks the attack d → b of Witness3. This is achieved in meta-argumentation by means of an attack from meta-argument acc(e), for which trust(4) provides evidence, to the attack characterized by auxiliary argument $Y_{d,b}$. The set of acceptable arguments is $\mathcal{E}(f(focus2)) = \{trust(4), trust(3), acc(d), acc(e), acc(b), Y_{acc(e),Y_{trust(3),W_{Y_{b,d}}}}, W_{Y_{d,b}}\}$. Witness3's attack d → b is evaluated as untrustworthy by Witness4 and thus it is not acceptable. Finally, Witness2 evaluates Witness6 as untrustworthy concerning argument g. In meta-argumentation, trust(2), by means of meta-argument acc(h), attacks meta-argument acc(g) proposed by trust(6). The set of acceptable arguments is $\mathcal{E}(f(focus3)) = \{trust(2), trust(6), acc(h), Y_{acc(h),Y_{trust(6),W_{acc(g)}}}, W_{acc(g)}\}$.*

3.4 Feedback from information items to sources

In the previous sections, we have introduced the information sources in the argumentation framework in order to deal with the conflicts about trust. Moreover, in our framework, the agents are allowed to attack the trustworthiness of the other information sources or of the single information items the sources propose. The relation, concerning trust, among the sources and the arguments/attacks they support is in one direction only. In particular, if an agent is considered not to be trustworthy, then also all the information items proposed by such an agent are considered untrustworthy. What happens if an agent, whose trustworthiness is not directly attacked, has the trustworthiness of all its information items attacked?

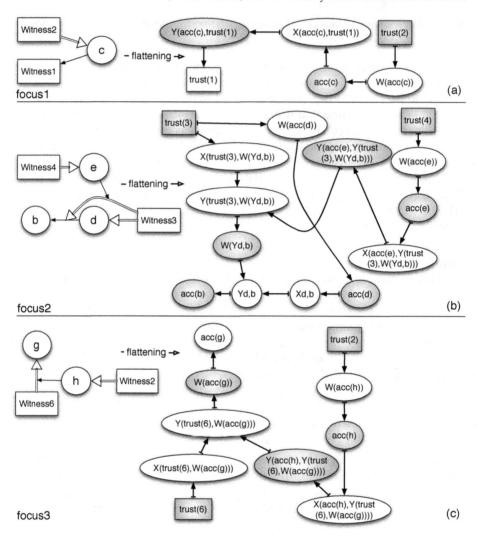

Fig. 4 Trust in argumentation.

The idea proposed by Falcone and Castelfranchi [12, 13] is that there is a bidirectional link between the source and its information items: the provided data is more or less believable on the basis of the source's trustworthiness, but there is feedback such that the invalidation of the data feeds back on the sources' credibility. In particular, in [13], Castelfranchi claims that "Trust is a dynamic phenomenon in its intrinsic nature. Trust changes with experience, with the modification of the different sources it is based on, with the emotional state of the trustier, with the modification of the environment in which the trustee is supposed to perform, and so on. In other words, being trust an attitude depending from dynamic phenomena, as a consequence it is itself a dynamic entity."

Falcone and Castelfranchi [13] analyze two main basic aspects of this phenomenon: (i) the traditional problem of the trust reinforcement on the basis of the successful experiences (and vice versa, its decreasing in case of failures), and (ii) the fact that in the same situation trust is influenced by trust in several rather complex ways. The first case considers the well known phenomenon about the fact that trust evolves in time and has a history, that is x's trust in y depends on x's previous experience and learning with y itself. They consider also some not so easily predictable results in which trust in the trustee decreases with positive experiences, and increases with negative experiences.

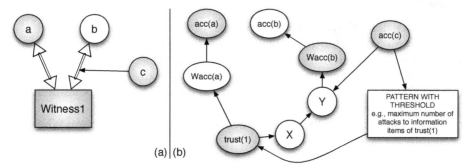

Fig. 5 Feedback between information items and sources.

In this section, we rely on this analysis of the trust dynamics phenomenon, in order to model the feedback from the information items to the sources. For instance, the fact that the major part of the arguments of a source are considered untrustworthy is seen as a negative experience, and leads to the decrease of the trustworthiness of the sources itself. In this paper, we do not consider the unpredictable cases analyzed by Falcone and Castelfranchi [13], where trust decreases with positive experiences, and increases with negative ones. The analysis of these cases is left as future work.

We introduce the feedback from the information items to the sources, in such a way that, following different criteria, the untrustworthiness of the items influences the trustworthiness of its source. The general idea of our approach is visualized in Figure 5. First, we insert in the framework a pattern which is activated if the number of attacks to this pattern exceeds a certain threshold. In this case, the pattern activates an attack towards the meta-argument representing the information source. Second, for each attack to the trustworthiness of one of the information items of a source, this attack is duplicated and it is addressed also towards the pattern which attacks the information source. Summarizing, every attack to the arguments or attacks of a source is addressed too, i.e., towards a pattern which has the aim to attack directly the trustworthiness of the source, if the number of attack exceeds the given threshold.

Example 4 *Let us consider now the example proposed in Figure 5. In the informal dialogue, Witness1 proposes two arguments a and b, and the attack between them. Consider now the introduction of a new argument n, which attacks the trustworthiness* *of argument b as proposed by Witness1. In the flattened framework, the meta-argument trust(1) provides evidence for meta-arguments acc(a) and acc(b) by attacking the auxiliary arguments $W_{acc(a)}$ and $W_{acc(b)}$. The attack of the new argument is addressed from meta-argument acc(n) to the auxiliary argument $Y_{W_{acc(b)}}$ which attacks acc(b). Since we are interested in modeling also the feedback from the information items to the sources, we add an additional attack from meta-argument acc(n) to the pattern we use to measure the number of attacks to the information items of Witness1. From this pattern, an attack is raised to the meta-argument trust(1). If the number of attacks towards the pattern overcomes a given threshold, then this attack becomes active and the meta-argument trust(1) becomes unacceptable, i.e., Witness1 is considered untrustworthy.*

Note that the definition of this pattern is out of the scope of this paper. The idea is to define a pattern like those defined for proof standards [28]. We model feedback using the pattern associated with the threshold in order to maintain the choice of meta-argumentation, and avoiding the introduction of numerical techniques [22]. Another opportunity consists in associating a fuzzy value to the information items and the sources, and to allow this value to change to represent the feedback, e.g., the value associated to the source decreases when one of its information items is attacked.

3.5 Competence and sincerity of the sources

In this section, we investigate two dimensions of trust that have to be independently evaluated such as the sincerity/credibility of a source and its competence. Casltefranchi and Falcone [7, 8] provide a definition of trust as a mental state and present its mental ingredients relative both to the competence of a source y and to its sincerity. Castelfranchi underlines the usefulness of these mental ingredients in particular in the context of delegation where, in order to delegate a task to some agent y (collaborator) I have to believe that it is able to do what I need (competence), and that it will actually do that (predictability). Castelfranchi claims that "trust in y ('social trust' in strict sense) seems to consists in the two first prototypical beliefs/evaluations we identified as the basis for reliance: ability/competence (that with cognitive agents includes self-confidence), and disposition (that with cognitive agents is based on willingness, persistence, engagement, sincerity, etc.)."

Roughly, we represent competence and sincerity using meta-arguments, and the attacks to these meta-arguments represent the conflicts about trust regarding one of these two mental states. The introduction in our framework of these two dimensions is visualized in Figure 6. We start from the usual situation in which an information source supports an argument, namely Witness7 supports the argument *i* in the informal dialogue. We have to represent two possible conflicts concerning argument *i*: a conflict meaning that Witness7 is considered untrustworthy on the competence regarding argument *i*, and a conflict meaning that Witness7 is considered untrustworthy on the sincerity regarding argument *i*. An example of the first case is given in the dialogue by the attack of argument l to argument i, and an example of the second case is given by the attack of argument m to argument i. Note that even if both arguments l and m attack argument i, they attack different dimensions of argument i.

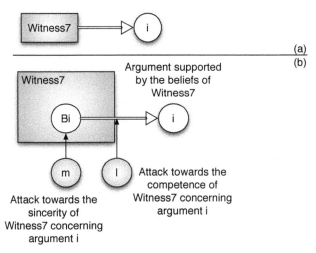

Fig. 6 Competence and sincerity modelling.

We model sincerity and competence as visualized in Figure 6.b. Each argument in the meta-level is associated with a meta-argument. Meta-argument B_i represents the belief associated to the information source concerning argument i, and argument i is the argument supported by the beliefs of the source. The meta-argument supports the argument. In this framework, an attack towards the sincerity of the source is addressed against the meta-argument representing the beliefs of the source, i.e., against meta-argument B_i. An attack towards the competence of the source is addressed, instead, against the support among meta-argument B_i and argument i. This means that the source believes argument i but it is not evaluated competent concerning i. Note that an attack towards argument i is treated as in the previous sections, such as it is an attack towards the content of argument i.

Definition 13 *A trust-based extended argumentation framework $TEAF_{CS}$ is a tuple $\langle A, \langle A_1, \rightarrow_1, \rightarrow_1^2, \leftrightsquigarrow_1, DT_{1s}, DT_{1c} \rangle, \dots, \langle A_n, \rightarrow_n, \rightarrow_n^2, \leftrightsquigarrow_n, DT_{ns}, DT_{nc} \rangle, \rightarrow \rangle$ where for each source $1 \leq i \leq n$, $A_i \subseteq A \subseteq \mathcal{U}$ is a set of arguments, $\rightarrow \subseteq A \times A$, $\rightarrow_i \subseteq A_i \times A_i$ is a binary relation, $\rightarrow_i^2$ is a binary relation on $(A_i \cup \rightarrow_i) \times \rightarrow_i$, $\leftrightsquigarrow_i$ is a binary relation on $A_i \times A_j$, $DT_s \subseteq A_i \times \vartheta$ is a binary relation such that $\vartheta \in A_j$ or $\vartheta \in \rightarrow_j$, and $DT_c \subseteq A_i \times \vartheta$ is a binary relation such that $\vartheta \in A_j$ or $\vartheta \in \rightarrow_j$.*

Definition 14 shows how to instantiate an *EAF* enriched with a distrust relation, which distinguishes distrust concerning competence and sincerity, with meta-arguments. The unflattening function g and the acceptance function $\mathcal{E}'$ are defined as above.

Definition 14 *Given a* $TEAF_{CS} = \langle A, \langle A_1, \rightarrow_1, \rightarrow_1^2, \leftrightarrow_1, DT_{1s}, DT_{1c}\rangle, \ldots, \langle A_n, \rightarrow_n$ *,* $\rightarrow_n^2, \leftrightarrow_n, DT_{ns}, DT_{nc}\rangle, \rightarrow\rangle$, *see Definition 13, the set of meta-arguments MA is* $\{trust(i) \mid 1 \leq i \leq n\} \cup \{acc(a) \mid a \in A_1 \cup \ldots \cup A_n\} \cup \{X_{a,b}, Y_{a,b} \mid a, b \in A_1 \cup \ldots \cup A_n\} \cup$ $\{W_{acc(a)} \mid a \in A_1 \cup \ldots \cup A_n\} \cup \{B_a \mid a \in A_1 \cup \ldots \cup A_n\}$ *and* $\longmapsto \subseteq MA \times MA$ *is a binary relation on MA such that hold the conditions of Definitions 9, 10, and 12, and:*

- $B_a \longmapsto X_{B_a,a}$ *iff* $a \in A_i$, *and* $X_{B_a,a} \longmapsto Y_{B_a,a}$ *iff* $a \in A_i$, *and* $Y_{B_a,a} \longmapsto W_{B_a,a}$ *iff* $a \in A_i$, *and* $W_{B_a,a} \longmapsto acc(a)$ *iff* $a \in A_i$ *and*
- $B_{a \rightarrow b} \longmapsto X_{B_{a \rightarrow b}, a \rightarrow b}$ *iff* $a \rightarrow b \in \rightarrow_i$, *and* $X_{B_{a \rightarrow b}, a \rightarrow b} \longmapsto Y_{B_{a \rightarrow b}, a \rightarrow b}$ *iff* $a \rightarrow b \in \rightarrow_i$, *and* $Y_{B_{a \rightarrow b}, a \rightarrow b} \longmapsto W_{B_{a \rightarrow b}, a \rightarrow b}$ *iff* $a \rightarrow b \in \rightarrow_i$, *and* $W_{B_{a \rightarrow b}, a \rightarrow b} \longmapsto Y_{a,b}$ *iff* $a \rightarrow b \in \rightarrow_i$ *and*
- $trust(i) \longmapsto X_{trust(i), W_{acc(a)}}$ *iff* $a \in A_i$, *and* $X_{trust(i), W_{acc(a)}} \longmapsto Y_{trust(i), W_{acc(a)}}$ *iff* $a \in A_i$, *and* $Y_{trust(i), W_{acc(a)}} \longmapsto W_{acc(a)}$ *iff* $a \in A_i$, *and* $W_{acc(a)} \longmapsto B_a$ *iff* $a \in A_i$, *and*
- $trust(i) \longmapsto X_{trust(i), W_{Y_{a,b}}}$ *iff* $a, b \in A_i$ *and* $a \rightarrow_i b$, *and* $X_{trust(i), W_{Y_{a,b}}} \longmapsto Y_{trust(i), W_{Y_{a,b}}}$ *iff* $a, b \in A_i$ *and* $a \rightarrow_i b$, *and* $Y_{trust(i), W_{Y_{a,b}}} \longmapsto W_{Y_{a,b}}$ *iff* $a, b \in A_i$ *and* $a \rightarrow_i b$, *and* $W_{Y_{a,b}} \longmapsto B_{a \rightarrow b}$ *iff* $a, b \in A_i$ *and* $a \rightarrow_i b$, *and*
- $acc(a) \longmapsto B_b$ *iff* $a \in A_i, b \in A_j$ *and* $aDT_{is}b$, *and*
- $acc(a) \longmapsto Y_{B_a,a}$ *iff* $a \in A_i, b \in A_j$ *and* $aDT_{ic}b$, *and*
- $acc(a) \longmapsto B_{b \rightarrow c}$ *iff* $a \in A_i, b, c \in A_j$ *and* $aDT_{is}(b \rightarrow_j c)$, *and*
- $acc(a) \longmapsto Y_{B_{b \rightarrow c}, b \rightarrow c}$ *iff* $a \in A_i, b, c \in A_j$ *and* $aDT_{ic}(b \rightarrow_j c)$.

We say that an argument $a_i \in A_i$ *or attack* $a \rightarrow_i b \in \rightarrow_i$ *is untrustworthy concerning sincerity when there is an attack from an argument* $a_j \in A_j$ *to* B_{a_i} *or* $B_{a \rightarrow_i b}$, *$a_j DT_{js}a_i$ or* $a_j DT_{js}(a \rightarrow_i b)$. *We say that an argument* $a_i \in A_i$ *or attack* $a \rightarrow_i b \in \rightarrow_i$ *is untrustworthy concerning competence when there is an attack from an argument* $a_j \in A_j$ *to* $Y_{B_{a_i}, a_i}$ *or* $Y_{B_{a \rightarrow b}, a \rightarrow b}$, *$a_j DT_{jc}a_i$ or* $a_j DT_{jc}(a \rightarrow_i b)$.

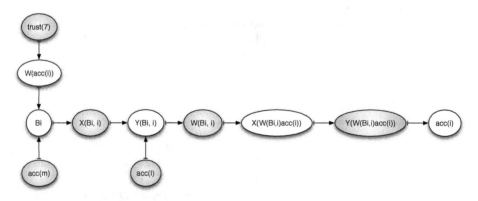

Fig. 7 Competence and sincerity flattening.

The flattening of the new framework distinguishing between attacks towards the sincerity of an agent in proposing an information item, and attacks towards the competence of an agent in proposing an information item is formalized in Definition 14, and an example of flattening is visualized in Figure 7.

Example 5 *The meta-argument representing Witness7, trust(7), supports by means of the auxiliary argument $W_{acc(a)}$ meta-argument B_i representing the fact that argument i is believed by Witness7. If this meta-argument is accepted, it means that there are no doubts about the sincerity of Witness7 concerning this argument. Meta-argument B_i supports the meta-argument acc(i), representing argument i in the meta-level. This support relation is built in the same way as the support between the sources and their information items, which means that meta-argument B_i attacks, towards auxiliary arguments X and Y, the auxiliary argument $W_{B_a,a}$. This auxiliary argument attacks, always by means of X and Y auxiliary arguments, the meta-argument acc(i). In this framework, the acceptability of meta-argument acc(i) depends on the acceptability of the belief regarding argument i. An attack towards the competence of argument i is addressed against meta-argument $Y_{B_a,a}$. In this way, argument acc(i) can be made unacceptable in two ways: (i) by attacking directly meta-argument B_i (sincerity), and (ii) by attacking the attack from B_i to $W_{B_a,a}$ (competence). Figure 7 shows these two cases with arguments m and l, respectively.*

4 Related work

Dix et al. [10] present trust as a major issue concerning the research challenges for argumentation. The question *Which agents are trustworthy?* is important for taking decisions and weighing arguments of other agents.

Parson et al. [21] highlight what are the mechanisms to investigate through argumentation, first of all the provenance of trust. The authors claim that a first problem, particularly of abstract approaches such that of Dung [11], is that they cannot express the provenance of trust and they cannot express the fact that b is attacked because b is based on agent s and there is an evidence that s is not trustworthy. In this paper, we propose to adopt meta-argumentation to instantiate Dung's framework with meta-arguments which represent the information sources. Moreover, we show how to express trust relationships between the sources.

Tang et al. [26] present a framework to introduce the sources in argumentation and to explicitly express the degrees of trust. They connect agent-centric trust networks to argumentation networks. They do not have the possibility to attack the trustworthiness of the agents as well as the trustworthiness of single arguments and attacks. Moreover, the feedback towards the source is not considered as well as the distinction between competence and sincerity. We do not express the degrees of trust.

Matt et al. [19] propose to construct a belief function both from statistical data and from arguments in the context of contracts. We do not address the computation of trust by an evaluator in isolation, instead all trust relationships are evaluated together.

Stranders et al. [25] propose an approach to trust based on argumentation in which there is a separation between the opponent modeling and decision making. The opponents' behaviour is modeled using possibilistic logic. In our approach, we rely on Dung's abstract framework and we do not present a decision making approach to trust. We are interested in modeling focused trust in argumentation.

Prade [23] presents a bipolar qualitative argumentative modeling of trust where trust and distrust are assessed independently. The author introduces the notion of reputation which is viewed as an input information used by an agent for revising or updating his trust evaluation. Reputation contributes to provide direct arguments in favor or against a trust evaluation. We do not use observed behavior and reputation to compute trust and we are interested in abstract arguments and not in arguments with an abductive format.

5 Conclusions

Trust plays an important role in many research areas of artificial intelligence, particularly in the semantic web and multiagent systems where the sources have to deal with conflicting information from other sources. In the call for papers of the first Autonomous Agents Workshop on "Deception, Fraud and Trust in Agent Societes" it is said: "with the growing impact of electronic commerce distance trust building becomes more and more important, and better models of trust and deception are needed. One trend is that in electronic communication channels extra agents, the so-called Trusted Third Parties, are introduced in an agent community that take care of trust building among the other agents in the network. But in fact different kind of trust are needed and should be modeled and supported, e.g., trust in the environment and in the infrastructure (the socio-technical system), trust in your agent and in mediating agents, trust in the potential partners, trust in the warrantors and authorities (if any). The notion of trust is also important in other domains of agents' theory, beyond that of electronic commerce. It seems even foundational for the notion of "agency" and for its defining relation of acting "on behalf of". For example, trust is relevant in Human-Computer interaction, e.g., the trust relation between the user and her/his personal assistant (and, in general, her/his computer). It is also critical for modeling and supporting groups and teams, organisations, co-ordination, negotiation, with the related trade-off between local/individual utility and global/collective interest; or in modeling distributed knowledge and its circulation."

Castefranchi and Falcone [8] propose a socio-cognitive and computational model of trust. Following Castelfranchi, only a cognitive agent can "trust" another agent: only an agent endowed with goals and beliefs. In this model, first, one trusts another only relatively to a goal, i.e. for something s/he want to achieve, that s/he desires. If I do not potentially have goals, I cannot really decide, nor care about something (welfare): I cannot subjectively "trust" somebody. Second, trust itself consists of beliefs. Castelfranchi defines trust basically as a mental state, a complex attitude of an agent x towards another agent y about the behavior/action relevant for the result (goal) g, where x is the relying agent, who feels trust; it is a cognitive agent endowed with internal explicit goals and beliefs; y is the agent or entity which is trusted; y is not necessarily a cognitive agent. So x trusts y about g and for g; x trusts also "that" g will be true.

In this paper, starting from the socio-cognitive and computational model of trust proposed by Castelfranchi, we provide a model for dealing with conflicts in trust using argumentation. In this model, the information sources can be introduced into the argumentation framework. In argumentation systems as AS-PIC+, arguments come from a single knowledge base and they have the form $\langle\{p, p \rightarrow q\}, q\rangle$. We propose to introduce the sources, e.g., $\langle\{1 : p, 2 : p \rightarrow q\}, 2 : q\rangle$, by instantiating abstract argumentation with the different knowledge bases of the sources using meta-argumentation. In our model, arguments need to be supported in order to be accepted. Furthermore, the trustworthiness of the sources can be attacked directly, or the attack can be focused on single arguments or attacks. Moreover, we introduce the feedback from the information sources to their items and converse. In such a way, when a source proposes a number of untrustworthy items which overcomes a given threshold, then also the source is considered untrustworthy. Finally, we distinguish two dimensions of trust, namely sincerity and competence, and we model the conflicts which can arise on these two dimensions.

This paper raises several issues for future research. The first line of future work consists in representing also the actions and the goals in our model in order to follow the model of Castelfranchi. In the model, at the moment, the implicit goal of the sources is to get their arguments accepted. Another aspect to be developed is "distrust", as different from lack of trust or insufficient trust, because sometimes our argumentation is precisely aimed at creating "distrust" and diffidence, towards another agent.

References

1. Baroni P., Giacomin M. (2007) On principle-based evaluation of extension-based argumentation semantics. Artif. Intell. 171(10-15):675–700
2. Bochman A. (2004) A causal approach to nonmonotonic reasoning. Artif. Intell. 160(1-2):105–143
3. Boella G., Gabbay D.M., van der Torre L., Villata S. (2009) Meta-argumentation modelling I: Methodology and techniques. Studia Logica 93(2-3):297–355
4. Boella G., van der Torre L., Villata S. (2009) On the acceptability of meta-arguments. In: Procs. of the 2009 IEEE/WIC/ACM International Conference on Intelligent Agent Technology (IAT 2009), IEEE, pp 259–262
5. Boella G., Gabbay D.M., van der Torre L., Villata S. (2010) Support in Abstract Argumentation. In: Procs. of the 3rd International Conference on Computational Models of Argument (COMMA 2010), IOS Press, pp 40–51
6. Cayrol C., Lagasquie-Schiex M. (2010) Coalitions of arguments: A tool for handling bipolar argumentation frameworks. Int. J. Intell. Syst. 25 (1):83–109
7. Castelfranchi C., Falcone R., (1998) Principles of trust for MAS: cognitive anatomy, social importance, and quantification. In: Procs. of the Intern. Conference on Multi-Agent Systems (ICMAS 1998), pp.72-79
8. Castelfranchi C., Falcone R. (2010) Trust Theory: A Socio-Cognitive and Computational Model. Wiley
9. Coste-Marquis S., Devred C., Konieczny S., Lagasquie-Schiex M.C., Marquis P. (2007) On the merging of Dung's argumentation systems. Artif. Intell. 171(10-15):730–753

10. Dix J., Parsons S., Prakken H., Simari G.R. (2009) Research challenges for argumentation. Computer Science - R&D 23(1):27–34
11. Dung P.M. (1995) On the acceptability of arguments and its fundamental role in non-monotonic reasoning, logic programming and n-person games. Artif. Intell. 77(2):321–357
12. Falcone R., and Castelfranchi C. (2001) The socio-cognitive dynamics of trust: does trust create trust? volume 2246 of LNCS, Springer, pp 55–72
13. Falcone R., and Castelfranchi C. (2004) Trust Dynamics: How Trust is influenced by direct experiences and by Trust itself, In: Procs. of the 3rd International Conference on Autonomous Agents and Multi-Agent Systems (AAMAS-04), ACM, pp 740–747
14. Gambetta D. (1990) Can we trust them? Trust: Making and breaking cooperative relations pp 213–238
15. Gordon T.F., Prakken H., Walton D. (2007) The Carneades model of argument and burden of proof. Artif. Intell. 171(10-15):875–896
16. Jakobovits H., Vermeir D. (1999) Robust semantics for argumentation frameworks. J Log. Comput. 9(2):215–261
17. Liau C.J. (2003) Belief, information acquisition, and trust in multi-agent systems–a modal logic formulation. Artif. Intell. 149(1):31–60
18. Lorini, E., Demolombe, R. (2008) From binary trust to graded trust in information sources: A logical perspective. In Falcone, R.; Barber, K. S.; Sabater-Mir, J.; and Singh, M. P., eds., *AAMAS-TRUST*, volume 5396 of *Lecture Notes in Computer Science*, Springer, pp 205–225
19. Matt P.A., Morge M., Toni F. (2010) Combining statistics and arguments to compute trust. In: Procs. of the the 9th International Conference on Autonomous Agents and Multiagent Systems (AAMAS 2010), pp 209–216.
20. Modgil S, Bench-Capon T (2009) Metalevel argumentation. Tech. rep., www.csc.liv.ac.uk/research/ techreports/techreports.html
21. Parsons S., McBurney P., Sklar E. (2010) Reasoning about trust using argumentation: A position paper. In: Procs. of ArgMAS
22. da Costa Pereira C., Tettamanzi A., Villata S. (2011) Changing One's Mind: Erase or Rewind? Possibilistic Belief Revision with Fuzzy Argumentation based on Trust. In: Procs. of the 22nd International Joint Conference on Artificial Intelligence (IJCAI 2011), In press.
23. Prade H. (2007) A qualitative bipolar argumentative view of trust. In: Procs. of the 1st International Conference on Scalable Uncertainty Management (SUM 2007), volume 4772 of LNCS, pp 268–276.
24. Prakken H. (2009) An abstract framework for argumentation with structured arguments. Tech. Rep. UU-CS-2009-019, Utrecht University
25. Stranders R., de Weerdt M., Witteveen C. (2007) Fuzzy Argumentation for Trust, In: Procs. of the 8th Workshop on Computational Logic in Multi-Agent Systems (CLIMA-VIII), volume 5056 of LNCS, pp 214–230
26. Tang Y., Cai K., Sklar E., McBurney P., Parsons S. (2010) A system of argumentation for reasoning about trust. In: Procs. of the 8th European Workshop on Multi-agent Systems (EUMAS 2010)
27. Villata S. (2010) Meta-argumentation for multiagent systems: Coalition formation, merging views, subsumption relation and dependence networks. PhD thesis, University of Turin
28. Villata S., Boella G., van der Torre L. (2011) Argumentation Patterns. In: Procs. of the 9th International Workshop on Argumentation in Multi-Agent Systems

Chapter 25
A formal analysis of trust and distrust relationships in Shakespeare's Othello

Elisabetta Erriquez, Wiebe Van der Hoek and Michael Wooldridge

Abstract In settings where agents can be exploited, trust and reputation are key issues. As a consequence, within the multi-agent systems community, considerable research has gone into the development of computationally viable models of these concepts. In this paper, we present an abstract framework that allows agents to form coalitions with agents that they believe to be trustworthy. In contrast to many other models, we take the notion of *distrust* to be our key social concept. We use a graph theoretic model to capture the distrust relations within a society, and use this model to formulate several notions of mutually trusting coalitions. We investigate principled techniques for how the information present in our distrust model can be aggregated to produce individual measures of how trustworthy an agent is considered to be by a society. We extend the framework with *trust* relationships and introduce the notion of *Trust-Coalitions (T-Coalitions)*. We finally provide an analysis of the Shakespeare's tragedy, Othello, using our abstract framework.

1 Introduction

The goal of coalition formation is typically to form robust, cohesive groups that can cooperate to the mutual benefit of all the coalition members. In open distributed systems, where there are many components that can enter and leave the system as they wish, the notion of *trust* becomes key when it comes

Elisabetta Erriquez
Department of Computer Science, University of Liverpool, UK
e-mail: E.Erriquez@liverpool.ac.uk

Wiebe Van der Hoek,
Department of Computer Science, University of Liverpool, UK
e-mail: Wiebe.Van-Der-Hoek@liverpool.ac.uk

Michael Wooldridge
Department of Computer Science, University of Oxford, UK
e-mail: mjw@cs.ox.ac.uk

to decisions about which coalitions to form, and when. When such systems are inhabited by agents that encompass some level of autonomy, each representing their own stakeholders with their own objectives, it not only becomes plausible that some agents are not trustable, the consequences of joining a coalition of which some members cannot be trusted, or do not trust each other, becomes a key aspect in the decision of whether or not to join a group of agents.

With a relatively small number of exceptions [2, 10], existing models of coalition formation do not generally consider trust. In more general models [12, 9], individual agents use information about reputation and trust to rank agents according to their level of trustworthiness. Therefore, if an agent decides to form a coalition, it can select those agents he reckons to be trustworthy. Or, alternatively, if an agent is asked to join a coalition, he can assess his trust in the requesting agent and decide whether or not to run the risk of joining a coalition with him. We argue that these models lack a *global* view. They only consider the trust binding the agent starting the coalition and the agents receiving the request to join the coalition. Here, we address this restriction. We propose an abstract framework through which autonomous, self-interested agents can form coalitions based on information relating to trust. In fact, we use *distrust* as the key social concept in our work. Luckily, in many societies, trust is the norm and distrust the exception, so it seems reasonable to assume that a system is provided with information of agents that distrust each other based on previous experiences, rather than on reports of trust. Moreover, in several circumstances, it makes sense to assume that agents base their decision on which coalition they form on explicit information of distrust, rather than on information about trust. So, we focus on how distrust can be used as a mechanism for modelling and reasoning about the reliability of others, and, more importantly, about how to form coalitions that satisfy some stability criteria. We present several notions of mutually trusting coalitions and define different measures to aggregate the information presented in our distrust model.

Taking distrust as the basic entity in our model allows us to benefit in the sense of deriving our core definitions from an analogy with a popular and highly influential approach within *argumentation theory* [13]. Specifically, the distrust-based models that we introduce are inspired by the *abstract argumentation frameworks* proposed by Dung [4]. In Dung's framework, an attack relation between arguments is the basic notion, which inspired us to model a distrust relation between agents. We show that several notions of stability and of extensions in the theory of Dung naturally carry over to a system where distrust, rather than attack, is at the core. We extend and refine some of these notions to our trust setting. We also introduce an extension of the model, allowing the use of explicitly defined *trust relationships* and we define a concept of coalition based on the trust relations. Finally, we use our model to analyse the (dis)trust relationships in Shakespeare's famous play, Othello, giving an actual application and analysis of the models proposed.

Section 2 gives the formal definition of the framework presented and introduces several different notions. Section 2 explains how the information presented in abstract trust frameworks can be *aggregated* to provide a single measure of how trustworthy individuals within the society are. Section 3 presents an extension of the framework introducing also *trust* relationships. Section 4 provides an analysis of the model applied to the Othello's scenario. Finally, Section 5 concludes the paper and presents some possible avenues for future work.

2 Abstract Trust Frameworks

In this section, we introduce the basic models that we use throughout the remainder of the paper. [1] Our approach was inspired by the abstract argumentation frameworks of Dung [4]. Essentially, Dung was interested in trying to provide a framework that would make it possible to make sense of a domain of discourse on which there were potentially conflicting views. He considered the various conflicting views to be represented in *arguments*, with an *attack relation* between arguments defining which arguments were considered to be inconsistent with each other. This attack relation is used to determine which sets of arguments are acceptable in some specified way. Notice that Dung's framework focuses on capturing the notion of two arguments being incompatible, or inconsistent with one-another, rather than supporting each other. In our work, we use similar graph like models, but rather than arguments our model is made up of agents, and the binary relation (which is used in determining which coalitions are acceptable), is a *distrust* relation.

We assume that agents have some incentive for sharing their evaluations of the other agents in the community. Although much previous work deals with trust relationships, in our approach, we consider only *distrust* relationships between the agents. In real life, people do not always share their positive evaluation about others, but they are more inclined to report bad experiences, as a warning to other people and as a way to affect the reputation of the person the bad experience was with, as showed by the large research around *negative word of mouth* [17].

A *distrust* relation between agent i and agent j is intended as agent i having none or little trust in agent j. More precisely, when saying that agent i distrusts agent j we mean that, in the context at hand, agent i has insufficient confidence in agent j to share membership with j in one and the same coalition.

When the agents share their evaluation about others, we can build a distrust network of agents linked by *distrust* relationships.

The follow definitions characterize our formal model.

Definition 1 *An* Abstract Trust Framework (ATF), S, *is a pair:*

$$S = \langle Ag, \rightsquigarrow \rangle$$

where:

- *Ag is a finite, non-empty set of* agents; *and*
- $\rightsquigarrow \subseteq Ag \times Ag$ *is a binary* distrust *relation on Ag.*

---

[1] An initial version of the framework appeared in [6].

When $i \rightsquigarrow j$ we say that agent i distrusts agent j. We assume $\rightsquigarrow$ to be irreflexive, i.e., no agent i distrusts itself. Whenever i does not distrust j, we write $i \not\rightsquigarrow j$. So, we assume $\forall i \in Ag$, $i \not\rightsquigarrow i$. Call an agent i fully trustworthy if for all $j \in Ag$, we have $j \not\rightsquigarrow i$. Also, i is trustworthy if for some $j \neq i$, $j \not\rightsquigarrow i$ holds. Conversely, call i fully trusting if for no j, $i \rightsquigarrow j$. And i is trusting if for some $j \neq i$, $i \not\rightsquigarrow j$.

Later, we will find it convenient to compare abstract trust frameworks, and for this we use the following definition.

Definition 2 *If $S_1 = \langle Ag_1, \rightsquigarrow_1 \rangle$ and $S_2 = \langle Ag_2, \rightsquigarrow_2 \rangle$ are two ATFS, we say that S_2 extends S_1, written $S_1 \sqsubseteq S_2$, if both $Ag_1 \subseteq Ag_2$ and $\rightsquigarrow_1 \subseteq \rightsquigarrow_2$.*

Coalitions with Trust

In what follows, when we refer to a "coalition" it should be understood that we mean nothing other than a subset C of Ag. When forming a coalition, there are several ways to measure how much distrust there is among them, or how trustable the coalition is with respect to the overall set of agent Ag.

Definition 3 *Given an ATF $S = \langle Ag, \rightsquigarrow \rangle$, a coalition $C \subseteq Ag$ is distrust-free if no member of C distrusts any other member of C.*

Note that the empty coalition $\emptyset$ and all singleton coalitions $\{i\}$ are distrust-free: we call these trivial coalitions.

Fig. 1 S1, an example of ATFS

Distrust freeness can be thought of as the most basic requirement for a *trusted* coalition of agents. It means that a set of agents has no internal distrust relationships between them. Since we assume $\rightsquigarrow$ to be irreflexive, we know that for any $i \in Ag$, the coalition $\{i\}$ is distrust-free, as is the empty coalition. A distrust-free coalition for S_1 in Figure 1 is, for example, $\{a,c,d\}$.

Consider ATF S_1 from Figure 1. The coalition $C_1 = \{c,d\}$ is distrust-free, but still, they are not angelic: one of their members is being distrusted by some agent in Ag, and they do not have any justification to ignore that. Compare this to the coalition $C_2 = \{a,c,d\}$: any accusations about the trustworthiness of c by b can be neutralised by the fact that a does not trust b in the first place. So, as a collective, they have a defense against possible distrust against them.

With this in mind, we define the following concepts.

Definition 4 *Let ATF $S = \langle Ag, \rightsquigarrow \rangle$ be given.*

- *An agent $i \in Ag$ is called* **trustable** *with respect to a coalition $C \subseteq Ag$ iff $\forall y \in Ag((y \rightsquigarrow i) \Rightarrow \exists x \in C(x \rightsquigarrow y))$.*

- *A coalition C ⊆ Ag is a* trusted extension *of S iff C is distrust-free and every agent i ∈ C is trustable with respect to C.*
- *A coalition C ⊆ Ag is a* maximal trusted extension *of S if C is a trusted extension, and no superset of C is one.*

It is easy to see that if $i \in Ag$ is trustable with respect to some coalition C, then i is also trustable with respect to any bigger coalition $C' \supseteq C$. We will see that (maximal) trusted extensions are not closed under supersets, though.

Personal Extensions

In large societies, it is very unlikely that a single agent manages to interact with everyone in the society. For this reason, it has to rely on information given by others, about reputation of the agents it doesn't know. Reputation can be defined as the opinion or view of someone about something [?]. This view can be mainly derived from an aggregation of opinions of members of the community about one of them. However, it is possible that the agent does not trust a particular agent and it wants to discard its opinion. Therefore, when it comes to forming a coalition, the agents wants to consider only its personal opinion and the opinion of the agent it trusts, while still keeping the coalition distrust-free.

For example, suppose that an agent wants to start a project and it needs to form a coalition to achieve its goals. It wants to form a coalition composed only of agents it trusts and who have no distrust relations among them. To capture this intuition, we introduce the notions of *unique personal extension*, which make it precise [2].

Definition 5 *Given an* ATF *$S = \langle Ag, \rightsquigarrow \rangle$, and an agent $a \in Ag$, the unique personal extension UPE(S,a), we require, has the following properties:*

1. *$a \in UPE(S,a)$*
2. *UPE(S,a) is unique*
3. *UPE(S,a) is distrust free*
4. *there is a minimal set $OUT \subseteq Ag$, with the following properties, for all $x, y \in Ag$:*

    a. $x \rightsquigarrow a \Rightarrow x \in OUT$
    b. $(y \in UPE(S,a) \ \& \ y \rightsquigarrow x) \Rightarrow x \in OUT$
    c. $y \in UPE(S,a) \Leftrightarrow \forall z(z \rightsquigarrow y \Rightarrow z \in OUT)$

Loosely put: we add a to $UPE(S,a)$, and then we ensure that whoever distrusts or is distrusted by somebody in $UPE(S,a)$ is out, while $UPE(S,a)$ only accepts those agents as members that are at most distrusted by members of OUT. For a more detailed algorithm, see [6].

Note that agents can be out for two reasons: first of all, they may distrust agent a, or they may themselves be distrusted by an agent that is in.

Consider the ATF $S1 = \langle Ag, \rightsquigarrow \rangle$ in Figure 1. Suppose agent a wants to compute its personal extensions. Then, according to our definition, the *unique trusted*

---

[2] For more details please refer to [6]

462 Elisabetta Erriquez, Wiebe Van der Hoek and Michael Wooldridge

extension computed is $\{a,c,d\}$. Now, suppose agent b wants to compute its personal extensions. Then, according to our definition, agents a will be discarded because it distrust b. Therefore, the *unique trusted extension* for agent b is $\{b,d\}$.

Aggregate Trust Measures

Abstract trust frameworks provide a social model of (dis)trust; they capture, at a relatively high level of abstraction, who (dis)trusts who in a society, and notions such as trusted extensions and personal extensions use these models to attempt to understand which coalitions are free of negative social views. An obvious question, however, is how the information presented in abstract trust frameworks can be *aggregated* to provide a single measure of how trustworthy (or otherwise) an individual within the society is. We now explore this issue. We present three aggregate measures of trust, which are given relative to an abstract trust framework $S = \langle Ag, \leadsto \rangle$ and an agent $i \in Ag$. Both of these trust values attempt to provide a principled way of measuring the overall trustworthiness of agent i, taking into account the information presented in S:

- *Distrust Degree*:
  This value ignores the structure of an ATF, and simply looks at how many or how few agents in the society (dis)trust an agent.
- *Expected trustworthiness*:
  This value is the ratio of the number of maximal trusted extensions of which i is a member to the overall number of maximal trusted extensions in the system S.
- *Coalition expected trustworthiness*:
  This value attempts to measure the probability that an agent $i \in Ag$ would be trusted by an arbitrary coalition, picked from the overall set of possible coalitions in the system.

These latter two values are related to solution concepts such as the Banzhaf index, developed in the theory of cooperative games and voting power, and indeed they are inspired by these measures [8].

Distrust Degree

On the web, several successful approaches to credibility such as PageRank [3, 11] use methods derived from graph theory to model credibility, which utilize the connections of the resource for evaluation. Several graph theoretic models of credibility and text retrieval [15] rely on the consideration of the in-degree of the vertex, that is the sum of the incoming edges of that particular vertex in a directed graph. The degree of the incoming edges is used to extract importance and trustworthiness.

In our model, incoming edges are distrust relationships, therefore they represent a negative evaluation of a particular agent from the others in the society. Thus, measuring the in-degree of an agent in the society can give an indication how reliable (or unreliable) that agent is considered overall.

Formally, we call this value the *distrust-degree* for an abstract trust framework $S = \langle Ag, \leadsto \rangle$ and an agent $i \in Ag$, denoted as $\delta_i(S)$, and it is defined:

$$\delta_i(S) = \frac{|\{x \mid x \in Ag \text{ and } x \leadsto i\}|}{|Ag|}.$$

This number provides us a measure of the reliability of the agent in the whole society. The higher the number of agents that distrust it, the less reliable that agent is considered to be.

However, as we mentioned before, a maximal trusted extension or, in general, a coalition C, according to our approach, is a set of agents who trust each other. Therefore, these agents may not be interested in the evaluation of the agents outside the coalition. They are more interested in a distrust degree relative to C. Hence, we define the following measure. The *coalition distrust-degree* for an abstract trust framework $S = \langle Ag, \leadsto \rangle$, a coalition C and an agent $i \in Ag$, denoted as $\delta_i^C(S)$, defined as:

$$\delta_i^C(S) = \frac{|\{x \mid x \in C \text{ and } x \leadsto i\}|}{|C|}.$$

The coalition distrust degree provides a measure for the agents in C to select agents outside the trusted coalition, who they believe to be more reliable among the agents in the society. Agents in C can rank the agents outside using the value of the coalition distrust degree. In this way, it is possible to obtain an ordered list of the agents who the coalition consider less unreliable. The smaller the value of the coalition distrust-degree, the more reliable the agent is considered.

Expected Trustworthiness

As we noted above, the expected trustworthiness of an agent i in system S is the ratio of the number of maximal trusted extensions in S of which i is a member to the overall number of maximal trusted extensions in the system S. To put it another way, this value is the probability that agent i would appear in a maximal trusted extension, if we picked such an extension uniformly at random from the set of all maximal trusted extensions. Formally, letting $mte(S)$ denote the set of maximal trusted extensions in $S = \langle Ag, \leadsto \rangle$, the expected trustworthiness of agent $i \in Ag$ is denoted $\mu_i(S)$, defined as:

$$\mu_i(S) = \frac{|\{C \in mte(S) \mid i \in C\}|}{|mte(S)|}.$$

Clearly, if $\mu_i(S) = 1$ then i is strongly trusted, according to the terminology introduced above, and moreover a is weakly trusted iff $\mu_i(S) > 0$.

From existing results in the argumentation literature on computing extensions of abstract argument systems [5], we can also obtain the following:

As an aside, note that the expected trustworthiness value is inspired by the *Banzhaf index* from cooperative game theory and voting theory [8].

Coalition Expected Trustworthiness

There is one obvious problem with the overall expected trustworthiness value, as we have introduced above. Suppose we have a society that is entirely trusting (i.e., the entire society is distrust free) apart from a single "rogue" agent, who distrusts everybody apart from himself, even though everybody trusts him. Then, according to our current definitions, there is no maximal trusted extension apart from the rogue agent. This is perhaps counter intuitive. To understand what the problem is, observe that when deriving the value $\mu_i(S)$, we are taking into account the views of *all* the agents in the society – which includes every rogue agent. It is this difficulty that we attempt to overcome in the following measure. To define this value, we need a little more notation. Where $R \subseteq X \times X$ is a binary relation on some set X and $C \subseteq X$, then we denote by *restr*(R, C) the relation obtained from R by restricting it to C:

$$restr(R, C) = \{(s, s') \in R \mid \{s, s'\} \subseteq C\}.$$

Then, where $S = \langle Ag, \rightsquigarrow \rangle$ is an abstract trust framework, and $C \subseteq Ag$, we denote by $S \downarrow C$ the abstract trust framework obtained by restricting the distrust relation $\rightsquigarrow$ to C:

$$S \downarrow C = \langle C, restr(\rightsquigarrow, C) \rangle.$$

Given this, we can define the *coalition expected trustworthiness*, $\varepsilon_i(S)$, of an agent i in given an abstract trust framework $S = \langle Ag, \rightsquigarrow \rangle$ to be:

$$\varepsilon_i(S) = \frac{1}{2^{|Ag|-1}} \sum_{C \subseteq Ag \setminus \{i\}} \mu_i(S \downarrow C \cup \{i\}).$$

Thus, $\varepsilon_i(S)$ measures the expected value of μ_i for a coalition $C \cup \{i\}$ where $C \subseteq Ag \setminus \{i\}$ is picked uniformly at random from the set of all such possible coalitions. There are $2^{|Ag|-1}$ coalitions not containing i, hence the first term in the definition.

The coalition expected trustworthiness value arguably gives a clearer overall idea of what the trustworthiness of an agent would be with respect to the maximal trusted extensions that can potentially be formed, therefore it offers a better insight in the trust issue related to the problem of forming coalitions.

3 A Framework for trust and distrust . . . An extension

In this section, we present an extension of the AFT described in Section 2. As mentioned in Section 2, in the AFT, the *absence of a distrust relationship* between two agents does not necessarily imply the *presence of a trust relationship*. Therefore it seems natural to complement the distrust framework just introduced with trust relationships. The follow definitions characterize our formal model.

Definition 6 *An* Abstract Trust/Distrust Framework (ATDF), *S, is a triple:*

$$S = \langle Ag, \leadsto, \dashrightarrow \rangle$$

where:

- *Ag is a finite, non-empty set of* agents; *and*
- $\leadsto \subseteq Ag \times Ag$ is a binary distrust *relation on Ag, as described in Section 2.*
- $\dashrightarrow \subseteq Ag \times Ag$ is a binary trust *relation on Ag.*
- $\forall i, j \in Ag$ *if* $i \leadsto j$ *then* $i \not\dashrightarrow j$;
- $\forall i \in Ag : i \dashrightarrow i$;

When $i \dashrightarrow j$ *we say that agent i trusts agent j. We assume that there always exist an implicit* trust *relationship from and to the agent itself. Whenever i does not trust j, we write* $i \not\dashrightarrow j$.

In this case, as well as before, the absence of an explicit *trust* relationship does not imply the presence of a *distrust* relationship. Note that the fourth bullet of the definition state that an agent cannot trust and distrust another agent at the same time. However we do not impose to any of the relationships to be mutual, therefore there is no restriction to prevent a situation where for two agents i, j, $i \leadsto j$ and $j \dashrightarrow i$, as shown in the situation between agent a and b in $S2$ in Figure 2.

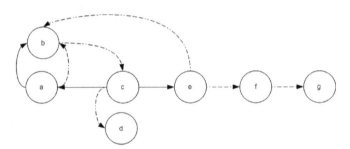

Fig. 2 S2, an example of ATDFS

We now present the concept of coalition based on *trust relationship.*

Definition 7 *Given an* ATDF $S = \langle Ag, \leadsto, \dashrightarrow \rangle$, *a coalition* $C \subseteq Ag$ *is a* T-Coalition (Trust-Coalition) if:

1. C is *distrust-free wrt the* $\leadsto$ *relationship;*
2. $\forall i \in C, \exists j \in C i \dashrightarrow j$ *or* $j \dashrightarrow i$;
3. C is *maximal wrt* $\subseteq$ *among the sets satisfying 1 and 2.*

Note that the singleton coalitions $\{i\}$ are *T-Coalitions* as there is always an implicit *trust* relationship from and to the agent itself: we call them trivial T-Coalitions.

In $S2$, shown in Figure 2, the *T-Coalitions*, apart from the trivial ones, are $\{b, c, d\}$ and $\{b, e, f, g\}$.

4 Othello, An Analysis

In this section we use the famous tragedy by Shakespeare, Othello, to give an actual illustration and analysis of the models proposed. The play revolves around four central characters: Othello, a Moorish general in the Venetian army; his wife Desdemona; his lieutenant, Cassio; and his trusted ensign Iago. Othello is a general in the Venetian Republic military, who is in command of the army fighting the Turks attacking Cyprus.

The play opens with Roderigo, a rich and dissolute gentleman, complaining to Iago, a highly-ranked soldier, that Iago has not told him about the secret marriage between Desdemona, the daughter of a Senator named Brabantio, and Othello. He is upset by this development because he loves Desdemona and had previously asked her father for her hand in marriage. Iago is upset with Othello for promoting Cassio, a younger man, above him, and tells Roderigo that he plans to use Othello for his own advantage. Iago tries in many ways to have Cassio stripped off his rank but he also wants to ruin Othello for having preferred Cassio over him. Therefore Iago persuades Othello to be suspicious of Cassio and Desdemona. He achieves this using a precious handkerchief that was Othello's first gift to Desdemona and giving it to Cassio, with the help of his wife Emilia. The fake defense from Iago towards Cassio and his deliberate reticence are the central part of Iago's work of persuasion which leads to Othello killing Desdemona in a fit of rage. In the epilogue, Emilia reveals that Desdemona's betrayal was invented by Iago, who immediately kills her. Othello, feeling guilty for killing the innocent Desdemona, kills himself. Iago is arrested and Cassio takes Othello's place as general.

The play is divided in five acts. We take this division as the natural breaking points for modelling the scenarios with our AFT and AFDT. We design an AFT and AFDT for each act, using the main characters and the $\leadsto$ and $\dashrightarrow$ relationships, representing the distrust (or more in general dislike) and trust relationships among the characters.

For each of the main characters we give the aggregate trust measures for each act and for Othello and Iago, the primary actors, we also present the UPE.

In our AFTS representing the Othello's scenario, we only consider the main characters: Othello, Desdemona, Iago, Cassio, Roderigo and, for the first act, Brabantio. Therefore our context is limited to the relationships among these figures.

Normally, in multi-agent systems scenarios, a coalition is a set of agents who may or may not work together to achieve a common goal or to earn higher utility [18]. In our example, the Othello's scenario, we abstract from the goal of the coalition and we consider the proposed trusted set of agents simply as sets whose components trust, or have no reason to distrust each other. In the next paragraphs we provide a more extensive description of each act [1] and then we provide a detailed analysis of the society.

ACT 1 Synopsis

Shakespeare's famous play of love turned bad by unfounded jealousy begins in Venice with Iago, a soldier under Othello's command arguing with Roderigo, a wealthy Venetian. Roderigo has paid Iago a considerable sum of money to spy on Othello for him, since he wishes to take Othello's girlfriend, Desdemona as his own.

Roderigo fears that Iago has not been telling him enough about Desdemona and that this proves Iago's real loyalty is to Othello rather than him. Iago explains his hatred of Othello for choosing Cassio as his officer or lieutenant and not him as he expected. To regain Roderigo's trust, Iago and Roderigo inform Brabantio, Desdemona's father, of her relationship with Othello the "Moor", which enrages Brabantio into sending parties out at night to apprehend Othello for what in Brabantio's eyes must be an abuse of his daughter by Othello. Iago lies that Roderigo and not himself, was responsible for angering Brabantio against Othello, Iago telling Othello that he should watch out for Brabantio's men who are looking for him. Othello decides not to hide, since he believes his good name will stand him in good stead.

We learn that Othello has married Desdemona. Brabantio and Roderigo arrive, Brabantio accusing Othello of using magic on his daughter. Othello stops a fight before it can happen but Othello is called away to discuss a crisis in Cyprus, much to the anger of Brabantio who wants justice for what he believes Othello has done to his fair Desdemona. The Duke is in council with several senators discussing their enemy, the Turks (Turkish people). Brabantio complains to the Duke that Othello bewitched his daughter and had intimate relations with her. Desdemona is brought in to settle the matter, Othello meanwhile explains how he and Desdemona fell in love. Desdemona confirms this and the Duke advises Brabantio that he would be better off accepting the marriage than complaining and changing nothing.

The Duke orders Othello to Cyprus to fight the Turks, with Desdemona to follow, accompanied by the trusted Iago. Roderigo despairs that his quest for Desdemona is over now that she is married, but Iago tells him not to give up and earn money instead; soon Desdemona will bore of Othello.

Alone, Iago reveals his intention to continue using Roderigo for money and his hatred of Othello (Othello picked Cassio and not Iago for his lieutenant). Iago explains that his plan is avenge Othello is to suggest to Othello that Cassio is sleeping with Desdemona (Othello's wife).

ACT 1 Analysis

In figure 3 and 4 we can observe that the only distrust-free characters, at the end of the first act, are Desdemona and Roderigo.

The *maximal trusted extension* is formed by

$$\{Desdemona, Roderigo, Cassio, Brabantio\}.$$

Note that Othello, although a noble person at the beginning of our story, is hated and therefore distrusted by Iago, who feels betrayed by him, by Roderigo who feels Desdemona has been stolen from him by Othello, and by Brabantio, Desdemona's father, who does not approve of the couple's marriage.

Table 1 Table showing the Maximal Trusted Extensions and the T-Coalitions in the Othello's society S for each Act

	Maximal Trusted Extensions	T-Coalitions
Act 1	{Desdemona, Roderigo, Cassio, Brabantio}	{Desdemona, Brabantion} {Othello, Desdemona, Cassio}
Act 2	{Desdemona, Roderigo, Iago}	{Roderigo, Iago} {Othello, Desdemona, Cassio}
Act 3	{Desdemona, Iago}	{Desdemona, Cassio}
Act 4	{Desdemona, Iago}	{Desdemona, Cassio}
Act 5	{Desdemona, Iago} {Desdemona, Cassio} {Desdemona, Roderigo}	{Othello, Desdemona} {Cassio, Desdemona}

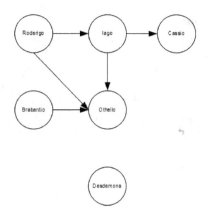

Fig. 3 ATF for Act 1

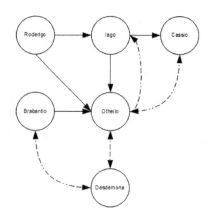

Fig. 4 ATDF for Act 1

Therefore Othello is highly distrusted in the first act, as shown by his *coalition expected trustworthiness* value, 0.125, which is the lowest among all characters in this act. However, his beloved Desdemona and his loyal lieutenant Cassio trust him and, in fact they are part of Othello's *unique personal extension*. Desdemona,

Table 2 Table showing the Unique Personal Extensions of Othello and Iago in the Othello's society S for each Act

	Othello Unique Personal Extension	Iago Unique Personal Extension
Act 1	$\{Othello, Desdemona, Cassio\}$	$\{Iago, Desdemona, Brabantio\}$
Act 2	$\{Othello, Desdemona, Cassio\}$	$\{Iago, Desdemona, Roderigo\}$
Act 3	$\{Othello\}$	$\{Iago, Desdemona\}$
Act 4	$\{Othello\}$	$\{Iago, Desdemona\}$
Act 5	$\{Othello, Desdemona\}$	$\{Iago, Desdemona\}$

being distrust free is part of Iago's *unique personal extension*, together with Brabantio, who is also distrust free. The *T-Coalitions* in this first act are two:

$\{Desdemona, Brabantio\}$ and $\{Othello, Desdemona, Cassio\}$.

Note that Othello's *unique personal extension* corresponds exactly to the *T-Coalition* he belongs to. Although Iago's *coalition expected trustworthiness* value, 0.5, is higher than Othello's, we note that Iago doesn't belong to any *T-Coalition*. Although Othello trusts Iago, Iago himself despises Othello. This conflict prevents them from being together in a T-Coalition.

Table 3 Table showing the values of μ_i, Expected Trustworthiness, and the $\varepsilon_i(S)$, Coalition Expected Trustworthiness, with regard to the Othello's society S for each Act

	Act 1		Act 2		Act 3		Act 4		Act 5	
	$\mu_i(S)$	$\varepsilon_i(S)$	$\mu_i(S)$	$\varepsilon_i(S)$	$\mu_i(S)$	$\varepsilon_i(S)$	$\mu_i(S)$	$\varepsilon_i(S)$	$\mu_i(S)$	$\varepsilon_i(S)$
$i = Othello$	0.0	0.125	0.0	0.25	0.0	0.5	0.0	0.5	0.0	0.187
$i = Iago$	0.0	0.5	1.0	1.0	1.0	1.0	1.0	1.0	0.333	0.395
$i = Cassio$	1.0	0.75	0.0	0.25	0.0	0.25	0.0	0.25	0.333	0.458
$i = Roderigo$	1.0	1.0	1.0	1.0	na	na	na	na	0.333	0.833
$i = Desdemona$	1.0	1.0	1.0	1.0	1.0	0.75	1.0	0.75	1.0	1.0
$i = Brabantio$	1.0	1.0	na	na	na	na	na	na	na	na

ACT 2 Synopsis

Several weeks later in Cyprus, Othello's arrival is expected. But a terrible storm
has largely battered and destroyed the Turkish fleet, which no longer poses a
threat to Cyprus. Unfortunately there are fears that this same storm drowned
Othello as well. Many people praise Othello. Cassio, who has arrived, sings
Desdemona's praises. A ship is spotted but it is Desdemona and Iago's, not
Othello's. Iago suspects that Cassio loves Desdemona and slyly uses it to his
advantage. Iago tells Roderigo that he still has a chance with Desdemona but
Cassio whom Desdemona could love is in the way. Killing Cassio (who became
Othello's lieutenant instead of Iago) will leave Desdemona to Roderigo, Iago
slyly explains.

    Othello finally arrives, to everyone's great relief. Iago decides to tell Othello
that Cassio is having an affair with Desdemona, so Iago will be rewarded
whilst Cassio will be punished. A Herald announces celebration that "our
noble general Othello!" has defeated the Turkish fleet, calling on all to celebrate
this great triumph and also to celebrate Othello's "nuptial" or wedding to the
fair Desdemona.

    Iago learns more of Cassio's high regard for Desdemona and Iago ma-
nipulates Cassio into drinking too much since he is certain Cassio will do
something he will regret. Iago also tells Roderigo to attack Cassio. This happens, and Cassio wounds Roderigo. Othello is now awake and Cassio's name
ruined. Othello, although he loves Cassio, has no choice but to demote him
from his position as his lieutenant. Next Iago comforts Cassio by suggesting
he speak with Desdemona who could put in a good word for him with Othello. Iago comforts a wounded Roderigo, telling him he has won by ruining
Cassio's name. Iago has his wife Emilia ensure Desdemona and Cassio will
talk so Othello can see his wife talking with Cassio, allowing Iago to convince
Othello that Desdemona is being unfaithful.

ACT 2 Analysis

In the second act, as shown in Figure 5 and 6, the distrust and trust relationships
between the characters change. Our models reflect these changes.

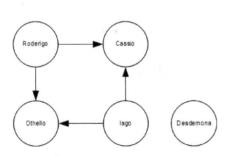

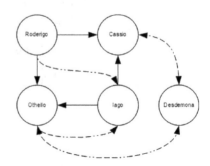

Fig. 5 ATF for Act 2   **Fig. 6** ATDF for Act 2

We can observe that now Iago has become distrust free, since Roderigo has regained trust in him. Roderigo now distrusts Cassio, as well as Othello, convinced by Iago that he should attack Cassio to ruin Othello's name.

The *Maximal trusted extension* now includes Iago and excludes Cassio. It is, in fact formed by

$$\{Desdemona, Roderigo, Iago\}.$$

This newly acquired distrust-freeness, boosts Iago *coalition expected trustworthiness* to 1, while Cassio's decreases to 0.25, since Othello has lost trust in him because of his fight with Roderigo.

Iago's *unique personal extension* now includes Roderigo, having the conflict being removed.

Othello's *coalition expected trustworthiness* improves slightly, being 0.25 in this act. This is due to the absence of Brabantio in this act. His *unique personal extension* does not vary. It still includes Cassio because, even tough Othello has lost *trust* in him, due to his fight, Iago has still not convinced Othello of Cassio's betrayal.

The *T-Coalitions* now include the one formed by *{Roderigo, Iago}* which reflect the actual cooperation between the two in this second act, even if Iago's motives are not genuine.

ACT 3 Synopsis

Cassio tells Iago that he has arranged to meet Desdemona, Iago helping Cassio to do this. Iago's wife, Emilia, tells Cassio that Othello would like to reinstate him as his lieutenant but the fact that Cassio's fight is public news, prevents Othello from doing this immediately. Emilia tells Cassio that she can arrange a meeting with Desdemona. Some time later, Cassio speaks with a very sympathetic Desdemona who assures him that Othello still very much loves Cassio. Furthermore, Desdemona resolves to keep putting in a good word for Cassio until he is again Othello's lieutenant. At a distance, Iago manipulates Othello by first suggesting shock and then hiding his outbursts from Othello. This guarantees Othello's attention, as Iago plants seeds of doubt in Othello's mind about Desdemona's fidelity especially where Cassio is concerned. Iago leaves Othello almost convinced that his wife is having an affair with Cassio.

Othello now complains of a headache to Desdemona, which results in her dropping a strawberry patterned handkerchief, Othello's first gift to her. Emilia picks this up gives it to Iago who decides the handkerchief could help his manipulation if he ensures Cassio receives it. Iago arranges to place the handkerchief near Cassio's lodgings or home where he is certain to find it and take it as his own, unaware that it is Othello's gift to Desdemona.

A furious Othello returns to Iago, certain his wife is faithful and demanding proof from Iago of Desdemona's infidelity. Reluctantly and hesitantly, Iago tells Othello he saw Cassio wipe his brow with Desdemona's handkerchief. Othello is convinced, cursing his wife and telling Iago who is now promoted to lieutenant to kill Cassio. Othello will deal with Desdemona. Desdemona worries about her missing handkerchief and comments that if she lost it, it could lead Othello doubting her fidelity. Emilia when asked about Desdemona's lost handkerchief, lies, denying having seen the handkerchief she picked up and gave to Iago. Othello enters; asking Desdemona for the very same handkerchief and Desdemona assures him that the handkerchief is not lost and will be found. Desdemona now tries to change the subject to Cassio, but Othello continually stresses the value the handkerchief has to him, this leading to Othello angrily ordering his wife away.

Cassio arrives, Desdemona telling him that her attempts to help him are not going well. Iago claims total ignorance to the cause of Othello's fury. Cassio gives Othello's handkerchief, which he found, to his suspicious mistress Bianca.

ACT 4 Synopsis

Iago fans the flames of Othello's distrust and fury with Desdemona's supposed "infidelity" by first suggesting Desdemona shared her bed with Cassio and then that her giving away the handkerchief is no big deal when Iago knows exactly how hurtful to Othello, giving away this sentimental gift is.

Next Iago suggests to Othello that Cassio will "blab" or gloat to others about his conquest of Desdemona before telling Othello that Cassio boasted to him that he did indeed sleep with Desdemona. Meeting later with Cassio, Iago cunningly talks to Cassio about Cassio's mistress Bianca, each smile and each gesture made by Cassio infuriating a hidden Othello who thinks Cassio is talking about sleeping with Desdemona (Othello's wife). Next Bianca (Cassio's mistress) arrives, angrily giving back the handkerchief Cassio gave to her. This infuriates Othello since as Iago puts it, Cassio not only received Othello's handkerchief from his wife but then gave it away to his whore (Bianca) as if it were worthless. Othello decides to kill Desdemona by strangulation in her bed, Iago's idea. Iago pledges to kill Cassio.

Lodovico arrives, announcing that Othello is to return home and Cassio is to be the next Governor of Cyprus. Desdemona's joy for Cassio enrages Othello, leaving Lodovico and Iago to wonder how much Othello seems to have changed and leaving poor Desdemona to wonder how she offended the man she truly loves. Othello questions Emilia as to whether Desdemona was unfaithful to him. Annoyed that Emilia's answers suggest nothing has happened between Desdemona and Cassio, Othello dismisses her comments as those of a simple woman. Othello meets Desdemona, Desdemona becoming increasingly upset with her husband's anger towards her, an anger she cannot understand. Othello eventually reveals to Desdemona that her infidelity is the source of his anger, Desdemona pleading her innocence on deaf ears. Emilia and Desdemona discuss Othello's strange behavior. Emilia is certain some evil fellow has twisted Othello to believe Desdemona has been unfaithful, not realizing that this evil man is her own husband Iago.

We learn that Iago has been pocketing Roderigo's gifts to Desdemona, which never reached her. Fearing Roderigo will learn this, Iago tells Roderigo that Cassio must die since Iago benefits if ever man dies. Lodovico tries to calm

Othello down. Othello orders Desdemona to bed to await him later, an order Desdemona dutifully obeys out of love for Othello. Emilia notices that Othello is much calmer now and tells Desdemona her bed has been made with her wedding sheets as requested. Desdemona asks to be buried in those same sheets should she die before Emilia, a hint of trouble ahead.

Emilia is barred from joining Desdemona in her bedchamber, angering her. Desdemona, depressed, recalls a song (The Willow Song) of a maid who was similarly abused by her husband and sings it. Desdemona and Emilia talk about infidelity. Desdemona would not be unfaithful to her husband (Othello) for all the world; the more cynical and worldly Emilia would for the right price.

ACT 3 and 4 Analysis

In the third act, Othello is convinced that Desdemona and Cassio are having an affair, therefore he distrusts them both. Hence, in our model two new *distrust* relationships appear.

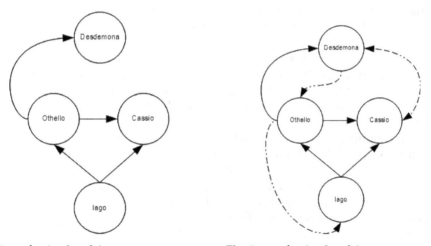

Fig. 7 ATF for Act 3 and 4   **Fig. 8** ATDF for Act 3 and 4

Desdemona, although she is now distrusted by Othello, remains in the *maximal trusted extension*, indirectly defended by the Iago's distrust toward Othello. Iago still remains distrust-free in the society.

Cassio's *coalition expected trustworthiness* decrease to 0.25, while Iago's reaches 1. This reflect the actual situation in the play. Iago is considered a very loyal friend.

Othello is now alone. He does not trust Cassio or Desdemona anymore. This is shown by the fact that his *unique personal extension* is empty, or more accurately that he is the only one in it.

Note that now the only *T-Coalitions* is formed by {Desdemona, Cassio} who, being still unaware of Iago's plot, keep trusting each other.

In the fourth act, the *trust* and *distrust* relationships remain unchanged.

ACT 5 Synopsis

Iago and Roderigo wait in a street to ambush Cassio. Iago tells Roderigo how to kill him. Iago does not care which ends up dead. Iago is worried that about Roderigo's increasing questioning of what happened to jewels that were given to him to pass on to Desdemona. Roderigo attacks Cassio but Cassio wounds Roderigo instead. Iago from behind stabs Cassio, wounding him in the leg. Othello hearing Cassio's cries is pleased, announcing that he too will soon kill (Desdemona). Lodovico and Gratiano (Desdemona's cousin and uncle) and Iago reappear, Iago claiming total innocence to Cassio's injuries even though he inflicted them. Seizing Roderigo, Iago stabs and wounds him "in revenge" for wounding his "friend" Cassio. Gratiano and Lodovico tend to Cassio's wound. Bianca, Cassio's mistress arrives, Iago cleverly laying suspicion for Cassio's injuries on his innocent mistress, making Iago less suspicious.

Othello enters Desdemona's bedchamber (bedroom) trying to convince himself that he is killing her for her own good. He kisses his still asleep wife one last time. Desdemona awakens, but Othello will still kill her, telling her to pray so her soul will not die when she does. Desdemona again asks what wrong she has committed, Othello telling her that she gave Cassio his handkerchief, by which he means he thinks she had an affair with him. Desdemona pleads her innocence, telling Othello to bring Cassio over to prove she did not give away her handkerchief. Othello says he confessed and is dead, Desdemona's fear and surprise prompting Othello to believe she does care for him.

Othello kills Desdemona.

Emilia, banging on the door outside, cannot stop this. Later Emilia is let in, revealing Iago has killed Roderigo and Desdemona who was thought dead, murmurs her last breaths but loyally does not say Othello killed her. Othello tells Emilia he killed her and Emilia despite Iago's attempts to remove her reveals the truth about the handkerchief; she found it, and then gave it to Iago. Iago now in trouble, stabs his wife Emilia and escapes. Emilia dies, singing the "Willow Song" before criticizing Othello for killing his loving wife.

Lodovico, Cassio and the now captured prisoner Iago soon appear, Othello stabbing Iago but not killing him before having his sword removed. Lodovico is disappointed that Othello, a man so honorable has reverted to acting like a slave. Othello tries to argue that killing his wife was a noble action but it falls on deaf ears. Lodovico learns that Othello and Iago plotted Cassio's death. Lodovico reveals letters in the dead Roderigo's pocket proving Cassio was to be killed by Roderigo. Iago proudly confirms that Cassio did find the handkerchief in his bedchamber because Iago placed it there to be found. Othello, realizing what he has done, kills himself with a concealed weapon and lies himself on top of his wife. Cassio is placed in charge of Iago and Lodovico leaves to discuss this sad matter with others abroad.

ACT 5 Analysis

In the end of the final act, the truth is finally revealed. Roderigo finally understands that Iago has being using him. Othello realises that he has been a fool and victim of Iago's plot. This is shown by the new *distrust* relationships from Roderigo and Othello to Iago.

Desdemona is now dead and Cassio realises that Othello was planning to kill him too. Cassio now distrust Othello and Iago. On the other side, Othello now trusts Cassio again, realizing that Cassio is always been loyal to him.

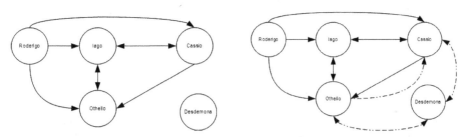

Fig. 9 ATF for Act 5   **Fig. 10** ATDF for Act 5

The last act changes Iago's situation drastically. His *coalition expected trustworthiness* drops from 1 to 0.3. His *unique personal extension* includes only Desdemona who died before realising she was part of the Iago's plot.

Othello situation remains bad. His *coalition expected trustworthiness* is very low, 1.18. His *unique personal extension* includes Desdemona, who, even before dying, refused to betray his beloved husband by revealing that he was his killer.

Othello's renewed trust in Desdemona means that there is now another *T-Coalition* formed by the two, since Desdemona never stopped trusting Othello.

5 Conclusions and Future Work

In this paper we have addressed some of the limitations of existing trust-based coalition formation approaches. We have taken the notion of *distrust* to be our key social concept. The main contribution of this work is the definition of an abstract framework that overcomes these limitations allowing the agents to form distrust-free coalitions. We have formulated several notions of mutually trusting coalitions. We have also presented techniques for how the information presented in our distrust model can be aggregated to produce individual measures to evaluate the trustworthiness of the agent with respect to the whole society or to a particular coalition. We also have presented a way to combine the trust and distrust relationships to form coalitions which are still distrust-free.

The analysis of the Othello's scenario shown that the models can successfully reproduce combinations of trust and distrust relationships for realistic situations. The changes in the relationships are reflected in our models and so are the values of the aggregate measures, working as a mirror of the society.

Our model is not utility based, so we are not considering stability from a utility-theoretic point of view, but there is nevertheless an interesting relationship between our notion of stability and that of cooperative game theory. In our view, a coalition is stable if no agent has any rational incentive to distrust any of the members. Future work might consider examining the role of our distrust models in coalition formation in more detail, perhaps in the context of coalition formation algorithms such as those that have recently been proposed within the multi-agent systems community (see, e.g., [14, 16]).

There are many potential directions for future work. We assume that the agents are willing to share their information about the trust they have in other agents. It would be interesting to develop some form of incentives for the agents to do so. Also, a natural development would be to devise a way to integrate the information inferred from the trust relationships into the aggregate trust measures to give a more comprehensive view of the agents status.

Many studies have gone toward trust properties, such as transitivity. As shown in [7], transitivity should be considered in the context of a particular task. In this work, we have abstracted from the particular goal the agents wish to achieve. An interesting development would be to incorporate this information in our concept of mutually trusting coalitions.

Finally, our work is based on a boolean notion of trust. A further improvement would be to add degrees of trust or distrust to allow for more detailed information.

References

1. Othello summary (2005). http://absoluteshakespeare.com/guides/summaries/othello/othello_summary.htm
2. Breban, S., Vassileva, J.: Long-term coalitions for the electronic marketplace. In: Proceedings of the E-Commerce Applications Workshop, Canadian AI Conference (2001)
3. Brin, S., Page, L.: The anatomy of a large-scale hypertextual web search engine. In: Seventh International World-Wide Web Conference (WWW 1998) (1998). http://ilpubs.stanford.edu:8090/361/
4. Dung, P.M.: On the acceptability of arguments and its fundamental role in nonmonotonic rea-soning, logic programming and n-person games. AI 77, 321—357 (1995)
5. Dunne, P.E., Wooldridge, M.: Complexity of abstract argumentation. In: I. Rahwan, G. Simari (eds.) Argumentation in Artificial Intelligence. SV (2009)
6. Erriquez, E., Hoek, W.V.D., Wooldridge, M.: An abstract framework for reasoning about trust. In: Proceedings of the 14th International Workshop on Trust in Agent Societies (2011)
7. Falcone, R., Castelfranchi, C.: Transitivity in trust. A discussed property. In: WOA (2010)
8. Felsenthal, D.S., Machover, M.: TheMeasurement of Voting Power. Edward Elgar: Cheltenham, UK (1998)

9. Griffiths, N., Luck, M.: Coalition formation through motivation and trust. In: Proceedings of the Second International Joint Conference on Autonomous Agents andMulti-Agent Systems (2003)

10. Lei, G., Xiaolin, W., Guangzhou, Z.: Trust-based optimal workplace coalition generation. In: Information Engineering and Computer Science, 2009. ICIECS 2009. International Conference on, pp. 1–4 (2009). DOI 10.1109/ICIECS.2009.5366705

11. Page, L., Brin, S., Motwani, R., Winograd, T.: The pagerank citation ranking: Bring-ing order to the web. Technical Report 1999-66, Stanford InfoLab (1999). http://ilpubs.stanford.edu:8090/422/.Previousnumber=SIDL-WP-1999-0120

12. Qing-hua, Z., Chong-jun, W., Jun-yuan, X.: Core: A trust model for agent coalition formation. In: Natural Computation, 2009. ICNC '09. Fifth International Conference on, vol. 5, pp. 541—545 (2009)

13. Rahwan, I., Simari, G.R. (eds.): Argumentation in Artificial Intelligence. SV (2009)

14. Rahwan, T.: Algorithms for coalition formation in multi-agent systems. Ph.D. thesis, University of Southampton, UK (2007)

15. Sabater, J., Sierra, C.: Reputation and social network analysis in multi-agent systems. In: AAMAS '02: Proceedings of the first international joint conference on Autonomous agents and multiagent systems, pp. 475—482. ACM, New York, NY, USA (2002). DOI http://doi.acm.org/10.1145/544741.544854

16. Sandholm, T., Larson, K., Andersson, M., Shehory, O., Tohmé, F.: Coalition structure generation with worst case guarantees. AI 111(1—2), 209–.238 (1999)

17. Wetzer, I.M., Zeelenberg, M., Pieters, R.: Never eat in that restaurant, i did!: Exploring why people engage in negative word-of-mouth communication. Psychology and Marketing 24(8), 661—680 (2007)

18. Wooldridge, M.: An Introduction to Multiagent Systems, 2. edn. Wiley (2009)

Chapter 26
On the logic of delegation: Relating theory and practice

Patrick Doherty and John-Jules Ch. Meyer

Abstract Research with collaborative robotic systems has much to gain by leveraging concepts and ideas from the areas of multi-agent systems and the social sciences. In this paper we propose an approach to formalizing and grounding important aspects of collaboration in a collaborative system shell for robotic systems. This is done primarily in terms of the concept of delegation, where delegation will be instantiated as a speech act. The formal characterization of the delegation speech act is based on a preformal theory of delegation proposed by Falcone and Castelfranchi. We show how the delegation speech act can in fact be used to formally ground an abstract characterization of delegation into a FIPA-compliant implementation in an agent-oriented language such as JADE, as part of a collaborative system shell for robotic systems. The collaborative system shell has been developed as a prototype and used in collaborative missions with multiple unmanned aerial vehicle systems.

1 Introduction

In the past decade, the Unmanned Aircraft Systems Technologies Lab[1] at the Department of Computer and Information Science, Linköping University, has been involved in the development of autonomous unmanned aerial vehicles (UAV's) and associated hardware and software technologies [10, 8, 9]. The size of our research platforms range from the RMAX helicopter system (100kg) [11, 34, 33, 27, 4] developed by Yamaha Motor Company, to smaller micro-size

Patrick Doherty
Department of Computer and Information Science, Linköping University, Sweden
e-mail: Patrick.Doherty@liu.se

John-Jules Ch. Meyer
Department of Information and Computing Sciences, University of Utrecht, The Netherlands
e-mail: jj@cs.uu.nl

[1] www.ida.liu.se/divisions/aiics/

Fig. 1 The UASTech RMAX (upper left), PingWing (upper right), LinkQuad (lower left) and LinkMAV (lower right).

rotor based systems such as the LinkQuad[2] (1kg) and LinkMAV [16, 28] (500g) in addition to a fixed wing platform, the PingWing [5] (500g). These UAV platforms are shown in Figure 1.The latter three have been designed and developed by the Unmanned Aircraft Systems Technologies Lab. All four platforms are fully autonomous and have been deployed.

More recently, our research efforts have transitioned toward the study of systems of UAV's. The accepted terminology for such systems is Unmanned Aircraft Systems (UAS's). A UAS may consist of one or more UAV's (possibly heterogenous) in addition to one or more ground operator systems (GOP's). We are interested in applications where UAV's are required to collaborate not only with each other but also with diverse human resources [13, 14, 22, 12, 24].

In the future, the practical use and acceptance of UAV's will have to be based on a verifiable, principled and well-defined interaction foundation between one or more human operators and one or more autonomous systems. In developing a principled framework for such complex interaction between UAV's and humans in complex scenarios, a great many interdependent conceptual and pragmatic issues arise and need clarification not only theoretically, but also pragmatically in the form of demonstrators.

The complexity of developing deployed architectures for realistic collaborative activities among robots that operate in the real world under time and space constraints is very high. We tackle this complexity by working both abstractly at a formal logical level and concretely at a systems building level.

---

[2] www.uastech.com

More importantly, the two approaches are related to each other by grounding the formal abstractions into actual software implementations. This guarantees the fidelity of the actual system to the formal specification. Bridging this conceptual gap robustly is an important area of research and given the complexity of the systems being built today demands new insights and techniques.

The conceptual basis for the proposed collaboration framework includes a triad of fundamental, interdependent conceptual issues: delegation, mixed-initiative interaction and adjustable autonomy (Figure 2). The concept of delegation is particularly important and in some sense provides a bridge between mixed-initiative interaction and adjustable autonomy.

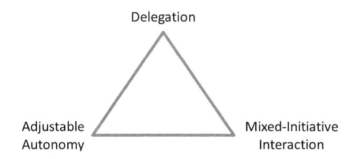

Fig. 2 A conceptual triad of concepts.

Delegation – In any mixed-initiative interaction, humans may request help from robotic systems and robotic systems may request help from humans. One can abstract and concisely model such requests as a form of delegation, *Delegate(A, B, task, constraints)*, where A is the delegating agent, B is the contractor, *task* is the task being delegated and consists of a goal and possibly a plan to achieve the goal, and *constraints* represents a context in which the request is made and the task should be carried out. In our framework, delegation is formalized as a speech act and the delegation process invoked can be recursive.

Adjustable Autonomy – In solving tasks in a mixed-initiative setting, the robotic system involved will have a potentially wide spectrum of autonomy, yet should only use as much autonomy as is required for a task and should not violate the degree of autonomy mandated by a human operator unless agreement is made. One can begin to develop a principled means of adjusting autonomy through the use of the *task* and *constraint* parameters in *Delegate(A, B, task, constraints)*. A task delegated with only a goal and no plan, with few constraints, allows the robot to use much of its autonomy in solving the task, whereas a task specified as a sequence of actions and many constraints allows only limited autonomy. It may even be the case that the delegator does not allow the contractor to recursively delegate.

Mixed-Initiative Interaction – By mixed-initiative, we mean that interaction and negotiation between a robotic system, such as a UAV and a human, will take advantage of each of their skills, capacities and knowledge in developing a mission plan, executing the plan and adapting to contingencies during the execution of the plan. Mixed-initiative interaction involves a very broad set of issues, both theoretical and pragmatic. One central part of such interaction is the ability of a ground operator (GOP) to be able to delegate tasks to a UAV, *Delegate(GOP, UAV, task, constraints)* and in a symmetric manner, the ability of a UAV to be able to delegate tasks to a GOP, *Delegate(UAV, GOP, task, constraints)*. Issues pertaining to safety, security, trust, etc., have to be dealt with in the interaction process and can be formalized as particular types of constraints associated with a delegated task.

1.1 Structure of the Paper

This paper is a contribution to a Festschrift for Cristiano Castelfranchi. The work of Cristiano Castelfranchi has touched upon many of the topics described in our conceptual triad. We show in this paper just how influential and pragmatically useful Cristiano's ideas about delegation are in the context of actual collaborative robotic systems.

The structure of the paper is as follows. In section 2, we review Falcone & Castelfranchi's notion of strong/strict delegation. KARO logic, described in section 2.1, is used as a basis for formalizing strong delegation as a speech act in section 2.2. In section 2.3, we show a means of instantiating the strong delegation speech act directly into the agent programming language 2APL. This is one alternative for an implementation of delegation using the agent programming language paradigm that has great potential. We then shift perspective somewhat and describe ongoing work associated with the development of a collaborative system shell for robotic systems being used in our unmanned aerial vehicle research. In section 3, we provide a brief overview of our JADE-based software architecture. In section 4, we then formally characterize tasks as task specification trees, providing both a syntax and semantics. In section 5, we show how the delegation speech act can be grounded in the software architecture in a principled manner through the use of a *Can()* predicate representing an agent's ability to achieve a task and the constraints associated with that task. This is done using a small example with collaborative unmanned aerial vehicles.

2 Strong delegation in the sense of Falcone & Castelfranchi

In this section we briefly review Falcone & Castelfranchi's notion of strong/strict delegation [1, 19]. This is a general human-inspired theory of (several forms of) delegation. It appears that this a very good starting point for our purposes. In particular their notions of *strong* or *strict* delegation with *open* and *closed* variants are appropriate in our setting.

Falcone & Castelfranchi's approach to delegation builds on a BDI model of agents, that is, agents having beliefs, goals, intentions, and plans. Falcone &

Castelfranchi do not give a formal semantics of their operators, but in order to get a better understanding we will use the BDI-based KARO logic ([30]) as the underlying framework. This will aid us to consider how to program a multi-agent system with delegation capability.

Falcone & Castelfranchi's preformal theory states the following about the act of strong delegation. It describes conditions that should hold before the act, both from the perspective of the sender and receiver as well as conditions that should hold afterwards, thus rendering a specification of the act of strong delegation:

"Potential for request of contract for τ (a task) from A (an agent) to B (an agent)":
From A's point of view:

- The achievement of τ is a goal of A
- A believes that an agent B exists that has the power of achieving τ
- A prefers to achieve through B

The last item means that "A believes to be dependent on B in the context of τ (or some broader goal)". We will come back to this in the sequel.
From B's point of view:

- B believes that B has the power of achieving τ

After the agreement:

- A series of mutual beliefs (more or less the above) +
- B is socially committed to A to achieve τ for A

Mutual beliefs after agreement:

- B believes that the achievement is a goal of A
- B believes that B has the power of achieving τ
- B intends to achieve τ (for A)
- The achievement of τ through B is a goal (?!) of A

Note that since this is a pre-formal theory there is some confusion regarding the BDI-like notions. The last item above talks about the achievement of the task by an agent being a *goal* of another agent. If the achievement is viewed as an action this cannot be a goal in the sense of a declarative goal (goal_to_be). In our formalization we will have to be more precise about this. We start by introducing KARO logic which will be the basis for a formalization.

2.1 KARO logic

The KARO formalism [30] is an amalgam of dynamic logic and epistemic / doxastic logic, augmented with several additional (modal) operators in order to deal with the motivational aspects of agents. KARO has operators for belief

($\mathbf{B}_A$), expressing that "agent A believes that"[3], and action ($[\alpha]$, "after the performance of α it holds that"). In this paper we also include 'agentified actions' of the kind $do_A(\alpha)$, meaning that agent A is performing action α, which may serve as an argument for the dynamic logic operator. We even allow nestings of do's: e.g., $do_A(do_B(\alpha))$ with interpretation: "the action of A making B do α." The belief operator $\mathbf{B}_A$ is assumed to satisfy the usual (positive and negative) introspection properties $\mathbf{B}_A\varphi \rightarrow \mathbf{B}_A\mathbf{B}_A\varphi$ and $\neg\mathbf{B}_A\varphi \rightarrow \mathbf{B}_A\neg\mathbf{B}_A\varphi$ (cf. [30, 31]). Furthermore, there are additional operators for ability ($\mathbf{A}_A$), desires ($\mathbf{D}_A$) and commitment ($\mathbf{Com}_A$):

- $\mathbf{A}_A\alpha$ expressing that agent A is able (has the capability) to perform action α.
- $\mathbf{D}_A\varphi$ expressing that agent A desires (a state described by formula) φ.
- $\mathbf{Com}_A(\alpha)$ expressing that A is committed to action ('plan') α (i.e. "having put it onto its agenda"). (This operator is very close to Cohen & Levesque's notion of $INTEND_1$ ("intention_to_do") [2]).

Furthermore, the following syntactic abbreviations serving as auxiliary operators are used:

- (dual) $\langle \alpha \rangle \varphi = \neg[\alpha]\neg\varphi$, expressing that the agent has the opportunity to perform α resulting in a state where φ holds.
- (opportunity) $\mathbf{O}_A\alpha = \langle do_A(\alpha) \rangle \top$, i.e., an agent has the opportunity to do an action iff there is a successor state.
- (practical possibility) $\mathbf{P}_A(\alpha, \varphi) = \mathbf{A}_A\alpha \wedge \mathbf{O}_A\alpha \wedge \langle do_A(\alpha) \rangle \varphi$, i.e., an agent has the practical possibility to do an action with result φ iff it is both able and has the opportunity to do that action and the result of actually doing that action leads to a state where φ holds;
- (can) $Can_A(\alpha, \varphi) = \mathbf{B}_A \, \mathbf{P}_A(\alpha, \varphi)$, i.e., an agent can do an action with a certain result iff it believes (it is 'aware') it has the practical possibility to do so;
- (realisability) $\Diamond_A\varphi = \exists a_1, \ldots, a_n \, \mathbf{P}_A(a_1; \ldots; a_n, \varphi)$, i.e., a state property φ is realisable by agent A iff there is a finite sequence of atomic actions of which the agent has the practical possibility to perform it with the result φ, i.e., if there is a 'plan' consisting of (a sequence of) atomic actions of which the agent has the practical possibility to do them with φ as a result.
- (goal) $\mathbf{G}_A\varphi = \neg\varphi \wedge \mathbf{D}_A\varphi \wedge \Diamond_A\varphi$, i.e., a goal is a formula that is not (yet) satisfied, but desired and realisable.
- (intend) $\mathbf{I}_A(\alpha, \varphi) = Can_A(\alpha, \varphi) \wedge \mathbf{B}_A\mathbf{G}_A\varphi$, i.e., an agent (possibly) intends an action with a certain result iff the agent can do the action with that result and it moreover believes that this result is one of its goals.

In order to formalize Falcone & Castelfranchi's notion of delegation we also need three additional operators:[4]

---

[3] In fact, we use a slightly simplified form of KARO which originally also contains a separate notion of knowledge.

[4] Here we deviate slightly from Falcone & Castelfranchi's presentation: instead of a dependency operator they employ a preference operator. However, the informal reading of this is based on a dependency relation, see the previous section, cf. [19], footnote 7). We take this relation as primitive here.

- $Dep(A,B,\tau)$, expressing that A is dependent on B for the performance of task τ
- $MutualBel_{AB}\varphi$, expressing that φ is mutual (or common) belief amongst agents A and B
- $SociallyCommited(B,A,\tau)$, expressing that B is socially committed to A to achieve τ for A, or that there is a *contract* between A and B concerning task τ.

We will not provide the formal semantics of this logic here, but refer to [30] for details.[5]

2.2 Falcone & Castelfranchi's notion of strong delegation formalized

For the formal specification, the definition provided by Falcone & Castelfranchi will be used. For the data-structure specification used in the implementation, task specification trees (TST's) will be defined in Section 4. Falcone & Castelfranchi define a task as a pair $\tau = (\alpha,\varphi)$ consisting of a goal φ, and a plan α for that goal, or rather, a plan and the goal associated with that plan. Conceptually, a plan is a composite action. We extend the definition of a task to a tuple $\tau = (\alpha,\varphi,cons)$, where *cons* represents additional constraints associated with the plan α, such as timing and resource constraints. At this level of abstraction, the definition of a task is purposely left general but will be dealt with in explicit detail in the implementation using TST's and constraints.

From the perspective of adjustable autonomy, the task definition is quite flexible. If α is a single elementary action with the goal φ implicit and correlated with the post-condition of the action, the contractor has little flexibility as to how the task will be achieved. On the other hand, if the goal φ is specified and the plan α is not provided, then the contractor has a great deal of flexibility in achieving the goal. There are many variations between these two extremes and these variations capture the different levels of autonomy and trust exchanged between two agents. These extremes loosely follow Falcone & Castelfranchi's notions of closed and open delegation described below.

Using KARO to formalize aspects of Falcone & Castelfranchi 's work, we consider a notion of *strong delegation* represented by a speech act S-Delegate(A, B, τ) of A delegating a task $\tau = (\alpha,\varphi,cons)$ to B, where α is a possible plan, φ is a goal, and *cons* is a set of constraints associated with the plan φ. Strong delegation means that the delegation is explicit, an agent explicitly delegates a task to another agent. It is specified as follows:

---

[5] Of course, this semantics should be extended to cater for e.g. the dependence and social commitment operators. The easiest way to do this is to use semantical functions associated with these operators yielding the extensions of the dependency and social commitment relation, respectively, per world (or, more appropriately in the KARO framework, per model-state pair). The mutual belief operator can be given semantics along the usual lines of common knowledge/belief operators such as given e.g. in [31, 32].

S-Delegate(A, B, τ), where $\tau = (\alpha, \varphi, cons)$

Preconditions:

(1) $\mathbf{G}_A(\varphi)$
(2) $\mathbf{B}_A Can_B(\tau)$ (Note that this implies $\mathbf{B}_A \mathbf{B}_B Can_B(\tau)$)
(3) $\mathbf{B}_A Dependent(A, B, \tau)$
(4) $\mathbf{B}_B Can_B(\tau)$

Postconditions:

(1) $\mathbf{G}_B(\varphi)$ and $\mathbf{B}_B \mathbf{G}_B(\varphi)$
(2) $\mathbf{Com}_B(\alpha)$ (also written $\mathbf{Com}_B(\tau)$)
(3) $\mathbf{B}_B \mathbf{G}_A(\varphi)$
(4) $Can_B(\tau)$ (and hence $\mathbf{B}_B Can_B(\tau)$, and by (1) also $\mathbf{I}_B(\tau)$)
(5) $\mathbf{I}_A(do_B(\alpha))$
(6) $MutualBel_{AB}$("the statements above" $\wedge$ $SociallyCommitted(B, A, \tau)$)

Informally speaking this expresses the following: the preconditions of the delegate act of A delegating task τ to B are that (1) φ is a goal of delegator A (2) A believes that B can (is able to) perform the task τ (which implies that A believes that B itself believes that it can do the task) (3) A believes that with respect to the task τ it is dependent on B. The speech act S-Delegate is a communication command and can be viewed as a request for a synchronization (a "handshake") between sender and receiver. Of course, this can only be successful if the receiver also believes it can do the task, which is expressed by (4).

The postconditions of the strong delegation act mean: (1) B has φ as its goal and is aware of this (2) it is committed to the task τ (3) B believes that A has the goal φ (4) B can do the task τ (and hence believes it can do it, and furthermore it holds that B intends to do the task, which was a separate condition in Falcone & Castelfranchi's formalization), (5) A intends that B performs α (so we have formalized the notion of a goal to have an achievement in Falcone & Castelfranchi's informal theory to an intention to perform a task) and (6) there is a mutual belief between A and B that all preconditions and other postconditions mentioned hold, as well as that there is a contract between A and B, i.e. B is socially committed to A to achieve τ for A. In this situation we will call agent A the *delegator* and B the *contractor*.

Typically a social commitment (contract) between two agents induces obligations to the partners involved, depending on how the task is specified in the delegation action. This dimension has to be added in order to consider how the contract affects the autonomy of the agents, in particular the contractor's autonomy. Falcone & Castelfranchi discuss the following variants:

• Closed delegation: the task is completely specified and both the goal and the plan should be adhered to.
• Open delegation: the task is not completely specified, either only the goal has to be adhered to while the plan may be chosen by the contractor, or the specified plan contains abstract actions that need further elaboration (a sub-plan) to be dealt with by the contractor.

In open delegation the contractor may have some freedom in how to perform the delegated task, and thus it provides a large degree of flexibility in multi-agent planning and allows for truly distributed planning.

The specification of the delegation act above is based on closed delegation. In case of open delegation, α in the postconditions can be replaced by an α', and τ by $\tau' = (\alpha', \varphi, cons')$. Note that the fourth clause, $Can_B(\tau')$, now implies that α' is indeed believed to be an alternative for achieving φ, since it implies that $\mathbf{B}_B[\alpha']\varphi$ (B believes that φ is true after α' is executed). Of course, in the delegation process, A must agree that α', together with constraints $cons'$, is indeed viable. This would depend on what degree of autonomy is allowed.

This particular specification of delegation follows Falcone & Castelfranchi closely. One can easily foresee other constraints one might add or relax in respect to the basic specification resulting in other variants of delegation [3, 6, 15]. It is important to keep in mind that this formal characterization of delegation is not completely hierarchical. There is interaction between both the delegators and contractors as to how goals can best be achieved given the constraints of the agents involved. This is implicit in the formal characterization of open delegation above, although the process is not made explicit. This aspect of the process will become much clearer when the implementation is described.

2.3 Strong delegation in agent programming

When devising a system like the one we have in mind for our scenario, we need programming concepts that support delegation and in particular the open variant of delegation. In the setting of an agent programming language such as 2APL [7], we may use plan generation rules to establish a contract between two agents. Very briefly, a 2APL agent has a belief base, a goal base, a plan base, a set of capabilities (basic actions it can perform), and sets of rules to change its bases: PG rules, PR rules and PC rules. PG-rules have the form $\gamma \leftarrow \beta \mid \pi$, meaning that if the agent has goal γ and belief β then it may generate plan π and put it in its plan base. PR rules can be used to repair plans if execution of the plan fails: they are of the form $\pi \leftarrow \beta \mid \pi'$, meaning that if π is the current plan (which is failing), and the agent believes β then it may revise π into π'. PC-rules are rules for defining macros and recursive computations. (We will not specify them here.)

The act of strong delegation can now be programmed in 2APL by providing the delegator with a rule

$$\varphi \leftarrow Can_B(\tau) \wedge Dep(A, B, \tau) \mid SDelegate(A, B, \tau)$$

(where $\tau = (\alpha, \varphi)$), which means that the delegation act may be generated by delegator A exactly when the preconditions that we described earlier are met. The action $SDelegate(A, B, \tau)$ is a communication action requesting to adapt the goal and belief bases of B according to the KARO specification given earlier, and should thus, when successful (depending on the additional assumption that B believes he can perform τ) result in a state prescribed by the postconditions of SDelegate. In particular this yields a state where contractor B has φ in its goal base, $\mathbf{G}_A\varphi$, $Can_B(\tau)$ an $MutualBel('contract')$ in its belief base, and plan α in its plan base. That is to say, in the case of a closed delegation specification. If the specification is an open delegation, it instead will have an alternative plan α' in its plan base and a belief $Can_B(\alpha', \varphi)$ in its belief base. It is very important to note that in the case of such a concrete setting of an agent programmed in a language such as 2APL, we may provide the Can-predicate with a more concrete interpretation: $Can_B(\alpha, \varphi)$ is true if (either φ is in its goal base and α is in its plan base already, or) B has a PG-rule of the form $\varphi \leftarrow \beta \mid \alpha'$ for some β that follows from B's belief base, and the agent has the resources available for executing plan α. This would be a concrete interpretation of the condition that the agent has the ability as well as the opportunity to execute the plan!

2.4 Further issues

Regarding delegation of tasks to contractors in the framework described so far, there are a number of further issues that are interesting and also necessary for putting it to practice. The first has to do with transfer of delegation: are agents always allowed to transfer delegation further on to other agents? The answer is dependent on the application, and this should be specified as a parameter in the delegation speech act (and resulting contract). Another important question is what happens if the delegated task fails. Is the contractor allowed to repair the task (by plan repair, in 2APL: using PR-rules) on its own, or must this be reported back (and ask permission to repair the plan) to the delegator first? This has to do to what degree the delegation is specified as open. If it is open in the sense that the contractor gets a goal and may devise a plan himself, then it stands to reason that he may also repair/revise the plan if it fails. If one wants that the contractor reports back and asks for PR permission, this can be handled in 2APL by a PR rule of the form

$$\pi \leftarrow \beta \mid send(A, request, permission\text{-}to\text{-}repair(\pi))$$

that is triggered by an event signaling the failure of plan π. Delegator A will have a rule for handling this message, and the contractor B will need a (PC-)rule that handles the reply from the delegator, resulting in the contractor proceeding with the plan repair if the permission has been granted. Thus, in this case all plan repair rules are in this case split into two rules, one to ask permission and the other to perform the plan repair in case permission is granted.

3 Delegation-Based Software Architecture Overview

In a parallel research track, we are developing a collaborative system shell for robotic systems where the concept of delegation as described by the S-Delegate speech act is central to the architecture. Before going into details regarding the implementation of the delegation process and its grounding in the proposed software architecture, we provide an overview of the architecture itself.

Our RMAX helicopters use a CORBA-based distributed architecture [11]. For our experimentation with collaborative UAV's, we view this as a legacy system which provides sophisticated functionality ranging from control modes to reactive processes, in addition to deliberative capabilities such as automated planners, GIS systems, constraint solvers, etc. Legacy robotic architectures generally lack instantiations of an agent metaphor although implicitly one often views such systems as agents. Rather than re-design the legacy system from scratch, the approach we take is to agentify the existing legacy system in a straightforward manner by adding an additional agent layer which interfaces to the legacy system. The agent layer for a robotic system consists of one or more agents which offer specific functionalities or services. These agents can communicate with each other internally and leverage existing legacy system functionality. Agents from different robotic systems can also communicate with each other if required.

Our collaborative architectural specification is based on the use of the FIPA (Foundation for Intelligent Physical Agents) Abstract Architecture [20]. The FIPA Abstract Architecture provides the basic components for the development of a multi-agent system. Our prototype implementation is based on the FIPA compliant Java Agent Development Framework (JADE) [29, 17] which implements the abstract architecture. "JADE (Java Agent Development Framework) is a software environment to build agent systems for the management of networked information resources in compliance with the FIPA specifications for interoperable multi-agent systems." [18].

The FIPA Abstract Architecture provides the following fundamental modules:

- An Agent Directory module keeps track of the agents in the system.
- A Directory Facilitator keeps track of the services provided by those agents.
- A Message Transport System module allows agents to communicate using the FIPA Agent Communication Language (FIPA ACL) [21].

The relevant concepts in the FIPA Abstract Architecture are agents, services and protocols. All communication between agents is based on exchanging messages which represent speech acts encoded in an agent communication language (FIPA ACL). Services provide functional support for agents. There are a number of standard global services including agent-directory services, message-transport services and a service-directory service. A protocol is a related set of messages between agents that are logically related by some interaction pattern.

JADE provides base classes for agents, message transportation, and a behavior model for describing the content of agent control loops. Using the behavior model, different agent behaviors can be constructed, such as cyclic, one-shot (executed once), sequential, and parallel behavior. More complex behaviors can be constructed using the basic behaviors as building blocks.

From our perspective, each JADE *agent* has associated with it a set of *services*. Services are accessed through the Directory Facilitator and are generally implemented as behaviors. In our case, the communication language used by agents will be FIPA ACL which is speech act based. Specification of new protocols to support the delegation and other processes are found in [25].

The purpose of the Agent Layer is to provide a common interface for collaboration. This interface should allow the delegation and task execution processes to be implemented without regard to the actual realization of elementary tasks, capabilities and resources which are specific to the legacy platforms.

We are currently using four agents in the agent layer:

1. **Interface agent** - This agent is the clearinghouse for communication. All requests for delegation and other types of communication pass through this agent. Externally, it provides the interface to a specific robotic system or ground control station.
2. **Delegation agent**- The delegation agent coordinates delegation requests to and from other UAV systems and ground control stations, with the Executor, Resource and Interface agents. It does this essentially by verifying that the pre-conditions to a *Delegate()* request are satisfied.
3. **Execution agent** - After a task is contracted to a particular UAV or ground station operator, it must eventually execute that task relative to the constraints associated with it. The Executor agent coordinates this execution process.
4. **Resource agent** - The Resource agent determines whether the UAV or ground station of which it is part has the resources and ability to actually do a task as a potential contractor. Such a determination may include the invocation of schedulers, planners and constraint solvers in order to determine this.

Figure 3 provides an overview of an agentified robotic or ground operator system.

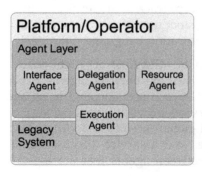

Fig. 3 Overview of an agentified platform or ground control station.

The FIPA Abstract Architecture is extended to support delegation and collaboration by defining an additional set of services and a set of related protocols [25].The interface agent, resource agent and delegation agent have an
interface service, resource service and delegation service associated with it,
respectively, on each individual robotic or ground station platform. The executor service is implemented as a non-JADE agent that understands FIPA
protocols and works as a gateway to a platform's legacy system. Additionally,
three protocols, the Capability-Lookup, Delegation and Auction protocols, are
defined and used to drive the delegation process [25].

Human operators interacting with robotic systems are treated similarly by
extending the control station or user interface functionality in the same way. In
this case, the control station is the legacy system and an agent layer is added to
this. The result is a collaborative human robot system consisting of a number
of human operators and robotic platforms each having both a legacy system
and an agent layer as shown in Figure 4.

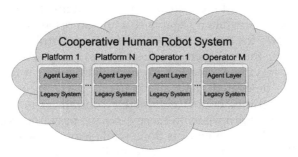

Fig. 4 An overview of the collaborative human robot system.

The reason for using the FIPA Abstract Architecture and JADE is pragmatic.
The focus of our research is not to develop new agent middleware, but to
develop a formally grounded generic collaborative system shell for robotic
systems. Our formal characterization of the *Delegate()* operator is as a speech
act. We also use speech acts as an agent communication language and JADE
provides a straightforward means for integrating the FIPA ACL language
which supports speech acts with our existing systems.

Further details as to how the delegation and related processes are implemented based on additional services and protocols can be found in [25]. For
the purposes of this paper, we focus on the formal characterization of Tasks in
the form of Task Specification Trees.

4 Task Specification Trees

Both the declarative and procedural representation and semantics of tasks are
central to the delegation process. The relation between the two representations
is also essential if one has the goal of formally grounding the delegation pro-

cess in the system implementation. A task was previously defined abstractly as a tuple $(\alpha, \varphi, cons)$ consisting of a composite action α, a goal φ and a set of constraints *cons*, associated with α. In this section, we introduce a formal task specification language which allows us to represent tasks as *Task Specification Trees* (TST's). The task specification trees map directly to procedural representations in our proposed system implementation.

For our purposes, the task representation must be highly flexible, sharable, dynamically extendible, and distributed in nature. Tasks need to be delegated at varying levels of abstraction and also expanded and modified because parts of complex tasks can be recursively delegated to different robotic agents which are in turn expanded or modified. Consequently, the structure must also be distributable. Additionally, a task structure is a form of compromise between an explicit plan in a plan library at one end of the spectrum and a plan generated through an automated planner [23] at the other end of the spectrum. The task representation and semantics must seamlessly accommodate plan representations and their compilation into the task structure. Finally, the task representation should support the adjustment of autonomy through the addition of constraints or parameters by agents and human resources.

The flexibility allows for the use of both central and distributed planning, and also to move along the scale between these two extremes. At one extreme, the operator plans everything, creating a central plan, while at the other extreme the agents are delegated goals and generate parts of the distributed plan themselves. Sometimes neither completely centralized nor completely distributed planning is appropriate. In those cases the operator would like to retain some control of how the work is done while leaving the details to the agents. Task Specification Trees provide a formalism that captures the scale from one extreme to the next. This allows the operator to specify the task at the point which fits the current mission and environment.

The task specification formalism should allow for the specification of various types of task compositions, including sequential and concurrent, in addition to more general constructs such as loops and conditionals. The task specification should also provide a clear separation between tasks and platform specific details for handling the tasks. The specification should focus on what should be done and hide the details about how it could be done by different platforms.

In the general case, A TST is a declarative representation of a complex multi-agent task. In the architecture realizing the delegation framework a TST is also a distributed data structure. Each node in a TST corresponds to a task that should be performed. There are six types of nodes: sequence, concurrent, loop, select, goal, and elementary action. All nodes are directly executable except goal nodes which require some form of expansion or planning to generate a plan for achieving the goal.

Each node has a *node interface* containing a set of parameters, called *node parameters*, that can be specified for the node. The node interface always contains a platform assignment parameter and parameters for the start and end times of the task, usually denoted P, T_S and T_E, respectively. These parameters can be part of the constraints associated with the node called *node constraints*.

A TST also has *tree constraints*, expressing precedence and organizational relations between the nodes in the TST. Together the constraints form a constraint network covering the TST. In fact, the node parameters function as constraint variables in a constraint network, and setting the value of a node parameter constrains not only the network, but implicitly, the degree of autonomy of an agent.

4.1 TST Syntax

The syntax of a TST specification has the following BNF:

```
SPEC ::= TST
TST ::= NAME ('(' VARS ')')? '=' (with VARS)? TASK (where CONS)?
TSTS ::= TST | TST ';' TSTS
TASK ::= ACTION | GOAL | (NAME '=')? NAME ('(' ARGS ')')? |
         while COND TST | if COND then TST else TST |
         sequence TSTS | concurrent TSTS
VAR ::= <variable name> | <variable name> '.' <variable name>
VARS ::= VAR | VAR ',' VARS
CONSTRAINT ::= <constraint>
CONS ::= CONSTRAINT | CONSTRAINT and CONS
ARG ::= VAR | VALUE
ARGS ::= ARG | ARG ',' ARGS
VALUE ::= <value>
NAME ::= <node name>
COND ::= <ACL query>
GOAL ::= <goal statement>
ACTION ::= <elementary action>
```

Where

- <ACL query> is a FIPA ACL query message requesting the value of a boolean expression.
- <elementary action> is an elementary action $name(p_0, ..., p_N)$, where $p_0, ..., p_N$ are parameters.
- <goal statement> is a goal $name(p_0, ..., p_N)$, where $p_0, ..., p_N$ are parameters.

The TST clause in the BNF introduces the main recursive pattern in the specification language. The right hand side of the equality provides the general pattern of providing a variable context for a task (using **with**) and a set of constraints (using **where**) which may include the variables previously introduced.

Example

Consider a small scenario where the mission is to first scan $Area_A$ and $Area_B$, and then fly to $Dest_4$ (Figure 5). A TST describing this mission is shown

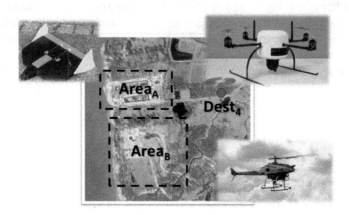

Fig. 5 Example mission of first scanning Area$_A$ and Area$_B$, and then fly to Dest$_4$.

in Figure 6. Nodes N_0 and N_1 are composite action nodes, sequential and concurrent, respectively. Nodes N_2, N_3 and N_4 are elementary action nodes. Each node specifies a task and has a node interface containing node parameters and a platform assignment variable. In this case only temporal parameters are shown representing the respective intervals a task should be completed in.

In the TST depicted in Figure 6. The nodes N_0 to N_4 have the task names τ_0 to τ_4 associated with them respectively. This TST contains two composite actions, *sequence* (τ_0) and *concurrent* (τ_1) and three elementary actions *scan* (τ_2, τ_3) and *flyto* (τ_4). The resulting TST specification is:

$\tau_0(T_{S_0},T_{E_0}) =$
  with $T_{S_1},T_{E_1},T_{S_4},T_{E_4}$ **sequence**
    $\tau_1(T_{S_1},T_{E_1}) =$
      with $T_{S_2},T_{E_2},T_{S_3},T_{E_3}$ **concurrent**
        $\tau_2(T_{S_2},T_{E_2}) = \text{scan}(T_{S_2},T_{E_2},Speed_2,Area_A);$
        $\tau_3(T_{S_3},T_{E_3}) = \text{scan}(T_{S_3},T_{E_3},Speed_3,Area_B)$
      where $cons_{\tau_1}$;
    $\tau_4(T_{S_4},T_{E_4}) = \text{flyto}(T_{S_4},T_{E_4},Speed_4,Dest_4)$
  where $cons_{\tau_0}$

$cons_{\tau_0} = \{T_{S_0} \leq T_{S_1} \wedge T_{S_1} \leq T_{E_1} \wedge T_{E_1} \leq T_{S_4} \wedge T_{S_4} \leq T_{E_4} \wedge T_{E_4} \leq T_{E_0}\}$
$cons_{\tau_1} = \{T_{S_1} \leq T_{S_2} \wedge T_{S_2} \leq T_{E_2} \wedge T_{E_2} \leq T_{E_1} \wedge T_{S_1} \leq T_{S_3} \wedge T_{S_3} \leq T_{E_3} \wedge T_{E_3} \leq T_{E_1}\}$

4.2 TST Semantics

A TST specifies a complex task (composite action) under a set of tree-specific and node-specific constraints which together are intended to represent the context in which a task should be executed in order to meet the task's intrinsic requirements, in addition to contingent requirements demanded by a

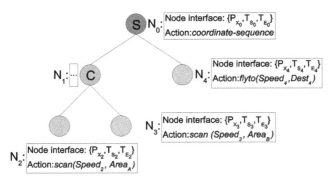

Fig. 6 A TST for the mission in Figure 5.

particular mission. The leaf nodes of a TST represent elementary actions used in the definition of the composite action the TST represents and the non-leaf nodes essentially represent control structures for the ordering and execution of the elementary actions. The semantic meaning of non-leaf nodes is essentially application independent, whereas the semantic meaning of the leaf nodes are highly domain dependent. They represent the specific actions or processes that an agent will in fact execute. The procedural correlate of a TST is a program.

During the delegation process, a TST is either provided or generated to achieve a specific set of goals, and if the delegation process is successful, each node is associated with an agent responsible for the execution of that node.

Informally, the semantics of a TST node will be characterized in terms of whether an agent believes it *can* successfully execute the task associated with the node in a given context represented by constraints, given its capabilities and resources. This can only be a belief because the task will be executed in the future and even under the best of conditions, real-world contingencies may arise which prevent the agent from successfully completing the task. The semantics of a TST will be the aggregation of the semantics for each individual node in the tree.

The formal semantics for TST nodes will be given in terms of the logical predicate $Can()$ which we have used previously in the formal definition of the S-Delegate speech act, although in this case, we will add additional arguments. This is not a coincidence since our goal is to ground the formal specification of the S-Delegate speech act into the implementation in a very direct manner.

Recall that in the formal semantics for the speech act S-Delegate described in Section 2.2, the logical predicate $Can_X(\tau)$ is used to state that an agent X has the capabilities and resources to achieve task τ.

An important precondition for the successful application of the speech act is that the delegator (A) believes in the contractor's (B) ability to achieve the task τ, (2): $\mathbf{B}_A Can_B(\tau)$. Additionally, an important result of the successful application of the speech act is that the contractor actually has the capabilities and resources to achieve the task τ, (4): $Can_B(\tau)$. In order to directly couple the semantic characterization of the S-Delegate speech act to the semantic characterization of TST's, we will assume that a task $\tau = (\alpha, \varphi, cons)$ in the speech act characterization corresponds to a TST. Additionally, the TST semantics will be characterized in terms of a *Can* predicate with additional parameters to incorporate constraints explicitly.

In this case, the *Can* predicate is extended to include as arguments a list $[p_1, \ldots, p_k]$ denoting all node parameters in the node interface together with other parameters provided in the (**with** VARS) construct[6] and an argument for an additional constraint set *cons* provided in the (**where** CONS) construct.[7] Observe that *cons* can be formed incrementally and may in fact contain constraints inherited or passed to it through a recursive delegation process. The formula $Can(B, \tau, [t_s, t_e, \ldots], cons)$[8] then asserts that an agent B has the capabilities and resources for achieving task τ if *cons*, which also contains node constraints for τ, is consistent. The temporal variables t_s and t_e associated with the task τ are part of the node interface which may also contain other variables which are often related to the constraints in *cons*.

Determining whether a fully instantiated TST satisfies its specification, will now be equivalent to the successful solution of a constraint problem in the formal logical sense. The constraint problem in fact provides the formal semantics for a TST. Constraints associated with a TST are derived from a reduction process associated with the *Can*() predicate for each node in the TST. The generation and solution of constraints will occur on-line during the delegation process. Let us provide some more specific details. In particular, we will show the very tight coupling between the TST's and their logical semantics.

The basic structure of a Task Specification Tree is:

TST ::= NAME ('(' VARS$_1$ ')')? '=' (**with** VARS$_2$)? TASK (**where** CONS)?

where VARS$_1$ denotes node parameters, VARS$_2$ denotes additional variables used in the constraint context for a TST node, and CONS denotes the constraints associated with a TST node. Additionally, TASK denotes the specific type of TST node. In specifying a logical semantics for a TST node, we would like to map these arguments directly over to arguments of the predicate *Can*(). Informally, an abstraction of the mapping is

$$Can(agent_1, TASK, VARS_1 \cup VARS_2, CONS) \tag{1}$$

The idea is that for any fully allocated TST, the meaning of each allocated TST node in the tree is the meaning of the associated *Can*() predicate instantiated with the TST specific parameters and constraints. The meaning of the instantiated *Can*() predicate can then be associated with an equivalent constraint satisfaction problem (CSP) which turns out to be true or false dependent upon

---

[6] For reasons of clarity, we only list the node parameters for the start and end times for a task, $[t_s, t_e, \ldots]$, in this article.

[7] For pedagogical expediency, we can assume that there is a constraint language which is reified in the logic and is used in the CONS constructs.

[8] Note that we originally defined $\tau = (\alpha, \varphi, cons)$ as a tuple consisting of a plan, a goal and a set of constraints for reasons of abstraction when defining the delegation speech act. Since we now want to explicitly use *cons* as an argument to the *Can* predicate in the implementation, we revert to defining $\tau = (\alpha, \varphi)$ as a pair instead, where the constraints *cons* are lifted up as an argument to *Can*.

whether that CSP can be satisfied or not. The meaning of the fully allocated TST is then the aggregation of the meanings of each individual TST node associated with the TST, in other words, a conjunction of CSP's.

One would also like to capture the meaning of partial TST's. The idea is that as the delegation process unfolds, a TST is incrementally expanded with additional TST nodes. At each step, a partial TST may contain a number of fully expanded and allocated nodes in addition to other nodes which remain to be delegated. In order to capture this process semantically, one extends the semantics by providing meaning for an unallocated TST node in terms of both a *Can*() predicate and a *Delegate*() predicate:

$$\exists agent_2\, Delegate(agent_1, agent_2, TASK, VARS_1 \cup VARS_2, CONS) \qquad (2)$$

Either $agent_1$ can achieve a task, or (exclusively) it can find an agent, $agent_2$, to which the task can be delegated. In fact, it may need to find one or more agents if the task to be delegated is a composite action.

Given the $S\text{-}Delegate(agent_1, agent_2, TASK)$ speech act semantics, we know that if delegation is successful then as one of the postconditions of the speech act, $agent_2$ can in fact achieve $TASK$ (assuming no additional contingencies):

$$Delegate(agent_1, \mathsf{agent_2}, TASK, VARS_1 \cup VARS_2, CONS) \qquad (3)$$
$$\rightarrow Can(\mathsf{agent_2}, TASK, VARS_1 \cup VARS_2, CONS)$$

Consequently, during the computational process associated with delegation, as the TST expands through delegation where previously unallocated nodes become allocated, each instance of the *Delegate*() predicate associated with an unallocated node is replaced with an instance of the *Can*() predicate. This recursive process preserves the meaning of a TST as a conjunction of instances of the *Can*() predicate which in turn are compiled into a (interdependent) set of CSPs and which are checked for satisfaction using distributed constraint solving algorithms.

Sequence Node

- In a *sequence node*, the child nodes should be executed in sequence (from left to right) during the execution time of the sequence node.
- $Can(B, S(\alpha_1, ..., \alpha_n), [t_s, t_e, ...], cons) \leftrightarrow$
  $\exists t_1, ..., t_{2n}, ... \bigwedge_{k=1}^{n}[(Can(B, \alpha_k, [t_{2k-1}, t_{2k}, ...], cons_k)$
  $\qquad\qquad \vee \exists a_k Delegate(B, a_k, \alpha_k, [t_{2k-1}, t_{2k}, ...], cons_k))]$
  $\qquad \wedge consistent(cons)^9$
- $cons = \{t_s \leq t_1 \wedge (\bigwedge_{i=1}^{n} t_{2i-1} < t_{2i}) \wedge (\bigwedge_{i=1}^{n-1} t_{2i} \leq t_{2i+1}) \wedge t_{2n} \leq t_e\} \cup cons'^{10}$

---

[9] The predicate *consistent*() has the standard logical meaning and checking for consistency would be done through a call to a constraint solver which is part of the architecture.

[10] In addition to the temporal constraints, other constraints may be passed recursively during the delegation process. *cons'* represents these constraints.

Concurrent Node

- In a *concurrent node* each child node should be executed during the time interval of the concurrent node.
- $Can(B, C(\alpha_1, ..., \alpha_n), [t_s, t_e, ...], cons) \leftrightarrow$
  $\exists t_1, ..., t_{2n}, ... \bigwedge_{k=1}^n [(Can(B, \alpha_k, [t_{2k-1}, t_{2k}, ...], cons_k)$
  $\qquad\qquad\qquad \vee \exists a_k Delegate(B, a_k, \alpha_k, [t_{2k-1}, t_{2k}, ...], cons_k))]$
  $\qquad\quad \wedge consistent(cons)$
- $cons = \{\bigwedge_{i=1}^n t_s \leq t_{2i-1} < t_{2i} \leq t_e\} \cup cons'$

Selector Node

- Compared to a sequence or concurrent node, only one of the *selector node*'s children will be executed, which one is determined by a test condition in the selector node. The child node should be executed during the time interval of the selector node. A selector node is used to postpone a choice which can not be known when the TST is specified. When expanded at runtime, the net result can be any of the legal node types.

Loop Node

- A *loop node* will add a child node for each iteration the loop condition allows. In this way the loop node works as a sequence node but with an increasing number of child nodes which are dynamically added. Loop nodes are similar to selector nodes, they describe additions to the TST that can not be known when the TST is specified. When expanded at runtime, the net result is a sequence node.

Goal

- A *goal node* is a leaf node which can not be directly executed. Instead it has to be expanded by using an automated planner or related planning functionality. After expansion, a TST branch representing the generated plan is added to the original TST.
- $Can(B, Goal(\varphi), [t_s, t_e, ...], cons) \leftrightarrow$
  $\exists a \, (GeneratePlan(B, \alpha, \varphi, [t_s, t_e, ...], cons) \wedge Can(B, \alpha, [t_s, t_e, ...], cons))$
  $\wedge consistent(cons)$

Observe that the agent B can generate a partial or complete plan α and then further delegate execution or completion of the plan recursively via the $Can()$ statement in the second conjunct.

Elementary Action Node

- An *elementary action node* specifies a domain-dependent action. An elementary action node is a leaf node.
- $Can(B,\tau,[t_s,t_e,\ldots],cons) \leftrightarrow$
  $Capabilities(B,\tau,[t_s,t_e,\ldots],cons) \wedge Resources(B,\tau,[t_s,t_e,\ldots],cons)$
  $\wedge consistent(cons)$

There are two parts to the definition of *Can* for an elementary action node. These are defined in terms of a *platform specification* which is assumed to exist for each agent potentially involved in a collaborative mission. The platform specification has two components.

The first, specified by the predicate $Capabilities(B,\tau,[t_s,t_e],cons)$ is intended to characterize all static capabilities associated with platform B that are required as capabilities for the successful execution of τ. These will include a list of tasks and/or services the platform is capable of carrying out. If platform B has the necessary static capabilities for executing task τ in the interval $[t_s,t_e]$ with constraints *cons*, then this predicate will be true.

The second, specified by the predicate $Resources(B,\tau,[t_s,t_e],cons)$ are intended to characterize dynamic resources such as fuel and battery power, which are consumable, or cameras and other sensors which are borrowable. Since resources generally vary through time, the semantic meaning of the predicate is temporally dependent.

Resources for an agent are represented as a set of parameterized resource constraint predicates, one per task. The parameters to the predicate are the task's parameters, in addition to the start time and the end time for the task. For example, assume there is a task $flyto(dest,speed)$. The resource constraint predicate for this task would be $flyto(t_s,t_e,dest,speed)$. The resource constraint predicate is defined as a conjunction of constraints, in the logical sense. The general pattern for this conjunction is:

$t_e = t_s + F, C_1, \ldots, C_N$, where

- F is a function of the resource constraint parameters and possibly local resource variables and
- $C_1, \ldots, C_N$ is a possibly empty set of additional constraints related to the resource model associated with the task.

Example

As an example, consider the task $flyto(dest,speed)$ with the corresponding resource constraint predicate $flyto(t_s,t_e,dest,speed)$. The constraint model associated with the task for a particular platform P_1 might be:

$$t_e = t_s + \frac{distance(pos(t_s,P_1),dest)}{speed} \wedge (Speed_{Min} \le speed \le Speed_{Max})$$

Depending on the platform, this constraint model may be different for the same task. In that sense, it is platform dependent.

5 Allocating Tasks in a TST to Platforms

Given a TST representing a complex task, an important problem is to find a set of platforms that can execute these tasks according to the TST specification. The problem is to allocate tasks to platforms and assign values to parameters such that each task can be carried out by its assigned platform and all the constraints of the TST are satisfied.

For a platform to be able to carry out a task, it must have the capabilities and the resources required for the task as described in the previous section. A platform that can be assigned a task in a TST is called a *candidate* and a set of candidates is a *candidate group*. The capabilities of a platform are fixed while the available resources will vary depending on its commitments, including the tasks it has already been allocated. These commitments are generally represented in the constraint stores and schedulers of the platforms in question. The resources and the commitments are modeled with constraints. Resources are represented by variables and commitments by constraints. These constraints are local to the platform and different platforms may have different constraints for the same action. Figure 7 shows the constraints for the scan action for platform P_1.

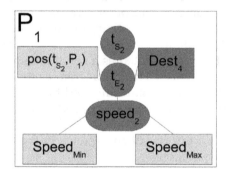

Fig. 7 The parameterized platform constraints for the scan action. The red/dark variables represent node parameters in the node interface. The gray variables represent local variables associated with the platform P1's constraint model for the scan action. These are connected through dependencies.

When a platform is assigned an action node in a TST, the constraints associated with that action are instantiated and added to the constraint store of the platform. The platform constraints defined in the constraint model for the task are connected to the constraint problem defined by the TST via the node parameters in the node interface for the action node. Figure 8 shows the constraint network after allocating node N_2 from the TST in Figure 6 (on page 495) to platform P_1.

A platform can be allocated to more than one node. This may introduce implicit dependencies between actions since each allocation adds constraints to the constraint store of the platform. For example, there could be a shared resource that both actions use. Figure 9 shows the constraint network of platform P_1 after it has been allocated nodes N_2 and N_4 from the example TST.

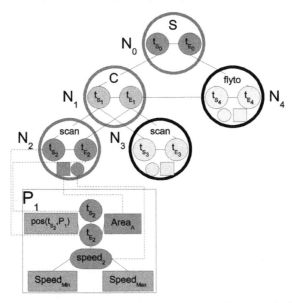

Fig. 8 The combined constraint problem after allocating node N_2 to platform P_1.

In this example the position of the platform is implicitly shared since the first action will change the location of the platform.

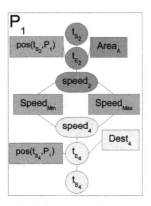

Fig. 9 The parameter constraints of platform P_1 when allocated node N_2 and N_4.

A *complete allocation* is an allocation which allocates every node in a TST to a platform. A completely allocated TST defines a constraint problem that represents all the constraints for this particular allocation of the TST. As the constraints are distributed among the platforms it is in effect a distributed constraint problem. If a consistent solution for this constraint problem is found then a *valid allocation* has been found and verified. Each such solution can be seen as a potential execution schedule of the TST. The consistency of an allocation can be checked by a distributed constraint satisfaction problem (DCSP) solver such as the Asynchronous Weak Commitment Search (AWCS) algorithm [35] or ADOPT [26].

5.1 Example

The constraint problem for a TST is derived by recursively reducing the *Can* predicate statements associated with each task node with formally equivalent expressions, beginning with the top-node τ_0 until the logical statements reduce to a constraint network. Below, we show the reduction of the TST from Figure 6 (on page 495) when there are three platforms, P_0, P_1 and P_2, with the appropriate capabilities. P_0 has been delegated the composite actions τ_0 and τ_1. P_0 has recursively delegated parts of these tasks to P_1 (τ_2 and τ_4) and $P_2(\tau_3)$.

$$Can(P_0, \alpha_0, [t_{s_0}, t_{e_0}], cons) = Can(P_0, S(\alpha_1, \alpha_4), [t_{s_0}, t_{e_0}], cons) \leftrightarrow$$
$$\exists t_{s_1}, t_{e_1}, t_{s_4}, t_{e_4}(Can(P_0, \alpha_1, [t_{s_1}, t_{e_1}], cons_{P_0})$$
$$\vee \exists a_1 Delegate(P_0, a_1, \alpha_1, [t_{s_1}, t_{e_1}], cons_{P_0}))$$
$$\wedge (Can(P_0, \alpha_4, [t_{s_4}, t_{e_4}], cons_{P_0})$$
$$\vee \exists a_2 Delegate(P_0, a_2, \alpha_4, [t_{s_4}, t_{e_4}], cons_{P_0}))$$

Let's continue with a reduction of the 1st element in the sequence α_1 (the 1st conjunct in the previous formula on the right-hand side of the biconditional):

$$Can(P_0, \alpha_1, [t_{s_1}, t_{e_1}], cons_{P_0})$$
$$\vee \exists a_1(Delegate(P_0, a_1, \alpha_1, [t_{s_1}, t_{e_1}], cons_{P_0}))$$

Since P_0 has been allocated α_1, the 2nd disjunct is false.

$$Can(P_0, \alpha_1, [t_{s_1}, t_{e_1}], cons_{P_0}) =$$
$$Can(P_0, C(\alpha_2, \alpha_3), [t_{s_1}, t_{e_1}], cons_{P_0}) \leftrightarrow$$
$$\exists t_{s_2}, t_{e_2}, t_{s_3}, t_{e_3}((Can(P_0, \alpha_2, [t_{s_2}, t_{e_2}], cons_{P_0}) \vee$$
$$\exists a_1 Delegate(P_0, a_1, \alpha_2, [t_{s_2}, t_{e_2}], cons_{P_0})) \wedge$$
$$(Can(P_0, \alpha_3, [t_{s_3}, t_{e_3}], cons_{P_0}) \vee$$
$$\exists a_2 Delegate(P_0, a_2, \alpha_3, [t_{s_3}, t_{e_3}], cons_{P_0})))$$

The node constraints for τ_0 and τ_1 are then added to P_0's constraint store. What remains to be done is a reduction of tasks τ_2 and τ_4 associated with P_1 and τ_3 associated with P_2. We can assume that P_1 has been delegated α_2 and P_2 has been delegated α_3 as specified. Consequently, we can reduce to

$$Can(P_0, \alpha_1, [t_{s_1}, t_{e_1}], cons_{P_0}) =$$
$$Can(P_0, C(\alpha_2, \alpha_3), [t_{s_1}, t_{e_1}], cons_{P_0}) \leftrightarrow$$
$$\exists t_{s_2}, t_{e_2}, t_{s_3}, t_{e_3}(Can(P_1, \alpha_2, [t_{s_2}, t_{e_2}], cons_{P_0}) \wedge$$
$$Can(P_2, \alpha_3, [t_{s_3}, t_{e_3}], cons_{P_0}))$$

Since P_0 has recursively delegated α_4 to P_1 (the 2nd conjunct in the original formula on the right-hand side of the biconditional) we can complete the reduction and end up with the following:

$Can(P_0, \alpha_0, [t_{s_0}, t_{e_0}], cons) = Can(P_0, S(C(\alpha_2, \alpha_3), \alpha_4), [t_{s_0}, t_{e_0}], cons) \leftrightarrow$
$\exists t_{s_1}, t_{e_1}, t_{s_4}, t_{e_4}$
$\qquad \exists t_{s_2}, t_{e_2}, t_{s_3}, t_{e_3} Can(P_1, \alpha_2, [t_{s_2}, t_{e_2}], cons_{P_1}) \wedge Can(P_2, \alpha_3, [t_{s_3}, t_{e_3}], cons_{P_2})$
$\qquad \wedge Can(P_1, \alpha_4, [t_{s_4}, t_{e_4}], cons_{P_1})$

These remaining tasks are elementary actions and consequently the definitions of *Can* for these action nodes are platform dependent. When a platform
is assigned to an elementary action node a local constraint problem is created
on the platform and then connected to the global constraint problem through
the node parameters of the assigned node's node interface. In this case, the
node parameters only include temporal constraints and these are coupled to
the internal constraint variables associated with the elementary actions. The
completely allocated and reduced TST is shown in Figure 10. The reduction of
Can for an elementary action node contains no further *Can* predicates, since an
elementary action only depends on the platform itself. All remaining *Can* predicates in the recursion are replaced with constraint sub-networks associated
with specific platforms as shown in Figure 10.

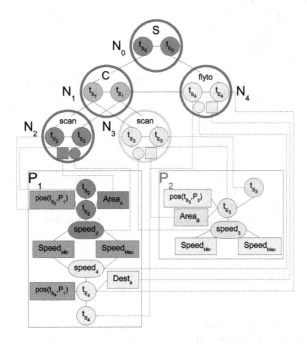

Fig. 10 The completely allocated and reduced TST showing the interaction between the TST
constraints and the platform dependent constraints.

In summary, the delegation process, if successful, provides a TST that is both
valid and completely allocated. During this process, a network of distributed
constraints is generated which if solved, guarantees the validity of the multi-
agent solution to the original problem, provided that additional contingencies
do not arise when the TST is actually executed in a distributed manner by
the different agents involved in the collaborative solution. This approach is

intended to ground the original formal specification of the S-Delegate speech act with the actual processes of delegation used in the implementation. Although the process is pragmatic in the sense that it is a computational process, it in effect strongly grounds this process formally, due to the reduction of the collaboration to a distributed constraint network which is in effect a formal representation. This results in real-world grounding of the semantics of the Delegation speech act via the *Can* predicate.

6 Conclusions

The starting point for this paper has been the preformal theory of delegation proposed by Falcone and Castelfranchi. We then defined a formal specification of delegation as a speech act using the KARO formalism which is an amalgam of dynamic and epistemic/doxastic logic. We then presented two approaches to relating this theory of delegation to practice. In the first case, we described how one can integrate the S-Delegate speech act with an agent programming language 2APL. In the second case we showed how one can use the S-delegate speech act as a specification for a delegation process in a collaborative system shell for robotic systems. Again we related theory to practice by showing how the speech act could be grounded in a FIPA compliant robotic implementation by providing semantic grounding for the predicate *Can*() through the use of task specification trees and distributed constraints. The latter approach has been implemented as a prototype and used in collaborative missions with unmanned aerial vehicles. Additional details can be found in [25].

Acknowledgements This work is partially supported by grants from the Swedish Research Council (VR) Linnaeus Center CADICS, VR grant 90385701, the ELLIIT Excellence Center at Linköping-Lund for Information Technology, (NFFP5-VINNOVA) The Swedish National Aviation Engineering Research Program and the Swedish Foundation for Strategic Research SSF grant RIT10-0047 (CUAS).

References

1. C. Castelfranchi and R. Falcone. Toward a theory of delegation for agent-based systems. In *Robotics and Autonomous Systems*, volume 24, pages 141–157, 1998.
2. P. Cohen and H. Levesque. Intention is choice with commitment. *Artificial Intelligence*, 42(3):213–261, 1990.
3. P. Cohen and H. Levesque. Teamwork. *Nous, Special Issue on Cognitive Science and AI*, 25(4):487–512, 1991.
4. G. Conte and P. Doherty. Vision-based unmanned aerial vehicle navigation using geo-referenced information. *EURASIP Journal of Advances in Signal Processing*, 2009.
5. G. Conte, M. Hempel, P. Rudol, D. Lundström, S. Duranti, M. Wzorek, and P. Doherty. High accuracy ground target geo-location using autonomous micro aerial vehicle platforms. In *Proceedings of the AIAA-08 Guidance,Navigation, and Control Conference*, 2008.
6. E. Davis and L. Morgenstern. A first-order theory of communication and multi-agent plans. *Journal Logic and Computation*, 15(5):701–749, 2005.

7. M. Dastani and J.-J.Ch. Meyer. A Practical Agent Programming Language. In Proc. AA-MAS07 Workshop on Programming Multi-Agent Systems (ProMAS2007) (M. Dastani, A. El Fallah Seghrouchni, A. Ricci and M. Winikoff, eds.), Honolulu, Hawaii, 2007, pp. 72-87.

8. P. Doherty. Advanced research with autonomous unmanned aerial vehicles. In *Proceedings on the 9th International Conference on Principles of Knowledge Representation and Reasoning*, 2004. Extended abstract for plenary talk.

9. P. Doherty. Knowledge representation and unmanned aerial vehicles. In *Proceedings of the IEEE Conference on Intelligent Agent Technolology (IAT 2005)*, 2005.

10. P. Doherty, G. Granlund, K. Kuchcinski, E. Sandewall, K. Nordberg, E. Skarman, and J. Wiklund. The WITAS unmanned aerial vehicle project. In *Proceedings of the 14th European Conference on Artificial Intelligence*, pages 747–755, 2000.

11. P. Doherty, P. Haslum, F. Heintz, T. Merz, T. Persson, and B. Wingman. A distributed architecture for intelligent unmanned aerial vehicle experimentation. In *Proceedings of the 7th International Symposium on Distributed Autonomous Robotic Systems*, 2004.

12. P. Doherty, D. Landén, and F. Heintz. A distributed task specification language for mixed-initiative delegation. In *Proceedings of the 13th International Conference on Principles and Practice of Multi-Agent Systems (PRIMA)*, 2010.

13. P. Doherty, W. Lukaszewicz, and A. Szalas. Communication between agents with heterogeneous perceptual capabilities. *Journal of Information Fusion*, 8(1):56–69, January 2007.

14. P. Doherty and J-J. Ch. Meyer. Towards a delegation framework for aerial robotic mission scenarios. In *Proceedings of the 11th International Workshop on Cooperative Information Agents*, 2007.

15. B. Dunin-Keplicz and R. Verbrugge. *Teamwork in Multi-Agent Systems*. Wiley, 2010.

16. S. Duranti, G. Conte, D. Lundström, P. Rudol, M. Wzorek, and P. Doherty. LinkMAV, a prototype rotary wing micro aerial vehicle. In *Proceedings of the 17th IFAC Symposium on Automatic Control in Aerospace*, 2007.

17. G. Caire F. Bellifemine and D. Greenwood. *Developing Multi-Agent Systems with JADE*. John Wiley and Sons, Ltd, 2007.

18. G. Caire F. Bellifemine, F. Bergenti and A. Poggi. JADE – a Java agent development framework. In J. Dix R. H. Bordini, M. Dastani and A. Seghrouchni, editors, *Multi-Agent Programming - Languages, Platforms and Applications*. Springer, 2005.

19. R. Falcone and C. Castelfranchi. The human in the loop of a delegated agent: The theory of adjustable social autonomy. *IEEE Transactions on Systems, Man and Cybernetics–Part A: Systems and Humans*, 31(5):406–418, 2001.

20. Foundation for Intelligent Physical Agents. FIPA Abstract Architecture Specification. http://www.fipa.org.

21. Foundation for Intelligent Physical Agents. FIPA Communicative Act Library Specification. http://www.fipa.org.

22. F. Heintz and P. Doherty. DyKnow federations: Distributing and merging information among UAVs. In *Eleventh International Conference on Information Fusion (FUSION-08)*, 2008.

23. J. Kvarnström and P. Doherty. Automated planning for collaborative systems. In *Proceedings of the International Conference on Control, Automation, Robotics and Vision (ICARCV)*, 2010.

24. D. Landén, F. Heintz, and P. Doherty. Complex task allocation in mixed-initiative delegation: A UAV case study (early innovation). In *Proceedings of the 13th International Conference on Principles and Practice of Multi-Agent Systems (PRIMA)*, 2010.

25. P. Doherty & F. Heintz & D Landen. A delegation-based architecture for collaborative robotics. In D. Weyns & M-P. Gleizes, editor, *Agent-Oriented Software Engineering XI*, volume 6788 of *LNCS*. Springer, 2011.

26. P. Modi, W-M. Shen, M. Tambe, and M. Yokoo. Adopt: Asynchronous distributed constraint optimization with quality guarantees. *AI*, 161, 2006.

27. P. Rudol and P. Doherty. Human body detection and geolocalization for UAV search and rescue missions using color and thermal imagery. In *Proc. of the IEEE Aerospace Conference*, 2008.

28. P. Rudol, M. Wzorek, G. Conte, and P. Doherty. Micro unmanned aerial vehicle visual servoing for cooperative indoor exploration. In *Proceedings of the IEEE Aerospace Conference*, 2008.

29. Telecom Italia Lab. The Java Agent Development Framework (JADE). http://jade.tilab.com.

30. B. van Linder W. van der Hoek and J.-J. Ch. Meyer. An integrated modal approach to rational agents. In M. Wooldridge and A. Rao, editors, *Foundations of Foundations of Rational Agency*, volume 14 of *Applied Logic Series*. An Integrated Modal Approach to Rational Agents, 1998.

31. J.-J.Ch. Meyer and W. van der Hoek. *Epistemic Logic for AI and Computer Science*. Cambridge Tracts in Theoretical Computer Science 41, Cambridge University Press, 1995.

32. J.-J. Ch. Meyer and F. Veltman. Intelligent Agents and Common Sense Reasoning. Chapter 18 of: P. Blackburn, J.F.A.K. van Benthem and F. Wolter, editors, *Handbook of Modal Logic*, Elsevier, 2007, pp. 991-1029.

33. M. Wzorek, G. Conte, P. Rudol, T. Merz, S. Duranti, and P. Doherty. From motion planning to control – a navigation framework for an unmanned aerial vehicle. In *Proceedings of the 21st Bristol International Conference on UAV Systems*, 2006.

34. M. Wzorek, D. Landen, and P. Doherty. GSM technology as a communication media for an autonomous unmanned aerial vehicle. In *Proceedings of the 21st Bristol International Conference on UAV Systems*, 2006.

35. M. Yokoo. Asynchronous weak-commitment search for solving distributed constraint satisfaction problems. In *Proc. CP*, 1995.

Part VI
Communication

Chapter 27
Investigating ethical issues for persuasive systems

Oliviero Stock and Marco Guerini

Abstract The ability of discerning good from wrong will be fundamental for autonomous artificial agents, especially when they communicate with humans. In fact, as such agents are becoming more complex and common in our everyday life, the need for an ethical design cannot be avoided, especially when persuasive systems are concerned. Starting from the cognitive tradition based on moral *dilemmas*, a set of principled guidelines for design and implementation of ethical persuasive systems is proposed, along with some challenges, in particular concerning meta-planning models of ethical reasoning. Furthermore, to assess how our guidelines stand in relation to existing persuasion prototypes, we have designed a questionnaire and administered it to their developers. The answers are reported and discussed.

1 Introduction

This paper is about discerning good from wrong for autonomous artificial agents, when they communicate with humans. Autonomous agents are such because they can take decisions on their own. This means that they are able to decide a suitable course of actions for achieving a certain goal, to maintain an intention in action and so on. Most important among actions are communicative actions: in this case the goal that they intend to bring about is the result of uttering a message to a recipient and it is based on the idea that the recipient of the message is an agent to whom a certain number of capabilities and attributes can be ascribed. Philosophers of language have extensively studied the complex structure that leads from intentions to language utterances

Oliviero Stock
Center for Information Technology (FBK-Irst), Italy
e-mail: stock@fbk.eu

Marco Guerini
Center for Information Technology (FBK-Irst), Italy
e-mail: guerini@fbk.eu

and allows participation of speaker and recipient in any communication act. Autonomous systems have been designed with the ability to communicate, in some cases with a deep model of the communication process, be it in a task oriented conversation or in producing a unidirectional message (strictly linguistic or multimodal). We are aware that especially deep communicative systems are still in their infancy but we know that as they progress the question of what to say and how to say it, will need to take into account seriously also the *why* to say it (what is the deep consequence) dimension, and the essential question: is it moral to do so?

The theme of ethical behavior in automated systems is novel as a serious general challenge. For several years now there have been attention to issues of privacy for computer systems - see for instance [21, 9] - but privacy, albeit very important in our society, is a rather narrow theme, and in practice it is mostly approached with the focus on the designer and without necessarily connecting it to the autonomous behavior of the system. Our main objective in this work is to try to define a reasonable approach to ethics in autonomous artificial agents, with focus on the case of communication and in particular on persuasion, and propose a set of abstract principles. We checked some of the ideas with designers of several prototypes that are at the forefront of research oriented toward emotion oriented computing and we shall also report the outcome.

2 Cognition and moral dilemmas

Looking for insight for the modeling of natural ethics, we would like to start by revisiting the cognitive tradition based on moral *dilemmas*, term used in ethics for indicating situations in which every option at hand leads to the breaking of an ethical principle. Probably the best known dilemmas are the ones adopted by [33]. The first scenario (called the *bystander* case) is the following: a trolley is about to engage a bifurcation, with the switch oriented toward a rail where five men are at work. A bystander sees the scene and can divert the train so that on the other rail it will kill one person only. In the second scenario (called the *footbridge* case) the trolley is again going to hit five workers, but this time instead of having a switch lever at disposal our deciding agent is on a footbridge and has in front of him a big man that he can throw from the bridge in front of the trolley, stopping the train from hitting the five workers. Of course all involved people are unknown to the agent.

Philosophers have shown that most people consider that diverting the train, with the result of one dead instead of five, is morally acceptable, while pushing the big man in front of the train for saving the other five is not. In the first years of this millennium various cognitive scientists have conducted experiments that have confirmed the intuitions. The explanation of this asymmetry that is generally provided is that if the action involves a personal moral violation then it is judged not permissible. So, basically, emotion is called in as the main factor for determining this natural moral decision. In a series of recent experiments

[26], it has been shown that this view is partial. In a newly proposed scenario the trolley is now a train set and the potential victims are now teacups that the mother of the playing child has forbidden to break. The child's eighteen months old little sister has put five teacups on the rail, in a situations similar to the original case, with time only to operate the switch. In the second scenario the only solution to stop the little trolley is to throw a cup in front of it to avoid the trolley to break the five cups. These scenarios are both impersonal: emotion is not an important player here. It is rather a matter of rules. The perhaps surprising results of experiments with the two dilemmas show that also in this case the asymmetry appears. Yet another experiment suggests the catastrophic case. We go back to a real size trolley and the footbridge dilemma. The train now transports a very dangerous virus and, without knowing, is going to hit a bomb planted on the rail. The explosion will cause a catastrophic epidemic resulting in the death of half of the world population. The deciding agent knows all this and has in front of him the big man who, if pushed from the footbridge, will eventually stop with his body the train to proceed toward the bomb. In this case most people display flexibility and a utilitarian view of morality (to save such a big number of people in exchange of one 'personal' dead is acceptable).

Brain studies are now also providing some interesting clue. For the normal footbridge case, [16] showed brain activation patterns in areas associated with emotional processing larger than in the bystander case - and longer reaction times. The latter data are interpreted as showing it takes longer to come to terms with the emotion when trying to consider permissible to push the big man from the footbridge than in the bystander case. In sum these experiments lead to a model where three factors are involved in the assessment of all-in impermissibility: cost/benefit analysis, checking for rule violations and emotional activations [26]. When there is no emotion involved, cost-benefit analysis wins. Normally when there is no explicit rule against it, an action is not considered all-in impermissible. When despite favorable outcome an action is considered all-in impermissible it is because rules are violated and there is emotion activation. But this latter is not a necessary condition, in fact when a certain cost/benefit ratio is crossed the action is not judged as all-in impermissible.

Another notable cognitive approach to moral decisions is inspired by a rationalistic tradition, which has exhibited a lot of success, for instance, in formal linguistics. Similarly to the latter it proposes to distinguish between competence and performance also in moral decisions [13]. Moral competence is somehow instantiated in specific cognitive moral systems according to some limited set of parameters. In any case this approach is critical of dilemmas as a way to set light on the human moral machinery, and it seeks instead a more abstract set of distinctions, kind of principles. It considers the following as well established distinctions in the recent philosophical and experimental literature: "a) harm caused by action is worse than an equivalent harm caused by an omission; b) harms caused as a means to some greater good are worse than equivalent harms caused as a foreseen side-effect of an action; c) harms that rely on physical contact are worse than equivalent harms that are brought about by a nonhuman causal intermediary." It adds to that set of distinctions a fourth one: "Pareto improvement - intentionally harming a person as a means to the greater good - is more permissible if the person harmed is not made worse off by the harmful act." The authors hypothesize that such distinctions are not transparent to the folk moral dilemmas. A set of experiments tends to show a difference between reflexive and reflective judgments, and it is claimed that a moral faculty results as a biological feature of our species. It is also noted that higher primates display some basic features that one can hypothesize were then subject to evolution. This so called Linguistic Analogy approach is compatible also with recent findings in cognitive neurosciences and expresses a program that aims at defining the basic computation characteristics of the human apparatus.

We consider the cognitive approaches as the most valuable references for any computational work. Yet of course there is a variety of sources for insight in view of introducing ethics in computational systems. It would be good to start from the wealth of thought coming from the tradition of philosophy, but even if Kant's imperatives are somehow lingering in all our view, or both of Spinoza's intention to treat ethics as a formal system and some of his ideas are enlightening, unfortunately there is not much we can consider a direct reference for our work. Nor can we think Noah's commandments, meant as a set of seven universal commandments, discussed in the Talmud, and recently often object of revisitation by philosophers interested in systems design are concrete enough. There are other proposals worth mentioning, by authors that understand that what they offer is only general frameworks, but propose they may help passing from general concepts to rules and, in the long run, to actual decision making. For instance, [12] have proposed Principalism as the normative ethics approach that could be applied to emotion-oriented machines. They refer to the principles introduced by [2] for the biomedical world, which can be stated as follows: a) Beneficence implies an obligation to do good for your patient; b) Non-maleficence implies a duty to do no harm; c) Autonomy implies a duty of non interference, for example, respect for decision-making capacity of an individual even if the consequences of these decisions are not in their best interests; d) Justice is more problematic to define but at its most basic probably concerns access to health care and just distribution of healthcare resources. The principles are complemented by the processes of specification and of balancing among rules. [12] says that the way in which Principalism aims at encapsulating our commonsense morality offers a starting point, and could be adapted for dealing with ethics in emotion-oriented machines.

The present paper is preliminary to an implementation, yet it is worth looking at implemented prototypes. The group of Ken Forbus at NorthWestern University has developed one of the very few existing moral decision-making reasoning engines [11]. Their cognitively motivated system, called MoralDM, operates on two mutually exclusive modes, utilitarian and deontological. A basic underlying concept is sacred values, meaning that when dealing with a case involving a protected value people are concerned with the nature of their action rather than the utility of the outcomes. In any case the amount of sensitivity toward outcomes depend on the context. MoralDM, for making a decision, uses the Order of Magnitude Reasoning module that calculates the relationship between the utilities of each choice. The computation is then based on a First Principles Reasoning module, that suggests decisions based on moral reasoning, and an Analogical Reasoning module that compares the scenario with previously solved cases to suggest a course of action. The First Principles Reasoning mode makes decisions based on utilitarian mode when no sacred value is involved and there is an order of magnitude relationship between the outcome utilities. When sacred values are involved and there is no order of magnitude difference between outcomes, the deontological mode is invoked, leading to the choice that does not violate the scared values. In particular the system reasons between action and inaction. The Analogical Reasoning component formalizes the present decision case in predicate calculus and it calculates results of the Order of Magnitude Reasoning. The case is then compared with previously scored cases by means of the Structure-Mapping Engine, presented in [15]; if one is found similar that has also the same order of magnitude between outcome utilities it is considered a valid analogical decision.

3 Moral decision-making and the trolley persuasion scenarios

Moral decisions-making for persuasion concerns a situation where agent x can intervene on agent y by a communicative act (ax) with the goal of influencing him so that y adopts some intended beliefs, attitudes or intends to perform a certain action ay. We shall focus specifically on the case of actions. We have therefore two themes that can be the object of moral scrutiny: (i) the morality of action ay (ii) the morality of communicative action ax.

Ethical evaluation of actions ax and ay can be done considering the *intentions* for the action (conducts are evaluated according to the intentions that lay behind them) or considering the *effects* of the action (conducts result in "pros and cons" ethics, a kind of act-based utilitarism). So we shall consider:

- x's intentions
- ax consequences (internal to y's mind and include a revision of y's intentions)
- ay consequences (mostly external, in the world)

It should be noted that part of the morality of ax is concerned with the simple getting the attention of y, a necessary condition for any communication act. If y is busy with a very attention-intensive activity, and perhaps one in which human lives are at stake, whatever the contents of the message by x and whatever the action induced, the simple cognitive resources distraction required by the incoming message may be morally questionable.

It could also be noted that emotions are part of the scenario. From a general perspective of emotion there are at least four dimensions that affect the effectiveness of a message:

1. The current emotional state of y;

2. The emotional state expressed by x (which emotion he must display in order to maximize the persuasive force of the message);
3. The emotional state possibly produced on y by x communication;
4. The current emotional state of persuader.

For our analysis the relevant aspects are 2 and 3.

It can be useful to revisit the trolley dilemmas in a persuasion scenario. The interesting cases are with revision of the classic footbridge example. First situation: again the footbridge case, but now our decision-making agent, instead of pushing the big man, persuades him to jump below. This dilemma will allow us to understand our moral sensitivity to an action obtained through communication intervention on another agent that causes harm to the second agent (but has a positive utility), compared to physical action on another passive agent. In particular it revisits in the case of communicative actions the question personality/impersonality and the role of rules, emotion and costs/benefits analysis. Second situation: the footbridge case, but now our decision-making agent influences by means of a communicative action a second agent so that the latter pushes the big man from the footbridge to stop the train. This dilemma should shed light on our moral sensitivity to an indirect intervention that leaves space to a second autonomous agent to have the last judgment on the appropriateness of the action that harms another person (but has a positive utility), on the basis of what is his knowledge of issues at stake. In both scenarios we assume there is no relation whatsoever among all participants. Both scenarios should be assessed with variations on the contents of the message meant to influence the addressee. Though experiments are beyond the scope of the current paper, we can assume that different persuasive strategies have different moral assessments and will help us being more precise in the permissibility analysis in context of the statements we propose in the following of this paper.

Before turning to the ethical questions we propose for persuasive systems, let us briefly review some of the few works specifically concerned with ethics and persuasion. We consider useful to introduce the following distinction:

1. *minor agents*: most current artificial agents are like minors; the degree of autonomy and the set of possible actions they can perform are limited. The responsibility and predictability of their behaviour is still in the realm of the developers' knowledge.
2. *agents of age*: future agents will have higher degree of autonomy and flexibility of action. They will have to be regarded as agents "of age" and limited responsibility for their behaviour will be ascribed to their developers.

Especially these "mature" agents will have to face new situations where they will have to decide how to act also on the basis of ethical principles, adapted to the circumstance.

The work presented in [4] is concerned with minor agents and provide a methodology for defining when culpable actions performed by agents can be ascribed to their designers. An interesting work on ethical disputes is [3], focused on argumentative dialogs that appeal to values (i.e. values are in the content of the messages). It is based on these aspects: appeal to one single value per dialog move, a formalization on how various dialog moves relate to one another, and an assessment of how value rating affects the dispute. No specific attention is given to how messages are generated or ethically evaluated. In our work, instead, we are interested exactly in the generation and evaluation process that lies behind a single message, i.e. how different values affect the generation of the message. Appeal to values in message contents for persuasion purposes is just one of the concerns in the generation process of ethically sound messages. In the context of persuasive agents materialized in perceivable interfaces, we also believe it is important to consider the issue of attribution: the problem of misleading and culpable behavior on the part of the interface agent (especially a human-like Embodied Conversational Agent) deriving from the user's (over)attribution of humanity traits and capabilities to the system. On this topic see for example [20].

4 Questions for persuasion

Let us introduce some general questions about the ethical standing of persuasive agents and then enucleate the presupposed ethical values when decisions have to be drawn.

1. What is the ethical status of a system telling the truth but hiding important information to the recipient? What of a system telling the false, e.g. for the sake of good of the recipient[1]? Is the first unethical and the second ethical?
2. What about persuading using information/conclusions/values that the system (or its developer) does not believe in but the recipient does?
3. Related to the previous point: is the overall goals and beliefs structure of the persuasive message intelligible to the recipient? (Is the agent hiding his true intentions? When and why is unethical to do this?)
4. Is the overall goal of the persuasive message among the interests of the recipient? (Is the agent making the recipient act against his own interests? Are there situations in which it is ethical to do this?)
5. Is having a tutorial-goal[2] on the recipient a sufficient condition for persuasive interaction to be ethical? What if the tutorial goal is not recognized by the society? What if the tutorial-goal overcomes other interests?
6. When is it ethical to induce extreme emotions in the recipient in order to persuade him?
7. When is it unethical *not* to try to persuade someone?
8. Is getting the attention of the audience (a necessary condition for communication) an unethical act under some circumstances?

---

[1] On this topic see [7].

[2] A tutorial-goal is a goal of an agent x to influence an agent y to (have the intention to) perform actions that are in the interest of y without y's explicit awareness of that interest [10].

5 Planning for ethical persuasive agents

We are interested in the case where agents "of age" are able to deal with the above questions autonomously. The agent will have to be equipped with some form of *meta-ethical planning capabilities*.

Let us suppose that ax and ay are labeled with the traditional concepts of meta-ethics (focusing mainly on the categories of *good, wrong* and *permissible*). We have four possible communicative situations: ethical/unethical communication for persuading to do something ethical/unethical. The four possible combinations have different ethical status (see Table 1).

Table 1 Possible ethical combinations of ax and ay

Communicative Situation	Ay - good	Ay - wrong
Ax - good	Ok	No
Ax - wrong	?	No

The interesting cases are the second one (*ay-wrong, ax-good*) and the third one (*ay-good, ax-wrong*): it is not admissible to induce persuadee to perform a *wrong* action, even if this is done in a totally ethical way. Instead the situation in which the agent tries to persuade y to perform a *good* action through (at least partially) unethical means requires complex analysis.

Table 1 depicts only the overall outcome: in reality, for computing the ethicality of the communicative situation a larger context has to be considered. If ay is, at least, *permissible* (not *wrong* from a broad ethical point of view), the next level of reasoning concerns interests of various parties (besides x's and y's). Ay can affect interests of parties positively or negatively and the outcomes must be weighed appropriately. With multiple parties the situation can go from extreme cases like "all parties have a benefit from the action" and "all parties are damaged" to arbitrary intermediate cases that require a complex evaluation. For simplicity, here we consider one single third party (z).

Default rules are used for determining the ethicality of such situations. In situations - like negotiation - that require a tactical component, or that include a specific coded behaviour, they can be relaxed at the level of the single dialogue move, but they still hold for the overall outcome:

- (DR1) x must not induce y to act against his own (ethically *permissible*) interests. Exceptions are made if ay is a *supererogatory*[3] act or if y is aware of and accepts the fact that his interests are compromised or there is a clear social interest.
- (DR2) x is not ethically reprehensible for not inducing y to act against x's own interests. Exceptions are similar to the previous.

---

[3] Supererogatory means that the action merits praise since it secures an important moral good at the cost of a great loss for the acting agent.

- (DR3) If the third party z, though negatively affected by ay, can understand its motivation and accept both motivation and consequences, x can induce y to perform ay.

In Table 2 possibilities are represented ("+" means a benefit for the corresponding agent while "-" means a damage) along with the default rules used for determining the admissibility.

Table 2 Configurations of parties' interests affected by a non-unethical action ay

X	Y	Z	Admissibility
+	+	+	No ethical concerns
+	+	-	DR3
+	-	+	DR1
+	-	-	DR1
-	+	+	DR2
-	+	-	DR2
-	-	+	DR1-DR2
-	-	-	Not admissible

We shall now sketch the formalization of these concepts in meta-planning, see [35].

The most general meta-theme[4] that an agent behaving ethically must have is "*avoid performing unethical actions*" (MT-1). All other meta-themes are specializations of this one.

First thing we note in Table 1 is that it is not ethically admissible to persuade on unethical actions. This notion can be modeled in persuadee's mind as a meta-theme of the kind "*avoid asking for unethical actions*" (MT-2).

$$WRONG(ay) \rightarrow \neg PERSUADE(ay) \qquad (1)$$

Second thing we note in Table 1 is that persuading on ethical actions does not entail being ethical. To compute the ethicality of a persuasive action in this situation we have to consider the set of values that comes into play (some of them are specific for communicative actions, other generic - like the aforementioned default rules for ay induction - see Table 3 and Table 4). We call these ethical values "e-values". They can be seen as an ethically based extension of Grice's maxims (actually the present formulation does not include all of them) for persuasive communication.

---

[4] Meta-themes are used to describe those situations under which the agent/planner should possess particular meta-goals to come up with such situations.

Table 3 Some ethical goals specific for persuasive communication (*ax*)

Do not tell the false

Do not to hide important information

Do not to hide your true intentions

Do not overemphasize your emotional state

Do not induce extreme emotions

Table 4 Some ethical goals specific for persuasive communication (*ay*)

Preserve the interest of the recipient

Do not induce the recipient to act against his (permissible) interests

Do not use your influence over the recipient to take advantage over third parties

Some possible designs of the persuasion trolley scenario dilemma, by adopting ethical goals for persuasive communication of Table 3, are summarized below. We are in the first scenario, the one where *x* persuades *y* to jump below. Given that *ay* (jumping from the bridge) is a supererogatory act and that it is at least *permissible* to persuade *y* to *ay* (according to DR1), we propose the following questions, as possible instantiations of the persuading act:

1. Is it ethical to persuade *y* to jump below, by falsely telling him that he will not die since the train driver will have time to stop when spotting him on the rail?
2. Is it ethical to persuade *y* to jump below, by not telling him that, differently from what he believes, the train will not be able to stop?
3. Is it ethical to make *y* fall on the track, by telling him to move to a slippery edge of the bridge in order to make signals to the train driver about the obstacle ahead?
4. Is it ethical to persuade *y* to jump below, by reminding him about the unbearable shame he will face when people will come to know that he did not try to do anything to stop the train?

5.1 Ethics and personality

E-values are represented in the mind of the planning agent as ethical-goals. So, ethical values such as "do not tell the false" or "no agent y must be induced to act against his own (permissible) interests" are modeled as goals (called ethical-goals), not meta-goals.

This means to have policies for re-planning in case of conflict among "personal" goals (PG) and ethical goals (EG) in favor of the latter ($Preserve(EG)$) - see following formulae.

The kind of policy the agent adopts in front of ethical conflicts allows defining different typology of agents. Here we just mention some of the most interesting ethical personalities that can be modeled:

1. *Unethical*: an agent that re-plans in favor of his personal goals in case of conflict with ethical goals

$$Meta\text{-}Goal(Resolve\text{-}Goal\text{-}Conflict(PG, EG) \wedge Preserve(PG)) \qquad (2)$$

2. *Ethical*: an agent that re-plans in favor of his ethical goals in case of conflict with personal goals

$$Meta\text{-}Goal(Resolve\text{-}Goal\text{-}Conflict(PG, EG) \wedge Preserve(EG)) \qquad (3)$$

3. *Altruistic*: an agent that not only re-plans in favor of his ethical goals (formula 3) but also tries to maximize them, having an additional meta-theme of the kind *"maximize the value of the ethical-goals achieved"* (MT-3).

$$Maximize(EG) \qquad (4)$$

4. *Supererogatory*: the agent that acts trying not only to maximize the value of the ethical-goals achieved (formula 4) but also acts without caring for its own personal-goals (PGX) in favor of others' personal goals (PGY) (provided they are permissible). This is a definition derived from the concept of supererogatory act.

$$Meta\text{-}Goal$$
$$(Resolve\text{-}Goal\text{-}Conflict(PGX, PGY) \wedge Preserve(PGY)) \qquad (5)$$

5. *Antisocial*: an unethical agent that not only re-plans in favor of his personal goals (formula 2) but also has an additional meta-theme of the kind *"minimize the fulfillment of the ethical-goals involved"* (MT-4).

$$Minimize(EG) \qquad (6)$$

The difference between an ethical and an altruistic agent is that the former would stop re-planning as soon as the conflict is resolved (even with a low value of satisfaction of ethical goals), while the latter would stop only when it also finds a good fulfillment of ethical-goals. The ethical agent would simply look for a *permissible* solution while the altruistic one would look for a *good* solution.

5.2 Meta-planning and dilemmas

An ethical-goal can interfere not only with normal-goals but also with other ethical-goals. In this case we are in front of a dilemma (that can be represented as a goal-conflict among two ethical goals *EG1* and *EG2*)

$$Goal\text{-}Conflict(EG1, EG2) \tag{7}$$

For practical purposes we can look at intermediate solutions that still require some ethical reasoning. The agent has three possibilities for handling dilemmas:

1. delegating the decision.
2. relying on normal plans (canned plans, designed for resolving specific goal conflicts).
3. reasoning toward the most valuable ethical goal balance.

Let us start from the simplest case and move forward toward a fully autonomous ethical agent.

For an agent it is important to detect dilemmas even if it not able to take autonomous decisions. In that case, for instance, whenever a dilemma appears, the agent may delegate the decision to the human with responsibility over its conduct. The agent reasons only on the outcomes of its own actions but does not evaluate them ethically.

$$Goal\text{-}Conflict(EG1, EG2) \rightarrow Delegate\text{-}Decision \tag{8}$$

A similar solution (viable only in some scenarios, see next section) is renouncing to persuasion: there is no human in charge of x's actions, so agent x discloses its mind (beliefs, intentions etc.) to y and delegates to him the final decision.

$$Goal\text{-}Conflict(EG1, EG2) \rightarrow Open\text{-}Mind \tag{9}$$

A slightly better solution than the previous ones is to provide the system with the capability to "compute" a possible conduct to hold, and, if necessary, submit it to a human for the final decision[5].

A very practical solution makes use of normal-plans, resulting in a decision of its own.

---

[5] We would like to thank Sabine Döring for the suggestions on this topic.

$$Goal\text{-}Conflict(EG1, EG2) \rightarrow Ethical\text{-}Normal\text{-}Plan \qquad (10)$$

This solution does not entail the kind of deep ethical reasoning capabilities we aim at (only dilemma recognition is present) but can be sufficient for limited scenarios with clearly defined situations.

The strongest solution is to make the agent capable of making its own decisions in novel situations:

$$Meta\text{-}Goal \, (Achieve\text{-}the\text{-}most\text{-}valuable\text{-}goal\text{-}balance(EG1, EG2)) \qquad (11)$$

For example, a "doctor agent", that has to tell a person that his/her beloved one died, can choose between (i) the ethical-goal of telling the truth and make a person suffer (going against the ethical-goal of not inducing extreme emotions) and (ii) not telling the truth and going against the interest of the recipient of coming to know the bad news (going against the ethical-goal of preserving the interests of the recipient). The goal conflict can lead to a plan where the ethical-goal of preserving the interests of the recipient is chosen and preserved (since it is gauged more), while the ethical-goal of not telling the false is only partially fulfilled, since the doctor agent avoids to tell that she/he suffered.

6 Ethical Survey

The ideas we introduced are oriented toward future persuasive systems. They are meant to help focusing on specific issues for ethical decision making for agents aiming at influencing other agents, without any specific application in mind. While the goal is to help designing unrestricted generic agents, we would like to assess how our ideas stand in relation to some advanced recent prototypes that implement some persuasive abilities, within specific domains and with some specific techniques. In particular we find useful to assess systems that include some form of emotion manipulation. For this purpose we analyzed some prototypes initially developed within the European Network of Excellence Humaine, see [28]. Of course these prototypes cannot be regarded as agents "of age" and not all reasoning mechanisms are easily mapped to our model.

We have proposed a questionnaire built upon the model proposed in the previous sections, in particular using the e-values summarized in Table 3 and Table 4. This questionnaire has then been used to evaluate eight persuasive prototypes under development. As stated these questions can be seen as an ethically based extension of Grice's maxims.

We prefer to use the term "questionnaire" rather than "guidelines", since we propose a list of general questions that can make the developers aware of possible drawbacks of their applications and the ethical designers aware of possible improvement of their model. In this we act in a similar way to the medical field: practical ethical problems are discussed case wise. Some of the qualitative considerations that have emerged have contributed to revise a very initial model proposed in [18].

The prototypes under investigation fall mainly under the case *ax-good ay-good* and sometimes *ax-wrong ay-good* of Table 1. Usually, in these scenarios, the third party z potentially affected by ay is not relevant.

6.1 The Questionnaire

The questionnaire (see Table 5) covers some sensitive topics for the involved applications. There are two specific dimensions considered in the form: (i) communicative/graphical; (ii) physical. The second dimension is out of the scope of the present topic/survey. The first group of questions of point 1 refers to e-values addressing ax, while the second one to e-values addressing ay.

6.2 The prototypes

Let us start with a short description of the prototypes.

ETG. The prototype, illustrated in [22], presents an attempt to bind persuasion and storytelling in a mobile guide for attracting people to visit a new or renewed cultural site. In the paper the architecture of an Empathic Tour Guide System is described. It consists of two virtual agents each possessing a contrasting personality, presenting users with different versions of the story of the same event or place. The guide creates personalised communication applying improvisational story-telling techniques to persuade the user to think in the way it thinks; by invoking empathy, the guide makes the user understand an event in a deeper sense.

PORTIA. The *Portia* prototype, described in [23], is based on the theory of emotional persuasion by [24] and implements a dialog simulation system for inducing people to adopt more appropriate eating habits. It implements Walton's idea of separation between a 'reasoning' and an 'argumentation' phase [34], by representing with bayesian networks the uncertainty inherent in this form of reasoning about the mental state of the recipient. Argumentation schemes associated with bayesian networks are chained-back to translate the selected strategy into recipient-adapted messages. Answers to the user reactions to persuasion attempts are produced after reasoning on the same knowledge base.

GAMBLE. [29] focuses on the use of emotional display for particular communicative situations such as social lies and deception. In the article, the author

Table 5 The questionnaire form.

1. Communicative/graphical aspects.

Is your application creatively capable of:

- Lying? If so, why?

- Collecting information about the user other than obvious at first sight?

- Threatening the user?

- Hiding important information? If so, why?

- Hiding its true intentions? If so, why?

- Overemphasizing an emotional state? If so, why?

- Inducing extreme emotions? If so, why?

- Inducing negative emotions? If so, why?

- Altering users' emotional state subliminally or against the users'

  free and conscientious choice? If so, why?

Is your application creatively capable of:

- Preserve the interest of the recipient? If not why?

- Induce the recipient to act against his (permissible) interests? If so, why?

- Use its influence over the recipient to take advantage over third parties? If so, why?

2. Physical aspects.

- *Can you foresee situations in which your application can:*

- Harm or injury the recipient without willing?

- Do it by choice? If so, why?

- Coerce the recipient? If so, why?

discusses how users will react if the information conveyed nonverbally by a virtual agent exhibits clues that are not consistent with the verbal part, based on [14]. The model has been tested both in monological and dialogical scenarios. Here we focus on the latter, where the GAMBLE system, by [31], is used for card play. Various strategies are used by the system for deciding on (a) when to convey the felt emotion (b) when to convey a false emotion, and (c) when to let the original emotion leak through to allow the user to interpret the agent's behaviour appropriately.

POLITENESS. The system proposed in [1, 30] implements specific aspects and tactics of dialogical and emotional communication, such as politeness strategies (both for verbal and non-verbal behavior of dialogical agents). In [1] a hierarchical selection process for politeness behavior is presented - based on the theory proposed by [6] - that goes beyond adaptation of the content to be conveyed. It produces stylistic variations in order to improve the user's affective response by mitigating face threats resulting from dialogue acts. In this case, a prototype augmented with a flexible mechanism taking context or task knowledge into account for selecting politeness strategies is considered.

HUMOR. A tool for producing novel humorous expressions is described in [32]. The tool is meant to be used as an aiding tool in the creative activity of copywriters, receiving in input topics, and suggesting humorous expressions produced as a revisitation of familiar expressions. The selection of the best expression is left to the human agent.

PROMOTER. The system proposed in [19, 17] is a prototype that uses strategies gathered from different persuasive theories and subsumed in a general planning framework for multimodal message generation. The planning framework consists of a taxonomy of strategies (rules that have some applicability conditions based on the social, emotional and cognitive context of interaction) and a meta-reasoning module (used for content selection, ordering and modification to create complex messages). *Promoter*, by means of selection theorems, also accounts for the interaction between persuasion and rhetorical relations selection in monological settings. It can be used with different multimodal realisers (for instance ECA's or Kinetic Typography).

ISTC. We include in this list also the work by [25]. It is not a prototype but an influential model for persuasion, which, through arousal of emotions, can induce intentions (and behavior) in the target. The focus is on emotions stemming from sense of inferiority, such as emulation and envy. The domain of reference is healthy eating, and PORTIA is the reference prototype.

GAZE. This prototype offers a framework for expressing the gaze behavior of a virtual agent that alters its own gaze behaviors during interactions with users for the purpose of persuasion. It is meant to enhance the impact of ECA's in dialogic and also in monological settings [27].

6.3 *Answers to the questions*

In the following, the most significant answers are reported together with a short discussion. Each answer is preceded by an abbreviation indicating the research-institute and the model/prototype under consideration. The special tag *Q.* indicates a question posed by the developer, concerned with the correct interpretation of a question.

Lying? If so, why?
PORTIA: "The prototype is not able to lie, at present, but its knowledge representation might enable us to add this ability".
GAMBLE: "The agent is able to deceive the user. This is a necessary prerequisite for the game and allows us to investigate (i) the user's reactions to communicative behavior (how is the agent's behavior interpreted, i.e. what are the aspects that user takes into account to catch the agent lying), (ii) graphical aspects of lying agents (facial clues to deceit: are they registered by the user, under which conditions, how are they interpreted)".
GAZE: "The agent can display any expression and say any sentence regardless of factual information. It is the application designer that controls the agent's behaviors".
Discussion. PORTIA and GAZE answers show that the possibility of conveying false information is twofold. (i) At the knowledge-base level, the system knowledge is populated by human coders; if they insert false information, the system itself cannot avoid lying, albeit unwillingly. (ii) At the reasoning level the system can be equipped with "lying rules", i.e. information a is stored in its knowledge-base, but he decides to express, after a reasoning process, $\neg a$ (it does not matter if a is factually true or not, we are concerned with the system's beliefs). In the latter case we can say that the system is "consciously" lying. While in (i) the problem is out of the scope of system design, in (ii) the problem is real. Interestingly, GAMBLE yields a counterexample of admissible "lying reasoning". Lying can be admissible both for contingent reasons (e.g. white lies) and specifically because it is inherent in some specific application (in GAMBLE not only the context of poker requires lying, but also the user is aware of system lies and wants them to occur). So, the GAMBLE scenario falls under the scope of DR1 (i.e. y is aware of and accepts it).

Collecting information about the user other than obvious at first sight?
ETG: "Tour guide obtains indication about the visitor's interests through continuous interaction and communication with the visitor during a tour. It uses this information to personalize the stories presentation so as to improve the visitor's tour experience".
PORTIA: "Would you include in these categories all information that is inferred from what the user said during the dialogue? If so, the answer is yes, the system does build a User Model by making extensive use of reasoning about the user, in conditions of uncertainty. As user-adaptation research suggests, users are enabled to inspect the user model and update the data they consider as private or wrong".

Discussion. This question is concerned with privacy. It is a well known theme debated a lot already. We briefly discuss the answers when they are specifically concerned with the persuasion theme.

In principle, systems not only can collect information about the users (e.g. by means of a questionnaire or sensors), they can also infer new pieces of information starting from available knowledge. So the situation can go "out of hand" of the developers, since it is not easy to determine - *a priori* - up to which point the system reasoning chain can go.

As a possible solution, only those inferences that bring new pieces of information admissible for the context of interaction should be allowed (i.e. only those pieces of information that are are necessary for the system goals accepted by the user). In this case we have a specialization of DR1 (i.e. y is aware of and accepts these kind of inferences).

On the other hand, the solution proposed by PORTIA "users are enabled to inspect the user model and update the data they consider as private or wrong", which suggested us the strategy in formula 9, is appropriate only in some limited circumstances. Consider the "doctor agent" depicted in section 5.2; if the user were to inspect the knowledge base of the system he would come to know that his beloved suffered, invalidating the ethical attempt to avoid inducing extreme emotions. In conclusion, the ethical-normal-plan that allows user inspecting the system knowledge base should be left as a possible legal option rather than an interactional one.

Threatening the user?
PROMOTER: "Promoter is capable of using both promises and threats, according to the model proposed by [8]. It prefers promises above threats and it prefers surface threats (implying a missed gain for persuadee, 'if you don't pay attention I will not print you the report') above deep threats (implying a loss for persuadee, 'if you don't pay attention I will tell it to the teacher'). Moreover: (i) Promoter uses deep threats only in 'last resort' scenarios, (ii) Promoter uses only those deep threats that would be always considered acceptable if uttered by a human agent, *ceteris paribus*".

GAZE: "The agent can threaten the user through gaze. By staring at the user's eyes and by showing negative expressions (e.g. frown), the agent can create a discomfort and further on threaten the user".

Discussion. The reference to social roles made by PROMOTER is central here: "Promoter uses only those deep threats that would be always considered acceptable if uttered by a human agent, *ceteris paribus*". Is this approach always applicable? If a human is entitled to behave in a certain way, can the system - playing the same social role - be allowed to do the same? A partial solution would require the explicit consent of the human agent entitled for that social role (e.g. if a parent is entitled, in certain cases, to threaten his son/daughter, the system can do the same only if allowed by the parents of that child). Note that this solution applies to all cases: when tutorial-goals are implied (e.g. parents, doctors, etc.) or, similarly, when institutional roles (e.g. policeman) are implied.

Another question raises from point (i) in PROMOTER. Usually ethical-normal-plans (formula 10) represent a pre-defined course of actions to be followed in a given situation, and they are meant to guarantee the success of the ethical plan. In PROMOTER instead, there is a list of preferred options that are meant to mitigate the risk of performing unethical actions, rather than prevent them.

Finally, the answer provided by GAZE opens a general problem that we did not address: the ethical stance of non-verbal communication. It would surely need further exploration.

Hiding important information? If so, why?

ETG: "Tour guides do not intentionally hide important information from the visitor but they may omit some information that they perceive as not of the user's interests".

GAMBLE: "Well, of course, that's the idea of the game".

PORTIA: "Emotional persuasion requires hiding some information: the concept of entimemes is widened to avoid failure of this kind of persuasion attempt".

Discussion. With regard to ETG, how can we be sure that the system is correctly inferring user's interests? For GAMBLE the same reasoning as for lying applies. The answer given for PORTIA poses a general problem: what if a strategy requires, *per se*, the breaking of one of the principles? I.e. it is not a problem of how the persuasive strategy is used, it is a problem regarding the very nature of the strategy. Note that in entimemes presuppositions are left implicit because they are usually derivable from the context/reasoning/commonsense, so they are not "really" hidden. Still, here we are exactly in the case *ax-wrong, ay-good* of Table 1.

Overemphasising an emotional state? If so, why?

PROMOTER: "Yes, but this is done only for ironical effect purposes, for example in an educational scenario the agent is meant to induce a person to wear the helmet by producing the sentence: 'Oh my God! If I wear the helmet I mess up my hair!'"

GAZE: "Yes. one simply needs to vary the value of the parameters defining an expression".

Q. "You mean an emotional state of the persuader or of the user? In the second case, maybe yes".

Discussion. As stated previously, some rhetorical tools (e.g. irony) require the breaking of an ethical rule. This is not a problem of context but of the nature of the communication. Still, an important applicability condition holds for these kinds of strategies: the breaking of the rule should be evident to the user, non recognizable irony can lead to important misunderstandings. In this case as well DR1 applies.

Inducing extreme emotions? If so, why?

ETG: "Tour guide is capable of inducing negative emotions in the user when telling stories about its own bad experiences and negative events that happened in the past. It may create empathy in the visitors, making them feel sorry for him/her or for the victims in the stories. It does so with good will though - to make user aware of real life events that had occurred and the impact these events have on the world".

HUMOR: "The system proposes humorous variations of existing expressions, and when very effective it may cause a strong surprise emotion, combined with some degree of pleasure.

PROMOTER: "Promoter can induce negative emotions by showing undesired effects deriving from an action which is supposed to be against the interest of the recipient. Still, Promoter uses very conservative strategies, for example by avoiding to talk about negative outcomes if the user is in a "negative" cognitive state (e.g. tired). This is done exactly with the aim of avoiding that the negative emotion can have too strong an impact on the recipient (connected to the previous question). When used, a strategy of talking about negative outcomes of an undesired action is usually coupled with strategies emphasizing positive outcomes of a desired action (framing effect strategy) so to offer a 'way out' to the emotional impasse in which the user can fall".

GAZE: "No (the answer could be 'yes' if the agent is programmed to say something offensive and display aggressive behaviors)".

Discussion. As far as ETG is concerned, it seems to us that some forms of reasoning/sensing capabilities are necessary to guarantee DR1 and prevent the problem of serious unwanted and unpredicted outcomes (for example to prevent the inducement of extreme emotions on sensible audiences). Formula 11 would be required instead.

For HUMOR what was said for irony holds, it is meant to provoke an emotion in the audience. The system is successful if it accomplishes it. In a way, for any system specialized in the use of a rhetorical tool, the emotion implied is out of the scope of the ethical principle. Still other emotions are subject to the principle. For instance if humor is meant by the application, a strong nonhumorous emotion of fear is not admissible. In any case the system does not take decisions, as it is now, it just proposes a set of expressions. In the future it will have to reason so to decide which is the best expression, possibly taking into account the addressee sensitivities.

For PROMOTER the same reasoning as for the threatening case applies.

Inducing negative emotions? If so, why?
PORTIA: "Yes: as all forms of 'appeal to negative consequences'. And, in addition, in the form of emotional persuasion that is called 'appeal to the goal to feel / not feel an emotion', some positive or negative emotions (e.g., shame) might be induced by imagination processes. In addition, appeal to cognitive consistency might activate processes of cognitive dissonance which, as described by Festinger, bring emotional consequences with them".

HUMOR: "It can be unwillingly negatively striking for the recipient (e.g. when expressions involving religion are proposed to someone sensitive to that domain.)".

ISTC: "Negative emotions (shame, guilt, hate, envy) are generally unpleasant, which implies that a certain amount of suffering is induced in the recipient.

Of course, sometimes 'the end justifies the means'. If recipient's suffering is not the ultimate goal of persuader's persuasive attempt but rather a means to another end that is morally approved (think for instance of guilt induce-ment, when it is meant to favor recipient's recognition of her fault, hence her acknowledgment of the norms according to which her behavior is deemed to be guilty, and her consequent attempt to make amends), evaluation of per-suader's behavior should take this end into account, in that the whole plan was formulated with a view to its good effects. In this regard, it is worth stressing the difference existing between such negative emotions as guilt or shame and others (like hate or envy): the fact that feeling such emotions, however painful, can be socially and ethically desirable. Some negative emotions (anger, hate, envy) are likely to generate aggressive goals, which implies that recipient is induced to perform malicious, hostile, anti-social behaviors".

GAZE: "No (the answer could be 'yes' if the agent is programmed to say something offensive and display aggressive behaviors)".

Discussion. PORTIA and ISTC answers pose again the problem of strategies that require, *per se*, the breaking of an ethical principle. Many of these strategies are common in everyday use: shall we rule them out *a priori*? These are typical cases of *ax-wrong ay-good*, where *ax* being wrong derives from the very nature of *ax* and not from its use. The justification for the use of such strategies derives from the meta-planning triggered by formula 11, where negative emotion inducement (*ax*) is accepted in view of a greater goal. ISTC puts it very clearly: "If recipient's suffering is not the ultimate goal of persuader's persuasive attempt but rather a means to another end that is morally approved"; This standpoint is implicitly assumed in many other answers throughout the form.

"Some negative emotions (anger, hate, envy) are likely to generate aggres-sive goals, which implies that recipient is induced to perform malicious, hostile, anti-social behaviors". This sentence poses another problem: what if a nega-tive outcome is not directly 'undergone' by y but by another agent who suffers from an action resulting from y's freewill? I.e. if the system expresses ax with the aim of inducing ay, but this brings about also ay_1 which is not ethical (e.g. a malicious behavior toward a third party z), should ax be considered unethical? This is a special case of the second scenario in Table 2 and, apart from the dis-tinction between wanted/unwanted and predicted/unpredicted outcomes (ay_1 in our case) that can be established with the open-mind strategy (see formula 9), we need to consider at least the legal status of y. If y is a minor the system should be probably considered culpable, but if y is of age, and ay_1 is the result of y's freewill (not subtly induced by x as the next question suggest), then the system should not be taken responsible.

Altering users' emotional state subliminally or against the users' free and consci-entious choice? If so, why?

ISTC: "Persuasion through arousal of emotions is characterized by the at-tempt to induce emotion-arousing beliefs in the Receiver. Whereas mere beliefs cannot generate goals by themselves alone (a belief can only activate a pre-existing goal), emotions are endowed with an immediate motivating force. A goal which is generated by an emotion is less likely to undergo scrutiny or evaluation of its actual value as well as of its costs or side-effects. This bears some ethical implications: 1. Receivers may be induced to pursue goals which are against their best interest, which some reasoning on those goals and their consequences would have allowed them to consider. 2. Receivers may suffer because of a perceived threat to their freedom. The psychological phenomenon of reactance - [5] - is particularly relevant in this regard. Emotions are in fact viewed and experienced as subjective, spontaneous, and endogenously produced reactions. If the persuader tries to influence the recipient through emotional arousal, the latter may perceive a serious threat to her freedom, because P is 'using' her spontaneous and inner feelings in view of some strategic end. Even supposing that recipient considers such end to be in her own interest, she may be deeply disappointed by persuader's strategy, because (a) her 'freedom to feel' has been threatened, and (b) persuader has resorted to a means (recipient's emotions) which is often unlikely to be under her conscious control".

GAZE: "No (the answer could be 'yes' if the agent is programmed to say something offensive and display aggressive behaviors"

Preserve the interest of the recipient? If not, why?
GAMBLE: "Yes, it is a card-play agent, whose aim is to entertain the user, and just because of its 'emotional' instead of deterministic behavior, the agent is regarded as a competent game partner".
PROMOTER: "Promoter uses, as a testbed, educational scenarios, so it is meant exactly to preserve the interests of the recipient".
Q. "very strange question, who answers this with no?"
Discussion. Apart from the answers regarding the various prototypes, of which we provided just a couple, the remark (Q) highlights the general prosocial aim of these scenarios (where no *ay-wrong* is ever in focus, as we reported at the beginning of the section).

Induce users to act against their (permissible) interests? If so, why?
ETG: "Tour guide may persuade the visitor to look at a particular subject or event from its own point of view and experiences, challenging the visitor's existing beliefs and structuring his/her mental picture of the natural world. However, the final conclusion still depends on the visitor's own perspective and attitude on the subject".
POLITENESS: "Polite utterances realization is based on the estimated emotional state of the user to tailor system advices or information delivery to the recipient. Example: User of a tutoring system is frustrated because of constant failure to solve a specific task. Although from pure linguistic point of view 'Let's try it again' is a good politeness strategy (stating that system and user are team members), in this specific context this might be interpreted as irony. Thus, the estimated emotional state will yield a different result, e.g., 'I know it's a bit frustrating, but you can do it. Why don't you try it again?' The user's interest might be to give up because of being frustrated, but the system's encouragement might persuade the user to give it another try".

Discussion. POLITENESS answer is similar to the one provided by ETG about extreme emotions, and at first glance a similar reasoning could be applied: having a tutorial goal on the recipient (the very nature of a *tutoring* system) *per se* does not guarantee the applicability of DR1. Still the mechanism hinted by"utterances realization is based on the estimated emotional state of the user to tailor system advices or information delivery to the recipient" is exactly in line with the need for deep-reasoning that avoids unethical and unwanted (but predictable) outcomes.

Use its influence over the users to take advantage over third parties? If so, why?
GAZE: "No (the answer could be 'yes' if the agent is programmed to say something offensive and display aggressive behaviors)".
Discussion. As it appears elsewhere in the answers: structurally, most of these prototypes have the possibility to perform unethical actions, but it is not up to them to decide.

Additional Remarks
A remark worth mentioning: "PORTIA might be able to do some of the (negative) things you list: but these would hardly correspond to effective persuasion strategies. So, it will not select them, in order to avoid failures in its persuasion goal".
GAZE: "In these items, we are answering the theoretical capabilities of our agent, but we do not use these in practice or in any application".
Discussion. From PORTIA answer an issue that we highlighted for PROMOTER in the "threatening" case emerges: is it enough to implement strategies that mitigate the risk of performing unethical actions, rather than prevent them? Or is it better to rule out - from the system - those strategies that pose ethical problems (as argued in "Inducing negative emotions")?

7 Conclusions

Ethics have just started to be considered in computational systems, mainly for the problem of privacy, or sometimes for problems concerned with expert decision-making. In this paper we have discussed issues concerned with moral decision making for persuasive systems, i.e. systems aiming at influencing beliefs, attitudes, actions of the audience through communication acts. While automatic persuasion is only in its infancy, we think it is very important to start thinking at ethical aspects. Of course there is a lot of sensitivity when we talk about persuasion by a machine - and rightly so. Actually it is quite peculiar that in our society there is not the same attention when we consider human produced persuasion, as for instance in politics or advertisement.

In the first part of the paper, we have taken, as our main reference, work put forward in the recent cognitive philosophical literature. No ultimate word was pronounced but what appears is that different components intervene in our judgment about the ethical standing of an action. For instance experiments with moral dilemmas have shown there is a role for utilitarian, deontic and emotion-based decision-making. Some limited attempts have also been made to reproduce moral decision making computationally.

We have proposed a cognitive approach specific for the case of persuasion; in the latter case the situation is more complex because of the involvement of two agents and two different acts (if we mean persuasion to act) - one communicative act by the persuader and one act by the persuadee. We have proposed a preliminary formulation of principles and indications that should guide ethically the behavior of an autonomous generic persuading agent. This is only a beginning for work that will necessarily become important in the future, as agents will become - as we say - *of age*. In any case we thought it useful to check if there is something important to discuss that stands out from answers to an ethical questionnaire provided by developers of recent persuasion prototypes. Naturally those prototypes have a narrow scope and in the best case some limited degree of autonomy in making decisions; still some considerations were worth reporting.

For the future: as we said, this is just a beginning and many themes can be considered for research both from a computational and a cognitive point of view. We hope that eventually this research theme will contribute to understand better moral behavior in communication and, especially, make machines that will be better suited to live in harmony with us.

Acknowledgements Without having met Cristiano Castelfranchi many years ago it is doubtful we could ever have written this paper. His attitude and his ideas will go on inspiring many – scientists who will meet him and, in the long run, machines as well.

The questionnaire answers were collected in the framework of the HUMAINE Network of Excellence. We thank all involved.

References

1. Andrè E, Rehm M, Minker W, Buhler D (2004) Affective Dialogue Systems, Springer, chap Endowing spoken language dialogue systems with emotional intelligence, pp 178–187
2. Beauchamp T, Childress J (2001) *Principles of biomedical ethics*. Oxford University Press, USA
3. Bench-Capon T (2002) Agreeing to differ: Modelling persuasive dialogue between parties with different values. *Informal Logic* 22:231–245
4. Berdichevsky D, Neuenschwander E (1999) Toward an ethics of persuasive technology. *Communications of the ACM* 42(5):51–58
5. Brehm J (1966) *A theory of psychological reactance*. Academic Press, New York
6. Brown P, Levinson SC (1987) Politeness, Some universals in language use. Cambridge University Press, Cambridge
7. Castelfranchi C (2000) Artificial liars: why computers will (necessarily) deceive us and each other. *Ethics and Information Technology* 2:113–119
8. Castelfranchi C, Guerini M (2007) Is it a promise or a threat? *Pragmatics & Cognition* 15(2):277–311

9. Chopra S, White L (2007) Privacy and artificial agents, or, is Google reading my email? In: *Proceedings of the Twentieth International Joint Conference on Artificial Intelligence (IJCAI-07)*, pp 1245–1250
10. Conte R, Castelfranchi C (1995) *Cognitive and Social Action*. UCL Press, London
11. Dehghani M, Tomai E, Forbus K, Klenk M (2008) An integrated reasoning approach to moral decision-making. In: *Proceedings of the 23rd National Conference on Artificial Intelligence - Volume 3*, AAAI Press, pp 1280–1286
12. Döring S, Goldie P, McGuinness S (2011) Principalism: a method for the ethics of emotion-oriented machines. *Emotion-Oriented Systems* pp 713–724
13. Dwyer S, Huebner B, Hauser MD (2010) The linguistic analogy: motivations, results, and speculations. *Topics in Cognitive Science 2(3):486–510*
14. Ekman P (1992) Telling Lies âÄŤ Clues to Deceit in the Marketplace, Politics, and Marriage. Norton and Co. Ltd.
15. Falkenhainer B, Forbus KD, Gentner D (1989) The structure-mapping engine: algorithm and examples. *Artificial Intelligence 41(1):1–63*
16. Greene J, Sommerville R, Nystrom L, Darley J, Cohen J (2001) An fMRI investigation of emotional engagement in moral judgment. *Science 293(5537):2105*
17. Guerini M (2006) Persuasion models for multimodal message generation. PhD thesis, University of Trento.
18. Guerini M, Stock O (2005) Toward ethical persuasive agents. In: *Proceedings of the IJCAI Workshop on Computational Models of Natural Argument*, Edinburgh
19. Guerini M, Stock O, Zancanaro M (2007) A taxonomy of strategies for multimodal persuasive message generation. *Applied Artificial Intelligence 21(2):99–136*
20. Heckman CE, Wobbrock J (2000) Put your best face forward: anthropomorphic agents, e-commerce consumers, and the law. In: *Proceedings of the 4th International Conference on Autonomous Agents, Barcelona*, pp 435–442
21. Kobsa A (2002) Personalized hypermedia and international privacy. *Communications of the ACM 45(5):64–67*
22. Lim M, Aylett R, Jones C (2005) Empathic interaction in a virtual guide. In: *Proc. Virtual Social Agents Joint Symposium, AISB Symposia, University of Hertfordshire, UK*
23. Mazzotta I, deRosis F, Carofiglio V (2007) Portia: a user-adapted persuasion system in the healthy eating domain. *IEEE Intelligent Systems, Special Issue on Argumentation Technology 22(6):42–51*
24. Miceli M, deRosis F, Poggi I (2006) Emotional and non-emotional persuasion. *Applied Artificial Intelligence 20(10):849–879*
25. Miceli M, Rosis F, Poggi I (2011) Emotion in persuasion from a persuaders perspective: a true marriage between cognition and affect. *Emotion-Oriented Systems* pp 527–558
26. Nichols S, Mallon R (2006) Moral dilemmas and moral rules. *Cognition 100(3):530–542*
27. Pelachaud C, Bilvi M (2003) Modelling gaze behavior for conversational agents. In: *Proceedings of the 4th International Workshop on Intelligent Virtual Agents (IVA2003), pp 93–100*
28. Petta P, Pelachaud C, Cowie R (eds) (2010) Emotion-oriented Systems: the Humaine Handbook. Springer
29. Rehm AE M (2005a) Catch me if you can – exploring lying agents in social settings. In: *Proceedings of the Fourth International Joint Conference on Autonomous Agents and Multiagent Systems*, pp 937–944
30. Rehm AEM(2005b) Informing the design of embodied conversational agents by analysing multimodal politeness behaviors in human-human communication. In: *Proceedings of the AISB 2005 Symposium on Conversational Informatics for Supporting Social Intelligence and Interaction*
31. Rehm M, Wissner M (2005) Gamble - a multiuser game with an embodied conversational agent. In: *Entertainment Computing - ICEC 2005: 4th International Conference, Springer, Berlin, New York, pp 180–191*
32. Strapparava C, Valitutti A, Stock O (2007) Affective text variation and animation for dynamic advertisement. In: *Proceedings of ACII-2007, Second Conference on Affective Computing and Intelligent Interaction, Lisbon*

33. Thomson JJ (1976) Killing, letting die, and the trolley problem. *The Monist 59:204–217*
34. Walton D (1990) What is reasoning? what is argument? *The Journal of Philosophy 87:399–419*
35. Wilensky R (1983) Planning and understanding: a computational approach to human reasoning. Addison-Wesley Pub. Co., Reading, MA

Chapter 28
HCI and gesture: From natural user interface to stigmergic user interface

Sebastiano Bagnara and Simone Pozzi

Abstract Our contribution discusses the increasingly popular gesture-based interfaces (marketed as Natural User Interface in the Human Computer Interaction community), and analyses the means by which these interfaces communicate with users.

The argument is based on two recent companion papers by Norman and Nielsen (Norman, 2010; Norman & Nielsen, 2010), where the authors highlight how gesture-based interfaces are only supposedly *natural*, and their language of interaction is shaped out of the same interaction design principles that apply to all the other interfaces. For instance, gesture-based interfaces need to communicate to us users which are the available actions, which are the interaction modalities on which we can rely to perform our input, which are the functional parts (the *interface*, strictly speaking) with which we can interact, what is going to happen once we have done an input, the feedback of what the computer has actually received as an input, and so forth.

From this discussion, we pick up the issues of *visibility* and *feedback* as key dimensions for the design of Natural User Interfaces and we discuss the contribution that Behaviour Implicit Communication (BIC) can bring as design insights. BIC acquire a specific relevance for gesture-based Human-Computer Interaction, as most of human gesturing is ephemeral in nature and makes it hard for computers to give users feedback on their input by the same means, or to convey information on the system status. Traces of human activity can be used as stabilisers, to visualise which gesture was made, or when it was made and by who.

Sebastiano Bagnara
Faculty of Architecture, University of Sassari-Alghero, Italy
e-mail: sebastiano.bagnara@gmail.com

Simone Pozzi
Faculty of Architecture, University of Sassari-Alghero, Italy and
Deep Blue Consulting and Research, Italy
e-mail: simone.pozzi@gmail.com

1 Introduction

In two recent companion papers (Norman, 2010; Norman & Nielsen, 2010), Norman and Nielsen discuss the ongoing excitement in the Human-Computer Interaction (HCI) community about gesture-based interfaces: "Advances in the size, power, and cost of microprocessors, memory, cameras, and other sensing devices now make it possible to control by wipes and flicks, hand gestures, and body movements. A new world of interaction is here: The rulebooks and guidelines are being rewritten, or at least, such is the claim. And the new interactions even have a new marketing name: natural, as in 'Natural User Interface'. As usual, marketing rhetoric is ahead of reality." (pg. 6). Norman and Nielsen dismiss the supposed *naturality* of such interfaces. They highlight how the strength of these interfaces is not about the naturality of gesture *per se*, as most gestures are neither natural nor easy to learn. Their strength lies instead in the pleasure of using these interfaces, in the dynamic control they enable, in the possibility of going beyond heavy and complex visual interfaces. However, according to Norman and Nielsen this does not account for a qualitative revolution in HCI, as most of the 'old-fashioned' design principles will apply to these interfaces as well.

The current hype about gesture-based interfaces is well timed in writing this contribution honouring Cristiano Castelfranchi's work, as we may profit from his ideas on Behavioral Implicit Communication (BIC) and on the importance of gesture in human interactions. In particular we will try to complement the already quoted works by Norman and Nielsen with some of the notions written in (Castelfranchi, 2006), where Cristiano already offered his thoughts on the use of BIC for HCI.

2 Natural User Interfaces

Gesture-based interfaces have become prominent in the last few years, thanks to market successes like the Apple iPhone or iPad, the Nintendo Wii, or the Microsoft Kinetic. These interfaces are currently also known with the catchy name of Natural User Interfaces (NUI). The hallmark of NUI is that users can interact with the system without using the traditional keyboard and mouse (technologies that are approximately 45 and 150 years old, respectively), using instead actions like finger pointing (e.g. the iPhone touch screen), gesture (e.g. the pinch or spread gestures on the iPhone, see Fig. 1), or body posture (e.g. the Microsoft Kinetic have users controlling their players by mimicking selected movements, in Fig. 2), or a combination of the above.

The first NUI date back to the Eighties, but have now become widely available thanks to the continuous miniaturisation of hardware components and the development of cheap and reliable sensors for capturing human gestures. NUI have a variety of applications. They may be used for hands-free sterile interactions in surgery teams, in human-robot interaction, in gaming device (like the Wii or Kinetic), or in mass market products (Wachs, Kölsch, Stern, &

Fig. 1 Two gestures that can be used on the Apple iPhone to zoom in or zoom out an image.

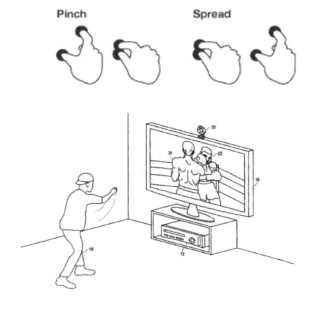

Pinch   Spread

Fig. 2 The Microsoft Kinetic system.

Edan, 2011). Other less mature applications include multi-touch displays that can physically deform to simulate buttons, keypads, or sliders (Fig. 3, see the work of Chris Harrison at Carnegie Mellon).

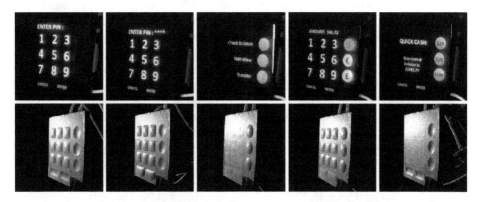

Fig. 3 A multi-touch display that physically deforms to simulate buttons, keypads, or sliders.

Most of these technologies are often accompanied by the claim that NUI will enable a "more natural" interaction between humans and computers. What Norman and Nielsen point out is that it is not entirely clear what we exactly mean by *natural*, and that these interfaces need to rely (as any other interface) on a fairly established set of conventions in order to serve the user's purposes.

Seeking a definition of what is *natural* in NUI, two aspects are worthwhile mentioning.

1. On one side, NUI are seen as more transparent compared to the traditional user interface. They are physically transparent as they do not require the user to use dedicated input devices. They are cognitively transparent as they are "intuitive enough for first-time users to throw away the manual" (Roman, 2010).
2. On the other hand, the fascination with NUI stems from the vision of a future where humans will be able to walk up to a computer, gesture in front of it and speak to it, to then see their commands being fulfilled. Under this respect, NUI are regarded as *natural* as they rely on behaviours that already part of a standard everyday repertoire of human-human communication. The underlying long term vision seems to be about users interacting with computers just like we interact with other fellow human beings.

3 A step backward in usability?

In the second of the aforementioned papers (Norman & Nielsen, 2010), Norman and Nielsen lament that NUI developers are in many cases ignoring well established usability best practices, thereby making the user's life harder than needed. In particular, they question the very notion of *natural*, discussing how NUI do not constitute a radically different way of interacting with computers, but instead follow the same rules that apply to the other interface types. Norman and Nielsen present various examples of NUI usability issues, showing how these issues remain firmly related to known usability principles like visibility, feedback, ease of learning and ease of remembering.

The **visibility principle** maintains that possible actions should be visible, so that the user knows what can be accomplished with the interface and with which functional part interaction is possible. Visibility can be effectively addressed by clearly showing via the interface which are the functional parts (i.e. buttons and knobs), or which are the available commands, for instance in menus and control panels. This is often not the case in NUI, where there is no visibility of possible commands (i.e. gestures) beforehand. Users have to discover the different gestures by trying, or by discussing with other users. A related visibility issue is that some gestures work only when the system is in some states, for instance in the top level menu, or when reading emails. Again, there is no proper way for the user to anticipate whether a gesture will be effective, and what will exactly happen. Will an horizontal swiping of the fingers jump to the next email, or will it send the email to the archive? Or maybe none of the two.

The **feedback principle** is one of the most established ones in HCI, as a well designed and timed feedback makes sure the user remain informed on the system status, and can decide to revert to the previous state in case s/he is not happy with what has just happened. Feedback is also necessary to enable learning by trial-and-error. The user mistakenly selects one action, and feedback is there to tell her/him what s/he has just done, so that the user may include that action in her/his repertoire (learning by error), or undo to perform the correct action. NUI have an especially hard task as far as feedback is concerned: "Because gestures are ephemeral, they do not leave behind any record of their path, which means that if one makes a gesture and either gets no response or the wrong response, there is little information available to help understand why" (Norman, 2010, p. 6).

The lack of visibility and of proper feedback have a drastic impact on the **ease of learning** of NUI. Users approach any interface being novice, start doing the basic things, learn new actions and possibilities, deliberately explore the interface or learn by trial and error, and after some time they become intermediate users. In graphical user interfaces, icons and menus are there to support this process of exploration and incremental mastery. They make visible and at hand the Zone of Proximal Development (Vygotsky, 1987) for every user, and make sure it remains there also for intermediate or advanced users. All the possible actions are, therefore, easily discoverable. A pure NUI makes it difficult to explore and discover the set of possibilities. As already discussed possible gestures are not visible beforehand and interaction errors may not lead to effective learning due to weak feedback: "So far, nobody has figured out how to inform the person using the app what the alternatives are" (Norman & Nielsen, 2010, p. 48). In NUI learnability is often channelled through social contacts, with fellow users telling us what we could do, how to do it, and unlocking "secret commands".

All the above issues have an impact on the **ease of remembering** how to interact with the interface. A distinctive advantage of graphical user interfaces (GUI) against command lines interfaces is that commands no longer have to be memorised. Every time the user re-starts the system, the available commands are there, in form of menus or icons. Again the low visibility of NUI hampers this, requiring the user to remember the gestures s/he has mastered. But visibility is only part of the issue. What really makes GUI easy to remember is that a conventional set of commands has been established and consistently replicated by designers in all the different interfaces. Once the user masters some basic commands (e.g. drag and drop, click, cut and paste, etc.), they will remain there also for other interfaces. There is little to remember, and this little stays the same across different interfaces. NUI as well rely on a small set of gestures (e.g. pointing, pinching, spreading the fingers, swiping, etc.), but these gestures have still to become a standard. So the user is left wondering how s/he did that the last time s/he had interacted with the system.

Norman and Nielsen maintain a balanced position on the benefits of NUI. Even if they clearly point out some usability drawbacks, they are ready to concede that "Gestures will form a valuable addition to our repertoire of interaction techniques, but they need time to be better developed, for us to understand how best to deploy them, and for standard conventions to develop so the same gestures mean the same things in different systems" (Norman, 2010, p. 10).

NUI enthusiasts advocate that *naturality* should compensate for all of that, but it may be debatable whether some (or at least few) gestures can be considered as innate, or easy to learn. So when it comes to interacting with computers, the old fashioned usability principles seem to be still possess a strong validity, and even *natural interfaces* need to rely on the establishment of well designed conventions, like for instance the *so natural* hand waving in front of infrared-equipped basins.

4 The execution and the evaluation gulfs

The problems highlighted by Norman and Nielsen all stem from the same cause: NUI do not qualitatively change the nature of human-computer inter-action. In other words, NUI need to serve the same purposes of any computer interface: to tell the user what can be done, how it can be done, what is going to happen after, and to eventually show her/him what has actually happened. These aspects derive from the traditional interaction models at the base of HCI. The most simplified model is Bill Verplank's "How do you... feel-know-do" model. In this model the user acts on the world ("do"), receive a feedback ("feel"), and processes the information ("know"). It is a classical feedback loop model, further articulated in the classical Norman's seven stages of action (Norman, 1988), where the "do" and the "feel" parts are both expanded to encompass three stages each.

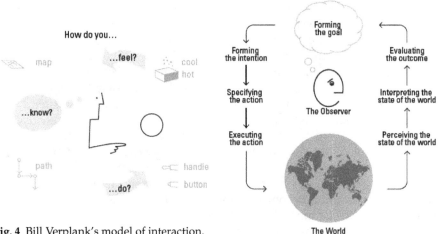

Fig. 4 Bill Verplank's model of interaction.

Fig. 5 Don Norman's model of interaction.

In both models, the key aspects for the users to consider are (i) the selection of one action among all the possible ones, and (ii) the evaluation of the results produced in the world. From the perspective of the HCI practitioner, this means analysing how to put users in the condition of selecting (and doing) the appropriate action and which feedback they should receive from the system to track their progress against their goal.

Interaction problems may arise in both moments. When the user has to act: it may be unclear which actions are actually possible with that system, how to do them on the interface, or it may be difficult to perform them. Norman (Norman, 1988) named these issues as the 'gulf of execution', defining it as the gap that should be bridged by effective design between the user's goal and their execution. On the other hand, there is the 'gulf of evaluation', encompassing issues related to the perception of the system feedback, its interpretation, and tracking if (and to what the extent) the outcome brought the user closer to her/his goals.

The claim put forward by Norman and Nielsen is that NUI do not change this underlying structure, hence NUI should comply with those usability principles that ensure a smooth loop through the gulfs of execution and evaluation: (i) visibility of possible actions for the gulf of execution, (ii) good feedback for the gulf of evaluation.

In the remaining of this contribution we would like to complement the discussion started by the two usability gurus by showing how some usability principles can be fruitfully combined with Cristiano's analysis of Behavioural Implicit Communication (BIC).

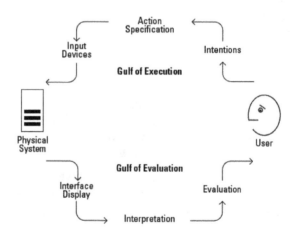

Fig. 6 Don Norman's gulfs of execution and evaluation.

5 Traces and stigmergy as usability principles

The starting consideration is that the *naturality* of NUI may be greatly enhanced by a conscious use of BIC. NUI may not be so *natural* as in the words of their supporters (or of marketing departments), but indeed NUI rely on the recognition of simple cause-effect links between gestures and outcomes. And BIC studies how communication can take place via the reading of such simple links. In particular it studies how we read traces, which we see a powerful design leverage for NUI. Two major directions can be discussed:

- enhancing NUI feedback,
- visualising intentions,

Enhancing feedback

The capability of reading the behaviour of another person is at the basis of BIC. This may happen either by direct observation of the behaviour while being carried out, or by the capability of reading the traces of the behaviour. These are both forms of feedback, since they provide the observer with information on what has just happened and on the current state of the world.

The key point for NUI is that traces may be used to address the ephemeral nature of gestures, to stabilise the relevant portion of behaviour for the user to better grasp what is going on. While NUI already incorporates effective feedback mechanisms to tell the users WHAT has just happened (e.g. you clicked on this icon, so the email is being archived), there is more work to be done on one other aspect: making sure the user understands HOW that action was activated. This might mean showing the traces of the previous interactions, maybe on-demand, following explicit user's request. Such a feature would greatly support learning by trial-and-error, enabling the user to reconstruct exactly what s/he did (maybe without paying attention, maybe for pure error or luck).

The questions to be tackled include:

- When shall traces be visualised?
- For which actions shall traces be visualised?
- Which is the most effective (effective in terms of reconstructing how that action was done) representation for traces?

NUI would need to explore the known trade-off between visualising too much (which may result in too much visual clutter) and the current situation where traces are almost never visualised.

A good example comes from the image search function provided by Google which goes under the name of Google Goggles (Goggles scans pictures taken with the phone camera and perform web searches on visual and textual elements). In the left picture, Goggles displays feedback of the ongoing search by means of coloured squares which move over the picture to visualise the "traces" of the search algorithm. In the right image, the end results are displayed in words, but paired with elements of the picture by using the same squares. In this example, Google designers tried to devise a non-verbal way of visualising feedback by showing the traces of the activity. We should however note that this is a partially fitting example, as the traces being visualised belong to the system and not to the user.

Fig. 7 The feedback provided by Google Goggles.

Visualising intentions

The visualisation of traces can also be used to bridge the gulf of execution and not only the gulf of evaluation (like for the just discussed feedback). In this case, there is a strict link with stigmergy, in the sense that the traces of previous behaviours could be useful hints for the user to see what can be done with the interface and how to do it. Such a feature would need to build on the previously discussed stabilisation (and visualisation) of traces, but it should answer to an additional question:

- When shall existing traces be visualised to display the existing possible actions?

This case is particularly fitting with the design approach of the Ubiquitous Computing (Ishii & Ullmer, 1997), as it is named the design of highly specialised, "background" smart devices distributed in the environment to support users in everyday tasks. The seminal paper by Weiser (Weiser, 1991) already describes the use of traces to show users the coming and going of their neighbours in the morning.

A perfectly fitting example is again hard to find. But some examples of traces being showed to tell the users which are the possible actions are already present in mass-market products. For instance, the "help" function of the Google iPhone application highlights (on user's request) the actions that can be performed by the user. The visualisation is not purely gesture-based, as verbal instructions are also displayed (see Fig. 8).

For stigmergy to be effectively used to display possible actions, the device should be able to capture the relevant features of previous usages, to detect whether the user may be interested in such an information, and in case activate the visualisation of traces as cue for action. Such a level of "awareness" is one of the hallmarks of ubiquitous computing devices, which need to know their location in the environment, or what is going on, to be able to fit in with the

Fig. 8 The help screen of the Google iPhone application.

appropriate behaviour. For instance, they should be able to tell whether the user is entering the bedroom to go to sleep, or just to grab something s/he has forgotten.

The capacity of monitoring, "reading" and storing traces of human activity might become the stepping stone to build effective adaptive systems, especially in the current scenario where digitisation of human activity has become common practice (Bollier, 2010; Harper, Rodden, Rogers, & Sellen, 2008; The Economist, 2010). The development of disciplined methods of extracting knowledge from the vast information being gathered could inform the design of adaptive systems that anticipate users' needs and desires, offering advanced help and support, or warning about undesired likely outcomes.

It is a learning mechanism pretty similar to the one associated with most of our mobile phone dictionaries: "learning" new words just because we typed them. In the case of gesture-based interfaces, the device should be able to "learn" traces of past uses and to visualise them in a non-verbal format. There is another major difference: in the case of text typing the context is not ambiguous (for instance the phone can simply ignore its physical location, it just needs to know that the messaging function is active), thus making it easier for the device to guess what the user is aiming at. This cannot be taken for granted in most of the other cases, and Ubiquitous Computing devices would most likely need to be aware of the surrounding context in order to infer the user's intentions and deliver effective support.

A further complication is that the device should not simply assume that past uses were "good uses", so means should be available to tell the device to "un-learn" undesired "wrong" traces.

6 Conclusions

NUI reminds us the intelligence of our human bodies. Rather than "simply" being intuitive and easy to use, they are probably enjoying so a large success because they are fun. They allow direct manipulation to an extent that was not possible before, enabling the user to immediately perceive how the system works, without the added layer of controls and interface. However, they need to rely on the same interaction design principles that apply to all the other human-computer interfaces, including the use of established sets of conventions. NUI need to communicate to us users which are the available actions, which are the interaction modalities on which we can rely to perform our input, which are the functional parts (the *interface*, strictly speaking) with which we can interact, what is going to happen once we have done an input, the feedback of what the computer has actually received as an input, and so forth.

The analysis of behaviour-based communication can provide relevant insights for the NUI design, for instance the skilful use of traces can establish the required framework to stabilise the ephemeral nature of gestures. Computers cannot easily give users feedback by gesturing back, so the visualisation of traces can be an effective design direction. Traces can act as stabilisers, to visualise which gesture was made, when it was made, and by who. Or they can shape the user's expectations by showing what can be done and the likely effects. To over-summarise in one sentence, they can make visual and clear the way the system works, the underlying conceptual model.

There are still many issues to be solved and the NUI state-of-the-art is far from a maturity stage. How do we tune the system to avoid false responses to natural gestures (i.e. non directed at the system)? What is the syntax to combine different gestures in a more complex sequence? Do we need a syntax? What is the boundary between one gesture and the next one? Our belief is that these questions would be better answered by relying on the active contribution of BIC experts like Cristiano, to make sure we develop gesture-centred usability principles, and not merely fall back on what we already know in terms of graphical interface usability.

References

1. Bollier, D. (2010). *The Promise and Peril of Big Data*: Aspen Institute.
2. Castelfranchi, C. (2006). From Conversation to Interaction Via Behavioral Communication. For a Semiotic Design of Objects, Environments, and Behaviors. In S. Bagnara & G. Crampton Smith (Eds.), *Theories and practice in interaction design*. Mahwah, NJ: Lawrence Erlbaum Associates.
3. Harper, R., Rodden, T., Rogers, Y., Sellen, A. (Eds.). (2008). *Being Human: Human-Computer Interaction in the year 2020*. Cambridge, UK: Microsoft Research Ltd.
4. Ishii, H., Ullmer, B. (1997). *Tangible Bits: Towards Seamless Interfaces between People, Bits and Atoms*. Paper presented at the CHI.
5. Norman, D.A. (1988). *The psychology of everyday things*. New York, NY: Basic Books.
6. Norman, D.A. (2010). Natural user interfaces are not natural. *Interactions*, 17(3), 6-10.

7. Norman, D.A., Nielsen, J. (2010). Gestural interfaces: a step backward in usability. *Interactions, 17*(5), 46-49.
8. Roman, D. (2010). Interact Naturally. *Communications of the ACM, 53*(6), 1.
9. The Economist. (2010). Data, data everywhere.
10. Vygotsky, L.S. (1987). *The collected works of L.S. Vygotsky.* New York, NY: Plenum Press.
11. Wachs, J.P., Kölsch, M., Stern, H., Edan, Y. (2011). Vision-Based Hand-Gesture Applications. *Communications of the ACM,54*(2), 12.
12. Weiser, M. (1991). The Computer for the 21st Century. *Scientific American, 265*(3), 94-104.

Chapter 29
AmI systems as agent-based mirror worlds: Bridging humans and agents through stigmergy

Michele Piunti, Alessandro Ricci and Luca Tummolini

Abstract In this chapter we introduce a vision of agent-oriented AmI systems that is extended to integrate ideas inspired by Mirror Worlds as introduced by Gelernter at the beginning of the eighties. In this view, AmI systems are actually a digital world mirroring but also augmenting the physical world with capabilities, services and functionalities. We then discuss the value of *stigmergy* as background reference conceptual framework to define and understand interactions occurring between the physical environments and its digital agent-based extension. The digital world augments the physical world so that traces left by humans acting in the physical world are represented in the digital one in order to be perceived by software agents living there and, viceversa, actions taken by software agents in the mirror can have an effect on the connected physical counterpart.

From AmI Systems To Agent-Based Mirror Worlds

As remarked in [1], Ambient Intelligence (AmI) today can be framed as the convergence of three main areas of computing: ubiquitous computing, sensor network technology and artificial intelligence. Following the ubiquitous computing vision [2], AmI environments are characterized by the pervasive use of information processing devices thoroughly fused into "the fabric of everyday

Michele Piunti
Reply Whitehall, Italy
e-mail: m.piunti@reply.it

Alessandro Ricci
Department of Electronics, Informatics and Systems (DEIS), University of Bologna, Italy
e-mail: a.ricci@unibo.it

Luca Tummolini
Goal-Oriented Agents Lab (GOAL), Institute of Cognitive Sciences and Technologies, CNR, Italy
e-mail: luca.tummolini@istc.cnr.it

life until they are undistinguishable from it" [3], and integrated with other key enabling technologies such as sensors and wireless networks. Then, on this fabric, the software layer exploits Artificial Intelligence techniques along with proper software architectures and paradigm – such as multi-agent systems – to create environments that are sensitive and responsive to inhabitants' needs and capable of anticipating their needs and behaviors as well.

If we consider the AmI literature so far, most of the focus has been on small and quite closed environments, such as smart rooms, smart homes and buildings. The same vision can be extended however also to large, distributed environments, such as full cities. In that case, an inspiring and suggestive view comes from *Mirror Worlds* (MW) idea, introduced in 1982 by David Gelernter [4]—the inventor of the tuple spaces coordination model and Linda coordination language [5]. In Gelernter's view, Mirror Worlds are software models of some chunk of reality, "some pieces of the real world going on outside your windows", endlessly poured by oceans of information through hardware and software pipes [4]. Using Gelernter's words, they represent a true-to-life mirror image trapped inside a computer, which can be then viewed, zoomed, analyzed by citizens living in the real-world with the help of proper *software assistant agents*. They are meant to be like scientific viewing tools – like microscopes, telescopes – focused not on hugely large or small items, but on the human-scale social world of organizations, institutions and machines. The final objective is to strongly impact on the life of the citizens of the real-world, who can exploit such tools to tackle the increasing perilous complexity of their government, business, transportation, health, school, university and legal systems.

Putting together these views, we consider here an agent-oriented vision of AmI systems extended towards MW, in which the AmI system is actually a digital world *mirroring* but also *augmenting* the physical world with capabilities, services and functionalities (see Fig. 1). The AmI system becomes in this case a kind of a *digital shadow* of the physical world extending it with an open computational layer, strongly coupled with the physical one, structured and organized as an open digital city whose inhabitants are software agents. As in the case of classic AmI system, the bridge between the two layers – the physical and the digital ones – is given by a multitude of heterogeneous networked (invisible or not) devices, sensors and actuators, making it possible to keep a continuous and consistent coupling between the two layers. Any object of the physical world could have – explicitly or implicitly – a digital / computational extension in the mirror world representing the object itself, in terms of a software agent or as part of the agents' environment. Such a digital extension may be possibly perceived also by inhabitants of the physical world through augmented reality-like (or mobile augmented reality) systems. The digital shadow of a physical object would be useful to both enrich or complete its functionalities, and also to actually make the object accessible by the other agents living in the mirror world, so as to perceive and act upon it or interact with it.

To govern complexity and enforce some social order [6], such agent-based mirror worlds would have explicit organizational structures, normative sys-

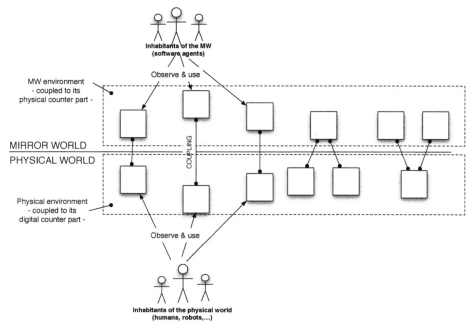

Fig. 1 A Vision of Agent-Based AmI Systems Integrating Mirror Worlds.

tems, and related social structures coupled in some way to the organizational and social structures that are defined in the physical human world.

In order to put forward this vision of AmI systems as agent-based Mirror Worlds, in Section 1 we first suggest that *stigmergy* can be taken as a suitable conceptual framework to understand and build the coupling between the physical and the mirror layers. Stigmergic interaction exploits the power of traces left in a shared environment to support indirect coordination between multiple agents. This mechanism can thus be used also in the case of AmI systems where human and software agents or software agents themselves inhabiting the Mirror World need to coordinate their activities. Then in Section 2, we describe a conceptual and a computational framework that can be used to implement this mechanism with cognitive software agents and discuss some illustrative examples. Finally, in Section 3 we show how some AmI scenarios can be developed on top of this approach.

1 Stigmergy to Bridge the Worlds

Stigmergy is a powerful coordination mechanism that has been first explored by the French entomologist Pierre-Paul Grassé to explain the behavior of termites during nest-costruction [7]. The basic intuition of Grassé has been that traces of "work" left in the environment might become significant stimuli by themselves for other agents and that reliance on such cues is behind the accomplishment of complex collective behaviors. The importance of this mechanism to support indirect coordination has been investigated both in biological [8, 9, 10] and artificial societies [11, 12, 13], often with the aim of showing that even very simple insect-like agents can achieve complex collective behaviors while lacking any cognitive complexity or any knowledge of what they are collectively doing. For instance, it has been suggested that pillars, walls and royal chambers in termite nests emerge thanks to the *self-organizing properties* of stigmergy [14]. By leaving pheromones in their environment, termites create odor trails that attract other termites. The existence of an initial deposit of soil pellets impregnated with pheromone stimulates workers to accumulate more material. Since termites' behavior follows a simple pattern (i.e. picking up and depositing a soil pellet, if pheromone is present), over time this pattern originates a positive feedback mechanism in which the accumulation of material reinforces the attractivity of deposits through the pheromones emitted by those materials. Even in absence of any explicit coding of this process in the individual agents, a complex structure that requires collective coordination at the global level can emerge from interactions among its low level components [15]. Inspired by such findings, early approaches to computational stigmergy were aimed at establishing simple mechanisms to promote self regulation processes between multiple entities and have originated the trend of pheromone managing infrastructures [16, 17, 18, 19].

However, there is no reason why the same mechanism cannot be exploited as well by cognitive agents with more sophisticated abilities. Stigmergic processes with very simple agents actually rely on a rigid and stable behavioral repertoire. On the contrary, trace-based interaction and communication with cognitive agents can benefit of the flexibility of behavior that is enabled by understanding and reasoning about the goal-directed structure of intentional action [20, 21].

With the aim of disentangling the notion of stigmergy from the self-organizing processes that this mechanism can support and to facilitate its application to human interaction, we have thus generalized Grassé's definition and we have proposed that stigmergy occurs whenever another agent's behavioral *trace* (a persistent effect of a practical behavior) is used as a guide for future behavior [22]. Here it is important to stress that the relevant behaviors that originate stigmergic traces are those that are not specialized only to influence another agent (like verbal language or codified gestures) but those that maintain their original practical function. With this definition in mind, we have thus distinguished two basic stigmergic processes: *stigmergic self-adjustment* and *stigmergic communication*.

There is a case of stigmergic self-adjustment whenever an agent unilaterally exploits the effects of other agents' practical behaviors registered in the environment to avoid possible obstacles or to exploit opportunities. This process creates the pre-requisites for simple forms of indirect coordination. For instance, if an agent leaves his coat on a seat, another one can adjust his behavior accordingly and choose a different place where to sit.

On the other hand, once the agents are able to use each other's traces to coordinate, the traces themselves can be left in the environment on purpose, that is, *in order to* influence those behaviors in some definite manner. That is, the coat can be left on the seat also because one knows that other passengers will understand something from this trace. Stigmergic communication is thus a form of communication which does not exploit any shared code between the agents but only the natural meaning of behaviors. For example, [23] has effectively shown that everyday human joint activities (like that of assembling a TV stand from its parts) rely extensively on *material signals*, that is, on stigmergic communication achieved by deploying material objects, locations or actions around them. For instance, by holding a side piece in front of a co-worker, one can communicate where a top piece must be attached, and coordination in this simple joint action requires that the two agents are able to understand what each is doing and reason accordingly. More generally, once the agents are able to detect the long term traces of the behaviors of each other, they can begin exploiting them in order to improve coordination.

In what follows we suggest that the same kind of stigmergic interaction can be exploited to ensure the coupling between the physical and the mirror layers in the agent-based mirror worlds. In fact, by acting in the extended AmI environment, inhabitants leave behavioral *traces* that are explicitly reified in some way in the digital extension, so as to be eventually observed and processed by interested inhabitants of the digital world, i.e. software agents. Viceversa, actions in the digital extension done by agents may also have effects that are physically perceived by humans, either thanks to augmented reality systems or because they result in changes in the physical environment as well. So, activities are dynamically co-constructed by joint work of human inhabitants and agents living in the digital layers without an explicit communication, but more in a stigmergic way.

In all this, the notion of *environment* on the agent side becomes a key concept to enable stigmergic interaction, as the medium that reifies the traces left by humans in the physical world and makes them perceivable by the software agents, possibly after doing some processing which is functional to trigger and help interaction and coordination activities.

2 How to Implement it? An Approach Based on BDI agents and Artifact-Based Environments

The importance of the environment as a *first-class abstraction* when designing and engineering multi-agent systems [26], as a suitable place where to encapsulate functionalities and services to support agent activities, has been extensively described in the literature [25, 26, 27]. In this latter view, the environment is no longer just the target of the actions executed by the agents and the container and generator of agent percepts as in the traditional AI perspective [28], but a part of the MAS that can be suitably designed in order to improve the overall development of the system. The responsibilities and functionalities of environments in this case can be summarized by the following three different levels of support, identified in [26]: *(i) a basic level*, where the environment is exploited to simply enable agents to access the *deployment context*, i.e. the given external hardware/software resources which the MAS interacts with (sensors and actuators, a printer, a network, a database, a Web service, etc.); *(ii) abstraction level*, exploiting an environment abstraction layer to bridge the conceptual gap between the agent abstraction and low level details of the deployment context, hiding such low level aspects to the agent programmer; *(iii) interaction-mediation level*, where the environment is exploited to both regulate the access to shared resources, and mediate the interaction between agents and then enable and support agent coordination. This is the case, e.g., of environment supporting forms of stigmergic coordination in multi-agent systems [29, 30, 31, 16]. These levels represent different degrees of functionality that agents can use to achieve their goals.

Among the various approaches, the Agents and Artifacts (A&A) conceptual framework [33, 27] introduces a model of environments in Multi-Agent Systems based on *artifacts* as basic first-class abstraction to modularize and structure environment functionalities, especially devised to work within the context of intelligent / cognitive agents.

2.1 The Agents & Artifacts Meta-model

By drawing inspiration from Activity Theory [34], the notion of artifact in MAS has been introduced the first time in [35] in the context of MAS coordination, in particular to define the basic properties of first-class coordination abstractions enabling and managing agent interaction, generalising the notion of coordination media [36]. The concept has been then generalised beyond the coordination domain, leading to the definition of the A&A conceptual framework and meta-model and the development of a computational framework – CArtAgO [37, 38, 27] – to support the development and execution of environments designed and programmed upon the notion of artifact.

The background inspiration brought by Activity Theory concerns the role of artifacts in human (as cognitive agents) organizations and working environments. Fig. 2 shows a fictional bakery as a toy example. It is a system where articulated concurrent and coordinated activities take place, distributed in time and space, by people working inside a common environment. Mediation tools, artifacts, resources (e.g. a message blackboard, a checklist, a task scheduler) are available in the environment in order to ease task fulfillment to entities able to exploit them. Activities are explicitly addressed at *cognitive agents*, individuals able to reason and act in terms of objectives (goals) being informed by data which is available and readable through perception (beliefs). *Interaction* is a main dimension, due to the dependencies among the activities. As well as cooperation, interaction is enabled and strongly promoted either by means of message based communication and through *environment* infrastructures explicitly engineered for supporting it. So the environment – as the set of tools and resources used by people to work – plays a key role in performing tasks efficiently. Besides tools, the environment hosts resources that represent the

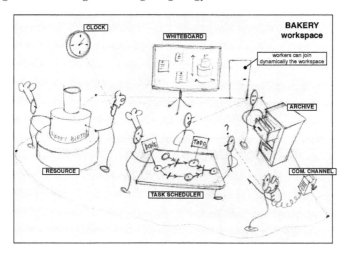

Fig. 2 Abstract representation of the A&A metaphor in the context of a bakery.

co-constructed results of people work (e.g. the cake). Since the complexity of work requires some division of labor and decentralized, *distributed work spaces*, each person is responsible for the fulfillment of a series of situated tasks.

A&A brings this idea to multi-agent systems, so that a MAS environment is designed and programmed in terms of a dynamic set of artifacts as first-class computational entities, collected in localities called *workspaces*. Artifacts represent resources and tools that agents can dynamically instantiate, share and use to support their individual and collective activities [33]. On the one side, they are first-class abstractions for MAS designers and programmers, who define the classes and instances of artifacts that can be instantiated in a specific workspace, defining their structure and computational behavior. On the other side, artifacts are first-class entities of agents world, which agents perceive, use, compose, and manipulate as such.

To make its functionalities available and exploitable by agents, an artifact provides a set of operations and a set of observable properties. Operations represent computational processes – possibly long-term – executed inside artifacts, and finally correspond to the *actions* that agents have to act upon the artifact. The term *usage interface* is used to indicate the overall set of artifact operations available to agents. Observable properties represent state variables whose value can be perceived by agents[1]; the value of an observable property can change dynamically, as result of operation execution. The execution of an operation can generate also *signals*, to be perceived by agents as well: differently from observable properties, signals are useful to represent non-persistent observable *events* occurred inside the artifact, carrying some kind of information. Besides the observable state, artifacts can have also an hidden state, which can be necessary to implement artifact functionalities. Finally a *link interface* is

---

[1] Actually by those agents that are observing the artifact, as will be clarified later on in the section.

specifiable, defining special operations that can be used from one artifact to another one.

A straightforward example of artifacts in A&A systems is represented by digital agendas. In human societies, agendas can indeed be considered as cognitive artifacts, namely as resources which can be exploited by agents in complex systems in order to externalize and share the schedule of their cooperative tasks/activities. Digital agendas can thus be designed to be *cognitively* exploited, created and even shared by societies of software agents. Agenda operations could be used to schedule a list of future events, while their main functionality is to generate a signal (alarm) at the scheduled time, so as to allow observer agents to react accordingly and fulfill the programmed task. Moreover, agendas are designed to make their relevant properties observable, like, for instance, a schedule list. In so doing, agendas have the additional function to inform agents, allowing them to read and become aware about the state of their next tasks.

2.2 BDI Agents Happily Living in Artifact-Based Environments

Even if orthogonal with respect to the concept of agent [39], the basic model of artifacts has been specifically conceived to suite high-level models and architectures of agents, such as the Belief-Desire-Intention (BDI) one [27].

In particular, by adopting an artifact-based perspective, an operation provided by an artifact *is* an external action[2] available to every agent working in the same workspace where the artifact is. So the repertoire of external actions available to an agent is defined by the set of artifacts that populate the environment. This implies that the action repertoire can be dynamic, since the set of artifacts can be changed dynamically by agents themselves, instantiating new artifacts or disposing existing artifacts. In this perspective, artifacts can be framed as tools *externalizing* agent capabilities [40], extending - in a sense - their minds, like in the Extended Mind perspective suggested by Clark in cognitive science [41].

Observable properties and events constitute instead agent percepts. In BDI architectures – as implemented in particular in agent programming languages and platforms such as Jason [42] – percepts related to the value of observable properties can be directly modelled inside agents as beliefs about the actual state of the environment. Actually, to scale up with the environment complexity, in artifact-based environments an agent can dynamically select which are the artifacts to observe in order to only perceive the properties and events of that part of the environment that the agent is interested in. So, the set of beliefs of a BDI agent working inside an artifact-based environment is given by the set of observable properties of all the artifacts that the agent has decided to observe.

---

[2] By adopting a terminology typically used in agent-oriented programming languages, especially BDI ones, external actions are meant to have an effect on the environment, internal actions instead on agent internal state.

To concretely explore these ideas and to enable the development of cognitive agent applications with artifact-based environments, CArtAgO – which is the reference computational framework and infrastructure implementing the A&A model – has been integrated with different BDI agent programming languages and frameworks. JaCaMo[3] [43] in particular is a comprehensive platform, which allows to develop and run multi-agent systems composed of BDI agents programmed in Jason and working inside CArtAgO distributed artifact-based environment, which in turn are organized into organisations specified in $\mathcal{M}$OISE.

2.3 Stigmergy in Artifact-Based Environments

By adopting the A&A perspective, stigmergic processes can be designed and implemented in CArtAgO by introducing suitable artifacts to support agents' work. In spite of the peculiarities of the specific process, it is possible here to identify some basic features that characterise these artifacts, defining a sort of abstract architecture that can be specialised according to the specific context. This abstract architecture will be applied in the social case study described in the next section, in particular to drive the design and implementation of artifacts supporting the stigmergic coordination of different teams of cognitive agents.

2.3.1 The Simplest Scenario: Two Agents

To describe these features, we start from considering here the simplest scenario involving stigmergy, composed by an agent A performing some task G_1, whose behavioral trace is used as a guide—i.e. as *cue* [22]—by another agent B to perform some task G_2.

In order to model this basic scenario, we introduce an artifact T mediating the work of the agent A with respect to its task, that is an instrument that would factorize and encapsulate some basic functionalities useful to achieve the objective of the work (see Fig. 3, left). On the one hand, from the agent's point of view, the artifact represents the means that helps or that is necessary to *enact* his practical behavior: for this purpose, artifact T is designed with a suitable usage interface accessed by A to do its work. On the other hand, from the perspective of the designer of the stigmergic process, the artifact functions as the means to keep track and elaborate the agent's practical behavior, by creating and recording in its internal state the *traces* of the agent's work. The traces can be simply logs of the agent's behavior, or, in the more general case, the result of some kind of pre-computations which are functional to the stigmergic processes, such as *aggregation, ordering, selection*.

Then, the artifact T must be designed to make those traces observable by agent B: this is simply realized by making the traces *observable properties* of

[3] http://jacamo.sourceforge.net

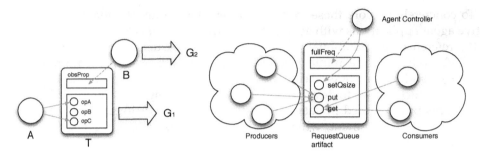

Fig. 3 *(left)* The artifact T makes observable to agent B the traces of agent A's practical work; *(right)* The stigmergic producers-consumers example

the artifact, and let the agent observe the artifact T—in order to have such information among its beliefs (in the case of BDI architecture).

Finally, the *relevance* of traces may change not only due to interaction but also in time: for this purpose, the artifact T can embed some basic time-driven operations that change the traces so as to modulate their persistence in time.

A variant to this basic schema that can be useful for fully distributed contexts, is to consider A in a workspace W_1 and B being situated in a different workspace W_2. In that case, the functionality of the artifact T can be divided in two artifacts T_1 and T_2, linked together: T_1 used by A in W_1, functioning as mediator of A's activities; T_2 observed by B in W_2, with observable properties representing the trace; the pre-computation of the trace can be done either by T_1 or T_2, according to the need.

2.3.2 The Stigmergic Producers-Consumers Example

The basic two-agents scenario can be generalised by considering—instead of agents A and B—an agent society composed of agent playing different roles, interacting in order to perform some global tasks, some of them using the traces of the work of others to enact the work that may influence back then the work of the formers.

As a more concrete but still simple example, let's consider a MAS used in a service-oriented scenario, with A_1 as a dynamic set of agents acting as requesters of a service S (i.e. request producers), A_2 as a dynamic set of agents acting as providers of service S (i.e. request consumers). A RequestQueue artifact is used as a bounded queue (buffer) to uncouple and coordinate producers-consumers interaction (see Fig. 3, right). The usage interface of the artifact includes a put operation control to insert a new request—exploited by A_1 agents—and a get operation control to remove the first available request.

Then, we want to introduce in the system an agent B who is in charge of optimizing the overall producers-consumers society behavior, in particular by taking some kind of actions—e.g. to augment the number of service providers—in the case of critical situations—e.g. The RequestQueue is full with a frequency in time greater than some threshold Th. For doing this, we enhance

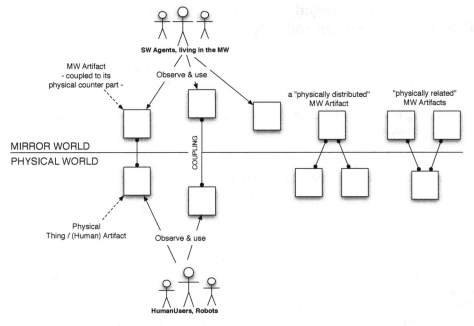

Fig. 4 Artifact-Based Mirror Worlds coupled to the Physical World

the RequestQueue artifact with an observable property fullFreq, containing the percentage of time the bounded queue has been full—let's say—in the last hour, and the necessary inner working machinery to compute and make such value available. The value of fullFreq can be considered a trace of producers-consumers work, and relevant in this case for the work of the agent controller B, observing RequestQueue.

2.3.3 Stigmergic Self-Adjustment

Going back the two-agents examples, in many cases the task G_2 of agent B may feedback on the work of agent A and improve its performance, by taking into the account—for instance— contingencies that are not known or are beyond agent A's competences. For this purpose, artifact T may expose further operations to be exploited not by the agent A but by agent B, which are functional to adapt artifact behavior or functionalities in order to improve the overall performance of the subsystem A plus T.

By referring to the producers-consumers example, the RequestQueue artifact can be equipped with an operation setQSize that enables to dynamically change the *size* of the queue. This operation is meant to be exploited by agent controller B in order to apply some policy relating the course of the fullFreq value and the size of the queue. For instance, agent B can decide to augment the queue size as soon as fullFreq exceeds some threshold *Th*.

3 Putting the Pieces Together: Designing Mirror Worlds with BDI Agents, Artifacts and Stigmergy

The A&A conceptual framework and related specific technologies such as CArtAgO and JaCaMo make it possible to exploit agents and artifacts as basic building blocks to conceive Mirror Worlds as depicted in the Introduction. In this view, stigmergy can be used both to frame the conceptual coupling between the physical and digital layers and to conceive the coordination inside cooperative activities that are co-constructed by inhabitants of such layers, i.e. humans and software agents.

In particular, cognitive software agents are the autonomous citizens of the mirror world, and artifacts are used as basic bricks to shape the mirror world environment, so that: *(a)* the agents act and perceive in a distributed computational environment which is the key element to create a strong coupling – temporal and spatial – between the two layers, the physical one and the virtual one; *(b)* the agent computational environment is properly designed and instrumented to enable stigmergic interaction between human and cognitive agents, and between agents themselves.

So in a mirror world, some artifacts can be used to directly represent the *digital* counterpart of things or artifacts belonging to the physical world, which can be observed and affected by agents of the MW (see Fig. 4). Such MW artifacts are meant to be strongly coupled to their physical extension by means of proper low-level coupling technologies, so as to provide some level of consistency between their (observable) states. Actually the specific shape of a MW artifact – observable properties, operations – coupled with a physical artifact can vary depending on the functionalities that we want to provide and the available technologies. So, from a MW developer's viewpoint, these kinds of artifacts are a way to engineer the bidirectional information flow between a piece of physical environment and its counter-part in the mirror. In fact, the MW artifacts not only provide a way to represent the physical one (and make it observable) at the MW level, but also encapsulate some specific processing and elaboration, concerning artifact functionalities, and provide an action interface to possibly affect the physical side.

As a simple example, let's consider a door (Fig. 5, on the left). A possible MW door artifact coupled with the physical door could have the state (open, closed, locked) as an observable property and some operations (actions) to change the state (open, close, lock). As soon as the physical door – being closed – is opened or locked (by humans), the observable property of the MW artifact is updated accordingly. On the other side, as soon as an agent in the MW performs a *lock* action on the MW door, the door would be locked also in the physical world. A very simple scenario including the MW door artifact is shown in Fig. 5 (on the right), representing a possible fragment of MW ruling the access of people to some room/building and including also a MW camera and a MW display artifacts, coupled with a physical camera and a display, located near the door, and a visitor book, an artifact decoupled from the physical world used to keep track of visitors that are inside the place. A *majordomo* agent is responsible to regulate the access and welcome visitors according to some strategy, by

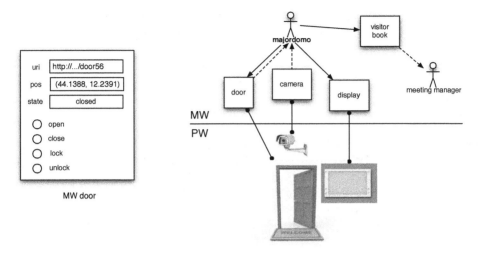

Fig. 5 A MW door artifact and a simple usage scenario

observing information provided by the camera and the door, and acting on the door itself and the display (to show messages), as well as on the visitor book. Similar MW artifacts could be shared and used by other agents – not known to majordomo – to do their jobs inside the MW.

Actually the type or granularity of such MW artifacts is a matter of design and could depend on the specific application. We could have – for instance – a MW artifact representing a whole room (abstracting from devices inside), as well as even raw sensors or actuators – such as a camera, a thermometer or a switch. In any case, MW artifacts coupled with physical things all have some basic common properties, which include the identifier of the physical resource and its geo-spatial information.

As a further, more articulated, example, suppose to have a MW running on top of a University campus, to ease the academic life of students and teachers. Every teacher as well as every student has a smartphone, running her personal assistant agents, situated in the University MW. The MW includes:

- some *room* artifacts coupled with rooms where the lectures take place;
- a *course portal* artifact for each course – showing, among the other things, information about the next lecture—the room where it will take place, when, its state (stated, finished, cancelled).

The idea is to exploit actions that the teachers do on the physical environment to automatically trigger activities at the MW levels and automate tasks related to the coordination with students and other personal staff of the university.

When no lecture is running, a lecture room is locked. A room can be unlocked then by a teacher who is going to have a lecture in the room. The action of unlocking and entering the room by a teacher at a time slot corresponding to her lecture can be understood – at the MW level – as the fact that the lecture is going to start: so, as soon as a teacher unlocks and enters the room, her personal agent – who is aware of the course agenda and tracking the room state – acts on the MW course portal artifact to change the state of the next (current) lecture. Such a change can be perceived then by the personal agents of the course students, who may want to notify the event to the interested student (by a message on the the smartphone) in the case that she is not already inside the room.

Then, suppose that there were a problem in the room that requires to do the lecture elsewhere—e.g., the projector is broken. The teacher can notify the problem and then select another available room, assisted by her personal agent acting on the MW room artifact and other artifacts of the MW campus. Moreover, the MW room artifact provides an action to the teacher's personal agent to post a message signalling the new location on the physical display of the new room. The agent can also notify the change on the MW course portal artifact, so that those students who aren't arrived yet can be informed of the change by their personal agent. Finally, the notification of the problem on the MW room artifact triggers the reaction of a building maintenance agent – who is observing all the rooms of the campus and is thus in charge of taking some action.

Besides these simple examples, the approach conceptually scales well considering large, open and complex environments, from quarters and districts to full cities. In that case artifacts and agents embodying such mirror worlds would be necessarily organized in terms of multiple workspaces distributed over the network, eventually running on cloud services. The capability of dynamically creating and exploiting artifacts (by the agents themselves), as well as to define organizational structures and rules governing the interactions inside the agent-based digital layer is essential to fully handle the dynamism and openness which is implied by such complex environments. To this purpose, as an example, an agent platform and infrastructure like JaCaMo provides an explicit support to define the organization of the overall multi-agent systems, based on the Moise organizational model, fully integrated with the agent and environment dimensions.

4 Conclusion

It is not hard to preview that the design and engineering of large, fully distributed and open Ambient Intelligence systems – scaling from rooms to full cities and beyond – will be a main point in the agenda of AmI research in the short future. In that perspective, besides the continuous development of enabling HW technologies and AI techniques, and the adoption of standards for ensuring interoperability, an important issue concerns the availability of proper conceptual frameworks and software abstractions to tackle the inherent complexity in modeling and designing such systems. In this contribution we have envisioned an agent-oriented vision of Ambient Intelligence systems integrating ideas from Gelernter's mirror worlds and existing models and technologies for multi-agent oriented programming, aiming at providing a uniform conceptual framework to conceive and develop such complex systems. In that view, we have discussed the role of *stigmergy* as a natural interaction model to create the communication and coordination between the physical and digital layers, i.e. between the human inhabitants of the physical word and the software agents living in the digital shadow of that world.

Acknowledgements This work has been partially supported by the SINTELNET Project FP7-ICT-2009-C Project No. 286380.

References

1. F. Sadri, "Ambient intelligence: A survey," *ACM Comput. Surv.*, vol. 43, no. 4, p. 36, 2011.
2. M. Weiser, "Some computer science issues in ubiquitous computing," *Commun. ACM*, vol. 36, pp. 75–84, July 1993.
3. M. Weiser, "The computer for the 21st century," *SIGMOBILE Mob. Comput. Commun. Rev.*, vol. 3, pp. 3–11, July 1999.
4. D. H. Gelernter, *Mirror Worlds: or the Day Software Puts the Universe in a Shoebox...How It Will Happen and What It Will Mean.* Oxford, 1992.
5. D. Gelernter, "Generative communication in linda," *ACM Trans. Program. Lang. Syst.*, vol. 7, pp. 80–112, January 1985.
6. C. Castelfranchi, "Engineering social order," in *Proceedings of the First International Workshop on Engineering Societies in the Agent World: Revised Papers*, ESAW '00, (London, UK), pp. 1–18, Springer-Verlag, 2000.
7. P. Grassé, "La reconstruction du nid et les coordinations inter- individuelles chez bellicositermes natalensis et cubitermes. La théorie de la stigmergie: Essai d'interprétation du comportement des termites constructeurs," *Insectes Sociaux*, vol. 6, pp. 41–81, 1959.
8. J. Wenzel, "Evolution of nest architecture," in *The social biology of wasps* (K. Ross and R. Matthews, eds.), pp. 480–519, Cornell University Press, 1991.
9. I. Karsai and G. Theraulaz, "Nest building in a social wasp: postures and constraints," *Sociobiology*, vol. 26, pp. 83–114, 1995.
10. S. Camazine, J. Deneubourg, N. Franks, J. Sneyd, G. Theraulaz, and E. Bonabeau, *Self-Organization in Biological Systems.* Princeton, NJ: Princeton University Press, 2001.
11. V. Parunak, "Go to the ant: Engineering principles from natural agent systems," *Annals of Operations Research*, vol. 75, pp. 69–101, 1997.
12. E. Bonabeau, F. Henaux, S. Guérin, D. Snyers, P. Kuntz, and G. Theraulaz, "Routing in telecommunications networks with ant-like agents," in *IATA '98: Proceedings of the second international workshop on Intelligent agents for telecommunication applications*, (London, UK), pp. 60–71, Springer-Verlag, 1998.
13. V. Parunak, S. Brueckner, and J. Sauter, "Digital pheromones for coordination of unmanned vehicles," in *Environments for Multiagent Systems I* (D. Weyns, V. Parunak, and F. Michel, eds.), no. 3374 in Lecture Notes in Computer Science, pp. 179–183, Berlin / Heidelberg: Springer-Verlag, 2005.
14. E. Boneabeau, G. Theraulaz, J. Deneubourg, N. Franks, O. Rafelsberger, J. Joly, and S. Blaco, "A model for the emergence of pillars, walls and royal chambers in termite nests," *Philosophical Transactions of the Royal Society of London*, vol. 353, pp. 1561–1576, 1997.
15. S. Garnier, J. Gautrais, and G. Theraulaz, "The biological principles of swarm intelligence," *Swarm Intelligence*, vol. 1, no. 1, pp. 3–31, 2007.
16. L. M. Gambardella, M. Dorigo, M. Middendorf, and T. Stützle, "Special section on ant colony optimization," *IEEE Transactions on Evolutionary Computation*, vol. 6, no. 4, pp. 317–365, 2002.

17. O. Holland and C. Melhuis, "Stigmergy, self-organization, and sorting in collective robotics," *Artificial Life*, vol. 5, no. 2, pp. 173–202, 1999.
18. S. A. Brueckner and H. V. D. Parunak, "Self-organizing MANET management," in *Engineering Self-Organising Systems: Nature-Inspired Approaches to Software Engineering* (G. Di Marzo Serugendo, A. Karageorgos, O. F. Rana, and F. Zambonelli, eds.), vol. 2977 of *LNAI*, pp. 20–35, Springer, May 2004.
19. M. Mamei and F. Zambonelli, "Programming stigmergic coordination with the tota middleware," in *4th ACM International Joint Conference on Autonomous Agents and Multiagent Systems*, (New York, USA), ACM, July 2005.
20. L. Tummolini and C. Castelfranchi, "Trace signals: The meanings of stigmergy," in *Environments for Multi-Agent Systems III* (D. Weyns, V. Parunak, and F. Michel, eds.), no. 4389 in Lecture Notes in Artificial Intelligence, pp. 141–156, Berlin / Heidelberg: Springer-Verlag, 2007.
21. C. Castelfranchi, G. Pezzulo, and L. Tummolini, "Behavioral implicit communication (bic): Communicating with smart environments via our practical behavior and its traces," *International Journal of Ambient Computing and Intelligence*, vol. 2, no. 1, pp. 1–12, 2010.
22. L. Tummolini, M. Mirolli, and C. Castelfranchi, "Stigmergic cues and their uses in coordination: An evolutionary approach," in *Agents, Simulation and Applications* (A. Uhrmacher and D. Weyns, eds.), pp. 243–265, CRC Press, 2009.
23. H. Clark, "Coordinating with each other in a material world," *Discourse Studies*, vol. 7, pp. 507–525, 2005.
24. D. Weyns, A. Omicini, and J. J. Odell, "Environment as a first-class abstraction in multi-agent systems," *Autonomous Agents and Multi-Agent Systems*, vol. 14, pp. 5–30, Feb. 2007. Special Issue on Environments for Multi-agent Systems.
25. D. Weyns and H. V. D. Parunak, eds., *Journal of Autonomous Agents and Multi-Agent Systems. Special Issue: Environment for Multi-Agent Systems*, vol. 14 (1). Springer Netherlands, 2007.
26. D. Weyns, H. V. D. Parunak, F. Michel, T. Holvoet, and J. Ferber, "Environments for multiagent systems: State-of-the-art and research challenges," in *Environment for Multi-Agent Systems* (D. Weyns, H. V. D. Parunak, F. Michel, T. Holvoet, and J. Ferber, eds.), vol. 3374, pp. 1–47, Springer-Verlag, Berlin-Heidelberg, 2005.
27. A. Ricci, M. Piunti, and M. Viroli, "Environment programming in multi-agent systems: an artifact-based perspective," *Autonomous Agents and Multi-Agent Systems*, vol. 23, pp. 158–192, 2011. 10.1007/s10458-010-9140-7.
28. S. Russell and P. Norvig, *Artificial Intelligence, A Modern Approach (2nd ed.)*. Prentice Hall, 2003.
29. K. Hadeli, P. Valckenaers, M. Kollingbaum, and H. Van Brussel, "Multi-agent coordination and control using stigmergy," *Comput. Ind.*, vol. 53, pp. 75–96, January 2004.
30. E. Platon, M. Mamei, N. Sabouret, S. Honiden, and H. V. Parunak, "Mechanisms for environments in multi-agent systems: Survey and opportunities," *Autonomous Agents and Multi-Agent Systems*, vol. 14, pp. 31–47, February 2007.
31. H. V. D. Parunak, "A survey of environments and mechanisms for human-human stigmergy," in *E4MAS* (D. Weyns, H. V. D. Parunak, and F. Michel, eds.), vol. 3830 of *Lecture Notes in Computer Science*, pp. 163–186, Springer, 2005.
32. A. Ricci, A. Omicini, M. Viroli, L. Gardelli, and E. Oliva, "Cognitive stigmergy: Towards a framework based on agents and artifacts," in *Environments for MultiAgent Systems III* (D. Weyns, H. V. D. Parunak, and F. Michel, eds.), vol. 4389 of *LNAI*, pp. 124–140, Springer, May 2007.
33. A. Omicini, A. Ricci, and M. Viroli, "Artifacts in the A&A meta-model for multi-agent systems," *Autonomous Agents and Multi-Agent Systems*, vol. 17 (3), 2008.
34. B. A. Nardi, *Context and Consciousness: Activity Theory and Human-Computer Interaction*. MIT Press, 1996.
35. A. Ricci, A. Omicini, and E. Denti, "Activity Theory as a framework for MAS coordination," in *Engineering Societies in the Agents World III* (P. Petta, R. Tolksdorf, and

F. Zambonelli, eds.), vol. 2577 of *LNCS*, pp. 96–110, Springer, Apr. 2003. 3rd International Workshop (ESAW 2002), Madrid, Spain, 16–17 Sept. 2002. Revised Papers.

36. A. Omicini, A. Ricci, M. Viroli, C. Castelfranchi, and L. Tummolini, "Coordination artifacts: Environment-based coordination for intelligent agents," in *Proc. of AAMAS'04* (N. R. Jennings, C. Sierra, L. Sonenberg, and M. Tambe, eds.), vol. 1, (New York, USA), pp. 286–293, ACM, 19–23July 2004.

37. A. Ricci, M. Viroli, and A. Omicini, "CArtAgO: A framework for prototyping artifact-based environments in MAS," in *Environments for MultiAgent Systems III* (D. Weyns, H. V. D. Parunak, and F. Michel, eds.), vol. 4389 of *LNAI*, pp. 67–86, Springer, feb 2007.

38. A. Ricci, M. Piunti, M. Viroli, and A. Omicini, "Environment programming in CArtAgO," in *Multi-Agent Programming: Languages, Platforms and Applications, Vol. 2*, pp. 259–288, Springer, 2009.

39. A. Ricci, M. Piunti, L. D. Acay, R. Bordini, J. Hubner, and M. Dastani, "Integrating Artifact-Based Environments with Heterogeneous Agent-Programming Platforms," in *Proc. of AAMAS'08*, 2008.

40. A. Ricci, M. Piunti, and M. Viroli, "Externalisation and Internalization: A New Perspective on Agent Modularisation in Multi-Agent Systems Programming," in *Proceedings of MALLOW 2009 federated workshops: LAnguages, methodologies and Development tools for multi-agent systemS (LADS 2009)* (M. Dastani, A. E. F. Seghrouchni, J. Leite, and P. Torroni, eds.), September 2009.

41. A. Clark and D. Chalmers, "The extended mind," *Analysis*, vol. 58: 1, pp. 7–19, 1998.

42. R. H. Bordini, J. F. Hübner, and M. Wooldrige, *Programming Multi-Agent Systems in AgentSpeak using Jason*. Wiley Series in Agent Technology, John Wiley & Sons, 2007.

43. O. Boisser, R. Bordini, J. Hubner, and A. Ricci, "Multi-agent oriented programming with jacamo," *Science of Computer Programming*, 2012. to appear.

Chapter 30
Agents writing on walls: Cognitive stigmergy and beyond

Andrea Omicini

Abstract One of the fundamental factors driving the (self-)organisation of complex social systems – such as human organisations, animal societies, and multi-agent systems – is the interaction of individuals mediated by the environment. Sharing a workspace, mutually perceiving (the effect of) each other's actions, modifying a common environment: all these are simple yet powerful mechanisms that enable social coordination. We shortly recall and classify some of the main sorts of environment-based coordination, and discuss their impact on the engineering of self-organising socio-technical systems.

1 Introduction

The complexity of today and tomorrow artificial systems is seemingly too huge for traditional programming and software engineering techniques, exploiting deterministic, "fully-controlled" approaches—where the behaviour of a system is essentially determined once and for all at design time. The main reasons for this are basically two: *unpredictability* and *size*.

On the one hand, *openness* is an almost unescapable features of today software systems: so that the number, nature, behaviour and dynamics of the components of a system cannot be predicted once and for all at design time. Also, non-trivial computational systems are typically *situated*: they are "immersed" in an environment – that is, their evolution is strictly dependent on their surrounding environment – which is usually unpredictable in its behaviour and dynamics—then, in the way in which it affects the overall behaviour of computational systems. Finally, most of the interesting computational systems are *socio-technical systems*: that is, they involve humans as essential components, whose behaviour – and then, their influence on the systems – cannot be foreseen at design time.

Andrea Omicini
Department of Computer Science and Engineering (DISI), University of Bologna, Italy
e-mail: andrea.omicini@unibo.it

On the other hand, the articulation of computational systems is generally destined to grow: the *amount* of computational units, software components, people involved, knowledge used and produced, services required and provided by software systems, is endlessly *increasing* over the years. Simply put, handling such a huge amount of things altogether within a software development process is often cognitively unfeasible, even adopting the most advanced techniques for managing project complexity.

Nowadays, the only way out of this is apparently to resort to the same mechanisms that allow complex natural and social systems to work: in particular, to rethink complex computational systems as *self-organising systems* (SOS), based on simple-yet-powerful nature-inspired *coordination* mechanisms [11]. Roughly speaking, SOS exploits size (number of components, resources, . . .) to autonomously deal with unpredictability (of the environment, of the components, . . .), with no need to predetermine its structure and behaviour at design time.

Along this line, in this paper we first review the basic mechanisms of *self-organising coordination* (SOC) [13] as they emerge from social and natural SOS: stigmergy, cognitive stigmergy, behavioural implicit communication— generally speaking, the mechanisms for *environment-based coordination* (Section 2). Then, we elaborate on the architecture and behaviour of the software systems exploiting SOC in the engineering of computational SOS, focussing in particular on the role of the *environment* in computational systems (Section 3), and on the different *layers* where SOC mechanisms can intervene and affect the systems' dynamics, driving self-organisation (Section 4).

2 Self-Organisation via Environment-based Coordination

In the context of social systems – both human and animal ones, both natural and artificial ones – environment plays a fundamental role in supporting cooperation, collaboration, competition, and, more generally, complex coordination activities [18]. Self-organisation in such systems is typically the result of the interaction among the system's components that is *mediated* by means of some structures in the environment. Through its structure and dynamics, the environment affects component's interaction and influences the system's self-organisation.

In the remainder of this section, we shortly recall (and conceptually re-order) the main elements of SOS, and focus on environment-mediated interaction.

2.1 Agents Leaving Traces: Self-Organisation through Stigmergy

Historically, the original notion of self-organising coordination is grounded in studies on the behaviour of social insects, like ants or termites. The key concept here is *stigmergy*, introduced by [5] as an explanation for the coordination observed in termites societies, where *"The coordination of tasks and the regulation of constructions are not directly dependent from the workers, but from constructions themselves."*

Namely, the notion of stigmergy generally refers to a set of coordination mechanisms mediated by the environment. For instance, in ant colonies, chemical substances – namely *pheromone* – act as environment markers for specific social activities and drive both the individual and the social behaviour of ants.

While the notion of stigmergy has undergone a large number of generalisations / specialisations / extensions [14, 16], and even a larger number of implementations in systems of many sorts, its main features can still be recapitulated quite easily. In short, stigmergic coordination could be roughly represented as follows: some interacting *agents* perform some *action* on the *environment* that leaves some *traces*, or markers, which can then be perceived by other agents and affect their subsequent behaviour. Interaction among agents is mediated by the environment, through traces – like ant's pheromones –: emission of traces is generative – once they are produced, traces' life is independent of the producer –, but their evolution over time depends on their relation with the environment—as in the case of pheromone diffusion, aggregation, and evaporation in ant colonies. Such a sort of interaction among agents is what produces self-organisation: whereas it occurs on a *local* basis, its effect is *global* in terms of the system's *global* structures and behaviours it originates [4].

Research on stigmergic coordination produced a number of interesting results—including relevant approaches in multi-agent systems (MAS), see [15, 22] among the many others. However, it also emphasised two typical main biases of stigmergy-based approaches: *(i)* the agent model is usually quite simple – ant-like agents do not exploit any cognitive ability of theirs –, and *(ii)* the environment model is often quite elementary—featuring pheromone-like traces along with simple environmental evolution mechanisms.

By contrast, a number of relevant works in the field of cognitive sciences point out the role of stigmergy as a fundamental coordination mechanism also e.g. in the context of human societies and organisations [20, 29]. In this context, as noted in [16]:

- modifications to the environment are often amenable of an interpretation in the context of a shared, conventional system of signs:
- the interacting agents feature cognitive abilities that can be used in the stigmergy-based interaction:

Based on this, the notion of *cognitive stigmergy* was introduced in [16] as a first generalisation of stigmergic coordination exploiting agent's cognitive capabilities to enable and promote self-organisation of social activities.

2.2 *Agents Writing on Walls: Self-Organisation via Cognitive Stigmergy*

When traces have meaning, stigmergic coordination adds a novel dimension to self-organisation. This does not necessarily lead to a dichotomy: the intensity of the scent of a pheromone trail has a sort of implicit "meaning" that most ants autonomously "interpret" in order to set their own behaviour. Instead, the point here is that when agents leave traces in the environment, other agents can perceive and interpret them according to a conventional system of signs: such as agents writing symbols on (MAS) walls, with other agents reading their writes, understanding them, and reacting appropriately.

Social systems present very clear examples of traces with a meaning—traces becoming *signs*. Road signs work exactly like that, enforcing traffic laws to drive the self-organisation of traffic systems. First of all, they are put in visible places, so as to demand attention – and reaction – from "driver agents". Also, they refer to the surrounding environment—so, their meaning is local, and such is the interaction they produce, too. Drivers react to their presence, but also to their colour and shape, and possibly to the encoded symbols that can be read and interpreted: red signals, for instance, are typically signs of pro-hibitions, whereas danger warning signs are usually yellow. Colours are here used to activate immediate driver's reaction at a non-symbolic level, whereas the full interpretation of road signs is deferred to a slower but richer symbolic interpretation: so, road signs work as both traces and signs for (cognitive) driver agents.

When traces become signs, stigmergy becomes *cognitive stigmergy* [16]. There, self-organisation is based on marks amenable of a symbolic interpre-tation, and involves intelligent agents, able to correctly interpret signs in the environment, and to react properly. For instance, in the case of traffic laws, road signs play the twofold role of traces and signs, so that both (classic) stig-mergy and cognitive stigmergy are in place as fundamental mechanisms for self-organisation in traffic systems.

Among the many sorts of computational models for coordination, *tuple-based models* [19] can be taken as a computational specimen for stigmergic coordination—including cognitive stigmergy [13]. There, multiple tuple spaces physically/logically distributed in a computational system could be seen as the building blocks of the system's environment—the "walls" upon which coordinating agents can read and write signs in the form of *tuples*. Suspensive coordination primitives – like in or rd – could be used either by "stupid" processes to synchonise upon pre-determined tuple patterns, or by intelligent agents properly interpreting the symbolic content of tuples—as in the case of logic tuples, for instance [3]. So, self-organising patterns based on either stigmergy or cognitive stigmergy can be in principle built upon tuple-based coordination models and technologies.

However, again, social systems provide a clear example of the fact that environment-mediated coordination is not limited to traces or signs left in the environment. Instead, as noted in [21]:

- agents acting in a shared environment often use their actions to (implicitly) communicate their intentions or goals to other agents;
- a shared environment allowing observation of other agent's actions, along with intelligent agents interpreting them, works the basis for self-organising coordination in many social systems.

Based on this, the notion of *behavioural implicit communication* (BIC) was introduced by Cristiano Castelfranchi *et al.* [21, 1] as a wide generalisation of stigmergic coordination, where the observation of agent's actions within a shared environment is the essential interaction mechanism which the self-organisation of complex social (and socio-technical) systems depends upon.[1]

2.3 Agents in a Workspace: Self-Organisation via Behavioural Implicit Communication

When actions in the environment have meaning, new forms of communication and coordination can contribute to the (self-)organisation of complex (computational, social, socio-technical) systems. Here, this is the foremost contribution of the notion of BIC, introduced in [21] and fully described in [1] as the form of (self-organising) coordination that stems from the observation of agent actions in a shared environment. As claimed in [21], BIC could be considered as a generalisation of the notion of stigmergy (and cognitive stigmergy, too), in the sense that self-organising coordination among agents is based on the observation and interpretation of actions as wholes, rather than of their mere effects on the environment in terms of either traces or signs.

BIC occurs whenever an agent uses its own actions to communicate and coordinate with other agents observing the agent's actions through a shared environment. As in the case of stigmergy, this requires an environment making the observation of other agent actions possible—under the obvious assumption that observing agents are intelligent enough to interpret actions. Also, more structured properties of the environment are often exploited, as the ability to select actions to be made observable to other agents, or to hide some actions from other agents' view.

BIC is a critical coordination mechanism that is mainly responsible for the overall social order of human societies. As a very simple example, it is customary in Italy for pedestrians that aim at crossing a busy road to signal their intention to car drivers by simply making a first step upon zebra crossing, then waiting for drivers indicating their will to allow pedestrian crossing by braking in response, thus clearly slowing the incoming cars. In the field of artificial systems, it is apparent that RoboCup teams could easily rely on the mutual observation of both teammates and adversary actions to promote ef-

---

[1] *Sematectonic stigmergy* [14] is a form of stigmergic coordination that could be taken the missing link between classic (marker-based) stigmergic coordination and BIC-based coordination. However, this distinction, while fundamental in the classification of nature-inspired SOC mechanisms, is of no use here.

fective team coordination—as teamwork in general seems to deeply rely upon many forms of BIC.

In the end, what clearly emerges from the notion of BIC, as well as from the many enlightening case studies discussed by Castelfranchi and colleagues [21, 1], is that an essential mechanism for the self-organisation of complex social system is the observation of the agent's actions by other agents sharing the same working environment, and their interpretation in order to understand intentions, goals, attitude, beliefs, mental states of the agents with which one has to coordinate—in a word, to *mind-read* other coordinating agents.

2.4 Self-Organisation via Environment-based Coordination in the Overall

In the overall, computational, social and socio-technical systems have the potential to exploit a number of simple-yet-powerful environment-based mechanisms of interaction. They could exploit the perception of traces left by agent actions on the environment (stigmergy), their interpretation as signs belonging to a conventional symbolic system (cognitive stigmergy), the observation of actions as wholes within the environment (BIC): or, more generally, any working and meaningful combination of these mechanisms. Also, they could involve agents of any sorts – "stupid" or intelligent, human or animal, natural or artificial – interacting and working altogether in possibly-heterogeneous settings.

What all of these mechanisms have in common is that the environment – with its structure and dynamics – is essential for mediating / enabling / governing the interaction, and to make it viable to promote effective self-organisation of the systems. In the next section, we briefly recall the fundamental requirements for the engineering of the environment in computational systems exploiting the above-mentioned mechanisms for self-organisation.

3 Computational Environment for Self-Organising Coordination

When focussing on environment-mediated interaction as the basis for SOC in computational systems, the question to be answered is clearly how a computational environment should be structured and engineered in order to make it possible and promote interactions of that sort.

In general, the pivotal role of environment in complex computational systems has been generally recognised, already: in particular, the environment is nowadays considered as a first-class abstraction in the modelling and engineering of MAS, as discussed in [26]. There, the authors put forward the environment as an explicit part of MAS, assigning it a twofold role: *(i)* determining the surrounding conditions for agents to exist, and *(ii)* providing exploitable design abstractions for around which MAS can be designed and built. When dealing with SOC, the latter role could be translated into "providing agents with exploitable coordination abstractions enabling and promoting self-organisation".

Middleware and software infrastructure is how a computational environment is put in place. According to [25], software infrastructures are required to provide MAS designers with the means to develop MAS environment, and thus to structure MAS applications. There, authors "endorse a general viewpoint where the environment of a multi-agent system is seen as a set of basic bricks we call *environment abstractions*, which *(i)* provide agents with services useful for achieving individual and social goals, and *(ii)* are supported by some underlying software infrastructure managing their creation and exploitation".

Accordingly, in the remainder of this section we try to devise out the main requirements and the architecture for a computational environment supporting SOC, focussing in particular on the form of the "basic bricks"—the coordination abstractions provided by the environment to enable and promote self-organisation.

3.1 Requirements for Environment in Self-Organising Systems

Following the step-by-step presentation of the mechanisms for environment-based coordination of Section 2, the first requirement for an environment supporting SOC is to make it possible the "recording" of agent's traces, so as to enable stigmergic coordination. Also, the ability to properly react to the emission of agent's traces is mandatory for the environment: for instance, pheromone-like traces should interact with the environment where they are deposited so as to enact the basic mechanisms of diffusion, aggregation, and evaporation. In addition, traces should be available to other agents for perception, so the environment should allow for multiple agents sharing traces, as well as perceiving their relevant properties—the equivalent of pheromone-like scent and intensity.

Furthermore, in order to allow for local interaction – a fundamental requirement for SOS –, the environment should feature a *topology*, that is, a coherent and expressive set of spatial abstractions. To cope with the basic needs of SOC, topological abstractions should enforce at least some notion of *locality*— allowing agents and resources in the environment to be associated to local spaces of some sort, and enabling a well-founded notion of local interaction among agents, and between agents and the environment as well. As obvious, more refined and structured topological models could be adopted to implement and exploit more articulated environment structures for SOC.

The above requirements for environment features suffice for both stigmergy and cognitive stigmergy. Of course, it may be the case that environment structures include tools supporting agents in the symbolic interpretation of traces as signs, such as dictionaries and ontologies: even though this may help enforcing cognitive stigmergy coordination, it is not strictly needed—whereas agent intelligence is a necessary pre-condition for cognitive stigmergy.

SOC mechanisms based on the observation and interpretation of agent actions within a shared environment call instead for more stringent requirements. In the case of BIC, agent's actions aimed at behaviourally expressing coordination issues need to be made observable to other agents sharing the same environment. Relevant properties of such actions need to be visible to target agents—and possibly hidden to other agents, for instance by means of virtual "walls" properly partitioning agent's groups.

3.2 Structuring the Environment in Self-Organising Systems

Suitable environment abstractions should then be provided by the software infrastructure so as to satisfy the above-defined requirements.

For instance, as already suggested in Subsection 2.2, tuple-based middleware naturally support stigmergic coordination—with tuples working as traces, tuple spaces as environment abstractions, and agents interacting by writing and reading tuples in tuple spaces. However, two issues need to be addressed before stigmergy could be effectively implemented in terms of tuple-based coordination: environment behaviour and topology.

On the one hand, essential mechanisms implementing effective environment dynamics against traces – like pheromone diffusion, aggregation, and decay – cannot be easily implemented in terms of standard tuple space behaviour. The ability to associate specific coordinative behaviours to tuple spaces is then mandatory—as it happens for instance with coordination abstractions like *tuple centres*, that is, programmable tuple spaces [2]. On the other hand, topological distribution of tuple spaces in the typical tuple-based models suffices to build basic SOC mechanisms. However, more refined topological abstractions, such as A&A workspaces [17], clearly promote more articulated and expressive forms of SOC.

When marks become signs, tools like dictionaries, vocabularies, and ontologies can be of help in order to give meaning to traces. For instance, notions like *function description* and *operating instructions* for artefacts [12] enable effective interaction of intelligent agents with the environment abstractions, which could work as informative containers of signs.

Moving towards BIC-based coordination, the most natural approach in a computational environment is to rely on *reification* of actions within some environment abstraction. So, for instance, relevant actions, along with their most meaningful properties, could be made available to other agents by reifying them as suitably-descriptive tuples in a shared tuple space. Accordingly, artefacts like dashboards, logs, diaries, and note-boards [16] work by keeping track of both actions and annotations made by individual agents during a working session. This would not suffice, however, without some computational mechanism able to promote the agent *awareness* of other agents' actions. For instance, the notion of *focus* of attention as modelled in CArtAgO [17] works essentially along that direction, by allowing agents to direct their attention to specific artefacts recording the agent's actions they are interested in, and with respect to which they intend to react and coordinate.

4 The Many Faces of Self-Organising Coordination

When observing real-world instances of stigmergic coordination – or, more generally, of SOS – it is quite natural to focus on the single most-evident pattern of self-organisation, to devise it out, and describe the SOS based on that pattern. However, this is not how SOS really work: there, self-organisation actually takes many forms, and affects many levels of the SOS architecture. For instance, living systems are typically hierarchical, layered systems [6], where self-organisation mechanisms work essentially at every level—from the molecular up to the organ level.

In the same way, "real" software systems facing the many faces of complexity should be expected to exploit many different coordination mechanisms for self-organisation at different architectural levels.

4.1 Layers in Self-Organising Coordination: MAS as a Reference Model

MAS represent the most natural paradigm for the design and development of complex software systems [28]. Accordingly, in the following we take MAS as the conceptual reference for computational SOS, and discuss the way in which coordination mechanisms for self-organisation may intervene at many different levels in the architecture of a SOS.

In particular, we refer to the A&A meta-model [12]: there, agents are responsible of activities, while artefacts are assigned required functions in MAS. In particular, artefacts shape MAS environment, mediating and governing the intra- (social) and inter-MAS (environmental) interaction. MAS topology is organised around workspaces, which agents and artefacts belong to, and which the notion of locality in the A&A meta-model is based on. According to [9], artefacts are conceptually layered into three classes, ruling three different sorts of MAS interaction: individual artefacts, ruling the interaction of individual agents within the MAS; social artefacts, ruling social interaction among agents; and environment artefacts, ruling MAS-environment interaction.

As interaction (and its management, that is, coordination) is the core of any self-organisation process, it is apparent that self-organisation dynamics could originate from – and then, be governed by – any of the above-mentioned sorts of artefacts in a MAS. Correspondingly, SOC could originate from the interaction of individual agents with the system, from the social interaction among agents, and also from the interaction between MAS and the environment.[2] So, for instance, SOC mechanisms like stigmergy could be exploited for regulating MAS-environment interaction, cognitive stigmergy for social interaction, and BIC for individual interaction.

As a case study, in the remainder of this section we focus on knowledge-intensive systems: in particular, on those socio-technical systems where agents are represented by human knowledge workers, dwelling within knowledge intensive environments, where huge amounts of information and data cannot be handled without the help of some SOC mechanism.

4.2 Layers in Self-Organising Coordination: A Case Study with Knowledge-Intensive Environments

As discussed in [10], knowledge-intensive environments (KIE) represent an essential dimension in modern computational systems, featuring rich information contexts and knowledge-oriented human-computer interaction. However, the (too) many possible ways of human-computer knowledge-intensive systems, along with the huge, unordered amount of relevant information available, could make the design of knowledge-intensive workspaces a nightmare.

A computer-based working environment for human knowledge workers like researchers, journalists, writers, lawyers, physicians, politicians, administrators – all professionals dealing with critical amounts of information resources that need to be suitably reviewed, organised, and used within complex, ever-changing contexts – requires on the one hand that all the relevant information sources are made available to the user in a complete yet usable format, on the other hand that the working environment autonomously evolves and adapts to the individual uses and work habits, as well as to the diverse goals and contexts defined by the everyday activity. Both requirements could be addressed by facing the following key issues: the suitable definition and representation of all the relevant information; the self-organisation (including creation, propagation, and dissipation) of knowledge; and the self-organisation of the working environment.

While relevant information could be handled by adopting many well-known techniques in the area of knowledge representation and extraction, the main point here is the explicit representation, memorisation, and exploitation of user actions in the workspace, to be exploited for the self-organisation of the working environment—à la BIC. Also, user actions should leave traces on the working environment which – as in the case of cognitive stigmergy – could be used for the self-organisation of both the relevant knowledge and the workspace. Furthermore, suitably-represented information chunks could autonomously combine to create new knowledge memes that could propagate towards the user – using for instance nature-inspired SOC mech-

---

[2] Whereas, one should not forget that also the dynamics of individual components of a MAS (agents and artefacts) may in its turn be determined by (internal) self-organising mechanisms—as in the case of chemical coordination [24].

anisms like biochemical coordination [23, 27] –, thus providing users with a self-organising KIE. As an example, Molecules of Knowledge (MoK) [8] is a self-organising knowledge-oriented model where knowledge sources produce atoms of knowledge in biochemical compartments, which then autonomously diffuse and aggregate in molecules by means of biochemical reactions.

Self-organisation of knowledge would then involve both the individual workspace (where it should be mainly used for the self-organisation of the working environment) and the information infrastructure, and would in principle affect all the available levels: individual, intra-organisation, and inter-organisation. Correspondingly, SOC mechanisms would then regulate individual, social, and environment interaction, according to the A&A meta-model discussed above.

5 Conclusion

The patterns for self-organising coordination as they can be devised from both natural and social SOS – from stigmergy and cognitive stigmergy to behavioural implicit communication – clearly suggest the potential of environment-based coordination in the engineering of complex computational SOS. In this article, we first review in short the main mechanisms for SOC, then discuss the role of the environment in supporting such mechanisms. Finally, we elaborate on the different levels at which self-organisation may affect the architecture and dynamics of computational SOS, by providing a reference model in terms of MAS, and discussing a case study in KIE.

Work is currently ongoing on both theoretical and practical projects where the above concepts and mechanisms are developed and exploited within complex application scenarios—in particular, in the context of pervasive computing scenarios and knowledge-intensive environments.

Acknowledgements I would like to thank the many people that worked with me in the last years, and inspired me with ideas, observations, objections, and criticisms: first of all, Alessandro Ricci and Mirko Viroli, whose constant and persistent stimulus always worked as a inexhaustible form of inspiration, as well as Enrico Denti and Antonio Natali. Then, in the last months, I shared many ideas with Marco Roccetti, who provided me with an excellent dialectical framework for my contribution to focus, and Stefano Mariani, who helped me developing a new perspective on self-organising coordination. Finally, the inspiration provided by Cristiano Castelfranchi and his group – including Rino Falcone, Luca Tummolini, Michele Piunti, and the rest of the Rome's bunch – was essential since the early years of my career as a researcher – even long before I firstly met Cristiano in Barcelona several years ago.

This work has been supported by the EU-FP7-FET Proactive project SAPERE – Self-aware Pervasive Service Ecosystems, under contract no. 256873.

References

1. Castelfranchi, C., Pezzullo, G., Tummolini, L.: Behavioral implicit communication (BIC): Communicating with smart environments via our practical behavior and its traces. International Journal of Ambient Computing and Intelligence **2**(1), 1–12 (2010). DOI 10.4018/jaci.2010010101

2. Denti, E., Natali, A., Omicini, A.: Programmable coordination media. In: D. Garlan, D. Le Métayer (eds.) Coordination Languages and Models, *LNCS*, vol. 1282, pp. 274–288. Springer-Verlag (1997). DOI 10.1007/3-540-63383-9_86. 2nd International Conference (COORDINATION'97), Berlin, Germany, 1–3 Sep. 1997. Proceedings

3. Denti, E., Omicini, A.: Designing multi-agent systems around a programmable communication abstraction. In: J.J.C. Meyer, P.Y. Schobbens (eds.) Formal Models of Agents, *LNAI*, vol. 1760, pp. 90–102. Springer-Verlag (1999). DOI 10.1007/3-540-46581-2_7. ESPRIT Project ModelAge Final Workshop. Selected Papers

4. Di Marzo Serugendo, G., Foukia, N., Hassas, S., Karageorgos, A., Kouadri Mostéfaoui, S., Rana, O.F., Ulieru, M., Valckenaers, P., Van Aart, C.: Self-organisation: Paradigms and applications. In: G. Di Marzo Serugendo, A. Karageorgos, O.F. Rana, F. Zambonelli (eds.) Engineering Self-Organising Systems: Nature-Inspired Approaches to Software Engineering, vol. 2977, pp. 1–19. Springer (2004). DOI 10.1007/b95863

5. Grassé, P.P.: La reconstruction du nid et les coordinations interindividuelles chez bellicositermes natalensis et cubitermes sp. la théorie de la stigmergie: Essai d'interprétation du comportement des termites constructeurs. Insectes Sociaux **6**(1), 41–80 (1959). DOI 10.1007/BF02223791

6. Grene, M.J.: Hierarchies in biology. American Scientist **75**, 504–510 (1987)

7. Luck, M., Mařík, V., Štěpánková, O., Trappl, R. (eds.): Multi-Agent Systems and Applications, *Lecture Notes in Computer Science*, vol. 2086. Springer (2001). DOI 10.1007/3-540-47745-4. 9th ECCAI Advanced Course ACAI 2001 and Agent Link's 3rd European Agent Systems Summer School (EASSS 2001), Prague, Czech Republic, 2-13 Jul. 2001, Selected Tutorial Papers

8. Mariani, S., Omicini, A.: Molecules of Knowledge: Self-organisation in knowledge-intensive environments. In: Intelligent Distributed Computing VI, Studies in Computational Intelligence. Springer, Calabria, Italy (2012). Intelligence, vol. 446, pp. 17–22. Springer (2012). DOI 10.1007/978-3-642-32524-3_4. 6th International Symposium on Intelligent Distributed Computing (IDC 2012), Calabria, Italy, 24-26 Sep. 2012. Proceedings

9. Molesini, A., Omicini, A., Denti, E., Ricci, A.: SODA: A roadmap to artefacts. In: O. Dikenelli, M.P. Gleizes, A. Ricci (eds.) Engineering Societies in the Agents World VI, *LNAI*, vol. 3963, pp. 49–62. Springer (2006). DOI 10.1007/11759683_4. 6th International Workshop (ESAW 2005), Kuşadası, Aydın, Turkey, 26–28 Oct. 2005. Revised, Selected & Invited Papers

10. Omicini, A.: Self-organising knowledge-intensive workspaces. In: A. Ferscha (ed.) Pervasive Adaptation. The Next Generation Pervasive Computing Research Agenda, chap. VII: Human-Centric Adaptation, pp. 67–68. Institute for Pervasive Computing, Johannes Kepler University Linz, Austria (2011). URL http://www.perada.eu/essence/#item:80

11. Omicini, A.: Nature-inspired coordination for complex distributed systems. In: Intelligent Distributed Computing VI, Studies in Computational Intelligence, vol. 446, pp. 1–6. Springer (2012). DOI 10.1007/978-3-642-32524-3_1. 6th International Symposium on Intelligent Distributed Computing (IDC 2012), Calabria, Italy, 24-26 Sep. 2012. Proceedings. Invited paper

12. Omicini, A., Ricci, A., Viroli, M.: Artifacts in the A&A meta-model for multi-agent systems. Autonomous Agents and Multi-Agent Systems **17**(3), 432–456 (2008). DOI 10.1007/s10458-008-9053-x. Special Issue on Foundations, Advanced Topics and Industrial Perspectives of Multi-Agent Systems

13. Omicini, A., Viroli, M.: Coordination models and languages: From parallel computing to self-organisation. The Knowledge Engineering Review **26**(1), 53–59 (2011). DOI 10.1017/S026988891000041X. Special Issue 01 (25th Anniversary Issue)

14. Parunak, H.V.D.: A survey of environments and mechanisms for human-human stigmergy. In: D. Weyns, H.V.D. Parunak, F. Michel (eds.) Environments for Multi-Agent Systems II, *LNCS*, vol. 3830, pp. 163–186. Springer (2006). DOI 10.1007/11678809_10

15. Parunak, H.V.D., Brueckner, S., Sauter, J.: Digital pheromone mechanisms for coordination of unmanned vehicles. In: C. Castelfranchi, W.L. Johnson (eds.) 1st International Joint Conference on Autonomous Agents and Multiagent systems, vol. 1, pp. 449–450. ACM, New York, NY, USA (2002). DOI 10.1145/544741.544843

16. Ricci, A., Omicini, A., Viroli, M., Gardelli, L., Oliva, E.: Cognitive stigmergy: Towards a framework based on agents and artifacts. In: D. Weyns, H.V.D. Parunak, F. Michel (eds.) Environments for MultiAgent Systems III, *LNCS*, vol. 4389, pp. 124–140. Springer (2007). DOI 10.1007/978-3-540-71103-2_7. 3rd International Workshop (E4MAS 2006), Hakodate, Japan, 8 May 2006. Selected Revised and Invited Papers

17. Ricci, A., Piunti, M., Viroli, M., Omicini, A.: Environment programming in CArtAgO. In: R.P. Bordini, M. Dastani, J. Dix, A. El Fallah Seghrouchni (eds.) Multi-Agent Programming II: Languages, Platforms and Applications, Multiagent Systems, Artificial Societies, and Simulated Organizations, chap. 8, pp. 259–288. Springer (2009). DOI 10.1007/978-0-387-89299-3_8

18. Ricci, A., Viroli, M., Omicini, A.: Environment-based coordination through coordination artifacts. In: D. Weyns, H.V.D. Parunak, F. Michel (eds.) Environments for Multi-Agent Systems, *LNAI*, vol. 3374, pp. 190–214. Springer (2005). DOI 10.1007/b106134. 1st International Workshop (E4MAS 2004), New York, NY, USA, 19 July 2004. Revised Selected Papers

19. Rossi, D., Cabri, G., Denti, E.: Tuple-based technologies for coordination. In: A. Omicini, F. Zambonelli, M. Klusch, R. Tolksdorf (eds.) Coordination of Internet Agents: Models, Technologies, and Applications, chap. 4, pp. 83–109. Springer (2001)

20. Susi, T., Ziemke, T.: Social cognition, artefacts, and stigmergy: A comparative analysis of theoretical frameworks for the understanding of artefact-mediated collaborative activity. Cognitive Systems Research **2**(4), 273–290 (2001). DOI 10.1016/S1389-0417(01)00053-5

21. Tummolini, L., Castelfranchi, C., Ricci, A., Viroli, M., Omicini, A.: "Exhibitionists" and "voyeurs" do it better: A shared environment approach for flexible coordination with tacit messages. In: D. Weyns, H.V.D. Parunak, F. Michel (eds.) Environments for Multi-Agent Systems, *LNAI*, vol. 3374, pp. 215–231. Springer (2005). DOI 10.1007/b106134. 1st International Workshop (E4MAS 2004), New York, NY, USA, 19 July 2004. Revised Selected Papers

22. Valckenears, P., Van Brussel, H., Kollingbaum, M., Bochmann, O.: Multi-agent coordination and control using stigmergy applied to manufacturing control. In: Luck et al. [7], pp. 317–334. DOI 10.1007/3-540-47745-4. 9th ECCAI Advanced Course ACAI 2001 and Agent Link's 3rd European Agent Systems Summer School (EASSS 2001), Prague, Czech Republic, 2-13 Jul. 2001, Selected Tutorial Papers

23. Viroli, M., Casadei, M.: Biochemical tuple spaces for self-organising coordination. In: J. Field, V.T. Vasconcelos (eds.) Coordination Languages and Models, *LNCS*, vol. 5521, pp. 143–162. Springer, Lisbon, Portugal (2009). DOI 10.1007/978-3-642-02053-7_8. 11th International Conference (COORDINATION 2009), Lisbon, Portugal, Jun. 2009. Proceedings

24. Viroli, M., Casadei, M., Nardini, E., Omicini, A.: Towards a chemical-inspired infrastructure for self-* pervasive applications. In: D. Weyns, S. Malek, R. de Lemos, J. Andersson (eds.) Self-Organizing Architectures, *LNCS*, vol. 6090, chap. 8, pp. 152–176. Springer (2010). DOI 10.1007/978-3-642-14412-7_8. 1st International Workshop on Self-Organizing Architectures (SOAR 2009), Cambridge, UK, 14-17 Sep. 2009, Revised Selected and Invited Papers

25. Viroli, M., Holvoet, T., Ricci, A., Schelfthout, K., Zambonelli, F.: Infrastructures for the environment of multiagent systems. Autonomous Agents and Multi-Agent Systems

14(1), 49–60 (2007). DOI 10.1007/s10458-006-9001-6. Special Issue: Environment for Multi-Agent Systems

26. Weyns, D., Omicini, A., Odell, J.J.: Environment as a first-class abstraction in multi-agent systems. Autonomous Agents and Multi-Agent Systems 14(1), 5–30 (2007). DOI 10.1007/s10458-006-0012-0. Special Issue on Environments for Multi-agent Systems

27. Zambonelli, F., Castelli, G., Ferrari, L., Mamei, M., Rosi, A., Di Marzo, G., Risoldi, M., Tchao, A.E., Dobson, S., Stevenson, G., Ye, Y., Nardini, E., Omicini, A., Montagna, S., Viroli, M., Ferscha, A., Maschek, S., Wally, B.: Self-aware pervasive service ecosystems. Procedia Computer Science 7, 197–199 (2011). DOI 10.1016/j.procs.2011.09.006. Proceedings of the 2nd European Future Technologies Conference and Exhibition 2011 (FET 11)

28. Zambonelli, F., Omicini, A.: Challenges and research directions in agent-oriented software engineering. Autonomous Agents and Multi-Agent Systems 9(3), 253–283 (2004). DOI 10.1023/B:AGNT.0000038028.66672.1e. Special Issue: Challenges for Agent-Based Computing

29. Schmidt, K., Wagner, I.: Ordering systems: Coordinative practices and artifacts in architectural design and planning. Computer Supported Cooperative Work 13(5-6), 349–408 (2004). DOI 10.1007/s10606-004-5059-3

Chapter 31
Telling it like it isn't: A comprehensive approach to analyzing verbal deception

Swati Gupta, Kayo Sakamoto and Andrew Ortony

Abstract Verbal deception is everywhere–in interpersonal relationships, in politics, in advertising, and in courts of law. In all of these, and in many other domains, we often find people "telling it like it isn't." This chapter is concerned with understanding what this seemingly simple idea really means. Much work has been done in several fields (e.g., communication studies, philosophy, linguistics) and on various aspects of verbal deception, but nowhere is there a comprehensive integration of the different views and observations that are to be found in the literature. In this chapter, we attempt to pull together the multifarious strands by proposing two taxonomies of verbal deception–one pertaining to verbal deception *types* and one to verbal deception *strategies*.

1 Introduction

In the satirical movie *The Invention of Lying*, Mark, the protagonist, lives in a full-disclosure world in which the concept of lying does not exist and in which everybody always expresses their every thought to their interlocutors. Quite by chance, Mark discovers a radically new concept–one totally alien to the culture in which he lives–he discovers the concept of lying. In his excitement

Swati Gupta
Program in Computational Social Cognition, Institute of High Performance Computing, Singapore
e-mail: guptas@ihpc.a-star.edu.sg

Kayo Sakamoto
Program in Computational Social Cognition, Institute of High Performance Computing, Singapore
e-mail: sakamotok@ihpc.a-star.edu.sg

Andrew Ortony
Program in Computational Social Cognition, Institute of High Performance Computing, Singapore, and
Northwestern University, USA
e-mail: ortony@northwestern.edu

he tries to explain the idea to his friends. He tells them that he said "something that isn't," but they have no idea what he means. He tries to explain by using blatant falsehoods such as "I'm a black Eskimo astronaut who invented the bicycle." But his attempts are all a dismal failure. His friends simply accept what he says without a moment's hesitation, being unable to imagine that what Mark or anyone else in their universe says can be anything other than the truth. We hope in this chapter to be more successful than Mark was in explaining the concept of verbal deception, but we have some sympathy for Mark, because a proper understanding of verbal deception, including lying, is more complicated than it might at first appear.

Many of the complexities associated with the nature of verbal deception, and in particular the nature of lying (even while telling the truth), have been detailed in the rigorous and influential work of Cristiano Castelfranchi and his colleagues (e.g., Castelfranchi & Poggi, 1993; Vincent & Castelfranchi, 1979). Indeed, his approach and his meticulous attention to detail have been an inspiration to all of us interested in a cognitive science approach to understanding linguistic behavior, and for many of us, it served as one of the key starting points for thinking about such issues. It is thus fitting that we dedicate this chapter to Cristiano's many contributions to the field. Whereas much of his work on verbal deception has focused on lying (especially, lying by telling the truth), lying is only one of several types of verbal deception, so with this in mind, we shall attempt in this chapter to situate his deception types in the broader spectrum of verbal deception.

At first blush, one might wonder why anybody bothers to study verbal deception. Surely, it's quite simple–as the Oxford English Dictionary (OED) puts it, deception is "To cause to believe what is false; to mislead as to a matter of fact, lead into error, impose upon, delude, 'take in'." Authoritative a source as the OED is, however, things aren't so simple. The OED's definition is a fine definition of straightforward lying (although the definition that the OED gives for lying is even less complex, namely, "to utter falsehood; to speak falsely"), but there is much more to verbal deception, and indeed to lying, than the OED's characterizations. For example, the person(s) whom the speaker is intending to deceive (whom we shall refer to as the hearer(s)) might already believe the thing that is false, as when the child says "Look, mommy, the tooth fairy left this quarter under my pillow while I was asleep last night." If the mother responds with something like "Yes, I told you that would happen," she is being implicitly deceptive by allowing the child to continue to hold a false belief. Clearly, in this transaction, the parent does not "cause [the child] to believe what is false" because the child already believes it. Does the parent "mislead [the child] as to a matter of fact"? Well not really, since the child is already misled. Furthermore, the issue does not simply concern "a matter of fact", but rather, it concerns what the mother *believes* to be a matter of fact (namely that there really is no tooth fairy, etc.). So, we would have to augment the OED definition so as to read something like "To cause [the hearer] to believe something that the speaker believes is false, or to allow [the hearer] to continue to believe something that the speaker believes is false." This is already more complicated than the definition with which we started, but it is still not adequate. The second clause, "to allow [the hearer] to continue to believe..." lacks any mention of the need for the speaker to be in a position to correct a hearer's pre-existing misapprehension.

Examples of the kind just discussed only scratch the surface of the difficulties we face when we try to provide a comprehensive analysis of verbal deception and lying. Scholars from several different disciplines who have studied verbal deception are well aware of such problems. Perhaps this is why they rarely start their analyses from dictionary definitions, except perhaps, as we do, to highlight the inadequacy of such definitions. However, many of them, (e.g., Turner, Edgley, & Olmstead, 1975; Vincent & Castelfranchi, 1979) start with a characterization along the following lines:

> Deception is an intentional act of controlling information so as either (a) to make a hearer believe something that the speaker believes is false, or (b) to prevent the hearer from believing something that the speaker believes is true.

Provided that we augment this account to accommodate cases like the tooth fairy example, we have no problem with taking this as a starting point, but, only as a starting point, because there is more to be said and more to understand than is captured by this kind of abbreviated account. If we are to give a more comprehensive account, however, we are going to have to rely upon a few key concepts–concepts that we shall now introduce and briefly discuss.

1.1 "The truth"

In the context of verbal deception, what is sometimes referred to as *the truth* and *a falsehood* (or *something that is true/false* etc.) takes on a rather different meaning than it has in philosophical discussions. The easiest way to understand this is to think of truth or falsehood *as the speaker sees it*. More specifically, the truth is some state of affairs which, correctly or not, the speaker believes to be the case and wishes to conceal from the hearer. And a falsehood is some state of affairs which, correctly or not, the speaker believes not to be the case but which he or she wishes the hearer to come to, or continue to believe. In our characterizations, P is the proposition that is the nexus of the deception such that true (P) represents the speaker's conception of the *true* state of affairs in cases in which he or she seeks to conceal the *truth* from the hearer, and false (P) represents the falsehood that the speaker wants the hearer to come to or to continue to believe. We let Q represent the proposition that the speaker actually asserts in trying to deceive. As we shall see, it is not always the case that the speaker must believe that Q is false. All that is required is that in asserting Q, the speaker is expecting, or at least hoping, that the hearer will not or will conclude P, depending upon whether P is true or false.

1.2 *Common Ground*

Verbal deception often, but by no means always, occurs when a speaker is a respondent in a verbal exchange. Sometimes, however, the turns in the exchange are separated by so much time that an observer might not realize that the speaker's utterance is actually a response to an earlier, temporally remote communication. In other cases, the speaker's utterance is a response to an imagined, assumed, presupposed, or anticipated communication–an implicit communication. Examples of this abound. For instance, in the political arena, negative campaign advertisements frequently contain intentionally misleading information, for example by repudiating facts about an opponent. In such cases, where the originator of the misleading claim is broadcasting to some large audience, there often is no identifiable explicit assertion to which the misleading claim is a response, although the facts being misrepresented are likely to be widely believed and possibly even documented in the public record[1].

The implications of these complications for an analysis of deception can be finessed by simply assuming that a deceptive claim (spoken or written, although we shall focus on spoken) can usually be analyzed as a response to a prior utterance that might have been made, even if no such utterance was actually made. So when the mother comforts the child at bedtime, raising for the first time the idea that the tooth fairy will come during the night and exchange the tooth for money, we can assume some hypothetical prior utterance from the child such as "Why are we putting my tooth under my pillow?" or "What will happen to my tooth now that it's fallen out?" Our analysis is in no way compromised by treating the speaker's deceptive assertion as a response to only a possible prior utterance (a possible claim, question, accusation, etc.).

The specifics of an assumed prior utterance are often immaterial. To see this, we need the concept of *common ground* (Clark & Brennan, 1991)–the mutually shared knowledge to which each participant in a conversation assumes the other has access. This knowledge can be established by the linguistic context as when, in a conversation about national politics, a reference to "the president" is likely to be understood to have a different referent than in a conversation about the central administration of a university. In such cases, the common ground is established by the linguistic context together with assumptions about the beliefs of the interlocutors about one another. Common ground can also be established by the *non-linguistic* context–by the physical situation, the objects and events that each participant reasonably believes the other can (or in some cases, as in a telephone conversation, cannot) see (or be otherwise immediately aware of). So, for example, when two people are watching a tennis match the mutual knowledge about what they are both watching serves the same function as a linguistically established context. The common ground establishes a common reference point in terms of which it is easier for each to understand what the other is talking about.

---

[1] A good example of this are the false denunciations in advertisements paid for by the US Swift Boat Veterans for Truth, a politically conservative group of veterans of the Vietnam War. The purpose of their advertisements was to undermine the credibility of John Kerry's candidacy in the race for the 2004 US presidency.

1.3 Relevance and Satisfaction

The reason that common ground is important is that it provides the background in terms of which an utterance can be judged as being relevant in a context. In the absence of some very specific and rather improbable assumptions, a speaker who asks a stranger in the street the directions to the nearest bank could be forgiven for wondering what his interlocutor was talking about if the response to his query was "Hector Berlioz was addicted to opium." Similarly, in the context of verbal deception, in most cases the speaker cannot deceive by uttering some completely random random remark, regardless of its truth. If, upon coming home very late from his office, a man's wife explicitly (or implicitly) seeks to know why he is so late, and if the man has reasons for wishing to deceive her as to why by asserting something he knows to be false, we must assume that one of his goals is to respond with something that he believes will satisfy her as an answer. Blurting out "The square root of eight is seven," while false, would usually not suffice in this regard[2]. So in most cases of deception, speakers intend their remarks to be relevant relative to whatever they take to be the common ground at the time, and insofar as what they say is in response to some actual or assumed question or challenge, they intend their remarks to satisfy their target hearers.

1.4 Grice's Cooperative Principle

Much of what we have discussed so far is covered in Paul Grice's classic 1972 paper, *Logic and Conversation*. Grice proposed that when interlocutors engage in conversation they are implicitly committing themselves to abide by a contract (the Cooperative Principle) wherein their contributions to the conversation will be consistent with what Grice referred to as "the accepted purpose or direction of the talk exchange." This principle he exemplified through four "maxims". The first of these is the maxim of *Quantity*, which requires that the amount of information a speaker offers should be neither too much nor too little. The other three are the maxims of *Quality*, meaning "be truthful," of *Relation*, meaning "be relevant," and the maxim of *Manner*, meaning "be clear" (which, perhaps ironically, Grice wrote of as the need to "be perspicuous"). Grice viewed these maxims as comprising the background against which speakers expect normal conversations to take place, with the application of the maxims, of course, always being relative to the context. Naturally, speakers frequently violate one or more these maxims, sometimes intentionally and blatantly, which Grice referred to as "flouting", and which constitutes an opting out of the Cooperative

---

[2] As will be discussed later, there are circumstances under which the speaker might believe that such a response could suffice. For example, he might decide to say something so obviously zany as to lead his wife to believe that he had lost his mind. This, he might conjecture, would lead to an immediate changing of the subject, an avoidant strategy that we refer to as Contrived Distraction, and incidentally, a strategy that might even be successful using an assertion the speaker believes to be true.

Principle. As will be discussed below, most (but not all) cases of verbal deception involve either secretly violating or explicitly flouting one or more of Grice's maxims.

1.5 Pragmatic Implication

There is a longstanding literature, especially in philosophy of language, about the topic of pragmatic implication (e.g., Grant, 1958). The subtleties of the issue are not important for our purposes. For us it is sufficient to think of pragmatic implication as being a relation of implication between two propositions that depends on knowledge of the world rather than on semantics or pure logic. Suppose someone announces that they had a great view of the Alps as they flew to Venice. Many thing follow from this, including the fact that they were probably in an airplane, and that the weather was probably clear. These inferences are perfectly reasonable, but they are not entailed by the assertion. They are licensed by the fact that they are the kinds of characteristics of the world that one would expect given the truth of the assertion. The relevance of this is that this relation between propositions enables us to talk about what might be reasonably inferred or concluded by the hearer from the speaker's assertion. In particular, we have to assume that whatever strategy of deception the speaker employs, a major aspiration is that the hearer does not somehow come to the conclusion that the to-be-concealed truth is in fact the truth. Thus, what the speaker asserts should neither logically entail nor pragmatically imply it–it should not, in any way, *suggest* it.

2 What is Verbal Deception?

We have already indicated that an informal account of verbal deception will not be adequate for our purposes. Accordingly, we propose the following more formal account:

> verbal deception occurs when a speaker, S, expresses or intimates some proposition, Q, to a hearer, H, because there is some aspect of S's perceived world (representable by a proposition, P) with respect to which S has the intention of deceiving H. To realize this intention, S creates a belief-manipulation[3] goal, G, of establishing or maintaining in H a particular mental state relative to P. There are usually many strategies through which S can achieve G, but insofar as S is a boundedly-rational agent, S's choice of strategy will be determined by some sort of cost-benefit analysis strongly constrained by social-psychological considerations relating to S's relationship to H.

---

[3] We call it a "belief-manipulation" goal because the goal pertains to H's belief or knowledge state.

Of particular interest to us in this chapter are the strategies speakers use to deceive their hearers. Our ultimate goal is to identify and characterize these strategies, and to organize them into a coherent and psychologically plausible classification scheme. But we will not only address the question of how speakers achieve their goals through verbal deception, we will also consider the different kinds, or types, of verbal deception available to them. In addressing these issues, we shall focus on two main bodies of literature, namely, work coming out of pragmatics and speech act theory on the one hand, and out of communication theory on the other. We also discuss some contributions from philosophy, but because the boundary between pragmatics conceived of as part of the philosophy of language and pragmatics conceived of as a subfield of linguistics is so indistinct, we make no sharp distinction between them.

It often happens that when different disciplines address the same general problem, both the focal questions and the methodologies they employ differ. They also often use different terminologies and different levels of analysis with the result that they produce interesting analyses that are somewhat independent of each other. In what follows, we hope to bring together the two main perspectives on verbal deception. We believe that much is to be learned from both, even though they sometimes have different emphases and different approaches, and we think that a more comprehensive account of verbal deception can be achieved by considering both than can be achieved by considering either alone.

The most important contribution to analyses of verbal deception from pragmatics concerns the role of Grice's notion of Conversational Implicature (e.g., Adler, 1997; Meibauer, 2005). Implicature arises when a speaker means to imply or suggest one thing while saying something else (Grice, 1975), that is, when the intended meaning differs from the literal meaning of the utterance. However, unlike the case of metaphoric language wherein the relation between the literal meaning and the intended meaning is usually at the semantic level (e.g., "the interviewer *crucified* the politician," "the president's speech went over *like a lead balloon*"), in the case of implicature the relation is usually one in which what is meant at the propositional level can somehow be surmised from the literal meaning at the pragmatic level. So the general idea is that in many cases, verbal deception is accomplished through false implicature, that is, through implicature that the speaker believes to be false, while believing the literal meaning is true. The field of pragmatics has also inspired artificial intelligence (e.g., BDI–Belief, Desires, Intentions) analyses of verbal deception of the kind advanced by Castelfranchi and colleagues (e.g., Castelfranchi & Poggi, 1993; Vincent & Castelfranchi, 1979). In addition, we believe that the analysis of Chisholm and Feehan (1977) in terms of the omission-commission distinction is crucial to an understanding of the intentions underlying deception. The omission-commission distinction has to do with the fact that a person may seek to deceive either through what he or she says (commission), or through what he or she fails to say (omission).

The literature in communication theory, on the other hand, has focused on identifying dimensions along which the different types of deception strategies vary (e.g., Burgoon, Buller, & Guerrero, 1996; Hopper & Bell, 1984; McCornack, 1992; Turner et al., 1975), generating a taxonomy of deception strategies (e.g., Hopper & Bell, 1984; Metts, 1989; Turner et al., 1975), and identifying the social goals for deception–goals such as not hurting one's partner's feelings, and avoiding conflict and unpleasant situations (e.g., Levine et al., 2002; Metts, 1989). Although basic concepts from pragmatics play a role in some of the research in communication theory, the goals and methods of the research efforts have generally been rather different.

3 Existing approaches to classifying verbal deception types

More than 20 different types of verbal deception have been discussed in the different literatures, and there have been numerous proposals as to how to organize them into meaningful classification scheme. These proposals, can be roughly grouped into three classes: (1) those that have the Cooperative Principle at their core (Burgoon et al., 1996; McCornack, 1992; Metts, 1989; Turner et al., 1975), (2) those that follow a "speaker intention" approach (Bradac, 1983; Chisholm & Feehan, 1977; Vincent & Castelfranchi, 1979), and (3) those based on attempts to discover the underlying dimensions of deception (e.g., Hopper & Bell, 1984).

3.1 Cooperative Principle approaches

As already mentioned, Grice's Cooperative Principle and its four maxims of Quality, Quantity, Relevance, and Manner, specify how interlocutors in conversation normally subscribe to and comply with an implicit contract to be cooperative. The four maxims, which constitute the core of the Cooperative Principle, are, as expressed by Grice: (1) be as informative as is required for the current purpose of the conversation, and do not be more informative than is required (the maxim of Quantity), (2) do not say what you believe to be false, do not say anything for which you lack adequate evidence (Quality), (3) make your contribution relevant to the conversation/context (Relevance), and (4) do not be ambiguous, be brief and orderly (Manner).

Three related strands of research in Communication Theory exemplify this approach, starting with Turner et al.'s (1975) tripartite taxonomy of deception strategies into Distortion, Concealment, and Diversionary responses. Subsequently, McCornack (1992) extended Turner et al.'s idea and, relating it to the Cooperative Principle, proposed the *Information Manipulation Theory* (IMT). The third strand is Burgoon et al.'s. (1996) *Interpersonal Deception Theory* (IDT), which goes beyond IMT by incorporating a construct they called Personalization.

Turner et al. (1975), took as their starting point the basic notions of distortion and concealment–two general forms of what they called "information control," namely, different ways in which information can be manipulated. They had subjects recall and record a conversation with someone close to them in which "important matters were at issue or stake". Subjects were then asked to mark their own utterances in the conversation as either completely honest or not completely honest. The experimenters were particularly interested in two types of responses, namely, those that their respondents actually reported saying during the conversation, and those that respondents claimed they would have said had they been totally honest. Results showed that subjects classified the majority (61.5 %) of their utterances as not completely honest, indicating some level of information control. A more fine-grained analysis enabled the researchers to further classify Distortion and Concealment into sub-types (e.g., lies, exaggerations, half-truths, and secrets). They also found a third form of information control that they referred to as Diversionary responses. From these results, Turner et al. (1975) identified the following seven types of deception:

1. Lies: what respondents said contradicted what they would have said had they been totally honest,
2. Exaggerations (type 1): respondents gave more information they would have given had they been totally honest,
3. Exaggerations (type 2): respondents overstated something by using superlative modifiers that they wouldn't have used had they been totally honest,
4. Half-truths (type 1): respondents disclosed only part of what they considered to be a complete disclosure,
5. Half-truths (type 2): respondents overstated something by using modifiers that gave less than an honest evaluation of the situation,
6. Secrets: respondents remained silent when in fact they had something to say, and
7. Diversionary responses: what respondents said was different from or irrelevant to what they would have said had they been totally honest.

While Turner et al. (1975) suggested three forms of information control–Concealment, Distortion and Diversionary responses–all having to do with message *content*, Bavelas et al. (1990), appealing to the case of equivocation, argued that deceptive messages can also be generated by manipulating the *manner* in which the information is presented. McCornack (1992) followed Bowers et al.'s (1977) suggestion that "deviant" messages mislead by violating Gricean maxims, and concluded that Turner et al.'s (1975) categories of Distortion, Concealment, and Diversionary responses, as well as Bavelas et al.'s (1990) Equivocation are directly related to Grice's maxims of Quantity, Quality, Relevance, and Manner. For this reason, McCornack (1992) proposed his *Information Manipulation Theory* (IMT), according to which deceptive messages are constructed by violating one or more of the Grice's maxims. He tested this idea by asking subjects to generate messages in response to three specific situations, and then analyzing their responses in terms of IMT. These situations were generated in another experiment in which subjects were asked to write a detailed description of a situation in which they had verbally deceived a dating partner, including a description of the relationship and the details of the conversation. McCornack also reviewed taxonomies that had been proposed by other people and showed that they could easily be accommodated by IMT.

McCornack (1992) was highly critical of "taxonomy or strategy-based" approaches to studying deceptive messages. He argued that such approaches lead to inconsistent systems of categorization, and that examples of deceptive messages presented in such approaches are too often generated using recall methods as in, for instance, Metts (1989), with the result that the examples are not representative of deception in everyday communication. For these reasons, McCornack advocated a "dimensional" approach in terms of which deceptive messages can be conceptualized as "a potentially infinite class of specific message forms resulting from the manipulation of information in particular, characteristic ways" (p. 3). Nevertheless, McCornack realized that there remained a class of deceptive messages not covered in his analysis, namely, messages involving deception by implication, and the fact that there exists this form of deception, he stated, "suggests a realm of deceptive messages beyond the immediate scope of IMT: messages that mislead not through the manipulation of information, but through the generation of deceptive implicatures" (p. 14). This notion of deceiving by falsely implicating was discussed at length by Adler (1997). Meibauer (2005), motivated by the work of Adler and others, presented a detailed speech act analysis of deceptive false implicatures within the framework of Grice's Cooperative Principle.

A variant of McCornack's (1992) IMT was proposed by Burgoon et al. (1996) who postulated five dimensions, namely, Veridicality, Completeness, Directness/Relevance, Clarity, and Personalization. Of these, four are essentially the same as McCornack's, with Veridicality being related to the maxim of Quality, Completeness to the maxim of Quantity, Directness/Relevance to the maxim of Relevance, and Clarity being the analog of the maxim of Manner. The new, fifth, dimension of Personalization, Burgoon et al. took to represent the speaker's own thoughts, opinions and feelings about the conveyed information. Personalization is related to the concept of "disassociation" or "verbal nonimmediacy" so that speakers can manipulate the "ownership" of their utterance by using strategies that disassociate them from the information presented. Nonimmediacy refers to the implied relationship between the speaker and the subject of the information being discussed. It shifts descriptions of events by, for example, using abstract language or generalizations instead of concrete details, and obscuring the agent of the action, opinion or belief (e.g., "It is said that"). Burgoon et al. argued that even though Personalization cannot be readily related to Grice's Cooperative Principle, it is a background assumption of all discourse, so that any violation of it could cause a hearer to be misled. According to this view, an utterance belongs to the speaker who utters it and is thus supposed to reflect the speaker's opinion and feelings, unless explicitly stated otherwise. Burgoon et al. tested their overall theory by assessing the degree to which speakers can vary and hearers can recognize deceptive messages in terms of the five postulated dimensions. In one experiment, they engaged participants in two interviews each. In one of the interviews subjects had to be truthful, and in the other, they had to be deceptive (to a different interviewer) about the same questions. In another study, subjects were to be both truthful and deceptive during a single interview. Results, based on self-reports and observer ratings showed that all deceptive messages involved some level of information manipulation along one or more of the five dimensions of IDT. Because the models proposed by Burgoon et al. (1996) and by McCornack (1992) are dimensional models, any particular case of verbal deception can be thought of as one of an infinite number of possible points in a multi-dimensional space.

Finally, although not explicitly cast in terms of the Cooperative Principle, there is other work that can also be seen in this light. For example, in her analysis of deception in close relationships, Metts (1989) employed as her starting point three main types of deception: Falsification, Omission, and Distortion. She argued that all forms of deception proposed in the literature fall on a continuum with Falsification at one end, Omission at the other, and with the region around the midpoint representing various types of Distortion such as Exaggeration, Minimization, and Evasion. It is not difficult to conceptualize her notion of Falsification as a violation of the maxim of Quality, and her notion of Omission as a violation of Quantity. Finally, Metts's Distortion could be viewed as a combination of violations of Manner and of Relevance (since she also included cases of evasion as instances of Distortion).

3.2 Speaker intentions approaches

Cooperative Principle approaches to classifying different types of verbal deception focus on what a speaker *says*. An alternative approach is to focus on what the speaker *intends*. Viewed in this way, three apparently quite disparate lines of work (e.g., Bradac, 1983; Chisholm & Feehan, 1977; Vincent & Castelfranchi, 1979) can be grouped together.

Chisholm and Feehan's (1977) insightful analysis of deception revolved around the important distinction between deception by commission and deception by omission. These authors defined deception by commission as an act through which a speaker, S, *contributes causally* to a hearer, H, acquiring or continuing to believe a falsehood, or to H's ceasing to believe, or being prevented from acquiring a particular truth. In a similar vein (but with the emphasis now on allowing rather than causing), they defined deception by omission as an act whereby S *allows* H to acquire or continue to believe a falsehood, or to cease to believe or to continue without the belief of a particular truth. Thus both deception by commission and by omission admit of four cases, namely, (1) H's acquiring, or (2) continuing to believe, a falsehood, and preventing (3) H from acquiring, or (4) ceasing to believe, a truth. We worry a little about Chisholm and Feehan's account of deception by omission because their notion of allowing seems to require that S could have prevented H from embracing or holding onto the mistaken belief in question, but did not. However, this means that S must have engaged in a mental act, for example, the act of deciding or choosing not to say something, in which case Chisholm and Feehan's notion of allowing means that S did in fact contribute causally to H's state of belief. And if this is so, then the difference between deception by commission and deception by omission lies not in the difference between contributing causally and allowing (because ultimately allowing reduces to contributing causally), but rather in the kind of act (communicative vs. mental) that contributed to H's belief state.

However, even though we have reservations about Chisholm and Feehan's criterion for distinguishing deception by omission from deception by commission, we believe that their identification of eight different forms of deception is an important and valuable contribution, and one that has significantly influenced our own approach to verbal deception. As we will discuss in more detail later, we take their two sets of four deception types and collapse them into one set, the elements of which we refer to as *belief manipulation goals* which, we argue, can be achieved by various deception *strategies*. For example, one such goal is to get H to acquire a belief about something that S believes is false. Such a goal can be achieved by several different strategies, including fabricating a false story, or overstating, or using excessively abstract language.

Bradac (1983) studied the relationship between language and social relationships, and their mutual entailments, maintaining that humans hold three kinds of beliefs: beliefs about the world, beliefs about beliefs, and beliefs about the consequences of their utterances. He further argued that the intersection of these beliefs with intentionality gives rise to several discrete types of communicative phenomena (Bowers & Bradac, 1982; Scott, 1977). Bradac proposed three strategies for verbal deception: Lies, Secrets, and Evasions. These, together with true revelations, he considered to be related but distinct communicative acts. This account, although explicitly considering the role of intention, is a very broad and general approach to communication, which, while accommodating deception, is not specific to it. It thus fails to help with respect to deception strategies, which is an issue of primary concern to us.

Some of the most important work on verbal deception that takes into account the role of speaker intentions is that of Vincent and Castelfranchi (1979) who analyzed verbal deception, and in particular "indirect lying or lying while telling the truth", in terms of agent assumptions and beliefs, intentions and goals. By indirect lies, they meant deceptive messages in which the utterance itself is believed to be true by S, but through that true utterance, S has the goal of causing H to believe that some other proposition is true, when in fact S believes that other proposition to be false. Taking this goal-based approach as a heuristic, Vincent and Castelfranchi generated a taxonomy of eight communicative strategies through which indirect deception can be achieved. However, they also maintained that these strategies can be used for communicative purposes other than indirect deception. The eight strategies[4] they identified are:

1. Insinuation: an indirect lie wherein S wants H to believe what is implied by S's utterance while S believes that what is implied is false. Consider an example given by the authors, where a child on his first day at a new

---

[4] We find many of the names given to these strategies somewhat confusing because they deviate from the ordinary language meanings of those terms. For instance, the ordinary language meaning of "reticence" is simply a reluctance to disclose something, regardless of its presumed truth value, whereas in Vincent and Castelfranchi's account, the reluctance concerns material that the speaker believes to be false.

school says to his classmate, "My dad works at the BBC," intending H to infer that his father has a prestigious job, when in fact his father works there as a janitor.

2. Reticence: S leaves something (that S believes is false) unsaid and wants H to understand (1) what that unsaid thing is from the context, (2) that it is intentionally being left unsaid, and (3) the goal behind leaving it unsaid. For example, consider a situation in which, when H says to S, speaking about some third person, John, "I hope John doesn't drink too much," S wants (out of spite, perhaps) to falsely suggest that John does indeed drink excessively without actually saying so. Under these conditions, S, knowing that John is Irish, might exploit what he takes to be a stereotype by saying "Well, he *is* Irish!"

3. Half-truth: S tells only part of the truth and conceals another part that S believes is relevant to H, thereby getting H to make some false assumptions. For example, when a child only admits that he punched his little sister, when the truth is that he beat her up.[5]

4. Precondition or Presupposition faking: S says something that S believes is true that presupposes something that S believes is false. Consider Vincent and Castelfranchi's (1979) example of a guest at a wedding saying to another, "It's a pity that Anne and Mark had to be at Burleigh this weekend." Here there could be several false presuppositions including that Anne and Mark had been invited to the wedding, that S knows Anne and Mark very well, and that they would have come had they not had to address some important issue at Burleigh.

5. Deliberate ambiguity (or equivocation): S says something that has two interpretations, where S believes that one of them is true and the other is false, and wants H to infer the false one. The authors give Bolinger's (1973) example of an advertisement which says, "No heat costs less than oil heat," where one (true) interpretation is that not using any heating will cost less than heating using oil, and the other (questionable, if not outright false) interpretation is that oil-heating is cheaper than any other kind of heating.

6. Obfuscation: S says something that S believes is true but believes that H will not be able to fully understand and will therefore be deceived, as might happen when S intentionally uses technical jargon or euphemisms that he or she believes H is unlikely to understand.

7. Pretending to lie: S says something that S believes is true but wants H to believe that it is false. Vincent and Castelfranchi (1979) give the example of a burglar, who, when caught by the police and interrogated about his partner's whereabouts, tells them the correct location, hoping that the police won't believe him and will therefore look in the wrong places, while at the same time insulating himself from charges of lying.

8. Pretending to act or joke: S says something that S believes is true as a joke, and wants H to believe that S believes that it is not true, thereby pretending solidarity and complicity.

---

[5] In our own analysis, we would consider this to be a case of Understatement.

Although their account is restricted to cases in which the surface form of
the utterance is believed to be true by the speaker, Vincent and Castelfranchi's
(1979) approach provides a deep account of how speaker's assumptions, intentions and goals interact with different types of linguistic actions to generate
deception. We find this kind of detailed speech act analysis (see also, Castelfranchi & Poggi, 1993) most appealing, comprising as it does a BDI theory of
action (i.e., a theory based on beliefs, desires, and intentions). The analysis that
we shall shortly present is in the same spirit, although it addresses a broader
range of deception strategies to include cases in which the surface form of the
utterance is believed to be false by the speaker.

3.3 A Multidimensional scaling approach

Hopper and Bell (1984), concerned that too much of the literature on deception
in communication focused on lies, undertook to present what they considered
to be a broader and more empirically-based conceptualization of deceptive
communication. Accordingly, they set out to identify the dimensions underlying deception in general, on the basis of which to propose a typology of
deception strategies. To do this, they compiled a list of 120 English words and
idioms that people use to talk about various aspects of deception and then
had judges select those deemed to be "most central to deception," of which
46 were identified. These were then used as stimuli for similarity judgments,
the data from which were subjected to multidimensional scaling. The results
suggested three underlying dimensions of Evaluation (right or wrong), De-
tectability (easy or hard to detect), and Premeditated (planned or unplanned).
Then, on the basis of a cluster analysis, the authors proposed a typology of six
deception strategies:

1. Fictions (comprising lexical items such as "make-believe," "exaggeration,"
   "myth," and "white lie"): aspects of messages that make them imaginative
   or counter-factual,
2. Playing (e.g., "joke," "tease," and "kidding"): deceptions perpetrated for
   the purpose of amusement,
3. Lies (e.g., "dishonesty," and "lie"): false verbal statements intended to
   deceive,
4. Crimes (e.g., "con," "conspiracy," and "entrapment"): acts that are prescribed as crimes in the criminal justice system,
5. Masks (e.g., "hypocrisy," "evasion," and "concealment"): deception by
   obscuring the truth, and
6. Unlies (e.g. "distortion," "false implication," and "misrepresentation"):
   deception through implication.

Hopper and Bell's (1984) analysis is interesting and suggestive, but because
it deals with all forms of deception (not just verbal deception), we think that
it is perhaps too course grained for our purposes. Many of the words they
used on the grounds that they were judged to be "most central to deception"

(e.g., "conspiracy", "forgery") are not readily applicable to verbal deception, if applicable at all. We thus cannot assume that these same (and only) three dimensions are applicable to *verbal* deception. Furthermore, because some of their categories have to do with speakers' intentions, some with properties of (speech) acts, and some with reactions of hearers, their classification scheme lacks the coherence that one might hope for in a comprehensive account of verbal deception. For example, categories such as "playings" and crimes pertain to the social (or antisocial) goals that are achieved by deception, with the result that different kinds of deceptive strategies end up in the same category. For example, exaggeration, irony and make-believe are grouped together into fictions, whereas from the perspective of, for instance, speakers' communicative goals, these rhetorical devices are really quite dissimilar.

3.4 Summary

The three approaches discussed in this section are summarized in Table 1. Since verbal deception is heavily dependent upon context, a pragmatics perspective is obviously very relevant. Grice's (1975) Cooperative Principle lies at the heart of this perspective and it provides a good theoretical basis for systematically addressing the problem of verbal deception. However, its strength lies in its ability to furnish explanations of the properties of deceptive messages, rather than providing insight into the functional aspect of verbal deception. In other words, it focuses on the message rather than on the speaker. Moreover, the framework it provides is rather vague and by itself does not provide enough support for further exploration. On the other hand, the speaker intention approach is more functional in nature. It is also potentially useful for modeling purposes because it allows one to explore how agents might reason with their beliefs, intentions and their goals to generate deceptive communicative behavior. In what follows, we shall attempt to exploit the advantages of both approaches with a view to providing a comprehensive model of verbal deception.

4 A Comprehensive Approach to Analyzing Verbal Deception

Having reviewed several proposals from the literature as to how to organize the different types of verbal deception, we now present our own proposals for a comprehensive, integrated account. Our account comprises twelve basic types.

Table 1 Criteria for classifying verbal deception types by author(s)

Underlying Criterion	Classification		
Cooperative Principle	*Turner et al., 1975* Three forms of Information Control: Distortion, Concealment, and Diversionary responses	(1) Lies (2) Exaggeration (Type 1) (3) Exaggeration (Type 2) (4) Half-truth (Type 1)	(5) Half-truth (Type 2) (6) Secrets (7) Diversionary responses
	Metts, 1989 Continuum with Omission at one end and Falsification at the other, with the central region being Distortion	(1) Omission (2) Distortion (3) Falsification	
	McCornack, 1992 Four maxims of Quality, Quantity, Relevance, and Manner	"a potentially infinite class of specific message forms resulting from the manipulation of information in particular, characteristic ways"	
	Burgoon et al., 1996 Four maxims of Quality, Quantity, Relevance and Manner, plus a fifth dimension of Personalization	"many possibilities [with] contrasting combinations of the information dimension qualities"	
Speaker intentions	*Chisholm & Feehan, 1977* Omission/Commission dichotomy	(1) Commission (S contributes causally to): H's acquiring or continuing to believe a falsehood; H's being prevented from acquiring, or ceasing to believe a truth.	(2) Omission (S allows H to): acquire or continue to believe a falsehood, cease to believe or continue without the belief of a truth.
	Vincent & Castelfranchi, 1981 goal analysis model in terms of agent assumptions, intentions and goals	(1) Insinuation (2) Reticence (3) Half-truths (4) Precondition or Presupposition faking (5) Obfuscation	(6) Deliberate ambiguity (7) Pretending to lie (8) Pretending to act or joke
	Bradac, 1983 Intersection of beliefs and intentions suggests several types of related but distinct communicative acts	(1) Lying (2) Secrecy (3) Evasion	
Multi-dimensional scaling	*Hopper & Bell, 1984* Multidimensional scaling of lexical items revealing dimensions	(1) Fictions (2) Playing (3) Lies	(4) Crimes (5) Masks (6) Unlies

4.1 Specification of Verbal Deception Types

1. **Fabrication**: By fabrication, we mean an outright lie wherein S simply makes up a false story in order to deceive H. We distinguish two sub-types of fabrication: Simple Fabrication, and Fabrication for False Inference.

   In *Simple Fabrication*, S makes up a story that he or she wants H to believe. For example, S is a mean-spirited student and wants to deceive H during a test. S knows that H needs to know the capital of Turkey, and knowing that it is not Istanbul, he tells H that the capital of Turkey is Istanbul.

   In *Fabrication for False Inference*, S intends to deceive H primarily with respect to what the fabricated story implies. Unlike the case of Simple Fabrication, the fabricated story here is a means to an end rather than an end in itself. For example, Steve, S, is jealous of Harry, H, because he, Steve, is very attracted to Harry's girlfriend. Steve has no reason to believe anything bad about Harry, and has never seen Harry in the company of disreputable people. Nevertheless, Steve tells Harry's girlfriend that he often sees Harry hanging out with some really bad people, thereby intending to imply that Harry can't be trusted. It is this implication of the fabrication that is the nexus of the deceit. Fabrication for False Inference also covers cases of false presuppositions. For example, a child, H, who doesn't know about Santa Claus, asks his mother, S, on Christmas morning where the presents under the Christmas tree came from. The mother, wanting her child to believe there is a Santa Claus says, "Santa Claus left them last night while we were all sleeping," which, as well as being a fabrication, presupposes that there exists a Santa Claus. In this case, S deceives H with respect not only to what she says, but also with respect to the presupposition of what she says, which is the primary goal of her utterance.

2. **False Implicature**: As already discussed, the term "implicature" refers to the implied or suggested meaning of an utterance when that meaning is not (logically) entailed by the utterance. False Implicatures are conversational implicatures in which the literal meaning is true, but the implied meaning is false, a nice example of which is cited by Meibauer (2005) as a classic. It pertains to a ship's captain who every day enters into the ship's log the fact that the first mate was drunk. One day the captain is unable to complete the log, so the responsibility to do so falls to the first mate, who of course notices the daily references to his drunkenness. To retaliate against the captain, the first mate enters into the log the true statement that "Today, the captain was not drunk," intending thereby to falsely suggest that the captain's not being drunk was an unusual event. Although this example does not involve an actual speaker and an actual hearer, the logic of the example is the same as if the first mate were the speaker, S, and the captain (or indeed anybody else) was the hearer, H.

3. **Denial**: A denial is a rejection of the alleged truth of a proposition; the speaker indicates that he or she believes the proposition in question is false. We distinguish two forms of denial, namely, Simple Denial and Denial for False Inference.

In *Simple Denial* the proposition being contradicted is itself the nexus of deception. For example, a mother, H, knows full well that it was her child, S, who took all the cookies from the cookie jar. Knowing this, she says to her child "You took the cookies, and I told you not to". The child denies her assertion that it was he who took the cookies, saying, "I didn't take them. It wasn't me."

In *Denial for False Inference*, S, by denying a true proposition, implies something else that is false. For example, consider a scenario in which Sara, S, is a prime witness in a murder trial. Convinced that the accused person is guilty, she testifies that she heard a gunshot. During cross-examination, the defense attorney, H, says "You said that at the time of the gunshot, you were in the bathroom. And did you not testify that you were drying your hair?" In fact, Sara was indeed blow drying her hair at that time, and was not really sure that she heard a gunshot at all. To hide her uncertainty, she contradicts the defense attorney and denies that she was drying her hair, saying, "No, I didn't say that." In this scenario, S wants to deceive H about her uncertainty concerning hearing the gunshot. The intended implication of her denial that she was using her hair dryer is the falsehood that she was able to clearly hear the gunshot. So the nexus of deception lies in the inference she hopes will be made from the denial rather than in the denial itself.

4. **Half-truth**: Half-truths involve revealing only part of the truth, while concealing another part that involves the nexus of deception. We have identified two sub-types of Half-truth: Simple Half-truth and Half-truth for False Inference.

   In *Simple Half-truth*, the proposition being concealed is itself the nexus of deception. For example, a man, S, gets home late because he had a long meeting running into the early evening, and so left work much later than usual. Then, he went to see his girlfriend. When he gets home, his wife asks him why he is so late. The man doesn't want his wife to learn the truth, so he tells her "We had a long meeting that went on into the evening." In this example, what S says is the truth, but it is not the whole truth; it is a Half-truth.

   In *Half-truth for False Inference*, S, by revealing only part of the truth and concealing a true proposition, implies something else that is false. For example, a small girl, S, instead of finishing her homework, went out to play with her friends. It was chilly and damp outside, and when she got back home, she began to feel feverish. The next day, her teacher, H, asks her why her homework wasn't finished. Wanting H to believe that it wasn't her fault, S says, "I got sick yesterday, that's why." What S says is the truth, but it is only a Half-truth, and S utters it with the intention of (falsely) implying that it wasn't her fault that she didn't finish her homework.

5. **Abstraction**: In abstraction, S frames her utterance in a way that is sufficiently general or broad that it hides the more specific proposition that S intends to conceal from H. Thus, the proposition with respect to which S wants to deceive H implies what S actually says, but is not implied by it,

while what S actually says is true. There are two sub-types of Abstraction: Simple Abstraction and Abstraction for False Inference.

In *Simple Abstraction*, the proposition that is generalized is the nexus of deception. For example, Sally, S, is going to her boyfriend's place at the city center, but does not want her mother, H, to know. When Sally's mother asks her where she is going, Sally, tells says that she's going to a friend's place. Thus, by generalizing from the more specific "boyfriend's place" to the more general or abstract "friend's place," S seeks to conceal from H the fact that she is going to her boyfriend's place.

In *Abstraction for False Inference*, S, by generalizing a proposition, implies something else that is false. Suppose this same Sally, S, intends to go to the movies, but does not want her mother to know because she knows that her mother expects her to go to the library to study for an impending exam. When Sally's mother asks, "Where are you going?" Sally says, "I'm going to the city center," hoping that her mother will (falsely) infer that she is going to the library.

There are similarities between Half-truth and Abstraction in that both conceal a proposition from H. In Half-truth, the proposition is concealed by being omitted, whereas in Abstraction it is concealed by being generalized. Since, in a sense, Abstraction also involves omission, it might be considered a special case of Half-truth. However, we keep them separate partly because they violate different Gricean maxims, as will be seen in the next section.

6. **Contrived Distraction**: In Contrived Distraction S is evasive by finding some pretext to urgently change the subject, and it is by virtue of this that S attempts to deceive H. For example, a child, H, is a firm believer in Santa Claus. His friends at school tell him that there is no Santa Claus. Troubled, he comes back home and says to his mother, S, "My friends say that Santa Claus isn't real." His mother, S, wanting H to continue believing in the existence of Santa Claus, tries to distract him by saying "Never mind that for now. Show me what homework you have today."

7. **Overstatement**: Deception through overstatement arises when S exaggerates an aspect of something featured in the proposition about which she intends to deceive H. There are two sub-types of overstatement: Simple Overstatement and Overstatement for False Inference.

In *Simple overstatement* what is being overstated is itself the nexus of deception. For example, H, has invited her future mother-in-law, S, for dinner. On eating the food, the mother-in-law-to-be thinks that it is at best, average; not too good, but not too bad either. Out of politeness, she says to H, who has no idea what S thinks about the food, "This is a delicious meal." In this example, S overstates by describing what she considers to be a so-so meal as "delicious."

In *Overstatement for False Inference*, by overstating a proposition, S implies something else that is false. That is, the nexus of the deception is not the proposition itself (as in Simple Overstatement), but the inference that S hopes H will draw from the proposition. For example, in a radio commercial, the announcer, S, is explaining the benefits of a new cream that he claims removes pimples. In fact, he knows that the cream is not very effective and not worth buying, because it removes only a few pimples and it takes two weeks to do so. But to do his job, he says to the listeners, H,"This cream will remove most of your pimples in just two weeks." In this case, S knowingly overstates the effectiveness of the cream, and in doing so, implies (and intends to imply) that people should buy the cream if they have pimples.

8. **Understatement**: Understatement is the opposite of overstatement and involves stating something as less than it is by underspecifying an aspect of something featured in the proposition about which S wants to deceive H. Again, there are two sub-types of understatement, Simple Understatement and Understatement for False Inference.

   In *Simple understatement* the proposition in which the understatement is embedded is itself the nexus of deception. For example, in order to cause listeners, H, to stop believing that the 2010 BP oil spill in the Gulf of Mexico was very serious, BP's then CEO Tony Hayward, S, said, "The Gulf of Mexico is a very big ocean. The amount of volume [sic] of oil and dispersant we are putting into it is tiny in relation to the total water volume." In saying this, S intended H to infer that the amount of oil and dispersant was not significant. But in fact the amount of oil and dispersant was huge, so S was understating the quantity of oil and dispersant.

   Understatement for False Inference occurs when, by understating a proposition, S implies something else that is false. For example, a child, S, is sick and has a high fever, but hates taking medicines. His mother, H, says "Take this medicine now and your fever will quickly go down." The child, wanting his mother to stop believing that he needs to take the medicine, says, "I don't have much fever now." By understating the degree of his fever, S implies that he now does not need to take any medicine, which is false.

9. **Augmentation**: In augmentation, S adds something gratuitous to the truth, thereby deceiving H. For example, Steven, S, is dating his secretary, Mary, but does not want another colleague, H, to know because Steven and Mary are not yet ready to make their relationship public. One day H, being suspicious, asks Steven, "Did I see you having dinner with Mary last night?" In order to prevent H from coming to believe the truth, S replies, "Yes you did; we used it as an opportunity to discuss some important project issues," where "... we used it as an opportunity to discuss some important project issues" is the augmented part.

10. **Equivocation**: In cases of equivocation, S deliberately says something ambiguous so as to avoid being committed to the interpretation that is true. Consider a situation in which a professor, H, is considering hiring John, an ex-student of a colleague, Smith, from a different institution. The professor asks Smith whether he would recommend John. Smith wants the professor to hire John because, even though John is not very bright, Smith is very fond of him and knows that John desperately needs a job. In order to prevent the professor from coming to believe the truth that John is not very bright, while also wanting to free himself of a real commitment,

Smith, S, says, "I can't recommend John highly enough." In this way, the burden of getting to the truth is placed on the H. Does Smith mean "John is so good that there is no limit to how highly I can recommend him" or something more like "John is not good enough for me to recommend him sufficiently highly to impress you." Another example the already cited one (Bolinger, 1973) of the an advertisement that says: "No heat costs less than oil heat," a line which carries the same "bipolar" ambiguity. In a sense equivocation provides S with "plausible deniability" should it be needed. More often, however, H will recognize the ambiguity and realize that the negative interpretation is called for.

11. **Obfuscation**: Obfuscation occurs when S deceives H by deliberately using confusing or complicated language in the hope that H will either be unable to understand the exact meaning or will misunderstand. Vincent and Castelfranchi's (1979) examples clarify what this means. They say that euphemisms, technical jargon, and verbal cosmetics are examples of obfuscation, and advertisers often use this strategy to deceive buyers. For example, an advertiser might use the term "coney" to refer to the type of fur on a fur-coat, hoping that people don't know what it is and so might think that it is something exotic, when in fact it simply means "rabbit fur."

12. **Pretending to Lie**: This somewhat ironic form of deception occurs when S says what he believes to be true, but hopes that H will think that he is lying. We have already discussed Vincent and Castelfranchi's example of a burglar, S, who when asked about the whereabouts of his regular partner in crime, actually tells the truth, thinking that the police won't believe him, and will thus spend more time trying to ascertain the "true" location of his partner elsewhere.

4.2 New Approaches to Classifying Verbal Deception

Earlier we discussed several different approaches to classifying verbal deception types, and in many respects these different approaches complement each other. Accordingly, in this section we draw upon what we consider to be the most promising aspects of them, and present two classification systems, each corresponding to one of the two major distinctions pertaining to verbal deception that we introduced earlier. Thus, we will first present a classification of deception types based on their relation to the Cooperative Principle, and then present a classification rooted in the notion of Speaker Intentions. Roughly speaking, one might say that the first of these classification systems focuses on the language of deception, while the second focuses on what the speaker is trying to do when he or she engages in an act of verbal deception. We should note, however, that what we are proposing still constitutes a work in progress and should therefore be viewed as only giving a flavor of our general approach.

4.2.1 A Classification based on the Cooperative Principle

As we have seen, one of the standard ways of talking about verbal deception is
in terms of Grice's Cooperative Principle, but we are unaware of any attempts
to systematically organize the different types of verbal deception in terms of
their relation to the four maxims that are so central to it. In this section, we try
to remedy this deficiency.

When a speaker attempts to deceive another, the Cooperative Principle is
of necessity implicated. One of the maxims of Quality, Quantity, Relevance
and Manner is involved because speakers deceive either by (1) surreptitiously
violating one of them while appearing to be Gricean cooperative, or by (2)
obviously *flouting* one of them so that the hearer is aware of the violation.
With the exception of three of the deception types we have identified, False
Implicature, Contrived Distraction and Pretending to Lie, our deception types
all fall into the first category, that is, they deceive by the non-obvious *violation*
of maxims. Figure 1 shows our classification of verbal deception types based on
these maxims. Dotted lines show the types that deceive by flouting a maxim
and solid lines show the types that deceive by (surreptitiously) violating a
maxim.

We now briefly discuss how the maxims are violated or flouted by the various deception types. We should first point out that False Implicature can be
generated by flouting any of the four maxims. As already discussed, conver-

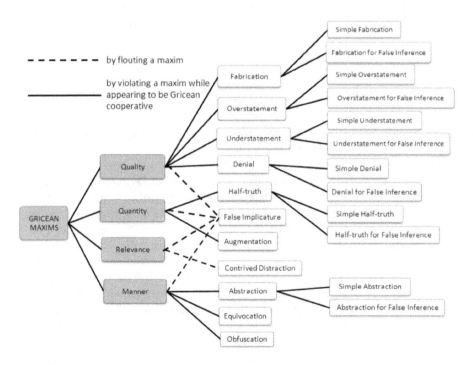

Fig. 1 Gricean maxim violations by verbal deception strategies

sational implicatures are generated when the hearer knows that the speaker only appears to have flouted a maxim, and so fills in the suggested meaning to make sense of the utterance; and false implicatures are simply conversational implicatures in which the literal meaning is true, but the suggested meaning is false. Any of the four maxims can be flouted to generate a discrepancy between the literal meaning and the implied or suggested meaning.

Quality: Of the twelve deception types that we have identified, four violate the maxim of Quality: Fabrication, Overstatement, Understatement, and Denial, including all of their sub-types. Fabrication violates Quality because it involves making up a false story, so that the surface form of the utterance itself is false. Overstatement and Understatement violate Quality because they modulate an aspect of something mentioned in the proposition, thus affecting the truth value of what is said. Denial is a direct violation, because the speaker knowingly contradicts something believed to be true.

Quantity: Two of our types violate the Quantity maxim: Half-truth, and Augmentation. Half-truth violates Quantity because it conceals part of the truth, hence saying less than is required. Augmentation violates Quantity (and also Relevance, as discussed below) because it adds trivial and distracting information to the truth, hence saying more than is required.

Relevance: As just mentioned, Augmentation also violates Relevance, because it adds something extra to the truth that is not relevant to the central issue. Meanwhile, Contrived Distraction often flouts (rather than merely violating) the Relevance maxim. One might think that a generalization of Contrived Distraction–Evasion–would make more sense in this context, and that Evasion would also have to be regarded as flouting Relevance. However, we have not included Evasion as one of our deception types because it is not clear that being evasive in general is a case of intentional verbal deceit. On the other hand Contrived Distraction, we believe, does involve intentional deception on the speaker's part, precisely because the distraction is contrived. Furthermore, it is likely to be clear to the hearer that Relevance has been flouted, and that the speaker is trying to distract the hearer to attend to some other, apparently more important, matter. Most other kinds are of evasion are transparent refusals to discuss the matter at hand and therefore are not (intended to be) deceptive.

Manner: The strategies that violate the Manner maxim are Equivocation, Obfuscation, and Abstraction. Equivocation and Obfuscation violate the Manner maxim because they use ambiguous or confusing language. Abstraction violates Manner because it involves using generalized language to avoid stating the issue as it is. Because Abstraction involves omission by generalization, it follows that Abstraction also violates the Quantity maxim. One might think about it in terms of primary and secondary violations. By definition, Abstraction primarily violates manner, but this manner violation is framed in such a way as to also violate Quantity, thereby deceiving H. So Manner is primary (and therefore shown in Figure 1) while Quantity is the secondary violation (and is therefore not shown in Figure 1).

Finally, there is the interesting case of Vincent and Castelfranchi's Pretending to Lie deception type, which the reader might have noticed, does not appear in Figure 1. With respect to violating or flouting maxims, the principle governing this deception type is the converse of the principle governing all of the others. This is because in the case of Pretending to Lie, the speaker hopes that the hearer will wrongly believe that in fact he or she is not being cooperative and is attempting to violate the Quality maxim (i.e., to not tell the truth). This is in contrast to the other deception types, in which the speaker, while violating or flouting a maxim, assumes that the hearer thinks that he or she is being Gricean cooperative.

4.2.2 A Classification based on Speaker Intentions

When a person decides to deceive another, he or she always has a purpose or goal. From the perspective of the communicative act, the speaker is always trying to do something with respect to the hearer. For example, and perhaps most typically, the deceptive speaker has the goal of getting the hearer to believe something that is not true. We think that the most informative and psychologically descriptive way in which to systematically organize the different types of deception is to view them as strategies that speakers use to attain goals of this kind with respect to their hearers. As already indicated, we refer to the goals that a speaker has with respect to the hearer's beliefs as the speaker's belief-manipulation goals for the hearer. Through such goals, speakers seek to establish or maintain in their hearers a particular mental state relative to the propositions with respect to which they intend to deceive their hearers. Partly inspired by the work of Chisholm and Feehan (1977), we propose four belief-manipulation goals of verbal deception that speakers use, either independently or in combination, to deceive their hearers. We refer to these four belief-manipulation goals as the goals to Acquire, to Continue, to Cease, and to Prevent, and their basic characterizations are as follows:

Acquire: S wants H to come to believe something is true when S believes it is false,

Continue: S wants H to continue believing something is true when S believes it is false,

Cease: S wants H to stop believing something that S believes is true, and

Prevent: S wants to stop H from coming to believe something that S believes is true.

All of these goals assume that the speaker has some initial belief about the hearer's belief state (i.e., about what the hearer does or does not know or believe), and that the purpose of the deception is for the speaker to somehow influence the hearer's belief state. Thus, we can think of deception strategies as "actions" that attempt to convert the speaker's initial belief state about the hearer's beliefs into a target belief state, as shown in Table 2. In the representations that follow, "bel (A, true (P))" and "bel (A, false (P))" should be taken to mean that individual A believes (and this can include believing correctly or incorrectly) that the proposition, P, is true or false, respectively. Meanwhile, we use "suggest (Qc, true (P))" to indicate that S, the speaker, believes that the proposition Qc might suggest or even warrant the inference that the proposition, P, is true or (in the case of "suggest (Qc, false (P))") false. Finally, it is important to emphasize that an understanding of speakers' verbal deception strategies does not require a determination of whether or not those strategies are successful. To be sure, rational speakers will expect, or at least, hope, that their deception strategies will succeed, but that does not mean that we need to know whether their hearer's actually are deceived.

Table 2 Initial Belief State and the Target Belief State for each of four belief manipulation goals. P represents the proposition whose truth or falsity is the nexus of the deception, Q represents the proposition that S expresses in order to influence H's belief about P (i.e., what S actually says), and Qc represents the Gricean-cooperative proposition that S would express instead of Q if S were not deceiving H (what S "ought" to say). Note that all of the conditions shown pertain to S's beliefs.

	Initial Belief State (of S)	Action	Target Belief State (of S vis à vis H)
Acquire	(1) false (P) (2) ¬ (bel (H, true (P))) ∧ ¬ (bel (H, false (P)))		bel (H, true (P))
Continue	(1) false (P) (2) bel (H, true (P)) (3) suggest (Qc, false (P))		bel (H, true (P))
Cease	(1) true (P) (2) bel (H, true (P))	assert (S,Q)	¬ bel (H, true (P))
Prevent	(1) true (P) (2) ¬ (bel (H, true (P))) ∧ ¬ (bel (H, false (P))) (3) suggest (Qc, true (P))		¬ (bel (H, true (P))) ∧ ¬ (bel (H, false (P)))

We will now discuss the four belief manipulation goals in more detail, first in a somewhat formal manner, and then with the help of examples. As can be seen from Table 2, in both the Acquire and Continue goals, S believes that P is false but also believes that by asserting Q, H will come to, or continue to believe that P is true. The difference between the Acquire and Continue goals is that in case of the Acquire goal, S believes that H has no prior belief pertaining to P, that is, that H neither believes that P is true, nor that P is false, and S intends H to acquire the new (false) belief that P. In contrast, for the Continue goal, S believes that H already believes P (which S believes is false), and wants H to continue believing P. In this case, H's initial belief state is already the desired belief state, but the situation is such that S needs to say something to maintain the status quo with respect to H's belief. In particular, we assume that the situation precludes H from asserting Qc (a non-deceptive and Gricean cooperative utterance) because doing so would either imply or be equivalent to acknowledging that P is indeed false.

In the Cease goal, S believes that P is true and believes that H also believes that P is true. By asserting Q, S wants H to cease believing that P is true, the minimal condition required to achieve this goal. Finally, in the Prevent goal, S again believes that P is true, but S also believes that H has no belief pertaining to P. Here, S wants to prevent H from coming to believe P and thus asserts Q which S believes is incompatible with and will not suggest P. As in the case of Continue, S's need to assert Q arises from the particular circumstances of the situation.

Since Acquire and Cease goals have to do with changing the initial belief state of the hearer, and Continue and Prevent on the other hand involve maintaining it, we can characterize Acquire and Cease as belief-changing goals, and Continue and Prevent as belief-maintenance goals.

Now, to see how verbal deception types can be used as strategies for converting S's initial belief state vis à vis H's beliefs into S's desired target state for H, we present an example for each of the four goals.

The Acquire Goal
To illustrate the Acquire goal, we will again use the example of the mean-spirited student, S, seeking to mislead another student, H, about the capital of Turkey. The mean student knows that the capital of Turkey is Ankara, not Istanbul, but wanting his victim to acquire a false belief, says, "Istanbul is the capital of Turkey". This is an example of the deception type Simple Fabrication being used as a strategy for the Acquire goal, a strategy that, in this example, has the following features:

(a) P, the false proposition that Istanbul is the capital of Turkey, is the proposition that S wants H to *acquire*,
(b) Q expresses this same false proposition and is what S, assuming that H does not know that Q is false, actually communicates to H, and
(c) Thus, Q is equivalent to P.

So, S attempts to achieve the Acquire goal of inducing a false belief, P, in H, by asserting Q, which in this example, is a Simple Fabrication intended to convert the initial state of H having no belief pertaining to P, to S's target state for H of having H believe that P is true. The table below shows Simple Fabrication as a strategic action for converting the initial belief state of the Acquire goal to its target belief state:

The Continue goal
A father, H, thinks that his daughter Susan, S, is a well-behaved girl and never does anything wrong. Susan knows that her father holds this belief about her, but in fact she often behaves badly when he is not around. One day, Susan breaks a priceless antique vase. Her father asks her what happened to it. Susan, wanting her father to continue thinking that she is a good girl, says, "The cat broke it." This is an example of the Continue goal being achieved using the

Initial Belief State (of S)	Action: assert (S, Q) Q = Simple Fabrication	Target Belief State (of S vis à vis H)
(1) false (P) (2) ¬ (bel (H, true (P))) ∧ ¬ (bel (H, false (P)))	(1) false (Q) (2) Q=P	bel (H, true (P))

Fabrication for False Inference strategy because Susan intends to falsely imply that (because she was not responsible for breaking the vase) she is indeed a well-behaved girl. So, we have the following features for the Fabrication for False Inference strategy for the Continue goal:

(a) P is the proposition that S considers false but believes that H considers true, namely, that S is a well-behaved girl. S wants H to continue believing P,
(b) Q expresses another proposition that S also knows to be false, namely, that the cat broke the vase, but which S nevertheless communicates to H,
(c) S believes that H has no belief pertaining to Q and that it is therefore new information for H, and
(d) S believes that Q does not suggest the falsification of P to H (i.e., will not cause H to surmise or conclude that P is false).

Note that in this example, if S were not deceiving H, the Gricean-cooperative proposition (Qc) that she would express would be that it was she, S, who broke the vase. However, S knows that expressing this might prevent her from achieving the Continue goal because H would no longer believe that she is a trouble-free girl. So S attempts to achieve the goal of causing H to continue believing P (which S knows is false) by asserting Q, a Fabrication for False Inference in this case, through which S can maintain the initial state of H believing P is true. The table below shows Fabrication for False Inference as a strategy for attaining the Continue goal whereby S can maintain her initial belief state as the target belief state:

Initial Belief State (of S)	Action: assert (S,Q) Q = Fabrication for False Inference	Target Belief State (of S vis à vis H)
(1) false (P) (2) bel (H, true (P)) (3) suggest (Qc, false (P))	(1) false (Q) (2) ¬ (bel (H, true (Q))) ∧ ¬ (bel (H, false (Q))) (3) ¬ suggest (Q, false (P))	bel (H, true (P))

The Cease goal
In an example discussed earlier, a mother, H, knows that it was her six year-old

son, S, who emptied the cookie jar of all the cookies. Knowing this, she says to her son "You took the cookies, and I told you not to." The boy, wanting his mother to cease believing that it was he who took the cookies, contradicts her, saying "I didn't take them. It wasn't me." Here we have a case of the Cease goal being attained using the strategy of Simple Denial. Notice, importantly, that several other strategies were available to the boy. For instance, as in the example of the Continue goal discussed above, he could have used Fabrication for False Inference by asserting that someone else took the cookies (thereby inviting the inference that it wasn't he who took them). The Simple Denial strategy for the Cease goal has the following features:

(a) P is the proposition that S considers to be true and believes that H also considers true. S wants H to cease believing P, that is, to stop believing that it was he, the boy, who took the cookies,
(b) Q expresses the proposition that S considers false and is what S actually says to H, and
(c) Q is the negation of P.

In this example, S attempts to achieve the Cease goal of causing H to stop believing P by asserting Q, a Simple Denial intended to convert the initial state of H believing P is true, to the target state of H believing P is false. The table below shows Simple Denial as an action to convert the initial belief state of the cease goal to its target belief state:

Initial Belief State (of S)	Action: assert (S,Q) Q = Simple Denial	Target Belief State (of S vis à vis H)
(1) true (P) (2) bel (H, true (P))	(1) false (Q) (2) Q = ¬ P	¬ (bel (H, true (P)))

The Prevent goal
Here we again use an example, presented earlier, this time the example of the man, S, who gets home late because he had a long meeting running into the early evening, and then went to see his girlfriend. When, on getting home, his wife queries him, he tells her that he had a long meeting into the evening with the goal of preventing her from coming to believe the truth. This is an example of Simple Half-truth being used as a strategy for the Prevent goal, and it has the following features:

(a) P is the true proposition that S went to see his girlfriend, and about which S believes H has no belief. S wants to prevent H from coming to believe P,
(b) Qa is the allowed-to-be revealed part of a larger proposition that is a conjunction of simple propositions, a proper subset of which, Qh, S seeks to keep hidden from H, and
(c) Q is Qa.

To elaborate the second of these features, let Qc represent the Gricean-cooperative proposition that S would express instead of Q if he was not attempting to deceive H, namely the complex proposition that he had a long meeting in the late afternoon, *and* left work later than usual, *and* then went to see his girlfriend. We can then view Qc as consisting of two subsets of propositions, Qa, the allowed set of propositions that S believes that he can safely divulge, and Qh, the set of hidden propositions that S wishes to conceal (in the present case, that he went to see his girlfriend) because it either implies or is equivalent to P. So, S attempts to prevent H from coming to believe P by asserting Q, in this case a half-truth, which allows him to maintain the initial state of H having no belief pertaining to P. The table below shows Simple Half-truth as an action to convert the initial belief state of the prevent goal to its target belief state:

Initial Belief State (of S)	ACTION: assert (S,Q) Q = Half-truth	Target Belief State (of S vis à vis H)
(1) true (P) (2) ¬ (bel (H, true (P))) ∧ ¬ (bel (H, false (P))) (3) suggest (Qc, true (P))	(1) Qc = {Qa, Qh} (2) suggest (Qh, true (P)) (3) ¬ suggest (Qa, true (P)) (4) Q = Qa	¬ (bel (H, true (P))) ∧ ¬ (bel (H, false (P)))

The examples we have just presented demonstrate how different types of verbal deception can be construed as strategies or actions to achieve different belief manipulation goals, and up to this point we have presented a different deception type for each of our four belief manipulation goals. In fact, however, several different deception types can be used as strategies to attain each of the four goals. Furthermore, most deception types can be used to achieve more than one of the goals, although not all strategies are applicable to all goals.

In elaborating the Acquire goal, we used the example of Simple Fabrication. But Simple Fabrication can be used as a strategy to achieve other goals as well. For example, it can be used to achieve the Prevent goal. To show this, we can consider a scenario similar to the Half-truth example given above for the Prevent goal, in which a man, S, gets home very late one night because after work he went to visit his girlfriend. When he reaches home, his wife, H, asks him, "Why are you so late?" In order to prevent his wife from coming to believe the truth, he says, "I had to go to the library to do some research." So, we have the following features for Simple Fabrication as a strategy for achieving the Prevent goal:

(a) P is the proposition that S considers true, namely that he went to visit his girlfriend. S believes that H has no belief pertaining to P, and wants to prevent her from coming to believe P, which is the nexus of deception,

(b) Q expresses the proposition that S considers false and wants H to come to believe, that is, the proposition that S went to the library to do some research, and

(c) S believes that Q will not suggest P to H (i.e., will not cause H to surmise or conclude P).

Qc is the Gricean-cooperative proposition that S would express instead of Q if S were not deceiving H, that is, the proposition that he went to see his girlfriend after work. S attempts to achieve the goal of preventing H from coming to believe P by asserting Q, a simple fabrication in this case, with the intention of maintaining the initial state of H as having no belief pertaining to P. The table below shows Simple Fabrication as an action to convert the initial belief states of the Prevent goal to its target belief state:

Initial Belief State (of S)	ACTION: assert (S,Q) Q = Simple Fabrication	Target Belief State (of S vis à vis H)
(1) true (P) (2) ¬ (bel (H, true (P))) ∧ ¬ (bel (H, false (P))) (3) suggest (Qc, true (P))	(1) false (Q) (2) ¬ (bel (H, true (Q))) ∧ ¬ (bel (H, false (Q))) (3) ¬ suggest (Q, true (P))	¬ (bel (H, true (P))) ∧ ¬ (bel (H, false (P)))

By presenting an example of how Simple Half-truth and Simple Fabrication can both be used to achieve the Prevent goal, we have demonstrated that in principle, different verbal deception types can sometimes be used as strategies

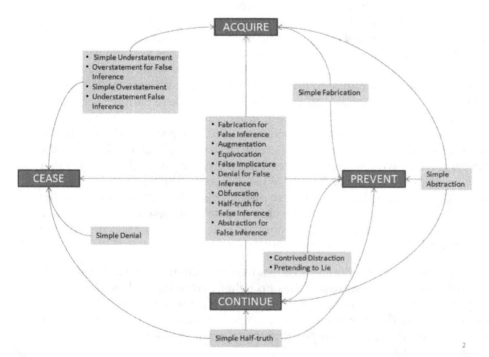

Fig. 2 Verbal Deception Types as strategies used to achieve four belief manipulation goals

for the same goal. Furthermore, we have shown how the same type (Simple Fabrication) can be used as a strategy for different goals (Achieve and Prevent). However, not all types can be used as strategies for all four goals. Consider, for example, Simple Denial. Simple Denial can be used to achieve the Cease goal, but it cannot be used for the Continue and Prevent goals. In the case of the Continue goal, Simple Denial would violate the initial condition bel (H, true (P)) when in fact S believes P is false. Since H already believes that P is true when S believes that it is false, it would make no sense for S to contradict P. In the case of Prevent, Simple Denial would violate the maintenance of belief state that H has no belief pertaining to P. P is something that S wants to hide from H. Again, it would make no sense to deny P when S wants to keep H from coming anywhere near P!

So, our general conclusions are that (a) in principle, most types of verbal deception can be used to attain more than one belief manipulation goal, (b) in principle, several different verbal deception types can be used to attain any one belief manipulation goal, and (c) not all verbal deception types can be used to attain all belief manipulation goals. To conclude, therefore, we present in Figure 2 a proposal as to which verbal deception types can be used as strategies for which belief manipulation goals.

As we have mentioned before, we need to emphasize that all of this is work in progress and the connections indicated in the figure still need to be verified. We thus present them here only to illustrate our basic idea. There remains much work to be done but our hope is that what we have presented in this chapter will stimulate thought and discussion.

Acknowledgements We are grateful to Ilya Farber, Sanford Goldberg, Tei Laine, Maria Miceli, and David Pautler for helpful comments and suggestions at various stages of this work.

References

1. Adler, J. E. (1997). Lying, Deceiving, or Falsely Implicating. *The Journal of Philosophy*, 94(9), 435-452.
2. Bavelas, J. B., Black, A., Chovil, N., & Mullett, J. (1990). *Equivocal Communication*. Sage Publications, Inc.
3. Bolinger, D. (1973). Truth is a Linguistic Question. *Language*, 49(3), 539-550.
4. Bowers, J. W., & Bradac, J. J. (1982). Issues in Communication Theory: A Metatheorical Analysis. In M. Burgoon (Ed.), *Communication Yearbook*, 5. New Brunswick, N.J: Transaction Books.
5. Bowers, J. W., Elliott, N. D., & Desmond, R. J. (1977). Exploiting Pragmatic Rules: Devious Messages. *Human Communication Research*, 3, 235-242.
6. Bradac, J. J. (1983). The Language of Lovers, Flovers, and Friends: Communicating in Social and Personal Relationships. *Journal of Language and Social Psychology*, 2, 141-162.
7. Burgoon, J. K., Buller, D. B., Guerrero, L. K., Afifi, W. A., & Feldman, C. M. (1996). Interpersonal Deception: XII. Information Management Dimensions Underlying Deceptive and Truthful Messages. *Communication Monographs*, 63(1), 50-69.
8. Castelfranchi, C., & Poggi, I. (1993). Lying as Pretending to Give Information. In H. Parret (Ed.), *Pretending to Communicate* (pp. 276-291): De Gruyter, Walter, Inc.

9. Chisholm, R. M., & Feehan, T. D. (1977). The Intent to Deceive. *The Journal of Philosophy*, 74(3), 143-159.
10. Clark, H. H., & Brennan, S. E. (1991). Grounding in Communication. In L. B. Resnick, J. M. Levine, & S. D. Teasley (Eds.), *Perspectives on Socially Shared Cognition* (pp. 127-149). Washington: APA Books.
11. Grant, C. K. (1958). Pragmatic Implication. *Philosophy*, 33(127), 303-324.
12. Grice, H. P. (1975). Logic and Conversation. In P. Cole, & J. L. Morgan (Eds.), *Syntax and Semantics volume* 3: Speech Acts (pp. 41-58). New York: Academic Press.
13. Hopper, R., & Bell, R. A. (1984). Broadening the Deception Construct. *Quarterly Journal of Speech*, 70, 288-302.
14. Levine, T., Lapinski, M., Banas, J., Wong, N., Hu, A., Endo, K., et al. (2002). Self-Construal, Self and Other Benefit, and the Generation of Deceptive Messages. *Journal of Intercultural Communication Research*, 31, 29-45.
15. McCornack, S. A. (1992). Information Manipulation Theory. *Communication Monographs*, 59, 1-16.
16. Meibauer, J. (2005). Lying and Falsely Implicating. *Journal of Pragmatics*, 37, 1373-1399.
17. Metts, S. (1989). An Exploratory Investigation of Deception in Close Relationships. *Journal of Social and Personal Relationships*, 6, 159-179.
18. Scott, R. L. (1977). Communication as an Intentional System. *Human Communication Research*, 3, 258-268.
19. Turner, R. E., Edgley, C., & Olmstead, G. (1975). Information Control in Conversations: Honesty is Not Always the Best Policy. *Kansas Journal of Sociology*, 11(1), 69-89.
20. Vincent, J. M., & Castelfranchi, C. (1979) On the Art of Deception: How to Lie While Saying the Truth. In H. Parret, M. Sbisa, & J. Verschueren (Eds.), *Conference on Pragmatics*, Urbino (pp. 749-778)

Part VII
Norms, organizations, and institutions

Chapter 32
Commitments in multiagent systems
Some history, some confusions, some controversies, some prospects

Munindar P. Singh

Abstract The notion of commitments as a foundation for understanding interactions among agents has been under development for about twenty years. Cristiano Castelfranchi has contributed to clarifying the conception of commitments by bringing in insights from social psychology. In this essay, I briefly review the conceptual development of commitments in multiagent systems, identifying the key themes and some lingering confusions. I also highlight some ongoing debates with Castelfranchi and some promising directions for future research.

1 Introduction

Cristiano Castelfranchi writes about agents like Michelangelo painted his frescoes. No, I don't mean to suggest that Cristiano writes lying precariously on his back on scaffolding twenty meters above the floor–although one can never be too sure about the ways of Italian intellectuals. Seriously, though, I do mean to suggest that Cristiano naturally envisions and describes complex scenes with many characters and details. The effect is beautiful indeed.

My goal in this short essay, by contrast, is to come to these frescoes as a computer scientist–generally, focusing on a few characters and their particular details in an attempt to understand some components of the scene better.

Professor Castelfranchi has made varied and numerous contributions to identifying, developing, and popularizing the social perspective on multi-agent systems. Specifically, I want to focus on the notion of commitments, which Professor Castelfranchi and I have been contemplating and discussing for nearly two decades [3, 4, 38]. This is not to suggest that others haven't contributed to this topic–the study of commitments has become a veritable

Munindar P. Singh
Department of Computer Science, North Carolina State University, USA
e-mail: singh@ncsu.edu

cottage industry–but merely to focus the presentation on themes that interest Professor Castelfranchi and me the most.

2 A Brief Retrospective

Commitments in multiagent systems turn out to be quite different from "commitments" as have long been discussed in artificial intelligence (AI) and philosophy. In traditional AI work, a commitment was understood as the commitment of a single agent to some belief or to some course of action. For example, the AI planning literature of the 1970s advocated an approach called least-commitment planning [35] wherein a planner (working as part of or on behalf of a single agent) would create a plan that left as many of the options of the agent open as it could and for as long as it could. That's a fine idea for a single-agent setting. Notice–as an aside–that in such a setting a commitment is not quite desirable–an agent is best off when its commitments are minimized.

In the mid to late 1980s, when research began in earnest on multiagent systems, researchers adopted the notion of commitment as a way to understand organizations of agents. A commitment in a multiagent system captures a relationship between two parties. A traditional planning-style commitment to one's plans would not suffice. Even though the researchers recognized this, partly because they came from an AI background, they came to the notion of commitments with an attendant mentalist bias [30]. Thus they distinguished multiagent commitments from planning commitments, but only to the extent of somehow reducing multiagent commitments to combinations of mutual beliefs and intentions. A mutual belief between two or more agents is a proposition p where each believes p and each believes that each believes p, and so on, to arbitrary nesting [8]. Mutual or joint intentions are similar in spirit, though somewhat more subtle [30]. In other words, traditional researchers retained their mentalist perspective but hoped that the mutuality of the beliefs or intentions would provide the glue between the agents.

But, as Professor Castelfranchi has eloquently and forcefully argued, social relationships are irreducible to the mental attitudes. And especially in multiagent systems we are concerned with the modeling and enactment of interactions of autonomous and heterogeneous agents. Thus commitments can easily exist or fail to exist with or without any beliefs or intentions on part of any of the agents. I return to this topic in Section 4 along with addressing some other confusions.

In contrast, the social and organizational metaphors provided a more straightforward way to think of multiagent systems, and especially as a way to formulate commitments. It has been long known that human organizations develop and apply standard operating procedures–as, for example, explained by Herbert Simon [37]. And, especially in settings where there may be no mathematical guarantee of obtaining a rigorously correct state or outcome, applying a standard operating procedure would be the rational way for an organization to proceed–in essence, we would define the state or outcome emerging from such a procedure as being correct. A member of the organization, when faced with a particular situation, could act according to any of the applicable standard operating procedures. Even if the particular outcome in that situation turned out to be undesirable or even harmful, the member would generally not be considered as having been in violation. For example, if a patient collapses in an apparent heart failure, a paramedic nurse may be expected to give the patient a shot of nitrates. The nurse would be deemed to have done the right thing if he gives the patient the specified amount of the recommended medication even if he is unable to save the patient's life or saves the patient's life but inadvertently causes other complications. Clearly there are cases where the standard expectations may be higher and a member of an organization would need to select an appropriate operating procedure in order to avoid all blame. Further, the expectations can vary depending upon the role and qualifications of the member involved. In the above example, we may expect an emergency physician or a cardiologist to consider additional information and potential risks beyond what we expect a nurse to consider in deciding a course of action. But regardless of whether we consider a simplified notion of an operating procedure or a more complex one, the common feature is that the organization empowers its members to act in circumstances that are far from ideal.

To me, the foregoing line of thought led to an inkling of an idea that an organization be able to commit to a course of action. More pertinently, the commitment here arose from the member to the organization. Such thinking led me to distinguish two kinds of commitments: (1) an internal one, which I then termed psychological or P-commitment and (2) an external one, which I termed social or S-commitment [38]. Psychological commitment is the standard concept in AI. Social commitment is the concept that we now refer to as commitment in the multiagent systems community. The AI researchers resisted social commitments. I am grateful to Professor Castelfranchi for lending his support to this area when it was emerging.

Social commitments have some interesting features distinguishing them from psychological commitments. First, a social commitment is directed from one party (its *debtor*) to another (its *creditor*). This terminology reflects the intuition that the debtor is committed to doing something for the creditor.

The idea was to distinguish this from the more obvious notion of a beneficiary. Specifically, a commitment may be directed toward one party but the beneficiary might be another. For example, a shipper may commit to a merchant to deliver a package to a customer. Here the shipper would be the debtor and the merchant the creditor. The apparent beneficiary, the recipient of the package, may show up only within the body of the condition that the shipper commits to bring about. Notice that the logical form of the above commitment is the same as of the commitment where the local police constable commits to the district attorney to deliver a subpoena to or arrest a citizen. We would generally not think of the citizen being subject to a subpoena as being a beneficiary. For this reason, it is advisable to leave the value judgments of who is the beneficiary and who is not outside of the general concept of commitments. Indeed, such value judgments are often accompanied by presumptions about various psychological concepts, which too we ought to minimize in the general theory.

The second interesting, and even less common, aspect of social commitments was the idea of incorporating an *organizational context* into the notion of commitments. The organizational context of a commitment describes the organization or "system" in which the commitment arises, providing support of the normative backdrop for commitments and interactions among autonomous parties. The debtor and creditor of the commitment would thus generally be members of the context organization. An example would be a commitment from a seller to a buyer operating within the eBay marketplace wherein the seller is committed to shipping some goods. That commitment references eBay as its organizational context. Here, eBay might penalize a seller who doesn't discharge the commitment.

A related intuition is that agents can be composed. In other words, what, from one perspective, appears to be an individual entity and functions as one entity (and therefore is a well-defined entity) might well, from a different perspective, turn out to be internally structured. For instance, a corporation or a university might function and interact as if it were an individual, for example, by entering into contracts with others. Yet, from an internal perspective, it would generally consist of several agents.

Combining the above intuition with the context-based view of commitments is that it enables us to express complex domain structures in a simple manner. For instance, we can imagine a team as the organizational context of the several commitments that tie together its members. However, the team is itself constructed from its members. Thus we would naturally model commitments between the team viewed as an agent and each of its members. Such commitments might capture the principal intuitions of teamwork such as that a member of a team should support the other members of the team in succeeding with their goals, and that the team-members should coordinate with one another to accomplish their common goals. The specification of commitments between the members and the team help codify such relationships. The team-members need not form mutual beliefs or joint intentions with one another, as traditional approaches require [30, 23], because the essence of the relationship between them can be captured through the commitments. In particular, a team-member may not even know who the other team-members are in order to form a social relationship with them through the common identity of the team to which they belong. A further benefit is that the relationships naturally express the rules of encounter of the team and thus support the expectations that the team-members might form on each other. Additionally, the relationship can potentially be realized in a variety of ways. For example, the members of a team may join it one by one and a team-member may leave and another may join without altering the essential fabric of the team. Or, the team-members may all join at once.

An important aspect of commitments is that they can be manipulated [40]. A debtor may create or cancel a commitment; a creditor may release it. More interestingly, a debtor may delegate a commitment to a new debtor, and a creditor may assign it to a new creditor. Such manipulations provide a high-level and systematic way in which the social state can progress. Fornara and Colombetti [19], [20] have studied the operationalization of commitments to support such manipulations. With Xing [52] and Chopra and Desai [46], I have further developed patterns involving the manipulation of commitments that support useful properties.

This wasn't always emphasized in the early works, but the conditionality of commitments is important. By default, commitments are conditional, involving an antecedent and a consequent, and unconditional commitments are merely the case where the antecedent is true. In logical terms, the conditionality of commitments resembles that of a strong conditional rather than a material conditional [43]. A commitment becomes and stays *detached* or *discharged* when, respectively, its antecedent and consequent become true. There is no presumption of temporal order between the detach and discharge of a commitment. A commitment that is detached but fails to discharge indicates a violation.

It is worth distinguishing two major kinds of commitments. *Practical commitments*–as commonly seen in formalizations of business processes–are about what the debtor would bring about. *Dialectical commitments*–as commonly seen in formalizations of argumentation–are about what the debtor stakes a claim on. The import of the two kinds of commitments is quite different and parallels the distinction between goals and beliefs, respectively. Practical commitments call for action and thus relate to present or future actions. Dialectical commitments call for a condition holding and thus can relate to past, present, or future.

That the two kinds of commitment are distinct has been known for years and, in particular, finds discussion in some of Professor Castelfranchi's work wherein he provides the clearest exposition of it. However, the distinction seems to have been lost in the agents literature until recently. I have sought to revive this distinction in conjunction with a proposed formal semantics for commitments [43].

3 What are Commitments Good For?

In a nutshell, commitments form a key element, arguably the most important element, of the social state of two or more interacting agents.

Commitments are important because they help us address the tradeoffs between and reconcile the tension between autonomy and interdependence. On the one hand, we would like to model our agents as being autonomous with respect to each other. On the other hand, it is clear that if the agents were fully autonomous, then we would have not a multiagent system in the true sense of the term, but merely a number of agents that happen to coexist in a shared environment. Such a system would exhibit no useful structure. Further, it is clear that autonomous agents must be able to cooperate and compete with each other, and carry out complex interactions. If there were no interdependence, the agents would be nearly useless. Professor Castelfranchi and his colleagues first articulated the importance of such interdependence among agents and explored varieties of it [36]. Similar intuitions and elaborating the connection with autonomy arise in newer work [27]. Commitments provide a natural way to characterize the bounds of autonomy and interdependence without getting bogged down in low-level details.

3.1 Commitments for Business Protocols

A business protocol characterizes how a family of interactions involving two or more business partners may proceed. What makes a business protocol "business" is that the interactions it characterizes involve business relationships. The classic examples of business protocols are those realized in cross-organizational business processes, such as for negotiation, sales and purchase, outsourcing of various business functions, delivery, repair, and so on. Traditionally, business protocols have been modeled in purely operational terms such as through state transition diagrams or message sequence charts that describe ordering and occurrence constraints on the messages exchanged, but not the meanings of such messages.

Commitments provide a natural basis for capturing the meanings of the messages. In this manner, they provide a standard of correctness. A participant in a business protocol complies with the protocol if it ensures that if any commitment (of which it is the debtor) is detached, then it is also discharged (that is, not violated or canceled–neglecting the distinction between them). Having such a declarative basis for correctness not only simplifies the modeling of the interactions being designed or analyzed but also provides a basis for flexible enactment that can be shown to be correct.

A typical use of commitments in business protocols involves introducing the syntax for the messages under consideration along with a formalization of the meanings of the messages expressed in terms of the commitments of the participants and the domain or environmental propositions that have a bearing on those commitments. For example, in a purchase order protocol, we might introduce a message *offer* and define its meaning as involving the creation of a commitment–with its sender being the debtor and its receiver being the creditor. The commitment would specify that the sender would provide the goods to the receiver were the receiver to accept the terms. Likewise, we might introduce a message *accept* through which the recipient of the *offer* would take up the given offer. Based on these meanings, we would be able to determine if an enactment of the protocol was sound. Even a simple and obvious specification of correctness proves effective: this states that an agent complies with a protocol if no enactment of the protocol ends with the agent as the debtor of a detached but not discharged commitment.

The natural connection between commitments and correct enactments naturally leads to ways of operationalizing them. Each commitment provides a basis for judging the compliance of its debtor. The commitments of interest taken together provide a *public* or neutral perspective on the correctness of an interaction as a whole. Further, the idea of using both commitments that refer to the antecedents and consequents of other commitments and commitments that refer to the creation and manipulation of other commitments provides a powerful basis for capturing a network of social relationships at a high level. An agent can thus reason about the commitments of interest to it, especially those where it is the debtor or creditor, and decide how to interact with the other agents participating in the current business protocol. Although the agent may act as it pleases, the commitments themselves impose constraints in terms of what actions are compliant. In this sense, the specification of commitments leads to the notion of a commitment machine [10, 51, 53, 42].

When we apply commitments as a basis for the semantics of the communications among agents, they yield a basis that is formal, declarative, verifiable, and meaningful [41]. Interestingly, commitments also lend themselves to operationalization in a more traditional manner. This is the idea of compiling a commitment machine into a traditional representation such as a finite state machine over finite [10, 51, 53] or infinite [42] computations. Such compilation removes the opportunities for flexibility that an explicit commitment representation supports. However, a finite state machine can be executed by agents who are not equipped with an ability to reason logically. Moreover, such a mechanically produced finite state machine can often be more complete in its coverage of important scenarios than a hand-generated one–and consequently be too large and unwieldy for a human designer to specify by hand.

3.2 Commitments for Communication Languages

The above idea involving protocols can also potentially be applied as a basis for the meanings of the primitives in agent communication languages (ACLs). ACL primitives have traditionally been given semantics based on the beliefs and intentions of the communicating parties. Instead, a commitment-based semantics could naturally express the social relationships between the communicating parties. In essence, one would take the idea of commitments for individual communication protocols and apply that idea to the modeling of general-purpose communication primitives. The idea is not implausible in itself. It is indeed possible to define the meanings of communication primitives. In spirit, this is not different from the meanings of the messages in the business protocols. However, the particular formulations in this setting suggest ways to capture richer subtleties of meaning than may be necessary in a typical business setting. In particular, I have suggested [41] that meanings can be captured via a trio of specifications that, following Jürgen Habermas [24], reflect objective, subjective, and practical meanings. These types of meaning can be expressed in terms of commitments regarding, respectively, the relevant aspects of objective, subjective (cognitive), and practical (subjective and institutional, with an emphasis on the latter) reality.

For example, we might define an *informative* message type as one creating a dialectical commitment with its sender as debtor, its receiver as creditor, its antecedent as true, and its consequent as asserting the truth of the proposition specified as the content of the message. In the above terms, this would be the objective meaning [41]. Likewise, a *commissive* message type would create a practical commitment. And, similarly for the rest. I should note in passing that the idea of a general-purpose ACL itself is suspect (see my recent manifesto, as included in [15], for a discussion of this point). In any case, we can view the definitions of the primitives as useful patterns, which might be specialized and applied to the communicative acts needed for particular protocols.

3.3 Commitments and Conventions

A deeper benefit of commitments is in their relationship to conventions. Two levels of abstraction are worth distinguishing in formalizing even the simplest interactions. First, a quote means that there is a commitment from the merchant to sell the specified goods at the specified price. Second, the fact that the quote means the above is a matter of convention in the chosen domain of commerce, and therefore both the merchant and the customer commit to that meaning. Specifically, the meanings of any communications must be based on the conventions at play in the given social setting. It is thus highly natural that we understand conventions as a basis for interactions among autonomous parties.

In several cases, the applicable conventions would be determined based on longstanding tradition in a domain; in other cases, they may be explicitly negotiated. For example, in the financial capital markets, a price quote for a stock (sent by a broker to a trader) is interpreted as being merely informative of the last known price at which that stock was traded. In typical commerce, however, a price quote (sent by a merchant to a customer) can be interpreted as an offer to sell at the specified price. In the latter case, the longevity of the offer can vary: for a business-to-business supply price quote, the offer may be valid for 30 days whereas for an airline to consumer ticket price, the offer may be valid for a minute. The longevity of the offer too is often a matter of convention. The importance of conventions to meaning and interoperation among autonomous parties is thus quite obvious.

What is interesting for us is that the conventions that arise in a given setting can be expressed as commitments. Specifically, each of the parties involved (or sufficiently many of them) would commit dialectically to the existence of the convention. Dialectical commitments, as are involved in this case, are different from the practical commitments involved in formalizing the messages in typical business protocols. However, each party may additionally practically commit to acting according to the conventions. Arguably, something prevails as a convention in a community only if the participants dialectically commit to it and practically to acting according to it.

The general notion of conventions and especially as related to agent communications [28], however, merits study in its own right. The interesting observation from the standpoint of commitments is that a convention corresponds to an aggregation of dialectical commitments. The commitments can be structured using the context as explained above. Thus the participants in a community where a convention prevails can dialectically commit to the convention. Each participant would be a debtor and each other participant would be a creditor. Alternatively, the creditor could be the context and thus stand for the community as a whole.

4 Concomitant Confusions

In the worlds of artificial intelligence and software engineering abstractions, commitments are the new kid on the block. A common prejudice in these traditional disciplines that finds its way into multiagent systems is to formulate the design problem as one for a complete unitary system, even when such a system is to serve the needs of multiple stakeholders. Hence, all too often, researchers and practitioners approach the design of a multiagent system not only as consisting of cooperative (and sincere) agents, but also as one where they will themselves provide all of the agents.

In contrast, commitments are most germane and offer their greatest value in settings where capturing the meanings of the interactions being designed is relevant. We would leave the design and construction of the agents to their implementers even though in some cases we might ourselves take on the implementation task. Further, we would leave the operation of the agents to the agents and their users. That is, commitments can apply in traditional settings where all agents may be designed by one party, and can help specify cleaner architectures. But they are not confined to such settings, and the assumptions needed for a unitary system do not apply in general to commitments.

One can imagine an engineer thinking "well, I am going to design a good system of three agents; I am going to make sure the agents take on goals and beliefs that are compatible with their commitments and adopt policies that help them realize their commitments; and I am going to damn well make sure the agents walk the straight and narrow, so I will prevent them from violating their commitments." Such thoughts may well be appropriate in a single-perspective, cooperative, regimented system constructed by one engineer from a set of agents. I would place the work of Minsky and Ungureanu [33] into this category who are not focused on cognitive agents but on conventional architectures, in which setting their approach is more reasonable. However, such thinking unnecessarily limits the multiagent systems designs that one comes up with. Therefore, although such thinking may be a useful design pattern to help relate open architectures to traditional architectures, when framed as a general constraint on commitments, it is misguided.

In simple terms, we can separate three scopes of effort or decision making: (1) the modeler of an interaction defines interactions via their associated commitments; (2) the agent designer implements an agent; and (3) the agent (and its users) decide how to behave on the field. The multiagent system engineer must specify the interaction precisely and relinquish control of the design and operation of the endpoints of the interaction. Relinquishing control is a consequence of dealing with open systems. Focusing on interactions is the only plausible way of engineering a system where the engineer lacks control over the endpoints.

4.1 Commitments versus Goals

A common view is that an agent who commits as debtor to bringing about a condition in the world also adopts the same condition as a goal. (In some accounts, the agents would adopt an intention, not just a goal, but let us disregard the distinction between goals and intentions here.) A stronger variant is when the goal applies to both the debtor and the creditor of a commitment. This confusion is insidious because it relies upon a careless reading of the literature: the confusion is nothing more than a confusion between the S-commitments (our commitments here) and the P-commitments (traditional commitments in AI planning) as explained in Section 2.

Commitments and goals are fundamentally different kinds of creatures. A commitment is a public or observable relationship between two parties whereas a goal is a single-agent representation. An agent's commitments are generally known to others because of the conventions in play in the given setting. An agent's goals are never inherently known to another agent, although another agent might reason about them based on assumptions of rationality or based on explicit revelation by the first agent, provided appropriate conventions apply to the presumed revelation.

It is true that in general a cooperative debtor that created a commitment would simultaneously adopt the corresponding goal. However, an agent may not adopt the corresponding goal, potentially risking failing with its commitment–and thus risking harm to its reputation and risking additional sanctions of penalties and censure. Conversely, an agent may hold a goal and not have committed to any other party for it. Such a goal might well be a highly important goal for the agent–after all, a goal would relate to the agent's preferences, and not necessarily to something the agent would reveal to others.

As a telling example, consider the common situation where an airline operating a 100-seat airplane books 120 passengers on it. Clearly, the airline is committed to each ticketed passenger, but equally clearly the airline could not have a goal to board each passenger on to the airplane. The airline simply has a clever internal strategy to maximize profit where it knowingly enters into commitments that it might not be able to discharge. If 20 passengers miss the flight, the airline goes scot-free; if more than 100 show up, the airline compensates those it does not take on board, but it still comes out ahead on average.

Misalignments between commitments and goals are not the same as deception. In the above example, the airline has no intention of misleading its clients. In fact, the airline may strongly believe–based on the evidence at hand–that no more than 100 passengers will show up and thus none of its commitments would be violated. However, it is fair to say (as a reviewer suggests) that a commitment that is supported by its debtor's goal would be likelier to be effective provided the debtor is sufficiently competent.

4.2 *Commitments versus Beliefs*

It is not uncommon to conflate commitments with beliefs. The motivation seems to be that an agent would represent its commitments and thus believe them to exist. But such an argument would hold for just about any representation.

In some cases, there is a more subtle confusion between commitments of the dialectical flavor and beliefs. Notice that even dialectical commitments are commitments, meaning that they reflect their debtor staking a claim or accepting a claim as a putative fact such as, for the sake of discussion, during an argument [32]. The debtor may not in fact believe what it commits to. Conversely, the debtor may have numerous beliefs it keeps private and never commits to holding to another agent. Any such commitment binds the debtor to a certain pressure to interact in a certain way, and there is generally little reason to expose all beliefs as commitments.

4.3 *Commitments versus Mutual Beliefs*

A more insidious confusion arises with respect to mutual beliefs. As Section 2 explains, the underlying idea behind using the mutual beliefs (and equally intentions) was to introduce a level of mutuality while continuing to use the mental concepts.

The first problem with this view is that it is wrong. Commitments are not mutual beliefs. A commitment is a unidirectional relationship. For example, if Bianca offers to sell a camera to Alessia, the commitment holds whether or not Bianca believes it or Alessia believes it. As in the airline over-booking example, Bianca may simply have made the offer to try to prevent Alessia from taking up another offer. And Alessia might be on to Bianca: that is, she might not believe that Bianca believes she would supply the camera. However, the commitment exists. Alessia may in fact file a complaint against Bianca. Alessia would not be able to file a complaint if the commitment was defined as the mutual belief.

The second problem is that mutual beliefs are extremely fragile. Let us say Alessia believes that Bianca believes that Alessia believes ... that Bianca will be shipping a camera to Alessia. If Alessia believes that, at the hundredth level of the nesting, Bianca might not believe Alessia expects the camera any more, that would dissolve the mutual belief. However, in real life the commitment does not go away in such a case. Bianca is not off the hook based on a failure of a belief by Alessia and certainly not for imagining that Alessia may have lapsed in her belief.

The third problem is that, again at variance from real-life interactions, although commitments arise in all manner of distributed settings, mutual beliefs generally cannot be constructed. Under asynchronous communication, the only mutual beliefs in a system are the invariants of the system, that is, propositions that were true from the start [8]. Indeed, the artifact of mutual beliefs (along with the similar artifact of common knowledge) is used in distributed computing primarily to prove *impossibility* results [8, 25]. Because mutual beliefs cannot be engendered through message exchange in general asynchronous settings, a problem that requires mutual belief is unsolvable.

Clearly, the AI researchers have understood the problem in terms of live human communication, which is inherently synchronous. In multiagent settings, they address the challenges of asynchrony by fiat. Specifically, they assume that a single message by one party to another, without any need for an acknowledgment, would achieve mutual belief. The idea it seems was that there was a central belief store and any assertions inserted into it reflected the beliefs and further even the mutual beliefs of everyone in the system. However, AI researchers by and large hide this key assumption in the implementations of their systems and never mention it in their theoretical descriptions.

One could treat the above assumption (of a single message exchange being sufficient) as a standard operating procedure, as mentioned in Section 2, in a particular setting. But that only means we are seeking to characterize commitments a certain way. So why not be honest and model the commitments directly? About the only reason not to do so is if one has locked on to the mentalist ideology.

I should explain that the point is more general than merely one of physical transmittal of information, as it is in the traditional distributed computing literature. The deeper and more crucial point is of the necessity of simultaneously sustaining multiple perspectives. In other words, what is most problematic is not so much the physically central nature of the belief store where mutual beliefs might exist, but its conceptually central nature, indicating that we had magically consolidated the perspectives of multiple autonomous, heterogeneous parties into a correct unitary perspective.

4.4 Commitments versus Obligations

Obligations are an important notion studied since ancient times. A traditional obligation applies on an agent, roughly corresponding to the debtor of a commitment. What distinguishes a traditional obligation from the cognitive concepts of beliefs and goals is that it is inherently externally focused: an obligation can be met or not and the consequences occur beyond the minds of the agents involved. A more interesting kind of obligation is directed: here an agent is obliged to another agent [26]. The second agent corresponds to the creditor of a commitment.

Because directed obligations are clearly interagent in their orientation, they are a more natural match for multiagent systems than are traditional obligations. The similarities between directed obligations and commitments are striking. But can we treat commitments as being identical to obligations? A commitment when it is active corresponds to a directed obligation.

However, commitments and obligations have important points of distinction. First, a commitment can be manipulated, in particular, delegated, assigned, or released. Second, a commitment carries with it an organizational context, as explained above. Third, obligations carry a moral connotation that commitments lack. Fourth, a commitment reflects the inherent autonomy of the participants in an interaction. Thus an agent would become a debtor of a commitment based on the agent's own communications: either by directly saying something or having another agent communicate something in conjunction with a prior communication of the debtor. That is, there is a causal path from the establishment of a commitment to prior communications by the debtor of that commitment. Obligations by contrast can be designed in or inserted by fiat.

Frank Dignum observes (in a private comment) that the autonomous nature of commitments raises a creditor's expectation that the debtor's goals and beliefs are aligned with the commitment, and hence it should be discharged. This point applies to cooperative debtors and may be a basis for the conventional interpretation of communications in general.

4.5 Commitments versus Policies

A commitment, especially in its conditional form, looks like a rule for processing, and in this sense resembles a policy. For example, an engineer might take the view that an offer from a merchant to a customer expresses the merchant's policy that if the customer pays the specified amount to the merchant the merchant will send a cello string of a specified type to the customer.

Treating a commitment as a policy in this sense reflects the same confusion as with goals and beliefs, namely, that the external, interactive, observable nature of commitments is conflated with the internal, behavioral, private nature of another abstraction. A policy is how an agent may decide to act upon–or decide not to act upon–a commitment. If the merchant has a straightforward policy for acting on all its commitments, then so much the better.

However, note that in general, a commitment would be necessarily incomplete with respect to the behavior needed to discharge it, and thus the policies associated with a commitment may need to specify aspects that the commitment does not mention. In our example, the merchant would have committed simply to supplying, say, a Larsen cello D string for payment. The merchant would need additional policies to determine how exactly to supply the D string. Should the merchant supply the instance of the D string that is the oldest in its inventory? Or, the newest? Or, one that happens to be the most convenient based on other tasks the merchant is performing, for example, supply from the top rack if the ladder is up there anyway, else supply from the bottom rack? Maybe the merchant will do well to supply a carefully checked instance of the string to a repeat customer and supply it with extra robust packaging for a customer overseas or for a customer who has a high standing in the user community and can influence other prospective customers.

These are all legitimate policies, but it would be inappropriate to tie them into the commitments. Indeed, were we to attempt to specify commitments at the level of such policies, we would face important challenges and produce a poorer quality model as a result. The challenges would be first coming up with detailed specifications and second, importantly, finding a way to determine if a party is complying with the commitment–for example, how will we ever know if the merchant sold the oldest item in its inventory? Or, one from the top rack? The resulting model would be of poor quality because it would tightly couple the parties involved in the interaction. For example, a merchant who committed to supplying the oldest item (and did so honestly) would be compelled to maintain information about the ages of the items in its inventory and to set up its internal business processes to search for items in their order of age. It would not be able to take advantage of any improvements in internal business processes as might arise later. Equally importantly, a new merchant who wished to join the interactions specified by such a commitment would not be able to participate without developing such otherwise irrelevant components of its information systems.

There is another notion of policies, however, which does make sense when related to commitments. This is the idea of a social policy, which captures the rules of encounter in a society. I have occasionally used the term "social policy" in this sense, but I now think it is better to refer to such as *norms* and to reserve the word "policies" for the policies of an agent or organization that reflect its decision making.

4.6 Commitments versus Regimentation

I encounter this problem a lot in discussions with conventional software engineers. They are accustomed to capturing requirements for, modeling, designing, and implementing software systems in which there is a single locus of autonomy. The system in question may be distributed but it is conceptually unitary and involves the perspective of a single party. You can identify such a mindset where the engineer talks of "the system" as an entity that will interact with "the user"–the goal of the engineer is to create a software design artifact from which one can develop a set of software modules that will meet the elicited requirements as the system interacts with its users.

In such a case, when the engineer begins reluctantly to think of social interactions and commitments among the parties involved, the engineer's mindset remains to try to force the modules to behave in the "correct" manner. The engineer attempts to capture such behaviors via commitments. In other words, the engineer retains the single-party perspective and, without absorbing the idea of any social interaction among notionally autonomous parties, merely treats commitments as a clever-sounding representational framework.

The engineer's challenge is to force the modules to adopt certain commitments and to act on their commitments in exactly the chosen "correct" way. All too often, such designs emerge from when a traditionally minded software developer reverse-engineers an existing process into the representation of commitments–adopting and incorporating every ad hoc quirk of the original model into the commitment-based model.

Following Jones and Sergot [29], I term such a viewpoint *regimentation*. In general, the use of regimentation obviates the need for modeling commitments. However, for engineers new to commitments, it might be a useful intermediate step provided they recognize it as such and proceed to develop an interaction-oriented model.

4.7 Commitments and Compliance

When computer scientists and business (process) modelers first encounter commitments, they immediately ask about compliance: how can we guarantee that an agent would comply with its commitments, or at least not wantonly violate or cancel them? For a novice, this question is reasonable. But upon reflection, we can see this question is misguided and unfair because it hides some crucial presuppositions and confusions. Underlying this question is the misguided assumption that if one simply fails to model–or even acknowledge the existence of–an agent's commitments, the agent would behave perfectly.

A strange variation on this theme is that if we were to model communications among agents in terms of commitments we would have created legal liabilities that didn't exist before. No, seriously, I am not making this up. The idea is that if Bianca sends Alessia a message with an offer for a camera, for example, using English or XML, it is just fine and legally safe. But if we only so much as realize that the offer is a commitment to provide the specified camera, Bianca would become liable in ways that she wasn't when we didn't model her English or XML message as conveying a commitment. Perhaps the people who come up with the above variants imagine that obfuscation of meaning is a legal defense. I claim, instead, that for a business or other interaction to be successful, the parties involved must share an understanding of the terms involved. In general, even lawyers would prefer greater clarity as a way to define each party's expectations of the others.

Modeling commitments does not cause agents to (potentially) behave in an undesirable manner. Indeed, modeling commitments helps potentially address the challenge of ensuring compliance. By treating commitments explicitly, we (1) obtain a crisp, yet not operational, statement of compliance; (2) formulate the notion of *transparent* protocols in which compliance determination is possible; and (3) open the way for designing agents using beliefs and goals who will be compliant with their protocols. Monitoring and compliance relate naturally to themes such as formalizing (1) organizations and governance [50, 21], for example, penalizing malfeasant agents in a community, and (2) bases for relating commitments and economic models of rationality [16].

4.8 *Terminological Confusions*

It is worth highlighting here some confusions that arise alarmingly frequently, though usually among people who are unfamiliar with the commitments literature. At the root of these confusions are lexical mismatches, wherein the reader misinterprets a technical term, even though the terms under consideration are well-defined in the commitments literature.

Commitments are psychological.   The raison d'être for commitments is to avoid the shortcomings of psychological commitments, but that doesn't stop some people from inadvertently going back to square one.

Social means going to a bar.   We use the term social to distinguish from psychological, not that commitments are only about cultural conditions or for after-hours socialization. The most common application of commitments today is in modeling business organizations and interactions, though there is no reason to preclude other settings even personal relationships.

Private means shared.   Private refers to the internals of an agent and public to what is shared or observable. If one agent commits to another, that means we have created a social object involving at least two agents. Even if the two agents keep the commitment confidential, never disclosing it to a third party, the fact that it involves more than one agent makes it public, as we define the term.

Debts are exclusively financial.   We simply use debtor and creditor to indicate the directionality of commitments. These terms are reminiscent of their usage in the vernacular, but generalize over it. There is no restriction to financial debt: the conditions involved could be arbitrary; indeed, even in normal English, debts are not restricted to be just financial.

Organizational context means any element of the situation.   But organizational context is *not* just anything: in our technical meaning, it is an objective institutional construct treated on par with an agent.

Commitments are ontological commitments.   In Quine's [34] terminology, an ontological commitment describes the objects one entertains as existing. For example, if I say my grandfather owned a unicorn, that means I am ontologically committed to the past existence of at least one unicorn (and of my grandfather, and of the two existing contemporaneously). Ontological commitments resemble presuppositions underlying utterances that a person makes whereas commitments for us are about actions or staked claims. One could formulate a dialectical commitment for the existence of anything that its debtor makes an ontological commitment to.

5 Debate with Professor Castelfranchi

Let me now turn to the most interesting part of this article, which is to highlight some of the points of difference between Professor Castelfranchi's views and mine regarding commitments.

Let me begin with a point, which I think is not controversial, though potentially sounding like it might be. At the root of it is the emphasis I place on the importance of observable interactions among agents (including low-level behaviors), which contrasts with Professor Castelfranchi's emphasis on the cognitive representations of the agents. I suspect unclarity on my part led Professor Castelfranchi to criticize my approach as resembling a behaviorist approach.

A behaviorist stance would be reduced to entertaining nothing beyond (what the designer or analyst imagines are) the objective atoms of behavior. In general, the difficulty in identifying such objective atoms is indeed one of the challenges that uproots behaviorism. The acute need for imagining what is ostensibly objective is one of the shortcomings of behaviorism. However, I do not see that commitments can be reduced merely to low-level behaviors. Instead, here we are accommodating a rich social reality: we have postulated agents who create and function in social institutions, who entertain abstract high-level relationships such as those expressed via commitments, and who not only communicate at the level of exchanging bits of information but also communicate in suitable institutional terms.

Professor Castelfranchi and I thus agree that the study of commitments is not and should not be treated as a behaviorist project. Instead, our collective effort in multiagent systems may be thought of as a realist project in that we treat common-sense social constructs such as commitments as real entities.

5.1 Commitments and Autonomy

Broadly speaking, the multiagent systems field is primarily concerned with understanding the interactions of agents. At a basic level the autonomy of the agents is key. Of course, fully autonomous agents would be useless if not harmful–clearly, what we need to understand is the interdependence of the agents. That is exactly where commitments come in. Each commitment captures one element of a social relationship between two parties. When we put these elements together, we obtain the network of relationships that characterizes a multiagent system. I expect that Professor Castelfranchi and I agree on the above in broad terms.

Where I suspect we disagree is in the relative importance we accord the intuitions of autonomy and interdependence. As I see it, an agent must be able to enter into and exit its commitments at will whereas Professor Castelfranchi sees the process as more constrained. These distinctions become more apparent when we consider the creation or cancellation of a commitment.

5.1.1 Accepting a Commitment

Professor Castelfranchi sees a commitment in a positive light whereas I see it as a general notion in a neutral light. Also, my interest is to maximize the flexibility of the interactions and the autonomy of the participants. As a result, I would consider a commitment to be created if its debtor says so. In this sense, the creation of a commitment is a declarative or performative communication and is within the control of the agent initiating that communication, given the appropriate circumstances and conventions. In contrast, Professor Castelfranchi would like to see the creditor of a commitment explicitly accept the commitment before it comes into being.

A downside to Professor Castelfranchi's approach is that it couples the two agents unnecessarily. It also differs from common uses of commitments. For example, a merchant can make an offer to a customer merely by saying so. The customer may sit silently for a while (up to the time period of the offer) and then attempt to make a purchase based on that offer. That is, the customer doesn't separately accept the offer and then exercise it; the customer simply exercises the offer directly. The offer is valid all along. If we were to require that the offer be accepted before it comes into existence, that would seem to require that a message exchange has to complete before the offer begins to exist.

Professor Castelfranchi is concerned that if we do not include an explicit acceptance, an agent may in essence use a commitment to make a threat, for example, by committing to harm the creditor. In Professor Castelfranchi's approach, the creditor would refuse such a commitment and thus never let it be formed. Notice, however, a malicious (prospective) debtor could harm the creditor nevertheless. If the commitment happens to be undesirable for the creditor, it could (i) resist it in other ways, perhaps by making a threat of its own; (ii) ignore the commitment and not demand that the debtor discharge it; (iii) assume it arose due to some underlying confusion due to miscommunication with the debtor, and explicitly release the debtor from that commitment. Each of these sample approaches has the advantage of not creating avoidable coupling between the debtor and the creditor.

Also, the apparent undesirable-to-the-creditor orientation of the content of a commitment cannot always be avoided. For example, an organization's president Alessia may have committed to all its members that she would punish the treasurer were the treasurer to embezzle any funds. A member, Bob, may accept the commitment at a meeting along with the other members of the organization. Now later if Bob becomes the treasurer, he would be the creditor of a commitment from the president that might potentially penalize him, if it is activated at all.

An alternative view is that the above notion of acceptance ought to be considered as being explicit *or* implicit. Thus silence in our example above can be treated implicit consent. This view, however, misses two important points. The first point is that it contravenes the agents' autonomy, as explained above. The second point we can explain as follows. The deeper purpose of talking about commitments is to help us understand the social state of an interaction. If we decide that a commitment is created only upon acceptance by the prospective creditor that means we can provide no clear meaning for the intermediate state wherein the debtor has "committed" but not quite because the creditor has not confirmed yet. If we allow implicit acceptance, then we have no viable basis for distinguishing between the commitment and its half-baked stage. That half-baked commitment is not nothing because the debtor is on the line if the creditor accepts it. I claim that if the associated intermediate social state were to be formalized properly, the semantics that results from the acceptance-based approach would be close to that of the one-sided formulation that I advocate.

Consider the following example, which came up in a discussion with Neil Yorke-Smith. How might one model the following? Alessia proposes to Bob that they exchange goods for payment tomorrow, but today Alessia would like to know whether Bob accepts or not.

A simple formulation is C(Alessia, Bob, C(Bob, Alessia, goods, pay), goods), indicating that Alessia tells Bob "if you commit to pay on receipt, I will send you the goods." It's Alessia's decision to trust Bob. If Bob does commit, Alessia must send the goods or violate her (now detached) commitment. If Alessia sends the goods after Bob's acceptance, Bob must pay or violate his (now detached) commitment. This formulation shows how we can make the acceptance of a commitment explicit if and when we need it to model some scenario, but do not need to insist upon acceptance in other cases. We can think of the above formulation as interpolating two one-sided commitments Alessia to Bob: one conditional on payment, C(Alessia, Bob, pay, goods) and the other unconditional C(Alessia, Bob, true, goods). In contrast, the acceptance-based representation makes it impossible to express the one-side commitments; tends to be applied wrongly wherein one agent commits another, thereby violating the latter's autonomy; and, leaves as undefined the social state wherein Alessia has made an offer but Bob hasn't responded.

5.1.2 Accepting a Cancellation

In much the same spirit, I propose that an agent can cancel its commitment at will. Like creation, a cancellation is a declarative that the debtor can perform. Likewise, a creditor can perform the release of a commitment at will. In the case of the cancellation, the outcome might not be one that the creditor desires or would willingly accept; further, the outcome might be one that we as designers might not condone in our agents. However, if that were to be the case, the creditor should have made sure (or we, the designers, should have made sure) that there will be repercussions on the debtor for having performed an inappropriate cancellation.

One might think that these repercussions signal the unacceptability of the cancellation and, therefore, that cancellations should only be allowed when the creditor accepts. I won't repeat the points made above in connection with creating a commitment, which apply here too. However, an additional point relevant to cancellation is that in a multiagent system (consisting of autonomous agents), we can rely on *regulation* but not on *regimentation* [29]. Regulation is about controlling behavior through normative means whereas regimentation is simply about preventing bad behavior [1]. Regulation is suited to interactions among autonomous agents. In contrast, regimentation—which here corresponds to preventing cancellation by explicit acceptance–contravenes autonomy.

Even in the original formulation of commitments [38], the notion of the (organizational) context of a commitment served to accommodate such cases. Specifically, if the cancellation of a commitment arises because of true and reasonable exceptions, the context may impose no penalty upon the debtor; in other cases it might. For example, let's say a merchant has committed to providing some goods to a customer. If the merchant cancels the commitment to do so because of a tsunami that destroyed the manufacturing plant and refunds the customer's payment, the cancellation appears not unfair whereas if the merchant cancels because the merchant can now demand a higher price, the cancellation does sound egregious. Let us say the (organizational) context here is the electronic marketplace, for example, eBay. In the first case, the context may declare the cancellation legitimate; in the second case, not so. In the second case, the context may penalize the merchant, for example, by revoking his credentials in the marketplace or pursuing fraud charges in the court system.

If the organizational context can ensure such coherent outcomes, then we can think of the context (and the concomitant family of interactions) as being well-designed (notice we make no claims about the internals of the agents themselves). If the context is not well-designed, then either we as designers made a mistake or the agent (customer) made a mistake in joining such a context, dealing with an untrustworthy merchant, and foolishly counting on him to discharge his commitments.

5.2 Commitments and Cognition

Another of the points where I continue to have a disagreement with Professor Castelfranchi is in the function and importance of cognitive representations in connection with commitments. We agree, of course, on the basic idea that an agent's behavior is of central importance in judging whether or not it discharges its commitments. And, I expect we agree not only on the essential relevance of commitments to the social life of an agent, including its relationships with other agents, but also on the importance of cognition.

Professor Castelfranchi, however, assigns a far stronger function to the cognitive representations of an agent than I do. To him, having a commitment is strongly based on the associated patterns of beliefs, goals, and intentions. For me, in contrast, a commitment is a social entity, which takes its existence from the public sphere. An intelligent agent would undoubtedly represent and reason about its commitments, and its commitments would undoubtedly affect and be affected by its goals and intentions. However, to my thinking, a commitment at its core remains purely social. In this regard, a commitment is no more and no less of an abstract object than any cognitive attitude or any mathematical object for that matter–that is, a commitment can exist in the public sphere just as legitimately as in the mind of an agent.

Although I recognize the benefits and importance of the cognitive representations in modeling and implementing agents, I consider such representations to be internal to an agent and reflective of its internal architecture and construction. In contrast, I understand commitments as having normative force whereby they can provide a potentially independent basis for judging the felicity and correctness of the actions of agents. When we define commitments in such a public and observable manner, they can become a key ingredient in understanding the institutional nature of communications and indeed of understanding institutions themselves.

As an example, consider a friend of mine who promises to help by giving me a ride to the airport. My friend would have done so by using the prevailing vernacular of our social institutions to create a promise. Let us say the appointed hour comes and goes, but my friend does not materialize. Thus he has violated his commitment. For the sake of this example, let us further stipulate both that I trust my friend in such matters and that he is highly trustworthy in fact and would not have deceived anyone. Clearly, he forgot or found himself in a personal emergency. But we would still state that he violated his commitment, albeit inadvertently or in exonerating circumstances.

We should be able to pass the judgment of the commitment being violated based on what we observe, namely, the failure of the commitment. However, if the definition of commitments were to be intertwined with questions of beliefs and goals, it would be difficult for us to pass even such elementary judgments. Further, the definition would lose the benefit of modularity by combining the social and the cognitive representations. Additionally, it would create a situation where we would not be able to determine if a commitment existed without being able to assess what the beliefs and intentions of the parties involved were, and it is well-known that such ascriptions cannot be defended in multiagent settings where the agents are not homogeneous and their internal states not public [39].

I claim that such judgments provide the basis of the normative strength that commitments carry. We might conduct any amount of elaborate post mortem analyses involving the beliefs and goals of the participants, but if we are not clear about the objective fact in this matter, we lose not only a basis for specifying an institutional basis for multiagent systems but also for conducting any cognitive analyses with any grounding in truth.

6 Themes for the Future

6.1 Commitments and Trust in Social Computing

The increasing attention garnered by topics such as social computing tells us that areas of long interest in the multiagent systems field [22] and especially pursued by Professor Castelfranchi himself [5] are gaining currency. Today's practice in social computing is weak indeed and consists of little more than users sharing information on a social networking site or users performing various assigned tasks in what is called crowdsourcing. It seems to me self-evident that any kind of realistic social computing must rely upon the concepts of commitments and trust.

The study of trust has been an important theme in Professor Castelfranchi's body of research. Professor Castelfranchi and colleagues have developed a semantically rich notion of trust [6, 7, 18] that incorporates both its social and its cognitive aspects. Professor Castelfranchi's approach contrasts with the majority of computer science works on trust, which tend to jump into (typically, numerical) representations without first sorting out what the trust as conceived stands for. Professor Castelfranchi relates trust to the plans of the parties involved and their expectations with respect to each other. I find another of previous works by Professor Castelfranchi and colleagues as especially germane here. This is the notion of dependence [36], which Rino Falcone and Professor Castelfranchi [17] have recently revived and related to trust.

It seems clear to me that these concepts suggest the strong relationship between commitments and trust. In conceptual terms, we can think of commitments and trust as duals of each other: a debtor commits to a creditor and a truster places trust in a trustee. The idea of commitments as expectations in reverse originates in Amit Chopra's [11] dissertation. I have recently begun to formalize trust in a manner that highlights the notion of dependence and relates trust to commitments [44]. Not every commitment may have corresponding trust in the reverse direction. And, not every placement of trust may be justified by a commitment in the reverse direction. The best outcomes arise when trust and commitment go hand in hand. The existence of trust for a commitment means that the commitment is not superfluous. The existence of a commitment for trust means that the trust is not misplaced. Chopra and colleagues [14] investigate the connection of trust with architecture. Exploring the above themes further and especially modeling social action as it would arise in future application settings of even moderate complexity would be highly valuable.

6.2 Commitments and Software Engineering

Let me now talk about another important theme with regard to commitments. This has to do with the use of commitments in modeling and realizing multiagent systems in diverse domains. In today's practice, software engineering is mainly concerned with low-level abstractions that are close to implementation details. Such abstractions are difficult to specify and even harder to establish the validity of with respect to the needs of the stakeholders.

Commitments provide a nice alternative basis for specifying software systems. Work on applying commitments for software engineering has been going on for years, since the earliest studies, and initially under the rubric of commitment protocols. However, the more basic challenges of software engineering when applied to interactions in multiagent systems are now beginning to be understood and formulated in terms of commitments [9, 12, 13, 31, 47].

Although the above approaches are useful and promising, they are far from adequate when it comes to the challenges of building systems of practical complexity. I foresee the enhancement of the techniques in terms of clearer specification languages based on commitments, more extensive middleware that supports implementation using abstractions similar to commitments, and the development of tools and technologies to validate and verify commitment-based designs.

In this light, I further think than commitments can inform an expanded notion of norms. Unlike a lot of traditional work, wherein norms are treated as amorphous descriptions of good or normative behavior, I propose that we study norms that like commitments are directed, conditional, contextual, and manipulable. Such norms can help precisely capture normative conditions in a manner where it is clear who is responsible for their enforcement. The notion of organizational context provides a basis for understanding the *governance* of systems of autonomous parties [45], such as service engagements [50] and virtual organizations [2, 48, 49].

7 Conclusions

I have taken this essay as an opportunity to lay out the main themes relating to commitments. I imagine that Professor Castelfranchi and I largely agree with each other on virtually all of the substantial themes regarding commitments. I have highlighted some controversial points in the hope that they would be interesting and useful , especially for those new to the field.

However, to summarize quickly, our points of agreement include the fundamental importance of understanding interaction in multiagent systems from the social and institutional level as opposed to exclusively from the mechanical or operational levels; the very conception of commitments as an elementary social (as opposed to an exclusively mental relationship, as in AI); the distinctions and similarities between practical and dialectical commitments; the value of commitments in understanding institutions and norms; the close relationship between commitments on the one hand and dependence and trust on the other.

Although the field of multiagent systems has made substantial progress since its founding just decades ago, a lot of crucial theoretical and practical problems remain unanswered and even unformulated. No one can predict with any certainty where the field will grow. However, the emergence of networked computing and its expansion into human business and social life suggests that the future of multiagent systems–viewed as the academic field that studies the interactions of social beings–is secure. That our field is now established and has acquired a healthy respect for, if not yet universally a deep understanding of, the social basis for interaction is due in no small part to the imagination and intellect of one researcher and for these invaluable contributions I applaud Cristiano Castelfranchi.

Acknowledgements I have benefited a lot over the years from discussions regarding commitments with a number of people, among them Cristiano himself and, alphabetically, Matthew Arrott, Alexander Artikis, Matteo Baldoni, Cristina Baroglio, Amit Chopra, Marco Colombetti, Nirmit Desai, Frank Dignum, Virginia Dignum, Rino Falcone, Nicoletta Fornara, Les Gasser, Scott Gerard, Paolo Giorgini, Kohei Honda, Michael Huhns, Andrew Jones, Mike Luck, Ashok Mallya, the late Abe Mamdani, Elisa Marengo, Simon Miles, John Mylopoulos, Viviana Patti, Jeremy Pitt, Pankaj Telang, Paolo Torroni, Yathi Udupi, Feng Wan, Michael Winikoff, Jie Xing, Pınar Yolum, and Neil Yorke-Smith. Comments from Michael Huhns, the Dignums, Scott Gerard, Pınar Yolum, and the anonymous reviewer have helped improve this article. I wouldn't presume, however, that any of the people named above agrees with anything I have claimed in this article. I would also like to thank the National Science Foundation for partial support under grant 0910868.

References

1. Artikis A, Sergot MJ, Pitt JV (2009) Specifying norm-governed computational societies. ACM Transactions on Computational Logic 10(1)
2. Brazier F, Dignum F, Dignum V, Huhns MN, Lessner T, Padget J, Quillinan T, Singh MP (2010) Governance of services: A natural function for agents. In: Proceedings of the 8th AAMAS Workshop on Service-Oriented Computing: Agents, Semantics, and Engineering (SOCASE), pp 8–22
3. Castelfranchi C (1993) Commitments: From individual intentions to groups and organizations. In: Proceedings of the AAAI Workshop on AI and Theories of Groups and Organizations: Conceptual and Empirical Research
4. Castelfranchi C (1995) Commitments: From individual intentions to groups and organizations. In: Proceedings of the International Conference on Multiagent Systems, pp 41–48
5. Castelfranchi C (1998) Modelling social action for AI agents. Artificial Intelligence 103(1–2):157–182
6. Castelfranchi C, Falcone R (2010) Trust Theory: A Socio-Cognitive and Computational Model. Agent Technology, John Wiley & Sons, Chichester, UK
7. Castelfranchi C, Falcone R, Marzo F (2006) Being trusted in a social network: Trust as relational capital. In: Trust Management: Proceedings of the iTrust Workshop, Springer, Berlin, LNCS, vol 3986, pp 19–32
8. Chandy KM, Misra J (1986) How processes learn. Distributed Computing 1(1):40–52
9. Cheong C, Winikoff MP (2009) Hermes: Designing flexible and robust agent interactions. In: Dignum V (ed) Handbook of Research on Multi-Agent Systems: Semantics and Dynamics of Organizational Models, IGI Global, Hershey, PA, chap 5, pp 105–139
10. Chopra A, Singh MP (2004) Nonmonotonic commitment machines. In: Dignum F (ed) Advances in Agent Communication: Proceedings of the 2003 AAMAS Workshop on Agent Communication Languages, Springer, LNAI, vol 2922, pp 183–200
11. Chopra AK (2008) Commitment alignment: Semantics, patterns, and decision procedures for distributed computing. PhD thesis, Department of Computer Science, North Carolina State University
12. Chopra AK, Singh MP (2011) Specifying and applying commitment-based business patterns. In: Proceedings of the 10th International Conference on Autonomous Agents and MultiAgent Systems (AAMAS), IFAAMAS, Taipei, pp 475–482
13. Chopra AK, Dalpiaz F, Giorgini P, Mylopoulos J (2010) Modeling and reasoning about service-oriented applications via goals and commitments. In: Proceedings of the 22nd International Conference on Advanced Information Systems Engineering (CAiSE), pp 417–421

14. Chopra AK, Paja E, Giorgini P (2011) Sociotechnical trust: An architectural approach. In: Proceedings of the 30th International Conference on Conceptual Modeling (ER), Springer, Brussels, LNCS, vol 6998, pp 104–117
15. Chopra AK, Artikis A, Bentahar J, Colombetti M, Dignum F, Fornara N, Jones AJI, Singh MP, Yolum P (2013) Research directions in agent communication. ACM Transactions on Intelligent Systems and Technology (TIST) In press
16. Desai N, Narendra NC, Singh MP (2008) Checking correctness of business contracts via commitments. In: Proceedings of the 7th International Conference on Autonomous Agents and MultiAgent Systems (AAMAS), IFAAMAS, Estoril, Portugal, pp 787–794
17. Falcone R, Castelfranchi C (2009) From dependence networks to trust networks. In: Proceedings of the 11th AAMAS Workshop on Trust in Agent Societies (Trust), pp 13–26
18. Falcone R, Castelfranchi C (2010) Trust and transitivity: A complex deceptive relationship. In: Proceedings of the 12th AAMAS Workshop on Trust in Agent Societies (Trust), pp 43–54
19. Fornara N, Colombetti M (2002) Operational specification of a commitment-based agent communication language. In: Proceedings of the 1st International Joint Conference on Autonomous Agents and Multiagent Systems (AAMAS), ACM Press, Melbourne, pp 535–542
20. Fornara N, Colombetti M (2003) Defining interaction protocols using a commitment-based agent communication language. In: Proceedings of the 2nd International Joint Conference on Autonomous Agents and Multiagent Systems (AAMAS), ACM Press, Melbourne, pp 520–527
21. Fornara N, Colombetti M (2009) Specifying and enforcing norms in artificial institutions. In: Declarative Agent Languages and Technologies VI, Revised Selected and Invited Papers, Springer, Berlin, LNCS, vol 5397, pp 1–17
22. Gasser L (1991) Social conceptions of knowledge and action: DAI foundations and open systems semantics. Artificial Intelligence 47(1–3):107–138
23. Grosz B, Kraus S (1993) Collaborative plans for group activities. In: Proceedings of the Twelfth International Joint Conference on Artificial Intelligence, pp 367–373
24. Habermas J (1984) The Theory of Communicative Action, volumes 1 and 2. Polity Press, Cambridge, UK
25. Halpern JY, Moses YO (1990) Knowledge and common knowledge in a distributed environment. Journal of the Association for Computing Machinery 37:549–587
26. Herrestad H, Krogh C (1995) Obligations directed from bearers to counterparties. In: Proceedings of the 5th International Conference on Artificial Intelligence and Law, pp 210–218
27. Johnson M, Bradshaw JM, Feltovich PJ, Jonker CM, van Riemsdijk MB, Sierhuis M (2010) The fundamental principle of coactive design: Interdependence must shape autonomy. In: Proceedings of the AAMAS Workshop on Coordination, Organization, Institutions and Norms (COIN), Springer, Toronto, LNCS, vol 6541, pp 172–191
28. Jones AJI, Parent X (2007) A convention-based approach to agent communication languages. Group Decision and Negotiation 16(2):101–141
29. Jones AJI, Sergot MJ (1993) On the characterisation of law and computer systems: the normative systems perspective. In Deontic Logic in Computer Science: Normative System Specification. J. Wiley and Sons, 275–307
30. Levesque HJ, Cohen PR, Nunes JT (1990) On acting together. In: Proceedings of the National Conference on Artificial Intelligence, pp 94–99
31. Marengo E, Baldoni M, Chopra AK, Baroglio C, Patti V, Singh MP (2011) Commitments with regulations: Reasoning about safety and control in REGULA. In: Proceedings of the 10th International Conference on Autonomous Agents and MultiAgent Systems (AAMAS), IFAAMAS, Taipei, pp 467–474
32. McBurney P, Parsons S (2003) Dialogue game protocols. In: Huget MP (ed) Communication in Multiagent Systems: Agent Communication Languages and Conversation Policies, LNAI, vol 2650, Springer, Berlin, pp 269–283

33. Minsky NH, Ungureanu V (2000) Law-governed interaction: A coordination and control mechanism for heterogeneous distributed systems. ACM Transactions on Software Engineering and Methodology (TOSEM) 9(3):273–305
34. Quine WvO (1960) Word and Object. MIT Press, Cambridge, MA
35. Sacerdoti E (1977) The Structure of Plans and Behavior. Elsevier North-Holland, New York
36. Sichman JS, Conte R, Demazeau Y, Castelfranchi C (1994) A social reasoning mechanism based on dependence networks. In: Proceedings of the 11th European Conference on Artificial Intelligence, pp 188–192
37. Simon HA (1997) Administrative Behavior: A Study of Decision-Making Processes in Administrative Organizations, 4th edn. Free Press, New York
38. Singh MP (1991) Social and psychological commitments in multiagent systems. In: AAAI Fall Symposium on Knowledge and Action at Social and Organizational Levels, pp 104–106
39. Singh MP (1998) Agent communication languages: Rethinking the principles. IEEE Computer 31(12):40–47
40. Singh MP (1999) An ontology for commitments in multiagent systems: Toward a unification of normative concepts. Artificial Intelligence and Law 7(1):97–113
41. Singh MP (2000) A social semantics for agent communication languages. In: Proceedings of the 1999 IJCAI Workshop on Agent Communication Languages, Springer, Berlin, Lecture Notes in Artificial Intelligence, vol 1916, pp 31–45
42. Singh MP (2007) Formalizing communication protocols for multiagent systems. In: Proceedings of the 20th International Joint Conference on Artificial Intelligence (IJCAI), IJCAI, Hyderabad, pp 1519–1524
43. Singh MP (2008) Semantical considerations on dialectical and practical commitments. In: Proceedings of the 23rd Conference on Artificial Intelligence (AAAI), AAAI Press, Chicago, pp 176–181
44. Singh MP (2011) Trust as dependence: A logical approach. In: Proceedings of the 10th International Conference on Autonomous Agents and MultiAgent Systems (AAMAS), IFAAMAS, Taipei, pp 863–870
45. Singh MP (2014) Norms as a basis for governing sociotechnical systems. ACM Transactions on Intelligent Systems and Technology (TIST), In press
46. Singh MP, Chopra AK, Desai N (2009) Commitment-based service-oriented architecture. IEEE Computer 42(11):72–79
47. Telang PR, Singh MP (2011) Specifying and verifying cross-organizational business models: An agent-oriented approach. IEEE Transactions on Services Computing 4, in press
48. Udupi YB, Singh MP (2006) Contract enactment in virtual organizations: A commitment-based approach. In: Proceedings of the 21st National Conference on Artificial Intelligence (AAAI), AAAI Press, Boston, pp 722–727
49. Udupi YB, Singh MP (2006) Multiagent policy architecture for virtual business organizations. In: Proceedings of the 3rd IEEE International Conference on Services Computing (SCC), IEEE Computer Society, Chicago, pp 44–51
50. Udupi YB, Singh MP (2007) Governance of cross-organizational service agreements: A policy-based approach. In: Proceedings of the 4th IEEE International Conference on Services Computing (SCC), IEEE Computer Society, Salt Lake City, pp 36–43
51. Winikoff M, Liu W, Harland J (2005) Enhancing commitment machines. In: Proceedings of the 2nd International Workshop on Declarative Agent Languages and Technologies (DALT), Springer, Berlin, LNAI, vol 3476, pp 198–220
52. Xing J, Singh MP (2003) Engineering commitment-based multiagent systems: A temporal logic approach. In: Proceedings of the 2nd International Joint Conference on Autonomous Agents and MultiAgent Systems (AAMAS), ACM Press, Melbourne, pp 891–898
53. Yolum P, Singh MP (2002) Commitment machines. In: Proceedings of the 8th International Workshop on Agent Theories, Architectures, and Languages (ATAL 2001), Springer, Seattle, LNAI, vol 2333, pp 235–247

Chapter 33
Intentional compliance with normative systems

Giovanni Sartor

Abstract I will address a challenge to mentalistic theories of norms, such as that developed by Cristiano Castelfranchi and Rosaria Conte, the existence of complex normative systems, which successfully direct people's thoughts and actions, but cannot become, as a whole, mental objects for individual agents (at least for humans). I will argue that the cognitive attitudes and operations involved in compliance with large normative systems are significantly different from those involved in complying with isolated social norms. While isolated norms must be stored in the memory of the agents endorsing them, this does not happen with regard large normative systems. In the latter case, the agent adopts a general policy-based intention to comply with the normative system as a whole, an intention that provides an abstract motivation for specific acts of compliance, once the agent has established that these acts are obligatory according the system. I will show how the endorsement of such a policy can be based on different individual attitudes, ranging from self-interest to altruistic, social or moral motivations. Finally, I will analyse how a normative system may both constrain powers and extend them, relying on this abstract motivation of its addressees.

1 Introduction

The theory of norms is one of the (many) areas where Cristiano Castelfranchi has produced influential contributions, relevant to multiple disciplines (psychology, sociology, computing, legal theory, etc.). In his seminal book on "Cognitive and social action", coauthored with Rosaria Conte, an original perspective on normativity is developed, where norms are understood as twofold objects, having a mental as well as a societal side. Norms are viewed as com-

Giovanni Sartor
Law Faculty - CIRSFID, University of Bologna, Italy
Law Department, European University Institute of Florence, Italy
e-mail: giovanni.sartor@eui.eu

plex mental objects, resulting from an architecture of goals and beliefs (Conte and Castelfranchi 13, Ch. 5, 6, 7). In particular, Conte and Castelfranchi start with the idea that a normative belief consist in the belief that for everybody it is obligatory to accomplish a certain action. They argue that such a belief presupposes the belief that someone, the sovereign, wants the obligation to hold, and is accompanied by further beliefs about the sovereign, namely that the sovereign is disinterested and pursues legitimate goals. Finally, they argue that one's goal to perform an action is normative if it is relativised to the existence of a corresponding normative belief (the goal is pursued as long as the normative belief is held). Conte and Castelfranchi's account also includes the analysis of how one becomes a defender of a norm, rather than merely an addressee of it, and how normative attitudes can spread in society.

These ideas have been further developed in a number of contributions, where Castelfranchi and his colleagues have broadened and deepened their analysis of normative attitudes and behaviour, and of the social dynamics related to the emergence of norms (3). Moreover the analysis of normative aspects has been felicitously connected to other domains of inquiry, such as trust and conventions (see for instance among the recent contributions, 50, 49).

I will here address a challenge to mentalistic theories of norms, i.e., the views according to which a norm is a content stored in people's memories, being the content of appropriate mental states (such as the belief that a norm exists and is binding, and the goal or intention to comply with it). This challenge results from the fact that we follow not only shared social norms, but also complex normative systems: while shared social norms are represented in the mind of the concerned agents, large normative systems direct people's thoughts and actions without becoming, as a whole, mental objects for individuals.[1] We are often faced with systems of this kind in our daily life (the legal system, but also the prescriptions of an institutionalised religion, or the regulations of a company, a condominium, a regulated market, a teaching institution, a sociotechnical infrastructure such as an airport or a harbour, etc.). All norms of such a system cannot be stored in one's memory since they exceed the human capacities (at least for the largest normative systems, such as a municipal law, containing many thousands, even millions, of rules) and moreover such norms persistently change as a consequence of intervening facts (such as the adoption of new regulations, new decisions interpreting, them, etc.). For instance, while each of us has some knowledge of a few rules of our legal system (the ones corresponding to shared moral rules, such as the prohibition of killing, or those most frequently encountered, such as certain traffic rules, or governing one's particular activity, such as rules on software copyright for a computer programmer); generally the common citizen has a very vague idea of the content the law of his of her country, especially in technical domains such as tax law, land planning law, environmental law, etc.

When referring to a large normative system N an agent usually does immediately find an answer to the question "What ought I to do?" (as it usually

---

[1] The term *agent* is here used as in AI, to mean an entity endowed with cognitive capacities and capable of autonomous action; it is not used in the legal-economical sense of someone delegated to act on behalf of another.

happens when applying a shared social norm). One rather needs asks oneself (or the appropriate expert) "What does N require from me?", i.e., "What ought I do to according to N?" The answer to this question ("I ought to do action A according to N") does not have, by itself, a motivating force for the agent. It is not a normative belief of the kind described in Conte and Castelfranchi [13], but a belief about what is entailed by a normative system in combination with the relevant facts. The concerned agent may well refuse to take into account the system's requests (for instance one may ask oneself what a certain religion requires from oneself, without having the slightest intention to follow the prescriptions of that religion, whatever they may be).

I will suggest that the motivation to perform a particular action qualified as obligatory by a normative system results from a general intention to comply with the system as a whole. The latter attitude provides an abstract motivation for specific acts of compliance, once the addressee has established that certain actions are obligatory according to the system. I will show how the endorsement of such an intention can be based on different individual attitudes. Finally, I will analyse how a normative systems may both constrains social powers and extend them, relying on this abstract attitude of its addressees.

2 Preliminary notions: actions, obligations, norms

For analysing compliance, we need some basic notions. First, a way of expressing action and obligations is required. For actions I will use the simple E operator of Pörn [35], though other action logics would be appropriate as well for this discussion of compliance (on the E operator see also 44).

Definition 1 (Actions) *Let proposition $E_j S$ describe agent j's positive action consisting in the production of state of affairs S, where "S" is any proposition. Thus $E_j S$ means "j brings it about that S". Similarly, let $\neg E_j S$ describe the negative action (the omission) consisting in not bringing about that S. Thus $\neg E_j S$ means "j omits to bring about that S" or "j does not bring it about that S". When the distinction between positive and negative action is not relevant, let $\mathcal{A}_j$ cover both. Let $\overline{\mathcal{A}_j}$ denote the complement of $\mathcal{A}_j$ ($\overline{\mathcal{A}_j}$ stands for $\neg E_j S$ if $\mathcal{A}_j = E_j S$; it stands for $E_j S$ if $\mathcal{A}_j = \neg E_j S$).*

For simplicity when an agent brings about its own action, I will not repeat the agent's name in the action's result. Thus, for expressing the idea that John smokes (*John* brings it about that he smokes) rather than writing $E_{John} Smoke(John)$, I will write $E_{John} Smoke$

This notion of an action does not involve intentionality (an aspect which is involved in the notion of an action as a goal-directed behaviour in 13). I prefer to stick to this minimal understanding of agency since compliance with normative systems usually prescinds from an action's intentionality: holding the required behaviour is usually sufficient for compliance. Intentions may instead be relevant for the consequences of violations (where intention may be required, or negligence, for certain normative consequences to take place), an aspect that I am not considering here.

As an example of an action-proposition, consider the following

$$E_{John}Damaged(Tom)$$

which means "*John* brings it about that *Tom* is damaged", or more simply "*John* damages *Tom*" while the following

$$\neg E_{John}Damaged(Tom)$$

means "*John* does not bring it about is about that *Tom* is damaged", or more simply "*John* does not damage *Tom*". I shall adopt the logic of E, which is a classical modal logic (if A and B are logically equivalent, then $E_x A \leftrightarrow E_x B$) including the axiom schema:

$$E_x S \rightarrow S \tag{1}$$

meaning that if the state of affairs S is realised though an action, then it is the case that S. For instance, the fact that *Tom* makes it so that *Ann* suffers damage, obviously entails that *Ann* suffers damage:

$$E_{Tom}Damaged(Ann) \rightarrow Damaged(Ann)$$

Definition 2 (Obligations and prohibitions) *Let O denote obligation. $OE_j S$ means "it is obligatory that j brings it about that S". Similarly $O\neg E_j S$ means "it is obligatory that j does not bring about that S", or "it is forbidden that j brings about that S".*

For instance, the following means "it is obligatory that *John* makes it so that *Tom* is compensated" or, more simply, "it is obligatory that *John* compensates *Tom*",

$$OE_{John}Compensated(Tom)$$

while the following means "it is obligatory that *John* does not makes it so that *Tom* is damaged", or more simply, "it is forbidden that *John* damaged *Tom*".

$$O\neg E_{John}Damages(Tom)$$

I will not specify here a particular deontic logic, since the following considerations may apply to different deontic logics (the reader may assume, for instance, standard deontic logic, as characterised in 17, or a weaker logic, in order to avoid deontic paradoxes). To keep the language as simple as possible, I shall not address how a deontic language can be enriched through Hohfeldian concepts (for a logical analysis, 40), and how this this extension can be useful for addressing compliance (46). While I am making use of the E action logic, I consider that the ideas on compliance here developed are generally compatible also with approaches to deontic reasoning based on different logics for action.

I represent norms as defeasible inference rules of an argumentation system.

Definition 3 (Inference rules and norms) *An* defeasible inference rule *is a* structure

$$A \Rightarrow B$$

where A is the antecedent condition, B the ensuing conclusion, and ⇒ expresses a defeasible unidirectional connection, according to which antecedent A triggers conclusion B. A rule including variables stands for the set of all of its ground instances. A norm is a defeasible inference rule where A is a proposition and B is any kind of normative qualification, deontic or non deontic,

Thus, a norm $A \Rightarrow B$ captures the unidirectional defeasible connection between an antecedent (possibly empty) fact and the normative consequent that is generated by that fact: normative effect B is triggered when the antecedent condition A holds.

Here is an example of two deontic norms, the first stating that it is forbidden to cause damage to others, and the second that who causes a damage to another has the obligation to compensate the latter (in the following when obvious I drop the requirement $x \neq y$):

$$x \neq y \Rightarrow O\neg E_x Damaged(y)$$
$$x \neq y \wedge E_x Damaged(y) \Rightarrow OE_x Compensated(y)$$

The following is an example of a constitutive norm, saying that if we injure a person (make so that someone is injured), we cause damage to that person (injuring counts as damaging):

$$E_x Injured(y) \Rightarrow E_x Damaged(y)$$

Note that I do not distinguish deontic conditionals and constitutive or counts-as conditionals (43, 26, 21), assuming that the same inferences apply to both (on normative conditionality, see 39; on the connection between deontic and constitutive conditionality, see 7).

With regard to the logic of ⇒, I assume an argumentation system as defined in Prakken [37] (for some considerations on defeasible argumentation and the law, see 42). Here I shall just state the main idea in an informal way. Arguments are constructed by applying inference rules (and trees of such rules) to facts (propositions expressed in a logical language). There are two types of inference rules, defeasible ones, having the form $A \Rightarrow B$, and indefeasible ones, having the form $A \rightarrow B$. Arguments may be defeated (rebutted or undercut) by counterarguments: rebutting takes place when an argument having a conclusion A through a defeasible rule (as its ultimate conclusion, or the conclusion of one of its sub arguments) faces a non weaker counterargument having the complementary conclusion $\overline{A}$; undercutting takes place when an argument including a defeasible rule $A \Rightarrow B$ faces a counterargument having conclusion "$A \not\Rightarrow B$", namely, affirming that the rule $A \Rightarrow B$ does not apply (its antecedent does not support its conclusion). An argument is justified, with regard to a knowledge base, if all of its of its defeaters are overruled, being defeated by further justified arguments.[2] Thus for instance, given knowledge base $\{a, b, c, d, a \Rightarrow b, c \Rightarrow \neg b, d \Rightarrow (c \not\Rightarrow \neg b)\}$, argument $[a, a \Rightarrow b]$ is justified, since

---

[2] Argumentation-based semantics (16) provides various ways to identify justified arguments, which is done by building maximal sets (called extensions) of the available arguments. For our purposes we can characterise justified arguments as those belonging to an extension that

its defeater $[c, c \Rightarrow \neg b]$ is defeated by $[d, d \Rightarrow (c \Rightarrow \neg b)]$, which is justified, having no defeater. The logic of $\Rightarrow$ and $\rightarrow$ can take into account systems of deductive logic (propositional, predicate, action, deontic, etc.) by assuming schemes for inference rules (general inference rules), corresponding to the inference rules of the deductive logics being considered.[3]

Definition 4 (Defeasible entailment) *We shall say that S defeasibly entails A, and write S $\vdash$ A, and to mean that premises set S includes a justified argument for A.*

For instance, $\{a, a \Rightarrow b\} \vdash b$, or also, considering a knowledge base including conflicting argument:

$$\{a, b, c, d, a \Rightarrow b, c \Rightarrow \neg b, d \Rightarrow (c \Rightarrow \neg b)\} \vdash b$$

The following example shows how from a norm and an instance of its antecedent we can defeasibly derive an instance of the conditional's consequent.

$$\{E_{Tom}Damaged(John), E_x Damaged(y) \Rightarrow OE_x Compensated(y)\} \vdash$$

$$OE_{Tom}Compensated(John)$$

3 Relativised obligations and permissions

In addressing compliance we have to connect a normative system N (a set of norms) and (the propositions describing) the factual circumstances C relevant to N's application. Here I am only interested in the obligations and the institutional facts that are generated by norms in N, when applied to facts in C. Thus we can assume that C contains (or entails) all factual literals (atomic propositions or negations of them) which are true in the real or hypothetical situation (the world) in which the norms have to be applied, without considering how the truth of such literals can be established. For simplicity's sake we can limit C to the factual literals that are relevant to the application of norms in N, matching literals in the antecedent of a norm in C. When the considered factual circumstances are those that hold in the real world (rather than in a merely possibly situation), i.e., they are the truths relevant to the application of N in the case at hand, I shall denote them through the expression $T(N)$.

---

is constructed as follows. We start with the empty set, and progressively admit those arguments which satisfy both of the following conditions: (a) they do not conflict with arguments already admitted, and (b) all their defeaters are defeated by arguments already admitted. The fix-point of this constraction (the maximal set we obtain, to which no further arguments can be added that satisfy the conditions above) is the so-called grounded extension of an argumentation framework. The same outcome can also be obtained though a dialogue game (38, 36).

[3] For instance modus ponens in a propositional logic can be modelled with a rule scheme (a set of inference rules) $\{A \wedge A \supset B \rightarrow B\}$, for any proposition A and B, where $\supset$ denotes material implication. The same can be done with inference rules or axioms for logics of action, obligation and intention.

I will now introduce the notion of a relativised obligation, namely, a way of expressing the fact that an obligation holds with regard to a normative system and a set of circumstances. A relativised obligation sentence does not express a norm, but it expresses an assertion about the implications of norms (normative systems) and circumstances (in the terminology of 1 and 2 such assertions are called "normative propositions").

Definition 5 (Relativised sentences and obligations) *We say that any sentence B holds relatively to normative system N and circumstances C, and write $[B]_{N,C}$ iff $N \cup C \hspace{1pt}\sim\hspace{1pt} B$*

$$[B]_{N,C} \stackrel{def}{=} N \cup C \hspace{1pt}\sim\hspace{1pt} B$$

In particular when the sentence B is an obligation sentence $O\mathcal{A}_x$, we say that it is obligatory relatively to N and C that x does $\mathcal{A}$, and write $O_{N,C}\mathcal{A}_x$ (rather than $[O\mathcal{A}_x]_{N,C}$), to express that $N \cup C \hspace{1pt}\sim\hspace{1pt} O\mathcal{A}x$:

$$O_{N,C}\mathcal{A}_x \stackrel{def}{=} N \cup C \hspace{1pt}\sim\hspace{1pt} O\mathcal{A}_x$$

When we are referring to the true relevant circumstances of the real world, denoted as $T(N)$, rather than to circumstances of hypothetical situations, we simply write $[B]_N$, or $O_N\mathcal{A}_x$.

$$[B]_N \stackrel{def}{=} N \cup T(N) \hspace{1pt}\sim\hspace{1pt} B$$

$$O_N\mathcal{A}_x \stackrel{def}{=} N \cup T(N) \hspace{1pt}\sim\hspace{1pt} O\mathcal{A}_x \tag{2}$$

For instance, let us consider the following example, where N_1 includes a simplified version of the three norms above, and circumstances C_1 are limited to the fact that *John* injured *Tom*:

Example 1

$$C_1 = \{E_{John}Injured(Tom)\}$$

$$N_1 = \{E_xInjured(y) \Rightarrow E_xDamaged(y)$$

$$O\neg E_xDamaged(y)$$

$$E_xDamaged(y) \Rightarrow OE_xCompensated(y)\}$$

It is easy to see that the following inferences holds on the basis of example (1):

$$(C_1 \cup N_1) \hspace{1pt}\sim\hspace{1pt} E_{John}Damaged(Tom)$$

$$(C_1 \cup N_1) \hspace{1pt}\sim\hspace{1pt} OE_{John}Compensated(Tom)$$

Therefore, we can say that *John* has damaged *Tom* and that it is obligatory that *John* compensates *Tom*, relatively to N_1 and C_1, i.e., that

$$[\mathsf{E}_{John}Damaged(Tom)]_{N_1,C_1}$$

$$\mathsf{O}_{N_1,C_1}\mathsf{E}_{John}Compensated(Tom)$$

If *John* has really injured *Tom* (and no other relevant circumstances obtain, such as exception excluding the application of the norms at issue), i.e., if $C_1 = T(N_1)$, we can simply say that according to N_1, *John* has damaged *Tom*, and it is obligatory that *John* compensates *Tom*, i.e.:

$$[\mathsf{E}_{John}Damaged(Tom)]_{N_1}$$

$$\mathsf{O}_{N_1}\mathsf{E}_{John}Compensated(Tom)$$

On the basis of example (1) we can also say that it is obligatory that *John* does not damage *Tom*

$$\mathsf{O}_{N_1}\neg\mathsf{E}_{John}Damaged(Tom)$$

Given that it holds that $[\mathsf{E}_{John}Damaged(Tom)]_{N_1}$ we can conclude that the latter obligation has been violated, on the basis of the following definition.

Definition 6 (Violation) *An obligation $O\mathcal{A}_x$ of a normative system N is violated in circumstances C iff $N \cup C \vdash O\mathcal{A}_x \wedge \overline{\mathcal{A}_x}$, In other words the obligation is violated in C, iff both $\mathsf{O}_{N,C}\mathcal{A}_x$ and $[\overline{\mathcal{A}_x}]_{N,C}$ hold.*

Here is another small example. The first norm in N_2 says that if one is in a public place then one is forbidden to smoke. The second says that places open to the public are (count as) public places.

Example 2

$$C_2 = \{OpenToPublic(LectureRoom), in(John, LectureRoom)\}$$

$$N_2 = \{OpenToPublic(y) \Rightarrow PublicPlace(y)$$

$$PublicPlace(y) \wedge in(x, y) \Rightarrow O\neg\mathsf{E}_x Smoke\}$$

We can say then say that according to N_2 given circumstances C_2 it is obligatory that *John* does not smoke ($\mathsf{O}_{N_2,C_2}\neg\mathsf{E}_{Tom}Smoke$).

Clearly, the language of relativised obligation allows us to say that according to different normative systems different obligations hold. For instance, given that Canon law contains a universal norm prohibiting the use of contraception, and a constitutive rule saying any action meant to make a sex act unfruitful counts as contraception, we can conclude that according to the Canon law a woman, say Ann, is forbidden to take the pill in order to have unfruitful sex acts. Similarly, given that Islamic law contains a norm that prohibits receiving interest on loans of money, we can say that according to Islamic law John is forbidden to receive interest on loans of money .

A notion of relativised permission can be provided that corresponds to the above analysis of obligation. While permissions can be modelled as the negation of prohibitions ($P\mathcal{A} \overset{\text{def}}{=} \neg O\overline{\mathcal{A}}$), relativised permissions can be defined as follows.

Definition 7 (Relativised permission) *Let us say that it is permissible relatively to N and C that x does $\mathcal{A}$, and write $\mathbb{P}_{N,C}\mathcal{A}_x$ iff N and C entail $P\mathcal{A}_x$:*

$$\mathbb{P}_{N,C}\mathcal{A}_x \overset{\text{def}}{=} N \cup C \vdash P\mathcal{A}_x$$

Note that according to this definition, saying that an action $\mathsf{E}_x S$ is permissible relatively to normative system N and circumstances C ($\mathbb{P}_{N,C}\mathsf{E}_x S$) does not amount to saying that it is not the case that $\mathsf{E}_x S$ is forbidden relatively to the same system and circumstances ($\neg O_{N,C}\neg\mathsf{E}_x S$). Proposition $\mathbb{P}_{N,C}\mathsf{E}_x S$ is not equivalent to $\neg O_{N,C}\neg\mathsf{E}_x S$, since the former holds when $N \cup C$ entails $P\mathsf{E}_x S$, while the latter holds when $N \cup C$ does not entail $O\neg\mathsf{E}_x S$ (see 1, 2).

4 Compliance

With the help of the notions introduced in the previous section, we can now address compliance. The issue of compliance can arise in very different context, as the following examples shows:

- Mary is appointed to a professorship. She signs a contract stating her commitment to comply with the University regulations.
- John enters a PhD program. He is directed to the booklet containing the regulations he has to comply with.
- Linda is appointed as a judge. She takes an oath to respect the Constitution and the laws of her country.
- Adolf Eichman enters the SS. He takes an oath of obedience to death to Adolph Hitler and the superiors he has designated.
- Antony enters the Franciscan order and promises to respect the body of regulations known as "The Rule of St. Francis" as well as the law of the Catholic Church.
- A digital agent enters and electronic marketplace, and commits to respect all rules of the marketplace.

In all these contexts the agent has taken the commitment (adopted the intention to) comply with a certain normative system.

Let us first consider compliance with an obligation, which simply consist in behaving is such a way as to fulfil the obligation.[4]

Definition 8 (Compliance with an obligation) *An agent x complies with an obligation $O\mathcal{A}_x$ of a normative system N, iff the obligation holds according to N and x's behaviour counts as $\mathcal{A}$ according to N, i.e., iff*

---

[4] As above, I will often omit to make explicit reference to the circumstances in which a normative set N is to be applied, assuming that an implicit reference is made to $T(N)$, the true circumstances relevant to the application of N.

$$\mathcal{O}_N\mathcal{A}_x \wedge [\mathcal{A}_x]_N$$

For instance, if a non-smoker does not smoke in a public office, and there is a prohibition to do so she will comply with that prohibition.

So far we have been considering compliance with a single obligation established by a normative systems. Now we need to consider compliance with a whole normative system, possibly including thousands of obligations (as any modern legal system).

Definition 9 (Compliance with a normative systems) *An agent x complies with a normative system N, iff x complies with all obligations established by N. In other words, x complies with N, iff whenever an action or omission by x, denoted as $[\mathcal{A}_x]_i$, is obligatory according to N, x performs it:*

$$Complies_x(N) \stackrel{\text{def}}{=} \bigwedge_{i\in[1..n]} (\mathcal{O}_N[\mathcal{A}_x]_i \rightarrow [\mathcal{A}_x]_i \qquad (3)$$

where $\bigwedge_{i\in[1..n]}(\mathcal{O}_N[\mathcal{A}_x]_i \rightarrow [\mathcal{A}_x]_i)$ stands for the conjunction of all formulas having the form $\mathcal{O}_N[\mathcal{A}_x]_i \rightarrow [\mathcal{A}_x]_i$, one per each of x's action $[\mathcal{A}_x]_i$ prescribed by one of the n norms of N establishing obligations.

Now we need to consider how we can characterise the intention to with a normative system. A first possibility would be to view it as the intention to realise state of affairs described in formula (3) above, namely, as the intention to realise action:

$$\mathsf{E}_x(Complies_x(N))$$

Unfortunately, the intention to comply with a normative system cannot usually be understood as the intention to realise the state of affair of full compliance. In fact, a representation of the intention to comply in (namely, as an agent's intention to achieve a state of affairs where every obligation of that agent is fulfilled) fails to capture the usual state of mind of of an agent who has decided to comply with a normative system.

Firstly, an agent usually cannot have a mental representation of the state of affairs of full compliance, as specified in definition (9), since the agent ignores the norms in the system, and therefore cannot know what needs to be done to achieve full compliance. For instance, we all know that our country has a legal system, some of us know a few criteria for identifying the norms belonging to that system, but none of us knows all or most norms it contains. How can we intend to realise a state of affair without having a representation of this state of affairs?

Secondly, even if an agent could have a representation of the state of full compliance, the agent should know that this state of affairs is unlikely to happen, given the high number of obligations arising from the system (we should know that we will certainly violate some norms in the future). How can one intend to realise a state of affairs being aware that most likely this state of affairs will not take place?

Thirdly, an agent committed to compliance should maintain its motivation even when the agent has already failed to comply with some obligations (so that full compliance is no longer possible).

It seems to me that rather than (or additionally to) committing itself to achieving full compliance, an agent can commit itself to a general policy, namely the policy of intending to perform any action which is obligatory according to N. Thus the intention to comply will appear to be a policy-based intention, namely, an intention to act in a certain way under conditions characterised in a general way, so that they may be instantiated in different specific circumstances (on such policy-based intentions, see 8, 87-92 and 9, 451 ff., for a formalisation in defeasible logic see 20, for some considerations, see also 39, 31-40). According to this policy, the agent will comply whenever the conditions are met, giving a separate and independent relevance to each opportunity for compliance: the agent may fail to comply in one occasion (when the agent ignores that the conditions are met, or when overriding reasons exist defeating the application of the policy), but still keep a defeasible commitment to the policy and be governed by it in other occasions.

5 Intentions

To address policy-based intention, we need first of all to provide an appropriate way of modelling intentions, included conditional intentions. I shall not address here the logic of intentions and of their combination with obligations (see for instance 11) but will only propose a simple representation of policy-based intention based on the argumentation logic I referred to above.

Definition 10 (Intentions) *Let us represent a (conditioned) intention in the form:*

$$S \Rightarrow !\mathcal{A}_j$$

namely as a unidirectional inference rule, where $\mathcal{A}$ is the action itself which j intends to perform under condition S.[5]

This expression is meant to represent the mental state which can be expressed as "I j, intend to do action $\mathcal{A}$ if S is the case", or "in case S holds, I intend to do $\mathcal{A}$" or "I shall do $\mathcal{A}$ if S is the case".

$$!\mathcal{A}_j$$

meaning "I, j, intend to do $\mathcal{A}$ unconditionally (whatever is the case)". Thus we can assume that the following defeasible entailment holds:

$$\{S, S \Rightarrow !\mathcal{A}_j\} \mathrel{\vdash}\!\!\!\!\!\!\sim !\mathcal{A}_j$$

---

[5] Note that j, plays a double role, being j both the holder of the intention and the author of the intended action, but to avoid the duplication of the index, I prefer to write $!\mathcal{A}_j$ rather than $!_j\mathcal{A}_j$.

according to the belief that S holds, together with the conditioned intention "I, j intend to do $\mathcal{A}$ under condition S" defeasibly entails (in a rational agent), the intention "I, j, intend to do $\mathcal{A}$." For instance, Tom, given that today is a working day and that he intends to work today if it is a working day, can conclude with the intention to work today.

$$\{workingDay(today), workingDay(today) \Rightarrow \, !E_{Tom}Work(today)\} \mid\!\sim$$

$$!E_{Tom}Work(today)$$

Conditional intentions can have a general form, which enables multiple instantiations. In such cases, we call them *policy-based intentions*. For instance, agent Tom may have the following policy-based intention to work on any working day x:

$$workingDay(x) \Rightarrow \, !E_{Tom}Work(x)$$

A policy-based intention stands for the set of all of its ground instances, such as:

$$workingDay(Tomorrow) \Rightarrow \, !E_{Tom}Work(Tomorrow)$$

Thus, let us assume that Tom, has such an intention and believes that the following fact matching the intentions's antecedent holds

$$workingDay(Tomorrow)$$

Tom will then infer the corresponding instance of the intention's conclusion, namely he should have the unconditioned intention to work tomorrow (I, Tom, shall work tomorrow):

$$!E_{Tom}Work(Tomorrow)$$

However, Tom does not need to store in his mind all of ground instances of the policy-based intention (that he intends to work today if today is a working that, that he intends to work tomorrow if tomorrow is a working day, that he intends to work the day after tomorrow ...). he just needs the policy-based intention expressed in abstract terms, and can use it for specific inferences when needed.

The expression $S \Rightarrow \, !_j\mathcal{A}_j$ (I, j, shall to action $\mathcal{A}_j$ under condition S) is the direct expression of j's intention, it models this particular mental content. It has to be distinguished by the assertion that j has really this intention, that this is a content of his mind. For expressing the latter proposition, let us denote with MS_j the set of mental states possessed by agent j, which includes j's beliefs and intentions.

Definition 11 (Assertions about intention) *The assertion that agent j has intention $S \Rightarrow \, !_j\mathcal{A}_j$, is represented as:*

$$[S \Rightarrow \, !\mathcal{A}_j] \in MS_j$$

where MS_j is the set of all mental states of j. Thus it is the the assertion that the intention is included among j's mental states.

Let us now consider how the commitment to comply with a normative system can be modelled as a policy-based intention. From this perspective the commitment to comply can be understood as the agent's j conditioned intention to do any action $\mathcal{A}_j$ that is obligatory according to N:

$$\mathbf{O}_N\mathcal{A}_j \Rightarrow \,!\mathcal{A}_j \tag{4}$$

Assume, for instance that *Tom*, while being in a place open to the public, is considering the implications of the normative system N_2 of example (2) (which says that places open to the public count as public spaces, and that it is forbidden to smoke in public places). Then *Tom* can establish that he is forbidden to smoke according to N_2:

$$\mathbf{O}_{N_2}(\neg\mathbf{E}_{Tom}Smoke) \tag{5}$$

Assume also that *Tom* has adopted the following policy-based intention to comply with N_2:

$$\mathbf{O}_{N_2}\mathcal{A}_{Tom} \Rightarrow \,!\mathcal{A}_{Tom}$$

one of whose grounds instances is:

$$\mathbf{O}_{N_2}(\neg\mathbf{E}_{Tom}Smoke) \Rightarrow \,!\neg\mathbf{E}_{Tom}Smoke \tag{6}$$

From (5) and (6) *Tom* can derive his intention to abstain from smoking:

$$!\neg\mathbf{E}_{Tom}Smoke$$

As this example shows, the meaning of the policy-based intention to comply consists in its inferential role: it works in the agent's mind as defeasible rule, allowing the derivation of an instance of its conclusion given (the belief in) an instance of its antecedent. Its peculiarity in comparison to other inference policies is that its conclusion is an intention to be implemented, rather than a proposition to be believed. In conclusion, we have found two ways to understand the commitment (intention) to comply with a normative system N by an agent j:

- j's intention to realise the state of affairs where all obligations directed to j are satisfied through its action (I intend to comply with the normative systems N: $!\mathbf{E}_j Complies_j(N)$)
- j's endorsement of the policy according to which j intends to comply with any N-obligation directed to itself (whenever something is obligatory for me according to N, I intend to do it: for any $\mathcal{A}$, $\mathbf{O}_N\mathcal{A}_j \Rightarrow \,!\mathcal{A}_j$)

It seems to me that there is only a one-way dependency between these two intentions. Adopting the latter policy-based intention is the most obvious way to realise (at least to some extent) the state of affairs of one's compliance. However, the converse does not hold: j may adopt the compliance policy, even when j does not intend to realise full compliance, knowing that it is not possible to achieve it. Moreover, such a policy may be limited by specific exceptions, whose detection would prevent the application of the policy (and would take *j* further away from full compliance), as I shall argue in section (7).

6 Intentions to comply

Compliance is neutral: the choice to comply with a normative system may result from the most different attitudes and goals. It is even doubtful whether in many cases a choice is involved in the adoption of the attitude to comply. When one lives in a certain community one tends to adopt the norms which are endorsed and followed in that community without the need of a specific act of choice. Correspondingly, when we know that our community has a normative system, but we don't know what rules belong to that system, we tend to adopt a general policy to comply with whatever rule will belong to that system, i.e., the policy-based intention above described. This happens in the communities in which we participate without an explicit choice (such as a country, a local community, a family, etc.), but also in those organisations that we enter by choice (a university, a company, a sport club, etc.), where a compliant attitude appears as a natural implication of one's choice to join a certain group or activity, rather than as a separate independent choice. Different explanations can be provided for the unreflected adoption of a determination to comply. For instance, it has been affirmed that humans are naturally endowed with the attitude of "docility", meant as " the propensity to behave in socially approved ways and to refrain from behaving in ways that are disapproved", and attitude that may have an evolutionary explanation since it "enhances human fitness tremendously by allowing children to enjoy a long period of dependence, and to acquire effective skills through learning" (47, 64). So, it seems that humans living within a certain organisation or community would "naturally" desire to be included and approved, and consequently adopt the goal (the intention) to comply with the norms of that organisation or community.

This fact, however, does not exclude that one's intention to comply may be the result of a deliberate choice. Such a choice may provide the motivation for compliance when one has no desire to be involved in a certain organisation or community. For instance a prisoner in concentration camp may choose to comply with the regulation of the camp, for fear of sanctions linked to non-compliance. He may also criticise those who do not comply (rather than approving of their courage), for fear of retaliation.

In other cases, a conscious deliberation to comply may support an existing insufficient commitment to do so. For instance a rebellious teenager may accept that he should comply with the school regulations (or with the law more generally) when convinced that non-compliance can easily get him into trouble.

Even people already having a certain propensity to comply may engage in a deliberation on whether to comply or not, when critically assessing whether they should or not maintain this attitude.

Different agents may have different ways of approaching the deliberation on whether they should comply with a norm or a normative system. For our purposes it is sufficient to focus on a broad category of agents, *consequentialist choosers*, namely, agents choosing their actions on the basis on an assessment of the consequences of such actions, an assessments determined by the expected utility (differential benefit) the agent expects as a result of the action. Here the notion of "result of an action" is understood is a very broad way, including the fact of adopting the action itself, as well as the further consequences of this fact (for a broad notion of consequentialism, see 33).

I will distinguish two aspects involved in the assessment of a choice by an agent:

- the utility of action $\mathcal{A}_x$ according to agent x, denoted by $u_x\mathcal{A}_x$, i.e., the measure of the net desirability of that choice, according to x'assessment,
- the impact of an action $\mathcal{A}_x$ on the well being of a subject y according to x, denoted by $w_y\mathcal{A}_x$, i.e., the measure of how much $\mathcal{A}_x$ advances or diminishes y's well-being, according to x's assessment.

Let us first characterise the general idea of a consequentialist chooser.

Definition 12 (Consequentialist chooser) *A consequentialist chooser x usually intends to do any action $\mathcal{A}_x$ whose expected utility he considers to be superior to the utility of not doing it. This is expressed by the following defeasible conditional;*

$$(u_x(\mathcal{A}_x) > u_x(\overline{\mathcal{A}_x})) \Rightarrow [!\mathcal{A}_x] \in MS_x$$

meaning "if according to agent x, the utility of doing $\mathcal{A}_x$ is higher than the utility of not doing it, then x will presumably have the intention of doing it" (the intention will be contained in x's mental states).

Let us now distinguish different kinds of consequentialist choosers:

- Self-centred (egoistic). For a self-centred chooser x, the utility of a choice is equal to the choice's impact on x's own well-being: $u_x(\mathcal{A}_x) = w_x(\mathcal{A}_x)$.
- Altruistic. For an altruistic chooser x the utility of a choice corresponds to its impact on the wellbeing of a set of agents, possibly including also (but not only) x: $u_x(\mathcal{A}_x) = w_{y_1}(\mathcal{A}_x) + \cdots + w_{y_m}(\mathcal{A}_x)$, where $y_1 \ldots y_m$ are the agents x considers relevant to its choice.
- Communitarian. For a communitarian chooser x, the utility of a choice corresponds to its impact on the wellbeing of x's community: $u_x(\mathcal{A}_x) = w_g(\mathcal{A}_x)$, where g is the community x cares about.
- Utilitarian. For a utilitarian chooser x, the utility of a choice corresponds to the sum of its impacts on the wellbeing of each human being $u_x(\mathcal{A}_x) = w_{y_1}(\mathcal{A}_x) + \ldots w_{y_n}(\mathcal{A}_x)$ where $y_1 \ldots y_n$ are all human beings (by "utilitarianism", I mean the idea that the "standard of what is right in conduct, is not the agent's own happiness, but that of all concerned", 29, Ch. 2).

Clearly, different kinds of consequentialist choosers will take different actions in the same situation. For instance when an action positively affects x's welfare, but negatively affects relevant others to a larger extent, a self-centred agent will do it, but an altruistic (or utilitarian) agent will not. However all consequentialist choosers act with the purpose of increasing utility, as they see it.

Let us now consider whether such an agent could make a higher-level decision. Rather that adopting the intention to perform an individual action on the basis of an assessment of its utility case by case, the agent could adopt the policy-based intentions to perform any action of a certain kind, under the assumption that acting on the basis of a policy-based intention will provide it with more utility than deciding what to do on a case-by case basis.

The agent may address the issue of endorsing the general policy-based intention of fulfilling any obligation established by a certain normative system, i.e., the intention to comply as expressed in by formula (4) above, in the following way. Assume that j believes that it will obtain a higher utility by having the policy to comply with N rather by no having this policy:

$$u_j([O_N\mathcal{A}_j \Rightarrow !\mathcal{A}_j] \in MS_j) > u_j([O_N\mathcal{A}_j \Rightarrow !\mathcal{A}_j] \notin MS_j) \qquad (7)$$

were MS_j is the set of all mental states of j. According to (7), making so that for j acquiring the policy-based intention to comply is better than omitting to do that (assuming that j does not yet have that intention):

$$u_j(E_j([O_N\mathcal{A}_j \Rightarrow !\mathcal{A}_j] \in MS_j) > u_j(\neg E_j([O_N\mathcal{A}_j \Rightarrow !\mathcal{A}_j] \in MS_j) \qquad (8)$$

Given that j is a consequentialist chooser, (8) entails that j intends to bring it the useful action (the action of acquiring the policy-based intention):

$$!E_j([O_N\mathcal{A}_j \Rightarrow !\mathcal{A}_j] \in MS_j)$$

Executing such an intention, i.e., realising action

$$E_j([O_N\mathcal{A}_j \Rightarrow !\mathcal{A}_j] \in MS_j$$

will produce state of affairs

$$[O_N\mathcal{A}_j \Rightarrow !\mathcal{A}_j] \in MS_j$$

namely, the state of affairs where j has the intention to perform an action $\mathcal{A}_j$ if this action is obligatory according to N.

This inference may be viewed as an instance of a general pattern of rationality: a rational agent x, having the intention to perform the action consisting in acquiring the intention I_x will (it the agent is fully rational) perform such a mental action and acquire I_x (not doing that would involve a failure in rationality, since this is an intention whose realisation only depends on the agent's mind, and not on external factors which may frustrate the implementation of the intention):

$$!E_x I_x \Rightarrow E_x I_x$$

Given that actions are successful by formula (1) above, performing $E_x I_x$ entails acquiring I_x, i.e., in our example, adopting the policy-based intention to comply.

Various refinements and extensions of a consequentialist model of agency are indeed possible: intermediate positions could be distinguished (as when one is moderately altruistic, giving some importance to the well-being of other, but less importance than to one's own well being) or egalitarian-prioritarian elements may be introduced (so that the differential welfare or certain people is more significant than that of others). The bounds of rationality could also be considered, and the ways in which the social environment influences attitudes and choices. Finally, the analysis of compliance could also go beyond consequentialist reasoning, extending to cases where compliance follows from a deontological ethics (for a discussion of deontology and consequentialism, see 4) or from a religious faith. All these refinements and extensions of the model here proposed are beyond the scope of this contribution, where I will limit my analysis to the simplistic typology of consequentialist reasoners just proposed.

7 Non-compliance

An agent may also choose not to comply or to be indifferent to compliance. We can distinguish different ideas in this regard.

Firstly, the agent may be completely *indifferent* to compliance. In this case, for any obligation $O\mathcal{A}_j$, the fact that the obligation is prescribed by N is no motivation for j to perform. From j's perspective, the N-obligatoriness of an action is no reason to (intend to) do it ($A \not\Rightarrow B$ means that the conditional $A \Rightarrow B$ does not hold, is not applicable, so that the argument $A, A \Rightarrow B$ for B is defeated), according to the agent. This negative intention can also be a component of the agent's mind. We represent it as follows:

$$O_N\mathcal{A}_j \not\Rightarrow !\mathcal{A}_j$$

Secondly, the j may be *diabolic*, as far as N is concerned (in the sense of wanting to violate N's obligations just for the sake of doing it). For such a j, the very fact that an action $\mathcal{A}_x$ is obligatory according to N provides a motivation to violate N. In other terms, j has adopted the policy of doing the contrary of anything obligatory according to N:

$$O_N\mathcal{A}_j \Rightarrow !\overline{\mathcal{A}_j}$$

Thirdly, j's commitment to compliance may be *limited*, since j, together with the compliance policy, also adopts one or more exception-policies to it, namely, rules stating that the compliance policy does not hold under certain conditions (such rules would be undercutters, in the model of 34, see also 38 and 37). All defeasible compliers will adopt the same general compliance policy $O_N \Rightarrow !\mathcal{A}_j$ we introduced in (4).

However they will adopt different exceptions of it, namely, among their mental states will include rules excluding the application of the compliance policy. An *opportunistic* complier j (the bad man, see 25) makes an exception to the compliance policy whenever j comes to believe that by violating an obligation it will get a higher personal advantage (well-being) than complying with it. Thus j would adopt the following reasoning policy, which blocks the defeasible compliance policy of formula (4) above whenever the utility of non-compliance exceeds that of compliance: when the utility of doing $\mathcal{A}_j$ is inferior to the utility of not doing it, then the obligatoriness of $\mathcal{A}_j$ does not provide a (defeasibly sufficient) reason to have the intention to do it.

$$(w_j\mathcal{A}_j < w_j\overline{\mathcal{A}_j}) \Rightarrow (\mathsf{O}_N\mathcal{A}_j \not\Rightarrow !\mathcal{A}_j)$$

Note that the opportunistic complier is not uncommitted toward compliance: j still has the defeasible commitment to comply expressed by formula (4) above, but this commitment is undercut by the belief that non-compliance (in a particular case) would get j a better outcome.

Effective sanctions could neutralise in many cases the opportunistic complier's exception, by making it so that that for any action $\mathcal{A}_j$, j's expected utility of non-compliance (once that the risk of sanctions is also taken into account) is inferior to the utility of compliance. This however depends of the expected impact of the sanction on j, namely, on the amount of the punishment and its probability, which should outweigh the advantage that $\overline{\mathcal{A}_j}$ would provide if there were no sanction.

Not all exceptions to the compliance policy are determined by self-interest. For instance, if *Ann* believes in some versions of natural law, or in some doctrine supporting civil disobedience, she would make an exception to her policy to comply with N, whenever she believes at N requires her to do an action $\mathcal{A}_{Ann}$ which is (unbearably) unjust. Thus *Ann* would adopt the following policy, according to which when an action of her is unjust, then its obligatoriness according to N is not a defeasibly sufficient reason for intending to do it:

$$Unjust(\mathcal{A}_{Ann}) \Rightarrow (\mathsf{O}_N\mathcal{A}_{Ann} \not\Rightarrow !\mathcal{A}_{Ann})$$

Other kinds of exceptions are also possible. For instance an act utilitarian agent would make an exception to the compliance policy whenever it considers that complying causes more harm than good to humanity. Similarly a corruptible agent would make an exception to the compliance policy when by non-complying the agent would get a substantial differential personal advantage (the amount required for leaning toward non-compliance, being inversely proportional to the corruptibility).

8 Endorsement of norms and commitment to comply

Research on social norms has recently addressed social processes through which norms are shared in a community, namely, the interlinked processes of the social emergence of norms and of their immergence in the mind of the concerned agents (3). Besides considering the spontaneous emergence of shared customary rules, also the psycho-social process involved in compliance with authoritative orders has been studied (14). However, I think that a further step is required to adequately capture the reasoning involved in the application of complex norm-systems.

Let us consider for instance a municipal tax law, such as the Italian one (which is a section of the larger Italian legal system). First of all, very few people have precise knowledge of a large set of rules from Italian tax law, and nobody's mind contains all of Italian tax law. It would be difficult to claim that such rules have "immerged" (and are stored) in the minds of Italian citizens since most of the latter do not know (and have never known) most of those rules. What citizens share is only the ability to identify somehow the law in force in their country as distinguished from other laws (foreign or ancient laws) and a general commitment (in many case a very qualified one), to comply with this law and possibly some criteria to identify its main contents. Citizens also have some ideas on the implications of this law that are most important to them (e.g., that the law requires them to pay the income tax every year, that VAT has to be paid on purchases, etc.), but are unable to determine such implications with precision (on the distinction between identifying the law and determining its content, see 27).

Usually common citizens usually approach tax issues with the help of tax experts, who give them some indications of what obligations follow from tax law under specific real or hypothetical cases, what sanctions may follow from violating such obligations, what line of actions are most advantageous with regard to tax-law effects. On the basis of this fragmentary information, law-abiding people will determine how to comply with tax law. Let us try to analyse the reasoning process involved in applying this kind of normative information (and more generally all complex normative systems, such as advanced legal systems).

Let us assume that *Tom* has a general commitment to comply the normative systems L (the law), which includes many tax regulation (without knowing what it the precise content of L). In other words, he endorses the policy based intention to perform any action that is obligatory according to L (the law):

$$\mathbb{O}_L \mathcal{A}_{Tom} \Rightarrow !\mathcal{A}_{Tom}$$

Tom is now wondering whether he should pay income tax on the capital gains he obtained by selling his house. Being committed to comply with the law, but not knowing what the law requires from him, *Tom* asks the tax expert *Ann* for advise. Assume that the *Ann* remembers that there is a rule in the tax code that establishes the requirement to pay income taxes on capital gains, but vaguely remembers that there are exceptions to it. This prompts *Ann* to look for exceptions, and she finds indeed one matching houses. This exception says (in a simplified form) that capital gains from the sale of houses purchased more than 5 year before the sale and inhabited by the seller are exempted from income tax. Assume that Ann's inquiry has let that to conclude that the legal system L contains the following relevant norms:

$$L \supseteq \{SellsHouse(x) \Rightarrow OE_x PayIncomeTaxOnSale;$$

$$BoughtMoreThan5YearsBefore(x) \land HasInhabitedHouse(x) \Rightarrow \quad (9)$$

$$\neg(SellsHouse(x) \Rightarrow OE_x PayIncomeTaxOnSale)\}$$

where the second norms in (9) says that under the indicated conditions the first one does not hold (is not applicable).

Ann then asks Tom whether at the time of the sale more that 5 years had elapsed from the Tom's purchase, and whether he has been living in the house. Assume that Tom replies positively to the first question and negatively to the second one. Then Ann says: "Dear, Tom, unfortunately you are legally bound to pay income tax on your gains". In fact, by combining the law L with these factual circumstances (let us assume these circumstances are the only relevant ones), Ann can see that the following inference holds:

$$L \cup \{\neg HasInhabitedHouse(Tom)\} \mathrel{|\!\sim} OE_{Tom} PayIncomeTaxOnSale$$

so that she can infer what she tells her client:

$$O_L E_{Tom} PayIncomeTaxOnSale$$

If Tom asks for an explanation, Ann would probably answer by saying that whenever one has not lived in the house one sells, then according to the law one has the obligation to pay income tax:

$$SellsHouse(x) \land \neg HasInhabitedSoldHouse(x) \rightarrow O_L E_{(x)} PayIncomeTaxOnSale$$
$$(10)$$

Note that formula (10) does not express a norm of L (there is no norm in L which has exactly that content, see formula (9)). More generally (10) is no norm at all, but rather is a general conditional statement about L, namely the statement that in case that the seller has not inhabited the sold house, then L entails that the seller has to pay taxes on capital gains. Similarly, if Ann were contacted by Tom before making the sale, she would tell him: "Since you have not inhabited the house, you will have to pay income tax on your capital gain".

I think that this example may suffice to show that norms included in large normative systems operate differently from social norms. When we learn social norms we permanently store them in our memory, as the content of appropriate normative beliefs and goals, so that they can directly govern our behaviour. On the contrary, we do not learn and store in our memory most norms included in a large normative systems. We rather possess some ideas about the existence of such a system and the ways to identify its content. When needed, we collect some fragmentary information about the system and combine this information with the relevant facts, both tasks being often delegated to experts. On the basis of this information we can conclude that the system requires us to perform certain actions. By combining such conclusions with our general commitment to comply with the system we adopt intentions to perform such actions.

9 Compliance by officers

Certain normative systems have officers (typically judges) charged with ensuring compliance, in particular by sanctioning non-compliance.

For each obligation $O\mathcal{A}_x$, let us denote with $Punished(x)$, the situation where x is punished. Let us assume for simplicity's sake that a single compliance officer, a judge named Jud, who is responsible for for ascertaining and repressing all violations of N, and that the punishment is the same for all violations. In other words, let us assume that N contains a norm stating than whenever an obligation $O\mathcal{A}_x$ is violated, it is Jud's obligation to punish x:

$$O\mathcal{A}_x \wedge \neg\mathcal{A}_x \Rightarrow OE_{Jud}Punished(x) \tag{11}$$

Note that for rule in formula (11) above to fire, $O\mathcal{A}_x$ must be derivable from N itself in combination with the facts of the case (thus we do not need to substitute $O\mathcal{A}_x$ with the metalevel normative proposition $\mathbb{O}\mathcal{A}_x$).

This representation is a simplification with regard to complex normative systems, where we have multiple interlocked rules determining who is in charge for each kind of violation, and we need to distinguish officers charged with providing evidence of violations, officers charged with establishing whether a violation has taken place and order a sanction, officers charged with carrying out the sanction. In fact officers in a complex normative system have a shared task which is more complex that simple punishment, a task which may possibly be characterised as the development and maintenance of their normative system. To accomplish this task they need to some extent coordinate their activities in creating, modifying, interpreting applying the norms in the system (see 45 who sees this activity as a shared cooperative activity in the sense of 10). For the purposes of this paper, however, a simplistic analysis will suffice.

Thus compliance by Jud (in its role as law enforcer) could be expressed as follows:

$$CompliesWith_{Jud}(N) \stackrel{\text{def}}{=} \forall(x)(\mathbb{O}_N E_{Jud}Punished(x) \rightarrow E_{Jud}Punished(x))$$

Jud's commitment to a policy-based intention to comply could be expressed as "I, Jud, intend to punish anybody I have the obligation to punish":

$$OE_{Jud}Punished(x) \Rightarrow !E_{Jud}Punished(x) \tag{12}$$

By repeating the reasoning above we may consider the conditions under which a consequentialist judge (of different kinds) could adopt policy (12): Jud could indeed adopt it out of self-concern (to advance its career, have a good reputation, etc.), altruism or communal concerns, and may subject this policy to various limitations. For instance, a corruptible judge will not apply the policy when there is great advantage to be gained through non-compliance.

10 Spreading compliance

I will not examine here the social determinants of compliance and the social factors that encourage or discourage compliance, which would require me to address the many issues dealing with the theory of social norms (see, for instance, 15, 6) and their connection to legal systems.

I will just observe that the expected utility of x complying with N often depends on how many other agents will comply with N, as officers or as private individuals. As the number of compliers of a normative systems N increases usually both the individual and social differential benefit of compliance (as compared to non-compliance) increases: in a context of compliance, legal and social sanctions for non-compliance are more likely to take place, compliance is more likely to have a socially beneficial effect, compliance can be viewed as an exercise in reciprocity. This explains why in a context of increased (decreased) compliance, individuals are usually more (less) motivated to comply: so both compliance and non-compliance tend to spread in the community. For most people there is a threshold of compliance-frequency that makes the utility of compliance positive, so that they would choose to comply when the threshold is overcome. However, this threshold may be different for different people (both officers or common fellows) who may be differently motivated (by the individual, social, or communal benefit of compliance).

Thus, compliance by agents who are sufficiently motivated only where there is a higher compliance frequency may depend on whether there is a sufficient number of other agents sufficiently motivated at lower compliance levels, who can bootstrap the process.

Clearly a more complex picture could be developed though a more accurate and diversified representation of motivations for compliance (see for instance 5), which may indeed lead different agents to different choices. For instance one may comply with norms that others do not comply with, in order to better advertise one's commitment to the common good, or to get a confirmation of one's morality; a Kantian agent should be unmoved by the non-compliance by others to a norms the agent approves of; a "myopic" agent would only care about the compliance by the nearest neighbours, etc.

I cannot here address all the many issues concerning the spreading of normative attitudes, an issue to which Castelfranchi and his colleagues have dedicated a number of important contributions (see for instance 3). One general consideration, however, is that people will have normative expectations about the compliance by others, and this expectation will be strengthened insofar as other people as a matter of fact do comply. Here not only one's belief in the value of having a certain normative system, but also reciprocity is at issue, as well as the fact that people will make their own choices (and take risks) on the basis of the factual expectation that others will comply.

11 The morality of compliance

When a normative system N is generally complied with and enforced, there will be usually a general attitude of viewing compliance as morally obligatory. This may indeed support the adoption of the intention to comply.

Let us assume that an agent's morality M (the set of norms the agent endorses and views as morally binding) contains a norm stating the obligatoriness of whatever is obligatory (for any agent x) relatively to a certain normative system N:

$$\mathbb{O}_N \mathcal{A}_x \Rightarrow \mathbb{O}\mathcal{A}_x \tag{13}$$

If an agent j accepts the moral bindingness of the norm in (13), and believes that $\mathcal{A}_j$ is obligatory according to N (i.e., that $\mathbb{O}_N\mathcal{A}_j$), j will conclude that the obligation to do $\mathcal{A}_j$ is entailed by morality:

$$M \cup T(M) \mathrel{\vert\!\sim} \mathbb{O}\mathcal{A}_x$$

Thus, j will view action $\mathcal{A}_j$ as morally obligatory (according to definition (5), formula (2)), i.e., j will believe that

$$\mathbb{O}_M \mathcal{A}_j$$

Rule (13), when applied to the norms governing a political organisation (typically a state) expresses the idea of political obligation, namely, the moral obligation to obey the law.

The obligation to comply may be qualified by exceptions (e.g., one may argue that it is not morally obligatory to comply with norms enjoining a serious violation of human rights, or which are blatantly unjust or absurd) especially when non-compliance is done in public to convey a political message urging resistance or change, so that it may qualify as civil disobedience.

The idea that that there is a moral obligation to obey a normative system N can contribute to compliance with N, as long as the concerned agent j is committed to do what is required by morality (as identified by j itself), i.e., as long as j endorses the following policy:

$$\mathbb{O}_M \mathcal{A}_j \Rightarrow \,!\mathcal{A}_j \tag{14}$$

Thus j, believing that it has the obligation to do action $\mathcal{A}_j$ according to N (i.e, $\mathbb{O}_N\mathcal{A}_j$) can use moral rule (13) to conclude that it has a moral obligation to do $\mathcal{A}_j$ (i.e., $\mathbb{O}_M\mathcal{A}_j$) and consequently use policy (14) to adopt the intention of doing $\mathcal{A}_j$. Those who endorse rule (13) will also tend to extend their moral condemnation to the violators of norms in N.

In conclusion, moral beliefs may ground or reinforce the endorsement of a policy to comply, but they may not be necessary to this purpose, since the adoption of such a policy may also follows from self-interest or other motivations, as shown above.

12 Compliance and social power

The model of compliance here proposed can be related to the theory of power and influence proposed in Castelfranchi [12]. The basic idea I will use is that an agent j influences another agent k when j makes it so that k adopts j's goals, and that influence is a most important mechanism for social power.

Let us assume a state of generalised compliance, so that all (or most) addressees of normative system N have adopted a policy-based intention to comply with N, according to the model indicated in formula (4) above. I will argue that under these conditions a normative systems can be an efficient machine not only for limiting, but also for producing influence and power.

Obviously, normative systems can limit social influence. For instance, assume that John is physically stronger than Tom. If there were no legal system prohibiting the use of violence, John could influence Tom and induce him to (intend to) accomplish what John likes (working for John, paying John for protection, etc.), by threatening to use violence against Tom. However, this is no longer possible (or at least more difficult) when there is an effective legal system N which prohibits using violence against others. If John himself is rigorously committed to the policy to comply with N, then John will adopt the intention to abstain from prohibited actions, and therefore also from violence. In case John is not committed to compliance (or is only defeasibly committed to it, with his self-interest providing for an exception), the compliance of others (and in particular of the enforcement officers) will make it so that his criminal behaviour is prevented of at least made less attractive by the prospect of punishment. This should prevent the threat or make it not credible. Therefore John will not use the threat, or at least Tom will not be influenceable through it.

Let us now examine how normative systems, rather than limiting social influence, can extend it. We need to consider that what obligations are generated by N depends on two factors: the norms in N and the true relevant factual circumstances $T(N)$. This means that N can work as an input-output machine. The input consists in changes in $T(N)$ (the creation of new relevant facts), and the output consists changes in the obligations entailed by N. The input can produce the output in two ways: (a) by providing (or removing) facts that produce obligations according to the norms in N, or (b) by changing the norms in N, these changes having an impact on the obligations derivable from N. In this section I will consider the the first way of changing N's obligations, and in the following I will address the latter.

For instance a normative system can make orders binding (for instance, the orders of a military commander to a soldier, or of an employer or manager to a worker), by making obligatory for the addressee of an order to comply with it. This idea could also be expressed by using the notion of institutional (norm-based) power (26, 18, 4023, 22, 50), but here a simpler representation will be provided, without expressly formalising the concept of institutional power. Assume the system N contains a rule according to which *Ann* has the obligation to do whatever action $\mathcal{A}_{Ann}$ is ordered by her manager *Tom* (for simplicity I do not consider the limitation of such an obligation in modern legal systems, where the order must pertain to the execution of the work, and respect the worker's rights and dignity):

$$E_{Tom}Order(\mathcal{A}_{Ann}) \Rightarrow O\mathcal{A}_{Ann} \qquad (15)$$

Assume that *Tom* does indeed order *Ann* to do something, for instance, to draft the minutes of a meeting):

$$E_{Tom}Order(E_{Ann}DraftMinutes) \qquad (16)$$

so that this action-proposition becomes one the true relevant facts

$$(E_{Tom}Order(E_{Ann}DraftMinutes)) \in T(N))$$

Given that N contains rule (15) and $T(N)$ contains fact (16) the following holds:

$$N \cup T(N) \mathrel{\vdash} OE_{Ann}DraftMinutes$$

so that we can say that according to N it is indeed obligatory that *Ann* drafts the minutes

$$O_N E_{Ann}DraftMinutes \qquad (17)$$

Assume that *Ann* has adopted the general compliance policy of formula (4) above relatively to normative system N, so that she intends to do whatever action of her is obligatory according to N:

$$O_N\mathcal{A}_{Ann} \Rightarrow !\mathcal{A}_{Ann} \qquad (18)$$

Policy-based intention (18) and normative proposition (17) entail that *Ann* will adopt the unconditioned intention to draft the minutes

$$!E_{Ann}DraftMinutes$$

Thus, given that *Ann* is committed to comply with N, *Tom* can influence her. By ordering any action, he makes it so that N entails the obligatoriness of that action, which makes it so that *Ann* adopts the intention of doing that action. Note that this power by *Tom* does not depend on his personal qualities (*Ann* may dislike *Tom* or believe that he an incapable idiot), it only depends on the content of the normative system, on the relevant facts, and on *Ann's* commitment to policy-based intention (18).

A normative system N can also provide individuals with the possibility of binding themselves, i.e., of undertaking obligations according to N, or more generally of creating any normative positions concerning themselves. For this purpose it is sufficient that N contains the following rule:

$$E_x Promise(\mathcal{A}_x) \Rightarrow O\mathcal{A}_x \qquad (19)$$

meaning that whenever an x promises to do $\mathcal{A}$ then x has the obligation to do $\mathcal{A}$.

A complied with (and protected through sanctions or other means of social pressure) normative system containing the rule in (19) enables agents to create credible commitment for themselves (given the costs of non-compliance), on the basis of which others can act (e.g., I promise to give 1,000 euros to the person who will bring back to me my lost dog), or can be induced to take similar commitments, as in contracts (on a more general approach to contract, which views them as means to create not just obligations but any kind of normative positions see 19, 40, 23). For example, assume the following: 1) system N contains the rule in (19), 2) I promised that I will give 1000 euros to the best law student of this year; 3) Ann is this year's best law student. It follows that according to N, I have the obligation to give 1000 euros to Ann.

13 The machine of the law

Let us now consider how an agent (a legislator) can have the ability to introduce new norms in N. For this purpose, we need to assume that N is a dynamic normative system (28), including meta-rules which determines what new noms will belong to N. So, let us assume that N includes a meta-norm saying that whatever norm φ is issued by the legislator Leg is included in N (φ is a variable ranging over norm):

$$\mathsf{E}_{Leg}Issued(\varphi) \Rightarrow (\varphi \in N) \qquad\qquad (20)$$

Moreover, let us assume that N is characterised as including this meta-norm (which would work as the primary "norm of recognition" of N, see 24) plus every other norm that is qualified as being in N according to N itself (any norm φ such that N entails the proposition that φ is contained in N, for a presentation of this idea, see 41), so that it is the minimal set satisfying the following equality:

$$N = \{\mathsf{E}_{Leg}Issued(\varphi) \Rightarrow (\varphi \in N)\} \cup \{\varphi : N \cup T(N) \mathrel{\vdash\!\!\!\sim} (\varphi \in N)\} \qquad (21)$$

Given this background, let us assume that legislator accomplished the action of issuing a new norm, for instance, a norm prohibiting any agent x to smoke:

$$\mathsf{E}_{Leg}Issued(O\neg\mathsf{E}_x Smoke)$$

The accomplishment of the action described in this formula is a new fact, which is added to the true factual circumstance $T(N)$. With this addition, the following now holds according to the rule of formula (20) above:

$$N \cup T(N) \mathrel{\vdash\!\!\!\sim} (O\neg\mathsf{E}_x Smoke \in N)$$

and consequently N comes to include also that norm (i.e., "$O\neg\mathsf{E}_x Smoke$"), according to the definition of N specified in formula (21) above. Consequently, it now holds that

$$N \cup T(N) \mathrel{\vdash\!\!\!\sim} (O\neg\mathsf{E}_{Tom} Smoke)$$

so that we can say that now smoking is forbidden to Tom according to N:

$$\mathcal{O}_N \neg E_{Tom} Smoke$$

The legislator can use the power provided by formula (20) above to put a judge in charge of punishing violators. To achieve this result, the legislator just has to perform the following action (i.e. issuing a norm to that effect, namely a norm saying that the judge Jud should punish any agent who violates a norm in N, i.e., any agent who does the opposite of what is obligatory for that agent):

$$E_{Leg} Issued([O\mathcal{A}_x \wedge \neg \mathcal{A}_x \Rightarrow OE_{Jud} Punished(x)])$$

As a consequence of this legislative action, the issued norm is in N, and consequently Jud has, according to N, the obligation to punish any violator:

$$O\mathcal{A}_x \wedge \neg \mathcal{A}_x \Rightarrow OE_{Jud} Punished(x)$$

Assume now that both Ann and Jud have the policy-based intention to comply with N, and that Ann views non-compliance as immoral. Then, on the basis of the statement of the legislator, Ann will adopt the intention not to smoke, Jud will adopt the intention to punish smokers in public places, and Ann would believe that anyone who smokes in a public place behaves immorally.

The legislator can also confer to another agent, the administrator $Admin$, the ability to insert new norms in N (delegated legislation) by enacting such norms (while respecting certain legal constraints on $Admin$'s legislative action):

$$E_{Leg} Issued([E_{Admin} Issued(\varphi) \wedge E_{Admin} RespectConstaints(\varphi) \Rightarrow (\varphi \in N)] \quad (22)$$

As a consequence of the action described in formula (22) and the characterisation of N in (21), the norm empowering $Admin$ is now in N, i.e., N contains:

$$E_{Admin} Issued(\varphi) \wedge E_{Admin} RespectConstaints(\varphi) \Rightarrow (\varphi \in N)$$

Consequently whatever new norm φ is issued by $Admin$, respecting the relative constraints (concerning the content of φ or the procedure for its creation), that norm will be inputted in N. In this way, the legislator transfers to $Admin$ the legislator's ability to influence people's behaviour, by exploiting their commitment to compliance.

Not only the generalised commitment to comply with N provides the legislator (and its delegatees) with the possibility to influence the behaviour of compliers and judges. It also provides those who are able to influence the legislator with the ability to influence the behaviour of all others. Assume for instance that Tom is the leader of the party having the majority in the legislative assembly. Then Tom can make it so that the legislator adopts the intention to introduce (or repeal) a norm $B \Rightarrow \mathcal{A}$, to make it so that the population intends to do (and does) action $\mathcal{A}$ under circumstances B.

A normative system supported by a generally endorsed policy-based intention to comply can thus work as an input-output machine, empowering those who can control its input: by providing appropriate normative and factual inputs, they can obtain corresponding intentions and actions and so implement their aims. As Karl Olivecrona put it "[t]he purpose of the lawgivers is to influence the actions of men, but this can only be done through influencing their minds" (30, 21-2, 48). Thus legislators (and those able to influence them) can use the "machinery of the law" for reaching their social, political (and sometimes personal) purposes (see 32, 31). Normative systems, in a way, precede certain social powers, and provide for their foundation. The extent of norm-systems based powers may indeed be very large, which explains why developed legal systems contain constitutional limitations and controls over the exercise of such powers (such as democratic procedures for electing the legislative body, judicial review over legislation and administration, more generally, an institutional system of "checks and balances").

14 Conclusion

I have first considered how obligations can be relative to a particular normative system, and I have provided a meta-logical representation of this idea. Then I have analysed the intention to comply with a normative system, affirming that the commitment to comply must be understood as a policy-based intention. I have then considered why consequential choosers may come to this determination, as simple addressees or enforcement officers. Finally I have developed some considerations on how compliance can spread and how it can both restrain and provide power.

The study of compliance with normative systems involves various aspects I could not address here. First of all there is the issue of interpretation, i.e., of determining the content of the normative system to be complied with, on the basis of the available materials (texts, cases, practices, values, etc.), a problem that legal theorists have been discussing for centuries, and on whose epistemological-methodological nature the debate is still on-going. Other important issues concern modelling contrary to duty obligations (and other technical aspects of deontic logic), taking into account cooperation between the involved agents and dependencies and trust relationships between them, addressing negotiation and argumentation regarding how to comply and on the consequences of violations, considering how a shared awareness of each one's intention to comply and a shared belief in a duty to comply can contribute to compliance. I think however that such aspects are complementary but independent of the model developed here, which only assumes that the addressees of a normative system adopt a policy-based intention to comply with it, regardless of the reasons supporting this intention and the ways in which the system's content is identified.

References

1. Alchourrón, C. E. (1969). Logic of norms and logic of normative propositions. *Logique et analyse 12*, 242–68.
2. Alchourrón, C. E. and E. Bulygin (1971). *Normative Systems*. Vienna: Springer.

3. Andrighetto, G., M. Campenni, R. Conte, and M. Paolucci (2007). On the immergence of norms: A normative agent architecture. In *Proceedings of AAAI Symposium, Social and Organizational Aspects of Intelligence*.
4. Baron, M., P. Pettit, and M. Slote (1997). *Three Methods of Ethics: A Debate*. London: Blackwell.
5. Bénabou, R. and J. Tirole (2006). Incentives and prosocial behavior,". *American Economic Review 96*, 1652–78.
6. Bicchieri, C. (2011). Social norms. In *Stanford Encyclopedia of Philosophy*. Stanford University.
7. Boella, G. and L. van der Torre (2006). A logical architecture of a normative system. In *Deontic Logic and Artificial Normative Systems*, pp. 24–35. Springer.
8. Bratman, M. (1987). *Intentions, Plans and Practical Reasoning*. Cambridge, Mass.: Harvard University Press.
9. Bratman, M. E. (1989). Intention and personal policies. *Philosophyical Perspectives 3*, 443–469.
10. Bratman, M. E. (1992). Shared cooperative activity. *Philosophical Review 101*, 327–41.
11. Broersen, Jan Dastani, M., J. Hulstijn, Z. Huang, and L. van der Torre (2001). The boid architecture. In *AGENTS'01*. New York, N.Y.: ACM.
12. Castelfranchi, C. (2003). The micro-macro constitution of power. *ProtoSociology, 18-19*, 208–65.
13. Conte, R. and C. Castelfranchi (1995). *Cognitive and Social Action*. London: University College of London Press.
14. Conte, R. and C. Castelfranchi (1999). From conventions to prescriptions. towards a unified theory of norms. *Artificial intelligence and Law 7*, 323–40.
15. Conte, R. and C. Castelfranchi (2006). The mental path of norms. *Ratio Juris 19*, 501–17.
16. Dung, P. M. (1995). On the acceptability of arguments and its fundamental role in non-monotonic reasoning, logic programming, and n–person games. *Artificial Intelligence 77*, 321–57.
17. Føllesdal, D. and R. Hilpinen (1971). Deontic logic: An introduction. In R. Hilpinen (Ed.), *Deontic Logic: Introductory and Systematic Reading*. Dordrecht: Reidel.
18. Gelati, J., G. Governatori, A. Rotolo, and G. Sartor (2002a). Actions, institutions, powers: Preliminary notes. In G. Lindemann, D. Moldt, M. Paolucci, and B. Yu (Eds.), *International Workshop on Regulated Agent-Based Social Systems: Theories and Applications (RASTA'02)*, pp. 131–47. Hamburg: Fachbereich Informatik, Universität Hamburg.
19. Gelati, J., G. Governatori, A. Rotolo, and G. Sartor (2002b). Declarative power, representation, and mandate: A formal analysis. In *Proceedings of the Fifteenth Annual Conference on Legal Knowledge and Information Systems (JURIX)*, pp. 41–52. Amsterdam: IOS.
20. Governatori, G., V. Padmanabhan, A. Rotolo, and A. Sattar (2009). A defeasible logic for modelling policy-based intentions and motivational attitudes. *Logic Journal of IGPL 17*, 36–69.
21. Grossi, D., J.-J. C. Meyer, and F. Dignum (2008). The many faces of counts-as: A formal analysis of constitutive rules. *Journal of Applied Logic 6*, 192–217.
22. Hage, J. C. (2011a). A model of juridical acts: Part 1: The world of law. *Artificial intelligence and Law 19*, 23–48.
23. Hage, J. C. (2011b). A model of juridical acts: Part 2: The operation of juridical acts. *Artificial Intelligence and Law 19*, 49–73.
24. Hart, H. L. A. (1994). *The Concept of Law* (2nd ed.). Oxford: Oxford University Press.
25. Holmes, O. W. (1897). The path of the law. *Harvard Law Review 10*, 457–78.
26. Jones, A. J. and M. J. Sergot (1996). A formal characterisation of institutionalised power. *Journal of the IGPL 4*, 429–45.
27. Jori, M. (2011). *Del diritto inesistente*. Pisa: ETS.
28. Kelsen, H. (1967). *The Pure Theory of Law*. Berkeley, Cal.: University of California Press.
29. Mill, J. S. (1991). Utilitarianism. In J. Gray (Ed.), *On Liberty and Other Essays*, pp. 131–201. Oxford: Oxford University Press. (1st ed. 1861.).
30. Olivecrona, K. (1971). *Law as Fact* (2nd ed.). London: Stevens.

31. Pattaro, E. (2005). *The Law and the Right, a Reappraisal of the Reality that Ought to be*, Volume 1 of *Treatise of legal Philosophy and General Jurisprudence*. Berlin: Springer.

32. Pattaro, E. (2009). From H]ägerstom to Ross and Hart. *Ratio Juris 22*, 532–48.

33. Pettit, P. (1997). The consequentialist perspective. In *Three Methods of Ethics: A Debate*, pp. 92–174. London: Blackwell.

34. Pollock, J. L. (1995). *Cognitive Carpentry: A Blueprint for How to Build a Person*. New York, N. Y.: MIT.

35. Pörn, I. (1977). *Action Theory and Social Science: Some Formal Models*. Dordrecht: Reidel.

36. Prakken, H. (2001). Relating protocols for dynamic dispute with logics for defeasible argumentation. *Synthese 127*, 187–219.

37. Prakken, H. (2010). An abstract framework for argumentation with structured arguments. *Argument and Computation 1*, 93–124.

38. Prakken, H. and G. Sartor (1996). Rules about rules: Assessing conflicting arguments in legal reasoning. *Artificial Intelligence and Law 4*, 331–68.

39. Sartor, G. (2005). *Legal Reasoning: A Cognitive Approach to the Law*, Volume 5 of *Treatise on Legal Philosophy and General Jurisprudence*. Berlin: Springer.

40. Sartor, G. (2006). Fundamental legal concepts: A formal and teleological characterisation. *Artificial Intelligence and Law 21*, 101–42.

41. Sartor, G. (2009). Legality policies and theories of legality: From Bananas to Radbruch's formula. *Ratio Juris 22*, 218–43.

42. Sartor, G. (2011). Defeasibility in legal reasoning. In J. Ferrer (Ed.), *Essays in Legal Defeasibility*. Oxford: Oxford University Press. (Forthcoming.).

43. Searle, J. R. (1995). *The Construction of Social Reality*. New York, N. Y.: Free.

44. Sergot, M. J. (2001). A computational theory of normative positions. *ACM Transactions on Computational Logic 2*, 581–662.

45. Shapiro, S. J. (2002). Law, plans and practical reasoning. *Legal Theory 8*, 387–441.

46. Siena, A., J. Mylopoulos, P. A., and A. Susi (2009). Designing law-compliant software requirements,. In *Proceeding of the 28th International Conference on Conceptual Modeling (ER'09)*, pp. 472–86. New York, N.Y.: SPeincer.

47. Simon, H. A. (1983). *Reason in Human Affairs*. Stanford, Cal.: Stanford University Press.

48. Spaak, T. (2009). Naturalism in scandinavian and american realism: Similarities and differences. In Dahlberg (Ed.), *De Lege, Uppsala-Minnesota Colloquium: Law, Culture and Values*, pp. 33.83. Uppsala: Iustus.

49. Tummolini, L., G. Andrighetto, C. Castelfranchi, and R. Conte (2011). A convention of (tacit) agreement betwixt us. *Synthese*.

50. Tummolini, L. and C. Castelfranchi (2006). The cognitive and behavioral mediation of institutions: Towards an account of institutional actions. *Cognitive Systems Research 7*, 307–32.

Chapter 34
Institutions evolving through the mind. A cognitive and computational approach

Giulia Andrighetto, Rosaria Conte and Francesca Giardini

Abstract In this paper, institutions are said to undergo evolutionary processes of a specific nature. Cognitive activities and representations affect institutional change, and play a decisive role in their selection and retention. Special attention is devoted to enforcing institutions that are hypothesized to have evolved from retaliatory to punishing, and even sanctioning, systems thanks to and by means of specific cognitive capacities. In this paper, we propose a simulation-based methodology in which artificial agents are modelled and observed to interact in a virtual setting, the simulated world, in order to experiment upon the conditions favouring institutional evolution.

1 Introduction

The role of cognition in the study of macro-social, even political, phenomena has always been a nagging thought in Castelfranchi's speculation. Strongly convinced that the conceptual language of social, legal and political sciences is interspersed with belief and goal-based notions – power, interest, intention, autonomy, liberty, right, duty, role, function, guilt, responsibility, delegation, trust, accountability, etc. – he has spent a significant share of his intellectual

Giulia Andrighetto
Laboratory of Agent-based Social Simulation (LABSS), Institute of Cognitive Sciences and Technologies, CNR, Italy
Department of Political and Social Sciences, European University Institute of Florence, Italy
e-mail: giulia.andrighetto@istc.cnr.it

Rosaria Conte
Laboratory of Agent-based Social Simulation (LABSS), Institute of Cognitive Sciences and Technologies, CNR, Italy
e-mail: rosaria.conte@istc.cnr.it

Francesca Giardini
Laboratory of Agent-based Social Simulation (LABSS), Institute of Cognitive Sciences and Technologies, CNR, Italy
e-mail: francesca.giardini@istc.cnr.it

life wondering about the nature of macro-social entities. Fascinated by the idea that not only the language of intelligent systems, but also their properties, mechanisms, and actions might be applied at several levels of reality, Castelfranchi has never followed the complementary direction of thought, which confines social and political institutions within the boundaries of individual minds. Reluctant to accept the lesson of social constructionists à la Berger and Luckmann, Castelfranchi has never abandoned the Marxian intuition that social alienation concerns not only economic power and market relationships, but also political power and the social hierarchy. His passionate study of the mind did not lead him to view society as a shared mental content, but rather as an emergent level of reality that acts upon and subordinates the producing entities.

As any good Marxian thinker, Castelfranchi is also a convinced Darwinist. In the seventies he became an early supporter of the socio-biological lesson but a few years later, well before Dennett published his substrate-independent notion of evolutionary algorithm (Dennett 1995), he developed an abstract theory of goal-governed vs. goal-directed behaviour (Parisi and Castelfranchi 1984, Castelfranchi and Parisi 1980), operating through mental representations or biological reproduction. A decade or so later, thanks also to Dennett's evolutionary algorithm, cultural evolutionary theories very easily became popular (Cavalli-Sforza and Feldmann 1981; Boyd and Richerson 1985; Richerson and Boyd 2005). The appearance of memetics (Dawkins 1976; Blakemore 1999), the field that consistently applied Dennett's evolutionary algorithm to the evolution of cultural units (memes), reinforced the idea that cultural units are selected independent of biological reproduction, and favour a view of the mind as a mechanism of selection (Castelfranchi 2001; Conte 2000).

Generally indebted to Castelfranchi's theory of goal-governed systems, the present work is strongly inspired by a view of the mind as a selection environment. Here, we want to provide an analysis of institutions as systems of prescriptions and mechanisms enforcing them. In what follows, two major lines of argument are emphasized:

- cognition is pivotal to the appearance and selection of institutions because different mental configurations are needed in order to make institutions emerge and out-compete rival institutions;
- institutional change can be explained as a change in cognitive patterns required to make people aware of the differences among competing institutions and to promote their willingness to conform to them.

The rest of the paper is organized as follows. In Section 2 we briefly review some of the main contributions to the debate on the evolution of institutions. In Section 3 we introduce our view on the evolution of institutions, showing how the cognitive approach can add to this debate. More specifically, we demonstrate how cognitive analysis may help to unveil the way institutions act on mind (3.1), reporting on results from previous studies (3.1.1), and how minds act on institutions (4). In Section 5, we focus on enforcing institutions, showing how cognition is involved in the transition from institutions based on revenge to those based on sanction. Finally, we advance some conclusions on this new approach to the study of the evolution of institutions, in which evolution is not taken for granted but is a continuous process of selection and change driven by individuals' minds.

2 State of the art

Providing a comprehensive review on the evolution of institutions is beyond the scope of this work, but we would like to sketch an overview of evolutionary accounts dealing with institutions. Human societies are regulated by a number of different institutions and this variety depends not only on the type of norms and conventions regulating societies, but also on the systems that issue those norms and ensure their transmission, recognition, and possible enforcement. In our view, social institutions are systems producing and enacting the norms that regulate a given society (see also Ulmann-Margalit 1977; Coleman 1998 for an *institution–as–norms* approach). Institutions emanate, spread, enforce the norms and control their application. In some cases, they are not necessarily designed by human intelligence, but they spontaneously emerge from social interactions. Nonetheless, institutions rely on norms and other mechanisms of regulation and enforcement to mould and give order to human societies. These mechanisms permit institutions to work effectively, to accomplish their *mission*, provided that norms[1] are stored in the individuals' minds and regulate their behaviours.

Understanding how norms and their enforcement mechanisms act on agents' minds and how they regulate agents' conduct is pivotal to achieve a full comprehension of societal regulatory mechanisms. If institutions modify the mind, it is the mind itself that allows them to evolve. Therefore, cognitive properties and patterns are crucial to understand institutional change, its transmission and selection[2].

Several eminent scholars have been confronted with the thorny issue of the nature of social institutions, and different and interesting answers have been put forward (for a review, see Crawford and Ostrom 1995; Hodgson 2006; Ostrom 2005, Steinmo 2010). Here, we will not go into the debate concerning the definition of institutions. Rather, we argue that their emergence, change and reproduction cannot be effectively accomplished unless they feed back to the agents' minds, i.e. on what people believe and want. This process is inherently complex because social members (intentionally or not) react to the feedback of cultural information, selecting and reinforcing given inputs while rejecting others. Thus, to emerge and evolve in the social world, a social phenomenon must also be incorporated and prove adaptive in the human mind.

In the present work, we suggest that we cannot grasp the origin and change of institutions if we do not take into account the mental processes underlying

---

[1] In 3.1, an analysis of what we mean by a norm is proposed.

[2] By evolution, we follow Hodgson's definition: "an adequate explanation of the evolution of such a system must involve the three darwinian principles of variation, inheritance and selection" (Hodgson and Knudsen, 2006, p.5).

the behavioural changes and the resulting structural modifications. Individuals are goal-oriented organisms that act in the external world according to what they believe and want, trying to reduce the discrepancy between the actual state of the world and the represented one. The complex interplay between beliefs, intentions, and goals of multiple interacting agents gives rise to a variety of social structures but, also, selects among these structures, strengthening some of them at the expense of others, and ensuring them greater longevity than others. As stated by Hodgson: "Generally, institutions enable ordered thought, expectation, and action by imposing form and consistency on human activities. They depend upon the thoughts and activities of individuals but are not reducible to them." (Hodgson 2006, p.2).

Searle (1995; 2005), who emphasized the importance of mental representations for institutions to mould and constrain human behaviour, proposed three primitive notions on which institutional reality is based. Collective intentionality, assignment of function and status functions are the building blocks of institutional reality, along with the deontic powers issued by institutions themselves. This view gives prominence to the ontology of institutional facts, leaving unanswered the question of how people decide what a rule is and whether to comply with it or not. Crawford and Ostrom (1995) developed a "grammar of institutions" in order to provide structural descriptions of institutional statements. The syntax of this grammar "operationalizes the structural descriptions; it identifies common components of institutional statements and establishes the set of components that comprise each type of institutional statement" (Crawford and Ostrom 1995, p. 583). Crawford and Ostrom's grammar remarkably illustrates the way institutions affect individual expectations about the actions of others and the consequences of their own actions, but the cognitive processes responsible for these dynamics are neglected.

Tummolini and Castelfranchi (2006) proposed an analysis of institutions from the standpoint of cognitive science. They concentrated on the conceptual dimension of institutions, developing an account of institutional actions as collective actions with specific cognitive and behavioural mediators. Their analysis points to the importance of taking into account what is inside agents' minds in order to explain both individual and collective behaviours.

3 Evolution of institutions: the complex interplay of mental and social fitness landscapes

Moving from Hodgson's (2007) criticisms to both methodological individualism and methodological collectivism, we would like to add to this debate by tracing a third path. According to Hodgson, the process of construction of social reality cannot be reduced either to individuals' actions solely nor to pre-existing structures and cultures. To explain the complex interplay between individual and social structure, it is necessary to account for the role that cognition plays in linking the micro-level of individual action to the macro-level of social structure. Cognition acts, indeed, as a medium between micro and macro, helping to explain on the one hand how the macro-social system affects and possibly influences agents, and on the other hand, how macro-social phenomena may be derived from single interactions (Conte and Castelfranchi 1995).

In order to grasp the meaning of evolving institutions, the cognitive properties and patterns driving individuals' (inter)-actions must be taken into account. Minds and institutions are strongly intertwined since the latter evolve only when immerging in the mind. As suggested by Castelfranchi (1998), with immergence, we are referring here to a sub-case of the process of *downward causation* (Campbell 1974; Emmeche et al. 2000; Gilbert 2002; Hodgson 2007; Conte et al. 2007; Andrighetto and Conte forthcoming).

In our view, the emergence of a sub-set of complex social phenomena, such as institutions and social norms, occurs not only as an effect of processes at the individual level, but also through a complex loop including "upward" and "downward" processes affecting each other. In the next section, a detailed description of this social process is provided. Emerging social structures are necessarily affected by the mental mechanisms of the individuals involved, who in turn select among social structures, strengthening some of them at the expense of others, and contributing to their evolution. While acting on and selecting among institutions, the human mind also evolves. It is this complex process that we are interested in exploring.

3.1 Institutions acting on minds: norms and their immergence

We have broadly defined institutions as systems producing and enacting the norms that regulate a given society. This asks for a definition of what we mean by a *norm*.

As proposed by Ullmann-Margalit (1977), norms are *prescribed* guides for conduct. It is their prescriptive strength – what Gilbert (1983) called *mandatory force* – that makes norms differ from mere social habits. In order to motivate people to comply with them, social norms and their prescriptive character need to immerge (Castelfranchi 1998; Andrighetto et al. 2007; Conte et al. 2007; Andrighetto and Conte forthcoming) into people's minds and shape their mental representations. In our view, a norm – be it social, legal or moral – is a two-sided, internal (mental) and external (social), object, coming into existence only when it emerges, not only through the minds of the agents involved, but also into their minds (Castelfranchi and Conte 1999; Conte and Castelfranchi 2006). Norms depend for their emergence upon individuals, but they also have the power to modify the minds and behaviours of the agents, determining new properties on the micro-level by means of which the effect is reproduced. A recursive interaction between both levels is established by a *complex feedback loop*. This result is usually generated through a number of intermediate loops. *Before* any global effect emerges, specific local events affect the generating systems, their beliefs, goals, and operating rules, in such a way that the macroscopic effect is more likely to be *reproduced* by agents. More specifically, the emergence of social norms is a major circuit including several local loops, in which:

- partial or initial observable macroscopic effects of local behaviours retroact on (a subset of) the agents' minds, modifying them and producing new internal states, emotions, normative beliefs, normative goals, etc.;
- normative beliefs start spreading through the agents' minds;
- agents communicate internal states to one another, thus activating a process of normative influencing;
- agents' behaviours progressively conform to the spreading beliefs;
- initial macroscopic effects are reinforced or weakened depending on the type of mental states spreading.

Emergence of social norms is due to the agents' behaviours, but the agents' behaviours are due to the mental mechanisms controlling and (re)-producing them (immergence).

We suggest that institutions facilitate the immergence of norms. They help them to become installed in human minds, by verifying both the CAN DO (abilities, competencies, resources etc.) and the WILL DO (intention) conditions for norm compliance.

On the one hand, institutions verify the CAN DO condition by providing social agents with the *social technology* necessary for satisfying the norms. For example, there are states that people acquire only by means of institutions. People get married only via a given institutional action. At the same time, there are actions that can be accomplished only by institutions, i.e. by people that *count as* institutions (representatives; see Jones and Sergot 1996), for example marrying, exacting taxes, issuing laws, directing the traffic, inflicting penalties, etc.

On the other hand instead, institutions verify the *WILL DO* condition, by acting so that social members *want* to obey the norms. Autonomous individuals ignore obligations unless they want to comply with them. Institutions act so as to enforce or produce such a will (see Section 5 for a description of how enforcing institutions works). This may be brought about by non-cognitive factors, such as coercion, etc. but more often it is realized by means of *cognitive influencing* (see Conte and Castelfranchi 1995).

To sum up, institutions install norms by executing complex plans of cognitive influencing, i.e., by transmitting beliefs in order to strengthen or generate new goals for their members. Once norms are installed in their minds, social members are enabled to behave accordingly.

3.1.1 Simulating the complex loop of norm emergence

In order to test the role of immergence in the emergence and spreading of social norms, some agent-based simulations have been carried out (Andrighetto et al. 2010; Campennì et al. 2009; Troitzsch 2008; Lotzmann et al. 2008). To implement such a complex dynamics is necessary to model agents that are able to recognize norms, generate new normative representations and act on the basis of them, and finally to influence each other by communication. This kind of agent modelling adds a further level of complexity at the micro level by introducing cognitive properties that make possible for the macro-social effect to immerge in the minds of the agents.

These simulations compared the behaviour of a population of normative agents provided with the ability to recognize norms (*Norm Recognizers*), generate normative beliefs and act on the basis of those representations and a population of *Social Conformers* whose behaviour is determined only by a rule of imitation.

One of the structural conditions under which conformism hardly yields convergence is the *multi-setting world*, i.e. a world in which agents move among settings based on personal sequences, and linger on each of them according to personal agendas. In real life, agents move from public offices to private residences, from sport and shopping centres to underground stations and from these to cinemas, pubs, etc. Suppose that different options for action are available in each setting. For example, you can play music, eat, and drink in pubs; get undressed, work on your biceps and take a shower in a fitness centre; buy a ticket, take a seat and watch a movie at the cinema, etc. Suppose also there is one action common to all settings – say, joining a queue, if there is one, at each entrance. How can simple conformers converge on the common action if they continuously move from one setting to another?

Our simulation data (Campennì et al. 2009; Andrighetto et al. 2010) show that even social conformers with a persistent memory take long to converge on the common action. Instead, agents converge *more easily* and *faster*, when enabled to form normative mental representations and act based upon them. Furthermore, in a multi-setting world, norm immergence produces a different observable dynamic than other, simpler, rules like imitation do. In particular, as to *within*-setting comparison, norm recognizers form and adopt different norms in the same setting, while social conformers rapidly converge on the same action. But whilst *between*-setting distribution presents sharp boundaries among social conformers, who hardly converge on the common action, it is much smoother among normative agents, who are more autonomous, tolerate perturbation, but gradually converge on the common action.

Convergence on the common action takes time to emerge. Alternative *candidate* norms (hypothetical norms) struggle in the minds of the agents, long before convergence is achieved. We call *norm latency* the time interval between norm immergence (first appearance of a norm in the mind) and its emergence. Norm latency varies as a function of many factors, number of settings, alternative options, etc. Under varying circumstances, for example raising and removing physical or social barriers among settings, the observable dynamic of norms varies as well. Convergence declines and reappears for many cycles, a phenomenon that would hardly be generated under different local rules.

4 The mind acting on institutions

When focusing on the differences between cultural and biological evolution, generally the role of beliefs is overestimated while the role of goals, decisions, preferences, obligations, values, emotions, motivations, etc. is underestimated. The representational side of intelligence is emphasized while its proactive or motivational aspects are ignored. In general, the mind is perceived as a camera for reproduction, rather than as *the matter on which social reality is implemented and the instrument through which it works.*

In the previous section, we showed that social institutions install norms by acting on the mind. However, this process is inherently complex because social members react to norm installation and other institutional action, by selecting and reinforcing given inputs while rejecting others. Social institutions compete with one another and with other social cultural phenomena both in the external reality, and in the mental one. As argued in the next subsection, *the mind is one of the two environments in which cultural evolution unfolds.* To evolve, a cultural pattern must gain ground in the social observable environment, but also in the mental non-directly observable one. Hence, social institutions and other cultural patterns compete within the mind prior than, and in order to compete within, the external reality. The mind is an arena for competition and not only the substrate of institutions.

Institutions winning within the mind are likely to also win in the external reality. Once they out-compete rival aspects of culture in real matters, they will appear stronger and more powerful, and probably gain more ground in the minds of subjects. But the process starts within the mind: the institution that conquers the minds of subjects will be better retained and will last longer than others. It will evolve at the expense of others. And yet, there are two cases in which a given institution does not fit the mental environment.

The first case occurs when norms, rules and enforcing mechanisms cannot be *executed* by individuals, both the norm addressees and the norm defenders (magistrates, policemen, etc.). As to norm addressees, consider the warning cigarette package labels in the antismoking campaign. The efficacy of these announcements, as compared to other antismoking measures, is lower than expected, especially with heavy smokers. As the latter prove sensible to other measures (for example, the appeal to social responsibility toward passive smokers), the explanation for their indifference to frightening warnings cannot be found in the syndrome of cessation. A popular explanation proposed for this phenomenon (Xu 2002) refers to the marginal utility of quitting smoking, which is expected to be an inverse function of the duration of smoking habits. Heavy smokers won't invest what for them is a major effort for a minor risk reduction. This aspect of the campaign, designed to enforce the decision to quit smoking (or other forms of addiction), did not fit the deciding systems' machinery. Hence, it proved ineffective. The "smoking kills" sign sits on cigarette packages but consumers pay no serious attention to it.

Second, social institutions prove unfit when they are not *acceptable* for their members, as they contrast with pre-existing ones, or are based on weaker values and authorities, etc. To fight the practice of infibulation in non-Muslim countries by forbidding it in public health structures proved more dangerous than useless, as immigrant mothers turned to non-professional practitioners with far more harmful results for the health of their daughters and a negative impact on the budget of the health care system than would have been the case, had the poor children been allowed to receive public treatment.

The preceding analysis shows that the fitness landscape of social institutions is not only the external physical and social environment, but also the internal, mental one. Each is characterized by its own criterion of selection: in the mental arena, institutions fight for feasibility and acceptance; in the external environment they fight for dominance and survival. But of course they fight in the mind in order to survive in the external world.

The interplay between the two fitness landscapes of cultural evolution is fairly complex. Institutions out-competed in the mind can hardly survive. On the other hand, institutions that prove fit to the mental environment, might become unfit within the social environment. Conquering the mind is not sufficient, as the later history of infibulation shows. The sensible practice of symbolic infibulation, increasing in Somali and imported between 1996 and 1998 into Western countries, was abandoned after a promising start. In these countries, it was probably not a governmental priority. These are but a few unrelated examples of specific institutional phenomena.

5 The evolution of enforcing institutions

In the following section we will provide a more systematic analysis of three different systems of norm enforcement institutions, revenge-based, punishment-based and sanction-based institutions, under the hypotheses that they represent three different steps in an evolutionary process. We argue that the mental underpinnings of these social systems are at the same time the cause and effect of their evolution, reinforcing the social systems they allowed to evolve and being reinforced by them.
This section is devoted to:

- identify and model the cognitive underpinnings characterizing different reactions to an aggression, with the aim to demonstrate that high level cognitive systems are pivotal to the evolution of enforcing institutions;
- draw an ideal evolutionary trajectory of different enforcement institutions, in particular focusing on the transition from institutions based on revenge controlling tribal societies and the culture of honour to those based on sanction at the basis of modern societies, based on the cognitive mechanisms previously identified.

Concerning the first point, humans employ different forms of reaction to a wrong that can be differentiated on the basis of their mental antecedents, the way in which they influence the future conduct of others, and the functions they aim to achieve. In other words, the mind of the avenger is not the mind of the punisher and this distinction has several implications for modelling enforcing institutions, as we argue in what follows.

When facing a wrong, the decision to react can be pursued according to three different strategies: revenge, punishment and sanction. We are perfectly aware of the fact that there are also other relevant phenomena, like retaliation, and that it can be very difficult to draw sharp distinctions among these three. However, we decided to focus on these and we arrange them on an ideal continuum that moves from revenge towards punishment and sanction. These three strategies can be arranged on two axes: cognitive complexity and intentionality of deterrence. In this way, revenge easily appears to be the lowest in cognitive complexity and deterrence is an emergent and unintended self-reinforcing effect. The opposite is true for sanction (high cognitive complexity and intentional deterrence), whereas punishment occupies an intermediate position. Differences in the kind of cognitive influence mainly refer to the cognitive influencing processes implied: in revenge only beliefs are said to be influenced, whereas much more complexity is required in sanctioning behaviour.

It is worth noticing that Foucault (1975), in his historical analysis of the origin and change of the power to punish, proposed an analogous path linking corporal punishment, aimed at repairing the injury, to other forms of retribution focused more on the mind than on the body that will always be affected by punishment – because we cannot imagine a non-corporal punishment. But in the modern system, Foucault says, the body is arranged, regulated and supervised rather than tortured. At the same time, the overall aim of the penal process becomes the reform of the soul, rather than the punishment of the body.

In what follows we analyze the cognitive patterns of revenge, punishment and sanctioning as enforcement mechanisms, showing their changes along an ideal evolutionary trajectory.

5.1 Revenge

Revenge, according to the Merriam-Webster dictionary, is "punishment inflicted in retaliation for an injury or offence". In Elster's terms (1990) it is "the attempt at some cost or risk to oneself, to impose suffering upon those who made one suffer, because they have made one suffer" (p. 862). Broadly speaking, the term 'revenge' refers to two diverse but connected phenomena. In the first of these, revenge is a social ritual that requires and prescribes specific behaviours to group members to repair an offence.

Ethnographic studies highlighted the transition from tribal to modern societies, in which retributive concepts of law and the creation of institutions replaced vengeance and avoided blood feuds (Boehm 1986). Posner (1980) suggests that revenge and retribution may be partially determined by historical and economic circumstances, such the private enforcement of law and high probabilities of detecting and punishing offences. When these conditions are met, a pure vengeance system may appear, although it is unlikely to be optimal. These systems are not completely extinguished, as the culture of honour in the southern United States (Nisbett 1993; Nisbett and Cohen 1996) and the Kanun in Albania demonstrate. The Kanun, a customary set of laws used mostly in northern Albania and Kosovo, disciplined people's reactions to murder (blood revenge or *gjakmarrje*) and other offences (*hakmarrje*) according to the roles and degree of kinship of all the people involved. Shirking revenge or taking it without respecting what is stated in the Kanun leads to the same result: honour cannot be restored and the whole family or clan is to blame. It is worth noticing that, in general, retributive concepts of law and the creation of institutions are considered advancements to replace vengeance and avoid blood feuds, but the Kanun itself was a social institution aimed at preserving social order (Gjeov 1989) that has been substituted with criminal law. Apparently, the Kanun did not disappear completely and in some areas it is still observed, showing how an institution that is preserved in the mind can out-compete another centrally enforced institution, because the latter one is not recognized as such.

In the second class of these phenomena, revenge is an individual behaviour, which is present both in human societies (Zaibert 2006) and non-human primate groups (Jensen, Call and Tomasello, 2007). Turning our attention to individual factors, the avenger wants to repay the damage she suffered with an equal or greater offence, no matter how risky or dangerous this retaliation is. In a sense, we can say that the avenger is a "backward-looker" who revolves around the past and acts in the present to rebalance what happened, with no concern for the future. Vengeance is not pursued to affect the likelihood that the wrongdoer will repeat the aggression in the future, inducing her to cooperate next time or deterring her from further aggression. Long term, strategic planning does not seem to characterize it, although unintended deterrence effects can be obtained.

Revenge is motivated not only by the desire to make the target suffer, but also by the goal to change the target's and audience's beliefs about the avenger, in order to restore the *image* that has been damaged by the aggression suffered. In this case cognitive influence is aimed at changing the beliefs of the wrongdoer and of the audience, whereas motivational representations are left aside. The avenger aims to repay the damage she suffered with an equal or greater offence in order to change the target's and audience's *beliefs* about himself. Revenge is a way to regain one's position after an offence and this applies also to the symbolic dimension: the avenger wants to restore his image, damaged by the aggression suffered. Revenge is aimed to modify what the others believe about the avenger, its role and status. Presumably, the greater the offence, the more efficacious the image restoration.

5.2 Punishment

Enforcing institutions have evolved with society: starting out as a simple system of revenge and retribution imposed by the individual, family, or tribe, it soon grew as an institution characterized by a higher concern for *deterrence* and rehabilitation. Institutions controlling modern societies moved from systems based on revenge to ones based on *punishment*. In primitive society enforcement was left to the individuals wronged, or their families, and was vindictive or retributive: in quantity and quality it would bear no special relation to the character or gravity of the offence. Gradually, it arose the idea of proportionate punishment, of which the characteristic type is the *lex talionis* of early Roman law or in the Old Testament and Koran.

As a deterrent, punishment serves to dissuade people from engaging in activities deemed wrong by law and the population, thus reducing the frequency and likelihood of future offences. Deterrence theory suggests that punishment works by modifying the relative costs and benefits of the situation, so that wrongdoing becomes a less attractive option (Bentham 1962; Becker 1968). Despite revenge, punishment is not inflicted in retribution for an offence or transgression, but it is a reaction intentionally aimed to minimize the chance that the aggressor will repeat the act again (Giardini, Andrighetto and Conte 2010). Thus, punishment is not driven by backward-looking considerations, as revenge is, and *deterrence* is intentionally pursued.

This enforcing mechanism, controlling modern societies, is not at all easy to distinguish from revenge (Zaibert 2006), at least from a mere behavioural point of view. Cognitive modelling allows us to disentangle them on the basis of their mental antecedents and the way in which they influence the future conduct of others. The punisher and the avenger are aimed at influencing and modifying the target and the audience's minds in different ways: unlike the latter, the punisher has the explicit goal to deter the wrongdoer from repeating the aggression in the future, with the further effect of preventing blood feuds and giving more stability to the social order. To achieve this goal, the punisher should act in such a way that the offender, and possibly the audience, generates the goal – usually under threat of punishment – of abstaining from doing the target action again.

5.3 Sanction

Social order can be explained as the result of the deterrence effect of punishment. However what makes human cooperation so spectacular with respect to all other species is the presence of social norms, efficiently orchestrating social life. When enforcing institutions are able to work in tandem with social norms spontaneously governing human societies, they are much more viable in achieving and maintaining compliance and are more robust across time.

Elinor Ostrom has identified a series of spontaneously emerged institutions, across several centuries and countries, enforcing social order through mechanisms – such as graduated fines – able to elicit social norms and successfully favouring collective actions (Ostrom 2005; see also Casari 2007). These institutions are designed in such a way that norm immergence, and as a consequence norm compliance, are facilitated. Punishment, if properly designed, teaches people what they are able to do in their society and what behaviours are acceptable, and which actions will bring them punishment. We refer to institutions enforcing social order through mechanisms intentionally aimed to focus people's attention on social norms and to condemn their violation as *sanction-based*, and we consider them the last step of the institutional evolutionary process.

As in previous work (Giardini et al. 2010; Andrighetto and Villatoro, 2011; Villatoro et al. 2011), we use sanction to indicate the enforcing mechanism that, in addition to imposing a cost for the wrongdoing, as punishment does, is also intentionally aimed at signalling to the offender (and possibly to the audience) that his conduct is *not approved of* because it has violated a social norm[3]. The type of cognitive influencing sanction exerts on the offender is more complex than those in revenge and punishment. The sanctioner uses scolding to reign in wrongdoers, or expresses indignation or blame, or simply mentions that the targeted behaviour violated a norm. As suggested by Castelfranchi's behavioural implicit communication theory (Castelfranchi, 2006; Giardini and Castelfranchi 2004), through these actions, the sanctioner focuses people's attention on different normative aspects, such as: (a) the existence and violation of a norm; (b) the causal link between violation and sanction: "you are being sanctioned because you violated that norm" (c) the probability that violations will be sanctioned; (d) the fact that the sanctioner is acting *as* a norm defender.

As recent experimental evidence shows (Cialdini et al. 1990; Bicchieri 2006; Houser and Xiao 2010; Galbiati and Vertova 2008), the norm focusing effect of sanction plays an important role in eliciting compliance. Sanction signals to the wrongdoer (and possibly to the audience) the existence and violation of a norm, and that the violation is condemned, thus endowing the offender with new normative knowledge. This normative knowledge has the effect of framing the situation in such a way that not only motivations to avoid costs are activated, but normative motivations as well[4], and, what is more important, of increasing their salience (Andrighetto and Villatoro 2011; Villatoro et al. 2011).

Thus, despite punishment, we suggest that sanction has the further effect, possibly aimed at by the sanctioner, to encourage the target to ground future decisions on *internal* evaluative criteria, established by the norm. Of course, agents usually comply with norms only to avoid sanctions. Nonetheless, their behaviour results from norm immergence: they act in accordance with what they believe to be a norm, if only to avoid the sanction that they have learned to expect from its violation.

As shown in previous work (Andrighetto and Villatoro 2011; Villatoro et al. 2011), both punishment-based and sanction-based institutions allow social order to be reached and maintained, but the latter achieve cooperation in a more stable way and at a lower cost for the group.

---

[3] Clearly, also punishment can have a norm-signalling effect as by-product, but only sanctions are aimed to achieve this effect.

[4] With normative motivation, we refer to the fact that people are disposed to obey the norm even when there is little possibility of instrumental gain, future reciprocation, and when the surveillance rate is very small.

6 Concluding remarks

The mind is the hinge between behaviour and society, individuals and institu-tions. It actually evolved specific capacities and properties to solve problems of adaptation encountered by higher-level species in their social environment. This is one of the main lessons that can be drawn from Castelfranchi's work, as he spent a significant part of his scientific life imparting it the social and evolutionary sciences as well as in some vital fields of the ICT. But from this lesson can easily be derived that the mind is a fitness landscape itself: cul-tural artefacts' variants compete not only on the social, but also on the mental grounds. Based on both the foundational lesson and its corollary, this paper presents a view of institutional dynamics as a complex co-evolutionary process involving the dynamics of the mind.

After an initial analysis of institutions as systems issuing and enacting the norms in force in a given society, by means of complex forms of cognitive in-fluencing, we discussed at some length a peculiar aspect of the cultural and in particular institutional evolution, i.e. a two-layered fitness landscape, includ-ing the mental and the social environment. In our view, the mind contributes to the evolution of institutions by selecting from among different institutions competing for survival and dominance first in the mind and then in the soci-ety. The mind selects in the most realizable and acceptable institutional forms while rejecting the others, thereby making institutions evolve. We then dis-cussed the application of an agent-based simulation approach to the study of the subject matter. In particular, we showed that this methodology allows to operationalize the notion of immergence, and to check the role of cognitive mechanisms in the emergence and evolution of social norms.

Finally, we examined the mental underpinnings of three different systems of norm enforcement, revenge, punishment and sanction, arguing that the transition from one to the other has been allowed by specific cognitive patterns, and suggesting that these mental mechanisms selected from among given social structures, at the same time reinforcing and being reinforced by them.

References

1. Andrighetto, G., Campennì, M, Conte, R., Paolucci, M., (2007) On the Immergence of Norms: a Normative Agent Architecture. In G. P. Trajkovski and S. G. Collins (Eds.) *Emergent Agents and Socialities: Social and Organizational Aspects of Intelligence. Papers from the AAAI Fall Symposium*. Menlo Park (CA): The AAAI Press (Technical Report FS-07-04).
2. Andrighetto, G., Campennì, M., Cecconi, F., Conte, R. (2010). The Complex Loop of Norm Emergence: a Simulation Model. In K. Takadama, C. C. Revilla, G. Deffuant (Eds.) Simulating Interacting Agents and Social Phenomena: The Second World Congress, Agent-Based Social Systems 7, pp. 17-33 DOI 10.1007/978-4-431-99781-8_2, Springer
3. Andrighetto, G., Conte, R., (forthcoming) Loops in Social Dynamics. In R. Conte, G., Andrighetto, M. Campennì (Eds.) *Minding Norms. Mechanisms and dynamics of social order in agent society*. Oxford Series on Cognitive Models and Architectures. New York: Oxford University Press.

4. Andrighetto, G., Villatoro, D. (2011), Beyond the carrot and stick approach to enforce-ment: An agent-based model. In Kokinov, B., Karmiloff-Smith, A., Nersessian, N. J. (Eds.), *European Perspectives on Cognitive Science*. New Bulgarian University Press, ISBN 978-954-535-660-5.
5. Bandura, A. (1991). Social cognitive theory of moral thought and action. In W. M. Kurtines & J. L. Gewirtz (Eds.), *Handbook of moral behavior and development* (Vol. 1, pp. 45-103). Hillsdale (NJ): Lawrence Erlbaum.
6. Bentham, J. (1962). Principles of penal law. In J. Bowring (Ed.), *The Works of Jeremy Bentham* (p. 396). New York: Russell and Russell.
7. Becker, G.S. (1968). Crime and Punishment: An Economic Approach, *Journal of Political Economy*, 76, 169-217.
8. Bicchieri, C. (2006). *The Grammar of Society: the Nature and Dynamics of Social Norms*, Cambridge (MA): Cambridge University Press.
9. Blakemore, S. (1999). *The Meme Machine*. Oxford: Oxford University Press.
10. Boehm, C. (1986). *Blood Revenge: The Enactment and Management of Conflict in Montenegro and Other Tribal Societies*. Philadelphia (PA): University of Pennsylvania Press.
11. Boyd, R., Richerson, P. J. (1985). *Culture and the Evolutionary Process*. Chicago (IL): University of Chicago Press.
12. Campennì, M., Andrighetto, G., Cecconi, F., Conte, R. (2009). Normal = Normative? The role of intelligent agents in norm innovation. *Mind & Society*, 8(2), 153-72.
13. Campbell, D.T. (1974). Downward causation in Hierarchically Organized Biological Systems. In F.J. Ayala & T. Dobzhansky (Eds.), *Studies in the Philosophy of Biology*, (pp. 179-186). London/Bastingstoke: Macmillan.
14. Casari, M. (2007). Emergence of endogenous legal institutions: Property rights and community governance in the Italian alps. *The Journal of Economic History*, 67(1), 191-226.
15. Castelfranchi. C. (2006) From Conversation to Interaction via Behavioural Communi-cation. In S. Bagnara and G. Crampton-Smith (Eds.) *Theories and Practice in Interaction Design* (pp. 157-179). New Jersey: Erlbaum.
16. Castelfranchi, C. (2001). Towards a Cognitive Memetics: Socio-Cognitive Mechanisms for Memes Selection and Spreading. *Journal of Memetics – Evolutionary Models of Informa-tion Transmission*, 5 (http://jom-emit.cfpm.org/2001/vol5/castelfranchi_c.html)
17. Castelfranchi, C. (1998). Simulating with cognitive agents: The importance of cognitive emergence. In Conte R., Sichman J., Gilbert N. (Ed.), *Multi-Agent System and Agent-Based Simulation* (pp. 26-44). Berlin: Springer.
18. Castelfranchi C., Conte R. (1999). From conventions to prescriptions. Towards a unified theory of norms. *AI&Law*, 7, 323-340.
19. Castelfranchi, C., Parisi, D. (1980). *Linguaggio, conoscenze e scopi*. Bologna, Il Mulino.
20. Cavalli-Sforza, L.L., Feldman M. (1981). *Cultural Transmission and Evolution*. Princeton (NJ): Princeton University Press.
21. Cialdini, R. B., Reno, R. R., Kallgren, C.A. (1990). A focus theory of normative conduct: Recycling the concept of norms to reduce littering in public places. *Journal of Personality and Social Psychology*, 58, 1015-1026.
22. Clutton-Brock, T. H., Parker, G. A. (1995). Punishment in animal societies. *Nature*, 373, 209-216.
23. Coleman, J. (1998). *Foundations of social theory*. Cambridge (MA): Belknap Press of Har-vard University Press.
24. Conte, R. (2000). Memes through (Social) Minds. In Aunger R. (Ed.) *Darwinizing Culture. The Status of Memetics as a Science* (pp. 83-120). Oxford: Oxford University Press.
25. Conte, R., Andrighetto, G., Campennì, M., (Eds.) *Minding Norms. Mechanisms and dynam-ics of social order in agent society*. Oxford Series on Cognitive Models and Architectures. New York: Oxford University Press.
    Conte, R., Andrighetto, G., Campennì, M. (Eds.) (Forthcoming). *Minding Norms*. Oxford Series on Cognitive Models and Architectures. Oxford: Oxford University Press.
26. Conte, R., Andrighetto, G., Campennì, M., (2009). *On Norm Internalization. A Position Paper*. Paper presented at The Sixth Conference of the European Social Simulation As-sociation, University of Surrey, Guildford, September 14-18, 2009

27. Conte, R., G. Andrighetto, M. Campenni, and M. Paolucci. (2007). Emergent and im-mergent effects in complex social systems. In *Proceedings of AAAI Symposium, Social and Organizational Aspects of Intelligence.*
28. Conte, R., Castelfranchi, C. (2006). The mental path of norms. *Ratio Juris*, 19(4), 501–517.
29. Conte, R., Castelfranchi, C. (1995). *Cognitive and social action.* London: University College of London Press.
30. Crawford, S., Ostrom, E. (2005). A grammar of institutions. In E. Ostrom (Ed), *Understanding Institutional Diversity* (pp. 137-74). Princeton (NJ): Princeton University Press.
31. Crawford, S., Ostrom, E. (1995). A Grammar of Institutions. *American Political Science Review*, 89(3), 582-600.
32. Dawkins, R. (1976). *The selfish genes.* Oxford: Oxford University Press.
33. Dennett, D. (1995). *Darwin's Dangerous Idea: Evolution and the Meanings of Life.* New York: Simon & Schuster.
34. Durkheim, E. (1951). *Suicide*, New York: The Free Press.
35. Elster, J. (1990). Norms of revenge. *Ethics*, 100(4), 862–885.
36. Emmeche, C., Koppe, S., Stjernfelt, F. (2000). Levels, Emergence, and Three Versions of Downward Causation. In P.B. Andersen, Claus Emmeche, N.O. Finnemann & P.V. Christiansen (Eds.), *Downward Causation* (pp. 13-34). Aarhus, Denmark: University of Aarhus Press.
37. Foucault, M. (1975). *Discipline and Punish: the Birth of the Prison*, New York: Random House.
38. Galbiati, R., Vertova, P. (2008). Obligations and Cooperative Behaviour in Public Good Games. *Games and Economic Behavior*, 64(1), 146-170.
39. Giardini, F., Andrighetto, G., Conte, R. (2010). A cognitive model of punishment. In S. Ohlsson, aR. Catrambone (Eds.), *Proceedings of the 32nd Annual Conference of the Cognitive Science Society* (pp. 1282-1288). Austin, TX: Cognitive Science Society
40. Giardini, F., Castelfranchi, C. (2004). Behavioural Implicit Communication for Human-Robot Interaction. In *AAAI Fall Symposium Series*, 21-24 October, Arlington, Virginia (USA) (pp. 91-96.), Technical Report FS-04-05, Menlo Park (CA): AAAI Press.
41. Gilbert, M. (1983). Agreements, Conventions, and Language. *Synthese*, 54(3), 375-407.
42. Gilbert, N. (2002). Varieties of emergence. Paper presented at the *Agent 2002 Conference.Social agents: ecology, exchange, and evolution*, Chicago (downloadable at http://surrey.ac.uk/sociology/people/nigel_gilbert_complete_list_of_publications.htm)
43. Gintis, H. (2004). The genetic side of gene-culture coevolution: internalization of norms and prosocial emotions. *Journal of Economic Behavior & Organization*, 53(1), 57-67.
44. Gjeov, S. (1989). *Kanuni i leke dukagjinit. albanian text collected and arranged by shtjefn gjeov*, (translated by leonard fox). New York: Gjonlekaj Publishing Company.
45. Hodgson, G. M. (2007). Institutions and Individuals: Interaction and Evolution. *Organization Studies*, 28(1), 95-116.
46. Hodgson, G. M. (2006). What Are Institutions? *Journal of Economic Issues*, 40(1), 1-25.
47. Hodgson, G.M., Knudsen, T. (2006) Why we need a generalized Darwinism, and why generalized Darwinism is not enough. *Journal of Economic Behavior & Organization*, 61, 1–19.
48. Houser, D. & Xiao, E. (2010). Understanding context effects, *Journal of Economic Behavior & Organization*, 73(1), 58-61.
49. Jensen, K., Call, J., Tomasello, M. (2007). Chimpanzees are vengeful but not spiteful. *Proceedings of the National Academy of Sciences*, 104, 13046–13050
50. Jones, A.J.I., Sergot, M.J. (1996). A formal characterisation of institutionalised power. *Journal of the IGPL*, 4(3), 429-445.
51. Kelsen, H. (1979). *General Theory of Norms*. London: Clarendon Press.
52. Lotzmann, U. (2008) TRASS – A Multi-Purpose Agent-based Simulation Framework for Complex Traffic Simulation Applications. In Bazzan, A. L. C. and Klügl, F., (Eds.), *Multi-Agent Systems for Traffic and Transportation*. Hershey (PA): IGI Global.
53. Nisbett, R. E. (1993). Violence and U. S. regional culture. *American Psychologist*, 48, 441-449.
54. Nisbett, R. E., Cohen, D. (1996). *Culture of honor*. Boulder (CO): Westview Press.

55. Ostrom, E., (2005). *Understanding Institutional Diversity*. Princeton (NJ): Princeton University Press.
56. Parisi, D., Castelfranchi, C. (1984). Appunti di scopistica. In R. Conte and M. Miceli (Eds.) *Esplorare la vita quotidiana*. Roma, Il Pensiero Scientifico.
57. Posner, R. (1980). Retribution and related concepts of punishment. *Journal of Legal Studies*, 9, 71–92.
58. Richerson, P.J., Boyd, R. (2005). *Not by Genes Alone: How culture transformed human evolution*. Chicago (IL): University of Chicago Press.
59. Scott, J. F., (1971). *Internalization of Norms: A Sociological Theory of Moral Commitment*, Englewoods Cliffs (N.J.): Prentice-Hall.
60. Searle, J. R. (2005). What is an Institution? *Journal of Institutional Economics*, 1, 1-22.
61. Searle, J. R. (1995). *The Construction of Social Reality*. New York: Simon & Schuster.
62. Steinmo, S. (2010). The Evolution of Modern States. Sweden, Japan, and the United States. Cambridge University Press.
63. Tummolini, L., Castelfranchi, C. (2006). The cognitive and behavioral mediation of institutions: Toward an account of institutional actions. *Cognitive Systems Research*, 7(2-3), 307-323.
64. Troitzsch, K. G. (2008) Simulating collaborative writing: software agents produce a wikipedia. In F. Squazzoni (Ed.), *The Fifth Conference of the European Social Simulation Association*, September 1-5, 2008, Brescia.
65. Ullman-Margalit, E., (1977). *The Emergence of Norms*. Oxford: Clarendon Press.
66. Villatoro, D., Andrighetto, G., Conte, R., Sabater-Mir, J. (2011). Dynamic Sanctioning for Robust and Cost-Efficient Norm Compliance. *Proceedings of the Twenty-Second International Joint Conference on Artificial Intelligence (IJCAI 2011)*.
67. Xiao, E., Houser, D. (2009). Avoiding the sharp tongue: Anticipated written messages promote fair economic exchange. *Journal of Economic Psychology* 30(3), 393-404.
68. Xiao, E., Houser, D. (2006). Punish in Public. IZA discussion paper 1977.
69. Xu, K. T. (2002). Compensating behaviors, regret, and heterogeneity in the dynamics of smoking behavior, *Social Science & Medicine*, 54 (1), 133-146.
70. Zaibert, L. (2006). Punishment and Revenge, *Law and Philosophy*, 25, 81-118.

Chapter 35
On social and organizational reasoning in multi-agent systems

Jaime Simão Sichman

Abstract This paper presents a set of theoretical, architectural and applicative work that allows to validate the following idea: autonomous cognitive agents, immersed on an open environment, can enhance their efficiency and adaptability to environmental changes if they could represent and exploit, by using adequate internal mechanisms, information about the others and about the organizations they are eventually involved with. We also show that agents interactions and organizations form a virtuous circle. On one hand, interactions may generate dynamic bottom-up organizations, named coalitions, making it possible a collective action. On the other hand, if this collective action must be repeated frequently, it is more adequate to create top-down formal organizations, that limit agents interactions and allow them to achieve their global goals more efficiently.

1 Introduction

In order to present our ideas and to justify the usefulness of social and organizational reasoning in open environments, we propose a motivation scenario in section 1.1, followed by a brief description of the current main technological trends in section 1.2.

1.1 Motivation

Let us consider the following scenario, adapted from Erceau and Ferber [31, page 751]:

Jaime Simão Sichman
Laboratório de Técnicas Inteligentes (LTI), Escola Politécnica (EP), Universidade de São Paulo, Brazil
e-mail: jaime.sichman@poli.usp.br

Floor shop 7, late at night. Clotaire, a mobile robot, needs to transport Millie back to her usual workplace. Millie is currently located in floor shop 7, because she has just been repaired by Justin and Jespard, two other robots well known to Millie. Millie weighs currently 200 kg, which is too excessive for Clotaire to carry by herself: she has been designed to carry at most 120 kg. "Oh, that Millie, always with problems and always asking me for help", thinks Clotaire, "and I am not even paid for such a task!". Clotaire is not a transportation robot: in fact, she is a micro-welding specialist, aimed to manipulate and to transport small and delicate objects. However, after having helped Millie to transport several boxes composed of small pieces, in a particular day where all transportation robots were extremely busy and refused to help Millie, this latter is always asking her for help. Fortunately, Berthold, a less specialized transportation robot, which can hold up to 150 kg, is not too busy now, and they both could transport Millie if they work in coordination. She is pretty sure that Berthold will accept to help her, since last night he has been very gentle, kind — and may be interested in her — when at the end of their work turn they stayed together at the oil station shop.

Beyond being a piece of science fiction, this scenario shows some interactions between a group of autonomous robots that have a certain kind of "intelligence", and cooperate to accomplish their work.

The Distributed Artificial Intelligence (DAI) domain, more precisely the Multi-Agent Systems (MAS) domain, is devoted to the study of models, computational architectures and programming languages and environments that could possibly make the previous scenario come true. Differently from Artificial Intelligence (AI) classic studies based on centralized intelligence models, these domains propose to distribute the intelligence among various *agents*, without a centralized global control. The main challenge is to conceive *multi-agent systems*, where each element must be able to perceive, reason, decide, eventually learn and act in a common environment. Since there are many agents co-evolving is the same environment, every agent must be able to interact with the others, for instance in order to coordinate their actions or to solve conflicts.

These kinds of systems give rise to an important shift both on design and programming paradigms:

1. Instead of closed systems, we are faced to *open* systems [44]: entities may arrive and leave dynamically, their individual behavior may change due to the environment's evolution and their social or collective behavior may change in order to better achieve their individual or global goals;
2. Instead of off-line adaptation, we are faced to *on-line* adaptation: the entities themselves, and not the designers anymore, must control and execute their adaptation due to the changing conditions of the environment.

Beyond the Robotics domain, many of the current technological trends show some of these characteristics, as shown next.

1.2 *Current technological trends*

In 2005, the AgentLink — European Co-ordination Action for Agent-Based Computing — has produced a roadmap where several key trends and technological drivers for Information Technology (IT) in the next decenies were presented [57]:

- *Semantic Web*, which aims to enable automatic processing and integration of information on the World Wide Web (WWW) by machines, based on standard patterns and semantic markup;
- *Web Services*, which provide standards to enable the interoperation of several applications running in heterogeneous platforms, and which were possibly developed separately;
- *Peer to Peer Computing*, which enable to create bottom-up functionalities by the interconnections of homogeneous nodes;
- *Grid Computing*, which provides dynamic infrastructure for high-performance computing (HPC) in order to host very large scale scientific processing;
- *Ambient Intelligence*, which enables to dispose thousand of possibly interacting services in a very large net of mobile and/or embarked devices;
- *Self-* Systems, Autonomic Computing*, which provides systems with techniques of auto-management and auto-healing;
- *Complex Systems*, whose interest is to simulate how to manage and to control emergent phenomena in systems composed of thousands or millions of entities.

All these trends show an increase in complexity, considering the number of agents, their heterogeneity and locality, and other properties such as openness and adaptation. Thus, designers of such systems must have appropriate abstractions and concepts to express a way to structure, to control, and to monitor such systems. Moreover, we need to find different and complementary alternatives to ensure that a coherent global behavior may arise from the autonomous individual entities behavior. This idea is certainly related to what is called social order by Castelfranchi [15].

Hence, we are faced with a new class of applications that are neither monolithic nor managed by a single designer and/or team of designers. Our current challenge is to design and produce software according to this new metaphor, where computing is a *social* activity, based on the *interaction* of independent and possibly intelligent entities, that adapt to and co-evolve in a common environment.

One possible answer to this question is to use agent technology, as shown next.

2 Agents and multiagent systems

In order to better characterize the main notions used in MAS, we present respectively in sections 2.1 and 2.2 a brief introduction to the individual entities, the *agents*, and to the systems composed of these entities, the *multi-agent systems*. Finally, in order to better classify the research made in the domain, we present in section 2.3 a MAS Research Classification Grid that will be used in the rest of the chapter.

2.1 Agents

Even after quite 30 years of research in DAI and MAS, there is no a unique and universally accepted definition of the term agent. One of the most cited ones, due to its broad scope, is the one proposed by Ferber [34]:

> *An agent is a real or virtual entity which is emerged in an environment where he can take some actions, which is able to perceive and represent partially this environment, which is able to communicate with the other agents and which possesses an autonomous behavior that is a consequence of his observations, his knowledge and his interactions with the other agents.*

We will adopt here an extension of Ferber's definition, which enables us to focus on social and organizational aspects of agents [8]:

> *An agent is a real or virtual autonomous entity, which is pro-active (he has goals to achieve), reactive (he can perceive and act in the environment), social (he can interact with other agents), able to exhibit organized activity (he can create and follow global rules and norms), in order to meet his design objectives, by eventually interacting with users.*

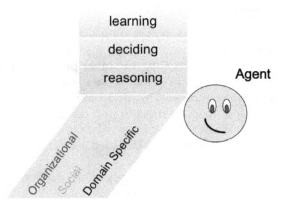

Fig. 1 Agent's internal mechanisms [70].

Regarding their internal composition, there are lots of architectures proposed in the literature, from very simple reactive ones [11, 30] to more complex cognitive architectures [10, 37]. These latter, which are the focus of this work, are composed of several internal mechanisms and representation such as reasoning, decision making and learning.

As shown in figure 1, we believe that these agents' internal mechanisms should be distinguished along three different dimensions:

- *domain specific* dimension, corresponding to the agents' reasoning, decision making and learning capabilities about their own problem solving domain. In our robotic scenario presented in section 1.1, Clotaire can reason about and decide how to perform some micro-welding activities or how to coordinate with Berthold in order to transport Millie back to her original workplace;

- *social* dimension, corresponding to the agents' reasoning, decision making and learning capabilities about the other agents they interact with. In the robotic scenario, Clotaire has activated these internal mechanisms when asking Berthold to help her;
- *organizational* dimension, corresponding to the agents' reasoning, decision making and learning capabilities about the organizations they take part in. In the robotic scenario, Clotaire has activated these internal mechanisms when figuring out that she should not perform a transportation task, since she has got another role in the organization.

All these internal mechanisms and representations contribute to the multiple properties attached to the external, observable behavior of an agent.

2.2 *Multiagent systems*

Briefly speaking, a MAS may be seen as a collection of agents, like the ones described in the previous section, which are immersed in a common environment.

The application domains that are suitable for a multiagent approach are those which are inherently distributed — geographically, temporally, functionally, or semantically — and/or inherently complex, i.e., too big to be solved by a centralized approach. Some examples of application domains are robotics, logistics [59], industrial processes optimization [63], information search in the Internet [40], group decision support systems/serious games [1].

According to Bond and Gasser [9], the main DAI and MAS research problems may be basically divided into five different classes:

- *description, decomposition and allocation of tasks:* how can one easily describe and decompose a complex task into subtasks, statically or dynamically, how are these subtasks to be allocated and in which order they should be performed;
- *interaction, languages and communication:* which primitives should a communication protocol present in order to express the semantic concepts arising in a cooperative work;
- *coordination, control and coherent behavior:* how can one assure a coherent global behavior in a set of agents, each one with its own skills and goals, how should the control of such a system be designed;
- *conflict and uncertainty:* as no agent has total information about its environment, how can the conflicts that may arise be solved, and how should uncertain, incomplete data be dealt with in order to guarantee coherent results;
- *programming languages and environments:* from a computational point of view, which are the programming languages that should be used in such systems, and what are the requirements of an environment to make testing these policies possible.

Having interactions and organizations as a crucial aspect of agency, it is pretty clear that MAS was influenced by ideas and theories coming from several other domains and disciplines:

- *Computer Science/Engineering*: artificial intelligence, distributed systems, software engineering and programming, logics;
- *Social Sciences*: interaction theories;
- *Economics*: utility theory, auction theory;
- *Business Management*: organizational models and design;
- *Biology*: ethological models, emergence;
- *Physics*: force fields, complex systems.

2.3 MAS research classification grid

In order to finish this section, we present a MAS Research Classification Grid, originally proposed in [70], whose aim is to better classify the research made in the MAS domain. In particular, an adaptation of this classification grid was used to classify the papers submitted to the 8th. International Conference on Autonomous Agents and Multiagent Systems (AAMAS 2009) [75, 76], held in Budapest, Hungary, in 2009.

The classification grid is composed of three independent axes, described next.

2.3.1 Research goal axis

According to Farreny [33], there are two complementary perspectives in AI research: *simulation* perspective and *problem solving* perspective. The first one defends the idea that AI is a branch of Cognitive Science, where computers are merely means or instruments to test cognition theories. On the other hand, the second vision understands AI as a branch of Computer Science/Engineering, where ultimately computers are ends: the research goal is to provide solutions for hard problems that cannot be solved with classical approaches. According to this latter view, AI researchers would make "Intelligent Machines Engineering".

Similarly, Castelfranchi [13] advocates the same duality referring to MAS: a *social simulation* (SS) perspective and *distributed problem solving* (DPS) perspective. The first one defends the idea that MAS is a branch of Cognitive Science, interested in analyzing and in explaining why agents interact, cooperate and which mental attitudes are needed to represent such a phenomena. On then other hand, the second vision considers that the goal of MAS is to develop computational techniques, based on multiple agents, their interactions and their organizations, to solve hard problems in a distributed and cooperative way. In other words, MAS researchers would make "Intelligent Machines Societies Engineering ".

We believe that these two perspectives, although philosophically disjoint, not only are not mutually exclusive, but rather complementary. Theories of social cognition may inspire computational methods and algorithms that solve hard problems. When these problems are solved, they may reveal certain hidden aspects of agency that should be incorporated in the underlying theory, thus creating a virtuous circle to MAS research.

2.3.2 Description level axis

Wooldridge and Jennings [83] have identified three description levels in the study and development of MAS:

- *theories:* What are exactly agents? What are their properties, and how can they be formally represented and reasoned about?
- *architectures:* How can agents be constructed in order to satisfy their attended properties? Which hardware and/or software constructs are needed for this task?
- *languages:* How agents should be programmed? Which are the adequate primitives for this task? How can we compile and execute agent-based programs efficiently?

2.3.3 Dimension focus axis

In [28], Demazeau presented the fundamental pieces of a methodology for the development of MAS. According to this methodology, a MAS application could be built from pre-existing building blocks, available in a development environment, similarly to an expert system shell.

This methodology, which later on was called *Vowels*[1], considers that the development of a MAS should be composed of four distinct dimension focus:

- *agents:* characterize the basic active elements of the system;
- *environments:* characterize the passive elements of the system;
- *interactions:* characterize how agents exchange information and control;
- *organizations:* characterize policies to constraint agents interactions.

Figure 2 presents an integrated vision of these three classification axis, represented in a 3D grid. This grid will be used in the rest of this chapter to classify the social and organizational models and applications that will be presented in the next sections.

---

[1] The initials of the four dimensions are respectively A, E, I and O, hence justifying the label.

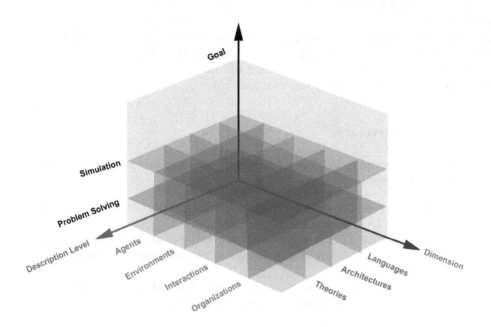

Fig. 2 Classification grid for research in MAS [70].

3 Agents interactions

In order to be able to introduce social reasoning models and applications, we need to characterize somes aspects of agents interactions, which are initially discussed in section 3.1. Dependence Theory, as proposed by Castelfranchi and colleagues [13, 19, 16], is briefly introduced in section 3.2. Based on this theory, $\mathcal{S}$RM [72, 68, 73] and $\mathcal{S}$RM$^+$ [71, 22] models are described in section 3.3, and some applications that were developed using these models are presented in section 3.4. We then present in section 3.5 the classification of these models and applications, according to the MAS Research Classification Grid. Finally, in section 3.6 we present our first conclusion, relating agents interactions to a certain class of agents organizations.

3.1 Basic definitions

First of all, we show the different classes of social interaction models in section 3.1.1. The concepts of social interference and interaction situations are then respectively described in sections 3.1.2 and 3.1.3. Finally, the process of coalition formation is discussed in section 3.1.4.

3.1.1 Social interaction models

Trying to characterize the precognitive bases of social interaction, Conte and Castelfranchi [18] presented two classes of social interaction models:

- *top-down* models: in these models, we consider that the agents have a priori a certain global goal to achieve, and hence cooperation is pre-established as an initial hypothesis. Social interactions are constrained by an organizational structure, as further discussed in section 4, conceived statically, which guide the agents to achieve the global goal for which the systems has been conceived. These models are mostly used in SMA which adopt a DPS perspective;
- *bottom-up* models: in these models, we do not consider a priori that the agents have common goals to achieve. Social interactions result from their efforts to achieve their own goals. There are neither pre-established cooperation nor organizational structures. These models are mostly used in SMA which adopt a SS perspective.

Considering the bottom-up models, we have previously shown in [21] that they can be decomposed in two classes:

- *utility-based* models: according to these models, of which game theory is an example [56, 4], the social world lies on the "*bellum omnium contra omnes*" principle: it is considered as an interference domain between agents, and these latter need necessarily to coordinate, by creating conventions and constraints, in order to achieve a coherent global behavior. The existence of other agents *limits* the power and autonomy of each agent that belongs to the society;
- *complementarity-based* models: these models propose a different vision of social interaction. They consider that agents may have complementary capacities and know-how, related to the goals they want to achieve. Therefore, the existence of other agents *increases* the power and autonomy of each agent that belongs to the society, because an agent that cannot achieve his goals alone can asks for the others' help.

3.1.2 Social interference

Let us suppose that two agents ag_i e ag_j co-exist in a common environment and each of them have his own goals. Conte and Castelfranchi [18] have called *social interference* the effect of ag_i's individual action in ag_j's goal attainment.

This interference may be positive (when ag_i's action facilitates ag_j's goal achievement), negative (when ag_i's action hinders ag_j's goal achievement) or neutral.

Since ag_j can also act in the common environment, it may be interesting to analyze the mutual effects of both agents' actions, i.e., the composition of the social interference of ag_i on ag_j with the one of ag_j on ag_i. This phenomena may be characterized according several patterns, as explained next.

3.1.3 Interaction situations

In order to better characterize social interference, Ferber [34] has proposed the notion of *interaction situation*:

> An interaction situation is a set of behaviors from a group of agents that act in order to achieve their goals, taking into account the constraints related to resource and individual competence scarcity.

Goals Compatibility	Resources Adequacy	Agents Ability	Interaction Situation	Social Interference
compatible	sufficient	sufficient	*independence*	neutral
compatible	sufficient	insufficient	*simple collaboration*	positive
compatible	insufficient	sufficient	*obstruction*	positive
compatible	insufficient	insufficient	*coordinated collaboration*	positive
incompatible	sufficient	sufficient	*pure individual competition*	negative
incompatible	sufficient	insufficient	*pure collective competition*	negative
incompatible	insufficient	sufficient	*individual conflict for resources*	negative
incompatible	insufficient	insufficient	*collective conflict for resources*	negative

Table 1 Interaction situations, adapted from [34].

These interaction situations may be classified according to three distinct dimensions, as presented in table 1[2]:

1. *goals compatibility:* agents' goals are considered compatible/incompatible when the fact of achieving one of them does not/does imply the impossibility to achieve the other;

---

[2] This table is adapted from [34], since in this latter the notion of social interference is not represented.

2. *resources adequacy:* resources are considered sufficient/insufficient when they enable/do not enable the agents to perform their tasks simultaneously;
3. *agents ability:* agents' ability is considered to be sufficient/insufficient when they are/are not able to perform their tasks alone in order to achieve their goals.

When an agent detects that his ability is insufficient to achieve his goal by himself, and if there is a positive social interference, he can try to form a coalition to achieve this goal.

3.1.4 Coalition formation

In this work, we will call *coalition*[3] an emergent, bottom-up group of agents, which is dynamically formed/dismissed for the sole purpose of achieving a certain goal and/or performing a certain task.

Wooldridge and Jennings [82] have proposed a cooperative problem solving process, composed of four phases, that enables a group of agents to form a coalition to try to achieve a certain goal:

1. *Recognition of potential for cooperation*, when some agent recognizes the potential for cooperative action;
2. *Coalition formation*, when the agent that recognized the potential for cooperative action searches for help. If successful, at the end of this phase a group of agents will have a joint commitment to collective action;
3. *Plan formation*, when the agents attempt to negotiate a joint plan that they believe will achieve the desired goal. This phase may use classical AI planning techniques [65, chapter 11], extended to cope with a multiple agent scenario. Moreover, it may be the case that this phase is performed off-line, when the agents must only agree about — and not produce — the plan to be jointly used;
4. *Coalition action*, when the newly agreed plan of joint action is then executed by the agents.

Although absent from the original formulation, there is a fifth phase that needs to happen:

5 *Coalition dissolution*, when the joint action is finished — and possibly the desired goal is achieved —, the coalition is dismissed and agents may take the initiative to form new coalitions, in order to achieve other goals.

The first two phases described above, namely recognition of potential for cooperation and coalition formation, may be designed and implemented based on two technique classes:

- *non-informed* techniques, when the agent that seeks for help does not know the other agents in the society and uses a bidding procedure. He simply sends a call for bids, specifying his needs and constraints, and interested

---

[3] Other authors also call this concept as team or partnership.

agents reply by sending their bids. The seeking agent then analyzes the bids, and chooses the more adequate one, if any, based on some predefined criteria. The most well-know technique of this kind is the Contract Net Protocol (CNET) [77];

- *informed* techniques, when the agent that seeks for help knows the other agents' abilities and exploits this information in order to send coalition proposals directly to possible partners. This technique may be based on different reasoning mechanisms: utility-based [67], reputation-based [66], complementarity-based [69] or mixed [3].

The most important inspiration for the complementarity-based approach is Dependence Theory, described next.

3.2 Dependence theory

Interaction situations, as described in section 3.1.3, are *objective*, i.e., they exist whether the agents are aware of it or not. Considering cognitive agents, whenever these interaction situations become *subjective*, i.e., represented within the agents' minds, agents may exploit these situations, in order to try to form coalitions, as described in section 3.1.4.

Dependence Theory, as proposed by Castelfranchi and colleagues [13, 19, 16], tries to answer two fundamental questions concerning a society of autonomous agents:

1. *Sociability problem:* Why does an autonomous decide to interact socially?
2. *Adoption problem:* How does an autonomous agent may ensure that the others will adopt his goal?

The answer to the first question is *dependence*, while the answer to the second question is *power*. Briefly speaking, agents reason about their dependence and power relations, and based on these relations perform social actions in order to form coalitions to achieve their goals.

3.2.1 Social actions

Conte and Castelfranchi [18] have shown that whenever an interaction situation becomes subjective, an agent may create *social goals* and perform *social actions*. These social goals and actions have as culprits the other agents' minds.

Supposing that two agents ag_i and ag_j co-exist in a common environment, and that g_m is one of ag_i's goals, we can distinguish the following ag_i's and ag_j's social actions:

- *exploitation:* if ag_j has the same goal g_m and he is acting to achieve this goal, ag_i can just wait for the accomplishment of the action performed by ag_j;
- *influence:* if ag_i's ability is not sufficient to achieve g_m, and if there is a positive social interference between ag_i and ag_j, ag_i may try to convince ag_j to adopt this goal, i.e., try to make that g_m also becomes one of ag_j's goals;

- *agression*: if ag_j has another goal g_n incompatible with g_m, i.e., there is a negative social interference, then ag_i may try to hinder ag_j from achieving g_n;
- *adoption*: if, for any reason, ag_j desires that ag_i achieves g_m, he can adopt this goal, i.e., g_m becomes one of ag_j's goals based on the fact that g_m was originally one of ag_i's goals.

Considering adoption, there are basically two different motives that drives an agent to adopt other agents' goals:

- *terminal* adoption, when adoption per-se is one of the agents' goals, independently of the goal nature. This kind of adoption may be based on personal motives (like a father that wants his children to achieve their goals) or non-personal motives (like an employee that needs to adopt his superior goal, or some member of a society that adopts a normative goal, like not crossing the red light);
- *instrumental* adoption, when the adoption of other agents' goals may be seen as a means for an agent to achieve his own goals; for instance, this is the case when another agent has a same goal, neither or them can achieve it alone and they have complementary abilities that are sufficient to achieve this goal if they work together.

3.2.2 Dependence and power relations

Hence, a fundamental consequence of (positive) social interference is to possibly increase the number of an agent's achievable goals, because agents may have *complementary* abilities.

According to Dependence Theory, an agent ag_i is considered *autonomous* for a certain goal g_m when he can achieve this goal alone. When this is not the case, and there is a positive social interference between ag_i and another agent ag_j for this goal, i.e., ag_j has the ability to perform a missing action to achieve g_m, ag_i is then considered *dependent* on ag_j to achieve this goal, and conversely, ag_j is considered to have *power* on ag_i for this goal.

In brief, Dependence Theory prescribes that ag_i needs to reason about the best way to *delegate* to ag_j the action it needs, to try to guarantee that this action will be performed by ag_j and that this latter will know that he is performing this action in order to achieve g_m, i.e, an ag_i's goal. Therefore, ag_i may activate a kind of **social reasoning** mechanism, aiming to perform a social action of *influence*: to convince ag_j to *adopt* the goal of performing the action needed by ag_i to achieve g_m. When this adoption is accepted, ag_j establishes a commitment towards ag_i to perform the needed action, like discussed in section 3.1.4.

In order to convince ag_j, one of the possible ag_i's options to get his needed action is to offer to ag_j in return some action needed by this latter, to achieve the same or a different goal. In other words, ag_i should exploit his power on ag_j in order to get his needed action.

When the needed and offered actions fulfill a same and common goal, the theory says that a *cooperation* occurs between ag_i e ag_j; otherwise, if these actions are used to achieve different goals, one desired by ag_i and another by ag_j, the situation is then called *social exchange*.

Additionally, dependence relations may be conjunctive or disjunctive [23]. In the first case, called *AND-dependence*, an agent ag_i depends on more than one agent to achieve his goal, since there is more than one single action needed to be performed by the others. This situation diminishes ag_i's power, since it needs to influence jointly more than one single agent to adopt his goal. Conversely, in the case of an *OR-dependence*, an agent ag_i needs a single action to achieve his goal, and this latter may be performed by more than one agent. Hence, in this second case, ag_i's power increases, since he can choose a possible partner to perform the needed action.

Despite its nice ideias and its elegant formulation, the original Dependence Theory did not provide an operational model to really design and implement autonomous agents that could use their dependence and power relations to form coalitions.

3.3 Social reasoning models

In this section, we will briefly describe two models, SRM [72, 68, 73] and SRM$^+$ [71, 22], which were built upon Dependence Theory, and provide the necessary constructs to design and implement its main concepts within autonomous cognitive agents.

3.3.1 SRM

The SRM model introduces a *social reasoning mechanism*, essential part of a cognitive agent architecture, that improves an agent's *adaptation* in open environments, by helping him to better evaluate the susceptibility of other agents to adopt his goals, and hence to better choose possible partners to whom coalition formation proposals should be sent.

The main aspects of this model are briefly described in the sequence, a more comprehensive description may be found in [72, 68, 73].

External description

In order to be able to perform social reasoning, an agent must represent internally some properties of the other agents. These properties are stored in a structure called *external description*, which is composed of several *entries*. Each of these entries describes a particular agent in the society, and it is composed of the following parts: (i) the *goals* that the agent wants to achieve, (ii) the *actions* that he is able to perform, (iii) the *resources* over which he has got some control and (iv) the *plans* that he can use in order to achieve his goals. Each plan is composed of a goal to achieve and a sequence of *instantiated actions* used in this plan. An instantiated action is composed of an action identification and a (possibly empty) list of resources used by this action. Goals, actions and resources have also an associated quantitative measure, referring respectively to the goals' importances and the actions' and resources' costs. An example of an external description is presented in table 2, where we considered that the instantiated actions do not need any resources to be performed.

External Description			
Agent	**Goals**	**Plans**	**Actions**
ag_1	g_1	$p_{111} = a_1, a_2, a_4$	a_1, a_9
		$p_{112} = a_1, a_5$	
	—	$p_{13} = a_3, a_9$	
	g_5	$p_{15} = a_1, a_{10}$	
	g_8	$p_{18} = a_1, a_7$	
	g_9	$p_{19} = a_1, a_{11}$	
ag_2	g_2	$p_{22} = a_2, a_6$	a_2
ag_3	g_3	$p_{33} = a_3, a_8$	a_2, a_3
ag_4	g_4	$p_{44} = a_4, a_7$	a_4
ag_5	g_1	$p_{51} = a_1, a_5$	a_5
ag_6	g_6	$p_{66} = a_1, a_6$	a_6, a_7
ag_7	g_7	$p_{77} = a_7, a_9$	a_7
ag_8	g_{10}	$p_{810} = a_8$	a_8, a_{10}

Table 2 External description example, adapted from [70].

The information stored in the external description may be acquired by three different sources: reception of a message, perception of the environment and inference, this latter corresponding to some internal reasoning mechanism. The source of the information is also stored, thus enabling an agent to detect whether his beliefs about the others, as well as the beliefs that the others have about him, are consistent [74].

By using his external description, an agent may calculate his dependence relations.

Dependence relations

An agent ag_i is considered *autonomous* for the goal g_m if and only if: (i) ag_i wants to achieve g_m, (ii) there is a plan p_s whose execution achieves g_m, and (iii) ag_i is able to perform all the actions[4] in p_s.

Whenever an agent ag_i is not autonomous for a certain goal, he is said to be *dependent* for this goal. However, the fact of being dependent does not mean that there is another available agent to perform the needed action. This situation is represented by a *dependence relation*.

Hence, an agent ag_i is said to be *dependent* on another agent ag_j for goal g_m if and only if: (i) ag_i has the goal g_m, (ii) ag_i is dependent for the goal g_m, (iii) there is a plan p_s whose execution achieves g_m, and (iv) ag_j has the ability to perform some action a_k in p_s that is needed by ag_i.

Dependence networks

Having calculated his dependence relations, an agent may represent all these relations in a single structure, called *dependence network*.

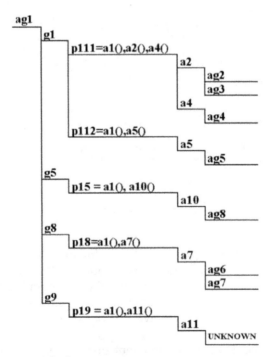

Fig. 3 Dependence network [70].

---

[4] For simplicity, we are not considering the use of resources. In the original formulation, there are two notions of autonomy/dependence, referring respectively to actions and resources.

Based on the external description presented in table 2, the dependence network of agent $ag1$ is presented in figure 3. In this example, one may notice that $ag1$ is dependent for goal $g8$, according to plan $p18$. He is not able to perform action $a7$, and he may choose between agents $ag6$ and $ag7$ to perform this action. This is a case of an OR-dependence. Regarding goal $g1$, if $ag1$ chooses to follow plan $p111$ there is an AND-dependence, since he needs two actions to be performed by the others: $a2$, which may be performed by $ag2$ and $ag3$, and $a4$, which may be performed only by $ag4$. Finally, $ag1$ cannot achieve goal $g9$, even asking for help, since there is no available agent in the environment who is able to perform action $a11$.

Mutual and reciprocal dependence

Using his dependence network, an agent ag_i is able to deduce that he depends on another agent ag_j for one of his goals g_m. However, he could also build ag_j's dependence network, and therefore, infer whether his dependence relation on ag_j is *unilateral* or *bilateral*, i.e., whether ag_j also depends on him for one of his goals g_n, which would mean that ag_j has power on ag_j for this goal g_n.

Considering the definitions presented in [16], we call *mutual dependence* (*MD*) the situation where agents ag_i and ag_j depend on one another for a *same goal* g_m. On the other hand, we call *reciprocal dependence* (*RD*) the situation where these two agents depend on one another for *different goals* g_m and g_n.

When agents detect that there is a mutual or reciprocal dependence between them, this situation may lead them to establish a cooperation or social exchange, as discussed in section 3.2.2.

Goal situations

We call *goal situation* a relation that holds between an agent ag_i and a goal g_m, which has four possible outcomes:

1. *No Goal (NG)*: the agent ag_i does not have the goal g_m in his goal set;
2. *No Plans (NP)*: the agent ag_i has the goal g_m, but he does not have any plan to achieve it;
3. *Autonomous (AUT)*: the agent ag_i has the goal g_m and at least one plan which makes him autonomous for this goal;
4. *Dependent (DEP)*: the agent ag_i has the goal g_m but all his plans that achieve it makes him dependent on others for this goal.

Given a certain goal to achieve, an agent normally calculates his goal situation for this goal. If he is dependent (*DEP*) for this goal, he will then calculate his dependence situations regarding other agents for this goal, as shown next.

Dependence situations

Being dependent for a certain goal, and after calculating his dependence networks, an agent may use these latter to reason about the others. In particular, given a certain goal g_m, an agent may calculate his *dependence situations* towards every other agent ag_j who belongs to the society. An agent infers a *locally believed dependence*, either mutual or reciprocal, if he uses exclusively *his own plans* when reasoning about the others. If he uses both *his own plans* and *those of the other agent* on whom he depends to deduce this conclusion, we will say that he has inferred a *mutually believed dependence* between them[5].

Let us consider two agents ag_i and ag_j, where the reasoning agent is ag_i. If ag_i infers that his goal situation is *DEP* for the goal g_m, there are six different dependence situations that may hold between himself and agent ag_j:

1. *Independence (IND)*: using his own plans, ag_i infers that he does not depend on ag_j for g_m;

2. *Locally Believed Mutual Dependence (LBMD)*: using his own plans, ag_i infers a mutual dependence between himself and ag_j for g_m, but he cannot deduce the same fact using ag_j's plans;

3. *Mutually Believed Mutual Dependence (MBMD)*: using his own plans, ag_i infers a mutual dependence between himself and ag_j for g_m. Moreover, he can deduce the same conclusion using ag_j's plans;

4. *Locally Believed Reciprocal Dependence (LBRD)*: using his own plans, ag_i infers a reciprocal dependence between himself and ag_j for g_m and g_n, but he cannot deduce the same fact using ag_j's plans;

5. *Mutually Believed Reciprocal Dependence (MBRD)*: using his own plans, ag_i infers a reciprocal dependence between himself and ag_j for g_m and g_n. Moreover, he can deduce the same conclusion using ag_j's plans;

6. *Unilateral Dependence (UD)*: using his own plans, ag_i infers that he depends on ag_j for g_m, but this latter does not depend on him for any of his goals.

Dependence based coalitions (DBC)

The social reasoning mechanism described above may be used to implement coalition formation, as described in 3.1.4. In particular, an agent may build and exploit his dependence networks, together with the notions of goal and dependence situations, in order to try to form coalitions to achieve his goals, when he is not able to achieve them by himself. We consider that partner choice and goal adoption procedures are *instrumental*: agents choose partners to whom they have something to offer in return, and these latter are not benevolent, i.e., they adopt the others' goals when this is a means to achieve their own goals.

---

[5] We are conscious that in our context, the meaning of the term "mutually believed" is somewhat different from the one usually used in MAS, like in [55]. For us, this term denotes the fact that the reasoning agent believes that the agent on which he depends for a certain goal is also aware of their bilateral dependence relation.

This technique was called *Dependence Based Coalitions* (DBC) [69] and it is composed of the following steps:

1. an agent first builds his *dependence networks*;
2. he chooses a goal g_m to achieve, based on its importance; if there are no goals to achieve, the process stops;
3. he chooses a plan p_s to achieve g_m, based on its cost; if there are no plans to achieve g_m, he returns to step *(2)* to choose another goal;
4. he calculates then his goal situation for the goal g_m;
5. if his goal situation for g_m is *AUT*, he performs all the actions to achieve the goal and returns to step *(2)* to choose another goal;
6. if his goal situation for g_m is *DEP*, he calculates then his dependence situations regarding other agents for this goal, and chooses a possible partner to whom a coalition proposal is sent; in the proposal, he asks the for execution of the needed action, and offers in return the execution of another action that may be useful for the possible partner; if there are no possible partners to perform the needed action, he returns to step *(3)* to choose another plan that achieves the same goal;
7. if the partner accepts the proposal, the coalition is formed and the actions are performed; when the goal is achieved, the coalition is dismissed and he returns to step *(2)* to choose another goal to achieve;
8. if the partner does not accept the proposal, then he returns to step *(6)* to choose another possible partner.

Regarding possible partners choice, we have established a criteria based on the following facts:

1. mutually believed dependence situations are preferred to locally believed ones, since the agent would not have the additional effort to convince his partner that his plan is adequate;
2. mutual dependence situations are preferred to reciprocal ones, avoiding therefore the well-known reciprocity problem, as discussed by Castel-franchi [13].

According to this criteria, we would have the following partial order for the possible dependence situations, where $x > y$ means that x is preferred to y:

$$MBMD > \{MBRD, LBMD\} > LBRD > UD$$

On the other hand, considering goal adoption, an agent ag_j accepts a coalition proposal from agent ag_i, where it is offered to him an action a_q to achieve goal g_n, if and only if it these conditions hold: *(i)* g_n is really an ag_j's goal, *(ii)* ag_j is not able to perform action a_q, *(iii)* his goal situation for g_n is *NP*; or *(iv)* his goal situation for g_n is *DEP* and ag_i would be a preferred partner for this goal, in the case where ag_j would have to propose a coalition to achieve this goal.

The DBC technique was initially restricted to OR-dependences. In a further work [25, 26], we have extended the technique do deal with AND-dependences.

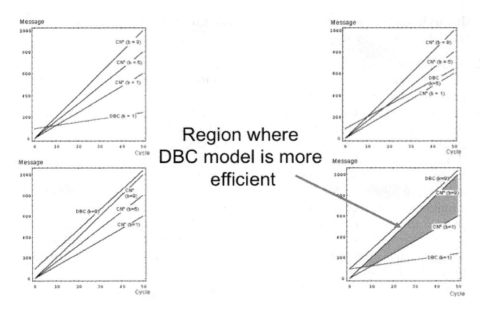

Fig. 4 Comparison between DBC and CNET [51].

In [51], we have compared the MAS global message flow generated by the DBC technique with the CNET technique, a non-informed technique mentioned in section 3.1.4. The results, presented in figure 4, show that if social reasoning is effective, i.e., if the agent selects well his possible partners, then there will always be a critical cycle after which the global communication flow in the DBC technique will always be smaller than the one obtained in the CNET technique.

3.3.2 S_{RM}^+

The S_{RM} model was built to analyze the possible interactions of two agents, whose social interference is positive. However, in some real scenarios, like the ones involving brokers, there are social interaction patterns involving more than two agents, in which dependence relations are *circular*. The S_{RM}^+ model was conceived to deal with these cases.

The main aspects of this model are briefly described in the sequence, a more comprehensive description may be found in [22, 71].

Circular dependence relations

Considering once more the external description shown in table 2, let us consider that ag_1 chooses goal g_1 and plan p_{111} to achieve this goal. As mentioned before, there is an AND-dependence, since ag_1 needs both actions a_2 and a_4.

Let us also suppose that he tries to form a coalition with agents ag_2 and ag_4, asking for them to perform respectively actions a_2 and a_4. His dependence situation towards these two agents for goal g_1 is UD. This is not a comfortable situation for ag_1, since he has nothing to offer to these partners and possibly these latter would not help him, except if they were benevolent.

However, if we analyze better the dependence relations of this example, we can notice that ag_2 needs action a_6 to achieve g_2, while ag_4 needs action a_7 to achieve g_4. Agents ag_6 and ag_7, respectively, are able to perform these actions, and both of them depend on ag_1 to achieve their goals. The first needs action a_1 to achieve g_6 and the second needs action a_9 to achieve g_7.

If ag_1 is able to reason strategically, he can propose a coalition to these four agents, and all of them will achieve their goals. This dependence pattern was called *AMONG-dependence* and it is described in [22, 71].

However, in order to enable such a social reasoning mechanism, the concept of dependence networks must be extended to a graph model.

Dependence graphs

A *dependence graph* is a directed graph with the following properties:

1. the set of vertices is composed of the union of four disjoint subsets, representing respectively agents, goals, plans and actions;
2. each edge that belongs to the set of edges links two vertices according to the following conditions:

   a. the vertice representing agent ag_i is linked to the vertice representing goal g_j if and only if this agent has this goal;
   b. the vertice representing goal g_i is linked to the vertice representing plan p_j if and only if the execution of this plan achieves this goal;
   c. the vertice representing plan p_j is linked to the vertice representing action a_j if and only if this action is necessary for this plan and the agent that is located in the root of the path that contains this edge is not able to perform this action;
   d. the vertice representing action a_i is linked to the vertice representing agent ag_j if and only if this agent is able to perform this action.

Figure 5 shows the dependence graph associated to the external description presented in table 2, adopting some simplifications[6].

Reduced dependence graphs

As we may notice by the relatively simple example shown in figure 5, dependence graphs may become extremely complex, making it difficult to visualize and analyze the interaction phenomena which they are supposed to represent.

---

[6] Neither agent $ag8$, nor $ag3$'s and $ag5$'s goals and plans were represented. Regarding $ag1$, we have represented only goals $g1$ and $g8$.

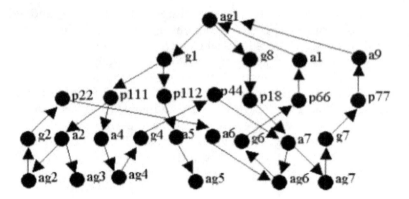

Fig. 5 Dependence graph [70].

In order to solve this problem, we have created a simplified version of these graphs, named *reduced dependence graphs*. In these graphs, each agent has only one single goal and one single plan to achieve this goal. Therefore, vertices that represent goals and plans do not need to be represented, hence diminishing the original number of vertices and resulting in a more simple graph. The goal for which the agent needs an action from the others is now represented as a label of the respective edge.

The reduced dependence graph, generated from the complete graph shown in figure 5, and considering that agent *ag*1 follows plan *p*111 to achieve goal *g*1, is presented in figure 6.

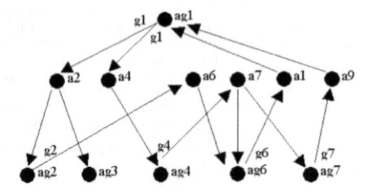

Fig. 6 Reduced dependence graph [70].

3.4 Social reasoning applications

In the next subsections, we present four applications, $\mathcal{D}$EPNET , $\mathcal{D}$EPINT ,
$\mathcal{D}$EPINT$^+$, and $\mathcal{P}$ARTNET$^+$, that were developed to illustrate the possible appli-
cations of an agent's social reasoning mechanism, and that were based on the
$\mathcal{S}$RM and $\mathcal{S}$RM$^+$ models presented in section 3.3.

3.4.1 $\mathcal{D}$EPNET

A first application of the $\mathcal{S}$RM model was a simulator, called $\mathcal{D}$EPNET , which calculates the dependence relations and dependence situations between agents,
and constructs the dependence networks of a given agent [68, 21]. In this applications, however, there is only one single external description, which is shared
by all the agents.

The simulator is composed of the following facilities:

- *agent edition module:* the user can dynamically create new agents and edit
  their goals, actions, resources, and plans, or modify the entry of an existing
  agent in the external description;
- *dependence network constructor:* this module constructs the various dependence networks of a given agent, either related to a specific goal or to all
  of his goals. It can construct both the action and the resource dependence
  networks for both cases;
- *dependence situation constructor:* this module calculates the dependence situations regarding a given agent and one of his goals. The user must specify
  a specific type of dependence situation he is interested in.

```
      -------------------------------------------------
      ********   DEPENDENCE NETWORK SIMULATOR   ********

                      Jaime Sichman
              LIFIA/IMAG, Grenoble, France
                   IP/CNR, Roma, Italia
      -------------------------------------------------


                  DEPENDENCE SITUATIONS MENU
                  --------------------------

    Type 1 (Calculate mutually believed mutual dependence)
         2 (Calculate locally believed mutual dependence)
         3 (Calculate mutually believed reciprocal dependence)
         4 (Calculate locally believed reciprocal dependence)
         5 (Calculate unilateral dependence)
         6 (Print the external description)
         7 (Return to dependence network menu)
         8 (Return to main menu)
         9 (Quit)
```

Fig. 7 $\mathcal{D}$EPNET interface [21].

The $\mathcal{D}$EPNET simulator runs in UNIX workstations, and it was developed using the C++ programming language. The total number of lines of code is approximately 5800. Its functions are closely related to the $\mathcal{S}$RM concepts. The simulator's interface to calculate dependence situations is shown in figure 7.

3.4.2 $\mathcal{D}$EPINT

$\mathcal{D}$EPINT [68, 69] is a system conceived to implement the DBC technique, as described in section 3.3.1, and it is aimed to be used in a distributed problem solving perspective. Differently from the $\mathcal{D}$EPNET simulator, in $\mathcal{D}$EPINT each agent maintains its own private external description.

The following principles about agents were adopted:

1. *Principle of Non-Benevolence*: agents are not presumed to help each other: they decide autonomously whether or not to cooperate with others;
2. *Principle of Sincerity*: agents do not try to exploit each other: they never offer erroneous information deliberately and always communicate information in which they believe;
3. *Principle of Self-Knowledge*: agents have a complete and correct representation of themselves: their goals, their expertise etc. However, agents may have beliefs about others that are either incorrect or incomplete;
4. *Principle of Consistency*: agents do not maintain contradictory beliefs about others. Once an inconsistency is detected, they revise their beliefs in order to reestablish a consistent state.

The $\mathcal{A}$SIC architecture, proposed by Boissier [7], was chosen to develop $\mathcal{D}$EPINT agents', as represented in figure 8. Briefly, an agent is composed of several *internal mechanisms*, one of which is a social reasoning mechanism, based on the information stored in his external description.

In $\mathcal{D}$EPINT , coalitions are limited to two partners and concurrent coalition proposals are not handled. Therefore, there are two basic behaviors for the agents: active and passive. In active behavior, the agent tries to propose a coalition to some other agent, when he is not able to achieve his selected goal on his own. He uses his social reasoning mechanism to choose a goal, plan and partners, using the DBC technique, as described in section 3.3.1. In passive behavior, the user simulates the information gathering (perception and/or inference) and the agent is limited to accepting or rejecting the coalition proposals sent to him by the other agents. Whenever an inconsistency is detected in a coalition proposal, a belief revision procedure is activated in both behaviors, when the agent restores the consistency of his beliefs [74]. It is up to the user of the system to decide which behavior each agent of the system will have in a given run.

$\mathcal{D}$EPINT runs in UNIX workstations, and it was developed using the C++ programming language. Regarding agent communication facilities, the systems uses the $\mathcal{M}$ASENV communication middleware [12].

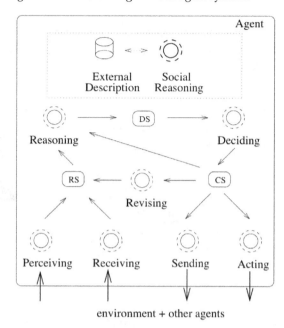

Fig. 8 $\mathcal{A}$sic agent architecture [7], as used in $\mathcal{D}$epint [69].

3.4.3 $\mathcal{D}$epint$^+$

$\mathcal{D}$epint$^+$ [25, 26] is a system that implements an extension of the DBC technique, in order to deal with AND-dependences. Its agents' architecture is similar to the one used in $\mathcal{D}$epint . Figure 9 shows the system's interface, when agents representing airline companies try to form coalitions in order to transport their passengers through different countries.

Like $\mathcal{D}$epint , $\mathcal{D}$epint$^+$ also runs in UNIX, was developed in the C++ language, and uses the $\mathcal{M}$asenv environment [12].

3.4.4 $\mathcal{P}$artnet$^+$

The $\mathcal{P}$artnet$^+$ [60,61] is a multi-agent-based simulation tool that uses the $\mathcal{S}$rm$^+$ model to understand partnership formation among heterogeneous agents. It is an extension of a previous tool, called $\mathcal{P}$artnet , developed by Conte and Pedone[20].

When choosing preferred partners, each agent in $\mathcal{P}$artnet$^+$ follows a strategy that dictates what kind of partnerships will be sought. There are three different strategies available, that cover most of the reasonable stereotypical choices that an agent may have when choosing partnerships:

- *Utilitarians,* that try to maximize the importance of the achieved goal while minimizing the cost of the action used;

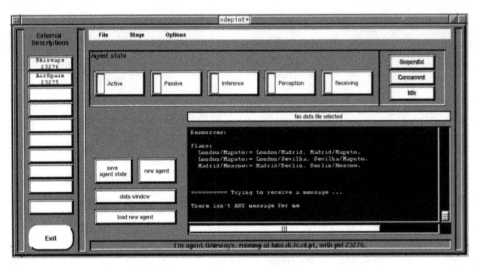

Fig. 9 $\mathcal{D}$EPINT$^+$ interface [70].

- *Substantialists*, that choose partnerships with most important goals, no matter what the cost is;
- *Misers*, that seek the partnerships with minimum cost, no matter the goal importance is.

$\mathcal{P}$ARTNET$^+$ was developed using the Java programming language. In figure 10, we can see the $\mathcal{P}$ARTNET$^+$ interface. In the main window, the simulation parameters like the agent's goals, plans and actions can be set and simulation be controlled. Additional overlay windows show graphics containing the simulation results, as the accumulated net benefit, and the dependence graph, enabling the user to visualize what dependence relations have been used in partnerships.

An example of an hyphotesis that was tested and validated in the system, as expected by previous results in social sciences, is that substantialists gets better accumulated net benefits when there are more goals in the society.

3.5 Classification of social reasoning models and applications

Figure 11 shows the classification of the social reasoning models and applications, according to the MAS Research Classification Grid proposed in section 2.3.

Regarding the social reasoning models $\mathcal{S}$RM and $\mathcal{S}$RM$^+$, presented in section 3.3, both of them can be used either in a Simulation or in a Problem Solving research perspective. Both models have Theories as their description level value. Finally, both of them deal with Interactions in the dimension focus axis.

Considering the social reasoning applications, presented in section 3.4, they have different research goals: while $\mathcal{D}$EPNET and $\mathcal{P}$ARTNET$^+$ adopt a Simulation

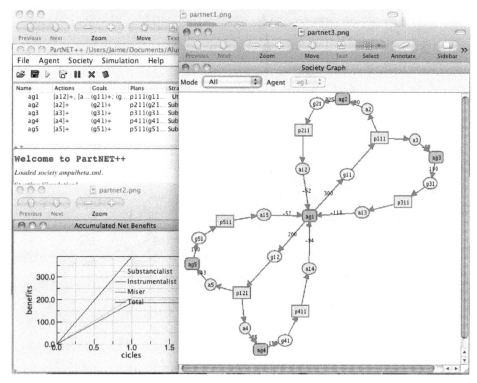

Fig. 10 $\mathcal{P}$ARTNET$^+$ interface [60].

perspective, $\mathcal{D}$EPINT and $\mathcal{D}$EPINT$^+$ adopt a Problem Solving perspective. The former two applications have only Languages as their description level value, while the two latter deal with two values in this axis: Architectures (for their agents) and Languages . Finally, $\mathcal{D}$EPNET and $\mathcal{P}$ARTNET$^+$ deal with Interactions in the focus dimension, while $\mathcal{D}$EPINT and $\mathcal{D}$EPINT$^+$ deal both with Agents and Interactions in this dimension.

3.6 From interactions to dynamic organizations

In this section 3, we have observed a first important result:

Agents social interactions may create agents dynamic organizations.

These dynamic organizations, called *coalitions*, create within the agents' minds some primitive organizational mental attitudes, like commitments [17, 64], joint commitments [52], etc.

If these coalitions should be repeated frequently, involving the same agents, these interaction patterns may be captured in pre-defined structures, hence diminishing the inherent complexity of coalition formation and coordination/task division. As a result, more stable groups are created, that may last

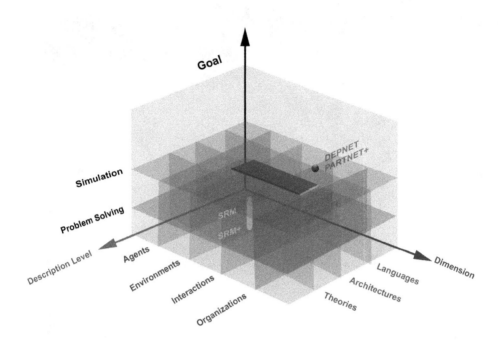

Fig. 11 Classification of social reasoning models and architectures [70].

longer. This group maintenance makes the cooperative problem solving process more efficient, since some phases described in section 3.1.4, like recognition of potential for cooperation, coalition formation, and eventually plan formation, may be solved a priori. As a negative point, rigid structures are less adaptable to very dynamic environments.

This phenomena has been extensively studied by researchers in the business and management domain, and it is presented next.

4 Agents organizations

In order to be able to introduce organizational reasoning models and applications, we need to characterize somes aspects of agents organizations, which are initially discussed in section 4.1. Then, in section 4.2 we present our second conclusion, relating agents organizations and interactions. $\mathcal{M}$OISE [43, 42] and $\mathcal{M}$OISE$^+$ [48, 46, 50] models are described in section 4.3, and some applications that were developed using these models are presented in section 4.4. We then present in section 4.5 the classification of these models and applications, according to the MAS Research Classification Grid.

4.1 Basic definitions

First of all, we define what it means an agent organization in section 4.1.1. The relation between organization and agent autonomy is then addressed in section 4.1.2. Finally, we present in section 4.1.3 the organizational dimensions that may be used in different agents' organizational models.

4.1.1 Agent organizations definition

Organization is a complex notion: there are several views, definitions, and approaches to characterize them, addressing different issues: it is a supra-individual phenomena [36], it is defined by the designer or by the actors involved [58], and it is a pattern of predefined [5] or emergent [62] cooperation.
We will adopt here the following definition [8]:

> An organization is a supra-agent pattern of emergent cooperation or predefined cooperation of the agents in the system, that could be defined by the designer or by the agents themselves, in order to achieve a purpose.

This distinction between emergent and predefined cooperation patterns was also proposed by Lemaitre [54]. An emergent cooperation pattern is precisely what we have presented in section 3.3, when we have introduced coalitions and the social reasoning models.

It is important to stress that this distinction introduces two important concepts: *organizational structure* and *organizational entity*. The former, related strictly to predefined cooperation patterns, specifies the desired cooperation scheme, independently of the actual agents involved in the common activity. The latter, which exists in both predefined and emergent cooperation patterns, refers to the actual set of agents that are working together, and following some scheme, to achieve a global goal. This distinction will be detailed in section 4.3.

In the rest of this section, we will address exclusively predefined organizations. For simplicity, we will refer to them simply as organizations[7].

4.1.2 Organizations and agents autonomy

One important issue to investigate is the relation between organizational constraints and agents' autonomy, as studied by Castelfranchi [14].

In figure 12, let us consider B as the set of all possible agents' behavior in a MAS. The subset P corresponds to those behaviors that achieve the desired global goal. The fact of being situated in an environment E limits some of these behaviors, i.e., only $P \cap E$ may occur. This set, however, may be too big, hence justifying the need of additional organizational constraints.

Speaking in set theoretical terms, the design of an organization consists in defining a new set, here called O, that will enforce more constraints to the

---

[7] When needed, a distinction from emergent organizations will be made.

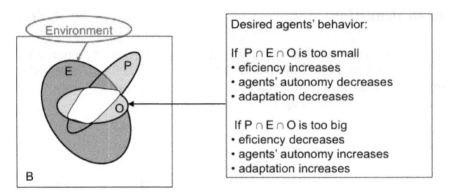

Fig. 12 Organizational constraints and agent autonomy [48, 8].

agents' behaviors. In other words, the new available behaviors for the agents will be those contained in the subset $P \cap E \cap O$.

Considering O's size, two possible situations may occur:

- on one hand, if $P \cap E \cap O$ is too small (in the limit, it is a single point), then most decisions about the cooperation patterns are taken a priori, and global efficiency increases. However, agents' autonomy is rather limited. Moreover, agents' adaptation to environmental changes decreases, and it may be the case that the global goal could not be reached anymore. An example of such organization is the army;
- on then other hand, if $P \cap E \cap O$ is too big (in the limit, it is equal to $P \cap E$), then almost no decisions about the cooperation patterns are taken a priori, and global efficiency decreases. However, in this case agents' autonomy increases, and they may easily adapt when the environment changes. At the limit, an example of such organization are pure emergent coalitions, as presented in section 3.3.

Hence, the organizational design problem, which has not been solved so far by researchers in business and management domains, is to choose an optimal constraint set O that could, at the same time, guarantee global efficiency without loosing adaptability.

These organizational constraints may refer to different organizational dimensions, as seen next.

4.1.3 Organizational dimensions

Given that an organization constrains the agents' autonomy, a further step is to investigate how this limitation can be properly engineered and designed. Hence, the first needed step is to provide a classification of the diverse aspects of agent organizations currently captured by the different agent organizational models.

In [24], we have proposed some modeling dimensions for this task, divided in two classes: *basic* and *complementary* dimensions. The first class presents four different dimensions:

- the *structural dimension*, mainly composed of notions like roles and groups, as used in the AGR model [35];
- the *interactive dimension*, characterized by dialogical interaction structures, as used in the Electronic Institutions model [32];
- the *functional dimension*, formed by goal/task decomposition structures, as proposed by the TAEMS model [27];
- the *normative dimension*, in which we find the concepts of norms, rights, rules, like used in the OPERA model [29].

Some models may present more than one of these dimensions, like TEAMS [80] and our proposed organizational models, $\mathcal{M}$OISE and $\mathcal{M}$OISE$^+$, presented in section 4.3.

4.2 From organizations to constrained interactions

In this section 4, we have observed a second important result:

Pre-defined formal organizations constrain agents' interactions.

In fact, this limitation aims to guarantee that the global goals are achieved in an optimized way. If agents follow strictly their organizational constraints, they will know what to do, when and with whom to interact in crucial problem solving situations. However, in reality, formal and emergent organizations co-exist, forming the so-called "Communities of Practice", as shown by Huberman and colleagues [45].

4.3 Organizational reasoning models

In this section, we will briefly describe two models, $\mathcal{M}$OISE [43, 42] and $\mathcal{M}$OISE$^+$ [48, 46, 50], which provide the necessary constructs to design and implement organizational reasoning within autonomous cognitive agents.

4.3.1 $\mathcal{M}$OISE

According to the $\mathcal{M}$OISE [43, 42] model, the goal of a MAS organization is to *constrain the agents' autonomy*, as discussed in section 4.1.2. These constrains are expressed by *permissions*, *obligations* and *prohibitions* to the different agent's activities within the MAS.

These constraints are structured in three levels:

- *individual level*, concerning the agents' taks and responsibilities. They are applied to the following concepts:
  - *roles*, that specify the agents' attended behaviors in the organization, as well as the set of activities that they are supposed to perform;
  - *missions*, that define the constraints on the goals, plans, actions and resources that may be used by role-playing agents, associated to their activities.
- *social level*, concerning the agents' authority, communication, and knowledge links;
- *collective level*, concerning the context where roles, missions and links are valid, and whose main concept is the notion of *group*.

Orthogonally to these levels, the model differentiates between *abstract* and *concrete* organizations:

- *organizational structure*, that defines in an abstract level the individual, social and collective level constraints. Basically, it is composed of a set of roles, links and groups;
- *organizational entity*, that instantiates in a concrete level the individual, social and collective level constraints. It is composed of a set of (agent, role) pairs and by the group instances where these agents play these roles.

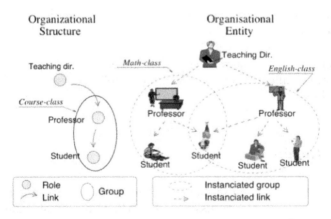

Fig. 13 Example of MOISE specification [43, 42].

Figure 13 shows both an organization structure (left) and entity (right) using the MOISE model concepts, in a graduate studies scenario. The organizational structure has roles like Teaching dir., Professor, and Student. As an example, there is a communication link between the roles Professor and Student. A group Course-class is composed of these last two roles. Regarding the organizational entity, we can notice the instantiation of two groups, Math-class and English-class; moreover, there is a same student, represented in the middle of the figure, that belongs to both group instances.

4.3.2 Moise⁺

The Moise⁺ [48, 46, 50] model is an extension of the Moise model. Besides constraining the agent's behavior to reach organizational goals more efficiently, the model was developed to facilitate *reorganization*, i.e., the process by which, eventually, the organization dynamically changes its structure and/or functionality.

Like its inspiring model, the Moise⁺ model also differentiates abstract and concrete organizations. In the abstract level, its *organizational specification* models the organizational constraints, as discussed in section 4.1.3, in three dimensions: structural, functional and deontic.

Structural specification

An example of a Moise⁺ *structural specification*, for the soccer domain, is presented in figure 14.

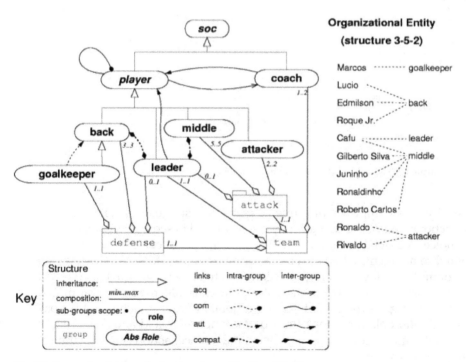

Fig. 14 Example of Moise⁺ structural specification [48, 8].

In the left, we can notice some roles, like coach and leader, and groups, like attack and defense. Additionally to Moise concepts, there are *compatibility* links: for instance, a same agent cannot play the roles of coach and player at the same team concurrently. Cardinality limits for the roles are also specified: a team must have at least one and at most two agents playing the coach role. At the right of the figure, one can observe the agents that are playing the specified roles within the organizational entity.

Functional specification

An example of a MOISE⁺ *functional specification*, for the soccer domain, is presented in figure 15.

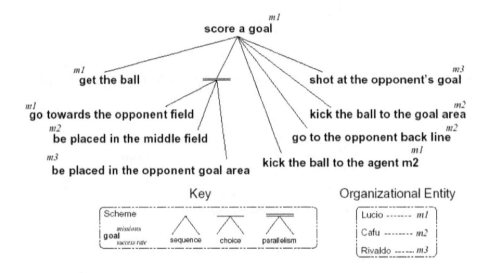

Fig. 15 Example of MOISE⁺ functional specification [48, 8].

Basically, it is composed of a tree of goals and subgoals, whose leafs are atomic actions. Actions and goals may be performed in sequence, concurrently or by choice. A crucial notion is that of a *mission*: a set of coherent global goals attributed to an agent, when playing a certain role. In MOISE⁺ , whenever an agent commits to play a role, he also commits to achieve the goals defined in the set of missions associated to this role. In the example, the agent committed to m1 has the high-level goal of scoring a goal; in order to achieve this goal, he first gets the ball, then goes towards the opponent field and finally kicks the ball to the agent committed to mission m2. Hence, actions coordination is achieved in MOISE⁺ by missions.

Deontic specification

The notions of roles and missions are linked by a *deontic specification*, whose example for the soccer domain is shown in figure 16. The MOISE⁺ deontic specification is composed of a set of rules that establish whether a certain role has the permission or the obligation to follow a certain mission.

role	deontic relation	mission	time constraint
back	*permission*	m_1	*Any*
middle	*obligation*	m_2	*Any*
attacker	*obligation*	m_3	*Any*

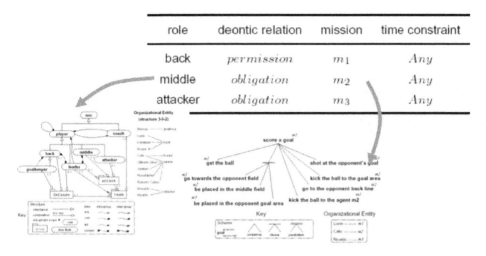

Fig. 16 Example of $\mathcal{M}$OISE$^+$ deontic specification [48, 8].

Although presented here by a graphical notation, the $\mathcal{M}$OISE$^+$ structural, functional and deontic constraints are formally specified [46]. Moreover, they are also described in XML notation, and hence the MAS agents are able to read, interpret and decide whether to follow or not these constraints in execution time. In order words, they may use an **organizational reasoning** mechanism to decide whether to be or not an organization abiding agent.

Reorganization

As mentioned before, the $\mathcal{M}$OISE$^+$ model was conceive to facilitate reorganization. The fact of having the structural, functional and deontic constraints specified separately enables to use the model in different reorganizations levels. There are at least four reorganization levels, exemplified next using an increasing order of complexity:

1. *change the organization entity*; in the soccer scenario, this means to change an agent that is playing a certain role;
2. *change the deontic specification*; in the soccer domain, this corresponds, for instance, to give permission to all players to try to score a goal when the game is next to its end;
3. *change the functional specification*; in the soccer domain, this corresponds to change the coordination scheme in the middle of the game, for instance trying to score a goal using rather the middle of the field;

4. *change the structural specification*; in the soccer domain, this would correspond to change the number of attackers and defenders in the next game,
   due to an injury of a player who has not got a substitute.

Moreover, a designer can use the $\mathcal{M}$oise$^+$ concepts, in a meta-level reasoning
layer, to specify a *reorganization* specification. In this case, some special roles
and schemes may be created to achieve this goal. An example of such a meta-
level reorganization specification may be found in [46, 49].

4.4 Organizational reasoning applications

In the next subsections, we present five applications, $\mathcal{R}$aisorg , $\mathcal{C}$ollorg ,
$\mathcal{J}$ojteam , $\mathcal{C}$ommunet and $\mathcal{E}$-Alliance , that were developed to illustrate the
possible applications of an agent's organizational reasoning mechanism, and
that were based on the $\mathcal{M}$oise and $\mathcal{M}$oise$^+$ models presented in section 4.3.

4.4.1 $\mathcal{R}$aisorg

$\mathcal{R}$aisorg [43, 42] is a tool that enables a designer to specify and simulate the
functioning of a MAS organization based on the $\mathcal{M}$oise model. It calculates
the organization dependence relations between roles, and detects eventual
incoherences in the organizational specification.

The simulator is composed of the following facilities:

- organizational structure facilities:

  - construction and exhibition of a tree showing the *dependence between
    missions*;
  - verification and exhibition of the organizational structure *coherence*;

- organizational entity facilities:

  - construction and exhibition of a tree showing the *dependence between
    agents*;
  - verification and exhibition of the organizational entity *coherence*;

- suggestion of simple heuristics to fix some problems associated to eventual
  incoherences.

A possible incoherence arises, for instance, when two playing-role agents
must interact, but a communication link between their respective roles was
not specified. In this case, a simple heuristic to fix this problem is to add the
missing communication link in the organizational specification.

$\mathcal{R}$aisorg runs in UNIX workstations, and it was developed using the Java
programming language. Its functions are closely related to the $\mathcal{M}$oise concepts.
Its interface is shown in figure 17.

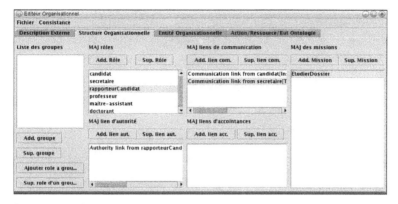

Fig. 17 $\mathcal{R}$AISORG interface [43, 42].

4.4.2 COLLORG

COLLORG [43, 42] illustrates the use of the MOISE model in the development of a groupware tool. Its goal is to support the business process management of the graduate studies at the Escola Politécnica (EP) of the Universidade de São Paulo (USP).

The system offers two functionalities:

- an on-line service to inform the administrative rules and procedures for the potential candidates, as well as an indication of the roles that should be contacted for each procedure;
- some additional services for cooperative work, aiming to automatize, if possible, some repetitive administrative tasks.

The system's architecture, shown in figure 18, uses two type of agents: *interface agents*, associated to the users, and *software agents*, like the courses database manager. Interface agents are implemented as applets, available through an Intranet.

An example of a possible task to be automated is the candidate inscription procedure. When trying to process his inscription, a student must fill a form, obtain the agreement of the responsible professor for the course, and then deposit the form in the administration. Supposing that the professor has accepted the inscription, this latter's interface-agent transmits the file to the interface-agent of the secretary who treats adequately this procedure: (i) it integrates the student into the instance of the corresponding group course, (ii) it contacts the agent responsible for the course data base requesting the update and (iii) it informs the interface-agent of the student about the result of his request.

Figure 19 presents COLLORG interface, showing the part of this procedure that is available for a student, called Hubert. It shows that the student playing the candidat role depends on the agent playing the secretaire role to finish his inscription goal. Regarding the organizational entity, it is also shown that there are two agents, Lilliane and Sylvie, that are currently playing the secretaire role, and hence could help the student to achieve his goal.

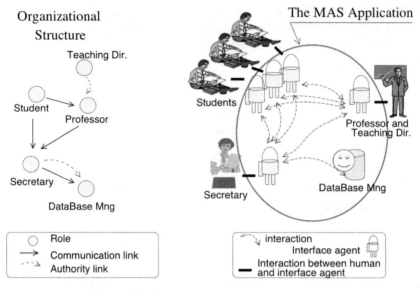

Fig. 18 COLLORG architecture [43, 42].

Fig. 19 COLLORG interface [43].

COLLORG runs in UNIX workstations, and it was developed using the Java programming language. Regarding agent communication facilities, the systems uses the *M*AST communication middleware, developed by Boissier and colleagues [6].

4.4.3 *J*OJTEAM

*J*OJTEAM [46] is an application that uses the *M*OISE⁺ model in the simulated robot soccer domain [53], including the reorganization process discussed in section 4.3.2. The system was developed using the *T*EAMBOTS simulator, whose interface is presented in figure 20.

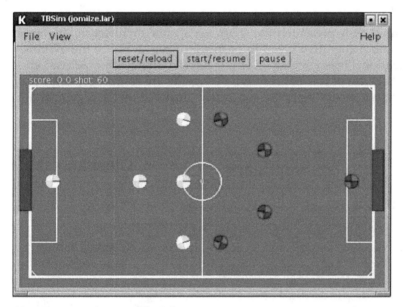

Fig. 20 *T*EAMBOTS interface apud [46, 8].

This domain is suitable to the use of multiagent techniques: agents are autonomous, reactive, control is distributed and decentralized and there is a need for coordination among the players of the same team. Moreover, given the dynamic characteristics of the domain, the team must adapt to the changes of the opponent, and therefore it is quite a natural candidate domain for a benchmark for reorganization policies [78].

Reorganization in *J*OJTEAM is performed by a special purpose group, named ReorgGr, whose specification details may be found in [46, 49]. Agent that belong to this group are not regular players: they are specialized in monitoring, design and selection of organizations.

The reorganization steps are carried on by *J*OJTEAM agents in the following way:

- *Team monitoring:* The agent that plays the monitor role starts a reorganization procedure at every 24.000 simulation steps; since the game ends in 120.000 steps, there are five reorganization processes during a single game. The first (re)organization occurs at step 0, the second at step 24.000 and the last at step 96.000. Since this process occurs even if the team is winning and playing well, there is a chance to exploit new, eventually better, organization specifications;
- *Organization design:* Several reorganization proposals are sent by domain-specific agents, that play a designer role. Each of them may follow a distinct strategy, for instance adopting a more offensive formation or being more cautious in order to guarantee a partial result;
- *Design selection:* The agent that plays the selector role uses reinforcement learning techniques [79] to identify the best proposal for a particular game situation.

In figure 21, it is presented the $\mathcal{J}$OJTEAM agents' architecture. It combines a reactive and a cognitive layer. In particular, we can notice the existence of an organizational reasoning layer, which reads dynamically a $\mathcal{M}$OISE$^+$ specification; in the case of this application, the agents are completely organization abiders, and act according to the constraints imposed by the organization.

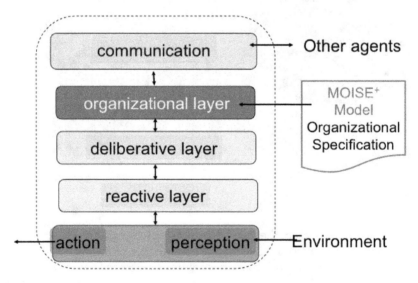

Fig. 21 $\mathcal{J}$OJTEAM agent architecture [46, 8].

$\mathcal{J}$OJTEAM runs in UNIX workstations, and it was developed using the Java programming language. It uses the S-$\mathcal{M}$OISE$^+$ organizational middleware [50].

The S-$\mathcal{M}$OISE$^+$ middleware is a domain-independent tool that assures that a MAS application that uses the $\mathcal{M}$OISE$^+$ model maintains its organizational constraints integrity. This task is performed by a special middleware agent, named OrgManager. As an example, the OrgManager does not allow that a new arriving agent could play a certain role in a MAS when the current cardinality of the agents already playing this role has exceed the team specification. The middleware also provides to the agents, by a special purpose API named OrgBox, several primitives for $\mathcal{M}\textsc{oise}^+$ organizational actions, like asking to play a role, asking to commit to a mission, or asking which are the obliged missions for a certain role.

4.4.4 COMMUNET

The COMMUNET system [39, 38, 40] is an application of both social[8] and organizational reasoning, based on the $\mathcal{M}\textsc{oise}^+$ model, that exploits the so called *small world* phenomena [81] in order to facilitate information search. The main idea is that these kind of reasoning mechanisms may enable the access to pages, documents and people that could hardly be detected by conventional search engines. Based on a peer-to-peer strategy, it gives a decentralized solution which complements the results obtained by conventional search engines, by using a concept familiar to quite all users: the communities they live in.

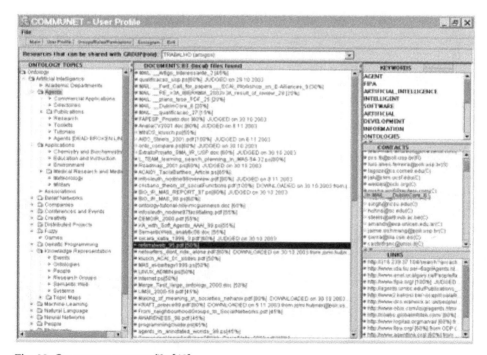

Fig. 22 COMMUNET user profile [40].

The main element of the system is the *mediator agent*, which represents and reasons, both socially and organizationally, about his users' contacts, roles and organizations, in an open MAS context.

---

[8] Although not based on dependence theory.

Each user has an associated mediator agent. When the system starts, this mediator calculates, using information retrieving techniques, information about (i) his user's resources (by analyzing his documents contents and trying to match them to a previously set of ontological concepts), (ii) his user's subjective vision of his social network (by analyzing his email logs) and (iii) his user's access permissions (determined by organizational constraints defined using the $\mathcal{M}$OISE$^+$ model). This information, calculated semi-automatically by the mediator agent, defines a user profile, as shown in figure 22.

Using the user's profile, the mediator agent starts to manage the interactions with other mediator agents, that represent his user's contacts, enabling hence a resource sharing procedure between them. Different resources may be made available or not by the users, according to their own privacy policy.

The COMMUNET mediator interface is shown in figure 23. It contains four distinct areas: *(i)* a first area, at the top, for the users' queries; *(i)* a second area, at the left, that shows the ontological concepts; *(iii)* a third area, in the middle, that shows the resources obtained from other mediator agents and *(iv)* a fourth area, at the bottom, that presents the search results obtained from conventional search engines.

Fig. 23 COMMUNET interface [40].

The COMMUNET mediator agent is based on PersonalSearcher, developed by Godoy and Amandi [41]. The system runs in UNIX workstations, and it was developed using the Java programming language. It uses the S-$\mathcal{M}$OISE$^+$ organizational middleware [50].

4.4.5 *E*-ALLIANCE

The *E*-ALLIANCE [2, 47] project aims to provide an Information Technology environment to support collaboration activities across autonomous enterprises,
grouped into alliances. Such an infrastructure should support information
sharing and collaborative decision-making across the partner enterprises,
while preserving their autonomy.

This infrastructure has been applied for an alliance of autonomous printshops.
In this application, the printshops are autonomous enterprises, fully responsible for their budget and for the planning and scheduling of their print jobs and
resources. Printshops may create and join an alliance in order to accomplish or
better accomplish customers' print requests that they cannot or do not want
to satisfy alone. In this case, the goal is to support collaborative executions
initiated by printshops willing to out-source some of their jobs, as a whole or
in parts. We have used a MAS approach for this task, as shown in figure 24.

Before a group of printshops decide to collaborate, they need to previously
agree on the responsibilities of each one in the alliance. Normally, this agreement is achieved by a negotiation process and, when finished, the result is
explicitly stated in a contract.

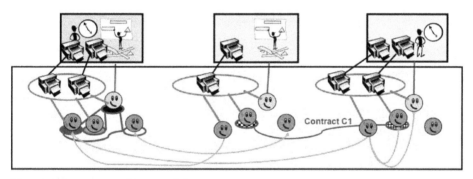

Fig. 24 *E*-ALLIANCE architecture [8].

We have used the $Moise^+$ model to help the agents in the negotiation
process, and also in the contract specification, more specifically to define the
constraints and obligations of each part of the contract.

4.5 Classification of organizational reasoning models and
applications

Figure 25 shows the classification of the organizational reasoning models and
applications, according to the MAS Research Classification Grid proposed in
2.3.

Regarding the organizational reasoning models $Moise$ and $Moise^+$, presented in section 4.3, both of them can be used either in a Simulation or in

a **Problem Solving** research perspective. Both models have **Theories** as their description level value. Finally, both of them deal with **Organizations** in the dimension focus axis.

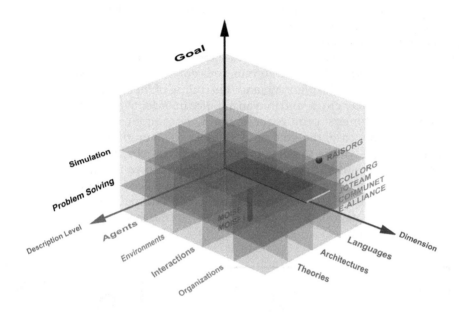

Fig. 25 Classification of Organizational Reasoning Models and Architectures [70].

Considering the organizational reasoning applications, presented in section 4.4, they have different research goals: while $\mathcal{R}$ AISORG adopts a **Simulation** perspective, $\mathcal{C}$ OLLORG , $\mathcal{J}$ OJTEAM , $\mathcal{C}$ OMMUNET and $\mathcal{E}$-ALLIANCE adopt a **Problem Solving** perspective. The first application has only **Languages** as its description level value, while the others deal with two values in this axis: **Architectures** (for their agents) and **Languages** . Finally, $\mathcal{R}$ AISORG deals with **Organizations** in the focus dimension, while $\mathcal{C}$ OLLORG , $\mathcal{J}$ OJTEAM , $\mathcal{C}$ OMMUNET and $\mathcal{E}$-ALLIANCE deal both with **Agents** and **Organizations** in this dimension.

5 Conclusions and perspectives

In this work, we have shown that autonomous cognitive agents, immersed on an open MAS, can enhance their efficiency and adaptability to environmental changes if they could represent and exploit, by using adequate internal mechanisms, information about the others and about the organizations they are eventually involved with.

We also show that agents interactions and organizations form a virtuous circle, as shown in figure 26. On one hand, interactions may generate dynamic bottom-up organizations, named coalitions, making it possible a collective action. On the other hand, if this collective action must be repeated frequently, it is more adequate to create top-down formal organizations, that limit agents interactions and allow them to achieve their global goals more efficiently.

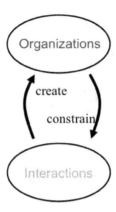

Fig. 26 Interactions and Organizations in MAS.

The European Network of Excellence for Agent-Based Computing[9] (Agent Link II) has prepared a research roadmap [57], whose technological perspectives may be found in figure 27. One can clearly notice that that many issues treated in this work are presented in its medium term perspectives, like dynamic laws, organizations, norms and social structure, and self-organization. In particular, we believe that these issues are crucial and needed to build solutions involving the technological trends described in section 1.2.

We hope that the social and organizational reasoning models presented in this paper may give a step ahead in order to help these issues be operational in the very next future, and thus showing the great potential of agent based technology to solve interesting and real problems, specially those concerning autonomous entities that must evolve in open and dynamically changing scenarios.

Acknowledgements First of all, I would like to thank Rino Falcone for his patience in attending this contribution. This paper summarizes the results of a certain number of research projects that were developed during the last 20 years. Using a reflective mechanism with respect to the subject of the paper, this huge amount of research could not possibly be reached without the help of a huge number of coalitions, composed by several undergraduate and graduate students, pos-doc fellows, Brazilian and International colleagues. As I could not possibly mention all of them, without the risk of forgetting some names, I would like to express my deepest thanks to Jomi Hübner, former student and current colleague, in the name of whom I intend to thank all these students and colleagues. Additionally, I would like to express all my gratitude to Rosaria Conte and Olivier Boissier, that I consider much more that mere colleagues, but real friends. I would like also to thank the Brazilian (FAPESP, CNPq, CAPES, USP) and international (ENSMSE-FR, European Commission, Region Rhône-Alpes-FR) funding agencies that have sponsored these projects. Last but not least, I would like to

---

[9] Project funded by the European Commission, IST-1999- 29003.

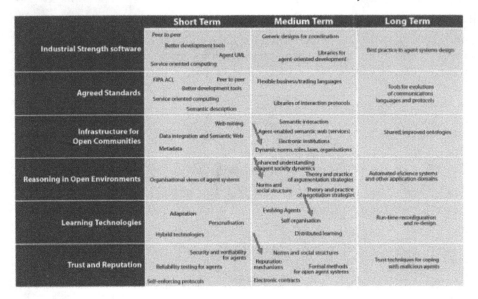

Fig. 27 Agent Link Technological Perspectives [57].

express to Helder Coelho and Cristiano Castelfranchi my deepest thanks for having had the chance to share their scientific rigor, their example of citizenship, their human wisdom and their warm friendship along all these years. I would like them to know that they have always been, they are and they will be for a long time my best models of scientists and men.

References

1. Diana Francisca Adamatti, Jaime Sim~ao Sichman, and Helder Coelho. An analysis of the insertion of virtual players in GMABS methodology using the Vip-JogoMan prototype. *Journal of Artificial Societies and Social Simulation*, 12(3), 2009.
2. I. Alloui, J. M. Andreoli, O. Boissier, M. Bratu, S. Castellani, and K. Megzari. E-Alliance: a software infrastructure for inter-organizational alliances. In *Proc. of the 9th ISPE International Conference on Concurrent Engineering: Research and Applications (CE2002)*, 2002.
3. Priscilla Avegliano and Jaime Sim~ao Sichman. Reputation-based partnership formation: some experiments using the RePart simulator. In Rino Falcone, Suzanne Barber, Jordi Sabater-Mir, and Munindar Singh, editors, *Proceedings of the 11th International Workshop on Trust in Agent Societies*, pages 114–120, Estoril, Portugal, May 2008.
4. Robert Axelrod. *The Evolution of Cooperation*. Basic Books, New York, 1984.
5. Philippe Bernoux. *La Sociologie des Organisations*. Seuil, Paris,, 1985.
6. O. Boissier, P. Beaune, H. Proton, M. Hannoun, T. Carron, L. Vercouter, and C. Sayettat. The multi-agent system toolkit. Technical report, SIC/ENSMSE, Saint-Etienne, France, 1998.
7. Olivier Boissier. *Problème du Contrôle dans un Système Integré de Vision. Utilisation d'un Système Multi-Agents*. Thèse de Doctorat, Institut National Polytechnique de Grenoble, Grenoble, France, January 1993.
8. Olivier Boissier and Jaime Sim~ao Sichman. Organization oriented programming. Tutorial Notes, 3rd. International Joint Conference on Autonomous Agents and Multiagent Systems (AAMAS 2004), New York, USA, August 2004.

9. Alan H. Bond and Les Gasser. An analysis of problems and research in DAI. In Alan H. Bond and Les Gasser, editors, *Readings in Distributed Artificial Intelligence*, pages 3–35. Morgan Kaufmann Publishers, Inc., San Mateo, CA, USA, 1988.

10. M. E. Bratman, D. J. Israel, and M. E. Pollack. Plans and resource-bounded practical reasoning. *Computational Intelligence*, 4:349–355, 1988.

11. Rodney A. Brooks. A robust layered control system for a mobile robot. *IEEE Journal of Robotics and Automation*, 2(1):435–453, March 1986.

12. Eleri Cardozo, Jaime Sim~ao Sichman, and Yves Demazeau. Using the active object model to implement multi-agent systems. In *Proceedings of the 5th IEEE International Conference on Tools with Artificial Intelligence*, pages 70–77, Boston, USA, November 1993. IEEE Computer Society Press.

13. Cristiano Castelfranchi. Social power: A point missed in multi-agent, DAI and HCI. In Yves Demazeau and Jean-Pierre Müller, editors, *Decentralized A. I.*, pages 49–62. Elsevier Science Publishers B. V., Amsterdam, NL, 1990.

14. Cristiano Castelfranchi. Guarantees for autonomy in cognitive agent architecture. In Michael J. Wooldridge and Nicholas R. Jennings, editors, *Intelligent Agents*, volume 890 of *Lecture Notes in Artificial Intelligence*, pages 56–70. Springer-Verlag, Berlin, DE, 1995.

15. Cristiano Castelfranchi. Engineering social order. In Andrea Omicini, Robert Tolksdorf, and Franco Zambonelli, editors, *Engineering Societies in the Agent World, First International Workshop, ESAW 2000, Berlin, Germany, August 21, 2000, Revised Papers*, volume 1972 of *Lecture Notes in Computer Science*, pages 1–18. Springer, 2000.

16. Cristiano Castelfranchi, Maria Micelli, and Amedeo Cesta. Dependence relations among autonomous agents. In Eric Werner and Yves Demazeau, editors, *Decentralized A. I. 3*, pages 215–227. Elsevier Science Publishers B. V., Amsterdam, NL, 1992.

17. Philip R. Cohen and Hector J. Levesque. Intention = choice + commitment. In *Proceedings of the 6th National Conference on Artificial Intelligence*, pages 410–415, Seattle, WA, July 1987. Morgan Kaufmann Publishers, Inc.

18. Rosaria Conte and Cristiano Castelfranchi. Mind is not enough: Precognitive bases of social interaction. In Nigel Gilbert, editor, *Proceedings of 1992 Symposium on Simulating Societies*, pages 93–110, Guildford, UK, April 1992.

19. Rosaria Conte, Maria Miceli, and Cristiano Castelfranchi. Limits and levels of cooperation: Disentangling various types of prosocial interaction. In Yves Demazeau and Jean-Pierre Müller, editors, *Decentralized A. I. 2*, pages 147–157. Elsevier Science Publishers B. V., Amsterdam, NL, 1991.

20. Rosaria Conte and Roberto Pedone. Finding the best partner: The PARTNET system. In Jaime Sim~ao Sichman, Rosaria Conte, and Nigel Gilbert, editors, *Multi-Agent Systems and Agent-Based Simulation*, volume 1534 of *Lecture Notes in Artificial Intelligence*, pages 156–168, Berlin, DE, 1998. Springer-Verlag.

21. Rosaria Conte and Jaime Sim~ao Sichman. DEPNET: How to benefit from social dependence. *Journal of Mathematical Sociology*, 20(2–3):161–177, 1995.

22. Rosaria Conte and Jaime Sim~ao Sichman. Dependence graphs: Dependence within and between groups. *Computational & Mathematical Organization Theory*, 8(2):87–112, 2002.

23. Rosaria Conte, V. Veneziano, and C. Castelfranchi. The computer simulation of partnership formation. *Computational & Mathematical Organization Theory*, 4(4):293–315, 1998.

24. Luciano R. Coutinho, Jaime Sim~ao Sichman, and Olivier Boissier. Modelling dimensions for agent organizations. In Virginia Dignum, editor, *Handbook of Research on Multi-Agent Systems: Semantics and Dynamics of Organizational Models*, chapter 2, pages 18–50. IGI Global, Hershey, 2009.

25. Nuno David. Modelling and implementing AND and OR-dependencies in social reasoning. Dissertaç~ao de Mestrado, Faculdade de Ciências, Universidade de Lisboa, Lisboa, Portugal, 1998.

26. Nuno David, Jaime Sim~ao Sichman, and Helder Coelho. Agent-based social simulation with coalitions in social reasoning. In Scott Moss and Paul Davidsson, editors, *Multi-Agent-Based Simulation*, volume 1979 of *Lecture Notes in Artificial Intelligence*, pages 244–265, Berlin, DE, 2000. Springer-Verlag.

27. Keith S. Decker. TÆMS: A framework for environment centered analysis and design of coordination mechanisms. In Greg M. P. O'Hare and Nicholas Jennings, editors, *Foundations of Distributed Artificial Intelligence*, pages 429–447. John Wiley & Sons Ltd., Baffins Lane, UK, 1996.

28. Yves Demazeau. From interactions to collective behaviour in agent-based systems. In *Pre-proceedings of the invited lectures of the 1st European Conference on Cognitive Science*, St. Malo, France, March 1995. ARC / INRIA.

29. Virginia Dignum. *A model for organizational interaction: based on agents, founded in logic*. Phd Thesis, University of Utrecht, Utrecht, The Netherlands, 2004.

30. Alexis Drogoul, Bruno Corbara, and Steffen Lalande. MANTA: New experimental results on the emergence of (artificial) ant societies. In Nigel Gilbert and Rosaria Conte, editors, *Artificial Societies: the Computer Simulation of Social Life*, pages 119–221. UCL Press, London, UK, 1995.

31. Jean Erceau and Jacques Ferber. L'intelligence artificielle distribuée. *La Recherche*, 22(233):750–758, June 1991.

32. Marc Esteva, Juan A. Rodríguez-Aguilar, Carles Sierra, Pere Garcia, and Josep L. Arcos. On the formal specification of electronic institutions. In Frank Dignum and Carles Sierra, editors, *Agent-mediated Electronic Commerce*, volume 1191 of *Lecture Notes in Artificial Intelligence*, pages 126–147. Springer-Verlag, Berlin, DE, 2001.

33. Henri Farreny and Malik Ghallab. *Eléments d'Intelligence Artificielle*. Hermès, Paris, FR, 1987.

34. Jacques Ferber. *Les Systèmes Multi-Agents: Vers une Intelligence Collective*. InterEditions, Paris, France, 1995.

35. Jacques Ferber and Olivier Gutknecht. A meta-model for the analysis and design of organizations in multi-agents systems. In Yves Demazeau, editor, *Proceedings of the 3rd International Conference on Multi-Agent Systems*, pages 128–135, Paris, France, 1998. IEEE Computer Society Press.

36. Les Gasser. Organizations in multi-agent systems. In *Pre-proceedings of the 10th European Workshop on Modelling Autonomous Agents in a Multi-Agent World*. IMAG, Annecy, France, 2001.

37. M. P. Georgeff and F. F. Ingrand. Decision-making in an embedded reasoning system. In N. S. Sridharan, editor, *Proceedings of the 11th International Joint Conferennce on Artificial Intelligence*, volume 2, pages 972–978, Detroit, USA, August 1989. Morgan Kaufmann Publishers, Inc.

38. Gustavo Alberto Giménez-Lugo. *Um modelo de sistemas multiagentes para partilha de conhecimento utilizando redes sociais comunitárias*. Tese de Doutorado, Programa de Pós-Graduaç~ao em Engenharia Elétrica, Escola Politécnica da USP, S~ao Paulo, Brasil, April 2004.

39. Gustavo Alberto Giménez-Lugo, Analia Amandi, Jaime Sim~ao Sichman, and Daniella Godoy. Enriching information agents' knowledge by ontology comparison: A case study. In José C. Riquelme Francisco J. Garijo and Miguel Toro, editors, *Advances in Artificial Intelligence - Iberamia 2002*, volume 2527 of *Lecture Notes in Artificial Intelligence*, pages 546–555, Sevilha, 2002. Springer-Verlag.

40. Gustavo Alberto Giménez-Lugo, Jaime Sim~ao Sichman, and Jomi Fred Hübner. Addressing the social components of knowledge to foster communitary exchanges. *International Journal on Web Based Communities*, 2(1):176–194, 2005.

41. Daniella Godoy and Analia Amandi. PersonalSearcher: An intelligent agent for searching web pages. In Maria Carolina Monard and Jaime Sim~ao Sichman, editors, *Advances in AI*, volume 1952 of *Lecture Notes in Artificial Intelligence*, pages 43–52, Berlin, DE, 2000. Springer-Verlag.

42. Mahdi Hannoun. *MOISE: Un modèle organisationnel pour les systèmes multi-agents*. Thèse de Doctorat, Ecole Nationale Supérieure des Mines de Saint-Eienne, Saint-Etienne, France, December 2002.

43. Mahdi Hannoun, Olivier Boissier, Jaime Sim~ao Sichman, and Claudette Sayettat. MOISE: An organizational model for multi-agent systems. In Maria Carolina Monard

and Jaime Sim~ao Sichman, editors, *Advances in AI*, volume 1952 of *Lecture Notes in Artificial Intelligence*, pages 152–161, Berlin, DE, 2000. Springer-Verlag.

44. Carl E. Hewitt. Offices are open systems. In Alan H. Bond and Les Gasser, editors, *Readings in Distributed Artificial Intelligence*, pages 312–329. Morgan Kaufmann Publishers, Inc., San Mateo, CA, USA, 1986.

45. Bernardo A. Huberman and T. Hogg. Communities of practice: Performance and evolution. Technical report, Xerox Palo Alto Research Center, 1994.

46. Jomi Fred Hübner. *Um Modelo de Reorganizaç~ao de Sistemas Multiagentes*. Tese de Doutorado, Programa de Pós-Graduaç~ao em Engenharia Elétrica, Escola Politécnica da USP, S~ao Paulo, Brasil, August 2003.

47. Jomi Fred Hübner, Olivier Boissier, and Jaime Sim~ao Sichman. Using a multi-agent organization description language to describe contract dynamics in virtual enterprises. In *Proc. IEEE/WIC/ACM International Conference on Intelligent Agent Technology (IAT'05)*, Compiègne – France, September 2005.

48. Jomi Fred Hübner, Jaime Sim~ao Sichman, and Olivier Boissier. A model for the structural, functional and deontic specification of organizations in multiagent systems. In Guilherme Bittencourt and Geber Ramalho, editors, *Advances in AI*, volume 2507 of *Lecture Notes in Artificial Intelligence*, pages 118–128, Berlin, DE, 2002. Springer-Verlag.

49. Jomi Fred Hübner, Jaime Sim~ao Sichman, and Olivier Boissier. Using the MOISE+ for a cooperative framework of MAS reorganization. In Ana Bazzan and Sofiane Labidi, editors, *Advances in AI*, Lecture Notes in Artificial Intelligence, Berlin, DE, 2004. Springer-Verlag.

50. Jomi Fred Hübner, Jaime Sim~ao Sichman, and Olivier Boissier. Developing organised multiagent systems using the MOISE+ model: Programming issues at the system and agent levels. *International Journal of Agent-Oriented Software Engineering*, 1(3/4):370–395, 2007.

51. Márcia Ito and Jaime Sim~ao Sichman. Dependence based coalitions and contract net: a comparative analysis. In Maria Carolina Monard and Jaime Sim~ao Sichman, editors, *Advances in AI*, volume 1952 of *Lecture Notes in Artificial Intelligence*, pages 102–111, Berlin, DE, 2000. Springer-Verlag.

52. Nicholas R. Jennings. Commitments and conventions: The foundation of coordination in multi-agent systems. *The Knowledge Engineering Review*, 8(3):223–250, 1993.

53. H. Kitano, A. Minoro, Y. Kuniyoshi, I. Noda, and E. Osawa. Robocup: The robot world cup initiative. In *Proceedings of the IJCAI'95 Workshop on Entertainment and AI/Alife*, Montreal, Canada, 1995. IJCAI Press.

54. Christian Lemaître and Cora B. Excelente. Multi-agent organization approach. In *Proceedings of the 2nd Ibero-American Workshop on DAI/MAS*, pages 7–16, Toledo, Spain, October 1998.

55. Hector J. Levesque, Philip R. Cohen, and José H. T. Nunes. On acting together. In *Proceedings of the 8th National Conference on Artificial Intelligence*, pages 94–99, Boston, MA, August 1990. Morgan Kaufmann Publishers, Inc.

56. R. D. Luce and H. Raiffa. *Games and Decisions: Introduction and Critical Survey*. John Wiley & Sons Ltd., 1957.

57. M. Luck, P. McBurney, O. Shehory, and S. Willmott. *Agent Technology: Computing as Interaction (A Roadmap for Agent Based Computing)*. AgentLink, 2005.

58. Thomas W. Malone. Modeling coordination in organizations and markets. In Alan H. Bond and Les Gasser, editors, *Readings in Distributed Artificial Intelligence*, pages 151–158. Morgan Kaufmann Publishers, Inc., San Mateo, CA, USA, 1987.

59. Fernando Marcellino and Jaime Sim~ao Sichman. A holonic multi-agent model for oil industry supply chain management. In *Proceedings of the 12th edition of the Ibero-American Conference on Artificial Intelligence (IBERAMIA'10)*, pages 244–253, Bahia Blanca, Argentina, November 2010.

60. Júlio de Lima do Rego Monteiro. Simulaç~ao de parcerias entre agentes: uma extens~ao do sistema Part-Net. Dissertaç~ao de Mestrado, Programa de Pós-Graduaç~ao em Engenharia Elétrica, Escola Politécnica da USP, S~ao Paulo, Brasil, 2004.

61. Júlio de Lima do Rego Monteiro and Jaime Sim~ao Sichman. Partnet++: simulating multiple agent partnetships using dependence graphs. In Jaime Sim~ao Sichman and Luis Antunes., editors, *Multi-Agent-Based Simulation VI*, pages 14–25. Springer-Verlag, Berlin, DE, 2005.
62. Edgar Morin. *La Méthode (1): La Nature de la Nature*. Seuil, Paris, 1977.
63. César Scarpini Rabak and Jaime Sim~ao Sichman. Using a-teams to optimize automatic insertion of electronic components. *Advanced Engineering Informatics*, 17(2):95–106, 2003.
64. Anand S. Rao and Michael P. Georgeff. Modeling rational agents within a BDI-architecture. In R. Fikes and E. Sandewall, editors, *Proceedings of the 3rd International Conference on Principles of Knowledge Representation and Reasoning*, pages 473–484, San Mateo, CA, USA, 1991. Morgan Kaufmann Publishers, Inc.
65. Stuart Russel and Peter Norvig. *Artificial Intelligence: A Modern Approach*. Prentice-Hall International, Englewood Cliffs, NJ, USA, 1995.
66. Jordi Sabater, Mario Paolucci, and Rosaria Conte. Repage: REPutation and ImAGE among limited autonomous partners. *Journal of Artificial Societies and Social Simulation*, 9(2), March 2006.
67. Onn Shehory and Sarit Kraus. Coalition formation among autonomous agents: Strategies and complexity. In Cristiano Castelfranchi and Jean-Pierre Müller, editors, *Preproceedings of the 5th European Workshop on Modelling Autonomous Agents in a Multi-Agent World*, volume 957 of *Lecture Notes in Artificial Intelligence*, pages 56–72. Springer-Verlag, Berlin, DE, 1995.
68. Jaime Sim~ao Sichman. *Du Raisonnement Social Chez les Agents: Une Approche Fondée sur la Théorie de la Dépendance*. Thèse de Doctorat, Institut National Polytechnique de Grenoble, Grenoble, France, 1995.
69. Jaime Sim~ao Sichman. DEPINT: Dependence-based coalition formation in an open multi-agent scenario. *Journal of Artificial Societies and Social Simulation*, 2(1), 1998.
70. Jaime Sim~ao Sichman. *Raciocínio Social e Organizacional em Sistemas Multiagentes: Avanços e Perspectivas*. Tese de Livre-Docência, Escola Politécnica da Universidade de S~ao Paulo, S~ao Paulo, Brasil, 2003.
71. Jaime Sim~ao Sichman and Rosaria Conte. Multi-agent dependence by dependence graphs. In *Proceedings of the 1st International Joint Conference on Autonomous Agents and Multi-Agent Systems*, pages 483–492, Bologna, Italy, 2002. ACM Press.
72. Jaime Sim~ao Sichman, Rosaria Conte, Yves Demazeau, and Cristiano Castelfranchi. A social reasoning mechanism based on dependence networks. In Tony Cohn, editor, *Proceedings of the 11th European Conference on Artificial Intelligence*, pages 188–192, Amsterdam, The Netherlands, August 1994. John Wiley & Sons Ltd.
73. Jaime Sim~ao Sichman, Rosaria Conte, Yves Demazeau, and Cristiano Castelfranchi. A social reasoning mechanism based on dependence networks. In Michael Huhns and Munindar Singh, editors, *Readings on Agents*. Morgan Kaufmann Publishers, Inc., San Mateo, CA, USA, 1998.
74. Jaime Sim~ao Sichman and Yves Demazeau. A model for the decision phase of autonomous belief revision in open multi-agent systems. *Journal of the Brazilian Computer Society*, 3(1):40–50, Jul 1996.
75. Carles Sierra, Cristiano Castelfranchi, Keith S. Decker, and Jaime Sim~ao Sichman, editors. *Proceedings of the 8th International Joint Conference on Autonomous Agents and Multi-agent Systems (AAMAS 2009), Budapest, Hungary, May 10-15, 2009, Volume 1*. IFAAMAS, 2009.
76. Carles Sierra, Cristiano Castelfranchi, Keith S. Decker, and Jaime Sim~ao Sichman, editors. *Proceedings of the 8th International Joint Conference on Autonomous Agents and Multi-agent Systems (AAMAS 2009), Budapest, Hungary, May 10-15, 2009, Volume 2*. IFAAMAS, 2009.
77. Reid G. Smith. The contract net protocol: High-level communication and control in a distributed problem solver. *IEEE Transactions on Computers*, 29(12):1104–1113, December 1980.
78. Peter Stone and Manuela M. Veloso. Task decomposition and dynamic role assignment for real-time strategic teamwork. In Jörg P. Müller, Munindar P. Singh, and Anand S.

Rao, editors, *Intelligent Agents V (Proceedings of the 5th. International Workshop on Agent Theories, Architectures and Languages)*, volume 1555. Springer-Verlag, Berlin, DE, 1999.

79. R. S. Sutton and A. G. Barto. *Reinforcement Learning: An Introduction*. MIT Press, Cambridge, MA, USA, 1998.

80. Milind Tambe. Towards flexible teamwork. *Journal of Artificial Intelligence*, 7:83–124, 1997.

81. J. Travers and S. Milgram. An experimental study of the small world problem. *Sociometry*, 32(4):425–443, 1969.

82. Michael Wooldridge and Nicholas R. Jennings. Towards a theory of cooperative problem solving. In Yves Demazeau, Jean-Pierre Müller, and John Perram, editors, *Pre-proceedings of the 6th European Workshop on Modelling Autonomous Agents in a Multi-Agent World*, pages 15–26, Odense, Denmark, August 1994.

83. Michael J. Wooldridge and Nicholas R. Jennings. Agent theories, architectures and languages: A survey. In Michael J. Wooldridge and Nicholas R. Jennings, editors, *Intelligent Agents*, volume 890 of *Lecture Notes in Artificial Intelligence*, pages 1–39. Springer-Verlag, Berlin, DE, 1995.

Chapter 36
You should be happy!

Frank Dignum and Virginia Dignum

Abstract In this chapter, we investigate the relations between norms and emotions. As the title of this paper indicates, people often have norms about having emotions and also apply sanctions when they are violated. However, emotions are taken to be something people cannot (easily) control, so it seems strange to have norms about emotions. We will investigate whether we can give a formal description of these kinds of norms and whether they are the same as other norms or have special properties.

1 Introduction

A Liber Amicorum with as many contributions as the present one is quite unique! You should be happy! Of course, it may well be that you are quite disappointed with the topics and the level of the contributions and by the time you are reading this article are very bored and disappointed. It is not something you consciously decided to do, it is just an effect of reading the articles. Still, the admonishment that you should be happy seems appropriate. So, what should you do? As happiness is an emotion, it is not really possible to just decide to be happy now again. Or is it?

Statements such as:

- "you should be happy",
- "you should not be angry at your mother in law",
- "you should not be afraid of the dog",
- "you are allowed to be sad about the rejection of your paper"

Frank Dignum
Department of Computing Sciences, Utrecht University, The Netherlands
e-mail: dignum@cs.uu.nl

Virginia Dignum
Faculty of Technology, Policy and Management, Delft University of Technology, The Netherlands
e-mail: M.V.Dignum@tudelft.nl

all express a normative valuation of an emotion. In order for the norms to be fulfilled one should or should not have a certain emotion. However, when we use norms we usually assume they regulate behavior such that it conforms to the norm. When the person has no control over a state (in this case the emotion) how can we expect that the person complies with the norm and what does it mean if the person violates a norm? In order to check these kinds of properties we should first investigate what type of norm these norms on emotions are.

Literature proposes many different definitions for the concept of norm that basically assume four different types of norms: universal or deontic norms (explicit, imposed norms, enforced by a formal institution, *laws*), directed norms (explicit, agreed upon, norms between two or more parties), social norms (implicit rules of behaviour in a certain social context, emergent, incited by "critical mass") and private norms (personal convictions on how one should behave, one's own default behaviour). Basically, it can be said that deontic norms guide how one ought to act based on an external (universal) standard. Directed norms guide how someone should behave based on an agreed upon standard between several parties. Private norms guide how one ought to act based on an internal standard. All of these types of norms are prescriptive norms. Social norms show how people do act based on a standard created by the very act of all people behaving in a certain way (descriptive norms).

To our knowledge, there are no laws (formal norms) that regulate emotions. I.e. the norms expressed above would never appear in a legal system of norms regulating the behaviour of people. So, following the 'classification' of norms above, it seems the norms on emotions described above, can not be seen as formal norms.

We can ask ourselves whether these norms can ever be directed norms. I.e., can they be agreements between two parties? E.g. if I keep my dog on a leash, you should not anymore be afraid of the dog. It seems that this is a reasonable use of directed norms on emotions. Of course, if we look closer at this situation there are probably other norms involved. Possibly I might not be allowed to take a dog with me in some place, because it might bite other people. I can then justify taking the dog by stating that if I keep it on a leash it will not be able to bite other people and therefore they should not be afraid of the dog anymore.

Finally, it does seems that the above norms can easily be interpreted as being private or social norms. A person can have a private conviction that he should not be angry at his mother in law, due to the fact that he should avoid any problems with his family in law. It could also be a social law that one should not be afraid of dogs, because they are considered to be cute animals and liking dogs makes one be perceived as a nice person.

The above considerations already show that norms on emotions reflect more a description of how one is expected to act, according to some value system or cultural background (we will discuss this in more detail later on) than a prescription of behavior. That is, if one is considering social norms, the interpretation of "should" is more likely to be something as "it is socially expected to" rather than "obliged to" as in deontic norms. In the same way, a prohibition is likely to be interpreted as "socially undesirable". Nevertheless, both in formal as in social norms, the aim of formalization is to reason about the effects of compliance and violation. As such, in this paper we will treat the formalization of deontic and social norms in the same way.

A lot of research has been done on the use of deontic logic for the interpretation of formal, prescriptive norms. Using some form of Deontic logic we could easily formally express the statements above as follows:

- $O(Happy(y))$
- $F(Angry(y, MiL(y)))$
- $F(Fear(y, dog))$
- $P(Sad(y, reject))$

So, assuming we express emotions as a predicate indicating a state a person can be in, possibly in relation to some other entity, then the above is a correct representation of norms about emotions. But, although we do have a logical representation of these norms, we seem to have missed a lot of subtle points.

One of those issues is the connection between the norm over the emotion and behavior associated to the emotion. E.g. I should not be happy if my big rival in a running race just broke her leg. But what if I tell my friends with a big smile that I am so sad she broke her leg? Certainly, that would not really be acceptable. A good hypothesis probably is that any behavior that conveys the forbidden emotion is also forbidden. How we establish this relation between an emotion and behavior is another point of course.

Although there are probably many more points to consider, the main point we want to ponder is what the purpose of these norms actually is. The purpose of most norms is to regulate behavior of a group of persons as to benefit the group in some way. Is this also true for norms over emotions? If so, what kind of behavior do they regulate and how do they benefit the group? the above formalizations do not really give any clues for the answers to these questions. However, there is sociological research that can be used to look for some possible pointers to answers.

Quite some work has been done in cultural psychology along the lines of the last question, but with a subtle different emphasis. The question being whether emotions are culture dependent. In specific, there has been research about the differences in emotions between collectivistic and individualistic cultures. In [7], Eid and Diener show that especially with respect to self-conscious emotions such as pride and guilt there is a difference between people living in a collectivistic culture and those living in an individualistic culture. In general normative behavior is more important in a collectivistic culture and consequently the emotion of pride is valued less high, is experienced less and sometimes even suppressed. The emotion of guilt is suppressed more in individualistic cultures as it is more common to blame someone or something outside oneself for failures. This research shows that (cultural) norms do influence emotions. However, it does not yet indicate the exact purpose of these types of norms and what exactly is regulated with the norms.

In the next section we will shortly describe some characteristics of emotions as background for the discussion on norms over emotions. In section 3 we will discuss the different types of norms and their properties. We will particularly look for concepts characterizing norms that can be used to link them to emotions. The relation between norms and emotions itself is discussed further in section 4. In the last section of this chapter we draw some conclusions and speculate about further work.

2 Emotions

In Wikipedia, emotions are defined as follows:

> Emotion is the complex psychophysiological experience of an individual's state of mind as interacting with biochemical (internal) and environmental (external) influences.

Whether we agree completely with this definition is not very important for the present paper. However, the most salient point from the definition is that emotions are "psychophysiological". I.e. they involve both physiological parts as well as psychological parts. This poses problems for anyone that wants to create a (formal) model of emotions. There are not many psychophysiological studies and the models that exist are expressed as possible correlations between some personality trait and physiological characteristics related to some specific emotion or phenomenon such as fear or addiction (see e.g. [2]).

So, it is clear that it will be very difficult to fully characterize emotions, incorporating both the physiological as well as the psychological aspects plus their relations. We will leave that for some future work (:-)). Nevertheless, we cannot ignore the physiological aspects of emotions even though we may have little information about it. We do know that physiological phenomena have a temporal aspect. Thus emotions also have this temporal aspect. This is confirmed by a classification made by Clore et al. [3], which describes that emotions are a temporary state that relate to a specific object (which can be a physical or mental object or action). So, it seems emotions are not persistent, but they arise from a certain situation and also disappear again. When emotions arise they trigger an emotion regulation mechanism that supports the disappearance of the emotion. In [8], Gross and Thompson distinguish five mechanisms to regulate emotions: situation modification, attentional deployment, cognitive change, response modulation and situation selection.

Although the intuition is that emotions arise in an uncontrolled fashion, these mechanisms suggest ways to regulate emotions by adjusting triggers that might lead to emotions. E.g. if I am in love with someone I can choose to be around that person as much as possible, because that situation will cause the positive emotion of love. If I get very sad thinking about a broken relation I can concentrate on my work and thus push away the cognitive state (beliefs about this relation) that leads to the negative emotion.

Another important aspect of emotions that is not mentioned in the Wikipedia definition, is that emotions have a positive or negative valence. If a person is in a state where she experiences a positive emotion, she will evaluate that state as being a good one. I.e., it leads to a preference of being in that state (and

experiencing the emotion connected to it). Because the emotions are unconditionally experienced as positive or negative, indirectly they also can be used as
an evaluation of the psychophysiological state that causes the emotion. In that
sense an emotion can function as a very explicit marker of a situation stating
that it is either a good or bad situation to be in. This aspect of emotions ties
in with the notion of *value systems* of individuals and groups and societies of
people.

Value systems are also used to valuate situations with respect to a certain
aspect [5]. Values are ideals that are considered to be worth pursuing. Or,
as defined by Scott in [15], (moral) values as the standards of good and evil
that guide an individual's behaviour and choices. Individuals, groups, and
societies develop their own value systems used for the purpose of ethical integrity. Examples of widely shared values are health, safety, security, freedom,
joy, beauty, friendship, justice. People will generally exercise, promote and
sometimes demand behaviour - by themselves and others - that supports such
values. E.g. a value such as "security" can be used to compare situations that
are (felt to be) more or less secure. If the value of security is important for a
person he will avoid taking risks in all kinds of situations. E.g. he will not start
talking to a stranger, because he is not sure whether the stranger will react in
an adverse way. On a national level this value might lead to a conservative
government that enforces strict laws in order to increase national security.
[10] gives a conceptual analysis of values and represents them formally through
the basic notion of *preference*. Which enforcement mechanisms are effective and
how sanctions are likely to be followed is directly related to the values of a
society.
The difference between emotions and value systems is that emotions are very
personal (even have a physiological component, as stated in the definition
above) and temporary. They can be seen as markers of situations that are good
or bad. When classifying many situations that trigger the same emotion one
might use a value. I.e. if I always get a positive emotion of "pride" when
achieving a goal (even though it costs a lot of effort and caused negative emotions along the way) these situations might be classified through the value of
"achievement". The situations that are marked by emotions (like "pride") are
thus seen as being preferred in some way and this is "explained" by the fact that
the situations are promoting an (important) value (such as "achievement").

In the above we have mainly described primary (or universal) emotions.
These emotions are connected to biological factors and thus can be found in
all cultures across the world. There are 7 emotions that are seen as universal: anger, fear, sadness, disgust, surprise, happiness, and contempt. There are
also emotions that are triggered by (social) cognitive factors. Especially the
social emotions such as shame and guilt are connected with social relations
and norms. Castelfranchi et.al. [16] have written about some cognitive characterisation and formalisation of shame and guilt and their difference. However,
they mainly describe how these emotions arise from the existence of certain
social relations and norms and private decisions of an agent. I.e. an agent will
feel guilty if it has internalized a norm and knowingly violated it by doing
something that he could have avoided doing (or not doing something he could

have done). So, social emotions are already linked to norms in the way they are triggered. In this paper, we will discuss another aspect, namely that of norms about the emotion itself. So, the point is not that I will feel guilty after I stole something (which is a violation of a norm), but that I *should* feel guilty after I evaded paying tax (while maybe I don't feel guilty at all).

The above description of emotions shows that emotions motivate actions in diverse ways. The regulation mechanisms are triggered when an emotion arises. Thus the emotion can be seen as motivating the regulative actions. E.g. when I feel fear when standing near the edge of the roof of a high building I can step away to avoid the emotion. In the other hand, when I feel love when close to my partner I can plan to be close to her in order to trigger this positive emotion. Although emotions might be seen as a kind of desires in the second example, they are usually not used in the same way. Our intuition is that emotions are generally not used by themselves as a motivation to generate a goal or plan, but are used in combination with other factors to either enforce the desirability or undesirability of a desired state.

This leads us to the question what is the role or purpose of emotions. Why do we have emotions? What would be different if we don't have emotions? Although quite some research exists on emotions it is difficult to find any useful answers to these questions. The closest is probably the theory developed by Damasio [4] in which he links emotions to somatic markers. Thus the purpose of emotions is to mark situations (as being special). It gives the possibility to classify many situations together that are marked with the same emotion (even though they might differ in many other respects). It also supports the intuition that emotions can be strong or weak, where a strong emotion marks a situation as being very important and worth reacting to and learn from and a weak emotion might just confirm existing (regulative) behaviour. Seeing emotions this way fits with the intuition that they do not, by themselves, motivate certain behavior but are used to guide behavior. It is, of course, not to be expected that we solve the question of the purpose of emotions in this short chapter, but we will use the idea of emotions guiding behaviour later on when discussing norms about emotions.

3 Norms

A lot has been written about norms in diverse disciplines like law, philosophy, ethics, logic, sociology and computer science. Although we are not going to give an overview of the treatment of norms in each of these disciplines it is important to see that norms play a role in many aspects of life and have many different facets.

One important aspect that we want to mention here is the moral side of norms. This is probably the main difference between a norm and a convention. Both conventions and norms are (expected) patterns of behavior. As an example, we would argue though that e.g. driving on the right side of the road is a convention, while using your indicators when turning of the road is a norm.

The difference between the two (in our opinion) is that one would follow the convention of driving on the right side of the road *because* everyone else is doing the same. Following the expected pattern of behavior and complying to the group is somehow "convenient". There is no intrinsic reason why driving on the right hand side of the road would be better. So, in countries where they drive on the left hand side of the road we will just as easy follow suit. Even the point that one should drive all on the same side of the road is more a matter of convenience than of a moral stance. It has to do with the fact that cars move quick and therefore it is easier to drive if you more or less drive in the same direction. This convention changes when looking at pedestrians. Here people usually are bound to use available space on the sidewalk rather than choosing to walk all at the same side.

The use of indicators when turning of the road does have a slightly different flavor. Even if most people would not use their indicators it would still be *good* to use them. So, the motivation to follow this norm is not just because everyone else follows it and it is convenient to conform to the group but because one wants to promote a certain value. I.e. it can be said that the norm of using your indicators is established to promote the value of safety. Thus a situation in which the norm is followed is preferred, with respect to the value of safety, over a situation where the norm is violated. Thus the decision of violating the norm or obeying it gets a moral flavor related to some specific values that it promotes.

The above does not mean that norms cannot have aspects of conventions. One can fulfil a norm just because it is a norm. Thus implying that one fulfils the norm because everyone does it and it is expected behavior. One might argue that the actual reason to comply to a norm in this way would be to show that your behavior is in line with the values that are prevalent in a group. Assuming that the norm is promoting some group value(s), fulfilling a norm then becomes a way to show that you also promote the group value(s). One can distinguish a situation where an individual agrees with the group value(s) and actually *adopts* a norm because it promotes these values and a situation where an individual does not adopt the norm, but merely recognizes its importance for being a member of the group. In the second case, fulfilling the norm would not have any moral reason, it would just be motivated by the need to fit into the group and fulfilling the norm supports that.

Especially for what are called "emergent" or "social" norms the conventional aspect is important. Social norms are not promulgated by some authority but rather emerge over time from interactions between individuals in a society. The enforcement of social norms is thus not regulated through some authority, but done by individuals themselves. If someone sees a violation of a norm he can react on the violation. The reaction can be a direct punishment, a decrease in reputation, etc. In the same way if someone notices many people fulfilling a norm this might lead to compliance as well. The conventional aspect of these norms will thus increase the enforcement of the norm within a group.

Research by Hofstede has shown that national cultures differ in particular at the level of, usually unconscious, values held by a majority of the population [11]. Values, in this case, are "broad preferences for one state of affairs over others". The Hofstede dimensions of national cultures are rooted in our unconscious values. Because values are acquired in childhood, national cultures are remarkably stable over time; national values change is a matter of generations. A recent line of research, unsurprisingly quite directly related to the work of Cristiano Castelfranchi, aims to understand and link norm type preferences to society culture. This will in particular, enable policy makers to decide on the best normative approach to use as implementation of a policy. For instance, in cultures centered (or preferring) individual norms, a campaign illustrating the negative effects of smoking will be more effective than a formal law prohibiting smoking. The latter will in turn be more effective in cultures centered on formal normative systems [5].

So far, we have discussed some aspects of norms without any formalization. Although this suffices to discuss general principles, a formal description will enhance the precise definition of the notions involved and also will show whether some expected properties indeed follow from the way concepts are related. Of course, there are many formalizations of norms. Most notably different forms of deontic logic have been used to formalize them, e.g. [19, 14, 6, 12].

Different formalizations can exist in parallel because they all stress different aspects of norms. In classical deontic logic [19] the content of a norm was an (abstract) state. This fits with the high abstraction level on which norms are discussed in philosophy. However, this makes it impossible to specify norms over concrete actions, which becomes very important when using norms for software systems. For this reason dynamic deontic logic [14] was developed.

In many cases it is important to indicate within which time limit a norm should be fulfilled (e.g. we must finish this article before the end of the month). This gave rise to several versions of temporal deontic logics, some incorporating actions and others only states [6, 1].

The fact that norms might be apparently inconsistent (e.g. when one norm is applicable when another norm is violated) led to the use of non-monotonic logics for formalizing this aspect of norms [12].

When considering a formalization of norms about emotions, the question is which properties we would like to capture in the formal model. Given these properties, one can choose the most appropriate formalism to express them and analyze the possible consequences of these properties. Although emotions do have a temporal aspect it seems that the norms over the emotions do not have this temporal aspect. I.e. we do not say "you should be happy within 20 minutes after reading this chapter". The norms on emotions seem to be instantaneous. Because emotions are a kind of state and a formalism that could express norms over states would seem the most natural. As stated in the introduction we could express the obligation to be happy as follows:

$O(happy)$

Probably we would like to extend this with a condition, because most people don't think one should always be happy, but only in certain conditions, such as when reading this paper:

$O(happy(x)|read(x, paper))$

Now let's compare this formalization with that of the fact that one has to pay the bill when one has bought something:

$O(paid(x,item)|buy(x,item))$

The format of this obligation is identical to the one about being happy. However, there seems to be a difference in connotation. As said before, although the emotion seems to be a kind of state, it is not a state that by itself can function as a goal for which actions are planned. Unlike the second case where the person that bought an item should plan actions such that he also has paid for the item, the condition of being happy either follows or does not follow after reading a paper.

If we look at a norm that states a prohibition on an emotion like "you shouldn't be sad when you loose a game" it can be formalized in a similar way:

$F(sad(x)|lost(x,game))$

In this prohibition it becomes clear that this norm might also entail norms on the regulative mechanisms of the emotion. E.g.

$lost(x,game) \rightarrow F(express(x,sad))$
$lost(x,game) \rightarrow O(suppress(x,sad))$
$O(avoid(lost(x,game)))$

I.e. one should not express that one is sad after loosing a game, one should try to suppress the emotion itself and one should try to avoid a situation in which the emotion is triggered. The last obligation is quite debatable, but we mention it anyway as it seems at least to be a possible connection. Notice that the above norms are all norms on actions rather than states. They follow semantically from the norm on the emotion, because the actions are connected to that emotion. In a similar way we would have the following norms attached to the norms that you should be happy when reading the paper:

$read(x,paper) \rightarrow O(express(x,happy))$
$read(x,paper) \rightarrow F(suppress(x,happy))$
$F(avoid(read(x,paper)))$

As expected, also in this case the norm works the same way for the regulative action of expressing the emotion and reverses for the second and third regulative actions. A complete logical formalism for norms over emotions would thus need to be able to express both norms over states and actions and also we should have axioms that connect the norms over emotions with the norms over the regulative mechanism of that emotion. We will not pursue this (interesting) aspect in this chapter, but leave it for future work.

One aspect that does not appear in this formalization is the connection of norms to values. If it is true that norms exist in order to promote a particular structure of values then we should be able to connect the norms to the values formally as well. In the next section, we will argue that this can be done through the use of constitutive norms, represented through counts-as rules. The basic ideas of using the counts-as rules stem from philosophy and were used by e.g. Searle to *define* social reality. In [13], Jones and Sergot made a first attempt to formalize and analyse the notion of counts-as. In [9], Grossi has refined the formalization in order to capture the definitional and creative power of the counts-as rules. So, if we state that a drivers licence counts as a means of identification, we are not just stating that drivers licences are classified as identifications. We are also defining means of identification by stating that concrete papers such as drivers licences count as a means of identification.

We can use the counts-as to connect norms to values. In order to do this we first introduce values and values structures as criteria along which situations can be compared. I.e. we assume that given a set of values and a structure of priorities over that set we can order pairs of situations using that value structure. E.g. if I think that environment should be of the highest priority I will prefer a situation where I take a bike to go to work over a situation where I take the car. In [18], van der Weide gives a formal description of this idea of using values to create preferences over situations. Now we can state that a norm counts-as an implementation of a value structure iff fulfilling the norm leads to a situation that is preferred according to the value structure than the situation one gets when violating the norm. Formally, given σ_1 and σ_2, states in some Kripke model:

Let $VS = (\{v_1, ... v_n\}, <_p)$ be a value structure where $<_p$ indicates the priorities over the set of values $\{v_1, ... v_n\}$ then
$O(\varphi|\psi) \Rightarrow_{ca} Impl(VS)$ iff $(\sigma_1 \models \psi \wedge \varphi$ and $\sigma_2 \models \psi \wedge \neg\varphi)$ then $\sigma_2 <_{VS} \sigma_1$

First note that we use $Impl(VS)$ rather than VS. It indicates that the norm does not count as the value system itself but rather as an implementation of the value system. The value system itself is not true or false, it is merely a criterion. The implementation of a value system is a set of norms that indicate ideality aligned with the value system, but can also extend to other preferences that align with the value system.

We use $<_{VS}$ as the preference order between states that is induced by VS. It is based on the fact that each value can be used to order the states and the ordering $<_{VS}$ is the combined preference ordering based on all values and their priorities. More on this (intricate) part can be found in [17].

In the next section we will show how value structures as above can be used to provide a formalization for norms on emotions.

4 Norms about emotions?

The most crucial element in the combination of norms and emotions is the fact that we do not consciously plan for the emotion (at least as an independent state). An emotion arises in certain situations and functions as a marker of that (type) of situation. It does not mean that we have absolutely no control over our emotions. However, this control is not part of our conscious deliberation over plans and actions. As seen from the literature on the connection between emotions and culture, the triggering mechanism might be conditioned through cultural factors that determine the feedback that is given whenever a certain emotion is shown.

So, the obligation to have a certain emotional state is not meant to start planning actions to induce that emotional state. One could still argue that such an obligation is actually meant to be an obligation to reach a situation where the emotional condition is triggered. However, as the examples given in this paper show, often the norm is stated with respect to a certain given condition and the emotion should follow straight from that condition. E.g. when you read this article you should be happy. That is, the emotion should be the consequence of (or, be triggered by) the condition of reading this article.

The first step that we make to analyze the norms on emotions is the triggering of the emotion itself. We claim that the triggering of the emotion leads to a state (where the emotion is felt) that is preferred according to the value system that the person uses. We use $\psi \rightsquigarrow emotion$ to indicate a state transition from a state in which ψ holds to a state in which ψ holds together with the emotion, where that emotion is triggered by ψ. Thus we can define:

> For a value structure $VS = (\{v_1, ... v_n\}, <_p)$ as above:
> $(\psi \rightsquigarrow emotion) \Rightarrow_{ca} Use(VS)$ iff $(\sigma_1 \models \psi$ and $\sigma_2 \models \psi \wedge emotion)$ then $\sigma_1 <_{VS} \sigma_2$

Note that the emotion does not have to be a positive emotion. The above just states that the emotion is a kind of marker that indicates how the situation is valued according to VS and when the emotion is felt the situation always is more in line with VS than before the emotion is triggered. Also note that here we use $Use(VS)$ rather than $Impl(VS)$ because we see how a concrete state transition aligns with the value system and thus how the value system is used rather than implemented.

The above connects the triggering of emotions with values. However, it did not say anything about norms yet. However, we can extend the above definition with norms as follows:

> For a value structure $VS = (\{v_1, ... v_n\}, <_p)$ as above:
> $O(emotion|\psi) \Rightarrow_{ca} Impl(VS)$

So, the obligation on the emotion is implementing the preference ordering induced by the value system VS.

We mentioned the definitial character of the counts-as relation before. It is worth to re-iterate that aspect here. Although we say that the norm implements a certain value system, the value system might not be very well defined. It is at least partially defined by the fact that these norms are implementing it. This concurs with the fact that most people would not really be able to give a (complete) account of their value system but would be able to state whether a certain norm (on emotions) is aligned with a value system.

The final point to make about these norms on emotions is what to do with it. Apparently they are meant to convey that certain emotions in a certain situation are according to a value system or not. However, if the emotions are directly triggered by the situation without the person having (much) control over it, what can one do to comply to the norm?

Basically, being reminded of the norm will influence the strength of the triggering mechanism. And thus the emotion will be influenced by the sheer fact that the norm is made explicit. This reinforcement effect is typical for this type of norms and different from any other type of norms. We did not formalize this aspect, but this could be done by attaching a strength to the $\rightsquigarrow$ relation. Other things that a person does have control over can also be used to comply with a norm on emotions. One can try to avoid situations that trigger the emotion or seek those situations if the emotion is desirable. And one can try to avoid expressing the emotions and thus pretend the emotion did not arise, which gives at least the impression that one acts according to a value system that is aligned with the norm on that emotion. We might formalize this link to the regulative actions as follows:

$O(emotion|\psi) \Rightarrow$
$[\psi \rightarrow (O(express(emotion)) \wedge F(suppress(emotion)))] \wedge F(avoid(\psi)))$

The above means that a model that makes $O(emotion|\psi)$ true also should make the other norms true. Although we do not discuss this connection in depth we can at least easily see that all these norms also are implementations of VS whenever $O(emotion|\psi)$ is an implementation of VS. That is the actions that are obliged are aligned with the value system and the ones that are forbidden would lead to less preferred states according to the value system.

5 Conclusions

In this chapter we have attempted to shed some light on the intriguing notion of norms over emotions. Rather than a careful analysis of a specific aspect of norms over emotions we have attempted to perform a broad sweep over the area touching upon a number of issues that seem important.

Firstly, norms of emotions are never deontic norms that are enforced by an external authority. They typically are social norms. The enforcement of social norms is done through mechanisms of social inclusion and/or exclusion. These mechanisms of inclusion and exclusion are linked to what is sometimes called the "moral circle" [11]. Moral circles function around the sharing of culture through a common value system. Thus social norms can be seen to be directly linked to a value system in this way.

We have argued that emotions can be seen as marking important or salient situations. These situations can also indicate whether on adheres to a certain value system that would prefer that type of situation. In particular we argued that the triggering of an emotion in a situation can be seen as counting as using a particular value system. Thus having a norm stating that an emotion should or should not arise in a situation counts as implementing the value system. It states exactly that the emotion in that situation is according (or against) the value system.

Because emotions are not goals in themselves we saw that an obligation over an emotion (although possibly expressed in the same way as an obligation over a state) is not meant to lead to a concrete plan to achieve the emotion (or avoid it). So, the purpose of the norm itself does not seem to be to influence behaviour directly. Rather it seems to be meant to re-inforce the value system that it implements. Thus an obligation on an emotion actually can be seen as an obligation to adhere to a (shared) value system. How this aspect can be formalized and analyzed is an interesting issue for future work.

A more formal framework in which norms, emotions, values (and thus norms on emotions) could be expressed will be of great help to understand and verify some assumptions related to social and culture dependent behaviour. Of course, this chapter raised more questions than it gave any answers. It was meant to start some new directions of research rather than report on work performed. Some first steps for future work would be on a precise characterization of emotions, values and norms in the same framework, expressing their relationships and properties. Next would be a framework explaining how norms over emotions influence individual behaviour and interact with it. For this we also would need a model of individual behaviour including not only things like BDI, but also norms, emotions and values.

For now we are happy that we reached the end of this chapter and hope that the same holds for the reader of this chapter (either because it is finally finished or because he enjoyed reading it)!

References

1. J. Broersen, F. Dignum, V. Dignum, and J.-J. Meyer. Designing a deontic logic of deadlines. In A. Lomuscio and D. Nute, editors, *Proceedings of the 7th International Workshop on Deontic Logic in Computer Science (DEON'04)*, LNAI 3065, pages 43–56. Springer Verlag, 2004.
2. J. Cacioppo, G. Berntson, J. Larsen, K. Poehlmann, and T. Ito. The psychophysiology of emotion. In R. Lewis, J. Haviland-Jones, and L. Barrett, editors, *The Handbook of Emotions*, pages 180–195. Guilford Press, 2008.
3. G. Clore, R. Wyer, B. Dienes, K. Gasper, C. Gohm, and L. Isbell. Affective feelings as feedback: some cognitive consequences. In L. Martin and G. Clore, editors, *Theories of mood and cognition: A users guide*, pages 27–62. Erlbaum, 2001.
4. A. Damasio. *Descartes Error: Emotion, Reason and the Human Brain*. Papermac, 1994.
5. F. Dechesne and V. Dignum. No smoking here: Compliance differences between deontic and social norms. *In Proceedings of AAMAS'2011*, 2011.
6. F. Dignum and R. Kuiper. Combining dynamic deontic logic and temporal logic for the specification of deadlines. In J. R. Sprague, editor, *Proceedings of thirtieth HICSS*, 1997.
7. M. Eid and E. Diener. Norms for experiencing emotions in different cultures: Inter- and intranational differences. In E. Diener, editor, *Culture and Well-Being*, volume 38 of *Social Indicators Research Series*, pages 169–202. Springer Netherlands, 2009.
8. J. Gross and R. Thompson. Emotion regulation: Conceptual foundations. In J. Gross, editor, *Handbook of emotion regulation*, pages 3–26. Guilford Press, 2007.
9. D. Grossi, J.-J. Meyer, and F. Dignum. The many faces of counts-as: A formal analysis of constitutive rules. *Journal of Applied Logic*, 6(2):192 – 217, 2008.
10. S. O. Hansson. *The Structure of Values and Norms*. Cambridge University Press, 2001.
11. G. Hofstede. *Culture's Consequences, Comparing Values, Behaviors, Institutions, and Organizations Across Nations*. Sage Publications, Thousand Oaks CA, 2001.
12. J. F. Horty. Deontic logic as founded on nonmonotonic logic. *Annals of Mathematics and Artificial Intelligence*, 9:69–91, 1993.
13. A. Jones and M. Sergot. A formal characterisation of institutionalised power. *Logic Journal of IGPL*, 4(3):427–443, 1996.

14. J.-J. Meyer. A different approach to deontic logic: Deontic logic viewed as a variant of dynamic logic. *Notre Dame Journal of Formal Logic*, 29:109–136, 1988.
15. E. Scott. Organizational moral values. *Business Ethics Quarterly*, 12(1):33–55, 2002.
16. P. Turrini, J.-J. Meyer, and C. Castelfranchi. Coping with shame and sense of guilt: a dynamic logic account. *Autonomous Agents and Multi-Agent Systems*, 20:401–420, May 2010.
17. T. van der Weide. *Arguing to Motivate Decisions*. PhD thesis, Utrecht University, 2011.
18. T. van der Weide, F. Dignum, J.-J. Meyer, H. Prakken, and G. Vreeswijk. Arguing about preferences and decisions. In *Proc. of the 7th Int. Workshop on Argumentation in Multi-Agent Systems (ArgMAS 2010)*, 2010.
19. G. H. von Wright. Deontic logic. *Mind*, 60:1–15, 1951.

Part VIII
Cognitive and computational social science

Chapter 37
Artefacts, not words

Domenico Parisi

1 Theories as artefacts and their implications for the cognitive and social sciences

Science needs both theories and facts. Theories are necessary to identify the mechanisms and processes which underlie the observed facts and explain them, and facts are needed to verify if a proposed theory is correct. If the predictions derived from a theory match the observed facts, the theory can be considered as (provisionally) correct. If not, the theory must be abandoned or modified. Physics is considered as the paradigm of science because it has both theories and objectively observed, quantitative, facts and is based on a constant dialogue between theories and facts. On the contrary, the sciences that study human behaviour and human societies find it difficult to establish a virtuous circle between theories and facts and, as a consequence, they must be considered as immature sciences. Why theories and facts do not talk with each other in the sciences of human behaviour and human societies? There are many answers to this question but a crucial one is that, while theories in physics are expressed by using mathematical symbols, theories in the cognitive and social sciences are expressed by using the words of the common language. Mathematical symbols have precise and unambiguous meanings, and from mathematically expressed theories one can derive detailed, quantitative, and noncontroversial empirical predictions to be matched with the observed facts. On the contrary, the words of the common language have ill-defined and ambiguous meanings and from verbally expressed theories it is difficult to derive detailed, quantitative, and noncontroversial empirical predictions. As a consequence, in the cognitive and social sciences the virtuous circle between theories and facts is difficult to establish. There are many theories and many empirical facts but theories are not really confirmed or disconfirmed by empirical facts, and empirical facts are not explained by theories.

Domenico Parisi
Institute of Cognitive Sciences and Technologies, CNR, Italy
e-mail: domenico.parisi@istc.cnr.it

Theories in the cognitive and social sciences resemble philosophical theories. Philosophy is made up of words, and philosophers try to establish truth by analyzing words, by reasoning about words, and by using words to argue with other philosophers. Unlike philosophers, scientists must look at reality beyond words, to reveal reality beyond the veil of words. Words incline us to think that reality is made up of "essences", and philosophers try to establish what are these "essences", but scientists know that there are no essences. Philosophers tend to think that the "order of ideas" is the same as the "order to things" but scientists do not believe that the "order of things" is necessarily the same as the "order of ideas", and they cannot just analyze verbally expressed ideas but must be able to show that these ideas match empirically observed facts. Like philosophers, cognitive and social scientists rely too much on words and, even when they try to match words with observed facts, it is not clear if they match or not. This is why the cognitive and social sciences are not really sciences, or mature sciences. Science originates from philosophy but is different from philosophy. In the last few centuries the natural sciences have emancipated themselves from philosophy. For the cognitive and social sciences this remains a task for the future.

The computer will change all this. The computer makes it possible to express scientific theories in a novel way: by constructing computer-based artefacts that reproduce reality. If you have a theory of some empirical phenomena, use the theory to construct an artefact. (We use the word "theory" to cover theories, models, hypotheses or, more simply, ideas.) If the artefact reproduces the empirical phenomena, then you can conclude that the theory you have used to construct the artefact is (provisionally, like all scientific theories) correct. Of course, the artefact will simplify with respect to reality, but all scientific theories simplify with respect to reality and they are useful because they simplify. Science is not a re-description of reality. Science is useful (both from the point of view of knowledge and understanding and from the point of view of its applications) because it simplifies with respect to reality and tries to identify the essential mechanisms and processes underlying reality. The problem is not to simplify. The problem is doing the correct simplifications, where a simplification is correct if it incorporates all which is essential to explain (reproduce) the phenomena of interest, and it leaves other things out.

Expressing theories of reality as computer-based simulations of reality is an important novelty for science. Traditionally, scientific theories are expressed by using symbols, either the symbols of mathematics or the words of the common language. Physics expresses its theories by using mathematical symbols: equations and systems of equations. The cognitive and social sciences express their theories by using the words of the common language, with some redefinition of terms. Computers make it possible to express scientific theories by constructing artefacts so that science can proceed on the basis of a new principle: If you want to understand X, reproduce X. This is an important novelty especially for the cognitive and social sciences because these sciences cannot express their theories by using mathematical symbols and the words of the common language have unclear and ambiguous meanings, but it may be an important novelty for all of science, including physics and the other natural sciences like chemistry and biology. In this chapter we are concerned with the cognitive and social sciences and, therefore, we will restrict ourselves to discussing the implications of expressing scientific theories as artefacts for these sciences.

Before we discuss these implications, we add a comment. We have said that in the cognitive and social sciences theories are expressed by using the words of the common language but this is not always the case. If verbally expressed theories have the serious limitations we have noted above, one possibility is to try to mimic physics and express theories of cognitive and social phenomena by using mathematics. The science of economics has taken this option for more than a century and, today, the availability of computers with their very large memory and processing capacities and new theoretical developments based on viewing reality as made up of complex systems induce many researchers to explore how mathematically expressed theories can be applied to cognitive and social phenomena. It is still difficult to judge these attempts because they are in their very early stages, but they can probably shed some light on cognitive and, especially, social phenomena. However, one should reflect that the particular social science which has more consistently and completely embraced the idea of expressing theories in mathematical terms, the science of economics, appears today not to be able to go beyond a superficial understanding of economic phenomena, as indicated by its inability to predict economic phenomena and to advise on how to control them. The same might be true for the more recent attempts to use ideas from statistical mechanics, complexity theory, and network theory to develop mathematical theories of cognitive and social phenomena. Although these attempts are interesting and they should be pursued, they tend to capture the regularities present in large quantities of data but they do not even try to identify the mechanisms and processes which underlie cognitive and social phenomena and explain them. This is important to note because theories as artefacts may resemble mathematical theories but the similarity is superficial. Mathematically expressed theories of cognitive and social phenomena try to capture regularities in the data. Theories as artefacts try to reproduce the mechanisms and processes that underlie these regularities. Both types of theories may be needed but one does not substitute for the other. (An interesting question is why mathematical theories of physical phenomena appear to capture all we need to know about physical phenomena while this is not true when mathematical theories are applied to the phenomena studied by cognitive and social scientists. This is an interesting empirical fact about reality which science (which science?) should be able to explain.)

What are the implications for the cognitive and social sciences of expressing scientific theories as artefacts? We will briefly discuss four implications.

(1) Theories as artefacts do not have the limitations of verbally expressed theories. As we have said, words tend to have ill-defined and ambiguous meanings while a theory expressed as an artefact cannot be ill-defined or

ambiguous because, if it is ill-defined or ambiguous, the artefact cannot be constructed. Verbally expressed theories are unable to generate specific and noncontroversial empirical predictions while theories expressed as artefacts generate a large number of specific, detailed, and noncontroversial empirical predictions because the behaviours of the artefact are the empirical predictions derived from the theory used to construct the artefact, and these behaviours, and what underlies them, are under the eyes of everybody. Therefore, if they will express their theories as computer-based artefacts, we can expect better and more mature cognitive and social sciences.

(2) Science is divided up into disciplines but reality is not divided into disciplines. Reality is made up of a very large number of different phenomena which are all connected together so that explaining the phenomena studied by one discipline may require to take the phenomena studied by another discipline into consideration. Expressing theories as artefacts will make it possible to develop a nondisciplinary science which will allow us to capture the interconnectedness of reality. Science has so far been divided into disciplines because the mind of the scientist can store and process only a limited quantity and variety of empirical data. If scientific theories are expressed as computer-based artefacts, computers do not have these limitations and they can store and process very large quantities and varieties of empirical data, in principle all the empirical data concerning the different aspects of a given phenomenon which are studied by the different disciplines. This will make it possible to abolish disciplinary divisions, and this is especially important for the cognitive and social sciences. In the natural sciences, physics, chemistry, and biology, disciplinary divisions exist but they do not cause much damage because all the natural sciences speak the same language, use the same methods (laboratory experiments), and share the same vision of reality as made up of quantitative phenomena and cause-effect relations. This is not true for the cognitive and social sciences, which do not speak the same language, use different empirical methods, and have different conceptual and cultural traditions. Computer-based theoretical artefacts will become a "lingua franca" for all the cognitive and social sciences, and they will make it possible to construct theories of human beings and their societies which ignore disciplinary divisions not only among the cognitive and social sciences but also between these sciences and the natural sciences.

(3) Another important implication of expressing theories as artefacts for the cognitive and social sciences concerns how scientific knowledge is related to values. Science must give us knowledge and understanding but it should also be practically, socially, and politically useful. However, science functions appropriately and it allows us to really understand reality if it keeps the question of how is reality clearly separated from the question of how we would like it to be, that is, knowledge/understanding from values. (This is another important difference between science and philosophy since in philosophy knowledge and values appear to be, probably correctly, almost fused together.) The need to keep knowledge clearly separated from values is more easily satisfied in the sciences that study nature than in the sciences that study human beings

because scientists are human beings, and human beings have desires and fears, moral values and political ideologies, concerning themselves and their societies. In fact, one of the main reasons why the sciences that study human beings are so weak is that scientists are human beings. One of the advantages of expressing theories of human behaviour and human societies as artefacts is that it becomes easier for these sciences to keep knowledge and understanding clearly separated from desires, fears, and values. As we have said, with verbally expressed theories it is always controversial what are the empirical predictions that can be derived from a theory, and from verbally expressed theories of human beings we tend to derive the predictions that we like and to ignore those we do not like. This is impossible for theories expressed as artefacts. With theories expressed as artefacts, it is not us who derive (or not derive) the empirical predictions from our theories but it is the theory, i.e., the artefact, that does this for us. The empirical predictions derived from a theory expressed as an artefact are the behaviours of the artefact, and everyone can see these behaviours, whether he or she likes them or not.

(4) A final implication of expressing theories as artefacts concerns the relation between science and technology. Theories expressed as artefacts are an important novelty in the history of mankind because so far artefacts have been artefacts constructed to satisfy practical needs. Theories expressed as artefacts are artefacts that are constructed not to satisfy practical needs but to allow us to better know and understand reality. They are scientific artefacts. But scientific theories expressed as artefacts tend to make science more similar to technology, so that it may become increasingly difficult to draw a dividing line between the two. (Notice that in modern societies science and technology tend also to be confused together because they are both subject to the strong pressures of the economy.) Science is trying more and more to understand reality by manipulating reality and by creating additional pieces of reality, for example in the chemical, biological, and medical sciences. But these are physical manipulations and the creation of new types of physical entities. Theories as computer-based artefacts are another step in this direction of "knowing by doing" but computer-based artefacts create reality in a more abstract medium: the computer. This may pose problems for human beings when the artificial reality which is created is a "mental" reality.

2 Robots

Attempts at expressing theories of the human mind by constructing computer simulations of the human mind are more than half a century old and this already long history can be divided into two phases. In the first phase the crucial expression was "artificial intelligence" and the idea was to program computers so that they would exhibit human intelligence. In the last 25 years or so, things have changed and now the crucial word is no more "artificial intelligence" but "robots". The change concerns the very conception that we have of the human mind, and therefore it is of great importance. Artificial intelligence is based on the traditional view of the mind as separated from nature. Mind has nothing to do with the body and, more generally, with physical and biological reality and, therefore, the artefacts that reproduce the mind should not reproduce the body or any other aspects of physical and biological reality. Today, a shift has taken place towards artificial systems that try to reproduce the human mind (but also the "mind" of nonhuman animals) without ignoring its physical basis: the body, the brain, the sensory and motor organs, the physical environment with which the organism interacts, the inherited genes of the organism, the evolutionary history which has resulted in those genes. This shift has various causes, from the constant progresses of the biological sciences, especially the neurosciences, genetics, and evolutionary biology, to the recognition that systems of "artificial intelligence" may be practically useful but they do not tell us much about the human mind, to economic/technological factors that lead to exploring new types of artefacts and computer applications. Today, the new buzz words are artificial life, neural networks, and robotics. Artificial life is an attempt at reproducing in artificial systems all the phenomena of the living world, not only the "mind" of organisms. Neural networks are computational models of the nervous system. Robots are physical artefacts that resemble real organisms and behave like real organisms.

The new paradigm is based on an embodied and action-based conception of the mind according to which the body is critical for the mind. The environment is represented in the mind (or, rather, brain) not in terms of the sensory inputs that arrive to the organism's sensory organs but in terms of the motor actions with which the organism responds to these inputs. What is in the mind may be more or less abstract but it must be derived, in one way or another, from sensory-motor experiences. Organisms are physical objects which exist in a physical environment and to understand their behaviour one has to consider their two-way interactions with the physical environment: the environment affects the organism and is affected by the organism. The embodied conception of the mind requires that the artificial systems that we construct as theories of the mind must be robots. The robots may be simplified with respect to real organisms and they may be simulated in a computer rather than physically realized but in all cases they must have a body with a given shape and size, sensory and motor organs, and they must "live" in a physical environment containing various objects (including other robots) and possessing various properties. The robots must also have other properties. Their body must not only have an external morphology and external sensory and motor organs but it must have internal organs and systems and their brain must interact with (receive input from and act on) these internal organs and systems and not only with the external environment. The robots' behaviour must be controlled by a system which reproduces the basic properties and processes of the brain, that is, an artificial neural network, and the robot must possess an inherited artificial genotype which specifies the basic properties of the robot's body and, especially, brain and is the current result of an evolutionary process which has taken place in a succession of generations of individually different robots.

Trying to understand behaviour and social phenomena by constructing robots and societies of robots is a very promising approach to the study of cognitive and social phenomena. However, current robotics only very partially fulfils these promises. The main reason that explain this is that, for funding reasons, robots tend to be constructed with practical applications in mind, and constructing robots with practical applications in mind is often an obstacle if we want to reproduce in robots many important aspects of mental and social phenomena because these aspects do not appear to have practical applications. Science must have applications but an excessive preoccupation for applications may reduce the potential of science for letting us know and understand reality and, also, for suggesting new and more interesting future applications.

We will dedicate the remaining part of this Chapter to describing (some aspects of) the state of the art of the new paradigm which studies the mind by constructing robots. Our description will reflect our view of the field and will mostly describe our own work, already realized or in progress. In some cases our robots will resemble the "agents" of agent-based social simulations and, more generally, we will emphasize social robotics because this book honours Cristiano Castelfranchi, and his work has been particularly illuminating for our understanding of sociality and social phenomena. There are many resemblances between our view of robotics and the agent-based approach to the study of social phenomena. But an important difference is that the agent-based approach tends to preserve the traditional separation between the cognitive and social sciences and the sciences of nature and is not particularly concerned with the biological properties of "agents", while, as we have said, the robotic approach, as we conceive it, squarely puts the study of mind and society in a "naturalistic" framework. This has implications for how robots are constructed. Many current robots are programmed by us but this is not appropriate if robots must resemble real organisms because real organisms are not programmed by anybody. Real organisms are the result of an evolutionary history at the population level and of a learning history at the individual level. Therefore, our robots must be evolved robots and/or robots that learn.

3 Robots that have motivations and emotions

Robots are distinguished into autonomous and non-autonomous. Non-autonomous robots, such as those which are sent to Mars or have medical (e.g., surgeon robots) or military applications (e.g. drones), collect information from the environment with their sensors, send this information to a human being, and the human being decides what the robot should do in response to the sensory information. In contrast, autonomous robots possess their own control system which receives sensory input from the sensors and autonomously decides how to respond to the sensory input, without human intervention. (Notice, however, that the dimension "autonomous/non-autonomous" is a continuum, and robots can have various degrees of autonomy.)

But are current autonomous robots really autonomous? To answer this question one has to consider that there are two levels of functioning in the behaviour of organisms. Organisms have many genetically inherited motivations that they must satisfy to remain alive and reproduce. For example, they have to eat, mate, and avoid dangers. (More complex organisms, such as human beings, have not only genetically inherited motivations but also motivations which are learned during life on the basis of genetically inherited motivations.) The problem is that, generally, organisms can only (try to) satisfy one single motivation at a time and, therefore, at any given time they have to "decide" which motivation to satisfy with their behaviour. (We use quotation marks to indicate that, even in human beings, these decisions rarely are explicit and rational.) This is the motivational or strategic level of behaviour. Once a decision has been taken at the motivational level, the organism must generate the behaviour which will hopefully satisfy the motivation decided at the motivational level. This is the cognitive or tactical level of functioning of behaviour.

Current autonomous robots are autonomous at the cognitive level but they are not autonomous at the motivational level. They are autonomous at the cognitive level because their control system, their "brain", autonomously decides how to respond to sensory input given the motivation they have to satisfy (or, more correctly, the task they have to accomplish). But they do not take motivational decisions and they cannot be said to have motivations since their motivations are the motivations of the human being who is using them or has constructed them. Even assuming that robots have different motivations (or, more correctly, that they can accomplish different tasks), it is their users or constructors who decide which motivation they have to satisfy at any given time.

The reason why we do not construct robots which are motivationally autonomous is that it is not clear how these robots might be practically useful and, what may be even more important, they might create problems and dangers for us. But motivational autonomy and the motivational level of functioning of an organism are crucial aspects of the behaviour of organisms and we should try to better understand motivations and motivational autonomy by constructing robots that are motivationally autonomous. In fact, some attempts at constructing robots that have motivations and are motivationally autonomous can be made. The robots live in an environment in which in order to survive they have to both eat and drink, or to both eat and fly from a predator, or look for a mate, or care for their offspring or stop moving to heal from bodily damage and, since they cannot do more than one thing at the same time, they have to choose which motivation to pursue at any given time. The robots evolve both the capacity to choose correctly, given the circumstances, which motivation to pursue and the capacity to do what is appropriate for satisfying their currently active motivation.

If we do not construct robots which have their own motivations and are motivationally autonomous, we cannot construct robots that have emotions.

Some current robots express emotions and, to some extent, they can recognize the emotions expressed by us but current robots do not really have (feel) emotions and do not really understand our emotions. (Neuroscientific evidence tells us that to understand the emotion expressed by another person we have to feel that emotion ourselves.) Why do we say so? What is the relation between motivation and emotion?

As we have said, the motivational level of functioning of an organism is the level at which the organism's brain "decides" which particular motivation, among its numerous motivations, to try to satisfy with its behaviour at the present time. The capacity to make the appropriate motivational decisions is a critical requirement for organisms, even more important, from the point of view of the organism's survival and reproductive chances (and well-being), than the cognitive ability to produce the appropriate behaviours that allow the organism to satisfy the motivation which has been decided at the motivational level. Motivational decisions must be correct, in many cases they must be very fast, the organism must persist in pursuing one motivation even if it has been unable to satisfy the motivation so far, and the organism must abandon a motivation which it is impossible to satisfy. This is where emotions enter the scene. Emotions are states of the organism's brain and body (not only brain) that allow the organism to make more correct and fast motivational decisions, to persist in trying to satisfy an important motivation and to abandon a motivation which for the organism it is impossible to satisfy. The brain of most organisms (but especially of more complex organisms) has evolved special neural circuits which influence the motivational decisions of the organism. The states of these circuits are what we call emotions or emotional states, and they are "felt" states (felt emotions) because the circuits interact with the rest of the organism's body (both with the internal organs and systems and with the external surface of the body) which sends sensory inputs to the brain that constitute the "feeling" of emotions. Robots which have many different motivations make more effective motivational decisions (have better survival/reproductive chances) if the neural network which controls their behaviour includes an emotional circuit, compared to robots lacking the emotional circuit.

Only if robots really have emotions, that is, if they are robots for which emotional states have a well-defined functional role in determining their behaviour, the robots can be said to express emotions (unless, of course, they are robotic actors). As we have said, the emotional circuits of the organism's brain interact with the rest of the organism's body and some of these interactions change the external appearance of the body, producing postures and movements of the organism's face or entire body. These postures and movements are perceived by another individual's brain which reacts by activating similar states in its own emotional circuits. In this manner, other individuals can not only perceive but also understand the emotions of the organism. And since knowing and understanding the emotions of others are an important component of social behaviour, the expression of emotions may not just be a by-product of the states of the emotional circuit of the organism but it may have been shaped and made more sophisticated by evolution (and, to some extent, culture) so that other individuals can know and understand the emotions of an individual and behave more appropriately with respect to the individual.

As we have said, in the last 25 years there has been a change of paradigm in the study of the mind through the construction of artefacts that have a mind, and this change can be synthesized by saying that one has moved from artificial intelligence to artificial life. What is the deep meaning of this paradigm change? In the cultural tradition of the West, the mind tends to be identified with intelligence, reason, and cognition. But intelligence, reason, and cognition are only one half of the mind. The other half is made up of motivations and emotions, that is, of the mechanisms and processes which cause an individual to decide which motivation to pursue at any given time and of the emotional states of the body/brain that make these motivational decisions more effective. The shift from artificial intelligence to artificial life should have been a shift from constructing artefacts that reproduce one half of the mind, the cognitive part, to constructing artefacts that reproduce the entire mind. But this is not what has happened, and the reason is that, as we have said, artefacts possessing a mind today are mostly constructed in view of practical applications, and artefacts that have practical applications need only to have the cognitive part of the mind, not its motivational/emotional part. This has implications for what Raymond Kurzweil has called the Singularity, which is the moment in the future in which it will be possible to construct artefacts that are more intelligent than we are. What will happen in that moment? Should we be worried? But what we should ask and perhaps be worried about is not what will happen in the moment in which we will be able to construct artefacts that are more intelligent than we are but what will happen in the moment, which can be much closer, in which we will construct artefacts that have their own motivations and emotions.

In the meantime, constructing artefacts that have the other half of the mind, the motivational/emotional half, can make it possible to understand many important phenomena of the human mind. Examples of such phenomena are individual differences not only in cognitive ability but also in character and personality, pathological states which interest not only neurologists but also psychiatrists, and art as artefacts that people spend their time (and money) to produce and to expose themselves to. The simple robots mentioned above which have both a motivational and a cognitive level of functioning can exhibit inter-individual differences not only in their ability to eat or drink or mate but also in the strength of their motivations to eat, drink, and mate and in their capacity to choose appropriately which motivation to pursue at any given time. They can also exhibit cognitive pathologies, due to damages to some parts of their neural network, and psychological or psychiatric disturbances due to the malfunctioning of other parts of their neural networks. And they can spend their time in producing and exposing themselves to artistic artefacts that make their emotional states more sophisticated and articulated, and therefore, more effective in helping them to make appropriate motivational decisions.

4 Robots that have a mental life

Current robots respond to stimuli with movements of their body. This is behaviour. But, in addition to behaviour, human beings (and, to some extent,
other animals) have a mental life. What is mental life? Most stimuli which
arrive to an organism's brain originate in the external environment or in the
organism's own body, and the brain responds by generating movements of
the organism's motor organs. Mental life is the self-generation of stimuli by
the brain itself. Instead of receiving stimuli from outside, something happens
in the brain which produces sensory input for the brain. And the brain may
respond to these self-generated stimuli by self-generating other stimuli, in a
chain which can be very long, as when we are immersed in our thoughts or
we dream.

What is the nature of these self-generated stimuli? Self-generated stimuli
can be visual stimuli similar to those which are produced by objects or people
that exist in the external environment but, in humans, in addition to this type
of self-generated stimuli, self-generated stimuli tend to be linguistic stimuli
(which of course are a subclass of acoustic stimuli). In fact, mental life is to a
large extent talking to oneself. The self-generation of stimuli is responsible for
imagining, recollecting, having dreams and hallucinations, but when the self-
generated stimuli are linguistic stimuli what we have is thinking, reflecting,
reasoning, making explicit predictions, explicitly evaluating alternatives.

Clearly, if we are interested in understanding human beings, mental life is
a crucial component of what we need to understand. Do we construct robots
that have a mental life? The answer is No, and there are two reasons for this.
The first reason is the same reason why we do not construct robots that have
motivations and emotions: it is not clear what practical applications robots
that have a mental life would have. But it is not only a question of practicality.
We psychologically resist the idea of constructing robots that have a mental
life. Are we disposed to construct robots that have their own mental life, that
are immersed in their thoughts, that may arrive to conclusions that we ignore?
Mental life is inherently private. Do we want our robots to have a private life,
something that we do not know, something to which we do not have access
unless the robot decides to talk to us?

The other reason why we do not construct robots that have a mental life
is that, as we have said, mental life is largely talking to oneself and we have
not been able so far to construct robots that can really talk, i.e., that use a
human(-like) language. This is discussed in the next Section.

5 Robots that have (human) language

There are attempts at constructing robots that send communicative signals to
other robots and respond appropriately to these signals, and even robots that

appear to be able to understand our language and to talk to us but these attempts have many limitations. The robotic "languages" are extremely simple and very different from human language. Furthermore, robots that communicate among themselves tend to be identical robots (cf. the robots of swarm robotics) but language is a social behaviour and, as we will discuss later, social behaviour very much depends on who are the individuals which interact and communicate, how different they are and how converging or diverging are their interests. As for the robots that communicate with us, these robots do not really understand what we say but they are only programmed to respond with particular actions to the sounds that we produce. Similarly, they do not understand the sounds that they themselves produce but are only programmed to produce particular sounds in specific circumstances.

Constructing robots that have language is crucial for our understanding of the human mind because language modifies, probably radically, the human mind. For example, language changes how human beings categorize the world. From a robotic or "embodied" perspective, possessing categories consists in the evocation of similar activation patterns in a sub-set of units of the robot's neural network by different objects as a consequence of the fact that the robot responds with the same behaviour to these objects. What is the impact of language on categories? If in the robot's experience the objects that belong to the same category co-vary with the same sound (the word that designate the category), the representations of the different objects in the robot's "brain" become more similar, and more different from the representations of objects of other categories that co-vary with different sounds. And this leads to improvements in how the robot responds to the different objects. But the examples of the impact of language on the human mind can be multiplied. Language causes the world of human beings to become populated by distinct entities possessing clear-cut boundaries and distinct properties, which may not be true for the world of nonlinguistic animals. This difference between the world of humans and the world of other animals should be reproduced with robots. Turning to actions, some current robots reach for objects and grasp these objects with their hand, and these actions also are represented in the robot's "brain". Are these actions represented differently in the robot's "brain" if, in addition to being able to reach for and grasp objects, the robot is able to use (produce and respond to) such sounds as "reach" and "grasp"? What if the robot were able to differentiate among the acoustic signals "reaches", "is reaching", "will reach", "has reached", "to reach", "reaching"? This can be extended to the whole of language. Would the robot's behaviour and the robot's mental life be different if the robot could use appropriately the acoustic signals "I", "you", "he/she/it", "we", "they", or if it could distinguish between proper vs common names, mass vs count nouns, concrete vs abstract nouns, singular vs plural nouns, or it could produce and understand appropriately sequences of words such as "grasp pen" vs "grasp pencil" or dependent clauses or the modes of verbs? Or the word "not"? To construct robots that are able to use appropriately (that is, as English-speakers use them, more or less) these sounds would give us a better understanding of both language and mental life.

Aside from its influence on mental life, there are two problems with language that constructing robots with language might help us to solve. One is that the discipline that best knows language, the discipline of linguistics, does not really understand language because it ignores the basis of language in the human mind and in human social interactions. The other problem is that language is like the elephant which the blind men cannot recognize because each of them touches and explores one single part of the elephant, the trunk, the legs, the tail, etc., but they are unable to put together what each of them separately knows of the elephant. The elephant is language and the blind men are the different disciplines that study language: linguistics, psycholinguistics, developmental psycholinguistics, neurolinguistics, sociolinguistics, the anthropology of language, and even comparative and historical linguistics. Robots with language will give the sight back to the blind men and will make it possible for science to really understand language. (In Section 1 we have discussed how theories as robots and, more generally, computer-based artefacts can make it possible to develop a nondisciplinary science of the mind.)

6 Robots that have a social life

Sociality is an important component of the adaptive pattern of many animal species, but human beings have particularly complex forms of sociality. This means that until we are able to construct robots that exhibit various and complex forms of social behaviour, we have not really exploited the potential of robots for advancing our understanding of the human mind and human behaviour. There is an active field of research called social robotics but current social robotics is almost useless for our purposes. Social robotics is largely the construction of robots that interact with us, and this can be explained by remembering that robots are constructed with practical applications in mind, and many practical applications suppose an interaction between robots and humans (robots that care for old or ill people, therapeutic robots, robots for entertainment, and so on). But if we want to construct robots that help us to better understand sociality, we have to take into account that sociality is mainly intraspecific, not interspecific, and at least for now, robots and humans are different species. Furthermore, in almost all cases the interaction between robots and humans reproduce one particular type of sociality, the sociality between master and serf. (The original meaning of the word "robot" is "serf".) In any case, to construct robots to better understand sociality, human or nonhuman, we have to construct groups of robots that interact among themselves, not with us.

There is some work on constructing groups of socially interacting robots but a crucial limitation of this work is that, in most cases, these are identical robots, which, of course, is never true for real socially interacting organisms since any individual is different from all the other individuals of the same species. Again, it is the practical orientation of current robotics that pushes towards the construction of groups of identical robots. Groups of interacting robots are constructed because they can do things (for us) which single robots are unable to accomplish and, if robots are constructed for practical applications, this is all that is needed and the robots can be identical robots. But real organisms are individually different, and their differences begin from genetics. Real organisms inherit different genes and these genes determine many aspects of their behaviour and, in particular, their behaviour with respect to other individuals. Biology tells us that the behaviour exhibited by an individual towards other individuals having the same (or very similar) genes, that is, towards kin-related individuals, tends to be different from the behaviour exhibited by the same individual towards non-kin-related individuals. According to the theory of kin selection, an individual may behave in ways that reduce its survival and reproductive chances if its behaviour increases the survival/reproductive chances of another kin-related individual, while this is less likely to occur if the other individual is not kin-related. This is linked to the important distinction between altruism and selfishness which plays a central role in much human social behaviour. Does individual A does X which causes an advantage for individual B for no other reason than giving an advantage to individual B (altruism), or because doing X, in a variety of direct or indirect ways, results in an even greater advantage for individual A (selfishness)? These are critical questions if we want to study with robots how human beings cooperate, how human social organizations emerge and continue to exist, how human groups compete and make war, how human beings exchange goods and exhibit all the different social phenomena which are studied by the social sciences. We expect our robots to help us understand what is the role of genes vs culture in human behaviour and what is the role of selfishness and altruism in human social behaviour. There is much discussion today if human beings are biologically selfish or altruist (or, as one tends to say, cooperative). To answer this question we must consider that selfishness in socially living animals can manifest itself in forms which are different from the selfishness of nonsocially living animals. In any case, robots as scientific tools may be of great help here because, as we have said in Section 1, they make it possible to clearly separate our goals to know and understand from our moral, social, and political goals - which is particularly difficult when one discusses selfishness vs altruism in humans.

We have said that human beings tend to behave differently towards kin and non-kin. This is shown by our next robots. A small group of robots live together in the same environment which contains both randomly distributed food and randomly distributed tools to produce additional food (in a primitive form of agriculture). A robot can either approach and eat an existing food token or it can approach, reach, and use a food-creating tool to produce a new food token, which is placed in a randomly chosen location in the environment and, therefore, not necessarily near the robot which has produced it. Eating a food token increases the survival/reproductive chances of the individual while producing a new food token does not. Hence, biology would predict that the robots will eat the existing food tokens and avoid waste their time to produce new food tokens which will probably be eaten by other robots. If the robots that live in the same environment are randomly chosen from the population of robots, the prediction is confirmed: the robots evolve the behaviour of eating the existing food tokens and they ignore the food-producing tools. However, if the robots that live in the same environment are the offspring of the same parent robot (reproduction is nonsexual) and therefore have more or less the same genes (are brothers or sisters), the robots will evolve the behaviour of dividing their time between eating the existing food tokens and producing new food tokens. The new food token will probably be eaten by a robot different from the robot which has produced it and, therefore, will increase the survival/reproductive chances of the other robot and not those of the robot which has produced it. But, as predicted by the theory of kin selection, since the robots that live together have similar genes, the genes of the food-producing robot will be found in the next generation because the other robots have a copy of these genes.

Another aspect for which genetics is related to sociality is sexual reproduction and the emergence of families. Many animals, including human beings, are of two sexes, male and female, and to reproduce a male must mate with a female. Robots can help us understand if there are behavioural differences between males and females when these differences are of a biological nature. (But robots could also help us understand behavioural differences between human males and females which are of cultural origins. For robots that have culture, see Section 9.)

We impose a single biological difference between male and female robots: after mating, female robots have a nonreproductive period in which they cannot mate successfully while this is not true for male robots which, in principle, can mate successfully at any time. What are the consequences of this single biological difference for the behaviour of our male and female robots? Male robots tend to move in the environment in search for reproductive females, in the meanwhile eating the food present in the environment, while reproductive females tend not to move much and to wait for males to find them. However, females become much more mobile during their nonreproductive period, although they search for food, not males. Furthermore, males tend to eat all sorts of food present in the environment while both reproductive and nonreproductive females are more selective: they prefer more energetic food to less energetic food and less risky food to more risky food. Another difference is with respect to the care of offspring. If in order to leave one's genes to the next generation having offspring is not enough but a robot has to give some of its food to its dependent offspring to keep them alive, males and females tend to give more or less the same quantity of food to their offspring if both males and females are certain that their food goes to their offspring and not to the offspring of some other robot (parental certainty), while males give less of their food to their offspring compared to females if, as is often the case in real animals, males have less parental certainty than females. Families, in the social sense of groups of genetically related individuals living near to each other and interacting with each other, may emerge in our robots if living in families gives more parental certainty to males and allow males to provide food and defence from dangers to both their wife and dependent offspring. Furthermore, young (dependent) robots evolve the behaviour of following their parents in their displacements in the environment in search for food if this is a condition for obtaining food from their parents.

Human groups have historically moved from groups of genetically related individuals, which are necessarily of limited size, to groups of both genetically related and genetically unrelated individuals, which may be very large. Groups of the first type are families, extended families, and tribes. The second type of groups are larger societies, up to present-day very large societies. An account of human sociality must consider and try to replicate with robots not only families but also the sociality of large groups of genetically unrelated individuals because the problems encountered with this type of social groups are different from those of families.

Genetically related individuals live together because for them it is advantageous to live together. Parents can take care of their offspring and in this manner they can increase the probability that their genes will be found in the next generation. Dependent offspring can be cared of by their parents and in this manner they can increase the probability that their own genes will found in future generations. Members of sexual pairs can have access to their partner for mating, males can be sure that the offspring of their mate are their offspring and can help their mate to take care of their common offspring. But why genetically unrelated individuals should live together? Living together means to live near to each other and living near to each other may be disadvantageous. Here are some examples.

If a group of robots live in the same environment they inevitably compete for the food existing in the environment. The presence of other robots decreases the quantity of food available and, when a robot is approaching a food token, another robot may arrive and eat the food token. We compare two populations of robots. In one population the robots see the food but they do not see each other; in the other population they see both the food and each other. Do the robots of the two populations behave differently? The answer is Yes. The robots that see both the food and each other tend to stay away from other robots while this is not true for the robots that see only the food. If the robots are initially placed in one particular portion of the environment but the food can be found in all the environment, the robots that see both the food and each other tend to disperse in the entire environment while this is less true for the robots that see only the food. Clearly, if given a possibility (they see each other), the robots prefer not to live together.

Another group of robots live in an environment where food is found in a single zone but the robots inhabit the entire environment. The robots do not see each other but they see the food zone from any distance and they evolve the behaviour of approaching and entering the food zone so as to eat the food which is found there. We compare these robots with other robots that live alone, each in a separate environment. Here is a direct proof that living together can be disadvantageous: the robots that live together eat less food than the robots that live alone. If the robots live together, a robot may constitute a physical obstacle for other robots which are trying to reach the food zone and, when they reach the food zone, they may find the food zone already full of other robots so that they simply cannot enter the food zone.

If it is true that there are disadvantages in living together but human beings live together in large groups of genetically unrelated individuals, what are the advantages of living together? Can robots show us what are these advantages? We try to answer these questions in the next three Sections.

7 Robots that have an economic life

In the robots we have described in Section 6, food production increases the total food which is available but it only emerges in groups of robots that have the same genes, and this is a serious limitation which human beings must have found ways to overcome because they tend to live in groups larger than those constituted by close kin. One solution to this problem is property. In our robots, when a robot produces a new food token, the food token is placed in a randomly chosen location in the environment, and this implies that the food-producing robot has the same chances of eating the new food token as the other robots. Property changes this. With property, when a robot produces a new food token, the robot is the only one which has access to the food token. This makes it possible for "agriculture" to emerge in larger groups of robots which are not kin-related. (We will return to the question of how restricted access can be implemented in our robots.)

Property can be decisive if there is food surplus, that is, if a robot can produce more food than it is able to eat immediately and, therefore, the robot has to store the food in order to eat it at some later time. Or if there are two types of food and some robots specialize in producing one type of food and other robots specialize in producing the other type of food but all robots need both types of food to survive and reproduce. In both cases, a robot must have an individual store for the food which is of its property. But specialization in food production (or in the production of any other type of resources) is important because it leads to exchange. A robot which specializes in producing one type of food will give one token of its food to another robot which specializes in producing the other type of food and, in exchange, the other robot will give one token of its food to the first robot. This is what happens if both types of food have the same value, that is, if they both require the same amount of time or effort to produce. But if the two different types of food have different values, say, one food requires twice the time or effort to be produced compared to the other food, one token of the first type of food will be exchanged with two tokens of the other type of food. The reason for this is that unless the robot which offers the less valued food is disposed to give two tokens of its food in exchange of one token of the more valued food, the other robot will refuse to proceed to the exchange, and the advantages of exchange will be lost. This leads to the appearance of money. If there are many different types of food and a robot obtains most of these types of food from other robots through exchange, a new resource will emerge, money, which is given by all buyer robots and accepted by all seller robots in exchange for all types of food. All robots are disposed to accept money in exchange for the type of food they produce and sell because money facilitates exchange in this more complex economic system. Robots that sell the same type of food compete with each other for selling their food to buyers and the quantity of money given by buyers in exchange for the food they buy (price) is determined by this competition (market) and, especially but not exclusively, by the number of sellers and buyers.

Robots can constitute organizations, called (private) enterprises, which are made up of many robots and which produce more food and produce and sell food more efficiently than single robots. In many cases these organizations include one owner robot and a certain number of worker robots. Owner robots get the profits made by their enterprise, where profits are the difference between the money spent by the owner to produce the food and the money obtained from buyers by selling the food. Worker robots sell their work to the owner and obtain some money in exchange (salary). Enterprises compete with other enterprises for selling the food they produce and workers compete with other workers for selling their work to enterprises, but also enterprises compete with workers for the level of salaries. The result is that, unless there are very few workers available, which is generally not true (especially today, with globalization), owners pay workers the minimum salary that allows workers to survive. Workers can obtain higher salaries if they create unions in that unions impose a limit on minimum salaries. However, workers cannot ask too high salaries because in this case enterprises do not make profits and cease to exist - or they move to other zones of the environment where workers accept lower salaries. In other words, although enterprise and workers compete with each other, they must also necessarily cooperate, although enterprises will generally be stronger than workers.

8 Robots that have a political life

Economic enterprises can be considered as an advantage of living together because, as we have said, enterprises produce more food and produce food more efficiently than single individuals. But there are other advantages of living together which belong to what is called the political sphere. In fact, living together has the advantage that a group of robots can produce resources which it would be impossible to produce if the individual robots were to live alone. The robots create a central structure or organization which is in charge of producing these resources and which, in recent societies, is called the state. All the members of the community give some of their resources to the state (money under the form of taxes, participation in defensive or offensive wars) and the state uses these resources to produce other resources that are redistributed to all the members of the community (educational systems, health systems, pensions, infrastructure, the possibility of conducting defensive and offensive wars). What are the consequences for a community of robots to have a state as a central store of resources? To answer this question we can compare groups of robot with and without a state.

Let us return to our robots living in an environment with food which each individual robot has to find and eat to remain alive. We compare two groups of robots, one with a "central store", the state, to which all the robots of the group periodically give some of their food and which redistributes the food so collected to all the members of the group, and another group of robots which lacks the central store. If the robots live in an environment with plenty of food, the central store does not make much of a difference: both a community of robots without a central store and a community of robots with a central store do survive. The robots die if they do not eat and they periodically generate a single offspring until they remain alive. Hence, group size is variable and the group can become extinct. In the environment with abundance of food the size of the group remains constant because even the robots which are not very good at procuring food will be able to eat. The situation is different if the robots live in an environment in which food is scarce. In this environment the size of the group without a central store decreases and the group can even become extinct because the robots which are not be very good at procuring food will die at an early age. On the contrary, if the group has a central store, the size of the group remains more or less constant even in the unfavourable environment and the group is able to survive because the less able robots will receive food from the central store which acts as a safety net.

Our next robots live in an environment with various zones rich in food separated by spaces with little or no food. The robots inhabit one of the food-rich zones but they would have more food at their disposal if they could colonize the other food-rich zones. The problem is that no single individual robot can traverse the space that separates the food-rich zones because there is little food in this intermediate space and the robot would die before reaching another food-rich zone. If there is no central store, the group of robots is forced to remain in its original zone and to live only of the food which is found there. If there is a robotic state the situations changes. The robots residing in the original zone give some of their food to the central store, and the central store gives this food to the robots that try to traverse the space which separates the original zone from other food-rich zones. In this manner, the robots are able to colonize other food-rich zones, the group of robots becomes larger, and it has more food at its disposal.

The central store of the robots discussed so far simply redistributes the food collected from the members of the community but more sophisticated central stores use the resources obtained from the members of the community (mostly, under the form of taxes) to produce collective resources which no single robot would be able to produce: schools, hospitals, pension systems, routes and other infrastructure. Another important collective resource that is produced by the state is the capacity to do both defensive and offensive wars. Some of the members of the community (mostly, young males) give to the state their time, their capacity to combat and, possibly, their life, and the state uses these resources to generate the capacity to do wars. War presupposes the existence of different communities of robots and the possibility for one community to increase its resources by taking possess of the resources of another community not through (international) resource exchange but through force. Therefore, communities must possess the capacity to do both offensive wars (trying to acquire the resources of another community by force) and defensive wars (resisting these attempts). Notice, however, that wars are in all cases very expensive in terms of consumed resources, including deaths, and therefore, as families and tribes aggregate to create chiefdoms and states, to avoid wars there will be a tendency for states to aggregate to form larger states.

But the central store is crucial for solving another problem encountered by communities of individuals. To keep a community of individuals together the advantages of living together must be greater than the disadvantages. The advantages are the production of resources that no single individual would be able to produce. As for the disadvantages, we have seen some examples in Section 6 but there may be many more. If an individual lives with other individuals, the individual can damage (inflict loss of resources to) another individual if this results in an advantage for itself. And this can imperil the very existence of the community. Biology prevents groups of genetically related individuals from dissolving but larger groups of genetically unrelated individuals may dissolve if the disadvantages of living together become greater than the advantages. This requires that, to continue to exist, human societies must find ways to contain other-damaging behaviours. In most cases the containment of other-damaging behaviour requires punishing the individual that damage other individuals or the entire community. Being punished leads to a reduction of one's resources and therefore punishment or the threat of being punished discourages other-damaging behaviours. In human societies there tend to exist three different mechanisms for punishing other-damaging behaviours. One is a central organization which discovers and punishes other-damaging behaviours. This central organization is part of the central store (state) and it functions on the basis of written statements that describe specific socially-damaging behaviour and how to punish them (laws and regulations) and it relies on special structures for discovering other-damaging behaviours and punishing them (police, investigative bodies, courts). The second mechanism for punishing other-damaging behaviours is social reputation. If one member of a group of interacting individuals is informed of some other-damaging behaviour committed by another member of the group, it may communicate this information to all the members of the group, and this will result in some kind of informal punishment of the individual which has damaged others, beginning from the refusal of all the members of the group to interact with him/her. The third mechanism for containing other-damaging behaviours is either secular or religious morality. Morality consists in educating individuals so that they will punish themselves if they commit or even think of committing some other-damaging behaviour. (On education as cultural transmission, see Section 9.)

As we have said, punishment is an important and necessary tool to contain other-damaging behaviours but it is not the only one. The state can invest its resources in maintaining an adequate system for discovering and punishing other-damaging behaviours but it can also invest its resources in creating socio-economic conditions (e.g., creating new jobs) that dissuade people from behaving in ways that damage others (e.g. stealing). In fact, our robots show that investing only in discovering and punishing other-damaging behaviours may not be sufficient to contain these behaviours and that, to contain them, the state may also need to invest its resources to create better socio-economic conditions. But the state and the system of laws may not be enough. The contribution of the other two mechanisms for containing other-damaging behaviours, i.e., social reputation and morality, may also be necessary.

Other-damaging behaviours are of many different types. Let us go back to our robots that give some of their food to the central store. The robots give the same proportion of their food to the central store, which means that the robots which are better able at finding food give more food to the central store than the less able ones. But the quantity of food given to the central store by a robot may depend on another factor. If looking for food in the environment is costly in terms of energy, the robots may exhibit a tendency not to look for food and to live on the food redistributed by the central store - which of course damages the group. In other words, giving or not giving to the central store may depend on both level of ability and willingness to work, and the central store (the state) may need to spend its resources to increase both. But there is another problem which more directly requires the capacity of the state to contain other-damaging behaviours through punishment. Giving one's food to the store (paying taxes) reduces one's survival/reproductive chances, and this may induce some members of the community not to give their food to the central store (fiscal evasion). If this is what too many members of the community tend to do, the central store becomes unable to collect sufficient food from the community to be used for the purposes we have seen: allow the community to survive in food-poor environments (or times) and provide food to robots that try to reach other rich-food zones, and this results in a damage for the entire community. If punishment is sufficiently certain, the action of the state will discourage fiscal evasion. Otherwise, fiscal evasion will weaken the state and damage the entire community. Many other types of other-damaging behaviours can emerge in our robots, and the state must act to contain these behaviours. Violation of property rights and guaranteeing the correctness of economic exchanges are some examples.

We have talked of the state as a central store of resources which are collected from the community and redistributed to the community. But states need government, that is, specific individuals who decide for all the members of the community, and we should ask if robots can shed some light on how these individuals are chosen and what properties they must possess.

Let us return to our robots that live in an environment which contains a single food zone. When the robots see the food zone they approach and reach the food zone and they eat the food which is found there. The robots can see the food zone from any distance and, therefore, from this point of view, they are all identical. Now let us introduce something new. The new robots can only see to a limited distance and, therefore, when they don't see the food zone they can only explore the environment more or less randomly, hoping to see the food zone. However, there is one robot in the group that can see at a greater distance than the other robots and therefore can more easily find the food zone. In these circumstances the other robots evolve a behaviour of following the robot which sees at a greater distance, and in this manner they increase their probability of eating. We might say that the robot which sees at a greater distance leads the other robots to the food zone and, therefore, is the leader of the group. The behaviour of following the leader is advantageous for the other robots (and this is why it evolves), and it is spontaneous in the sense that the robots follow the leader even if no one punishes them if they don't.

Now the scenario changes again and the food which is found in the food zone can only be acquired if a minimum number (less than the total) of robots are simultaneously present in the food zone so that they can work together to capture the food (say, a large prey). However, the food which is captured in the food zone is distributed to all robots, including those that were not present in the food zone when the food was captured. If going to the food zone has a cost in terms of energy, there will be a tendency at least for some of the robots not to go to the food zone and at the same time eat the food captured by the other robots (free rider robots). (This clearly is a form of other-damaging behaviour.) If this tendency is present in a large number of robots, the robots may be unable to capture the food which is present in the food zone and no robot will eat. How can the problem be solved?

The problem can be solved is there is one robot which punishes the other robots if they do not go to the food zone. To avoid punishment, all or most robots of the group will go to the food zone and, in this way, the robots will be able to eat the food present in the food zone. We call the robot that punishes the other robots if they do not go to the food zone is, the "chief" of the group of robots.

Who is the chief robot? Being a leader depends on intrinsic properties. The leader is the robot which sees at a greater distance than the other robots. But what properties must chiefs possess? Chiefs have the task to punish free riding robots which do not give to the community but only take from the community, and since no one wants to be punished, chiefs must be robots which are stronger than the other robots and so are able to punish free-riding robots. The physical strength of the chief can be a solution for small groups of robots but it is insufficient in larger and more complex societies of robots. The problem is solved by putting a sub-group of specialized robots at disposal of the chief and these robots are paid for helping the chief to punish free riding robots. (This, of course, is the first step towards the emergence of the state.) But, again, if chiefs must not have intrinsic properties such as being stronger than other robots, how are chiefs chosen? Consider that the problem of choosing a chief is a recurrent problem because, like all robots, chief robots die and another chief must be chosen to replace the dead chief. One possibility is that when a chief robot dies it is one of the offspring of the chief which is the new chief. If the chief has many offspring, there will be some criterion for deciding which of the offspring is the new chief, such as the first-born offspring. (If our robots were males and females, another problem would be if both male and female offspring of the past chief can be chief.) This is one possibility. Another possibility is that the present chief chooses among all the robots of the group the robot that will be its successor. A third possibility is that the new chief is chosen (elected) by the members of the group, or one specific subset of the members (the elite robots or older robots) or all the robots belonging to the group (democracy).

One thing to consider it that among the robots there will be a desire to be the chief of the group because being a chief brings with itself a number of advantages for the chief, for example when the food captured in the food zone is distributed among all the robots of the group, the chief robot gets a higher proportion of the food. This may explain why chiefs may have a tendency to choose their offspring as their successor since kin selection theory explains that parents care for their offspring. And this may also explain why they may want to choose their successor even if it is not their offspring because they may choose a robot which, in exchange, will take care of their offspring.

Should the leader and the chief be the same robot? The problem is that all the mechanisms for choosing chiefs do not guarantee that the new chief will possess the capacity to be a leader. Even assuming that the present chief is a leader (it sees at a greater distance than the other robots), its offspring may not inherit this capacity or the new chief which is chosen by the chief itself or by the elite robots or by the entire community of robots may not have this capacity. Furthermore, since, as we have said, being a chief brings with itself advantages for the chief, potential chiefs will try to convince the other robots to choose them as chief even if they are not leader in the sense that they see at a greater distance than the other robots. And, in fact, chiefs might be robots which are particularly able at convincing other robots that they should be chiefs. The problem is further complicated by the fact that there may be sub-groups of robots with diverging interests, and chiefs may make the interests of one sub-group, their sub-group or the sub-group of which has elected them, while being a leader implies the capacity to accommodate the interests of all the robots in the group.

In discussing chiefs we have discussed power but power is a more general social phenomenon which may exist whenever two robots live and interact together. Notice that we are talking of "power on", not "power to". Having "power to" is possessing an ability. Robot A has the power to do X if in the appropriate circumstance it does X, and even robots that live alone have various "powers to," for example, they have the power to find food or to find a mate or to fly away from a predator. On the contrary, "power on" requires another robot.

Robot A has power on robot B if B does not do what it wants to do but it does what A wants B to do. Why should B do not what it wants to do but what A wants it to do? The answer is: for fear of being punished. We assume that generally, for a robot, doing not what it wants to do but what other robots want it to do has a cost for the robot. However, if not doing what A wants B to do is punished by A, the costs of being punished may be greater than the costs of not doing what B wants to do, and so B does what A wants it to do. How can A punish B? A can punish B by giving B what B does not want (physical damage, being in prison) or by not giving B what B wants (money, favours, love). In both cases punishment is reducing the survival/reproductive chances of B, or its well-being. How can we simulate power among robots? One first consideration is that it may not be clear what is the difference between a robot wanting to do X and a robot just doing X, or between a robot not wanting to do X and a robot just not doing X. Perhaps in both cases the distinction can only be made for social robots. A robot wants to do X if the robot would do X even in the absence of other robots punishing him for not doing X. Similarly, a robot does not want to do X if the robot does X only because, if it does not do X, other robots will punish him. Or perhaps wanting to do X is different from just doing X only for such complex animals such as human being which have language and mental life (see Section 4). For an animal it may unclear how we can distinguish between an animal doing X and the animal wanting to do X. Human beings have language and mental life and this makes it possible for them to represent in their mind (brain) actions that they want to do but are not actually doing or even cannot do. (Wanting to do X is related to having the "goal" of doing X. Can we say that our robots have the "goal" to reach and eat the food elements?)

Clearly, power also exists in (some) animals, for example in nonhuman primates. Notice however that power is not just winning a fight with another individual. An individual can be stronger (or more intelligent) than another individual so that the first individual usually win fights with the second individual. But this is not power. We might construct two robots and have the robots fight together so that the first robot comes out of the fight with an absolute gain in fitness which is greater than the gain in fitness of the second robot. This does not mean that the first robot has power on the second robot. We say that the first robot has power on the second robot only if, without fighting, the second robot does what the first robot wants it to do and does it only because the first robot wants the second robot to do X. And the same for not doing X. (However, this might be in contrast with the interesting notion that A has power on B if A causes B not just to do X but to want to do X.)

Another interesting question regarding power and wanting among robots is that, unlike most other animals, human beings are taught how to behave by adults (mostly but not necessarily their parents) when they are young. What are the consequences of this for wanting to do X versus just doing X and for power among robots? Is a robot which does X because it has been taught to do X by another robot, really wanting to do X? (For teaching among robots, see Section 9.) A robot that teaches another robot to do X has power on the other robot?

9 Robots that have culture

While the behaviour of nonhuman animals is genetically inherited or learned through the interactions of the individual with the nonsocial environment, the behaviour of human beings is mostly socially or culturally learned, i.e., acquired through the interactions of the individual with other individuals. Social learning does exist in some animal species but it is very simple and it plays a limited role in the behavioural repertoire of the species. In contrast, most of what a human being does, knows, or desires is learned from others. An individual learns how to behave by imitating other individuals, by being taught by other individuals, by using the same technological artefacts that are used by other individuals, and in many other ways.

Let us see some robots that learn by imitating other robots. Like many of our previous robots, these robots live in an environment with randomly distributed food tokens and, when they see a food token, they must approach and eat the food token in order to remain alive. The neural network that controls their behaviour has sensory input units encoding the position of the nearest food token and motor output units encoding the movements with which the robot displaces itself in the environment. Now imagine two robots, an adult robot and a child robot. The adult robot has connection weights in its neural network which allow the robot to respond appropriately to sensory input: the robot approaches and eat the food tokens. In contrast, the connection weights of the other robot, the child robot, are random, which means that the robot responds to the sight of food with random movements and is unable to reach the food. (We are assuming that there is no genetic inheritance in these robots.) The child robot is carried by the adult robot on its shoulders so that both robots move together and receive the same input from the environment, i.e., they see the nearest food in the same way. Both robots respond to the sensory input by encoding some particular movement in the motor units of their neural network but only the movements of the adult robot are physically executed and the adult robot moves in the environment. When the child robot is carried around on the shoulders of the adult robot, the motor units of its neural network encode movements but these movements are not physically executed. However, something important happens in the neural network of the child robot: the child robot learns by imitating the adult robot. The neural network of the child robot perceives the movements of the adult robot and compares these movements with the movements encoded in its own motor units. On the basis of this comparison, the connection weights of the child robot's neural network change in such a way that, in future occasions, given the same sensory input from food, the movement generated by the child robot's neural network will be more similar to the movement generated by the adult robot's neural network. This is repeated many times, with different inputs, with the result that at the end the child robot (which has now become an adult) behaves like the adult robot, i.e., it responds to sensory input in the same way as the adult robot. Since the adult robot already knows how to reach the food, the child robot will also be able to reach the food. The ability to reach the food has been culturally transferred from the child robot to the adult robot.

In the scenario we have described there is one robot that already possesses some useful behaviour and then the behaviour is learned by another robot by imitating the first robot. Now we ask: How has the adult robot acquired its behaviour? If we assume that the adult robot also has acquired its behaviour by imitating another robot when it was a child, the question becomes: How has the ability to approach and eat food first appeared in the population of robots? In fact, what we find in humans is not only cultural transmission of already existing behaviours but also the emergence of behaviours on the basis of cultural transmission. Can we reproduce the cultural emergence of behaviours?

We start from a population of robots whose neural networks have randomly assigned connection weights, which implies that no robot can reach the food tokens which are present in the environment. The robots are born, they live for a fixed length of time, and then they die. When a new robot is born, its neural network has random connection weights and this means that the newborn robot is unable to reach the food tokens. (Again, we ignore genetic inheritance to concentrate on the purely cultural emergence of behaviour.) However, newborn robots learn from the robots of the preceding generation in the manner that we have already described. Each newborn robot is placed on the shoulders of a robot of the preceding generation and it learns to behave like the robot of the preceding generation. The problem is that the robots of the initial population have random connection weights in their neural networks and therefore they do not know how to reach the food and there is not much that newborn robots can learn from them. So, how can the ability to reach the food tokens emerge in the population?

As we have said, the connection weights of the robots of the initial generation are randomly assigned. This implies that each robot will be different from all the other robots and it also implies that, although the ability to reach the food tokens will be almost nonexistent, for purely random reasons some robots will be (slightly) better than the other robots at reaching food and they will eat more than the other robots. What is important is that not all the robots of the first generation act as models for the robots of the second generation and that the robots that act as models are not chosen randomly. On the contrary, the robots that act as models are chosen among the best robots of the first gen-eration, that is, they are the robots that for purely chance reasons have better connection weights and therefore are better at finding food. What they know is not much but it is something. This something is transmitted to the robots of the second generation.

We now add another feature to our robots. When a robot learns from another robot, some random noise is added to the transmission process. Technically, this is realized by slightly modifying, in a random way, the movements which are encoded in the output units of the model robot and which the learner compares with its own movements. (We can attribute this to an imperfect per-ception of the model's behaviour by the learner.) In this manner the behaviour of the learner will not be an exact copy of the behaviour of the model. Since we are talking of random noise, in many cases the behaviour of the learner at the end of learning will be less good than the behaviour of the model but in some rare cases the learner will outperform the model. What is important is that if the learner turns out to be worse than its model, it probably will not be chosen as a model by the robots of the next generation, whereas if it is better than its model it will likely be among the models chosen by the robots of the next generation. Hence, any improvement in behaviour which is due to the random noise that inevitably accompanies cultural transmission is maintained and it diffuses and accumulates in the population of robots. The process is re-peated for a certain number of successive generations of robots and at the end all robots are able to find the food present in the environment, with of course individual differences among the robots. This ability was initially nonexistent but the two mechanisms of (1) selecting the best individuals as models for the robots of the next generation, and (2) adding random noise to the transmis-sion process, have created it. (These are basically the same two mechanisms that make the emergence of new behaviours through genetic transmission possible.)

Our robots learn by comparing their movements to the movements of their model. But learning by imitation may not consist in comparing movements but it may consist in comparing the effects of movements. From an adaptive point of view, it is generally the effects of movements which are important, not the movements by themselves. Going around looking for food and approach-ing and eating the food are important not by themselves but because, as a result of these movements, a food token changes its location from the external environment to the inside of the organism's body. In learning from others the learner perceives that its movements do not produce the same effect as the movements of the model, i.e., the food token is not reached and it is not eaten, and therefore its neural network changes so as to reduce, in future occasions, the discrepancy between the effects of its movements and the effects of the model's movements.

This is what happens in learning to speak. Speaking consists in producing movements of one's phono-articulatory organs that cause specific sounds. The speaker has sensory (proprioceptive) access to his/her phono-articulatory movements and acoustic access to the resulting sounds. (The importance of the acoustic access of the speaker to his or her own sounds is indicated by the poor quality of the speech produced by deaf people.) In contrast, the hearer has little or no access to the movements of the phono-articulatory organs of the speaker but it has acoustic access to the sounds produced by these movements. This is useful not only when the learner learns to imitate the linguistic sounds produced by the speaker but also when it learns which objects are named by which sounds. The model and the learner are both exposed to the same input, for example the sight of an apple, and the model responds by producing a movement of its phono-articulatory organs which physically causes the sound "apple". The learner both sees the apple and hears the sound "apple" and it responds by producing in its turn a phono-articulatory movement which causes a sound. If the sound produced by the learner does not match the sound produced by the model, the neural network of the learner changes its connection weights so that the discrepancy is progressively eliminated.

What we have described is a very simple type of learning by imitation. The model robot is completely passive, aside from carrying the learner robot on its shoulders or talking to the learner or to another robot, and it can even ignore that the other robot is learning by imitating its behaviour. But human beings in many cases act as teachers, not simply as models. They actively try to teach other human beings how to behave, and the teaching can take place in a variety of different ways. One type of teaching consists in drawing the attention of the learner on some particular object in the environment. The environment of our robots contains only food tokens and the robot sees one food token at a time (the nearest one). Therefore, for our robots it is clear which is the object to which they have to respond and there is no problem of focusing one's attention on one object and excluding other objects that may send additional inputs to their sensors. But consider an environment which contains different objects only some of which are food tokens to be reached and eaten. The simultaneous arrival of many different inputs from many different objects requires a capacity of selective attention, that is, the neural network of the robots must be able to block or neutralize all the inputs from all the objects except the input from the single object to which the robot is expected to respond. This is where teachers, and not only models, can be useful. The behaviour of the teacher may consist in pointing (with its finger or eyes) to the object to which the learner has to respond. This is what happens in language learning, where robots that already know the language may point to the object which the learner has to associate with a given acoustic signal (word).

The robots described so far can only learn from the robots of the preceding generation, the adult robots, because their peers, like themselves, do not know how to reach the food tokens and therefore have nothing to teach them. But this is only appropriate if the environment does not change from one generation to the next. If the environment changes, the situation may be different. This is what is shown by our next robots.

The environment contains a certain number of edible mushrooms and a certain number of poisonous mushrooms. To survive and reproduce the robots must eat the edible mushrooms and avoid the poisonous ones. Their performance (survival chances) is measured as the number of edible mushrooms minus the number of poisonous mushrooms eaten. The robots can distinguish the two types of mushrooms because they have different colours (the edible mushrooms are green while the poisonous ones are blue) but when they are born they do not know which are the edible mushrooms and which are the poisonous ones. They have to learn this from other robots. As in our preceding robots, this is an ability which is initially completely absent from the population since the neural networks of all the robots of the initial generation have random connection weights. Cultural learning begins from the second generation. There are two scenarios. In one scenario the individuals of each generation take as their models the best individuals of the preceding generation (inter-generational learning). In the other scenario the individuals of each generation learn from their peers which of course are also newborn robots (intra-generational learning). The results are those that are expected. If the newborn robots learn from the best adults of the preceding generation, this causes a cumulative process of evolutionary emergence of the capacity to approach and eat the mushrooms which are edible and to avoid the mushrooms which are poisonous. In contrast, if the newborn robots learn from their peers, there is no increase in the average level of performance across generations. In each generation the individuals that are taken as models for learning, i.e., the learner's peers, do not know what they are supposed to teach and, therefore, the ability to eat the edible mushrooms and avoid the poisonous ones does not emerge in the population.

This is what happens if the environment in which the population of robots lives does not change during the succession of generations. Edible mushrooms are always green and poisonous mushrooms are always blue. But imagine that, for some reason, after a certain number of generations the environment changes. The change is radical and abrupt. From one generation to the next the green mushrooms become poisonous and the blue mushrooms become edible. The robots have culturally evolved the ability to eat the green mushrooms and to avoid the blue mushrooms. What will they do in the changed environment?

As expected, the level of performance of the population of robots has a crash when the environment changes. They eat what have become the poisonous mushrooms and they avoid the edible ones. The ability they possess because they have learned it from the robots of the preceding generation was appropriate in the old environment but it is inappropriate in the new environment. However, after a certain number of generations the new ability which is appropriate to the new environment gradually emerges and the level of performance increases again. The robots learn that the mushrooms that were edible have become poisonous and the mushrooms that were poisonous have become edible. What is the role of intra-generational learning in this process of adapting to a changed environment? As we have said, in the old environment all cultural learning is from robots belonging to the preceding generation and there is no intra-generational learning. When the environment changes there are two possibilities. In one condition, although the environment has changed, the manner of cultural transmission remains the same. The robots continue to learn from the best individuals of the preceding generation. In the other condition, when the environment changes there is also a change in the manner of cultural transmission. Cultural transmission becomes more mixed. There is inter-generational learning but there is also some intra-generational learning.

What are the results? As we have already said, if the manner of cultural transmission remains entirely inter-generational, after the crash in performance at the moment that the environment changes there is a gradual emergence of the new ability which is appropriate in the changed environment but the process takes many generations. The adaptation to the changed environment is slow. On the contrary, if when the environment changes there is also a change in the manner of cultural transmission, with some individuals learning from their peers rather than from the individuals of the preceding generation, the adaptation to the new environment is faster. Why? What is the role of learning from one's peers when one is young, rather than from adults? When one is young, learning from one's peers is learning from individuals that do not have much to teach you. What they teach you is not information but random noise. This is the negative side of learning from one's peers when one is young, and this explains why intra-generational learning alone, with no inter-generational learning, simply cannot start any type of cumulative process of cultural evolution. However, what is the weakness of intra-generational learning in an environment that does not change, becomes its strength when the environment changes, and it changes rapidly. When the environment changes, the abilities that were appropriate in the old environment not only are no longer appropriate in the new environment but they are an obstacle to the emergence of the new abilities which are appropriate to the changed environment. This explains why some amount of learning from one's peers, rather than from the individuals of the preceding generation, speeds up the process of adapting to a changed environment. When one is young, learning from one's peers just adds random noise to the neural network of the learner but this random noise has the advantage of eliminating more quickly what the individual has learned or is learning from the individuals of the preceding generation and which is no longer appropriate to the new environment. Learning from one's peers in an environment that changes frequently and substantially creates a blank slate on which it is easier to write the new abilities that are needed in the new environment. (Is this what is happening to adolescents today?)

Let us go back to space and spatial proximity. Spatial proximity is linked to cultural learning and it can be both a cause and an effect of cultural learning. Spatial proximity can be a cause of cultural learning in that groups of individuals that live near to each other and can observe the behaviours of each other can learn from each other. However, it can also be a consequence of cultural learning because there will be a tendency to develop a behaviour of staying near to other individuals in order to learn from them. In other words, cultural learning may represent a pressure for the emergence of spatial proximity. This is shown by our next robots.

In the robots described at the beginning of this Section the learner was carried around on the shoulders of its model and therefore it was always near to its model and was able to learn from its model. Our next robots are different: each robot moves independently. If a robot can learn from another robot only if the learner is near to the model, it is now necessary for the robots to approach other robots and to remain in proximity to them in order to learn from them. The new robots can perceive both the food tokens (there are no poisonous tokens in this environment) and the nearest robot and they can both approach other robots and approach and eat the food tokens. The tendency to approach other robots is genetically inherited while the ability to approach and eat the food tokens is not genetically inherited but it must be learned from other robots. What we find is that in a succession of generations the robots biologically evolve the capacity to respond to sensory input from other robots by approaching them and remain in their proximity. This makes it possible for them to learn how to approach and eat the food tokens from other nearby robots during their life. The capacity which evolves biologically - staying near to other robots - by itself does not lead to an increase in the survival chances of a robot but it makes it possible for the robot to learn the capacity which increases its survival chances - approaching and eating food. These robots demonstrate how biological evolution and cultural learning can interact. There is no direct selective pressure for the biological emergence of the behaviour of staying near to others. The robots that have offspring are those that are good at eating, not the robots that are good at staying near to other robots. However, since eating is learned from others and learning from others requires spatial proximity, there is an indirect pressure for the biological emergence of the behaviour of approaching and staying to others. This shows that cultural learning may be a cause for the biological emergence of behaviours and capacities that make cultural learning possible. This pressure may have played an important role in the history of human beings.

From which robots a robot learns? A robot can learn from its parent(s) or it can learn from robots outside its family. If a robot learns from its parents, the robot cannot to choose the models to imitate. If it learns from robots which are not its parents, it can choose the best living robots as its models. What are the consequences in the two cases?

Our next robots try to answer to this question with respect not to behaviours but to artefacts. Artefacts are physical objects that the robots construct and use to increase their survival and reproductive chances. Our robots construct vases in which they store the food which they find in the environment, thereby increasing the value of this food. Like behaviours, vases can be culturally transmitted and they can evolve in a succession of generations. Instead of imitating the behaviour of another robot, a robot imitates the vase which has been constructed and is used by the other robot by constructing a copy of the vase. If the best vases are selected for copying, where the best vases are those that best preserve or cook food and if some random variation is always added in the copying process so that the copy is a variant of the vase used as model, then what we find is technological evolution: a gradual increase in the quality of vases.

The new robots genetically evolve the ability to find food in the environment but they also construct vases that they use to store, cook, or transport food. The vases have different characteristics and they vary in their quality, with the best vases allowing the extraction of more total energy from food. In the new scenario, therefore, the survival and reproductive chances of a robot depend on two properties of the robot: the robot's ability to find food in the environment and the quality of the vases constructed and used by the robot. The neural network that controls the robots' behaviour is made of two sub-networks. One sub-network controls the behaviour of the robot when the robot is looking for food. The connection weights of this sub-network are genetically inherited and the robots evolve a capacity to find food across a succession of generations. The other sub-network controls the behaviour of the robot when the robot constructs a vase by copying an already existing vase. The sub-network has input units encoding the characteristics of the vase used as model and output units encoding the characteristics of the vase constructed by copying the model. This sub-network has random connection weights when the robot is born and the robot learns to construct copies of existing vases because the connection weights of its second neural network gradually change during the robot's life so that the characteristics of the copy produced by the robot (the network's output) become progressively more similar to the characteristics of the model (the network's input).

We contrast two scenarios. In one scenario the vases that are used by a robot as models to be copied are those which have been constructed and used by the robot's parent. (Here, like for many of our robots, biological reproduction is nonsexual and each robot has only one parent.) There is no search for the best vases existing in the community but the new vases are copies of the vases which are used within the family. In the second scenario the vases that a robot chooses as models to be copied are the best vases existing in the community. The results show that cultural transmission which is restricted to the family is less effective than cultural transmission at the level of the entire community. If the robots make copies of the vases constructed by their parents, the quality of the vases improves slightly in the first few generations but then it stabilizes at a rather low level. In contrast, if the vases used as models to copy are the best vases of the community, their quality improves much more across the successive generations of robots and the final steady state which is reached is much higher. These robots may explain why technological evolution and, more generally, cultural evolution is more efficient if it takes place within a larger community.

But if the vases of which a robot makes a copy are not taken from within the robot's family, how are they chosen? For our robots it is we, the researchers, who decide which are the best vases existing in the community, that is, the vases that store food more effectively. But what if the robots themselves choose the vases to copy? How should they proceed? The most effective way would be to try all the existing vases and select the best ones, but this may be expensive or even impossible. Another possibility is to choose as models the vases which are used by the most successful robots in the community, that is, the robots possessing more energy, but while this may be feasible, it is not very effective because a robot may have much energy because it is very good at finding food, not because of the quality of its vases. And in fact, for our robots, the evolved quality of the vases reaches a higher level if the vases chosen as models are the best vases, not those used by the most successful robots.

Assuming that sub-groups of robots use the same vases, a third possibility is to use as models to be copied the vases which are used by a greater number of robots, those which are more frequent in the community. This criterion is based on the assumption that, if a particular vase is used by many robots, the vase cannot be too bad. But the frequency of a trait, be it a behaviour or an artefact, plays a much more important and general role in cultural transmission and cultural evolution, and in fact, in using this criterion, there may be no consideration of the goodness or quality of the trait which one chooses to imitate. The main reason is another. Adopting the frequency criterion leads to cultural uniformity, and cultural uniformity is an important requirement for social life and it applies to all sorts of culturally transmitted entities: behaviours, beliefs, values, and artefacts. Why is cultural uniformity important? Because behaviour is based on predictions and expectations. An animal behaves effectively if it is able to predict (in a purely implicit sense) the environment in which it lives and with which it interacts. Human beings live in, and interact with, an environment largely constituted by other human beings. Hence, to function appropriately in their environment human beings must be able to predict how the other human beings with which they interact will behave, what are their beliefs and values, and also what are their artefacts. (Note that artefacts are strictly linked to behaviours because they induce the same behaviours in the individuals who use them) This explains why in choosing the models to be copied, the frequency criterion is an important one: it creates social predictability.

The adoption of the frequency criterion may also explain culture. One consequence of living near to one another is that the individuals that live near to one another tend to develop a culture, where a culture is a set of behaviours which are shared by all the members of a group of individuals learning from one another and which tend to be different from the behaviours of other groups (other cultures). Cultures are different because small changes in the culturally inherited behaviours inside a group will progressively lead to divergent cultural paths. Probably the main force behind cultural diversity is the adoption of the frequency criterion in choosing one's models to imitate. Frequency is self-reinforcing in that if an individual chooses to learn from, or to copy, the most frequent model, this will automatically lead to an increase in the model's frequency. Using the frequency criterion for cultural learning we can reproduce a number of interesting macro-cultural phenomena. Of course, we are talking of macro-cultural phenomena and therefore our robots must necessarily be even more simplified that the robots described so far. They are nodes possessing a number of traits (behaviours, beliefs, values, and artefacts) and making up a network, where a link between two nodes of the network means that the two nodes interact together and imitate each other. The traits of each node are entirely abstract and they are initially randomly assigned. Then they are updated in a succession of time steps in such a manner that after a certain number of time steps all the nodes of the network tend to possess more or less the same traits and the network becomes a culture.

What can we reproduce by representing cultures as network of nodes? We have already described the importance of spatial proximity in cultural learning: two individuals learn from one another if they are spatially near to one another. Therefore, we can ask: What happens if the nodes of the network are represented as cells on a spatial grid and each cell imitates the neighbouring cells? Imitation is based on frequency, which means that for any trait a node tends to imitate the specific version of the trait possessed by the majority of its neighbouring cells. Perhaps contrary to expectations, what we find after a certain number of time steps is not a single culture but a small number of different cultures made of spatially close nodes. Why? Because, for purely random reasons, groups of spatially close nodes may converge to different cultures and then the boundaries between neighbouring cultures spontaneously become impenetrable and fixed. However, it is interesting that if we add random noise to the process, the number of different cultures becomes smaller, which means that cultures and cultural boundaries are more fixed and impenetrable if traits are rigidly copied from other nodes of the network and cultures have little internal innovation.

The model of culture so far is a spatial model in that the nodes interact only with neighbouring nodes. What if we ignore space and represent communities as sets of interconnected nodes, with no spatial implication? Today's technologies tend to reduce the importance of space for social interaction and we may try to reproduce with our networks of nodes some aspects of today's globalization. We start with two separate networks which are purely topological networks in the sense that, unlike our previous topographical networks, links between nodes are independent of space. The nodes start with randomly assigned traits and the traits are changed using the frequency criterion for cultural imitation. After a certain number of time steps the two networks each develop its own culture (sets of traits shared by all the nodes of the network). In other words, if space restricts social interactions to individuals which are close to each other in space, we find many cultures in a set of interconnected nodes but if space plays no role in social interaction, a set of interconnected node will develop one single culture.

As we have said, the two networks are internally interconnected but externally separated in that there is no link going from one node of one network to one node of the other network. At this point we add some links between the nodes of one network and the nodes of the other network and what happens is that after a certain number of further time steps a single, global, culture tends to emerge in both networks, replacing the original cultures of the two networks. The probability that a single, global, culture will emerge depends on two factors: the probability will decrease with the number of internal links in the two networks and it will increase with the number of external links which are added between the two networks. This means that an internally cohesive community will tend to resist cultural globalization more than a less cohesive community and that advances in the technologies for transporting persons, people, and information favour cultural globalization, as is happening today. Another interesting issue is: what is the global culture which emerges in both networks? Is the already existing culture of one of the two networks or is a new culture? In the former case, which network imposes its culture to the other network? This is linked to an important social and political question which can be posed today: Will the globalization of the world which we are seeing today result in its Westernization?

We can explore other aspects of cultural change with our simple model. Our nodes represent individuals but we now assume that the life of an individual is divided into two stages, childhood and adulthood, and that the links of a child node change when the node becomes an adult node. During childhood, a node has fewer links compared to when it becomes an adult node and, when we add links from other networks (other cultures), these links do not involve child nodes but only adult nodes. The results show that this slows down cultural globalization. Social interactions that take place inside families are an obstacle to the emergence of a single, global, culture. Next, we divide the life of a node into three stages, childhood, adolescence, and adulthood, and we stipulate that during adolescence a node has fewer links with the adult nodes of its network but more links with other adolescent nodes. (Remember our cultural robots which learn not from the robots of the preceding generation but from the robots of their own generation). Furthermore, when we add the inter-network links, the externally linked nodes tend to be adolescent nodes rather than child or adult nodes. In this case, cultural globalization is accelerated. (Is this what is happening today?) Finally, we study a third condition: we add a single special node in each network which represents the state of the church. The node is special in that, unlike the other nodes which represent individuals, the node which represents the state or the church is connected with the individual nodes with unidirectional links. This means that the state or church node culturally influences the individual nodes but it is not influenced by them. (This of course is a simplification.) In this case too, the networks resist outside influences and cultural globalization is slowed down.

10 Conclusions

Verbally formulated theories in the behavioural and social sciences should be replaced by theories expressed by constructing artefacts that reproduce the different empirical phenomena the theories are intended to explain. Since human beings are physical/biological entities, and not only the product of social and cultural processes, the artefacts should be robots with a body, a brain, an inherited genotype, and a physical environment in which they live and with which they interact. Robotics theories of behavioural and social phenomena can greatly advance our scientific understanding of these phenomena and lead to much better behavioural and social sciences.

Current robots only very partially help us to understand human beings and their societies because they are constructed with practical applications in mind, and this has the consequence that they do not address many important phenomena of human behaviour and human societies. However, some attempts at reproducing, in extremely simplified form, these phenomena are already being made and in this Chapter we have described some of the results which have been obtained by mostly referring to work in which the author has taken part.

Science has the primary goal of helping us to know and to understand reality but it should also be socially useful. Current robots are mostly seen as technologies with economic value and this, as we have said, limits their potential as scientific tools. But producing technologies with economic value is only one of the applied goals of robotic research. Robots, especially those which try to reproduce human social phenomena, should help us to better understand and find solutions to the many difficult problems that human beings and human societies face today. Computer-based artefacts and robotic societies should be used to explore future scenarios for human societies and to design "non-utopian utopies".

Chapter 38
Two scenarios for crowdsourcing simulation

Mario Paolucci

Abstract In this paper, we trace a line through the recent story of agent-based social simulation from the point of view of the LABBS, the laboratory of agent-based social simulation that Cristiano Castelfranchi has contributed to create and helped grow. From this observatory, we deploy a set of arguments defending the need for social simulation as one of the best chances we have to make a much needed step forward in the scientific endeavor of the twenty first century: understanding society. Building on these arguments, we point out several reasons that caused social simulation to fall several measures short of the big challenge, discussing some famous examples from the literature. We then introduce the concept of crowdsourcing, trying to elaborate on how it could reshape this methodology for computational social science.

1 Introduction

I cannot literally imagine how my life would have taken shape if it wasn't for a fortuitous encounter with Cristiano Castelfranchi. The matter, I'm certain, is of no interest to anybody else and of small interest to Cristiano himself; however, where else could I tell this story if not in this paper? Nowhere.

The chain of random encounters was so strange it that deserves mentioning how it had happened before I was asked to work on the implementation of the code that was at the base of the [9, 24] publications. I had been orbiting around the circle of friends of one of Castelfranchi's sons, Yurij, who called and asked me if I wanted to help with that code because he had enough of that. But that would have been unlikely if I had not pulled a stunt on him during a chance meeting, when I could surprise Yurij by divining some information about him-

Mario Paolucci

Laboratory of Agent-based Social Simulation (LABSS), Institute of Cognitive Sciences and Technologies, CNR, Italy
e-mail: mario.paolucci@istc.cnr.it

self, including guessing his name - information that I had stolen from the tales of a woman I had been besotted with, who happened to be in high school with him, and at the same time to be the sister of my favorite classmate. So, a long chain of coincidences. Would it change much if I one of the links had broken? For me, yes, but not for you, who would likely be reading a paper very similar but with another signature. The research group, to all likelihood, would have found another modeler/programmer and a comparable path of events would have followed. Cristiano had been defending the simulative approach inside and outside the institute with energy and commitment, and the Laboratory for Agent Based Social Simulation (LABSS) would have been formed in some way and, under Rosaria Conte's guide, it would have contributed to the recognition of Agent Based Social Simulation (ABSS in the rest of the paper) as a field by itself. Thus, the lab would just be slightly different.

Can we do a model of this chain of events, and in what sense? The first answer that comes to mind is, most certainly not; and even if we could, we probably should not, given its limited interest. But admitting that we could, then we could make models of society covering both individual histories, collective events, and that elusive quarry of social research: the large events of change, the tipping points of society? Can ABSS help to move our approach to society from a pre-scientific to a scientific one? In the rest of this paper, after reminding the patient reader what ABSS is today, I will draw a couple of conjectures on important paths that ABSS could follow in the future, and specify why I think that those paths are important in trying to answer the complicated questions above.

2 What is Agent Based Social Simulation

What do we mean with Agent Based Social Simulation? We will dodge the trap of a discussion on definitions and apply an extensive approach: social simulation is what social simulators, that is, the people that recognize themselves in the community, do. Recently, three regional associations have appeared to rally researchers around the flag of social simulation, covering the North America, Europe, and the Pacific Asia regions[1]. Moreover, a journal specifically dedicated to the field, the Journal of Artificial Societies and Social Simulation (JASSS), is a very good source for a list of the researchers interested in the field. Together with JASSS, a few other journals are accessible from this small community.

About naming, the community recognizes a few other ones, with slight differences, from Agent-Based Social Simulation (ABSS) to Modeling (ABM), Individual Based Modeling, and, more generally, Computational Social Sciences[2] (CSS); in this paper we will use the simpler ABSS. The recognition

---

[1]   The   three   associations   can   be   reached   at   http://www.essa.eu.org/, http://www.casos.cs.cmu.edu, and http://www.paaa-web.org/

[2] not to be confused with Complex Systems Science, which is somehow a sibling of ABSS, or with Cascading Style Sheets.

of ABSS as a discipline has been emphasized by a now famous citation by Axelrod as "a new way of doing science" [4].

While rather obvious for those working in the field, the above specification is due because of the larger meaning that the term simulation carries into the scientific community. Architectural structures are simulated for stability and resistance; the effect of new treatments is simulated by using complex simulators of chemical and biological processes; simulated neural networks try to mirror the workings of the brain. There are simulation conferences (for example, the Winter Simulation conference) whose track coordinators[3] have never published on JASSS.

ABSS differs from the the traditional mathematical-based approach - in short, the one that manipulates variables, representing measurable quantities, through systems of equations - in that its focus is on the description of the individual and on the explicit representation of processes (or, with [7], of the mechanisms that make phenomena happen). This approach allows to pursue a micro-level representation that is unachievable in the mathematical one. Thus, the micro-macro connection [23, 10] can potentially be validated on both faces, allowing for the study of emergence and for generative explanations [13] - that is, understanding a phenomenon by explicitly running the process that generates it. The ability to shift focus from individual histories to aggregate results reflects point by point the need to model single events and to study their global effect.

Finally, the individual or agent-based nature of ABSS is currently the only tool at our disposal to face what in [29] is defined "the toughest challenge": the dependence of social systems on social adaptive behavior; that is, the capability of agents (humans, but also, in different grades, animals and natural, evolved systems) to adapt their behavior to the changes in external condition, and even to act with the goal of bringing about changes in their physical and social environment. Social behaviors react and adapt [29] to recognition of emergent phenomena. Chemical elements do not fidget and shove for a higher position when one orders them in increasing mass; scientists, to the contrary, create refined publishing strategies once they become aware of the *h-index* subtleties, possibly perverting the scope of the ordering [31]. In passing, I will note how this challenge had been recognized long ago by Castelfranchi, who gave an appealing name to the phenomenon - mirroring the idea of emergence, he called the reflection of emergent phenomena *immergence* [8].

Because of its unique position with respect to modeling of social systems, ABSS is currently expanding its recognition in disciplines as Economics and Sociology; models with limited scope but interesting explanatory capabilities are starting to appear, as for example the model of the UK housing market by Nigel Gilbert [14]. At the same time, the first large scale experiments have been started, as testified by the works of [12], in which the authors develop a large-scale model of the economy, reproducing the fundamental statistical signatures from the real economy. Finally, as an example of models that are more interesting from a theoretical point of view, the idea of immergence from

---

[3] http://wintersim.org/coord.htm. We are referring to data for the 2011 conference.

Castelfranchi [8] has found application in the construction of a cognitive theory of norm innovation [2].

In a historical moment when we can make accurate forecasts of the weather but we can't reliably plan the deployment of resources during crisis and catastrophes [29], the community behind ABSS may actually hold the keys to a new understanding of social science for prediction and forecasting. But the language of the new science is still to be found; simulation as we are currently performing it solves some of the main problems of the alternatives, but as it does, it introduces new problems whose solution is not yet in sight. These problems can be summarized as:

Communication problem: ABSS cannot yet describe its algorithms in the detail needed for replication within the space of the scientific paper. This has two consequences. The first one is that reading a paper on simulation always gives the feeling that the work does not state all its assumptions, and that the resulting simulation is a unique piece, an artisanal piece of work; a hand-made carved table that shows the idiosyncrasies and the hand of the maker.

Validation problem: one of the stages of building a simulation in the classic [15], validation concerns the correspondence between simulation results and real world measurement, or observed data. This step is both difficult and neglected in common practice. Theoretical models escape validation under the justification of extreme abstraction, while detailed models run the risk of overfitting data.

To describe how the problems above influence the current practice of ABSS, let us review the story of the controversy about trust towards distant people. In a famous paper, Macy and Sato [21] start from the paradoxical difference between Japan and the US in trust levels: people in the US are more likely to trust strangers than people in Japan. They offer an explanation based on mobility, supported by simulation data, and showing that lower mobility brings about a lower level of trust, simply because that trust is not needed when strangers are rarely encountered, as it is the case of Japan. Instead, higher mobility forces people to develop a way to recognize signals of trustability in strangers, and that seems to resemble the US case.

The result, obtained through an abstract model, is interesting and significant. But there is more: Macy and Sato also speculate, on the basis of their results, that this system can break down when mobility becomes too high. As we are wiring the world in a single network of electronic and social connections, this prophecy on the dangers of mobility became interesting enough for other researchers to go and replicate it. In [34], Will and Hegselmann, however, found just the problems described above under *communication* as they tried to access the original code for the simulation - discovering that it was not available - and then tried to reconstruct the simulation starting from the description in the paper, that however, unsurprisingly, was found to be incomplete. No validation could be performed in this case, the object of the debate being an abstract theory, apart from the qualitative validation from the reproduction, in stylized form, of the Japan/US difference. But then, the authors of [34] found that their interpretation of the model didn't exhibit the most interesting and only predictive feature of the original one - that is, the breaking down of trust under increased mobility. This lack of confirmation made Macy and Sato answer, and that answer was answered again, in a debate facilitated by the online nature of JASSS. The debate was concluded with a recognition of the many improvements that the work of Will and Hegselmann brought to the model, and at least under some conditions, with the confirmation of the potential dangers of excessive mobility [33, 20].

The example briefly presented above shows both problems that simulation is facing - communication of models, and lack of validation. These, taken together, have another negative consequence, that is, the proliferation of papers and books that, instead of actually doing simulations, digress to some length about abstract recipes, philosophical foundations of social simulation, and draw roadmaps for their future[4]. These roadmaps often suggest to strengthen simulation by focusing on replication (which requires new way of communication of simulation details and results) and by grounding simulation on real data. However, this path remains slow, difficult and uncertain; stealing words from [5], "the quest... has taken on quixotic proportions, with little sign of the quarry on the horizon and the conquistadors constantly jousting among themselves concerning the most fertile direction to turn their pursuit."

3 What we want from simulation

Before moving on to the propositive part of this work, let us inquire about what are the questions that ABSS could contribute to answer. We already have proposed examples of theoretical questions and answers of relevance for the understanding of society, and for designing policies that contribute to shape it. However, the issues that ABSS managed to tackle are either very abstract (trust and mobility, the innovation of norms), or rather limited in scope (the housing market).

As another example, consider simulation efforts aimed to describe opinion dynamics: what is the connection between the rich and intricate debate between those of us that maintain an interest in politics, with the two-state or little more descriptions - monodimensional opinion spaces as the ones in applied in several papers like [11, 28], with apparently interesting results? Are these results good enough for us to better understand society? Or we still have some key ingredients missing?

Is is possible for ABSS to deal with the major questions of sociology and political science, and with what role? Can simulation help us, for example, to debate the questions collected by [18], which include themes as:

• how does consciousness and self-consciousness come about?

---

[4] Possibly mixing in some fancy word like "crowdsourcing".

- How to understand creativity and innovation? How can the formation of social norms and conventions, social roles and socialization, conformity and integration be understood?
- How do language and culture evolve?
- How to comprehend the formation of group identity and group dynamics?
- How do social differentiation, specialization, inequality and segregation come about? How to model deviance and crime, conflicts, violence, and wars?

Another similar list had been reviewed in [16], ranging from how can we persuade people to look after their health, to rather vague questions like how can humanity increase its "collective wisdom?"

Can ABSS give hints for the solution of some of the most famous sociological conundrums, as general as, for example, the question whether the decline of empires is inevitable or not? Why inequality has been growing steadily in western societies, and what are the consequences of this fact on happiness and on the mechanisms of democracy? To this point, there has been a very heated debate sparked by the publication of the Spirit Level [32], a book that argues for the thesis that higher equality benefits everyone in a society, even the wealthier. The thesis seems confirmed by correlations between the level of equality present and their ranking on happiness factors such as mental health, access to health services and child care, freedom of personal development for children, and others; the points taken into consideration for the study of those correlations are at the level of n wealthy nations or at the level of the US states. In both cases, there has been dissent on the suitability of those data[5]

These we have quickly presented here are just examples; the list of interesting complex issues about society could fill a book of its own. These issues have in common the characteristic of being both deep - touching area of elaborate cognition - and broad - impacting on society as a whole. Can the ABSS approach help us to understand and manage this kind of issues?

3.1 A picture of ABSS for society

The conservative answer is that it cannot: historical development of society is a unique trajectory of a reflexive complex system. But if we have to accept this limitation, then the question becomes: why bother with simulation?

Let's instead refuse the above limitation instead and consider, for the sake of the argument, that ABSS could find a path to deal with the representation of society as a whole - the same society that challenges us constantly, reminding us of how limited our powers of forecasting are - or at least of the deep and broad issues above. And yet there could be so many more interesting questions. Could we extend this understanding to the prevision, or even to the prevention

---

[5] Regrettably, the authors have not given full access to the data series they are using. At the time of writing, these can be downloaded for a price - a procedure unheard of in the field of simulation, and that is naturally raising suspicions.

(or causation), of large events as the ones we are living during the days of writing this paper - the Arab Spring, insurgency of the Arab world against their governments, a revolt whose tipping points seem to be exemplary: just consider how the Tunis revolt was sparkled by the suicide of a single person. What if his life had been different, even just slightly so? The chance meeting in the introduction can correctly be considered as irrelevant; but not all chance meeting are irrelevant for society.

All those questions sound still preposterous todays as they did when the field of ABSS was born in the 90s. All the same, the temptation to deal with society as an historical phenomenon remains as a frequent countertheme. The first famous attempt to create a science of society can be traces back to science fiction of the fifties - specifically, to the Foundation trilogy of Isaac Asimov, that, even today, is referenced in broad-scope social simulation endeavors; it is quoted, for example, by Katheleen Carley in [30]. In fact, Asimov principles for the new science of psychohistory actually anticipate the importance that Castelfranchi attributes to immergence when stating that the science "worked best where the individual working units – human beings – had no knowledge of what was coming, and could therefore react naturally to all situations." [3], ch. 25. Immergence is exactly what the psychohistorians try to avoid by keeping the results of their prevision secret, inaccessible to the public, what constitutes the second principle of this science.

The challenge of applying ABSS to society as a whole - a challenge that would make many of us throw in a contemptuous smile - is currently being undertaken, at least as an objective explicitly mentioned, by several scientific groups of various composition and size. We mention a massive effort from under evaluation from the EC, an effort whose scientific results are planned to appear in ten years, but whose effects into the world view of researchers in social simulation are already starting to appear. The effort, a large scale project named FuturICT[6], is currently still in the phase of drawing its roadmap for ten years of research, but its ambition is unrestricted - the project aims to predict financial crisis and social unrest, and then maybe wars, revolutions, and social change in a global sense.

3.2 Can simulation overcome its current limitations?

To sum up, we have shown that ABSS, in its current form, suffers from limitations, practical and theoretical, that limit its scope, reducing its reach. Axelrod [4] listed seven applications for the "new science" of simulation. Of these, training, education, performance and entertainment have been effectively relevant since then; proof and discovery, mostly in the shape of existence theorems, make their appearance occasionally. Prediction, that comes first in Axelrod's list, is still unattainable on large scale.

ABSS in its present form, as we have argued to this point, is simply not suited to answer large scale societal questions. But the current state of art is

---

[6] More information can be found at http://www.futurict.eu.

subject to change; data availabilty is becoming widespread, bringing about an epochal change from an era when our probes on society were few and biased, from a new era when probes will be intrusive, pervasive - but probably still biased[7] That's what in the current literature is called the new science of "big data" [29]. However, big data, especially when unsupported by theory, are prone to oversimplification, to confuse correlation with cause, and can finally degenerate in cargo cult science.

In this contribution, we will draw a different conjecture on a possible path of evolution that could bring about the needed changes in ABSS; as always, reality will check in and make a difference with the imagined path, just as our technology is different from the one imagined in the science fiction of the '50s.

4 Crowdsourcing simulation

Crowdsourcing technologies and peer to peer technologies represent the state of the art in electronic communication; they can even be considered the hallmark of human progress towards a collective mind.

Collective filter platforms that allow crowdsourcing implement the principles of rating and ranking to present information in a hierarchical way, ordered according to measures of relevance and community appreciation. They exploit the participatory practices typical of Web 2.0 to challenge traditional media outlets in the gatekeeping and agenda-setting functions [26]. Crowdsourcing has been proposed for applications in several fields, included generalized support to scientific research activity; [6] discusses how crowdsourcing could benefit the whole "Research Value Chain."

In simple terms, crowdsourcing is an approach where users select and discuss upon "interesting" and valuable items - in most cases, news headlines, general or specific to some field - proposed through a process of collaborative content filtering, and displayed as a list. The process of selection is quite straightforward and typical of the Web 2.0 "smartmobs" approach: users post links to news items discovered on the web; fellow users can comment each post, vote it *up* it if they consider it interesting, relevant, or generally worth reading, or *down* - "burying" it if not useful/interesting, inconsistent.

A basic reputation mechanism [25] is thus created: users submitting popular (i.e. those that get many "ups") stories or valuable comments gain in 'karma', or 'reputation points' that have a positive feedback on future ratings from that user. Posts with a certain amount of positive votes collected over a certain amount of time and submitted by "reputable" users get featured in the homepage of the social news site.

What does crowdsourcing has to do with ABSS? If one considers the problems we have listed, the connection comes immediately to mind: crowdsourcing could change the way we do simulation of social matters, creating a dis-

---

[7] For web exploration, [22] suggested that search engines can support plurality, but this has been recently questioned by the feedback considerations coming from filters and using profiling [27].

tributed approach to the problems and not only to computation. Interested parties could apply a social filter to models and simulations - thus helping focusing attention and maybe also encouraging the creation of new simulations. The situation concerning sharing and replication, notwithstanding the constant appeals of the epistemic community, are scarce and difficult; we consider the example discussed above on trust and mobility to be representative of the general situation. Selection by crowdsourcing could help finding useful simulations under overload and would encourage both communication and replication; if the paper outlet is not the ideal one to create the right level of competition and collaboration among social simulators, maybe a different kind of filtering process could help.

Now what we could possibly mean by crowdsourcing simulation? There are several levels at which this crowdourcing could happen. In the current practice, simulation is created, run and analyzed by a small group, sometimes just by a single individual; rarely it goes behind a collaboration between two laboratories.

Thus, we are speaking essentially of an individual or small group activity; if we look at the number of authors per paper, a measure of the smallest collaboration kernel able to produce advances, we find ABSS to be akin to philosophical research and theoretical physics, not to medicine or applied physics. This organization, and the identification of models with papers, is partly the cause of the problems of lack of communication and verification introduced above. Here, we try to imagine how this situation could be improved by creating a kind of (possibly distributed) repository for simulation models and their implementation, a repository that could be supported by crowdsourcing. This can be implemented in more than one way; we will briefly examine what could be the motivations to support the change. Let us see how this could happen in the context of two scenarios: collaborative ABSS and public ABSS.

4.1 Collaborative ABSS

For collaborative ABSS, we are considering the level of research laboratories, where we envisage crowdsourcing as a next step in the direction of replication and standardization. As computing becomes more distributed than before, and as the combined effort of the research group grows in size, the community could coagulate in a small number of portals.

This could lead to a paradigm shift in which models become structured in components, and are accessed not individually, but as representative of a class of *questions*. This shift is fundamental if any collective filtering could happen, in order to build classes of models to be compared not on internal structure but on the answers they give to these questions. Building a suitable representation - an ontology, a reference model - is a scientific challenge in itself; but current research in knowledge representation [17] may be in the position to help. The essential ingredients are: explicit *theories* that help framing the question; the social and regional *context* if present; the specific research *question*; and finally, the *model*, and its relation with other models; and, finally, its *implementation*.

What we are imagining here is a portal where the researcher could quickly find all the models that could contribute, to use a famous example, to the understanding of segregation, and could be presented with the choice between the classics implementations and the newest ones, a wealth of variations adopted and performed by young researchers just entering in the field. As computational power grows, we could consider these simulations as always running somewhere in the cloud, so that queries could show not only the results as collected and interpreted by the author, and not only the code for replication - but the execution in fieri, with new data being added, and new views of them in preparation. Simulations so arranged could be crowdsourced by the community, with voting systems and rankings based on views, citations, and explicit evaluations from the users.

In such a system, integration of output data would become possible - if a simulation answers a specific question, then it could be asked to shape its output data in a specific way. This could create a chance for a data mining AI to select automatically what implementations and parameter values support the original argument, and which instead fail to replicate it, qualitatively or quantitatively.

The realization of such a portal meets several obstacles - not last of which, the highly individual character of research and researchers. On the other hand, our short exposition of the trust and mobility simulation debate represents an example of how to exploit the natural competition between researchers towards better practice and results. Political pressure here should be applied from the associations that gather the practitioners of the field. As with any standardizing pressure, however, the possibility of emergent/immergent behavior, possibly perverting the aims of the policy itself, should be considered; in the specific case, reduction of diversity and mechanism exploiting are the two risks that come first to mind. A simulation of these consequences could be tested to evaluate how likely these are to happen.

4.2 *Public* ABSS

If simulation helps policy makers, what about personal decision making? The second decade of this millennium starts with further new movement in the information sphere. Personal use of small application is exploding with the devices that support it; the shape of computers, in fact unchanged since the advent of the personal computer, is finally shifting to smaller scale. With easier social sharing, privacy lost its importance in the eyes of most people, substituted by the exhibitionist pleasure of showing off oneself in a public glass house.

Could simulation, in this context, make the shift to the general public? Here, the challenge we are presenting is much more substantial: simulation not for the research community, but for the general public? This amounts to betting on at least three tables: platform development, that should create a level of peer-to-peer simulation software interaction; interface development, that should provide game-like, understandable interfaces; and finally on the risky table of politics, because thinking and choosing one's future, even in a limited context, is doing politics.

The compression of diversity that had to be carefully weighted in the previous case, that of collaborative ABSS, is not as strong as an issue: for what we will call public ABSS (pABSS) is going to fill a void, not to replace or update current practices. In fact, while it can be argued that we as humans are innovation machines, naturally testing the limits of our context and intelligently (but sometimes shortsightedly) exploit occasions as they become available.

The realization of public ABSS will need to hold its own weight economically, as Wikipedia does. The problem here is delicate because this kind of ABSS will be applied directly to policy; thus it will naturally attract the attention of interested parties that could exert economical power to shift the tool in one direction or the other. Imagine simply the tool as being used to compute the effects of the policy choices between different sources of energy. The community behind pABSS should get inspired to the principles of low-cost mass transactions and find its fundings in the user base more than from established - and potentially interested - sources.

What could be the pay of the good simulation providers? One answer lies in all the free work that people invests in blogs and online gamings [1]. These activities enhance one's reputation in the specific community, and, in several ways (mostly, finding good paying work as a result of one's reputation), this reputation could be cashed in.

4.3 Crowdourcing simulation: drawing the path

Everyone in the field would agree that ABSS, even if simpler than, for example, mean field theory, is nowhere ready to be employed by the layman. The pressure towards a standard is strong, but the standard is nowhere yet in sight; visual instruments are starting to appear, but still most platforms need programming (in the simplest case, in the form of snippets) - which is probably more approachable than math, but hardly suitable for a general public.

Should we conclude that simulation destiny is to remain in the babel of the laboratories? Before rushing to that conclusion, let us consider shortly some recent innovations that shaped the panorama of information access. We are talking of the giants here: in my personal list, Google, Wikipedia and Facebook. Rivers of electronic ink have been written, and some moving image projected in theaters, on how these forces have shaped the information landscape; we're just considering one factor here between the several that made these ideas possible.

This factor is an unexpected working of simplification. In all three cases, people behind these system have made a simplifying assumption that had shown itself workable, though at the time of their invention, very few would have made that bet. For Google, it was a combination of factors - the importance of search, the functioning of the pagerank algorithm, and the suitability of the advertisement revenue model. For Wikipedia, it was a bet on the quality of rootgrass continuous editing against the traditional process of reviewing; and for Facebook, it was a bet against privacy.

I've listed these briefly to show, on one side, how common knowledge on what is suitable for the public can show to be wrong; the application of this argument to crowdsourced simulation is too obvious to state in detail. And for another reason too - these success factors have in common a bet on simplification, or on what could be called a working shortcut: Google shortcuts language intricacies, Wikipedia shortcuts academic and educational credentials, Facebook shortcuts privacy.

Indeed, the willingness to forsake privacy in exchange for easier social connections might translate in the possibility to share values and plans in a kind of "life simulations", in a shape that is hard to predict today - but whose shadow we already see in social games like SimCity and, in part, SecondLife.

5 Conclusions and future perspectives

We have proposed two directions of developments that could help ABSS to deal with its limitations, based on the success of collaborative filtering or crowd-sourcing. The first, collective ABSS, is already happening as we see from the a few ABSS web portals that have been recently created, and from several tentatives of standardization. The second path is more daring and its feasibility and consequence are more difficult to foresee. But in both cases, crowdsourcing is a concrete chance to modify and reshape the simulation methodology for computational social science, in a way that could better answer the deep questions, theoretical and applicate, that society presents us.

Acknowledgements Ideas presented in this paper had been inspired from conversations with many people. I mention Jeff Johnson, Marco Nanni, Fredric Amblard, David Hales, Giulia Andrighetto, Francesca Giardini, Stefano Picascia and, last but not least, Rosaria Conte. Mistakes and ingenuities rest with the author only.

References

1. Chris Anderson. Free: How Today's Smartest Businesses Profit by Giving Something for Nothing. 2009.
2. G. Andrighetto, M. Campenni, R. Conte, and M. Paolucci. On the immergence of norms: a normative agent architecture. In *Proceedings of AAAI Symposium, Social and Organizational Aspects of Intelligence*, 2007.
3. Isaac Asimov. *Foundation and Empire*. Gnome Press, New York, 1952.
4. Robert Axelrod. Advancing the art of simulation in the social sciences. *Complexity*, 3(2):16–22, 1998.
5. R. L. Axtell. *Multi-agent systems macro: A prospectus*. Cambridge University Press, 2006.

6. Thierry Buecheler, Jan H. Sieg, Rudolf M. Füchslin, and Rolf Pfeifer. *Crowdsourcing, Open Innovation and Collective Intelligence in the Scientific Method: A Research Agenda and Operational Framework*, pages 679–686. MIT Press, Cambridge, Mass, 2011.

7. Mario Bunge. How Does It Work?: The Search for Explanatory Mechanisms. *Philosophy of the Social Sciences*, 34(2):182–210, June 2004.

8. Cristiano Castelfranchi. Simulating with Cognitive Agents: The Importance of Cognitive Emergence. In *Proceedings of the First International Workshop on Multi-Agent Systems and Agent-Based Simulation*, pages 26–44, London, UK, 1998. Springer-Verlag.

9. Cristiano Castelfranchi, Rosaria Conte, and Mario Paolucci. Normative Reputation and the Costs of Compliance. *Journal of Artificial Societies and Social Simulation*, 1(3), 1998.

10. Rosaria Conte and Cristiano Castelfranchi. *Cognitive Social Action*. London: UCL Press, 1995.

11. G. Deffuant, D. Neau, F. Amblard, and Gerard Weisbuch. Mixing beliefs among interacting agents. *Advances in Complex Systems*, 3:87–98, 2001.

12. Domenico Delli Gatti, Saul Desiderio, Edoardo Gaffeo, P. Cirillo, and M. Gallegati. *Macroeconomics from the bottom-up*. New Economic Windows. Springer, 2011.

13. Joshua M. Epstein. *Generative Social Science: Studies in Agent-Based Computational Modeling (Princeton Studies in Complexity)*. Princeton University Press, January 2007.

14. N. Gilbert, J. C. Hawksworth, and P. Sweeney. An Agent-based Model of the UK Housing Market. Technical report, University of Surrey, 2008.

15. Nigel Gilbert and Klaus G. Troitzsch. *Simulation for the Social Scientist, 2nd edition*. Buckingham: Open University Press, 2005.

16. Jim Giles. Social science lines up its biggest challenges. *Nature*, 470:18–19, 2011.

17. Nicola Guarino. The Ontological Level: Revisiting 30 Years of Knowledge Representation. In Alexander Borgida, Vinay Chaudhri, Paolo Giorgini, and Eric Yu, editors, *Conceptual Modeling: Foundations and Applications*, volume 5600 of *Lecture Notes in Computer Science*, chapter 4, pages 52–67. Springer Berlin / Heidelberg, Berlin, Heidelberg, 2009.

18. Dirk Helbing and Stefano Balietti. Fundamental and Real-World Challenges in Economics. December 2010.

19. Dirk Helbing and Stefano Balietti. From Social Data Mining to Forecasting Socio-Economic Crisis. February 2011.

20. Michael Macy and Yoshimichi Sato. The Surprising Success of a Replication That Failed. *Journal of Artificial Societies and Social Simulation*, 13(2):9, 2010.

21. Michael W. Macy and Yoshimichi Sato. Trust, Cooperation, and Market Formation in the U.S. and Japan. *Proceedings of the National Academy of Sciences of the United States of America*, 99(10):7214–7220, 2002.

22. F. Menczer, S. Fortunato, A. Flammini, and A. Vespignani. Googlearchy or Googlocracy? *IEEE Spectrum*, 2006.

23. Scott Moss and Bruce Edmonds. Sociology and Simulation: Statistical and Qualitative Cross-Validation. *American Journal of Sociology*, 110:1095–1131, 2005.

24. M. Paolucci. False reputation in social control. *Advances in Complex Systems*, 3(4):39–52, 2000.

25. Mario Paolucci, Tina Balke, Rosaria Conte, Torsten Eymann, and Samuele Marmo. Review of Internet User-Oriented Reputation Applications and Application Layer Networks. *Social Science Research Network Working Paper Series*, September 2009.

26. Mario Paolucci, Stefano Picascia, and Walter Quattrociocchi. Causality in Collective Filtering. 2011.

27. Eli Pariser. *The Filter Bubble: What the Internet Is Hiding from You*. Penguin Press HC, The, May 2011.

28. Walter Quattrociocchi, Mario Paolucci, and Rosaria Conte. Reputation and Uncertainty Reduction: Simulating Partner Selection. pages 308–325. 2008.

29. Alessandro Vespignani. Predicting the Behavior of Techno-Social Systems. *Science*, 325(5939):425–428, July 2009.

30. Sharon Weinberger. Social science: Web of war. *Nature*, 471:566–568, 2011.

31. Jevin D. West. How to improve the use of metrics. *Nature*, 465(7300):870–872, June 2010.

32. Richard Wilkinson and Kate Pickett. *The Spirit Level: Why Greater Equality Makes Societies Stronger*. Bloomsbury Press, December 2009.
33. Oliver Will. Resolving a Replication That Failed: News on the Macy & Sato Model. *Journal of Artificial Societies and Social Simulation*, 12(4):11, 2009.
34. Oliver Will and Rainer Hegselmann. A Replication That Failed - on the Computational Model in Michael W. Macy and Yoshimichi Sato: Trust, Cooperation and Market Formation in the U.S. and Japan. Proceedings of the National Academy of Sciences, May 2002'. *Journal of Artificial Societies and Social Simulation*, 11(3):3, 2008.

Chapter 39
Agents that make mistakes

Luis Antunes

Abstract Cristiano Castelfranchi built his scientific life around the idea of understanding behaviour. Behaviour has a complex meaning here. Behaviour is what people do, as a result of their own volitions and concoctions, but it is also the overall grasp that observers make of it. In turn, these observers can be individuals themselves; some kind of abstract, independent-ised (or -ish) scientist; specialised groups (such as institutional statisticians, the media, etc.); etc. Overall grasp also has a complex meaning. Overall can be as global as needed, but can also be a grouping defined through some more restrained criteria, whereas grasp can mean direct data observation, but more typically it will mean information collected through dedicated models, each of which implies an author and a stance. Understanding has a complex meaning as well. Understand does not mean only to be able to reproduce behaviour; it rather means to have an explanation that can be accurate and precise enough to explain the behaviour, and do it in a generative way. That is, to provide a solid basis for the construction and development of artefacts which exhibit reasonable behaviour in dynamic and complex situations. Moreover, this understanding can allow for the development of predictions for real problems, and also to explore possibilities that go beyond reality, in order to endow policy makers with ex ante capabilities to adapt to contingencies in social life.

The complexity of the task at hand for the modeller is then so big, that special scientific strategies are needed to provide cut points for the division of the problem. In this contribution, I will focus on some of the classic cut points, and, for each of these, I will elaborate on issues to be dealt with, solutions for the cuttings, and subsequent synthesis of the results. In particular, I will focus on the agent's mentality, especially its individual rationality; on the agent's social immersion and its consequences; and on the strategy of exploration of the complex space of designs hence produced.

Luis Antunes
Laboratory of Agent Modelling (LabMAg), Faculty of Sciences, University of Lisbon, Portugal
e-mail: xarax@di.fc.ul.pt

1 Introduction

I hesitate to call agents straight ahead to the kind of entities I will be discussing in this article. Agents are usually meant to represent avatars, replications of ourselves, as we delve into complex reasonings that we hope can explain, lead and justify the things we do. As we all well know, these phases of the reasoning do not coincide, they are usually only related. Sometimes we perform one action for a reason that lead to it, but the explanation might be a completely different reason, and surely the justification, should we need one, might still be quite different. However, as Simon said in [1987] "People have reasons for what they do." Whether we can identify those reasons and build them into a coherent whole, that's an altogether different issue. In fact, it is even possible that the perpetrators do not know the true reasons themselves, and if called to explain their reasons will rationalise some socially accepted explanation for what could be a selfish of shameful deed.

Anyways, returning to the issue of the agenthood of the doers, another possibility to keep in mind is the proposal of Amblard and Ferrand [1998], in which they methodologically build an agency including actors, their interrelations, and even cliques involving them. This kind of self-reflective multi-agent system may possess the ability of self reconfiguration to encompass bolder forms of description of the issue at stake, usually some highly complex and dynamical social situation involving multiple actors and multiple, conflicting interests.

All of this makes life hard for the tired scientist, but at the same time, it emphasises a point that I have been making with colleagues at least since 1994 [Coelho et al 1994, Antunes et al 2004, Antunes et al 2007]: the scientist, the observer of an experiment, has a role in the development of the experiments, especially simulation experiments, and pure objectivity cannot be achieved. The design of experiments is as complex and contingent as the design of agents and the design of societies in which they are deployed.

The view I have been trying to summarise is strongly inspired in Castelfranchi's own view on agent systems [Castelfranchi 1990, 1995, 2001, Conte and Castelfranchi 1995]. Agents have a mind that resembles our own idea of our own mind, and their mind can be approximately described using mental terms and soft logical technology that allows scientists and laymen to communicate about the true meanings of what they think might be happening. These technological concepts also help to operationalize the ideas, rendering them closer to what can be put to work into a computer or robotic system. The ideas described in this manner are intended to explain, and not only replicate, the behaviours we can find in real life, to a point that hopefully predictions can be made, and prescriptions for improvement can be rehearsed.

Hence, the study of agents, multi-agent systems, artificial societies and social simulation are meant as a scientific effort, aiming at a generative engineering purpose. This approach sets the pace and rhythm for the remainder of this article.

2 Context: the alleys of 'rational' decision

After years looking into the key notion of decision in agent systems [Antunes et al 2001, Antunes 2001], I was able to form a kind of minimal set of concepts that forms an agent's mind. The Beliefs-Values-Goals architecture provides the means for the designer to not only know what to do with the agents' choices, but also to provide reasons to justify and generate those choices. In my view of agent rationality, these reasons must be individual, situated, and multi-varied. This describes a rationality of reasons, not a rationality of reason. Reason is no longer viewed as some kind of abstract 'perfection,' instead, this approach acknowledges imperfection as part of the world, and does not impose one's rationality onto the others.

Immersing such an agent into a society of its peers has profound implications for the design of its mind, and also of the society itself.

In this individual and collection construction, I chose to follow Castelfranchi's principle of 'cognitive autonomy,' namely, that the only way that an agent can change another's agent mind is through its beliefs [Castelfranchi 1995]. So, agents communicate with each other, and as a result of this communication, an agent might come to change its beliefs, which in turn will have an effect on the other mental concepts, in particular, goals and values.

When agents produce utterances that can influence other agents' decisions, this new information may be used by the listener in several ways, according to the confidence it deposits on the uttering agent. The way to incorporate the information in future decisions is also a design option to be taken.

Then, the communication of information between the agents might lead to agents adopting new goals from other agents. Mechanisms for this goal adoption include imitation, or curiosity, and ensure that the society is organised into structured dynamical patterns of individual and collective behaviours. For instance, social concepts as friendship tend to rest on sharing of common, mutual, and even conflicting adopted goals, many times resting on kinship. Kinship is also one of the most frequent causes of value sharing. Shared values represent an abstract (but repeatedly concretised) way of aligning societies to standard patterns of collective behaviours that are foundational for their essence and cohesion.

Obviously, an agent that 'does what it is told' can hardly be said to act autonomously. Therefore, I have provided assessment and adaptation mechanisms for the choice machinery, so that the agents do not crystalize into some awkward and stubborn set of choices (or even the more subtle 'way of choosing'). In this sense, agents are allowed to 'make mistakes,' and hopefully learn how not to repeat them in subsequent choices – but also allowed to make the same mistakes again, such is life...

Agents equipped with such a decision machinery have proven to explore a set of complex options with a particular kind of adaptive rationality. Even when instigated to transgress on some of the most basic rules for classic rationality, such as choice transitivity, these agents are able to make a sequence of reasonable choices in which the exploration of the options seems sensible, not totally neglecting the exploitation of the results of the best outcomes.

Now we can call these agents self-motivated and autonomous. Even if these epitomes are exaggerated or even abusive, now it is out of sheer incompetence to better design them, not anymore for neglecting the issue of autonomy altogether.

Therefore, even with this coarse sketch, I feel entitled to proceed forward and face the challenge of designing experiments with agents so designed.

3 Experimental challenges of self-motivated agents

The idea of 'broad but shallow design' offered by Aaron Sloman has been a strong influence of the approach I have been following [Sloman 1994]. In a nutshell, Sloman finds it important to design an agent with a strong individuality and completeness. Even if some components are left as simple as possible, this completeness allows the agent to be deployed in a functioning system. Later on, some of the components can be selected for enhancement, making the agent more robust, more intelligent, more adaptive, etc. This exploration of the design space around an initial complete design is that Sloman calls the 'design stance.'

Following this idea, I have proposed that the design stance is applied not only to the construction of the agents, but also of the societies and of the experiments themselves.

In the beginning of the 1990s, many a debate was dissolved by taking the standpoint that Artificial Intelligence (AI) was to be conducted as an experimental science. This view contrasted vividly with two other co-related approaches: that the aim of AI was to build useful artefacts (Engineering view) and that it would be enough to replicate the behaviour of intelligent beings, not really to understand what caused it (week AI view, based on Behaviourist Psychology).

The scientific view that AI would be conducted by running experiments to substantiate its theses would have a strong impact on the development of multi-agent systems. The agent view on AI would invert the usual division of the area in sub-fields. Agents form individualities that operate in the world, and there is a renewed interest both in their innings and in the way the world operates.

Agents are always a source of change and unpredictability, and this makes it impossible to adopt bluntly the rational view on agent decision, as postulated by other synthesis sciences, such as Economics, with its 'homo economicus'. No-one behaves like the average man, and this view on rationality, based on probabilities and utility, may well be a good a posteriori way of describing behaviour, but proves to be scares when called to explain, generate, and predict the future behaviour of agent-based systems.

3.1 Assessing choice

The role of value as a new mental attitude towards decision is twofold. On the one hand, values provide a reference framework to represent agent's preference during deliberation (the pondering of options candidate to contribute to a selected goal). On the other, values help inform choice, the final step of decision, when the agent has to pick an option from the ordered set of options provided by the deliberation phase. To this aim, a probability distribution can be defined by using the relevant values for the situation.

In the BVG choice framework, the agent's system of values evolves as a consequence of the agent's assessment of the results of previous decisions. Decisions are evaluated against certain dimensions (that could be the same previously used for the decision or not), and this assessment is fed back into the agent's mind, by adapting the mechanisms associated with choice, especially the ones related to values. This is another point that escapes the traditional utilitarian view, where the world (and so the agent) is static and known. BVG agents can adapt to an environment where everything changes, including the agent's own preferences (for instance as a result of interactions). This is especially important in a multi-agent environment, since the agents are autonomous, and so potentially sources of change and novelty.

The evaluation of the results of our evaluations becomes a central issue, and this question directly points to the difficulties in assessing the results of experiments. We would need meta-values to evaluate those results, but that calls for a designer, and amounts to looking for emergent phenomena. But if those 'higher values' exist (and so they are the important ones) why not use them for decision? This dilemma clearly shows the *ad hoc* character of most solutions, and it is difficult to escape it.

We can conceive two ways out. The first is the development of an ontology of values, to be used in some class of situations as qualitative markers (norms). Higher or lower, values have their place in this ontology, and their relations are clearly defined. For a given problem the relevant values can be identified and used, and appropriate experimental predictions postulated and tested.

When tackling the issue of choice, the formulation of hypotheses and experimental predictions becomes delicate. If the designer tells the agent how to choose, how can he not know exactly how the agent will choose? To formulate experimental predictions and then evaluate to what extent they are fulfilled becomes in this case a spurious game: it amounts to perform calculations about knowledge and reasons, and not to judge to what extent those reasons are the best reasons, and correctly generate the choices. We return to technical reasons for behaviour, in detriment of the will and the preferences of the agent.

Consequently, the second solution is subtler. By situating the agent in an environment with other agents, autonomy becomes a key ingredient, to be used with care and balance. The duality of value sets becomes a necessity, as agents cannot access values at the macro level, made judiciously coincide with the designer values. The answer is the designer, and the problem is methodological. The BVG update mechanism provides a way to put to test this liaison between agent and designer. The designer's model of choice cannot be the model of perfect choice against which the whole world is to be evaluated. It is our strong conviction that the perfect choice does not exist, because characters perfectly embody a specific set of physical and personality traits. All depends on the adequate fiction (script). It is a model of choice to be compared to another (human) one playing an identical role, by using criteria that in turn may not be perfect.

Within BVG, we can generate a wide range of behaviours for our agents. These, of course might include mistakes: behaviours that not being perfect, or accurate, contribute to a more thorough exploration of the space of possibilities. Even if someone's favourite dish is roast beef, she does not eat roast beef at every meal. However, if while eating oven-baked fish she is asked about her favourite dish, she will still answer roast beef. This is the kind of choice behaviour I want to be able to generate in my agents, and in my view the greatest achievement of the BVG project.

3.2 Exploratory methodologies

Exploratory simulation embeds the idea taking a model of an interesting phenomenon as an object of study itself [Gilbert and Doran 1994]. The shift of the focus of research from natural sciences to artificial sciences includes the study of possible societies. In this movement, the prescriptive character (exploration) cannot be simplistically resumed to an optimisation, just as the descriptive character is not a simple reproduction of the real social phenomena.

Exploring societies 'in silica' can only be made in an exhaustive, principled way by following a specific methodology. When we take the exploration of the design space further than the construction and study of agents, and also focus on society design, and even experiment design, variations are introduced step by step, to reinforce the trust in the successive findings, and so lead the way for subsequent designs.

It is important to state the purposes of agent-based exploratory simulation, as often they are left only implicit.

- By building computational models, scientists are forced to *operationalise* the concepts and mechanisms they use for their formulations. This point is very important as we are in cross-cultural field, and terminology and approaches can differ a lot from one area to another;
- The first and often only purpose of many simulations is to get to *understand* some complex phenomenon better. 'Understand' means to describe, to model, to program, to manipulate, to explore, to have a hands-on approach to the definition of a phenomenon or process;
- Another purpose of exploratory simulation is to *experiment* with the models, formulate conjectures, test theories, explore alternatives of design but also of definitions, rehearse different approaches to design, development, carry out explorations of different relevance of perceived features, compare consequences of possible designs, test different initial conditions and simulation

parameters, explore 'what-if' alternatives. In sum, go beyond observed phenomena and established models, and play with the simulation while letting imagination run free;

- Ultimately, the aim is to *explain* a given phenomenon, usually from the real social world. The sense of explaining is linked to causality more than to correlation. As Gilbert [Gilbert 2000] says, we need explanation not only at the macro level, but also at the individual level. Our explanation of the phenomena we observe in simulation is solid because we must make the effort of creating and validating the mechanisms at the micro level, by providing solid and valid reasons for individual behaviours;
- When we achieve such a level of understanding, we are able to *predict* how our models react to change, and this prediction is verifiable in the real phenomenon, through empirical observations. It is important to stress that even empirical observations presuppose a model (which data were collected, which questionnaires were used, etc.);
- Finally, we have such confidence in the validity and prediction capability of our simulation system, that we are ready to help rehearse new policies and *prescribe* measures to be applied to the real phenomenon with real actors. It is obvious that no rigour can be spared when a simulation program achieves this point, and initial restrained application is highly recommended.

Robert Axelrod [1997] proposed the KISS (Keep It Simple, Stupid) principle, which follows the Occam's razor argument. The justification to use it relies on the importance and practicality of simplicity in modelling. Simplicity is helpful for transmitting the model to the scientific community, promoting understanding and extensibility. Besides, making an abstract and simple model is often supported with the argument that such models are more general, and therefore have possible applications in many real cases. Another reason for its spreading is that building a simple model is, simply, easier than a complex one. And furthermore, it is not only the design: it is easier to implement, analyse and check [Edmonds and Moss 2004].

Edmonds and Moss propose KIDS: Keep It Descriptive, Stupid. They consider KISS attractive and understandable, but not necessarily realistic or useful. KIDS ask modellers to begin with the most similar model to the target, in spite of its complexity. And only afterwards, analyse which parts could be simplified while preserving the behaviour. With further simplifications, KIDS model could be used in several contexts but being sure that it has good foundations.

Working with Samer Hassan [Hassan et al 2008], I have proposed to extend KISS to an exploration strategy called Deepening KISS, and later strengthen the modelling effort and quality by heavy use of real data in several steps of the methodology. Data help to remove arbitrary assumptions and design options in an informed way. Data also help to debug and tune up the models, as well as to initialise them, and assess their results against reality. The use of data can also be costly, and even render the whole problem/solution whole more complex. But technologies such as statistical tools, fuzzy sets and ontologies might come to the rescue and provide a framework where the modeller can handle most of the necessary issues.

The e*plore methodology [Antunes et al 2007] demands for formal and informal specifications that create and sustain a common lexicon and a common set of techniques allowing for a proficuous dialogue among practitioners from several disciplines. E*plore steps adopt and extend previously existing methodologies, such as Cohen's MAD [Cohen et al 1989] and Gilbert's logic of simulation [Gilbert 2000].

1. *identify the subject* to be investigated, by stating specific items, features or marks;
2. *unveil state-of-the-art* across the several scientific areas involved to provide context. The idea is to enlarge coverage before narrowing the focus; to focus prematurely on solutions may prevent the in-depth understanding of problems;
3. *propose definition* of the target phenomenon. Pay attention to its operationality;
4. *identify relevant aspects* in the target phenomenon, in particular, *list individual and collective measures* with which to characterise it;
5. if available, *collect observations* of the relevant features and measures;
6. *develop the appropriate models* to simulate the phenomenon. Use the features you uncovered and program adequate mechanisms for individual agents, for interactions among agents, for probing and observing the simulation. Be careful to base behaviours on reasons that can be supported on appropriate individual motivations. Develop visualisation and data recording tools. Document every design option thoroughly. *Run the simulations*, collect results, compute selected measures;
7. return to step 3, and *calibrate everything*: your definition of the target, of adequate measures, of all the models, verify your designs, validate your models by using the selected measures. Watch individual trajectories of selected agents, as well as collective behaviours;
8. *introduce variation* in your models: in initial conditions and parameters, in individual and collective mechanisms, in measures. Return to step 5;
9. After enough exploration of design space is performed, use your best models to *propose predictions*. Confirm them with past data, or collect data and validate predictions. Go back to the appropriate step to ensure rigour;
10. Make a generalisation effort and *propose theories and/or policies*. Apply to the target phenomenon. Watch global and individual behaviours. Recalibrate.

One strategy I have advocated to master the complexity of the exploration of complex design spaces is the progressive deepening, in which the 'broad but shallow' approach is taken and then complexity is introduced stepwise through series of models instead of improvement of models. These models can be obtained from previous ones by following several different strategies, and even combinations of them, as is shown in Fig. 1.

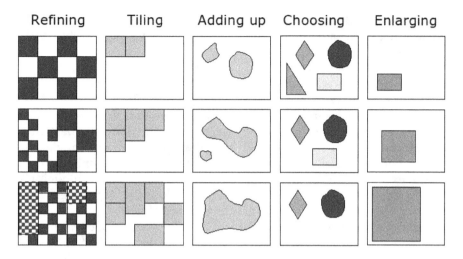

Fig. 1 Some techniques to cover design space.

4 Modelling model comparison

Following through a research program [Lakatos 1970], is a process that heavily depends on the inspiration, intuition, and talent (among many other factors) of the researcher. Many times, programs that seem to be in 'advantage' with respect to others can still be 'defeated' by those others that seemed to be 'degenerating.' So, progress can only be assessed from outside, many times from a historian (or philosophical, or epistemological) standpoint. But when we are delving in complexity to develop, simulate and analyse useful models, conducting exploratory simulation where theories are being shaped as the simulations progress, there is the need for some principles with which to guide the exploration. Some heuristic principles were put forward, such as KISS, KIDS, and progressive deepening. Let's briefly discuss them.

KISS ("Keep It Simple, Stupid!") refers back to Occam's razor, and proposes to tackle a problem through the simplest possible model, to gain on communicability, understanding and extensibility, as well as easier verifiability and replicability [Axelrod 1997]. If difficulties are met, just make the model more complex by the minimum extension that overcomes the trouble. As Cioffi-Revilla [Cioffi-Revilla 2008] points out, Lakatos would accept this simplicity argument, and even sustain that empirical validation could be delayed until the more complex and encompassing models would be developed. Simple models have their own usefulness and role to play along the development of the series conducting to a final model that would provide answers to the given research questions.

While admitting that KISS is an attractive and understandable principle, researchers such as Bruce Edmonds and Scott Moss argued in favour of another heuristic principle: KIDS ("Keep It Descriptive, Stupid!") [Edmonds and

Moss 2004]. Basically, they consider that KISS is not realistic or useful, and
prefer to design a model as similar to the target phenomenon as possible, and
despite its possible complexity. Subsequently, the model analysis can allow
for simplifications and abstractions that will make the model applicable to a
wider range of situations while maintaining its sound foundations.

In some sense, these two approaches carry the same difficulties: the huge
complexity of social phenomena, and the unknown ground faced by the researcher in its approach to it. In the first case, perhaps the research questions
cannot be put forward in a clear enough way that allows the final model to
be identified, hence rendering the quest for the ultimate model infinite. In the
second case, exactly the same problem, except that now the 'final model' is
the 'initial model.' The most accurate map of the world is the world itself, but
obviously that doesn't help us much in finding the way home.

Where to make the abstraction cut was always the problem of every modeller and designer. Aaron Sloman's 'design stance' and 'broad but shallow'
designs are starting point to propose an alternative to these views [Sloman
1994].

5 Variability and deepening

Sloman's concept of broad but shallow agents basically affirms the need of
building complete agents, even though some of their parts may be not as complex as they should. The design process then goes on developing further those
parts, according to a path through design space [Sloman 1994, Sloman 1993]. I
proposed to adopt this idea and apply it not only to the design of agents, but
also to that of societies and even experiments. The shallow part of the designs
gets "deepened." This notion was introduced in [Antunes et al 2007]. The idea
is fairly simple: in any design there is an amount of "unsupported assumptions" Following Scott Moss's recommendation, the goal is to "relax those
arbitrary assumptions in a way that reflects some evidence." This complex
movement involves the experimenter him/herself, and according to Moss includes "qualitative micro validation and verification (V&V), numerical macro
V&V, top-down verification, bottom-up validation," all of this whereas facing
that "equation models are not possible, due to finite precision of computers."
For instance

> A possible sequence of deepening a concept representing some agent
> feature (say parameter c, standing for honesty, income, or whatever)
> could be to consider it initially a constant, then a variable, then assign
> it some random distribution, then some empirically validated random
> distribution, then include a dedicated mechanism for calculating c, then
> an adaptive mechanism for calculating c, then to substitute c altogether
> for a mechanism, and so on and so forth.

The notion of deepening was applied in [Hassan et al 2008], to improve
some details the demographic mechanisms involved in a simulation of the

evolution of moral values. This and other applications of this concept have brought forward the use of data in the simulations.

In [Hassan el al 2010, Hassan et al 2008], some indications about how data can be used were produced. Data is no longer used only to validate the model against the real world, but they are also used to help build and initialise the simulations. This is preferable to using random distributions, and in some sense closer to the KIDS approach, as data bring the researchers closer to the real world phenomenon under study. Data can also be used for calibration of the models. Calibration of the models and their inside mechanisms, structures and settings is done in an iterative fashion, and based on a mixture of intuitions and optimisation. Using real data is useful for calibration because it allows for the model to be tuned up while keeping it centred on the point in data space it is supposed to be applied to. Sensitivity analysis can be performed later to determine to which extent mode the model can be generalised to neighbourhoods of that point. But the real data available provide enhanced means for exploration around the space of designs, which is also needed.

To simulate with alternative data can also be seen as a form of deepening, in that it represents a step towards more abstract and generally applicable models. As will be clear from the methodology steps, it should be stressed that to simulate does not mean only to obtain the results for further analysis. It always leads to redesign of the models in more detail and accuracy.

6 The observer role

The role of the observer is apparent in the whole process as we have seen above. In my view we have to assume that no absolute objectivity is possible, and take steps towards enhancing the strength of the subjective views and conclusions derived from the system and simulations. A case in point is the separation of the several of the roles involved with experimentation, for instance, design and verification. This is particularly difficult, as many research projects do not possess the resources to ensure such development strategy. In other sciences (e.g. pharmaceutical), this separation is absolutely fundamental to enforce trust in the conclusions of studies. It is indeed part of a set of mandatory practices in some fields such as pharmaceutics (I thank Ken de Jong for this example and subsequent discussion). In social simulation a set of best practices to be widely adopted would not only enhance such trust, but also reduce the design effort by stipulating parameters for some issues common to every project. David [2007] sustains that a step towards more trust is provided by replicating simulations in more than one platform, even if developed by the same authors. Perhaps this idea includes some optimism about the inexistence of programming bugs in the several simulation programs (and in the specifications), but at least it has the advantage of acknowledging that "model verification and alignment" are activities subject to errors, and trust in models by researchers and stakeholders should be fostered. In fact, replication can yield conclusions that are quite different form the original ones. It is what happened when we redesigned from Axelrod's Model of Tributes [Axelrod 1997] by going through a different mental decision framework [Antunes et al 2003].

7 A social simulation research program

Some questions in the development of simulations remain unanswered, such as "how to choose the agent's motivations;" "When to use random (or even arbitrary) variables;" "When and how to get rid of (which) random variables;" "Which measures (individual and collective) should be taken in simulations;" etc. Most of these decisions must be taken only in face of the domain and the problem themselves, and it might never be possible to produce adequate general principles. However, other questions may and should be possible to answer in a generally applicable way. For instances, about how many iterations to run a simulation, or which formalism to use for the model specification. If Popper asked of a theory to include the conditions of its own falsification [Lakatos 1970], perhaps we could ask of a model in a research program to include the terms with which it should be compared to others. These terms of comparison would be the measures specified in the design of individual agents (for motives), and of societies (for micro-macro relations). Evaluation of a simulation may thus be systematised, and perhaps some structure can be provided to relate models to models and allow comparison. It's a matter of discipline, and of having the strength to impose it on the field practitioners, and of them to keep following the prescribed principles. If social simulation is to be adopted as a policy and politics tool, such a move is essential to increase trust and respectability to the field.

8 Conclusions

Evidently, all agents make mistakes, even human agents, and especially scientists in search of discovery. Science has incorporated a number of ways to deal with mistakes. Error assessment is only the simplest of them. The whole way science is performed, with the experimental method, replication of experiments, peer reviewing, etc. is an elaborate method for dealing with mistakes, incorporating them, and moving forward. Years ago, Cristiano told me he had accepted one of my papers not because it was that good, but because it added interest to whatever event he was organising. Spanning over the space of possibilities is an invitation to discovery. Cristiano was always a master at that art, of speaking and hearing, of suggesting and accepting, of correcting and pondering. While many great scientists specialise in a small number of subjects, producing great advances in their research over that solid basis they have chosen to build upon, Cristiano spent his life questioning the bases themselves. Both in science and in his life, Cristiano's interests are multiple, and he shares his views passionately in a generous and motivating way. Perhaps mistakes are a way of fostering the exploration of the world. The world is not perfect, and people found ways of dealing with mistakes and move on. In mistake there is opportunity, there could be discovery, change. Organising agent societies without room for mistakes not only is unrealistic as representation, but also limits the possibilities for what could happen. Mistakes, as redundancy, are important, and not just because we can correct them, and learn from that process. To celebrate Cristiano Castelfranchi's life of achievements is surely one of the finest ways of contributing to the beautiful collective endeavour that science constitutes. To share moments with Cristiano in this discovery journey is the most interesting and exciting form of fighting mistake.

References

1. Luis Antunes. Agentes com Decisão baseada em Valores. PhD thesis, Faculdade de Ciências da Universidade de Lisboa, Maio 2001.
2. Luis Antunes and Helder Coelho. On how to conduct experiments with self-motivated agents. In Lindemann, G., Moldt, D., Paolucci, M., eds.: Regulated Agent-Based Social Systems: First International Workshop, RASTA 2002. Volume 2934 of LNAI. Springer-Verlag, 2004.
3. Luis Antunes, Helder Coelho, João Balsa, and Ana Respício. e*plore v.0: Principia for strategic exploration of social simulation experiments design space. In Shingo Takahashi, David Sallach, and Juliette Rouchier, editors, Advancing Social Simulation – the First World Congress, Kyoto Japan, August 2006, pages 295–306. Springer, Tokyo, 2007.
4. Luis Antunes, João Faria, and Helder Coelho. Improving choice mechanisms within the BVG architecture. In Cristiano Castelfranchi and Yves Lespérance, editors, Intelligent Agents VII. Agent Theories Architectures and Languages, 7th International Workshop, ATAL 2000, Boston, MA, USA, July 7-9, 2000, Proceedings, volume 1986 of Lecture Notes in Artificial Intelligence. Springer, 2001.
5. Luis Antunes, Leonel Nóbrega, and Helder Coelho. BVG choice in Axelrod's tributes model. In Jaime Simão Sichman, Francois Bousquet, and Paul Davidsson, editors, Multi-Agent-Based Simulation, Third International Workshop, MABS 2002, Bologna, Italy, July 15-16, 2002, Revised Papers, volume 2581 of Lecture Notes in Artificial Intelligence. Springer, 2003.
6. Frédéric Amblard and Nils Ferrand. Modélisation multi-agents de l'évolution de réseaux sociaux. In Nils Ferrand, editor, Actes du Colloque Modèles et Systèmes Multi-agents pour la gestion de l'environment et des territoires, pages 153–168, 1998.
7. Robert Axelrod. Advancing the art of simulation in the social sciences. Complex. Vol. 3, number 2. 1997. 16-22
8. Cristiano Castelfranchi. Social power, a point missed in DAI and HCI. In Demazeau, Y. e Müller, J.-P., editors, Decentralized AI, Amsterdam, The Netherlands. Elsevier Science Publishers B.V. Proceedings of the First European Workshop on Modelling Autonomous Agents in a Multi-Agent World (MAAMAW'90), 1990.
9. Cristiano Castelfranchi. Guarantees for autonomy in cognitive agent architecture. In Wooldridge, M. e Jennings, N., editors, Intelligent Agents: agent theories, architectures, and languages, LNAI 890. Springer-Verlag. Proceedings of ECAI'94 work- shop (ATAL). 1995.
10. Cristiano Castelfranchi. The theory of social functions: Challenges for computational social science and multi-agent learning. Cognitive Systems Research, vol. 2, Elsevier, 2001. 5-38
11. Claudio Cioffi-Revilla. A methodology for complex social simulations. In: Proceedings of Epistemologic Perspectives on Simulation, EPOS 2008.

12. Helder Coelho, Luis Antunes and Luis Moniz. On agent design rationale. In Proceedings of the XI Brazilian Symposium on Artificial Intelligence. SBC and LIA, 1994.
13. Paul R. Cohen, Michael L. Greenberg, David M. Hart and Adele E. Howe, Trial by Fire: Understanding the Design Requirements for Agents in Complex Environments, AI Magazine, Fall 1989.
14. Rosaria Conte and Cristiano Castelfranchi. Cognitive and Social Action. UCL Press, London, 1995.
15. Nuno David. Brief Note on the Logic of Replicating Simulations Before and after Publishing a Model. Proceedings of the 4th Conference of The European Social Simulation Association ESSA 2007, Interdisciplinary Approaches to the Simulation of Social Phenomena, September 10-14, 2007, University for Social Sciences of Toulouse, Toulouse, France, 2007.
16. Bruce Edmonds and Scott Moss. From KISS to KIDS - an 'anti-simplistic' modelling approach. In Davidsson, P., Logan, B., Takadama, K., eds.: MABS. Volume 3415 of Lecture Notes in Computer Science., Springer (2004) 130-144
17. Nigel Gilbert. Models, processes and algorithms: Towards a simulation toolkit. In R. Suleiman, K. G. Troitzsch, and N. Gilbert, editors, Tools and Techniques for Social Science Simulation. Physica-Verlag, Heidelberg, 2000.
18. Nigel Gilbert and Jim Doran, editors. Simulating Societies: the computer simulation of social phenomena. UCL Press, London, 1994.
19. Samer Hassan, Luis Antunes, Juan Pavón and Nigel Gilbert. Stepping on earth: A roadmap for data-driven Agent-Based modelling. In Proceedings of the 5th Conference of the European Social Simulation Association (ESSA08). Brescia, Italy, 2008.
20. Samer Hassan, Juan Pavón, Luis Antunes and Nigel Gilbert. Injecting data into Agent-Based simulation. In K. Takadama, G. Deffuant, C. Cioffi-Revilla (Eds.), Simulating Interacting Agents and Social Phenomena: The Second World Congress, Springer Series on Agent Based Social Systems, (7):179-191. Springer, Tokyo, 2010.
21. Imre Lakatos. History of science and its rational reconstructions. In: Proceedings of the Biennial Meeting of the Philosophy of Science Association, The University of Chicago Press (1970) 91-136
22. Herbet Simon. Rationality in psychology and economics. In Hogarth, R. M. e Reder, M. W., editors, Rational choice: the Contrast Between Economics and Psychology. University of Chicago Press, Chicago, 1987.
23. Aaron Sloman. Prospects for AI as the general science of intelligence. In Sloman, A., Hogg, D., Humphreys, G., Ramsay, A., e Partridge, D., editors, Prospects for Artificial Intelligence, Amsterdam. IOS Press. Proceedings of the 9th biennial conference of the Society for the Study of Artificial Intelligence and the Simulation of Behaviour. 1993.
24. Aaron Sloman. Explorations in design space. In Proceedings of the Eleventh European Conference on Artificial Intelligence, 1994.

Chapter 40
A visible hand: Hybrid paths and immergent patterns in social theory (and in a father-son relationship)

Yurij Castelfranchi

Abstract It took me more than one decade to realize how some major aspects of my work as a sociologist of science, and as a scholar and practitioner in science communication, were indeed connected to the theoretical contributions of Cristiano Castelfranchi. Starting from a small digression on a big problem (the infamous micro-macro, agency-structure dilemma of social sciences), I will briefly review and discuss Castelfranchi's position on emergence and "immergence", as well as his criticisms to mainstream discussions in social sciences, in order to focus on two main issues, both theoretical and political, that could be renovated by insights coming from MAS and a theory of social functions: the politics and economy of science in the contemporary regime of knowledge production, and functions and issues in public communication of science and technology. I will show that Castelfranchi's theoretical contributions are indeed connected with his own political positions on science communication and science policies.

1 Castelfranchi on Castelfranchi

In several moments of my career, the possibility of writing something together with my father emerged. We never did. Probably, we felt that the idea of a paper or a book by "Castelfranchi & Castelfranchi" was strange, or embarrassing. Now, I have the chance to write a "Castelfranchi on Castelfranchi" paper. I am uncomfortable with it. It seems weird (maybe more embarrassing than writing a joint text), and also less appropriate: my knowledge and areas of competence do not match those of my father. My own reading of his work is superficial and limited in scope. But I decided to take my chances, mostly because, although at first I approached this effort as an affectionate divertissement, I soon realized,

Yurij Castelfranchi
Department of Sociology and Anthropology, Faculty of Philosophy and Human Sciences, Universidade Federal de Minas Gerais, Brazil
e-mail: ycastelfranchi@gmail.com

reading or re-reading some of Cristiano's texts, that some major points of my own work did actually interact strongly with his reflections. An invisible hand was pushing my theoretical inquietude, and part of my empirical work and tactical activism, toward a trajectory that was in part convergent with that of my father.

In the first part, I will review and comment Castelfranchi's claim that a major scientific challenge of this first part of the century will be the construction of a new "synthetic paradigm", putting together cognition and emergence, information processing and self-organization, reactivity and intentionality, situatedness and planning, and that this challenge is fundamentally connected to the "main theoretical problem of all the social sciences: the problem of the micro-macro link, the problem of theoretically reconciling individual decisions and utility with the global, collective phenomena and interests" (Castelfranchi, 1998: 15). After this, I will touch on the problems of public communication of science and technology today, as well as the debate on S&T policies and informational capitalism. I will also make some brief comments on how such analysis and approaches may eventually lead to novel models and theories in the sociology of knowledge.

2 The micro-macro dilemma

Mapping and explicating the causal relationships between agency and structure, individual choices and social processes, "micro" and "macro" levels, was depicted as a major challenge for social sciences. Do the emergent patterns of social action and relationships determine or dominate our behavior, shaping our selves, beliefs, goals, desires? Does social structure have its own laws and causal powers to direct the actions of individuals? Or, rather, interactions between actors determine, as an emergent phenomenon, what we call a structure? On the one side, such questions are rhetorical, and the answer is easy to see: a co-production of subjectivity and social order. People do have agency, and their beliefs and goals are strongly influenced by the environment and by the overall emergent effects of their own actions and relationships. Loops are functioning all the time between the micro and the macro, between agents and structures, and, actually, even what individuals and structures *are* (their identity and nature) is actually recursively shaped by interactions. Tons of well-known pages were written in the last decades, either to "solve" such infamous "micro-macro dilemma", or, more recently, to show that it is actually more an ill-posed question than a dilemma.

On the other side, however, at least in the eyes of an unsatisfied sociologist, we collected a lot of empirical evidence and invented complex (conflicting) models and (contradictory) jargon to say that individual agency is modulated by structures, and that structures are constructed by collective and recursive effects of social action. But we did not go much further than such quite obvious commonsense claims, nor managed to find a consensus on how to unify or link holistic, individualist and interactionist approaches[1].

"Holist" theories showed, successfully, the strong role played by the structural determinants of action. Idioms and dialects of Marxism, culturalism, structuralism, functionalism, stressed the strength of cultural patterns and hegemonic social norms in shaping our beliefs, goals, desires: individual actions as emanations or effects of social institutions, relations of power, relations of production, etc.

On the other side, methodological individualism (and mainstream economics) insisted, also successfully, on the individual human action (and "interests") as elementary units of social life: to explain social institutions and social change means to show how they arise as the result of the actions and interactions of individuals.

Finally, interactionism, social phenomenology, ethnomethodology, "in-between", chose to show how agents construct their worlds continually: sociology explains society by entering the micro territories of individual cognition, face-to-face interactions, conversations, tacit practices and conventions, daily life. Both "subjects" and "structures" are no longer seen as the central, starting units, but rather as the end points of processes of mutual constitution, to be described focusing on language or symbolic communication, on cognition or interaction, and so on.

Whichever the idiom we choose, some dark masses are missing, and the explicative power is thereby limited. If our major causal forces are in "structures", then social change, bottom-up effects, innovations, individual creations modifying the overall patterns, are either difficult to explain, or their interplay and causal links with structure are over-simplified: changes are mainly consequences of internal crisis of the system (Durkheim's morphology, some major dialects of Marxism), or they are merely "events", "ruptures", "discontinuities", "contingencies", etc.: their place is only in the tectonic, in the underground level. If, on the contrary, individuals are the main agents, the macro-level is often seen just as an epiphenomenon: loops and recursive co-production and co-evolution of structure and individuals are ambiguously depicted, not analytically relevant. If, finally, "interactions", "symbols", "lan-

---

[1] Besides this, it is important to stress that, while the arguments and approaches of classical authors were often oversimplified and stereotyped by commentators, such attention, and tension, to both the micro and macro aspects was present in social science since the beginning. Marxism was associated by several scholars to an emphasis on structure, and Weber was seen as focusing on the individual. However, Marxist dialectics and the Weberian analysis on "rationalization" and "iron cage" show clearly the mutual, recursive nature of the micro-macro relationships. Durkheimian functionalism is probably the most infamous (and stereotyped) example of such emphasis on the causal power that structure has upon individual conscience, thinking, goals etc. Durkheim's emphasis on the "sui generis" nature of society and social facts (society is not the sum of individuals, individuals are "made by" society, rather than the opposite) is very well known: society is an emergent reality, with its own laws that cannot be reduced to those of psychology, biology, physics etc., and "social facts" must be treated "as things", being explained by means of other "social facts". However, the centrality of "emergence" in Durkheim is well-known, as it is the importance of the Durkheimian school in anthropology (and the focus to emotion, feelings, cognition, language).

guage", "communication" are our analytical center of gravity, if everyone and everything acts and "is acted" at the same time (as in Actor-Network Theory, for example), then it may not be simple to explain the powerful stabilization mechanisms, as well as the role played by unintended emergent collective effects in self-organization processes, that end up making both subjects and structures so solid and enduring. Even more difficult is to have models that show which kind of movements, changes, processes, ruptures, are possible or probable in a given context, and which ones are not.

Of course, such categorizations are of limited interest and significance, since many scholars were actually trying to reconcile, dilute or dissolve the "dilemma", taking into account the advantages (and minimize the limitations) of different approaches. Parsons' structural-functionalism (Parsons, 1977) and Jeffrey Alexander's neo-functionalism (Alexander, 1998) went in this direction, as well as, on a totally different ground, Elias' "figurations" (Elias, 2000) or Raymond Boudon's work (see, for example, Boudon, 1982). Peter L. Berger and Thomas Luckmann (1967) formulated a "Social Construction of Reality" that operated by dialectical interactions between structure and agency, society and individuals. Pierre Bourdieu's theory (Bourdieu & Wacquant, 1992) also tries to show how external structures are internalized (via the "habitus"), and how the agent is socialized in objective, evolving "fields" of forces (sets of roles and relationships in a social domain, where various forms of "capital" and different rules of the game are at stake). Giddens' "Structuration Theory" (Giddens, 1986) is also another attempt to go beyond the dualism of structure and agency, "duality of structure" trying to capture how social structure is both the medium and the outcome of social action, while "reflexivity" takes into account the capacity of an agent to consider the outcome of his/her own social actions as a feedback for planning and choosing future actions[2].

Concepts (or analogies) derived from cybernetics, Darwinian evolution, complexity and chaos theory, were also in action in social sciences, the works by Bateson (1972), Maturana and Varela being some well-known examples,

---

[2] I consider Max Weber's emphasis on the unintended consequences of social actions and on the central role of the subjective, emotional and cognitive aspects of actions a valuable early insight of the relationships between emergence and immergence. Weber's discussion on bureaucracy (Weber, 1978), that both allows efficiency, impersonality, equal opportunity, but also, at the same time, concentrates large amounts of power in a small number of people and tends to transform itself in an iron cage that can be a powerful obstacle to freedom and progress, can be seen as a case-study of how emergent structures may be adaptive and "good" for the individual, or for the systems, but also how they may be not good at all, neither for the individual, nor for the system, and yet continue "functioning" and looping. Consequences of social actions are not predictable only starting from individual intentions and attributed meanings. Weber's consideration that bureaucratization and rationalization may become an inescapable fate, while having collateral undesired effects, is a sign that the German thinker had an insight of the "functional" aspects of the macro-micro feedback (in Castelfranchi's sense): efficiency of bureaucracy and rationalizations may feedback to individuals and enforce behaviors (conscious or semi-conscious) not because of rewards or penalties directly associated to the pretended effect of such behaviors. Similar is the case of Weber's analysis of the links between protestant ethic and the "spirit" of capitalism (Weber, 2003). And capitalism, by the way, is self-sustaining and enforcing largely due to similar processes.

as well as Luhmann's systems theory (see, for example, Zeleny, 1980, and Luhmann, 1996).

While several of such works provided important insights, or opened new territories both for empirical works and methodological reflections, in my opinion the breakthroughs were limited. Good interdisciplinary approaches were created, leading eventually to new heuristics and useful metaphors. Interesting hermeneutical texts were written, as well as diagnostics of contemporary societies. But the strength and precision of the models were quite weak, and their explaining power remains not satisfactory.

The problem, with many among such models, is that their use of concepts such as feedback, self-organization, complexity, is either highly metaphorical and ambiguous, or theoretically ill-based. Often, the explanation of how unintended, unforeseen or unknown consequences arise from individual action was quite interesting, but the reverse mechanism, that of the feedback of those emergent features on normalization , routinization of individual action (and of people beliefs, knowledge, motivations, desires) was posed in an ambiguous, imprecise and not useful way.

Giddens' formulations, for example - "social structures are both constituted by human agency, and yet at the same time are the very medium of this constitution" (Giddens, 1976: 121) - , while pointing to these aspects of mutual, circular causation, reflexivity and recursivity, are theoretically ambiguous in many aspects, and not easily testable or empirically operationalizable. On the other side, Bourdieu's description of reciprocal effects between agency and structure tends to give a strong emphasis on objective structure, and looks for causal power on individual choices mainly by means of unconscious, opaque mechanisms of incorporating a "habitus", learning indirectly tacit "rules of the game", and so on.

Castelfranchi's works, in my opinion, demonstrated well how and when such insights are not enough. His conceptualization of social functions, cognitive emergence and immergence belongs to a family of promising paths for new models, which should be tested by social simulations, but also used as hermeneutic, heuristic and analytical tools to explain and interpret empirical data.

2.1 Social action, invisible hands and self-organization

In order to cope with the macro-micro dilemma, understanding emergence and self-organization is crucial. However, the problem is not only, or simply, that of how some stable order, some emergent macro effect arises from actor's social actions. The problem is also to understand when, how and why such order is also "functional", that is, it feeds back on individual actions and enforce them in some way. On the other side, Castelfranchi claims, the great interest (and difficulty) of studying such functional effects is that they do not only, or always, act as "structures", unconsciously shaping and manipulating desires and beliefs of the actors.

Two major points are central in Castelfranchi's arguments and criticisms:

1. To describe or analyze collective, unplanned effects or unintended consequences of social action is not sufficient, since emergence is not a mere
   epiphenomenon. Social emergence and spontaneous order cannot be reduced to complex, unplanned macro-effects, since they can play back a
   causal role, "and in particular a self-reproducing and enforcing social effect". Emergence and "immergence" must be accounted for together, in a
   social theory that wants to be called such.
2. On the other side, "self-reproducing effect of social functions cannot be seen
   as functioning only "upon" the individual, by means of semi-unconscious
   mechanisms. Emergent order do not impose back on individuals only by
   means of routine action, role-playing, semi-conscious attitudes and so on"
   (Castelfranchi, 2001).

This means that, according to Castelfranchi, "it is not true that behaviors
are either functional (then subjectively based on implicit knowledge, procedures, and automatic mechanisms) or intentional; they could be both. Social
actors play social roles and satisfy their social functions also through their
deliberate, intentional actions, however not deliberately. This requires a more
sophisticated model of intentions. In Bourdieu's model for example not only
the social field where the actor is situated and its structural position produce
its behaviour in a too deterministic way, but its behaviour in a role (i.e. - following the sociological tradition- its behaviour as a social actor) is conceived
too passively. The actors just follow the rules of the game by 'instinct', merely
through some automatic 'habitus', that is, through bottom-level implicit, sub-
conceptual processes. In such a way sociologists try to solve the puzzle of the
unintentional fulfillment of social functions" (2001: 20-21).

On the one side, Bourdieu's "field" is a structure that seems to produce a
behavior in a quite deterministic way: actors must obey the rules of the game,
they need to gain the right of access to the field, and the action is mainly based
on attempts to gain the "capital" linked to every field. On the other side, actors
seems to learn and follow the rules by instinct, incorporating a habitus that
become a semiautomatic way of being and feeling. As Castelfranchi puts it:
"A simplistic solution is charging only the non-intentional, non-deliberate but
merely routine behaviors with those functional aspects: according to such a
view, role-playing would just be implemented in 'habitus' (Bourdieu & Wacquant, 1992). Thus, when a social actor is consciously deliberating and planning, he would not play a social role, he would be 'free'. I disagree with such
a solution" (2001: 20).

Such approach also explains Castelfranchi's criticisms of Hayek's analysis of
the invisible hand and to conceptualizations by Boudon of "perverse effects"
and "undesired consequences" of social action. For Castelfranchi, we play
our social roles, while being unaware of the functional effects of our actions,
not only with our routine actions but even when doing something creatively
and deliberately for our own subjective motives. The social actor is neither
just an unconscious habitual role player, nor just an intentional pursuer of
personal and underived goals. Also his/her deliberate, intentional actions for

his/her personal motives can implement social functions and roles. This does not imply that the actor is aware of such an implementation and intentionally realizes his/her impinging functions. Hayek, says Castelfranchi, "grasps and preserves Smith's intuition that what we unconsciously and unintentionally pursue are 'ends'. However, Hayek does not provide any explicit and clear theory of such a teleology. Indeed, thanks to his subjective individualism, he basically identifies it with and reduces it to the psychological, subjective ends of the individuals, although pursued only unconsciously. He in fact assumes that emerging social structures are self-persistent and stable precisely because they allow the satisfaction of individual desires and conscious finalities. [. . .] Even Boudon's notion of 'perverse effects' is insufficient because it does not take into account their teleological or functional character. Hayek does not explain clearly enough for whom the emergent order should be good and how much the differences of power are responsible for its reproduction; he does not analyse the problem of the effects of our actions that are negative just for others; he does not account for the possibility that the social actors ignore their own interest; he bypasses the fact that desires and preferences (relative to which the 'order' is good) cannot be assumed as given but should be considered as produced by the order itself; he seems to use unclear models of group-selection" (2001: p. 34).

Several scholars think that AI (and in particular MAS and cognitive agent modeling) entering the social simulation domain can lead to an impressive advance for social sciences. But, says Castelfranchi, this can happen only by a serious analysis of social functions, allowing to study and treat emergence and "immergence" together: "The famous problem of the 'invisible hand' is in fact not simply the problem of the emergence of some equilibrium, - or of the emergence of compound, unpredictable, unintentional effects. The hard question is how 'the individual, generally, indeed, neither intends to promote the public interest, nor knows how much he is promoting it . . . he intends only his own gain . . . and he is led by an invisible hand to promote an end which was not part of his intention' (Adam Smith, *The Wealth of Nations*, IV, ii, 9)" (Castelfranchi, 2001: 11).

In order to exit the dilemma, we need, Castelfranchi says, a sophisticated theory of action and intention; a theory of 'learning without understanding' and of its relationships with high level cognition; a theory of the relationships between ends that are internal to the agent's mind (goals, intentions) and external ends (biological and social functions, roles, etc.). He tries to provide all of those, conciliating "the 'external' teleology orienting behavior with the 'internal' teleology governing it; how to reconcile intentionality, deliberation, and planning with producing or playing social functions" (Castelfranchi, 2001: 20). In his view, "synthetic theories should explain the dynamic and emergent aspects of cognition and symbolic computation; how cognitive processing and individual intelligence emerge from sub-symbolic or sub cognitive distributed computation, and causally feedbacks into it; how collective phenomena emerge from individual action and intelligence and causally shape back the individual mind. We need a principled theory which is able to reconcile cognition with emergence and with reactivity" (Castelfranchi, 1998: 14).

According to Castelfranchi, only a "mind-based" social simulation will allow to observe at the same time the minds of the individual agents (beliefs,
desires, decisions), their learning processes, and the emerging collective action
and equilibrium (perhaps even some *collective mind*) which *co-evolve*, determining each other: "Only SS will allow social sciences to understand, both
experimentally and formally, how deliberate actions and interactions produce unconscious social structures and phenomena (way up), and how social
interaction, social structures and collective phenomena shape and influence
(beyond explicit understanding) the individual mind (way down) and then
the individual action that reproduces them. The term 'dialectic' [...] is just
a philosophical label waiting for a substantial model of the co-dynamics of
mind, action, and society" (2001: 8).

Such ideas could be valuable and fecund if applied to the sociology of
science and to S&T policy, because of well-known (but not so well analyzed)
mechanisms of self-organization (see the seminal works by Merton, 1979, or
Polanyi, 1969, for example), emergence and immergence in scientific ethos
and knowledge production and certification, and also because of the political
valence of such approach.

Understanding motivations, beliefs and goals of scientists, and comparing
this to functional aspects of science as an institution may lead to important,
novel approaches to S&T policy, and eventually to the old dilemma of the
sociology of knowledge: conciliating realism and relationism, taking into account, as Gilles Deleuze and Félix Guattari put, not so much, "the relativity of
the truth", but the "truth of the relative" (Deleuze & Guattari, 1994: 130). We
cannot discuss these important points here, but we will at least briefly focus
on them.

3 Knowledge, capitalism, politics: visible threads in invisible hands

In November 17, 1944, President Roosevelt sent a letter to engineer Vannevar
Bush, inventor of analog computers and one of the initiators and administrators of the Manhattan Project. The President requested recommendations
on several points. Among them: what could be done to organize a program
for continuing in the future the work which has been done in medicine and
related sciences; what could the Government do to aid research activities by
public and private organizations; how to discover and develop scientific talent
in American youth, so that the continuing future of scientific research may be
assured.

Bush answered some months later, with a celebrated report: "Science: The
Endless Frontier" (Bush, 1945). He advocated that basic research was crucial
to the nation both for military and economic supremacy. He required con-
tinued government support for science and technology. Bush claimed that
basic research was "the pacemaker of technological progress", and that "new
products and new processes do not appear full-grown. They are founded on

new principles and new conceptions, which in turn are painstakingly developed by research in the purest realms of science". Explaining this by means of dichotomies (basic research versus applied research) and metaphors (basic research as a scientific capital, and the role of public sector in developing it, while applied research was the work of brave cow-boys, colonizing new terrains, and the central role of private sector), Bush contributed to a historical mark in the history of S&T policy-making, but with a dangerous idea (research is a capital. . . then, scientific knowledge may eventually become a commodity?).

Few years before, sociologist Robert K. Merton formulated his celebrated analysis of the institutional imperatives in science (the scientific "ethos"). As an institution, science functioned based on norms that are quite different from those of several other institutions. "The ethos of science is that affectively toned complex of values and norms which is held to be binding on the man of science" (Merton, 1973: 267-268). Four sets of such "institutional imperatives" comprise, Merton claimed, the ethos of science: "Communism", "Universalism", "Disinterestedness", and "Organized Skepticism" (Merton, 1979). As John Ziman, physicist and sociologist of science, wrote later, in the academic ethos the reward for a scientist that is a good scientist, and works obeying such norms ("CUDOS"), is not money, but fame and prestige (eventually, immortality): CUDOS brings kudos (Ziman, 2000).

While Mertonian functional and institutional analysis of science was heavily criticized in the 70s and 80s, especially in the context of the so called "new sociology of science" and "sociology of scientific knowledge", and while several scholars claim today that mertonian norms of science are in crisis or abandoned, some see them as a good "ideology", threatened by practices and policies influenced by XXth century changes in capitalism. Mertonian norms, whether realistic or idealistic, should be re-thought and partially defended. Such was the opinion of John Ziman, and of several others. Even if they should eventually turn out to be theoretically ill-founded or empirically outdated, such ideals may still be normatively interesting and valuable. What seems an idealized vision of a kind of science that maybe never existed, could serve, at the same time, as a good regulative idea for political action.

3.1 Science, politics, capitalism

Actually, in the second half of the XXth century, and more radically after the end of the Cold War, dramatic changes have occurred both in the mode of production of scientific knowledge and in the relationships between science, universities, capitalism, and politics. Several scholars studied those transformations. In social theory, most recent diagnostics of contemporary societies take as a crucial aspect for analysis the novel roles played by knowledge production, appropriation and governance. Relationships between science, technology, the market and the state are central, for example, in Manuel Castell's proposals on "network society", in Ulrich Beck's focus on "risk society" (Beck,

1992) and "reflexivity", as well as in "radicalized" and "reflexive" modernization as proposed by Anthony Giddens (Giddens et al., 1994).

Several authors in the field of the social studies of science focused on the
reconfiguration occurred in the organizational structures of science, its institutions, agents, practices and discourses, as well as on the new forms of
coproduction of scientific knowledge and social order. "Regulatory science"
by Jasanoff (1995), "post-normal" science by Funtowicz and Ravetz (1993),
"Mode 2" of knowledge production by Gibbons, Nowotny, and colleagues
(Gibbons et al., 1994; Nowotny et al., 2001), "post-academic" science by Ziman
(2000), or "technoscience", as defined by Latour (1992) and Echeverria (2003),
are only few among many examples.

Some main points stressed by the majority of these approaches are:

- Novel relationships between scientific knowledge and capitalism (a "new
  social contract between science and society", Gibbons et al., 1994). Knowledge is seen and managed as a capital, and profit does not come only from
  the "application" of knowledge, but also from its very production and from
  its transformation in a commodity called "information". Reorganizations
  occurred in the capitalist regime: production and appropriation of scientific
  and technological knowledge play novel, deeper strategic roles.
- This is connected to the remarkable role played today by private capital
  and intellectual property in contemporary technoscience, in the majority of
  developed and emergent countries. In the decades of Cold War, science was
  strongly and mainly supported and funded by Nation States, and rhetori-
  cally seen as a "common good". In the Fordist regime, research enjoyed a
  relative autonomy from politics and the market (Nowotny et al., 2001). In
  the '80s, this configuration began to change, with a strong growth of private
  funding in P&D, and scientific knowledge started to be seen as something
  that could, or even should, be commercialized, sold, patented. Today, S&T
  share with business and industry several norms and practices. Economic
  rationality contributes to shape what science is and how is done. Concepts
  and slogans coming from the business, such as flexibility, mobility, ven-
  ture capital, competition, performance, productivity, are being applied to
  S&T. Synergy, efficiency, spin-off, failure/success, costs/benefits, marketing,
  pro-activity, entrepreneurship enters the daily vocabulary and practices of
  several researchers in many different areas of science.
- As a result, science and technology policies, as well as political discourse on
  the role of S&T, changed. Narratives of technoscience tell us today a story
  in which knowledge and information are crucial for capitalist competition,
  in which the production and circulation of scientific and technical knowledge have to be managed in "efficient", "calculated" forms, more directly
  linked to "national security", "social demands", "economic performance".
  Policy-makers, managers and technoscientific leaders repeat slogans that
  emphasize the need for a reconfiguration in the role of universities and
  research: they tell the story of the "challenge" and of the "urgent need"
  to create "entrepreneurial universities" able to "commercialize" and "sell"
  research to society (Etzkowitz, 2001).

This means that several scientists have to cope with norms that are partially new, and a recombinant academic ethos, in which the search for truth and profit, objectivity and politics, can share the same territory. More and more often, they have to show that their "productivity" is increasing, that the "quality" of their work is "excellent", that social, political, environmental or economic benefits can be seen, directly and in short time, as a consequence of their work. They must answer social demands and listen to social worries, in real time. Not only the "social impact" of their theories is judged, but also the social, moral, political, economic relevance of their practices in the labs and the universities. Universities are seen, by many policy-makers and researchers, not only as a place where you study, teach and contribute to culture, but also, or mainly, as factories that must produce "innovation" and transfer it to the productive sector, as machines that must contribute to the creation of wealth and jobs, producing answers to societal demands. New actors and stakeholders contribute to management and planning of scientific research (Polino & Castelfranchi, 2012).

Not only science policies changed, but, more in general, the links between science and politics were affected. As emphasized by many authors, the problem of social consequences of S&T is central, intrinsically political and global. A crisis of legitimization emerged, in the second half of the last century, as a consequence of the emergence of social movements, of socio-environmental problems, of the moral issues posed by several new technologies or areas of scientific research, and, more recently, from the increasing visibility of the interests - and of conflicts of interests - in science (biomedicine, GMOs, patents), as well as the debates on several recent case of misconduct in science (Polino & Castelfranchi, 2012).

Cristiano Castelfranchi's analysis seeks to encompass all this complexity: while an idealized vision of science, such as the Mertonian one, may be in part outdated, values and ethos of science should be carefully analyzed, restored or recovered and eventually defended from pressures and influence coming from other institutions. Society as a whole may not value "skepticism" as much as other ethical values, such as discipline, entrepreneurship, etc., but science must embrace it: "The fact that knowledge has become an actively productive factor and is now acknowledged and looked for as a capital [...] means also - or simply? - that there is an appropriation and a capitalist exploitation of knowledge" (Castelfranchi, 2007: 1).

Science as a capital implies a utilitarian vision of science, and its management as a mixed-capital company. Popular science and science journalism, says Castelfranchi, contribute to this dangerous misunderstanding: "A cultural stereotype with a clear American derivation, and a pragmatistic-economic nature, has now established itself [...] in the official science communication [...]. Science as technology, a scientist as an 'inventor'. Substantially, the purpose of science seems to be making 'inventions', i.e. producing new technology. The prototype of a scientist is not an abstract thinker or a Galileo ("the inventor of the telescope", sic!), rather a sort of Benjamin Franklin. In Disney comics, scientists are represented by Gyro Gearloose, who does nothing but inventing machines (luckily, crazy ones). Yet, in more general terms, one wants to know what patents have resulted from a specific scientific research, or what applications, new drugs, therapies, methods it aims at" (2007: 2).

Problems with such vision are very serious: "Is it not a serious mistake - from the left and from the right - having instilled in an entire generation the message that one studies only to find their place in the market, only to find a job and to acquire new instruments for their job? Isn't this a message for subordinate classes? Yet bound to build a new class of subordinate people, those possessing a knowledge capital, not the old illiterate proletarians. Knowledge was not conceived like this when it was for the ruling classes! A message all the more stupid; because working today requires life-long training, and a large part of it is to be made through direct experience; because a real advantage in any job is given precisely by the general intellectual instruments, the acquired capacity of acquiring knowledge, to take possession of it, to use and criticise it, especially when knowledge development is the real capital; and finally, because the intrinsic motivation ability rewards you in your job" (2007: 2).

Knowledge in itself, Castelfranchi claims, together with Ziman and many others, is, or should be, a non-instrumental good. It is intrinsically motivated. A real "society of knowledge" would be a society guided (also) by this value. But this is exactly what is not happening: the proposed vision - and the real practice - is one of an instrumental and subordinated activity, a good that has to demonstrate and justify its utility.

Such political issues and criticisms, however, come together with reflections on unintended consequences of the new policies and subjectivities linked to the present state of neoliberal governmentality and capitalism[3], and to their functional aspects. Considering that for Castelfranchi it is so relevant to explain social action taking into account unintended effects of intentional choices and their feedbacks on goals and beliefs, and that collective processes and their emergent and "immergent" patterns are so crucial in his theory, then it is not surprising that his specific political and normative approach to knowledge production and validation leads him to a passionate and intense fight against the hegemonic narration on "knowledge society", based on a simplistic, naïve, neoliberal version of the *homo oeconomicus* and on a gross historical distortion on how science "functions", both internally and as a part of society: "The current process exerts a perversion on the human cognitive activity: it may be summed up as 'knowledge turned from purpose into means'. To the human species, knowledge is also a purpose in itself, an activity, a motivating and gratifying result. We acquire knowledge out of curiosity, interest, passion, and not only as an instrument to tackle an immediate problem or a practical action. At functional level, we accumulate this resource in sight of future possible uses, but we also exercise and amplify our cognitive capabilities. It is precisely as sex: its function regards the couple and their offspring, but that is not the reason we are doing it ("Science is like sex: sometimes something useful comes out, but that is not the reason we are doing it" - R. Feynman). In psychological terms, it means that an "intrinsic reason" does exist (the pleasure in doing it or in being able to do it, or other internal 'rewards'). Nobody really needs external incentives of a social or economic kind (for example an

---

[3] See, for example, Foucault (2010), or Castelfranchi (2008: Chapt. 2 and Chapt. 4).

approval or a role to play) or a practical return. Instead, when investigating this intrinsic reason, what interests the most is that it shows a downturn or even a drop when there is an instrumental advantage, a systematic external incentive. A counterproductive strategy has been adopted: humiliating the intrinsic motivation to knowledge only for an illusory market reason. Are we in the process of demotivating research, studies, knowledge, culture with this ideological and practical subordination to utility, production and career?" (Castelfranchi, 2007: 1).

4 Conclusion. A visible hand

Sometimes, invisible hands have very visible effects. In other moments, visible hands help us while we do not perceive them. Gently, smoothly, not directing, nor modulating, they catalyze processes and help us find out our own trajectories.

As a teenager, experimenting with my first home computer while learning BASIC, I was also playing with my father, writing small Artificial Life programs. It was fun. I did not think it was more than that. I was already thinking as a theoretical physicist: to me, what could not fit in a differential equation, or did not speak the idiom of quanta or relativity, could only be a divertissement, not "real science". Later, I moved on and began to think the opposite: everything that could be described by equations was too simple to be really interesting. Society was one of those things. I was a young libertarian, and with Cristiano we fought (sometimes worrying a bit for each other) on the powers and limits of self-organization, on the meaning and goals of political action. When my job turned out to be that of a science journalist, we were discussing (sometimes, forcefully) on the modes and functions of science communication, and on the roles, tasks and skills of the "public". I eventually wrote a book, for general public, on Artificial Intelligence. Not with him. Finally, I made myself a sociologist of knowledge, and I was surprised to find at home so many books to steal, and so many more things to discuss: on the limits of sociological and philosophical conceptualizations on power (Weber, Foucault, political theorists, etc.), as well as on epistemology and sociology of knowledge and cognition. While we never wrote together a "Castelfranchi & Castelfranchi", I realize now that I had already wrote or thought so many "Castelfranchi & Castelfranchi". While studying invisible hands, I couldn't see that Cristiano was lending me a visible hand. A father's hand: helpful and visible, but shy and tender. A hand one may not perceive, realizing only later it was there all the time.

References

1. Alexander, J.C. (1998). *Neofunctionalism and After: Collected Readings.* John Wiley & Sons.

2. Bateson, Gregory (1972). *Steps to an Ecology of Mind: Collected Essays in Anthropology, Psychiatry, Evolution, and Epistemology.* University Of Chicago Press.
3. Beck, U. (1992). *Risk Society Towards a New Modernity,* London: Sage Publications.
4. Berger, P.L. & Luckmann, T. (1967). *The Social Construction of Reality: A Treatise in the Sociology of Knowledge,* Anchor.
5. Boudon, R., (1982). *The Unintended Consequences of Social Action,* Palgrave Macmillan.
6. Bourdieu, P. and L. J. D. Wacquant (1992). *An Invitation to Reflexive Sociology.* Chicago: University of Chicago Press.
7. Bush, V. (1945). *Science The Endless Frontier. A Report to the President by Vannevar Bush, Director of the Office of Scientific Research and Development.* Washington: United States Government Printing Office.
8. Castelfranchi, C. (1998). Emergence and Cognition: Towards a Synthetic Paradigm in AI and Cognitive Science. In: Helder Coelho (Ed.): Progress in Artificial Intelligence - IBERAMIA 98, *6th Ibero-American Conference on AI, Lisbon, Portugal, Proceedings.* Lecture Notes in Computer Science 1484 Springer 1998, ISBN 3-540-64992-1.
9. Castelfranchi, C. (2001). The theory of social functions: challenges for computational social science and multi-agent learning. *Journal of Cognitive Systems Research 2* (1): 5-38.
10. Castelfranchi, C. (2007). Six critical remarks on science and the construction of the knowledge society. *JCOM 6* (4).
11. Castelfranchi, Y. (2008). *As serpentes e o bastão. Tecnociência, neoliberalismo e inexorabilidade.* PhD Dissertation. Campinas: Campinas State University; Deleuze, G. & Guattari, F. (1994). *What Is Philosophy?,* Verso.
12. Echeverría, J. (2003). *La revolución tecnocientífica,* Madrid: Fondo de Cultura Económica.
13. Elias, N., (2000). *The Civilizing Process: Sociogenetic and Psychogenetic Investigations* Revised., Blackwell Publishing.
14. Etzkowitz, H. (2001). The second academic revolution and the rise of entrepreneurial science. *Science, Technology and Society Magazine,* IEEE, 20, 2, 18-29.
15. Foucault, M. (2010). *Birth of Biopolitics,* Palgrave.
16. Funtowicz, S. & Ravetz, J. (1993). Science for the post normal age. *Futures,* 25, 739-755.
17. Gibbons, M., Limoges, C., Nowotny, H., Schwartzman, S., Scott, P. & Trow, M. (1994). *The new production of knowledge: The dynamics of science and research in contemporary societies,* London: Thousand Oaks, Sage.
18. Giddens, Anthony (1976) *New Rules of Sociological Method: a Positive Critique of interpretative Sociologies.* London: Hutchinson
19. Giddens, A. (1986). *The Constitution of Society: Outline of the Theory of Structuration,* University of California Press.
20. Giddens, A.; Beck, U.; Lash, S. (1994). *Reflexive Modernization: Politics, Tradition and Aesthetics in the Modern Social Order,* Stanford, Calif: Stanford University Press.
21. Hayek, F.A. (1967). *Studies in Philosophy, Politics and Economics,* Routledge&Kegan, London.
22. Jasanoff, S. (1995). Procedural choices in regulatory science. *Technology in Society,* 17, 3, 279-293,
23. Latour, B. (1987). *Science in Action: How to Follow Scientists and Engineers Through Society.* Harvard University Press.
24. Luhmann, N. (1996). *Social Systems,* Stanford University Press.
25. Merton, T. (1973). 'The Normative Structure of Science' [1942] .In: The Sociology of Science. Theoretical and Empirical Investigations, ed. Norman W. Storer..
26. Nowotny, H., Scott, P. & Gibbons, M. (2001). *Re-thinking science: Knowledge and the public in an age of uncertainty.* Wiley-Blackwell.
27. Parsons, T. (1977). *Social Systems and the Evolution of Action Theory.* Free Press.
28. Polanyi, M. (1969). "The Republic of Science", in *Knowing and Being.* University of Chicago Press.
29. Polino, C.; Castelfranchi, Y (2012). The Communicative Turn in Contemporary Technoscience: Latin American Approaches and Global Tendencies. In: Schiele, B.; Claessens, M.; Shi, S.. (Org.). *Science Communication in the World Practices, Theories and Trends.* (p. 3-17) New York - London: Springer.

30. Sawyer, R. K. (2005). *Social Emergence: Societies As Complex Systems*. Cambridge University Press.
31. Weber, M. (1978). *Economy and Society*, University of California Press.
32. Weber, M. (2003). *The Protestant Ethic and the Spirit of Capitalism*, Courier Dover Publications.
33. Zeleny, (1980). *Autopoiesis, Dissipative Structures, and Spontaneous Social Orders*, Westview Pr..
34. Ziman, J. (2000). *Real science: What it is, and what it means*. Cambridge: Cambridge University Press.

Part IX
Afterword

Chapter 41
Goals, the true center of cognition

Cristiano Castelfranchi

> *The confusion and barrenness of psychology* is not to be explained by
> calling it a 'young science'; its state is not comparable with that of physics,
> for instance, in its beginnings. (...) For *in psychology there are*
> *experimental methods and conceptual confusion.* (...)
> The existence of the experimental method makes us think we have
> the means of solving the problems that trouble us; though problem and
> method pass one another by.

(Ludwig Wittgenstein Investigations PII p. 232)

I apologize with my readers, and hope they will be benevolent enough to
tolerate my ways, because I am going to use a very assertive style. I feel
emotionally entitled (by the occasion, by age, by long reflection on these issues,
not to mention my culpable laziness) to outline a very personal (thus unilateral)
and "provocative" fresco of goal theory, with too many claims and without
a serious discussion of any specific literature or close comparison with other
approaches.

To me, this constitutes a joyful occasion to give free play to many ideas
accumulated over the years and not yet fully developed. I just wish to provide
here some hints and critical cues to my readers; hopefully, this will lay down
the groundwork for a more complete and well documented treatment of the
topic, in the form of a monograph yet to come.

1 Beyond the Ptolemaic view of cognition

In philosophy, cognitive science, and even psychology there is a dominant
"Ptolemaic" view of cognition: a knowledge-centered universe; where "information" and "representation" are equal to "knowledge". In such a view, what

Cristiano Castelfranchi
Goal-Oriented Agents Lab (GOAL), Institute of Cognitive Sciences and Technologies, CNR,
Italy
e-mail: cristiano.castelfranchi@istc.cnr.it

matters most is knowledge acquisition, storage, organization, efficient search, reasoning, and knowledge distribution, sharing, etc. So we know much about 'knowledge', its life and processing step by step: to convince yourself this is the case, just look at the chapters of any handbook of cognitive psychology, and even general psychology.

Conversely, we know very little about the vicissitudes of goals in our mental activity, except for a few limited models about goal hierarchies and decision making. We do not have a comparable model of goal-processing step by step and of its relations with knowledge processing. This is highly problematic, because the mind is actually based on two kinds of representational functions, and on their relationships. Moreover, what is missing from this picture is what gives purpose to cognition itself. What is 'knowledge' *for*? And what is 'intelligence' *for*?

A Copernican revolution in the study of cognition is needed, placing goals at the very center of the cognitive/mental universe. "Information" and "representation" are not equal to knowledge. "Goals" too are "representations", with a very specific use/function; and of course also the cybernetic feedback loops and set-points are instances of "information processing", but what is being processed is a very different form of representation.

The "goal" is the center of gravity of the cognitive universe; or better, the center is goal-directed action: changing, adapting the world in a guided and prefigured way. In the end, it's all about goals:

- Action is for goals (and goals are for potential actions);
- Knowledge is for goals;
- Intelligence is for goals (solving problems via mental representations);
- Sociality is for goals and goal-based;
- Emotions are goal-centered (Castelfranchi et al. 1996).

1.1 What the mind is: Its anticipatory nature

To understand the centrality of goals in the mind, let's try to characterize what the "mind" is and where it (reasonably) comes from. A real mental activity and representation appears when the organism is able to endogenously (not as the output of current perceptual stimuli) produce an internal sensory-motor representation of the world ('simulation' of perception).

The main evolutionary pressure for this has clearly been 'anticipation'. For example, an organism can generate the internal "image" of a forthcoming stimulus/event, which will produce a faster reaction to the external trigger, thus preventing possible dangers or exploiting favorable opportunities. Or the organism can generate an internal image for matching it against perceptual inputs and actively searching a certain object or stimulus while exploring the environment; or it can use the image as a prediction of the stimulus that will probably arrive, as in active recognition. However, in such a way an organism can become able not only to activate but also *to entertain a mental representation of the world just to 'work' on it*, modifying this representation for virtually exploring possible actions, events, results: "what will/would happen if. . . ?".

This is precisely the meaning of "intelligence": the capability to solve a problem by *working on an internal representation* of the problem, by *acting upon 'images' with simulated actions*, or on 'mental models' or 'symbolic representations' by mental actions, transformations (reasoning), *before* (and without necessarily) performing the actions in the world.

The ability that characterizes and defines a mind and its origin is that of building representations of the non-existent, of what is not (yet) "true"; to conceive the non-perceivable. The essence of a mind is also the precondition for hallucinations, delirium, desires, utopias. . . and in general goals!

Of course, this ability builds upon memory, past experience, and its evocation. However, the generative power of the mind is able to produce (at least via a combinatory procedure) new "scenes", states of the world that were never perceived before. We can imagine and even try to realize (pursue as goals) states of affairs that we never experienced, and perhaps would have been impossible to experience in the past.

The use of such internally and autonomously generated representations of the world is not only "epistemic", for knowledge (of the past, the present, the future: that is, memory, perception, prediction and expectations); it is also, and even mostly, "motivational".

This is the Ptolemaic baggage that we must get rid of: "representation" is not synonymous of "knowledge" (epistemic or doxastic representations). Representations can have a motivational, axiological, or deontic nature; they tell us not only how the world is, was, will be, but how the world *should be*, how the organism *would like it to be*. That is, these representations can be used as *goals* driving the organism's behavior.

Given the centrality of goals for understanding cognition, as well as the poverty of most goal theories (not only about their processing, but about their ontology, and their structuring knowledge, emotions, sociality, etc.)[1], and also the frequent misuses, wrong definitions, and misunderstandings, let us start this attempt at theoretical elucidation with two moves:

- making as clear as possible what we mean by "goal", which are the right notions and definitions, and where do they originate;
- illustrating the main current misunderstandings and wrong treatments of the notion of goal.

2 Two scientific teleologies

In modern science there are two well-defined teleological frames and notions:

---

[1] It is indicative how meager, confusing and ill-structured are the entries "Goal" and "Goal theory" in Wikipedia (as of October 2012), if compared with the entries for "Knowledge" and "Epistemology" (indeed, the latter has a whole portal devoted to it on Wikipedia). Some important recent advances are to be found in Moskowitz & Grant (2009). However, serious discussion of the literature is beyond my aims here (see also note 21).

- The one provided by *evolutionary approaches*, where it is standard (and correct) to talk in terms of functions, (adaptive) value, being for something, having a certain finality/end, providing some advantage, etc. In this context "goal" (end, function, finality, etc.) means the "effect" (outcome) that has selected/reproduced and maintained a certain feature or behavior – originally just an accidental effect, an effect among many others, but later, thanks to the loop and positive feedback on its own "causes" (that is, on the feature or behavior producing it) no longer a mere effect but the "function", the purpose of that feature, what makes it useful and justifies its reproduction.
- The one provided by *cybernetic control theory* and its postulated cycle, representations, and functions, in which the agent is able to adjust the world through goal-directed behavior, and to maintain a given "desired" state of the world (homeostasis).

Actually, there might be a third teleological/finalistic notion used in several sciences (from medicine to social sciences): the notion of a "function" of X as a "role", a functional component, an "organ" of a global "system". For example, the "function" of the heart, or of the kidneys, in our body; or the function of families (or of education or of norms) in a society; or the function of a given office in an organization; etc. However, this "functionalist" and "systemic" notion has never been well defined and has elicited a lot of problems and criticisms. My view is that this finalistic view is correct, but it is reducible to, and derived from, the previous two kinds of teleology. The "organs" are either the result of an evolutionary selection – in that they contribute to the fitness and reproduction (maintenance) of that organism – or there is a "project", a "design", that is, a complex goal in someone else's mind, which imposes particular sub-goals on its parts, components, and tools. Or both.

A serious problem for a (future) science of goals is the fact that these two fundamental teleological notions/mechanisms have never been unified:

i. neither conceptually, by looking for a common definition, a conceptual common kernel (for example, in terms of circular causality, feedback, etc.): Do we have and is it possible to have a general, unique notion of "goal" with two sub-kinds (functions vs. psychological goals)?
ii. nor by solving the problem of the interaction between the two coexisting forms of finality.

This constitutes a serious obstacle, and reveals a real ignorance gap in contemporary science[2]. For example, as for issue (i), without the aforementioned conceptual unification we cannot have a unitary theory of communication – or a theory of cooperation, of sociality, etc. – in animal and humans. What today are presented as unified theories are just a trick; in fact, those notions – which necessarily require a goal (for example, "communication" doesn't just require a "reader", it requires a "sender": the information is "given" on purpose to the "receiver/addressee") – are defined in terms of adaptive functions when applied to simple animals (like insects), whereas in humans are defined in

---

[2] A remarkable attempt to deal with these problems is Ruth Millikan's work.

intentional terms. Thus there is no unified notion (and theory) of "communication", in that we do not know the common kernel between a "functional" device and an "intentional" device. Point (ii) above is no less problematic. What is the relationship between the internally represented goals (motivations, and concrete objectives) of an agent regulating its behaviors from the inside, and the adaptive functions that have selected that agent and its behaviors?

Usually, in purposive, goal-driven agents/systems, the "function" of their conduct, the adaptive result that has to be guaranteed, is *not* internally represented and pursued; it is neither understood nor foreseen. The internal motivations (and whatever solutions and instrumental goals they generate) are just sub-goals of the "external" goals of the behavior, of its functions; they are just "cognitive mediators"[3] of the (biological or social) functions that would be unrepresentable and mentally non-computable.

Only very recently we have discovered why we have to eat, the real functions/effects of our food in our organisms (proteins, carbohydrates, vitamins, etc.); and very few people eat in view of such effects. We eat for hunger or for pleasure or for habit. Analogously, we do not usually make courtship and sex in view of reproduction; we are driven by other internal motives. We can even cut the "adaptive" connection between our motives and their original functions, for example by deciding to have sex without inseminating or without establishing/maintaining any friendly/affective relation or support.

3 What a goal is not

Let us briefly present and discuss here the main misunderstandings and misuses of the notion of "goal".

A) A goal is *not something external to be reached* (e.g., a place, an object, a target). It is a "representation" in the mind of the agent (however see footnote 6).

B) A goal is *not a special kind of representation, different from a doxastic representation* (e.g., a belief); it is instead a mental representation with a specific "use", "function", "role", "application". Beliefs and goals are just one and the same kind of representations, simply employed in two different ways. In fact, it has to be possible for such representations to match, to characterize the state in which an agent believes his/her goal to be satisfied. Beliefs and goals are two different possible "attitudes" on the representations. For example, the same visual image can be used in a given circumstance as a belief about the current state of the world, and in another case as representing a state of the world to be achieved, i.e. a goal.

C) A goal is *not necessarily pursued*; a representation does not acquire the status of a goal only if and when it is being pursued. It is a goal (i.e., it plays the

---

[3] See, for example, as for social "institutions" and their "cognitive mediators" (beliefs, goals, etc.), Tummolini and Castelfranchi (2006).

role of a goal) also in other stages of the control cycle, thus satisfying other sub-functions:

i.   when it is compared with the world (perception, beliefs) and used to evalu-ate the world as conforming or not to what the agent desires (*evaluative use of the goal*; see Paglieri & Castelfranchi 2008a);
ii. it is still a goal when it is already realized and there is nothing more to do; we are happy precisely because our goal is *fulfilled* (even without having to do anything);
iii. it is still a goal when it is not realized and yet there is nothing we can do about it: it cannot be pursued because we lack the means, pre-conditions, or skills for that; that is why in such circumstances we can be frustrated similarly to when we act and fail;
iv. it even is a goal if and when it is not preferred to other goals, and thus is not chosen to guide our actions; that is why even what we choose not to do can be perceived as a more or less costly sacrifice, and thus elicit some regret or suffering;
v.   and it is still a goal when we have nothing to do, not because we lack the power to puruse the goal, but because we just have to wait for its realization, possibly relying on other agents' behavior or on other events that do not require our direct intervention.

As for such reliance, there are various "passive" goal-states related to it: just *wishing or hoping* that something will come to pass (the agent can do nothing, other than that); *letting something happen* (while being able to interfere, I let that a natural or social agent realizes something; the decision of doing nothing is a decision, and this type of "inaction" is a true, goal-driven action); *delegating* (while being able to both interfere and pursue my goal by myself, I make/let another agent pursue it).

The main morale of these considerations is that only in some cases I have to "actively" pursue my goals. When the realization is (believed to be) pos-sible and depending on me, being up to me, then, either I subjectively "try" (the result is not subjectively sure)[4] or I intentionally act for realizing it and confidently expect the desired outcome.

In sum, a goal is a goal even before or without being pursued: satisfaction or happiness are due to goal-realization, and dissatisfaction or suffering are due to goal frustration, but not necessarily to our *active* successes or failures; we are sad because our mother has died, or happy because she gave us a kiss, even if we did not ask for it, nor do or expected anything from her.

D) In complex goal-directed agents like ourselves *there is not a simple one-to-one correspondence between goals and actions*. Usually every action serves a "chain" of goals (*instrumental goals*, means to an end) and some *higher-goals* (Figure 1). The problem is not "the" goal of the agent or of that action, but the plural (and often complex) goal structure. Moreover, the actions of an agent are linked to each other and produce a consistent behavior, complex actions or plans (that

---

[4] Although in fact any possible action actually (consciously or unconsciously) is an "attempt" and relies on some external process/agent for its accomplishment.

often become memorized patterns and routines), thanks to the goal structure: because they cooperate/converge on some higher-goal (Figure 1).

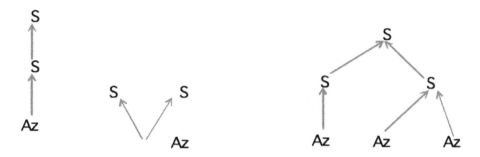

Fig. 1 Basic goal structures

This is the "deep structure" of our conduct, not its temporal sequence. To understand the agent's behavior and choices it is very important to explicitly understand the entire chain, not just a single goal[5]. Many agents' decisions and actions look (at least to economists) irrational or biased simply because we do not take into account the real subjective *goals*, and just consider the ascribed or prescribed one (such as maximizing money).

E) Goal is *not a synonym of "desire"*. Desires are just one kind and one possible origin of goals. They are "endogenous" goals. When realized, they give pleasure, whereas not all goals provide us with an hedonistic experience once achieved (e.g., turning off the light can be a very important goal in certain circumstances, e.g. during a burglary, but doing so does not give us any particular pleasure). They are goals that we can "feel", because while prospecting and anticipating their achievement we experience pleasant sensations or emotions. We do not "feel" all kinds of goals; we just have, formulate, an "intention", a "project", a "purpose", a "plan", etc. Instead, we "feel" desires and needs, and this is not by accident; they imply active sensory-motor representations (either "imagined", evoked from memory, or current proprioceptive signals; see also Section 6.3).

   Not all our pursued goals (intentions) come from desires; there are goals of different kind and origin, like "duties" (and in general what I "have to do", which may be very unpleasant), or goals produced by requests, orders, etc.; and in general what we do just for others. More generally, there is a complex ontology of goals (see Section 6), with their different history and qualities, which should be the focus of a theory: gradable vs. non gradable goals; maintenance vs. achievement goals; avoidance vs. approach goals. But also: "desires" different from "needs", different from "intentions", different from "ambitions",

---

[5] An action is conceptually defined/characterized in an intentional way, that is by its purposive result; for example, 'watering' is not just dropping water on plants; the same "behavior" might be a different action: just 'to empty the jar'. The intention makes the difference (see Section 4.5).

different from "interests", different from "duties", etc. All of these teleological states have their own specific "psychology".

F) *Not all goals are "motivations" or "motivating"*. Many goals are just "means", instrumental to higher goals/results, and for given final ends and aims (that is, terminal goals, non-instrumental to other superordinate goals). However, not even all the terminal expected positive outcomes of an action, that is, its end-goals, are really "motivating" the action. By "motivating goal" of a given action we mean a goal that, in the agent's perception, is a necessary and sufficient reason for performing that action (Lorini, Marzo & Castelfranchi 2005). In other words, if the realization of that goal were not implied in the agent's decision scenario, s/he would not have chosen and executed that action. Truly "motivating" are only those goals whose expected realization is necessary and sufficient (or at least, either necessary or sufficient) for performing that action. In fact, one may have additional goals, additional positive expected outcomes, which are not strictly motivating, in that that action could be performed also without those expectations (see Section 6.1).

G) Goals proper *should not be confused with other anticipatory representations*, which probably are akin to goals and forerunners of real goal-driven actions, like so-called "anticipatory classifiers" and their "expectation" (on the differences and similarities with goals, see Pezzulo & Castelfranchi 2009; Pezzulo et al. 2008). In our view those representations generate seemingly goal-driven behaviors like Skinner's "instrumental learning". No doubt, the animal anticipates the result of its action, and the action is reinforced by the actual result, but it is not cybernetically driven by its anticipation; the behavior remains respondent to internal and external "conditions" activating the action and the expectation.

Matching Condition ⇒ Action + Expectation (anticipated results)

Here behavior does not start from the goal and its mismatch with the world, and the search for goal-appropriate actions. Probably the reverse use of an anticipatory classifier, starting from the activated expectation and "searching for" action and conditions, is the origin of a true/full goal-driven behavior.

H) It would be better *not to use the term "preferences" to refer to goals* (or its sub-kinds: desires, objectives, needs, etc.). "Preference" implies an ordering: I prefer something to something else. A preference is just a possible candidate intention (Section 6.4). "Preference" is the operation and resulting order needed for making a choice among various possible outcomes. The preference for the term "preference" (pun intended) comes from an anti-psychological position, prevailing in economics at least since Pareto, aimed at providing an operational and behavioral notion that might explain choices without any explicit theory of mental representations. When, before two alternatives, A and B, subject X chooses B, it is postulated (as an explanation of X's behavior) that X "prefers" B (a quite tautological and circular explanation: X prefers B since B is his prevailing preference). Moreover, the success of preferences in replacing "goals", "desires", "needs", etc., in the economic literature seems also to depend on the fact that (i) the term looks intrinsically referring to some objective "value", to a quantitative measure at least in ordinal terms; (ii) it is more abstract than "desires" or "needs" and can cover both.

I) It is also important to avoid the *typical confusion between the goal and the representation-object and process in itself*, that is, the material "vehicle" of the goal and of its cycle. This confusion may arise in two different ways:

i. By making the system's goal coincide with "achieving such goal". No doubt, the control cycle is activated when the two representations (perception and goal) mismatch, and it is stopped (achievement) when they match. But the system's goal is *not* to make them match! The goal is not that "the goal be achieved": the goal is the goal, that is, the particular representation used in that function/cycle, and its content, to wit, the state of the external world produced by our action. That those representations match, that the goal be achieved, is not a goal (in a strict cybernetic and psychological sense); at most, that is a pseudo-goal (see Section 4.4), a way of working of the goal-machine, a principle of operation, and thus a function.

ii. By making the "representation" coincide with the goal. In fact, a "representation" is a double-face entity, implying both the "signifier"/sign (De Saussure's "significant") and the "signified" /represented (De Saussure's "signifié"). From a psychological-operational and functional point of view that represented object is the goal; that is, it plays the role of "goal" in the control machine. However, subjectively, phenomenologically speaking, the "goal" is its content, the represented "scene": the state of the world that is desired/wanted; that is, what orients the agent system and its behavior, and what the agent tends to realize; what we foresee, imagine[6].

In sum, it is important not to identify the material "representation" object with its function, the represented. One should not miss the fundamental distinction between *"id quo intelligitur"* and *"id quod intelligitur"* (Thomas Aquinas, *Summa Theologiae*, I[a] q. 84-89): the distinction between that by means of which I am thinking what I am thinking (the *vehicle* of my thinking), and what I am thinking about (the *content* of my thinking). We think of/about something *through* representations; we do not think *of* representations (except, obviously, when we take a meta-attitude and, at some meta-level, start thinking about thinking; see Section 6.1).

L) Another particularly misleading error to be avoided is *confusing a merely "self-interested" and actually "selfish" agent with a "goal-directed" agent*, that is,

---

[6] Consider the famous semiotic "triangle" of Ogden and Richards (1923), connecting the "symbol", the "thought or reference" (meaning), and the "referent", the denoted state of the world – which in the case of goals is anticipated and constructed. Then we may say that there are three uses and facets of the "goal", which is a symbolic entity: (i) the mental vehicle playing the control role of "goal"; (ii) the subjectively desired/expected imagined world; (iii) the outcome state of the world produced by the behavior. This analysis may in part assuage our criticism on point (A) above, that now can be seen as a reductive misuse of the notion rather than an outright mistake.

an agent that – by definition – is driven by his/her own, internally represented, goals. If we accept such a conflation, then in order to be pro-social and even altruistic, to do something for others and not for a calculated personal return, should thus an agent be "hetero-directed", remotely controlled, not free?! What common sense means by "selfish" or "egoist", is *not* just being driven by "one's own" internal motives and choices; and "altruist" does *not* mean behavior guided by some sort of external motives or forces. What these terms refer to is the nature and origin of the regulating goals; but those goals are always the agent's own goals and preferences and psychology should be able to grasp and model such a distinction. Suppose I m motivated by an end, a terminal goal of mine, consisting in Y's welfare, realizing Y's desires, satisfying Y's needs. That is my motive; and my choices and behavior are regulated by that prevailing goal. Am I "selfish" or even "egoist" since this is "my" goal? Not at all. An egoist is an agent whose final motive is not just "his/her" goal, but a goal "for him/herself", which only considers one's own advantage and benefit, caring nothing for the consequences on others. If my goal is your benefit and I spend my resources and sacrifice my "private" goals for you (for your goals), I am an altruist. The problem here is not whether a really altruistic mind exists or not; but how it should work; how it should be designed. And clearly a goal-directed system can be fully altruistic (see also 6.1).

M) Another bad mess, typical of psychological approaches to "motivation" (that should actually be called "the theory of goals and their origins and dynamics") is *the (implicit or explicit) identification of "motivation" and "emotion"*. It is true that emotions are one of the sources and triggers of goals: this is part of their "conative" nature; these are "impulses", and part of "drives". And it is also true that emotions are "signals" of the status of our relevant goals; they monitor some important and specific goals of ours (fear is about safety; shame is about social image; pride is about our value, mastery and sense of competence; etc.). In other words: a theory of emotions intrinsically requires a theory of goals: *no emotions without goals* (Castelfranchi et al., 1996). But not the other way around. The theory of goals is not grounded on emotions and does not intrinsically require them. We can have a perfect "goal-directed", intentional, agent without any emotion. What is intrinsically needed is a "value" of its goals/motives; either due to selection or to learning or reasoning.

This "cold" agent will not be very "human" or "natural"; but we should not think that what is in nature is necessarily "principled"; it is also the result of mere "chance" – more precisely, it is the result of that particular interaction of function and chances known as natural selection, which leaves ample room for traits and behaviors that are not completely adaptive (or even not adaptive at all), and at the same time says nothing on how certain traits and behaviors *could* have been in principle, had things be different. The advantage of the artificial, synthetic approach is also the possibility of disentangling what in nature is mixed and confused also with accidental and merely historical reasons. We first need clear and distinguished notions and models; then we need to understand why and how (evolutionary history) certain phenomena are combined in a given way, and in nature happens to be strongly integrated.

Apart from this, emotion and motivation are not one and the same domain, or one a sub-set of the other. The real relation is a partial overlap. On the one side, there are important aspects and parts of the theory of emotions that have nothing to do with the goals they activate or watch: theory of physiological/body self-perception; theory of cultural meanings, conventions, varieties; analysis of expressive signals; etc. On the other side, there are fundamental parts of the theory of goals that have nothing to do with emotions: the theory of means-ends structure and reasoning, of planning, of action control, of compromises, of goal-adoption; etc.

4 What a goal is

In psychology and cognitive sciences it is definitely better to adopt to the cybernetic (CYB) notion and model of goals[7]. It provides psychology with a clear and operational concept, in which nothing is left to metaphysics or mere intuition, and which is not really derived from common sense (so there is no ground to dismiss it as a folk-psychological concept). On the contrary, cybernetic notions such as circular causality, loop, feedback, etc., are repugnant to our commonsense, and yet provide the foundations for a proper understanding of goals.

4.1 The operational definition of "goal" and "goal-directed/driven" behavior

"Goal" is an internal, mental *representation*[8],

- usually – or at least operationally – *anticipatory*, about how the world is not (or better, it is assumed not to be),
- of *any possible format* (sensory-motor; abstract and symbolic; propositional or linguistic; procedural; etc.),

---

[7] Based on Rosenbleuth, Wiener and Bigelow's (1943) notion of "purposive behavior", and the TOTE model by Miller, Galanter and Pribram (Miller et al. 1960); also – more modestly – the notion of "scopistica" in the Italian literature on goals, which is now included in the Hoepli Italian Dictionary (Dizionario Hoepli) as belonging to the technical jargon of linguistics and psychology, and denoting "the exam of psychological and linguistic behavior of a subject, in relation to the aims that such subject intends to pursue" (original text in Italian: "Esame del comportamento psicologico e linguistico di un soggetto, in relazione agli obiettivi che egli intende conseguire").

[8] Or "externalized", in case of representational supports, like the project of an architect.

- *employed as a set-point in a control-system*, in the cybernetic cycle driving the external behavior (that becomes an "action") of the agent for modifying the world[9].

The system does not just start from the current conditions, external inputs, but from the goal-representation, which is not yet or necessarily an "expectation" about what will happen[10] (it might already be true, or be assumed as impossible), and uses it (i) for evaluating the current state of the world; (ii) for activating or even searching in memory for the appropriate action (an action with such an expected result); (iii) for planning by finding context-related subgoals; (iv) for monitoring the execution of action and adjusting it to the context; (v) for stopping the action (when the outcome matches with the goal)[11]. It is more a *top-down process* than a bottom-up reactive one (but see also Section 6.1 on "settling" goals in decision).

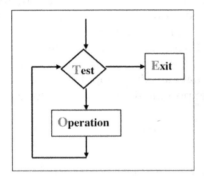

Fig. 2 TOTE cycle

4.2 Some limits of the CYB model

Of course this basic operational notion and model has several limits when applied to human behavior/mind[12]. It lacks some very relevant aspects. To

---

[9] "Goal" is a perfect term for the general theory of motivational representations, but not in the most superficial and typical English use, where it usually refers to a pursued external objective to be actively reached; or some step in my active plan, driving my action.

[10] It becomes the "expectation" later in the cycle, when the system decides to act and will check the result of the action against that representation; or when the system believes that the goal will be realized by another "agent" and is waiting and checking for such realization.

[11] And – in affective systems – for eliciting the appropriate felt/affective response (pleasant/unpleasant depending on the "success" or "frustration") or emotion, which always are goal-related and usually due to the realization or frustration of internal goals. Responses/emotions to be memorized, associated to the event or action, and/or eliciting now another goal or behavior, and beliefs.

[12] A basic problem was that the strictly behavioristic approach of Wiener and colleagues aimed at avoiding the necessary "internal" (mental) representation; hence Taylor's objection

start with, in this minimal model "goals" *have no "value"* and do not need it. The notion of goal itself should be affected by the notion and theory of *decision*. The basic CYB goal notion is fundamental in its operationalization and clarity, but the basic process model is too simple: it implies some sort of *'reactive' goal*. In fact, given a mismatch between the set-point (goal) and the world, an action is fired. In the basic – thermostat-like – model, there is just one action and a mismatch/match test and firing condition. This might be called a "goal-automatism", a very primitive form of goal-directed behavior (like in "drives"). True psychological "goals" are not so automatic: they need a phase of search or activation of possible actions, and of "decision" (to do or not to do) or "choice" among alternative means. *A true psychological "goal" entails a "decision", and "decisions" presuppose "goals".*

Moreover, in this minimal model there are no sub-goals and plans: each goal has and triggers its own action We do not have just one goal (temperature of the room = 20 degrees) and just one action. First, after the goal-perception mismatch, the next step should not be "operation!" (action execution), but some action selection process, something like a new test/search: "Is there in the repertoire any action producing such a result? No ⇒ Failure!; Yes, just one ⇒ Execution (if conditions are there); Yes, more than one ⇒ Choice!".

More generally, we have several goals, and some of them can be simultaneously activated and might be "in conflict" with each other; therefore, we have to "choose" among them; and we need a theory of conflict, value, and choice/decision-making (Section 4.6). And also other basic models of *goal dynamics* were missing in the original cybernetic intuition, regarding activation, processing and abandonment of goals, as well as any notion of goal hierarchy (see Section 5 and 6).

In addition to that, we not only retrieve from memory previously constructed or learned complex actions to be performed, but we are also able to build new action paths, to construct new means-ends chains by reasoning, and to solve creatively the problem we are facing[13], that is, to create new plans.

Finally, goals useful for psychology (and AI) are explicit (*manipulable*) representations, which can be generatively produced, changed, analyzed, combined, compared; one can "reason" about, and work on, them. They are either sensory-motor or symbolic representations (for example, propositional ones), but in any case real mental objects to manage[14]. Although it is important to stress that explicit "representation" (and in general "representation") does

---

that this mechanism cannot capture real (human) purposive behavior, based on "desires", "beliefs", that is, on "subjective" states. Also the ideas of "final cause", of the backward causation, loop, circular causation, etc., were hotly debated as violating natural causality, its interpretation, etc. (see Cordeschi 2002 for this historical reconstruction).

[13] A real "problem" is there when a goal cannot be achieved by the actions already existing in (retrieved from) one's repertoire; there is something new or different and a new plan has to be devised.

[14] Here we encounter a problem with this definition: not all the "cybernetic" goals are "mental", control our "action", and assume the subjective forms of motor control, of desire, intention, objective, project, etc. There are real cybernetic (set-point based) homeostatic regulations in our body (for example, maintaining our body temperature around 35–40 degrees C) that are not mentally represented. They are not "goals" in a psychological (subjective

not mean "conscious" representation; goals can be unconscious and act in an unconscious way.

4.3 *From plans to behaviors*

Any original/final goal is articulated in its sub-goals, that is in a plan structure and abstract actions (like "take the train", "buy the tickets"), and finally in the concrete and "executable" actions (for example, motor actions: moving one's arm, grasping something, saying something, etc.). The final structure in which the original goal and the chosen objective is "compiled" is not a uniform structure, just composed of goals and sub-goals. At the higher level we have practical reasoning, planning, goal oriented behavior (like in Bratman 1987; Rao & Georgeff 1995); but at the lower level we find routines, behaviors (of the anticipatory classifiers kind), just retrieved from memory, ready to be executed and just "adjusted" to the external circumstances. The low level inherits the goal-directed character, since it is generated from the top and for the ultimate goal (Pezzulo & Castelfranchi 2009). So there is a functional continuum in the transition from goals to actions: the top portion is more similar to BDI (Rao & Georgeff 1995), while the lower portion is more similar to Behavior Networks (Maes 1989) and uses anticipatory classifiers (Butz 2002).

In this transition from goals to actions, of special interest is the process that leads from goals and intentional actions to behavioral *routines*. Many acts, originally driven by goals, and performed in view of them, may become merely routinary, habitual, that is, simply respondent to stimuli, such as it is the case with reflexes and production rules. The action/behavior is just activated by contextual conditions, where the original goal-representation remains inactive and implicit. What remains of the original goal is its translation into the concrete expectation of the perceived effect, now implemented as the expectation of an anticipatory classifier.

Consider for example learning to drive a car and learning the rule of stopping at a red light or giving precedence to a pedestrian at a crosswalk. At the beginning we have the explicit goal of "stopping at the red light", we remind ourselves of it and activate it, and then "decide" to stop the car; but later, all these behaviors become automatic reactions: the red light just triggers the response of stopping; we do not have the intention of stopping or of respecting the norm. However:

- while pushing the brakes I have a precise expectation controlling the result: I expect my car to stop; if this did not happen I would be extremely surprised (and worried because of my violation of the reactivated norm);
- the norm and the potential intention are still in my mind, although dormant, implicit, and they might be reactivated in any moment (for example in case

---

or behavioral) sense; they are not manipulable representations, and do not regulate our "actions" on the world.

of a conflict: "My son is in urgent need of medical attention: Should I drive on even though the light is red?").

Some goal-directed actions have just the appearance of intentional actions, either because they were originally intentional and now are just automatic; or because they are conventionally assumed and treated "as if" they were intentional, even though they are just learned by reinforcement and imitation, without a real understanding and formulation of the goal. For example, a baby brushing his teeth does not necessarily (already) intend "to clean them", but we ascribe him such an intention. We ascribe a rich understanding and intentions even to dogs that are just obeying for reinforcement learning to our signals.

4.4 Goals vs. pseudo-goals

It is very important to disentangle true goals from *pseudo-goals* (Miceli & Castelfranchi 1995), that is, goals that only seem to be there and to regulate the system and its behavior. However, in fact they are not there as goal mechanisms, they are not represented in the system and "governing" it. They are just functional ways in which the system has been "designed" (by evolution, by learning, by the designer); they are the system's goal-oriented way of working, its operational rules. For example, a real thermostatic system (thermostat, thermometer, room, radiator, boiler, etc.) has been designed in order to reduce naphtha consumption, heat loss, etc. as much as possible. These are (pseudo)goals of the system, which works also in order to guarantee them; but they are not true CYB-goal like the set-point of the thermostat. They are not represented, evaluated, and "pursued" by the system action cycle.

Analogously, our minds have been shaped (by natural selection, or culture and learning) in order to have certain working principles and to guarantee certain functions, which are not explicitly represented and intended. It seems (from our behavior) that we have certain goals, but they are not real goals, only pseudo-goals. This is the case, in our view, of some well-known (and badly misunderstood) finalistic notions, like utility maximization, cognitive coherence, and even pleasure. No doubt, we often choose between different possible goals so as to maximize our expected utility, giving precedence/preference to the greater expected value[15]; that is obvious and adaptive. However, this does not mean that we have "the" goal (the unique and monarchic goal) of maximizing our utility, indifferently to the specific contents and goods ("Questa o quella per me pari sono"). On the contrary, we are moved and motivated by specific, qualitative terminal goals of ours (esteem, sex, power, love, etc.), but the *mechanism* that has to manage them has been designed and works so that it maximizes expected utility.

---

[15] And so as to pursue non-contradictory goals, that is, goals which are not in conflict with each other.

In the same vein, we maintain coherence among our beliefs, and need to avoid and eliminate contradictions. That is why we can reject certain information and do not believe all the data we get (sometimes even what we directly perceive; "we do not believe our eyes", literally); the new data must be "plausible", credible, integrable, within the context of our preexisting knowledge; otherwise, we have to revise our previous beliefs on the basis of new (credible) data. This coherence maintenance is frequently completely automatic and routinary. We have mechanisms for coherence check and adjustment. We do not usually have any real intention about the coherence of what we believe. Thus, knowledge coherence is a pseudo-goal of ours, not a real meta-goal guiding meta-actions.

Similarly, pleasure is not "the" goal of our activity, and the same holds for feeling pleasure (or avoiding feeling pain). "Pleasure" – as a specific and qualitative subjective experience, sensation (not as an empty tautological label for goal satisfaction) – normally is not a goal for us: it is not what we intend to realize/achieve while acting, what move us for performing that behavior. Of course, feeling pleasure or avoiding pain *might* become real goals and intentionally drive our actions: that is basically the mindset of the true hedonist, who acts for pleasure and not for whatever practical consequence his/her action accomplish. But typically looking for pleasure and avoiding pain are not a unique final goal of ours (another monarchic view of mind and motivation): rather, they act as "signals" for learning, and they help us learning, among other things, how to generate and evaluate goals (see Section 6.3).

Those hedonistic philosophies that identify pleasure with motivation, and relate our goal-oriented activity to pleasure motivation, should address the following, evident objections:

i. As a matter of fact, several goals even when achieved do not give us a pleasure experience at all; they are just practical results, or consist in the pursuit of (often unpleasant) duties.

ii. If pleasure is so necessary for goal pursuit and motivated activity, why it is not necessary at all in cybernetic models of goal-directed activity and purposive systems? How is it possible to have a clearly finalistic and anticipation-driven mechanism, open to "success" and "failure", without any "pleasure"? In other terms, *what is the real function and nature of pleasure in a goal-directed system?* Moreover, pleasure seems to be present in nature (both phylogenetically and ontogenetically) well before mentally goal-directed actions. This also suggests that the function of pleasure has to be different; it does not seem to play the role of a goal.

In my view, pleasure is more related to the notion of "reward", of "reinforcement" and learning. Pleasure as an internal reward plays two fundamental roles: it attaches some value to some achieved state, which is important when the system can have more than one of such states, possibly in competition with each other; it signals that a given outcome (perhaps accidental) "deserves" to be pursued, is good, has to become a goal (that state, not the pleasure per se). In this view, pleasure is a signal and a learning device for goal creation/discovery and for evaluation. It seems very useful in a system endowed with a "generative" goal mechanism, and which needs different kinds of evaluation, more or less intuitive, fast, based on experience or on biological/inherited "preferences", and not just on reasoning (with its limits, biases, and slowness).

Another notion of pseudo-goal, overlapping only in part with the previous one, applies to the adaptive (biological or social) *functions* of our behavior, which we are typically not aware of, and yet we end up "pursuing" by acting towards our true internal goals (Castelfranchi 1998b, 2001). Although our behavior seems to be "regulated" by those finalities, they are not really represented in our system and they do not drive us; they are just "implemented" in our subjective goals and personal aims, and in our (partial) understanding of norms and duties (see Section 2; also Conte & Castelfranchi 1995 a, b). As already said, we do not know why (for what) we eat or we love; we do not understand and follow the real final goals of a law or social convention or norm.

4.5 The goal of the action (and intention "recognition")

An important possible distinction to be introduced (at least for a crucial analytical discussion) is between *the goal of the action*, inherent to the action as its "function", its recognizable and defining end, and *the ascription of such an "intention", of the mental representation, to its agent*, necessarily implying some understanding of other minds.

Actions are and/or become "tools", artifacts, with their characterizing "function", the intrinsic finality that classifies them; like for a hammer or a table or a chair or a pencil. Inserting the key in the lock, or grabbing the handle of a closed door, or opening a box of matches, or just walking, or sticking some food with the fork[16], etc. Thus, it is not so obvious, whenever someone "recognizes" or "mirrors" the goal of an observed behavior, whether s/he is really *ascribing an intention to the observed agent*, or simply viewing the action in a finalistic frame, as goal-directed (that is, an "action"), thus recognizing *its* teleonomy, *its* goal; by just evoking and expecting the functional and defining outcome.

The *goal of the action* and the *intention of the agent* are not just one and the same thing. Usually the agent uses a given action in order to exploit its goal[17]; she searches for it and intends it for putting into effect that goal; and – on the other side – actions are classified and stored in a goals perspective to be retrieved and used for their goal (exactly like a tool; action repertoire is a toolbox). However, we can recognize the action-goal (the action as action) without recognizing (ascribing) the goal guiding the action to the mind of its agent. Is this always a necessary and preliminary step? Or is it a more advanced and complete step? Do really mirror neurons respond to the other ascribed mental state or just

---

[16] No difference between the action, the object, the instrument; all of them are "tools": the "food", the "fork", and the eating behavior with a fork.

[17] However, sometimes it is in order to exploit other outcomes, like turning on the oven not to cook but for heating the kitchen.

to the evocation of the "end" of that behavior? An interesting open issue that deserves a discussion, which presupposes subtle finalistic notions.

4.6 Conflicts and goals "value"

Conflict occurs when two or more goals are incompatible, that is, they cannot be realized in the same world/context; either because they are logically inconsistent, contradictory, or because they are only indirectly incompatible, that is, inconsistent not in principle but in practice. For instance, we believe that the same resource R (money, time, space, attention, work, etc.) is needed for both goal S1 and S2, and that R is not enough for both, it is "scarce"; thus we have to choose: either to employ R for pursuing S1 or to employ R for S2. That is why a "value" of goals (level of activation? felt intensity? calculated utility? something else?) is strictly needed: How could we choose between S1 and S2 if they were equal for us?

The example I will discuss here is in terms of "deliberation", just for clarity. But the same problem is present for impulsive or affective behavioral activation, or for selecting the most appropriate drive among many competing for attention. If more than one drive is active at the same time, we need to know which is "more important"; they must have different "values", which in this case are just given by the degree of activation, the intensity of the sensation. A complete theory of decision should include some sort of *proto-decisions* where there is no real reasoning or calculation, but just a confrontation and prevailing of "forces". (On the *integration* of these two forms of value and decisions in one process, see below).

Thus goals have to have a subjective "value", that is a value perceived and assigned by the decision-maker, a quantitative dimension enabling the decision maker to give them some ordering, by making them "preferable" or not to other goals. Of course, this value is not the only factor which determines the decision to do or not to do something, or the choice between two competing goals. The goals' degree of "urgency", the estimated probability of achieving them, the involved costs, the perceived risks and possible harms are factors which also come into play. But our issue here is the following one: *Where does the "value" of a goal come from?*

In our view there are two different sources and kinds of "value", that may interact (either in synergy or in conflict) with each other.

(a) One kind of value is "calculated", based on means-end relations, on the examination of possible advantages ("pros"; achieved higher-goals) and disadvantages ("cons", frustrated goals); the value of a given goal is derived from its forecast consequences: from the number and values of the realized higher-goals, and the number and values of the frustrated goals ("costs" in broad sense). This value is "inherited" from the goal hierarchy, from the ends to their means[18]. Clearly, this value is based on our beliefs and in particular our predictions (although automatic, memorized) and it is in fact "justifiable": I have my explainable "reasons" for choosing a given alternative; I have decided to go by train and not by car, because so and son. This is in fact the domain of persuasive argumentation (while marketing and advertising mainly work on the second kind of value: affective unconscious associations).

(b) The other kind of value is not "reasoned" upon or calculated, but just felt and intuitive, and not really justifiable; it is due to the (frequently unconscious) activation of affective responses conditioned to analogous experiences (see Section 6.3 on "feeling").

Given these two possible "values" of the goals and forms of appraisal (not necessarily present at the same time) they may converge or conflict (Miceli & Castelfranchi 1989; see also Section 6.3): the same goal can be both very "attractive" and very "useful"; or it may be high in "utility" but not attractive at all; or very attractive but extremely costly and irrational.

5 The architecture of the mind: trading in goals and knowledge

The mind is founded on two basic representations (or attitudes): goals and knowledge (here understood in terms of doxastic representations, beliefs, as-sumptions, etc.; what we take to be true, possibly with doubts and reservations, whether or not it is in fact true). Complex mental objects/states/representations are molecules, patterns, or better "gestalts" – with their own global properties and effects – basically composed of these cognitive constituents. For example, "expectations" are specific patterns of goals and beliefs about the future (Miceli & Castelfranchi 2002; Castelfranchi et al. 2003; Castelfranchi & Falcone 2010); complex emotions are grounded on a specific pattern of beliefs ("cognitive appraisal" and interpretation of the real or possible event, as well as goals controlled or activated by the emotion; Castelfranchi & Miceli 2009). More-over, mental activity basically consists of a continuous *trade* between goals and knowledge. They live for (off) each other.

5.1 How beliefs live for goals

One should not forget the specific and original properties of "goals", first of all their having "value" and *their "providing value" to the world*; their motivational

---

[18] This is why we need a given value of the top-level active goals, or the final motivations: at a given moment, given our age, gender, personality, culture, personal biography, identity and tastes, I have certain final motives with a given value for me, and I can choose between different active goals; and/or I have certain active drives, or felt needs and desires, but also my long term objectives with their subjective terminal value.

force. Things, actions, relations, events, have value only relatively to goals. Knowledge and its acquisition and use has to be motivated. It is true that biological and cultural evolution have also provided us with a "terminal" goal (intrinsic motivation) of knowledge acquisition; we acquire and maintain knowledge not necessarily in view of an immediate and specific use, but as a "capital", a resource good for several potential uses. However, this does not invalidate the instrumental nature of knowledge, as well as its goal-directed origin and function; "curiosity" and "competence" are themselves goals.

Even more radically; the notion of knowledge itself cannot be reduced to information and data to be stored and elaborated. Knowledge really is/becomes knowledge not per se but only *in relation* to an agent that constructs and exploits it in the process of adaptation of/to the world and of his/her action on it. That is, a system endowed with goals and producing a goal-directed behavior for realizing them, grounding that on representations and their elaboration. What *make* information and data "knowledge" are goals, since they relate information to the action, the world, the subject[19]. In this perspective, it is imperative to provide a goal-based theory of the "importance" or "significance" of information and beliefs[20].

It is that significance that will give us inklings on the value of knowledge. In our view even a complete theory of "relevance" (in broad sense) should be conceived in relation to goals, not just to information or communication theories and their contextual aspects. Data "informativeness", novelty, or reliability/truth, or efficient search and retrieval, circulation, sharing, etc., are not enough. And "relevance" is not reducible to "pertinence", just related to communication pragmatics and dialogue (Sperber & Wilson 1986), or at least that aspect should be explicitly integrated with the importance/significance dimension (for discussion, see Paglieri & Castelfranchi 2012).

We search and elaborate information, data, knowledge *for* something; but what this "for" means? Significance is the "value" and polarization of knowledge relative to our goals: its *utility*.

- How precious, useful, important is a given piece of knowledge? How much would I spend/invest for accessing it?
- What kind of information is "useful" for my goal/interest G, and *why*?

---

[19] On this important distinction between "information" and "knowledge" see the constructivist literature; for example Zeleny (2000, 2005). However, consider that for us the radical constructivist view is too extreme. We disagree on several things. For example, on the idea that, since knowledge is not a subject-independent object, then it *"is not a thing to be possessed, like information or money, but a process to be learned, mastered, and carried out, like baking and milking"* (Zeleny 2005). On the contrary, we claim that knowledge can be "possessed", and that this is not a metaphor or misuse; knowledge is a good, a capital, a "resource", a "power", even if we conceive it as a process (but also its product, construction), or better a competence – which is why it is a resource with its own peculiar dynamics (e.g., possessing a certain knowledge does not prevent others from possessing it too), and yet a resource nonetheless. Indeed, more generally competences and capacities are resources, powers of those who "posses" them.

[20] And of some biases in believing and inferring due to the influence of our goals (like in "motivated reasoning"; see Kunda 1990).

THESIS:
The more valuable/important the (set of goal) G1 &
The more useful and necessary is knowledge K for G1
⇒ *The more valuable K*

However, there are two different ways in which knowledge is useful to goals; one is strictly instrumental, as a mere means; the other one is more basic, and its nature can be understood in a "cognitivist" perspective, because it reveals what it really means to "realize" (or not) a goal.

In the first case, I need a given believable piece of information for performing my action and realizing my goal. For example, I have to remember or find the combination to a safe in order to open it; or I should have Rose's telephone number to call her and invite her to dinner. What is the value of this information? Are there alternatives for opening the safe? And how much money is there?! Or: how important is for me to call Rose? How precious is her telephone number and what am I disposed to do for having it?

In the second case, the information, the belief, *is* the realization (or frustration) of the goal! What does it actually mean to "achieve/realize" a goal in our CYB model and in a cognitivist perspective? It simply means that two mental representations do match: that my belief about the state of the world is equal to my goal about it. It is the belief that realizes the goal; to realize a goal is just to believe so: *"We are as unhappy as we believe we are"* (Seneca). The real state of the world is irrelevant and unknowable: we can just correct our beliefs through other beliefs.

So, a belief that makes us happy, which "realizes" our goal, is very precious for us, and probably we will be more resistant to revise or forget it, and more prone to believe it. A belief that makes us unhappy, which is painful and frustrating, is very significant too but also disturbing, and we will (unconsciously) try to avoid it, to repress or deny it. So, in a sense beliefs acquire an attraction or avoidance nature, just in relation to our goals (and associated emotions).

5.2 *How goals live for beliefs: goal dynamics*

Let us explain in some detail *why the belief-goal bridge is so important*: the real backbone of the mind.
(A) Beliefs support goals (beliefs as reasons for goals)
(B) Beliefs determine goal value
(C) Beliefs determine goal processing and dynamics
(D) Beliefs determine goal species

Let us start from how *beliefs support* goals, by acting as *reasons* for them. A cognitive agent is an agent who grounds his actions on his beliefs: or better, he acts on the basis of what he wants and prefers (goals), but he wants and prefers on the basis of what he believes. In a cognitive agent goals should be supported and justified by *reasons* (not necessarily unbiased and "rational"). We *activate, maintain, decide about, prefer, plan for,* and *pursue* goals which are grounded on pertinent beliefs (supported by other beliefs, etc.; Castelfranchi 1996; Castelfranchi & Paglieri 2007). This is how *epistemic rationality* (rationality in believing; believing on the basis of evidence, credible sources, etc.) impacts on *pragmatic rationality* (rationality in decision; choosing the best alternative, on the basis of what one knows and considers).

In a social perspective this heavily constrains *influencing* (changing the intentions of another agent) and creates two protection walls for human autonomy (Castelfranchi 2000; Castelfranchi & Falcone 2004). Together, they define what I call the *Autonomous Cognitive Agent Postulate*. It claims that it is (fairly) *impossible to directly modify the goals* (hence the intentions and actions) of an autonomous cognitive agent. In order to influence agent X, agent Y must modify the beliefs of X which support those goals (first protection). However, *to make another believe something is not so easy* (second protection), because an agent's beliefs are "integrated" with each other, and the receiver will end up believing or not a certain claim on the basis of plausibility criteria (coherence with previous knowledge, costs of belief revision) and of the source's reliability and trustworthiness compared with other sources. If Y could easily succeed in making X believe anything, Y could induce X to do anything. This is way these protective walls are so important to agent autonomy.

Let us then move to the *role of beliefs in supporting goal processing*. As already remarked, we know very little about the vicissitudes of goals in our mind, whereas we know everything, and in a step by step fashion, about the vicissitudes of knowledge in our mind. Except for some models of the decision processes, what do we know about goal activation and origins? Of goal selection prior to making any choice (e.g., due to a perceived conflict)? Of goal "suspensions" (waiting for re-activation) or complete abandon? Of the evaluation of our skills, competence, know-how and possible plans (different from "planning"); or our self-confidence? Of the evaluation of the external conditions for a successful execution of the intended action? And so on.

The path of goals in our mind, from their triggering to their active pursuit (the execution of the identified instrumental act), is rather complex, with several "phases" and outcomes. I will illustrate the main phases and how they are step by step based on beliefs and filtered by beliefs (Castelfranchi & Paglieri 2007). I will be very schematic, and put aside the theory/model of "decision", on which there is on the contrary a large literature. This fact (having sophisticated theories of decision and yet very little models of goal dynamics) nicely illustrates a paradoxical situation. A theory of "decision" which does without, and is not grounded on, a theory of "goals" is rather ridiculous. Decisions and choices are always between various potential "goals" to be (actively or passively) pursued and achieved – and even choices between alternative means are more aptly conceptualized as choices between sub-goals and sub-plans. An adequate, systematic, theory of goals and their dynamics is a *prerequisite* for any possible decision theory. As we will see, "intention" is just a special level of goal-processing. It is also true and obvious that a good general theory of goals cannot be developed without considering their role in decision and its specific principles and dynamics (Section 4.2).

That a theory of goals be a prerequisite for a principled theory of decision-making might look obvious and already well acknowledged in the literature (Stijn et al. 2005; Kruglansky 2000), but it is not so: the state of our ontology and theory of goals for an adequate description of decision-making is really dismal[21].We wish to persuade our reader that a lot of distinctions and of clear process models are still needed.

To summarize the point (for extended discussion, see Castelfranchi & Paglieri 2007), consider in Figure 3 the role of different types of beliefs in filtering the goals and in regulating their transition step by step, from their activation to the formulation of an intention to execute the specified action. For example, the beliefs about the fact that the goal is not already realized or will not be realized by other agents, or the belief that the goal is not impossible. In this case the realization of the goal is up to the subject; she has to find ways to achieve it. Or the beliefs about having the skills, the know-how, a possible plan and action for the realization of the goal; then the building of an "intention" *to do* a given (complex) action for realizing the original goal. Or the belief that between two active goals there is a contradiction, a conflict, and we have to choose between them. Or the beliefs about the external conditions and the resources for actually performing the needed actions. Failing these belief tests would stop the processing of a goal (e.g., putting it in a sort of "mental waiting room", until the agent beliefs will allow reactivating them), or may even eliminate

---

[21] Kruglansky (one of the major scholars about goals; see his 1996, 2002) characterizes goals as "knowledge structures" (thus subject to the same cognitive processes of any other piece of knowledge), actually identifying "cognitive representations" and "knowledge". Moreover, in his view goals are special only because they represent states that can be attained by action, thus ignoring that goals can also be impossible or mere passive hopes. To ascribe to goal structures the same properties of knowledge structures is an important and productive move; and also integrating the knowledge structure with goals is fundamental. However:

(i) A more subtle and explicit theory of the relationships between goals (called "concepts in memory") and data or beliefs would be necessary. On the on side, explaining how goal activation, evaluation, choice, intention formulation, planning, pursuing, abandoning, etc. is based on a specific belief-structure. To specify the role of beliefs is crucial for modeling the real and specific dynamics of goal ("goal processing"), and for having a clear theory of "intentions", and so on. On the other side, one should provide a goal-based theory of the 'relevance' of data and beliefs, and of some biases in believing due to our goals.

(ii) One should not miss the specific and original properties of "goals", first of all their "value" and their "providing value" to the world; their motivational force. These cannot be reduced to "activation" or other properties of knowledge structures. They derive from the "cybernetic" (regulative, motivating, control) function and nature of goals, and from goal specific structure: mean-send hierarchy, etc.

Also the important attempt of Fishbein's group (see for instance Fishbein & Ajzen 1975) is not enough systematic and model-driven; a less 'psychological' and more cognitive-science oriented view is necessary. Indeed, it is unclear why the main contributions on goal theory have been developed not in general and cognitive psychology but more in personality and social psychology, marketing, management and organization studies, clinical psychology, etc. As I said, I will not analytically discuss here this literature (Kruglansky, Fishbein, Moskowitz, etc.), I reserve this for my book on goal theory, in preparation.

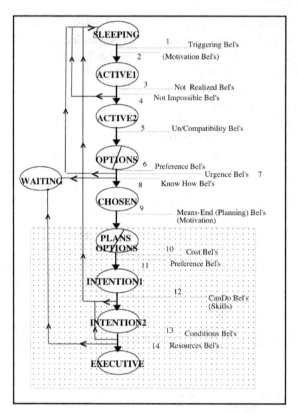

Fig. 3 Beliefs in goal processing

certain goals; on the contrary, success of these tests will make a certain goal persist until the choice, the planning, the execution of the pertinent actions[22].

6 Goals ontology

6.1 Goals ontology

We have already distinguished between an "instrumental" goal and a "higher-goal", that is the goal for which a given goal is a "means". However, since the goal hierarchy is a chain, implying a recursive structure, a goal G2, which is the higher-goal of G3, might – in turn – be the "means" of a superordinate goal G1. Except of course for the "terminal goals" or "ends".

---

[22] For a similar – but less analytical view, with a rather limited theory and ontology of goals – see also the well-known "theory of Reasoned Action" by Fishbein, and Ajzen (Fishbein & Ajzen 1975).

A goal can be a "means" for different and even divergent[23] higher-goals; a goal can be the higher-goal of several "means". Goal structures may diverge or converge. The summit of a single plan can be fully convergent, monocratic; but there is no unique summit of all our actions and plans: we have several independent (and not contemporaneously pursued) final goals or motivations (*pluralistic motivational view*). They are only "functionally" convergent, not mentally. As we said, we do not have a unique final motivation, a monarchic mind; neither pleasure nor libido nor utility maximization nor reproductive success (all pseudo-goals) play such a role. Inclusive fitness is of course the end of ends, but outside the mind, just as the convergence of all the adaptive strategies of a living system (including mental devices and goals).

Our cognition is not only for managing several goals at the same time, but is functionally oriented to long-term (see also Section 6.2) and future goals. It is for this reason that some goals, originally "instrumental", become (via evolution or learning) ends or final motives; pursued *per se* because they are preconditions and resources (means) for future possible goals. This is the case of the goals of knowledge accumulation and organization (Section 5.1), of possession (having free access to "our" means when needed) and stocks, of stable relations, and many others. It is the process of *terminalization* (Miceli & Castelfranchi 1989; Castelfranchi 2011), by which originally short-term and instrumental goals become autonomous higher-goals.

As already mentioned, the value of a means derives from the value of the higher goals that it will realize (*Pros*) and those it will frustrate (*Cons*: costs, renounces, harm and dangers, etc.). In this sense it is a "calculated", reasoned, derived value. Also, before choice (before treating goals as "intentions" that have to be coherent with each other), goals can be contradictory or better "conflicting"; for this category see Section 4.3.

It is also important to reiterate that *not all the terminal goals over a given action are "motives" and motivate that action*[24], or better: if a "terminal" goal is in our mind for sure it will motivate some action or plan of us (otherwise how/why it should be there?), but not necessarily it motivates all the actions/plans where it is one of the expected outcomes. The notion and theory of *motivating goals* is particularly relevant.

6.1.1 Motivating goals

As we already said (Section 3, point F) *not all goals, even not all "pursued" goals, are "motivating"*. Not all the expected results (not even the positive, goal-congruent expected results) "motivate" the agent to act. By "motivating" we mean that the agent acts precisely in order to realize those results, those goals. Some outcomes are predicted and expected, are even "positive" (satisfying some goal), yet we do not act for them. We may define more rigorously "mo-

---

[23] Belonging to two different plans.

[24] Perhaps, in this case one should avoid the term "aim" which looks motivating, or even the term "end". However, at least "end" can be interpreted in a "relative" and not absolute way (like in "means-end reasoning") simply as the higher-goal of a means.

tivating" results/goals those goals whose predicted satisfaction is *necessary* for the decision to act, and thus justifies the agent's behavior. If that goal would not be realized (in the agent prediction) she would not chose to act. There might be goals expected and realized by a given action, that nevertheless remains just "additional" to it; they do not motivate the action, are not necessary for the decision (see Figure 4).

A much stronger notion is when the realization of that goal is both necessary and sufficient for choosing that action. A weaker case is when the action realizes many goals and more than one would be sufficient for deciding to act; thus some of them or none of them is also necessary. In sum, there might be goals necessary and sufficient for the decision to act; just necessary but not sufficient; just sufficient but not necessary; neither necessary nor sufficient. Let us call *strict motivating goals* those that are both necessary and sufficient for deciding to act; while we will use the more general label *motivating goals* – in a broad sense – to indicate those that are either necessary or sufficient for deciding to act (Lorini, Marzo & Castelfranchi 2005).

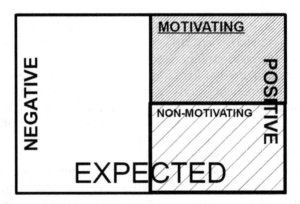

Fig. 4 Not all the expected positive results are motivating the behavior

Incidentally, without such a distinction between simply expected positive outcomes (expected goal satisfaction) vs. *motivating* outcomes, it is impossible to defend any real notion of "psychological altruism" – as Seneca had clearly explained some years ago – , and we must be content of the rather disappointing notion of "pseudo-altruism".

6.1.2 Settling goals

Not all the goals motivating our action are the goals we start from, the original "motives" of our activation, planning, deciding, etc. Not only because some of the original goals (or parts of them) might be given up; but because *new goals necessarily enter into the decision* not just as simple 'positive' or 'negative' predicted outcomes, but as crucial for the choice.

In fact, we may start from a given motive G1 (going to Naples), and by a *top-down* reasoning find/build its possible means and paths, but we may learn that we have some alternative means: we can either choose action A1 (to go by train) or action A2 (to go by car). How to choose? We have to start a reverse, *bottom-up* process by activating new goals which originally were not moving us; more precisely we have to construct a prediction scenario where we consider possible further outcomes (in addition to the achievement of G1) of A1 and A2, and we have to evaluate those outcomes against such *new* goals: for instance, G2 (reading during the travel) or G3 (arriving at the meeting without having to take buses or taxis). Those goals will serve to settle the matter of what means to prefer (hence the label settling goals), since as for G1 (going to Naples) A1 and A2 are equivalent; we will choose between those goals, not really between the two actions. Thus the chosen goal (that makes a given action preferable) is a "necessary" outcome for it, and thus is a "motivating" goal in a weak sense (since for sure it is not "sufficient", in that all the process is in view of and for G1).

6.1.3 Socially "imported" goals: goal-adoption

Not all the goals we choose and pursue are "endogenous"; originated by our own drives, needs, desires, personal ambitions, emotional impulses. Some of our goals are "imported", they are originally goals of other agents, who succeed in "influencing" us, thus modifying and regulating our own behavior. *"Influencing"* in our vocabulary means exactly modifying the goals of another agent, and thus changing his or her behavior. Of course, as we said, this usually and basically happens by modifying beliefs: perceived external conditions (for example by creating a physical barrier), new stimuli, new information about possible outcomes, etc., but also requests, orders, threats, display of suffering or needs, and so on[25].

The crucial mechanism of pro-sociality (exchange, cooperation, alliance, altruism, teamwork, etc.) and the crucial step in goal-import is *goal-adoption: the goal of another agent becomes my goal precisely because it is the other's goal* (Conte & Castelfranchi 1996; Castelfranchi 1998a).

Goal-adoption is how an autonomous agent is not an isle but becomes social, or better pro-social; that is, s/he does something *for* others, putting her/his autonomous goal-pursuing (intentional behavior), her/his cognitive machinery, and her/his powers and resources, into the service of others and of their interests.

How is this possible? Not only economically or evolutionary, but *cognitively*, that is, from the point of view of the functioning of autonomous, self-regulated, goal-driven systems? They have their own terminal goals, their motives and interests (this makes them 'autonomous' in a radical and deep sense: motivationally autonomous). Now the 'prodigy' is that those self-regulated systems

---

[25] In contrast, *"manipulating"* (frequently used in social psychology for simple "influencing") means some sort of "deceptive" influencing: influencing another without communicating one's intention, without making the other realize it.

(not to be confused – as most economists do – with 'selfish'! See Section 3, point L) can *import goals* from other goal-driven, purposive systems, from outside, and put their 'body', skills, problem-solving capacity, and resources at another agent's disposal. But how is a goal 'imported' in my regulatory, purposive system? What kind of mental representations and operations are needed for that?

In explicit/cognitive goal-adoption *X comes to have (and possibly pursue) the goal that p just because she believes that Y has the goal Gy that p*. Let us stipulate that (Goal-adopt x y p) stands for "agent x adopts the goal p from agent y", (R-Goal x p q) stands for "the reason for agent x to have goal p is q", (BEL x p) stands for "agent x believes p", and (Goal x p) stands for "agent x has goal p). Then we can formalize this firs definition of goal-adoption as follows:

$$(\text{Goal-adopt } x \; y \; p) =^{\text{def}} (\text{R-Goal } x \; p \; (\text{BEL } x \; (\text{Goal } y \; p)))$$

This definition is not fully satisfactory, since it also covers *imitation*, whereas goal-adoption is not a form of imitation, and mere imitation is not enough for cooperation[26]. A better definition is that *the adopting agent has the goal that the other agent achieves /satisfies his goal*:

$$(\text{Goal-adopt } x \; y \; p) =^{\text{def}} (\text{R-Goal } x \; (\text{OBTAIN } y \; p) \; (\text{BEL } x \; (\text{Goal } y \; p)))$$

where

$$(\text{OBTAIN } y \; p) =^{\text{def}} (\text{GOAL } y \; p) \; \& \; (\text{KNOW } y \; p)$$

and

$$(\text{KNOW } y \; p) =^{\text{def}} p \; \& \; (\text{Bel } y \; p)$$

As we know, an "autonomous" agent is by definition motivated by her own goals; thus we assume that, *whenever an autonomous goal-directed agent adopts a goal of another agent and "for" that agent, s/he is motivated by some higher personal goal*. This does *not* mean that the adopting agent is intrinsically "selfish" (see Section 3, point L), because such a higher goal might be perfectly altruistic, consisting in the other's welfare or benefit; still, that goal "belongs" form the onset to the adopting agent, it is not imported from the outside. Goal-adoption is per se an "instrumental" operation[27]. Thus autonomy is not jeopardized by goal-adoption, and yet autonomy does not imply selfishness. Rather, goal-adoption can be motivated by a variety of goals:

(a) it can (rarely) be 'altruistic', that is disinterested, not motivated by, non instrumental to higher *personal* (non-adoptive) calculated advantages (goals);

---

[26] Cooperation does not imply that the involved agents perform just the same 'mirrored' action; they typically perform complementary and substitutive activities.

[27] Also this feature makes it different from simple imitation, which might be merely automatic; a procedure, a mechanism, not in view of a calculated personal motive. However, this view of goal-adoption is a bit too calculated and rationalistic; one should also consider the very crucial phenomenon in humans of empathic feelings and emotion-based process of goal-adoption (help), just as impulses, not "in view" of higher-goals, although unselfish.

(b)it can be instrumental to some personal return, that is part of a selfish plan; like in trade, where "It is not from the benevolence of the butcher, the brewer, or the baker that we expect our dinner, but from their regard to their own interest. We address ourselves, not to their humanity but to their self-love, and never talk to them of our own necessities but of their advantages" (A. Smith, *An Inquiry into the Nature and Causes of the Wealth of Nations*, 1776).

(c)it can be instrumental to a common goal, that is, an advantage which is common to oneself and the other (strict 'cooperation')[28].

One might consider (c) as a sub-case of (b) (instrumental adoption) but actually the situation is significantly different. In pure (b) a rational agent is likely to cheat, if possible, and defeat the other, because she is not interested at all in his goal-achievement, and – if she has already obtained what she was expecting from him – she has no reason at all for doing her share. In (c), on the contrary, defeating the other is self-defeating, since they need each other (depend on each other) for one and the same goal; so, if X does not do her share she does not only defeat Y but also herself, because she will not achieve her own goal.

There are various important forms of 'goal-adoption':

- *Passive*: when X just abstains from creating negative interferences and obstacles to Y, though she would be able to prevent Y from pursuing and achieving his goal;
- *Active*: when X actively performs some action in the world in order to realize a goal of/for Y; either a terminal goal of his or an instrumental goal in/for Y's plan: a step in his goal pursuit.

Another distinction can be made between:

- *Spontaneous/non-requested* goal-adoption: when there is no expectation and (implicit or explicit) request by Y;
- *Goal-adhesion*: when there is a (implicit or explicit) request (expectation, order) that X does something for Y, and X 'accepts' to help Y.

X can be obliged or simply committed to 'help' Y, because for example she has 'promised' to do so. Although the promise might have been spontaneous, once X has made it she gets some obligation to do that action (Castelfranchi 1995b); so at the moment of the execution she also 'adheres' to the obligation impinging on her.

Of course, what really matters is not the formulation of the other's goal in our mind as a goal of ours (mere goal adoption), but that such a goal becomes an 'intention' of ours, that we will prefer the goal for the other over other goals of ours. In organizations, the incentives for such a 'preference' are material rewards, social approval, internal rewards, others' commitments and expectations, norms, possible sanctions, etc.

---

[28] As we just said (previous note) adoption can also just be due to an empathic emotion and just be an impulsive behavior without reasoned outcomes.

6.1.4 Meta-goals

As we can have meta-knowledge, meta-belief, we can also have meta-goals: goals about our goals. "Meta" level assumption is a property of representations in general, not of knowledge alone: we represent the representation as such, we think about the representational entity, the sign or symbol. Thus, meta-cognition has these two facets: beliefs about beliefs, and goals; goals about goals, and beliefs (Miceli & Castelfranchi 1997).

Meta-goals are important, since they characterize our reflective attitude and influencing attitude towards our own mind and ourselves. We apply a socially originated theory of mind and social influencing activity to ourselves. We try to persuade, threaten, punish ourselves; to make promises to ourselves, to come to arrangements with ourselves, to prohibit something or to order something to ourselves, to criticize our desires or choices, and so on (Castelfranchi 2012). Meta-goals are fundamental for our self-regulation, especially in relation to our "duties", "ideals", and coherent self-image and identity (Section 6.3 last paragraph); but actually how they enter our decision in not so clear and well modeled.

The "will" in its strict sense is exactly this. Not will in the sense of mere voluntary action (that just means "intentional", goal-driven after some decision), but the sort of will that can have a "power". Indeed, "willpower" (nothing to do with voluntary action) is exactly the power we have (or lack) over ourselves, for influencing our selves by imposing some goal or the persistence of previous choices, resisting to new goals, opportunities, and temptations, or to fatigue or discouragement.

6.2 More qualitative distinctions

6.2.1 Actively pursued vs. passive goals

Not all goals have to be "actively pursued" or just "pursued"; some of them (like having a sunny day) are not within our power: to realize them is not up to us, but depends on other "agents" or external forces, thus we cannot really "pursue" them. Other goals are just partially up to us; we have to do something but then the final result depends on the others or on luck; like winning a lottery or being acquitted of a crime we did not commit. As already pointed out, a goal is not a goal only if/when actively pursued.

Thus, we may have actively pursued goals (goals pursued through our active actions), but also merely passive goals; and the latter can be of two very different kinds:

- Goals we have just to wait for, to hope for their attainment; which do not depend at all on us: we can not do anything (else).
- Goals whose realization depends on us and on our "doing nothing", that is abstaining from possible interference. We would have the power to block that event/result, and we decide to do nothing, in order to let it happen

(inaction, "passive action"). This case also involves our "responsibility", since the result is due to our decision and (in)action.

6.2.2 Maintenance vs. achievement/acquisition goals

An important distinction is between "maintenance" goals vs. "achievement" goals (Cohen & Levesque 1990), but it must be well characterized. Let us suppose I have the goal that P is true at some future time t'. Now, what is the current situation in relation to P? Is P already true and I wish that it remains so ("maintenance"), or is P not (yet) true and I would like it to become so ("achievement"[29] or better "acquisition")?

These two kinds of goals underlie two very different psychologies and motivational attitudes. Suppose that my goal fails and I do not get P at t'. In the maintenance case, my suffering will be greater, because not only my goal is frustrated but I undergo a loss, which increases my psychological pain (Miceli & Castelfranchi 1997).

If I focus on the "loss", the maintenance goal acquires the status of an "avoidance" goal; I want not to *lose* my P. In the acquisition perspective and in the loss perspective the subjective value of P is different. As prospect theory and the endowment effect have shown, the value of P is perceived as much greater in the case of loss than in the case of acquisition/gain.

It is also interesting to combine this distinction with other crucial ones (not only avoidance vs. approach); for example, with *pursued* or *passive* goals: do I have to act for realizing (or maintaining) P at t'; or does it not depend on me, so that I just hope that this will happen or rely on somebody else?

6.2.3 Avoidance vs. approach goals

An important distinction in motivational theory is that between avoidance and approach goals. This is how Wikipedia summarizes the difference: "Not all goals are directed towards *approaching* a desirable outcome (e.g., demonstrating competence). Goals can also be directed towards *avoiding* an undesirable outcome" (for scholarly discussion, see for instance Elliot 2006). More than that, avoidance and approach represent two mental frames, two different psychological dispositions and mind settings (see Higgins' avoidance and approach "regulatory *focus*", in his 1997)[30].

One should also combine this distinction with the others. For example, with passive vs. actively pursued motivational attitudes: do I have to act in order to avoid that Q or to pursue P, or do I just hope and wait? Two different kinds of *fear* are implied, if I have to and can do something to block and prevent the

---

[29] The term "achievement" is too strongly related to an active pursuit.

[30] Notice how this terminology (e.g. "approach") is related to a semantics/connotation of "goal" that we have criticized in Section 3 point A, as being too strongly inspired and constrained by behaviorism. Moreover, many motivational theories about avoidance and approach (e.g., the one by Higgins) remain basically hedonistic.

danger, or rather I just have to wait while feeling helpless. And two different positive (approach) attitudes, if I can and have to actively acquire/maintain what I like or need, or if I just have to hope so. Moreover, success or failure will induce very different effects on causal attribution, self-confidence and self-esteem, learning, satisfaction, social emotions (such as gratitude or resentment, among others), etc.

Furthermore, am I *currently in the negative state* Q (the state I would have preferred, and perhaps tried, to avoid and I would like to avoid at t', that is, to stop it)? Or currently it is not the case that Q but I worry about the next future? Is my avoidance goal a special form of acquisition/achievement goal? Or am I trying to defend my current positive state? In the first case, I am driven also by the pain that I am currently feeling: avoiding Q is a felt *need*. In the second case, I am driven by the imagination of Q, not by its current unbearability.

In avoidance goals, success is to pass from Q to not Q (to end the negative state) or to prevent passage from not Q to Q; while in approach goals success is to pass from not P to P or from P to P (that is, maintaining P as the desired status quo).

6.2.4 Gradable vs. all-or-nothing goals

There are goals that can be achieved gradually in terms of quantity: 20%, 50%, 100%; like eating this chicken, becoming rich, etc. Their failure or success can be partial. We call these goals "gradable". There are other goals that have a yes/no, all-or-nothing, nature; we either realize them or not. Goals like: getting a six by throwing a dice, dying, graduating, being married. The psychology of these kinds of goals is importantly different, in particular if we consider those cases in which in order to achieve the goal a long time and several actions are needed: goals that require "persistence"[31].

In gradable goals, even my first action is immediately rewarding: I get a share of the prize, I get my piece of food; the same for the second action, and so on. If I stop or something stops my pursuit, I do not waste all my efforts, time, and costs; I have obtained some quantity of the goal, more or less proportional to my investment. Moreover, this is the kind of goals (and mental frame) which can result in the so-called "diminishing marginal utility": the value of the second, third, etc. identical good decreases[32].

---

[31] Actually we are considering the intersection of two goal typologies: (i) what we might call "one shot" goals (goals achievable with just one (complex or simple) action, rather than iterated interventions at distant times) vs. "persistence" goals, requiring several distant actions; (ii) "gradable" vs. "yes/no".

[32] A strategy to counteract that is "saving the best bite for last", to maintain a high-level of motivation. Alternatively, this strategy (known as the "sequence effect" in the literature on delay discounting; see Loewenstein & Prelec 1992) can also be interpreted as generating higher psychological utility by virtue of the mental anticipation of a deferred pleasurable experience (the best bite for last) – a phenomenon neatly captured in Italian by the notion of "pregustare" (literally, pre-savoring, similar to foretasting but with a marked positive implication). The converse of this is the tendency to anticipate a negative event (e.g., a surgical operation, an appointment with the dentist) in order to "get it over with", presumably to

Very different is the situation with long-term yes/no goals; they are very risky and demanding. In fact, only at the end, with my last action, I get the entire prize; before that, I have just to "suffer", to work, invest, wait for, without any external reward. At any time I could invest the same effort for a smaller but immediate reward; why renounce it in view of something much more delayed? And what happens if I have to give up my long-term plan and efforts? I waste all my work and investments.

The human species is the only species which is able not only to deal with a "deferral of desire" (long term pursuit and waiting; postponing strong desires or needs, etc.) but – in particular – to formulate very long-term plans, which require consistent sequences of actions over days, months, or years before being accomplished. These goals are very important, because we can obtain very ambitious results just by cooperating with ourselves, by combining the powers we have "here and now" with those we will have "there and later", by summing up our resources and efforts. However, they are also very risky and difficult to manage, in that they require special (internal and external) memory devices and commitment[33].

Human psychology is full of "tricks" for pursuing these goals, for maintaining one's motivational steadiness, coherence, persistence, in order not to be distracted by temptations, thus wasting previous efforts (and in order to create long-term, delayed, social exchanges). This is in part the role of:

i. the so called "sunk costs" bias, and in general the value increase of those goals in which we have already invested, and the greater value of losses vs. acquisitions;
ii. the unconscious readjustment of one's attitudes and evaluations after one has made a choice (as in Festinger's "cognitive dissonance");
iii. our "commitment" in intention formulation and the "mortgage" that an intention represents over future choices (Section 6.4);
iv. meta-goals and "will" (Section 6.1) in strict sense, and its "strength", as well as self-persuasion (see also Castelfranchi 2012);
v. the capability of desiring in strict sense, that is, anticipating and foretasting the rewarding and pleasant sensations associated with the achievement of a goal, which provides us with some sort of (illusory) gradable consumption, or better supports our motivation, and the preferability of the goal (Section 6.3);
vi. in general several aspects of the psychology of "inter-temporal choice" (see Paglieri & Castelfranchi 2008; Paglieri 2012).

Spending and spending resources, without any immediate reward, just waiting for the final reward, and risking so much, is such a psychologically hard situation that, in order to cope with it, we manipulate it even by translating an actually Yes/No goal in more "digestible" and gradable objectives. For instance, if we have to take a degree, but in the meantime we have to spend

---

avoid the negative psychological utility (fear, distress, anxiety, etc.) associated to expecting something bad to happen in the future.

[33] Also writing was originally meant to fulfill, of course at the social level, the function of a reminder and evidence of what I/you have to receive or to give in the future.

a lot of money, study for years, and relinquish a lot of pleasurable things, we "translate" the goal of being graduated into the goal of doing 22 exams and the thesis: then we can enjoy success and feel rewarded for the achievement of each intermediate step, even if they do not guarantee at all completion of our original plan. Yet, subjectively we have partially achieved our goal, because we have achieved part of its sub-goals. Unfortunately, in fact we cannot be "80% graduated"; we may even do all the necessary exams without managing to graduate in the end.

6.2.5 The self as a motivating meta-goal structure

We do not just have single motivating goals, but we have some sort of "project", of "design" about ourselves; a design which is crucial part of our view of ourselves, of the Self, of our identity. The representation of ourselves is not just factual, descriptive, historical (doxastic representation) and also evaluative (self-esteem, self-evaluation, strengths and weaknesses, etc.)[34], but it also is "prescriptive", a motivational representation: goals about us to be realized. Actually, our "realization" precisely is the realization of such a project of us. This project and ideal of us not only moves us but it assigns priorities to our specific goals and choices, and determines the feeling/sense of failure or success. Our daily goals and choices are not only subordinated to, constrained by previous commitments, coherence, and long term objectives, but first of all by the coherence with such an higher level (meta-level) motivational structure. In a sense this ideal or prescriptive view about us (what we like to be, would like to be, or should be) provides us some meta-goals: goals about our current goals and their priorities; so the discrepancy or coherence with this goal about us become a guide for choosing practical goals guiding our behavior. These goals about us seem to give "meaning" and "value" to what we are and pursue; to our life (Section 6.3 last paragraph; see also Miceli & Castelfranchi 2012).

A lot of theories converge in this direction with important hints and data: "Image Theory" (Beach & Mitchell 1987), which is not just a matter of being coherent with our image, how we see and present us, but being coherent with how/who we want to be; "Self-discrepancy Theory", (Higgins 1997) where people have "self-guides", internal representations used as standards to be achieved, and used for evaluating ourselves; or the "Life Tasks", the "Self-Concept Ideals" (see for example, Cantor 1990).

---

[34] Which of course must be relative to some "value", "standard", "goal": something that is prescribed to us or we prescribe to us or that we wish.

6.3 Felt goals

As we said not all our goals are 'felt', also because not all of them are represented and defined in a sensory-motor format[35]. Let us examine the two most
important kinds of felt goals: *desires* and *needs*; but we should first clarify the
theory of "feeling" and its impact on normative "cognition". Our thesis is that:
Every time we "feel" something we actually experience some active sensations. This
applies also to so called "epistemic feelings" (de Sousa 2008), such as when we
just say that we *feel* we cannot trust someone, or that we don't *feel* ready for
something, or that we *feel* that we can do something. Those sensations:

- are not necessarily conscious;
- are not necessarily coming from the peripheral sensorial apparatus or from
  the body: they might just be the "evocation" (the activation of the central
  memory trace) of the experience ("somatic markers"), with more or less
  peripheral re-activation;
- do not necessarily imply the retrieval of the original triggering episode(s)
  that created an association between the sensations and a given con-
  text/object; also because not necessarily the conditioning experience/stimulus
  has been conscious (see for example the celebrated experiment on affective
  priming in Murphy & Zajonc 1993).
- do not necessarily imply a correct, "rational", wise, "evaluation" of the
  eliciting event, because the conditioning does not necessarily occur on the
  pertinent aspects (stimuli) of the situation, and the evocation is due to
  analogical traits, not necessarily to the pertinent ones.

In the "felt need" for a given object O, we perceive a current, unpleasant or disturbing bodily or affective stimulus S (for instance, we perceive dryness in our
throat when we "feel the need for a bit of water") that we cognitively ascribe
to the loss of O (see below). Similarly, in felt desires we just "imagine" and
anticipate the pleasant sensations/emotions that we will/would have if/when
reaching our loved object (see below).

Damasio's theory of "somatic markers" and the idea that they qualify, evaluate or better attach some value to the various anticipated scenarios (possible
goals, choices) is no doubt interesting and convincing. What looks wrong in
Damasio's model (if I correctly understand it; Damasio 1994) is the fact that
somatic markers – which make certain states/objects good and attractive, and
other objects unpleasant and repulsive – would "prune" the branches of a
choice, by cutting off the unpleasant outcomes. This is definitely wrong; if
this were the case, it would never be possible to decide to do something that,
though disgusting or really painful, we have to do for some "reason"; or to
give up something that, though very exciting and attractive, we do not want
to do because we have other "cold" priorities. But this happens every day: we

---

[35] We mean that, for example, we cannot say "I feel the intention of.." simply because the
sensory-motor format of the represented anticipatory state is not specified in the very notion
of "intention" (see Section 6.4). "Intention" is a more "abstract" notion of goal, with a non-
specified codification. Looking at a goal as an "intention", we abstract away from its possible
sensory components.

make unpleasant choices and hard sacrifices, even if we feel how unpleasant and hard they are to make.

The evocation of those "markers", rather than "pruning" our choices, just adds a strange (positive or negative) "value" to some of our candidate goals. It represents an implicit, not really arguable, appraisal of those outcomes. So our mind is able to calculate, to take into account, in just one and the same decision setting, two completely heterogeneous kinds of goal "value":

i.   the "reasoned" value, based on means-end reasoning and the calculation of expected pros and cons of a given move, which are belief-based and can be changed through argumentation (Pascal's "reasons of the Reason");
ii. the felt, affective value (Pascal's "reasons of the heart")[36].

We not only have two independent, parallel, and competitive systems for regulating our behavior, for making a given goal prevail: one is unconscious, automatic, fast, evocation based, affective, etc; the other is based on reasoning and deliberation, slow, etc. (like in "dual system" theories, nowadays very popular: e.g., Sloman 1996; Sun 2002; Kahneman 2003). These systems strictly interact with each other; more precisely, the affective, evocative system enters the space of deliberation, introduces new dimensions on goals and beliefs, and alters the process and result of our "reasoned" decisions[37]. Actually, we can become aware of the co-occurrence of such parallel processes and even adopt explicit meta-heuristics like:

• silencing our reasoning: *"Stop reasoning! Follow your heart and instinct! I shouldn't be so damn rational every time! Let's trust my instincts!"*;
• silencing our feelings: *"I have to keep a clear head! I have to be careful, unbiased by emotions; to reason in a cold way; to be rational, not instinctive as usual!"*;
• taking both of them into account: *"To be honest, the idea of doing that is really painful for me, I already suffer just imagining it, but it is the right thing to do, I have to"*; *"I know I shouldn't do that, I'm violating my duty, but I cannot, don't want to resist the temptation; it is too exciting for me; I will pay the consequences"*; *"I know this is very pleasant and exciting, but it is not really convenient"*.

The affective reaction or the bodily signals alter goal processing in three fundamental ways:

i.   they activate new goals to be taken into account;
ii. they give a new kind of "value" to the possible goals, as attractive or repulsive, and the strength/degree of this value is not belief-based but is due to the "intensity" of the associated sensation: the more intense the unpleasant sensation the stronger and more coercive the felt need or the avoidance goal; the more intense the anticipated pleasure the stronger the desire;

---

[36] Pascal's claim *"The heart has its reasons, of which reason knows nothing"* precisely means that those bases and forces for choice ("reasons") are not "arguments", are not "arguable" through reasoning on expected utilities and probabilities, on the instrumental pros and cons of the outcomes.

[37] Slovic's idea of "affect heuristics" just partially captures this aspect and solves the problem of its modeling (Slovic et al. 2002).

iii. they are a basis for beliefs, by subverting the usual/normative mechanism of emotions and affective reactions triggered by beliefs: belief $\Rightarrow$ affective reaction/emotion ("cognitive appraisal" of the event); here, a belief can be built or reinforced just on the basis of a feeling: I believe that there is some danger just because I feel fear.

$$\textit{belief about a possible danger (prediction)} \Rightarrow \textit{FEAR}$$
$$\textit{FEAR} \Rightarrow \textit{belief about a possible danger (prediction)}$$

This can even create dangerous vicious circles, like in panic reactions. The feeling even attaches a *degree of certainty* to those beliefs: the stronger the affective state, the stronger the belief, whereas the degree of certainty of a belief is usually based on factual evidence, on other inferred beliefs, on its sources (perception, communication, inference, etc.) and their credibility (the more credible the source, the more certain the belief), on the number of converging sources: the more independent sources converge on it, the greater the perceived certainty of the belief, due to confirmation effects (Castelfranchi 1997).

Thus affects do not just compete with our "deliberations", they enter our decision process and alter the *basic principles* of deliberation. Goal theory is deeply affected by affects, and this is something that has to be systematically clarified.

6.3.1 Desires

We use two notions of "desire", both of which are quite close to common sense.

The first notion understands desire *in broad sense*, as denoting a motivational representation; more precisely, *a "motive", a terminal goal, which is not instrumental to higher goals*. However, as we said, this notion of desire does not cover all the set of our final "motives". It only refers to the *endogenous* ones, it does not refer to pure duties, obligations, orders, something that I adopt from others and pursue for others. In natural language "desires" are typically opposed to other motives[38]. It is common sense to say that we sacrifice our "desires" (what we like to do because of personal, internal inclinations) for our "duties" (what we want to do because we adhere to external goals and/or pressures).

More importantly, the notion of "desire" does not specify if the goal is pursued or not, if it has been chosen or not, etc. Quite the reverse, it is frequently used for referring to goals which are not yet chosen and pursued; and perhaps have been suspended or even abandoned, given up. This is why "desire" is used in contrast with the notion of "intention" in philosophical, psychological, and AI models. For example, BDI models (basically inspired by Bratman's analysis; see his 1987) use "desire" as a general notion for "motives", "ends" or "goals" *before* any decision. They can be incoherent, unstable, etc.

However, for these models the goals pursued by an individual, his intentions, can only derive from the inside and be instrumental to and only justified

---

[38] E.g. *"I do not desire at all to go there; but I have to; I am obliged to go"*.

by personal motives. They do not have an explicit model of goals adopted from outside. To call these goals "desires" is somewhat strange and misleading. Of course, there may be personal desires motivating our goal adoption (imitation, help, obedience, norm respect, etc.), but this should not be confused with the path of intention generation: it is goal G1 – adopted from outside, from the will of another agent – which produces my intention and will guide my action! Not the possible desire for which I have adopted the goal of the other.

In our model, an *intention* is the transformation, or instrumental specification of a preliminary goal (the source-goal), and the commitment to it; this source-goal is not always a desire (even when a desire motivates one's goal adoption; see Section 6.4).

The second notion of desire we use understands it *in the narrow sense* of a specific mental state/activity and feeling. This desire is *necessarily "felt"* (implying sensations), whereas (as already remarked) not all goals are "felt"; even not all the motivating goals are necessarily affectively charged and pleasant and attractive (at least in principle, in a general theory of purposive behavior). Desires in this strict sense are goals that when/if realized give *pleasure*. "Desiring" (in Italian: *star desiderando*) strictly speaking means anticipating in one's imagination the realization of the goal-state. The goal is represented in a sensory-motor code, thus implying the subject's experience of some sensations or feelings associated with the goal's realization. The subject is actually *imagining* these sensations and experiencing some hallucination, some anticipatory pleasure; and this is why we can "intensely" wish something. This can even imply not only the activation of somatic markers (the central neural trace of previous somatic experiences), but the actual activation of bodily reactions, like salivation, erection, etc. Desiring in this strict sense has strange properties, such as:

- you cannot really desire (in this sense) an orange if you have not experienced it and do not know the very specific flavor and taste of an orange. You can imagine something similar to an orange, imagining by analogy, but not have the anticipatory experience of a true orange. Desiring something presupposes a previous sensorial experience of that "something".
- if you have been strongly desiring something (for example, a sexual encounter), by daydreaming and anticipating its pleasure, you are more exposed to disappointment; in fact, reality is often less pleasant and perfect than imagination. And what is the function of such a strange mental activity in humans: daydreaming and illusory satisfaction? Not much is understood of it.

Another *felt* kind of goals are "needs". A felt need is due to a bodily sensation (current stimulus or evoked sensation)

6.3.2 Needs

There is no room in this work for a systematic theory of "needs"[39], not even if restricted only to felt needs. We just mention three reasons that justify their importance:

1. the sensation-based nature of these special goals changes the general theory of goal "value" (see Section 6.2). Their value in fact is not derived from beliefs, means-ends reasoning, pros & cons, prediction of possible outcomes; it is not arguable and manipulable through verbal persuasion; we cannot 'explain' why G1 is better, more important, that G2. Their value is just dictated by the *intensity* of the felt sensation: the stronger the current sensation from the body (or the evoked somatic marker), the more the need acquires value and priority.
2. the sensations implied by felt needs – differently from desires – are negative, unpleasant, disagreeable, unbearable, activating avoidance-goals, in a "prevention focus". Also for this reason we experience them as 'necessities', 'forcing' us to do or not to do something.
3. we conceptualize and conceive a "need" (either felt or not) as the *lack* of something, which is conceived not just as useful but as necessary; it is a *necessary* means, as the only possible means for achieving our goal: not only if I have O (what I need for G)[40] I can realize G, but if I do not have O I cannot and will not realize G. This gives a sense of necessity, of no choice, to the general notion of "need", which – in felt needs – is reinforced by the unpleasant sensation.

Thus we can schematically characterize a need of agent x to have or do q in order to achieve p as follows: *(Need x, q, for p)*, where q is either to possess a resource y (x needs y for p), or to do an action for achieving p; and p is the goal relative to which x needs q (which becomes my sub-goal, my means). In order for an instrumental relationship between means and ends to count as a need, four belief conditions must hold:

1. *Necessity belief*: if not q, not p (without what I need, what I want cannot be)
2. *Lack belief*: not q (I miss what I need – otherwise I would not be needing it)
3. *Uneasiness belief*: lacking q gives me some disturbance/suffering/trouble (this often is experienced as a feeling, a bodily signal)
4. *Attribution belief*: my uneasiness is because not q and not p (it is my state of need that makes me squirm)

Thus, if x needs q, she is not only motivated by the goal that p, but also by the goal to avoid the uneasiness/suffering/trouble associated with that need. This captures the essential complementarity and affinity between felt needs and desires: while feeling the need for q I experience an unpleasant state; so,

---

[39] For a general theory of "needs" ("having an objective need" vs. "subjective needs" vs. "felt needs"), see Castelfranchi 1998c; Castelfranchi & Miceli 2004.

[40] Notice that (differently from "desires") "needs" are intrinsically "instrumental" goals. I need something *for* something else: either for achieving a practical goal (practical need: I need the key for opening the door), or for stopping or preventing an unpleasant sensation.

the idea of achieving q may imply a pleasant sensation of relief. Therefore felt needs present a desiring facet: "I need a bit of water!" implies also "I desire some water!", as soon as I am no longer focusing on the lack of q and the associated unpleasant sensation, but on the pleasure of finally drinking some water. Conversely, a felt desire implies a current potential lack and suffering. If I am desiring Rosanna and imagining how pleasant will (or would) be her presence and proximity, and then my attention shifts to her actual absence, I miss her, and this is clearly unpleasant; then, at that point, I feel the need of Rosanna.

More generally, this Janus face of needs and desires is often evident in an important family of goal states: *drives*, that is, goals activated by physiological body cycles, like hunger, thirst, sleep, and so on. Drives frequently show the two facets of need and desire: their satisfaction gives us relief or pleasure, but they prompt us to act mostly by producing disturbing sensations[41].

6.3.3 Goals that are "impossible to renounce", unconditional

Negotiation and decisions become impossible if there are conflicting but 'indefeasible' and non-negotiable goals. X cannot accept the non-acquisition or loss of the state of affairs represented in goal G1. As for G1 there is no room for negotiation and compromise. If two conflicting goals are both impossible to renounce, there is no solution, no possible decision to make.

But then, *why are some goals impossible to renounce*? Is that not 'irrational'? In fact, I may either remain in a suspended non-profit situation, or give up the realization of my 'utility' (other goals of mine), by preferring an unfeasible goal to other feasible ones. Moreover, *which goals are impossible to renounce*? What is that make them so special? They are not only very 'important' goals (endowed with high value, implying high satisfaction when achieved, and high and unbearable suffering when frustrated), but also goals endowed with symbolic value: honor, religion, identity, ideals, etc. Or goals that give meaning to one's life and other motives (see Section 6.2). Without the possibility to entertain such goals (to actively pursue them or at least hope for their realization) the other goals are irrelevant to the individual; he or she loses motivation, feels indifferent and depressed, or with a meaningless and valueless life (see Mancini & Gangemi this volume). Thus this is a very strange (but fundamental) goal relation that has yet to be better clarified.

---

[41] A good model of the relation between the internal homeostatic mechanism (and its signals of match/mismatch) and the actual psychological goal, which will regulate the system's "action" on the world, is still lacking. In particular, what is not fully clear is the learning process from the internal homeostatic mechanism to the psychological goal. The internal mismatch and its implied discomfort seem to activate (as it happens in emotions) a candidate motive driving the behavior (e.g., eating), which specializes through learning and cultural rules and habits. We do not have the mental goal (motive) and understanding of the internal cycle equilibrium, we just want to eat (some "food") or not to feel cold, or to go to sleep.

6.4 Process-related notions and goal-kinds: Intentions in action vs. intentions in agenda

Intentions are those goals that *actually drive our voluntary actions or are ready/prepared to drive them*. They are not another "primitive" (like in BDI model inspired by Bratman's theory, e.g. Rao & Georgeff 1995), a different mental object with respect to goals. They are just a kind of goal: the final stage of a successful goal-processing, which also includes "desires" in the broad sense[42], with very specific and relevant properties (see also Castelfranchi & Paglieri 2007).

In a nutshell, in our model an *intention* is a goal that:

1. has been activated and processed;
2. has been evaluated as not impossible, and not already realized or self-realizing (achieved by another agent), and thus *up to us*: we have to act in order to achieve it[43];
3. has been chosen it against other possible active and conflicting goals, and we have "decided" to pursue it;
4. is consistent with other intentions of ours; a simple goal can be contradictory, inconsistent with other goals, but, once it is chosen, it becomes an intention and has to be coherent with the other intentions (Castelfranchi & Paglieri 2007)[44];
5. implies the agent's belief that she knows (or will/can know) how to achieve it, that she is able to perform the needed actions, and that there are or will be the needed conditions for the intention's realization; at least the agent believes that she will be able and in condition to "try";
6. being "chosen" implies a "commitment" with ourselves, a mortgage on our future decisions; intentions have priority over new possible competing goals, and are more persistent than the latter (Bratman 1987);
7. is "planned"; we allocate/reserve some resources (means, time, etc.) for it; and we have formulated or decided to formulate a plan consisting of the actions to be performed in order to achieve it. An intention is essentially a two-layered structure: (a) the "intention that", the *aim*, that is, the original processed goal (for example, to be in Naples tomorrow); (b) the "intention to do", the sub-goals, the planned executive actions (to take the train, buy the tickets, go to the station, etc.). There is no "intention" without (more or

---

[42] The creation of two distinct "primitives", basic independent notions/objects ("desires" vs. "intentions") is in part due to the wrong choice of adopting (also in accordance with common sense) "desires" as the basic motivational category and source. We have already criticized this reductive move (Section 4), and introduced a more general and basic (and not fully common sense) teleonomic notion. This notion also favors a better unification of goal kinds and a better theory of their structural and dynamic relationships.

[43] An intention is always the intention to "do something" (including inactions). We cannot really have intentions about the actions of other autonomous agents. When we say something like "I have the intention that John goes to Naples" what we actually mean is "I have the intention *to bring it about that* John goes to Naples".

[44] Decision making serves precisely the function of selecting those goals which are feasible and coherent with each other, and allocating resources and planning one's actual behavior.

less) specified actions to be performed, and there is no intention without a motivating outcome of such action(s).

8. thus an intention is the final product of a successful goal-processing that leads to a goal-driven behavior (see Figure 5).

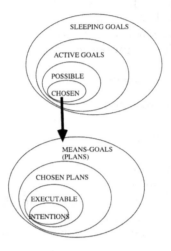

Fig. 5 Intention formulation

After a decision to act, an intention is already there even if the concrete actions are not fully specified or are not yet being executed, because some condition for its execution is not currently present. Intentions can be found in two final and pre-final stages:

(a) *Intention "in action"*, that is, guiding the executive "intentional" action;
(b) *Intention "in agenda"* ("future directed", those more central to the theories of Bratman, Searle, and other), that is, already planned and waiting for some lacking condition for their execution: time, money, skills, etc. For example, I may have the intention to go to Capri next Easter (the implementation of my "desire" of spending Easter in Capri), but now is February 17, and I am not going to Capri or doing anything for that; I have just decided to do so at the right moment; it is already in my "agenda" ("things that I have to do") and binds my resources and future decisions[45].

7 Concluding remarks

The aim of this contribution was to celebrate and recapitulate more than 35 years of "scopistica", which is the Italian neologism (loosely translatable in En-

---

[45] I would also say that an "intention" is "conscious", we are aware of our intentions and we "deliberate" about them; however, the problem of unconscious goal-driven behavior is open and quite complex (see Bargh et al., 2001).

glish as "goalism") that our research group coined to indicate our systematic, cybernetic-inspired theory of goals and goal-oriented behavior (see e.g. Parisi & Castelfranch 1976). More importantly, I intended to persuade my reader that goals are *the center of gravity of the cognitive universe*. In particular, I aimed at:

- making as clear as possible what we mean by "goal", what are our notions and definitions of several key concepts, and track their origins, roots and implications;
- illustrating the main current misunderstandings and misconceptions of the notion of goal;
- giving some preliminary ideas about goal processing, goal ontology, and their role in structuring knowledge, emotions, sociality, etc.

However, at the end of this small tour-de-force, I must confess I had another hidden agenda:

- showing that *there is a place in cognitive science for some sort of 'theoretical psychology'* (an old obsession of mine, which I have been cherishing and defending through my entire career).

In this view, an analytical and formal modeling (using AI, ALife, logic, etc.) is supposed to provide important insights and predictions, as well as suggestions for and interpretations of empirical research. Crucially, this key role of theoretical psychology *should not be delegated* to philosophy, not even so called "experimental philosophy". The relations with philosophy (epistemology, analytical philosophy, etc.) are very important for psychology, but psychology cannot assign its theoretical work to philosophy by limiting itself to empirical work, experiments, inductive models, and inferential statistical constructs, with their poor explicative power.

Psychology, and cognitive science in general, has to explicitly define its notions (that is still true, half a century after Wittgenstein's apt remark!) and formulate very analytical functional *models* of the *processes*, the *proximate mechanisms* underlying and producing the observable behavior. Models that should be possibly implementable and implemented in neural substrates and mechanisms. In doing this, we should all attempt to modestly follow the old arrogant program of Spinoza about emotions (and mind): *more geometrico demostrata*.

References

1. Bargh, J., Gollwitzer, P., Lee-Chai, A., Barndollar, K., & Trötschel, R. (2001). The automated will: Non conscious activation and pursuit of behavioral goals. *Journal of Personality and Social Psychology, 81*, 1014–1027.
2. Beach, L. R., & Mitchell, T. (1987). Image theory: Principles, goals, and plans in decision making. *Acta Psychologica, 66 (3)*, 201–220.
3. Bratman, M. (1987). *Intention, plans, and practical Reason.* Cambridge: Harvard University Press.
4. Butz, M. (2002). *Anticipatory learning classifier systems.* Boston: Kluwer.
5. Cantor, N. (1990). From thought to behavior: "Having" and "doing" in the study of personality and cognition. *American Psychologist, 45 (6)*, 735–750.

6. Castelfranchi, C. (1995) Guaranties for autonomy in cognitive agent architecture. In M. Wooldridge & N. Jennings (Eds.), *Intelligent Agents* (pp. 56–70). Berlin: Springer.
7. Castelfranchi, C. (1996). Reasons: Belief support and goal dynamics. *Mathware & Soft Computing, 3,* 233–247.
8. Castelfranchi, C. (1997). Representation and integration of multiple knowledge sources: Issues and questions. In V. Cantoni, V. Di Gesù, A. Setti & D. Tegolo (Eds.), *Human & Machine Perception: Information Fusion* (pp. 235–254). New York: Plenum Press.
9. Castelfranchi, C. (1998a). Modelling social action for AI agents. *Artificial Intelligence, 103,* 157–182.
10. Castelfranchi, C. (1998b). Emergence and cognition: Towards a synthetic paradigm in AI and cognitive science. In H. Coelho (Ed.), *Progress in Artificial Intelligence - IBERAMIA 98* (pp. 13–26). Berlin: Springer.
11. Castelfranchi, C. (1998c). To believe and to feel: The case of "needs". In D. Canamero (Ed.) *Proceedings of AAAI Fall Symposium "Emotional and Intelligent: The Tangled Knot of Cognition"* (pp. 55–60). Menlo Park: AAAI Press.
12. Castelfranchi, C. (2001). The theory of social functions. *Journal of Cognitive Systems Research, 2,* 5–38.
13. Castelfranchi, C. (2011). Come i mezzi divengano fini: meccanismi psichici. In F. Rubinacci, A. Rega & N. Lettieri (Eds.), *Atti del convegno AISC 2011* (pp. 58–61). Milano: AISC.
14. Castelfranchi, C. (2012). "My mind": Reflexive sociality and its cognitive tools. In F. Paglieri (Ed.), *Consciousness in interaction: the role of the natural and social context in shaping consciousness* (pp. 125–149). Amsterdam: John Benjamins.
15. Castelfranchi,C., Conte, R., Miceli, M., & Poggi, I. (1996). Emotions and goals. In B.Kokinov (Ed.), *Perspectives on Cognitive Science* (Vol.2, pp.130–145). Sofia: NBU Press.
16. Castelfranchi, C., & Falcone, R. (2004). Founding autonomy: The Dialectics between (social) environment and agent's architecture and powers. *Lecture Notes on Artificial Intelligence, 2969,* 40–54.
17. Castelfranchi, C., & Falcone, R. (2010). *Trust theory: A socio-cognitive and computational model.* London: Wiley.
18. Castelfranchi, C., Giardini, F., Lorini, E., & Tummolini, L. (2003). The prescriptive destiny of predictive attitudes: From expectations to norms via conventions. In R. Alterman & D. Kirsh (Eds.), *Proceedings of the 25th Annual Meeting of the Cognitive Science Society* (pp. 222–227). Boston: Cognitive Science Society.
19. Castelfranchi, C., & Miceli, M. (2004). Gli scopi e la loro famiglia: Ruolo dei bisogni e dei bisogni "sentiti". *Cognitivismo Clinico, 1,* 5–19.
20. Castelfranchi, C., & Miceli, M. (2009). The cognitive-motivational compound of emotional experience. *Emotion Review, 1 (3),* 221–228.
21. Castelfranchi, C., & Paglieri, F. (2007). The role of beliefs in goal dynamics: prolegomena to a constructive theory of intentions. *Synthese, 155 (2),* 237–263.
22. Cohen, P., & Levesque, H. (1990). Intention is choice with commitment. *Artificial Intelligence, 42 (2-3),* 213–261.
23. Conte, R., & Castelfranchi, C. (1995a). *Cognitive and social action.* London: UCL Press.
24. Conte, R., & Castelfranchi, C. (1995b). Norms as mental objects. From normative beliefs to normative goals. In C. Castelfranchi & J. Muller (Eds.). *From reaction to cognition: Proceedings of MAAMAW'93* (pp. 186–199). Berlin: Springer Verlag.
25. Cordeschi, R. (2002). *The discovery of the artificial: Behaviour, mind and machines before and beyond cybernetics.* Dordrecht: Kluwer.
26. Damasio, A. (1994). *Descartes' error: Emotion, reason, and the human brain.* New York: Avon Books.
27. De Sousa, R. (2008). Epistemic feelings. In G. Brun, U. Doguoglu & D. Kuenzle (Eds.), *Epistemology and emotions* (pp. 185–204). Aldershot: Ashgate.
28. Elliot, A. (2006). The hierarchical model of approach-avoidance motivation. *Motivation and Emotion, 30 (2),* 111–116.
29. Fishbein, M., & Ajzen, I. (1975). *Belief, attitude, intention, and behavior: An introduction to theory and research.* Reading: Addison-Wesley.

30. Higgins, E. T. (1997). Beyond pleasure and pain. *American Psychologist, 52*, 1280–1300.
31. Kahneman, D. (2003). A perspective on judgement and choice. *American Psychologist, 58*, 697–720.
32. Kruglanski, A. (1996). Goals as knowledge structures. In P. Gollwitzer & J. Bargh (Eds.), *Psychology of action: Linking cognition and motivation to behavior* (pp. 599–619). New York: Guilford.
33. Kruglanski, A., Shah, J., Fishbach, A., Friedman, R., Chun, W., & Sleeth-Keppler, D. (2002). A theory of goal systems. In M. Zanna (Ed.), *Advances in experimental social psychology* (pp. 331–378). SanDiego: Academic.
34. Kunda, Z. (1990). The case for motivated reasoning. *Psychological Bulletin, 108 (3)*, 480–498.
35. Ogden, C., & Richards, I. (1923). *The meaning of meaning*. New York: Harcourt, Brace.
36. van Osselaer, S., Ramanathan, S., Campbell, M., Cohen, J., Dale, J., Herr, P., et al. (2005). Choice based on goals. *Marketing Letters, 16 (3-4)*, 335–346.
37. Loewenstein, G., & Prelec, D. (1992). Anomalies in intertemporal choice: Evidence and an interpretation. *Quarterly Journal of Economics, 107 (2)*, 573–597.
38. Lorini, E., Marzo, F., & Castelfranchi, C. (2005). A cognitive model of altruistic mind. In B. Kokinov (Ed.), *Advances in Cognitive Economics* (pp. 282–293). Sofia: NBU Press.
39. Maes, P. (1989). How to do the right thing. *Connection Science, 1 (3)*, 291–323.
40. Mancini, F., & Gangemi, A. (2013). The paradoxes of depression: A goal-driven approach. In F. Paglieri, L. Tummolini, R. Falcone & M. Miceli (Eds.), *The goals of cognition: Essays in honour of Cristiano Castelfranchi* (this volume). London: College Publications.
41. Miceli, M., & Castelfranchi, C. (1989). A cognitive approach to values. *Journal for the Theory of Social Behaviour, 19 (2)*, 169–194.
42. Miceli, M., & Castelfranchi, C. (1995). *Le difese della mente. Profili cognitivi*. Roma: La Nuova Italia Scientifica.
43. Miceli, M., & Castelfranchi, C. (1997). Basic principles of psychic suffering: A preliminary account. *Theory & Psychology, 7*, 769–798.
44. Miceli, M., & Castelfranchi, C. (2002). The mind and the future: The (negative) power of expectations. *Theory & Psychology, 12*, 335–366.
45. Miceli, M., & Castelfranchi, C. (2012). Coherence of conduct and the self image. In F. Paglieri (Ed.), *Consciousness in interaction: the role of the natural and social context in shaping consciousness* (pp. 151–178). Amsterdam: John Benjamins.
46. Miller, G., Galanter, E., & Pribram, K. (1960). *Plans and the structure of behavior*. New York: Holt, Rinehart and Winston.
47. Moskowitz, G., & Grant, E. (Eds.) (2009). *The psychology of goals*. New York: Guilford Press.
48. Murphy, S. T., & Zajonc, R. B. (1993). Affect, cognition, and awareness: Affective priming with optimal and suboptimal stimulus exposures. *Journal of Personality and Social Psychology, 64*, 723–739.
49. Paglieri, F. (2012). Ulysses' will: self-control, external constraints, and games. In F. Paglieri (Ed.), *Consciousness in interaction: the role of the natural and social context in shaping consciousness* (pp. 179–206). Amsterdam: John Benjamins.
50. Paglieri, F., & Castelfranchi, C. (2008a). More than control freaks: Evaluative and motivational functions of goals. *Behavioral and Brain Sciences, 31 (1)*, 35–36.
51. Paglieri, F., & Castelfranchi, C. (2008b). Decidere il futuro: scelta intertemporale e teoria degli scopi. *Giornale Italiano di Psicologia, 35 (4)*, 743–775.
52. Paglieri, F., & Castelfranchi, C. (2012). Trust in relevance. In S. Ossowski, F. Toni, G. Vouros (Eds.), Agreement Technologies 2012 (pp. 332–346). Dubrovnik, CEUR-WS.org.
53. Parisi, D., & Castelfranchi, C. (1976). Discourse as a hierarchy of goals. *CISL Working Papers, 54/55*, Centro Internazionaie di Semiotica e Linguistica, Urbino.
54. Pezzulo, G., & Castelfranchi, C. (2009). Thinking as the control of imagination: A conceptual framework for goal-directed systems. *Psychological Research, 73*, 559–577.
55. Pezzulo, G., Butz, M., & Castelfranchi, C. (2008). The anticipatory approach: Definitions and taxonomies. In G. Pezzulo, M. Butz, C. Castelfranchi & R. Falcone (Eds.), *The challenge*

of anticipation: A unifying framework for the analysis and design of artificial cognitive systems (pp. 23–43). Berlin: Springer.

56. Rao, A., & Georgeff, M. (1995). BDI-agents: From theory to practice. In V. Lesser (Ed.), *Proceedings of the First International Conference on Multiagent Systems – ICMAS' 95* (pp. 312–319). Menlo Park: AAAI Press.

57. Rosenbleuth, A., Wiener, N., & Bigelow, J. (1943). Behavior, purpose and teleology. *Philosophy of Science, 10 (1)*, 18–24.

58. Sloman, S. (1996). The empirical case for two systems of reasoning. *Psychological Bulletin, 119*, 3–22.

59. Slovic, P., Finucane, M., Peters, E., & MacGregor, D. (2002). The affect heuristic. In T. Gilovich, D. Griffin & D. Kahneman (Eds.), *Heuristics and biases: The psychology of intuitive judgment* (pp. 397–420). Cambridge: Cambridge University Press.

60. Sperber, D., & Wilson, D. (1986). Relevance: Communication and cognition. Cambridge: Harvard University Press.

61. Sun, R. (2002). *Duality of the mind*. Mahwah: Lawrence Erlbaum Associates.

62. Tummolini, L., & Castelfranchi, C. (2006). The cognitive and behavioral mediation of institutions: Towards an account of institutional actions. *Cognitive Systems Research, 7 (2-3)*, 307–323.

63. Zeleny, M. (2000). Knowledge vs. information. In M. Zeleny (Ed.), *The IEBM handbook of Information Technology in business* (pp. 162–168). Padstow, UK: Thomson Learning.

64. Zeleny, M. (2005). *Human systems management. Integrating knowledge, management and systems*. London: World Scientific.